D1622684

DRAMA

ESSAYS

OTHER

CONNECTIONS

Literature for Composition

CONNECTIONS

Literature for Composition

Quentin Miller
Suffolk University

Julie Nash
University of Massachusetts Lowell

HOUGHTON MIFFLIN COMPANY Boston New York

Publisher: Patricia Coryell
Editor-in-Chief: Carrie Brandon
Marketing Manager: Tom Ziolkowski
Senior Development Editor: Martha Bustin
Senior Project Editor: Rosemary Winfield
Art and Design Manager: Jill Haber
Photo Editor: Jennifer Meyer Dare
Composition Buyer: Chuck Dutton
New Title Project Manager: Priscilla Manchester
Editorial Assistant: Katilyn Crowley
Marketing Associate: Bettina Chiu
Editorial Assistant: Andrew Laskey

Cover: Photograph of the interior of Grand Central Station, New York City, by Warren Wetmore, ca. 1903–1913. Copyright © CORBIS.

Credits continue on page 1453, which constitutes an extension of the copyright page.

Printed in the U.S.A.

Library of Congress Catalog Card Number 2006940953

2 3 4 5 6 7 8 9 - DOC – 11 10 09 08 07

Instructor's exam copy:
ISBN 10: 0-618-73210-1
ISBN 13: 978-0-618-73210-4.

For orders, use student text ISBNs:
ISBN 10: 0-618-48114-1
ISBN: 978-0-618-48114-9.

Brief Contents

Contents

List of Art, Photos, and Illustrations

Black and White Images

Color Insert

Preface for Instructors: A Letter from the Authors

Students Have Something to Say

In his poem "Introduction to Poetry," Billy Collins considers ways that people derive meaning from literature, and he recommends we hold a work "up to the light/like a color slide/or press an ear against its hive."

Our aim throughout the writing, editing, and class testing of *Connections* has been to encourage students to explore literature with this kind of close association and curiosity. Students clearly have a great deal to say when they connect what they read with their own complex and multifaceted lives and approach literature as a helpful, entertaining heritage that belongs to them.

A Literary Exploration of Human Nature

A literary exploration of human nature, this anthology invites students to make connections among

- age-old themes and the present,
- the genres of short fiction, poetry, drama, essays, and film,
- works of literature from different eras and cultures,
- literary selections and life experiences,
- the realms of literature and art, and
- recurring characters in literature and in life.

It has been our experience that students' critical thinking and writing skills improve in the course of making these connections and that students express important ideas and insights in their work.

A Rich Mix of Familiar and New Voices

Connections includes 170 diverse selections from different eras and cultures, forming a flexible but coherent array of short fiction, poetry, drama, and essays. Familiar selections are mingled with less familiar ones, and "old chestnuts" appear often in uncommon contexts, allowing fresh readings and interpretations. Roughly half of the included works are contemporary (1945 to the present), including many new voices that emerged during the past decade.

Flexible, Relevant Thematic Clusters and Strong Support Pedagogy

Flexible Themes

Students relate and respond to the flexible themes that are featured in Part 4 (Chapters 12–17) of *Connections*:

- obedience and rebellion,
- love and lust,
- honesty and deception,
- vengeance and forgiveness,
- industry and idleness, and
- greed, gluttony, and generosity.

Literature, like life, is open to interpretation and reinterpretation, despite our occasional preference for certainties and our tendency to see the world in terms of binary oppositions. The above themes are far from clear-cut and thus are rich topics for students' class discussion and writing.

Support Pedagogy

Support pedagogy was a priority in writing and class-testing *Connections*. We have taken care that the questions following literary works in Part 4 (Chapters 12–17) foster lively class discussions, creative and critical thinking, and improved writing. Three types of questions focus students' attention on

- Close Reading,
- Critical and Creative Reading, and
- Connections to Other Readings.

Additional questions about the book's four-color art program link the art images and literary selections.

"Common Characters" in Literature

In Part 4 (Chapters 12–17), *Connections* profiles six intriguing archetypes—that is, enduring "Common Characters" who fulfill important functions in the artistic imagination, in popular culture, and in reality. Students will recognize these archetypes and benefit from exploring them in literary contexts:

- Icarus (in Chapter 12, Obedience and Rebellion)
- Don Juan (in Chapter 13, Love and Lust)
- The Trickster Figure (in Chapter 14, Honesty and Deception)
- The Prodigal Son (in Chapter 15, Vengeance and Forgiveness)
- The Rags-to-Riches figure (in Chapter 16, Industry and Idleness)
- The Gambler (in Chapter 17, Greed, Gluttony, and Generosity)

The book's art program (described in detail below) extends the discussion of each literary archetype into the visual realm.

Concise Writing Instruction

We believe that students improve their analytical writing skills by engaging deeply with varied works of literature and by writing and revising their own essays. The eleven rhetorical chapters in *Connections* (Parts 1–3, Chapters 1–11) are written in a brief, practical, student-friendly style that emphasizes key skills and terms that students will find useful in this and later courses. Because instructors emphasize composition and literary analysis to varying degrees, these rhetorical sections are flexible. They do not have to be assigned in order.

- **Part I, Reading, Writing, and Argument (Chapters 1–3):** The first three rhetorical chapters introduce central concepts for reading, interpreting, writing, and constructing an argument.
- **Part II, Reading and Writing about Literary Genres (Chapters 4–8):** The next five chapters provide helpful vocabulary and ideas on reading and writing about fiction, poetry, drama, essays, and film.
- **Part III, Critical Strategies for Research (Chapters 9–11):** The final three rhetorical chapters look at critical approaches to literature and writing the research paper, with a step-by-step walkthrough of the research process.

Authentic Student Essays

Student essays appear throughout the rhetorical chapters (Parts 1–3, Chapters 1–11), with accompanying profiles and photos of each writer. These essays help students to prepare for peer review and demonstrate how students might incorporate important elements of writing such as thesis, evidence, and argument into their own writing.

Innovative Art Program

The art program in *Connections* goes beyond the usual offerings of artworks that were created in response to specific writings or pieces that were written in response to specific artworks. The striking and memorable art images in *Connections* instead aim to be

- open to various interpretations,
- good for stimulating discussion in class,
- a combination of familiar and unfamiliar works,
- well-supported by artist profiles, art history background, and study questions; and
- illuminating to the literary themes and recurring archetypes under consideration.

Connections is arranged to help students discover relevant, meaningful links among the collected short stories, poems, plays, essays, and visuals and between what they read and what they already know.

Connections' Approach to Better Discussion and Better Student Writing

Throughout its selections, rhetorical chapters, and supporting pedagogy, *Connections* helps students to see that literature is not static. One of the great pleasures of reading literature is its unfixed, open-ended quality. As we have all experienced, the meaning of a play or a work of fiction can change or deepen with time, especially when a familiar selection is set in a new and unexpected context. It can shift because of a discussion with a friend, the reading of a perceptive work of criticism, or an alteration in life's circumstances. Meaning evolves and develops as each reader considers the selection in the light of individual experiences and perspectives.

In *Connections*, students are urged to see that literature's ambiguity and openness to interpretation make it enjoyable and relevant to their deepest concerns. It is not, as students sometimes think, a maddening puzzle with one "right" solution or a simplified, binary realm that is inhabited by characters who are either good or bad, honest or deceptive, obedient or rebellious. *Connections* encourages students to grapple with the literature as they read, as they participate in class discussions, and as they work on their own writing. It is designed to help students find their voices and extend their already considerable interpretive and persuasive abilities.

Additional Resources for the Instructor

Connections' *Online Instructor's Resource Manual*

Designed and written for maximum helpfulness to busy instructors, the Online Instructor's Resource Manual offers the following for each literary selection:

- an extended author biography,
- discussion approaches and classroom tips,
- links to author podcasts with *teaching tips* and discussion *talking points*,
- critical reactions and controversies,
- additional discussion questions and prompts,
- related content (from other thematic units and from the visual art program),
- additional assignments (journal, quiz, and exam or essay assignments),
- print, film, and media resources, and
- a bibliography of key works of criticism.

Instructors' Website with Live Literary Links

The Instructors' Website lists film and stage adaptations, songs, shows, audio clips, and poetry readings, time lines, and other resources for the instructor. It is available at <college.hmco.com/pic/miller>.

Additional Resources for Your Students

Help your students hear, see, and interact with current authors using the following online resources, available at the Student Website, <college.hmco.com/pic/miller>:

- **Author podcasts**
- **The Poetic Voice:** Listen to poets like Michel Collier, Ron Slate, and current poet laureate Donald Hall as they read and discuss their own works on Houghton Mifflin's podcast The Poetic Voice, available at <http://www.houghtonmifflinbooks.com/features/poetry/poeticvoice>.
- **Meet the Authors:** Hear authors read selections from current fiction and nonfiction works and discuss their work and the creative process on Meet the Authors, available at <http://www.houghtonmifflinbooks.com/audio>.
- **Video Section:** Watch award-winning authors like Jhumpa Lahiri (winner of the 2000 Pulitzer Prize for her story collection *Interpreter of Maladies*) and Jonathan Safran Foer (finalist for the *Los Angeles Times*'s 2003 Art Seidenbaum Award for First Fiction for *Everything Is Illuminated*) read from and discuss their new books in Video Section, available at <http://www.houghtonmifflinbooks.com/audio/#video>.
- **Discussion Forums:** Ask questions and engage in dialogue with authors at the Discussion Forums site, available at <http://www.houghtonmifflinbooks.com/forums/index.jspa>.
- **Reader's Guides:** Discuss books, join an online reading group, or find additional works to read. Reader's Guides (in the categories of Featured, Fiction, and Nonfiction) provide discussion questions for each book as well as recommended further readings. The Reader's Guides are available at <http://www.houghtonmifflinbooks.com/readers_guides>.

You Choose

With *Connections*, choose one or any of the following at a discount packaged price:

Shakespeare plays For qualified adopters, any play by Shakespeare (in an edition drawn from *The Riverside Shakespeare*) can be added or substituted for the Shakespeare play that appears in *Connections: The First Part of Henry the Fourth*. Please speak to your sales representative or custom publishing editor.

Other suggested trade titles Other books by well-known Houghton Mifflin authors are also available for packaging at a discount. Reader's Guides are available for the following works and others. See <http://www.houghtonmifflinbooks.com/readers_guides/fiction.shtml>.

- Penelope Fitzgerald, *The Blue Flower*
- Penelope Fitzgerald, *The Bookshop*
- Jonathan Safran Foer, *Everything Is Illuminated*
- Jonathan Safran Foer, *Extremely Loud and Incredibly Close*
- Jhumpa Lahiri, *Interpreter of Maladies*
- Jhumpa Lahiri, *The Namesake*
- Carson McCullers, *The Heart Is a Lonely Hunter*
- Carson McCullers, *The Member of the Wedding*

***Blue Pills: A Positive Love Story* by Frederik Peeters (2007) (a graphic novel)** Selling over twenty thousand copies in France, this graphic novel by Frederik Peeters was called a "tour-de-force" by *Indy Magazine* and a "visual representation of the process of coping and adjusting that ranks among the best comics published anywhere in the world in the past few years."

The Best American Short Stories* and *The Best American Essays The top-selling Best American series allows you to bring timely and cutting-edge examples of genres covered in *Connections*. See, for example, the following:

- *The Best American Essays 2007*, edited by David Foster Wallace and Robert Atwan (contains support pedagogy)
- *The Best American Short Stories 2007*, edited by Stephen King and Heidi Pitlor

For more information about other titles in the Best American series, please contact your sales representative or visit <http://www.houghtonmifflinbooks.com>.

Acknowledgments

We extend our grateful thanks to the following colleagues who reviewed the manuscript at many stages and gave us invaluable feedback and advice:

Mark L. Amdahl, Montgomery County Community College
Clinton P. E. Atchley, Henderson State University
Lynnette Beers, Santiago Canyon College
B. Cole Bennett, Abilene Christian University
Robin W. Bryant, Phillips Community College of the University of Arkansas
Sharon Buzzard, Quincy University
Robert Cummings, University of Georgia
Bryan P. Davis, Georgia Southwestern State University
Christy Desmet, University of Georgia
Sarah H. Dustin, Florida Gulf Coast University
Monika Elbert, Montclair State University

Stacy Erickson Bourns, University of North Texas
Gayle L. Fornataro, Los Angeles Valley College
Linda G. Foss, Centralia College
Karen Gaffney, Raritan Valley Community College
Roy Neil Graves, University of Tennessee at Martin
Bill Hardwig, University of Tennessee
Curtis Harrell, NorthWest Arkansas Community College
Lee Harrison, Houston Community College Southwest
Elizabeth Howells, Armstrong Atlantic State University
Richard Kaplan, Harper College
Kelly Martin, Collin County Community College
Jim McKeown, McLennan Community College
Gerri McNenny, Chapman University
Alan Mitnick, Passaic County Community College
Jane Mushabac, New York City College of Technology, CUNY
John B. Padgett, Brevard College
Ann Reh, De Anza College
David Rollison, College of Marin
Tom Speer, Pima Community College
Frances Stallworth, Florida A&M University Tallahassee
Chris C. Stead, University of Mississippi
Jessica Lyn Van Slooten, State University of West Georgia
James G. Van Belle, Edmonds Community College
Anne K. Weed, Keuka College
Margaret Whitt, University of Denver
Susan Dara Wright, Montclair and William Paterson Universities

It has been a pleasure to work with the editorial and production team at Houghton Mifflin. Their enthusiasm for this project has been contagious, and their attention to detail and quality shows throughout each chapter. We would like to thank Pat Coryell, Carrie Brandon, Joann Kozyrev, Lisa Kimball, Michael Gillespie, Tom Ziolkowski, Bettina Chiu, Bruce Cantley, Katilyn Crowley, Daisuke Yasutake, Greg Fulchino, Kamali Thornell, Marsha Nourse, Ania Wieckowski, Maura Coughlin, Andrew Laskey, Anne Schroeder, Mary Dalton Hoffman, George McLean, Susan Zorn, Mary Kanable, Deborah Prato, and Bernice Eisen, and in particular, Martha Bustin and Rosemary Winfield. For her tremendous work assisting us with the preparation of the Instructor's Resource Manual, Margaret Toth deserves all the gratitude we can offer.

We are fortunate to work with talented and professional colleagues whose informal and formal discussions of teaching writing have been invaluable. We offer our thanks to the English departments at Suffolk University and the University of Massachusetts Lowell, especially to our department chairs, Anthony Merzlak and Melissa Pennell.

Special thanks for their insights into writing pedagogy and their suggestions for this text go to Paula Haines, Susan Kirtley, Marlowe Miller, Anthony Szczesiul, and Gigi Thibodeau at the University of Massachusetts at Lowell and to

Rich Miller, Brian Trabold, Lisa Celovsky, Jennie Barber, Fred Marchant, and Tom Connolly at Suffolk.

In addition, we would like to thank our writing students: their energy, curiosity, and intelligence inspired this book. We tested many of these selections on them, and their feedback helped shape the anthology for the better. We would especially like to thank the students who agreed to write essays for this volume: Sarah Himberger, Darryl Holliday, Lacey Perkins, George Scala, Kristin Seabolt, and Jinyeda Tapia.

We are also grateful for the support of our families, especially Robert and Sylvia Miller and Paul and Kathy Nash.

Finally, this book is dedicated with love to our children, Brennan and Owen Miller, the most important "connections" we'll ever make.

Quentin Miller, Suffolk University
Julie Nash, University of Massachusetts Lowell

CONNECTIONS

Literature for Composition

Part 1

Reading, Writing, and Argument

Chapter 1

Reading Literature

Only connect.
—E. M. Forster, *Howard's End* (1910)

Thinking Critically about Human Nature

Human beings define themselves as animals that laugh, cry, think, and remember. We try to distinguish ourselves from other animals by focusing on our special abilities. Perhaps we are humans partly because we have this ability to distinguish or define ourselves. As a species we have done an awful lot of defining in our attempts to understand our place in the mysterious universe. In the scientific classification of genus and species, we are *Homo sapiens*, or "knowing humans."

Literature is perhaps the most complex form of the endless process of defining what is human. We study literature largely because it reveals the intricacies of human nature. Why do people behave the way they do? Psychologists try to answer this question by studying behavior patterns, dreams, and events from childhood that lodge in people's memories. Sociologists might look at social forces like the effects of being crowded or of witnessing violence. Historians are likely to view human behavior as the product of broad movements such as political revolutions that sometimes overshadow the individual's ability to control his or her behavior. All of these approaches are valid, and in all of them we are constantly searching for new or compelling explanations.

Literary scholars and critics are also searching, but they work in different realms: the realm of language and the realm of the imagination. Although the literary imagination can invent worlds that do not include people, it is always concerned with some form of human behavior. For example, though there may be no direct evidence of humanity in a poem describing a flower garden, our perception of the poem raises questions that have to do with human nature: Why is the person describing the garden so interested in these flowers? Who was the gardener who planted and tended them? What is the reader's response to the language used to describe these flowers? The literary imagination always deals with humanity, and it does so through the medium of written language.

Communication through language takes many forms. An e-mail message might contain incomplete sentences, unconventional spellings, or even little punctuation marks that express emotion. A newspaper article usually contains quotations from some source. Even blunt means of communication have different conventions that distinguish them. We wouldn't trust a newspaper article that relied on emoticons in place of quotations.

One basic distinction is between spoken and written language. Spoken language can reveal as much about humanity as can written language. We tell stories daily ("You wouldn't believe what just happened to me!"), and we know that shouting, whispering, or swearing can have different effects on the listener. Like written language, spoken language follows certain conventions, and it can also become art, something more than strict communication. Singing and rapping, for instance, exploit some of the sound qualities of language to do more than simply communicate an idea.

Although verbal communication can be studied as literature, *literature* generally refers to written texts that can be interpreted in various ways. Literature is especially worthy of our attention because it is both a form of communication and an art form. Unlike speech, it also has a visual appeal because it produces an artifact: something tangible. You're holding it in your hands: a bundle of paper with ink impressions. The creation of paper and ink is an achievement that might be easy to overlook. Perhaps we should say that humans are animals that write and read literature—no monkey would argue with that.

Although literature always deals with human behavior, some writers deny that they are explaining anything, insisting that they're "only telling a story." The reader of literature, however, generally wants to learn something when she sits down with a book, even if her primary intention is to enjoy a good story. The author's intention takes a back seat to the reader's desire to derive *meaning* from a text. The Greek writer and philosopher Aristotle (384–322 BCE) once claimed that literature had two functions: to delight and to instruct. This has been a surprisingly enduring definition.

Literature has the capacity to be enjoyable and instructive at the same time. It can also instruct differently to different groups of readers or even to different individual readers. At various points throughout history and in various cultures, literature has attempted to teach readers a strictly defined moral system: behave this way and you are good, behave that way and you are bad. Literature that intends to teach a specific lesson is called **didactic.**

However, even didactic literature can be ambiguous. For example, Satan in John Milton's epic poem *Paradise Lost* is clearly the villain, yet many readers find him the most attractive and fully developed character in the poem. In Mark Twain's *Adventures of Huckleberry Finn*, the title character Huck deliberates long and hard about saving the life of the escaped slave Jim. Knowing he will be condemned by the slave-owning society in which he was raised, Huck proclaims, "All right, then, I'll go to hell!" and makes a decision that elevates him in the eyes of readers who are opposed to slavery. Hell and heaven, right and wrong, and vice and virtue are not clear-cut concepts in many works of literature.

Perhaps the most important way that literature teaches morality is by allowing us to make connections to other times and places. In "A Defense of Poetry," the Romantic poet Percy Bysshe Shelley wrote that "a man, to be greatly good, must imagine intensely and comprehensively; he must put himself in the place of another and of many others. . . . The great instrument of moral good is the imagination." The American South of *Huckleberry Finn* is a place we can only imagine, yet in Shelley's view our ability to imagine it and to connect with those who lived there makes us better people. Many of us have faced a crisis of conscience in which we have found ourselves questioning the values of the majority. We may not have to worry about betraying our friends into slavery, but we still connect with Huck because we've struggled with our own moral dilemmas. The literature in this anthology represents a wide variety of writers from different historical periods, countries, and backgrounds. Yet the so-called vices and virtues featured in this book are universal, as likely to be found in Restoration England as in contemporary China.

When Huck rejects the values of his society in favor of his own reasoned conclusions about right and wrong, he is thinking critically about the world around him. He has weighed the opinions of those who support slavery (including the opinions of people whom he loves and respects) against his own instinctive understanding that owning a fellow human being is morally wrong. Contemporary readers tend to cheer for Huck as he chooses the more difficult path for himself because they agree with his conclusions. Yet Huck does not congratulate himself. He is conflicted about his decision even to the point of believing that he will be damned for it. What readers see as a virtue in Huck (respecting the humanity of his friend as well as his own conscience) is viewed as a vice (disobedience) by his society. Through Huckleberry Finn, Mark Twain demonstrates that critical thinking—especially about matters of vice and virtue—can be difficult, frustrating, and even frightening at times. Yet the thought of living in a world in which we lack the ability to analyze and question ideas and information is even more frightening.

In a somewhat different manner, you will also engage in critical thinking as you read the literature in this text. *Critical thinking* involves thinking processes that go beyond mere recall. You read for *knowledge*, and then to think critically about a work of literature, you also read for *understanding;* finally, you must be able to *apply* what you have read to other situations. In his essay "The American Scholar," Ralph Waldo Emerson writes, "One must be an inventor to read well." The "invention" he alludes to involves the creation of new ideas inspired by the ones evident in the reading. To become an inventor in this way, you will exercise some of the "higher-order" critical thinking skills described by Benjamin Bloom in his classification of the types of thinking used in education: analysis, synthesis, and evaluation.

- *Analysis* calls on the thinker or reader to identify patterns, to understand the elements that constitute the patterns, and to recognize the meanings that might make sense of the patterns.

- *Synthesis* calls on the reader or thinker to bring together several areas of knowledge, to relate general ideas with specific ideas, and to draw conclusions through prediction or speculation.
- *Evaluation* might involve comparing ideas, assessing theories, developing a thesis based on a logical argument, or recognizing one's subjective perspective weighed against the perspectives of others.

All of these skills combine to allow critical thinkers to *interpret* literature. Chapters 2 through 9 build on this brief definition of critical thinking, and the questions following each literary selection in Chapters 12 through 17 can lead to critical thinking about literature.

The literature in this anthology seeks to present readers with complex representations of human behavior. As humans, we are involved in a constant battle between what our instinct (our animal side) tells us to do and the ways in which our wisdom (our human side) attempts to control those instincts. Literature allows these two sides to confront one another by prompting us to feel and think at the same time. The best literature does not seek to understand humanity by simply rewarding "good" characters and punishing "bad" characters. Rather, it shows humans struggling through language and with language, allowing readers to arrive at bold, complex interpretations of human nature. The seventeenth-century British philosopher John Locke once wrote that "reading furnishes the mind only with materials for knowledge; it is thinking that makes what we read ours." As you read the literature in this anthology, you can make it yours by thinking critically about its language, its characters, and its ideas.

Animal Nature: Reading Allegories

People cry, laugh, or write and read literature partly because they are animals—animals with big cerebral cortexes and opposable thumbs, but animals nonetheless. We often behave for the same reasons animals behave: we fight over territory, for instance, or we lash out when we feel cornered. Think of all the phrases that describe humans through analogies to animals: *sly like a fox*, *lionhearted*, *dirty rat*, and *lazy as a dog*. Now think of all of the stories about animals you've read from a young age. Your first picture books probably were about bunnies and cats, not people. You heard about Chicken Little, the gullible chick who thought the sky was falling, and you learned that the steady, plodding tortoise, not the fast, overconfident hare, would win the race. You developed the skill to recognize and be afraid of a wolf in sheep's clothing, a wolf trying to blow your house down, or a wolf disguised as a grandmother.

Children's stories—and occasionally adults' stories, too—reveal our animal nature by turning animals into characters. A story in which all the characters are animals who reveal human attributes is a type of **allegory,** a story in which every character and every action is meant to represent something else. Allegory relies heavily on **metaphor**—a figure of speech that associates qualities of one thing with another—and allows the meaning of the metaphor to evolve through the course of a story, or **narrative.**

An allegory often functions as a kind of **satire,** a mode of literature that attempts to expose and weaken a powerful and corrupt institution. George Orwell's novel *Animal Farm*, for instance, is an allegory of the Russian revolution. Art Speigelman's graphic novel *Maus* is an allegory describing the Nazi regime in Germany. These allegories are part of a literary tradition known as the beast epic, which in medieval Europe was used to satirize the church and the court and among African Americans in the nineteenth century was used to satirize slave owners who were unaware of the cleverness of their slaves.

Many readers are familiar with Aesop, the Greek writer who in his fables used animals to describe human nature. In these stories, foxes and crows or ants and grasshoppers act out dramas that carry lessons for humans. In case the reader or listener didn't get it, the lesson is spelled out as "the **moral** of the story." Unlike Aesop's fables, sophisticated stories usually do not supply their own morals—that's the reader's job—and if they did, most readers would probably resent the authors. Readers might want to be instructed somehow while they are being delighted; however, they probably do not want that instruction to be overbearing.

We begin our inquiry into human nature with a fable written by American satirist Mark Twain (1835–1910), a complex allegory of human nature that introduces the process of reading and interpretation in its "moral."

Mark Twain *(1835–1910)*

A Fable

Once upon a time an artist who had painted a small and very beautiful picture placed it so that he could see it in the mirror. He said, "This doubles the distance and softens it, and it is twice as lovely as it was before."

The animals out in the woods heard of this through the housecat, who was greatly admired by them because he was so learned, and so refined and civilized, and so polite and high-bred, and could tell them so much which they didn't know before, and were not certain about afterward. They were much excited about this new piece of gossip, and they asked questions, so as to get at a full understanding of it. They asked what a picture was, and the cat explained.

"It is a flat thing," he said; "wonderfully flat, marvelously flat, enchantingly flat and elegant. And, oh, so beautiful!"

That excited them almost to a frenzy, and they said they would give the world to see it. Then the bear asked:

"What is it that makes it so beautiful?" 5

"It is the looks of it," said the cat.

This filled them with admiration and uncertainty, and they were more excited than ever. Then the cow asked:

"What is a mirror?"

"It is a hole in the wall," said the cat. "You look in it, and there you see the picture, and it is so dainty and charming and ethereal and inspiring in its unimaginable beauty that your head turns round and round, and you almost swoon with ecstasy."

10 The ass had not said anything as yet; he now began to throw doubts. He said there had never been anything as beautiful as this before, and probably wasn't now. He said that when it took a whole basketful of sesquipedalian adjectives to whoop up a thing of beauty, it was time for suspicion.

It was easy to see that these doubts were having an effect upon the animals, so the cat went off offended. The subject was dropped for a couple of days, but in the meantime curiosity was taking a fresh start, and there was a revival of interest perceptible. Then the animals assailed the ass for spoiling what could possibly have been a pleasure to them, on a mere suspicion that the picture was not beautiful, without any evidence that such was the case. The ass was not troubled; he was calm, and said there was one way to find out who was in the right, himself or the cat: he would go and look in that hole, and come back and tell what he found there. The animals felt relieved and grateful, and asked him to go at once—which he did.

But he did not know where he ought to stand; and so, through error, he stood between the picture and the mirror. The result was that the picture had no chance, and didn't show up. He returned home and said:

"The cat lied. There was nothing in that hole but an ass. There wasn't a sign of a flat thing visible. It was handsome ass, and friendly, but just an ass, and nothing more."

The elephant asked:

15 "Did you see it good and clear? Were you close to it?"

"I saw it good and clear, O Hathi, King of Beasts. I was so close that I touched noses with it."

"This is very strange," said the elephant; "the cat was always truthful before—as far as we could make out. Let another witness try. Go, Baloo, look in the hole, and come and report."

So the bear went. When he came back, he said:

"Both the cat and the ass have lied; there was nothing in the hole but a bear."

20 Great was the surprise and puzzlement of the animals. Each was now anxious to make the test himself and get at the straight truth. The elephant sent them one at a time.

First, the cow. She found nothing in the hole but a cow.

The tiger found nothing in it but a tiger.

The lion found nothing in it but a lion.

The leopard found nothing in it but a leopard.

25 The camel found a camel, and nothing more.

Then Hathi was wroth, and said he would have the truth, if he had to go and fetch it himself. When he returned, he abused his whole subjectry for liars, and was in an unappeasable fury with the moral and mental blindness of the cat. He said that anybody but a near-sighted fool could see that there was nothing in the hole but an elephant.

Moral, by the Cat

You can find in a text whatever you bring, if you will stand between it and the mirror of your imagination. You may not see your ears, but they will be there.

(1909)

At first glance, Twain's fable sounds like many fables you've probably read before: it's about animals, it begins with "Once upon a time," and it ends with a moral. Yet this brilliant little tale can help to make us more aware of the process of reading and interpreting literature. The story begins with an artist, presumably a human artist, who paints a picture and puts a mirror across from it. Twain might be playing with an ancient definition of literature, reiterated by Prince Hamlet in Shakespeare's famous play *Hamlet, Prince of Denmark*, when the prince entreats actors to "hold up a mirror to nature" (III.iii.20). The artist in Twain's story creates art—holding up a mirror to nature—and then complicates his project by holding up a mirror to art.

Anish Kapoor, *Sky Mirror* (2001).

The artist disappears from the story and never returns. However, the mirror that he has placed across from his art causes a crisis of interpretation. The story is not about the artist; it is about what happens to his art when others regard it or, in this case, fail to regard it. The animals never get to see the artwork because they see only themselves in the mirror. The situation produces a crisis because none of the animals sees the same thing and they can't figure out why they all have such different interpretations of what they saw.

The animals in this story are much the same, except for three: the ass, who casts doubt on the housecat's wisdom; the elephant, who has the power to command others to arrive at interpretations before he does; and the housecat, who defines pictures and mirrors in the beginning and supplies the moral at the end. The cat has a special status, one of power and wisdom. We aren't sure that Twain's narrator admires the cat all that much, though. The cat, he says, "was greatly admired by them because he was so learned, and so refined and civilized, and so polite and high-bred, and could tell them so much which they didn't know before, and were not certain about afterward." The cat, in other words, is full of it: we can tell because he defines a painting as "a flat thing" and a mirror as "a hole in the wall." If we read the story as an allegory, the cat is clearly a critic. Twain may be blaming his readers (the other animals in the fable) for initially believing what the cat/critic has to say and further faulting them for not seeing an artwork directly because they are so wrapped up in themselves.

Although Twain doesn't necessarily like the cat/critic, he doesn't fault him either. The cat is given the last word, and the language of the moral is sufficiently complicated to make the reader raise questions. First, why does the cat get to supply the moral? Imagine if another character were allowed to supply the moral or meaning of the story:

Moral, by the artist: If you show people a mirror, they'll never look at your work.

Moral, by the ass: Never trust someone else to tell you about something you could see for yourself.

Moral, by the elephant: If you want something done right, do it yourself.

Moral, by Mark Twain: Animals have no business looking at human art.

The cat, however, provides a startling perspective. Let's take it one sentence at a time:

> "You can find in a text whatever you bring, if you will stand between it and the mirror of your imagination."

We refer to works of literature as texts throughout this book. The word *text* has a number of connotations, most of which involve printed words on a page. Today, many objects that are not strictly literary—such as photographs, television shows, and speech acts—are regarded as "texts" that can be "read." Chapter 8 of this book offers instruction about "reading" film. Twain's cat, though, is using the common 1909 definition of *text* as writing and is indicating that the text in the story—the mirror—is meant on some level to represent a piece of writing. We might assume that the text should be the painting, not the mirror, but the animals never see the painting.

The first part of the first sentence of the cat's moral sounds positive: "You can find in a text whatever you bring." This sounds like another way of saying that different readers will bring different perspectives to a work of literature and that they will all see something different in it. On some level, readers want to believe that is true: you might read a poem differently from the person sitting next to you in class. You might conclude that everyone sees what they want to see in literature and that all interpretations are equally valid.

However, the second part of the cat's sentence implies that the animals' interpretations are closed-minded: "if you will stand between [the text] and the mirror of your imagination." The text is still the mirror. The imagination must be the painting. The mirror is reality; the work of art is the imagination. If we follow that logic, the cat's moral means something like this: if all we can see in a text is ourselves, we have blinded ourselves to the beauty of the text *and* to our own imagination. Reality is flat and boring without the benefits of art and the imagination.

You can continue to pursue the implications of this interpretation of the first sentence of the moral individually or in class. We have two additional questions to ask as you do so:

1. What are the implications of the fact that this moral is delivered by the cat, a character who is separated from the others by his breeding and refinement and whose definitions are seen to be either inadequate ("a painting is a flat thing") or wrong ("a mirror is a hole in the wall")?
2. What might be meant by the second sentence of the cat's moral: "You may not see your ears, but they will be there"? Consider the relationship between seeing and hearing as they pertain to this story.

Twain's story is entertaining, challenging, puzzling, and complex. We aimed to show the following in our reading of Twain's story:

- Multiple morals are possible, depending on one's perspective. When you read, you presumably have a perspective, determined partially by the way you think and partially by the text itself. However, you might be surprised to find that your perspective is not constant.
- Morals are not stable. Morals represent wisdom, and wisdom varies with experience. It is far too easy to assume that a moral of a story (or a commandment or a law) is true and that it can be applied to every situation in life. Think of the precept that killing a person is wrong. What if you had the opportunity to prevent a mass murder by killing the mass murderer? Literature does not always package up conventional wisdom as a pill that readers can easily swallow, and neither does it always aim to subvert conventional wisdom. It offers any number of messages.
- We should be somewhat suspicious of what we find in texts, since they contain both wisdom and the potential for deception. Literature sometimes delights in

misleading readers by providing false clues or emphases. The best way to approach texts is to be both the cat and the ass: someone who is confident to define and understand something but also someone who is skeptical of how others define it.

The Nature of Reading

> Ts'ui Pe must have said once: "I am withdrawing to write a book." And another time: "I am withdrawing to construct a labyrinth." Every one imagined two works; to no one did it occur that the book and the maze were one and the same thing.
> —JORGE LUIS BORGES, "*The Garden of Forking Paths*" (1944)

"A Fable" by Mark Twain is the only story in this book that contains "a moral" at the end, ambiguous or otherwise. Most literature puts the reader in charge of defining the meaning of a work. However, the goal of interpretation is only partially to discover and summarize a meaning, a theme, or the essence of a text's "message." Literature is more than a crossword puzzle, and we can never assume that it requires a single, stable solution. When we read literature, we are encouraged to do something unlike what we do when we undertake most other intellectual tasks: we are encouraged to understand more than one thing at the same time.

In his 1938 essay "Poetry: A Note on Ontology," the poet and critic John Crowe Ransom writes, "The definition which some writers have given to art is: the reference of the idea to the image." Literature might be better defined as "a web of references connecting many ideas to many images." Picture yourself lounging in the grass on a sunny day. You focus on an ant climbing up a blade of grass. Yet somewhere in your field of vision you see tree branches bending in the wind, and beyond that a cloud moving across the sky. These are three distinct images, all characterized by motion. You could distill many ideas at the same time from this web of images—the instinctive struggle of the ant, the graceful resistance of the tree branches, the gentle indifference of the cloud—all of which might help you to define your mood on this sunny day. Similarly, in reading literature, although you may be able to focus on only one of the images or ideas at any given time, the others are all there, and they all contribute in some way to your "reading" of the scene.

You have already been trained to do certain things when you read literature: to search for something deep, something abstract, or something not entirely obvious. Whether or not you find what you were searching for, the point is that you have searched. Reading literature becomes a kind of quest. A good way to think of this quest is through a metaphor employed by the Argentine fiction writer Jorge Luis Borges, who wrote of literature as "a garden of forking paths." Too often readers treat literature like algebra and assume the problem has a single right answer. Literature invites you to search for something, but maybe not for *x*.

"Fine," you might say, "but how do I know what I'm looking for?" That's an excellent question. Every work of literature is unique. To approach all literature in search of the same thing is to deny that uniqueness. Your goal in college literature courses is to become somewhat flexible and supple as a reader. You accomplish that flexibility by listening carefully to what a work of literature has to say while at the same time questioning what it is saying. The nature of reading involves the mixture of these two roles: listener and questioner. You might do well to remember what it was like to be a five-year-old approaching a simple text: "sounding out" certain aspects that don't make sense (by underlining phrases, looking up words in a dictionary, rereading, and so forth) and recognizing others that seem familiar. Although your mind and the texts you encounter are more complex, the process is parallel. In a sense, we are always learning how to read.

The following poem, "Woman" by Nikki Giovanni (b. 1943), compares a woman and a man to a number of things in nature. The speaker also compares the woman to one artificial thing—a book. This kind of comparison is a literary *convention.* Different **genres,** or categories of literature, emphasize different conventions as a way of communicating their meaning. These conventions are discussed at length in the chapters on writing about fiction, poetry, drama, and essays, the four main genres covered in this book. The genre of poetry often emphasizes **figurative language,** the type of language that compares one thing to another directly (**metaphor**) or indirectly by using the word *like* (**simile;** see Chapter 5). As you read through the poem, contemplate what the comparisons tell you and whether they all tell you the same thing.

Nikki Giovanni *(b. 1943)*

Woman

she wanted to be a blade
of grass amid the fields
but he wouldn't agree
to be the dandelion

she wanted to be a robin singing
through the leaves
but he refused to be
her tree

she spun herself into a web
and looking for a place to rest
turned to him
but he stood straight
declining to be her corner

she tried to be a book
but he wouldn't read

she turned herself into a bulb
but he wouldn't let her grow

she decided to become
a woman
and though he still refused

to be a man
she decided it was all
right

(1978)

As noted earlier, children's stories often use animals to signify some human characteristic. Many poems written by and for adults attempt to understand how humans fit into nature's patterns. Nature is the source of life and death. It can devastate us with its power and comfort us with its beauty. Poets frequently turn to nature for *inspiration*, a word that means "to breathe life into." In "Woman," the poet's imagination is inspired by certain relationships in nature. These relationships are then used to explain something about the nature of a woman and a man.

Reading this poem involves understanding Giovanni's "point" about a man and a woman. The poem clearly has to do with the relationship between them, and we might conclude that men are stubborn and women should be self-reliant. The man resists the woman in every **stanza** (grouping of lines; see Chapter 5) of this poem, signified by the repetition of the word *but*. The formula is relatively simple: the woman wants something, but the man refuses. The rhythm of this formula is consistent. Except for the final stanza, each stanza seems to follow it: *she wanted . . . , but he wouldn't . . .* The poem, you might conclude, is about male resistance to female desires. In the end, she decides to be who she is despite who he is.

Although this explanation may seem satisfactory, reading involves a more careful examination of the words on the page and their potential meanings. All literature, and especially poetry, challenges you to read closely, noting patterns and the potential for language to slip, for meaning to become unstable. Though some complain that professors and some students are "reading too much into" a work of literature, it may not be possible to "read too much into" something, provided that the reading can be substantiated with evidence. It may be worse to read a work too superficially.

The assumption that "Woman" is about how a man suppresses a woman's desires holds for the first two stanzas:

> she wanted to be a blade
> of grass amid the fields
> but he wouldn't agree
> to be the dandelion

she wanted to be a robin singing
through the leaves
but he refused to be
her tree

In both of these stanzas, the man is associated with something in nature that stands tall, relative to the things around it. We might assume that the speaker is saying that men should be strong. Is a dandelion *strong?* It's stubborn, as anyone knows who has tried to pull one up by the root, but it is not conventionally strong. Also, consider what the relationship is between the dandelion and the blade of grass in the first stanza. In what way does the blade of grass depend on the dandelion? A robin that wants to sing through leaves needs a tree; however, in what way does grass need a dandelion? And can we assume that if the man refuses to be the dandelion, then he is also a blade of grass? We know only that he refuses to change. We might question whether a woman should demand that he change: a blade of grass cannot become a dandelion.

In the third stanza the woman actually does something: "she spun herself into a web" (line 9). The man in this stanza stands straight instead of being her corner. This is a tough pair of images: the man is clearly inflexible and denies the woman's desire, again. We are asking deeper questions of the poem now: How is it that the woman has the capacity for endless change? Or does she? And why does she feel that she needs him? Or does she? She has already spun herself into a web despite the fact that he doesn't become a corner to accommodate her. She could find another corner. Maybe it wasn't wise of her to spin herself into a web before she had found an appropriate corner.

The fourth stanza is unique because the woman is not compared to something from nature: "she tried to be a book / but he wouldn't read." What's interesting here is the man's degree of stubbornness: not only would he not read *her*, but he wouldn't read at all. And it is not that he *couldn't* read. The other noteworthy word is *tried.* Is the implication that she tried but failed to become a book? A book depends directly on its readers. Here we are sure what the relationship is between the man and the woman: she depends on him for her meaning. This is not true in the other stanzas.

The fifth stanza, like the third, showcases the woman's action: "she turned herself into a bulb." This is plant imagery, as in the first two stanzas. However, here the male character simply "wouldn't let her grow." The reader should ask a new question: who is the more powerful character? In the first four stanzas, the male character simply refuses to agree to change: "he wouldn't agree" (3), "he refused" (7), "declining to be" (13), "he wouldn't read" (15). His actions are all responses to hers; she is the active one: "she wanted" (1), "she wanted" (5), "she spun" (9), "she tried" (14), "she turned herself into a bulb" (16). In the fifth stanza, his action is much more aggressive and more sinister: "he wouldn't let her grow." How does he achieve this kind of power? In what way can he prevent her growth? The speaker of the poem pointedly does not tell us *how* he prevents her from growing. We are left to question the image itself: is there anything that can prevent a bulb from growing?

Bulbs are both the seed and the root of certain plants, like tulips or onions. Once they are planted in the ground, they need only water to live: they thrust up out of the dirt toward the light of their own accord. Several things could prevent them from growing: a rock could be placed above them, their water supply could be cut off, or they could never be placed in the ground in the first place. In any of these cases, preventing a bulb from growing is akin to preventing it from living. The image of the fifth stanza, then, is the least detailed and the most violent. The poet does not say "she turned herself into a bulb / but he became a rock and placed himself over her so she couldn't grow." Nor does she say, "she turned herself into a bulb / but he left her in the basement unplanted so she couldn't grow." Here the reader must put together associations to come up with a possible interpretation.

In the poem's final stanza, the woman again takes action: she decides to become a woman (18–19), and she also decides that it is all right that the man refuses to become a man (20–23). The original interpretation we advanced—that she has desires and that he is too stubborn to accommodate them—still holds. However, given what we have noticed about the fifth stanza—that he has the power to prevent her growth—does the poem suggest that it is "all right" because the woman has decided she doesn't depend on the man or because she has escaped his deadly power? Or are her final decisions tantamount to her giving up? In other words, has she simply resigned herself to her destiny? In this interpretation, she has given up her desire to be something lively and beautiful, like a robin singing or a blade of grass.

We originally suggested that the man is stubborn: he refuses to change to accommodate the woman's desires. Our closer reading discovered that he is more threatening than stubborn: he refuses to let her grow. Both readings render him dishonorable, and the poem's title "Woman" encourages us to focus on her rather than on him. The poem also begins and ends with her perspective. What has she learned over the course of the poem?

1. That a woman can be fulfilled even if her man won't change?
2. That a woman should give up her hopes to become something other than a woman?
3. That people can change themselves more easily than they can change others?
4. All of the above?

The nature of reading makes us want to choose 1, 2, or 3, but the nature of literature usually leads in the direction of 4: all of the above. Using Borges's metaphor, we could go down many paths, so the reader must make conscious choices to arrive at a unified interpretation (see Chapter 3 on argument). However, we need to recognize that we are making choices.

In the tentative interpretation above, we chose to emphasize the fifth stanza about the bulb that is not allowed to grow. We did not focus on lines 20 and 21, which contain the curious phrase "he still refused / to be a man," implying that he had been refusing to be a man for a long time. Perhaps Giovanni is saying something about manhood: that men should be agreeable, flexible, and nurturing. This one is not.

If we had focused on the last lines about being a man, we would have built a different argument than the one we did. The nice thing about a garden of forking paths is that you can retrace your steps and take a different path, even if you ultimately end up in the same place. This is an important concept when writing about literature. As you write about the literature in this book, you will often have to retrace your steps to formulate your **thesis**, or statement that will unify your essay. Retracing your steps through a written draft might indicate that you have changed your mind about your thesis or refined it. Such retracing is called **revision.** The next chapter discusses how to work through the drafting process to create a thesis statement and a unified paper.

Chapter 2

Writing about Literature

The desire to write grows with writing.
—DESIDERIUS ERASMUS, *Adagia* (1500)

Why Write?

As we discussed in Chapter 1, literature is usually defined as something written, especially great writing that continues to be meaningful over time. By writing about literature, you go beneath its surface and into its rich interior, like a diver exploring the depths of an ocean. Exploration can be a frightening prospect because you are entering an unknown realm, and many students are anxious about their writing abilities. The purpose of this chapter is to make the process of writing about literature seem exciting rather than daunting.

Why do you write about literature? The glib answer is that your instructor requires it. Most likely, you do not spend your spare time in this activity. However, your instructor does not require it for the sheer joy of reading student essays. He or she believes that the best way to elicit from you a sophisticated, sustained engagement with literature—an art form that is both accessible and endlessly challenging—is to encourage you to articulate your ideas in writing. Your instructor is not alone: the majority of colleges and universities in our vast country require an introduction to literature course with a writing component. In fact, our culture as a whole associates higher education with some grasp of literature combined with the experience of writing about it.

However, you may not be convinced by this argument because it may sound like a parent responding to a child's questions with "Because I said so." To approach your writing as simply something you have to do is to miss an opportunity, and though you may master the skill of pleasing your professor enough to get by with a passing grade for the course, you will have failed to make literature matter to you, to connect what you read to your life and to your values. The key is not to approach a literary text with the intention to "get it," but to approach it with the hope of getting something "out of it." You do that by making the literature yours; by writing carefully, passionately, and patiently; and by making connections, both among your readings and between your readings and your life.

Writing requires different thought processes than speech, and though you may come up with some brilliant insights during class discussion, they are ultimately fleeting. (This is why we study "great books" more often than we study "great talk shows": writing is more refined and more permanent than speech is.) Writing allows you to be patient because it offers the possibility to **revise,** to look again at what you've said and to improve on it.

When you write essays for this course, you are not writing literature; rather, you are writing an analysis of it. Although in some sense all writing is creative, this is not a creative writing course. The goal of your writing here is to deepen your understanding of literature by analyzing it. A good way to answer the question "Why write?" is with the answer "To understand, deeply."

What Do I Know?

Writing is not merely the *evidence* of your understanding; it is the *process through which* you understand. You can respond to the question "What do I know?" in two ways. You might say, "I don't know much." Or you might say, "What could I learn? How can I use that learning to articulate something taking shape in my mind?" Some people feel that they shouldn't bother to write about something that didn't make perfect sense to them when they first read it. Imagine yourself staring at a blank piece of paper or a blank computer screen as you begin your writing process about a certain poem. "I don't understand this poem," you might say. "How am I supposed to write about it?" The point is that you will only understand it *if* you write about it. If you are thinking about writing as the process through which you understand, you're more likely to begin. You have to develop the confidence to begin writing, and the only way to do that is to believe that writing itself can aid in your understanding.

One source of anxiety may be that the word *literature* sounds so formal and intimidating. Our culture and your teachers may have communicated that literature is more than plain writing, and to some degree it is (see Chapter 1). It is art, after all, and so seems removed from common experience, like those rare and inscrutable paintings we are told are beautiful or profound.

However, literature was never intended to gather dust in silent libraries, and visual art was not produced to be safely guarded in vaults underneath some chilly museum. At some level, literature is simply words on a page and paintings are simply pigmented oils on a canvas, not so removed from everyday life. Literature is written words: carefully chosen words, yes, artfully arranged words, probably—but still only words. Virginia Woolf and Ernest Hemingway had to face a blank piece of paper exactly like you do. They scratched out words and stormed away from their desk exactly like you might.

Odds are that you are not going to earn your living as a literary critic or scholar, though you might. At the same time, you are a kind of literary critic in this course, and part of the point of higher education is to develop your capacity to think like a critic. Contrary to the movie ratings you may read in the newspaper or see on television, critics do more than give two thumbs up or three-and-a-half stars.

When it comes to literature, critics *interpret*, as discussed in Chapter 1. A critic's interpretations should not aim to be completely subjective ("This poem reminds me of my Aunt Jane"), nor should they aim to fully explain the human condition ("As you can see, *Oliver Twist* solves all of the mysteries of life and death"). Somewhere between these two poles is an appropriate way to make meaning so that both you and your reader will benefit from the process. To answer the question "Why am I doing this?" you should think of yourself working with a literary text to make meaning.

Audience

You should also think of your writing as a kind of performance: you are making meaning for a specific audience. While continuing to ask questions that might help you think about the purpose of your writing, you also ask this fundamental question: "Who is my reader?" The evident answer is, again, "my instructor." This reader is a powerful one, indeed, because he or she evaluates your interpretation and attaches that evaluation to your name. Grading is a process that students inevitably regard as meaningful and that professors usually accept as necessary.

However, your main goal is not to get a certain grade but to feel more powerful and realize your potential. Your audience, the reader, already has some power, so it's natural for you to want some, too. You get that power by imitating someone who has learned to acquire it: your instructor. He or she has become powerful because he or she is a good reader: someone who likes to read, who appreciates original uses of language, and probably has written some good literary criticism.

Keeping in mind these assumptions, you can make a list of things you want to do and don't want to do when you hand in your essays. For instance,

- My instructor uses original language; therefore, I don't want to use clichés.
- My instructor likes to read good writing; therefore I want to produce a good paper that's thoughtful, clear, unified, and well organized.
- My instructor has read and written literary criticism; therefore I want to figure out what that is and master its conventions.

Students often complain that Professor X in history wants them to write one way while Professor Y in English wants them to write another. This often happens: different disciplines have different conventions, and certainly different professors value different qualities even within these disciplines. The key to being a powerful writer, then, is to be flexible so that you can meet these readers halfway between their expectations and your inclinations. You can do that without compromising your writerly soul: every great writer thinks about audience to some degree.

Unless you are writing a diary meant for your eyes alone, the point of writing is to communicate to someone else. The tension between what you want to write and what your reader wants to read can be a productive tension. As you are developing flexibility, you will also develop confidence and a voice. A few more assumptions should guide you as you think about this tension:

- If your reader doesn't "get" what you're trying to say, assume that he or she is still a good reader and that you can improve your writing more easily than you can change the way your reader reads. Your writing might be clear to *you*, but that doesn't mean it is clear to someone else who doesn't live within your skull.
- Assume that you *will* have something to say about a work of literature and that you care about your idea.
- Assume that all writers improve with practice and patience. Dozens of writers enter their first year of college believing that they are not (and never can be) good writers. Most revise that self-destructive idea by the end of the year.

Getting Started

Moving from blank screen to finished product is not a quick process, nor is it a neat one. You probably begin to "write" your paper even before you sit down to that blank screen. While reading either the text or the assignment, you initiate some thoughts that might turn into writing. If you read with a pen or a highlighter in your hand—a highly recommended practice—you begin writing *while* you are reading. Perhaps you are only marking up the text rather than writing words; that's okay: you are calling attention to what you found important on a first reading. Marks on a page become letters, letters become words, words become paragraphs, and paragraphs eventually become essays.

One reading of a text is never enough. The first impressions a text makes are valid, and you should not overlook them. However, good readers and writers must be willing to build on those impressions, and second and third readings allow for that building. One good model may be to read the first time without a pen or highlighter in your hand, allowing the text to speak to you, and then follow that reading immediately with a second reading, armed with a writing implement. Some good writers approach the text a few times with different colored pens so they can distinguish their first impressions from their later impressions.

These are all good writing habits; you will need to decide which works best for you. The point is that many writers begin writing instinctively, while reading. Others begin by reflecting on their reading. If this is your style, it still helps to have a pen in your hand while reflecting. You are going to produce a written document, after all, so you should start writing as soon as you can, even if that writing is rudimentary and incoherent.

The Reading Journal

Even if your instructor does not require a reading journal, he or she probably thinks it is a good idea. This journal can be useful both for class discussion and for writing. Record in it your initial responses to a work of literature so that you have a reference point when you return to that work. It is a neater, better organized, and more developed version of the notes you might take in the margin of this book. Moreover, the margins of this book are severely limited in terms of space; a reading journal is not. Here are some ideas for what to record in a reading journal:

- Words that you need to look up in a dictionary
- Names or places that you need to research
- Impressions of patterns in a work of literature (such as repeated phrases or rhymed words)
- Lines, speeches, or words that provoke a particularly strong reaction
- Your candid initial responses to a work of literature followed by a developed analysis of those reactions (example: "I really hate Daisy Buchanan: she reminds me of my sister. They're both so distant! Maybe her distance has been caused by something.")
- Questions about a work

The word *journal* derives from the French word for "day" (*jour*), implying that it is something you should write in daily. That may seem like a lofty ideal, but it would certainly make you a better writer as well as a more careful reader.

Outlining, Brainstorming, and Freewriting

Some students are not comfortable beginning their actual writing until they have an **outline,** a kind of blueprint for the essay. In its classic form, an outline is marked by headings and subheadings, topics and subtopics. It is an organizing device, and it may not be the most effective way to begin writing if you have difficulty structuring an entire argument before you have begun. It was designed in an earlier era when many essays were typed on a typewriter, or even handwritten. In those precomputer days, if you organized your paper in a confusing way, it was physically difficult to change its organization after writing it out by hand or typing it.

With the ability to move large chunks of text around—deleting, cutting, pasting, and inserting with little effort—preorganizing your thoughts is less important than it was thirty years ago. In fact, you might try creating an outline only after you have a working draft of your paper. At this later stage, you might be able to see a summary of your ideas and determine whether the paper is jumbled up or incomplete.

This said, you can still begin with an outline. If you want to be less orderly and thus allow for more creativity and spontaneity, however, you can try one of the following prewriting methods as an alternative.

Freewriting is a variation of what used to be called "automatic writing," a method to get in touch with ideas that are in your mind, struggling to surface. The key to freewriting is that you are producing only a draft that you are not going to hand in to anyone for a grade. Its purpose is to unlock some gated-up idea by initiating the physical process of writing before you feel mentally prepared to begin.

The process of freewriting is this: simply write. Don't worry about grammar, coherence, form, unity, or evidence; all of those can be taken care of in later stages of the drafting process. You are simply spilling words onto a page. Some freewriters force themselves to write for ten or fifteen minutes, without stopping. Much of what they produce can be nonsensical or nonproductive: "This is garbage, this is garbage, I don't know what I'm saying." Yet at some point an idea may surface. For example:

> This is garbage. Okay. Time to write. What do I think about Huck Finn? He's unlike me in every way and I can't imagine how I'm going to relate to him. He's a typical boy. The only time I could relate was when he dresses up like a girl and gets caught. I suppose that's because he's essentially a boy and even his gestures betray him.

Imagine this piece of freewriting as the beginning of an essay in which the author writes about authenticity in Twain's *Adventures of Huckleberry Finn*. Although the first few sentences of this freewriting sample do not seem to be leading in that direction, the author must work through them before arriving at the potentially useful idea that the protagonist of Twain's novel has a clear gender-based identity.

Brainstorming is another way to begin a paper. Like freewriting, brainstorming attempts to get in touch with some ideas that may not be evident before the writer puts them on paper. Freewriting can be done either with a pen and paper or on a word processor; brainstorming requires a pen and paper because it is often less linear than freewriting and will not take the form of sentences or lines of type. Picture the way some professors write words, phrases, and numbers on the board and connect them with arrows or circles and you can see what a brainstorming session might look like.

Brainstorming might begin with a word or phrase rather than with a sentence. You might find yourself scratching out words or phrases, drawing lines between some words or arrows between others. It can be messy, but it is a draft that others probably will never see and that they could hardly make sense of. Why bother? It is a proven, effective way to drop a bucket into the dark well of your mind and come up with something. Here's an example of what brainstorming might look like:

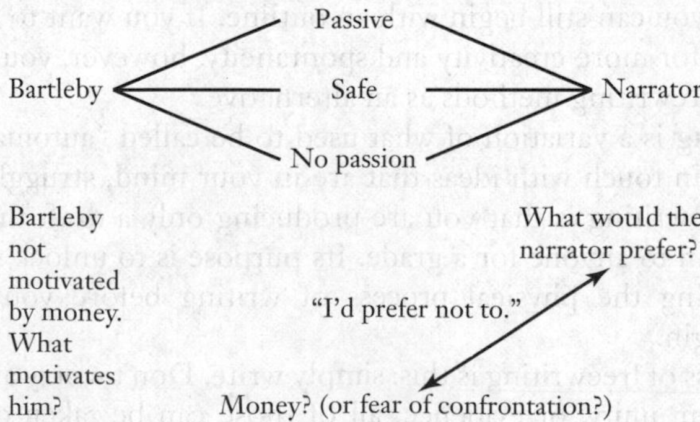

In this example, the student is analyzing Herman Melville's story "Bartleby the Scrivener" (see Chapter 16). She is attempting to see similarities between the story's unnamed first-person narrator and Bartleby, the mysterious title character. She comes up with common characteristics, and she also generates some questions that can lead to a deeper interpretation of the story. Like freewriting, brainstorming does not need to be eloquent or fully formed; it is the roughest of rough drafts. Its best function is to get you thinking about the crucial questions a work of literature provokes.

Journals, outlining, brainstorming, and freewriting can be useful methods to help you find a way into a text. No doubt you have many different responses to one work of literature, and some may not lead to important writing. Before you have invested much time in the drafting process, these prewriting activities can help you to eliminate some paths and pursue others.

Annotating and Questioning a Text

In addition to doing prewriting activities, you need to respond directly to the text itself so that you can be sure that what you want to say does indeed relate to that individual text. Outlining, freewriting, and brainstorming might help you narrow the scope of what you want to say, but they probably take place with the book closed. You also need to deal with the book itself.

Novelist Nicholson Baker wrote a book called *U & I* about his admiration for the elder, more prominent writer John Updike. This relationship takes place mostly in Baker's creative imagination and in his memory: the two writers met twice, only briefly. The book is an exercise in what Baker calls "memory criticism" or "closed-book examination": Baker attempts to re-create and describe his own progress as a writer by recalling passages of Updike he once read. Although he has an uncanny memory, when he later checks his memory against what Updike actually wrote, he is startled to discover that he often misquoted Updike. (At one point late in the book Baker declares, "What is wrong with me?" [155].)

There's nothing "wrong" with Baker's method, or with writing about one's memory of literature—at first. Since it is a written document, literature gives us the opportunity to make sure our impressions are accurate, to reread as we write. Writers have to examine the words of other writers directly, and when writing about literature you can only keep a book closed for so long.

One of the first processes of writing about literature is underlining or highlighting your text. An excellent next step is to **annotate** the text, either in the margin or on a separate piece of paper (or in your reading journal, if you're keeping one). This annotation takes many forms, from one-word summaries or reminders in the margins of your book (like "desire" or "description") to fuller phrases or sentences (such as "Here the speaker changes his mind about dreams").

Some of the most productive annotations are questions. Literature makes a wonderful subject for writing and critical inquiry because it always raises questions. Usually the reader must articulate what those questions are, and since every reader will raise different questions, each reader will always have something original to say. Writing about literature is responding to the questions you ask of texts and also to the questions texts ask of you.

Illustration of Prewriting: Colette's "The Other Wife"

The following short story by the French author Colette (1873–1954) can be used to illustrate the types of questions raised by a text and a reader. This story compresses a great deal of emotion and life experience into a brief space. It has a specific setting—a pricey restaurant in a coastal town in France at the beginning of the twentieth century—and yet its subject is timeless: the experience of falling out of love.

Colette *(1873–1954)*

Translated by Matthew Ward

The Other Wife

"Table for two? This way, Monsieur, Madame, there is still a table next to the window, if Madame and Monsieur would like a view of the bay."

Alice followed the maître d'.

"Oh, yes. Come on, Marc, it'll be like having lunch on a boat on the water . . ."

Her husband caught her by passing his arm under hers. "We'll be more comfortable over there."

5 "There? In the middle of all those people? I'd much rather . . ."

"Alice, please."

He tightened his grip in such a meaningful way that she turned around. "What's the matter?"

"Shh . . ." he said softly, looking at her intently, and led her toward the table in the middle.

"What is it, Marc?"

10 "I'll tell you, darling. Let me order lunch first. Would you like the shrimp? Or the eggs in aspic?"

"Whatever you like, you know that."

They smiled at one another, wasting the precious time of an overworked maître d', stricken with a kind of nervous dance, who was standing next to them, perspiring.

"The shrimp," said Marc. "Then the eggs and bacon. And the cold chicken with a romaine salad. *Fromage blanc?* The house specialty? We'll go with the specialty. Two strong coffees. My chauffeur will be having lunch also, we'll be leaving again at two o'clock. Some cider? No, I don't trust it . . . Dry champagne."

He sighed as if he had just moved an armoire, gazed at the colorless midday sea, at the pearly white sky, then at his wife, whom he found lovely in her little Mercury hat with its large, hanging veil.

"You're looking well, darling. And all this blue water makes your eyes look green, imagine that! And you've put on weight since you've been traveling . . . It's nice up to a point, but only up to a point!"

Her firm, round breasts rose proudly as she leaned over the table.

"Why did you keep me from taking that place next to the window?"

Marc Seguy never considered lying. "Because you were about to sit next to someone I know."

"Someone I don't know?"

"My ex-wife."

She couldn't think of anything to say and opened her blue eyes wider.

"So what, darling? It'll happen again. It's not important."

The words came back to Alice and she asked, in order, the inevitable questions. "Did she see you? Could she see that you saw her? Will you point her out to me?"

"Don't look now, please, she must be watching us . . . The lady with brown hair, no hat, she must be staying in this hotel. By herself, behind those children in red . . ."

"Yes. I see."

Hidden behind some broad-brimmed beach hats, Alice was able to look at the woman who, fifteen months ago, had still been her husband's wife.

"Incompatibility," Marc said. "Oh, I mean . . . total incompatibility! We divorced like well-bred people, almost like friends, quietly, quickly. And then I fell in love with you, and you really wanted to be happy with me. How lucky we are that our happiness doesn't involve any guilty parties or victims!"

The woman in white, whose smooth, lustrous hair reflected the light from the sea in azure patches, was smoking a cigarette with her eyes half closed. Alice turned back toward her husband, took some shrimp and butter, and ate calmly. After a moment's silence she asked: "Why didn't you ever tell me that she had blue eyes, too?"

"Well, I never thought about it!"

He kissed the hand she was extending toward the bread basket and she blushed with pleasure. Dusky and ample, she might have seemed somewhat coarse, but the changeable blue of her eyes and her wavy, golden hair made her look like a frail and sentimental blonde. She vowed overwhelming gratitude to her husband. Immodest without knowing it, everything about her bore the overly conspicuous marks of extreme happiness.

They ate and drank heartily, and each thought the other had forgotten the woman in white. Now and then, however, Alice laughed too loudly, and Marc was careful about his posture, holding his shoulders back, his head up. They waited quite a long time for their coffee, in silence. An incandescent river, the straggled reflection of the invisible sun overhead, shifted slowly across the sea and shone with a blinding brilliance.

"She's still there, you know," Alice whispered.

"Is she making you uncomfortable? Would you like to have coffee somewhere else?"

"No, not at all! She's the one who must be uncomfortable! Besides, she doesn't exactly seem to be having a wild time, if you could see her . . ."

"I don't have to. I know that look of hers."

"Oh, was she like that?"

He exhaled his cigarette smoke through his nostrils and knitted his eyebrows. "Like that? No. To tell you honestly, she wasn't happy with me."

"Oh, really now!"

"The way you indulge me is so charming, darling . . . It's crazy . . . You're an angel . . . You love me . . . I'm so proud when I see those eyes of yours. Yes, those eyes . . . She . . . I just didn't know how to make her happy, that's all. I didn't know how."

"She's just difficult!"

Alice fanned herself irritably, and cast brief glances at the woman in white, who was smoking, her head resting against the back of the cane chair, her eyes closed with an air of satisfied lassitude.

Marc shrugged his shoulders modestly.

"That's the right word," he admitted. "What can you do? You have to feel sorry for people who are never satisfied. But we're satisfied . . . Aren't we, darling?"

She did not answer. She was looking furtively, and closely, at her husband's face, ruddy and regular; at his thick hair, threaded here and there with white silk; at his short, well-cared-for hands; and doubtful for the first time, she asked herself, "What more did she want from him?"

And as they were leaving, while Marc was paying the bill and asking for the chauffeur and about the route, she kept looking, with envy and curiosity, at the woman in white, this dissatisfied, this difficult, this superior . . .

(Translated 1957)

Some stories ask direct questions of the reader and eventually answer them. In the murder mystery, the reader always knows "Who done it?" by the end, as well as how the murderer did it, where he did it, when he did it, and why he did it. However, most literature does not raise obvious questions; instead, the reader must both raise the questions and supply possible answers based on evidence, which comes in the form of specific examples and especially direct quotations (see Chapter 3). We have supplied some discussion questions following each piece in this anthology, and your instructor and classmates may provide others.

Part of the artistry of literature is the tension between what the writer includes and what the writer omits. In "The Other Wife," Colette includes some details that we might find helpful, such as the names of the two main characters, Alice and Marc. She does not include the name of Marc's chauffeur or of the restaurant's maitre d', because these men are only functionaries in the story. However, Marc's first wife, though also underdeveloped, is an important character. Why aren't we given her name?

The presence of the nameless former wife creates a mystery. We don't know her name, and she never says anything. For about the first one-third of the story, we don't even know why Marc chooses to sit in the middle of a crowded room instead of by the window. When Alice learns the reason, she is speechless, and Marc explains: "It's not important."

Marc hopes that this short statement will put things in perspective, allow his second wife to trust him, and enable the two of them to enjoy their lunch despite the fact that the situation is extremely uncomfortable. However, the statement "It's not important," coupled with the observation that Marc declines to use his former wife's name, should prompt us to raise some useful questions. Why is Marc the one who decides what is important? Where does he get this power? Is this power related to the reason Alice seems to change her mind about their giddy happiness in the story's final paragraphs?

What *is* important? This is the essence of any question you should ask as you prepare to write about a text. You might finish this story and ask questions such as "What are eggs in aspic? What's a Mercury hat look like? What does that French phrase *fromage blanc* mean?" However, these are factual questions that can easily be answered with a little research. The text asks some crucial *interpretive* questions of the reader that are not so easily answered. Here are a few examples:

- Why does the story emphasize comfort?
- Where does Marc get his power to determine what is important?
- Why does Alice seem to revise her opinion of her husband by the end of the story?

At the beginning of the drafting process you do not know whether these are the questions you will want to pursue. As you work through your drafts, you will discover whether they are or whether you should choose some others. Literature does not tend to ask one single question of its readers. Rather, it reveals gaps that allow readers to raise their own questions. Nevertheless, all good questions must relate to the text. Let's put it this way: "What important issue arises when a careful reader responds to the implied questions raised by a work of literature?"

Coincidentally, the characters in this story also ask many questions. The story begins with a seemingly meaningless question: "Table for two?" This question leads to the central **irony** of the story: Marc and Alice sit at a table for two, yet the presence of a third party, Marc's former wife, upsets the balance and serenity of this table. One can also compare the kinds of questions Alice and Marc ask. Alice asks pointed questions: "What's the matter?" and "What is it, Marc?" and "Why did you keep me from taking that place next to the window?" Marc seems to ask only trivial questions: "Would you like the shrimp? Or the eggs in aspic?"

In the center of the story, after Alice learns that Marc's former wife is in the restaurant, the narrator says, "[Alice] asked, in order, the inevitable questions. 'Did she see you? Could she see that you saw her? Will you point her out to me?'" Why are these questions "inevitable"? From whose perspective? We presume that the narrator thinks that the questions are inevitable because they're the questions the reader might expect. After a while Alice asks a question that neither Marc nor the reader expects: "Why didn't you ever tell me that she had blue eyes, too?" Marc's response is similar to his earlier comment about what's important: "Well, I never thought about it!" In both cases, he is selective.

In the dramatic final three paragraphs of the story, something clearly shifts. Two other questions are asked. Marc asks Alice, "But we're satisfied . . . Aren't we, darling?" (The answer should be, "Of course we are, darling," but it clearly isn't.) And Alice asks herself, "What more did she want from him?" For the first time, we are in Alice's head, with her thoughts about the situation. This is a change in *perspective*. Until now we have only heard Marc and Alice speak; now we are allowed to hear Alice think. The fact that Alice asks herself this question should clue the reader into something important about this story—perspective. In the above paragraphs, we dance between actual questions that the text raises and the types of questions a reader might ask of the text. The idea of perspective is a useful way to bridge the gap between the two sets of questions. The fact that Alice asks herself a question toward the end of the story signals a definite shift in perspective.

The final paragraph is a "silent" paragraph in a sense: the author includes no dialogue. Yet we learn that Marc is still talking, asking questions about directions, while Alice is gazing intently at Marc's former wife, silently drawing conclusions about the former wife and also about herself: the former wife may be "dissatisfied" and "difficult," as Marc has said, but Alice judges her as "superior" and regards her with "envy."

If we think some more about this shift in perspective, we also see that it means Marc has lost his power over his wife. Throughout most of the story, Marc's in control. He determines what's "important." He orders lunch for his wife according to what he wants. Yet what does Alice want? What does she find important? While we get a glimpse of her priorities through some of her earlier questions, only toward the end do we get a real sense of her feelings. And although Marc seems in control of little details, he can't control his wife's thoughts or feelings.

The Drafting Process

At this point you have asked several questions. You have narrowed down your topics and decided to write about perspective. What next?

You should not expect to move from this crucial stage to your final draft quickly, but you are in an excellent position to start drafting. Some writers need to have their introduction in place before they can continue; others need to simply start writing and might not even get to the introduction until they're done with the body of the paper. There is no perfect formula. Learn to know yourself as a writer and do not force anything at this early stage. Learn to be comfortable with producing a series of *drafts* rather than expecting that you will be able to jump from prewriting and questioning sessions to a final draft suitable to hand in to your instructor.

Personal computers have made the revision process much easier than it used to be. Still, writing can only reach its potential when you allow yourself time to revise it carefully. One draft, written the night before the due date, is not going to be your best work. You aren't likely to read much literature in this anthology that was written in one spontaneous draft.

Chapters 4 through 8, which discuss the conventions of writing about specific literary genres, will take you through student drafts. This chapter is intended more as a broad, theoretical overview of the process of prewriting, writing, and revising. We have already discussed the prewriting strategies of keeping a journal, freewriting, brainstorming, outlining, annotating, and questioning a text. The next stage—drafting your actual paper—is harder to describe because writers approach it in many different ways. Here are a few more strategies that you may want to try and a checklist of items that you should work toward throughout the drafting process.

The First Rough Draft

As you move from a set of questions to your first rough draft, you should feel comfortable in a mode that might be called *focused freewriting*. You roughly know that you are writing about perspective in the story "The Other Wife." Your paper is also going to say something about control, about speech versus silence, and maybe about gender since the story illustrates relationships between husbands and wives. Your goal here should be to generate a few paragraphs of material. They can be moved around, expanded, or deleted later; for now, think of yourself scooping up a few good handfuls of clay and throwing them on a potter's wheel: they will take shape eventually.

The Next Drafts

You can write any number of drafts before producing the final one. The number of drafts depends on how much time you have, how long the paper will be, how ambitiously you (or your instructor) has defined your context, and so forth. The key principle is that you should allow yourself some time between drafts. (Your instructor may or may not require that you hand in these drafts.)

Some instructors devote class time to *peer revision*, during which other students read your first drafts. The drafting process takes time, and your writing can benefit from a fresh pair of eyes, whether those eyes belong to someone else or to you, after you have rested. To gain more clarity, print your drafts before revising them: our eyes respond differently to words on paper copies than to words on computer screens. Moreover, if something goes wrong with your computer or with your disk, you still have a recent draft of your paper to show your instructor when you tell him or her about your computer problem. Your instructor may be skeptical that you are telling the truth: a printed draft can function as physical evidence.

Evidence

Always include direct quotations from the literature you are analyzing. These direct quotations are your most specific form of **evidence.** Summaries of plot elements or assessments of character can also constitute evidence, but papers with few or no quotations generally suffer from vagueness or inaccuracy.

You can also include too much evidence at the expense of your own analysis. An essay that contains more quotations from the primary text than your own writing is probably not analytical enough or does not develop an original idea that the reader can appreciate. In general, the evidence you select from the text should clearly illustrate the point you are making. You should avoid the too-common practice of allowing the quotation to speak for itself: in other words, discuss and analyze the quotations you include.

If your first rough draft contains no specific evidence from the text, do not feel too anxious, but begin to add that evidence to later drafts. This is a good time to return to the annotations you made while reading the text to figure out what aspects you want to focus on. Although you need not include everything you highlighted or underlined, certainly some of those passages will be essential to your argument.

As you add those quotations to your text, double-check their wording and remember to include the page numbers (or line numbers, in the case of poetry) where you found them. Indicate in which source you found a quotation and on what page. You can keep track of these sources more easily while you are writing these early drafts than while you're completing a final draft. Citation methods are discussed in detail in Chapter 10.

Much of the evidence you include in your essay should probably be concentrated in the body of your paper, described below. Though you can sometimes include quotations in your introduction or your conclusion, usually these beginning and concluding paragraphs are statements of your own original idea. If those paragraphs are dominated by evidence, your idea might become obscured. The body of your paper exists to prove the point you make in your introduction and your conclusion. As in a courtroom, the proof is illustrated through evidence.

Elements of the Final Draft: A Checklist

The following sections briefly describe the most basic components of a college essay. Chapters 4 through 8 illustrate the process through which some student writers advance from prewriting to the final draft.

The Introduction

Perhaps the most important paragraph(s) in your paper, your introduction generally contains a **context,** or way of approaching the main text, and your thesis, or main, unifying idea that includes both your argument and its conclusion. To lead the reader gently into the topic, you usually name the author (or authors) and work (or works) that will be discussed. At the same time, you firmly move the reader in a definite direction as you state your thesis.

The introduction to the paper entitled "Perspective in Colette's 'The Other Wife'" might look something like this:

The phrase "Beauty is in the eye of the beholder" is a well-known cliché that is usually taken to mean that everyone has different standards for beauty. It also makes clear that beholding, or looking at something carefully, can be a powerful activity that yields much meaning. In Colette's story "The Other Wife," simply looking at someone gives one of the main characters enough information to change her opinions about her husband.

While the husband Marc does a lot of talking and tries to control his second wife Alice, in the end the story abruptly shifts perspective to his wife's thoughts and reveals that the silence of Marc's former wife is more powerful than Marc's words. Alice sees the former wife, though silent, as "superior" at the story's conclusion, and the husband who thinks himself superior loses his stature in her eyes. *Through a shift in perspective, we learn that what Alice sees is more meaningful than what her husband says (and does not see).*

The Thesis

The final sentence of the sample introduction is the **thesis** of the paper (see also Chapter 3). The thesis has a number of functions:

- To advance the writer's interpretation
- To help unify the essay that will follow
- To frame the terms of the writer's argument
- To indicate the direction the paper will take
- To conclude something about the work being considered

This final point is crucial. The thesis is not as effective if it merely promises that an idea will form somewhere along the way. (Example: "In this paper, I will discuss perspective in Colette's story 'The Other Wife.'") That type of thesis does not give the reader the kind of intellectual direction you want to provide.

A thesis should be a statement of your opinion, or argument. As Chapter 3 explains, argument in this sense does not mean some hostile attack, but simply a line of reasoning. In other words, you probably don't want your thesis to scream at the reader: "Colette's story is about nothing less than the history of the systematic repression of women, and anyone who can't see that is a pig-headed fool." Even if you believe that, you need to express the idea nonaggressively.

The thesis is customarily part of the introduction, usually the final sentence. As you become more confident, you might attempt to modify your writing style and take certain chances with regard to the placement of your thesis. However, your reader is looking for a thesis somewhere around the final sentence of an introduction. If it is not there, your reader might not easily locate it.

The Conclusion

The final paragraph of your paper, or **conclusion**, is not, as some writers believe, simply the introduction reprinted and preceded with a phrase like "So, as you can see . . ." or "So, as I have argued . . ." Rather, it is an opportunity to extend your argument in a new direction, enlarging its context and applicability. Although you might find it necessary to summarize your argument in your conclusion, you can also use that space to consider some of the implications of your argument.

The Body

The **body** includes everything between the introduction and conclusion. (The introduction and conclusion are frequently one paragraph each, and sometimes more than that, as our example shows.) The body is made up of an undetermined number of paragraphs that follow one another in a logical manner. Each paragraph represents a coherent idea; each is a smaller version of the essay as a whole. Paragraphs can be any length: some ideas take longer to develop than others.

The organization of these paragraphs should allow you to create effective **transitions** between paragraphs. Transitions are devices that allow paragraphs to flow easily into one another so that the reader sees the logic in your organization. If you are having trouble creating transitions, you might need to reorganize your paragraphs, or you might need to add something. Transitions generally occur at the conclusion of one paragraph and the introduction of another, signaling logical connections between paragraphs (sometimes with words like *also, another,* or *moreover* to demonstrate relationships).

The heart of your paragraphs should be evidence in the form of specific examples or (especially) direct quotations from the work you are analyzing. If you include this evidence at the beginning or the end of your paragraphs, you will have a difficult time making transitions between your paragraphs, since direct quotations are not your ideas. So be extremely cautious about beginning or ending a paragraph with a direct quotation.

Works Cited

The final element to appear in your paper is usually the list of works that you made reference to or "cited" in the body of your paper. Provide full bibliographic information for your readers, allowing them to go back and find the books, articles, websites, and other works you used as sources. Citation methods are discussed in Chapter 10.

When you write about literature, you are analyzing it using the critical thinking methods discussed in Chapter 1 and the drafting methods discussed in this chapter. The next chapter, on argument, develops the ideas of these first two chapters and brings them together as a way of thinking deliberately about the way we write analytically.

Chapter 3

Constructing an Argument

Use soft words and hard arguments.
—ENGLISH PROVERB

This chapter further develops what you learned in Chapter 2, Writing about Literature, which encouraged you to think critically and to approach writing as a drafting process. In the course of developing a final draft to hand in to your instructor, you will naturally construct a rhetorical argument. This chapter will help you fine-tune your understanding of what an argument is.

In the context of college writing, an **argument** is an opinion-based analysis of a subject, not a hostile exchange. If your professor writes, "What's your argument?" at the end of your paper, he or she is asking for a clearer expression of your idea in relation to the topic rather than a vehement pronouncement of your disagreement with some idea. Good arguments contain balanced reasoning, a logical structure, and ample evidence. This chapter concentrates on the challenges of constructing an argument about a work of literature.

Matters of Opinion

A fact is a piece of information that cannot be disputed. Facts are provable. Opinions are expressions of truth that originate from a certain perspective rather than from scientific or objective knowledge. Budding critical thinkers are sometimes uncomfortable with stating their opinion or with believing that their opinions count for anything. An argument offers you the opportunity to discover your own opinions, to work them out in writing, and to measure them against the opinions of others.

Before you can convince your reader to accept your opinion of a text, you must be convinced that you have some credibility as a good reader. Otherwise you will never manage to persuade the reader of your essay (your professor) that your analysis matters. Conclusions written by beginning college writers often go something like this: "So from my perspective, Eliot's poem 'The Love Song of J. Alfred Prufrock' is a deep look into the soul of a man who never had the courage to communicate with the women he loved. But that is only my opinion—others may see it differently."

This kind of final sentence is disastrous to an argument; the writer is erasing everything he or she has said up to that point. Your reader understands that your analysis has its origins in your "opinion," or personal critical response; you don't need to emphasize that fact or to suggest that you don't know what you are talking about. (However, you must know what you are talking about, which is why we devote a whole chapter in this book to reading carefully and critically.)

When you analyze literature, you should not consider your opinion in terms of right and wrong, but rather in terms of **validity.** A valid opinion is informed and thoughtful, creative and substantial. For instance, if a writer analyzed "The Love Song of J. Alfred Prufrock" as a poem about the effects of the Great Depression on the individual, someone could point out that Eliot's poem was published in 1916, and the Depression began in 1929. It's easy to spot the invalid nature of that argument. Most judgments of an argument's validity have to deal with more complex issues.

We can take the cliché "Everyone is entitled to an opinion" and alter it for the purposes of college writing and critical thinking: "Even though everyone is entitled to an opinion, those opinions gain more substance when they are well informed and persuasively expressed." Many people consider an opinion to be an expression of their personal taste that is therefore invulnerable to criticism, such as "I like poems about nature more than I like poems about people." There's nothing here to criticize or judge; someone has merely expressed personal taste.

Rather than being statements of taste, opinions are expressions of judgment that depend on an analysis of **evidence,** or support (discussed below and in Chapter 2). Because they rest on evidence, they are open to debate and discussion by others. If someone expresses a purely personal opinion based on taste, such as "I like anchovy pizza," or "I hate Tom Cruise," you probably should not try to open up a discussion on the subject.

In literary analysis, therefore, you should aim for statements and analyses that your professors or classmates might be able to dispute; your statements should at least make readers curious about the way you arrived at your opinion. If your taste runs to poems about nature, you might end up with the following opinion: "The poem 'The Prairies' by William Cullen Bryant is one of the most engaging nature poems ever written because the poet recognizes the importance of connecting his subject to his form." The "because" clause contains the analysis, and you will prove it by citing evidence from the text showing that the poet connects his subject to his form. This is a significant development over what might be your initial reaction to the poem: "Wow! I liked that!"

Evidence: The Burden of Proof

Evidence is perhaps the most important element in an argument. In literary analysis, evidence generally includes your analysis and direct quotations from the work you are analyzing.

Even more important than finding evidence is the method of presenting it. You might go through a lengthy poem and find ten lines that express exactly what you are trying to say, but that is only half the task. You, the writer, still must discuss it. Consider what the word *evidence* means in a legal trial. The courtroom lawyer cannot simply point to Exhibit A—let's say a gun in a murder trial—and simply proclaim, "There you have it. It's his gun: the man's guilty." He will likely build a story around the gun, discuss the accused man's motives, reconstruct the scene of the crime, and scrutinize the gun itself for deeper evidence (fingerprints or DNA).

The same is true when you present evidence from your literary work: you must not only tell us where it comes from and how it functions within the poem; you must also tell us how it contributes to your argument and what its important features are.

Textual evidence comes in the form of direct **quotation** and of accurate **summary.** You have access to both, and as a writer you have to decide when to include quotations in your essay and when to summarize. If you are analyzing a short poem, you will probably have to give direct quotations because poetic language is so distilled. By "provide evidence," we mean *quote* from a work *in your essay.*

If you are analyzing a novel, you will also need to include direct quotations from time to time—again, because language is what you are analyzing and to some degree you will have to tell your reader, "This is what the text actually says: I'm not making this up." However, you will not be able to **explicate** (analyze in great detail) a novel the same way you explicate a poem: you might have to summarize large portions of a novel to get at your point. For example, if you were writing about Jane Austen's novel *Pride and Prejudice*, you might say, "In the long conversation between Elizabeth Bennett and Mr. Darcy, it is obvious that their discomfort is building." While you need not reprint the entire conversation here, you might follow up this statement with "For example . . ." followed by a quotation or two from the text that clearly reveals this discomfort.

There is no set formula for either the number or length of your quotations: you will learn to make these decisions over time, through trial and error. The important point is to be aware that your readers—your professor and your classmates—are looking for textual evidence and your opinion will not have much weight without it.

Audience

As already mentioned, your readers include your professor and, in some cases, your classmates. Some professors use peer revision to allow students to offer opinions and critiques of each other's written work before the professor sees the paper. In either case, you probably consider your professor as an especially powerful reader because, as discussed in Chapter 2, he or she assesses your work with a grade. Whether you are overly concerned with your grade or not, your professor is your primary **audience,** the reader for whom you are writing. He or she is well aware of the standards used to assess college writing and will evaluate your work based on his or her understanding of certain academic conventions.

However, professors in different disciplines might have different expectations. Your literature professor, your psychology professor, and your history professor, for instance, all view evidence differently. Your psychology professor might require a "review of existing scholarship" at the beginning of your paper, and she might want you to clearly state your intention at the beginning of your paper: "In this paper I will . . ." Your literature professor might discourage this kind of approach and ask you to draw up your thesis (discussed below) more subtly. He might also insist that you write about literature in the present tense (for example, you should write, "In this scene Hamlet *goes* (not *went*) to Wittenberg . . ."). Your history professor will probably say the opposite: write about history in the past tense. You need to be flexible and aware of different requirements.

It's a simple fact that audiences (or individual readers) are different: you speak differently to your parents, your friends, and your professors. You make these adjustments easily in speech, and you can do the same in writing. Even within a given discipline, you may find that your professors focus on different things: "Professor Miller hates it when a student writer uses the word *I* in a paper, but Professor Nash encourages me to use *I*. What should I do?" Adjust. This is not to say you should compromise your faith in your own opinions or style, or that you should simply write to please an individual professor like a well-trained dog; it is only saying that you should be well aware of the expectations of your audience. In the discipline of literary studies, the conventions are established and revised by an organization called the Modern Language Association, or MLA. The MLA regulates and assesses changes in the field: it is responsible for the citation guidelines described in our chapter on research (Chapter 10).

Here are a few conventions to remember when you are writing for an English class:

- Generally write about literature in the present tense.
- Include an appropriate amount of direct quotations from the primary text you are analyzing.
- Cite quotations from all sources with documentation.
- Be sensitive to the standards of conventional written English and to your instructor's specific directives.

Interpretation

Your job as a budding literary critic is to explain the meaning of a text from your perspective. As Chapter 9 discusses, that perspective may be informed by various ways of thinking: you may be searching for historical or cultural meaning when you read a literary text, or you may find the illustration of a psychological or philosophical truth in a poem, play, or story. However, you are probably not following a single theory or method for understanding literature; more often, your interpretation will be guided by specific questions raised by your instructor, by the editors of this book in our questions following each work, by your classmates during class discussion, or by you. In any of these cases, interpretation grows out of an inquiry: you are asking something of a text, and the answer to that question is the basis for your argument (see also Chapter 1).

Your professor will evaluate your interpretation according to a set of guidelines. He or she may include these criteria explicitly on your assignment sheet, or you may have to learn them by listening. Different instructors have different expectations: one professor may downgrade you for a misplaced semicolon, while another will not. However, you can assume that your professor values the following aspects of a good argument.

Organization and Coherence

A good argument is well organized. A well-organized argument has no set formula; generally one idea flows logically into another idea. Nothing is missing between the parts of a well-organized argument, and the reader does not think that the piece of the argument on page 6 really connects better to the piece of the argument on page 2.

Imagine that you are writing a paper on Wole Soyinka's play *Death and the King's Horseman* contained in Chapter 12. You are arguing that Elesin, the protagonist, is acting out of pure self-interest rather than fear when he refuses to commit suicide in accordance with his cultural duty. You have gathered the following evidence from the text:

- Elesin's speech to the praise-singer in which he emphasizes worldly luxury
- Elesin's physical desire for the young woman in the marketplace
- The death of Elesin's son as a consequence of his inaction
- Elesin's bitter discussion of cultural duty with Sergeant Pilkings

How to organize this evidence? Two of these bits of evidence involve Elesin's speech (the first and the fourth), so one would flow logically into the other. Also, the death of Elesin's son may be an important piece of evidence in this argument, but it is a consequence of Elesin's inaction rather than a cause of it. If the third piece of evidence does belong in the paper, it probably belongs toward the end of the paper rather than in the middle of it.

Even if you have not read the play, you should be able to see from these four pieces of potential evidence how the argument might be organized. If you are struggling with organization, you can mark your rough drafts with different colored highlighters, using a different color for each different idea. If the draft contains blocks of colors grouped together, it is probably fairly well organized; however, if pink paragraphs show up on pages 1 and 4 but not on pages 2 or 3, that's a sign that those similar ideas need to be grouped together.

Many scholars and thinkers have written about the best ways to structure an argument. We will only mention one to allow you to think about an argument's potential organization; we do not want to suggest that all arguments must follow the same structure, and your instructor might have specific ideas as well.

The British philosopher Stephen Toulmin, in his book *The Uses of Argument* (Cambridge University Press, 1969), identifies six components of a formal argument:

- The **claim** is the thesis or main point you are trying to make.
- Following the claim is your **support,** what we have been calling evidence, also referred to as "grounds" or "data" in the Toulmin model. The way you present your evidence is important: it is risky to use absolute statements that overgeneralize your case, such as "Men never ask for directions."
- For this reason, Toulmin's model calls for **qualifiers.** You might be better off qualifying generalized statements: "Many men tend to be reluctant to ask for directions."
- Every claim rests on underlying assumptions. Toulmin calls these **warrants.**
- The reader and writer know that these warrants are true, so they don't have to be proven; however, they may require some **backing,** or additional support.
- Toward the end of the argument, in Toulmin's formulation, you should include a **concession**—that is, an acknowledgment of the opposing argument. If you are arguing that Elesin in Soyinka's play acts out of self-interest rather than fear, and if you have found one particularly compelling piece of evidence from the text that would indicate that Elesin is fearful, you should acknowledge that piece of evidence and admit that other perspectives are valid, too.
- Finally, you should create a kind of **rebuttal** at the end of the argument that can show how the opposition's position is weak or invalid.

The Toulmin model is a tried-and-true method of argumentation and gives you a sense of the choices available as you are organizing your paper.

A good argument is coherent. To *cohere* roughly means to "hold together." Elements of an argument that do not seem to fit comfortably threaten to make an argument *incoherent* (a word that connotes "nonsense"). The coherence of your argument is a question of staying "on topic." You have defined the topic, perhaps in conjunction with your instructor, and the topic has a certain scope, or range. If an element of your argument falls outside of that scope or range, you risk incoherence.

It may be a relief to know that you don't have to account for every word in a work of literature (unless your instructor has asked for an explication). Moreover, the logic of your argument, rather than the structure of a text, should give shape to your essay; your argument does not need to mirror the structure of the work of literature you are analyzing.

One way to assess both the organization and the coherence of your argument is to summarize each paragraph of your rough draft in a succinct phrase. Seeing these summaries together might give you a sense of what belongs in a different place and what might not belong at all. Here is an example:

Paragraph 1: Introduction, including thesis
Paragraph 2: Elesin's speech to Praise-singer, emphasis on material world
Paragraph 3: Elesin's discussion with Pilkings, self-involvement
Paragraph 4: Praise-singer's use of metaphor
Paragraph 5: Elesin's assumptions about his son Olunde's decisions

Even if you have not read the play, you will probably notice that paragraph 4 does not fit comfortably with the argument. If paragraph 4 belongs in the paper, it should probably connect to the other paragraph that discusses the praise-singer, paragraph 2. Given the topic, though, paragraph 4 probably does not belong in the argument.

As Chapter 2 discussed, a graceful argument should contain **transitions** from one paragraph or idea to the next. Transitional phrases or sentences are logical "links" that demonstrate the relationship of ideas and the progression from earlier ideas to later ones. The author of the above draft probably would not have been successful in transitioning between paragraphs 3, 4, and 5 because paragraph 4 does not seem to have a logical place between paragraphs 3 and 5. The author may have to change his or her thesis, adjust the scope of the argument, or simply get rid of paragraph 4.

Two elements crucial to your essay's coherence are your introduction and conclusion. The introductory and concluding paragraphs of any argument receive more scrutiny than the body of the argument. In your introduction and conclusion you should be well aware of the context for your argument, the structure of the argument, the scope of the argument, and the importance of the argument. Beyond that, you should be able to make your reader aware of all of these dimensions of your argument.

The **context,** or issues surrounding the argument, is of supreme importance. It frames your argument and explains why your ideas are relevant. The context will affect the way you interpret a text. You might generate a context by connecting this work to another literary work to discover a common motif (such as the notion of duty) or from a discipline or method of thinking (such as the history of Nigeria). You will usually want to introduce the context at the beginning of your essay before stating your thesis. In your conclusion you then remind the reader of your context and, having laid out your argument, consider what "truth" you have advanced that the reader can take away and apply to the world outside.

Some writers copy their introduction at the end of their paper and call it a conclusion, maybe adding a phrase like "So, as I have shown" at the beginning. However, conclusions that are identical to introductions are weak because they imply that your argument has not taken you anywhere. On the other hand, if you have opened your paper with a personal anecdote or analogy, it makes sense to return to that image in your concluding paragraph. Think of your introduction as a descent from the world outside into the world of your essay and the conclusion as a reentry into the world outside from the world of your essay: your reader should be enlightened by what you have said.

Persuasion

An argument should be convincing. People who study **rhetoric,** or the art of persuasive communication, are keenly aware of the way arguments unfold. What follows are a few principles of persuasion.

The language of an argument must be clear. One of the frustrations of writing is the difference between what you intend to write and the actual words that end up on the page. Many writers have terrific arguments about a work of literature but then cannot express them in writing. Clarity and precision are two of the goals of written analysis.

Indirect phrasing is a common impediment to clarity. For instance, your instructors may indicate that you are writing in the **passive voice** rather than the **active voice.** This means that you are placing the subject of your sentence toward the end of the sentence rather than at the beginning: Instead of "The dog chased the ducks," the passive voice reads, "The ducks were chased by the dogs," or, more vaguely, "The ducks were chased." Sometimes the passive voice is best. For example, if you don't know who is doing the action, it makes sense to write in the passive voice: "We were robbed" is better than "A robber robbed us." However, usually the passive voice makes the writer seem less confident than he or she wants to be. The less confident you seem, the less convincing you will be.

The study of rhetoric as an art form dates back to ancient Greece. In Aristotle's *Poetics*, Aristotle distinguishes rhetoric from imaginative literature by saying that rhetoric is a way of presenting and organizing some true principle to convince the reader or listener of that truth. The truth, as the critic sees it, is based on a number of pieces of evidence, as already described: because A is true, and B is true, and C is true, and D is true, then X is also true. This formula sounds simple because C follows B and B follows A; however, in your argument, you have to decide what A, B, C, and D are. Organizing them according to this kind of logical progression can be tricky because the smaller pieces must fit together and build on one another.

As you develop your argument, consider whether it is strong or weak. Ask yourself, "Could someone argue with this?" If you are saying something important, someone should be able to present a counterargument. If you anticipate that counterargument, you will be able to account for it (this is Toulmin's concession and rebuttal). For instance, if you are arguing that a character sacrifices himself for love of his country and you read some passage suggesting that his motivations are not so noble, you have to deal with this problem: it could be argued that he sacrifices himself out of a desire for glory, or out of ignorance. Rather than pretend that those possibilities do not exist, you can account for them and still argue that your interpretation has some validity because your evidence outweighs the evidence of the opposition.

Rhetoricians value logic, clarity, and persuasion, and they also value creative and appealing uses of language. If your argument would benefit from an analogy, a metaphor, or a descriptive phrase, by all means include it. This is, again, a question of audience: if your instructor has written "Take chances!" on your assignment sheet, you might feel freer to indulge in creative language; if your instructor has written, "I will take five points off for every word that does not directly advance your argument," you need to be more careful.

Tone

Good arguments have a consistent and appropriate tone throughout. Since you are writing formal academic essays in college, you would not begin your paper this way: "Dude, I think this Soyinka guy is nuts." Writing is more formal than speech, and analytical college writing is more formal than other forms of communication such as e-mail. Your vocabulary should be appropriate to the level of formal analysis you are undertaking.

At the same time, you should be in command of the language you use and not be artificial. Do not be tempted, in other words, to use a thesaurus to replace every two-syllable word in your paper with a four-syllable word; since those are not your natural words, your paper might sound strange. Although your instructor values and understands the nuances of the English language, you can be true to your own "voice" while honoring the accepted conventions of this language.

This brief introduction to argument should make you aware of your obligations as a writer and your need to become attuned to the expectations of your audience. This chapter develops the practical advice offered in Chapter 2 (which also emphasized audience) and also connects to some of the more advanced ways of reading and researching that are addressed in Chapters 9, 10, and 11, chapters that demonstrate how a formal argument places you in relation to a larger community of thinkers. The next chapters (Chapters 4, 5, 6, 7, and 8) introduce some of the specialized vocabulary and ways of reading associated with different genres.

Part 2

Reading and Writing about Literary Genres

Chapter 4

Reading and Writing about Fiction

> Truth is stranger than fiction, but it is because fiction is obliged to stick to possibilities. Truth isn't.
> —MARK TWAIN, *Following the Equator* (1897)

Fiction tends to be a popular genre in literature courses, if not the favorite. Who doesn't like a good story? Even so, writing about fiction can be more difficult than writing about poetry and drama. A poem usually lasts only a page or two, so it is easier to see what is going on. Drama consists mostly of written speech, which is a more familiar and more accessible form of language than written narrative.

Fiction puts certain demands on a reader's memory. When we discuss or write about a story, we have to flip pages to make sure we are remembering it accurately. (This observation is especially true of longer fiction such as novels. Although much of this chapter applies to novels as well as short stories, this anthology includes only short stories.) Before writing about fiction, you need to reread it and take notes or annotate important passages.

This chapter provides a rudimentary vocabulary for discussing fiction and for recognizing its conventions. Understanding the conventions of fiction will help you derive meaning from stories. As with all literary genres, though, these conventions are merely a starting point for analysis: if you recognize foreshadowing in a story, for instance, that's a great first step toward understanding, but you also need to attach significance to that convention by analyzing it.

Elements of Fiction

Fiction is often described as "the lie that tells the truth." The word *lie* refers to the idea that fiction is a "made-up" story—unlike the essay, the prose genre discussed in Chapter 7. Yet this distinction is sometimes misleading, for while fiction is a work of the imagination rather than reality, it is also based closely on real events, sometimes events that happened to the author.

In a work of fiction, the **author** (the actual person who wrote the story) is not the same as the **narrator** (the voice that tells the story). Authors of stories maintain a distance from their characters. Sometimes that distance is obvious—for instance, if a male author writes a story from the point of view of a female character—and sometimes it is not so obvious, especially if we know something of the author's biography and if the story is clearly connected to events from that biography. Even so, it is a mistake to equate the author with his or her main character, even if the main character is also the narrator. Begin with the assumption that the events in the story, whether or not they resemble the events in an author's life, are part of the fictional world the author has created.

Point of View

A **narrative** is any work of literature that tells a story. Since some narrator is telling this story, you encounter the narrative **point of view** as soon as the story begins. You can begin your interpretation of every narrative by asking, "Who is telling this story? How is that person situated in relation to the story's action?" The narrator is sometimes a character in the story and at other times a disembodied voice that tells the story but does not participate in its action.

First-person narratives are told by a character ("I"). Sometimes the character introduces himself or herself right away, as in the opening sentence of Herman Melville's classic American novel *Moby-Dick:* "Call me Ishmael." In other cases it may be pages or chapters before you become aware that the narrator is a character rather than a storytelling voice. In first-person stories the narrator participates, to some degree, in the story he or she tells. Occasionally this participation may seem like little more than witnessing: Ford Madox Ford's novel *The Good Soldier* begins with the memorable sentence "This is the saddest story I have ever heard." The first-person narrator suggests that the sad story he is about to narrate is outside his experience: he has "heard" it, implying he was not directly involved. As with many first-person narratives, though, the story has more to do with the narrator than he initially leads us to believe.

We have to think carefully about the narrator's role in a story because he or she may not be completely honest or straightforward about his or her involvement in the action. A primary factor to scrutinize is motivation: *why* is the narrator telling the story? Again, it might not be obvious, but whether the narrator appears to be a major or a minor character, he or she is probably more major than we suspect. Factors like jealousy might cloud the narrator's ability to be completely honest with us about the events or the characters within a story. Critics and readers often refer to an **unreliable narrator**, one whom we cannot fully trust because of his or her unspoken involvement in the story. To some degree, all first-person narrators are unreliable because they all narrate from an individual perspective. In other words, someone telling a story cannot be completely neutral or objective. However, some narrators are more reliable than others.

Third-person narrators are not participants in the story they are narrating. Thus they are not exactly characters, though they occasionally might express an author's desires or perspective. For example, a third-person narrator may address the reader directly as though the narrator knows us and is toying with our expectations. Third-person narrators come in three distinct types:

- The *omniscient narrator* "knows everything" (as the word implies) about the characters in the story and can narrate or refrain from narrating details about any character—both internal details like a character's dreams and external details like a character's clothing. Whereas a first-person narrator might say, "I could see Jenna turning red and I knew she was about to scream," an omniscient third-person narrator might say, "Jenna felt her blood boiling and told herself to calm down, for screaming right now would be a bad idea."
- Whereas a fully omniscient narrator can float among the characters in a story, a *limited omniscient* narrator gives the story a narrower focus. Limited omniscient narrators often confine themselves to the inner life of only one character. Although these narrators are not the same as the focal character, they see the world largely through that character's eyes.
- A third-person narrator's omniscience might also be limited to the external details of a story: in this case, the narrator is often referred to as *objective*. Objective narrators are as free from perspective as they can be, much like the ideal journalist who only reports the facts.

Narrators rely heavily on dialogue (conversations between characters) and plot (or action) when they tell their stories; the reader must discern a character's motivation from what that character says and does.

Occasionally, but rarely, a story is narrated from a *second-person point of view*. In these stories, "you," the reader, are assumed to be one of the characters. The story is told to you as though you are involved in the action. This type of narrative assumes your willingness to play along, to assume the persona of a character in a story much as authors sometimes assume a persona to become a narrator. (A **persona** is a mask, or an assumed public identity. Sometimes an author maintains distance from the narrators or characters in a story by insisting on the difference between himself or herself and a persona.)

Plot

After realizing *who* is narrating, or perhaps even before, the reader is aware of *what* is being narrated. The events of a story are collectively referred to as the **plot.** Some types of stories favor the plot more than the other characteristics discussed here: action adventures, for instance, or even crime stories rely heavily on the details of what happens. Many works of literature, including those in this book, tend to balance plot with other elements, such as character development or an innovative use of language. Although these layers of storytelling give stories their weightiness, the plot is always an integral part of a story.

Some classic works of literature, such as Virginia Woolf's novel *Mrs. Dalloway* or James Joyce's novel *Ulysses,* have relatively little action: these two novels narrate the mundane events of a seemingly average day in the life of a London socialite and an average Dubliner, respectively. They are lengthy, ambitious novels that delve deep into the mind. If you were asked what they are "about," you might easily say, "Not much." They are more about thoughts and character than about action. Usually, however, the question of what a story is "about" is often a question about plot: what happened first, what happened next, and how one event affected the next event.

When you are writing about fiction, you need not be too detailed in your *plot summary*. Too much summary becomes meaningless if it is not connected to an analysis. You will develop an instinct for the amount of summary to include. As you analyze a story, you may need to refer to part of the plot, especially if something you say depends on the sequence of events.

For instance, in a discussion of Toni Morrison's short story "Recitatif," you might say, "After Twyla leaves the orphanage, she finds herself working as a waitress when she next encounters Roberta. At this point the crucial differences between the two friends become evident." The plot summary in the first sentence is needed for the analysis in the second sentence. An event-by-event account of the whole story is probably unnecessary. You can assume that your audience—in this case, your instructor—is familiar with the work under discussion. The writing assignment may explain how much summary to include; if you still have questions, it is always safer to consult with your instructor than to assume you know what she or he expects.

The *sequence* of the plot is not always straightforward: stories are not always told chronologically, or in a cause-and-effect order. Even if they are narrated chronologically, the reader may be aware of certain gaps in the plot: expanses of time that pass without our knowing what happened during them. These gaps have meaning: the plot includes both the events being narrated and the events *not* being narrated, and what happens in unnarrated time may hold the key to your interpretation of the story. If a story is not told in a conventional way—for instance, if the narrator goes back and forth in time—you shoulder more of the burden than you would otherwise. In these cases you need to reorder the story—either on your paper or in your mind—to clarify the relationship between the events of the story.

The order in which a story is told is as important as the events. Many short stories begin *in medias res*, or "in the middle of things." This type of story begins with an action that is central to the story's theme, then fills in the **back story,** also referred to as **exposition,** a term discussed in Chapter 6 on drama. Virtually all short stories are based on a **conflict,** or a tension between two opposing forces. The main character is either caught between those forces or is one of the forces. The main character is called the **protagonist,** and the character or forcehe or she is opposing is called the **antagonist.**

Often the conflict in a short story is multilayered: if the story centers around an argument, the conflict might seem to be between the two characters having the argument, but it may be much larger than the argument. If the two characters are living in poverty, then the conflict could be between those two characters and the society that has left them poor: the argument may simply reveal the stress that results from the broader conflict.

The structure of the short story is by no means fixed, and authors try to find innovative ways to tell their stories. As the short story form was developing in the United States in the middle of the nineteenth century, poet and short story writer Edgar Allan Poe (whose story "The Cask of Amontillado" can be found in Chapter 15) came up with an enduring definition of the short story in his review of a collection by Nathaniel Hawthorne. Poe wrote,

> A skilful literary artist has constructed a tale. If wise, he has not fashioned his thoughts to accommodate his incidents; but having conceived, with deliberate care, a certain unique or single *effect* to be wrought out, he then invents such incidents—he then combines such events as may best aid him in establishing this preconceived effect. If his very initial sentence tend not to the outbringing of this effect, then he has failed in his first step.

Poe emphasizes *unity* throughout his influential review. The short story, in his estimation, does not have the leisure to digress: every sentence, from the first through the last, contributes to the overall effect.

Often the narrator of a story is sensitive to the reader's desire for unity and helps the reader through devices such as **foreshadowing,** or details that clue the reader in to the outcome of the story. (Foreshadowing is also a common element of drama: Anton Chekhov famously observed that a gun that the audience sees in the first act of a play will be fired in the final act.) Instances of foreshadowing tend to be subtle but forceful enough to impress themselves on the mind of the reader. Imagine a story that ends with a character falling off a roof. Perhaps the narrator took time early in the story to relate the details of a pie falling off a kitchen counter and shattering; maybe one character tried in vain to catch the falling pie. Such events may seem trivial when the reader first encounters them, but they set the reader on edge and prepare him or her for what might happen later. When you encounter the falling pie, though, you cannot know its meaning until you have finished reading the story. Foreshadowing only works retrospectively.

The falling pie can also be regarded as a **symbol,** another way to unify a story. A symbol is a thing that suggests a meaning that goes beyond itself. The falling pie symbolizes something fragile, something that cannot be fixed once it has been broken, not unlike the human life it foreshadows. Symbols derive their meaning from their context, however: the pie in another context might signify something else (the phrase "American as apple pie" connotes something comforting and familiar). Some symbols are familiar to readers because they have been used repeatedly in a similar manner: if a character shows up with his pet snake draped around his neck, we probably are not going to assume he is a nice guy.

Character

Although short stories also do not have the leisure to introduce a large cast of characters, as a novel or a play might, **character** is one of the most important features of fiction. A character's thoughts, speech, and action become the point of contact between the reader and the story. Character is developed in short fiction against the backdrop of the story's setting, but more pointedly in relation to the story's plot. We know and evaluate a character through the way he or she acts or reacts to the events of the story.

Although stories are meant to entertain the reader on some level, they are also instructive: we are poised to sharpen our understanding of human nature by reading about characters, whether we want to be like them or to reject them. The word *character* can refer to one of the people in a story and also to the moral integrity of an individual (as in "he has real strength of character").

A character in a short story is often a recognizable type, sometimes called a *stock character* if it occurs repeatedly in literature, such as a mysterious stranger or a slippery salesman. (Since stock characters are based on a reader's preconceptions, they can easily become stereotypes.) Fiction writers have to communicate a character's type to us before they can begin to portray the character's individual circumstances. We might learn superficial characteristics such as a character's profession before we learn the more personal characteristics: a "typical lawyer" might be the first impression we have of a character, but she may develop over the course of the story as she faces an ethical dilemma, such as whether to defend a criminal she knows is guilty. Complicated, realistic characters are known as *round* characters. Both the characters in this chapter's story, "This Blessed House," are round characters because they struggle with real problems and are capable of change.

Setting

Along with plot, setting provides the backdrop for a character's development. **Setting** refers to both the physical place of a story (such as a city, an apartment, or a desert) and the time or period in which a story takes place (such as winter, or morning, or 1852). The details of the setting are all meaningful, and they contribute to the unity Poe speaks of in the quotation above, as well as to the story's overall effect. We can assume, for instance, that if a story takes place on a bitterly cold day, our response to it will be different than to a story with the same plot that takes place on a beautiful, comfortable summer day. Similarly, a story that takes place in a prison cell would not be the same story if it were set in a restaurant.

Theme

Although these conventions are important to any analysis of fiction, they do not constitute a "checklist" for writing about fiction. As you arrive at an interpretation of a story, some of these conventions will impress you more than others. You will see that identifying the conflict or getting a handle on the setting is only the first step.

In your education before college you were probably taught that the ultimate point of writing about a story was to discover its **theme**, and while interpretations generally lead to a statement of a story's theme, a story does not have a single theme that you have to "figure out." As earlier chapters discussed, the way you read a story depends largely on the context you select, perhaps in conjunction with your instructor or with the writing assignment.

The theme of a story is an abstract idea that is illustrated through the story's action and the development of the characters in relation to that action. When people ask each other what a story is "about," they're often looking for the plot ("It's about a guy who goes hunting and gets shot by his wife"). However, if your instructor asks you what a story is "about," he or she is probably looking for the theme. The theme is not the same thing as the topic: it is a statement about that topic. For instance, to say that a story is about death is not to state its theme; you would have to say that the story is about the way people ruin the lives of their loved ones when they deny their own fears of death, or something similar.

Stories can be about more than one thing. This is one of the characteristics that differentiates stories from essays: essays, as discussed in Chapter 7, usually explicitly state their underlying idea, which takes the form of a thesis.

Student Essay on Jhumpa Lahiri's "This Blessed House"

The following story appeared in Jhumpa Lahiri's book *Interpreter of Maladies*, a short story collection that won the Pulitzer Prize for fiction in 1999. Following the story is a brief discussion of the elements of fiction it uses. Following this discussion is a short student essay on the setting in the story, particularly the question of irony in the title: is the term "blessed house" ironic in that the house is actually cursed because of Sanjeev and Twinkle's marriage?

Jhumpa Lahiri *(b. 1967)*

This Blessed House

They discovered the first one in a cupboard above the stove, beside an unopened bottle of malt vinegar. "Guess what I found." Twinkle walked into the living room, lined from end to end with taped-up packing boxes, waving the vinegar in one hand and a white porcelain effigy of Christ, roughly the same size as the vinegar bottle, in the other.

Sanjeev looked up. He was kneeling on the floor, marking, with ripped bits of a Post-it, patches on the baseboard that needed to be retouched with paint. "Throw it away."

"Which?"

"Both."

"But I can cook something with the vinegar. It's brand-new." 5

"You've never cooked anything with vinegar."

"I'll look something up. In one of those books we got for our wedding."

Sanjeev turned back to the baseboard, to replace a Post-it scrap that had fallen to the floor. "Check the expiration. And at the very least get rid of that idiotic statue."

"But it could be worth something. Who knows?" She turned it upside down, then stroked, with her index finger, the minuscule frozen folds of its robes. "It's pretty."

"We're not Christian," Sanjeev said. Lately he had begun noticing the need to state the obvious to Twinkle. The day before he had to tell her that if she dragged her end of the bureau instead of lifting it, the parquet floor would scratch.

She shrugged. "No, we're not Christian. We're good little Hindus." She planted a kiss on top of Christ's head, then placed the statue on top of the fireplace mantel, which needed, Sanjeev observed, to be dusted.

By the end of the week the mantel had still not been dusted; it had, however, come to serve as the display shelf for a sizable collection of Christian paraphernalia. There was a 3-D postcard of Saint Francis done in four colors, which Twinkle had found taped to the back of the medicine cabinet, and a wooden cross key chain, which Sanjeev had stepped on with bare feet as he was installing extra shelving in Twinkle's study. There was a framed paint-by-number of the three wise men, against a black velvet background, tucked in the linen closet. There was also a tile trivet depicting a blond, unbearded Jesus, delivering a sermon on a mountaintop, left in one of the drawers of the built-in china cabinet in the dining room.

"Do you think the previous owners were born-agains?" asked Twinkle, making room the next day for a small plastic snow-filled dome containing a miniature Nativity scene, found behind the pipes of the kitchen sink.

Sanjeev was organizing his engineering texts from MIT in alphabetical order on a bookshelf, though it had been several years since he had needed to consult any of them. After graduating, he moved from Boston to Connecticut, to work for a firm near Hartford, and he had recently learned that he was being considered for the position of vice president. At thirty-three he had a secretary of his own and a dozen people working under his supervision who gladly supplied him with any information he needed. Still, the presence of his college books in the room reminded him of a time in his life he recalled with fondness, when he would walk each evening across the Mass. Avenue bridge to order Mughlai chicken with spinach from his favorite Indian restaurant on the other side of the Charles, and return to his dorm to write out clean copies of his problem sets.

"Or perhaps it's an attempt to convert people," Twinkle mused.

"Clearly the scheme has succeeded in your case."

She disregarded him, shaking the little plastic dome so that the snow swirled over the manger.

He studied the items on the mantel. It puzzled him that each was in its own way so silly. Clearly they lacked a sense of sacredness. He was further puzzled that Twinkle, who normally displayed good taste, was so charmed. These objects meant something to Twinkle, but they meant nothing to him. They irritated him. "We should call the Realtor. Tell him there's all this nonsense left behind. Tell him to take it away."

"Oh, Sanj." Twinkle groaned. "Please. I would feel terrible throwing them away. Obviously they were important to the people who used to live here. It would feel, I don't know, sacrilegious or something."

"If they're so precious, then why are they hidden all over the house? Why didn't they take them with them?"

"There must be others," Twinkle said. Her eyes roamed the bare off-white walls of the room, as if there were other things concealed behind the plaster. "What else do you think we'll find?"

But as they unpacked their boxes and hung up their winter clothes and the silk paintings of elephant processions bought on their honeymoon in Jaipur, Twinkle, much to her dismay, could not find a thing. Nearly a week had passed before they discovered, one Saturday afternoon, a larger-than-life-sized watercolor poster of Christ, weeping translucent tears the size of peanut shells and sporting a crown of thorns, rolled up behind a radiator in the guest bedroom. Sanjeev had mistaken it for a window shade.

"Oh, we must, we simply must put it up. It's too spectacular." Twinkle lit a cigarette and began to smoke it with relish, waving it around Sanjeev's head as if it were a conductor's baton as Mahler's Fifth Symphony roared from the stereo downstairs.

"Now, look. I will tolerate, for now, your little biblical menagerie in the living room. But I refuse to have this," he said, flicking at one of the painted peanut-tears, "displayed in our home."

Twinkle stared at him, placidly exhaling, the smoke emerging in two thin blue streams from her nostrils. She rolled up the poster slowly, securing it with one of the elastic bands she always wore around her wrist for tying back her thick, unruly hair, streaked here and there with henna. "I'm going to put it in my study," she informed him. "That way you don't have to look at it."

"What about the housewarming? They'll want to see all the rooms. I've invited people from the office."

She rolled her eyes. Sanjeev noted that the symphony, now in its third movement, had reached a crescendo, for it pulsed with the telltale clashing of cymbals.

"I'll put it behind the door," she offered. "That way, when they peek in, they won't see. Happy?"

He stood watching her as she left the room, with her poster and her cigarette; a few ashes had fallen to the floor where she'd been standing. He bent down, pinched them between his fingers, and deposited them in his cupped palm. The tender fourth movement, the *adagietto*, began. During breakfast, Sanjeev had read in the liner notes that Mahler had proposed to his wife by sending her the manuscript of this portion of the score. Although there were elements of tragedy and struggle in the Fifth Symphony, he had read, it was principally music of love and happiness.

He heard the toilet flush. "By the way," Twinkle hollered, "if you want to impress people, I wouldn't play this music. It's putting me to sleep."

Sanjeev went to the bathroom to throw away the ashes. The cigarette butt still bobbed in the toilet bowl, but the tank was refilling, so he had to wait a moment before he could flush it again. In the mirror of the medicine cabinet he inspected his long eyelashes—like a girl's, Twinkle liked to tease. Though he was of average build, his cheeks had a plumpness to them; this, along with the eyelashes, detracted, he feared, from what he hoped was a distinguished profile. He was of average height as well, and had wished ever since he had stopped growing that he were just one inch taller. For this reason it irritated him when Twinkle insisted on wearing high heels, as she had done the other night when they ate dinner in Manhattan. This was the first weekend after they'd moved into the house; by then the mantel had already filled up considerably, and they had bickered about it in the car on the way down. But then Twinkle had drunk four glasses of whiskey in a nameless bar in Alphabet City, and forgot all about it. She dragged him to a tiny bookshop on St. Mark's Place, where she browsed for nearly an hour, and when they left she insisted that they dance a tango on the sidewalk in front of strangers.

Afterward, she tottered on his arm, rising faintly over his line of vision, in a pair of suede three-inch leopard-print pumps. In this manner they walked the endless blocks back to a parking garage on Washington Square, for Sanjeev had heard far too many stories about the terrible things that happened to cars in Manhattan. "But I do nothing all day except sit at my desk," she fretted when they were driving home, after he had mentioned that her shoes looked uncomfortable and suggested that perhaps she should not wear them. "I can't exactly wear heels when I'm typing." Though he abandoned the argument, he knew for a fact that she didn't spend all day at her desk; just that afternoon, when he got back from a run, he found her inexplicably in bed, reading. When he asked why she was in bed in the middle of the day she told him she was bored. He had wanted to say to her then, You could unpack some boxes. You could sweep the attic. You could retouch the paint on the bathroom windowsill, and after you do it you could warn me so that I don't put my watch on it. They didn't bother her, these scattered, unsettled matters. She seemed content with whatever clothes she found at the front of the closet, with whatever magazine was lying around, with whatever song was on the radio—content yet curious. And now all of her curiosity centered around discovering the next treasure.

A few days later when Sanjeev returned from the office, he found Twinkle on the telephone, smoking and talking to one of her girlfriends in California even though it was before five o'clock and the long-distance rates were at their peak. "Highly devout people," she was saying, pausing every now and then to exhale. "Each day is like a treasure hunt. I'm serious. This you won't believe. The switch plates in the bedrooms were decorated with scenes from the Bible. You know, Noah's Ark and all that. Three bedrooms, but one is my study. Sanjeev went to the hardware store right away and replaced them, can you imagine, he replaced every single one."

Now it was the friend's turn to talk. Twinkle nodded, slouched on the floor in front of the fridge, wearing black stirrup pants and a yellow chenille sweater, groping for her lighter. Sanjeev could smell something aromatic on the stove, and he picked his way carefully across the extra-long phone cord tangled on the

Mexican terra-cotta tiles. He opened the lid of a pot with some sort of reddish brown sauce dripping over the sides, boiling furiously.

"It's a stew made with fish. I put the vinegar in it," she said to him, interrupting her friend, crossing her fingers. "Sorry, you were saying?" She was like that, excited and delighted by little things, crossing her fingers before any remotely unpredictable event, like tasting a new flavor of ice cream, or dropping a letter in a mailbox. It was a quality he did not understand. It made him feel stupid, as if the world contained hidden wonders he could not anticipate, or see. He looked at her face, which, it occurred to him, had not grown out of its girlhood, the eyes untroubled, the pleasing features unfirm, as if they still had to settle into some sort of permanent expression. Nicknamed after a nursery rhyme, she had yet to shed a childhood endearment. Now, in the second month of their marriage, certain things nettled him—the way she sometimes spat a little when she spoke, or left her undergarments after removing them at night at the foot of their bed rather than depositing them in the laundry hamper.

They had met only four months before. Her parents, who lived in California, and his, who still lived in Calcutta, were old friends, and across continents they had arranged the occasion at which Twinkle and Sanjeev were introduced—a sixteenth birthday party for a daughter in their circle—when Sanjeev was in Palo Alto on business. At the restaurant they were seated side by side at a round table with a revolving platter of spareribs and egg rolls and chicken wings, which, they concurred, all tasted the same. They had concurred too on their adolescent but still persistent fondness for Wodehouse novels, and their dislike for the sitar, and later Twinkle confessed that she was charmed by the way Sanjeev had dutifully refilled her teacup during their conversation.

And so the phone calls began, and grew longer, and then the visits, first he to Stanford, then she to Connecticut, after which Sanjeev would save in an ashtray left on the balcony the crushed cigarettes she had smoked during the weekend—saved them, that is, until the next time she came to visit him, and then he vacuumed the apartment, washed the sheets, even dusted the plant leaves in her honor. She was twenty-seven and recently abandoned, he had gathered, by an American who had tried and failed to be an actor; Sanjeev was lonely, with an excessively generous income for a single man, and had never been in love. At the urging of their matchmakers, they married in India, amid hundreds of well-wishers whom he barely remembered from his childhood, in incessant August rains, under a red and orange tent strung with Christmas tree lights on Mandeville Road.

"Did you sweep the attic?" he asked Twinkle later as she was folding paper napkins and wedging them by their plates. The attic was the only part of the house they had not yet given an initial cleaning.

"Not yet. I will, I promise. I hope this tastes good," she said, planting the steaming pot on top of the Jesus trivet. There was a loaf of Italian bread in a little basket, and iceberg lettuce and grated carrots tossed with bottled dressing and croutons, and glasses of red wine. She was not terribly ambitious in the kitchen. She bought preroasted chickens from the supermarket and served them with potato salad prepared who knew when, sold in little plastic containers. Indian food, she complained, was a bother; she detested chopping garlic, and peeling ginger, and could not operate a blender, and so it was Sanjeev who, on weekends, seasoned mustard oil with cinnamon sticks and cloves in order to produce a proper curry.

40 He had to admit, though, that whatever it was that she had cooked today, it was unusually tasty, attractive even, with bright white cubes of fish, and flecks of parsley, and fresh tomatoes gleaming in the dark brown-red broth.

"How did you make it?"

"I made it up."

"What did you do?"

"I just put some things into the pot and added the malt vinegar at the end."

45 "How much vinegar?"

She shrugged, ripping off some bread and plunging it into her bowl.

"What do you mean you don't know? You should write it down. What if you need to make it again, for a party or something?"

"I'll remember," she said. She covered the bread basket with a dishtowel that had, he suddenly noticed, the Ten Commandments printed on it. She flashed him a smile, giving his knee a little squeeze under the table. "Face it. This house is blessed."

The housewarming party was scheduled for the last Saturday in October, and they had invited about thirty people. All were Sanjeev's acquaintances, people from the office, and a number of Indian couples in the Connecticut area, many of whom he barely knew, but who had regularly invited him, in his bachelor days, to supper on Saturdays. He often wondered why they included him in their circle. He had little in common with any of them, but he always attended their gatherings, to eat spiced chickpeas and shrimp cutlets, and gossip and discuss politics, for he seldom had other plans. So far, no one had met Twinkle; back when they were still dating, Sanjeev didn't want to waste their brief weekends together with people he associated with being alone. Other than Sanjeev and an ex-boyfriend who she believed worked in a pottery studio in Brookfield, she knew no one in the state of Connecticut. She was completing her master's thesis at Stanford, a study of an Irish poet whom Sanjeev had never heard of.

50 Sanjeev had found the house on his own before leaving for the wedding, for a good price, in a neighborhood with a fine school system. He was impressed by the elegant curved staircase with its wrought-iron banister, and the dark wooden wainscoting, and the solarium overlooking rhododendron bushes, and the solid brass 22, which also happened to be the date of his birth, nailed impressively to the vaguely Tudor facade. There were two working fireplaces, a two-car garage, and an attic suitable for converting into extra bedrooms if, the Realtor mentioned, the need should arise. By then Sanjeev had already made up his mind, was determined that he and Twinkle should live there together, forever, and so he had not bothered to notice the switch plates covered with biblical stickers, or the transparent decal of the Virgin on the half shell, as Twinkle liked to call it, adhered to the window in the master bedroom. When, after moving in, he tried to scrape it off, he scratched the glass.

The weekend before the party they were raking the lawn when he heard Twinkle shriek. He ran to her, clutching his rake, worried that she had discovered a dead animal, or a snake. A brisk October breeze stung the tops of his ears as his sneakers crunched over brown and yellow leaves. What he reached her, she had collapsed on the grass, dissolved in nearly silent laughter. Behind an overgrown forsythia bush was a plaster Virgin Mary as tall as their waists, with a blue painted hood draped over her head in the manner of an Indian bride. Twinkle grabbed the hem of her T-shirt and began wiping away the dirt staining the statue's brow.

"I suppose you want to put her by the foot of our bed," Sanjeev said.

She looked at him, astonished. Her belly was exposed, and he saw that there were goose bumps around her navel. "What do you think? Of course we can't put this in our bedroom."

"We can't?"

"No, silly Sanj. This is meant for outside. For the lawn."

"Oh God, no. Twinkle, no."

"But we must. It would be bad luck not to."

"All the neighbors will see. They'll think we're insane."

"Why, for having a statue of the Virgin Mary on our lawn? Every other person in this neighborhood has a statue of Mary on the lawn. We'll fit right in."

"We're not Christian."

"So you keep reminding me." She spat onto the tip of her finger and started to rub intently at a particularly stubborn stain on Mary's chin. "Do you think this is dirt, or some kind of fungus?"

He was getting nowhere with her, with this woman whom he had known for only four months and whom he had married, this woman with whom he now shared his life. He thought with a flicker of regret of the snapshots his mother used to send him from Calcutta, of prospective brides who could sing and sew and season lentils without consulting a cookbook. Sanjeev had considered these women, had even ranked them in order of preference, but then he had met Twinkle. "Twinkle, I can't have the people I work with see this statue on my lawn."

"They can't fire you for being a believer. It would be discrimination."

"That's not the point."

"Why does it matter to you so much what other people think?"

"Twinkle, please." He was tired. He let his weight rest against his rake as she began dragging the statue toward an oval bed of myrtle, beside the lamppost that flanked the brick pathway. "Look, Sanj. She's so lovely."

He returned to his pile of leaves and began to deposit them by handfuls into a plastic garbage bag. Over his head the blue sky was cloudless. One tree on the lawn was still full of leaves, red and orange, like the tent in which he had married Twinkle.

He did not know if he loved her. He said he did when she had first asked him, one afternoon in Palo Alto as they sat side by side in a darkened, nearly empty movie theater. Before the film, one of her favorites, something in German that he found extremely depressing, she had pressed the tip of her nose to his so that he could feel the flutter of her mascara-coated eyelashes. That afternoon he had replied, yes, he loved her, and she was delighted, and fed him a piece of popcorn, letting her finger linger an instant between his lips, as if it were his reward for coming up with the right answer.

Though she did not say it herself, he assumed then that she loved him too, but now he was no longer sure. In truth, Sanjeev did not know what love was, only what he thought it was not. It was not, he had decided, returning to an empty carpeted condominium each night, and using only the top fork in his cutlery drawer, and turning away politely at those weekend dinner parties when the other men eventually put their arms around the waists of their wives and girlfriends, leaning over every now and again to kiss their shoulders or necks. It was not sending away for classical music CDs by mail, working his way methodically through the major composers that the catalogue recommended, and always sending his payments in on time. In the months before meeting Twinkle, Sanjeev had begun to realize this. "You have enough money in the bank to raise three families," his mother reminded him when they spoke at the start of each month on the phone. "You need a wife to look after and love." Now he had one, a pretty one, from a suitably high caste, who would soon have a master's degree. What was there not to love?

70 That evening Sanjeev poured himself a gin and tonic, drank it and most of another during one segment of the news, and then approached Twinkle, who was taking a bubble bath, for she announced that her limbs ached from raking the lawn, something she had never done before. He didn't knock. She had applied a bright blue mask to her face, was smoking and sipping some bourbon with ice and leafing through a fat paperback book whose pages had buckled and turned gray from the water. He glanced at the cover; the only thing written on it was the word "Sonnets" in dark red letters. He took a breath, and then he informed her very calmly that after finishing his drink he was going to put on his shoes and go outside and remove the Virgin from the front lawn.

"Where are you going to put it?" she asked him dreamily, her eyes closed. One of her legs emerged, unfolding gracefully, from the layer of suds. She flexed and pointed her toes.

"For now I am going to put it in the garage. Then tomorrow morning on my way to work I am going to take it to the dump."

"Don't you dare." She stood up, letting the book fall into the water, bubbles dripping down her thighs. "I hate you," she informed him, her eyes narrowing at the word "hate." She reached for her bathrobe, tied it tightly about her waist, and padded down the winding staircase, leaving sloppy wet footprints along the parquet floor. When she reached the foyer, Sanjeev said, "Are you planning on leaving the house that way?" He felt a throbbing in his temples, and his voice revealed an unfamiliar snarl when he spoke.

"Who cares? Who cares what way I leave this house?"

75 "Where are you planning on going at this hour?"

"You can't throw away that statue. I won't let you." Her mask, now dry, had assumed an ashen quality, and water from her hair dripped onto the caked contours of her face.

"Yes I can. I will."

"No," Twinkle said, her voice suddenly small. "This is our house. We own it together. The statue is a part of our property." She had begun to shiver. A small pool of bathwater had collected around her ankles. He went to shut a window, fearing that she would catch cold. Then he noticed that some of the water dripping down her hard blue face was tears.

"Oh God, Twinkle, please, I didn't mean it." He had never seen her cry before, had never seen such sadness in her eyes. She didn't turn away or try to stop the tears; instead she looked strangely at peace. For a moment she closed her lids, pale and unprotected compared to the blue that caked the rest of her face. Sanjeev felt ill, as if he had caten either too much or too little.

She went to him, placing her damp toweled arms about his neck, sobbing into his chest, soaking his shirt. The mask flaked onto his shoulders.

In the end they settled on a compromise: the statue would be placed in a recess at the side of the house, so that it wasn't obvious to passersby, but was still clearly visible to all who came.

The menu for the party was fairly simple: there would be a case of champagne, and samosas from an Indian restaurant in Hartford, and big trays of rice with chicken and almonds and orange peels, which Sanjeev had spent the greater part of the morning and afternoon preparing. He had never entertained on such a large scale before and, worried that there would not be enough to drink, ran out at one point to buy another case of champagne just in case. For this reason he burned onc of the rice trays and had to start it over again. Twinkle swept the floors and volunteered to pick up the samosas; she had an appointment for a manicure and a pedicure in that direction, anyway. Sanjeev had planned to ask if she would consider clearing the menagerie off the mantel, if only for the party, but she left while he was in the shower. She was gone for a good three hours, and so it was Sanjeev who did the rest of the cleaning. By five-thirty the entire house sparkled, with scented candles that Twinkle had picked up in Hartford illuminating the items on the mantel, and slender stalks of burning incense planted into the soil of potted plants. Each time he passed the mantel he winced, dreading the raised eyebrows of his guests as they viewed the flickering ceramic saints, the salt and pepper shakers designed to resemble Mary and Joseph. Still, they would be impressed, he hoped, by the lovely bay windows, the shining parquet floors, the impressive winding staircase, the wooden wainscoting, as they sipped champagne and dipped samosas in chutney.

Douglas, one of the new consultants at the firm, and his girlfriend Nora were the first to arrive. Both were tall and blond, wearing matching wire-rimmed glasses and long black overcoats. Nora wore a black hat full of sharp thin feathers that corresponded to the sharp thin angles of her face. Her left hand was joined with Douglas's. In her right hand was a bottle of cognac with a red ribbon wrapped around its neck, which she gave to Twinkle.

"Great lawn, Sanjeev," Douglas remarked. "We've got to get that rake out ourselves, sweetie. And this must be . . ."

"My wife. Tanima."

"Call me Twinkle."

"What an unusual name," Nora remarked.

Twinkle shrugged. "Not really. There's an actress in Bombay named Dimple Kapadia. She even has a sister named Simple."

Douglas and Nora raised their eyebrows simultaneously, nodding slowly, as if to let the absurdity of the names settle in. "Pleased to meet you, Twinkle."

"Help yourself to champagne. There's gallons."

"I hope you don't mind my asking," Douglas said, "but I noticed the statue outside, and are you guys Christian? I thought you were Indian."

"There are Christians in India," Sanjeev replied, "but we're not."

"I love your outfit," Nora told Twinkle.

"And I adore your hat. Would you like the grand tour?"

The bell rang again, and again and again. Within minutes, it seemed, the house had filled with bodies and conversations and unfamiliar fragrances. The women wore heels and sheer stockings, and short black dresses made of crepe and chiffon. They handed their wraps and coats to Sanjeev, who draped them carefully on hangers in the spacious coat closet, though Twinkle told people to throw their things on the ottomans in the solarium. Some of the Indian women wore their finest saris, made with gold filigree that draped in elegant pleats over their shoulders. The men wore jackets and ties and citrus-scented aftershaves. As people filtered from one room to the next, presents piled onto the long cherry-wood table that ran from one end of the downstairs hall to the other.

It bewildered Sanjeev that it was for him, and his house, and his wife, that they had all gone to so much care. The only other time in his life that something similar had happened was his wedding day, but somehow this was different, for these were not his family, but people who knew him only casually, and in a sense owed him nothing. Everyone congratulated him. Lester, another coworker, predicted that Sanjeev would be promoted to vice president in two months maximum. People devoured the samosas, and dutifully admired the freshly painted ceilings and walls, the hanging plants, the bay windows, the silk paintings from Jaipur. But most of all they admired Twinkle, and her brocaded *salwar-kameez*, which was the shade of a persimmon with a low scoop in the back, and the little string of white rose petals she had coiled cleverly around her head, and the pearl choker with a sapphire at its center that adorned her throat. Over hectic jazz records, played under Twinkle's supervision, they laughed at her anecdotes and observations, forming a widening circle around her, while Sanjeev replenished the samosas that he kept warming evenly in the oven, and getting ice for people's drinks, and opening more bottles of champagne with some difficulty, and explaining for the fortieth time that he wasn't Christian. It was Twinkle who led them in separate groups up and down the winding stairs, to gaze at the back lawn, to peer down the cellar steps. "Your friends adore the poster in my study," she mentioned to him triumphantly, placing her hand on the small of his back as they, at one point, brushed past each other.

Sanjeev went to the kitchen, which was empty, and ate a piece of chicken out of the tray on the counter with his fingers because he thought no one was looking. He ate a second piece, then washed it down with a gulp of gin straight from the bottle.

"Great house. Great rice." Sunil, an anesthesiologist, walked in, spooning food from his paper plate into his mouth. "Do you have more champagne?"

"Your wife's wow," added Prabal, following behind. He was an unmarried professor of physics at Yale. For a moment Sanjeev stared at him blankly, then blushed; once at a dinner party Prabal had pronounced that Sophia Loren was wow, as was Audrey Hepburn. "Does she have a sister?"

Sunil picked a raisin out of the rice tray. "Is her last name Little Star?"

The two men laughed and started eating more rice from the tray, plowing through it with their plastic spoons. Sanjeev went down to the cellar for more liquor. For a few minutes he paused on the steps, in the damp, cool silence, hugging the second crate of champagne to his chest as the party drifted above the rafters. Then he set the reinforcements on the dining table.

"Yes, everything, we found them all in the house, in the most unusual places," he heard Twinkle saying in the living room. "In fact we keep finding them."

"No!"

"Yes! Every day is like a treasure hunt. It's too good. God only knows what else we'll find, no pun intended."

That was what started it. As if by some unspoken pact, the whole party joined forces and began combing through each of the rooms, opening closets on their own, peering under chairs and cushions, feeling behind curtains, removing books from bookcases. Groups scampered, giggling and swaying, up and down the winding staircase.

"We've never explored the attic," Twinkle announced suddenly, and so everybody followed.

"How do we get up there?"

"There's a ladder in the hallway, somewhere in the ceiling."

Wearily Sanjeev followed at the back of the crowd, to point out the location of the ladder, but Twinkle had already found it on her own. "Eureka!" she hollered.

Douglas pulled the chain that released the steps. His face was flushed and he was wearing Nora's feather hat on his head. One by one the guests disappeared, men helping women as they placed their strappy high heels on the narrow slats of the ladder, the Indian women wrapping the free ends of their expensive saris into their waistbands. The men followed behind, all quickly disappearing, until Sanjeev alone remained at the top of the winding staircase. Footsteps thundered over his head. He had no desire to join them. He wondered if the ceiling would collapse, imagined, for a split second, the sight of all the tumbling drunk perfumed bodies crashing, tangled, around him. He heard a shriek, and then rising, spreading waves of laughter in discordant tones. Something fell, something else shattered. He could hear them babbling about a trunk. They seemed to be struggling to get it open, banging feverishly on its surface.

He thought perhaps Twinkle would call for his assistance, but he was not summoned. He looked about the hallway and to the landing below, at the champagne glasses and half-eaten samosas and napkins smeared with lipstick abandoned in every corner, on every available surface. Then he noticed that Twinkle, in her haste, had discarded her shoes altogether, for they lay by the foot of the ladder, black patent-leather mules with heels like golf tees, open toes, and slightly soiled silk labels on the instep where her soles had rested. He placed them in the doorway of the master bedroom so that no one would trip when they descended.

He heard something creaking open slowly. The strident voices had subsided to an even murmur. It occurred to Sanjeev that he had the house all to himself. The music had ended and he could hear, if he concentrated, the hum of the refrigerator, and the rustle of the last leaves on the trees outside, and the tapping of their branches against the windowpanes. With one flick of his hand he could snap the ladder back on its spring into the ceiling, and they would have no way of getting down unless he were to pull the chain and let them. He thought of all the things he could do, undisturbed. He could sweep Twinkle's menagerie into a garbage bag and get in the car and drive it all to the dump, and tear down the poster of weeping Jesus, and take a hammer to the Virgin Mary while he was at it. Then he would return to the empty house; he could easily clear up the cups and plates in an hour's time, and pour himself a gin and tonic, and eat a plate of warmed rice and listen to his new Bach CD while reading the liner notes so as to understand it properly. He nudged the ladder slightly, but it was sturdily planted against the floor. Budging it would require some effort.

"My God, I need a cigarette," Twinkle exclaimed from above.

Sanjeev felt knots forming at the back of his neck. He felt dizzy. He needed to lie down. He walked toward the bedroom, but stopped short when he saw Twinkle's shoes facing him in the doorway. He thought of her slipping them on her feet. But instead of feeling irritated, as he had ever since they'd moved into the house together, he felt a pang of anticipation at the thought of her rushing unsteadily down the winding staircase in them, scratching the floor a bit in her path. The pang intensified as he thought of her rushing to the bathroom to brighten her lipstick, and eventually rushing to get people their coats, and finally rushing to the cherry-wood table when the last guest had left, to begin opening their housewarming presents. It was the same pang he used to feel before they were married, when he would hang up the phone after one of their conversations, or when he would drive back from the airport, wondering which ascending plane in the sky was hers.

"Sanj, you won't believe this."

She emerged with her back to him, her hands over her head, the tops of her bare shoulder blades perspiring, supporting something still hidden from view.

"You got it, Twinkle?" someone asked.

"Yes, you can let go."

Now he saw that her hands were wrapped around it: a solid silver bust of Christ, the head easily three times the size of his own. It had a patrician bump on its nose, magnificent curly hair that rested atop a pronounced collarbone, and a broad forehead that reflected in miniature the walls and doors and lampshades around them. Its expression was confident, as if assured of its devotees, the unyielding lips sensuous and full. It was also sporting Nora's feather hat. As Twinkle descended, Sanjeev put his hands around her waist to balance her, and he relieved her of the bust when she had reached the ground. It weighed a good thirty pounds. The others began lowering themselves slowly, exhausted from the hunt. Some trickled downstairs in search of a fresh drink.

She took a breath, raised her eyebrows, crossed her fingers. "Would you mind 120
terribly if we displayed it on the mantel? Just for tonight? I know you hate it."

He did hate it. He hated its immensity, and its flawless, polished surface, and its undeniable value. He hated that it was in his house, and that he owned it. Unlike the other things they'd found, this contained dignity, solemnity, beauty even. But to his surprise these qualities made him hate it all the more. Most of all he hated it because he knew that Twinkle loved it.

"I'll keep it in my study from tomorrow," Twinkle added. "I promise."

She would never put it in her study, he knew. For the rest of their days together she would keep it on the center of the mantel, flanked on either side by the rest of the menagerie. Each time they had guests Twinkle would explain how she had found it, and they would admire her as they listened. He gazed at the crushed rose petals in her hair, at the pearl and sapphire choker at her throat, at the sparkly crimson polish on her toes. He decided these were among the things that made Prabal think she was wow. His head ached from gin and his arms ached from the weight of the statue. He said, "I put your shoes in the bedroom."

"Thanks. But my feet are killing me." Twinkle gave his elbow a little squeeze and headed for the living room.

Sanjeev pressed the massive silver face to his ribs, careful not to let the 125
feather hat slip, and followed her.

(1999)

"This Blessed House" is an example of third-person narration and uses a limited omniscient point of view. The narrator is not a character in the story but can communicate the characters' words, actions, and thoughts. The author of this story has chosen to limit the narrator's omniscience by confining it to the perspective of a single character: Sanjeev.

The plot builds toward one event: the party at the end of the story. Although it begins when Sanjeev and Twinkle move into the house, we learn about their lives prior to moving in through the exposition, or back story. Especially important in the exposition is their courtship, the fact that their marriage was partly arranged by their parents, and that, for a married couple, they haven't known each other very long (four months) by traditional American standards.

The setting of this story seems to be of particular importance: the story takes place entirely within the "blessed house" of the title, and the surprises and discoveries of the hidden Christian paraphernalia conflict with Sanjeev's obsessive efforts to fix up his dwelling. The story is largely about the way these two characters respond to the "blessed house" they have moved into.

The two main characters, Sanjeev and Twinkle, are depicted as nearly complete opposites: Sanjeev loves order and cleanliness, and he is keenly aware of what other people think. Twinkle is chaotic and sloppy; she follows her own rules.

These characters are drawn partially through symbols: Sanjeev listens to the elaborate, ordered music of Bach and Mahler, while Twinkle plays "hectic jazz" at the housewarming party. Sanjeev spends his time in the kitchen combining ingredients to make a "proper curry," while Twinkle throws a bunch of ingredients into a pot without measuring them. Other symbols include the Post-it notes that Sanjeev uses to mark imperfections in the baseboards, the dust on the mantle, Twinkle's shoes, and all of the religious icons they discover.

Irony is a literary convention that masks the appearance of reality. In irony, words mean the opposite of what they typically mean. Irony is, in this sense, the opposite of literal meaning. We gave a student, an English major at Suffolk University named Sarah Himberger, the following question as a writing assignment: "In 'This Blessed House' by Jhumpa Lahiri, is the word *Blessed* in the title ironic or literal? Based on your response to this question, what do you see as the future of Twinkle and Sanjeev's relationship?" We did not ask Sarah to deal with all the conventions of fiction; the question was focused so that Sarah could control her argument (see Chapter 3).

Student Essay

Sarah Himberger is originally from Cape Cod, Massachusetts. She received her bachelor's degree in English from Suffolk University in May 2005. Immediately after graduating, Sarah worked as a teaching assistant for the Suffolk University English Department and was a substitute teacher of English as a second language. She now works with people with developmental and cognitive disabilities. She plans to attend graduate school to study special education.

Himberger 1

Sarah Himberger

Final Draft

An Ironic Blessing

Jhumpa Lahiri's short story, "This Blessed House" begins as a newlywed couple begin to discover Christian knick-knacks hidden inside their newly purchased first home together. Almost as once, the

Himberger 2

irony of these findings is evident, as Sanjeev and Twinkle are not Christian but Hindu. Yet, as they start to discover more and more of this Christian memorabilia, the title of the story can be further analyzed. When one examines the relationship between Twinkle and Sanjeev, especially Sanjeev's anxiety and disgust at Twinkle's fascination with the Christian discoveries, one can conclude that the title plays both an ironic and literal role, but overall, "This Blessed House" is in fact an ironic title for the piece.

As soon as the reader is introduced to Sanjeev and Twinkle, they are already discovering their "blessed" paraphernalia. The story opens with the line "They discovered the first one in a cupboard above the stove, beside an unopened bottle of malt vinegar . . . a white porcelain effigy of Christ, roughly the same size as the vinegar bottle" (53). Within the first few paragraphs of the story the reader also realizes there is indeed irony to these findings. "'We're not Christian,' Sanjeev said. Lately he had begun noticing the need to state the obvious to Twinkle." To this, Twinkle replies, somewhat mockingly, "No, we're not Christian. We're good little Hindus" (54).

Within these statements there are two different levels of irony that are elaborated upon as the story develops. There is, of course, the surface irony that these two Hindu people are discovering Christian icons which they are entirely unfamiliar with, and now are attempting to deal with them. Yet, at the same time, there is a more developed irony, focusing on the relationship between Sanjeev and Twinkle. They are newlyweds, and in a time when "This Blessed House" should be literal, a time of happiness and newlywed bliss, it is quite the opposite. Sanjeev struggles to accept his wife as who she really is: someone completely and entirely different from himself.

One episode that illustrates all of these ironies occurs with the discovery of the lawn statue of the Virgin Mary. After Twinkle finds it behind a bush, she insists that it should be placed on the lawn. "No, silly Sanj. This is meant for outside. For the lawn" (59). Sanjeev is

Himberger 3

of course horrified, due to his preoccupation and anxiety concerning what others will think of him. "Twinkle, I can't have the people I work with see this statue on my lawn." At this moment, Twinkle becomes quite aware of Sanjeev's insecurities, as she asks him, "Why does it matter to you so much what people think?" (59). With each "blessed" discovery, the two newlyweds begin to discover something more, something about each other that is not necessarily positive.

The situation only gets worse as Sanjeev decides to dispose of the statue. "For now I am going to put it in the garage. Then tomorrow morning on my way to work I am going to take it to the dump" (60). Twinkle is devastated by this news, and she reacts emotionally to Sanjeev's threats. "'I hate you,' she informed him, her eyes narrowing at the word 'hate"' (60). Twinkle begins to cry, something Sanjeev has never seen. "In the end, they settled on a compromise: the statue would be placed in a recess at the side of the house, so that it wasn't obvious to passersby, but was still clearly visible to all who came" (61). The fact that this very dramatic moment between Sanjeev and Twinkle occurs because of the statue of the Virgin Mary emphasizes the irony of the story's title. A "blessed" figure only emphasizes the struggles and incompatibility Sanjeev and Twinkle are facing as they start their life together.

As the story ends, the reader is left with the image of Sanjeev following Twinkle, carrying the Christ bust discovered in the attic at the party. "Sanjeev pressed the massive silver face to his ribs, careful not to let the feather hat slip, and followed her" (65). Although it is difficult to predict the future of Sanjeev and Twinkle's relationship, perhaps this can be seen as an optimistic ending. Throughout the story, the differences in the personalities of the two are made quite evident: the structured, insecure mind of Sanjeev, and the care-free, easy-going, disorganized mind of Twinkle. Twinkle is "wow" while Sanjeev is dull. Yet, this is hope for these two, as Twinkle squeezes Sanjeev's elbow at

Himberger 4

the close of the story. There is something quite hopeful at the end, as Sanjeev follows Twinkle up the stairs, carrying yet another "blessed" item.

Work Cited

Lahiri, Jhumpa. "This Blessed House." In Connections: Literature for Composition. By Quentin Miller and Julie Nash. Boston: Houghton, 2008. 53–65.

In evaluating Sarah's response to Lahiri's story, consider the balance she attempts to strike between plot summary and direct textual evidence. Also, scrutinize her thesis to evaluate its strengths and weaknesses. Finally, is Sarah's argument about irony persuasive?

Although the conventions discussed in this chapter are relevant to fiction, they can also be found in other genres. Poetry, for instance, can also have a narrative (see Chapter 5), drama and fiction share the same desire to address (if not resolve) conflict (see Chapter 6), and narrative voice in a story is related to the essayist's voice (see Chapter 7).

Chapter 5

Reading and Writing about Poetry

> A poem should be wordless
> As the flight of birds.
> —ARCHIBALD MACLEISH, *"Ars Poetica"* (1926)

What Is a Poem?

In his poem "Ars Poetica" Archibald MacLeish makes a series of assertions about what a poem should be. In the above epigraph he hopes for wordlessness in poetry and combines this wish with the image of birds in flight. These two lines of poetry about what a poem *should be* serve as a good introduction to what poetry *actually is*.

First, they contain the impossible dreams of a poet: a poem should be wordless, but of course, it cannot be. A poem is words and, on a literal level, nothing but words. This yearning for something beyond normal human experience is what makes poets write poems. Second, these lines, like all lines in poetry, express an idea. In this poem the idea is explicit: the speaker responds to the question "What should a poem be?" by saying, "It should be this." In other poems, the poet may express an idea less overtly, by simply presenting certain images. American poet William Carlos Williams declared, "No ideas but in things," meaning that images of objects should be used to make an abstract idea come alive.

Third, MacLeish's lines use **imagery** and *figurative language* to communicate their idea. An *image* is a picture, in this case of birds in flight. The reader sees birds in flight and imagines something graceful, beautiful, and silent ("wordless"). This image is connected to the idea of poetry through the use of *simile*, a form of figurative language that implicitly or explicitly compares two things (a poem and birds in flight). Simile is discussed later in this chapter.

MacLeish's poem also shows that the essence of poetry is play. Because it is so carefully crafted, poetry, more than other forms of literature, might feel fragile in a student's hands, like an egg or a rare painting. To pick up a poem and start finding your way into it is to risk breaking it. But that view is likely to inhibit you.

Poems are just words, after all: words on a page or words chanted, spoken, or sung. It is natural for people to tell stories (fiction), to react emotionally to drama (plays, films), or to attempt to understand something by writing about it (essays). It is equally natural for people to play around with language. To combine two dissimilar things—poetry and birds—in this way is a form of invention that gives us joy. We begin to enjoy poetry even as toddlers. Before children have mastered their own language, they delight in rhyming words and making up words. Songs are poems, and you probably like to listen to them for their sound quality as well as their meaning. Poetry reimagines the world with the most creative language available: through both sounds and figurative language.

However, poetry is often serious, and its most common subjects are love and death. It is a record of a tough mind engaging with tough subjects, a map of a machete-wielding explorer cutting through a dense jungle. When you read poetry, you have an opportunity to hack your way through this same jungle.

Words into Lines

It is tempting to define poetry the same way the Supreme Court once defined pornography: tough to describe, but you know it when you see it. In the case of poetry, seeing it is only half the experience, though: hearing it is the other half. Fans of literature often go out to see and hear poets read their work in bookstores, coffee shops, or other public venues. Ancient poets chanted from mountaintops or pulpits; today they might be heard rapping in clubs. Less frequently, people read poems in books or magazines or on public monuments. Your experience in this course will probably combine the private act of seeing and reading a poem with the public act of speaking and hearing a poem. That is, your instructor will probably assign poems for you to read at home and he or she may read (or ask you to read) a poem or part of a poem in class at the beginning of your discussion.

A poem is formally defined as any grouping of words arranged as **verse** (writing involving metrical form; sometimes the word is used interchangeably with *poetry*). Like a florist or a musical composer who places flowers or notes in a particular order for a specific effect, a poet *arranges* words for a particular purpose. What makes these words *verse* is that they are arranged into **lines.** Whereas the paragraph is the fundamental unit of prose, the line is the fundamental unit of poetry. Poets may play with the notion of the line. If the poet leaves a good deal of white space on the page, he or she may want the reader to consider what that blank area signifies. Other poets, like Allen Ginsberg (see Chapter 17) and Walt Whitman (see Chapter 16), use long lines. Here is an example of a line of poetry from Whitman's "Song of Myself" that cannot be contained in one line on a standard page:

> Talkative young ones to those that like them . . . the recitative of fish-pedlars
> and fruit-pedlars . . . the loud laugh of workpeople at their meals,

By contrast, here is an example of an entire two-line poem by Ezra Pound:

IN A STATION OF THE METRO

The apparition of these faces in the crowd;
Petals on a wet, black bough.

(1916)

We see opposite extremes here: Whitman includes everything he observes in his poems (1,336 long lines), while Pound is much more restrained (2 short lines). Both poets are describing crowds of people: Whitman allows us to hear their individual voices while Pound converts them into a unified, silent image.

A final way to think about what a poem is and how it is arranged might be illustrated through the concept of *found poems*, which are fragments of language usually not arranged intentionally as verse. The poet does not invent these words but rather finds them somewhere and arranges them into a poem. The organization of lines makes a great deal of difference in a found poem. Imagine that a poet is flipping through the sports section of a newspaper and finds the following headlines: "Heat too much for Timberwolves," "Bears beaten by weakened Patriots," "Yankees dominate Indians." The poet decides that these headlines about sports teams constitute a poem and writes a poem called "American History" that looks like this:

AMERICAN HISTORY

Bears beaten
By weakened patriots.
Yankees dominate
Indians.
Heat
Too much
For
Timberwolves.

The found poem, arranged and titled this way, is about the ecological and human disaster of westward expansion. By the end of the poem we feel the oppressive, stifling condition of global warming, the latest in a series of human disasters, because of the way the poet gradually dwindles the lines to one or two words apiece. The poem is weary and plodding because of the arrangement of the lines: we can almost hear the timberwolves panting at the end of the poem. How would the effect of this found poem be different if the poet had arranged it into three lines, one for each newspaper headline?

Some poems rely heavily on the visual appeal of their lines: the seventeenth-century British poet George Herbert published a poem in 1633 titled "The Altar" and structured the lines on the page to resemble an altar:

George Herbert *(1593–1633)*

The Altar

A broken ALTAR, Lord, thy servant rears,
Made of a heart, and cemented with tears:
Whose parts are as thy hand did frame;
No workman's tool hath touched the same.

A HEART alone
Is such a stone,
As nothing but
Thy power doth cut.
Wherefore each part
Of my hard heart
Meets in this frame
To praise thy Name:

That, if I chance to hold my peace,
These stones to praise thee may not cease.
Oh let thy blessed SACRIFICE be mine,
And sanctify this ALTAR to be thine.

(1633)

In this poem Herbert is comparing his heart to an altar and devoting his love, as well as his poem, to God. The poem would not have the same effect if the lines began on the left-hand side of the page or if the poem extended for two pages. Herbert is not the only poet to arrange his lines into pictures: twentieth-century American poet Gregory Corso ordered the lines of his poem "Bomb" to look like the mushroom cloud left by the explosion of an atomic bomb. However, the vast majority of poems are more concerned with the way their words sound than with the way they look.

A common way to order the lines of a poem is to group them into **stanzas.** *Stanza* is Italian for "room": thus a poem is like a house with four or five "rooms." (If a poem comprises one long stanza, you might think of a house with one enormous room in it.) In discussing poetry, one always talks of stanzas rather than paragraphs.

In addition, the lines within a stanza often form certain patterns. A pair of rhymed lines (expressed as *aa* if the first pair of rhymed sounds in the poem, or *bb* if the second) is called a **couplet.** If the couplet follows a pattern of iambic pentameter, it is a *heroic couplet* (discussed in the next section). Three subsequent rhyming lines (*aaa*) constitute a triplet. Occasionally poems that consist almost entirely of heroic couplets contain an occasional **triplet,** highlighted with a bracket in the margins. A four-line stanza is known as a **quatrain.** A three-line stanza, far less common in English, is called a **tercet.**

Verse, Rhyme, Assonance, and Alliteration

Verse is often defined as "words composed in a metrical way." Each line of poetry is arranged and phrased according to its rhythm, or meter (discussed in more detail in the next section). However, that rhythm might not be predictable, even, or obvious. The word *verse* comes from the Latin *vertere,* meaning "to turn" (for complete explanations of the meaning of words, the best source is the *Oxford English Dictionary,* or *OED*). The poetic line "turns" to begin another line. *Vertere* is also the source for words like *reverse, versatile,* and *well-versed.* These related words have to do with changing or turning, too: *reverse* means to change direction, and *versatile* is defined in the *OED* as "Marked or characterized by changeability or inconstancy; subject to change or fluctuation; variable, changeable." When people use the cliché "poetry in motion," they may not be aware that poetry, simply by its definition as verse, is already in motion.

Like meter, the word *verse* also has a musical association. Each verse of a song is a new idea or exploration: after a verse or two has been sung or played, the song frequently returns to a repeated chorus. Poems, like songs, often rely on repetition (of a word, a sound, a line, or perhaps an entire stanza), and they appeal to our sense of hearing. Within the lines of poetry are sometimes surprising, sometimes predictable, principles of rhythm, meter, and rhyme. For instance, you can clap your hands or snap your fingers to the following lines from Edgar Allan Poe's 1849 poem "The Bells":

> Keeping time, time, time,
> In a sort of Runic rhyme,
> To the tintinnabulation that so musically wells
> From the bells, bells, bells, bells,
>   Bells, bells, *bells*—
> From the jingling and the tinkling of the bells.

The music Poe describes is reflected in the poem: we may not know what "tintinnabulation" means (Poe created this word for this poem), but we know how it sounds and can see that its sound fits into the way the poem keeps time. Some of the greatest poems in the English language are connected to song, such as William Blake's *Songs of Innocence* and *Songs of Experience* or Walt Whitman's "Song of Myself." For this reason, poetry is best appreciated if it is read aloud.

Rhyme is another basic sound feature of poetry, especially *end rhyme.* End rhyme is the convention of concluding the lines of a poem that are close to one another with words that rhyme. End rhyme most commonly occurs either in adjacent lines of poetry or in alternating lines. An example of rhymes in adjacent lines is the following excerpt from Alexander Pope's "An Essay on Criticism" published in 1709:

> 'Tis with our judgments as our watches, none
> Go just alike, yet each believes his own.
> In poets as true genius in but rare,
> True taste as seldom is the critic's share.

Pope's poem is written in **heroic couplets:** as already described, a couplet is a pair of rhymed lines, and these couplets are heroic because they contain ten syllables each, which was the form commonly used in English epic poetry. (The ten syllables in the heroic line follow an unstressed/stressed pattern that is described below as *iambic pentameter*.) Eighteenth-century British poets were fond of heroic couplets because tastes in art at that time favored order and symmetry. Heroic couplets dominated English poetry for a century or more.

In the English Renaissance, or Shakespeare's time (a century before Pope), rhyming in alternating lines was characteristic of poetry. An example is the following excerpt from Sir Philip Sidney's "Astrophil and Stella" published in 1591:

> Loving in truth, and fain in verse my love to show
> That the dear she might take some pleasure of my pain,
> Pleasure might cause her read, reading might make her know,
> Knowledge might pity win, and pity grace obtain . . .

Poems written in heroic couplets have a different flow than poems that rhyme alternating lines: heroic couplets operate in pairs, whereas alternating lines unfold four lines at a time. Poets play with these two basic patterns and often create variations of them. As mentioned, critics commonly use italicized letters to signify the patterns of end rhyme. Pope's poem can be described this way: *aabb*. Sidney's poem would be described as *abab*. As with figurative language, identifying the patterns or conventions of end rhyme is only the first step to writing about them. What are the different effects of the two excerpts above? Think about the subject matter as you consider that question: Pope is writing about literary criticism, and Sidney is writing about a man who longs for a woman.

Rhyme can also exist within a line of poetry: this is called *internal rhyme*. An example of internal rhyme can be seen in John Updike's poem "Player Piano": "My stick fingers click with a snicker / And, chuckling, they knuckle the keys." "Stick" and "click" in the first line constitute internal rhyme. "Snicker" reinforces that rhyme. Whether rhyme is at the end of a line or within a line, it can be inexact, a convention called *slant rhyme*. In Updike's poem, "chuckling" and "knuckle" *nearly* rhyme and so are internal slant rhymes. Another example of slant rhyme would be the words "page" and "face" placed at the end of two rhyming lines: close to end rhyme, but not exact. Slant rhyme gives the impression that a poem is somewhat slippery, controlled yet not rigid.

Nearly as common as rhyme are the conventions of assonance and alliteration in poetry. **Assonance** refers to repeated vowel sounds in words that are close to one another: the following line from Andrew Marvell's "To His Coy Mistress" has two examples of assonance, indicated by the underlined letters: "The grave's a fine and private place." "Grave" is connected to "place" and "fine" to "private" through assonance. The whole line is unified and balanced by these two pairs of words. **Alliteration,** a more familiar convention, refers to repeated consonants at the beginning of words that are near one another. Here is an example of alliteration from Christina Rosetti's "Goblin Market" (1862), contained in Chapter 12 of this book:

Figs to fill your mouth
Citrons from the South,
Sweet to tongue and sound to eye . . .

"Figs" and "fill" is one example of alliteration, but "Citrons," "South," Sweet," and "sound" is a more striking one. The reader is blanketed by delicious "s" sounds. The effect of this alliteration is to overwhelm the senses, which is the purpose of the poem.

Meter

The **meter** of a poem, briefly defined above, can be analyzed according to the number of syllables in each line and the recurrent patterns they follow. If we're thinking of poetry like music, meter is the beat. Literary scholars describe meter in terms of stressed and unstressed syllables. You may have had to complete exercises in which you marked the stressed syllables in a line of poetry with a slash (/) and unstressed syllables with a small curve that looks like a *u* (u) written above the syllables in a line. You can recognize fairly easily which syllables are stressed and unstressed by reading them aloud and determining where the natural emphasis would be. The greater challenge is to think about how the patterns of meter might contribute to the poem's overall effect.

The language used to describe meter can sound scientific or mathematical. We are talking about *numbers* of syllables, after all, and the *patterns* they form. Much like we measure length in feet, so do we measure poetry in feet: a **foot** is composed of a stressed syllable and one or two unstressed syllables; these syllables normally fall into one of the following patterns:

Anapest: two unstressed syllables, one stressed (as in "upside-down")
Dactyl: one stressed, two unstressed ("magazine")
Iamb: one unstressed, one stressed ("enough")
Trochee: one stressed, one unstressed ("purple")

Thus we describe poetry by stating what types of feet it has and the number of those feet that occur within a line. A line with one foot is called monometer; two feet, dimeter; three feet, trimeter; four feet, tetrameter; five feet, pentameter; six feet, hexameter; seven feet, heptameter; and eight feet, octameter. If we combine the number of feet in a line with the type of foot, we might get a description of a poem's meter like *dactylic trimeter* (a line of three dactyls, as in "Different magazines alternate") or *iambic pentameter* (a line of five iambs, as in "Shall I compare thee to a summer's day?"). If *iambic pentameter* sounds familiar, it's not only because Shakespeare used it, but also because the English language seems to fall naturally into this pattern. **Blank verse** is iambic pentameter that does not use end rhyme: it is how Shakespeare and his contemporaries wrote many of their plays. John Milton's epic poem *Paradise Lost* is composed in blank verse.

Identifying a poem's metrical scheme might not seem like the most exciting thing to do with a poem, but it can be a helpful step toward interpretation. The more you know about poetry and the more comfortable you become with the vocabulary used to discuss it, the more sophisticated your interpretation will be. A poem's meter might not be consistent throughout the poem, for instance. If you could identify the metrical shift in a poem and connect that shift to your interpretation of the poem, you would be in a position to present a good argument.

Form

If an entire poem falls into a particular, recognizable pattern, we say that it has a certain *form*. Probably the most recognizable form in English poetry is the **sonnet.** This is the form Shakespeare and his contemporaries used during the English Renaissance. It is a fourteen-line poem that follows one of two basic patterns: the Italian (or Petrarchan) sonnet and the English (or Shakespearean) sonnet.

The *Italian* (or *Petrarchan*) *sonnet* is divided into two parts: the *octave* (first eight lines) and the *sestet* (final six lines). The rhyme scheme varies, but most commonly the octave is rhymed *abbaabba* and the sestet *cdccdc*. Both classic sonnet forms are frequently used to advance a kind of argument, or the development of a central idea, that is made obvious by the sections of the poems. In the Italian sonnet, the octave generally presents the issue, or the problem; the sestet attempts to address it or somehow resolve it. Here is an Italian sonnet:

Sir Thomas Wyatt the Elder *(1503–1542)*

Farewell, Love

Farewell, Love, and all thy laws forever,
Thy baited hooks shall tangle me no more;
Senec and Plato call me from thy lore,
To perfect wealth my wit for to endeavor.
In blind error when I did persever,
Thy sharp repulse, that pricketh aye so sore,
Hath taught me to set in trifles no store

And 'scape forth since liberty is lever.°
Therefore farewell, go trouble younger hearts,
And in me claim no more authority;
With idle youth go use thy property,
And thereon spend thy many brittle darts.
For hitherto though I have lost all my time,
Me lusteth no longer rotten boughs to climb.

(1557)

The *English* (or *Shakespearean*) *sonnet* can be divided into three quatrains followed by a couplet. During the English Renaissance, when the form was most popular, the three quatrains were generally used to develop three points of an argument; the couplet often presented an ironic reversal that altered the meaning of the poem. The rhyme scheme is most often *abab cdcd efef gg*.

Many poets since the English Renaissance have used the sonnet form, too. The following example is from the Harlem Renaissance, a period of artistic outpouring from the early twentieth century during which African Americans developed a unique style and artistic idiom. While poets like Langston Hughes (whose poem is the subject of the student essay at the end of this chapter) developed his voice in conjunction with the musical form known as jazz, his contemporary Countee Cullen wrote in more traditional forms, such as the following Shakespearean sonnet "Yet Do I Marvel":

Countee Cullen *(1903–1946)*

Yet Do I Marvel

I doubt not God is good, well-meaning, kind,
And did He stoop to quibble could tell why
The little buried mole continues blind,
Why flesh that mirrors Him must some day die,
Make plain the reason tortured Tantalus
Is baited by the fickle fruit, declare
If merely brute caprice dooms Sisyphus
To struggle up a never-ending stair.
Inscrutable His ways are, and immune
To catechism by a mind too strewn
With petty cares so slightly understand
What awful brain compels his awful hand.
Yet do I marvel at this curious thing:
To make a poet black, and bid him sing!

(1925)

lever: More important.

The sonnet is one of the most common forms of poetry in English. You might have been introduced to the Japanese form **haiku** well before you ever heard of a sonnet. A haiku is a three-line poem containing a total of seventeen syllables: five in the first line, seven in the second, five in the third. This form is not long enough to sustain the type of argument one might encounter in a sonnet. Haikus are tightly contained images, reflecting other forms of Japanese classical art in their delicacy and attention to minute detail. Here is an example of haiku by Basho Matsuo (1644–1694), considered the first great haiku poet:

From all directions
Winds bring petals of cherry
Into the grebe lake.

Although the haiku form seems simple, it is not easy to compose one that is evocative and controlled. While a sonnet is used to express an idea, a haiku is more frequently the vehicle for an emotion expressed through an image.

Another short form, more common in English poetry, is the **epigram.** An epigram is designed to be witty and as short as possible: occasionally two lines. Although we are supposed to admire an epigram's cleverness, it does not hold up to the same scrutiny that we might devote to a sonnet or a longer form. Epigrams are often sharp and sarcastic. Here is an example by Ben Jonson (1572–1637), a swashbuckling playwright and poet of great renown whose imprisonment occasioned the following epigram about spies:

LIX: ON SPIES

Spies, you are lights in state, but of base stuff,
Who, when you've burnt yourself down to the snuff,
Stink, and are thrown away. End fair enough.

The final sentence is short, like the poem: the speaker cuttingly dismisses all spies and the worthlessness of their lives, which are more like the butt-ends of cheap candles than shining lights.

Some longer forms are defined as carefully as sonnets but are even more elaborate in their construction. The villanelle and the sestina are two such forms. A **villanelle** is a nineteen-line poem organized into six stanzas: five tercets followed by a quatrain. The rhyme scheme of the first tercet, *aba,* is repeated in the other four tercets; the final quatrain uses the same rhyme sounds organized *abaa*. The effect is a lilting poem with many repeated sounds: for an example, see the poem "Do Not Go Gentle into That Good Night" by Dylan Thomas in Chapter 12. Villanelles are tightly unified: the poet seems in full control of the poem's sound effect.

A *sestina* consists of six stanzas of six lines each followed by a concluding three-line stanza. The six words that conclude each line of the first stanza are repeated as the last words of each line in each of the following five stanzas in a different order. The final three-line stanza (the *envoy*) repeats each of those words again. A sestina is like a juggling act: we admire the technical expertise of the poet or juggler.

Not all poets write in specific forms, though they were much more likely to do so in Pope's time (the eighteenth century) or in Sidney's time (the late sixteenth century). In those eras, English poets were especially attuned to conventions of rhyme, meter, and form. A poem was considered a finely crafted work of art as much as a creative utterance or emotional outpouring; rhyme was a way to give that artwork its beauty, unity, and harmony.

Over time, poets began to experiment with these forms and even completely destroyed earlier conventions, much as musicians attempt to invent new styles. The relationship between the convention-bound poetry of earlier centuries and the loose improvisation of more recent centuries is similar to the relationship between a classical symphony and a work of avant-garde jazz.

The British Romantic poets of the late eighteenth and early nineteenth centuries mark a turning point away from strict adherence to poetic form. Some of the major figures of this movement are represented in this book, including John Keats and Lord Byron (Chapter 13), Samuel Taylor Coleridge (Chapter 15), and William Wordsworth (Chapters 16 and 17). Although the willingness to reject strict conventions has been much more common in the twentieth- and twenty-first centuries, the shift away from strict adherence to form began in English with the Romantic poets.

The type of modern poetry that rejects predetermined conventions is called **free verse** or *open form*. Robert Frost likened it to playing tennis without a net. A poet like Walt Whitman, whose sprawling lines are described above, would view rhyme and other conventions as inhibiting. At the same time, some contemporary poets, including Frost, view rhyme and other conventions as challenging and necessary.

Lyric, Epic, and Other Types

In addition to patterns of meter and rhyme, poetry can be classified according to its overall form and purpose. One basic distinction is between a lyric poem and an epic poem. A **lyric** expresses personal ideas, emotions, or observations, usually of a single speaker. An **epic,** a less common type, is a classical form of *narrative poetry*, or story in verse. Epics are typically long (even book length) and often center around the exploits of a hero: Homer's *Odyssey* or Milton's *Paradise Lost* are epics. The setting is typically wide-ranging, and most epics feature gods or other supernatural beings.

Some other types of narrative poetry are not necessarily epics: a narrative poem, as the name implies, tells a story. Samuel Taylor Coleridge's "The Rime of the Ancient Mariner" is a familiar example of a narrative called a **ballad:** you can find Coleridge's poem in Chapter 15. A ballad is a specific type of narrative poem that has its origins in song. Ballads frequently repeat one line from stanza to stanza (or from verse to verse, if we are thinking about them as songs). Many of Bob Dylan's songs take the form of ballads, and in fact ballads partake of oral traditions usually passed along in popular songs. Ballads employ repeated lines, or refrains, and frequently rhyme: if a ballad is written in four-line stanzas, the second and fourth lines often rhyme. Ballads also frequently contain multiple voices, characters in conversation with one another.

These features are evident in the following ballad by Dudley Randall entitled "Ballad of Birmingham," first published in 1969. The subject of the poem is a 1963 bombing of a church in Birmingham, Alabama, by the members of the Ku Klux Klan that caused the deaths of four African American girls.

Dudley Randall *(1914–2000)*

Ballad of Birmingham

(On the bombing of a church in Birmingham, Alabama, 1963)

"Mother dear, may I go downtown
Instead of out to play,
And march the streets of Birmingham
In a Freedom March today?"

"No, baby, no, you may not go,
For the dogs are fierce and wild,
And clubs and hoses, guns and jails
Aren't good for a little child."

"But, mother, I won't be alone.
Other children will go with me,
And march the streets of Birmingham
To make our country free."

"No, baby, no, you may not go,
For I fear those guns will fire.
But you may go to church instead
And sing in the children's choir."

She has combed and brushed her night-dark hair,
And bathed rose petal sweet,
And drawn white gloves on her small brown hands,
And white shoes on her feet.

The mother smiled to know her child
Was in the sacred place,
But that smile was the last smile
To come upon her face.

For when she heard the explosion,
Her eyes grew wet and wild.
She raced through the streets of Birmingham
Calling for her child.

A church in Birmingham, Alabama, 1963.

She clawed through bits of glass and brick,
Then lifted out a shoe.
"O, here's the shoe my baby wore,
But, baby, where are you?"

(1969)

In this ballad, the repetition of the words "baby" and "child" unify the poem and heighten our emotional response to it. Ballads are frequently retold to spread the word about a story of public interest or about a notorious or legendary figure.

Poems can also be classified according to their intent. An **ode** is a lyric poem that attempts to address a difficult philosophical subject, usually through serious tone and formal diction. The form goes back to Greek antiquity: Horace and Pindar were the two major figures associated with the ode. The form was revived during the English Renaissance and again during the Romantic period. British Romantic poet John Keats wrote many odes; you may be familiar with his "Ode to a Nightingale" or his "Ode on a Grecian Urn." Many odes are lengthy: we have selected a short one in the interest of preserving space. Here is Alexander Pope's "Ode on Solitude" (1717):

Alexander Pope *(1688–1744)*

Ode on Solitude

Happy the man whose wish and care
A few paternal acres bound,
Content to breathe his native air,
In his own ground.

Whose herds with milk, whose fields with bread,
Whose flocks supply him with attire,
Whose trees in summer yield him shade,
In winter fire.

Blest! Who can unconcernedly find
Hours, days, and years slide soft away,
In health of body, peace of mind,
Quiet by day,

Sound sleep by night; study and ease
Together mixed; sweet recreation
And innocence, which most does please,
With meditation.

Thus let me live, unseen, unknown;
Thus unlamented let me die;
Steal from the world, and not a stone
Tell where I lie.

(1717)

The poem begins by describing the happiness of a man who lives peacefully "in his own ground" and ends with the speaker projecting his own death, which would place him literally "in his own ground." The speaker's desire for peace and a lack of public scrutiny nearly amounts to a death wish by the poem's end: the imagery to prepare us for such an idea has been in the poem all along.

An **elegy** is a poem written in memory and in honor of someone who is dead, though this connotation of elegy has only existed since the English Renaissance: in ancient Greece, elegies, though generally solemn or stately, were not necessarily intended to mourn the deceased. The Greek origins of the word *elegy* also associate this mode with heroic couplets, defined above as rhymed pairs of lines written in iambic pentameter. Here is the beginning of an elegy including all of these associations, Thomas Carew's 1640 poem, "An Elegy upon the Death of the Dean of Paul's, Dr. John Donne" (the poet John Donne):

Can we not force from widowed poetry,
Now thou art dead, great Donne, one elegy
To crown thy hearse? Why yet did we not trust,
Though with unkneaded dough-bak'd prose, thy dust,
Such as the unscissor'd lect'rer from the flower
Of fading rhetoric, short-lived as his hour,
Dry as the sand that measures it, might lay
Upon the ashes on the funeral day?

The tone of this poem is somber: poetry is described as a widow now that Donne has died, and yet Carew "forces" one more poem that can act as a fitting tribute. In this way, living poetry seeks to offset the loss of the deceased poet.

Unlike the ode and the elegy, parody has a lighthearted tone. A **parody** is a poem that imitates another poem and at the same time ridicules it, generally following the same form, rhyme scheme, or meter as the original poem. Parodies are humorous, and although they imply criticism, they can also contain a certain degree of homage or respect for the original. In Chapter 13, Raleigh's "The Nymph's Reply to the Shepherd" is a parody of Marlowe's "The Passionate Shepherd to His Love." Mary Collier's poem "The Woman's Labour" in Chapter 16 is a parodic response to Stephen Duck's "The Thresher's Labour."

Figurative Language

Poetry's most salient features are the sound appeal of its words and its use of **figurative language.** Figurative language is the opposite of literal language; it stretches the boundaries of what language can do, rebelling against the idea that language simply supplies information. "A rose is a rose is a rose is a rose," Gertrude Stein wrote, expressing how dull and repetitive life would be if we never explored figurative language. In George Orwell's famous novel *1984* the oppressive government tries to do away with figurative language by introducing "newspeak," a flat, descriptive language that would eliminate rich, evocative words like *spectacular* and *fantastic* and replace them with *good* and, if something is better than good, *plus good.* In Orwell's chilling novel language is simplified to resemble math, which makes for a more efficient society. Figurative language resists such simplification.

The common forms of figurative language that are the heart of poetry are metaphor and simile. A **metaphor** is a direct comparison. "He's a bull in a china shop," you might say of a friend who tends to barrel into situations recklessly, unaware of the damage he is doing. This metaphor is a cliché, which means it is used so often that it is immediately familiar but also a little tired. You might say of the same friend, "He's a jackhammer in a jewelry store," which is a metaphor that tries to express the same thing in a less familiar phrase.

However, the **connotations** of the words *bull* and *jackhammer* are different. The connotations of a word are the associations it suggests in various contexts, in addition to its literal meaning, or **denotation.** *Dynamite* can be something destructive and potentially dangerous, but it also has the connotation of something alluring and fabulous. If you encountered the jackhammer metaphor in a poem, you might think about why the poet chose it instead of the familiar bull metaphor. One reason would be that poets dislike clichés. Another reason would be that the connotations of jackhammer are more fitting to the context. You would begin by thinking about those connotations. A bull is an animal; a jackhammer is mechanical. A bull is unpredictable; a jackhammer keeps pummeling regularly. A bull charges forward; a jackhammer digs. A bull is clumsy; a jackhammer is deliberately destructive. As you follow these connotations, you might determine that a "bull in a china shop" and a "jackhammer in a jewelry store" do not really mean, or connote, the same kind of character at all. Moreover, you may decide that the jackhammer metaphor does not work as well as the bull metaphor, after all.

Sometimes metaphors are less obvious: you may have to ask yourself if a word or phrase you encounter is metaphorical or not. In Robert Frost's familiar poem "The Road Not Taken," the speaker says, "Two roads diverged in a yellow wood" and wonders whether he should take the one that many travelers have gone down or the one that is less traveled. The metaphorical meaning of these paths is obvious: the speaker is contemplating the choices of his life. The road many have traveled is the path of conformity; the road fewer have traveled is the path of individual will, of exploration, discovery, and nonconformity. The speaker does not say, "My life choices are paths in the woods." The metaphor is implied.

Similes are closely related to metaphors, but the comparison in similes is indirect. Similes are recognizable by their use of the words *like* or *as*. In the Frost example, the simile version would be "My life choices are *like* paths in the woods." In the epigraph to this chapter, MacLeish uses a simile: "A poem should be wordless / *As* the flight of birds."

Metaphors and similes may seem like the same thing, only phrased differently. However, they produce different tones and therefore may have different functions. A simile, less blunt and direct than a metaphor, seems more tentative or exploratory. If one thing is like another thing, then the poet is acknowledging that, in some ways, it is also *not* like that thing. Shakespeare plays against a simile when he writes, "My mistress's eyes are nothing like the sun" (see his sonnet in Chapter 13). He is responding to what might be considered a poetic cliché: "My mistress's eyes are like the sun," which could imply that they are brilliant, radiant, hot, hard to look at, fiery, and so forth. By saying they're *not* like that, Shakespeare is commenting on popular poetic expression and perhaps ridiculing it, but he's also suggesting a possible new simile: if his mistress's eyes are nothing like the sun, what are they like?

Let's examine a familiar simile from a poem to see how it operates. T. S. Eliot's famous poem "The Love Song of J. Alfred Prufrock" (in Chapter 12) begins, "Let us go then, you and I, / When the evening is spread out against the sky / Like a patient etherised upon a table." In what way is an evening spread out against the sky like a patient etherised on a table? The meaning is far from obvious, but the effect is clear: we are led gently into the poem in its first line, which sounds lovely and formal, as though the speaker is leading the reader into a ball or a dinner. We are then arrested by the disturbing image of an unconscious patient on a table. We are still faced with the question of how the evening is like the patient. They are both paralyzed, or suspended. This connection forms a major theme of the poem and puts the reader into a certain frame of mind. We are not going to be charmed by what this speaker shows us. We may even feel a little sick, as one does under the influence of anesthesia ("etherized").

You might already know how to recognize a metaphor or a simile. In college writing, you will also discuss how they operate, what they mean, and why they're an important feature of a poem. The same is true of form, meter, and all the other features of poetry briefly introduced here: recognizing and understanding them is not an end in itself; it is a means toward interpreting the poem's meaning.

Student Essay on Langston Hughes's "The Weary Blues"

Poetry has many other features that have not been discussed here. This introduction can only highlight the most common ones. The student essay that follows illustrates one final point: that the speaking voice of the poem is not, as in fiction, called the "narrator." Although this voice is telling a story, and thus "narrating," it is usually called the *speaker* of the poem. Moreover, the speaker is not necessarily the same person as the poet. A middle-aged, white, male poet can write a poem from the point of view of a young, black, female speaker. Call a poetic speaker a speaker, and don't assume too much about the author.

Langston Hughes (1902–1967) was the most prominent writer during a period known as the Harlem Renaissance, also called the New Negro Renaissance. As mentioned earlier in this chapter, the Harlem Renaissance was a period of extraordinary literary and artistic output by African Americans whose artistic freedom had long been suppressed by slavery and its aftereffects (segregation, discrimination, and racism). During the Renaissance, which lasted roughly from the end of World War I until the end of the Great Depression (1919–1939), black artists discovered new outlets for creativity that had previously been unknown to them or unvalued by the rest of their society.

Jazz music is the most obvious and enduring product of the Harlem Renaissance. Jazz, which set the precedent for literature and visual art during this period, was a mixture of European traditional musical forms, African rhythms, Caribbean instrumentation, and African American history. Jazz developed at the beginning of the twentieth century in the American South—most notably in New Orleans—and traveled north during the period known as the Great Migration, which marked a huge demographic shift as blacks fled the rural, agrarian South for the urban, industrial North.

For a number of reasons, Harlem was a primary destination for blacks who had migrated north: it offered an abundance of housing and jobs, and also a

Aaron Douglas, *Play de Blues* (1926).

rapidly developing community of African Americans with a desire to fulfill their version of the American Dream. New York City and Harlem in particular became a center of political, musical, and literary expression.

Langston Hughes arrived in Harlem after being raised in the Midwest (Missouri, Kansas, and Ohio) and after sailing as a crew member to Africa via Europe. Like jazz, and like America itself, Hughes represents a transnational perspective. Although he also wrote fiction, nonfiction, and drama, he is primarily known as a poet, one of the greatest in U.S. literary history. His consistent aim was to write accessible lyrical poetry reflecting his experience and, by extension, the experiences of African Americans at this crucial period in history. Although his poems are easy to read, they frequently present complex challenges to the reader. To appreciate Hughes, we must read his poetry closely and carefully.

The following poem, "The Weary Blues," was first published in 1925 during the height of the Harlem Renaissance. (Lenox Avenue, referred to in line 4, is a major thoroughfare in Harlem.) It provides a number of interpretive challenges to the reader.

The blues is an offshoot of jazz characterized by a "blue note": the third, fifth, or seventh note of an eight-note scale is performed at a lower pitch. A singer might wail, a guitarist might press the string of the guitar up on the neck, and a trumpet player like Louis Armstrong might bring the note up or down a halftone by pressing his lips tighter or subtly loosening them. Blues music flourished during the twentieth century in the Mississippi Delta and in Chicago, and many music historians trace how it metamorphosed into rock-and-roll, which branched out into other popular forms. The more familiar connotation of "the blues" is mild depression, but in its classic form, the blues embodies both sadness and joy. (See the story "Sonny's Blues" by James Baldwin in Chapter 15.) The blues form developed out of work songs sung by slaves in the United States before the Civil War: this poem thus connects to Chapter 16: "Industry and Idleness." It might be productive to view the piano player as a worker in this poem and the poem's speaker as someone who benefits from that work.

We can think about the way Hughes uses the blues in this poem: how do the two sets of actual blues lyrics within the poem compare to one another, and what is noteworthy about the length of the two lyrics, their order, and the meanings they lend to the rest of the poem?

Langston Hughes *(1902–1967)*

The Weary Blues

Droning a drowsy syncopated tune,
Rocking back and forth to a mellow croon,
    I heard a Negro play.
Down on Lenox Avenue the other night
By the pale dull pallor of an old gas light
    He did a lazy sway . . .
    He did a lazy sway . . .
To the tune o' those Weary Blues.
With his ebony hands on each ivory key
He made that poor piano moan with melody.
    O Blues!
Swaying to and fro on his rickety stool
He played that sad raggy tune like a musical fool.
    Sweet Blues!
Coming from a black man's soul.
    O Blues!
In a deep song voice with a melancholy tone
I heard that Negro sing, that old piano moan—
    "Ain't got nobody in all this world,
    Ain't got nobody but ma self.
    I's gwine to quit ma frownin'
    And put ma troubles on the shelf."

Thump, thump, thump, went his foot on the floor.
He played a few chords then he sang some more—
"I got the Weary Blues
    And I can't be satisfied.
    Got the Weary Blues
    And can't be satisfied—
    I ain't happy no mo'
    And I wish that I had died."
And far into the night he crooned that tune.
The stars went out and so did the moon.
The singer stopped playing and went to bed
While the Weary Blues echoed through his head.
He slept like a rock or a man that's dead.

(1925)

The student writer Kristin Seabolt was given the following assignment: "Paying close attention to its poetic features, analyze 'The Weary Blues' in such a way that you answer the following questions: What is the relationship between the speaker and the piano player? What happens to the speaker by the end of the poem? What has happened to the piano player by the end of the poem?"

Student Essay

Kristin Seabolt is originally from San Diego, California, and she graduated with a BA in English from Suffolk University in 2006. When she's not busy reading, she designs jewelry and practices amateur photography. She plans to get her PhD in Czech literature with an eye toward writing and teaching full time.

Seabolt 1

Kristin Seabolt

Final Draft

Movement and Change in the Weary Blues

In "The Weary Blues," Langston Hughes uses several poetic devices to show the movement and changes of both the speaker and

Seabolt 2

the subject—the piano player—of the poem. In these thirty-five lines of poetry, Hughes shows a distinct change in the relationship of the speaker and the piano player. Both characters also change individually in the latter part of the poem. Through both end rhyme and alliteration, he gives the poem shape and rhythm. He guides the reader, through these devices, in how the poem should sound and feel.

When the speaker begins the poem, he is observing the piano player from the perspective of a member of his audience. The speaker seems to be taking pleasure from the piano player's blues. He continues to praise the blues in lines such as 11 and 14, saying "O Blues!" and "Sweet Blues!" The speaker also seems to note the sadness in the music. In line 1 he refers to it as "droning" and "drowsy." In line 10, the speaker calls the singer's instrument a "poor piano" that is moaning. The speaker also refers to the song as "sad," "raggy" and "melancholy." Although the speaker clearly enjoys what he is hearing, he takes great notice of the sorrow that is involved in everything about the music—from the piano itself to the song the player is singing. With all of these vivid descriptions of what the piano player is doing, it seems strange that the actual player himself is never described as anything but a "Negro." While the music has a rich personality, the actual player is given none.

While the speaker is listening and enjoying the music, the piano player does not seem to notice the speaker at all. This leads the reader to believe that the speaker is merely one face in the midst of the crowd of observers who are hearing this man play and sing. In fact, though the poem's subject is the piano player, not much is really learned about him. His voice is only heard twice, through lyrics of the song he is singing.

In the beginning of the poem, the speaker is enjoying the music on a personal level, seemingly on Lenox Avenue hearing this piano player, and seeing a snippet of the player's life. The speaker seems to be an actual person, bringing himself into the poem by saying in line 3, "I heard a Negro play." However, by the end of the poem, two changes have been

Seabolt 3

made to the speaker's voice. First, as a character he has left the poem entirely. He began the poem as present as the actual piano player, but after the second set of lyrics, the speaker leaves the poem entirely, no longer hearing or praising the music. Instead, the poem focuses in on the actual piano player, instead of the music, for the first time.

The second change has to do with the speaker's amount of knowledge. In the beginning, he was speaking about an experience he had, listening to the blues on Lenox Avenue. The only thing that the speaker knows is that the piano player "made that poor piano moan with melody," and that he, as the audience, enjoys it. He knows nothing of the piano player's life outside of the one moment in which he is singing Weary Blues. By the end of the poem, the speaker is no longer referring to the moment that he heard the piano player, but instead has become all-knowing and all-seeing, watching the piano player play until dawn, and then sleep "like a rock or a man that's dead."

The piano player also changes throughout the poem. He starts out singing Weary Blues, and the speaker associates everything he's doing with sadness and melancholy. "Swaying to and fro on his rickety stool / He played that sad raggy tune like a musical fool." Here, the "rickety stool" and "sad raggy tune" set the tone of the events that are unfolding. This also happens in lines 17 and 18. "In a deep song voice with a melancholy tone / I heard that Negro sing, that old piano moan." In these two lines, both the words "melancholy" and "old piano" reinforce the slow, sad tone that is being associated with the piano player and his song.

Contrastingly, at the end of the poem, the player is represented as lighter, happier, even whimsical. In lines 1 to 30, the speaker is slowly describing each detail about what he is seeing and hearing. The words are slow and lyrical, creating a song that weaves through the speaker's story of hearing the piano player. Then, almost instantly, in line 31, after the last line of lyrics, the poem picks up and seems to go more quickly, talking about how the piano player played into the night. While the

Seabolt 4

majority of the poem has been slowly diagramming the player during one song, in just one line, "The stars went out and so did the moon."

In this moment, the piano player becomes more than just a sad man playing a sad song for the speaker's audience. In these last lines, he becomes a real person who goes to bed and sleeps well. It is important that the speaker makes the reader aware that "He slept like a rock or a man that's dead." In this simile, two things can be seen clearly. The piano player is not as sad as the poem initially indicates. In contrast to words such as <u>pale</u>, <u>sad</u>, <u>dull</u>, <u>drowsy</u>, <u>old</u>, and <u>raggy</u>, the lines that seem to best represent the piano player in the end of the poem are part of the player's lyrics: "I's gwine to quit ma frownin' / And put ma troubles on the shelf." In the last five lines, there are no words that evoke sadness. The simile indicates that the piano player was sleeping soundly, because both a rock and a dead man "sleep" forever, since both are inanimate objects. Dead men and rocks have no worries, no blues. If the piano player is able to sleep as well as these objects, he has set down the sorrow that is suggested in his song.

Langston Hughes's use of rhyme is interesting. "With his ebony hands on each ivory key / He made that poor piano moan with melody." While this is in the midst of the poem's description of the piano player's song, it could also stand alone as one separate thought. Before this, the speaker is talking about how the player is swaying, and after these lines he says, "O Blues!"

Another example of this is in lines 31 and 32. "And far into the night he crooned that tune. / The stars went out and so did the moon." It is clear that these lines are connected, both referring to the night and how the piano player played until the morning. The lines before this are the song's lyrics, and the lines after talk about the player leaving his music to go to bed. Lines 31 and 32, while a part of the poem, are also one distinct thought.

Alliteration is another device that Hughes uses in order to set the tone of the poem from beginning to end. In the beginning, the repetitive consonants are plodding, causing the person who is reading or speaking the words to slow down. They set the rhythm of the first part of the poem. "Droning a drowsy syncopated tune." "By the pale dull pallor of an old gas light." In the first line, alliteration can be seen in the words "droning" and "drowsy." The D sound, as well as the other consonant sound of P in the words "pale" and "pallor," cause the mouth to slow down. It is appropriate that the words are those like "droning" and "drowsy" because the sounds of alliteration at the beginning of the poem give the poem a drowsy sound.

Toward the end of the poem, however, when the piano player is going home and the descriptions of sadness end to show the possibility that the player is perhaps not so sad, the alliteration helps the poem to pick up, quickening the reader while being wispy and whimsical. "The stars went out and so did the moon. / The singer stopped playing and went to bed." The words "stars," "so," "singer," and "stopped" all begin in S, a consonant that moves the reader along quickly through the last two lines of the poem.

Hughes uses these devices to add shape and rhythm to his poem. His end rhymes connect the lines together while separating thoughts about the player's fingers on the keys, his deep voice, or the tapping of his foot. Through alliteration, he guides the reader in the way the poem should be read, slow and melodic in the beginning, faster and blissful towards the end. With both end rhyme and alliteration, Hughes creates a moody poem that first describes the music and then the piano player, from both a personal and then an all-knowing point of view.

Work Cited

Hughes, Langston. "The Weary Blues." In Connections: Literature for Composition. By Quentin Miller and Julie Nash. Boston: Houghton, 2008. 88–90.

As you can see, Kristin discusses the poem's features as she answers the questions in the assignment. Rather than creating a laundry list of all of the poem's characteristics, she selects those that are most relevant to her argument.

Like poetry, all genres choose words carefully, and all of them employ (or can employ) literary devices like metaphor and alliteration. As in fiction, poems can tell stories or even enact drama through dialogue, as in plays. What is truly unique about poetry is its arrangement as verse and its essential connection to song, which might be why MacLeish wants it to be "wordless" in the epigraph to this chapter, or why Whitman's lengthy poem "Song of Myself" culminates in a sound he calls a "barbaric yawp."

Chapter 6

Reading and Writing about Drama

What is drama but life with the dull bits cut out?
—ALFRED HITCHCOCK (1960)

Unlike poetry and fiction, a written work of drama is rarely a finished artistic achievement. Although a novelist may revise parts of a text in response to suggestions from an editor, he or she ultimately remains in control of the book. A playwright, on the other hand, knows that the written work will undergo numerous interpretations before it reaches the ears and eyes of an audience. At a minimum, the words of the written text are affected by the way the director, the set designer, and the actors interpret the play.

By the time a play becomes a public performance, it may bear little resemblance to the work the author intended to write. In the 1980s, for example, William Shakespeare's *Macbeth* was set in South Africa during the era of apartheid, a racially segregated governing system that lasted from 1948 to 1994. Actors wore contemporary costumes, including army camouflage—a far cry from Elizabethan clothes. Although the director used Shakespeare's text, the new setting meant that the play would comment on a political situation that Shakespeare knew nothing about. Viewing Shakespeare's tragedy through the historical lens of 1980s apartheid led to an entirely new understanding of *Macbeth*.

When you study and write about drama in an introduction to literature or literature and composition class, you have both an advantage and a disadvantage compared to an audience member at a live performance. While you lose the total effect that good staging, acting, music, and costumes can produce, you have a better opportunity to study the language of the play and to see how the author uses the elements of literature to achieve an overall effect. For example, you can understand and analyze symbolism, foreshadowing, irony, and verbal wit in greater detail than an audience member can.

Since this book will be used primarily in introductory literature and composition courses, most of the discussion focuses on the literary rather than the performance aspect of plays. Even so, you should always keep performance in mind as you read and discuss the plays in this book. Also, see a live play whenever you get the chance. The more you experience the full effect of live drama, the more you are able to imagine the different ways a play can be interpreted and performed.

A Brief History of Drama

Many of today's young adults have seen few live theater performances because television and film have largely replaced the theater as the means through which we witness imaginary tragedies and comedies. Yet live drama is the oldest literary form. Drama as we know it has its roots in ancient religious rituals acted out to appease the gods and to bring together a community of believers. We trace the Western theater tradition back to ancient Greece, when people gathered to praise the god Dionysus during annual festivals. Crowds watched while a chorus of priests chanted songs that honored Dionysus. Over time individual actors began to act out scenes from the god's life story while the role of the chorus diminished.

Eventually, the subject matter for theater expanded to commemorate the lives of great heroes and important events. However, Athenian theater festivals were never secular affairs. They were always connected to worship and were accompanied by religious sacrifices. *Medea*, featured in Chapter 15, "Vengeance and Forgiveness," is an example of an ancient Greek tragedy that continues to horrify modern audiences.

Ancient Greek theater.

Although Christians in medieval Europe rejected the values of their classical predecessors (in fact, the theatrical traditions of ancient Greece and Rome were condemned), drama remained a vehicle for the worship of God. Priests originally acted out biblical scenes in Latin to celebrate religious seasons like Easter or Christmas. By the thirteenth century, "mystery plays" depicting the life of Christ in a series of cycles were being performed in the vernacular rather than in Latin. Actors in these plays included religious clergy as well as members of professional craft guilds (such as groups of bakers or smiths). The annual performance of the mystery cycles was a complicated and impressive celebration, with elaborate settings, costumes, music, and special effects that included fireworks and real water "floods." Other medieval dramas included miracle plays that celebrated the lives of saints, morality plays that addressed matters of vice and virtue, and eventually, more secular pageants that depicted folk traditions.

During the Renaissance period in England (from the early sixteenth to the early seventeenth centuries), the mystery cycles disappeared, possibly because of their association with Roman Catholicism, and theater became more a form of entertainment than a religious experience. In the sixteenth century, under the patronage of Elizabeth I of England, dramatists produced what many believe to be the theater's greatest works. William Shakespeare, Ben Jonson, Christopher Marlowe, and numerous other playwrights wrote stories of men and women involved in intrigue, mistaken identity, love, and revenge. These plays were performed in theaters in the round (that is, with the stage at the center of the theater, surrounded by the audience) to a mixed audience of dukes and paupers.

An exterior view of the Globe Theater today.

A model of the Globe Theater as it looked in Shakespeare's time.

Elizabethan plays reflect the concerns of their time: a deep awareness of the nuances of language, anxiety over changing social roles, and a preoccupation with art's relationship to death, to name only a few. This period of literary history remains important, and Elizabeth I was a powerful female patron of the arts. However, while Elizabethan theater included some of the most interesting and complex female characters on the stage, women were not allowed to perform publicly until the end of the seventeenth century. Before that time, female roles were performed by adolescent boys.

After the great period of playwriting in England during the late sixteenth and early seventeenth centuries, during which Shakespeare wrote his plays (see *I Henry IV* in Chapter 16), public drama disappeared for seventeen years. In 1642, England's new Puritan rulers closed all public stages and forbade public performances. When the theaters reopened after the restoration of Charles II to the throne in 1660, the stage would never be the same again. For the first time in history, professional female actors performed the roles written for women. Many of these women became stars, and playwrights created roles for them that tantalized male theatergoers. Restoration drama across Europe became known for its sexual innuendo and scandalous depiction of adultery and seduction as well as for its vicious satire: see, for example, Moliere's play *The Miser* in Chapter 17.

Although drama was still a viable form of entertainment in eighteenth-century England, the plays produced during that century were subject to state censorship following the Licensing Act of 1737. Before that time, theater had become a popular venue for social **satire,** a mode of literature that points out the flaws of character types or individuals, often wealthy people, monarchs, or politicians. With drama under censure, the novel became an important entertainment form. Its popularity was also due to the rise of literacy and the class of merchants, who hoped to earn respectability by developing their private libraries. Thus although drama did not disappear from England or other Western countries in the late eighteenth and nineteenth centuries, these eras are more noted for other forms of literary production, especially fiction.

The late nineteenth and twentieth centuries, however, saw a resurgence of drama as a potentially vital form well suited to modernist experimentation. Authors such as Henrik Ibsen (Norway), George Bernard Shaw (Ireland), and Eugene O'Neill (United States) revealed drama's potential for artistic innovation and for stirring up audiences. In Ireland's Abbey Theater in the early twentieth century, a number of prominent playwrights, including W. B. Yeats, Lady Gregory, Sean O'Casey, and John Millington Synge, were responsible for an Irish literary renaissance that showcased drama as one of its most vital forms: a play by Synge was responsible for a riot in Dublin. In the United States Eugene O'Neill was similarly at the vanguard of a new generation of playwrights who were willing to challenge the values and tastes of their audiences.

The mid-twentieth century saw the development of internationally respected drama in the United States for the first time: Arthur Miller, Tennessee Williams, and Edward Albee wrote plays that have been influential in the development of American drama. Williams's *Cat on a Hot Tin Roof* can be found in Chapter 13. Miller is the author of *Death of a Salesman*, a play well suited to his theory of "tragedy and the common man." Miller wrote an influential essay on this subject that links ancient definitions of tragedy based on the lives of kings to contemporary notions of tragedy based on the lives of everyday people.

After Miller the American theater was poised to include the lives of everyday people who are on the margins of American society: Lorraine Hansberry, David Henry Hwang, George C. Wolfe, August Wilson, and Tony Kushner are some playwrights who have brought into the limelight Americans who were previously hidden in the shadows. The twentieth century also saw drama that was increasingly experimental, beginning with the expressionist playwright Bertolt Brecht from Germany, followed by absurdist playwright Samuel Beckett from Ireland, and continuing with British experimenters Harold Pinter and Tom Stoppard as well as American Sam Shepard.

Playwrights who share in traditions that are not exclusively European, such as Wole Soyinka, a Nigerian poet, playwright, and essayist whose play *Death and the King's Horseman* can be found in Chapter 12, have also been prominent figures on the international stage. A host of non-Western traditions, such as Sanskrit theater in India and Noh drama and Kabuki theater in Japan, have flourished for centuries; because this is an introductory textbook that cannot include all traditions, we have space to only mention them here.

Although contemporary theater has lost the religious overtones that were once so integral to the genre, seeing a play remains a communal event. Whereas people read a novel or poem or watch a television show at home, they typically view plays in the presence of others. If the performance is successful, hundreds—even thousands—of people have come together to share an experience. It is a social opportunity to sympathize, condemn, cheer, or cry.

Elements of Drama

In general, the formal elements of drama overlap with those of fiction and poetry, although they differ in how they are experienced by the audience. A play's **setting**—the place and time period of its action on stage—is central to its interpretation. Playwrights use setting to establish the play's mood and to convey information about characters and situations. Compare the use of setting in the following descriptions by Irish playwrights Samuel Beckett and George Bernard Shaw. Here is Beckett's stage description for the opening of his absurdist play, *Endgame:*

Bare interior.
Grey light.
Left and right back, high up, two small windows, curtains drawn.
Front right, a door. Hanging near door, its face to wall, a picture.
Front left, touching each other, covered with an old sheet, two ashbins.
Center, in an armchair on castors, covered with an old sheet, Hamm.

For a stage designer on a tight budget, Beckett's set is a dream come true. This is not going to be a work that relies on elaborately designed scenery for its effect. Two windows, a door, a picture, a chair, and two dustbins are all we see on the stage. Try to imagine the effect that this sparse setting would have on an audience. What do dustbins connote? How about grey lighting? Even before the play begins, we realize that this work has a bleak, depressing theme. Few rooms look like this. In the case of *Endgame*, the setting prepares us for the subject and tone of the play.

Now look at the description of the opening setting for George Bernard Shaw's play, *Arms and the Man.* While Shaw is known for his detailed stage directions, this example is verbose even for him:

Night. A lady's bedchamber in Bulgaria, in a small town near the Dragoman Pass. It is late in November in the year 1885, and through an open window with a little balcony on the left can be seen a peak of the Balkans, wonderfully white and beautiful in the starlit snow. The interior of the room is not like anything to be seen in the east of Europe. It is half rich Bulgarian, half cheap Viennese. The counterpane and hangings of the bed, the window curtains, the little carpet, and all the ornamental textile fabrics in the room are oriental and gorgeous: the paper on the walls is occidental and paltry. Above the head of the bed, which stands against a little wall cutting off the right hand corner of the room diagonally, is a painted wooden shrine, blue and gold, with an ivory image of Christ, and a light hanging before it in a pierced metal ball suspended by three chains. On the left, further forward, is an ottoman. The washstand, against the wall on the left, consists of an enamelled iron basin with a pail beneath it in a painted metal frame, and a single towel on the rail at the side. A chair near it is Austrian bent wood, with cane seat. The dressing table, between the bed and the window, is an ordinary pine table, covered with a cloth of many colors, but with an expensive toilet mirror on it. The door is on the right; and there is a chest of drawers between the door and the bed. This chest of drawers is also covered by a variegated native cloth, and on it there is a pile of paper backed novels, a box of chocolate creams, and a miniature easel, on which is a large photograph of an extremely handsome officer, whose lofty bearing and magnetic glance can be felt even from the portrait. The room is lighted by a candle on the chest of drawers, and another on the dressing table, with a box of matches beside it. The window is hinged doorwise and stands wide open, folding back to the left. Outside a pair of wooden shutters, opening outwards, also stand open. On the balcony, a young lady, intensely conscious of the romantic beauty of the night, and of the fact that her own youth and beauty is a part of it, is on the balcony, gazing at the snowy Balkans. She is covered by a long mantle of furs, worth, on a moderate estimate, about three times the furniture of her room.

Her reverie is interrupted by her mother, Catherine Petkoff, a woman over forty, imperiously energetic, with magnificent black hair and eyes, who might be a very splendid specimen of the wife of a mountain farmer, but is determined to be a Viennese lady, and to that end wears a fashionable tea gown on all occasions.

In addition to a detailed vision of what the physical set should look like—down to information about the way the windows and doors should open—Shaw's description reveals much about his characters, two self-conscious women who are aware of the way they project themselves. Before the characters utter a word, we can assume a few things about this play. The detailed descriptions suggest that this play will be more consciously grounded in reality than Beckett's and will include characters whose motives and actions more closely resemble those of people we encounter in our everyday lives.

In addition, unlike in Beckett's play, there is no suggestion of bleakness. The room is ornately decorated, comically so, and candles cast warm lighting that complements the warmth suggested by the young woman's furs. The author takes an ironic approach to his characters, letting us know that while the message of the play may be serious (as it is), there will be light moments. Although Shaw's plays, like Beckett's, are plays of ideas, we can see from their settings alone that each writer will explore his ideas through different theatrical conventions.

While setting may be the first thing an audience notices in a drama, usually the characters and the plot drive the play. As in fiction, **characters** can be *round* (or realistic), such as the conflicted Mrs. Peters in *Trifles*, the play featured in this chapter. These characters, whether they are protagonists or antagonists, tend to have both positive and negative qualities. They are motivated by real problems and they speak and behave in ways that are consistent with human nature. Like the rest of us, round characters consist of a combination of vices and virtues, and they sometimes struggle to tell the difference between the two. These characters are often dynamic, changing over the course of the play. As the play opens, Mrs. Peters is the sheriff's wife, "married to the law" as another character describes her. By the end of the play, she has begun to separate the concept of "justice" from the legal system that her husband represents. The play is as much about the personal change experienced by Mrs. Peters as it is about the mystery of who killed Mr. Wright and why.

On the other hand, some playwrights rely on *flat* characters to embody a particular vice or virtue. These characters tend to be static and unchanging, and they lack the complex qualities possessed by real individuals. Flat characters commonly embody stereotypes—the drunken Irishman or the stupid hillbilly—and are used by playwrights for comic effect. On the seventeenth- and eighteenth-century British stage, flat characters often had names that signified their major characteristic: a sadistic husband is named "Pinchwife" in William Wycherly's 1688 comedy *The Country Wife*. Nearly a century later, Richard Brinsely Sheriden dubbed a malicious gossip "Lady Sneerwell" in *The School for Scandal*. These allegorical characters are not meant to represent complex human beings, but instead satirize a particular human characteristic.

In the play included in this chapter, Susan Glaspell's *Trifles*, Mr. Wright is a flat character. We never meet him directly because he is dead as the play opens. Cruel and stingy, he is the embodiment of the cold, uncaring husband. Nothing in the play suggests that he may have had inner struggles or that he was driven by complex motives. He's simply a mean person. Glaspell uses both round and flat characters in *Trifles:* since Mr. Wright is an entirely unpleasant person, we can better enter into the struggles of Mrs. Hale and Mrs. Peters as they decide what to do about their growing understanding of the motives behind his murder.

Unlike authors of fiction, who can narrate a character's thoughts, playwrights have to rely on other techniques to convey the complex inner drives and motivations of their creations. Since the audience cannot read minds, dialogue and the actors' body language must reveal the characters' inner thoughts. Although **dialogue**, or conversation between characters, occurs in many works of fiction and even in some poems and essays, it is the basic stuff of drama. A writer's challenge is to create realistic-sounding dialogue that provides ample background information for the audience.

Sometimes, however, an author cannot practically convey information to the audience through dialogue. Perhaps a character is discussing actions and feelings that he would never share with anyone. In this case, the author often uses a stage convention called a **soliloquy,** a speech directed at the audience that represents the character's inner thoughts. A playwright does not have the fiction writer's advantage of entering a character's head and reproducing his thoughts, and so we have Hamlet asking himself, loud enough so the audience can hear, whether it is better "to be or not to be." A soliloquy is a theatrical convention that violates the expectations of realism because few people talk to themselves in such profound and articulate ways, but most audiences are willing to accept this convention in the same way that audiences of musicals accept the fact that characters suddenly burst into song and dance.

In addition to telling the audience more about a character's motivations, dialogue and soliloquy are convenient ways for playwrights to move the **plot** forward. The plot consists of the actions of the play. Most plots follow a traditional pattern that holds true even when the plot is not presented in chronological order but instead uses **flashbacks,** or depictions of past events. As in fiction, a typical dramatic plot begins with the **exposition,** or background information. During this period the playwright explains the situation confronting the characters.

In *Trifles*, the exposition includes the opening dialogue in which the County Attorney asks for details about John Wright's death. Mr. Hale describes finding John Wright's body and being surprised by Mrs. Hale's unconventional response:

County Attorney: What—was she doing?
Hale: She was rockin' back and forth. She had her apron in her hand and was kind of—pleating it.
County Attorney: And how did she—look?
Hale: She looked queer.

In this example, the exposition serves two purposes. While Glaspell allows her characters to act out their roles of probing investigator and dutiful citizen, she is also giving her audience information that reveals Mrs. Wright's odd behavior in the wake of her husband's murder, information that might provide a clue to her guilt or innocence.

Once the exposition has established the play's situation, the plot usually becomes complicated in the **rising action.** During this part of the play, the conflict deepens and becomes more complex. A conflict can be described as internal—inside a single character, as in *Trifles*—or external—between a character and a larger force, or between two or more characters. In *Trifles*, Mrs. Hale and Mrs. Peters discuss the unhappy life of Minnie Wright and their own responsibility to her as women and as community members. The plot twists as each new discovery yields more information about Mrs. Wright's mental state at the time of her husband's murder. During the rising action, both the characters and the audience experience conflict, in this case because it is difficult to sift through competing notions of justice.

Finally, most plays, like most works of fiction and some poems, reach a **climax,** the moment of crisis or turning point in the drama. The rising action has been building to this point all along. In *Trifles*, the climax takes place at the end, when the County Attorney condescendingly asks the women whether Mrs. Wright was going to quilt or knot the quilt she had been working on. This is the moment of truth. Will Mrs. Peters stay "married to the law" and turn over the evidence she and Mrs. Hale have found, or will they remain quiet and protect the person they perceive to be the real victim in the Wrights' marriage?

The climax of a play is usually followed by the **denouement,** or unraveling of the threads that have led to the conflict. The denouement is the resolution of the conflict.

Plot development is similar in fiction and in drama, with some differences. Because a play's performance is enacted during a limited time period (usually one to three hours), not every significant event takes place on stage. In fact, playwrights often begin their plays after a significant event has occurred: Sophocles's *Oedipus Rex* opens after Oedipus has killed his father and married his mother. The play's conflict arises from his discovery of those deeds and their consequences.

Similarly, in Shakespeare's *Hamlet*, we never see the murder of Hamlet's father because it happens well before the play opens. When we do meet the former king of Denmark, he is a ghost, asking his son to avenge his murder. In *Trifles*, Mr. Wright is dead as the play opens. We learn about all of these events as they are recalled after the fact. Although fiction does not always depict every significant event in the plot either, drama is even more limited by timing and the difficulties of staging certain scenes.

Tragedy, Comedy, and Other Distinctions

Plays like *Death and the King's Horseman* in Chapter 12 and *Medea* in Chapter 15 are **tragedies**, a term defined by the Greek philosopher Aristotle in his influential work of criticism, *Poetics*, written in the third century BCE. According to Aristotle, a tragedy is a work of drama that depicts the downfall of a great person, occasioned by his or her own actions or character flaws and producing an emotional **catharsis** (a cleansing of feelings of pity and fear) in the audience. This catharsis is often brought on, according to Aristotle, by the spectacle of suffering on the stage. In a famous passage, Aristotle describes the "perfect" tragic plot and character:

> It follows plainly, in the first place, that the change of fortune presented must not be the spectacle of a virtuous man brought from prosperity to adversity: for this moves neither pity nor fear; it merely shocks us. Nor, again, that of a bad man passing from adversity to prosperity: for nothing can be more alien to the spirit of Tragedy; it possesses no single tragic quality; it neither satisfies the moral sense nor calls forth pity or fear. Nor, again, should the downfall of the utter villain be exhibited. A plot of this kind would, doubtless, satisfy the moral sense, but it would inspire neither pity nor fear; for pity is aroused by unmerited misfortune, fear by the misfortune of a man like ourselves. Such an event, therefore, will be neither pitiful nor terrible. There remains, then, the character between these two extremes—that of a man who is not eminently good and just, yet whose misfortune is brought about not by vice or depravity, but by some error or frailty. He must be one who is highly renowned and prosperous—a personage like Oedipus, Thyestes, or other illustrious men of such families.

While the definition has changed over time (we are now more accepting of tragedies involving everyday people rather than limiting them to "great" men), the essential qualities of tragedy have remained surprisingly consistent. Modern audiences are still drawn to tragedies in the classic sense of the term: the popularity of Mario Puzo's *The Godfather* and Dennis Lehane's *Mystic River*—novels turned into famous movies—attest to the power of tragedy in our lives today.

On the other hand, our definition of **comedy** has changed from ancient times to our own. We now think of a comedy as a work that makes us laugh, but traditionally a comic play was simply one with a "happy ending," frequently involving a marriage and the restoration of the social order (called a *romantic comedy*). Usually the lovers in romantic comedies—often pairs of lovers—have to overcome an impediment to their unions. Aristotle defined a comic work as one that featured "low" characters (characters from a lower social class), but Renaissance and Restoration comedies usually focused on the courtships and intrigues of the nobility.

We also speak of the *comedy of manners*, which focuses on the manners of high society, often employing witty dialogue. Oscar Wilde's play *The Importance of Being Earnest* in Chapter 14 is an example of both a romantic comedy and a comedy of manners. Although comedies may address serious issues, they generally have a lighter outlook and a positive resolution.

Critics also speak of *tragicomedies*, or hybrids of tragedy and comedy that generally begin with tragic presumptions yet end comically. These plays can lend themselves easily to absurdism or tragic farce.

The *theater of the absurd* refers to plays of the late twentieth century (such as the one by Samuel Beckett described above) that have abstract settings and that attempt to illustrate some philosophical principle about the nature of humanity. Like *surrealist* plays, absurd plays do not strive to represent reality on the stage.

Student Essay on Susan Glaspell's *Trifles*

The main divisions of a play are called **acts,** which are sometimes further divided into *scenes*. Susan Glaspell's one-act play *Trifles* features two characters, Mrs. Peters and Mrs. Hale, who must resolve an ethical dilemma that challenges the values of the world in which they live. As "good" women, dutiful wives and neighbors, these women come to see that the patriarchal system of justice to which one of them is literally wed is inadequate. By the end of the play, we (the audience) know that the women will choose to band with each other and deceive their husbands to protect an abused wife who killed her husband. What we may not know is how we feel about that fact. Such an ambiguous situation is perfect for constructing a written argument: is obedience to the law in this situation a virtue or a vice?

Susan Glaspell *(1876–1948)*

Trifles

SCENE

The kitchen in the now abandoned farmhouse of John Wright, *a gloomy kitchen, and left without having been put in order—unwashed pans under the sink, a loaf of bread outside the bread-box, a dish-towel on the table—other signs of incompleted work. At the rear the outer door opens and the* Sheriff *comes in followed by the* County Attorney *and* Hale. *The* Sheriff *and* Hale *are men in middle life, the* County Attorney *is a young man; all are much bundled up and go at once to the stove. They are followed by the two women—the* Sheriff's *wife first; she is a slight wiry woman, a thin nervous face.* Mrs. Hale *is larger and would ordinarily be called more comfortable looking, but she is disturbed now and looks fearfully about as she enters. The women have come in slowly, and stand close together near the door.*

County Attorney [*Rubbing his hands.*]: This feels good. Come up to the fire, ladies.
Mrs. Peters [*After taking a step forward.*]: I'm not—cold.
Sheriff [*Unbuttoning his overcoat and stepping away from the stove as if to mark the beginning of official business.*]: Now, Mr. Hale, before we move things about, you explain to Mr. Henderson just what you saw when you came here yesterday morning.
County Attorney: By the way, has anything been moved? Are things just as you left them yesterday?
Sheriff [*Looking about.*]: It's just the same. When it dropped below zero last night I thought I'd better send Frank out this morning to make a fire for us—no use getting pneumonia with a big case on, but I told him not to touch anything except the stove—and you know Frank.
County Attorney: Somebody should have been left here yesterday.
Sheriff: Oh—yesterday. When I had to send Frank to Morris Center for that man who went crazy—I want you to know I had my hands full yesterday. I knew you could get back from Omaha by today and as long as I went over everything here myself—
County Attorney: Well, Mr. Hale, tell just what happened when you came here yesterday morning.
Hale: Harry and I had started to town with a load of potatoes. We came along the road from my place and as I got here I said, "I'm going to see if I can't get John Wright to go in with me on a party telephone." I spoke to Wright about it once before and he put me off, saying folks talked too much anyway, and all he asked was peace and quiet—I guess you know about how much he talked himself; but I thought maybe if I went to the house and talked about it before his wife, though I said to Harry that I didn't know as what his wife wanted made much difference to John—
County Attorney: Let's talk about that later, Mr. Hale. I do want to talk about that, but tell now just what happened when you got to the house.
Hale: I didn't hear or see anything; I knocked at the door, and still it was all quiet inside. I knew they must be up, it was past eight o'clock. So I knocked again, and I thought I heard somebody say, "Come in." I wasn't sure, I'm not sure yet, but I opened the door—this door [*indicating the door by which the two women are still standing*] and there in that rocker—[*pointing to it*] sat Mrs. Wright.

[They all look at the rocker.]

County Attorney: What—was she doing?
Hale: She was rockin' back and forth. She had her apron in her hand and was kind of—pleating it.
County Attorney: And how did she—look?
Hale: Well, she looked queer.
County Attorney: How do you mean—queer?

Hale: Well, as if she didn't know what she was going to do next. And kind of done up.

County Attorney: How did she seem to feel about your coming?

Hale: Why, I don't think she minded—one way or other. She didn't pay much attention. I said, "How do, Mrs. Wright, it's cold, ain't it?" And she said, "Is it?"—and went on kind of pleating at her apron. Well, I was surprised; she didn't ask me to come up to the stove, or to set down, but just sat there, not even looking at me, so I said, "I want to see John." And then she—laughed. I guess you would call it a laugh. I thought of Harry and the team outside, so I said a little sharp: "Can't I see John?" "No," she says, kind o' dull like. "Ain't he home?" says I. "Yes," says she, "he's home." "Then why can't I see him?" I asked her, out of patience. "'Cause he's dead," says she. "*Dead?*" says I. She just nodded her head, not getting a bit excited, but rockin' back and forth. "Why—where is he?" says I, not knowing what to say. She just pointed upstairs—like that [*himself pointing to the room above*]. I got up, with the idea of going up there. I walked from there to here—then I says, "Why, what did he die of?" "He died of a rope round his neck," says she, and just went on pleatin' at her apron. Well, I went out and called Harry. I thought I might—need help. We went upstairs and there he was lyin'—

County Attorney: I think I'd rather have you go into that upstairs, where you can point it all out. Just go on now with the rest of the story.

Hale: Well, my first thought was to get that rope off. It looked . . . [*Stops, his face twitches*] . . . but Harry, he went up to him, and he said, "No, he's dead all right, and we'd better not touch anything." So we went back downstairs. She was still sitting that same way. "Has anybody been notified?" I asked. "No," says she, unconcerned. "Who did this, Mrs. Wright?" said Harry. He said it business-like—and she stopped pleatin' of her apron. "I don't know," she says. "You don't *know?*" says Harry. "No," says she. "Weren't you sleepin' in the bed with him?" says Harry. "Yes," says she, "but I was on the inside." "Somebody slipped a rope round his neck and strangled him and you didn't wake up?" says Harry. "I didn't wake up," she said after him. We must 'a looked as if we didn't see how that could be, for after a minute she said, "I sleep sound." Harry was going to ask her more questions but I said maybe we ought to let her tell her story first to the coroner, or the sheriff, so Harry went fast as he could to Rivers' place, where there's a telephone.

County Attorney: And what did Mrs. Wright do when she knew that you had gone for the coroner?

Hale: She moved from that chair to this one over here [*Pointing to a small chair in the corner*] and just sat there with her hands held together and looking down. I got a feeling that I ought to make some conversation, so I said I had come in to see if John wanted to put in a telephone, and at that she started to laugh, and then she stopped and looked at me—scared. [*The* County Attorney, *who has had his notebook out, makes a note.*] I dunno, maybe it wasn't scared. I wouldn't like to say it was. Soon Harry got back, and then Dr. Lloyd came, and you, Mr. Peters, and so I guess that's all I know that you don't.

County Attorney [*Looking around.*]: I guess we'll go upstairs first—and then out to the barn and around there. [*To the* Sheriff.] You're convinced that there was nothing important here—nothing that would point to any motive.

Sheriff: Nothing here but kitchen things.

[The County Attorney, *after again looking around the kitchen, opens the door of a cupboard closet. He gets up on a chair and looks on a shelf. Pulls his hand away, sticky.]*

County Attorney: Here's a nice mess.

[The women draw nearer.]

Mrs. Peters [*To the other woman.*]: Oh, her fruit; it did freeze. [*To the* Lawyer.] She worried about that when it turned so cold. She said the fire'd go out and her jars would break.

Sheriff: Well, can you beat the women! Held for murder and worryin' about her preserves.

County Attorney: I guess before we're through she may have something more serious than preserves to worry about.

Hale: Well, women are used to worrying over trifles.

[The two women move a little closer together.]

County Attorney [*With the gallantry of a young politician.*]: And yet, for all their worries, what would we do without the ladies? [*The women do not unbend. He goes to the sink, takes a dipperful of water from the pail and pouring it into a basin, washes his hands. Starts to wipe them on the roller-towel, turns it for a cleaner place.*] Dirty towels! [*Kicks his foot against the pans under the sink.*] Not much of a housekeeper, would you say, ladies?

Mrs. Hale [*Stiffly.*]: There's a great deal of work to be done on a farm.

County Attorney: To be sure. And yet [*With a little bow to her*] I know there are some Dickson county farmhouses which do not have such roller towels.

[He gives it a pull to expose its full length again.]

Mrs. Hale: Those towels get dirty awful quick. Men's hands aren't always as clean as they might be.

County Attorney: Ah, loyal to your sex, I see. But you and Mrs. Wright were neighbors. I suppose you were friends, too.

Mrs. Hale [*Shaking her head.*]: I've not seen much of her of late years. I've not been in this house—it's more than a year.

County Attorney: And why was that? You didn't like her?

Mrs. Hale: I liked her all well enough. Farmers' wives have their hands full, Mr. Henderson. And then—

County Attorney: Yes—?

Mrs. Hale [*Looking about.*]: It never seemed a very cheerful place.

County Attorney: No—it's not cheerful. I shouldn't say she had the homemaking instinct.

Mrs. Hale: Well, I don't know as Wright had, either.

County Attorney: You mean that they didn't get on very well?

Mrs. Hale: No, I don't mean anything. But I don't think a place'd be any cheerfuller for John Wright's being in it.

County Attorney: I'd like to talk more of that a little later. I want to get the lay of things upstairs now.

[He goes to the left, where three steps lead to a stair door.]

Sheriff: I suppose anything Mrs. Peters does'll be all right. She was to take in some clothes for her, you know, and a few little things. We left in such a hurry yesterday.

County Attorney: Yes, but I would like to see what you take, Mrs. Peters, and keep an eye out for anything that might be of use to us.

Mrs. Peters: Yes, Mr. Henderson.

[The women listen to the men's steps on the stairs, then look about the kitchen.]

Mrs. Hale: I'd hate to have men coming into my kitchen, snooping around and criticising.

[She arranges the pans under sink which the Lawyer had shoved out of place.]

Mrs. Peters: Of course it's no more than their duty.

Mrs. Hale: Duty's all right, but I guess that deputy sheriff that came out to make the fire might have got a little of this on. [*Gives the roller towel a pull.*] Wish I'd thought of that sooner. Seems mean to talk about her for not having things slicked up when she had to come away in such a hurry.

Mrs. Peters [*Who has gone to a small table in the left rear corner of the room, and lifted one end of a towel that covers a pan.*]: She had bread set.

[Stands still.]

Mrs. Hale [*Eyes fixed on a loaf of bread beside the breadbox, which is on a low shelf at the other side of the room. Moves slowly toward it.*]: She was going to put this in there. [*Picks up loaf, then abruptly drops it. In a manner of returning to familiar things.*] It's a shame about her fruit. I wonder if it's all gone. [*Gets up on the chair and looks.*] I think there's some here that's all right, Mrs. Peters. Yes—here; [*Holding it toward the window*] this is cherries, too. [*Looking again.*] I declare I believe that's the only one. [*Gets down, bottle in her hand. Goes to the sink and wipes it off on the outside.*] She'll feel awful bad after all her hard work in the hot weather. I remember the afternoon I put up my cherries last summer.

[She puts the bottle on the big kitchen table, center of the room. With a sigh, is about to sit down in the rocking-chair. Before she is seated realizes what chair it is; with a slow look at it, steps back. The chair which she has touched rocks back and forth.]

Mrs. Peters: Well, I must get those things from the front room closet. [*She goes to the door at the right, but after looking into the other room, steps back.*] You coming with me, Mrs. Hale? You could help me carry them.

[They go in the other room; reappear, Mrs. Peters *carrying a dress and skirt,* Mrs. Hale *following with a pair of shoes.]*

Mrs. Peters: My, it's cold in there.

[She puts the clothes on the big table, and hurries to the stove.]

Mrs. Hale [*Examining the skirt.*]: Wright was close. I think maybe that's why she kept so much to herself. She didn't even belong to the Ladies Aid. I suppose she felt she couldn't do her part, and then you don't enjoy things when you feel shabby. She used to wear pretty clothes and be lively, when she was Minnie Foster, one of the town girls singing in the choir. But that—oh, that was thirty years ago. This all you was to take in?

Mrs. Peters: She said she wanted an apron. Funny thing to want, for there isn't much to get you dirty in jail, goodness knows. But I suppose just to make her feel more natural. She said they was in the top drawer in this cupboard. Yes, here. And then her little shawl that always hung behind the door. [*Opens stair door and looks.*] Yes, here it is.

[Quickly shuts door leading upstairs.]

Mrs. Hale [*Abruptly moving toward her.*]: Mrs. Peters?

Mrs. Peters: Yes, Mrs. Hale?

Mrs. Hale: Do you think she did it?

Mrs. Peters [*In a frightened voice.*]: Oh, I don't know.

Mrs. Hale: Well, I don't think she did. Asking for an apron and her little shawl. Worrying about her fruit.

Mrs. Peters [*Starts to speak, glances up, where footsteps are heard in the room above. In a low voice.*]: Mr. Peters says it looks bad for her. Mr. Henderson is awful sarcastic in a speech and he'll make fun of her sayin' she didn't wake up.

Mrs. Hale: Well, I guess John Wright didn't wake when they was slipping that rope under his neck.

Mrs. Peters: No, it's strange. It must have been done awful crafty and still. They say it was such a—funny way to kill a man, rigging it all up like that.

Mrs. Hale: That's just what Mr. Hale said. There was a gun in the house. He says that's what he can't understand.

Mrs. Peters: Mr. Henderson said coming out that what was needed for the case was a motive; something to show anger, or—sudden feeling.

Mrs. Hale [*Who is standing by the table.*]: Well, I don't see any signs of anger around here. [*She puts her hand on the dish towel which lies on the table, stands looking down at table, one half of which is clean, the other half messy.*] It's wiped to here. [*Makes a move as if to finish work, then turns and looks at loaf of bread outside the breadbox. Drops towel. In that voice of coming back to familiar things.*] Wonder how they are finding things upstairs. I hope she had it a little more red-up up there. You know, it seems kind of *sneaking*. Locking her up in town and then coming out here and trying to get her own house to turn against her!

Mrs. Peters: But Mrs. Hale, the law is the law.

Mrs. Hale: I s'pose 'tis. [*Unbuttoning her coat.*] Better loosen up your things, Mrs. Peters. You won't feel them when you go out.

*[*Mrs. Peters *takes off her fur tippet, goes to hang it on hook at back of room, stands looking at the under part of the small corner table.]*

Mrs. Peters: She was piecing a quilt.

[She brings the large sewing basket and they look at the bright pieces.]

Mrs. Hale: It's log cabin pattern. Pretty, isn't it? I wonder if she was goin' to quilt it or just knot it?

[Footsteps have been heard coming down the stairs. The Sheriff *enters followed by* Hale *and the* County Attorney.*]*

Sheriff: They wonder if she was going to quilt it or just knot it!

[The men laugh, the women look abashed.]

County Attorney [*Rubbing his hands over the stove.*]: Frank's fire didn't do much up there, did it? Well, let's go out to the barn and get that cleared up.

[The men go outside.]

Mrs. Hale [*Resentfully.*]: I don't know as there's anything so strange, our takin' up our time with little things while we're waiting for them to get the evidence. [*She sits down at the big table smoothing out a block with decision.*] I don't see as it's anything to laugh about.

Mrs. Peters [*Apologetically.*]: Of course they've got awful important things on their minds.

[Pulls up a chair and joins Mrs. Hale *at the table.]*

Mrs. Hale [*Examining another block.*]: Mrs. Peters, look at this one. Here, this is the one she was working on, and look at the sewing! All the rest of it has been so nice and even. And look at this! It's all over the place! Why, it looks as if she didn't know what she was about!

[After she had said this they look at each other, then start to glance back at the door. After an instant Mrs. Hale *has pulled at a knot and ripped the sewing.]*

Mrs. Peters: Oh, what are you doing, Mrs. Hale?

Mrs. Hale [*Mildly.*]: Just pulling out a stitch or two that's not sewed very good. [*Threading a needle.*] Bad sewing always made me fidgety.

Mrs. Peters [*Nervously.*]: I don't think we ought to touch things.

Mrs. Hale: I'll just finish up this end. [*Suddenly stopping and leaning forward.*] Mrs. Peters?

Mrs. Peters: Yes, Mrs. Hale?

Mrs. Hale: What do you suppose she was so nervous about?

Mrs. Peters: Oh—I don't know. I don't know as she was nervous. I sometimes sew awful queer when I'm just tired. [Mrs. Hale *starts to say something, looks at* Mrs. Peters, *then goes on sewing.*] Well I must get these things wrapped up. They may be through sooner than we think. [*Putting apron and other things together.*] I wonder where I can find a piece of paper, and string.

Mrs. Hale: In that cupboard, maybe.

Mrs. Peters [*Looking in cupboard.*]: Why, here's a bird-cage. [*Holds it up.*] Did she have a bird, Mrs. Hale?

Mrs. Hale: Why, I don't know whether she did or not—I've not been here for so long. There was a man around last year selling canaries cheap, but I don't know as she took one; maybe she did. She used to sing real pretty herself.

Mrs. Peters [*Glancing around.*]: Seems funny to think of a bird here. But she must have had one, or why would she have a cage? I wonder what happened to it.

Mrs. Hale: I s'pose maybe the cat got it.

Mrs. Peters: No, she didn't have a cat. She's got that feeling some people have about cats—being afraid of them. My cat got in her room and she was real upset and asked me to take it out.

Mrs. Hale: My sister Bessie was like that. Queer, ain't it?

Mrs. Peters [*Examining the cage.*]: Why, look at this door. It's broke. One hinge is pulled apart.

Mrs. Hale [*Looking too.*]: Looks as if someone must have been rough with it.

Mrs. Peters: Why, yes.

[She brings the cage forward and puts it on the table.]

Mrs. Hale: I wish if they're going to find any evidence they'd be about it. I don't like this place.

Mrs. Peters: But I'm awful glad you came with me, Mrs. Hale. It would be lonesome for me sitting here alone.

Mrs. Hale: It would, wouldn't it? [*Dropping her sewing.*] But I tell you what I do wish, Mrs. Peters. I wish I had come over sometimes when *she* was here. I—[*Looking around the room*]—wish I had.

Mrs. Peters: But of course you were awful busy, Mrs. Hale—your house and your children.

Mrs. Hale: I could've come. I stayed away because it weren't cheerful—and that's why I ought to have come. I—I've never liked this place. Maybe because it's down in a hollow and you don't see the road. I dunno what it is, but it's a lonesome place and always was. I wish I had come over to see Minnie Foster sometimes. I can see now—

[Shakes her head.]

Mrs. Peters: Well, you mustn't reproach yourself, Mrs. Hale. Somehow we just don't see how it is with other folks until—something comes up.

Mrs. Hale: Not having children makes less work—but it makes a quiet house, and Wright out to work all day, and no company when he did come in. Did you know John Wright, Mrs. Peters?

Mrs. Peters: Not to know him; I've seen him in town. They say he was a good man.

Mrs. Hale: Yes—good; he didn't drink, and kept his word as well as most, I guess, and paid his debts. But he was a hard man, Mrs. Peters. Just to pass the time of day with him—[*Shivers.*] Like a raw wind that gets to the bone. [*Pauses, her eye falling on the cage.*] I should think she would 'a wanted a bird. But what do you suppose went with it?

Mrs. Peters: I don't know, unless it got sick and died.

[She reaches over and swings the broken door, swings it again, both women watch it.]

Mrs. Hale: You weren't raised round here, were you? [Mrs. Peters *shakes her head.*] You didn't know—her?

Mrs. Peters: Not till they brought her yesterday.

Mrs. Hale: She—come to think of it, she was kind of like a bird herself—real sweet and pretty, but kind of timid and—fluttery. How—she—did—change. [*Silence; then as if struck by a happy thought and relieved to get back to every day things.*] Tell you what, Mrs. Peters, why don't you take the quilt in with you? It might take up her mind.

Mrs. Peters: Why, I think that's a real nice idea, Mrs. Hale. There couldn't possibly be any objection to it, could there? Now, just what would I take? I wonder if her patches are in here—and her things.

[They look in the sewing basket.]

Mrs. Hale: Here's some red. I expect this has got sewing things in it. [*Brings out a fancy box.*] What a pretty box. Looks like something somebody would give you. Maybe her scissors are in here. [*Opens box. Suddenly puts her hand to her nose.*] Why—[Mrs. Peters *bends nearer, then turns her face away.*] There's something wrapped up in this piece of silk.

Mrs. Peters: Why, this isn't her scissors.

Mrs. Hale [*Lifting the silk.*]: Oh, Mrs. Peters—its—

*[*Mrs. Peters *bends closer.]*

Mrs. Peters: It's the bird.

Mrs. Hale [*Jumping up.*]: But, Mrs. Peters—look at it! Its neck! Look at its neck! It's all—other side *to.*

Mrs. Peters: Somebody—wrung—its—neck.

[Their eyes meet. A look of growing comprehension, of horror. Steps are heard outside. Mrs. Hale *slips box under quilt pieces, and sinks into her chair. Enter* Sheriff *and* County Attorney. Mrs. Peters *rises.]*

County Attorney [*As one turning from serious things to little pleasantries.*]: Well, ladies, have you decided whether she was going to quilt it or knot it?

Mrs. Peters: We think she was going to—knot it.

County Attorney: Well, that's interesting, I'm sure. [*Seeing the birdcage.*] Has the bird flown?

Mrs. Hale [*Putting more quilt pieces over the box.*]: We think the—cat got it.

County Attorney: [*Preoccupied.*] Is there a cat?

[Mrs. Hale *glances in a quick covert way at* Mrs. Peters.]

Mrs. Peters: Well, not *now.* They're superstitious, you know. They leave.

County Attorney [*To* Sheriff Peters, *continuing an interrupted conversation.*]: No sign at all of anyone having come from the outside. Their own rope. Now let's go up again and go over it piece by piece. [*They start upstairs.*] It would have to have been someone who knew just the—

[Mrs. Peters sits down. *The two women sit there not looking at one another, but as if peering into something and at the same time holding back. When they talk now it is in the manner of feeling their way over strange ground, as if afraid of what they are saying, but as if they can not help saying it.*]

Mrs. Hale: She liked the bird. She was going to bury it in that pretty box.

Mrs. Peters [*In a whisper.*]: When I was a girl—my kitten—there was a boy took a hatchet, and before my eyes—and before I could get there—[*Covers her face an instant.*] If they hadn't held me back I would have—[*Catches herself, looks upstairs where steps are heard, falters weakly*]—hurt him.

Mrs. Hale [*With a slow look around her.*]: I wonder how it would seem never to have had any children around. [*Pause.*] No, Wright wouldn't like the bird—a thing that sang. She used to sing. He killed that, too.

Mrs. Peters [*Moving uneasily.*]: We don't know who killed the bird.

Mrs. Hale: I knew John Wright.

Mrs. Peters: It was an awful thing was done in this house that night, Mrs. Hale. Killing a man while he slept, slipping a rope around his neck that choked the life out of him.

Mrs. Hale: His neck. Choked the life out of him.

[*Her hand goes out and rests on the bird-cage.*]

Mrs. Peters [*With rising voice.*]: We don't know who killed him. We don't *know.*

Mrs. Hale [*Her own feeling not interrupted.*]: If there'd been years and years of nothing, then a bird to sing to you, it would be awful—still, after the bird was still.

Mrs. Peters [*Something within her speaking.*]: I know what stillness is. When we homesteaded in Dakota, and my first baby died—after he was two years old, and me with no other then—

Mrs. Hale [*Moving.*]: How soon do you suppose they'll be through, looking for the evidence?

Mrs. Peters: I know what stillness is. [*Pulling herself back.*] The law has got to punish crime, Mrs. Hale.

Mrs. Hale [*Not as if answering that.*]: I wish you'd seen Minnie Foster when she wore a white dress with blue ribbons and stood up there in the choir and sang. [*A look around the room.*] Oh, I *wish* I'd come over here once in a while! That was a crime! That was a crime! Who's going to punish that?

Mrs. Peters [*Looking upstairs.*]: We mustn't—take on.

Mrs. Hale: I might have known she needed help! I know how things can be—for women. I tell you, it's queer, Mrs. Peters. We live close together and we live far apart. We all go through the same things—it's all just a different kind of the same thing. [*Brushes her eyes, noticing the bottle of fruit, reaches out for it.*] If I was you I wouldn't tell her her fruit was gone. Tell her it *ain't*. Tell her it's all right. Take this in to prove it to her. She—she may never know whether it was broke or not.

Mrs. Peters [*Takes the bottle, looks about for something to wrap it in; takes petticoat from the clothes brought from the other room, very nervously begins winding this around the bottle. In a false voice.*]: My, it's a good thing the men couldn't hear us. Wouldn't they just laugh! Getting all stirred up over a little thing like a—dead canary. As if that could have anything to do with—with—wouldn't they *laugh!*

[The men are heard coming down stairs.]

Mrs. Hale [*Under her breath.*]: Maybe they would—maybe they wouldn't.

County Attorney: No, Peters, it's all perfectly clear except a reason for doing it. But you know juries when it comes to women. If there was some definite thing. Something to show—something to make a story about—a thing that would connect up with this strange way of doing it—

[The women's eyes meet for an instant. Enter Hale *from outer door.]*

Hale: Well, I've got the team around. Pretty cold out there.

County Attorney: I'm going to stay here a while by myself. [*To the* Sheriff.] You can send Frank out for me, can't you? I want to go over everything. I'm not satisfied that we can't do better.

Sheriff: Do you want to see what Mrs. Peters is going to take in?

[The Lawyer *goes to the table, picks up the apron, laughs.]*

County Attorney: Oh, I guess they're not very dangerous things the ladies have picked out. [*Moves a few things about, disturbing the quilt pieces which cover the box. Steps back.*] No, Mrs. Peters doesn't need supervising. For that matter, a sheriff's wife is married to the law. Ever think of it that way, Mrs. Peters?

Mrs. Peters: Not—just that way.

Sheriff [*Chuckling.*]: Married to the law. [*Moves toward the other room.*] I just want you to come in here a minute, George. We ought to take a look at these windows.

County Attorney [*Scoffingly.*]: Oh, windows!

Sheriff: We'll be right out, Mr. Hale.

*[*Hale *goes outside. The* Sheriff *follows the* County Attorney *into the other room. Then* Mrs. Hale *rises, hands tight together, looking intensely at* Mrs. Peters, *whose eyes make a slow turn, finally meeting* Mrs. Hale's. *A moment* Mrs. Hale

holds her, then her own eyes point the way to where the box is concealed. Suddenly Mrs. Peters *throws back quilt pieces and tries to put the box in the bag she is wearing. It is too big. She opens box, starts to take bird out, cannot touch it, goes to pieces, stands there helpless. Sound of a knob turning in the other room. Mrs. Hale snatches the box and puts it in the pocket of her big coat. Enter* County Attorney *and* Sheriff.*]*

County Attorney [*Facetiously.*]: Well, Henry, at least we found out that she was not going to quilt it. She was going to—what is it you call it, ladies?

Mrs. Hale [*Her hand against her pocket.*]: We call it—knot it, Mr. Henderson.

(CURTAIN)

(1917)

As with poetry, when writing about drama you discuss its conventions only to support your thesis about a play. An essay that simply walked through a play like *Trifles* pointing out round and flat characters and explaining how dialogue forwards the plot would be both obvious and boring. Your essay needs to put forth an argument, an idea that is debatable and that you can support with evidence from the play's text.

Student writer Darryl Holliday carefully chooses passages from *Trifles* to advance his argument about whether or not situations exist in which the law can be ignored. Darryl quotes dialogue as it appears in the play. He gives a clear thesis at the end of his second paragraph, and he uses evidence from the text to support his argument.

Student Essay

Darryl Holliday is an English major at the University of Massachusetts, Lowell. In addition to studying, he enjoys writing poetry and playing guitar. In summing up his own life history to date, Darryl says, "He recently discovered the potential of his soul and is looking to make good use of it."

Holliday 1

Darryl Holliday

Final Draft

Trifles: Susan Glaspell's Social Theater

On a surface level, Trifles, by Susan Glaspell, presents the difficult moral dilemma of two women faced with the biased nature

Holliday 2

of a legal system they did not create. The overall idea presented by this play is this: can the law be justifiably ignored on the basis of morality? With so many factors to consider in such a conflicting decision, no one answer can be used for every situation. Whether we realize it or not, we all must confront these questions in some form at some point in our lives. Is it justifiable to steal food for the homeless from billion dollar corporations that exploit foreign countries? Is it acceptable for a person to break imposed speed limits in order to get his pregnant wife to a delivery room? Is it okay for impoverished people to raid oil pipelines when their government uses natural resources for their own profit? People face these situations and others like them every day.

The conflict arises when a commitment to one's morals and peers contradicts the imposing nature of a legal system created by fallible human beings. I don't have answers, but I do have an opinion. Like the women in Trifles, I often wonder if the law can be ignored when certain facts fail to reach the ears of those whose job it is to make sure these laws are followed. These are the problems that Mrs. Hale and Mrs. Peters struggle with in Glaspell's play. On a broader level, they represent those who are oppressed by laws and law enforcers who only see what they want to see. Can a biased law system always be fair to all? Susan Glaspell uses theater, drawing specifically on the use of dialogue, to argue that it cannot. Thus, the women are right in hiding evidence from the law.

Unfortunately for Mrs. Hale and Mrs. Peters, the legal system that they live within is biased from the beginning. Glaspell intentionally divides the plays' characters into men and women, characters who live in separate worlds even when they live in the same house. She uses dialogue to highlight the men's condescending attitudes toward their wives and their lack of understanding:

> Mrs. Peters: [To the other woman.] Oh, her fruit; it did freeze. [To the Lawyer.] She worried about that when it turned so cold. She said the fire'd go out and her jars would break.

Holliday 3

> Sheriff: Well, can you beat the women! Held for murder and worryin' about her preserves.
>
> County Attorney: I guess before we're through she may have something more serious than preserves to worry about.
>
> Hale: Well, women are used to worrying over trifles. (110)

Considering the evidence the men are looking for to convict Mrs. Wright, this last statement becomes somewhat ironic at the end of the play when such evidence is found among Mrs. Wright's sewing materials in the form of a dead bird. The men would probably consider such evidence to be "trifles," or trivial details, and therefore unimportant to the situation. Yet these trifles hold the key to the play's mystery. Glaspell creates a small, claustrophobic world to highlight a larger problem. In reality, this bias is sometimes shared by lawmakers and law enforcers even today. Unfortunately for all, opinions about gender, race, and other social categories sometimes come into play in what should always be a search for true justice as far as law is concerned. Does the unfair treatment of these people entitle them to ignore certain laws in order to even the playing field?

Glaspell uses these initial comments to emphasize that the men have already established their ideas as to Mrs. Wright's guilt. What they have not established is a clear understanding of an alternative point of view. By not fully utilizing the perspective of the people it is built to protect, the created laws and their enforcement will turn out one-sided. The men of Trifles do not view the women as important to their case, and consequently miss out on vital information from a useful perspective. Likewise, law sometimes does not take into account the views of certain society members. It is the right of these people to ignore these laws if necessary, and it is their duty to correct them when possible.

By not giving importance to the women's opinions, the men ignore possible motives for the crime. This becomes clear in an exchange between Mrs. Hale and the County Attorney:

Holliday 4

Mrs. Hale: [Looking about.] It never seemed a very cheerful place.

County Attorney: No—it's not cheerful. I shouldn't say she had the homemaking instinct.

Mrs. Hale: Well, I don't know as Wright had, either.

County Attorney: You mean that they didn't get along very well?

Mrs. Hale: No, I don't mean anything. But I don't think a place'd be any cheerfuller for John Wright's being in it.

County Attorney: I'd like to talk more of that a little later. I want to get the lay of things upstairs now. (110–11)

This is the second time that the County Attorney refuses to inquire about John Wright's personality with a "later" that will never be addressed in the play. While the women seem to sense something more than a murder going on, "the law" ignores their attempt at finding the truth. Intentionally on Glaspell's part, it is when the men leave the room and bypass the kitchen that Mrs. Hale and Mrs. Peters begin to discover the true story. The dialogue between the two women, even when they disagree, reflects a far deeper understanding of one another than either woman seems to share with her husband. They soon discover that the dead bird, a symbol of Mrs. Wright's caged life, is murdered in the same manner as Mr. Wright has been. The bird can also be a symbol of the buried truth that will never be found by the law. Mrs. Wright, though extreme in her method, has found her own justice when the law would not. After realizing this as a possibility, Mrs. Hale and Mrs. Peters are left with their decision.

We are all aware that no system of laws can be perfect for every situation, so should an imperfect law system be followed without hesitation or consideration to one's own moral values? Although the law does give a certain amount of order and stability to a society, there will always be situations where the law cannot do the best good for the most people. As in the case of Trifles, sometimes the law is biased, uncaring, and disconnected from the people it is meant to protect. It is in these times I say that it can and should be ignored for the sake of morality and fairness, and I believe that Glaspell felt the same way. As Mrs. Hale says, "We all go through the same things—it's all just a different kind of the same thing." To me, that says that to truly be a part of society and the world is to act based on what is good and fair for all, especially when the law is in the way.

Work Cited

Glaspell, Susan. Trifles. Connections: Literature for Composition. By Quentin Miller and Julie Nash. Boston: Houghton, 2008. (107–18).

Darryl's paper uses the elements of drama to forward a more general argument about justice. His thesis is clear and the examples he chooses from the text support that thesis. Close reading of dialogue is a real strength of this paper. Darryl follows up comments by the County Attorney with the observation that "this is the second time that the County Attorney refuses to inquire about John Wright's personality with a 'later' that will never be addressed in the play." Writing about a work of literature, even one you have read carefully, leads you to notice details like these and gives you the opportunity to make meaning out of those details. For Darryl, the fact that the County Attorney is so quick to dismiss the women justifies their decision to dismiss him, or at least what he represents—"the law."

Drama has been addressing questions about universal dilemmas like justice and morality since its religious beginnings. This anthology features classical and contemporary examples that connect this ancient literary form to other types of literature. Hopefully you will find them both provocative and relevant.

Chapter 7

Reading and Writing about Essays

> One writes out of one thing only—one's own experience. Everything depends on how relentlessly one forces from this experience the last drop, sweet or bitter, it can possibly give.
> —JAMES BALDWIN, *Autobiographical Notes* (1955)

The essay is often considered the poor relation of the other major literary genres. Living on the border between journalism (information) and fiction (imagination), essays are frequently overlooked. When they are taught, they are separated from literature: if a college student is required to take two semesters of English courses, he or she usually writes about essays during the first semester and literature (excluding essays) during the second. There are many reasons behind this scenario, and there is nothing inherently wrong with it, yet essays are a major genre. To regard them as separate from literature is to overlook their importance and to deny their ability to delight and instruct.

Essays in English developed at the time poetry and drama flourished: during the late English Renaissance—Shakespeare's time—at the end of the sixteenth century and the beginning of the seventeenth. (Fiction developed a century or so later: the modern novel arrived at the beginning of the eighteenth century.) The English author who first used the term *essay* was Francis Bacon (1561–1626), whose essay "On Revenge" can be found in Chapter 15 of this book. Bacon published a small book called *Essays* in 1597; he borrowed the term from the French author Michel de Montaigne, who invented it from the French verb *essayer*, meaning "to try," or "to attempt." Essays in this original context are synonymous with "attempts" at understanding. They frequently begin with the word *On*, as in Bacon's "On Revenge." We take Bacon's title to mean, "Here is my attempt when I reflect on the concept of revenge." Although Montaigne's and Bacon's essays set the precedent for the essays that followed, the genre developed in different directions over time.

Types of Essays

Montaigne's and Bacon's essays are short—usually only a few paragraphs—and they are prose (not verse). They are *reflective* or *meditative* essays, sometimes referred to as **belletristic essays** (after the French *belles lettres*, or "pretty writings"). Like most literature, reflective essays are carefully revised and crafted, yet they give the impression of a person thinking out loud. In other words, they are thoughtful and ruminative, and although they may have a point to prove, they seem like someone's "attempt" to understand something by following his or her thoughts wherever they lead. We are generally aware of both the author and the subject; the author does not pretend to be completely objective or removed from the subject, as a journalist might be; however, neither does the author shine the spotlight on his or her own experiences, as a diarist, autobiographer, or memoirist might. The result is a written record of a particular idea as perceived by a particular person at a particular moment in history.

Reflective essays have continued to be short, though few are as short as Montaigne's and Bacon's early attempts. The essay form became extremely popular in England in the eighteenth century, a time when rational thought and literacy were highly valued. After a pair of writers named Joseph Addison and Richard Steele wrote under the name "The Spectator," a number of similar pseudonyms cropped up: "The Tatler" and "The Rambler" in England and "Poor Richard" and "Common Sense" in the country that was about to become the United States. The writers behind these essays were among the most familiar literary figures of the day: Samuel Johnson, Benjamin Franklin, and Thomas Paine. They chose to write their essays with a certain **persona,** or literary mask. However, the persona of the essay writer is not too distant from the author. Whereas we can never assume that a character in a short story has anything in common with its author, we can usually assume that the persona of a reflective essay is roughly equivalent to its author.

The essay form remained relatively short in the eighteenth century. Essays were often published in small journals or newspapers, and they are still published in literary magazines like the *New Yorker*, the *Atlantic Monthly*, and *Harper's*. Yet the purpose, meaning, and even length of essays have changed over time. Although they are roughly the length of a short story, essays can be much more expansive. A twentieth-century master of the form, James Baldwin, published three book-length essays: *The Fire Next Time*, *No Name in the Street*, and *The Evidence of Things Not Seen*. Our definition of an essay as a work that makes you equally aware of an idea and of a particular person engaging with that idea still holds true for Baldwin's book-length essays. Although he enhances this basic formula with reportage and history, he stops short of providing statistical evidence or footnotes referencing other works, as you might do for a college essay.

In fact, the **argumentative** (or **persuasive**) **essay**—the type of paper you might write for college classes—grows out of the reflective essay tradition. Essays deal with ideas. When the author of an essay has a central point to make and is trying to convince readers of the validity of that point, he or she is writing an argumentative or persuasive essay (see Chapter 3). Like the essays Montaigne and Bacon wrote, this type of essay "attempts" to understand something, but it downplays voice and clever phrasing and is more focused on supplying **evidence** with footnotes, quotations, and facts. The more convinced an author is of her own opinion, the more likely she is to try to persuade the reader of that opinion's importance. The essayist might feel compelled to "prove" what she is saying, to bring forth evidence that will support it. Such evidence might take the form of footnotes or other documentation of research. A short version of the argumentative essay dominates the editorial pages of newspapers.

Essays come in several other types. The **expository essay** is concerned with informing the reader. It is less an attempt at understanding something and more a guide toward understanding. These essays are practical: the reader seeks information and the essayist provides it in a clear, well-organized manner.

The **descriptive essay** emphasizes an author's observations more than his or her interpretation of these observations. The author of a descriptive essay puts great stock in detail and is reluctant to give too much significance to the thing he or she describes: the reader can do that, or perhaps add more observations.

The **narrative essay** tells a story; however, it is not a "made-up" story, or fiction. Narrative is a way of ordering a series of events: first this, then that, and finally this. The author controls how we see an event by putting its parts in a certain order, selecting relevant details and omitting irrelevant details, even though he or she is describing something that happened. Although, like all essays, narrative essays are based on an idea, that idea may not be explicitly expressed. Rather, it is revealed through the details of the story.

Analyzing Essays

The essay forms described above are rarely absolute: many essays blend elements of reflection, persuasion, exposition, and narration. The first step in analyzing essays is to recognize these elements. One of the most important features of an essay is its **tone,** or the mood it creates. An author has many different ways to express tone, including *word choice*, or **diction.** An author who is relatively removed from a subject might begin with "*Apparently* x is true," whereas an author who feels passionately about a subject and is intent on persuading the reader might begin with something like "*Anyone with intelligence can see* that x is true" (see also Chapter 3 on argument). The second example has a more urgent tone. Diction also determines an author's voice, discussed below.

The *structure* of an essay is also a noteworthy feature. Some essays are divided into numbered sections the way poems are divided into sections or novels into chapters. Other essays are not clearly divided yet still follow a certain structure. To analyze an essay, you can summarize each of its paragraphs with a brief sentence or phrase and then think about how the author gets from one paragraph to another. What is the structural logic of a piece? In an argumentative essay, the essay is structured to highlight its ability to persuade. In a reflective essay some paragraphs may seem like digressions from the main topic; yet those digressions are part of the whole essay, and they may be the key to understanding it.

An essay was earlier defined as a written record of a particular idea as perceived by a particular person at a particular moment in history. Therefore, you can pay attention to the balance between the idea and the personality that expresses that idea: that is, the essay's theme and its voice. As with fiction, which rarely spells out its moral, the **theme** of an essay is not always explicit. It is most likely to be explicit in an argumentative essay, in which case it is called the **thesis.** In reflective, descriptive, or narrative essays, the reader may have to figure out the theme, and there may be more than one way of interpreting it.

The **voice** of an author is related to *tone* and also to the author's persona, or mask. The voice indicates the perspective of the author, in part by revealing something about his authority: how does he know what he is saying? Either he has observed something, or has read about a subject, or has studied it formally. In any of these cases, he will generally show how he has arrived at his perspective.

Voice can be illustrated by the following comparison. One essay might begin by using informal diction: "While sitting in a coffee shop the other day, I was struck by the number of people talking on cell phones." Another essay might begin, "Countless studies have shown that technology is turning our nation into a society of individuals rather than a community." We are more aware of the identity of the first writer: someone who sits in coffee shops watching his surroundings. His *voice* reveals something of his personality. The second essayist seems more removed from his subject; his diction or word choice is more formal. However, we can still learn something about him from his voice: he is someone who has read "countless studies" and learns by doing research. If these two sentences occurred in the same essay, we might be aware of a *shift* in the essayist's voice, which might be a good subject for analysis.

Student Essay on Sir Henry Taylor's "On Secrecy"

As with many essays, the subject of Sir Henry Taylor's "On Secrecy" is announced in its title. The essay is taken from Taylor's book *The Statesman*, an inquiry into the nature of government. You might ask what a work about government written in the nineteenth century has to do with you. This is precisely the question answered by Lacey Perkins, an English major at Suffolk University. Lacey was asked to consider the importance of keeping secrets in a society saturated with the type of technology that allows for instant and widespread sharing of information. What value does a secret have in the world of easily forwarded e-mail, blogs in which strangers spill the darkest details of their lives, and security cameras observing us in semiprivate situations? How does Taylor's essay either anticipate or fail to anticipate the status of secrecy in contemporary times?

Sir Henry Taylor *(1800–1886)*

On Secrecy

Whom a statesman trusts at all he should trust largely, not to say unboundedly; and he should avow his trust to the world. In nine cases out of ten of betrayed confidence in affairs of State, vanity is the traitor. When a man comes into possession of some chance secrets now and then—some one or two—he is tempted to parade them to this friend or that. But when he is known to be trusted with all manner of secrets, his vanity is interested, not to show them, but to show that he can keep them. And his fidelity of heart is also better secured.

A secret may be sometimes best kept by keeping the secret of its being a secret. It is not many years since a State secret of the greatest importance was printed without being divulged, merely by sending it to the press like any other matter, and trusting to the mechanical habits of the persons employed. They printed it piecemeal in ignorance of what it was about.

The only secrecy which is worthy of trust in matters of State—and indeed the same may be said of secrecy in private friendship—is that which not merely observes an *enjoined* silence, but which maintains a considerate and judicious reticence in matters in which silence is perceived to be expedient, though it have *not* been enjoined. Faithfulness to public interests and to official and to friendly confidence, demands a careful exercise of the judgment as to what shall be spoken and what not, on many occasions when there is no question of obedience to express injunctions of secrecy. And indeed, in dealing with a confidential officer or friend, a statesman would do well to avoid any frequency of injunction on this head on particular occasions, because it tends to impair, on the part of such officer or friend, that general watchfulness which is produced in a man who feels that he is thrown upon his own judgment and caution.

Secrecy will hardly be perfectly preserved unless by one who makes it a rule to avoid the whole of a subject of which he has to retain a part. To flesh your friend's curiosity and then endeavour to leave him with a *hûc usque*,[1] is exposing your faculty of reticence to an unnecessary trial.

The most difficult of all subjects to be kept secret are such as will furnish fair 5
occasion for a jest; and a statesman should regulate his confidence accordingly; being especially sparing of it in regard to such matters, and where he must needs impart them, taking care not to imp their wings by any jest of his own imparted along with them.

Shy and unready men are great betrayers of secrets; for there are few wants more urgent for the moment then the want of something to say. Such men may stand in need of the assurance given in Ecclesiasticus,—"If thou hast heard a word, let it die with thee: and be bold, it will not burst thee."

(1836)

[1]**hûc usque:** Hitherto; thus far.

Taylor's essay is argumentative: he means to persuade the reader of the importance of keeping secrets, and in the final sentence he connects that importance to bravery, or "boldness." The tone of the essay is somewhat formal yet also playful: he writes, for instance, "A secret may be sometimes best kept by keeping the secret of its being a secret," a clever sentence that you probably had to reread a couple of times. Word choice contributes to this serious yet playful tone: although he uses a Latin phrase and alludes to Ecclesiasticus, occasionally he also uses a colloquial phrase like "imp their wings" (a term from falconry that means "to improve the flight of a bird by engrafting feathers"). This is not a strictly scientific essay: he plays loosely with figures, speaking in the first paragraph of "nine cases out of ten" and "one or two" secrets. These are anecdotal estimates, not statistics.

Here is one student's response to the essay.

Student Essay

Originally from Sherman, Maine, Lacey Perkins is attending Suffolk University in Boston and has a double major in history and creative writing. She is the editor-in-chief of the school's literary and arts magazine, *Venture.* In her spare time, she enjoys writing poetry and fiction, going to concerts, and going on road trips with her friends. After graduating from Suffolk, she plans to attend graduate school and eventually to pursue a career in editing and publishing.

Perkins 1

Lacey Perkins

Final Draft

Secrecy in the Information Age

In the aftermath of the sex scandal between President Clinton and Monica Lewinsky, the subject of secrecy and politics might have invited giggles, especially given the fact that the tawdry details of the affair were immediately available on the Internet; but the terror attacks of September 11, 2001, have revealed the serious side of the delicate balance governments must face between revealing and concealing

Perkins 2

information. In his essay "On Secrecy," Sir Henry Taylor warns against how much information a statesman should divulge: "A statesman should regulate his confidence," he writes (127).

The contemporary world is filled with examples of politicians and business executives who either withheld sensitive information or failed to do so. In the aftermath of the 9/11 terror attacks, the American public has given a great deal of power to the FBI, the CIA, and the newly formed department of homeland security whose jobs are to discover sensitive information and use it to keep the public safe.

It is striking how willingly some people have given up their basic right to privacy, and the current political climate of fear is only one factor. The average citizen must also deal with the sensitive matter of keeping secrets. With networking sites, blogs, and online journals, it is increasingly hard to keep a secret. The medium is there, and many people—especially younger generations—are keen to spread their secrets across the globe instantly. Reality television has become one of the more popular, albeit voyeuristic, genres of TV.

Surely, secrecy has a place in society; it is just a matter of how to retain secrecy in a world driven to tell secrets. Taylor tackles this very issue in his essay, claiming that having a secret makes a man feel important; therefore, he must tell it. Throughout the essay, Taylor stresses the importance of being careful about who a man exposes his secrets to: "a statesman should regulate his confidence accordingly" (127). The reason people still inform the entire world of their secrets is related to a widespread need for attention.

Perhaps people are looking for the fifteen minutes of fame Andy Warhol predicted. But as Taylor writes, "vanity is the traitor" (127). Today, one can be the center of attention immediately, just by writing a blog or creating a profile that will be discovered by hundreds of other lonely Internet users. Soon, these same people have exposed their deepest secrets, conceivably led astray by vanity, just as Taylor suggests. In a world where so much is constantly happening, aided by the technological explosion, it seems as though some of these people exposing all their secrets may just be trying to get noticed. Then, if they are noticed, mere attention somehow makes them feel important—even if they unveil an unflattering secret.

Just the idea of having a secret is enough to make one feel important. But if no one knows there is a secret, then how does that equal importance? This may be where the urge to spill one's secrets originates. "When a man comes into possession of some chance secrets now and then—some one or two—he is tempted to parade them to this friend or that," Taylor writes (127). This idea seems more true today than ever, with people splashing their innermost secrets across the Internet, or exposing their darkest moments to the world on talk shows or reality television.

Although it may seem like many people have no desire to keep a secret anymore, perhaps we are lacking the kind of filter we need to protect our privacy. Taylor defines keeping secrets as "a careful exercise of the judgment as to what shall be spoken and what not" (127). Just as Taylor explains, judgment seems to be the key to secrecy today. As compelling as it may be to offer personal facts about oneself in an online profile, one should first consider exactly what one wants the world to know. Such an unleashing of secrets can make one vulnerable.

If one chooses to use discretion, as Taylor suggests, things that one may not want others—such as coworkers, family, and significant others—to know will be kept private. Drunken nights, relationships, personal problems like anorexia or self-mutilation, and family problems are just some of the secrets that have flooded cyberspace and even television in the form of reality TV. Once-personal secrets are now in living rooms across the world, or on computer screens. Maybe the age of information has gone so far that people even want deep secrets at their immediate disposal.

Perkins 4

However, keeping secrets, no matter how big, small, important, or minute they seem, makes one human. It is only natural to keep some things hidden from certain people because it secures our personal sense of importance rather than the less reliable public fame we might seek in our weaker moments. Taylor gives his advice: "A secret may be sometimes best kept by keeping the secret of its being a secret." If one does not acknowledge that a secret is such a secret, then perhaps a scandal-hungry public would not clamor to read blogs or watch reality TV and the audience for such vanity would be eliminated.

But one cannot blame websites or blogs for leaking secrets; the websites and blogs merely exist as media to showcase secrets. It is truly up to the individual to decide what he or she chooses to expose to the public. Getting caught up in the fifteen minutes of fame that blogs and websites allow everyone to have access to may cause people to feel the urge to blab every intimate detail of their lives, but there are certain things in a person's life that would seem to be things that one would want only close friends or family to know—if at all.

Work Cited

Taylor, Sir Henry. "On Secrecy." Connections: Literature for Composition. Ed. Quentin Miller and Julie Nash. Boston: Houghton, 2008. 127.

As you evaluate Lacey's essay, consider the degree to which she relies on her own observations rather than her reading of Taylor's essay: is her primary purpose to persuade us or to illuminate Taylor's essay? Does she ever deviate from that purpose?

Chapter 8

Reading and Writing about Film

> The words *Kiss Kiss Bang Bang*, which I saw on an Italian movie poster, are perhaps the briefest statement imaginable of the basic appeal of movies. This appeal is what attracts us, and ultimately what makes us despair when we begin to understand how seldom movies are more than this.
> —PAULINE KAEL (1968)

Movies that go beyond the repetitive appeal to sex and violence described in critic Pauline Kael's assessment can be rich texts to interpret, just like any literature. Some films even provide models for the viewers need to think critically. In Alfred Hitchcock's classic 1954 film *Rear Window*, L. B. "Jeff" Jeffries (played by James Stewart) spends his days watching his neighbors come and go while he recovers from a broken leg. After witnessing some mysterious activities in an apartment across the courtyard from his window, Jeff becomes convinced that his neighbor, Lars Thorwald, has murdered his wife. While he tries to convince his girlfriend Lisa (played by Grace Kelly) that Thorwald's actions cannot be easily explained away, she dismisses him initially, wishing that Jeff would devote as much attention to her as he does to the strangers in nearby apartments. Yet Lisa eventually begins to suspect Thorwald and becomes caught up in the drama, asking Jeff to "start at the beginning." She says, "Tell me everything you saw, and what you think it means."

As spectators to the domestic drama seen through their apartment's rear window, the characters Jeff and Lisa can be compared to viewers of a film. (They even have a "soundtrack": the music being composed by a piano-playing neighbor.) Like the spectators of a film, Jeff and Lisa have a "text" (in this case the actions of Thorwald) that they will have to "read" correctly to gain meaning. "Telling everything you saw" is the easy part, a simple recall of the plot. Figuring out "what you think it means" is more complicated, requiring a combination of close reading, interpretation, and critical thinking. If Jeff and Lisa are unable to convince others to share their reading of the events across the courtyard, the results could be deadly for them.

Still from *Rear Window* (1954).

Fortunately, the stakes are not quite as high when you are writing about film for a class; even the worst papers are unlikely to get you killed. Writing about film is a lot like writing about any text, and you can review the other writing chapters in this book for tips on constructing an argument and supporting it with evidence (see especially Chapters 2 and 3). Like short stories or plays, films are composed of characters, plots, settings, and dialogue. Although films may resemble poems by using poetic language, symbolism, and imagery, the medium of film differs from other literary media. Like peeping Toms looking through a rear window, we enter the world of film by watching carefully crafted scenes that have been created through the joint efforts of a screenwriter, a director, actors, and set designers, to name only a few people responsible for bringing the cinema to life.

Characters

Films, like plays and fiction, may be populated by flat **characters,** round characters, or a combination of flat and round characters (see also Chapter 6). Our reading of a character is determined by that character's language and actions; however, unlike in a short story or a play that you merely read, much depends on the actor who is cast in a role. Francis Ford Coppola's casting of Marlon Brando in the title role of the classic Mafia movie *The Godfather* is an example of the impact an actor can have on a character. Brando's soft-spoken portrayal of Don Corleone came to embody the calm, reassuring leadership style of the "old" Mafia, which contrasted with the violent vengefulness of Al Pacino's Michael, Don Corleone's son and successor.

In hindsight, Humphrey Bogart seems an inevitable choice to play Rick Blaine in the 1942 classic film *Casablanca*; however, Ronald Reagan, the B-movie actor who later became U.S. president, was also a contender for the part. The decision to go with Bogart instead of Reagan altered film history forever (and possibly U.S. history as well!). As we all know, some casting decisions are made because the actor is right for the part. Other decisions are driven by financial considerations, or the star appeal of a given actor. How else to explain Keanu Reeves's unconvincing portrayals of British characters in Coppola's 1992 *Dracula* or Kenneth Branagh's 1993 *Much Ado about Nothing*? No matter how well a character may be portrayed in a film script, a poor casting job can negatively affect our view of the film, much like a great performance can help rescue a thin script.

Point of View and the Camera

As in other literary genres, films are told from a specific **point of view** (see also Chapter 4). If the viewer sees all the characters and events unfold without being limited to any individual perspective, the point of view is *omniscient*. Some films use the convention of the omniscient *voice-over*; a voice of someone telling the story who is not shown on screen. *Casablanca* opens with a voice-over in which the narrator provides the historical background for the movie's plot and sets the tone:

> With the coming of the Second World War, many eyes in imprisoned Europe turned hopefully, or desperately, toward the freedom of the Americas. Lisbon became the great embarkation point, but not everybody could get to Lisbon directly, and so, a tortuous, roundabout refugee trail sprang up. Paris to Marseilles, across the Mediterranean to Oran, then by train, or auto, or foot, across the rim of Africa to Casablanca in French Morocco. Here, the fortunate ones, through money, or influence, or luck, might obtain exit visa's and scurry to Lisbon, and from Lisbon to the New World. But the others wait in Casablanca—and wait—and wait—and wait.

This speech, spoken by an authoritative male voice, explains the presence of the diverse and desperate group of people who will constitute the film's cast. It also suggests the corrupt world the characters inhabit, one in which human lives are bought and sold cheaply. The final lines, emphasizing the seemingly endless wait for many of Casablanca's refugees, leave the viewer with a feeling of hopelessness and claustrophobia.

In most cases, however, the "narrator" of a film is the camera itself. The importance of the camera in determining our response to a film cannot be overemphasized. As a critical viewer, you can always ask yourself where the camera is in relation to the characters. How distant is it? What is the camera angle? How often does that angle change? Few directors use a single-shot approach; cameras move across scenes (or *pan*), or they *zoom* in for a *close-up*.

Directors cut from one scene or camera to another, often rapidly, an effect known as a *jump cut*. The eye of the camera is rarely stable for long.

If the viewer sees the events of the film from the perspective of only one or two characters, his or her position is *third-person limited*. Unlike with the omniscient point of view, the viewer does not have access to some perspectives. Sometimes a scene or a whole movie is filmed through the eyes of one character, and the viewer sees only what that character sees. The famous shower scene in Alfred Hitchcock's *Psycho* is shot in this way; its point of view is *first person*. The camera shoots from the killer's perspective, and the audience is in the terrifying position of identifying with the killer and seeing the murder through his eyes.

Point of view can have an important impact on the way we understand a work. When we see with a character's "eyes," as in first-person point of view, we form an intellectual and emotional connection with that character. When we know something a character does not know, as in the omniscient point of view, we are given an advantage over that character and sometimes feel distant from him or her.

Mise en Scène

Setting also plays a huge role in achieving a film's total effect. The **mise en scène** includes the film's location, sets, props, and costumes—everything that sets the scene for the characters to develop and the plot to unfold. In the film adaptations of the Harry Potter series, the mise en scène is the world of magic and wizardry. Hogwarts school, with its talking pictures, moving staircase, and enchanted banquet hall, is a world in itself. The house colors, the professors' capes, the Quidditch field, and the talking "sorting hat" are all part of an effective and memorable mise en scène. As a result, the "world" of the Harry Potter movies is as important as character and plot in drawing us into the films and creating a realistic universe in which magic is the norm. The same is true of the classic movie *The Wizard of Oz*. When Dorothy steps from the ordinary world of Kansas into the magical world of Oz, one of the most dramatic mise en scène shifts in cinematic history occurs: a transformation from black-and-white film to full color.

Editing

Sometimes a filmmaker has done such an effective job choosing a script, casting a film, and creating a mise en scène that we accept the film at face value and forget that each second is a carefully designed moment. Nothing in film appears by accident, and, as with writing, editing plays an important role in our appreciation of the final product. A film *shot* is a continuous, uncut slice of film, or a series of *frames* (essentially still pictures). When editing, a filmmaker splices shots together and cuts other shots out, deciding whether to call attention to the cutting from one shot to another or to make the transitions more seamless. When a movie cuts from the point of view of one character to that of another or shifts from a character to what that character sees, the editing helps us shift our own point of view.

You are also familiar with the convention of speeding up a film, which is almost always done for comic effect (one thinks of the Keystone Cops or the 1960s sitcom *The Monkees*), and of using slow motion for dramatic effect (a common method for heightening the significance of a particular moment, especially in films about sports like *Chariots of Fire*).

Sound

In editing, the filmmaker also decides whether to use *sound* or silence. Music, traffic noises, wind, and even screams can be edited in or out of a scene depending on the director's wish. A *soundtrack* includes all the music that provides the background mood for a film as well as the music that the characters might hear as they go through the film. At times the soundtrack dominates the "language" of the film: for instance, if two mild-mannered nuns enter a loud party, the blaring club music would make for a comic effect. In *Casablanca*, the song "As Time Goes By" accompanies the most intense scenes between Rick and Ilsa and reinforces the theme of lost love. Often the soundtrack is much subtler: we might be dimly aware of creepy music, scary music, or joyful music framing our response to a scene or sequence.

When you are asked to analyze film in your writing, pay close attention to the way music operates. Few contemporary films are devoid of music; if you encounter one, you can consider why it has no music and what effect the lack of a soundtrack has on the viewer.

Films Adapted from Books

Often in an introduction to literature class professors assign films that have been adapted from books. Whether the film is "like" the book is not always the important question to ask. Film and literature are different media, and changes from the book are inevitable. Adapting a 400-page novel with a huge cast of characters into a two-hour film necessitates eliminating subplots or minor characters, possibly combining certain scenes, and even omitting large chunks of dialogue. If a short story is adapted to film, some scenes and characters may have to be added.

For example, Andre Dubus's story "Killings" (in Chapter 15 of this anthology) was adapted as the 2001 movie *In the Bedroom*. The film added scenes that enabled us to know the characters better, and it fleshed out the character of the mother, played by Sissy Spacek. Unlike the blunt title "Killings," the film's title refers to the architecture of a lobster trap (one of the chambers of a lobster trap is called the "bedroom"), highlighting a potential symbol.

Do these changes amount to an unfaithful adaptation? That's a decision for you, as a critic, to make. Critics often look at the **theme** or **tone** of the fiction and the film. If these are consistent, then the adaptation is considered to be faithful. Another consideration is the work's **conclusion.** In George Bernard Shaw's play *Pygmalion*, a newly independent Eliza Doolittle tells her mentor Henry Higgins that she is leaving his household and starting a life for herself without him. Shaw felt so strongly about the conclusion to his play that he wrote a sequel explaining why Eliza makes her decision and emphasizing that she sticks with it. Yet in two film adaptations of the play (one made in 1938, the other made into the musical *My Fair Lady* in 1964), Eliza returns to Higgins within minutes of leaving him as he triumphantly asks her to fetch his slippers. While both adaptations borrow heavily from Shaw's original script, their deviation from his ending might leave some critics to conclude that the adaptation is unfaithful and—worse—that it undermines Shaw's entire message.

Be Specific

When writing about film, you can consider how film-specific terms interact with the traditional elements of literature to achieve a unique effect. A strong thesis is the key to your success. As you support your thesis with evidence, you will find you have a wealth of details to choose from.

As with any literary analysis, quoting **dialogue** is a great way to illustrate your point. You can also describe the mise en scène or discuss how point of view affects your understanding of the characters and events. As always, the more specific you can be, the better. Describe individual scenes, backgrounds, and costumes. What do they look like? If you take the time to describe an actor's facial expression or the way the wind blows through the curtains in a haunted house, your readers will have a better idea of why you have arrived at your critical conclusions and will be more likely to accept your argument.

Student Essay on *Casablanca*

Casablanca is a widely available classic that demonstrates the complex nature of vice and virtue. Neither Rick Blaine nor Ilsa Lund is wholly virtuous or wholly wicked. They are two lovers struggling to balance their own happiness against their duties to others and to their countries. Here are the final scenes from the script.

Julius J. Epstein, Philip G. Epstein, and Howard Koch *(1909–2000, 1909–1952, 1902–1995)*

Casablanca [excerpt]

CUT TO: INT. RICK'S CAFE—MAIN ROOM—NIGHT

Rick opens the door. Ilsa rushes in. Her intensity reveals the strain she is under. Rick grabs her by both arms and pulls her close.

Ilsa: Richard, Victor thinks I'm leaving with him. Haven't you told him?
Rick: No, not yet.

Scene from *Casablanca* (1942).

Ilsa: But it's all right, isn't it? You were able to arrange everything?
Rick: Everything is quite all right.
Ilsa: Oh, Rick!

She looks at him with a vaguely questioning look.

Rick: We'll tell him at the airport. The less time to think, the easier for all of us. Please trust me.

Ilsa pauses and looks at risk, unsure for a moment.

Ilsa: Yes, I will.

Laszlo comes in and closes the door behind himself.

Laszlo: Monsieur Blaine, I don't know how to thank you.
Rick: Oh, save it. We've still lots of things to do.

They all walk towards the bar. Laszlo deposits his hat on a nearby table.

CUT TO: INT. RICK'S CAFE—OFFICE—NIGHT

Renault opens the office door and peers down at the proceedings.

CUT TO: INT. RICK'S CAFE—MAIN ROOM—NIGHT

Laszlo: I brought the money, Monsieur Blaine.
Rick: Keep it. You'll need it in America.

Laszlo: But we made a deal.
Rick [*cutting him short*]: Oh, never mind about that. You won't have any trouble in Lisbon, will you?
Laszlo: No. It's all arranged.
Rick: Good. I've got the letters right here, all made out in blank.

He takes out the letters.

Rick: All you have to do is fill in the signatures.

He hands them to Laszlo, who takes them gratefully.

Renault: Victor Laszlo!

All three hear footsteps and turn to see Renault walking towards them from the bottom of the stairs.

Renault: Victor Laszlo, you are under arrest . . . (*as he walks toward them*) on a charge of accessory to the murder of the couriers from whom these letters were stolen.

Ilsa and Laszlo are both caught completely off guard. They turn towards Rick, bewildered. Horror is in Ilsa's eyes. Renault takes the letters.

Renault: Oh, you are surprised about my friend Ricky?

Obviously the situation delights Renault. He smiles as he turns toward Rick.

Renault: The explanation is quite simple. Love, it seems, has triumphed over virtue. Thank—

Suddenly the smile fades. In Rick's hand is a gun, which he levels at Renault.

Rick: —Not so fast, Louis. Nobody's going to be arrested. Not for a while yet.
Renault: Have you taken leave of your senses?
Rick: I have. Sit down over there.
Renault: Put that gun down.

Renault then walks toward Rick. Rick puts out his arm to stop him.

Rick: Louis, I wouldn't like to shoot you, but I will, if you take one more step.

Renault halts for a moment and studies Rick.

Renault: Under the circumstances, I will sit down.

He walks to a table and sits.

Rick [*sharply*]: Keep your hands on the table.

He takes out a cigarette case.

Renault: I suppose you know what you're doing, but I wonder if you realize what this means?
Rick: I do. We've got plenty of time to discuss that later.
Renault: Call off your watch-dogs you said.

Rick: Just the same, you call the airport and let me hear you tell them. And remember, this gun's pointed right at your heart.
Renault: That is my least vulnerable spot.

As Renault picks up the phone and dials, Rick takes back the letters.

Renault [*into phone*]: Hello, is this the airport? This is Captain Renault speaking. There'll be two letters of transit for the Lisbon plane. There's to be no trouble about them. Good.

CUT TO: INT. GERMAN CONSULATE—NIGHT

Strasser is on the phone.

Strasser: Hello? Hello?

He hangs up the receiver and presses a BUZZER on his desk. An officer quickly enters.

Strasser [*to officer*]: My car, quickly!
Officer [*saluting*]: Zu Befehl, Herr Major.

The officer exits and Strasser resumes on the telephone.

Strasser: This is Major Strasser. Have a squad of police meet me at the airport at once. At once! Do you hear?

He hangs up the receiver and, grabbing for his cap, hurriedly exits.

DISSOLVE TO: EXT. AIRPORT—NIGHT

The entire airport is surrounded by a heavy fog. The outline of the transport plane is barely visible.

CUT TO: INT./EXT. AIRPORT HANGAR—NIGHT

A uniformed ORDERLY uses a telephone near the hangar door. On the airfield a transport plane is being readied.

Orderly: Hello. Hello, radio tower? Lisbon plane taking off in ten minutes. East runway. Visibility: one and one half miles. Light ground fog. Depth of fog: approximately 500. Ceiling: unlimited. Thank you.

He hangs up and moves to a car that has just pulled up outside the hanger.

Renault gets out while the orderly stands at attention. He's closely followed by Rick, right hand in the pocket of his trench coat, covering Renault with a gun.

Laszlo and Ilsa emerge from the rear of the car.

Rick [*indicating the orderly*]: Louis, have your man go with Mr. Laszlo and take care of his luggage.
Renault [*bowing ironically*]: Certainly Rick, anything you say. [*to orderly*] Find Mr. Laszlo's luggage and put it on the plane.
Orderly: Yes, sir. This way please.

The orderly escorts Laszlo off in the direction of the plane. Rick takes the letters of transit out of his pocket and hands them to Renault, who turns and walks toward the hangar.

Rick: If you don't mind, you fill in the names. That will make it even more official.
Renault: You think of everything, don't you?
Rick [*quietly*]: And the names are Mr. and Mrs. Victor Laszlo.

Renault stops dead in his tracks, and turns around. Both Ilsa and Renault look at Rick with astonishment.

Ilsa: But why my name, Richard?
Rick: Because you're getting on that plane.
Ilsa [*confused*]: I don't understand. What about you?
Rick: I'm staying here with him 'til the plane gets safely away.

Rick's intention suddenly dawns on Ilsa.

Ilsa: No, Richard, no. What has happened to you? Last night we said—
Rick: —Last night we said a great many things. You said I was to do the thinking for both of us. Well, I've done a lot of it since then and it all adds up to one thing. You're getting on that plane with Victor where you belong.
Ilsa [*protesting*]: But Richard, no, I, I—
Rick: —You've got to listen to me. Do you have any idea what you'd have to look forward to if you stayed here? Nine chances out of ten we'd both wind up in a concentration camp. Isn't that true, Louis?

Renault countersigns the papers.

Renault: I'm afraid Major Strasser would insist.
Ilsa: You're saying this only to make me go.
Rick: I'm saying it because it's true. Inside of us we both know you belong with Victor. You're part of his work, the thing that keeps him going. If that plane leaves the ground and you're not with him, you'll regret it.
Ilsa: No.
Rick: Maybe not today, maybe not tomorrow, but soon, and for the rest of your life.
Ilsa: But what about us?
Rick: We'll always have Paris. We didn't have, we'd lost it, until you came to Casablanca. We got it back last night.
Ilsa: And I said I would never leave you.
Rick: And you never will. But I've got a job to do, too. Where I'm going you can't follow. What I've got to do you can't be any part of. Ilsa, I'm no good at being noble, but it doesn't take much to see that the problems of three little people don't amount to a hill of beans in this crazy world. Someday you'll understand that. Now, now . . .

Ilsa's eyes well up with tears. Rick puts his hand to her chin and raises her face to meet his own.

Rick: Here's looking at you, kid.

Cut to: Ext. Road—Night

Major Strasser drives at break-neck speed towards the airport. He HONKS his horn furiously.

Cut to: Int./Ext. Airport Hangar—Night

Laszlo returns. Rick walks into the hangar and Renault hands him the letters. He walks back out to Laszlo.

Laszlo: Everything in order?

Rick: All except one thing. There's something you should know before you leave.

Laszlo [*sensing what is coming*]: Monsieur Blaine, I don't ask you to explain anything.

Rick: I'm going to anyway, because it may make a difference to you later on. You said you knew about Ilsa and me.

Laszlo: Yes.

Rick: But you didn't know she was at my place last night when you were. She came there for the letters of transit. Isn't that true, Ilsa?

Ilsa [*facing Laszlo*]: Yes.

Rick [*forcefully*]: She tried everything to get them, and nothing worked. She did her best to convince me that she was still in love with me, but that was all over long ago. For your sake, she pretended it wasn't, and I let her pretend.

Laszlo: I understand.

Rick: Here it is.

Rick hands the letters to Laszlo.

Laszlo: Thanks. I appreciate it.

Laszlo extends his hand to Rick, who grasps it firmly.

Laszlo: And welcome back to the fight. This time I know our side will win.

On the airfield the airplane engine TURNS OVER and the propellers start turning. They all turn to see the plane readying for take-off.

Ilsa looks at Rick and he returns her stare with a blank expression. He then glances at Laszlo, as does Ilsa.

Then Laszlo breaks the silence.

Laszlo: Are you ready Ilsa?

Ilsa: Yes, I'm ready. [*to Rick*] Goodbye, Rick. God bless you.

Rick: You better hurry, or you'll miss that plane.

Rick watches as Ilsa and Laszlo walk very deliberately towards the plane.

Renault: Well I was right. You are a sentimentalist.

Rick: Stay where you are. I don't know what you're talking about.

Rick puts a cigarette in his mouth.

Renault: What you just did for Laszlo, and that fairy tale that you invented to send Ilsa away with him. I know a little about women, my friend. She went, but she knew you were lying.
Rick: Anyway, thanks for helping me out.
Renault: I suppose you know this isn't going to be pleasant for either of us, especially for you. I'll have to arrest you of course.
Rick: As soon as the plane goes, Louis.

The door to the plane is closed by an attendant and it slowly taxies down the field.
Suddenly a speeding car comes to a stop outside the hangar. Strasser alights from the car and runs toward Renault.

Strasser: What is the meaning of that phone call?
Renault: Victor Laszlo is on that plane.

Renault nods toward the field. Strasser turns to see the plane taxiing towards the runway.

Strasser: Why do you stand here? Why don't you stop him?
Renault: Ask Monsieur Rick.

Strasser looks briefly at Rick, then makes a step towards the telephone just inside the hangar door.

Rick: Get away from that phone.

Strasser stops in his tracks, looks at Rick, and sees that he is armed.

Strasser [*steely*]: I would advise you not to interfere.
Rick: I was willing to shoot Captain Renault, and I'm willing to shoot you.

Strasser watches the plane in agony. His eyes dart towards the telephone. He runs toward it and desperately grabs the receiver.

Strasser: Hello?
Rick: Put that phone down!
Strasser: Get me the Radio Tower!
Rick: Put it down!

Strasser, one hand holding the receiver, pulls out a pistol with the other hand, and SHOOTS quickly at Rick. The bullet misses its mark.
Rick now SHOOTS at Strasser, who crumples to the ground.
At the sound of an approaching car both men turn. A police car SPEEDS in and comes to a stop near Renault. Four gendarmes hurriedly jump out.
In the distance the plane turns onto the runway.
The gendarmes run to Renault. The first one hurriedly salutes him.

Gendarme: Mon Capitaine!
Renault: Major Strasser's been shot.

Renault pauses and looks at Rick. Rick returns Renault's gaze with expressionless eyes.

Renault: Round up the usual suspects.
Gendarme: Oui, mon Capitaine.

The gendarmes take Strasser's body away and then drive off.
Renault walks inside the hangar, picks up a bottle of Vichy water, and opens it.

Renault: Well, Rick, you're not only a sentimentalist, but you've become a patriot.
Rick: Maybe, but it seemed like a good time to start.
Renault: I think perhaps you're right.

As he pours the water into a glass, Renault sees the Vichy label and quickly DROPS the bottle into a trash basket which he then KICKS over.
He walks over and stands beside Rick. They both watch the plane take off, maintaining their gaze until it disappears into the clouds.
Rick and Louis slowly walk away from the hangar toward the runway.

Renault: It might be a good idea for you to disappear from Casablanca for a while. There's a Free French garrison over at Brazzaville. I could be induced to arrange a passage.
Rick: My letter of transit? I could use a trip. But it doesn't make any difference about our bet. You still owe me ten thousand francs.
Renault: And that ten thousand francs should pay our expenses.
Rick: Our expenses?
Renault: Uh huh.
Rick: Louis, I think this is the beginning of a beautiful friendship.

The two walk off together into the night. FADE OUT.

THE END

(1942)

The following student essay by Jineyda Tapia discusses how the elements of film work together in the final scene of *Casablanca.* (See the scene from the script, above, and if possible, view the scene in the movie itself to understand the combined effects of light, editing, and sound.) In her paper Jineyda refers to many details of lighting, camera work, and sound effects, "reading" the film as she would any work of literature. Her essay analyzes elements specific to film. Its thesis is implied but never stated directly. Do you think the essay would be stronger with a more explicit thesis statement? How so?

Student Essay

Jineyda Tapia was raised in the Dominican Republic and graduated with a degree in English from the University of Massachusetts–Lowell in 2006. She currently teaches high school English in Lawrence, Massachusetts.

Tapia 1

Jineyda Tapia

Final Draft

Classic Casablanca

The highly acclaimed American movie Casablanca, directed by Michael Curtiz, remains memorable even today for its powerful intermingling of war and romance. While the film created a number of classic moments in cinema, perhaps its most famous scene is the last one in which Rick and Ilsa part forever. This scene wraps up all the elements the film has been exploring and creates new tension: Who will stay with the beautiful Ilsa? Will Rick help the couple or run away with his lost love? Is there a solution to this dilemma that can make all parties (and the viewer) happy? It is through the help of scenery and music that these questions finally get answered.

First, a quick recap of the story is required to get us up to speed. It is World War II and resistance hero Victor Laszlo and his wife Ilsa Lund are trying to escape to Lisbon so that they can catch a plane to America. It just so happens that the only exit point is through French-occupied Casablanca, Morocco. However, it becomes impossible for them to leave, especially since the French Capitaine Louis Renault is in cahoots with the local Nazi leader, Strasser.

To further complicate this plot, it turns out that Ilsa and Rick (a.k.a. Richard), the owner of Casablanca's popular Rick's Café Americain, had had an affair in Paris several years before. Rick has two exit visas and is the only man who can help Ilsa and Victor escape, but his bitter feelings about Ilsa prevent him from extending himself. Thus amidst the political tensions in the movie, another is created: Rick, who was abandoned by Ilsa in Paris, now holds the key to their freedom.

It is in the last scene that we discover how these tensions resolve. Though the audience has primarily observed the events of the film through Rick's point of view, we are still ignorant as to what he will do. Our ignorance is compounded by the atmosphere, the mise en scène.

Tapia 2

In the scene leading up to the famous airport scene, Rick's Café is no longer a lively and crowded arena, but is empty and dark; the solitude is highlighted by the rows of empty tables and chairs. Rick has recruited Renault to set up Victor for buying illegal visas. However, just as Renault explains to the shocked Victor and Ilsa that "love, it seems, has triumphed over virtue" (140), he turns around to face Rick's gun. The camera shot is solely on the gun, aligning the audience to Renault's point of view, allowing us to share his shock at Rick's behavior.

The story now focuses on four characters: Victor, Ilsa, Rick, and Renault. They are on their way to the airport, where the plane is departing in ten minutes. The place is isolated and music plays in the background. The music heightens the tension when Rick reveals that the exit visas should be made to Mr. and Mrs. Victor Laszlo rather than to Rick and Ilsa, as the two lovers had discussed. Note that the camera shows Renault in the front shot, Rick in the middle, and Ilsa in the background. This sequence highlights Ilsa's nervousness as we see her pacing and looking around anxiously. As soon as she hears this she moves forward towards Rick, and the camera zooms in on them. For a moment only, there is no one else in the world.

As Rick is warning her of the dangers they would face if they stayed in Casablanca, the camera shows both of them in a profile shot. However, when the moment gets intimate, the camera alternates between Ilsa and Rick's faces. Then as "As Time Goes By" softly begins to play in the background, Rick reassures Ilsa that the right thing is for her to go "where you belong" (142). When Ilsa asks, "What about us?," Rick replies, "We'll always have Paris" to the swelling music that they first fell in love to. There are greater problems in the world, Rick acknowledges, other than the "problems of three little people" (142).

After this revelation all elements combine to make a successful shot. Teary-eyed Ilsa lowers her head, and the camera follows her. It continues to focus on her face as Rick touches her cheek while "As Time Goes By" plays in the background. He utters his famous line,

Tapia 3

"Here's looking at you, kid" (142). Both softly smile and there's a sense of peace, of resolution, as the camera lingers for seconds and finally shows Ilsa turn away. Suddenly, the music swells and the point of view shifts to reveal the Nazi Captain Strasser, violently interrupting this love scene. This sudden shift highlights the fact that Victor and Ilsa have to leave *now*. It is ironic that Rick and Ilsa's song is "As Time Goes By": they may want to stay frozen in the moment, but time and the events of their day always catch up with them.

Victor comes back into the picture and Rick feels that he has to clear things up. Ironically, the fog still shrouds the scene, suggesting that there is much these men will still fail to understand about the woman they love. Both men are facing each other and Ilsa is off to the side where she's wiping the tears off her face. Victor tells Rick, "And welcome back to the fight. This time I know our side will win" (143), and the moment is once again interrupted by a reminder of time's passing with the sound of the plane's engine propellers beginning to spin.

Ilsa looks at Rick, then at Victor, and Victor asks her if she is ready. With a final look to Rick, she moves to the side of her husband. The camera jumps from Ilsa, to Rick, to Victor and then finally readjusts itself to reveal Ilsa and Victor side by side as husband and wife facing Rick. These camera movements signal to the audience that it's over. There is no chance for Ilsa or Rick to be together. The married couple turn and walk into the mist, becoming smaller the further they move. Rick remains off to the side, a stagnant figure seeing his beloved walk away.

As the plane is leaving, heading into the fog, Strasser arrives. Rick shoots him after a tense confrontation, and suddenly a carload of officials arrives. Once again, the film highlights the importance of time. This time it is the self-serving Renault who must decide whether to hand his friend Rick over to the Gestapo or to risk his own position by protecting him. Like Rick and Ilsa before him, Renault does not have the luxury of time in which to weigh his decisions. The tension is finally released as Renault announces, "Major Strasser's been shot" (144).

Tapia 4

Then a brief moment of silence follows as everyone waits for his next words: "Round up the usual suspects" (144).

Both men look at each other and smile slightly. The body is carried out and nonchalantly Renault pours a drink of Vichy water. However, in an act that shows that he too is a sentimentalist and a patriot (as he had accused Rick of being), the camera zooms in on the bottle's label; with a look of disgust Renault tosses the bottle in the trash and kicks the can away from him, as the camera focuses on the trash can, suggesting that it is the proper receptacle for all things Vichy-related. This reminds the viewer that political tension still exists in the world despite the resolution of the film's romantic plot.

The camera then pans over to the lift-off of Victor and Ilsa's plane. Reminiscent of the first scenes of the movie, both men's views follow the plane toward the sky, toward the freedom of America. The camera then focuses exclusively on the plane, as it disappears into the fog and only the sound of engines can be heard.

In the film's final moments, Renault walks side by side with Rick away from the past and into the future. When Rick reminds Renault that he owes him 10,000 francs from a lost wager, Renault tells him that that money will go toward <u>their</u> expenses as they leave Casablanca and join the resistance. Here the camera shifts from their sides to their backs, as they walk toward the unknown future.

Meanwhile, the patriotic music of "La Marseillaise" plays in the background. When Rick finally utters the last line of the film, we know that the fates of the two friends have shifted forever: "Louis, I think this is the beginning of a beautiful friendship" (145). The scene ends with an alliance between both men to put aside their self-interest and join the fight against tyranny.

Throughout these last scenes of <u>Casablanca</u> the interplay of music and mise en scène reinforces the characters' dialogues and actions. It is fitting that the movie's theme song is "As Time Goes By" because time is exactly what these characters do not have in the film's final

Tapia 5

scenes. They must make life or death decisions in seconds. We share their tension and their confusion as the camera shifts its point of view and focuses sometimes rapidly, sometimes agonizingly slowly. While we remember the film for its remarkable plot and its convincing acting, it is also this combination of the foggy mise en scène, the effective camera work, and the haunting music that makes it a classic.

Works Cited

Casablanca. Written by Julius G. Epstein, Philip J. Epstein, and Howard Koch. Dir. Michael Curtiz. Perf. Humphrey Bogart and Ingrid Bergman. Warner Bros., 1942. DVD. MGM, 1998.

As you evaluate Jineyda's essay, notice how she describes the film scenes. How much detail is necessary for this type of analysis? Also, think of how she uses the vocabulary introduced in this chapter. As in earlier chapters, this chapter has mentioned only some of the terms that can be used to describe and write about film. You can also reflect on the terminology for writing about drama (Chapter 6), since film is, essentially, a version of drama adapted to twentieth- and twentieth-first-century technology.

Part 3

Critical Strategies for Research

Chapter 9

Critical Approaches to Literature

What if criticism is a science as well as an art?
—NORTHRUP FRYE, *Anatomy of Criticism* (1957)

As noted in Chapter 1, readers too often approach works of literature looking for the single "correct" interpretation and become frustrated when that one right answer eludes them. Remembering that there is more than one way to read a work of literature is helpful. Some of the most enthusiastic students in required literature and writing courses are engineering or math majors who enjoy coming to a class in which their own interpretations of literature, if supported by the text, are as valid as the instructor's. Permission to approach a text in a number of different ways is a refreshing change from the pressure of always coming up with the "right" answer. (However, we are all grateful that certain professions emphasize the need to arrive at the right answer from time to time. We would probably all agree that we want the people who design bridges, for example, to arrive at the correct mathematical formula before starting to build.) This does not mean, however, that "anything counts" when it comes to interpreting literature: few literature professors and critics feel that all interpretations are equally valid. Careful reading and textual evidence are important regardless of your critical approach.

Over the past few decades, professors have been attuned to *literary theory*, a term you probably didn't hear in high school English classes. Theory provides an intellectual framework, or **context**, for approaching literary texts. Critical readings of a text are never simply neutral interpretations of the words on the page, although understanding the way these words work together is central to such readings. All of us bring our assumptions to the literature we read, and those assumptions determine our critical strategies, whether or not we are aware of it. Theory helps make us more aware of both assumptions and strategies.

Most critics use a combination of approaches to interpret a literary text. All of these approaches begin with a close reading of the text itself. Regardless of your critical strategy, you must have a thorough understanding of what the work says and how it says it. As you read the literary selections in this book, begin with the close reading strategies discussed in other chapters. Once you have done so, you are ready to open up your initial interpretation, adding layers of possible meaning to the work.

This chapter introduces some critical approaches to literature. You may be surprised to find that the field of literary criticism often crosses over into other disciplines like history or psychology. As a way of illustrating these different strategies, we are going to interpret an apparently simple poem, Robert Herrick's "To the Virgins, to Make Much of Time," through a number of critical lenses.

Herrick's poem (published in England in 1648) may be familiar to you. It is frequently anthologized. Its rhyme scheme and meter are relatively simple and its message is relatively straightforward. Yet this poem can be read many different ways. As you read it for the first time, consider the poem's theme. How does Herrick use figurative language to convey his theme and achieve his overall effect?

Robert Herrick *(1591–1664)*

To the Virgins, to Make Much of Time

Gather ye rosebuds while ye may,
Old Time is still a-flying:
And this same flower that smiles to-day
To-morrow will be dying.

The glorious lamp of heaven, the sun,
The higher he's a-getting,
The sooner will his race be run,
And nearer he's to setting.

That age is best which is the first,
When youth and blood are warmer;
But being spent, the worse, and worst
Times still succeed the former.

Then be not coy, but use your time,
And while ye may, go marry:
For having lost but once your prime,
You may for ever tarry.

(1648)

A Formalist Approach to "To the Virgins, to Make Much of Time"

Whether you know it or not, you are already familiar with the formalist approach to literature. Formalist critics, sometimes called "new critics," value the kind of close reading exemplified in Chapter 1, which discussed Mark

Twain's "A Fable" and Nikki Giovanni's "Woman." Formalist approaches to literature focus on the unifying elements and tensions of the text itself. Formalists are less interested in the biographical background of an author or the historical or cultural forces that help to shape a work. They value the qualities of literature that help literary works stand alone, regardless of their place and time. A formalist pays close attention to the way a text's language and form work together to convey an overall theme or effect. Cleanth Brooks, an influential formalist critic, describes a good poem this way:[1]

> [T]he elements of a poem are related to each other, not as blossoms juxtaposed in a bouquet, but as the blossoms are related to the other parts of a growing plant. The beauty of the poem is the flowering of the whole plant, and needs the stalk, the leaf, and the hidden roots. If this figure seems somewhat high-flown, let us borrow an analogy from another art: the poem is like a little drama. The total effect proceeds from all elements in the drama, and in a good poem, as in a good drama, there is no waste motion and there are no superfluous parts.

According to Brooks, the elements of a poem are mutually dependent. He compares a good poem to a beautiful flower: while we may admire the blossoms of the flower and ignore the rather common-looking stem, the blossoms are dependent on the stem to bring them water and nutrients. Likewise, a poem may move its reader by sending a compelling message, but we cannot divorce that message from the structure or language of the poem itself.

Formalists usually define literature as a special form of language and describe a set of criteria by which it can be judged. The meaning of a text, according to formalists, is based on public standards of language. The text, in other words, is not a private product of an individual: the reader, not the author, is responsible for articulating the meaning. Usually formalists focus on the tensions or conflicts that exist and that are resolved by the end of the work.

Here is a list of questions you might ask when taking a formalist approach to a work of literature:

- What is the work's *structure?* Is it formal, like a **sonnet?** Or is its structure driven by the need to tell a story, like a **ballad?**
- How does the work use **figurative language (metaphor, symbolism)** to convey its meaning?
- Does the work contain any contradictions or ambiguities? If so, are they resolved?
- What is the function of **irony** (if any) in the text?

These questions indicate that formalist critics are primarily concerned with the artistic features of a work. Formalism has come under fire for being naive about the placement of art in our culture. Some critical theorists who oppose formalism argue that all works of literature are shaped by powerful historical and

[1]Cleanth Brooks, "Irony as a Principle of Structure," in Morton D. Zabel, ed., *Literary Opinion in America* (New York: Harper, 1951), 729.

cultural forces that cannot be ignored in trying to gain an understanding of a text. We will look at some of these theories later in this chapter; however, any theoretical approach to a work begins with a good close reading, something a formalist approach can accomplish very well.

A formalist critic would note that "To the Virgins, to Make Much of Time" is an example of a *carpe diem* poem, a Latin phrase that means "seize the day," or, roughly, capture the importance of the present moment. The poem's theme is clearly one of urgency: live life to the fullest now because we are all going to grow old and die. A formalist critic would also note the poem's structure: it is composed of four stanzas, each with four lines. The **rhyme** scheme is a simple *abab* and the **meter** appears to be regular as well. The poem has a musical quality, with the rhyme and meter working together to create a lyrical effect. In the first two stanzas, the meter would be irregular if we pronounced the words the way they sound in conversation (for instance, "flower" is two syllables). However, this poem expects us to compress "flower" into "flow'r" as one syllable, eliding, or slurring over, the "e."

Gather ye rosebuds while ye may, (8 syllables)
Old Time is still a-flying: (7 syllables)
And this same flower that smiles to-day (8 syllables, "flower" as "flow'r")
To-morrow will be dying. (7 syllables)

The glorious lamp of heaven, the sun, (8 syllables: "glorious" as two syllables, "heaven" as one)
The higher he's a-getting, (7 syllables)
The sooner will his race be run, (8 syllables)
And nearer he's to setting. (7 syllables)

This meter helps to reinforce the poem's unity, and its lighthearted tone is consistent with the carefree activity of gathering rosebuds. One line flows easily and musically into the next until lines 11 and 12: "But being spent, the worse, and worst / Times still succeed the former." Formalist critics might draw a parallel between the poem's theme of encroaching death and this faltering meter, which is akin to a skipped heartbeat.

We do not know who the poem's speaker is (and readers must always be wary of confusing the speaker with the poet), but we can assume that the speaker is not one of the young women being addressed given the frequent use of the pronoun "ye" (or "you") rather than the inclusive "we." A formalist critic might ask, "What is the relationship between the speaker and the young maidens he (or she) is imploring to make the most of their youth?" Why the urgency?

A formalist also looks at imagery to see how the text's theme is reinforced. In this case, the girls are encouraged to "gather . . . rosebuds." This suggestion can be taken literally, in the sense that picking flowers is a pleasurable, but relatively unproductive, way to spend time—something these girls may not have the leisure to do when they are older with more responsibilities. In addition, the rose is a rather delicate flower, one that doesn't last long and is difficult to grow.

Gathering the "smiling" buds, then, before they have had the chance to bloom means plucking them before they have a chance to "die," an occasion that might occur as quickly as "tomorrow."

As we move through the poem, we see additional layers of meaning. Clearly the speaker is not only referring to picking flowers. References to the passing sun, youth, and age make us realize that there is more at stake than having a nice bouquet on the table. The rosebuds are a symbol of romance and sex (an association that continues today). The speaker asks his listeners to "be not *coy*," a word that suggests sexual reticence, but "marry" while there's still time. In other words, "make the most of your youth and beauty, ladies, because you're not going to get any better than this." Like a rosebud, youth is in its first blossom only once, a time when both roses and maidens are most desirable. A bud turns into a bloom that all too soon turns into a dead rose. No one wants to gather that.

Historical Approaches to "To the Virgins, to Make Much of Time"

This work has been popular for over three hundred years, and its message of making the most of our short time on earth is no less relevant today than it was in Herrick's time. A formalist reading would emphasize this universal appeal. In contrast, a historical reading would view the poem through the lens of its place and time of composition and might also take into account the original audience of the poem. Some literary critics believe that no work of literature can truly be understood outside of its historical context. A group of critics known as *new historicists* broaden the traditional definition of "history" (the progress of significant public events) to include the everyday lives of ordinary people. These critics argue that history and literature are never definitively "knowable" because there are an infinite number of competing "truths" about any historical time period.

For example, Americans are now living during a specific historical period in which their country is fighting a "war on terror." In fifty years, historians might come across the following two documents from this period: a copy of the *New York Times* from March 20, 2003, the day the American-led coalition invaded Iraq, and a script from the show *Friends* that aired the same week. Which document is more valuable as a window into history? The new historicist would be reluctant to automatically choose one over the other and instead would view the two in conjunction with one another. Both provide important glimpses into the global events of the time and the impact of those events on popular culture. Both shed light on the fears and desires of people living in America in 2003.

A new historicist supplements his or her understanding of traditional history—the names of kings, dates of wars, and so forth—with documents that can shed light on the lives of everyday people from a given time period—diaries, letters, and newspaper articles. In a similar way, a literary text helps shed light on a historical period while our knowledge of the historical period helps shape our reading of a text.

Here is a list of questions you might ask when taking a historical approach to a work of literature:

- When was this work written? What do I know about the author?
- What major historical events are addressed directly in this work?
- How might this work indirectly reflect the impact of historical events?
- What does this work tell us about the everyday lives of average people during this period? Their needs and desires? Their values?
- How does this work reflect or comment on some of the power structures of the time?

Let's return to "To the Virgins, to Make Much of Time." When Herrick wrote this poem, he was serving (reluctantly) as a minister in a rural parish in England. He had lived through a brutal civil war at the end of which King Charles I, to whom Herrick was loyal, was beheaded in 1649 under the Puritan parliamentary leader Oliver Cromwell. Tensions between the Puritans and the royalists (as those loyal to the king were known) had been high for decades. One dispute between the two groups centered on the leisure pastimes of rural peasant life, which many Puritans correctly argued had their origins in pagan rituals. The Puritans discouraged and later forbade Sunday games and sporting events, Christmas parties, harvest fests, and May Day celebrations. In 1633, a Puritan named William Prynne laid out the Puritan position against these activities in a work known as "Histrio-Mastix," calling Christmas dancing, Easter celebrations, and May Day flower-gathering traditions "diabolical," "wanton," "whorish," and "sinful." The royal response to these accusations was swift: Prynne's books were burned and he was tortured and imprisoned.

King James I (who reigned from 1603 to 1625) and his successor Charles I both encouraged these rural pastimes, in part because they mitigated the harshness of peasant life, preventing insurrection. When Charles I reissued what came to be known as "The Book of Sports" in response to Prynne, the culture wars were on. In "The Book of Sports," the king proclaimed his approval of Sunday recreational activities and commanded that

> after the end of divine service our good people be not disturbed, letted [hindered] or discouraged from any lawful recreation, such as dancing, either men or women; archery for men, leaping, vaulting, or any other such harmless recreation, nor from having of May-games, Whitsun-ales, and Morris-dances; and the setting up of May-poles and other sports therewith used: so as the same be had in due and convenient time, without impediment or neglect of divine service: and that women shall have leave to carry rushes to the church for the decorating of it, according to their old custom.

In the intervening years between the publication of Prynne's work and that of Herrick's in 1648, the Puritan army had defeated Charles's royalist followers and the king was executed in 1649. The Puritans quickly shut down all theaters and sought to "purify" Anglican faith by simplifying church services and ridding religion of all its Catholic and pagan influences. Royalists were stripped of their political power and their property; many were executed, and others went into exile abroad.

With the help of "Histrio-Mastix" and "The Book of Sports," we can enhance our reading of "To the Virgins, to Make Much of Time." Read in light of its historical context, this seemingly simple poem is politically radical, a direct challenge to the dominant Puritan worldview. The gathering of rosebuds and other flowers was the type of rural custom that the Puritan leaders of Herrick's time associated with paganism. With this (and other poems from the same volume) Herrick celebrates the values of his murdered king and directly challenges the values of the Puritan usurpers. Herrick romanticizes the values and customs of rural life, viewing them as more life-affirming than the sterile Puritan outlook. Happiness comes to an end with the passage of time, and Herrick knew from his personal experience that "the worse, and worst / Times still succeed the former."

A historical critic might also wonder whether Herrick's depiction of these rural traditions is accurate. He or she might well ask, "How much time did peasant girls spend gathering rosebuds anyway? Didn't they have anything else to do?" Many historical critics take a *Marxist* perspective and focus on issues of economic and social class. Marxist critics view literature with an eye for class conflict. They try to assess whether a text subverts or affirms existing power structures associated with class.

A Marxist reading of "To the Virgins" would consider the realities of rural peasant life. Peasant girls certainly did their share of gathering, but they wouldn't have been gathering anything so frivolous as roses. A Marxist critic would point out that roses are completely impractical from the standpoint of industry. Not only are they merely decorative, but they are also hard to grow and die easily. In one sense, Herrick's exhortation to the women to gather roses is a subversive one: "Don't bother working too hard," he implies, "but have some fun while you still can." This is would hardly appear to be an attempt to keep the peasants laboring away while those in the manor relax.

On the other hand, if "To the Virgins, to Make Much of Time" were our only source, we might assume that country life in England was pleasant and at least gave women the option of gathering roses and picking out a husband. The fact that Herrick tells these women to gather roses would imply that this is a viable possibility for them. A little research, however, would challenge that theory. The real life of Herrick's country folk was, in the words of his contemporary Thomas Hobbes, "nasty, brutish, and short" (from his work *Leviathan*). Entire families farmed land owned by local squires, paying dearly for the privilege while living in squalid conditions, their lives often cut short by disease. In fact, the marriages that Herrick encourages might well have been death sentences, as childbirth often killed women along with their babies.

A Marxist critic would take note of these facts and ask, "Why might Herrick paint such a rosy picture (pun intended) of peasant life? Does his poem challenge the economic power structure or affirm it?" Despite our previous reading, the poem seems to affirm the economic power structure of the time. From this perspective, Herrick is romanticizing country life, telling the peasants, "You don't have it so bad. Have fun with your country rituals and fall in love and don't take up arms against the local lord. Things are fine here in the country." (In his life outside poetry, Herrick harbored no such illusions about country life. He felt stifled and longed for the excitement of London.)

As you can see, a historical reading adds a number of new insights to our original view of the poem. For one thing, we have seen how the poem is at once politically radical and economically conservative. Herrick's poetry is more than a pleasant little lyric (although it is that). It is also a vehicle for challenging a new world and expressing nostalgia for the traditional values of the past.

A Gender-Based Approach to "To the Virgins, to Make Much of Time"

Like historical criticism, gender-based criticism (including feminist criticism) reads a work of literature in a context that goes beyond the work itself. While many gender-based critics incorporate a historical approach, their focus is primarily on the impact of gender (the identity associated with maleness or femaleness) on the production or reception of a text.

As with historical criticism, there are a variety of gender-based approaches to literature. Some critics focus on the gender of the *reader*, arguing that the experience of being male or female inevitably alters the way we read a text (a form of reader-response criticism, discussed below). Other critics focus on the *author's* gender as in important factor in the production of a literary text. Still others might look at the historical literary representations of women and men and the way *cultures* have traditionally constructed gender.

For an example of the connection between culture and gender, try this brainstorming exercise. Write the headings *Masculine* and *Feminine* on a piece of paper. In one minute write down as many words for each category that you can think of. Chances are that under the word *Masculine* you have written words like *strong* and *powerful*, as well as some words with negative connotations like *aggressive* and *domineering*. Your answers for *Feminine* might include *delicate* and *nurturing* as well as the less-than-positive attributions of *weak* and *dependent*.

Thanks to feminism and other gender-based approaches, we know these categories to be stereotypes and can easily think of women and men who possess qualities traditionally associated with the "opposite" gender. Yet the ease with which you probably came up with these adjectives demonstrates how powerful these stereotypes are, despite the efforts of educators and other cultural leaders to debunk them. Gender-based criticism operates under the assumption that we are all influenced by these gender stereotypes; these critics look for evidence of gender stereotypes in literary texts, investigating the way literature challenges or reinforces these stereotypes and the oppression of women.

Gender-based theorists also challenge the traditional *canon*, the body of literature determined over the years to be "great" by scholars and critics. Feminist critics note that since men have traditionally had greater access to education and power, they have determined which works are considered masterpieces and which ones are taught and read throughout the ages. If, as many people assume, men and women are different (whether through biological or cultural influences), they bring different sets of assumptions and values to their reading. Thus, the assumptions and values that have been reinforced in the literary canon over the years have generally been masculine ones.

Feminist critics point out that even when women writers have been considered "great" traditionally, they have been uneasily incorporated into a male canon. For example, early-nineteenth-century authors Jane Austen and Maria Edgeworth were both featured in a series of great British "Men of Letters."

In *The Madwoman in the Attic*, feminist critics Sandra M. Gilbert and Susan Gubar suggest that you begin feminist criticism with some basic questions:[2]

> What does it mean to be a woman writer in a culture whose fundamental definitions of literary authority are both overtly and covertly patriarchal? If the vexed and vexing polarities of angel and monster, sweet dumb Snow White and fierce mad Queen, are major images literary tradition offers women, how does such imagery influence the ways in which women attempt the pen? If the Queen's looking glass speaks with the King's voice, how do its perpetual kingly admonitions affect the Queen's own voice? Since his is the chief voice she hears, does the Queen try to sound like the King, imitating his tone, his phrasing, his point of view? Or does she "talk back" to him in her own vocabulary, her own timbre, insisting on her own viewpoint? We believe these are questions feminist literary criticism—both theoretical and practical—must answer.

Gilbert and Gubar use the fairy tale "Snow White" to illustrate a larger concept (much like fairy tales are used in this book to illustrate different facets of human nature). They argue that literary depictions of women often fall into one of two stereotypes: angel or monster (or similar oppositions like virgin or whore, devoted mother or selfish career woman). Given that society is patriarchal (governed by men), what are women's options?

According to Gilbert and Gubar, the voice that tells the wicked queen that "Snow White is the fairest one of all" is that of the king, who represents male power. In other words, it is a masculine voice that tells women they aren't attractive enough or worthy enough. This voice pits one woman against another, making women perceive other women to be the enemy, when it is the king's voice that sends this destructive message. What options does the queen have? She can internalize the voice in the mirror and act to please the king by adopting his worldview and value system (as happens in the fairy tale), or she can reject the king (which means rejecting the values of patriarchal society and suffering the consequences).

Here is a list of additional questions you might ask when taking a gender-based approach to literature:

- What is the gender of the author?
- How does this work depict relationships between men and women?
- Does this work reinforce or challenge gender-based stereotypes?
- Is power held exclusively (or primarily) by male or female characters? What attitude does the work take toward powerful men and women?

[2]Sandra M. Gilbert and Susan Gubar, *The Madwoman in the Attic* (New Haven: Yale University Press, 1979), 46.

Robert Herrick's "To the Virgins, to Make Much of Time" can be read productively through a gender-based lens. Start with the title, "To the Virgins." We immediately know that Herrick is addressing women. Although virginity is not exclusive to women, it typically refers to females. The *Oxford English Dictionary* defines *virgin* as "An unmarried or chaste maiden or woman, distinguished for piety or steadfastness in religion, and regarded as having a special place among the members of the Christian church on account of these merits" and "A woman (esp. a young woman) who is, or remains, in a state of inviolate chastity; an absolutely pure maiden or maid." In both of these uses of the word, a *virgin* is a young woman who is defined by and valued for her chastity, her sexual purity.

The title might suggest that the speaker is trying to exhort his listeners to have sex while they still can, a common theme in *carpe diem* poems such as Andrew Marvell's "To His Coy Mistress" (see Chapter 13). However, Herrick writes, "Then be not coy, but use your time, / And while ye may, go marry." Marriage, not sexual amorousness, is the point. The next definition of *virgin* in the *OED* is "An old maid, a spinster," and the *OED* notes that *old maid* is a derogatory term. The theme of Herrick's poem, then, is that virgins should find a husband while they are still attractive or they will find themselves virgins in the least desirable sense of the word. (You might remember that children's card game in which the loser is left with the Old Maid card, the only card in the deck that doesn't have a match.)

The young girls in the poem, if not in reality, are having a good time gathering rosebuds and enjoying their warm-blooded youth. They might be tempted to extend this life of leisure indefinitely. Why settle down? Because, Herrick points out, time passes by. The sun won't stop rising and setting to wait for these girls who are in the prime of their life. Thus Herrick is hardly saying, "Girls only want to have fun"; he is saying, "Don't waste time before entering into a contractual agreement that will give you a secure form of happiness."

A critical gender-based reading might question the premise on which Herrick's argument is based and stress that it is written from a male point of view. Who says that "The age is best which is the first"? Is Herrick claiming that once women have lost their youth and beauty, they lose their value? Does his focus on *female* virgins mean that men can take their time, marry whenever they want to, but women had better hurry up? In addition, feminist critics might point out that marriage during this era was not bliss but was often a contractual agreement in which women had no legal rights and little say over their destiny.

A Psychological Approach to "To the Virgins, to Make Much of Time"

In some ways, the work of a literary critic is similar to the work of a psychotherapist. A therapist learns to "read" the words and actions of the patient so that he or she can interpret those words and actions and figure out what is going on beneath the surface. Similarly, the literary critic reads a text and tries to construct meaning from its details. In fact, literary critics have found psychological insights and techniques to be particularly useful in interpreting literature.

Most literary psychological critics have been influenced by the ideas of Sigmund Freud, even though many of his theories have been challenged in the century since he wrote. Perhaps Freud's most significant contribution to literary criticism is his discussion of the "unconscious mind," the notion that human beings have a wealth of repressed and unacceptable desires, memories, and motives that they are not even aware of. While people may be unable or unwilling to understand their unconscious mind (or the subconscious, as we say today), it manifests itself in dreams, art, and certain irrational behaviors and verbal gaffes (the "Freudian slip"). As Freud wrote, "He that has eyes to see and ears to hear may convince himself that no mortal can keep a secret. If his lips are silent, he chatters with his fingertips; betrayal oozes out of him at every pore."[3] In other words, nervous habits such as biting our fingernails or licking our lips can be as revealing (often more so) as anything we say.

Freud also popularized the Oedipus complex, what he described as men's unconscious wish to kill their father and marry their mother (and the corresponding Electra complex in which women wish to kill their mother and marry their father). Naturally, if you ask people to own up to these impulses, most will strongly deny that they desire any such thing, even though some psychologists see these forbidden impulses as powerful driving forces. They are not literal impulses: they are representations of the forces that influence our thought and action.

Literary critics often perform their own versions of Freudian analysis on characters in literature or even on authors. They read stories with an eye toward characters' childhoods, family relationships, or secret motives. If a character relates a dream or a recurring irrational thought, psychological critics pounce on that. Many productions of Shakespeare's *Hamlet* have played up Hamlet's Oedipus complex, staging scenes between Hamlet and his mother to maximize the sexual tension between them.

However, Freudian analysis is not the only possible psychological approach, either to psychology or to literature. A prominent psychological critic named Jacques Lacan, who is strongly influenced by Freud, reads literary texts by delving into various developmental "stages" or by looking deep into linguistic utterances rather than only characters' behavior.

Here is a list of questions you might ask when taking a psychological approach to literature:

- How might the events in this character's childhood influence his or her adult decisions?
- Does the work depict any dreams or dreamlike reveries? What kinds of symbols appear in these scenes? What significance might they have to the work as a whole?
- Do the anxieties or wishes reflected in this work reflect the anxieties or wishes of the author?

[3]Sigmund Freud, *The First Dream: Fragment of an Analysis of a Case of Hysteria* (1905), 77–78.

Although "To the Virgins, to Make Much of Time" does not have individual characters that we get to know in any depth, the poem still yields some interesting insights when approached through a psychological reading. For example, psychologists have long noted the powerful, mysterious forces of sex and death as explanations for human behavior and motivation. Psychological critics of this poem would identify both of these forces in the speaker's advice. They might see Herrick's advice to the virgins to "go marry" as a repressed way of encouraging them to indulge their sexual desires. Sex, and its consequence (children), are common ways to combat one's own mortality. The "Old Time" that is "flying" will lead each of us to our death. This fear of death motivates the speaker and, he hopes, the young women he is addressing.

A psychological critic might also wonder about Herrick's personal experiences with sex and death. In fact, Herrick's father killed himself when Herrick was only a baby. Thus, the notion of early and sudden death would possibly have haunted Herrick from childhood. Interestingly, Herrick himself never followed his own advice to "go marry," nor is there any evidence that he was sexually promiscuous. While his poetry often treats sexual themes rather frankly, by all accounts Herrick himself lived the respectable life of a minister in a small country village. A psychological critic might read Herrick's poetry in the same way a psychotherapist might interpret a dream, as a subconscious reflection of Herrick's own repressed desires.

A Reader-Response Approach to "To the Virgins, to Make Much of Time"

Each of these readings has no doubt helped you see things in the poem you might not have seen before. None of these approaches is more correct than the others because they all use the text to support their readings. One or two of these interpretations may have been more persuasive to you, however, and that's as it should be. Reader-response critics argue that any text is a meaningless set of ink marks on a page until a reader or group of readers inscribes it with meaning. (This is a departure from formalist critics, who believed that a privileged reader—the critic—could determine meaning.) The text's meaning emerges through the reader's act of interpretation. Thus reader-response criticism emphasizes the role of the reader in the process of deriving meaning from a text.

However, this does not mean that anything goes and that all readings are equally valid. A reader might have a difficult time writing an essay in which he claims that "To the Virgins" is a call for people to visit Mars via hovercraft. Reader-response critics sometimes disagree on the level of autonomy granted to the individual reader, some arguing that interpretation is completely in the reader's control, and others focusing more on the interaction between the reader and the text. For most, reader-response criticism *begins* with a personal reaction to a work, but a good reader interprets that reaction by looking closely at the reading, often using an additional critical strategy such as formalism or gender-based criticism.

Classroom discussions of a work of literature can always begin with students' initial reactions: "I loved it!" or "Why does the author say something in twenty pages that he could have said in three?" or "The ending was too unrealistic." Each of these opinions can be a useful pathway into an interpretation of the reading. If the ending seems unrealistic, what kind of ending do you think would have worked? Where in the text do you see evidence for that claim?

Reader-response theorists, like other theorists, departed from formalists in the late twentieth century. Wayne Booth's influential book *The Rhetoric of Fiction* began to emphasize the effect of a written text on a reader. Stanley Fish put even more emphasis on the reader, placing him or her in control of a text's meaning. In his influential work *Is There a Text in This Class?* he advances the idea of "interpretive communities" of readers that agree on the standards they will use to evaluate texts. (Think about whether this concept holds true in your class discussions, if your instructor uses that format.) The values and beliefs of interpretive communities change over time.

Here is a list of questions you might ask when taking a reader-response approach to a work of literature:

- What effect does this work have on me?
- What in the text is causing that reaction?
- What experiences or desires am I bringing to this reading that might be shaping the way I respond to it?

The authors of this book conducted a survey of relatives, students, and friends and asked for their response to the poem. The responses varied widely. Here are some examples:

> **From Susan, a young woman in her early twenties:** I really liked the poem. What I liked about it was the message it sent to me to use your time well while you have this gift of life. Robert Herrick was speaking to the young when he said, "Gather ye rosebuds," but I think that no matter how old a person is once you realize this truth about time you start living your life in a more meaningful way. I think I have this type of response to the poem because I have seen people at different ages in their life come to this awareness. For some strange reason when you are young you think you have all the time in the world, but as you get older you realize that time waits for no one. I remember reading this poem in college and sitting in class and trying to understand with my classmates what the verses meant. But now that I am out of college, I truly understand the depth of this poem. "Then be not coy, but use your time." To me I hear that even if you are not in your prime, you shouldn't just exist, but live life to its fullest.

> **From Frances, a mother of two in her late thirties:** Were I not happily married, I'd probably take great offense at Mr. Herrick's advice (and obviously, he would want to be addressed as Mr. Herrick and not the formal "Robert" or the less formal "Bob"). However, since I am not one of those whom he is warning, I find it rather humorous. I'd love to know what he considers to be an "aging" woman. Or it seems like a "pick-up poem" (instead of a pick-up line) to me: "A man walks into a bar and recites to the woman sitting next to him."

> **From Dan, a married man in his mid-thirties:** I didn't like the poem. It seems pretty simplistic and obvious. It's an old message and frankly not all that well done. Roses are a clichéd literary symbol by now.
>
> **From Anne, a woman in her early forties:** I agreed with the poem's message 100 percent. I thank God I had a great time when I was younger, playing the field and enjoying myself. The only thing I disagreed with was when he told the girls to get married. I'm going to encourage my daughters to take their time and keep having fun. I'm forty-two now and he's right: that old sun is moving all too quickly and as we get older, things just get worse.

Each of the above statements is a *response*, not an interpretation of the poem. Do any of these echo your own response to the work? Any one of these brief writings could become the foundation of a good critical interpretation, but in the interest of time, we'll take a look at Anne's. (As a writing exercise, you might try using one of the other responses as the basis of an interpretation.)

If one concentrates on the words "And while ye may, go marry," one might argue that Anne has missed the point: the poem makes it clear that Herrick is not telling the virgins to "play the field" but to settle down. A formalist reading would identify the poem's theme right away: seize the day and get married. But Anne barely picked up on that message. As someone who "played the field" in her youth, she approached the poem through the lens of her own experiences (as reader-response critics say we do). She later elaborated on her response:

> I focused on the plural noun, "roses," as in "more than one." If Herrick really wanted his virgins to get married, why would he ask them to gather "roses"? Wouldn't he say something like "Find a beautiful rose and pick it"? He talks about these girls being warm-blooded and tells them not to be coy which means sexually shy, doesn't it? I think he just adds that line about marriage at the end to make it respectable.

Anne has mined the text for support of her interpretation. She believes that the poem has two opposing themes—play the field and get married—and she believes Herrick privileges the "play the field" message. It comes in the first stanza and is supported by sexually suggestive words. Our trusted *Oxford English Dictionary* has several definitions of *coy*, one of which supports Anne's reading: "Displaying modest backwardness or shyness (sometimes with emphasis on the displaying); not responding readily to familiar advances; now *esp.* of a girl or young woman." Read this way, "be not coy" can mean, "do not resist when a man makes advances to you." Were Anne to turn her ideas into a critical paper, her thesis might read: "Although Robert Herrick's 'To the Virgins, to Make Much of Time' seems to urge young women to get married, the poem has a contradictory subtext that suggests a less committed sexual experience."

Anne's interpretation illustrates the different ways a text can be analyzed. Her focus on the gathering of rosebuds is important because it emphasizes pleasure, one of the poem's main **themes.** However, when she says that Herrick added the last line to make the poem "respectable," she's going outside the poem and attempting to explain the author's motives in writing it, a form of *psychological* analysis. A psychological (and even *gender-based*) analysis might give us some insight into Herrick's attitudes toward "playing around" versus marriage, and a *historical* analysis might tell us about the cultural attitudes in Herrick's time. We might then have a better idea of whether Anne's thesis is solid. You may or may not agree with Anne's reading of the poem (we're still not sure we do), but her reading has opened our eyes to interpretations we might have missed.

This chapter has introduced some important critical approaches to literature. Each of these approaches (and others that look at culture and race relations) can help you arrive at a valid interpretation of a text. The literature you will read in this anthology can be interpreted in many different ways, and your readings may be different from those of your classmates and your instructor. This is the ideal learning situation, and we hope you enjoy it.

Chapter 10

Writing the Literary Research Paper

If we knew what we were doing, it wouldn't be called research, would it?
—ALBERT EINSTEIN, *Albert Einstein: The Human Side* (1954)

While students sometimes dread the research paper, it can be a valuable and positive learning experience that gives you a feeling of mastery. Here are some reasons why it is often required in a literature course:

- **A research paper is an opportunity to understand a literary work from a different perspective.** Literary critics have published a staggering amount of work on the interpretation of literature. Occasionally these critics disagree with one another, much as you might find yourself disagreeing with a classmate during class discussion. Examining the differences between these points of view can help you determine your own opinion. (See also Chapter 9 on differing critical perspectives.)
- **A research paper helps you take charge of the many resources available to you.** Many college students are anxious about their college libraries, or even about more familiar research resources like the Internet. Often students are so intimidated by their college library that they avoid it as long as possible. But your college or university has poured a great deal of money into the library to provide you with a valuable resource. The knowledge that exists cannot be contained between the covers of your textbooks and within your classrooms and professors' offices. The research paper can help make you aware of how broad your horizons can become.
- **A research paper allows for discovery.** Searching for and finding something that might help you in some intellectual quest is genuinely exciting. Be willing to shout "Eureka!"
- **A research paper allows you to regard literature in a more sophisticated way.** Although what you, your professor, and your classmates say in class is helpful, written language and spoken language are not the same thing. Written interpretations of literature are usually well thought out and carefully revised and edited. Some are so complex that they require the same amount of

intellectual attention that literature requires. Though some may be dry and lifeless, others can be intellectually exciting.

- **A research paper allows you to be innovative and creative.** Many novice researchers think that research limits what they can say by tying it to what others have said; on the contrary, when done well, literary research allows you to branch out. Good research is more than adding a few quotations to a paper; rather, it involves following someone else's ideas and then discovering your own. Following a new path is the first step to clearing your own path.
- **Knowledge is power.** By completing literary research you access more knowledge, and thus you become more powerful.

To sum up, while a research paper can be hard work, it is also a tremendous opportunity for self-directed growth and learning. When completed, it rewards your effort with a solid feeling of accomplishment.

Getting Started

Understand the Assignment As a first step, make sure that you know what your audience (your instructor) expects of you (as discussed in Chapter 3). For instance, your instructor might require two sources in addition to the primary texts you are analyzing, or he or she might require twenty. This difference would certainly affect the way you conduct your research. Instructors also have different approaches to assigning research papers. One might say, "Write a research paper on the Oedipus complex and *Hamlet*," while another might say, "Choose an author who interests you, and write a research paper about him or her." Ascertain the specific details of the assignment and make sure you understand exactly what is required.

Plan the Research Project Anticipate exactly how much time you have and how you want to spend it. Let's say that you receive your paper assignment two weeks before it is due. You might come up with a timetable that looks like this:

Day 1: Panic! Reread assignment, talk to Professor Jones, think about a topic.

Day 2: Recover from panic; take twenty minutes to brainstorm about the topic and another twenty to make sense of the brainstorming. Spend another twenty minutes writing the very beginnings of a rough draft so that an idea begins to form.

Day 3: Visit the library. Never been there before. This is just to look around, familiarize myself with the place, check out the resources. One hour.

Days 4–5: Weekend.

Day 6: Continue rough draft and return to library to see if they have much about author X.

Day 7: Continue rough draft and actually locate five sources for the paper and read them. Two hours.

Day 8: Break. Bio exam.

Day 9: Locate five more sources and read them. Two hours.

Days 10–14 (including weekend): Evaluate sources, finish drafting the paper with the best four or five sources in mind.

This plan has several good features. One is that the student planned to find ten sources even though her professor only required four or five. That is because *a source is not necessarily valuable only because you found it*. If the source has little to do with what you want to say, it is worthless, and you might weaken your argument by attempting to jam a quotation from this source into your paper to show that you did some research. Good researchers find much more than they can use: the more you find, the more selective you can be.

Another feature of the plan is that the student visited the library more than once. This gave her the leisure to become familiar with it before diving into her research. It also gave her the feeling that maybe there was something interesting out there. A rushed trip to the library at midnight before the due date does not afford you the leisure to have these feelings.

Another feature of the above plan is that the student's drafting process and her research process are intertwined. This is a good idea for two related reasons: (1) you don't want your thesis to dictate your research (because you might not find anything directly related to your thesis), and (2) you don't want your research to dictate your thesis (because you might end up structuring your idea too much around what others have said).

What Is a Source?

More important than the number of sources in a research paper is the value of the sources you eventually use. So what is a "source," and how can you know which sources are valuable?

The types of sources available are discussed in the sections below entitled "Library Research" and "Internet Research"; this section focuses on what a source is or might be. A *source* is any reliable knowledge that can be cited in support of an argument. How broad can it be? Think creatively and critically about sources and, as always, consult with your instructor about the types of sources you will eventually use.

Literary criticism changes constantly. In one decade critics might write mostly about literature's formal features such as irony; in the next decade they might write more about class struggle as it is revealed in literature (see Chapter 9). The changing climate in literary schools of thought also means that the value and nature of sources will constantly change. At the moment, for instance, many literary critics are practicing "cultural criticism," which looks at cultural artifacts that seem far removed from the study of literature. These critics might use a grammar school textbook, for instance, to explain how a work of literature reflects the way literacy is related to social class. While this grammar textbook would not have been considered a useful source in past decades, now it could be.

A source might be a formal or informal work of literary criticism, or it might come from outside the field of literary criticism. Let's say that you are writing a paper on Tim O'Brien, a prominent American prose writer who is frequently associated with the Vietnam War, the subject of virtually all of his essays and fiction. Imagine you are writing a paper on "The Things They Carried," a short story that is included in his book *The Things They Carried*, and that you are focusing on the difference between the actual material things the soldiers in the story carry and the more abstract emotional things they carry. You hope to argue that the backdrop of the Vietnam War creates a landscape so unstable that the realistic material details, far from distracting from the story's "theme," provide that theme. In short, the things the soldiers carry give the story its weight and thus its meaning.

You decide to go about researching the actual duties and experiences of American foot soldiers in Vietnam. What did they have to transport with them as they walked around? You might consult:

- Your Uncle Jim, who served in Vietnam
- A biography of the story's author, Tim O'Brien
- A history of the Vietnam War based entirely on newspaper reports from that era
- A history of the Vietnam War written by a prominent historian
- A volume of essays about Vietnam War literature
- A critical study of the works of Tim O'Brien
- A website called "Vietnam Veterans for Peace"
- The *Wikipedia* entry on Tim O'Brien

The list could go on. In other words, by thinking creatively, you can gather a good number of valuable sources.

- Let's say your Uncle Jim was a foot soldier who kept a diary about the things he had to carry when he served in Vietnam. That would make him a better source than if he had been a helicopter pilot who never set foot on the ground, or someone whose memory is not reliable.
- How about O'Brien's biography? It might be an excellent resource for your argument, but let's say that the first half of the biography focused entirely on O'Brien's life before he became a writer, even before he went to Vietnam. Would you find anything important in that section? If not, you don't need to summarize it or provide details, like where O'Brien's mother was born and what her maiden name was.
- Let's say that you glanced through the table of contents of the volume on Vietnam War literature and found nothing about O'Brien. Would that automatically mean that you couldn't use it? There might be an article in there that says something about the way the Vietnam landscape distorts reality: you wouldn't want to overlook that.

• And let's take *Wikipedia*, or the ever-changing Internet in general: how accurate is this information?

You can be both selective and creative in figuring out which sources will be useful. Do not be afraid to ask for guidance from your instructor, a tutor, or a reference librarian.

In all good research, you will encounter sources you cannot (or should not) use in your paper. This does not mean that you will not learn something from them, and they might lead you in a new direction. (A book might have a bibliography that leads you to the perfect source, for instance, or a website might have a collection of links at the end that does the same thing.) Although research might seem like a maze in which you find yourself at a dead end from time to time, persistence almost always pays off.

Library Research

Library research differs from computer research in several ways: (1) the library is probably more intimidating than your home computer; (2) the library has everything your home computer has and much, much more; (3) libraries are often overlooked, valuable treasures. A theme of this chapter is discovery: exposing things that might have been hidden from sight.

Although not all libraries are equally useful, the information revolution of the past twenty years has transformed them. They are no longer dusty, cavernous, cold places where books are stacked in intimidating towers and where severe-looking women are paid to hiss at you to be quiet, but rather information centers, often with impressive electronic resources in addition to books. Research librarians are fabulous human resources, too: far from wanting you to be quiet, they anxiously await your questions and are generally eager to help you.

If your library offers an orientation tour, going on it can be a first step. If it does not, you might take the initiative to browse through the stacks yourself. Do not simply browse through the book stacks to research your paper. Though this can be an enjoyable and effective beginning to research, it is not scientific: you might miss a great number of possible sources. Instead, understand how librarians classify their materials before you begin to explore them. Most likely, your library's material holdings are divided into three main sections: reference works, periodicals, and books for circulation.

Reference works generally do not circulate (leave the library). They include books such as encyclopedias, dictionaries, and atlases, as well as more specialized works that might be useful for literary research (such as the *American Writers* series, or *Contemporary Literary Criticism*, or *The Dictionary of Literary Biography*). Reference works generally provide information or lead you to other sources; they can be great inroads into your research, but they are not likely to be the end of your research.

The section of *periodicals* includes scholarly journals, newspapers, and magazines. Periodicals, as the name implies, are published at regular intervals (daily, monthly, three times a year, and so forth). Part of a library's role is to *archive* these materials, or to preserve copies of them so that they can be consulted now and in the future. Because newspapers and magazines are heavy, difficult to store, and break down easily, libraries often find alternatives to archiving the paper versions of these texts. While microfilm has long been a popular choice, electronic media and storage devices like CD-ROMs are quickly replacing microfilm. Academic journals, as mentioned earlier, are often bound together by year and shelved as books. These, too, are now being replaced by electronic versions, and some journals exist only as "e-journals"—electronic resources that have no print version. Most frequently, journals exist in both print and electronic versions.

The *books for circulation* are probably shelved according to the *Library of Congress* classification system. Your hometown library might have used the Dewey Decimal System, which organizes fiction according to the last name of the author and sorts nonfiction books according to the subject by assigning them a *call number*. The more refined Library of Congress system sorts all books by subject beginning with a letter or pair of letters, followed by a number, more letters, and more numbers. If you are not familiar with this system, walk through the "P" section of your library to get a sense of how literature and literary criticism are sorted. You will notice how the system organizes literature by the nationality of the author and the era in which the author wrote.

You will also notice how the works written *by* an author (primary sources) and the works written *about* an author (secondary sources) are shelved together. If you were writing the sample paper topic on Tim O'Brien, his book *The Things They Carried* would be shelved as PS 3565.B75 T48 1991. Books about him would immediately follow. For instance, a book called *A Trauma Artist: Tim O'Brien and the Fiction of Vietnam* by Mark A. Heberle has the call number PS 3565.B75 Z65 2001.

Library Catalogs

How do you know what is out there? Like a detective, you have to be willing to redefine what you are looking for, or you may not recognize a "clue" when you stumble across one. You also have to believe that whether your library is the size of a classroom or a skyscraper with 2 million volumes, it has something you can use as a source in your paper. The place to begin is the library's catalog.

Almost all libraries have now cataloged their holdings electronically, and you can usually search the catalog using the categories of *Author*, *Title*, *Subject*, and *Keyword*. In searching for sources about Tim O'Brien, you might begin with an author search to see which books by O'Brien your library holds. You would select *Author* and then (in almost all cases, though your library may be an exception) you would type the author's last name (O'Brien), followed by a comma, followed by his first name. The catalog will provide you with the call numbers of the works owned by the library.

If you know the title of a particular work of criticism—for instance, if this title is listed in a reference entry on O'Brien or if you discovered it on a website or through a bibliography—you can select *Title* in your library's catalog and type it in: again, you will be given a call number.

The *Subject* and *Keyword* categories are the most general, and often the most useful ways to begin a search. You might initiate a subject search and type something like "Vietnam War literature." If the search yields too many sources, you will have to change the terms: say, "Vietnam War fiction" or "U.S. literature and Vietnam War." The *and* limits the search by looking for sources that are cross-listed under *both* "U.S. literature" and "Vietnam War." If you wrote, "U.S. literature OR Vietnam War," you would get sources for both subjects—probably a billion in this case. *OR* is easier to use if your terms are narrower. *AND* and *OR* are *Boolean operators*, meaning they determine where the search engine will find your sources. *NOT* is another Boolean operator: you might write "Vietnam War literature NOT poetry."

Libraries' Electronic Databases

These library catalog searches will lead you to books, collections of essays, or individual essays in books or journals held by your library. That is just one step, though. You might also be able to access journal articles that are in electronic databases. Many libraries have purchased databases that contain full-text journal articles from a number of different sources and journals. "Project Muse" or "Academic Search Premier" are examples of such databases, but many others exist. This might be a good time to consult with your reference librarian.

"Full-text" means that your computer screen will display the entire journal article: no need to find the journal in your library's stacks. However, if your library owns the journal and the article is not available in full-text format, resist laziness: find the source once you have figured out that it might be useful.

Internet Research

The Internet, or World Wide Web, was originally called "the Information Superhighway" when it was developed in the early 1990s. While many of its designers hoped it would be a free-flowing, high-speed source of information, it has become much more than that: an opportunity to market goods, for instance, or a place to chat with like-minded people. The Internet can still be an excellent source of information, but because it lacks editorial standards, it can also be an excellent source of *mis*information. For example, a quick Google search for the birthdate of an author of this textbook revealed four different dates *on the first page!* Since anyone with the right software can create a website, you cannot be sure what to trust on the Internet. While books and journals might also contain misinformation, a published work has been checked and rechecked by editors and so is less likely to have errors.

Nearly every famous author is represented on the Internet, many with their own websites. If you discover one of these websites, ascertain right away who is managing it. The author's agent? A fan? A professor? The author's publisher? Knowing this background will help you understand what the website is for and how reliable it might be. Also find out how recently the website was updated. A website that was updated last week indicates that it is active and probably more reliable than one created three years ago that hasn't been touched since.

Author websites often contain biographies and lists of works. If the author is long deceased and his or her works are in the "public domain," the website author might actually reprint the author's work on the website. You would do well to check these versions of the author's work against published versions. Website authors frequently type published versions onto their own computers, and they might make mistakes. You might also find a list of secondary sources on the website. Although this can be useful, it might not be a complete or comprehensive list. Finally, there might be links to other websites or even to articles on the author that are published on the Web. These links might be especially helpful, and a website author who has bothered to put links onto the website is probably well informed and more reliable than an author who has not. Websites must be cited along with all the other works you cite or consult (see the end of this chapter).

Avoiding Plagiarism

First, a background note: Plagiarism is a subject that we and other college professors take very seriously. Our colleagues are increasingly upset about plagiarism on college campuses: we discuss it at academic conferences, write about it in journals, and work hard to implement policies at our colleges and universities that take aim at the problem and address it vigorously. Your professor is most likely thoroughly exasperated, offended, and angered by plagiarism and is more than likely prepared to take action against it.

Plagiarism can be defined as any attempt to take credit for someone else's writing. The obvious forms of plagiarism are buying a paper from a so-called paper mill on the Internet and giving it to your professor as though you wrote it. However, plagiarism is sometimes more subtle: if you find a critic who has said something interesting, you might write or rewrite his or her words as part of your paper and forget to cite that source in your paper. From the point of view of your professor, you have plagiarized, even though you forgot to cite the source and even though you put it in your own words. You have still taken and reprinted someone else's ideas or language and failed to acknowledge that fact.

Plagiarism is a problem for several reasons:

- First, it is disrespectful. A plagiarist is saying that all the labor professors put into teaching students how to write a thoughtful college essay is a waste of time.

- Second, it is a betrayal of trust. When you hand in a paper, your professor accepts it as yours. If part of it is plagiarized, the professor will doubt your integrity.
- Third, it mocks the whole enterprise of literary criticism, which is about positioning original ideas in relation to the published ideas of others.

Finally, plagiarism usually does not work. Professors can recognize fairly easily that a paper was not written by one of their students, and they have the research skills to figure out where that paper came from.

Your professor understands that you are stressed out, busy, pressured to get decent grades, and not necessarily expert at managing your time. But your professor also does not see any of those circumstances as an excuse for plagiarizing. If you take your education seriously, do not even consider it.

Students occasionally plagiarize without realizing it. To avoid plagiarism, remind yourself of its most basic definition: any attempt to receive credit for written work that you didn't write. Bearing that in mind, be safe and cite everything you include *in any form* in your paper. Although putting something in your own words, or *paraphrasing*, may make it more original, it is not *fully* original, and therefore you must acknowledge its source. If a critic wrote, "John Updike is known for his often lurid tales of suburban lust," and you wrote in your paper, "John Updike is known for his tawdry tales of life in the suburbs," you *must* include a parenthetical citation, exactly as if you had reprinted every word of the quotation. In fact, this paraphrase is so close to the original version that it is unclear why you wouldn't include the quotation. To paraphrase without attribution is one of the most common forms of plagiarism, and many students think it is acceptable. However, it is still plagiarism.

Another common problem is that a writer forgets or misplaces the publication information for a source. You may find a quotation or a photocopied page among your research materials and you might have forgotten where it came from, or who wrote it. Each writer has to develop a method for keeping track of the bibliographic information of the sources he or she finds. Make sure that you write down all the bibliographic information as soon as you locate a source. You might write this down in a notebook or on an index card. You can also photocopy the articles you need and then write the bibliographic information on the first page of the photocopy. As long as your method is reliable and consistent, you will be in good shape.

Citing Sources

The following information is based on guidelines of the Modern Language Association (MLA). While this citation method may not be the only one you will be required to use in college, it is the most common system used in literature courses. Since different academic disciplines require different citation methods—footnotes, endnotes, bibliographies—simply follow the system of citation specified by your instructor. The information provided here is not comprehensive: your instructor might require a style manual in addition to this textbook.

The MLA updates its citation methods periodically. The method is not arbitrary: it is designed to make the text of the essay readable, with a minimum of cross checking between the body of the text and the sources cited at the bottom of a page or on another page (that is, footnotes or endnotes). The MLA has tried to streamline the process of citation so that the reader of a text is not distracted by an overabundance of information: the reader of an essay on literature wants to concentrate on what the author is saying. Within the body of a text, you are only required to provide the most basic information about a source in parentheses; you then give the full details on the **Works Cited** page at the end of your paper. If you mention the author and title of a source in your sentence, you only need to provide the page number in parentheses: for instance,

> In his book *A Trauma Artist*, Mark A. Heberle writes that "Vietnam was a disaster for many soldiers" (48).

In this example, note that the parentheses *follow* the quotation marks but *come before* the period. If you do not mention the author's last name in your sentence, you need to include it in the parentheses (Heberle 48). You do not need the word *page* or *P.* or *pp*. Your reader or professor understands that the number in the parentheses refers to a certain page and that if he or she wants to check, the quotation you cite can be found on page 48 of Heberle's book. The title, author, publisher, place of publication, and year of publication are all contained on your Works Cited page, explained below.

If you quote poetry, it is standard to refer to the *line numbers* of a poem in parentheses. Otherwise, the number within the parentheses is assumed to be a page number. These parentheses occur at the end of the sentence in which you quote from or summarize the work of another author. The parentheses follow the quotation marks (if it is a direct quotation) and precede the end of punctuation of your sentence.

To reiterate, within the text of your paper you do not need any footnotes or endnotes if you are using the MLA method; you do not need the word *page* or the letter *p* inside the parentheses. All bibliographic information occurs on your Works Cited page, which is the final page of your paper (usually its own page, separate from the body of your paper, though your instructor may specify otherwise). If your sentence clearly shows that the work is written by a certain author, you only need the page number in parentheses; if you do not make this clear, you need the last name of the author along with the page number (no comma separates them).

If you happen to have more than one work by the same author and your sentences do not make clear which work you are citing, you need to include a short word from the title of the work in parentheses. Let's say you are writing a sample paper on Tim O'Brien and you are including quotations from his books *Going after Cacciato* and *The Things They Carried*. If you quote from the second work in your paper, and if you make clear that O'Brien is the author of the quotation, the parentheses would say (*Things* 16). If you do not mention the author in your sentence, the parentheses would have to say (O'Brien, *Things* 16).

The Works Cited Page

This section of the chapter is based on the *MLA Handbook for Writers of Research Papers* (sixth edition) by Joseph Gibaldi (New York: Modern Language Association, 2003). This book will be especially helpful if you take literature classes beyond this introductory course: it contains comprehensive information about citation that goes well beyond what we can cover here, and it also extends our discussion of research and reviews the standards of grammar and punctuation.

Your Works Cited page appears at the end of your paper and lists all the sources you have used. Thus it positions you in a community of writers and critics by giving them access to your information and showing that you have support for what you say. If a reader wanted to verify that you had quoted accurately, the page number listed in parentheses would lead him or her to the exact page in your source. Finally, the Works Cited list is a quasi-legal document: if you forget to include it, you risk charges of plagiarism.

A Works Cited page is organized *alphabetically by the last names of the authors of individual works*. Each entry, with the exception of anonymous or Internet sources (discussed below), should begin with an author's or editor's last name.

Print Sources on the Works Cited Page

Books with One Author Book entries begin with the *author*, last name followed by first name. Next comes the *title*, then the *place of publication*, *name of publisher*, and *date of publication*. Place periods after the author's name and the title, as well as at the end of the entry. Place a colon after the place of publication and a comma after the name of the publisher. Take careful note of the way you punctuate these entries. Here's an example:

Hayles, N. Katherine. <u>How We Became Posthuman</u>. Chicago: U of Chicago P, 1999.

Books with Two or Three Authors If a book has more than one author, list the names in the same order they appear on the book's title page. The first author is listed last name first, and subsequent authors are listed in regular order. Example:

Baldwin, James, and Richard Avedon. <u>Nothing Personal</u>. New York: Atheneum, 1964.

Books with Four or More Authors If a book has more than three authors, list only the first author's name followed by "et al." (for *et alii*, which is Latin for "and others"). Example:

Lauter, Paul, et al. <u>The Heath Anthology of American Literature</u>. 5th ed. Boston: Houghton, 2006.

Translated Books If a book has a translator, list the author's name first, and include the translator's name, signified by the abbreviation "Trans." (for "Translated by") after the title. Example:

> Valenzuela, Luisa. Symmetries. Trans. Margaret Jull Costa. London: High Risk, 1998.

Edited Books Similarly, if an editor has published an edition of a work by another author, you include the editor's name, signified by "Ed." (for "Edited by") after the title. Example:

> Crafts, Hannah. The Bondwoman's Narrative. Ed. Henry Louis Gates, Jr. New York: Warner, 2002.

Anthologies The most common source for your Works Cited page in this class is the book you are holding in your hands, which is an anthology. An *anthology* is a book that collects works by many authors and frequently has one or more editors. To list a selection from an anthology, you need to include (1) the author and title of the individual selection, (2) the title of the anthology, (3) the editors and title of the anthology, (3) the city, publisher, and year of publication of the anthology, and (4) the page numbers of the individual work within the anthology. Here is the standard way to cite such entries in your list of works cited:

> Howells, William Dean. "Editha." Connections: Literature for Composition. Ed. Quentin Miller and Julie Nash. Boston: Houghton, 2008. 214–24.

Note that periods are used to end each element within the citation. The page numbers where the work can be found in the anthology go at the end of the entry.

Scholarly Journals An article in a scholarly journal is another common source. Again, the author's last name is the first part of the entry, followed by the article title, followed by the other publication information, which includes (in this case) the title of the periodical, the volume and number of the periodical, the date of the issue where you found the article (followed by a colon), and finally the pages of the article. Example:

> White, Ed. "Early American Nations as Imagined Communities." American Quarterly 56.1 (2004): 49–81.

The "56.1" in the above entry refers to the volume and number of this issue of *American Quarterly*.

Newspapers and Magazines An article in a newspaper or magazine might be useful in your research. The beginning of the entry is the same as for a journal: author's last name, first name, title of article, title of periodical. The final two parts of the entry are the date of publication and page numbers. Example:

Bandele, Asha. "I Need to Woman Up and Do This on My Own." New York Times 19 March 2006: 7.

Anonymous Works Occasionally the author's name of a work is not available. If a work is anonymous, use its title to organize it within the Works Cited page.

Electronic Sources on the Works Cited Page

Internet Sources While many Internet sources are anonymous, search for and list the author's name wherever possible. Electronic sources might also contain works you find on a CD-ROM, which are more likely to include authors' names. If you are using an Internet source, the URL (Web address) follows the other information you might include. You also need to include, if it is available, the most recent date the site was updated and the date you accessed the site. If you are writing a paper on John Updike and have found the Updike homepage, which is managed by James Yerkes and is titled *The Centaurian*, your entry would look like this:

Yerkes, James. The Centaurian. 28 Dec. 2007. 30 Dec. 2007 <http://userpages.prexar.com/joyerkes/>.

The second date is the date you accessed the site and is followed by the URL and a period. Since this is a personal site, the author's name is listed first. If the website you find is a collaborative site that is a scholarly project or a professional site, you would list the title of the site first and use the first word of the site to alphabetize this work within the Works Cited page. Example:

Voice of the Shuttle. Ed. Alan Liu. 10 March 2007. U of California, Santa Barbara. 3 April 2007 <http://vos.ucsb.edu/>.

Note that both of these entries contain the most recent date the website was updated followed by the date you accessed the site. On this second entry, the author has also included between those dates the name of the institution sponsoring the site. There are many authors on this site, so Alan Liu is named as the editor; James Yerkes is named as the author of the John Updike site because it is a personal site not sponsored by an institution. The URL is contained in angle brackets (< >). If you cannot find any of the required information (such as the website author's name), cite what you can find: alphabetize the entry by the title of the site, in that case, rather than by the author's last name.

CD-ROMs If you find a source on a CD-ROM in your library, begin with the author, followed by the article title, followed by the publication information for the print version (if one exists). The same information that follows an Internet source should then be included: the title of the site, the date of electronic publication or the last update, the name of the institution sponsoring the site (if any), the date you accessed the article, and the URL. Finally, you should include the vendor information if it is available.

If the source is only on a CD-ROM and does not contain a Web link, include as much bibliographic information as you have. Example:

> Magill, Frank N., ed. Masterplots Complete CD-ROM. Pasadena, CA: Salem P, 1997–.

Sample Works Cited Page

If you were to use all the sources listed above in your paper, here is what your Works Cited list would look like:

Works Cited

Baldwin, James, and Richard Avedon. Nothing Personal. New York: Atheneum, 1964.

Bandele, Asha. "I Need to Woman Up and Do This on My Own." New York Times 19 March 2006: 7.

Crafts, Hannah. The Bondwoman's Narrative. Ed. Henry Louis Gates, Jr. New York: Warner, 2002.

Hayles, N. Katherine. How We Became Posthuman. Chicago: U of Chicago P, 1999.

Howells, William Dean. "Editha." Connections: Literature for Composition. Ed. Quentin Miller and Julie Nash. Boston: Houghton, 2008. 214–24.

Lauter, Paul, et al. The Heath Anthology of American Literature. 5th ed. Boston: Houghton, 2006.

Magill, Frank N., ed. Masterplots Complete CD-ROM. Pasadena, CA: Salem P, 1997–.

Valenzuela, Luisa. Symmetries. Trans. Margaret Jull Costa. London: High Risk, 1998.

Voice of the Shuttle. Ed. Alan Liu. 10 March 2007. U of California, Santa Barbara. 3 April 2007 <http://vox.ucsb.edu/>.

White, Ed. "Early American Nations as Imagined Communities." American Quarterly 56.1 (2004): 49–81.

Yerkes, James. The Centaurian. 28 Dec. 2007. 30 Dec. 2007 <http://userpages.prexar.com/joyerkes/>.

In the following chapter, student George Scala takes us through his process of research culminating in his Works Cited page.

Chapter 11

A Step-by-Step Example of the Research Process

To illustrate the process of research described in Chapter 10, this chapter includes a sample paper by student author George Scala titled "'No Summer' for the Working Class: Rebecca Harding Davis and the Cohesion of Romantic and Realist Trends in 'Life in the Iron-Mills.'" His research log and research materials are also included.

George's research process and final paper are one model for research, but not the only one. Your instructor might want you to emphasize different types of sources from the ones George found, and your research paper might be either broader or narrower in scope. However, you can get some sense of how the process works, and, as in other chapters, you will have a sample essay to discuss in class.

George's primary text is Rebecca Harding Davis's story "Life in the Iron-Mills" (Chapter 16, "Industry and Idleness," page 1033). The story was published in the *Atlantic Monthly* in 1861 as the Civil War was beginning. The original audience of the story was probably middle class or upper middle class: magazine fiction was a popular genre in the mid-nineteenth century, and the *Atlantic Monthly*, published in Boston, was one of its most popular venues. You can see from the first few paragraphs of the story that the narrator is eager to invade the safe world of her readers. The literary movement known as *realism* that flourished during Davis's lifetime endeavored to ask difficult ethical questions of the reader without necessarily providing answers.

"Life in the Iron-Mills" raises provocative questions about work, art, social responsibility, religion, and immigration in America. George was asked to focus on realism and on the reality of ironworkers in the nineteenth century. However, he shaped his topic in accordance with what he discovered in his research and eventually focused on romanticism as well as realism. *Romanticism* was a popular mode of literature that flourished earlier in the nineteenth century than realism. Whereas realism emphasized social dilemmas and concrete details, romanticism emphasized personal experience and emotion. Davis's story is positioned somewhere between these movements.

To get the most out of this chapter, read Davis's "Life in the Iron-Mills" (page 1033), and then return to this chapter to see George's research log, copies of the articles he used, and his essay.

Nineteenth-century iron mill.

Research Log and Prewriting

Day 1

Looked over assignment sheet and notes that I took in the margin. Began brainstorming about topics (about one-half hour).

Began rereading Davis's story "Life in the Iron-Mills" (about one hour).

Day 2

Met with Professor Miller and discussed possible paper topics. He suggested ways to narrow the focus and further flesh out a working thesis (about twenty minutes).

Finished rereading "Life in the Iron-Mills" (about one hour).

Day 3

Used Suffolk's Sawyer Library webpage to do research and read some scholarly articles. I came across nine possibilities and will soon begin weeding out extraneous material (about an hour).

Freewriting (one-half hour). I tried to get some ideas out rather than producing a coherent section of the paper.

Day 4

Skimmed through the nine articles and decided that five would not help me in my final paper (one-half hour).

Close reading of the four remaining, more useful articles by Lasseter, Hesford, Hughes, and Silver (about two hours).

Day 5

Day off, but I thought about the project and even talked about my work with some friends. The name *research paper* is important to keep in mind, as I find that locating and evaluating sources and generally thinking about the topic/paper takes longer than the actual drafting process itself.

Day 6

Reviewed my notes and a few texts from a course that I took in literary theory; this provided me with two more sources (Brown and Cuddon) (about one hour).

Freewriting (one-half hour).

Day 7

Visited the Boston Public Library (Copley Branch) and found a useful text about Rebecca Harding Davis and her relationship to the rise of American realism (Harris's book *Rebecca Harding Davis and American Realism*). This may be my most valuable source. I also found a text that covers nineteenth-century American art that reminded me of an art history course I took three semesters ago (about one hour).

Freewriting (half an hour).

After looking through all of the information that I gathered, I began narrowing down a topic. Because Professor Miller gave me some leeway in this regard, I decided that the best way to choose a truly workable topic is to "work with what I've got." Rather than taking the tale at face value and doing a cut-and-dry textual analysis, I have decided that I would like to really examine issues and larger thematic concepts that surround the work itself. The themes of romanticism and realism seemed to be prevalent, in one way or another, in all of my sources. On further examination, the topic really seemed to come into focus and present itself.

Now that the topic is more concrete—"Life in the Iron-Mills" and its ties to romanticism and realism—I must eliminate the sources that will prove unhelpful for this particular assignment. Schocket's article is a clear example of an article that appeared to be quite interesting but ultimately proved to be extraneous.

After doing a close reading of Schocket's article, I realized that while it is interesting and quite cogent, it has very little to do with my proposed topic. While race relations and a subsequent "racial" reading of "Life in the Iron-Mills" is important to the world of scholarly criticism, it, again, will not enrich my paper. However, I should point out that the title of Schocket's article is somewhat deceiving: "'Discovering Some New Race': Rebecca Harding Davis's 'Life in the Iron-Mills' and the Literary Emergence of Working-Class Whiteness." Because the notion of class distinctions becomes such an important, central theme in "Life in the Iron-Mills," one would assume that this article would seriously enhance a reader's understanding of the idea of "class emergence"; yet the article thus becomes, quite literally, very "black and white."

Day 8

Off.

Day 9

Continued working on draft, now with my most applicable sources at hand.

Day 10

Again, I touched base with Professor Miller with some quick questions regarding the paper assignment. Also, I updated him with my progress thus far.

Continued working on draft.

Constructed a draft of the "works cited" page.

Days 11–14

Finished draft and "works cited" page.
Edited final draft.
Culminating discussion with Professor Miller.

Sources: Selected Criticism on Rebecca Harding Davis and "Life in the Iron-Mills"

Walter Hesford

From Literary Contexts of "Life in the Iron-Mills"

Rebecca Harding Davis's "Life in the Iron-Mills," published in the April, 1861 *Atlantic Monthly*, is the first notable work of fiction to concern itself with the life of the factory worker in an industrial American town.[1] In literary histories, the story is usually treated, if treated at all, as a forerunner or early example of American literary realism.[2] That it should receive such treatment is natural. Davis takes pains to initiate us into the knowledge of hitherto little acknowledged social realities; she seems a pioneer exploring a territory which, by the end of the nineteenth century, would be recognized as the new American wilderness. Yet the significance of "Life in the Iron-Mills" can better be appreciated, I think, by setting it in several other literary contexts: the achievement of Nathaniel Hawthorne, the writer to whom Davis owed most; the tradition of the social novel; the religious, apocalyptic bias of mid-nineteenth-century American literature. Set in these contexts, Davis's story comes to life not as a work which is admirable because it is almost realistic, but as a work which astonishes and informs its past and present readers because it shares in and extends the accomplishments of the romance.

In *Bits of Gossip*, a book of reminiscences, Davis recalls the world of romance she constructed as a child reading Bunyan and Scott in a tree-house.[3] One day

[1]Rebecca Harding Davis, "Life in the Iron-Mills," *Atlantic Monthly*, VII (April, 1861), 430–451. In 1972, Feminist Press (Old Westbury, New York), issued a reprint of the work, with a lengthy "Biographical Interpretation" by Tillie Olsen. For the sake of convenience, page references in the paper are to this reprint.

[2]See, for example, Arthur Hobson Quinn, *American Fiction* (New York, 1936), pp. 181–190; Robert E. Spiller and others, eds., *Literary History of the United States* (New York, 1960), pp. 880–881.

[3]Rebecca Harding Davis, *Bits of Gossip* (Boston, 1904), pp. 28–29.

she brought up into her private world a collection of "moral tales" for children, among which, she records,

> were two or three unsigned stories which I read over so often that I almost know every line of them by heart now. One was a story told by a town-pump, and another the account of the rambles of a little girl like myself, and still another a description of a Sunday morning in a quiet town like our sleepy village. There was no talk of enchantment in them. But in these papers the commonplace folk and things which I saw every day took on a sudden mystery and charm, and, for the first time, I found that they too belonged to the magic world of knights and pilgrims and fiends.[4]

Years later, when she discovered that the author of these tales was Hawthorne, Davis wrote a note of appreciation, which began a brief but substantial relationship.[5] What concerns us here is the life-long attraction Hawthorne's efforts held for Davis.

[4]Ibid., p. 30.

[5]Ibid., pp. 31–64. Tillie Olsen provides a perceptive commentary on this relationship. See "Biographical Interpretation," pp. 71, 89, 105–109. Olsen however, is apparently incorrect in suggesting that Hawthorne initiated the relationship because of his enthusiasm for "Life in the Iron-Mills."

Janice Milner Lasseter

From The Censored and Uncensored Literary Lives of "Life in the Iron-Mills"

Inasmuch as ye have done it unto one of the least of these, ye have done it unto me.
—Mitchell, quoting Jesus (Matt. 25.36; Davis, *Life in the Iron-Mills*)

Rebecca Blaine Harding (not yet Davis) must have been a bit dismayed when she read her first published story, *Life in the Iron-Mills*,[1] in its April 1861 *Atlantic Monthly* form. An entire paragraph had been excised from the manuscript (holograph) she had submitted in 1860.[2] When in 1972 Tillie Olsen reprinted *Life in the Iron-Mills*, she naturally used the *Atlantic Monthly* text, since she found it "in one of three water-stained, coverless volumes of bound *Atlantic Monthlys* . . . in an Omaha junkshop" (157). Ticknor and Fields published a new version of the story in an 1865 collection of fiction from the *Atlantic Monthly*.[3] Olsen's reprint and Cecelia Tichi's 1997 edition were both based on the *Atlantic*'s version of the story. Neither Olsen nor Tichi indicate awareness of the 1865 text. This 1865 version restores the substance of the holograph paragraph in two paragraphs, rather than one. The holograph and the 1865 texts contain Davis's full artistic

[1]Since the story has been published both as a story in a magazine and as a monograph, I am using italics for each mention of the title.

[2]This item is reproduced by permission of The Huntington Library, San Marino, California, FI 1170.

[3]The revised version, with identical content, appears in two separate collections. Throughout this essay I will refer to this version as the 1865 revision.

vision, though the holograph is the superior text. It offers internal coherence to the story and is stylistically superior—more poetic, more technically accurate, and less effusive and declamatory—than the 1865 version of the story which, nonetheless, surpasses the *Atlantic Monthly* text.

Because the story we have been reading is truncated, we have not been able to understand fully Davis's view of social justice. An examination of the various literary lives of *Life in the Iron-Mills* explains the way the publishing business attempted to mediate the vast social reform theories abounding in the mid-nineteenth century, including Davis's, and also discloses the "secret . . . that has lain dumb for centuries," the "terrible dumb question" at the heart of the story (13–14).[4] The holograph version and, less effectively, the 1865 text target the Evangelical Protestant church as the primary social institution which had failed at what she believed was its most elemental task—to allow "brotherly love" to inhere in the church and then suffuse American culture, thereby eliminating poverty.[5] Were that vision to be realized, the Evangelical Protestant Church would become the instrument of humanitarian reform needed to moderate an industrial, capitalist economy that was running amuck. If the "Christian" nation were genuinely to enact Christian charity in public policy, the American dream would be available to one and all.

[4]All quotations from the *Atlantic Monthly* version of the story are taken from Olsen's 1972 edition and are cited in the text solely by page numbers.

[5]Beth Maclay Doriani has argued much the same about the 1861 version. Davis's reform impulse, Doriani posits, may be traced to Jonathan Edwards's definition of "true virtue."

Andrew Silver

From "Unnatural Unions": Picturesque Travel, Sexual Politics, and Working-Class Representation in "A Night under Ground" and "Life in the Iron-Mills"

On December 19, 1860, the *Atlantic Monthly* arrived in Rebecca Harding Davis's hometown of Wheeling, West Virginia, including among its offerings a story entitled "A Night under Ground," an erotically charged picturesque travel narrative detailing one woman's liberating descent into the Cornish copper-mines of Michigan. "A Night under Ground," like most picturesque narratives routinely offered to readers in magazines like *Harper's*, the *Atlantic*, and *Putnam's Monthly*, only nominally concerns itself with working-class miners, instead using a site of working-class labor to provide a remarkable fantasy of escape for middle-class readers. Soon after the publication of "A Night under Ground," Davis sent her own story of the Cornish industrial working class to the *Atlantic Monthly*. Though "A Night under Ground" and "Life in the Iron-Mills" share many strikingly similar elements—both narratives portray five members of the upper-class traveling to an industrial site for business and amusement, both narratives have these travelers encounter and become briefly fascinated with one separate and unique working-class Cornish man, both narratives begin by employing elaborate metaphors of rivers as slaves, and both conclude with striking images of the dawn—the narratives could not be further apart as investigations of working-class sites and subjectivities. While "A Night under Ground" embodies the subjective and ahistorical concerns of the mid-nineteenth-century picturesque, Rebecca Harding Davis's "Life in the Iron-Mills" represents one of the first American critiques of the picturesque, arguing against the romanticization—and increasing eroticization—of the poor in picturesque narratives, contrasting upper-class tourists' mobility with the immobility of the working-class poor, and finally offering a new picturesque aesthetic that envisions a world in which the poor, rather than the rich, get to experience the newly moral edification of picturesque travel.

The picturesque, a loosely defined genre that first emerged in eighteenth-century landscape painting and was quickly popularized by hordes of middle-class tourists, has exerted a continuous influence upon literature, tourism, public parks and social reform policies since its birth in the desultory writings of landscape aesthetes in eighteenth-century England. That tourists still dutifully seek out ruined castles and collapsing barns, still delight in snapping photographs of quaintly decayed older urban vistas, and still continue to seek refuge from overdeveloped urban areas by traveling to seemingly wild open parks like Atlanta's Piedmont Park or New York's Central Park is a testament to the largely invisible influence of the picturesque. In the more than two hundred years since its birth, definitions of the picturesque have been as polymorphous as its influence. First embraced by a variety of landscape aesthetes and tourists in eighteenth-century England, the picturesque aesthetic arose in opposition to the uniform compositional elements that contribute to the aesthetic pleasures of the Burkean "sublime." Picturesque theorists argued that aesthetes and tourists should seek out aesthetic irregularity or ruggedness, refusing overarching displays of unified compositional authority, and allowing the spectator's eye instead to revel in the ironically playful associations of unlike and often fragmented elements. Rather than touring the continent in search of expansive, awe-inspiring vistas supplied by mountains, oceans, or meticulously ordered palatial gardens, the picturesque tourist turned to England's ruined abbeys, hilltop huts, and unenclosed parks for aesthetic inspiration.[1]

Produced by the leisured middle and upper classes in an increasingly industrialized Europe, the eighteenth-century picturesque studiously avoids squalid scenes of urban poverty and newly enclosed agrarian country-sides, returning its audiences to the pleasurable wild vistas and romanticized poverty of an earlier feudal era unmarked by modernization. The picturesque's geographic displacement finds its human correlative in the displacement of often impoverished rural figures, transformed by the highly metaphoric imagination of the picturesque

[1]For my discussion of the picturesque, I am indebted especially to the following works: Andrews, "The Metropolitan Picturesque"; Barrell, "Visualizing the Division of Labour"; Bermingham, *Landscape and Ideology* and "The Picturesque and Ready-to-Wear Femininity"; Copley, "William Gilpin and the Black-Lead Mine"; Michasiw, "Nine Revisionist Theses on the Picturesque"; and Price, "The Picturesque moment."

traveler into mythic figures of an idealized past and, in the transformation, rendered more acceptable objects for upper-class fantasy. Picturesque artists were especially fond of including rugged gypsies in their narratives, attracted by their status as pre-industrial wanderers and exiles from the quotidian pressures of commerce. William Gilpin, the foremost eighteenth-century picturesque theorist, recommends that pupils of picturesque landscape painting "deck thy scene / with figures suited to its style," even if this means expurgating actual figures altogether. "If rocky, wild, and awful, be thy views," he muses, "Low arts of husbandry exclude: The spade, / The plough, the patient angler with his rod, / Be banish'd thence; far other guests invite, / Wild as those scenes themselves, banditti fierce, / And gipsey-tribes, not merely to adorn, / But to impress that sentiment more strong, / Awak'd already by the savage-scene" (*Three Essays* 20). The kaleidoscopic displays of metaphoric virtuosity in picturesque texts—here farmers metamorphose into gypsies and fishermen into banditti—fragment any narrative outside the aesthete's own creative consciousness of the world, loosening the claims of historical reality upon upper-class imagination and, by banishing signs of contemporary poverty from the picturesque gaze, opening tabooed sources of visual pleasure in unconventional scenes and subjects. Ann Bermingham links the picturesque with a recovery of middle-class masculinity through the dominating "scopophilic gaze," arguing that the picturesque eye is not only "an aestheticizing eye, but a fetishising one as well" ("Picturesque" 92). Any sign of utility or the exploitive working conditions that accompany working-class labor would interrupt the picturesque text's wilful suspension of the real and so destroy the fantasy of domination at the heart of the picturesque. The picturesque eye, Gilpin explains, is "disgusted" by the "unnatural union" between working-class labor and upper-class picturesque fantasy; his phrase, normally reserved for sexual transgression, hints at the erotically enlivening spectacle of the working-class in these narratives, a voyeuristic fantasy which can only be indulged if properly displaced by the imagination of upper-class aesthetes.

By the mid-nineteenth century, when the presence of industrial work became an unavoidable feature of even rural life, the widely popular picturesque tour turned its objectifying eye on novel sites of working-class labor; recasting industrial work as pre-industrial play and transforming anonymous mechanized industry into ruggedly individualistic masculine sport.[2] Such displaced narratives of working-class industry became a staple of the mid-nineteenth-century American picturesque, providing a potent antidote to the constraints of urban middle-class life and transforming great anxieties about systemic industrialization and the discontent of working-class masses into subjective narratives of individual middle-class pleasure. The Missouri iron industry, in one picturesque narrative, becomes the "boyish sport" of "so many frolicsome demons stirring up the fires of Tartarus" ("Visit" 299–300); copper miners, in another narrative, are "wild

[2]"At the end of the eighteenth century," Andrews writes, "the picturesque was founded largely on the aesthetics of poverty, neglect, and decay. By the middle of the nineteenth century, in the great cities, such a taste was hard to indulge. Poverty was on one's doorstep, not loitering at the boundary of one's country estate" (287).

people" from Pandemonium (Smith 173); and lumbermen, in another picturesque tour, become "true worshiper[s] in the temple of the forest" likened to "copper-faced" Indians—the American equivalent of Gilpin's pre-industrial gypsies (Hallock 439). Workers in a newly industrial American economy, now favorably compared to effete members of the educated and idle urban bourgeoisie, become embodiments of an almost mythical masculine prowess for picturesque writers—Dionysian beings reminiscent of a pre-industrial age in which men were free and one with nature, even in the midst of intense and refreshingly perilous labor. "Picturesque variety and individuality," Malcolm Andrews explains of the mid-nineteenth-century picturesque, "was thought to have survived only outside the culturally dominant middle classes, and particularly amongst the poorer classes, where there were apparently no such homogenising cultural constraints" (287). Unlike the "irksome," "habitual," "shriveled," and sheltered life of the middle-class, industrial work in these middle-class fantasies is transformed into the "thrilling" and "exciting," "worship" of wildness, and working-class lives are themselves transformed into an extended "holiday," a "paradise"—an existence freer than "the flight of the eagle or the bound of the deer" (Hallock 439). The commodity value of the picturesque narrative comes from the transformation of working-class industry into middle-class pleasure, working-class routine into middle-class novelty, working-class immobility into middle-class liberation. "I am not certain but I might conscientiously recommend the 'Mine Holes' as a cheap summer resort" (Smith 171), one picturesque tourist concludes, his analogy bringing picturesque objectification to its logical conclusion by recasting mining life as an appealing antidote to the emasculating routine of white-collar work.

References

Andrews, Malcolm. "The Metropolitan Picturesque." Copley and Garside, *The Politics of the Picturesque* 282–98.

Barrell, John. "Visualizing the Division of Labour: William Pyne's Microcosm." *The Birth of Pandora and the Division of Knowledge*. By Barrell. London: Macmillan, 1992. 89–118.

Bermingham, Ann. *Landscape and Ideology: The English Rustic Tradition, 1740–1860*. Berkeley: U of California P, 1986.

———. "The Picturesque and Ready-to-Wear Femininity." Copley and Garside, *The Politics of the Picturesque* 81–119.

Copley, Stephen. "William Gilpin and the Black-Lead Mine." Copley and Garside, *The Politics of the Picturesque* 42–61.

Copley, Stephen, and Peter Garside, eds. *The Politics of the Picturesque: Literature, Landscape and Aesthetics since 1770*. Cambridge: Cambridge UP, 1994.

Gilpin, William. *Three Essays: On Picturesque Beauty; on Picturesque Travel; and on Sketching Landscape*. London: R. Blamire, 1962.

Hallock, Charles. "Life among the Loggers." *Harper's Monthly Magazine* 20 (1860): 437–54.

Michasiw, Kim Ian. "Nine Revisionist Theses on the Picturesque." *Representations* 38 (1992): 76–100.

Price, Martin. "The Picturesque Moment." *From Sensibility to Romanticism: Essays Presented to Frederick A. Pottle.* Ed. Frederick W. Hilles and Harold Bloom. New York: Oxford UP, 1965. 259–92.

Sheila Hassell Hughes

From Between Bodies of Knowledge There Is a Great Gulf Fixed: A Liberationist Reading of Class and Gender in "Life in the Iron-Mills"

Critics have recognized Rebecca Harding Davis's "Life in the Iron-Mills" as "radical"—calling it "a startling new experiment in literature and a pioneering document in American literature's transition from romanticism to realism."[1] Davis's tale was first published in the April 1861 issue of the *Atlantic Monthly*, during a period variously identified as Victorian, Romantic, or Sentimental.[2] By the time of the Civil War, after Transcendentalism's heyday and before the rise of the Social Gospel Movement, the popular moral ethos was something of a stew. If the roots of Puritan orthodoxy had been pretty much boiled away, and the orthopraxis emphasized by the social gospellers was yet to appear, then right feeling, or "orthosentimentum" was the distinguishing flavor. The mix still betrayed ingredients of Puritan and Romantic notions of individualism, intuition, and symbolism, but was now accompanied by a generous new dose of social conservatism. Distasteful hints of doctrine were sweetened by just the right amount of religious feeling. The radical utopian attempts of the Transcendentalists had been buried, but their view of the self as emotional subject lived on in Romantics such as Whitman, and was appropriated in the sentimentalism of popular culture as well.[3]

In this context, the bleak, gritty story of industrial laborers and capitalists emerged not only as anomalous, but also as antagonistic to Romantic and sentimental literary modes. Davis's voice is one of confrontation against what Ann C. Rose characterizes as the prevailing "mood of acquiesence to the ills of industrial capitalism, mixed with pride in its visible achievements."[4] Since conservative literary forms are complicit in this acquiesence, Davis's rejection judges them as well.

Scholars have generally found it difficult to reconcile Davis's radical form with the religious, specifically Christian, features of her tale. Two critics who have attempted to address this tension come to quite different conclusions. Sharon Harris reads the work as a critique of "passive Christianity," but her study of irony fails to address adequately the remaining constructive or stubbornly spiritual elements of "Life in the Iron-Mills."[5] William H. Shurr, on the other hand, reads the story as a conversion narrative. While his approach highlights more of the ambiguities in Davis's religious rhetoric, it depends upon a dichotomy between the political and the spiritual which does not do full justice to Davis's text either.[6] Harris's reading emphasizes the text's religious elements as an aspect of form that the political content ironically undoes, whereas Shurr tends to undermine the social aspects of the tale through his religious form criticism.

The challenge which remains, then, is to read Davis's novella in a way that takes seriously both its sociopolitical and religious critique as well as its spiritual vision. Because "Life in the Iron-Mills" begs to be read toward both political and personal transformation, it does not neatly categorize as realist, reformist, or religious. I will argue instead that the principle of "liberation" opens up the complexities of Davis's text in unique ways. The biblical cry for liberation can be heard in Davis's novella, which also prefigures developments by twentieth-century theologians in other contexts of class, race, and gender oppression. I will thus attempt a "religious reading"[7] which allows for the interplay and intertextuality of the political and spiritual, the critical and visionary in Davis's text—a tale that is radically political yet particularly Christian in its lineage and historical trajectory.

The story of one tragic night in the life of an iron mill laborer forms the core of Davis's "Life in the Iron-Mills." Hugh Wolfe is a Welsh immigrant who carves images in the scrap-iron "korl." His cousin Deb, gnarled and hunchbacked from her own labor in a cotton mill, harbors a secret love for Hugh, who is grateful for her domestic care but repulsed by her disfigurement. On the night in question, several bourgeois visitors appear to inspect the mill where Hugh is working and where Deb, having brought his dinner, now lies sleeping in a pile of ash. One of the visitors, Mitchell, is startled by a mysterious female figure in the dark, which turns out to be one of Hugh's statues. Mitchell's keen aesthetic sense is touched, and he is mesmerized by the groping, wolfish woman with hungry eyes. Wolfe is identified as the artist, and the two men discuss the meaning of the figure. Later, when Hugh is bemoaning the unbridgeable distance between his own state and Mitchell's, Deb reveals that she has stolen the visitor's wallet in order to help Hugh escape drudgery. Dismayed, Hugh sets out to return the money, but has an aesthetic epiphany at a church along his way and determines to follow Deb's plan after all. Soon, both Hugh and Deb are imprisoned. Having sunk lower still, Hugh is inconsolable, untouched by either the curious Mitchell's unhelpful visit or Deb's whispers from the next cell. He takes his life by carving into his own veins with the artist's tool. A Quaker woman visits the prison and rescues Deb, however, taking her away to live among green hills, where they bury Hugh.

Thirty years after the events of Hugh's demise, someone has returned to the house where the Wolfes rented cellar rooms. Tapping idly on the inside of a second-storey window pane, the mysterious stranger tells this story, asking readers if they can imagine life amid the grime below. The tale of one man's life, presented as a question itself, is meant to answer the inquiry. Having told Hugh's story, the narrator becomes self-conscious again, and we discover that the korl figure has been preserved and stands near the narrator, in a corner of her/his library. Its groping hand, it seems, now points to the east and "the promise of Dawn" (65).

Davis's "startlingly new experiment" is pioneering in its realism, but it relies on an ancient source: in her own words, time, place, and perspective, Davis retells the gospel parable of Lazarus and the rich man. She appropriates the parable for her own apparently secular purposes—a demythification and desentimentalizing of the rising capitalism—and reshapes and seemingly subverts it in the process. Both the genre of parable and the content of this particular parable, however, actually suit her ends well.

The content of the story is quite clearly a reworking of the original parable. In the original (Luke 16:19–31), the crippled beggar, Lazarus, is laid at the gates of a rich man, who passes him daily without even the slightest charity of longed-for crumbs. Only dogs, a sign of contamination, attend the beggar, licking his open sores.[8] When the two men die, angels carry Lazarus to Abraham's side, where he is comforted, but the rich man goes to Hell, where he looks up at Lazarus and cries to Abraham for pity.[9] The patriarch explains that Lazarus cannot be sent to "dip the tip of his finger in water and cool [the man's] tongue," because between them and him "there is a great gulf fixed" (Luke 16:24–26). Neither can Lazarus be sent back to warn the rich man's brothers—if they will not listen to Moses and the prophets, they certainly will not listen to one risen from the dead.

Many of these elements abide in Davis's version. The poor "dogged" Wolfe (who is left to lick his own wounds) and the rich capitalist Mitchell eye each other across a "great gulf never to be passed. Never!" (30). The tormenting inferno is the iron mill, whose demonic machines are alternatively "gods in pain" and "wild beasts" devouring their victims (19, 31). Its smoke rises continually, like the "eternal fire prepared for the devil" and for those who saw the Son of Man thirsty and "gave [him] nothing to drink" (Matthew 26:41–42). That the visiting capitalists invoke Dante to describe the scene at the mill only draws attention to the original biblical sources of both his and Davis's imagery. In addition, the specific forms of pain of both biblical characters appear in "Life in the Iron-Mills," conflated in the korl statue—drowning in fire and mad with hunger. The crucial plot development of Davis's version also reflects the parable. In both stories one man is judged and incarcerated while the other is set or remains free. Although, in her tale, the other man's visit is superficially achieved, it is just as ineffectual in fact, and the great gulf of class remains fixed. Finally, Abraham's bosom appears in the nineteenth-century version as the green hills of peace, to which the Quaker "angel" eventually carries the poor man's body.

What is most fascinating about this version however, is not the number of parallels to its biblical source, but the way in which these elements are inverted and subverted. Indeed, Davis reconfigures and reverses more than just the ultimate inversion. "Life in the Iron-Mills" essentially begins in hell, and descends through all its manifestations: from the dark cellar where the laborer lives, to the "city of fires" where he works, to the prison cell where he dies on his pallet, bleeding and "ironed," denied the freedom of the street-dog he envies (20, 51). The gates of the rich appear only briefly, as the gothic church in the middle of the tale, and they are the site of Hugh Wolfe's testing, not of the capitalist's (48–49). Mitchell enters this realm by descending into Hugh's torment—seeming to cross the gulf. Perhaps he will cool the suffering man's parched tongue. The drop of water he offers is neither a moment of physical refreshment, nor the hope of eternal life, however, but the tantalizing taste of cultural refinement and ethereal beauty. Hugh is blessed with the tip of a gentleman's hat instead of the watery tip of a saint's finger. And when Mitchell descends again, to visit the convict in prison, he grants no freeing pardon; he comes out of curiosity, not generosity.

Notes

1. Sharon M. Harris, *Rebecca Harding Davis and American Literary Realism* (Philadelphia, 1991): 56, and "Rebecca Harding Davis: From Romanticism to Realism," *American Literary Realism* 21 (Winter 1989): 4, respectively.
2. Ann Douglas identifies the American Victorian era as 1820–1875 in *The Feminization of American Culture* (New York, 1977); Harris, "Rebecca Harding Davis," 4; Douglas, *Feminization of American Culture*, 6.
3. For Transcendentalism, see Anne C. Rose, *Transcendentalism as a Social Movement, 1830–1850* (New Haven, Conn., 1981), vii–xi, 38–41; for Sentimentalism, see Douglas, *Feminization of American Culture*, intro.; for Romanticism, see Harris, "Rebecca Harding Davis."
4. Rose, *Transcendentalism as a Social Movement*, xi.
5. Harris, *Rebecca Harding Davis and American Literary Realism*, 50.
6. William H. Shur, "*Life in the Iron Mills:* A Nineteenth-Century Conversion Narrative," *American Transcendental Quarterly* 5 (Dec. 1991): 245–57. Shurr argues here that the bourgeois Mitchell is "an early convert to a kind of vague but intensely personal Christian utopianism" (250), which is more religious that either socialist (252) or social (254). He concludes that Mitchell is, in fact, the tale's anonymous narrator. As my discussion of both conversion and the political will show, I find this proposal untenable.
7. I draw here on Robert Detweiler's definition and exploration of religious reading as "indulg[ing] the pleasures of others" and otherness itself in the text, and his emphasis on "the irreducibility of form" in Detweiler, *Breaking the Fall: Religious Readings of Contemporary Fiction* (San Francisco, 1991): 126–27, 44.
8. Eduard Schweizer, *The Good News According to Luke*, trans. John Drury (Maryknoll, N.Y., 1984), 261.
9. "Hades" in Greek. Schweizer states: "In the Bible, the 'underworld' is never hell but the place of the dead awaiting judgment. . . . [B]eing with Abraham . . . on the other hand, describes a final state of peace" (Schweizer, *Good News*, 261). Whether or not the rich man's condition is eternal, it is depicted as one of suffering.

Notes and Quotations

Since George continuously revised on his computer, we have no drafts of his work, but here are some notes he took while researching:

Harris:

"Two factors in Davis's personal life forever changed her vision of what the function and form of literature should be: first, being raised in a rapidly growing mill town, and second, experiencing first hand the brutal realities of war." (Harris 1)

"Davis was a realist in that she insisted upon reporting quotidian American life, abandoning the 'rose-tinted' and homogenous perspective of that life and rendering her material so as to give her readers an illusion of actual experience; and further, she rejected many aspects of romanticism. . . ." (6)

"Davis synthesized many of these styles, most often using techniques of both romanticism and sentimentalism (as traditionally defined) to draw readers into stories wherein the realities of quotidian life were of primary significance; and she often insisted on a moral perspective, although not one defined by a particular religion." (7)

At seminary: she studied geometry, literature, music, and drawing, and even took courses in evidences of Christianity.

Avid interest in local history

Washington Female Seminary in Washington, Pennsylvania. (23)

"Later, Rebecca would become a newspaper correspondent, by becoming a contributing editor to the <u>New York Daily Tribune</u> and <u>The Independent</u>." (25)

Father's public involvement allowed her access to leading citizens in Wheeling. (24)

"Davis's inclusion of immigrants in her depiction of the mill town, and especially Irish immigrants, is a significant element of realism. Between 1815 and 1865, approximately five million immigrants had entered the United States." (30)

"Hugh also, even unwittingly, 'sees' the potential in the refuse to be remodeled. It is the same technique Davis suggests for re-shaping the lives of these victims who are the 'refuse' of industry: whittle away their filth and their silence and they become 'sometimes strangely beautiful.'" (36)

<u>Hughes:</u>

"Because 'Life in the Iron-Mills' begs to be read toward both political and personal transformation, it does not neatly categorize as realist, reformist, or religious." (113)

Biblical interpretation—Lazarus 114 parable, etc.

"This nineteenth-century fiction seeks to engage its audience—to question, test, perhaps accuse—in a biblically parabolic way." (115)

". . . requires the hearer's participation in it and aims at transforming the audience along with the fictive events, so the narrator of 'Life in the Iron-Mills' addresses the audience directly and invites imaginary participation—as a means to social reidentification rather than mere sentimental sympathy." (119)

"The text thus confronts its readers with a literary realism that threatens a radical personal and social import. It invites them/us to do something more than to hear or observe." (121)

"Davis's task is to pierce the privileged blindness of her audience with the intense and painful vision of her subjects—to do more than mark the upper-storey window-pane with grime from the streets below." (124)

Hugh—"he is torn between realism and romantic escape"

<u>Silver:</u>

"Though still immensely popular in the late 1850s and early 1860s, attempts to bring rural picturesque aesthetics to bear upon industrial sites came under increasing suspicion and scrutiny by authors and critics concerned especially with the cultural effects of popular representations of urban poverty." (Silver, 104)

Replaces "romanticized" idyllic view of urban scenarios.

Allows a certain distance . . .

<u>Lasseter:</u>

"Apprenticed to the newspaper's [<u>Wheeling Interpreter</u>] editor Archibald Campbell and later as the paper's assistant editor, Rebecca Harding had engaged professionally numerous utopian initiatives associated with a nascent socialism." (177)

A call to arms, but less abrasive than nonfiction works like this . . .

"unless we read this sentence as ironic, as does Harris, or parabolic, as does Doriani, we must conclude that Davis has tricked us into expecting general social reform, only to learn that the drastic reform needed to save the poor will happen not on earth, but in eternity." (180)

<u>Hesford:</u>

Is the first notable work of fiction to concern itself with the life of the factory worker in an industrial American town. (71)

"The narrator, though secluded above the crowd she observes from her window, shares with the crowd, with the men and women who work in the iron-mills, the stifling air, the stifling environment. Implicitly, she shares the life of those who concern her, who will concern us." (72)

"'Life in the Iron-Mills' evolves its significance, its evaluations and revelation, through a work of art." (75)

Both drawing from realist artistic style and also the idea of the unitarian artist, yet born with his artistic ability.

"Fiction 'with a purpose' and fictions which address the 'problem' or 'condition' of the working class are bound to introduce the reader to a certain quantity of socio-economic reality, which is the province of literary realism. Such literature, in probing the *meaning* of apprehended reality, in rendering resolutions, often reveals its affinity to the ideology and form of the romance." (76)

I however disagree. (77)

"Wolfe, however, like other working-class protagonists, only symbolically participates in the triumph implicit in the romantic resolution, in the promise of the countryside, of the dawn." (80)

Final Draft

Student Essay

A recent graduate of Suffolk University, George Scala III holds his BA in English literature and art history. In addition to his scholarly pursuits, he is an avid fiction writer and musician and works as an actor throughout the New England area. He also enjoys working out and playing tennis during the summer months. He is currently earning a master's degree in English at Northeastern University and eventually plans to earn his PhD. He hopes to teach literature and drama at the college level.

Scala 1

George A. Scala III

Professor Miller

English 101

7 April 2006

"No Summer" for the Working Class: Rebecca Harding Davis and the Cohesion of Romantic and Realist Trends in "Life in the Iron-Mills"

Since its first publication in an 1861 edition of The Atlantic Monthly, Rebecca Harding Davis's story "Life in the Iron-Mills" has

Scala 2

perplexed readers as it carefully straddles two apparently polar literary genres: romanticism and realism. Yet Harding (still using her maiden name before her marriage to L. Clarke Davis in 1863) stood at this dividing line and satisfactorily managed to create a work of literature that blends both romantic and realist elements.

Though the work calls for action to be taken directly by those who would have originally read it, the author cultivates this message not through the somewhat abrasive "news-article" approach that might be expected but through the medium of a short story, complete with a limited number of well-drawn and pathos-evoking characters. By using a romantic literary (and artistic) framework in which journalistic themes are addressed, Harding simultaneously holds the attention of her readers through fiction and allows the work's undeniable undertone of the unfair treatment and harsh lives of the mid-nineteenth-century working class to surface.

Though the terms "romanticism" and "realism" are quite broad with regard to their respective literary meanings, fundamental stylistic elements from each genre combine to make "Life in the Iron-Mills" a hybrid—both fictitious and moralizing. To use critic Sharon Harris's words, "Davis synthesized . . . these styles to draw readers into stories wherein the realities of quotidian life were of primary significance" (7). While literary romanticism arguably has a history that extends back much further than that of realism, by the late nineteenth century, the movement that takes as its main concern the truthful portrayal of contemporary life became the "main trend in fiction" (Cuddon 761). Furthermore, Cuddon reminds us that "realist novelists paid particular attention to exact documentation, to getting the facts right" (731).

Although the realist movement in literature and art began in France during the early to mid-1800s, American writers like Rebecca Harding Davis quickly adopted the realist mindset—most say because of increased industrialization and the state of the country around the time of the Civil War. Additionally, in 1848, the world saw the first

Scala 3

printing of Marx and Engels's Communist Manifesto, a work that ultimately called for a classless society, attainable only through the working class's willingness to revolt and overthrow the "oppressor of his [Marx's] own day, capitalists or bourgeoisie" (Hornstein 446).

One might wonder why Davis would ever concern herself with the conditions of poor workers, as she was born into a fairly well-off family and lived a middle-class lifestyle. She attended the Washington Female Seminary in Washington, Pennsylvania, where she developed a strong literary background, thus leading her to work as a newspaper correspondent in and around her hometown and as a contributing editor to both the New York Daily Tribune and The Independent (Harris 25).

However, Davis may have specifically been drawn to the idea of literature serving a moral purpose because she was "raised in a rapidly growing mill town" (Harris 1), where she undoubtedly saw the effects of working-class living firsthand. After all, "Life in the Iron-Mills" stands as "the first notable work of fiction to concern itself with the life of the factory worker in an industrial American town" (Hesford 71).

Hughes reminds us that because "'Life in the Iron-Mills' begs to be read toward both political and personal transformation, it does not neatly categorize as realist, reformist, or religious" (113). Though present-day literary critics sometimes attempt to compartmentalize individual works and view them through a single filter at a time, Davis's piece can be fully understood only when one accepts that she had to draw from many pools of inspiration to create a work with a romantic storyline and realist message. Modern distinctions (Marxist, feminist, cultural, historical, etc.) did not exist during the 1860s as they do today. The concepts, though present within (and necessary to understand) the text, precede the terminology.

However, because of its subject matter, as it essentially evokes issues of class, a "red flag" (no pun intended) should pop up in our minds, thus prompting us to address its Marxist undertone. At first glance, one may attempt to argue that a Marxist reading of "Life in

Scala 4

the Iron-Mills" is not possible because the work deals with a select number of main characters. In general, Marxist thought tends to shift focus from "the individual to the society" (Hornstein 447). However, on further examination, a careful reader will soon find that Marxist literary criticism "interprets writers in the light of their class origins and judges them chiefly by their attitude toward 'class struggle'" (Hornstein 447): "Life in the Iron-Mills" transcends mere fiction and assumes a didactic responsibility by "[inviting] us to do something more than to hear or observe" (Hughes 121).

Davis takes us on a journey of sorts, literally down into another place, somewhere unfamiliar and certainly out of our own sphere. We observe not only another locale, but another entire class itself: "Their lives were like those of their class: incessant labor, sleeping in kennel-like rooms, eating rank pork and molasses, drinking—God and the distillers only know what; with an occasional night in jail to atone for some drunken excess. Is that all of their lives?" (1162).

The message seems simple enough: a working-class life is nothing short of arduous. Throughout the rest of the story, Davis gives factual evidence regarding the population of the unnamed town, again establishing an overall sense of verisimilitude, perhaps to her own hometown of Wheeling, West Virginia.[1]

Nevertheless, Davis does not overwhelm the reader with sheer facts and details, clearly knowing that doing so would result in a general lack of interest in her story and, therefore, her attempts to reveal an austere social problem. Accordingly, most all scholarly criticism done on "Life in the Iron-Mills" at some point attempts to dissect the beginning of the tale itself and the reasons why Harding

[1]One "significant element of realism," neatly pointed out by Harris, can be found in Davis's choice to include immigrants (especially Irish) because "between 1815 and 1865, approximately five million immigrants had entered the United States" (30).

Scala 5

would have set up her novella in such a way. Right from the start, the omniscient yet detached narrator grabs hold of the reader and thrusts him or her into the story's central plot, that of "a furnace tender in one of Kirby & John's rolling-mills,—Hugh Wolfe" (1161). The reader can more fully see the problems that members of the working class had to face because Davis's characters are so three-dimensional. For example, in order for her work to function as a work of fiction, Davis individualizes Hugh's character by giving him an artistic soul underneath his rough exterior. Though Hugh "spent [his time] hewing and hacking with his blunt knife" (1166), we as readers are not to assume that all iron-workers moonlight as sculptors.

Davis is indeed asking us to align our sympathies with <u>all</u> members of the working class; she succeeds in creating a call for social reform that manifests itself through individual figures who represent larger groups in society, thus making for a better, easier to absorb, work of fiction. As industrialization swept over America during the nineteenth century, skilled labor and craftsmen were quickly replaced by those simply needing to work to live. He is not the artist of the patronage system; he is the artist "inborn," indulging only in his need to create so that his soul can endure:

> In the neighboring furnace-buildings lay great heaps of the refuse from the ore after the pig-metal is run. Korl we call it here: a light, porous substance,of a delicate, waxen, flesh-colored tinge. Out of the blocks of this korl, Wolfe, in his off-hours from the furnace, had a habit of chipping and moulding [sic] figures . . . hideous, fantastic enough, but sometimes strangely beautiful. (1166)

It is interesting to see how Davis blends ideas of both romanticism and realism in Hugh's work. His act of creation—creating art for its own sake—is nothing short of romantic. Yet the korl woman has an exterior as rough as Hugh's: we are able to see the work and the story's main character in a "warts and all" kind of way. Hugh also, like the korl woman, is "hungry . . . [for] summat to make [him] live" (1170)—a hunger satisfied only through art.

But ultimately, Davis mocks the all-too-romanticized ideas of the artist, specifically, the belief that an artist may surpass social status merely for having talent, or that all artists are directly connected with "high-brow" culture. The idea gets planted in Hugh's head that he should question his "worth" (1174) and his own place in life. He becomes almost dissatisfied with himself because the socially advanced make him feel like he is responsible for his own miserable place in society. When he is wrongfully jailed, art no longer serves an escape for Hugh and he takes his own life. Romantic fancies prove to be realistically ineffectual. Here, again, Davis is asking us to see this and further agree that action needs to be taken on the societal—not just individual—level.

Because art becomes such an important symbol in "Life in the Iron-Mills," Davis frames the entire work mockingly, referencing established romantic traditions:

> The sky sank down before dawn, muddy, flat, immovable. The air is thick, clammy with the breadth of crowded human beings. . . . The idiosyncrasy of this town is smoke. It rolls suddenly in slow folds from the great chimneys of the iron foundries, and settles down in black, slimy pools on the muddy streets. . . . A dirty canary chirps desolately in a cage beside me. Its dream of green fields and sunshine is a very old dream,—almost worn out. (1160)

This opening scene is anything but the idyllic pastures filled with pleasant and contented workers often depicted in contemporary picturesque paintings, a genre that "studiously avoids squalid scenes of urban poverty and newly enclosed agrarian country-sides, returning its audiences to the pleasurable wild vistas and romanticized poverty of an earlier feudal era" (Silver 95). Artists at this time would often show the working class in what can only be described as a sentimentalized way. Before the adoption of the realist mindset, lower-class figures were shown comfortable with, and even perhaps enjoying, the ease of a life at work. Specific (and certainly false) characteristics of such workers included clear, clean skin, feet, and hands, far-from-tattered clothes, and an overall air of satisfaction with their own lives.

Though this trend began in painting, it clearly translated to the literary world during Davis's time, as she herself points out that the reader may even be expecting "green fields and sunshine" (1160) on reading her work. Yet, as Silver notes, the tradition of bringing "rural picturesque aesthetics to bear upon industrial sites came under increasing suspicion and scrutiny by authors and critics concerned especially with the cultural effects of popular representations of urban poverty" during the late 1850s and 1860s (104).

The last line of the story, which calls for "The promise of a New Dawn" (italics mine), is probably one of the author's most chilling and complex. Biblical interpretations of this line all seem to dance around the same concept: although Hugh's life on earth was nothing but abhorrent, he has, through death, transcended to a better and more peaceful place. Hugh doesn't see the picturesque landscape in life but might in death; undoubtedly, such interpretations draw from the Christian promise of salvation in the afterlife. Yet, as Lasseter claims, this line functions more appropriately with regard to the overall thematic message of the story when it is taken as intentionally ironical (180).

"Life in the Iron-Mills" emerges out of a need for true investigation into the lives of the working class by a woman who assumed the roles of both fiction writer and social critic. Yet one of Davis's biggest obstacles undoubtedly revolved around the need to connect with her audience to cement her message effectively. Because little attention had been previously given to poor workers in literature, it is evident that Davis needed to find a delicate balance between interesting fiction and instructional prose. Again, to convey her "nonfiction" message of the need for social reform in a manner that would be more easily absorbed by readers, Davis paints an interesting picture concerning the poor furnace tender, framed by a decidedly non-working-class narrator. As

Hesford stresses, "the [genre of] romance gives dynamic, accessible import to Davis' social concerns" (85).

Again, it is quite important to the story's functionality that the narrator is closer in terms of class to Davis herself and, of course, readers of The Atlantic Monthly. Hesford asserts, "Davis assesses the condition of the worker from a strategic distance" (77). Thus, if the "outsider" narrator is able to recognize the plight of the working class, we as readers should be able to do the same; Davis cleverly places the reader and the narrator on the same level: casual observer, but with a powerful voice.

Works Cited

Cuddon, J. A. The Penguin Dictionary of Literary Terms and Literary Theory. 4th ed. London: Penguin, 1999.

Davis, Rebecca Harding. "Life in the Iron-Mills." Connections: Literature for Composition. By Quentin Miller and Julie Nash. Boston: Houghton, 2004. 1160–85.

Harris, Sharon M. Rebecca Harding Davis and American Realism. Philadelphia: U of Pennsylvania P, 1991.

Hesford, Walter. "Literary Contexts of 'Life in the Iron-Mills.'" American Literature 49.1 (1977): 70–85.

Hornstein, Lillian Herlands, G. D. Percy, and Calvin S. Brown, eds. The Reader's Companion to World Literature. 2nd ed. New York: Signet Classics, 2002.

Hughes, Sheila Hassell. "Between Bodies of Knowledge There Is a Great Gulf Fixed: A Liberationist Reading of Class and Gender in 'Life in the Iron-Mills.'" American Quarterly 49.1 (1997): 113–37.

Lasseter, Janice Milner. "The Censored and Uncensored Literary Lives of 'Life in the Iron-Mills.'" Legacy 20.1–2 (2003): 175–90.

Silver, Andrew. "'Unnatural Unions': Picturesque Travel, Sexual Politics, and Working-Class Representation in 'A Night under Ground' and 'Life in the Iron-Mills.'" Legacy 20.1–2 (2003): 94–17.

Part 4

Literary Explorations of Human Nature

Connections

A Collection of Art

The images in this color insert are discussed in Chapters 12, 13, 14, 15, 16, and 17. For exact page numbers, see the captions.

Marshall D. Rumbaugh, *Rosa Parks* (1983) (see page 389).

Wilfred Hildonen, *Punk* (2005) (see page 389).

Jules Adler, *Voice of the People* (1899) (see page 389).

Pieter the Elder Brueghel, *Fall of Icarus* (c. 1558–1566) (see page 400).

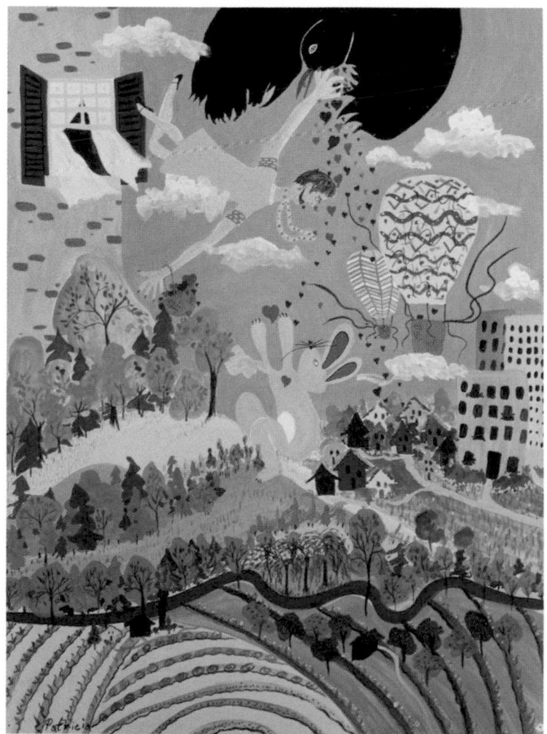

Patricia A. Schwimmer, *Flight to Freedom* (1994) (see page 400).

Jeanie Tomanek, *Icarus lands safely, only slightly singed* (2002) (see page 400).

Harold Harvey, *The Young Menage* (1932) (see page 579).

Ilya Efimovich Repin, *What Freedom!* (1903) (see page 580).

Rene Magritte, *The Lovers* (1928) (see page 580).

Iain Faulkner, *Blind Date* (2005) (see page 580).

Thomas Phillips, *George Gordon Byron (Lord Byron)* (1813) (see page 637).

Giuseppe Bernardino Bison, *Don Juan in Hell* (n.d.) (see page 637).

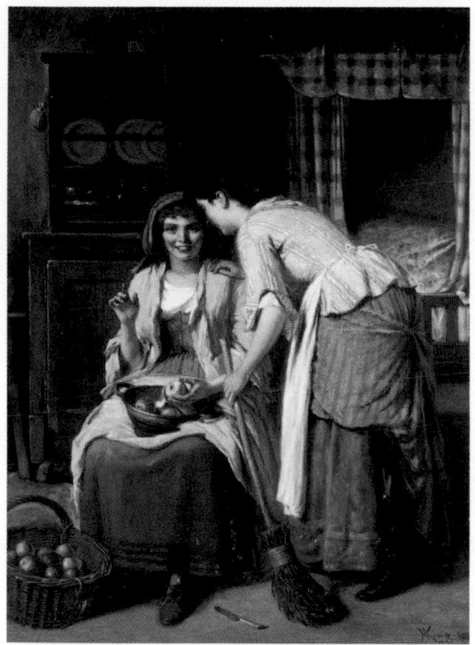

Haynes King, *A Great Secret* (n.d.) (see page 787).

Patricia A. Schwimmer, *Many Masks* (1995) (see page 787).

John Everett Millais, *Trust Me* (c. 1862) (see page 787).

Loki with His Fishing Net (18th century) (see page 811).

The Pied Piper Leading Away the Children of Hamelin (c. 1899) (see page 811).

Celia Washington, *Eden, the First Exodus* (1989) (see page 811).

Still of the Wicked Witch of the West from the film *The Wizard of Oz* (1939) (see page 980).

Jean Beraud, *Mary Magdalen at the House of the Pharisee* (1891) (see page 980).

Mark Copeland, *After the Fox?* (1997) (see page 980).

James Tissot, *The Return of the Prodigal Son* (1852) (see page 1014).

James Jacques Joseph Tissot, *The Prodigal Son in Modern Life: The Return* (c. 1882) (see page 1014).

James Hopkins, *Shelf Life* (2005) (see page 1425).

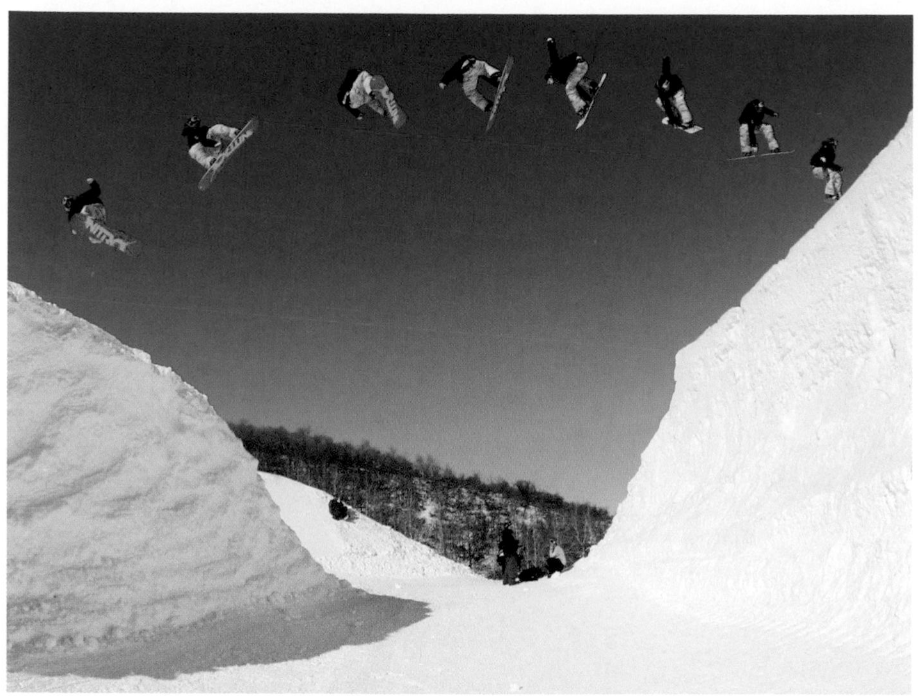

Dave Lehl, *Snowboarding Sequence* (2007) (see page 1443).

Stuart Luke Gatherer, *Doubledown* (2004) (see page 1443).

Greg Hargreaves, *Businessman on Branching Path* (n.d.) (see page 1443).

Chapter 12

Obedience and Rebellion

Think of all the familiar stories in which characters get in trouble for failing to do as they are told. Little Red Riding Hood, Bilbo Baggins in J. R. R. Tolkien's *The Hobbit*, and Dorothy in *The Wizard of Oz* are all told literally to "stay on the path," and they all find trouble when they step off the path. Adam and Eve in the Bible's Genesis section are told that they cannot eat the fruit from one tree only, yet they do. Countless children's stories have obedience as their theme, and the clear lesson is that children who do not listen to the directions of their elders are imperiling themselves.

Yet sometimes "doing as you're told" is not necessarily the best, or most desirable, idea. Resisting or defying authority is natural but also confusing. The world would be a more orderly place if everyone did what he or she was told to do. However, it would probably be a dull place. Moreover, if the people in power are corrupt, "doing as you're told" might be immoral. That is, rebellion can be a good thing, a necessary part of human growth. It involves belief in one's own ideas rather than thoughtless obedience to someone else's. It requires individual action.

Sometimes that action can involve a deeply moral decision. As pointed out in Chapter 1, the protagonist of Mark Twain's novel *Adventures of Huckleberry Finn* rebels against the teachings of his slave-owning society and risks "going to hell" (and probably to jail) to save the life of his best friend. At other times the rebel disobeys for reasons of survival rather than morality: Hansel and Gretel, to take another children's story, are told to trust their parents and not to follow them out of the woods, yet to obey these particular parents would mean death.

Neither rebellion nor obedience is necessarily the right response to all situations. Although the dutiful soldier who follows the orders of his superiors and the anti-authority street punk are clearly two distinct and opposite personalities, we would be ignoring subtleties if we simply preferred one personality to the other in all situations. If you value obedience, what do you do with the soldier who "only follows orders" when the orders are given by someone who is corrupt, or even criminal? If you value rebellion, what do you do when the seemingly noble street demonstrator overturns and burns your car?

As you read and interpret the literature in this chapter, you will be encouraged to consider rebellion and obedience from different perspectives and so will

Michael Hogue, Illustration from *The Hobbit* (1984).

need to work and rework your personal definitions of the two terms. Is a rebel someone who does not do as she's told merely for the sake of defying authority? Is she anything more or less than a nonconformist? Does she need to have some purpose, some cause, to be considered a rebel? Is obedience the same thing as "following orders"? Does the obedient young man have any responsibility to think for himself?

This chapter contains a rich variety of stories, poems, plays, essays, and images that address the related themes of rebellion and obedience. The fiction section begins with a story from the tradition of American realism, "Editha" by William Dean Howells, about a young woman who wants her man to participate in the glory of war before she can declare her love for him. The second story in the section, "The Lottery" by Shirley Jackson, illustrates what can happen when everyone in a community follows the traditions associated with a ritual. Albert Camus' "The Guest" puts a schoolteacher in an awkward position when he is told that he must deliver a prisoner, a convicted murderer, to another location. John Updike's story "A & P" places a young grocery store clerk in the position of defending the right of young women to wear what they want to wear. The final three stories in this section—Jamaica Kincaid's "Girl," Amy Tan's "Rules of the

Hansel and Gretel in the forest.

Game," and Elizabeth McKenzie's "Stop That Girl"—are about young women who are expected to operate within guidelines designed by their parents.

Three of the poems in this chapter—Felicia Hemans's "Casabianca," Alfred, Lord Tennyson's "The Charge of the Light Brigade," and Wilfred Owen's "Dulce et Decorum Est"—have war as their backdrop. War is a fitting context for examining obedience and rebellion because it is a disorienting world without clear rules (thus the expression "All's fair in love and war"). To counterbalance chaos and to achieve its difficult objectives, the military expects unquestioning obedience from those in its ranks, even if following orders will cost an individual his or her life.

The long allegorical poem "Goblin Market" by Christina Rossetti plays on the motif of "forbidden fruit" as two sisters decide whether to give in to the temptation of buying the sumptuous fruit offered by grotesque goblin men. Emily Dickinson's short poem "Much Madness is divinest Sense" inverts traditional values. Gregory Corso's poem "Marriage" considers with comic absurdity what would happen to the speaker if he decided to live a conventional, respectable, middle-class life. Corso's poem is the flip side of two poems about characters who follow convention throughout their lives: Auden's "The Unknown Citizen" and Thomas's "Do Not Go Gentle into That Good Night." Possibly the most famous "unknown citizen" in all of poetry is the subject of T. S. Eliot's famous poem "The Love Song of J. Alfred Prufrock," which delves into the mind of a bland man who wonders if the safe path he has chosen has made him insignificant.

Convention and respect are also at the heart of the play included in this chapter, but there is little comic relief in Wole Soyinka's *Death and the King's Horseman*. In Yoruba culture in Nigeria, the king's horseman, or most trusted servant, is expected to take his own life following the king's death. Although the ceremonies and rituals surrounding this event are ancient, in modern times the motivation to commit suicide in accordance with spiritual teachings is clearly less appealing. The protagonist of this play, Elesin, is faced with the decision between dying in fulfillment of his duties or living with the consequence that his already weakening culture may be completely destroyed.

The first essay in this chapter is "Civil Disobedience" by the great American thinker and writer Henry David Thoreau. Thoreau describes how he opposes the authority of his government, which condones slave ownership. George Orwell, author of "Shooting an Elephant," is a representative of his government, a colonial officer in Burma, who believes he must shoot an elephant that has gone on a rampage. The final essay, "Take the Cannoli," is by Sarah Vowell, a young woman who weighs her family's expectations and boyfriend's expectations against the code of behavior set forth in the classic American movie *The Godfather*.

The Common Characters section of this chapter focuses on Icarus. In this familiar myth, Icarus's father, Daedalus (pronounced "Dedalus"), creates a pair of wings for Icarus but warns him not to fly too close to the sun. Retellings of the Icarus story are represented here in paintings, poems, and a song lyric. Icarus is a fitting figure for this chapter because we are all familiar with the transgression of disobeying our father. What would you do if someone gave you a pair of wings but cautioned you against flying too high? Maybe you are sure you would obey, but what if Icarus had obeyed? The story would have a happy ending, but you might not want to read it.

Fiction

William Dean Howells

Editha

William Dean Howells (1837–1920) was one of the most influential writers of his time, not only because of his tremendous literary output (including a staggering thirty-eight novels) but also because of his central position in the literary world. He was the first president of the American Academy of Arts and Letters, the editor of the magazine *The Atlantic Monthly*, and a highly respected critic whose nod of approval could launch a young writer's career. One of the most prominent practitioners of the literary movement called "realism," Howells believed strongly that literary fiction should be "true" in the sense that it should frame the dilemmas that ordinary people face in real life. The following short story, "Editha," was published in 1905 in the wake of the Spanish-American war of 1898. As you read it, consider what elements of the story continue to seem "true" in this sense of the word today.

....

The air was thick with the war feeling, like the electricity of a storm which has not yet burst. Editha sat looking out into the hot spring afternoon, with her lips parted, and panting with the intensity of the question whether she could let him go. She had decided that she could not let him stay, when she saw him at the end of the still leafless avenue, making slowly up towards the house, with his head down and his figure relaxed. She ran impatiently out on the veranda, to the edge of the steps, and imperatively demanded greater haste of him with her will before she called aloud to him: "George!"

He had quickened his pace in mystical response to her mystical urgence, before he could have heard her; now he looked up and answered, "Well?"

"Oh, how united we are!" she exulted, and then she swooped down the steps to him. "What is it?" she cried.

"It's war," he said, and he pulled her up to him and kissed her.

She kissed him back intensely, but irrelevantly, as to their passion, and 5
uttered from deep in her throat, "How glorious!"

"It's war," he repeated, without consenting to her sense of it; and she did not know just what to think at first. She never knew what to think of him; that made his mystery, his charm. All through their courtship, which was contemporaneous with the growth of the war feeling, she had been puzzled by his want of seriousness about it. He seemed to despise it even more than he abhorred it. She could have understood his abhorring any sort of blood-shed; that would have been a survival of his old life when he thought he would be a minister, and before he changed and took up the law. But making light of a cause so high and noble seemed to show a want of earnestness at the core of his being. Not but that she felt herself able to cope with a congenital defect of that sort, and make his love for her save him from himself. Now perhaps the miracle was already wrought in him. In the presence of the tremendous fact that he announced, all triviality seemed to have gone out of him; she began to feel that. He sank down on the top step, and wiped his forehead with a handkerchief, while she poured out upon him her question of the origin and authenticity of his news.

All the while, in her duplex emotioning, she was aware that now at the very beginning she must put a guard upon herself against urging him, by any word or act, to take the part that her whole soul willed him to take, for the completion of her ideal of him. He was very nearly perfect as he was, and he must be allowed to perfect himself. But he was peculiar, and he might very well be reasoned out of his peculiarity. Before her reasoning went her emotioning: her nature pulling on his nature, her womanhood upon his manhood, without her knowing the means she was using to the end she was willing. She had always supposed that the man who won her would have done something to win her; she did not know what, but something. George Gearson had simply asked for her love, on the way home from a concert, and she gave her love to him without, as it were, thinking. But now, it flashed upon her, if he could do something worthy to have won her—be a hero, *her* hero—it would be even better than if he had done it before asking her; it would be grander. Besides, she had believed in the war from the beginning.

"But don't you see, dearest," she said, "that it wouldn't have come to this if it hadn't been the order of Providence? And I call any war glorious that is for the liberation of people who have been struggling for years against the cruelest oppression. Don't you think so, too?"

"I suppose so," he returned, languidly. "But war! Is it glorious to break the peace of the world?"

"That ignoble peace! It was no peace at all, with that crime and shame at our very gates." She was conscious of parroting the current phrases of the newspapers, but it was no time to pick and choose her words. She must sacrifice anything to the high ideal she had for him, and after a good deal of rapid argument she ended with the climax: "But now it doesn't matter about the how or why. Since the war has come; all that is gone. There are no two sides any more. There is nothing now but our country."

He sat with his eyes closed and his head leant back against the veranda, and he remarked, with a vague smile, as if musing aloud, "Our country—right or wrong."

"Yes, right or wrong!" she returned, fervidly. "I'll go and get you some lemonade." She rose rustling, and whisked away; when she came back with two tall glasses of clouded liquid on a tray, and the ice clucking in them, he still sat as she had left him, and she said, as if there had been no interruption: "But there is no question of wrong in this case. I call it a sacred war. A war for liberty and humanity, if ever there was one. And I know you will see it just as I do, yet."

He took half the lemonade at a gulp, and he answered as he set the glass down: "I know you always have the highest ideal. When I differ from you I ought to doubt myself."

A generous sob rose in Editha's throat for the humility of a man, so very nearly perfect, who was willing to put himself below her.

Besides, she felt, more subliminally, that he was never so near slipping through her fingers as when he took that meek way.

"You shall not say that! Only, for once I happen to be right." She seized his hand in her two hands, and poured her soul from her eyes into his. "Don't you think so?" she entreated him.

He released his hand and drank the rest of his lemonade, and she added, "Have mine, too," but he shook his head in answering, "I've no business to think so, unless I act so, too."

Her heart stopped a beat before it pulsed on with leaps that she felt in her neck. She had noticed that strange thing in men: they seemed to feel bound to do what they believed, and not think a thing was finished when they said it, as girls did. She knew what was in his mind, but she pretended not, and she said, "Oh, I am not sure," and then faltered.

He went on as if to himself, without apparently heeding her: "There's only one way of proving one's faith in a thing like this."

She could not say she understood, but she did understand.

He went on again. "If I believed—if I felt as you do about this war—Do you wish me to feel as you do?"

Now she was really not sure; so she said: "George, I don't know what you mean."

He seemed to muse away from her as before. "There is a sort of fascination in it. I suppose that at the bottom of his heart every man would like at times to have his courage tested, to see how he would act."

"How can you talk in that ghastly way?"

"It *is* rather morbid. Still, that's what it comes to, unless you're swept away by ambition or driven by conviction. I haven't the conviction or the ambition, and the other thing is what it comes to with me. I ought to have been a preacher, after all; then I couldn't have asked it of myself, as I must, now I'm a lawyer. And you believe that it's a holy war, Editha?" he suddenly addressed her. "Oh, I know you do! But you wish me to believe so, too?"

She hardly knew whether he was mocking or not, in the ironical way he always had with her plainer mind. But the only thing was to be outspoken with him.

"George, I wish you to believe whatever you think is true, at any and every cost. If I've ever tried to talk you into anything, I take it all back."

"Oh, I know that, Editha. I know how sincere you are and how—I wish I had your undoubting spirit! I'll think it over; I'd like to believe as you do. But I don't, now; I don't, indeed. It isn't this war alone; though this seems particularly wanton and needless, but it's every war—so stupid; it makes me sick. Why shouldn't this thing have been settled reasonably?"

"Because," she said, very throatily again, "God meant it to be war."

"You think it was God? Yes, I suppose that is what people will say."

"Do you suppose it would have been war if God hadn't meant it?"

"I don't know. Sometimes it seems as if God had put this world into men's keeping to work it as they pleased."

"Now, George, that is blasphemy."

"Well, I won't blaspheme. I'll try to believe in your pocket Providence," he said, and then he rose to go.

"Why don't you stay to dinner?" Dinner at Balcom's Works was at one o'clock.

"I'll come back to supper, if you'll let me. Perhaps I shall bring you a convert."

"Well, you may come back, on that condition."

"All right. If I don't come, you'll understand."

He went away without kissing her, and she felt it a suspension of their engagement. It all interested her intensely; she was undergoing a tremendous experience, and she was being equal to it. While she stood looking after him, her mother came out through one of the long windows onto the veranda, with a catlike softness and vagueness.

"Why didn't he stay to dinner?"

"Because—because—war has been declared," Editha pronounced, without turning.

Her mother said, "Oh, my!" and then said nothing more until she had sat down in one of the large Shaker chairs and rocked herself for some time. Then she closed whatever tacit passage of thought there had been in her mind with the spoken words: "Well, I hope *he* won't go."

"And *I* hope he *will*," the girl said, and confronted her mother with a stormy exultation that would have frightened any creature less unimpressionable than a cat.

Her mother rocked herself again for an interval of cogitation. What she arrived at in speech was: "Well, I guess you've done a wicked thing, Editha Balcom."

The girl said, as she passed indoors through the same window her mother had come out by: "I haven't done anything—yet."

In her room, she put together all her letters and gifts from Gearson, down to the withered petals of the first flower he had offered, with that timidity of his veiled in that irony of his. In the heart of the packet she enshrined her engagement ring which she had restored to the pretty box he had brought it her in. Then she sat down, if not calmly yet strongly, and wrote:

"GEORGE:—I understood when you left me. But I think we had better emphasize your meaning that if we cannot be one in everything we had better be one in nothing. So I am sending these things for your keeping till you have made up your mind.

"I shall always love you, and therefore I shall never marry any one else. But the man I marry must love his country first of all, and be able to say to me,

"'I could not love thee, dear, so much,
Loved I not honor more.'

"There is no honor above America with me. In this great hour there is no other honor.

"Your heart will make my words clear to you. I had never expected to say so much, but it has come upon me that I must say the utmost.

EDITHA"

She thought she had worded her letter well, worded it in a way that could not be bettered; all had been implied and nothing expressed.

She had it ready to send with the packet she had tied with red, white, and blue ribbon, when it occurred to her that she was not just to him, that she was not giving him a fair chance. He said he would go and think it over, and she was not waiting. She was pushing, threatening, compelling. That was not a woman's part. She must leave him free, free, free. She could not accept for her country or herself a forced sacrifice.

In writing her letter she had satisfied the impulse from which it sprang; she could well afford to wait till he had thought it over. She put the packet and the letter by, and rested serene in her consciousness of having done what was laid upon her by her love itself to do, and yet used patience, mercy, justice.

She had her reward. Gearson did not come to tea, but she had given him till 50
morning, when, late at night there came up from the village the sound of fife and drum, with a tumult of voices, in shouting, singing, and laughing. The noise drew nearer and nearer; it reached the street end of the avenue; there it silenced itself, and one voice, the voice she knew best, rose over the silence. It fell; the air was filled with cheers; the fife and drum struck up, with the shouting, singing, and laughing again, but now retreating; and a single figure came hurrying up the avenue.

She ran down to meet her lover and clung to him. He was very gay, and he put his arm around her with a boisterous laugh. "Well, you must call me Captain now; or Cap, if you prefer; that's what the boys call me. Yes, we've had a meeting at the town-hall, and everybody has volunteered; and they selected me for captain, and I'm going to the war, the big war, the glorious war, the holy war ordained by the pocket Providence that blesses butchery. Come along; let's tell the whole family about it. Call them from their downy beds, father, mother, Aunt Hitty and all the folks!"

But when they mounted the veranda steps he did not wait for a larger audience; he poured the story out upon Editha alone.

"There was a lot of speaking, and then some of the fools set up a shout for me. It was all going one way, and I thought it would be a good joke to sprinkle a little cold water on them. But you can't do that with a crowd that adores you. The first thing I knew I was sprinkling hell-fire on them. 'Cry havoc, and let slip the dogs of war.' That was the style. Now that it had come to a fight, there were no two parties; there was one country, and the thing was to fight to a finish as quick as possible. I suggested volunteering then and there, and I wrote my name first of all on the roster. Then they elected me—that's all. I wish I had some ice-water."

She left him walking up and down the veranda, while she ran for the ice-pitcher and goblet, and when she came back he was still walking up and down shouting the story he had told her to her father and mother, who had come out more sketchily dressed than they commonly were by day. He drank goblet after goblet of the ice-water without noticing who was giving it, and kept on talking, and laughing through his talk wildly. "It's astonishing," he said, "how well the worse reason looks when you try to make it appear the better. Why, I believe I was the first convert to the war in that crowd to-night! I never thought I should like to kill a man; but now I shouldn't care; and the smokeless powder lets you see the man drop that you kill. It's all for the country! What a thing it is to have a country that *can't* be wrong, but if it is, is right, anyway!"

Editha had a great, vital thought, an inspiration. She set down the ice- 55
pitcher on the veranda floor, and ran up-stairs and got the letter she had written him. When at last he noisily bade her father and mother, "Well, goodnight. I forgot I woke you up; I sha'n't want any sleep myself," she followed him down the avenue to the gate. There, after the whirling words that seemed to fly away from her thoughts and refuse to serve them, she made a last effort to solemnize the moment that seemed so crazy, and pressed the letter she had written upon him.

"What's this?" he said. "Want me to mail it?"

"No, no. It's for you. I wrote it after you went this morning. Keep it—keep it—and read it sometime—" She thought, and then her inspiration came: "Read it if you ever doubt what you've done, or fear that I regret your having done it. Read it after you've started."

They strained each other in embraces that seemed as ineffective as their words, and he kissed her face with quick, hot breaths that were so unlike him, that made her feel as if she had lost her old lover and found a stranger in his place. The stranger said: "What a gorgeous flower you are, with your red hair, and your blue eyes that look black now, and your face with the color painted out by the white moonshine! Let me hold you under the chin, to see whether I love blood, you tiger-lily!" Then he laughed Gearson's laugh, and released her, scared and giddy. With her wilfulness she had been frightened by a sense of subtler force in him, and mystically mastered as she had never been before.

She ran all the way back to the house, and mounted the steps panting. Her mother and father were talking of the great affair. Her mother said: "Wa'n't Mr. Gearson in rather of an excited state of mind? Didn't you think he acted curious?"

"Well, not for a man who's just been elected captain and has set 'em up for the whole of Company A," her father chuckled back.

"What in the world do you mean, Mr. Balcom? Oh! There's Editha!" She offered to follow the girl indoors.

"Don't come, mother!" Editha called, vanishing.

Mrs. Balcom remained to reproach her husband, "I don't see much anything to laugh at."

"Well, it's catching. Caught it from Gearson. I guess it won't be much of a war, and I guess Gearson don't think so, either. The other fellows will back down as soon as they see we mean it. I wouldn't lose any sleep over it. I'm going back to bed, myself."

Gearson came back again next afternoon, looking pale and rather sick, but quite himself, even to his languid irony. "I guess I'd better tell you, Editha, that I consecrated myself to your god of battles last night by pouring too many libations to him down my throat. But I'm all right now. One has to carry off the excitement, somehow."

"Promise me," she commanded, "that you'll never touch it again!"

"What! Not let the cannikin clink? Not let the soldier drink? Well, I promise."

"You don't belong to yourself now; you don't even belong to *me*. You belong to your country, and you have a sacred charge to keep yourself strong and well for your country's sake. I have been thinking, thinking all night and all day long."

"You look as if you've been crying a little, too," he said, with his queer smile.

"That's all past. I've been thinking, and worshiping *you*. Don't you suppose I know all that you've been through, to come to this? I've followed you every step from your old theories and opinions."

"Well, you've had a long road to hoe."

"And I know you've done this from the highest motives—"

"Oh, there won't be much pettifogging to do till this cruel war is—"

"And you haven't simply done it for my sake. I couldn't respect you if you had."

"Well, then let's say I haven't. A man that hasn't got his own respect wants 75
the respect of all the other people he can corner. But we won't go into that. I'm in for the thing now, and we've got to face our future. My idea is that this isn't going to be a very protracted struggle; we shall just scare the enemy to death before we fight at all. But we must provide for contingencies, Editha. If anything happens to me—"

"Oh, George!" She clung to him, sobbing.

"I don't want you to be foolishly bound to my memory. I should hate that, wherever I happened to be."

"I am yours, for time and eternity—time and eternity." She liked the words; they satisfied her famine for phrases.

"Well, say eternity; that's all right; but time's another thing; and I'm talking about time. But there is something! My mother! If anything happens—"

She winced, and he laughed. "You're not the bold soldier-girl of yesterday!" 80
Then he sobered. "If anything happens, I want you to help my mother out. She won't like my doing this thing. She brought me up to think war is a fool thing as well as a bad thing. My father was in the Civil War; all through it; lost his arm in it." She thrilled with the sense of the arm around her; what if that should be lost? He laughed as if divining her: "Oh, it doesn't run in the family, as far as I know!" Then he added, gravely: "He came home with misgivings about war, and they grew on him. I guess he and mother agreed between them that I was to be brought up in his final mind about it; but that was before my time. I only knew him from my mother's report of him and his opinions; I don't know whether they were hers first; but they were hers last. This will be a blow to her. I shall have to write and tell her—"

He stopped and she asked: "Would you like me to write, too, George?"

"I don't believe that would do. No, I'll do the writing. She'll understand a little if I say that the way to minimize it was to make the war on the largest possible scale at once—that I felt I must have been helping on the war somehow if I hadn't helped keep it from coming, and I knew I hadn't; when it came, I had no right to stay out of it."

Whether his sophistries satisfied him or not, they satisfied her. She clung to his breast, and whispered, with closed eyes and quivering lips: "Yes, yes, yes!"

"But if anything should happen, you might go to her and see what you could do for her. You know? It's rather far off; she can't leave her chair—"

"Oh, I'll go, if it's the ends of the earth! But nothing will happen! Nothing 85
can! I—"

She felt herself lifted with his rising, and Gearson was saying, with his arm still round her, to her father: "Well, we're off at once, Mr. Balcom. We're to be formally accepted at the capital, and then bunched up with the rest somehow, and sent into camp somewhere, and got to the front as soon as possible. We all want to be in the van, of course; we're the first company to report to the Governor. I came to tell Editha, but I hadn't got around to it."

She saw him again for a moment at the capital, in the station, just before the train started southward with his regiment. He looked well, in his uniform, and very soldierly, but somehow girlish, too, with his clean-shaven face and slim figure. The manly eyes and the strong voice satisfied her, and his preoccupation with some unexpected details of duty flattered her. Other girls were weeping and bemoaning themselves, but she felt a sort of noble distinction in the abstraction, the almost unconsciousness, with which they parted. Only at the last moment he said: "Don't forget my mother. It mayn't be such a walkover as I supposed," and he laughed at the notion.

He waved his hand to her, as the train moved off—she knew it among a score of hands that were waved to other girls from the platform of the car, for it held a letter which she knew was hers. Then he went inside the car to read it, doubtless, and she did not see him again. But she felt safe for him through the strength of what she called her love. What she called her God, always speaking the name in a deep voice and with the implication of a mutual understanding, would watch over him and keep him and bring him back to her. If with an empty sleeve, then he should have three arms instead of two, for both of hers should be his for life. She did not see, though, why she should always be thinking of the arm his father had lost.

There were not many letters from him, but they were such as she could have wished, and she put her whole strength into making hers such as she imagined he could have wished, glorifying and supporting him. She wrote to his mother glorifying him as their hero, but the brief answer she got was merely to the effect that Mrs. Gearson was not well enough to write herself, and thanking her for her letter by the hand of someone who called herself "Yrs truly, Mrs. W. J. Andrews."

Editha determined not to be hurt, but to write again quite as if the answer had been all she expected. Before it seemed as if she could have written, there came news of the first skirmish, and in the list of the killed, which was telegraphed as a trifling loss on our side, was Gearson's name. There was a frantic time of trying to make out that it might be, must be, some other Gearson; but the name and company and the regiment and the State were too definitely given.

Then there was a lapse into the depths out of which it seemed as if she could never rise again; then a lift into clouds far above all grief, black clouds, that blotted out the sun, but where she soared with him, with George—George! She had the fever that she expected of herself, but she did not die in it; she was not even delirious, and it did not last long. When she was well enough to leave her bed, her one thought was of George's mother, of his strangely worded wish that she should go to her and see what she could do for her. In the exaltation of the duty laid upon her—it buoyed her up instead of burdening her—she rapidly recovered.

Her father went with her on the long railroad journey from northern New York to western Iowa; he had business out in Davenport, and he said he could just as well go then as anytime; and he went with her to the little country town where George's mother lived in a little house on the edge of the illimitable cornfields, under trees pushed to a top of the rolling prairie. George's father had settled there after the Civil War, as so many other old soldiers had done; but they were Eastern people, and Editha fancied touches of the East in the June rose overhanging the front door, and the garden with early summer flowers stretching from the gate of the paling fence.

It was very low inside the house, and so dim, with the closed blinds, that they could scarcely see one another: Editha tall and black in her crapes which filled the air with the smell of their dyes; her father standing decorously apart with his hat on his forearm, as at funerals; a woman rested in a deep armchair, and the woman who had let the strangers in stood behind the chair.

The seated woman turned her head round and up, and asked the woman behind her chair: "*Who* did you say?"

Editha, if she had done what she had expected of herself, would have gone 95
down on her knees at the feet of the seated figure and said, "I am George's Editha," for answer.

But instead of her own voice she heard that other woman's voice saying "Well, I don't know as I *did* get the name just right. I guess I'll have to make a little more light in here," and she went and pushed two of the shutters ajar.

Then Editha's father said, in his public will-now-address-a-few-remarks tone: "My name is Balcom, ma'am—Junius H. Balcom, of Balcom's Works, New York; my daughter—"

"Oh!" the seated woman broke in, with a powerful voice, the voice that always surprised Editha from Gearson's slender frame. "Let me see you. Stand round where the light can strike on your face," and Editha dumbly obeyed. "So, you're Editha Balcom," she sighed.

"Yes," Editha said, sounding more like a culprit than a comforter.

"What did you come for?" Mrs. Gearson asked. 100

Editha's face quivered and her knees shook. "I came—because—because George—" She could go no further.

"Yes," the mother said, "he told me that he had asked you to come if he got killed. You didn't expect that, I suppose, when you sent him."

"I would rather have died myself than done it!" Editha said, with more truth in her deep voice than she ordinarily found in it. "I tried to leave him free"—

"Yes, that letter of yours, that came back with his other things, that left him free."

Editha saw now where George's irony came from. 105

"It was not to be read before—unless—until—I told him so," she faltered.

"Of course, he wouldn't read a letter of yours, under the circumstances, till he thought you wanted him to. Been sick?" the woman abruptly demanded.

"Very sick," Editha said, with self-pity.

"Daughter's life," her father interposed, "was almost despaired of, at one time."

Mrs. Gearson gave him no heed. "I suppose you would have been glad to 110
die, such a brave person as you! I don't believe *he* was glad to die. He was always a timid boy, that way; he was afraid of a good many things; but if he was afraid he did what he made up his mind to. I suppose he made up his mind to go, but I knew what it cost him by what it cost me when I heard of it. I had been through *one* war before. When you sent him you didn't expect he would get killed."

The voice seemed to compassionate Editha, and it was time. "No," she huskily murmured.

"No, girls don't; women don't, when they give their men up to their country. They think they'll come marching back, somehow, just as gay as they went, or if it's an empty sleeve, or even an empty pantaloon, it's all the more glory, and they're so much the prouder of them, poor things!"

The tears began to run down Editha's face; she had not wept till then; but it was now such a relief to be understood that the tears came.

"No, you didn't expect him to get killed," Mrs. Gearson repeated, in a voice which was startlingly like George's again. "You just expected him to kill some one else, some of those foreigners, that weren't there because they had any say about it, but because they had to be there, poor wretches—conscripts, or whatever you call 'em. You thought it would be all right for my George, *your* George, to kill the sons of those miserable mothers and the husbands of those girls that you would never see the faces of." The woman lifted her powerful voice in a psalmlike note. "I thank my God he didn't live to do it! I thank my God they killed him first, and that he ain't livin' with their blood on his hands!" She dropped her eyes, which she had raised with her voice, and glared at Editha. "What you got that black on for?" She lifted herself by her powerful arms so high that her helpless body seemed to hang limp its full length. "Take it off, take it off, before I tear it from your back!"

The lady who was passing the summer near Balcom's Works was sketching 115
Editha's beauty, which lent itself wonderfully to the effects of a colorist. It had come to that confidence which is rather apt to grow between artist and sitter, and Editha had told her everything.

"To think of your having such a tragedy in your life!" the lady said. She added: "I suppose there are people who feel that way about war. But when you consider the good this war has done—how much it has done for the country! I can't understand such people, for my part. And when you had come all the way out there to console her—got up out of a sick-bed! Well!"

"I think," Editha said, magnanimously, "she wasn't quite in her right mind; and so did papa."

"Yes," the lady said, looking at Editha's lips in nature and then at her lips in art, and giving an empirical touch to them in the picture. "But how dreadful of her! How perfectly—excuse me—how *vulgar*!"

A light broke upon Editha in the darkness which she felt had been without a gleam of brightness for weeks and months. The mystery that had bewildered her was solved by the word; and from that moment she rose from groveling in shame and self-pity, and began to live again in the ideal.

(1905)

Questions for Discussion and Writing

Close Reading

1. What do you assume "the war feeling" is like, and how does it affect Editha's words and actions?
2. How is Editha described physically in the story, and how does that physical description contribute to your sense of her character?

3. Both George Gearson and his mother can be "ironic" in their speech; what does the narrator mean by that, and what are some examples of it?
4. Discuss the role of Editha's letter to George in the story.

CRITICAL AND CREATIVE READING

5. What does Editha hope to gain by pressing George to act dutifully toward his country? Does she succeed?
6. Is George weak because he follows Editha's wishes instead of his own conscience?
7. The story ends with Editha's renewed commitment to living "in the ideal." What are the advantages and disadvantages of living in the ideal? What are some solid examples of "the real" and "the ideal" in this story?

CONNECTIONS TO OTHER READINGS

8. Like Waverly Jong in Amy Tan's story "Rules of the Game," Editha faces the disapproval of someone in the older generation. In both cases this disapproval comes from someone's mother. Yet Waverly is a rebellious figure and Editha is motivated by obedience. Despite this difference, are these two characters drawn similarly, with similar strengths and weaknesses?
9. Based on his essay "Civil Disobedience," how would Henry David Thoreau have counseled George to act when "the war feeling" was on the town and on his lover Editha?
10. The title character in Felicia Hemans's poem "Casabianca" waits for his father's permission to leave the deck of a burning ship. The speaker describes his faith in noble terms. Discuss the question of obedience and nobility in "Editha" and "Casabianca."

Shirley Jackson

The Lottery

Shirley Jackson (1916–1965) is best remembered as the author of the following story, "The Lottery," which was published in the *New Yorker* in 1948. She was a prolific fiction writer during her relatively brief life, publishing a half-dozen novels, essays, two memoirs, a handful of children's works, and over ninety stories. Some of her fiction that has been receiving attention lately is in the gothic/horror genre, such as her novel *The Haunting of Hill House*. "The Lottery" is a horrifying story, to be sure, yet would you call it a "horror story"? If not, how would you categorize it?

The morning of June 27th was clear and sunny, with the fresh warmth of a full-summer day; the flowers were blossoming profusely and the grass was richly green. The people of the village began to gather in the square, between the post office and the bank, around ten o'clock; in some towns there were so many people that the lottery took two days and had to be started on June 26th, but in this village, where there were only about three hundred people, the whole lottery took less than two hours, so it could begin at ten o'clock in the morning and still be through in time to allow the villagers to get home for noon dinner.

The children assembled first, of course. School was recently over for the summer, and the feeling of liberty sat uneasily on most of them; they tended to gather together quietly for a while before they broke into boisterous play, and their talk was still of the classroom and the teacher, of books and reprimands. Bobby Martin had already stuffed his pockets full of stones, and the other boys soon followed his example, selecting the smoothest and roundest stones; Bobby and Harry Jones and Dickie Delacroix—the villagers pronounced his name "Delacroy"—eventually made a great pile of stones in one corner of the square and guarded it against the raids of the other boys. The girls stood aside, talking among themselves, looking over their shoulders at the boys, and the very small children rolled in the dust or clung to the hands of their older brothers or sisters.

Soon the men began to gather, surveying their own children, speaking of planting and rain, tractors and taxes. They stood together, away from the pile of stones in the corner, and their jokes were quiet and they smiled rather than laughed. The women, wearing faded house dresses and sweaters, came shortly after their menfolk. They greeted one another and exchanged bits of gossip as they went to join their husbands. Soon the women, standing by their husbands, began to call to their children, and the children came reluctantly, having to be called four or five times. Bobby Martin ducked under his mother's grasping hand and ran, laughing, back to the pile of stones. His father spoke up sharply, and Bobby came quickly and took his place between his father and his oldest brother.

The lottery was conducted—as were the square dances, the teenage club, the Halloween program—by Mr. Summers, who had time and energy to devote to civic activities. He was a round-faced, jovial man and he ran the coal business, and people were sorry for him, because he had no children and his wife was a scold. When he arrived in the square, carrying the black wooden box, there was a murmur of conversation among the villagers, and he waved and called, "Little late today, folks." The postmaster, Mr. Graves, followed him, carrying a three-legged stool, and the stool was put in the center of the square and Mr. Summers set the black box down on it. The villagers kept their distance, leaving a space between themselves and the stool, and when Mr. Summers said, "Some of you fellows want to give me a hand?" there was a hesitation before two men, Mr. Martin and his oldest son, Baxter, came forward to hold the box steady on the stool while Mr. Summers stirred up the papers inside it.

5 The original paraphernalia for the lottery had been lost long ago, and the black box now resting on the stool had been put into use even before Old Man Warner, the oldest man in town, was born. Mr. Summers spoke frequently to the villagers about making a new box, but no one liked to upset even as much tradition as was represented by the black box. There was a story that the present box had been made with some pieces of the box that had preceded it, the one that had been constructed when the first people settled down to make a village here. Every year, after the lottery, Mr. Summers began talking again about a new box, but every year the subject was allowed to fade off without anything's being done. The black box grew shabbier each year; by now it was no longer completely black but splintered badly along one side to show the original wood color, and in some places faded or stained.

Mr. Martin and his oldest son, Baxter, held the black box securely on the stool until Mr. Summers had stirred the papers thoroughly with his hand. Because so much of the ritual had been forgotten or discarded, Mr. Summers had been successful in having slips of paper substituted for the chips of wood that had been used for generations. Chips of wood, Mr. Summers had argued, had been all very well when the village was tiny, but now that the population was more than three hundred and likely to keep on growing, it was necessary to use something that would fit more easily into the black box. The night before the lottery, Mr. Summers and Mr. Graves made up the slips of paper and put them in the box, and it was then taken to the safe of Mr. Summers's coal company and locked up until Mr. Summers was ready to take it to the square next morning. The rest of the year, the box was put away, sometimes one place, sometimes another; it had spent one year in Mr. Graves's barn and another year underfoot in the post office, and sometimes it was set on a shelf in the Martin grocery and left there.

There was a great deal of fussing to be done before Mr. Summers declared the lottery open. There were the lists to make up—of heads of families, heads of households in each family, members of each household in each family. There was the proper swearing-in of Mr. Summers by the postmaster, as the official of the lottery; at one time, some people remembered, there had been a recital of some sort, performed by the official of the lottery, a perfunctory, tuneless chant that had been rattled off duly each year; some people believed that the official of the lottery used to stand just so when he said or sang it, others believed that he was supposed to walk among the people, but years and years ago this part of the ritual had been allowed to lapse. There had been, also, a ritual salute, which the official of the lottery had had to use in addressing each person who came up to draw from the box, but this also had changed with time, until now it was felt necessary only for the official to speak to each person approaching. Mr. Summers was very good at all this; in his clean white shirt and blue jeans, with one hand resting carelessly on the black box, he seemed very proper and important as he talked interminably to Mr. Graves and the Martins.

Just as Mr. Summers finally left off talking and turned to the assembled villagers, Mrs. Hutchinson came hurriedly along the path to the square, her sweater thrown over her shoulders, and slid into place in the back of the crowd.

"Clean forgot what day it was," she said to Mrs. Delacroix, who stood next to her, and they both laughed softly. "Thought my old man was out back stacking wood." Mrs. Hutchinson went on, "and then I looked out the window and the kids was gone, and then I remembered it was the twenty-seventh and came a-running." She dried her hands on her apron, and Mrs. Delacroix said, "You're in time, though. They're still talking away up there."

Mrs. Hutchinson craned her neck to see through the crowd and found her husband and children standing near the front. She tapped Mrs. Delacroix on the arm as a farewell and began to make her way through the crowd. The people separated good-humoredly to let her through; two or three people said, in voices just loud enough to be heard across the crowd, "Here comes your Missus, Hutchinson," and "Bill, she made it after all." Mrs. Hutchinson reached her husband, and Mr. Summers, who had been waiting, said cheerfully, "Thought we were going to have to get on without you, Tessie." Mrs. Hutchinson said, grinning, "Wouldn't have me leave m'dishes in the sink, now, would you, Joe?" and soft laughter ran through the crowd as the people stirred back into position after Mrs. Hutchinson's arrival.

10 "Well, now," Mr. Summers said soberly, "guess we better get started, get this over with, so's we can go back to work. Anybody ain't here?"

"Dunbar," several people said. "Dunbar, Dunbar."

Mr. Summers consulted his list. "Clyde Dunbar," he said. "That's right. He's broke his leg, hasn't he? Who's drawing for him?"

"Me, I guess," a woman said, and Mr. Summers turned to look at her. "Wife draws for her husband," Mr. Summers said. "Don't you have a grown boy to do it for you, Janey?" Although Mr. Summers and everyone else in the village knew the answer perfectly well, it was the business of the official of the lottery to ask such questions formally. Mr. Summers waited with an expression of polite interest while Mrs. Dunbar answered.

"Horace's not but sixteen yet," Mrs. Dunbar said regretfully. "Guess I gotta fill in for the old man this year."

15 "Right," Mr. Summers said. He made a note on the list he was holding. Then he asked, "Watson boy drawing this year?"

A tall boy in the crowd raised his hand. "Here," he said. "I'm drawing for m'mother and me." He blinked his eyes nervously and ducked his head as several voices in the crowd said things like "Good fellow, Jack," and "Glad to see your mother's got a man to do it."

"Well," Mr. Summers said, "guess that's everyone. Old Man Warner make it?"

"Here," a voice said, and Mr. Summers nodded.

A sudden hush fell on the crowd as Mr. Summers cleared his throat and looked at the list. "All ready?" he called. "Now, I'll read the names—heads of families first—and the men come up and take a paper out of the box. Keep the paper folded in your hand without looking at it until everyone has had a turn. Everything clear?"

20 The people had done it so many times that they only half-listened to the directions; most of them were quiet, wetting their lips, not looking around. Then Mr. Summers raised one hand high and said, "Adams." A man disengaged

himself from the crowd and came forward. "Hi, Steve," Mr. Summers said, and Mr. Adams said, "Hi, Joe." They grinned at one another humorlessly and nervously. Then Mr. Adams reached into the black box and took out a folded paper. He held it firmly by one corner as he turned and went hastily back to his place in the crowd, where he stood a little apart from his family, not looking down at his hand.

"Allen," Mr. Summers said. "Anderson. . . . Bentham."

"Seems like there's no time at all between lotteries any more," Mrs. Delacroix said to Mrs. Graves in the back row. "Seems like we got through with the last one only last week."

"Time sure goes fast," Mrs. Graves said.

"Clark. . . . Delacroix."

"There goes my old man," Mrs. Delacroix said. She held her breath while her husband went forward.

"Dunbar," Mr. Summers said, and Mrs. Dunbar went steadily to the box while one of the women said, "Go on, Janey," and another said, "There she goes."

"We're next," Mrs. Graves said. She watched while Mr. Graves came around from the side of the box, greeted Mr. Summers gravely, and selected a slip of paper from the box. By now, all through the crowd there were men holding the small folded papers in their large hands, turning them over and over nervously. Mrs. Dunbar and her two sons stood together, Mrs. Dunbar holding the slip of paper.

"Harburt. . . . Hutchinson."

"Get up there, Bill," Mrs. Hutchinson said, and the people near her laughed.

"Jones."

"They do say," Mr. Adams said to Old Man Warner, who stood next to him, "that over in the north village they're talking of giving up the lottery."

Old Man Warner snorted. "Pack of crazy fools," he said. "Listening to the young folks, nothing's good enough for *them.* Next thing you know, they'll be wanting to go back to living in caves, nobody work any more, live *that* way for a while. Used to be a saying about 'Lottery in June, corn be heavy soon.' First thing you know, we'd all be eating stewed chickweed and acorns. There's *always* been a lottery," he added petulantly. "Bad enough to see young Joe Summers up there joking with everybody."

"Some places have already quit lotteries," Mrs. Adams said.

"Nothing but trouble in *that,*" Old Man Warner said stoutly. "Pack of young fools."

"Martin." And Bobby Martin watched his father go forward. "Overdyke. . . . Percy."

"I wish they'd hurry," Mrs. Dunbar said to her older son. "I wish they'd hurry."

"They're almost through," her son said.

"You get ready to run tell Dad," Mrs. Dunbar said.

Mr. Summers called his own name and then stepped forward precisely and selected a slip from the box. Then he called, "Warner."

"Seventy-seventh year I been in the lottery," Old Man Warner said as he went through the crowd. "Seventy-seventh time."

"Watson." The tall boy came awkwardly through the crowd. Someone said, "Don't be nervous, Jack," and Mr. Summers said, "Take your time, son."

"Zanini."

After that, there was a long pause, a breathless pause, until Mr. Summers, holding his slip of paper in the air, said, "All right, fellows." For a minute, no one moved, and then all the slips of paper were opened. Suddenly, all the women began to speak at once, saying, "Who is it?," "Who's got it?," "Is it the Dunbars?," "Is it the Watsons?" Then the voices began to say, "It's Hutchinson. It's Bill," "Bill Hutchinson's got it."

"Go tell your father," Mrs. Dunbar said to her older son.

People began to look around to see the Hutchinsons. Bill Hutchinson was standing quiet, staring down at the paper in his hand. Suddenly, Tessie Hutchinson shouted to Mr. Summers, "You didn't give him time enough to take any paper he wanted. I saw you. It wasn't fair!"

"Be a good sport, Tessie," Mrs. Delacroix called, and Mrs. Graves said, "All of us took the same chance."

"Shut up, Tessie," Bill Hutchinson said.

"Well, everyone," Mr. Summers said, "that was done pretty fast, and now we've got to be hurrying a little more to get done in time." He consulted his next list. "Bill," he said, "you draw for the Hutchinson family. You got any other households in the Hutchinsons?"

"There's Don and Eva," Mrs. Hutchinson yelled. "Make *them* take their chance!"

"Daughters draw with their husbands' families, Tessie," Mr. Summers said gently. "You know that as well as anyone else."

"It wasn't *fair*," Tessie said.

"I guess not, Joe," Bill Hutchinson said regretfully. "My daughter draws with her husband's family, that's only fair. And I've got no other family except the kids."

"Then, as far as drawing for families is concerned, it's you," Mr. Summers said in explanation, "and as far as drawing for households is concerned, that's you, too. Right?"

"Right," Bill Hutchinson said.

"How many kids, Bill?" Mr. Summers asked formally.

"Three," Bill Hutchinson said. "There's Bill, Jr., and Nancy, and little Dave. And Tessie and me."

"All right, then," Mr. Summers said. "Harry, you got their tickets back?"

Mr. Graves nodded and held up the slips of paper. "Put them in the box, then," Mr. Summers directed. "Take Bill's and put it in."

"I think we ought to start over," Mrs. Hutchinson said, as quietly as she could. "I tell you it wasn't *fair*. You didn't give him time enough to choose. Everybody saw that."

Mr. Graves had selected the five slips and put them in the box, and he dropped all the papers but those onto the ground, where the breeze caught them and lifted them off.

"Listen, everybody," Mrs. Hutchinson was saying to the people around her.

"Ready, Bill?" Mr. Summers asked, and Bill Hutchinson, with one quick glance around at his wife and children, nodded.

"Remember," Mr. Summers said, "take the slips and keep them folded until each person has taken one. Harry, you help little Dave." Mr. Graves took the hand of the little boy, who came willingly with him up to the box. "Take a paper out of the box, Davy," Mr. Summers said. Davy put his hand into the box and laughed. "Take just *one* paper," Mr. Summers said. "Harry, you hold it for him." Mr. Graves took the child's hand and removed the folded paper from the tight fist and held it while little Dave stood next to him and looked up at him wonderingly.

"Nancy next," Mr. Summers said. Nancy was twelve, and her school friends breathed heavily as she went forward, switching her skirt, and took a slip daintily from the box. "Bill, Jr.," Mr. Summers said, and Billy, his face red and his feet over-large, nearly knocked the box over as he got a paper out. "Tessie," Mr. Summers said. She hesitated for a minute, looking around defiantly, and then set her lips and went up to the box. She snatched a paper out and held it behind her.

65 "Bill," Mr. Summers said, and Bill Hutchinson reached into the box and felt around, bringing his hand out at last with the slip of paper in it.

The crowd was quiet. A girl whispered, "I hope it's not Nancy," and the sound of the whisper reached the edges of the crowd.

"It's not the way it used to be," Old Man Warner said clearly. "People ain't the way they used to be."

"All right," Mr. Summers said. "Open the papers. Harry, you open little Dave's."

Mr. Graves opened the slip of paper and there was a general sigh through the crowd as he held it up and everyone could see that it was blank. Nancy and Bill, Jr., opened theirs at the same time, and both beamed and laughed, turning around to the crowd and holding their slips of paper above their heads.

70 "Tessie," Mr. Summers said. There was a pause, and then Mr. Summers looked at Bill Hutchinson, and Bill unfolded his paper and showed it. It was blank.

"It's Tessie," Mr. Summers said, and his voice was hushed. "Show us her paper, Bill."

Bill Hutchinson went over to his wife and forced the slip of paper out of her hand. It had a black spot on it, the black spot Mr. Summers had made the night before with the heavy pencil in the coal-company office. Bill Hutchinson held it up, and there was a stir in the crowd.

"All right, folks," Mr. Summers said. "Let's finish quickly."

Although the villagers had forgotten the ritual and lost the original black box, they still remembered to use stones. The pile of stones the boys had made earlier was ready; there were stones on the ground with the blowing scraps of paper that had come out of the box. Mrs. Delacroix selected a stone so large she had to pick it up with both hands and turned to Mrs. Dunbar. "Come on," she said. "Hurry up."

75 Mrs. Dunbar had small stones in both hands, and she said, gasping for breath, "I can't run at all. You'll have to go ahead and I'll catch up with you."

The children had stones already, and someone gave little Davy Hutchinson a few pebbles.

Tessie Hutchinson was in the center of a cleared space by now, and she held her hands out desperately as the villagers moved in on her. "It isn't fair," she said. A stone hit her on the side of the head.

Old Man Warner was saying, "Come on, come on, everyone." Steve Adams was in the front of the crowd of villagers, with Mrs. Graves beside him.

"It ain't fair, it isn't right," Mrs. Hutchinson screamed, and then they were upon her.

(1948)

Questions for Discussion and Writing

Close Reading

1. List the rituals associated with "the lottery." Do you have a clear sense of how they developed?
2. When is Mrs. Hutchinson's character first introduced? Does anything separate her from the other characters before she selects the paper with the black mark on it?
3. Winning a lottery is generally considered a positive thing; how does the author of this story prepare us for the fact that this lottery is a sinister event?

Critical and Creative Reading

4. Is it completely incomprehensible that the people in a village would obediently follow the tradition of stoning one member of their community once a year? Think of examples of something people do routinely without thinking of the consequences to others.
5. What types of activities do people justify by saying, "That's the way it's always been done"? How powerful is our sense of ritual? What would be the cost of an individual rebelling against a ritual practiced by everyone else in a community?
6. The practice of sacrifice goes back to ancient civilizations. Are we more horrified by the sacrifice in this story because it seems to take place in modern times, or is the story only horrifying because we don't understand the purpose of the sacrifice?
7. Imagine that you are a character in this story, one person in the crowd who is expected to throw a rock at Tessie Hutchinson. Also imagine that the consequence of refusing to throw a rock is that you will be the next sacrificial victim. Would you throw the rock?

Connections to Other Readings

8. Wilfred Owen's poem "Dulce et Decorum Est" questions the notion that sacrificing oneself for one's country is a sweet and fitting death. Does Jackson's story also question the value of sacrifice? Does her story have the same emphasis as Owen's poem?

9. Wole Soyinka's play *Death and the King's Horseman* also calls on the main character, Elesin, to sacrifice his life because tradition has long dictated that the king's horseman must die after the king's death. Compare how Jackson's story and Soyinka's play handle the themes of sacrifice, duty to tradition, and the will to survive despite traditions.
10. George in William Dean Howells's story "Editha" dies in service to his country. Do you feel differently about his death than you feel about Tessie Hutchinson's death? Is your response due to the fact that war is more familiar than ritual sacrifice?

Albert Camus

Translated by Justin O'Brien

The Guest

Albert Camus (1913–1960) rose from a childhood of poverty in Algeria (then a colony of France) to literary prominence and was the recipient of the 1957 Nobel Prize for literature. Camus studied philosophy and worked as a journalist in Algeria until 1940, when he moved to France and extended the scope of his writing to include plays, essays, and fiction. He is associated with the French school of thought known as existentialism and with the literary movement known as absurdism, both of which were at their height in the mid-twentieth century in Paris. The dominant theme of these two movements is coming to terms with the potential absurdity of the human condition in a world devoid of religious meaning. Camus attacked questions of ethics throughout his fiction, examining how people behave in complex situations, and he was always aware of the power struggle between dominant groups (such as the wealthy or the colonizers) and subjugated groups.

The schoolmaster was watching the two men climb toward him. One was on horseback, the other on foot. They had not yet tackled the abrupt rise leading to the schoolhouse built on the hillside. They were toiling onward, making slow progress in the snow, among the stones, on the vast expanse of the high, deserted plateau. From time to time the horse stumbled. Without hearing anything yet, he could see the breath issuing from the horse's nostrils. One of the men, at least, knew the region. They were following the trail although it had disappeared days ago under a layer of dirty white snow. The schoolmaster calculated that it would take them half an hour to get onto the hill. It was cold; he went back into the school to get a sweater.

He crossed the empty, frigid classroom. On the blackboard the four rivers of France, drawn with four different colored chalks, had been flowing toward their estuaries for the past three days. Snow had suddenly fallen in mid-October after eight months of drought without the transition of rain, and the twenty pupils, more or less, who lived in the villages scattered over the plateau had stopped coming. With fair weather they would return. Daru now heated only the single room that was his lodging, adjoining the classroom and giving also onto the plateau to the east. Like the class windows, his window looked to the south too. On that side the school was a few kilometers from the point where the plateau began to slope toward the south. In clear weather could be seen the purple mass of the mountain range where the gap opened onto the desert.

Somewhat warmed, Daru returned to the window from which he had first seen the two men. They were no longer visible. Hence they must have tackled the rise. The sky was not so dark, for the snow had stopped falling during the night. The morning had opened with a dirty light which had scarcely become brighter as the ceiling of clouds lifted. At two in the afternoon it seemed as if the day were merely beginning. But still this was better than those three days when the thick snow was falling amidst unbroken darkness with little gusts of wind that rattled the double door of the classroom. Then Daru had spent long hours in his room, leaving it only to go to the shed and feed the chickens or get some coal. Fortunately the delivery truck from Tadjid, the nearest village to the north, had brought his supplies two days before the blizzard. It would return in forty-eight hours.

Besides, he had enough to resist a siege, for the little room was cluttered with bags of wheat that the administration left as a stock to distribute to those of his pupils whose families had suffered from the drought. Actually they had all been victims because they were all poor. Every day Daru would distribute a ration to the children. They had missed it, he knew, during these bad days. Possibly one of the fathers or big brothers would come this afternoon and he could supply them with grain. It was just a matter of carrying them over to the next harvest. Now shiploads of wheat were arriving from France and the worst was over. But it would be hard to forget that poverty, that army of ragged ghosts wandering in the sunlight, the plateaus burned to a cinder month after month, the earth shriveled up little by little, literally scorched, every stone bursting into dust under one's foot. The sheep had died then by thousands and even a few men, here and there, sometimes without anyone's knowing.

In contrast with such poverty, he who lived almost like a monk in his remote 5
schoolhouse, nonetheless satisfied with the little he had and with the rough life, had felt like a lord with his whitewashed walls, his narrow couch, his unpainted shelves, his well, and his weekly provision of water and food. And suddenly this snow, without warning, without the foretaste of rain. This is the way the region was, cruel to live in, even without men—who didn't help matters either. But Daru had been born here. Everywhere else, he felt exiled.

He stepped out onto the terrace in front of the schoolhouse. The two men were now halfway up the slope. He recognized the horseman as Balducci, the old gendarme[1] he had known for a long time. Balducci was holding on the end of a

[1]*gendarme:* A French soldier.

rope an Arab who was walking behind him with hands bound and head lowered. The gendarme waved a greeting to which Daru did not reply, lost as he was in contemplation of the Arab dressed in a faded blue jellaba,[2] his feet in sandals but covered with socks of heavy raw wool, his head surmounted by a narrow, short *chèche.*[3] They were approaching. Balducci was holding back his horse in order not to hurt the Arab, and the group was advancing slowly.

Within earshot, Balducci shouted: "One hour to do the three kilometers from El Ameur!" Daru did not answer. Short and square in his thick sweater, he watched them climb. Not once had the Arab raised his head. "Hello," said Daru when they got up onto the terrace. "Come in and warm up." Balducci painfully got down from his horse without letting go the rope. From under his bristling mustache he smiled at the schoolmaster. His little dark eyes, deep-set under a tanned forehead, and his mouth surrounded with wrinkles made him look attentive and studious. Daru took the bridle, led the horse to the shed, and came back to the two men, who were now waiting for him in the school. He led them into his room. "I am going to heat up the classroom," he said. "We'll be more comfortable there." When he entered the room again, Balducci was on the couch. He had undone the rope tying him to the Arab, who had squatted near the stove. His hands still bound, the *chèche* pushed back on his head, he was looking toward the window. At first Daru noticed only his huge lips, fat, smooth, almost Negroid; yet his nose was straight, his eyes were dark and full of fever. The *chèche* revealed an obstinate forehead and, under the weathered skin now rather discolored by the cold, the whole face had a restless and rebellious look that struck Daru when the Arab, turning his face toward him, looked him straight in the eyes. "Go into the other room," said the schoolmaster, "and I'll make you some mint tea." "Thanks," Balducci said. "What a chore! How I long for retirement." And addressing his prisoner in Arabic: "Come on, you." The Arab got up and, slowly, holding his bound wrists in front of him, went into the classroom.

With the tea, Daru brought a chair. But Balducci was already enthroned on the nearest pupil's desk and the Arab had squatted against the teacher's platform facing the stove, which stood between the desk and the window. When he held out the glass of tea to the prisoner, Daru hesitated at the sight of his bound hands. "He might perhaps be untied." "Sure," said Balducci. "That was for the trip." He started to get to his feet. But Daru, setting the glass on the floor, had knelt beside the Arab. Without saying anything, the Arab watched him with his feverish eyes. Once his hands were free, he rubbed his swollen wrists against each other, took the glass of tea, and sucked up the burning liquid in swift little sips.

"Good," said Daru. "And where are you headed?"

Balducci withdrew his mustache from the tea. "Here, son."

"Odd pupils! And you're spending the night?"

"No. I'm going back to El Ameur. And you will deliver this fellow to Tinguit. He is expected at police headquarters."

Balducci was looking at Daru with a friendly little smile.

[2]*jellaba:* A traditional robe worn by North African Arabs.

[3]*chèche:* A scarf fashioned into a turban.

"What's this story?" asked the schoolmaster. "Are you pulling my leg?"

"No, son. Those are the orders."

"The orders? I'm not . . ." Daru hesitated, not wanting to hurt the old Corsican. "I mean, that's not my job."

"What! What's the meaning of that? In wartime people do all kinds of jobs."

"Then I'll wait for the declaration of war!"

Balducci nodded.

"O.K. But the orders exist and they concern you too. Things are brewing, it appears. There is talk of a forthcoming revolt. We are mobilized, in a way."

Daru still had his obstinate look.

"Listen, son," Balducci said. "I like you and you must understand. There's only a dozen of us at El Ameur to patrol throughout the whole territory of a small department and I must get back in a hurry. I was told to hand this guy over to you and return without delay. He couldn't be kept there. His village was beginning to stir; they wanted to take him back. You must take him to Tinguit tomorrow before the day is over. Twenty kilometers shouldn't faze a husky fellow like you. After that, all will be over. You'll come back to your pupils and your comfortable life."

Behind the wall the horse could be heard snorting and pawing the earth. Daru was looking out the window. Decidedly, the weather was clearing and the light was increasing over the snowy plateau. When all the snow was melted, the sun would take over again and once more would burn the fields of stone. For days, still, the unchanging sky would shed its dry light on the solitary expanse where nothing had any connection with man.

"After all," he said, turning around toward Balducci, "what did he do?" And, before the gendarme had opened his mouth, he asked: "Does he speak French?"

"No, not a word. We had been looking for him for a month, but they were hiding him. He killed his cousin."

"Is he against us?"

"I don't think so. But you can never be sure."

"Why did he kill?"

"A family squabble, I think. One owed the other grain, it seems. It's not at all clear. In short, he killed his cousin with a billhook. You know, like a sheep, *kreezk!*"

Balducci made the gesture of drawing a blade across his throat and the Arab, his attention attracted, watched him with a sort of anxiety. Daru felt a sudden wrath against the man, against all men with their rotten spite, their tireless hates, their blood lust.

But the kettle was singing on the stove. He served Balducci more tea, hesitated, then served the Arab again, who, a second time, drank avidly. His raised arms made the jellaba fall open and the schoolmaster saw his thin, muscular chest.

"Thanks, kid," Balducci said. "And now, I'm off."

He got up and went toward the Arab, taking a small rope from his pocket.

"What are you doing?" Daru asked dryly.

Balducci, disconcerted, showed him the rope.

"Don't bother."

The old gendarme hesitated. "It's up to you. Of course, you are armed?"

"I have my shotgun."

"Where?"

"In the trunk."

"You ought to have it near your bed."

"Why? I have nothing to fear."

"You're crazy, son. If there's an uprising, no one is safe, we're all in the same boat."

"I'll defend myself. I'll have time to see them coming."

Balducci began to laugh, then suddenly the mustache covered the white teeth.

"You'll have time? O.K. That's just what I was saying. You have always been a little cracked. That's why I like you, my son was like that."

At the same time he took out his revolver and put it on the desk.

"Keep it; I don't need two weapons from here to El Ameur."

The revolver shone against the black paint of the table. When the gendarme turned toward him, the schoolmaster caught the smell of leather and horseflesh.

"Listen, Balducci," Daru said suddenly, "every bit of this disgusts me, and first of all your fellow here. But I won't hand him over. Fight, yes, if I have to. But not that."

The old gendarme stood in front of him and looked at him severely.

"You're being a fool," he said slowly. "I don't like it either. You don't get used to putting a rope on a man even after years of it, and you're even ashamed—yes, ashamed. But you can't let them have their way."

"I won't hand him over," Daru said again.

"It's an order, son, and I repeat it."

"That's right. Repeat to them what I've said to you: I won't hand him over."

Balducci made a visible effort to reflect. He looked at the Arab and at Daru. At last he decided.

"No, I won't tell them anything. If you want to drop us, go ahead; I'll not denounce you. I have an order to deliver the prisoner and I'm doing so. And now you'll just sign this paper for me."

"There's no need. I'll not deny that you left him with me."

"Don't be mean with me. I know you'll tell the truth. You're from hereabouts and you are a man. But you must sign, that's the rule."

Daru opened his drawer, took out a little square bottle of purple ink, the red wooden penholder with the "sergeant-major" pen he used for making models of penmanship, and signed. The gendarme carefully folded the paper and put it into his wallet. Then he moved toward the door.

"I'll see you off," Daru said.

"No," said Balducci. "There's no use being polite. You insulted me."

He looked at the Arab, motionless in the same spot, sniffed peevishly, and turned away toward the door. "Good-by, son," he said. The door shut behind him. Balducci appeared suddenly outside the window and then disappeared. His footsteps were muffled by the snow. The horse stirred on the other side of the wall and several chickens fluttered in fright. A moment later Balducci reappeared outside the window leading the horse by the bridle. He walked toward the little rise without turning around and disappeared from sight with the horse following him. A big stone could be heard bouncing down. Daru walked back toward the prisoner, who, without stirring, never took his eyes off him. "Wait," the schoolmaster said in Arabic and went toward the bedroom. As he was going through the door, he had a second thought, went to the desk, took the revolver, and stuck it in his pocket. Then, without looking back, he went into his room.

For some time he lay on his couch watching the sky gradually close over, listening to the silence. It was this silence that had seemed painful to him during the first days here, after the war. He had requested a post in the little town at the base of the foothills separating the upper plateaus from the desert. There, rocky walls, green and black to the north, pink and lavender to the south, marked the frontier of eternal summer. He had been named to a post farther north, on the plateau itself. In the beginning, the solitude and the silence had been hard for him on these wastelands peopled only by stones. Occasionally, furrows suggested cultivation, but they had been dug to uncover a certain kind of stone good for building. The only plowing here was to harvest rocks. Elsewhere a thin layer of soil accumulated in the hollows would be scraped out to enrich paltry village gardens. This is the way it was: bare rock covered three quarters of the region. Towns sprang up, flourished, then disappeared; men came by, loved one another or fought bitterly, then died. No one in this desert, neither he nor his guest, mattered. And yet, outside this desert neither of them, Daru knew, could have really lived.

When he got up, no noise came from the classroom. He was amazed at the unmixed joy he derived from the mere thought that the Arab might have fled and that he would be alone with no decision to make. But the prisoner was there. He had merely stretched out between the stove and the desk. With eyes open, he was staring at the ceiling. In that position, his thick lips were particularly noticeable, giving him a pouting look. "Come," said Daru. The Arab got up and followed him. In the bedroom, the schoolmaster pointed to a chair near the table under the window. The Arab sat down without taking his eyes off Daru.

"Are you hungry?"

"Yes," the prisoner said.

Daru set the table for two. He took flour and oil, shaped a cake in a frying-pan, and lighted the little stove that functioned on bottled gas. While the cake was cooking, he went out to the shed to get cheese, eggs, dates, and condensed milk. When the cake was done he set it on the window sill to cool, heated some condensed milk diluted with water, and beat up the eggs into an omelette. In one of his motions he knocked against the revolver stuck in his right pocket. He set the bowl down, went into the classroom, and put the revolver in his desk drawer. When he came back to the room, night was falling. He put on the light and served the Arab. "Eat," he said. The Arab took a piece of the cake, lifted it eagerly to his mouth, and stopped short.

"And you?" he asked.

"After you. I'll eat too."

The thick lips opened slightly. The Arab hesitated, then bit into the cake determinedly.

The meal over, the Arab looked at the schoolmaster. "Are you the judge?"

"No, I'm simply keeping you until tomorrow."

"Why do you eat with me?"

"I'm hungry."

The Arab fell silent. Daru got up and went out. He brought back a folding bed from the shed, set it up between the table and the stove, perpendicular to his own bed. From a large suitcase which, upright in a corner, served as a shelf for papers, he took two blankets and arranged them on the camp bed. Then he stopped, felt useless, and sat down on his bed. There was nothing more to do or to get ready. He had to look at this man. He looked at him, therefore, trying to imagine his face bursting with rage. He couldn't do so. He could see nothing but the dark yet shining eyes and the animal mouth.

"Why did you kill him?" he asked in a voice whose hostile tone surprised him.

The Arab looked away.

"He ran away. I ran after him."

He raised his eyes to Daru again and they were full of a sort of woeful interrogation. "Now what will they do to me?"

"Are you afraid?"

He stiffened, turning his eyes away.

"Are you sorry?"

The Arab stared at him openmouthed. Obviously he did not understand. Daru's annoyance was growing. At the same time he felt awkward and self-conscious with his big body wedged between the two beds.

"Lie down there," he said impatiently. "That's your bed."

The Arab didn't move. He called to Daru:

"Tell me!"

The schoolmaster looked at him.

"Is the gendarme coming back tomorrow?"

"I don't know."

"Are you coming with us?"

"I don't know. Why?"

The prisoner got up and stretched out on top of the blankets, his feet toward the window. The light from the electric bulb shone straight into his eyes and he closed them at once.

"Why?" Daru repeated, standing beside the bed.

The Arab opened his eyes under the blinding light and looked at him, trying not to blink.

"Come with us," he said.

In the middle of the night, Daru was still not asleep. He had gone to bed after undressing completely; he generally slept naked. But when he suddenly realized that he had nothing on, he hesitated. He felt vulnerable and the temptation came to him to put his clothes back on. Then he shrugged his shoulders;

after all, he wasn't a child and, if need be, he could break his adversary in two. From his bed he could observe him, lying on his back, still motionless with his eyes closed under the harsh light. When Daru turned out the light, the darkness seemed to coagulate all of a sudden. Little by little, the night came back to life in the window where the starless sky was stirring gently. The schoolmaster soon made out the body lying at his feet. The Arab still did not move, but his eyes seemed open. A faint wind was prowling around the schoolhouse. Perhaps it would drive away the clouds and the sun would reappear.

During the night the wind increased. The hens fluttered a little and then were silent. The Arab turned over on his side with his back to Daru, who thought he heard him moan. Then he listened for his guest's breathing, become heavier and more regular. He listened to that breath so close to him and mused without being able to go to sleep. In this room where he had been sleeping alone for a year, this presence bothered him. But it bothered him also by imposing on him a sort of brotherhood he knew well but refused to accept in the present circumstances. Men who share the same rooms, soldiers or prisoners, develop a strange alliance as if, having cast off their armor with their clothing, they fraternized every evening, over and above their differences, in the ancient community of dream and fatigue. But Daru shook himself; he didn't like such musings, and it was essential to sleep.

A little later, however, when the Arab stirred slightly, the schoolmaster was still not asleep. When the prisoner made a second move, he stiffened, on the alert. The Arab was lifting himself slowly on his arms with almost the motion of a sleepwalker. Seated upright in bed, he waited motionless without turning his head toward Daru, as if he were listening attentively. Daru did not stir; it had just occurred to him that the revolver was still in the drawer of his desk. It was better to act at once. Yet he continued to observe the prisoner, who, with the same slithery motion, put his feet on the ground, waited again, then began to stand up slowly. Daru was about to call out to him when the Arab began to walk, in a quite natural but extraordinarily silent way. He was heading toward the door at the end of the room that opened into the shed. He lifted the latch with precaution and went out, pushing the door behind him but without shutting it. Daru had not stirred. "He is running away," he merely thought. "Good riddance!" Yet he listened attentively. The hens were not fluttering; the guest must be on the plateau. A faint sound of water reached him, and he didn't know what it was until the Arab again stood framed in the doorway, closed the door carefully, and came back to bed without a sound. Then Daru turned his back on him and fell asleep. Still later he seemed, from the depths of his sleep, to hear furtive steps around the schoolhouse. "I'm dreaming! I'm dreaming!" he repeated to himself. And he went on sleeping.

When he awoke, the sky was clear; the loose window let in a cold, pure air. 100
The Arab was asleep, hunched up under the blankets now, his mouth open, utterly relaxed. But when Daru shook him, he started dreadfully, staring at Daru with wild eyes as if he had never seen him and such a frightened expression that the schoolmaster stepped back. "Don't be afraid. It's me. You must eat." The Arab nodded his head and said yes. Calm had returned to his face, but his expression was vacant and listless.

The coffee was ready. They drank it seated together on the folding bed as they munched their pieces of the cake. Then Daru led the Arab under the shed and showed him the faucet where he washed. He went back into the room, folded the blankets and the bed, made his own bed and put the room in order. Then he went through the classroom and out onto the terrace. The sun was already rising in the blue sky; a soft, bright light was bathing the deserted plateau. On the ridge the snow was melting in spots. The stones were about to reappear. Crouched on the edge of the plateau, the schoolmaster looked at the deserted expanse. He thought of Balducci. He had hurt him, for he had sent him off in a way as if he didn't want to be associated with him. He could still hear the gendarme's farewell and, without knowing why, he felt strangely empty and vulnerable. At that moment, from the other side of the schoolhouse, the prisoner coughed. Daru listened to him almost despite himself and then, furious, threw a pebble that whistled through the air before sinking into the snow. That man's stupid crime revolted him, but to hand him over was contrary to honor. Merely thinking of it made him smart with humiliation. And he cursed at one and the same time his own people who had sent him this Arab and the Arab too who had dared to kill and not managed to get away. Daru got up, walked in a circle on the terrace, waited motionless, and then went back into the schoolhouse.

The Arab, leaning over the cement floor of the shed, was washing his teeth with two fingers. Daru looked at him and said: "Come." He went back into the room ahead of the prisoner. He slipped a hunting-jacket on over his sweater and put on walking-shoes. Standing, he waited until the Arab had put on his *chèche* and sandals. They went into the classroom and the schoolmaster pointed to the exit, saying: "Go ahead." The fellow didn't budge. "I'm coming," said Daru. The Arab went out. Daru went back into the room and made a package of pieces of rusk, dates, and sugar. In the classroom, before going out, he hesitated a second in front of his desk, then crossed the threshold and locked the door. "That's the way," he said. He started toward the east, followed by the prisoner. But, a short distance from the schoolhouse, he thought he heard a slight sound behind them. He retraced his steps and examined the surroundings of the house, there was no one there. The Arab watched him without seeming to understand. "Come on," said Daru.

They walked for an hour and rested beside a sharp peak of limestone. The snow was melting faster and faster and the sun was drinking up the puddles at once, rapidly cleaning the plateau, which gradually dried and vibrated like the air itself. When they resumed walking, the ground rang under their feet. From time to time a bird rent the space in front of them with a joyful cry. Daru breathed in deeply the fresh morning light. He felt a sort of rapture before the vast familiar expanse, now almost entirely yellow under its dome of blue sky. They walked an hour more, descending toward the south. They reached a level height made up of crumbly rocks. From there on, the plateau sloped down, eastward, toward a low plain where there were a few spindly trees and, to the south, toward outcroppings of rock that gave the landscape a chaotic look.

Daru surveyed the two directions. There was nothing but the sky on the horizon. Not a man could be seen. He turned toward the Arab, who was looking at him blankly. Daru held out the package to him. "Take it," he said. "There are dates, bread, and sugar. You can hold out for two days. Here are a thousand francs too." The Arab took the package and the money but kept his full hands at chest level as if he didn't know what to do with what was being given him. "Now look," the schoolmaster said as he pointed in the direction of the east, "there's the way to Tinguit. You have a two-hour walk. At Tinguit you'll find the administration and the police. They are expecting you." The Arab looked toward the east, still holding the package and the money against his chest. Daru took his elbow and turned him rather roughly toward the south. At the foot of the height on which they stood could be seen a faint path. "That's the trail across the plateau. In a day's walk from here you'll find pasturelands and the first nomads. They'll take you in and shelter you according to their law." The Arab had now turned toward Daru and a sort of panic was visible in his expression. "Listen," he said. Daru shook his head: "No, be quiet. Now I'm leaving you." He turned his back on him, took two long steps in the direction of the school, looked hesitantly at the motionless Arab, and started off again. For a few minutes he heard nothing but his own step resounding on the cold ground and did not turn his head. A moment later, however, he turned around. The Arab was still there on the edge of the hill, his arms hanging now, and he was looking at the schoolmaster. Daru felt something rise in his throat. But he swore with impatience, waved vaguely, and started off again. He had already gone some distance when he again stopped and looked. There was no longer anyone on the hill.

Daru hesitated. The sun was now rather high in the sky and was beginning 105
to beat down on his head. The schoolmaster retraced his steps, at first somewhat uncertainly, then with decision. When he reached the little hill, he was bathed in sweat. He climbed it as fast as he could and stopped, out of breath, at the top. The rock-fields to the south stood out sharply against the blue sky, but on the plain to the east a steamy heat was already rising. And in that slight haze, Daru, with heavy heart, made out the Arab walking slowly on the road to prison.

A little later, standing before the window of the classroom, the schoolmaster was watching the clear light bathing the whole surface of the plateau, but he hardly saw it. Behind him on the blackboard, among the winding French rivers, sprawled the clumsily chalked-up words he had just read: "You handed over our brother. You will pay for this." Daru looked at the sky, the plateau, and, beyond, the invisible lands stretching all the way to the sea. In this vast landscape he had loved so much, he was alone.

(1957)

Questions for Discussion and Writing

Close Reading

1. Before Balducci and his prisoner enter Daru's school, the reader is given a description of the setting and of Daru's situation. How is this description important to the rest of the story?
2. Daru proclaims to Balducci that he will not follow the order to deliver the prisoner. Why not? And why is it significant that Balducci refers to him repeatedly as "son"?

3. Balducci gives Daru a revolver when he hands over the prisoner. Note the passages when we are made aware of the revolver: what might it symbolize?

Critical and Creative Reading

4. Daru declares that he will not do what Balducci has asked him to do. Is he a rebel or someone who doesn't want to get involved?
5. Daru gives the prisoner freedom of choice when he points out the two roads to him. Yet in giving the prisoner food and money, he has aided a known criminal. If the prisoner were to commit another crime, would Daru be responsible as an accomplice? Or would you say that the prisoner was not Daru's concern in the first place and therefore he could not be blamed for what the prisoner did?
6. Two moments of irony occur toward the end of the story: (1) the prisoner apparently decides to march toward prison and hand himself over to the authorities, and (2) Daru's life is threatened by guerrillas who think that Daru has handed the prisoner over when he has not. How do these ironies complicate the theme of this story? (As a way of clarifying your thought about this question, imagine the story with a different ending: the prisoner marches toward freedom and the guerrillas thank Daru for freeing him.)

Connections to Other Readings

7. In Wole Soyinka's play *Death and the King's Horseman* the character Olunde acts in a similar manner to Daru in "The Guest": both men try to make a better world by undoing the actions of someone "higher" than them. Examine this theme by commenting on the fate of Olunde and Daru.
8. Are Daru in this story and Waverly Jong in Amy Tan's "Rules of the Game" rebels, or are they people who want to rewrite the rules? (Is there a difference?)
9. Comment on the colonial setting of this story and of George Orwell's essay "Shooting an Elephant." Do Camus and Orwell share a perspective on the relationship between colonizers and colonial subjects? To what degree are these pieces critical of the colonial system?

John Updike

A & P

John Updike (b. 1932) is one of the most prolific American writers. Although he is best known for his novels of small town and suburban discontentment and infidelity—notably in the "Rabbit novels" and the 1968 novel *Couples*—Updike has written on a broad range of subjects and has set his novels all over the globe as well as in the past and the future. He has published an astonishing number of short stories, poems, and nonfiction works, in addition to nearly two dozen novels, and he is consistently recognized and rewarded for his talents, especially his glittering prose: two of the "Rabbit novels" won the Pulitzer Prize. The following story is from early in his career; it first appeared in the 1962 story collection *Pigeon Feathers*. The main character of this story—a well-intentioned young man consumed by sexual desire—is a common type for Updike, but the unsophisticated first-person voice is not typical of his stories. (See also his story "Wife-Wooing" in Chapter 13.)

In walks these three girls in nothing but bathing suits. I'm in the third checkout slot, with my back to the door, so I don't see them until they're over by the bread. The one that caught my eye first was the one in the plaid green two-piece. She was a chunky kid, with a good tan and a sweet broad soft-looking can with those two crescents of white just under it, where the sun never seems to hit, at the top of the backs of her legs. I stood there with my hand on a box of HiHo crackers trying to remember if I rang it up or not. I ring it up again and the customer starts giving me hell. She's one of these cash-register-watchers, a witch about fifty with rouge on her cheekbones and no eyebrows, and I know it made her day to trip me up. She'd been watching cash registers for fifty years and probably never seen a mistake before.

By the time I got her feathers smoothed and her goodies into a bag—she gives me a little snort in passing, if she'd been born at the right time they would have burned her over in Salem—by the time I get her on her way the girls had circled around the bread and were coming back, without a pushcart, back my way along the counters, in the aisle between the checkouts and the Special bins. They didn't even have shoes on. There was this chunky one, with the two-piece—it was bright green and all the seams on the bra were still sharp and her belly was still pretty pale so I guessed she just got it (the suit)—there was this one, with one of those chubby berry-faces, the lips all bunched together under her nose, this one, and a tall one, with black hair that hadn't quite frizzed right, and one of these sunburns right across under the eyes, and a chin that was too long—you know, the kind of girl other girls think is very "striking" and "attractive" but never quite makes it, as they very well know, which is why they like her so much—and then the third one, that wasn't quite so tall. She was the queen. She kind of led them, the other two peeking around and making their shoulders round. She didn't look around, not this queen, she just walked straight on slowly, on these long white primadonna legs. She came down a little hard on her heels, as if she didn't walk in bare feet that much, putting down her heels and then letting the weight move along to her toes as if she was testing the floor with every step, putting a little deliberate extra action into it. You never know for sure how girls' minds work (do you really think it's a mind in there or just a little buzz like a bee in a glass jar?) but you got the idea she had talked the other two into coming here with her, and now she was showing them how to do it, walk slow and hold yourself straight.

She had on a kind of dirty-pink—beige maybe, I don't know—bathing suit with a little nubble all over it and, what got me, the straps were down. They were off her shoulders looped loose around the cool tops of her arms, and I guess as a result the suit had slipped a little on her, so all around the top of the cloth there was this shining rim. If it hadn't been there you wouldn't have known there could have been anything whiter than those shoulders. With the straps pushed off, there was nothing between the top of the suit and the top of her head except just *her*, this clean bare plane of the top of her chest down from the shoulder bones like a dented sheet of metal tilted in the light. I mean, it was more than pretty.

She had a sort of oaky hair that the sun and salt had bleached, done up in a bun that was unravelling, and a kind of prim face. Walking into the A & P with your straps down, I suppose it's the only kind of face you *can* have. She held her head so high her neck, coming up out of those white shoulders, looked kind of stretched, but I didn't mind. The longer her neck was, the more of her there was.

She must have felt in the corner of her eye me and over my shoulder 5
Stokesie in the second slot watching, but she didn't tip. Not this queen. She kept her eyes moving across the racks, and stopped, and turned so slow it made my stomach rub the inside of my apron, and buzzed to the other two, who kind of huddled against her for relief, and then they all three of them went up the cat-and-dog-food-breakfast-cereal-macaroni-rice-raisins-seasonings-spreads-spaghetti-soft-drinks-crackers-and-cookies aisle. From the third slot I look straight up this aisle to the meat counter, and I watched them all the way. The fat one with the tan sort of fumbled with the cookies, but on second thought she put the package back. The sheep pushing their carts down the aisle—the girls were walking against the usual traffic (not that we have one-way signs or anything)—were pretty hilarious. You could see them, when Queenie's white shoulders dawned on them, kind of jerk, or hop, or hiccup, but their eyes snapped back to their own baskets and on they pushed. I bet you could set off dynamite in an A & P and the people would by and large keep reaching and checking oatmeal off their lists and muttering "Let me see, there was a third thing, began with A, asparagus, no, ah, yes, applesauce!" or whatever it is they do mutter. But there was no doubt, this jiggled them. A few houseslaves in pin curlers even looked around after pushing their carts past to make sure what they had seen was correct.

You know, it's one thing to have a girl in a bathing suit down on the beach, where what with the glare nobody can look at each other much anyway, and another thing in the cool of the A & P, under the fluorescent lights, against all those stacked packages, with her feet paddling along naked over our checkerboard green-and-cream rubber-tile floor.

"Oh Daddy," Stokesie said beside me. "I feel so faint."

"Darling," I said. "Hold me tight." Stokesie's married, with two babies chalked up on his fuselage already, but as far as I can tell that's the only difference. He's twenty-two, and I was nineteen this April.

"Is it done?" he asks, the responsible married man finding his voice. I forgot to say he thinks he's going to be manager some sunny day, maybe in

1990 when it's called the Great Alexandrov and Petrooshki Tea Company or something.[1]

What he meant was, our town is five miles from a beach, with a big summer colony out on the Point, but we're right in the middle of town, and the women generally put on a shirt or shorts or something before they get out of the car into the street. And anyway these are usually women with six children and varicose veins mapping their legs and nobody, including them, could care less. As I say, we're right in the middle of town, and if you stand at our front doors you can see two banks and the Congregational church and the newspaper store and three real estate offices and about twenty-seven old freeloaders tearing up Central Street because the sewer broke again. It's not as if we're on the Cape; we're north of Boston and there's people in this town haven't seen the ocean for twenty years.

The girls had reached the meat counter and were asking McMahon something. He pointed, they pointed, and they shuffled out of sight behind a pyramid of Diet Delight peaches. All that was left for us to see was old McMahon patting his mouth and looking after them sizing up their joints. Poor kids, I began to feel sorry for them, they couldn't help it.

Now here comes the sad part of the story, at least my family says it's sad, but I don't think it's so sad myself. The store's pretty empty, it being Thursday afternoon, so there was nothing much to do except lean on the register and wait for the girls to show up again. The whole store was like a pinball machine and I didn't know which tunnel they'd come out of. After a while they come around out of the far aisle, around the light bulbs, records at discount of the Caribbean Six or Tony Martin Sings or some such gunk you wonder they waste the wax on, six-packs of candy bars, and plastic toys done up in cellophane that fall apart when a kid looks at them anyway. Around they come, Queenie still leading the way, and holding a little gray jar in her hand. Slots Three through Seven are unmanned and I could see her wondering between Stokes and me, but Stokesie with his usual luck draws an old party in baggy gray pants who stumbles up with four giant cans of pineapple juice (what do these bums *do* with all that pineapple juice? I've often asked myself) so the girls come to me. Queenie puts down the jar and I take it into my fingers icy cold. Kingfish Fancy Herring Snacks in Pure Sour Cream: 49¢. Now her hands are empty, not a ring or a bracelet, bare as God made them, and I wonder where the money's coming from. Still with that prim look she lifts a folded dollar bill out of the hollow at the center of her nubbled pink top. The jar went heavy in my hand. Really, I thought that was so cute.

Then everybody's luck begins to run out. Lengel comes in from haggling with a truck full of cabbages on the lot and is about to scuttle into that door marked MANAGER behind which he hides all day when the girls touch his eye. Lengel's pretty dreary, teaches Sunday school and the rest, but he doesn't miss that much. He comes over and says, "Girls, this isn't the beach."

[1] *Great Alexandrov and Petrooshki:* "A & P" stands for "Atlantic and Pacific." The full name of this chain of grocery stores was "The Great Atlantic and Pacific Tea Company." The fear expressed here is that the Soviet Union, America's adversary during the cold war, would eventually triumph. The story takes place in the late 1950s.

Queenie blushes, though maybe it's just a brush of sunburn I was noticing for the first time, now that she was so close. "My mother asked me to pick up a jar of herring snacks." Her voice kind of startled me, the way voices do when you see the people first, coming out so flat and dumb yet kind of tony, too, the way it ticked over "pick up" and "snacks." All of a sudden I slid right down her voice into her living room. Her father and the other men were standing around in ice-cream coats and bow ties and the women were in sandals picking up herring snacks on toothpicks off a big glass plate and they were all holding drinks the color of water with olives and springs of mint in them. When my parents have somebody over they get lemonade and if it's a real racy affair Schlitz in tall glasses with "They'll Do It Every Time" cartoons stencilled on.

"That's all right," Lengel said. "But this isn't the beach." His repeating this 15
struck me as funny, as if it had just occurred to him, and he had been thinking all these years the A & P was a great big dune and he was the head lifeguard. He didn't like my smiling—as I say he doesn't miss much—but he concentrates on giving the girls that sad Sunday-school-superintendent stare.

Queenie's blush is no sunburn now, and the plump one in plaid, that I liked better from the back—a really sweet can—pipes up, "We weren't doing any shopping. We just came in for the one thing."

"That makes no difference," Lengel tells her, and I could see from the way his eyes went that he hadn't noticed she was wearing a two-piece before. "We want you decently dressed when you come in here."

"We *are* decent," Queenie says suddenly, her lower lip pushing, getting sore now that she remembers her place, a place from which the crowd that runs the A & P must look pretty crummy. Fancy Herring Snacks flashed in her very blue eyes.

"Girls, I don't want to argue with you. After this come in here with your shoulders covered. It's our policy." He turns his back. That's policy for you. Policy is what the kingpins want. What the others want is juvenile delinquency.

All this while, the customers had been showing up with their carts but, you 20
know, sheep, seeing a scene, they had all bunched up on Stokesie, who shook open a paper bag as gently as peeling a peach, not wanting to miss a word. I could feel in the silence everybody getting nervous, most of all Lengel, who asks me, "Sammy, have you rung up their purchase?"

I thought and said "No" but it wasn't about that I was thinking. I go through the punches, 4, 9, GROC, TOT—it's more complicated than you think, and after you do it often enough, it begins to make a little song, that you hear words to, in my case "Hello (*bing*) there, you (*gung*) hap-py *pee*-pul (*splat*)!"—the *splat* being the drawer flying out. I uncrease the bill, tenderly as you may imagine, it just having come from between the two smoothest scoops of vanilla I had ever known there were, and pass a half and a penny into her narrow pink palm, and nestle the herrings in a bag and twist its neck and hand it over, all the time thinking.

The girls, and who'd blame them, are in a hurry to get out, so I say "I quit" to Lengel quick enough for them to hear, hoping they'll stop and watch me, their unsuspected hero. They keep right on going, into the electric eye; the door flies open and they flicker across the lot to their car, Queenie and Plaid and Big Tall Goony-Goony (not that as raw material she was so bad), leaving me with Lengel and a kink in his eyebrow.

"Did you say something, Sammy?"

"I said I quit."

"I thought you did."

"You didn't have to embarrass them."

"It was they who were embarrassing us."

I started to say something that came out "Fiddle-de-do." It's a saying of my grandmother's, and I know she would have been pleased.

"I don't think you know what you're saying," Lengel said.

"I know you don't," I said. "But I do." I pull the bow at the back of my apron and start shrugging it off my shoulders. A couple of customers that had been heading for my slot begin to knock against each other, like scared pigs in a chute.

5309 10

your life," Lengel says, and I know that's true too, but remembering how he made that pretty girl blush makes me so scrunchy inside I punch the No Sale tab and the machine whirs "pee-pul" and the drawer splats out. One advantage to this scene taking place in summer, I can follow this up with a clean exit, there's no fumbling around getting your coat and earmuffs, I just saunter into the electric eye in my white shirt that my mother ironed the night before, and the door heaves itself open, and outside the sunshine is skating around on the asphalt.

I look around for my girls, but they're gone, of course. There~~'s nobody~~ (wasn't anybody) but some young married screaming with her children about some candy they didn't get by the door (of) a blue Falcon station wagon. Looking back in the big windows, over the bags of peat moss and aluminum furniture stacked on the pavement, I ~~can~~ (could) see Lengel in my place in the slot, checking the sheep through. His face ~~is~~ (was) dark gray and his back stiff, as if he'd just had an injection of iron, and my stomach kind of ~~falls~~ (fell) ~~as~~ I ~~realize~~ (felt) how hard the world~~'s~~ (was) going to be to me ~~hereafter~~ (then).

JOHN UPDIKE

Typewritten manuscript from John Updike's "A & P."

Lengel sighs and begins to look very patient and old and gray. He's been a friend of my parents for years. "Sammy, you don't want to do this to your Mom and Dad," he tells me. It's true, I don't. But it seems to me that once you begin a gesture it's fatal not to go through with it. I folded the apron, "Sammy" stitched in red on the pocket, and put it on the counter, and drop the bow tie on top of it. The bow tie is theirs, if you've ever wondered. "You'll feel this for the rest of your life," Lengel says, and I know that's true, too, but remembering how he made that pretty girl blush makes me so scrunchy inside I punch the No Sale tab and the machine whirs "pee-pul" and the drawer splats out. One advantage to this scene taking place in summer, I can follow this up with a clean exit, there's no fumbling around getting your coat and galoshes, I just saunter into the electric eye in my white shirt that my mother ironed the night before, and the door heaves itself open, and outside the sunshine is skating around on the asphalt.

I look around for my girls, but they're gone, of course. There wasn't anybody but some young married screaming with her children about some candy they didn't get by the door of a powder-blue Falcon station wagon. Looking back in the big windows, over the bags of peat moss and aluminum lawn furniture stacked on the pavement, I could see Lengel in my place in the slot, checking the sheep through. His face was dark gray and his back stiff, as if he's just had an injection of iron, and my stomach kind of fell as I felt how hard the world was going to be to me hereafter.

(1961)

Questions for Discussion and Writing

Close Reading

1. What kind of a place is the A & P store where Sammy works, based on the details of this story? How does the setting affect the story's theme?
2. Sammy repeatedly refers to the other customers as "sheep." What is the effect of this characterization? Do you notice any other animal imagery in the story?
3. What range of emotions does Sammy face after uttering the words "I quit"? How do these emotions make sense of his final observation in the story's last sentence?

Critical and Creative Reading

4. Would the story have a different meaning if the girls Sammy is defending heard him say "I quit"?
5. The story describes a fairly mundane scene—a teenager quits his dead-end job—yet there seems to be something larger at stake here: what is it?
6. Write a version of "A & P" from the perspective of "Queenie." Think about her personality and about the significance of Sammy in her eyes.

CONNECTIONS TO OTHER READINGS

7. Who is more rebellious: Sammy in "A & P" or Waverly Jong in "Rules of the Game"?
8. Consider the themes of marriage and middle-class respectability as they play out in "A & P" and in Gregory Corso's poem "Marriage."
9. Write an essay exploring communication and desire in "A & P" and in T. S. Eliot's poem "The Love Song of J. Alfred Prufrock."

Jamaica Kincaid

Girl

Jamaica Kincaid (b. 1949) is the author of essays, stories, and novels, though her work (like "Girl") is frequently difficult to categorize. A native of St. John's Island, Antigua, Kincaid now lives in the United States, and the subject of her writings is the sometimes contentious relationship between natives of the Caribbean islands and wealthy Americans who do not realize the value of Caribbean cultures. As you are reading "Girl," consider whether you would classify it as a short story. If not, what is it?

Wash the white clothes on Monday and put them on the stone heap; wash the color clothes on Tuesday and put them on the clothesline to dry; don't walk barehead in the hot sun; cook pumpkin fritters in very hot sweet oil; soak your little cloths right after you take them off; when buying cotton to make yourself a nice blouse, be sure that it doesn't have gum on it, because that way it won't hold up well after a wash; soak salt fish overnight before you cook it; is it true that you sing benna[1] in Sunday school?; always eat your food in such a way that it won't turn someone else's stomach; on Sundays try to walk like a lady and not like the slut you are so bent on becoming; don't sing benna in Sunday school; you mustn't speak to wharf-rat boys, not even to give directions; don't eat fruits on the street—flies will follow you; *but I don't sing benna on Sundays at all and never in Sunday school;* this is how to sew on a button; this is how to make a buttonhole for the button you have just sewed on; this is how to hem a dress when you see the hem coming down and so to prevent yourself from looking like the slut I know you are so bent on becoming; this is how you iron your father's khaki shirt so that it doesn't have a crease; this is how you iron your father's khaki pants so that they don't have a crease; this is how you grow okra—far from the house,

[1]*benna:* Calypso music, popular music not appropriate for church.

because okra tree harbors red ants; when you are growing dasheen,[2] make sure it gets plenty of water or else it makes your throat itch when you are eating it; this is how you sweep a corner; this is how you sweep a whole house; this is how you sweep a yard; this is how you smile to someone you don't like too much; this is how you smile to someone you don't like at all; this is how you smile to someone you like completely; this is how you set a table for tea; this is how you set a table for dinner; this is how you set a table for dinner with an important guest; this is how you set a table for lunch; this is how you set a table for breakfast; this is how to behave in the presence of men who don't know you very well, and this way they won't recognize immediately the slut I have warned you against becoming; be sure to wash every day, even if it is with your own spit; don't squat down to play marbles—you are not a boy, you know; don't pick people's flowers—you might catch something; don't throw stones at blackbirds, because it might not be a blackbird at all; this is how to make a bread pudding; this is how to make doukona;[3] this is how to make pepper pot; this is how to make a good medicine for a cold; this is how to make a good medicine to throw away a child before it even becomes a child; this is how to catch a fish; this is how to throw back a fish you don't like; and that way something bad won't fall on you; this is how to bully a man; this is how a man bullies you; this is how to love a man, and if this doesn't work there are other ways, and if they don't work don't feel too bad about giving up; this is how to spit up in the air if you feel like it, and this is how to move quick so that it doesn't fall on you; this is how to make ends meet; always squeeze bread to make sure it's fresh; *but what if the baker won't let me feel the bread?*; you mean to say that after all you are really going to be the kind of woman who the baker won't let near the bread?

(1978)

Questions for Discussion and Writing

Close Reading

1. The narrator of "Girl"—except for the phrases in italics—appears to be the girl's mother; how do we know this?
2. What phrases are repeated throughout the story? What is the effect of this repetition?
3. The final italicized phrase sets up the story's conclusion; what is the purpose of the first italicized phrase?

Critical and Creative Reading

4. Create a set of useful categories that could be used to classify all the phrases in "Girl." The number and type of categories are up to you; the key is to use them to say something interpretive about the story.

[2]*dasheen:* An edible tuber that is a staple food of some subtropical countries. Also called *taro*.

[3]*doukona:* A kind of spiced pudding.

5. If this story were entitled "Boy," what would have to change?
6. What is your dominant response to the mother character in this story? Do any phrases temper this response, or is it continually reinforced throughout?

Connections to Other Readings

7. Consider female rebellion in "Girl" and in McKenzie's story "Stop That Girl."
8. Write about the way mothers exert rhetorical power in "Girl" and in Amy Tan's "Rules of the Game."
9. Discuss the way female sexual appeal is treated in the following works: Jamaica Kincaid's "Girl," John Updike's "A & P," and Christina Rossetti's "Goblin Market." Why does society seem so concerned with the reputation of young women?

Amy Tan

Rules of the Game

Amy Tan (b. 1952) was born in Oakland, California, the daughter of Chinese immigrants. Following the tragic early death of her father and brother, Tan's mother brought the family to Switzerland, where Tan completed high school. She returned to California for college; in 1985 she wrote the following story, "Rules of the Game," for a writing workshop. The story developed into the first of her four novels, *The Joy Luck Club*, which won the National Book Award in 1989. She has also published books for children and a collection of essays, *The Opposite of Fate* (2004). Her intense relationship with her mother is evident in much of her work, including the following story. Note the way Tan uses language to characterize the narrator's mother as well as the narrator.

I was six when my mother taught me the art of invisible strength. It was a strategy for winning arguments, respect from others, and eventually, though neither of us knew it at the time, chess games.

"Bite back your tongue," scolded my mother when I cried loudly, yanking her hand toward the store that sold bags of salted plums. At home, she said, "Wise guy, he not go against wind. In Chinese we say, Come from South, blow with wind—poom!—North will follow. Strongest wind cannot be seen."

The next week I bit back my tongue as we entered the store with the forbidden candies. When my mother finished her shopping, she quietly plucked a small bag of plums from the rack and put it on the counter with the rest of the items.

My mother imparted her daily truths so she could help my older brothers and me rise above our circumstances. We lived in San Francisco's Chinatown. Like most of the other Chinese children who played in the back alleys of restaurants and curio shops, I didn't think we were poor. My bowl was always full, three five-course meals every day, beginning with a soup of mysterious things I didn't want to know the names of.

5 We lived on Waverly Place, in a warm, clean, two-bedroom flat that sat above a small Chinese bakery specializing in steamed pastries and dim sum. In the early morning, when the alley was still quiet, I could smell fragrant red beans as they were cooked down to a pasty sweetness. By daybreak, our flat was heavy with the odor of fried sesame balls and sweet curried chicken crescents. From my bed, I would listen as my father got ready for work, then locked the door behind him, one-two-three clicks.

At the end of our two-block alley was a small sandlot playground with swings and slides well-shined down the middle with use. The play area was bordered by wood-slat benches where old-country people sat cracking roasted watermelon seeds with their golden teeth and scattering the husks to an impatient gathering of gurgling pigeons. The best playground, however, was the dark alley itself. It was crammed with daily mysteries and adventures. My brothers and I would peer into the medicinal herb shop, watching old Li dole out onto a stiff sheet of white paper the right amount of insect shells, saffron-colored seeds, and pungent leaves for his ailing customers. It was said that he once cured a woman dying of an ancestral curse that had eluded the best of American doctors. Next to the pharmacy was a printer who specialized in gold-embossed wedding invitations and festive red banners.

Farther down the street was Ping Yuen Fish Market. The front window displayed a tank crowded with doomed fish and turtles struggling to gain footing on the slimy green-tiled sides. A hand-written sign informed tourists, "Within this store, is all for food, not for pet." Inside, the butchers with their bloodstained white smocks deftly gutted the fish while customers cried out their orders and shouted, "Give me your freshest," to which the butchers always protested, "All are freshest." On less crowded market days, we would inspect the crates of live frogs and crabs which we were warned not to poke, boxes of dried cuttlefish, and row upon row of iced prawns, squid, and slippery fish. The sanddabs made me shiver each time; their eyes lay on one flattened side and reminded me of my mother's story of a careless girl who ran into a crowded street and was crushed by a cab. "Was smash flat," reported my mother.

At the corner of the alley was Hong Sing's, a four-table café with a recessed stairwell in front that led to a door marked "Tradesmen." My brothers and I believed the bad people emerged from this door at night. Tourists never went to Hong Sing's, since the menu was printed only in Chinese. A Caucasian man with a big camera once posed me and my playmates in front of the restaurant. He had us move to the side of the picture window so the photo would capture the roasted duck with its head dangling from a juice-covered rope. After he took the picture, I told him he should go into Hong Sing's and eat dinner. When he smiled and asked me what they served, I shouted, "Guts and duck's feet and octopus gizzards!" Then I ran off with my friends, shrieking with laughter as we scampered across the alley and hid in the entryway grotto of the China Gem Company, my heart pounding with hope that he would chase us.

My mother named me after the street that we lived on: Waverly Place Jong, my official name for important American documents. But my family called me Meimei, "Little Sister." I was the youngest, the only daughter. Each morning before school, my mother would twist and yank on my thick black hair until she had formed two tightly wound pigtails. One day, as she struggled to weave a hard-toothed comb through my disobedient hair, I had a sly thought.

I asked her, "Ma, what is Chinese torture?" My mother shook her head. A 10
bobby pin was wedged between her lips. She wetted her palm and smoothed the hair above my ear, then pushed the pin in so that it nicked sharply against my scalp.

"Who say this word?" she asked without a trace of knowing how wicked I was being. I shrugged my shoulders and said, "Some boy in my class said Chinese people do Chinese torture."

"Chinese people do many things," she said simply. "Chinese people do business, do medicine, do painting. Not lazy like American people. We do torture. Best torture."

My older brother Vincent was the one who actually got the chess set. We had gone to the annual Christmas party held at the First Chinese Baptist Church at the end of the alley. The missionary ladies had put together a Santa bag of gifts donated by members of another church. None of the gifts had names on them. There were separate sacks for boys and girls of different ages.

One of the Chinese parishioners had donned a Santa Claus costume and a stiff paper beard with cotton balls glued to it. I think the only children who thought he was the real thing were too young to know that Santa Claus was not Chinese. When my turn came up, the Santa man asked me how old I was. I thought it was a trick question; I was seven according to the American formula and eight by the Chinese calendar. I said I was born on March 17, 1951. That seemed to satisfy him. He then solemnly asked if I had been a very, very good girl this year and did I believe in Jesus Christ and obey my parents. I knew the only answer to that. I nodded back with equal solemnity.

Having watched the older children opening their gifts, I already knew that 15
the big gifts were not necessarily the nicest ones. One girl my age got a large coloring book of biblical characters, while a less greedy girl who selected a smaller box received a glass vial of lavender toilet water. The sound of the box was also important. A ten-year-old boy had chosen a box that jangled when he shook it. It was a tin globe of the world with a slit for inserting money. He must have thought it was full of dimes and nickels, because when he saw that it had just ten pennies, his face fell with such undisguised disappointment that his mother slapped the side of his head and led him out of the church hall, apologizing to the crowd for her son who had such bad manners he couldn't appreciate such a fine gift.

As I peered into the sack, I quickly fingered the remaining presents, testing their weight, imagining what they contained. I chose a heavy compact one that was wrapped in shiny silver foil and a red satin ribbon. It was a twelve-pack of Life Savers and I spent the rest of the party arranging and rearranging the candy tubes in the order of my favorites. My brother Winston chose wisely as well. His present turned out to be a box of intricate plastic parts; the instructions on the box proclaimed that when they were properly assembled he would have an authentic miniature replica of a World War II submarine.

Vincent got the chess set, which would have been a very decent present to get at a church Christmas party, except it was obviously used and, as we discovered later, it was missing a black pawn and a white knight. My mother graciously thanked the unknown benefactor, saying, "Too good. Cost too much." At which point, an old lady with fine white, wispy hair nodded toward our family and said with a whistling whisper, "Merry, merry Christmas."

When we got home, my mother told Vincent to throw the chess set away. "She not want it. We not want it." she said, tossing her head stiffly to the side with a tight, proud smile. My brothers had deaf ears. They were already lining up the chess pieces and reading from the dog-eared instruction book.

I watched Vincent and Winston play during Christmas week. The chessboard seemed to hold elaborate secrets waiting to be untangled. The chessmen were more powerful than old Li's magic herbs that cured ancestral curses. And my brothers wore such serious faces that I was sure something was at stake that was greater than avoiding the tradesmen's door to Hong Sing's.

"Let me! Let me!" I begged between games when one brother or the other 20
would sit back with a deep sigh of relief and victory, the other annoyed, unable to let go of the outcome. Vincent at first refused to let me play, but when I offered my Life Savers as replacements for the buttons that filled in for the missing pieces, he relented. He chose the flavors: wild cherry for the black pawn and peppermint for the white knight. Winner could eat both.

As our mother sprinkled flour and rolled out small doughy circles for the steamed dumplings that would be our dinner that night, Vincent explained the rules, pointing to each piece. "You have sixteen pieces and so do I. One king and queen, two bishops, two knights, two castles, and eight pawns. The pawns can only move forward one step, except on the first move. Then they can move two. But they can only take men by moving crossways like this, except in the beginning, when you can move ahead and take another pawn."

"Why?" I asked as I moved my pawn. "Why can't they move more steps?"

"Because they're pawns," he said.

"But why do they go crossways to take other men? Why aren't there any women and children?"

"Why is the sky blue? Why must you always ask stupid questions?" asked 25
Vincent. "This is a game. These are the rules. I didn't make them up. See. Here in the book." He jabbed a page with a pawn in his hand. "Pawn. P-A-W-N. Pawn. Read it yourself."

My mother patted the flour off her hands. "Let me see book," she said quietly. She scanned the pages quickly, not reading the foreign English symbols, seeming to search deliberately for nothing in particular.

"This American rules," she concluded at last. "Every time people come out from foreign country, must know rules. You not know, judge say, Too bad, go back. They not telling you why so you can use their way go forward. They say, Don't know why, you find out yourself. But they knowing all the time. Better you take it, find out why yourself." She tossed her head back with a satisfied smile.

I found out about all the whys later. I read the rules and looked up all the big words in a dictionary. I borrowed books from the Chinatown library. I studied each chess piece, trying to absorb the power each contained.

I learned about opening moves and why it's important to control the center early on; the shortest distance between two points is straight down the middle. I learned about the middle game and why tactics between two adversaries are like clashing ideas; the one who plays better has the clearest plans for both attacking and getting out of traps. I learned why it is essential in the endgame to have foresight, a mathematical understanding of all possible moves, and patience; all weaknesses and advantages become evident to a strong adversary and are obscured to a tiring opponent. I discovered that for the whole game one must gather invisible strengths and see the endgame before the game begins.

I also found out why I should never reveal "why" to others. A little knowledge 30
withheld is a great advantage one should store for future use. That is the power of chess. It is a game of secrets in which one must show and never tell.

I loved the secrets I found within the sixty-four black and white squares. I carefully drew a handmade chessboard and pinned it to the wall next to my bed, where I would stare for hours at imaginary battles. Soon I no longer lost any games or Life Savers, but I lost my adversaries. Winston and Vincent decided they were more interested in roaming the streets after school in their Hopalong Cassidy cowboy hats.

On a cold spring afternoon, while walking home from school, I detoured through the playground at the end of our alley. I saw a group of old men, two seated across a folding table playing a game of chess, others smoking pipes, eating peanuts, and watching. I ran home and grabbed Vincent's chess set, which was bound in a cardboard box with rubber bands. I also carefully selected two prized rolls of Life Savers. I came back to the park and approached a man who was observing the game.

"Want to play?" I asked him. His face widened with surprise and he grinned as he looked at the box under my arm.

"Little sister, been a long time since I play with dolls," he said, smiling benevolently. I quickly put the box down next to him on the bench and displayed my retort.

Lau Po, as he allowed me to call him, turned out to be a much better player 35
than my brothers. I lost many games and many Life Savers. But over the weeks, with each diminishing roll of candies, I added new secrets. Lau Po gave me the names. The Double Attack from the East and West Shores. Throwing Stones on the Drowning Man. The Sudden Meeting of the Clan. The Surprise from the Sleeping Guard. The Humble Servant Who Kills the King. Sand in the Eyes of Advancing Forces. A Double Killing Without Blood.

There were also the fine points of chess etiquette. Keep captured men in neat rows, as well-tended prisoners. Never announce "Check" with vanity, lest someone with an unseen sword slit your throat. Never hurl pieces into the sandbox after you have lost a game, because then you must find them again, by yourself, after apologizing to all around you. By the end of the summer, Lau Po had taught me all he knew, and I had become a better chess player.

A small weekend crowd of Chinese people and tourists would gather as I played and defeated my opponents one by one. My mother would join the crowds during these outdoor exhibition games. She sat proudly on the bench, telling my admirers with proper Chinese humility, "Is luck."

A man who watched me play in the park suggested that my mother allow me to play in local chess tournaments. My mother smiled graciously, an answer that meant nothing. I desperately wanted to go, but I bit back my tongue. I knew she would not let me play among strangers. So as we walked home I said in a small voice that I didn't want to play in the local tournament. They would have American rules. If I lost, I would bring shame on my family.

"Is shame you fall down nobody push you," said my mother.

During my first tournament, my mother sat with me in the front row as I 40
waited for my turn. I frequently bounced my legs to unstick them from the cold metal seat of the folding chair. When my name was called, I leapt up. My mother unwrapped something in her lap. It was her *chang*, a small tablet of red jade which held the sun's fire. "Is luck," she whispered, and tucked it into my dress pocket. I turned to my opponent, a fifteen-year-old boy from Oakland. He looked at me, wrinkling his nose.

As I began to play, the boy disappeared, the color ran out of the room, and I saw only my white pieces and his black ones waiting on the other side. A light wind began blowing past my ears. It whispered secrets only I could hear.

"Blow from the South," it murmured. "The wind leaves no trail." I saw a clear path, the traps to avoid. The crowd rustled. "Shhh! Shhh!" said the corners of the room. The wind blew stronger. "Throw sand from the East to distract him." The knight came forward ready for the sacrifice. The wind hissed, louder and louder. "Blow, blow, blow. He cannot see. He is blind now. Make him lean away from the wind so he is easier to knock down."

"Check," I said, as the wind roared with laughter. The wind died down to little puffs, my own breath.

My mother placed my first trophy next to a new plastic chess set that the neighborhood Tao society had given to me. As she wiped each piece with a soft cloth, she said, "Next time win more, lose less."

"Ma, it's not how many pieces you lose," I said. "Sometimes you need to lose 45
pieces to get ahead."

"Better to lose less, see if you really need."

At the next tournament, I won again, but it was my mother who wore the triumphant grin.

"Lost eight piece this time. Last time was eleven. What I tell you? Better off lose less!" I was annoyed, but I couldn't say anything.

I attended more tournaments, each one farther away from home. I won all games, in all divisions. The Chinese bakery downstairs from our flat displayed my growing collection of trophies in its window, amidst the dust-covered cakes that were never picked up. The day after I won an important regional tournament, the window encased a fresh sheet cake with whipped-cream frosting and red script saying "Congratulations, Waverly Jong, Chinatown Chess Champion." Soon after that, a flower shop, headstone engraver, and funeral parlor offered to sponsor me in national tournaments. That's when my mother decided I no longer had to do the dishes. Winston and Vincent had to do my chores.

"Why does she get to play and we do all the work," complained Vincent. 50

"Is new American rules," said my mother. "Meimei play, squeeze all her brains out for win chess. You play, worth squeeze towel."

By my ninth birthday, I was a national chess champion. I was still some 429 points away from grand-master status, but I was touted as the Great American Hope, a child prodigy and a girl to boot. They ran a photo of me in *Life* magazine next to a quote in which Bobby Fischer[1] said, "There will never be a woman grand master." "Your move, Bobby," said the caption.

The day they took the magazine picture I wore neatly plaited braids clipped with plastic barrettes trimmed with rhinestones. I was playing in a large high school auditorium that echoed with phlegmy coughs and the squeaky rubber knobs of chair legs sliding across freshly waxed wooden floors. Seated across from me was an American man, about the same age as Lau Po, maybe fifty. I remember that his sweaty brow seemed to weep at my every move. He wore a dark, malodorous suit. One of his pockets was stuffed with a great white kerchief on which he wiped his palm before sweeping his hand over the chosen chess piece with great flourish.

In my crisp pink-and-white dress with scratchy lace at the neck, one of two my mother had sewn for these special occasions, I would clasp my hands under my chin, the delicate points of my elbows poised lightly on the table in the manner my mother had shown me for posing for the press. I would swing my patent leather shoes back and forth like an impatient child riding on a school bus. Then I would pause, such in my lips, twirl my chosen piece in midair as if undecided, and then firmly plant it in its new threatening place, with a triumphant smile thrown back at my opponent for good measure.

I no longer played in the alley of Waverly Place. I never visited the playground 55
where the pigeons and old men gathered. I went to school, then directly home to learn new chess secrets, cleverly concealed advantages, more escape routes.

But I found it difficult to concentrate at home. My mother had a habit of standing over me while I plotted out my games. I think she thought of herself as my protective ally. Her lips would be sealed tight, and after each move I made, a soft "Hmmmmph" would escape from her nose.

[1]*Bobby Fischer:* An American world chess champion who gained attention in the 1970s for his chess prowess and his ability to hold the spotlight while making outrageous statements. Fischer went into exile following his defeat of Russian grandmaster Boris Spassky.

"Ma, I can't practice when you stand there like that," I said one day. She retreated to the kitchen and made loud noises with the pots and pans. When the crashing stopped, I could see out of the corner of my eye that she was standing in the doorway, "Hmmmmph!" Only this one came out of her tight throat.

My parents made many concessions to allow me to practice. One time I complained that the bedroom I shared was so noisy that I couldn't think. Thereafter, my brothers slept in a bed in the living room facing the street. I said I couldn't finish my rice; my head didn't work right when my stomach was too full. I left the table with half-finished bowls and nobody complained. But there was one duty I couldn't avoid. I had to accompany my mother on Saturday market days when I had no tournament to play. My mother would proudly walk with me, visiting many shops, buying very little. "This my daughter Wave-ly Jong," she said to whoever looked her way.

One day after we left a shop I said under my breath, "I wish you wouldn't do that, telling everybody I'm your daughter." My mother stopped walking. Crowds of people with heavy bags pushed past us on the sidewalk, bumping into first one shoulder, than another.

"Aiii-ya. So shame be with mother?" She grasped my hand even tighter as she glared at me.

I looked down. "It's not that, it's just so obvious. It's just so embarrassing."

"Embarrass you be my daughter?" Her voice was cracking with anger.

"That's not what I meant. That's not what I said."

"What you say?"

I knew it was a mistake to say anything more, but I heard my voice speaking, "Why do you have to use me to show off? If you want to show off, then why don't you learn to play chess?"

My mother's eyes turned into dangerous black slits. She had no words for me, just sharp silence.

I felt the wind rushing around my hot ears. I jerked my hand out of my mother's tight grasp and spun around, knocking into an old woman. Her bag of groceries spilled to the ground.

"Aii-ya! Stupid girl!" my mother and the woman cried. Oranges and tin cans careened down the sidewalk. As my mother stooped to help the old woman pick up the escaping food, I took off.

I raced down the street, dashing between people, not looking back as my mother screamed shrilly, "Meimei! Meimei!" I fled down an alley, past dark, curtained shops and merchants washing the grime off their windows. I sped into the sunlight, into a large street crowded with tourists examining trinkets and souvenirs. I ducked into another dark alley, down another street, up another alley. I ran until it hurt and I realized I had nowhere to go, that I was not running from anything. The alleys contained no escape routes.

My breath came out like angry smoke. It was cold. I sat down on an upturned plastic pail next to a stack of empty boxes, cupping my chin with my hands, thinking hard. I imagined my mother, first walking briskly down one street or another looking for me, then giving up and returning home to await my arrival. After two hours, I stood up on creaking legs and slowly walked home.

The alley was quiet and I could see the yellow lights shining from our flat like two tiger's eyes in the night. I climbed the sixteen steps to the door, advancing quietly up each so as not to make any warning sounds. I turned the knob; the door was locked. I heard a chair moving, quick steps, the locks turning—click! click! click!—and then the door opened.

"About time you got home," said Vincent. "Boy, are you in trouble."

He slid back to the dinner table. On a platter were the remains of a large fish, its fleshy head still connected to bones swimming upstream in vain escape. Standing there waiting for my punishment, I heard my mother speak in a dry voice.

"We not concerning this girl. This girl not have concerning for us."

Nobody looked at me. Bone chopsticks clinked against the inside of bowls 75
being emptied into hungry mouths.

I walked into my room, closed the door, and lay down on my bed. The room was dark, the ceiling filled with shadows from the dinnertime lights of neighboring flats.

In my head, I saw a chessboard with sixty-four black and white squares. Opposite me was my opponent, two angry black slits. She wore a triumphant smile. "Strongest wind cannot be seen," she said.

Her black men advanced across the plane, slowly marching to each successive level as a single unit. My white pieces screamed as they scurried and fell off the board one by one. As her men drew closer to my edge, I felt myself growing light. I rose up into the air and flew out the window. Higher and higher, above the alley, over the tops of tiled roofs, where I was gathered up by the wind and pushed up toward the night sky until everything below me disappeared and I was alone.

I closed my eyes and pondered my next move.

(1989)

Questions for Discussion and Writing

Close Reading

1. List the differences between American "rules" and Chinese "rules" as they are depicted in the story. Is it possible to adapt to both sets of rules, or should the narrator choose one set to live by?
2. How do the lessons imparted by Lau Po, Waverly's chess-playing teacher in the park, differ from the lessons imparted by Waverly's mother?
3. How does the author use the wind as a metaphor throughout the story?

Critical and Creative Reading

4. Waverly's power comes through her mastery of chess and her ensuing fame. What is Waverly's mother's power? Who is more powerful?
5. What is the nature of the first lesson Waverly's mother teaches her in the first three paragraphs of the story? Does she forget that lesson, or does she consciously ignore it?

6. The words *rules* and *game* can be read many ways in this story. What is the best way to learn new rules: through observation, instruction, or experience? How does the story respond to this question?
7. Was it necessary for Waverly to reject her mother to develop her identity?

CONNECTIONS TO OTHER READINGS

8. "Rules of the Game" is based on a clash of cultures: American rules and Chinese rules. Compare this tension to the tension between traditional Yoruba society and British colonial society in Wole Soyinka's *Death and the King's Horseman*. Does the tension in both works lead to a similar or a different conclusion about the nature of rebellion?
9. Waverly Jong in "Rules of the Game" and Ann in Elizabeth McKenzie's story "Stop That Girl" are both young, female, first-person narrators. They both rebel against authority figures. Is this rebellion, in their cases, simply a way of asserting their individuality? Is it a necessary step toward maturity?
10. Discuss the effect that a parent's expectations have on a child in this story and in Wole Soyinka's play *Death and the King's Horseman*.

Elizabeth McKenzie

Stop That Girl

Elizabeth McKenzie (b. 1958) is an emerging American author who lives in Santa Cruz, California. She has published in a number of highly regarded literary journals and has worked as an editor for the *Atlantic Monthly*. The following story was selected for the *Best American Non-Required Reading* volume for 2002 and is collected in her book *Stop That Girl: A Novel in Stories*. Her frank descriptions and first-person narrative might make this story seem like a memoir, but it is fiction. What elements of fiction are evident throughout the story?

My mother and I lived alone then, in a pink bungalow in Long Beach, with a small yard full of gopher holes and the smell of the refinery settling over everything we had. Couldn't leave a glass on the shelf a week without it gathering a fine mist of oil. I thought we had a real life anyway, before my mother started over.

I had a stocky Yorkshire nanny, who walked me home from school past the barbershop with the unhappy mynah bird. "Kill me!" it suggested as we passed by.

I never knew my father. He was some frat boy who danced well. Mom believed I'd have a leveler head.

My mother worked in petroleum research. She was a geology major in college and went to field camps in Wyoming and was renowned for shooting a bobcat at a hundred yards while it was cuffing around her professor's beagle. For the company, she looked through telescopes at the moon, as if there might be something useful up there. Mom felt her job was a joke. When she came home at night, she locked herself in the bathroom for an hour, taking a hot bath filled with salts.

5 She was said to look like Lauren Bacall in those days and dated a number of different engineers from the refinery. While Mom went searching for her purse and coat, they would bribe me with something, like it was up to me to release her—Silly Putty, a magnet, a comic book, a stuffed pig with a music box in it.

There we are in Long Beach the fall I start fifth grade, when the nights have grown cooler and our gas wall unit bangs out its stale-smelling heat and we're on the brink of changes so vast it's hard to believe we don't see them coming. One Saturday evening, we receive a new visitor in the form of Roy Ransom, a real estate broker, a handsome talker with dimples, cowboy boots, and a rounded ruby ring that looks like a bloody eyeball. He brings a bouquet as big as a baby, and my mother holds it that way. He slips me a piece of Double Bubble. By the following week it's a Slip 'N Slide. I suspect he appeals to that secret Wild West part of my mother, but it's more. A few months later my mother tells me, "Roy's taking us both out for a drive today, Ann. We're going to see a house."

I sit in the back seat of Roy's Caddy as we leave Long Beach behind. We aim for the San Fernando Valley. "You mean we're going to buy a house out here?" I ask Mom. We're in the Encino Hills; compared with Long Beach it looks like paradise: huge ranch houses and big yards; rose bushes, hibiscus, banana trees, palms.

"Well, maybe," my mother says, turning around in her seat like she has something to tell me. "We might buy a house—with Roy."

"With Roy?"

10 "Yes. We might all live out here together."

"Annie-girl, sound like a plan?" Roy says, eyeing me in his mirror.

I realize what they're trying to tell me.

We pull up in front of a huge, shingled yellow house, as long as the entire row of bungalows in Long Beach. My mother looks stunned as we wander into the place. It has beamed ceilings, parquet floors, a kitchen with an island and a double range, a breakfast nook and bar, a family room, three bedrooms, three baths, two fireplaces, and a den. They show me the room that would be mine—it has sheer pink curtains and wallpaper with ballerinas on it, something for a well-defined girl. When we finish inspecting the place, Roy Ransom says, "Hey, Annie, hit me right here! As hard as you can!" He is pointing at his stomach.

I don't ask why. I just do it.

15 "I'm waiting." He winks at my mother.

My hand hurts. I kick him in the shin.

A year later Mrs. Ransom has retired from petroleum work, pregnant. In the afternoons, she sews clothes and toys and bedding for the baby, placing them in the nursery-to-be, while I'm thinking of names. Percy is the one I'm rooting for.

Quiet collects in the rooms of that big house more than anywhere I've ever lived. I often tell my mother it's a suburban tomb, and she says, "Ann, I love this man. But you are still the most important person in the world to me." The words I live for, and I skate around the parquet floor in my socks, still feeling like it's all just temporary. I still can't believe that an extended family of Kuwaitis has moved into the pink bungalow, and that Nana has gone back to Leeds, and that a few friends from my school in Long Beach write me real letters with stamps on them like I've moved across the world.

"How about a swim?" Mom asks me after school nowadays.

"Maybe."

I come out into the back yard after a while and see my mother, in her white, flowered bathing cap, doing graceful laps up and down the pool. This is no kidney-shaped job, as Roy would point out. It's a classic rectangle of crystal blue, and I'm impressed by my mother's sidestroke.

"Come on in," Mom calls to me.

To surprise my mother, I say, "Okay" and walk straight into the pool with all my clothes on. She laughs and doesn't get mad at me for possibly ruining my leather shoes.

It's in the afternoons after school when I know I still have an impact on her. Once Roy's home, she'll even offer to help him clean up Open Houses or gather garbage from yards. She acts like he's our savior. One evening he insists we accompany him to pound in some fresh For Sale signs, and I climb onto the roof of the Cadillac and won't get off.

"Get down, Ann," my pregnant mother says, waiting sway-backed by the car. Like a prehistoric lobster, Roy snaps at my ankles.

"From up here I can see the reservoir," I say. "I think boys are peeing into it."

"That's nice, but let's go."

"Is that, like, what we drink?"

Roy stalks around the car and I hop to the other side. He charges back and this time I slip off. I fall onto the concrete, and no matter how much it hurts I decide I won't cry. Instead, I pretend I'm in a coma. "Ann?" my mother says. "Ann, are you all right? Look what you did!" she yells at Roy Ransom. "Faker," he replies. He tickles me. I sink my teeth into his arm. He slaps me across the top of the head, and my mother tells Roy never to lay a hand on me again. Roy tells my mother I'm a spoiled brat, and then I sit up and hear myself saying, "And you're a home-wrecker."

And thus, the following weekend, it's decided I'm spending some time with The Frosts. They are my grandparents, but when we talk about them we always call them The Frosts. Until then, I'd only seen them once or twice a year, because my mother hates them. They don't seem to miss us. They are too young and too busy for grandparents—Otto's a patent lawyer, Liz a pediatrician. Mom grew up a lonely daydreamer with no brothers or sisters. That's her rationale for the new baby—so things will be different for me.

Friday afternoon Dr. Frost shows up to collect me. She looks like my mother, but is smaller and more efficient, never a moment to kill. I don't know her very well. "Put on a dress with a nice collar, Ann. And comb your hair. I want you to look pretty for your passport."

"Why do I need a passport?"

"Hasn't your mother told you about our trip?"

"Trip?"

"You're coming to Europe with me. I'm attending a medical conference. You're going to straighten out and learn your place in the world. Good deal?"

"Europe?" I say, looking at my mother. "When?"

"Next month," Dr. Frost says.

Next month is May. May is a big month. May is when my mother is having the baby.

"I can't go," I say. "I need to be here for the baby."

"You've been a big help already," my mother says.

"I need to help more!"

Dr. Frost says, "After we have your picture taken, let's go buy some new clothes, shall we? I'm going to need some new things myself."

"I don't need any new clothes."

"All right, then we'll just get your picture taken."

I'm speechless, but finally I say, "This is definitely bizarre and grotesque," my favorite expression in many situations. Then I add my other: "It's also grossly mutilated and hugely deformed."

"Ann, your grandmother has offered to take you to Europe. You're a very lucky girl."

Lucky? Who needs parquet floors and a pool. Who needs Europe with the very person who makes my mother scream or cry whenever they talk on the phone. I try to catch my mother's eye, the special eye that knows me better than anyone, and I say, "I don't want to go." But the eye doesn't blink. There's no hope. Though they disagree on everything else, they're together on this one. My mother tells me, "The baby might not even come while you're gone, who knows."

Roy can't make it to the airport. Neither can Otto. I hug my mother and pat her stomach, which looks square now, like a little house. "Tell Percy to wait," I croak out.

"I'll try," my mother says.

Our travels take us first to Copenhagen, city of copper domes turned green and raw beef. I'm in Europe. I'm excited. I tell myself I'll see yodelers and eat lots of chocolate and buy souvenirs for my mother and the people I'm meeting at my new school. Even Dr. Frost seems to have loosened up a little. She's humming and smiling without explaining why.

Our second night there, in a quaint hotel with floors tilted like a fun house, we receive a telegram from Roy Ransom. "Wonderful news STOP We have a daughter STOP Catherine Louise STOP Mother and baby fine."

"Who's we?" I say, grabbing the telegram. It hits me for the first time that my sister's father is Roy Ransom. "Can I call my mother at the hospital?"

This is 1964. It isn't so easy. Dr. Frost says we'll send a telegram instead.

"Can we go home now?"

"Ann, you don't want to see a newborn baby. They're ugly little things with red faces. They don't even open their eyes."

"Really?"

I slide on the bare floors in my socks all the way to the lower wall. Tivoli Gardens flashes brightly across the street. From her bag my grandmother hauls out a textbook she has brought on this trip to instruct me with. It contains pictures of every bone, every muscle, every ligament, the cardiovascular, the respiratory, the digestive system, the works. "Tell me about dissecting cadavers," I ask her.

"Nothing to it," Dr. Frost says.

"But you were cutting open dead bodies. Wasn't it bizarre and grotesque?"

"Ann, the body is an amazing machine. It's not bizarre and grotesque at all," 60
she says, pointing at a skeleton.

I want to hear interesting stories about guts, not her version of them. "Dead bodies are wonderful, newborn babies are really gross?"

"Goodnight, Ann," she says.

"Maybe we should go home," I murmur, but she ignores me in a different way, pretending not to hear. I pull the covers up around my neck and fall asleep hearing my grandmother listing bones.

The International College of Surgeons is meeting in Vienna, and we take three days driving there through Germany. I like stopping in towns and villages, jumping around cobblestone squares, dipping my hands in fountains, and eating pastries. I decide to stop thinking about home. The afternoon we arrive in Vienna, we check in at the Intercontinental across from the park, in plenty of time for the first night's event, and I'm fitting right in. Dr. Frost takes a long bath and changes into a blue chiffon dress, and I wear a green velvet frock with white gloves. We set out for our evening together in a taxi. She smells like hairspray and Windsong and talcum all mixed together. Her rings glint in the evening light. She taps her little heels.

We pull up at a real palace and proceed up a wide bank of marble steps. The 65
roar of the doctors from around the world deepens as we get closer. Dr. Frost grabs the list of those in attendance and scans it. When we cross into the ballroom, I look up at my grandmother and she has her nose at full tilt, her forehead high like a half-moon. A small orchestra is tuning up at the end of the room. Dr. Frost taps me on the shoulder and points to a tall, silvery-haired man standing alone in the crowd. "Go introduce yourself to that man," she urges me.

"Why?"

"Just do it," she whispers.

Luckily, I don't have to, because he turns and his face is radiant at the sight of Dr. Frost. "Liz," he says. He gives her a kiss and looks at her and laughs. "And this is your daughter?"

"My granddaughter."

"Impossible," he says, taking her hand. "You look wonderful." 70

"Ann, this is Dr. Von Allsberg."

I'm more interested in what we're having for dinner, and I locate our table next to the dance floor. Eventually, a doctor takes the seat next to me. While Dr. Frost talks to the man with the silver hair, my doctor has a waxed mustache and smells like varnish. His name is Dr. Witkovitch and he's an internist from a small village in the Julian Mountains. He tells me he breeds roller-pigeons, which come in all colors and are iridescent. They rocket high into the sky, then come rolling down to earth in a free fall. It's a stunt and they enjoy it. I realize that Dr. Witkovitch is actually a very young man; it's the stiff mustache, oiled hair, and musty jacket that make him seem outdated and old. I'm thinking Dr. Frost will be impressed to see that I've befriended someone so quickly, but she's not watching. We slice up thin wafers of veal.

Later, the orchestra plays Strauss and I watch while Dr. Von Allsberg waltzes with Dr. Frost. She moves like a swan, her head back and eyes fastened on him.

"How do you know Dr. Von Allsberg?" I ask her that night.

"I know many people here." 75

"Can we go to Dr. Witkovitch's roller-pigeon farm?"

"Hardly," she says, examining her eyes in the mirror. "We have plenty to do as it is."

"Not even for a day?"

"Where is it?"

"Yugoslavia." 80

"Ha!"

The next day Dr. Frost leaves me with a baby-sitting service at the hotel. Over the phone, arranging it, someone calls her Mrs. Frost. "No! It's Dr. Frost." She never lets that mistake slip by. "Whenever your grandfather makes reservations, and he says it's for a Dr. and Mr. Frost, they behave very strangely, because they assume your grandfather must be the doctor and therefore is married to a man. People would rather believe your grandfather is married to a man than think a woman is a doctor!"

I am shocked.

"Say, after the conference, we'll take a boat trip on the Danube, how would that be?" she asks me.

"Good." 85

"Better than a bunch of roller-chickens?"

"Pigeons!"

"Same difference."

The babysitter is a glum old Austrian woman who likes to say "It is not allowed!" as often as she can clear her throat, and I read all day, looking out a window at the park. She feeds me some hard salty meat in a broth with little dumplings swimming around in it. By pointing at the park and annoying her with long sentences she doesn't understand, I get her to take me out, but I'm in such a bad mood I end up throwing rocks at a swan. And I'm disappointed Dr. Witkovitch hasn't hunted me down to find out if I can go to his farm in Yugoslavia. The last night in Vienna, the night we are supposed to go to a special Hungarian restaurant and sample goulash, my grandmother breaks the news to me she's going to an opera with Dr. Von Allsberg instead.

"You can come too, of course, but I promise you, it will be very long and boring." 90

"In that case, I'd love to."

"Seriously, Ann, I don't think you'd enjoy it. I'm all for exposing you to cultural events, but you'll have a lot more fun running around here."

"Running around?" This makes me grind my teeth, and I close my eyes and imagine my grandmother being speared by head-hunters. "What's the opera, anyway?"

"*Der Rosenkavalier,*"[1] she tells me. Then she proceeds to offer up the whole story, which is about mistaken identities. If she already knows, why does she need to go? And I'm skeptical about the plot. People can't be tricked that easily. If I came home in a costume, my mother would still recognize me. It's changes on the inside she won't be able to see.

There's a different babysitter at night. An old bald man with only a pinkie and a thumb on his right hand. For some reason, whiling away the evening with him in the smoky TV room, I feel like crying for the first time in a long time. I'm not even sure why. The seven-fingered man bites the nail on his lonely thumb. I keep running to the window and looking out at the lamps in the park and at every cab that pulls up to see if my grandmother is returning. At last, very late, I see Dr. Frost and Dr. Von Allsberg strolling together out of the park, their heads close and crowned by lamplight. And it's bizarre and grotesque, because I can see that they're holding hands.

When the conference ends, I'm glad to see the last of Dr. Von Allsberg. My grandmother and I drive to a small village on the Danube, where we board the boat. It is a hot May day. We spend hours drifting past castles and abbeys and orchards, sitting on the deck in the sun eating little napoleons and drinking tea. This is what I've been waiting for.

"I wish there had been more women there for you to meet," my grandmother remarks. "You're to do great things. No man should stand in your way. And don't let Roy Ransom tell you otherwise! Think you'd like to be a doctor?"

"Maybe. What about industrial baking?"

"I want you to set your sights as high as you can. Your mother was sent to fine schools. I don't want you to think . . ." She pauses. "I happen to know that the man who was your father came from a very fine family."

I squint into the sun. "So what's a fine family like?"

"A fine family, Ann, is one with noble values and good ancestry. Like mine. Congressmen, attorneys and judges, officers in the Civil and Revolutionary Wars. Well educated and able to contribute to society."

"And did they get along with their kids?"

"I would think so."

I say, "That's good."

"Yes, it is good. I'm glad you and I are getting to know each other. Your mother was what they call a daddy's girl. Never liked me, truth be told. Even when she was a baby."

I look to see if Dr. Frost is kidding. "Babies always like their mothers."

"Not in this case. I'm afraid you've no idea what I'm talking about, coming from the spot she put you in."

[1]*Der Rosenkavalier:* A 1911 comic opera by Richard Strauss.

And I say, "Well, I'm afraid you have no idea what I'm talking about, because all you ever cared about was your job."

"I see," Dr. Frost snorts.

For the rest of the boat ride, when I'm not snapping pictures in every direction, I'm trying to make my grandmother forget what I've said. My new sister might entice her. "She's much nicer than I am," I say. "She has red hair and speaks many languages. She can do magic tricks and dance."

"There'll be no stopping you two," my grandmother replies.

And finally, the day reaches its inevitable conclusion when we get off the boat and Dr. Von Allsberg stands waiting on the dock with flowers. "Why didn't you tell me he was going to be here?"

"Seriously, Ann. Are you my keeper?"

I march behind them, filtering everything I see through a blaze of fury. Spears are flying, and Dr. Frost is being lowered into a boiling cauldron. Tears are filling my eyes, and I don't want anyone to see them. And suddenly I get a strange urge to run up behind her and jump on her back and scream, "Piggyback ride!" Wham. Her small efficient body tumbles and cracks down on the cobblestones.

"Ouch," she groans.

"Sorry," I say, standing up.

"What were you thinking?" Von Allsberg says.

"My arm is broken," Dr. Frost announces.

"You're faking," I say.

"Afraid not," she says.

We spend hours in a local clinic while they set her arm. It's a clean break. The ulna. Ulna, ulna, I hear Dr. Frost say again and again. A neurologist, Von Allsberg supervises the exam, pricking her fingertips and banging a tuning fork on his shoe and then pressing the cool metal to her elbow and palms. How could a bone break so easily? Lying on the table, in the yellow light of the clinic, she looks old, finally—the way a grandmother should.

Now everything is different. My grandmother can't drive the car—not with a gearshift and a broken right arm. So Dr. Von Allsberg offers to get us back to Copenhagen. We'll spend just a few more days in Germany and Holland. We'll get home early. I'm now stuck in the back seat, where I have to stare at their necks. They talk and laugh and occasionally toss comments back to me like tidbits for a lost dog. Dr. Frost has bumps and creases on her neck—does Dr. Von Allsberg realize? Somewhere along the way, Von Allsberg buys me a doll: an Alpine girl in a dirndl, clutching a little straw basket. I immediately detest her like I detest the ballerinas in my room at home. But I have to admit, she's in a beautiful box. The box is green and has a delicate pattern on it, and is lined with velvet.

Twelve hours ahead of us on the polar route, and we want to make sure Dr. Frost will be as comfortable as possible. There's no doubt her arm is hurting. She takes the window seat so she won't be jostled, and the cast rolls between us with no one's signature on it except mine. I can't wait to get home.

At last we land in Los Angeles. I'm so excited I forget my carry-on bag and have to run back into the plane. Finally, walking out of customs, beaming with my experiences, returning to my homeland, I spot my mother and Roy in the crowd. They are waving, watching our glorious arrival. They are standing with a buggy.

"Mom!" I yell, running to her.

"Hey Annie-girl!" Roy Ransom says, hugging me first.

I get to my mother. I had imagined her grabbing me and squeezing me like there was no tomorrow, but instead she looks strange, an imposter in my mother's clothes. "Mom?"

"Did you change your hair?" she asks me.

"No."

"Mother, your arm!"

"Hello, Helen," Dr. Frost says. "Is this my new granddaughter?"

"Mom, I have a present for you!" I say, digging into my bag.

Everyone's peering into the buggy. I decide to wait on the souvenirs and wiggle in for a look. I see my sister for the first time. She's very small, surrounded by the blankets my mother made. She's wearing the yellow cap I sewed the piping on. I reach in to pick her up.

"No, dear," my mother says. "Not now. She's sleepy. Just leave her there."

I want to hold her.

"Ann, pay attention to your mother," Roy says. "You don't know how to hold her yet."

By then I am holding her just fine. "Percy," I say.

"Let me have her," my mother says.

"Just a second."

"Ann, now."

That's it. I start to run. After carrying my suitcase all over Europe, she's only a tiny bundle.

My mother says, "Wait! Stop!"

It was the beginning of my future, and I had the thought at that moment that there was no one around who would ever understand my version of things. So I darted in and out of the crowd, holding my sister close to me. I heard my mother calling out, and Roy Ransom shouting, "Stop that girl!" But the people I ran by were hurrying off to their own destinations, and no one stood in my way.

After scurrying down a flight of stairs and rounding a few corners, I found a vacant phone booth and closed the two of us in. My sister wasn't frightened. Why should she be? I held her out carefully and looked at her puffy blue eyes. She was staring right at me. Like she really wanted to know who I was. Though she had almost no hair or eyebrows, she looked exactly the way I'd imagined her. She lifted a small fist to her mouth and started sucking on it. "It's me," I taught her. "It's Ann. Ann. Ann."

It was a good thing I was home. My sister was growing up.

(2002)

QUESTIONS FOR DISCUSSION AND WRITING

CLOSE READING

1. Pay attention to the way Ann characterizes everyone else in the story. Does she try to elicit sympathy for anyone except herself? How does she encourage the reader to share her perspective?

2. List the incidents in the story when someone gives Ann a direct order. Does she respond to these orders with any consistency?
3. Why does the narrator emphasize bodily harm, consciously or unconsciously? List the incidents of bodily harm in the story, and consider their function within the narrative.

CRITICAL AND CREATIVE READING

4. The title of the story is "Stop That Girl," and Ann does seem to be a volatile individual. However, does she need to be "stopped," or should she be allowed more freedom?
5. The story ends with Ann noticing that her baby sister is "growing up," which is ironic given that everyone in the story seems to think that Ann is the one who needs to grow up. Discuss the notion of rebellion as it pertains to maturity.
6. Is Ann experiencing anything more than typical sibling jealousy in this story? If not, does she express her feelings of jealousy in a predictable, conventional way?

CONNECTIONS TO OTHER READINGS

7. Are there any advantages to doing exactly as you're told to do even if the advice seems illogical? Discuss that question as it is illustrated in "Stop That Girl" as well as in Shirley Jackson's "The Lottery" and/or in Alfred, Lord Tennyson's "The Charge of the Light Brigade."
8. Use "Stop That Girl" and Amy Tan's story "Rules of the Game" or Jamaica Kincaid's "Girl" to discuss the notion of young girls either defying or living up to their parents' expectations.
9. Consider the idea that "doing as you're told" equals "being good" in both "Stop That Girl" and in Gregory Corso's poem "Marriage." Do the speaker of "Marriage" and the narrator of "Stop That Girl" resist convention for the same reasons?
10. Is it a coincidence that both Sarah Vowell in her essay "Take the Cannoli" and Ann in "Stop That Girl" learn something about their lives in America as they travel through Europe? Does travel represent the same thing to both of these young women?

Poetry

Felicia Dorothea Hemans

Casabianca

The subjects of patriotism and military service are common in the poetry of Felicia Hemans (1793–1835). Hemans's two brothers and husband served in the military, and Hemans lived during an era in which

England was almost constantly at war. The following poem, "Casabianca," was inspired by a real event that the poet describes in her footnote to the poem: "Young Casabianca, a boy about thirteen years old, son to the Admiral of the Orient, remained at his post (in the Battle of the Nile) after the ship had taken fire, and all the guns had been abandoned; and perished in the explosion of the vessel, when the flames had reached the powder." This battle took place near Alexandria, Egypt, between the British and the French as part of a series of wars known as the Napoleonic Wars (1803–1815).

The boy stood on the burning deck,
Whence all but he had fled;
The flame that lit the battle's wreck
Shone round him o'er the dead.

Yet beautiful and bright he stood,
As born to rule the storm—
A creature of heroic blood,
A proud, though childlike form.

The flames rolled on—he would not go
Without his father's word;
That father, faint in death below,
His voice no longer heard.

He called aloud:—"Say, father! say
If yet my task is done!"
He knew not that the chieftain lay
Unconscious of his son.

"Speak, father!" once again he cried,
"If I may yet be gone!"
And but the booming shots replied,
And fast the flames rolled on.

Upon his brow he felt their breath,
And in his waving hair,
And looked from that lone post of death
In still yet brave despair;

And shouted but once more aloud,
"My father! must I stay?"
While o'er him fast, through sail and shroud,
The wreathing fires made way.

They wrapped the ship in splendor wild,
They caught the flag on high,
And streamed above the gallant child
Like banners in the sky.

There came a burst of thunder sound—
The boy—O, where was he?
Ask of the winds that far around
With fragments strewed the sea!

With mast, and helm, and pennon[1] fair,
That well had borne their part;
But the noblest thing which perished there
Was that young faithful heart!

(1826)

Questions for Discussion and Writing

Close Reading

1. What adjectives does the speaker use to describe young Casabianca?
2. The boy Casabianca calls to his father three times to get his permission to leave the burning ship; what is the difference in tone between his three speeches?
3. Is the meter of the poem consistent throughout? If it is, comment on why it is appropriate that the meter be consistent; if it is not, comment on the poem's departures from a nearly consistent meter.

Critical and Creative Reading

4. Is the poem sentimental in that it encourages excessive feeling on the part of the reader? If so, how do you react to that sentimentality?
5. What do you suppose is the poet's motivation for writing this poem?
6. Imagine the relationship between Casabianca and his father before the event in the poem: do you think Casabianca was taught to be obedient or taught not to think for himself? (Is there any difference between these two terms?)

Connections to Other Readings

7. Think about the themes of obedience and nobility in this poem and in Tennyson's "The Charge of the Light Brigade." The situations are not exactly parallel—Tennyson's "noble six hundred" follow orders while Casabianca waits for orders that never come. Nevertheless, do the two poems convey similar ideas about obedience and nobility?

[1]*pennon:* A pennant or maritime flag.

8. Would you describe Casabianca's need for his father's commands in this poem and George's obedience to Editha's wishes in Howells's story "Editha" as tragic or pathetic? (Or is one an example of tragedy and the other an example of pathos?)
9. In the conclusion to Wilfred Owen's poem "Dulce et Decorum Est," the speaker calls the popular notion that sacrifice for one's country is sweet and fitting a lie; how does Hemans's poem comment on that same idea through Casabianca's death and, perhaps, his father's death?

Christina Rossetti

Goblin Market

Christina Rossetti (1830–1894) lived in an English household filled with verse: her father was an Italian expatriate who wrote poetry, and her brothers, Dante Gabriel and William Michael, were also poets. Rossetti is best known for the following poem, "Goblin Market," though she continued to publish throughout the three decades between the publication of her first collection of poems and her death. She never married, breaking two engagements because her affiliation with the Anglo-Catholic movement within the Anglican Church did not coincide with the religious views of her prospective husbands. "Goblin Market" clearly has religious overtones because of its theme of "forbidden fruit" (as in the Garden of Eden); however, the poem is more evidently about sensuality and sexuality.

Morning and evening
Maids heard the goblins cry:
"Come buy our orchard fruits,
Come buy, come buy:
Apples and quinces,
Lemons and oranges,
Plump unpecked cherries,
Melons and raspberries,
Bloom-down-cheeked peaches,
Swart-headed mulberries,
Wild free-born cranberries,
Crab-apples, dewberries,
Pine-apples, blackberries,
Apricots, strawberries;—

Dante Charles Gabriel Rossetti, Frontispiece of *Goblin Market and Other Poems* (1862).

All ripe together
In summer weather,—
Morns that pass by,
Fair eves that fly;
Come buy, come buy:
Our grapes fresh from the vine,
Pomegranates full and fine,
Dates and sharp bullaces,
Rare pears and greengages,
Damsons[1] and bilberries,
Taste them and try:
Currants and gooseberries,
Bright-fire-like barberries,
Figs to fill your mouth,
Citrons from the South,

[1] *damsons:* Along with bullaces and greengages, varieties of plums.

Sweet to tongue and sound to eye;
Come buy, come buy."

Evening by evening
Among the brookside rushes,
Laura bowed her head to hear,
Lizzie veiled her blushes:
Crouching close together
In the cooling weather,
With clasping arms and cautioning lips,
With tingling cheeks and finger tips.
"Lie close," Laura said,
Pricking up her golden head:
"We must not look at goblin men,
We must not buy their fruits:
Who knows upon what soil they fed
Their hungry thirsty roots?"
"Come buy," call the goblins
Hobbling down the glen.
"Oh," cried Lizzie, "Laura, Laura,
You should not peep at goblin men."
Lizzie covered up her eyes,
Covered close lest they should look;
Laura reared her glossy head,
And whispered like the restless brook:
"Look, Lizzie, look, Lizzie,
Down the glen tramp little men.
One hauls a basket,
One bears a plate,
One lugs a golden dish
Of many pounds weight.
How fair the vine must grow
Whose grapes are so luscious;
How warm the wind must blow
Thro' those fruit bushes."
"No," said Lizzie: "No, no, no;
Their offers should not charm us,
Their evil gifts would harm us."
She thrust a dimpled finger
In each ear, shut eyes and ran:
Curious Laura chose to linger
Wondering at each merchant man.
One had a cat's face,
One whisked a tail,
One tramped at a rat's pace,
One crawled like a snail,

One like a wombat[2] prowled obtuse and furry,
One like a ratel[3] tumbled hurry skurry.
She heard a voice like voice of doves
Cooing all together:
They sounded kind and full of loves
In the pleasant weather.

Laura stretched her gleaming neck
Like a rush-imbedded swan,
Like a lily from the beck,[4]
Like a moonlit poplar branch,
Like a vessel at the launch
When its last restraint is gone.

Backwards up the mossy glen
Turned and trooped the goblin men,
With their shrill repeated cry,
"Come buy, come buy."
When they reached where Laura was
They stood stock still upon the moss,
Leering at each other,
Brother with queer brother;
Signalling each other,
Brother with sly brother.
One set his basket down,
One reared his plate;
One began to weave a crown
Of tendrils, leaves and rough nuts brown
(Men sell not such in any town);
One heaved the golden weight
Of dish and fruit to offer her:
"Come buy, come buy" was still their cry.
Laura stared but did not stir,
Longed but had no money:
The whisk-tailed merchant bade her taste
In tones as smooth as honey,
The cat-faced purr'd,
The rat-paced spoke a word
Of welcome, and the snail-paced even was heard;
One parrot-voiced and jolly
Cried "Pretty Goblin" still for "Pretty Polly;"—
One whistled like a bird.

[2]*wombat:* A rodentlike Australian marsupial.
[3]*ratel:* A badgerlike South African mammal.
[4]*beck:* A brook.

But sweet-tooth Laura spoke in haste:
"Good folk, I have no coin;
To take were to purloin:
I have no copper in my purse,
I have no silver either,
And all my gold is on the furze[5]
That shakes in windy weather
Above the rusty heather."
"You have much gold upon your head,"
They answered all together:
"Buy from us with a golden curl."
She clipped a precious golden lock,
She dropped a tear more rare than pearl,
Then sucked their fruit globes fair or red:
Sweeter than honey from the rock.
Stronger than man-rejoicing wine,
Clearer than water flowed that juice;
She never tasted such before,
How should it cloy with length of use?
She sucked and sucked and sucked the more
Fruits which that unknown orchard bore;
She sucked until her lips were sore;
Then flung the emptied rinds away
But gathered up one kernel-stone,
And knew not was it night or day
As she turned home alone.

Lizzie met her at the gate
Full of wise upbraidings:
"Dear, you should not stay so late
Twilight is not good for maidens;
Should not loiter in the glen
In the haunts of goblin men.
Do you not remember Jeanie,
How she met them in the moonlight,
Took their gifts both choice and many,
Ate their fruits and wore their flowers
Plucked from bowers
Where summer ripens at all hours?
But ever in the noonlight
She pined and pined away;
Sought them by night and day,
Found them no more but dwindled and grew grey;
Then fell with the first snow,

[5]*furze:* Evergreen underbrush. Also called *gorse*.

While to this day no grass will grow
Where she lies low:
I planted daisies there a year ago
That never blow.
You should not loiter so."
"Nay, hush," said Laura:
"Nay, hush, my sister:
I ate and ate my fill,
Yet my mouth waters still;
Tomorrow night I will
Buy more:" and kissed her:
"Have done with sorrow;
I'll bring you plums tomorrow
Fresh on their mother twigs,
Cherries worth getting;
You cannot think what figs
My teeth have met in,
What melons icy-cold
Piled on a dish of gold
Too huge for me to hold,
What peaches with a velvet nap,
Pellucid grapes without one seed:
Odorous indeed must be the mead
Whereon they grow, and pure the wave they drink
With lilies at the brink,
And sugar-sweet their sap."

Golden head by golden head,
Like two pigeons in one nest
Folded in each other's wings,
They lay down in their curtained bed:
Like two blossoms on one stem,
Like two flakes of new-fall'n snow,
Like two wands of ivory
Tipped with gold for awful kings.
Moon and stars gazed in at them,
Wind sang to them lullaby,
Lumbering owls forbore to fly,
Not a bat flapped to and fro
Round their rest:
Cheek to cheek and breast to breast
Locked together in one nest.

Early in the morning
When the first cock crowed his warning,
Neat like bees, as sweet and busy,

Laura rose with Lizzie:
Fetched in honey, milked the cows,
Aired and set to rights the house,
Kneaded cakes of whitest wheat,
Cakes for dainty mouths to eat,
Next churned butter, whipped up cream,
Fed their poultry, sat and sewed;
Talked as modest maidens should:
Lizzie with an open heart,
Laura in an absent dream,
One content, one sick in part;
One warbling for the mere bright day's delight,
One longing for the night.

At length slow evening came:
They went with pitchers to the reedy brook;
Lizzie most placid in her look,
Laura most like a leaping flame.
They drew the gurgling water from its deep;
Lizzie plucked purple and rich golden flags,
Then turning homewards said: "The sunset flushes
Those furthest loftiest crags;
Come, Laura, not another maiden lags,
No wilful squirrel wags,
The beasts and birds are fast asleep."
But Laura loitered still among the rushes
And said the bank was steep.

And said the hour was early still,
The dew not fall'n, the wind not chill:
Listening ever, but not catching
The customary cry,
"Come buy, come buy,"
With its iterated jingle
Of sugar-baited words:
Not for all her watching
Once discerning even one goblin
Racing, whisking, tumbling, hobbling;
Let alone the herds
That used to tramp along the glen,
In groups or single,
Of brisk fruit-merchant men.

Till Lizzie urged, "O Laura, come;
I hear the fruit-call but I dare not look:
You should not loiter longer at this brook:

Come with me home.
The stars rise, the moon bends her arc,
Each glowworm winks her spark,
Let us get home before the night grows dark:
For clouds may gather
Tho' this is summer weather,
Put out the lights and drench us thro';
Then if we lost our way what should we do?"

Laura turned cold as stone
To find her sister heard that cry alone,
That goblin cry,
"Come buy our fruits, come buy."
Must she then buy no more such dainty fruit?
Must she no more such succous pasture find,
Gone deaf and blind?
Her tree of life drooped from the root:
She said not one word in her heart's sore ache;
But peering thro' the dimness, nought discerning,
Trudged home, her pitcher dripping all the way;
So crept to bed, and lay
Silent till Lizzie slept;
Then sat up in a passionate yearning,
And gnashed her teeth for baulked desire, and wept
As if her heart would break.

Day after day, night after night,
Laura kept watch in vain
In sullen silence of exceeding pain.
She never caught again the goblin cry:
"Come buy, come buy;"—
She never spied the goblin men
Hawking their fruits along the glen:
But when the noon waxed bright
Her hair grew thin and gray;
She dwindled, as the fair full moon doth turn
To swift decay and burn
Her fire away.

One day remembering her kernel-stone
She set it by a wall that faced the south;
Dewed it with tears, hoped for a root,
Watched for a waxing shoot,
But there came none;
It never saw the sun,

It never felt the trickling moisture run:
While with sunk eyes and faded mouth
She dreamed of melons, as a traveller sees
False waves in desert drouth
With shade of leaf-crowned trees,
And burns the thirstier in the sandful breeze.

She no more swept the house,
Tended the fowls or cows,
Fetched honey, kneaded cakes of wheat,
Brought water from the brook:
But sat down listless in the chimney-nook
And would not eat.

Tender Lizzie could not bear
To watch her sister's cankerous care
Yet not to share.
She night and morning
Caught the goblins' cry:
"Come buy our orchard fruits,
Come buy, come buy:"—
Beside the brook, along the glen,
She heard the tramp of goblin men,
The voice and stir
Poor Laura could not hear;
Longed to buy fruit to comfort her,
But feared to pay too dear.
She thought of Jeanie in her grave,
Who should have been a bride;
But who for joys brides hope to have
Fell sick and died
In her gay prime,
In earliest Winter time,
With the first glazing rime,
With the first snow-fall of crisp Winter time.

Till Laura dwindling
Seemed knocking at Death's door:
Then Lizzie weighed no more
Better and worse;
But put a silver penny in her purse,
Kissed Laura, crossed the heath with clumps of furze
At twilight, halted by the brook:
And for the first time in her life
Began to listen and look.

Laughed every goblin
When they spied her peeping:
Came towards her hobbling,
Flying, running, leaping,
Puffing and blowing,
Chuckling, clapping, crowing,
Clucking and gobbling,
Mopping and mowing,
Full of airs and graces,
Pulling wry faccs,
Demure grimaces,
Cat-like and rat-like,
Ratel- and wombat-like,
Snail-paced in a hurry,
Parrot-voiced and whistler,
Helter skelter, hurry skurry,
Chattering like magpies,
Fluttering like pigeons,
Gliding like fishes,—
Hugged her and kissed her,
Squeezed and caressed her:
Stretched up their dishes,
Panniers,[6] and plates:
"Look at our apples
Russet and dun,
Bob at our cherries,
Bite at our peaches,
Citrons and dates,
Grapes for the asking,
Pears red with basking
Out in the sun,
Plums on their twigs;
Pluck them and suck them,
Pomegranates, figs."—

"Good folk," said Lizzie,
Mindful of Jeanie:
"Give me much and many:"—
Held out her apron,
Tossed them her penny.
"Nay, take a seat with us,
Honour and eat with us,"
They answered grinning:
"Our feast is but beginning.

[6] *panniers:* Baskets.

Night yet is early,
Warm and dew-pearly,
Wakeful and starry:
Such fruits as these
No man can carry;
Half their bloom would fly,
Half their dew would dry,
Half their flavour would pass by.
Sit down and feast with us,
Be welcome guest with us,
Cheer you and rest with us."—
"Thank you," said Lizzie: "But one waits
At home alone for me:
So without further parleying,
If you will not sell me any
Of your fruits tho' much and many,
Give me back my silver penny
I tossed you for a fee."—
They began to scratch their pates,
No longer wagging, purring,
But visibly demurring,
Grunting and snarling.
One called her proud,
Cross-grained, uncivil;
Their tones waxed loud,
Their looks were evil.
Lashing their tails
They trod and hustled her,
Elbowed and jostled her,
Clawed with their nails,
Barking, mewing, hissing, mocking,
Tore her gown and soiled her stocking,
Twitched her hair out by the roots,
Stamped upon her tender feet,
Held her hands and squeezed their fruits
Against her mouth to make her eat.

White and golden Lizzie stood,
Like a lily in a flood,—
Like a rock of blue-veined stone
Lashed by tides obstreperously,—
Like a beacon left alone
In a hoary roaring sea,
Sending up a golden fire,—
Like a fruit-crowned orange-tree
White with blossoms honey-sweet

Sore beset by wasp and bee,—
Like a royal virgin town
Topped with gilded dome and spire
Close beleaguerred by a fleet
Mad to tug her standard down.

One may lead a horse to water,
Twenty cannot make him drink.
Tho' the goblins cuffed and caught her,
Coaxed and fought her,
Bullied and besought her,
Scratched her, pinched her black as ink,
Kicked and knocked her,
Mauled and mocked her,
Lizzie uttered not a word;
Would not open lip from lip
Lest they should cram a mouthful in:
But laughed in heart to feel the drip
Of juice that syruped all her face,
And lodged in dimples of her chin,
And streaked her neck which quaked like curd.
At last the evil people,
Worn out by her resistance
Flung back her penny, kicked their fruit
Along whichever road they took,
Not leaving root or stone or shoot;
Some writhed into the ground,
Some dived into the brook
With ring and ripple,
Some scudded on the gale without a sound,
Some vanished in the distance.

In a smart, ache, tingle,
Lizzie went her way;
Knew not was it night or day;
Sprang up the bank, tore thro' the furze,
Threaded copse and dingle,
And heard her penny jingle
Bouncing in her purse,
Its bounce was music to her ear.
She ran and ran
As if she feared some goblin man
Dogged her with gibe or curse
Or something worse:
But not one goblin skurried after,
Nor was she pricked by fear;

The kind heart made her windy-paced
That urged her home quite out of breath with haste
And inward laughter.

She cried "Laura," up the garden,
"Did you miss me?
Come and kiss me.
Never mind my bruises,
Hug me, kiss me, suck my juices
Squeezed from goblin fruits for you,
Goblin pulp and goblin dew.
Eat me, drink me, love me;
Laura, make much of me:
For your sake I have braved the glen
And had to do with goblin merchant men."

Laura started from her chair,
Flung her arms up in the air,
Clutched her hair:
"Lizzie, Lizzie, have you tasted
For my sake the fruit forbidden?
Must your light like mine be hidden,
Your young life like mine be wasted,
Undone in mine undoing
And ruined in my ruin,
Thirsty, cankered, goblin-ridden?"—
She clung about her sister,
Kissed and kissed and kissed her:
Tears once again
Refreshed her shrunken eyes,
Dropping like rain
After long sultry drouth;
Shaking with aguish fear, and pain,
She kissed and kissed her with a hungry mouth.

Her lips began to scorch,
That juice was wormwood[7] to her tongue,
She loathed the feast:
Writhing as one possessed she leaped and sung,
Rent all her robe, and wrung
Her hands in lamentable haste,
And beat her breast.
Her locks streamed like the torch

[7]*wormwood:* A bitter, spiny, pungent plant; absinthe is distilled from it.

Borne by a racer at full speed,
Or like the mane of horses in their flight,
Or like an eagle when she stems the light
Straight toward the sun,
Or like a caged thing freed,
Or like a flying flag when armies run.

Swift fire spread thro' her veins, knocked at her heart,
Met the fire smouldering there
And overbore its lesser flame;
She gorged on bitterness without a name:
Ah! fool, to choose such part
Of soul-consuming care!
Sense failed in the mortal strife:
Like the watch-tower of a town
Which an earthquake shatters down,
Like a lightning-stricken mast,
Like a wind-uprooted tree
Spun about,
Like a foam-topped waterspout
Cast down headlong in the sea,
She fell at last;
Pleasure past and anguish past,
Is it death or is it life?

Life out of death.
That night long Lizzie watched by her,
Counted her pulse's flagging stir,
Felt for her breath,
Held water to her lips, and cooled her face
With tears and fanning leaves:
But when the first birds chirped about their eaves,
And early reapers plodded to the place
Of golden sheaves,
And dew-wet grass
Bowed in the morning winds so brisk to pass,
And new buds with new day
Opened of cup-like lilies on the stream,
Laura awoke as from a dream,
Laughed in the innocent old way,
Hugged Lizzie but not twice or thrice;
Her gleaming locks showed not one thread of grey,
Her breath was sweet as May
And light danced in her eyes.

Days, weeks, months, years
Afterwards, when both were wives
With children of their own;
Their mother-hearts beset with fears,
Their lives bound up in tender lives;
Laura would call the little ones
And tell them of her early prime,
Those pleasant days long gone
Of not-returning time:
Would talk about the haunted glen,
The wicked, quaint fruit-merchant men,
Their fruits like honey to the throat
But poison in the blood;
(Men sell not such in any town:)
Would tell them how her sister stood
In deadly peril to do her good,
And win the fiery antidote:
Then joining hands to little hands
Would bid them cling together,
"For there is no friend like a sister
In calm or stormy weather;
To cheer one on the tedious way,
To fetch one if one goes astray,
To lift one if one totters down,
To strengthen whilst one stands."

(1862)

QUESTIONS FOR DISCUSSION AND WRITING

CLOSE READING

1. What are the specific arguments Lizzie and Laura make about whether they should buy fruit from the goblins? What forces control these arguments?
2. How are the goblins described by Lizzie, by Laura, and by the speaker? Look for adjectives in response to this question, but also for the actions of the goblins.
3. The poem is unified through end rhyme; does this rhyme scheme have a consistent pattern?

CRITICAL AND CREATIVE READING

4. Should you give in to your primal urges or desires despite common wisdom to the contrary, or restrain those desires? Use "Goblin Market" to illustrate your argument.

5. Would Lizzie and Laura have been better off if Laura had never tasted the goblins' fruit?
6. Consider what the "fruit" in the poem might be by thinking about forbidden pleasures. How does fruit operate as a metaphor? Can you think of other appropriate metaphors that represent something similar?

CONNECTIONS TO OTHER READINGS

7. The subjects of "Goblin Market" and of "The Charge of the Light Brigade" by Tennyson are considerably different, yet the poems share some poetic techniques. Compare these techniques to explore whether these two poems, written at roughly the same time, share a common sensibility.
8. Respond to the following statement using "Goblin Market" and either Soyinka's *Death and the King's Horseman* or Camus' "The Guest": Freedom of choice should never be taken away; the outcome of the choices we make is less important than exercising this freedom.
9. Make the case either for or against traditional notions of "being good" based on your reading of "Goblin Market" and Gregory Corso's poem "Marriage."

Alfred, Lord Tennyson

The Charge of the Light Brigade

One of the most popular and venerated poets of the nineteenth century, Alfred, Lord Tennyson (1809–1892) succeeded William Wordsworth as poet laureate of England in 1850. Tennyson's popularity led him to be associated with the voice of the people, a poetic equivalent to the fiction writer Charles Dickens. Although his reputation following his death has been uneven, Tennyson earned his legacy through the hard work of painstaking revision. Many of his poems, such as the ambitious *In Memoriam*, are studies in private, isolated melancholy, yet a significant number, including "The Charge of the Light Brigade," were in response to public events. The following poem was inspired by a cavalry charge at Balaclava (October 25, 1854) during the Crimean War (1853–1856), a war between Russia on one side and major European powers (especially Britain, France, and the Ottoman Empire) on the other, ostensibly over the influence of the Orthodox Church. The war became infamous because of the sloppy, mismanaged way it was conducted. The challenge of reading this poem, which was once a favorite recitation piece for schoolchildren, is in discerning the speaker's tone.

I

Half a league, half a league,
Half a league onward,
All in the valley of Death
Rode the six hundred.
"Forward the Light Brigade!
Charge for the guns!" he said.
Into the valley of Death
Rode the six hundred.

II

"Forward, the Light Brigade!"
Was there a man dismay'd?
Not tho' the soldier knew
Some one had blunder'd.
Theirs not to make reply,
Theirs not to reason why,
Theirs but to do and die.
Into the valley of Death
Rode the six hundred.

III

Cannon to right of them,
Cannon to left of them,
Cannon in front of them
Volley'd and thunder'd;
Storm'd at with shot and shell,
Boldly they rode and well,
Into the jaws of Death,
Into the mouth of hell
Rode the six hundred.

IV

Flash'd all their sabres bare,
Flash'd as they turn'd in air
Sabring the gunners there,
Charging an army, while
All the world wonder'd.
Plunged in the battery-smoke
Right thro' the line they broke;
Cossack and Russian
Reel'd from the sabre-stroke
Shatter'd and sunder'd.
Then they rode back, but not,
Not the six hundred.

V

Cannon to right of them,
Cannon to left of them,
Cannon behind them
  Volley'd and thunder'd;
Storm'd at with shot and shell,
While horse and hero fell,
They that had fought so well
Came thro' the jaws of Death,
Back from the mouth of hell,
All that was left of them,
  Left of six hundred.

VI

When can their glory fade?
O the wild charge they made!
  All the world wonder'd.
Honor the charge they made!
Honor the Light Brigade,
  Noble six hundred!

(1855)

Questions for Discussion and Writing

Close Reading

1. Discuss the use of repetition throughout "The Charge of the Light Brigade."
2. Although the poem is divided into six stanzas, they are not all the same length. Consider why Tennyson might have structured the poem this way.
3. Tennyson's use of sound in this poem is striking. List examples of assonance, alliteration, and end rhyme and discuss how the poem's sounds reinforce its themes.

Critical and Creative Reading

4. The poem contains the famous lines "Theirs not to make reply, / Theirs not to reason why, / Theirs but to do and die" (lines 13–15). This kind of obedience is the key element to military success; in this case, however, the soldiers are unaware that "Some one had blunder'd" (line 12). Is Tennyson saying a good soldier will always follow orders, even if someone has blundered? Is the situation Tennyson's speaker describes ironic or unfortunate, or does he allow for the possibility that the soldiers might have acted differently?
5. How do you reconcile the imagery and language of nobility in this poem with the fact that many of the six hundred soldiers died during this battle?

6. Discuss the distance between the speaker of this poem and the charge of the Light Brigade in the Crimean War, and consider why the "noble six hundred" are anonymous. Would the tone of the poem have been different if the speaker were an eyewitness to the battle or a participant in it?

Connections to Other Readings

7. The notion of sacrifice for one's country or community is central to several works in this chapter, such as Wilfred Owen's poem "Dulce et Decorum Est," Wole Soyinka's play *Death and the King's Horseman*, William Dean Howells's story "Editha," and Shirley Jackson's story "The Lottery." Discuss sacrifice as it pertains to Tennyson's poem and one or more of these other works.
8. Consider the notion of duty implied by the lines "Theirs not to make reply,/Theirs not to reason why, / Theirs but to do and die" in this poem and in the short story "The Guest" by Alfred Camus.
9. Would you want to live in a society in which all citizens accepted their duty without question, like the "noble six hundred" in Tennyson's poem, or in a society in which everyone questioned accepted wisdom, like the speaker of Gregory Corso's "Marriage" and/or the narrator of Elizabeth McKenzie's story "Stop That Girl"?

Emily Dickinson

Much Madness is divinest Sense (435)

A woman known in her lifetime as a mysterious recluse, Emily Dickinson (1830–1886) is now considered one of the greatest lyric poets in American literature, if not the greatest. Raised in a prominent family in picturesque Amherst, Massachusetts, Dickinson received an above-average education for a woman at that time and read widely, especially in the British literature of her time. Her quirky poetry with its trademark dashes and brilliant slippages was largely unpublished in her lifetime: following an early, strong desire to see her verse in print, Dickinson closed herself off from the publishing world and the world in general. Her more than 1,700 poems, published posthumously, continue to intrigue students and critics. (See also her poems "Tell all the Truth, but tell it slant" in Chapter 14 and "Mine Enemy is Growing Old" in Chapter 15.)

Much Madness is divinest Sense—
To a discerning Eye—
Much Sense—the starkest Madness—
'Tis the Majority

In this, as All, prevail—
Assent—and you are sane—
Demur—you're straightway dangerous—
And handled with a Chain—

(c. 1862)

Handwritten manuscript of Emily Dickinson's "Much Madness is divinest Sense."

Questions for Discussion and Writing

Close Reading

1. Where does the poet use alliteration? To what effect?
2. What is implied by the phrase "discerning Eye" in line 2?

Critical and Creative Reading

3. The word "divinest" in line 1 implies "godly" or "heavenly." Why do you suppose Dickinson selected (or created) that word for this poem?

4. What is the poet's attitude toward the "majority"? Does the speaker seem to take the opinions of others seriously?
5. In 1862, when the poem was written, slaves in the American South, prisoners, and insane people were all "handled with chains," a phrase from the poem's final line. Does the poem apply to all three of these marginalized groups?

CONNECTIONS TO OTHER READINGS

6. Is the speaker of this poem allied with Henry David Thoreau in his essay "Civil Disobedience"? Is she disobedient or merely observant?
7. Discuss the risks of acting against the opinions of the majority in this poem and in Shirley Jackson's story "The Lottery."
8. Compare the treatment of madness in Dickinson's poem and in Gregory Corso's poem "Marriage."

Wilfred Owen

Dulce et Decorum Est

The career of the British poet Wilfred Owen (1893–1918) will always be associated with World War I, the event that both catalyzed his development as a poet and took his life. Owen was initially an assistant to a country vicar, or minister, and his commitment to Christian beliefs made his decision to enlist a difficult one. He produced his finest poetry in 1917 while recovering from "shell shock," alternately called "battle fatigue," a condition resulting from the extreme stress and trauma of participating in and witnessing combat. The following poem, "Dulce et Decorum Est," a Latin phrase originally written by Horace, can be roughly translated in context (with the rest of the phrase "pro patria mori") as "It is sweet and fitting to die for one's country." Consider why Owen might have appropriated this title from an ancient Latin source, and think about what an alternative English title might have been.

Bent double, like old beggars under sacks,
Knock-kneed, coughing like hags, we cursed through sludge,
Till on the haunting flares we turned our backs,
And towards our distant rest began to trudge.
Men marched asleep. Many had lost their boots,
But limped on, blood-shod. All went lame, all blind;
Drunk with fatigue; deaf even to the hoots
Of gas-shells dropping softly behind.

Gas! GAS! Quick, boys!—An ecstasy of fumbling,
Fitting the clumsy helmets just in time,
But someone still was yelling out and stumbling
And floundering like a man in fire or lime.—
Dim through the misty panes and thick green light,
As under a green sea, I saw him drowning.

In all my dreams before my helpless sight
He plunges at me, guttering, choking, drowning.

If in some smothering dreams, you too could pace
Behind the wagon that we flung him in,
And watch the white eyes writhing in his face,
His hanging face, like a devil's sick of sin;
If you could hear, at every jolt, the blood
Come gargling from the froth-corrupted lungs,
Bitter as the cud
Of vile, incurable sores on innocent tongues,—
My friend, you would not tell with such high zest
To children ardent for some desperate glory,
The old Lie: Dulce et decorum est
Pro patria mori.

(1917)

QUESTIONS FOR DISCUSSION AND WRITING

CLOSE READING

1. How does the poem emphasize the sense of sight? What other senses does it appeal to?
2. Read the poem aloud, paying close attention to the way it sounds. Owen uses assonance, the repetition of internal vowel sounds as in "white eyes writhing" (line 19) or "sick of sin" (line 20). How pervasive is Owen's use of assonance? What other poetic devices use sound in this poem? What effect is the poet trying to achieve by making the poem sound this way?
3. The poem has several subjects: we, I, and you. Comment on the speaker's individual identity, his identity as one of the soldiers, and his relationship to his audience.

CRITICAL AND CREATIVE READING

4. Pay attention to the speaker's figurative language. To what does he compare himself and the other soldiers? How do these comparisons shape the poem's theme?

5. Clearly the speaker of this poem, like the poet, served in a war. In that sense he is obedient to his country's need, or dutiful. However, does his poem constitute a kind of rebellion? If so, is it surprising? If the poem is not a kind of rebellion, how would you describe it?
6. The poem says in no uncertain terms that war is ugly. But war can be ugly at the same time that it is noble, glorious, or necessary. Does the poem speak about any positive aspects of war, or does it only comment on its ugliness and its horrifying images?

CONNECTIONS TO OTHER READINGS

7. The short story "Editha" by William Dean Howells also calls into question the meaning of war. However, George's death in "Editha" is not described in the same detail as the death of the anonymous soldier in Owen's poem. Pay careful attention to the similarities and differences of these two works, and discuss whether they are both the same kind of work.
8. Wole Soyinka's play *Death and the King's Horseman* centers around the theme of duty to one's country. Could you say that Soyinka, like the speaker of "Dulce et Decorum Est," believes that the phrase "It is sweet and fitting to die for one's country" is a "lie"?
9. Does Felicia Hemans's poem "Casabianca" share the view of war expressed in Owen's poem "Dulce et Decorum Est"?

T. S. Eliot

The Love Song of J. Alfred Prufrock

Thomas Stearns Eliot (1888–1965) is undoubtedly one of the most influential poets of the twentieth century. A native of St. Louis, Missouri, who lived in England for most of his life, Eliot was a central figure in the international movement known as "modernism." Modernists responded to the historical upheavals of the early twentieth century (such as World War I, the mobility provided by the rise of the automobile and plane travel, and massive immigration from Europe to the United States) to reimagine the role of art in the contemporary world. Eliot's poems–as well as his essays and his drama–reflect both a deep tie to the past and a willingness to break from it. In "The Love Song of J. Alfred Prufrock," his most frequently read poem, beautiful language is coupled with disturbing imagery, as in the first three lines. The reader is shocked out of complacency and encouraged to pay attention to the deep meaning beneath the surface represented in works of art.

S'io credesse che mia risposta fosse
A persona che mai tornasse al mondo,
Questa fiamma staria senza più scosse.
Ma perciocche giammai di questo fondo
Non tornò vivo alcun, s'i'odo il vero,
Senza tema d'infamia ti rispondo.[1]

Let us go then, you and I,
When the evening is spread out against the sky
Like a patient etherised upon a table;
Let us go, through certain half-deserted streets,
The muttering retreats
Of restless nights in one-night cheap hotels
And sawdust restaurants with oyster-shells:
Streets that follow like a tedious argument
Of insidious intent
To lead you to an overwhelming question . . .
Oh, do not ask, "What is it?"
Let us go and make our visit.

In the room the women come and go
Talking of Michelangelo.

The yellow fog that rubs its back upon the window-panes,
The yellow smoke that rubs its muzzle on the window-panes,
Licked its tongue into the corners of the evening,
Lingered upon the pools that stand in drains,
Let fall upon its back the soot that falls from chimneys,
Slipped by the terrace, made a sudden leap,
And seeing that it was a soft October night,
Curled once about the house, and fell asleep.

And indeed there will be time
For the yellow smoke that slides along the street
Rubbing its back upon the window-panes;
There will be time, there will be time
To prepare a face to meet the faces that you meet;
There will be time to murder and create,
And time for all the works and days of hands
That lift and drop a question on your plate;
Time for you and time for me,
And time yet for a hundred indecisions,
And for a hundred visions and revisions,
Before the taking of a toast and tea.

[1]"If I thought my answer were directed to one who could return to the world forever, this flame would never move again; but since no one has ever returned alive from this depth, if what I hear is true, I answer you without fear of infamy." From Dante's *Inferno*.

In the room the women come and go
Talking of Michelangelo.

And indeed there will be time
To wonder, "Do I dare?" and, "Do I dare?"
Time to turn back and descend the stair,
With a bald spot in the middle of my hair—
(They will say: "How his hair is growing thin!")
My morning coat, my collar mounting firmly to the chin,
My necktie rich and modest, but asserted by a simple pin—
(They will say: "But how his arms and legs are thin!")
Do I dare
Disturb the universe?
In a minute there is time
For decisions and revisions which a minute will reverse.

For I have known them all already, known them all—
Have known the evenings, mornings, afternoons,
I have measured out my life with coffee spoons;
I know the voices dying with a dying fall
Beneath the music from a farther room.
  So how should I presume?

And I have known the eyes already, known them all—
The eyes that fix you in a formulated phrase,
And when I am formulated, sprawling on a pin,
When I am pinned and wriggling on the wall,
Then how should I begin
To spit out all the butt-ends of my days and ways?
  And how should I presume?

And I have known the arms already, known them all—
Arms that are braceleted and white and bare
(But in the lamplight, downed with light brown hair!)
Is it perfume from a dress
That makes me so digress?
Arms that lie along a table, or wrap about a shawl.
  And should I then presume?
  And how should I begin?

. . . . .

Shall I say, I have gone at dusk through narrow streets
And watched the smoke that rises from the pipes
Of lonely men in shirt-sleeves, leaning out of windows? . . .

I should have been a pair of ragged claws
Scuttling across the floors of silent seas.

. . . . .

And the afternoon, the evening, sleeps so peacefully!
Smoothed by long fingers,
Asleep . . . tired . . . or it malingers,
Stretched on the floor, here beside you and me.
Should I, after tea and cakes and ices,
Have the strength to force the moment to its crisis?
But though I have wept and fasted, wept and prayed,
Though I have seen my head (grown slightly bald) brought in upon a platter,
I am no prophet—and here's no great matter;
I have seen the moment of my greatness flicker,
And I have seen the eternal Footman hold my coat, and snicker,
And in short, I was afraid.

And would it have been worth it, after all,
After the cups, the marmalade, the tea,
Among the porcelain, among some talk of you and me,
Would it have been worth while,
To have bitten off the matter with a smile,
To have squeezed the universe into a ball
To roll it towards some overwhelming question,
To say: "I am Lazarus, come from the dead,
Come back to tell you all, I shall tell you all"—
If one, settling a pillow by her head,
  Should say: "That is not what I meant at all.
  That is not it, at all."

And would it have been worth it, after all,
Would it have been worth while,
After the sunsets and the dooryards and the sprinkled streets,
After the novels, after the teacups, after the skirts that trail along the floor—
And this, and so much more?—
It is impossible to say just what I mean!
But as if a magic lantern threw the nerves in patterns on a screen:
Would it have been worth while
If one, settling a pillow or throwing off a shawl,
And turning toward the window, should say:
  "That is not it at all,
  That is not what I meant, at all."

. . . . .

No! I am not Prince Hamlet, nor was meant to be;
Am an attendant lord, one that will do
To swell a progress, start a scene or two,
Advise the prince; no doubt, an easy tool,
Deferential, glad to be of use,
Politic, cautious, and meticulous;
Full of high sentence, but a bit obtuse;
At times, indeed, almost ridiculous—
Almost, at times, the Fool.

I grow old . . . I grow old . . .
I shall wear the bottoms of my trousers rolled.

Shall I part my hair behind? Do I dare to eat a peach?
I shall wear white flannel trousers, and walk upon the beach.
I have heard the mermaids singing, each to each.

I do not think that they will sing to me.

I have seen them riding seaward on the waves
Combing the white hair of the waves blown back
When the wind blows the water white and black.

We have lingered in the chambers of the sea
By sea-girls wreathed with seaweed red and brown
Till human voices wake us, and we drown.

(1915)

Questions for Discussion and Writing

Close Reading

1. Begin by listing the repetitions in the poem: what effect do they have?
2. Why would the poet begin with an Italian epigraph? How does this particular epigraph from Dante's *Inferno* prepare us for the themes of the poem?
3. The poem employs end rhyme, though not in a systematic way. Do you see patterns, if not a system, in the rhyme scheme? What is the effect of using rhyme as Eliot does here?
4. Choose one of the many metaphors in the poem (such as "coffee spoons" in line 51 or "ragged claws" in line 73) and explain how its meaning relates to the theme.

Critical and Creative Reading

5. Prufrock wonders, "Do I dare?" repeatedly through the poem; in line 122 he says, "Do I dare to eat a peach?" Why does he link his lack of daring to

something as mundane as eating a peach? What else might he have said to communicate the same idea?

6. Who are these women who come and go talking of Michelangelo, and why does the speaker single out one in particular who might say to him, "That is not what I meant at all"?
7. In line 104 Prufrock lets his guard down and reveals his frustration when he cries, "It is impossible to say just what I mean!" Discuss the theme of communication in the poem.

CONNECTIONS TO OTHER READINGS

8. The speaker of Eliot's poem and of Corso's poem "Marriage" both ask questions of themselves. Compare the personalities of the two speakers and speculate why they draw different conclusions about their situations. Could the speaker in Eliot's poem be wondering whether or not to propose marriage?
9. Compare the setting of this poem and that of John Updike's story "A & P": how do our circumstances affect the magnitude of our decisions, such as whether to obey or disobey society's dictates?

W. H. Auden

The Unknown Citizen

Wystan Hugh Auden (1907–1973) was one of a group of poets, including Stephen Spender and C. Day Lewis, who attempted to define a "new school" of British poetry in the 1920s and 1930s. Influenced by T. S. Eliot (see "The Love Song of J. Alfred Prufrock" preceding this poem), Auden and his contemporaries looked out at an English landscape and an English people ravaged by war and economic depression. Like Eliot, Auden was able to merge the language and concerns of popular culture with universal or mythological concerns. (See also Auden's poem "Musée des Beaux Arts" in the Icarus portfolio at the end of this chapter.)

(To JS/07/M/378
This Marble Monument
Is Erected by the State)

He was found by the Bureau of Statistics to be
One against whom there was no official complaint,
And all the reports on his conduct agree

That, in the modern sense of an old-fashioned word, he was a saint,
For in everything he did he served the Greater Community.
Except for the War till the day he retired
He worked in a factory and never got fired,
But satisfied his employers, Fudge Motors Inc.
Yet he wasn't a scab or odd in his views,
For his Union reports that he paid his dues,
(Our report on his Union shows it was sound)
And our Social Psychology workers found
That he was popular with his mates and liked a drink.
The Press are convinced that he bought a paper every day
And that his reactions to advertisements were normal in every way.
Policies taken out in his name prove that he was fully insured,
And his Health-card shows he was once in hospital but left it cured.
Both Producers Research and High-Grade Living declare
He was fully sensible to the advantages of the Instalment Plan
And had everything necessary to the Modern Man,
A phonograph, a radio, a car and a frigidaire.
Our researchers into Public Opinion are content
That he held the proper opinions for the time of year;
When there was peace, he was for peace; when there was war, he went.
He was married and added five children to the population,
Which our Eugenist[1] says was the right number for a parent of his
  generation,
And our teachers report that he never interfered with their education.
Was he free? Was he happy? The question is absurd:
Had anything been wrong, we should certainly have heard.

(1940)

Questions for Discussion and Writing

Close Reading

1. Trace the rhyme scheme of the poem, using letters to denote end rhyme (for example, *abab* or *aabb:* see Chapter 5 for a description of rhyme and how to represent it). What patterns do you notice, and what is the effect of writing the poem this way?
2. What is necessary to be "a modern man," according to the poem? How does this definition feed into the themes of the rest of the poem?
3. How does the epigraph function in this poem?

[1]*Eugenist:* Eugenics was a pseudo-science that gained some popularity in the early twentieth century. It was founded on a notion that the human race could be improved through genetic manipulation in future generations.

Critical and Creative Reading

4. How common is the type of person described in "The Unknown Citizen"? By what other names is he or she called?
5. Is it better to be a "known citizen" than an unknown citizen even if one is "known" for acts that are not valued by society?
6. Write an updated version of "The Unknown Citizen" set in the twenty-first century that describes a condition of anonymity brought about by our contemporary culture. How different is it from Auden's poem?

Connections to Other Readings

7. Compare the dehumanization of Auden's "unknown citizen" to Marge Piercy's poem "The Secretary Chant" (Chapter 16).
8. Write an essay in which you argue for or against the usefulness of considering J. Alfred Prufrock from T. S. Eliot's poem "The Love Song of J. Alfred Prufrock" as essentially the same character as that described in Auden's poem.
9. Based on his essay "Civil Disobedience," what would Henry David Thoreau have to say about both the individual and the society described in "The Unknown Citizen"?

Dylan Thomas

Do Not Go Gentle into That Good Night

The intense forces of life and death are at the heart of Dylan Thomas's poetry. Thomas (1914–1953) grew up in the coastal town of Swansea, Wales, and worked initially as a newspaper reporter. His poetry is passionate and marks a departure, in some ways, from the alienated poems of T. S. Eliot and W. H. Auden, whose poems immediately precede this one. Like the Romantic poets Byron, Shelley, and Keats, Dylan Thomas died young, reportedly after drinking excessive amounts of whiskey in a bohemian bar called the White Horse Tavern in Manhattan's Greenwich Village. This story probably feeds into the popular belief that folk-rock legend Bob Dylan took his stage name from Dylan Thomas, a legend that Bob Dylan has denied. While some critics describe Thomas as a Romantic and bohemian poet of the soul, other critics admire him for his careful poetic craftsmanship. Both critical responses are appropriate for the following villanelle (a 19-line poem in which lines 1 and 3 repeat alternately as a refrain throughout the later stanzas, according to a set pattern).

Do not go gentle into that good night,
Old age should burn and rave at close of day;
Rage, rage against the dying of the light.

Though wise men at their end know dark is right,
Because their words had forked no lightning they
Do not go gentle into that good night.

Good men, the last wave by, crying how bright
Their frail deeds might have danced in a green bay,
Rage, rage against the dying of the light.

Wild men who caught and sang the sun in flight,
And learn, too late, they grieved it on its way,
Do not go gentle into that good night.

Grave men, near death, who see with blinding sight
Blind eyes could blaze like meteors and be gay,
Rage, rage against the dying of the light.

And you, my father, there on the sad height,
Curse, bless, me now with your fierce tears, I pray.
Do not go gentle into that good night.
Rage, rage against the dying of the light.

(1951)

Questions for Discussion and Writing

Close Reading

1. This poem is an example of a villanelle, a relatively uncommon poetic form consisting of precisely 19 lines in six stanzas. Each stanza is a *tercet*, a three-line stanza in which the first and third lines rhyme. This pattern is repeated throughout the poem until the final stanza, which is a quatrain, or four-line stanza. What are the advantages of writing a poem according to such a strict form?
2. Except for the first and last stanzas, each stanza begins with an observation about a certain type of man. Is it clear what type of man the speaker's father most closely resembles?
3. Discuss the poem's imagery. How consistent is it? What is its overall effect?

Critical and Creative Reading

4. The poem mentions death only once, and not directly in connection with the speaker's father. Could the poem be about something other than death?
5. Many people express the desire to die peacefully, even during sleep. Why would this speaker want the opposite for his father?

6. In the final stanza, how are the speaker's father's "fierce tears" both a curse and a blessing?

CONNECTIONS TO OTHER READINGS

7. Compare attitudes toward life and death in this poem to those exhibited by Elesin in Soyinka's play *Death and the King's Horseman.*
8. Discuss the legacy of Auden's "Unknown Citizen" to the potential legacy of the speaker's father in this poem and to J. Alfred Prufrock in Eliot's poem.
9. What is the speaker's attitude toward accepted wisdom in this poem and in Emily Dickinson's "Much Madness is divinest Sense"?

Gregory Corso

Marriage

Gregory Corso (1930–2001) is usually associated with the "Beat Generation," a group of young American writers of the 1950s like Jack Kerouac and Allen Ginsberg who flouted conventional values and literary forms in favor of writing spontaneous prose and poetry. (See Ginsburg's poem in Chapter 17.) Corso began reading and writing literature during a three-year prison sentence beginning when he was sixteen, and he started publishing poetry when he was twenty-five. The "Beats" resisted the conformity of American society in the 1950s; Corso once wrote, "I'm not a square, you see a square is some guy who forces himself arbitrarily into a square auto-life mold, because squareness is not a shape that any living creature occurs in." Is he offering an alternative to "squareness" in the following poem, or does he simply resist it?

Should I get married? Should I be good?
Astound the girl next door with my velvet suit and faustus hood?
Don't take her to movies but to cemeteries
tell all about werewolf bathtubs and forked clarinets
then desire her and kiss her and all the preliminaries
and she going just so far and I understanding why
not getting angry saying You must feel! It's beautiful to feel!
Instead take her in my arms lean against an old crooked tombstone
and woo her the entire night the constellations in the sky—

When she introduces me to her parents
back straightened, hair finally combed, strangled by a tie,
should I sit knees together on their 3rd degree sofa
and not ask Where's the bathroom?

How else to feel other than I am,
often thinking Flash Gordon[1] soap—
O how terrible it must be for a young man
seated before a family and the family thinking
We never saw him before! He wants our Mary Lou!
After tea and homemade cookies they ask What do you do for a living?

Should I tell them? Would they like me then?
Say All right get married, we're losing a daughter
but we're gaining a son—
And should I then ask Where's the bathroom?

O God, and the wedding! All her family and her friends
and only a handful of mine all scroungy and bearded
just wait to get at the drinks and food—
And the priest! he looking at me as if I masturbated
asking me Do you take this woman for your lawful wedded wife?
And I trembling what to say say Pie Glue!
I kiss the bride all those corny men slapping me on the back
She's all yours, boy! Ha-ha-ha!
And in their eyes you could see some obscene honeymoon going on—
Then all that absurd rice and clanky cans and shoes
Niagara Falls! Hordes of us! Husbands! Wives! Flowers! Chocolates!
All streaming into cozy hotels
All going to do the same thing tonight
The indifferent clerk he knowing what was going to happen
The lobby zombies they knowing what
The whistling elevator man he knowing
The winking bellboy knowing
Everybody knowing! I'd be almost inclined not to do anything!
Stay up all night! Stare that hotel clerk in the eye!
Screaming: I deny honeymoon! I deny honeymoon!
running rampant into those almost climactic suites
yelling Radio belly! Cat shovel!
O I'd live in Niagara forever! in a dark cave beneath the Falls
I'd sit there the Mad Honeymooner
devising ways to break marriages, a scourge of bigamy
a saint of divorce—

But I should get married I should be good
How nice it'd be to come home to her
and sit by the fireplace and she in the kitchen
aproned young and lovely wanting my baby
and so happy about me she burns the roast beef

[1] *Flash Gordon:* A comic superhero known for his speed. Corso's allusion is absurd; he could have chosen any superhero.

and comes crying to me and I get up from my big papa chair
saying Christmas teeth! Radiant brains! Apple deaf!
God what a husband I'd make! Yes, I should get married!
So much to do! like sneaking into Mr Jones' house late at night
and cover his golf clubs with 1920 Norwegian books
Like hanging a picture of Rimbaud[2] on the lawnmower
like pasting Tannu Tuva[3] postage stamps all over the picket fence
like when Mrs Kindhead comes to collect for the Community Chest
grab her and tell her There are unfavorable omens in the sky!
And when the mayor comes to get my vote tell him
When are you going to stop people killing whales!
And when the milkman comes leave him a note in the bottle
Penguin dust, bring me penguin dust, I want penguin dust—

Yet if I should get married and it's Connecticut and snow
and she gives birth to a child and I am sleepless, worn,
up for nights, head bowed against a quiet window, the past behind me,
finding myself in the most common of situations a trembling man
knowledged with responsibility not twig-smear nor Roman coin soup—
O what would that be like!
Surely I'd give it for a nipple a rubber Tacitus[4]
For a rattle a bag of broken Bach records
Tack Della Francesca[5] all over its crib
Sew the Greek alphabet on its bib
And build for its playpen a roofless Parthenon

No, I doubt I'd be that kind of father
not rural not snow no quiet window
but hot smelly tight New York City
seven flights up, roaches and rats in the walls
a fat Reichian[6] wife screeching over potatoes Get a job!
And five nose running brats in love with Batman
And the neighbors all toothless and dry haired
like those hag masses of the 18th century
all wanting to come in and watch TV
The landlord wants his rent
Grocery store Blue Cross Gas & Electric Knights of Columbus
Impossible to lie back and dream Telephone snow, ghost parking—

[2] *Rimbaud:* French poet Arthur Rimbaud (1854–1891), who is known for his dark vision of love.

[3] *Tannu Tuva:* A small Siberian country that issued colorful, collectible stamps in the early twentieth century.

[4] *Tacitus:* Gaius Tacitus, a Latin historian from the first century.

[5] *Della Francesca:* Piero della Francesca, a Renaissance artist who painted in fifteenth-century Italy.

[6] *Reichian:* Based on the theories of German psychologist Wilhem Reich (1897–1957), who emphasized connections between the body and emotions and who placed particular emphasis on orgone, or accumulated energy. Reich connected sexuality and emotional behavior.

No! I should not get married I should never get married!
But—imagine If I were married to a beautiful sophisticated woman
tall and pale wearing an elegant black dress and long black gloves
holding a cigarette holder in one hand and highball in the other
and we lived high up a penthouse with a huge window
from which we could see all of New York and even farther on clearer days
No, can't imagine myself married to that pleasant prison dream—

O but what about love? I forget love
not that I am incapable of love
it's just that I see love as odd as wearing shoes—
I never wanted to marry a girl who was like my mother
And Ingrid Bergman[7] was always impossible
And there's maybe a girl now but she's already married
And I don't like men and—
but there's got to be somebody!
Because what if I'm 60 years old and not married,
all alone in a furnished room with pee stains on my underwear
and everybody else is married! All the universe married but me!

Ah, yet well I know that were a woman possible as I am possible
then marriage would be possible—
Like SHE in her lonely alien gaud waiting her Egyptian lover
so I wait—bereft of 2,000 years and the bath of life.

(1960)

QUESTIONS FOR DISCUSSION AND WRITING

CLOSE READING

1. Although certainly unconventional, this poem does use some conventions. Where does the poem employ end rhyme? If the end rhyme is not used evenly, why is it used at all?
2. Discuss the use of exclamation points and question marks in "Marriage."
3. Catalog the speaker's allusions to figures from antiquity and from contemporary popular culture. Are these allusions absurd, or do they support the poem's themes?

CRITICAL AND CREATIVE READING

4. One of the goals of Beat Generation writers was to capture the spontaneity of thought. These writers placed a higher value on performance than on revision. From a reader's point of view, what are the advantages and disadvantages of this method? Illustrate your response with examples from "Marriage."

[7] *Ingrid Bergman:* A Swedish film actress (1915–1982).

5. This poem is, or is intended to be, funny. Does Corso's humor deflect the seriousness of the questions that open the poem ("Should I get married? Should I be good?"), or is the humor meant to show that these questions are absurd?
6. Does Corso want to persuade the reader that the American dream of conventional, stable, middle-class, heterosexual union and child-rearing is ridiculous? Or is he conveying his personal opinion that such a lifestyle is simply not for him?

CONNECTIONS TO OTHER READINGS

7. Compare the speaker's resistance to conformity in "Marriage" to Ann's resistance to conformity in Elizabeth McKenzie's "Stop That Girl." Are both of these nonconformists also rebels? What is the difference, if there is one, between these two terms?
8. One of the questions informing Sarah Vowell's essay "Take the Cannoli" is a variation on Corso's question: "Should I get married? Should I be good?" What happens to this question in both of these pieces? Have Vowell's and Corso's speakers made up their minds before they start writing, or are they genuinely exploring those questions through their writing?
9. Shirley Jackson's story "The Lottery" describes the rituals surrounding the lottery, much as Corso describes the rituals surrounding a wedding in "Marriage." Although the works are different in tone and theme, do they lead the reader to similar conclusions about following the rituals of one's society?
10. Compare the methods and themes of this poem to that of another "Beat" writer, Allen Ginsberg, whose poem "C'mon Pigs of Western Civilization Eat More Grease" appears in Chapter 17.

Drama

Wole Soyinka

Death and the King's Horseman

Nigerian playwright Wole Soyinka (b. 1934) won the Nobel Prize in literature in 1986. Influenced by European literature and thought as well as by African drama, Soyinka was educated both in Nigeria and in England. He was held as a political prisoner for nearly two years (1967–1969) during the Nigerian civil war for publishing an appeal for a cease-fire. Since receiving the Nobel Price, he has remained a powerful literary and public figure. He continues to publish plays as well as poetry, and he is an eloquent spokesman for the rights of all people to determine their own fate and to make their own decisions.

The following play, *Death and the King's Horseman*, is rich and complex, influenced not only by Soyinka's personal history (in the figure of Olunde, who returns to his native Nigeria after leaving to be educated in England), but also by actual history: the play is based on events that took place in 1946 in Oyo, an ancient Yoruba city in Nigeria. (*Yoruba* refers to an indigenous tribe in Nigeria and also to the language they speak.) Like many countries in Africa, Nigeria–the most populous of Africa's countries—was a colony of a European nation (England) for much of the twentieth century. In 1960 Nigeria achieved formal independence from Great Britain and underwent a bloody and brutal civil war from 1967 to 1970. Although Soyinka's play was published after the civil war, it takes place during a time when Nigeria was still a British colony. The play focuses on the tension between Yoruba tradition and the British concept of the way things should be done, as well as on the tension between modernization and tradition in general. It is a classic but complex example of tragedy. Do not be put off by the language of the play, which is initially somewhat baffling because it is highly ritualized. As the play continues you are likely to feel the dramatic tension more acutely, and a second reading should be more rewarding than the first.

Author's Note

This play is based on events which took place in Oyo, ancient Yoruba city of Nigeria, in 1946. That year, the lives of Elesin (Olori Elesin), his son, and the Colonial District Officer intertwined with the disastrous results set out in the play. The changes I have

Scene from *Death and the King's Horseman* by Wole Soyinka performed at Washington State University.

made are in matters of detail, sequence and of course characterisation. The action has also been set back two or three years to while the war was still on, for minor reasons of dramaturgy.

The factual account still exists in the archives of the British Colonial Administration. It has already inspired a fine play in Yoruba (Oba Wàjà) by Duro Ladipo. It has also misbegotten a film by some German television company.

The bane of themes of this genre is that they are no sooner employed creatively than they acquire the facile tag of "clash of cultures," a prejudicial label which, quite apart from its frequent misapplication, presupposes a potential equality in every given situation *of the alien culture and the indigenous, on the actual soil of the latter. (In the area of misapplication, the overseas prize for illiteracy and mental conditioning undoubtedly goes to the blurb-writer for the American edition of my novel* Season of Anomy *who unblushingly declares that this work portrays the "clash between old values and new ways, between western methods and African traditions"!) It is thanks to this kind of perverse mentality that I find it necessary to caution the would-be producer of this play against a sadly familiar reductionist tendency, and to direct his vision instead to the far more difficult and risky task of eliciting the play's threnodic essence.*

One of the more obvious alternative structures of the play would be to make the District Officer the victim of a cruel dilemma. This is not to my taste and it is not by chance that I have avoided dialogue or situation which would encourage this. No attempt should be made in production to suggest it. The Colonial Factor is an incident, a catalytic incident merely. The confrontation in the play is largely metaphysical, contained in the human vehicle which is Elesin and the universe of the Yoruba mind—the world of the living, the dead and the unborn, and the numinous passage which links all: transition. Death and the King's Horseman *can be fully realised only through an evocation of music from the abyss of transition.*

W.S.

CHARACTERS

Praise-Singer	
Elesin	*Horseman of the King*
Iyaloja	*'Mother' of the market*
Simon Pilkings	*District Officer*
Jane Pilkings	*his wife*
Serjeant Amusa	
Joseph	*houseboy to the Pilkingses*
Bride	
H.R.H. The Prince	
The Resident	
Aide-de-Camp	
Olunde	*eldest son of Elesin*

Drummers, Women, Young Girls, Dancers at the Ball

The play should run without an interval. For rapid scene changes, one adjustable outline set is very appropriate.

1

A passage through a market in its closing stages. The stalls are being emptied, mats folded. A few women pass through on their way home, loaded with baskets. On a cloth-stand, bolts of cloth are taken down, display pieces folded and piled on a tray. Elesin Oba enters along a passage before the market, pursued by his drummers and praise-singers. He is a man of enormous vitality, speaks, dances and sings with that infectious enjoyment of life which accompanies all his actions.

Praise-Singer: Elesin o! Elesin Oba! Howu! What tryst is this the cockerel[1] goes to keep with such haste that he must leave his tail behind?

Elesin [*slows down a bit, laughing*]: A tryst where the cockerel needs no adornment.

Praise-Singer: O-oh, you hear that my companions? That's the way the world goes. Because the man approaches a brand-new bride he forgets the long faithful mother of his children.

Elesin: When the horse sniffs the stable does he not strain at the bridle? The market is the long-suffering home of my spirit and the women are packing up to go. That Esu-harrassed day slipped into the stewpot while we feasted. We ate it up with the rest of the meat. I have neglected my women.

Praise-Singer: We know all that. Still it's no reason for shedding your tail on this day of all days. I know the women will cover you in damask and *alari*[2] but when the wind blows cold from behind, that's when the fowl knows his true friends.

Elesin: Olohun-iyo!

Praise-Singer: Are you sure there will be one like me on the other side?

Elesin: Olohun-iyo!

Praise-Singer: Far be it for me to belittle the dwellers of that place but, a man is either born to his art or he isn't. And I don't know for certain that you'll meet my father, so who is going to sing these deeds in accents that will pierce the deafness of the ancient ones. I have prepared my going—just tell me: Olohun-iyo, I need you on this journey and I shall be behind you.

Elesin: You're like a jealous wife. Stay close to me, but only on this side. My fame, my honour are legacies to the living; stay behind and let the world sip its honey from your lips.

Praise-Singer: Your name will be like the sweet berry a child places under his tongue to sweeten the passage of food. The world will never spit it out.

Elesin: Come then. This market is my roost. When I come among the women I am a chicken with a hundred mothers. I become a monarch whose palace is built with tenderness and beauty.

Praise-Singer: They love to spoil you but beware. The hands of women also weaken the unwary.

[1]*cockerel:* A young rooster. The dialogue in this portion of the play is highly metaphorical.

[2]*damask and alari:* Fine fabrics.

Elesin: This night I'll lay my head upon their lap and go to sleep. This night I'll touch feet with their feet in a dance that is no longer of this earth. But the smell of their flesh, their sweat, the smell of indigo on their cloth, this is the last air I wish to breathe as I go to meet my great forebears.

Praise-Singer: In their time the world was never tilted from its groove, it shall not be in yours.

Elesin: The gods have said No.

Praise-Singer: In their time the great wars came and went, the little wars came and went; the white slavers came and went, they took away the heart of our race, they bore away the mind and muscle of our race. The city fell and was rebuilt; the city fell and our people trudged through mountain and forest to found a new home but—Elesin Oba do you hear me?

Elesin: I hear your voice Olohun-iyo.

Praise-Singer: Our world was never wrenched from its true course.

Elesin: The gods have said No.

Praise-Singer: There is only one home to the life of a river-mussel; there is only one home to the life of a tortoise; there is only one shell to the soul of man: there is only one world to the spirit of our race. If that world leaves its course and smashes on boulders of the great void, whose world will give us shelter?

Elesin: It did not in the time of my forebears, it shall not in mine.

Praise-Singer: The cockerel must not be seen without his feathers.

Elesin: Nor will the Not-I bird be much longer without his nest.

Praise-Singer [*stopped in his lyric stride*]: The Not-I bird, Elesin?

Elesin: I said, the Not-I bird.

Praise-Singer: All respect to our elders but, is there really such a bird?

Elesin: What! Could it be that he failed to knock on your door?

Praise-Singer [*smiling*]: Elesin's riddles are not merely the nut in the kernel that breaks human teeth; he also buries the kernel in hot embers and dares a man's fingers to draw it out.

Elesin: I am sure he called on you, Olohun-iyo. Did you hide in the loft and push out the servant to tell him you were out?

[Elesin executes a brief, half-taunting dance. The drummer moves in and draws a rhythm out of his steps. Elesin dances towards the market-place as he chants the story of the Not-I bird, his voice changing dexterously to mimic his characters. He performs like a born raconteur,[3] infecting his retinue with his humour and energy. More women arrive during his recital, including Iyaloja.]

Death came calling.
Who does not know his rasp of reeds?
A twilight whisper in the leaves before
The great araba falls? Did you hear it?
Not I! swears the farmer. He snaps
His fingers round his head, abandons

[3]*raconteur:* A storyteller.

A hard-worn harvest and begins
A rapid dialogue with his legs.

"Not I," shouts the fearless hunter, "but—
It's getting dark, and this night-lamp
Has leaked out all its oil. I think
It's best to go home and resume my hunt
Another day." But now he pauses, suddenly
Lets out a wail: "Oh foolish mouth, calling
Down a curse on your own head! Your lamp
Has leaked out all its oil, has it?"
Forwards or backwards now he dare not move.
To search for leaves and make *etutu*[4]
On that spot? Or race home to the safety
Of his hearth? Ten market-days have passed
My friends, and still he's rooted there
Rigid as the plinth of Orayan.

The mouth of the courtesan barely
Opened wide enough to take a ha'penny *robo*
When she wailed: "Not I." All dressed she was
To call upon my friend the Chief Tax Officer.
But now she sends her go-between instead:
"Tell him I'm ill: my period has come suddenly
But not—I hope—my time."

Why is the pupil crying?
His hapless head was made to taste
The knuckles of my friend the Mallam:
"If you were then reciting the Koran
Would you have ears for idle noises
Darkening the trees, you child of ill omen?"
He shuts down school before its time
Runs home and rings himself with amulets.

And take my good kinsman Ifawomi.
His hands were like a carver's, strong
And true. I saw them
Tremble like wet wings of a fowl
One day he cast his time-smoothed *opele*[5]
Across the divination board. And all because
The suppliant looked him in the eye and asked,
"Did you hear that whisper in the leaves?"
"Not I," was his reply; "perhaps I'm growing deaf—

[4]*etutu:* Seven days of funeral ritual atonement to send the deceased spirit into the next realm.
[5]*opele:* A string of nuts used to divine the future.

Good-day." And Ifa spoke no more that day
The priest locked fast his doors,
Sealed up his leaking roof—but wait!
This sudden care was not for Fawomi
But for Osanyin, courier-bird of Ifa's
Heart of wisdom. I did not know a kite
Was hovering in the sky
And Ifa now a twittering chicken in
The brood of Fawomi the Mother Hen.

Ah, but I must not forget my evening
Courier from the abundant palm, whose groan
Became Not I, as he constipated down
A wayside bush. He wonders if Elegbara
Has tricked his buttocks to discharge
Against a sacred grove. Hear him
Mutter spells to ward off penalties
For an abomination he did not intend.
If any here
Stumbles on a gourd of wine, fermenting
Near the road, and nearby hears a stream
Of spells issuing from a crouching form.
Brother to a *sigidi*,[6] bring home my wine,
Tell my tapper I have ejected
Fear from home and farm. Assure him,
All is well.

Praise-Singer: In your time we do not doubt the peace of farmstead and home, the peace of road and hearth, we do not doubt the peace of the forest.

Elesin: There was fear in the forest too.
Not-I was lately heard even in the lair
Of beasts. The hyena cackled loud Not I,
The civet twitched his fiery tail and glared:
Not I. Not-I became the answering-name
Of the restless bird, that little one
Whom Death found nesting in the leaves
When whisper of his coming ran
Before him on the wind. Not-I
Has long abandoned home. This same dawn
I heard him twitter in the gods' abode.
Ah, companions of this living world
What a thing this is, that even those
We call immortal
Should fear to die.

[6]*sigidi:* A nightmare, sometimes used by wizards to annoy or kill a man in his sleep. Also a carved figure endowed with these powers.

Iyaloja: But you, husband of multitudes?
Elesin: I, when that Not-I bird perched
Upon my roof, bade him seek his nest again,
Safe, without care or fear. I unrolled
My welcome mat for him to see. Not-I
Flew happily away, you'll hear his voice
No more in this lifetime—You all know
What I am.
Praise-Singer: That rock which turns its open lodes
Into the path of lightning. A gay
Thoroughbred whose stride disdains
To falter though an adder reared
Suddenly in his path.
Elsein: My rein is loosened.
I am master of my Fate. When the hour comes
Watch me dance along the narrowing path
Glazed by the soles of my great precursors.
My soul is eager. I shall not turn aside.
Women: You will not delay?
Elsein: Where the storm pleases, and when, it directs
The giants of the forest. When friendship summons
Is when the true comrade goes.
Women: Nothing will hold you back?
Elsein: Nothing. What! Has no one told you yet?
I go to keep my friend and master company.
Who says the mouth does not believe in
"No, I have chewed all that before?" I say I have.
The world is not a constant honey-pot.
Where I found little I made do with little.
Where there was plenty I gorged myself.
My master's hands and mine have always
Dipped together and, home or sacred feast,
The bowl was beaten bronze, the meats
So succulent our teeth accused us of neglect.
We shared the choicest of the season's
Harvest of yams. How my friend would read
Desire in my eyes before I knew the cause—
However rare, however precious, it was mine.
Women: The town, the very land was yours.
Elesin: The world was mine. Our joint hands
Raised houseposts of trust that withstood
The siege of envy and the termites of time.
But the twilight hour brings bats and rodents—
Shall I yield them cause to foul the rafters?
Praise-Singer: Elesin Oba! Are you not that man who
Looked out of doors that stormy day

The god of luck limped by, drenched
To the very lice that held
His rags together? You took pity upon
His sores and wished him fortune.
Fortune was footloose this dawn, he replied,
Till you trapped him in a heartfelt wish
That now returns to you. Elesin Oba!
I say you are that man who
Chanced upon the calabash of honour
You thought it was palm wine and
Drained its contents to the final drop.

Elesin: Life has an end. A life that will outlive
Fame and friendship begs another name.
What elder takes his tongue to his plate,
Licks it clean of every crumb? He will encounter
Silence when he calls on children to fulfill
The smallest errand! Life is honour.
It ends when honour ends.

Women: We know you for a man of honour.

Elesin: Stop! Enough of that!

Women [*puzzled, they whisper among themselves, turning mostly to Iyaloja*]: What is it? Did we say something to give offence? Have we slighted him in some way?

Elesin: Enough of that sound I say. Let me hear no more in that vein. I've heard enough.

Iyaloja: We must have said something wrong. [*Comes forward a little.*] Elesin Oba, we ask forgiveness before you speak.

Elesin: I am bitterly offended.

Iyaloja: Our unworthiness has betrayed us. All we can do is ask your forgiveness. Correct us like a kind father.

Elesin: This day of all days . . .

Iyaloja: It does not bear thinking. If we offend you now we have mortified the gods. We offend heaven itself. Father of us all, tell us where we went astray. [*She kneels, the other women follow.*]

Elesin: Are you not ashamed? Even a tear-veiled
Eye preserves its function of sight.
Because my mind was raised to horizons
Even the boldest man lowers his gaze
In thinking of, must my body here
Be taken for a vagrant's?

Iyaloja: Horseman of the King, I am more baffled than ever.

Praise-Singer: The strictest father unbends his brow when the child is penitent, Elesin. When time is short, we do not spend it prolonging the riddle. Their shoulders are bowed with the weight of fear lest they have marred your day beyond repair. Speak now in plain words and let us pursue the ailment to the home of remedies.

Elesin: Words are cheap, 'We know you for
A man of honour.' Well tell me, is this how
A man of honour should be seen?
Are these not the same clothes in which
I came among you a full half-hour ago?

[He roars with laughter and the women, relieved, rise and rush into stalls to fetch rich cloths.]

Woman: The gods are kind. A fault soon remedied is soon forgiven. Elesin Oba, even as we match our words with deed, let your heart forgive us completely.

Elesin: You who are breath and giver of my being
How shall I dare refuse you forgiveness
Even if the offence were real.

Iyaloja [*dancing round him. Sings*]:
He forgives us. He forgives us.
What a fearful thing it is when
The voyager sets forth
But a curse remains behind.

Women: For a while we truly feared
Our hands had wrenched the world adrift
In emptiness.

Iyaloja: Richly, richly, robe him richly
The cloth of honour is *alari*
Sanyan[7] is the band of friendship
Boa-skin makes slippers of esteem

Women: For a while we truly feared
Our hands had wrenched the world adrift
In emptiness.

Praise-Singer: He who must, must voyage forth
The world will not roll backwards
It is he who must, with one
Great gesture overtake the world.

Women: For a while we truly feared
Our hands had wrenched the world
In emptiness.

Praise-Singer: The gourd you bear is not for shirking.
The gourd is not for setting down
At the first crossroad or wayside grove.
Only one river may know its contents.

Women: We shall all meet at the great market
We shall all meet at the great market

[7]*sanyan:* A beige silken cloth.

He who goes early takes the best bargains
But we shall meet, and resume our banter.

[Elesin stands resplendent in rich clothes, cap, shawl, etc. His sash is of a bright red alari *cloth. The women dance round him. Suddenly, his attention is caught by an object off-stage.]*

Elesin: The world I know is good.
Women: We know you'll leave it so.
Elesin: The world I know is the bounty
Of hives after bees have swarmed.
No goodness teems with such open hands
Even in the dreams of deities.
Women: And we know you'll leave it so.
Elesin: I was born to keep it so. A hive
Is never known to wander. An anthill
Does not desert its roots. We cannot see
The still great womb of the world—
No man beholds his mother's womb—
Yet who denies it's there? Coiled
To the navel of the world is that
Endless cord that links us all
To the great origin. If I lose my way
The trailing cord will bring me to the roots.
Women: The world is in your hands.

[The earlier distraction, a beautiful young girl, comes along the passage through which Elesin first made his entry.]

Elesin: I embrace it. And let me tell you, women—
I like this farewell that the world designed,
Unless my eyes deceive me, unless
We are already parted, the world and I,
And all that breeds desire is lodged
Among our tireless ancestors. Tell me friends,
Am I still earthed in that beloved market
Of my youth? Or could it be my will
Has outleapt the conscious act and I have come
Among the great departed?
Praise-Singer: Elesin-Oba why do your eyes roll like a bush-rat who sees his fate like his father's spirit, mirrored in the eye of a snake? And all these questions! You're standing on the same earth you've always stood upon. This voice you hear is mine, Oluhun-iyo, not that of an acolyte in heaven.
Elesin: How can that be? In all my life
As Horseman of the King, the juiciest
Fruit on every tree was mine. I saw,

I touched, I wooed, rarely was the answer No.
The honour of my place, the veneration I
Received in the eye of man or woman
Prospered my suit and
Played havoc with my sleeping hours.
And they tell me my eyes were a hawk
In perpetual hunger. Split an iroko tree
In two, hide a woman's beauty in its heartwood
And seal it up again—Elesin, journeying by,
Would make his camp beside that tree
Of all the shades in the forest.

Praise-Singer: Who would deny your reputation, snake-on-the-loose in dark passages of the market! Bed-bug who wages war on the mat and receives the thanks of the vanquished! When caught with his bride's own sister he protested—but I was only prostrating myself to her as becomes a grateful in-law. Hunter who carries his powder-horn on the hips and fires crouching or standing! Warrior who never makes that excuse of the whining coward—but how can I go to battle without my trousers?—trouserless or shirtless it's all one to him. Oka-rearing-from-a-camouflage-of-leaves, before he strikes the victim is already prone! Once they told him, Howu, a stallion does not feed on the grass beneath him: he replied, true, but surely he can roll on it!

Women: Ba-a-a-ba O!

Praise-Singer: Ah, but listen yet. You know there is the leaf-nibbling grub and there is the cola-chewing beetle; the leaf-nibbling grub lives on the leaf, the cola-chewing beetle lives in the colanut. Don't we know what our man feeds on when we find him cocooned in a woman's wrapper?

Elesin: Enough, enough, you all have cause
To know me well. But, if you say this earth
Is still the same as gave birth to those songs,
Tell me who was that goddess through whose lips
I saw the ivory pebbles of Oya's river-bed.
Iyaloja, who is she? I saw her enter
Your stall; all your daughters I know well.
No, not even Ogun-of-the-farm toiling
Dawn till dusk on his tuber patch
Not even Ogun with the finest hoe he ever
Forged at the anvil could have shaped
That rise of buttocks, not though he had
The richest earth between his fingers.
Her wrapper was no disguise
For thighs whose ripples shamed the river's
Coils around the hills of Ilesi. Her eyes
Were new-laid eggs glowing in the dark.
Her skin . . .

Iyaloja: Elesin Oba . . .
Elesin: What! Where do you all say I am?
Iyaloja: Still among the living.
Elesin: And that radiance which so suddenly
Lit up this market I could boast
I knew so well?
Iyaloja: Has one step already in her husband's home. She is betrothed.
Elesin [*irritated*]: Why do you tell me that?

[Iyaloja falls silent. The women shuffle uneasily.]

Iyaloja: Not because we dare give you offence Elesin. Today is your day and the whole world is yours. Still, even those who leave town to make a new dwelling elsewhere like to be remembered by what they leave behind.

Elesin: Who does not seek to be remembered?
Memory is Master of Death, the chink
In his armour of conceit. I shall leave
That which makes my going the sheerest
Dream of an afternoon. Should voyagers
Not travel light? Let the considerate traveller
Shed, of his excessive load, all
That may benefit the living.
Women [*relieved*]: Ah Elesin Oba, we knew you for a man of honour.
Elesin: Then honour me. I deserve a bed of honour to lie upon.
Iyaloja: The best is yours. We know you for a man of honour. You are not one who eats and leaves nothing on his plate for children. Did you not say it yourself? Not one who blights the happiness of others for a moment's pleasure.
Elesin: Who speaks of pleasure? O women, listen!
Pleasure palls. Our acts should have meaning.
The sap of the plantain never dries.
You have seen the young shoot swelling
Even as the parent stalk begins to wither.
Women, let my going be likened to
The twilight hour of the plantain.
Women: What does he mean Iyaloja? This language is the language of our elders, we do not fully grasp it.
Iyaloja: I dare not understand you yet Elesin.
Elesin: All you who stand before the spirit that dares
The opening of the last door of passage,
Dare to rid my going of regrets! My wish
Transcends the blotting out of thought
In one mere moment's tremor of the senses.
Do me credit. And do me honour.
I am girded for the route beyond
Burdens of waste and longing.

Then let me travel light. Let
Seed that will not serve the stomach
On the way remain behind. Let it take root
In the earth of my choice, in this earth
I leave behind.

Iyaloja [*turns to women*]: The voice I hear is already touched by the waiting fingers of our departed. I dare not refuse.

Woman: But Iyaloja . . .

Iyaloja: The matter is no longer in our hands.

Woman: But she is betrothed to your own son. Tell him.

Iyaloja: My son's wish is mine. I did the asking for him, the loss can be remedied. But who will remedy the blight of closed hands on the day when all should be openness and light? Tell him, you say! You wish that I burden him with knowledge that will sour his wish and lay regrets on the last moments of his mind. You pray to him who is your intercessor to the other world—don't set this world adrift in your own time; would you rather it was my hand whose sacrilege wrenched it loose?

Woman: Not many men will brave the curse of a dispossessed husband.

Iyaloja: Only the curses of the departed are to be feared. The claims of one whose foot is on the threshold of their abode surpasses even the claims of blood. It is impiety even to place hindrances in their ways.

Elesin: What do my mothers say? Shall I step
Burdened into the unknown?

Iyaloja: Not we, but the very earth says No. The sap in the plantain does not dry. Let grain that will not feed the voyager at his passage drop here and take root as he steps beyond this earth and us. Oh you who fill the home from hearth to threshold with the voices of children, you who now bestride the hidden gulf and pause to draw the right foot across and into the resting-home of the great forebears, it is good that your loins be drained into the earth we know, that your last strength be ploughed back into the womb that gave you being.

Praise-Singer: Iyaloja, mother of multitudes in the teeming market of the world, how your wisdom transfigures you!

Iyaloja [*smiling broadly, completely reconciled*]: Elesin, even at the narrow end of the passage I know you will look back and sigh a last regret for the flesh that flashed past your spirit in flight. You always had a restless eye. Your choice has my blessing. [*To the women.*] Take the good news to our daughter and make her ready. [*Some women go off.*]

Elesin: Your eyes were clouded at first.

Iyaloja: Not for long. It is those who stand at the gateway of the great change to whose cry we must pay heed. And then, think of this—it makes the mind tremble. The fruit of such a union is rare. It will be neither of this world nor of the next. Nor of the one behind us. As if the timelessness of the ancestor world and the unborn have joined spirits to wring an issue of the elusive being of passage . . . Elesin!

Elesin: I am here. What is it?
Iyaloja: Did you hear all I said just now?
Elesin: Yes.
Iyaloja: The living must eat and drink. When the moment comes, don't turn the food to rodents' droppings in their mouth. Don't let them taste the ashes of the world when they step out at dawn to breathe the morning dew.
Elesin: This doubt is unworthy of you Iyaloja.
Iyaloja: Eating the awusa nut[8] is not so difficult as drinking water afterwards.
Elesin: The waters of the bitter stream are honey to a man
Whose tongue has savoured all.
Iyaloja: No one knows when the ants desert their home; they leave the mound intact. The swallow is never seen to peck holes in its nest when it is time to move with the season. There are always throngs of humanity behind the leave-taker. The rain should not come through the roof for them, the wind must not blow through the walls at night.
Elesin: I refuse to take offence.
Iyaloja: You wish to travel light. Well, the earth is yours. But be sure the seed you leave in it attracts no curse.
Elesin: You really mistake my person Iyaloja.
Iyaloja: I said nothing. Now we must go prepare your bridal chamber. Then these same hands will lay your shrouds.
Elesin [*exasperated*]: Must you be so blunt? [*Recovers.*] Well, weave your shrouds, but let the fingers of my bride seal my eyelids with earth and wash my body.
Iyaloja: Prepare yourself Elesin.

[She gets up to leave. At that moment the women return, leading the Bride. Elesin's face glows with pleasure. He flicks the sleeves of his agbada with renewed confidence and steps forward to meet the group. As the girl kneels before Iyaloja, lights fade out on the scene.]

2

The verandah of the District Officer's bungalow. A tango is playing from an old hand-cranked gramophone and, glimpsed through the wide windows and doors which open onto the fore-stage verandah are the shapes of Simon Pilkings and his wife, Jane, tangoing in and out of shadows in the living-room. They are wearing what is immediately apparent as some form of fancy-dress. The dance goes on for some moments and then the figure of a 'Native Administration' policeman emerges and climbs up the steps onto the verandah. He peeps through and observes the dancing couple, reacting with what is obviously a long-standing bewilderment. He stiffens suddenly, his expression changes to one of disbelief and horror. In his excitement he upsets a flower-pot and attracts the attention of the couple. They stop dancing.

[8]*awusa nut:* A bitter kola nut, believed to be an aphrodisiac.

Pilkings: Is there anyone out there?

Jane: I'll turn off the gramophone.

Pilkings [*approaching the verandah*]: I'm sure I heard something fall over. [*The constable retreats slowly, open-mouthed as Pilkings approaches the verandah.*] Oh it's you Amusa. Why didn't you just knock instead of knocking things over?

Amusa [*stammers badly and points a shaky finger at his dress*]: Mista Pirinkin . . . Mista Pirinkin . . .

Pilkings: What is the matter with you?

Jane [*emerging*]: Who is it dear? Oh, Amusa . . .

Pilkings: Yes it's Amusa, and acting most strangely.

Amusa [*his attention now transferred to Mrs Pilkings*]: Mammadam . . . you too!

Pilkings: What the hell is the matter with you man!

Jane: Your costume darling. Our fancy dress.

Pilkings: Oh hell, I'd forgotten all about that. [*Lifts the face mask over his head showing his face. His wife follows suit.*]

Jane: I think you've shocked his big pagan heart bless him.

Pilkings: Nonsense, he's a Moslem. Come on Amusa, you don't believe in all this nonsense do you? I thought you were a good Moslem.

Amusa: Mista Pirinkin, I beg you sir, what you think you do with that dress? It belong to dead cult, not for human being.

Pilkings: Oh Amusa, what a let down you are. I swear by you at the club you know—thank God for Amusa, he doesn't believe in any mumbo-jumbo. And now look at you!

Amusa: Mista Pirinkin, I beg you, take it off. Is not good for man like you to touch that cloth.

Pilkings: Well, I've got it on. And what's more Jane and I have bet on it we're taking first prize at the ball. Now, if you can just pull yourself together and tell me what you wanted to see me about . . .

Amusa: Sir, I cannot talk this matter to you in that dress. I no fit.

Pilkings: What's that rubbish again?

Jane: He is dead earnest too Simon. I think you'll have to handle this delicately.

Pilkings: Delicately my . . . ! Look here Amusa, I think this little joke has gone far enough hm? Let's have some sense. You seem to forget that you are a police officer in the service of His Majesty's Government. I order you to report your business at once or face disciplinary action.

Amusa: Sir, it is a matter of death. How can man talk against death to person in uniform of death? Is like talking against government to person in uniform of police. Please sir, I go and come back.

Pilkings [*roars*]: Now! [*Amusa switches his gaze to the ceiling suddenly, remains mute.*]

Jane: Oh Amusa, what is there to be scared of in the costume? You saw it confiscated last month from those *egungun*[9] men who were creating trouble

[9]*egungun:* The ancestral spirits of the people.

in town. You helped arrest the cult leaders yourself—if the juju didn't harm you at the time how could it possibly harm you now? And merely by looking at it?

Amusa [*without looking down*]: Madam, I arrrest the ring-leaders who make trouble but me I no touch *egungun.* That *egungun* inself, I no touch. And I no abuse 'am. I arrest ring-leader but I treat *egungun* with respect.

Pilkings: It's hopeless. We'll merely end up missing the best part of the ball. When they get this way there is nothing you can do. It's simply hammering against a brick wall. Write your report or whatever it is on that pad Amusa and take yourself out of here. Come on Jane. We only upset his delicate sensibilities by remaining here.

[Amusa waits for them to leave, then writes in the notebook, somewhat laboriously. Drumming from the direction of the town wells up. Amusa listens, makes a movement as if he wants to recall Pilkings but changes his mind. Completes his note and goes. A few moments later Pilkings emerges, picks up the pad and reads.]

Pilkings: Jane!

Jane [*from the bedroom*]: Coming darling. Nearly ready.

Pilkings: Never mind being ready, just listen to this.

Jane: What is it?

Pilkings: Amusa's report. Listen. "I have to report that it come to my information that one prominent chief, namely, the Elesin Oba, is to commit death tonight as a result of native custom. Because this is criminal offence I await further instruction at charge office. Sergeant Amusa."

[Jane comes out onto the verandah while he is reading.]

Jane: Did I hear you say commit death?

Pilkings: Obviously he means murder.

Jane: You mean a ritual murder?

Pilkings: Must be. You think you've stamped it all out but it's always lurking under the surface somewhere.

Jane: Oh. Does it mean we are not getting to the ball at all?

Pilkings: No-o. I'll have the man arrested. Everyone remotely involved. In any case there may be nothing to it. Just rumours.

Jane: Really? I thought you found Amusa's rumours generally reliable.

Pilkings: That's true enough. But who knows what may have been giving him the scare lately. Look at his conduct tonight.

Jane [*laughing*]: You have to admit he had his own peculiar logic. [*Deepens her voice.*] How can man talk against death to person in uniform of death? [*Laughs.*] Anyway, you can't go into the police station dressed like that.

Pilkings: I'll send Joseph with instructions. Damn it, what a confounded nuisance!

Jane: But don't you think you should talk first to the man, Simon?

Pilkings: Do you want to go to the ball or not?

Jane: Darling, why are you getting rattled? I was only trying to be intelligent. It seems hardly fair just to lock up a man—and a chief at that—simply on the er . . . what is that legal word again?—uncorroborated word of a sergeant.

Pilkings: Well, that's easily decided. Joseph!

Joseph [*from within*]: Yes master.

Pilkings: You're quite right of course, I am getting rattled. Probably the effect of those bloody drums. Do you hear how they go on and on?

Jane: I wondered when you'd notice. Do you suppose it has something to do with this affair?

Pilkings: Who knows? They always find an excuse for making a noise . . . [*Thoughtfully.*] Even so . . .

Jane: Yes Simon?

Pilkings: It's different Jane. I don't think I've heard this particular—sound—before. Something unsettling about it.

Jane: I thought all bush drumming sounded the same.

Pilkings: Don't tease me now Jane. This may be serious.

Jane: I'm sorry. [*Gets up and throws her arms around his neck. Kisses him. The houseboy enters, retreats and knocks.*]

Pilkings [*wearily*]: Oh, come in Joseph! I don't know where you pick up all these elephantine notions of tact. Come over here.

Joseph: Sir?

Pilkings: Joseph, are you a christian or not?

Joseph: Yessir.

Pilkings: Does seeing me in this outfit bother you?

Joseph: No sir, it has no power.

Pilkings: Thank God for some sanity at last. Now Joseph, answer me on the honour of a christian—what is supposed to be going on in town tonight?

Joseph: Tonight sir? You mean that chief who is going to kill himself?

Pilkings: What?

Jane: What do you mean, kill himself?

Pilkings: You do mean he is going to kill somebody don't you?

Joseph: No master. He will not kill anybody and no one will kill him. He will simply die.

Jane: But why Joseph?

Joseph: It is native law and custom. The King die last month. Tonight is his burial. But before they can bury him, the Elesin must die so as to accompany him to heaven.

Pilkings: I seem to be fated to clash more often with that man than with any of the other chiefs.

Joseph: He is the King's Chief Horseman.

Pilkings [*in a resigned way*]: I know.

Jane: Simon, what's the matter?

Pilkings: It would have to be him!

Jane: Who is he?

Pilkings: Don't you remember? He's that chief with whom I had a scrap some three or four years ago. I helped his son get to a medical school in England, remember? He fought tooth and nail to prevent it.

Jane: Oh now I remember. He was that very sensitive young man. What was his name again?

Pilkings: Olunde. Haven't replied to his last letter come to think of it. The old pagan wanted him to stay and carry on some family tradition or the other. Honestly I couldn't understand the fuss he made. I literally had to help the boy escape from close confinement and load him onto the next boat. A most intelligent boy, really bright.

Jane: I rather thought he was much too sensitive you know. The kind of person you feel should be a poet munching rose petals in Bloomsbury.

Pilkings: Well, he's going to make a first-class doctor. His mind is set on that. And as long as he wants my help he is welcome to it.

Jane [*after a pause*]: Simon.

Pilkings: Yes?

Jane: This boy, he was his eldest son wasn't he?

Pilkings: I'm not sure. Who could tell with that old ram?

Jane: Do you know, Joseph?

Joseph: Oh yes madam. He was the eldest son. That's why Elesin cursed master good and proper. The eldest son is not supposed to travel away from the land.

Jane [*giggling*]: Is that true Simon? Did he really curse you good and proper?

Pilkings: By all accounts I should be dead by now.

Joseph: Oh no, master is white man. And good christian. Black man juju can't touch master.

Jane: If he was his eldest, it means that he would be the Elesin to the next king. It's a family thing isn't it Joseph?

Joseph: Yes madam. And if this Elesin had died before the King, his eldest son must take his place.

Jane: That would explain why the old chief was so mad you took the boy away.

Pilkings: Well it makes me all the more happy I did.

Jane: I wonder if he knew.

Pilkings: Who? Oh, you mean Olunde?

Jane: Yes. Was that why he was so determined to get away? I wouldn't stay if I knew I was trapped in such a horrible custom.

Pilkings [*thoughtfully*]: No, I don't think he knew. At least he gave no indication. But you couldn't really tell with him. He was rather close you know, quite unlike most of them. Didn't give much away, not even to me.

Jane: Aren't they all rather close, Simon?

Pilkings: These natives here? Good gracious. They'll open their mouths and yap with you about their family secrets before you can stop them. Only the other day . . .

Jane: But Simon, do they really give anything away? I mean, anything that really counts. This affair for instance, we didn't know they still practised that custom did we?

Pilkings: Ye-e-es, I suppose you're right there. Sly, devious bastards.

Joseph [*stiffly*]: Can I go now master? I have to clean the kitchen.

Pilkings: What? Oh, you can go. Forgot you were still here.

[Joseph goes.]

Jane: Simon, you really must watch your language. Bastard isn't just a simple swear-word in these parts, you know.

Pilkings: Look, just when did you become a social anthropologist, that's what I'd like to know.

Jane: I'm not claiming to know anything. I just happen to have overheard quarrels among the servants. That's how I know they consider it a smear.

Pilkings: I thought the extended family system took care of all that. Elastic family, no bastards.

Jane [*shrugs*]: Have it your own way.

[Awkward silence. The drumming increases in volume. Jane gets up suddenly, restless.]

That drumming Simon, do you think it might really be connected with this ritual? It's been going on all evening.

Pilkings: Let's ask our native guide. Joseph! Just a minute Joseph. [*Joseph re-enters.*] What's the drumming about?

Joseph: I don't know master.

Pilkings: What do you mean you don't know? It's only two years since your conversion. Don't tell me all that holy water nonsense also wiped out your tribal memory.

Joseph [*visibly shocked*]: Master!

Jane: Now you've done it.

Pilkings: What have I done now?

Jane: Never mind. Listen Joseph, just tell me this. Is that drumming connected with dying or anything of that nature?

Joseph: Madam, this is what I am trying to say: I am not sure. It sounds like the death of a great chief and then, it sounds like the wedding of a great chief. It really mix me up.

Pilkings: Oh get back to the kitchen. A fat lot of help you are.

Joseph: Yes master. [*Goes.*]

Jane: Simon . . .

Pilkings: Alright, alright. I'm in no mood for preaching.

Jane: It isn't my preaching you have to worry about, it's the preaching of the missionaries who preceded you here. When they make converts they really convert them. Calling holy water nonsense to our Joseph is really like insulting the Virgin Mary before a Roman Catholic. He's going to hand in his notice tomorrow you mark my word.

Pilkings: Now you're being ridiculous.

Jane: Am I? What are you willing to bet that tomorrow we are going to be without a steward-boy? Did you see his face?

Pilkings: I am more concerned about whether or not we will be one native chief short by tomorrow. Christ! Just listen to those drums. [*He strides up and down, undecided.*]

Jane [*getting up*]: I'll change and make up some supper.

Pilkings: What's that?

Jane: Simon, it's obvious we have to miss this ball.

Pilkings: Nonsense. It's the first bit of real fun the European club has managed to organise for over a year, I'm damned if I'm going to miss it. And it is a rather special occasion. Doesn't happen every day.

Jane: You know this business has to be stopped Simon. And you are the only man who can do it.

Pilkings: I don't have to stop anything. If they want to throw themselves off the top of a cliff or poison themselves for the sake of some barbaric custom what is that to me? If it were ritual murder or something like that I'd be duty bound to do something. I can't keep an eye on all the potential suicides in this province. And as for that man—believe me it's good riddance.

Jane [*laughs*]: I know you better than that Simon. You are going to have to do something to stop it—after you've finished blustering.

Pilkings [*shouts after her*]: And suppose after all it's only a wedding. I'd look a proper fool if I interrupted a chief on his honeymoon, wouldn't I? [*Resumes his angry stride, slows down.*] Ah well, who can tell what those chiefs actually do on their honeymoon anyway? [*He takes up the pad and scribbles rapidly on it.*] Joseph! Joseph! Joseph! [*Some moments later Joseph puts in a sulky appearance.*] Did you hear me call you? Why the hell didn't you answer?

Joseph: I didn't hear master.

Pilkings: You didn't hear me! How come you are here then?

Joseph [*stubbornly*]: I didn't hear master.

Pilkings [*controls himself with an effort*]: We'll talk about it in the morning. I want you to take this note directly to Sergeant Amusa. You'll find him at the charge office. Get on your bicycle and race there with it. I expect you back in twenty minutes exactly. Twenty minutes, is that clear?

Joseph: Yes master. [*Going.*]

Pilkings: Oh er . . . Joseph.

Joseph Yes master?

Pilkings [*between gritted teeth*]: Er . . . forget what I said just now. The holy water is not nonsense. *I* was talking nonsense.

Joseph: Yes master. [*Goes.*]

Jane [*pokes her head round the door*]: Have you found him?

Pilkings: Found who?

Jane: Joseph. Weren't you shouting for him?

Pilkings: Oh yes, he turned up finally.

Jane: You sounded desperate. What was it all about?

Pilkings: Oh nothing. I just wanted to apologise to him. Assure him that the holy water isn't really nonsense.

Jane: Oh? And how did he take it?

Pilkings: Who the hell gives a damn! I had a sudden vision of our Very Reverend Macfarlane drafting another letter of complaint to the Resident about my unchristian language towards his parishioners.

Jane: Oh I think he's given up on you by now.

Pilkings: Don't be too sure. And anyway, I wanted to make sure Joseph didn't "lose" my note on the way. He looked sufficiently full of the holy crusade to do some such thing.

Jane: If you've finished exaggerating, come and have something to eat.

Pilkings: No, put it all away. We can still get to the ball.

Jane: Simon . . .

Pilkings: Get your costume back on. Nothing to worry about. I've instructed Amusa to arrest the man and lock him up.

Jane: But that station is hardly secure Simon. He'll soon get his friends to help him escape.

Pilkings: A-ah, that's where I have out-thought you. I'm not having him put in the station cell. Amusa will bring him right here and lock him up in my study. And he'll stay with him till we get back. No one will dare come here to incite him to anything.

Jane: How clever of you darling. I'll get ready.

Pilkings: Hey.

Jane: Yes darling.

Pilkings: I have a surprise for you. I was going to keep it until we actually got to the ball.

Jane: What is it?

Pilkings: You know the Prince is on a tour of the colonies don't you? Well, he docked in the capital only this morning but he is already at the Residency. He is going to grace the ball with his presence later tonight.

Jane: Simon! Not really.

Pilkings: Yes he is. He's been invited to give away the prizes and he has agreed. You must admit old Engleton is the best Club Secretary we ever had. Quick off the mark that lad.

Jane: But how thrilling.

Pilkings: The other provincials are going to be damned envious.

Jane: I wonder what he'll come as.

Pilkings: Oh I don't know. As a coat-of-arms perhaps. Anyway it won't be anything to touch this.

Jane: Well that's lucky. If we are to be presented I won't have to start looking for a pair of gloves. It's all sewn on.

Pilkings [*laughing*]: Quite right. Trust a woman to think of that. Come on, let's get going.

Jane [*rushing off*]: Won't be a second. [*Stops.*] Now I see why you've been so edgy all evening. I thought you weren't handling this affair with your usual brilliance—to begin with that is.

Pilkings [*his mood is much improved*]: Shut up woman and get your things on.

Jane: Alright boss, coming.

[Pilkings suddenly begins to hum the tango to which they were dancing before. Starts to execute a few practice steps. Lights fade.]

3

A swelling, agitated hum of women's voices rises immediately in the background. The lights come on and we see the frontage of a converted cloth stall in the market. The floor leading up to the entrance is covered in rich velvets and woven cloth. The women come on stage, borne backwards by the determined progress of Sergeant Amusa and his two constables who already have their batons out and use them as a pressure against the women. At the edge of the cloth-covered floor however the women take a determined stand and block all further progress of the men. They begin to tease them mercilessly.

Amusa: I am tell you women for last time to commot my road. I am here on official business.

Woman: Official business you white man's eunuch? Official business is taking place where you want to go and it's a business you wouldn't understand.

Woman [*makes a quick tug at the constable's baton*]: That doesn't fool anyone you know. It's the one you carry under your government knickers that counts. [*She bends low as if to peep under the baggy shorts. The embarrassed constable quickly puts his knees together. The women roar.*]

Woman: You mean there is nothing there at all?

Woman: Oh there was something. You know that handbell which the whiteman uses to summon his servants . . . ?

Amusa [*he manages to preserve some dignity throughout*]: I hope you women know that interfering with officer in execution of his duty is criminal offence.

Woman: Interfere? He says we're interfering with him. You foolish man we're telling you there's nothing there to interfere with.

Amusa: I am order you now to clear the road.

Woman: What road? The one your father built?

Woman: You are a Policeman not so? Then you know what they call trespassing in court. Or—[*Pointing to the cloth-lined steps.*]—do you think that kind of road is built for every kind of feet.

Woman: Go back and tell the white man who sent you to come himself.

Amusa: If I go I will come back with reinforcement. And we will all return carrying weapons.

Woman: Oh, now I understand. Before they can put on those knickers the white man first cuts off their weapons.

Woman: What a cheek! You mean you come here to show power to women and you don't even have a weapon.

Amusa [*shouting above the laughter*]: For the last time I warn you women to clear the road.

Woman: To where?

Amusa: To that hut. I know he dey dere.

Woman: Who?

Amusa: The chief who call himself Elesin Oba.

Woman: You ignorant man. It is not he who calls himself Elesin Oba, it is his blood that says it. As it called out to his father before him and will to his son after him. And that is in spite of everything your white man can do.

Woman: Is it not the same ocean that washes this land and the white man's land? Tell your white man he can hide our son away as long as he likes. When the time comes for him, the same ocean will bring him back.

Amusa: The government say dat kin' ting must stop.

Woman: Who will stop it? You? Tonight our husband and father will prove himself greater than the laws of strangers.

Amusa: I tell you nobody go prove anyting tonight or anytime. Is ignorant and criminal to prove dat kin' prove.

Iyaloja [*entering, from the hut. She is accompanied by a group of young girls who have been attending the Bride*]: What is it Amusa? Why do you come here to disturb the happiness of others.

Amusa: Madame Iyaloja, I glad you come. You know me. I no like trouble but duty is duty. I am here to arrest Elesin for criminal intent. Tell these women to stop obstructing me in the performance of my duty.

Iyaloja: And you? What gives you the right to obstruct our leader of men in the performance of his duty.

Amusa: What kin' duty be dat one Iyaloja.

Iyaloja: What kin' duty? What kin' duty does a man have to his new bride?

Amusa [*bewildered, looks at the women and at the entrance to the hut*]: Iyaloja, is it wedding you call dis kin' ting?

Iyaloja: You have wives haven't you? Whatever the white man has done to you he hasn't stopped you having wives. And if he has, at least he is married. If you don't know what a marriage is, go and ask him to tell you.

Amusa: This no to wedding.

Iyaloja: And ask him at the same time what he would have done if anyone had come to disturb him on his wedding night.

Amusa: Iyaloja, I say dis no to wedding.

Iyaloja: You want to look inside the bridal chamber? You want to see for yourself how a man cuts the virgin knot?

Amusa: Madam . . .

Woman: Perhaps his wives are still waiting for him to learn.

Amusa: Iyaloja, make you tell dese women make den no insult me again. If I hear dat kin' insult once more . . .

Girl [*pushing her way through*]: You will do what?

Girl: He's out of his mind. It's our mothers you're talking to, do you know that? Not to any illiterate villager you can bully and terrorise. How dare you intrude here anyway?

Girl: What a cheek, what impertinence!

Girl: You've treated them too gently. Now let them see what it is to tamper with the mothers of this market.

Girls: Your betters dare not enter the market when the women say no!

Girl: Haven't you learnt that yet, you jester in khaki and starch?

Iyaloja: Daughters . . .

Girl: No no Iyaloja, leave us to deal with him. He no longer knows his mother, we'll teach him.

[With a sudden movement they snatch the batons of the two constables. They begin to hem them in.]

Girl: What next? We have your batons? What next? What are you going to do?

[With equally swift movements they knock off their hats.]

Girl: Move if you dare. We have your hats, what will you do about it? Didn't the white man teach you to take off your hats before women?

Iyaloja: It's a wedding night. It's a night of joy for us. Peace . . .

Girl: Not for him. Who asked him here?

Girl: Does he dare go to the Residency without an invitation?

Girl: Not even where the servants eat the left-overs.

Girls [*in turn. In an 'English' accent*]: Well well it's Mister Amusa. Were you invited? [*Play-acting to one another. The older women encourage them with their titters.*]

—Your invitation card please?
—Who are you? Have we been introduced?
—And who did you say you were?
—Sorry, I didn't quite catch your name.
—May I take your hat?
—If you insist. May I take yours? [*Exchanging the policeman's hats.*]
—How very kind of you.
—Not at all. Won't you sit down?
—After you.
—Oh no.
—I insist.
—You're most gracious.
—And how do you find the place?
—The natives are alright.
—Friendly?
—Tractable.
—Not a teeny-weeny bit restless?
—Well, a teeny-weeny bit restless.
—One might even say, difficult?
—Indeed one might be tempted to say, difficult.
—But you do manage to cope?
—Yes indeed I do. I have a rather faithful ox called Amusa.
—He's loyal?
—Absolutely.
—Lay down his life for you what?
—Without a moment's thought.
—Had one like that once. Trust him with my life.
—Mostly of course they are liars.
—Never known a native tell the truth.
—Does it get rather close around here?
—It's mild for this time of the year.
—But the rains may still come.
—They are late this year aren't they?

—They are keeping African time.
—Ha ha ha ha
—Ha ha ha ha
—The humidity is what gets me.
—It used to be whisky.
—Ha ha ha ha
—Ha ha ha ha
—What's your handicap old chap?
—Is there racing by golly?
—Splendid golf course, you'll like it.
—I'm beginning to like it already.
—And a European club, exclusive.
—You've kept the flag flying.
—We do our best for the old country.
—It's a pleasure to serve.
—Another whisky old chap?
—You are indeed too too kind.
—Not at all sir. Where is that boy? [*With a sudden bellow.*] Sergeant!

Amusa [*snaps to attention*]: Yessir!

[The women collapse with laughter.]

Girl: Take your men out of here.
Amusa [*realising the trick, he rages from loss of face*]: I'm give you warning . . .
Girl: Alright then. Off with his knickers! [*They surge slowly forward.*]
Iyaloja: Daughters, please.
Amusa [*squaring himself for defence*]: The first woman wey touch me . . .
Iyaloja: My children, I beg of you . . .
Girl: Then tell him to leave this market. This is the home of our mothers. We don't want the eater of white left-overs at the feast their hands have prepared.
Iyaloja: You heard them Amusa. You had better go.
Girls: Now!
Amusa [*commencing his retreat*]: We dey go now, but make you no say we no warn you.
Girl: Now!
Girl: Before we read the riot act—you should know all about that.
Amusa: Make we go. [*They depart, more precipitately.*]

[The women strike their palms across in the gesture of wonder.]

Women: Do they teach you all that at school?
Woman: And to think I nearly kept Apinke away from the place.
Woman: Did you hear them? Did you see how they mimicked the white man?
Woman: The voices exactly. Hey, there are wonders in this world!
Iyaloja: Well, our elders have said it: Dada may be weak, but he has a younger sibling who is truly fearless.
Woman: The next time the white man shows his face in this market I will set Wuraola on his tail.

[A woman bursts into song and dance of euphoria—"Tani l'awa o l'ogbeja? Kayi! A l'ogbeja. Omo Kekere l'ogbeja." The rest of the women join in, some placing the girls on their back like infants, others dancing round them. The dance becomes general, mounting in excitement. Elesin appears, in wrapper only. In his hands a white velvet cloth folded loosely as if it held some delicate object. He cries out.]*

Elesin: Oh you mothers of beautiful brides! [*The dancing stops. They turn and see him, and the object in his hands. Iyaloja approaches and gently takes the cloth from him.*] Take it. It is no mere virgin stain, but the union of life and the seeds of passage. My vital flow, the last from this flesh is intermingled with the promise of future life. All is prepared. Listen! [*A steady drum-beat from the distance.*] Yes. It is nearly time. The King's dog has been killed. The King's favourite horse is about to follow his master. My brother chiefs know their task and perform it well. [*He listens again.*]

[The Bride emerges, stands shyly by the door. He turns to her.]

Our marriage is not yet wholly fulfilled. When earth and passage wed, the consummation is complete only when there are grains of earth on the eyelids of passage. Stay by me till then. My faithful drummers, do me your last service. This is where I have chosen to do my leave-taking, in this heart of life, this hive which contains the swarm of the world in its small compass. This is where I have known love and laughter away from the palace. Even the richest food cloys when eaten days on end; in the market, nothing ever cloys. Listen. [*They listen to the drums.*] They have begun to seek out the heart of the King's favourite horse. Soon it will ride in its bolt of raffia with the dog at its feet. Together they will ride on the shoulders of the King's grooms through the pulse centres of the town. They know it is here I shall await them. I have told them. [*His eyes appear to cloud. He passes his hand over them as if to clear his sight. He gives a faint smile.*] It promises well; just then I felt my spirit's eagerness. The kite makes for wide spaces and the wind creeps up behind its tail; can the kite say less than—thank you, the quicker the better? But wait a while my spirit. Wait. Wait for the coming of the courier of the King. Do you know friends, the horse is born to this one destiny, to bear the burden that is man upon its back. Except for this night, this night alone when the spotless stallion will ride in triumph on the back of man. In the time of my father I witnessed the strange sight. Perhaps tonight also I shall see it for the last time. If they arrive before the drums beat for me, I shall tell him to let the Alafin know I follow swiftly. If they come after the drums have sounded, why then, all is well for I have gone ahead. Our spirits shall fall in step along the great passage. [*He listens to the drums. He seems again to be falling into a state of semi-hypnosis; his eyes scan the sky but it is in a kind of daze. His voice is a little breathless.*] The moon has fed, a glow from its full stomach fills the sky and air, but I cannot tell

*"Who says we haven't a defender? Silence! We have our defenders. Little children are our champions".

where is that gateway through which I must pass. My faithful friends, let our feet touch together this last time, lead me into the other market with sounds that cover my skin with down yet make my limbs strike earth like a thoroughbred. Dear mothers, let me dance into the passage even as I have lived beneath your roofs. [*He comes down progressively among them. They make way for him, the drummers playing. His dance is one of solemn, regal motions, each gesture of the body is made with a solemn finality. The women join him, their steps a somewhat more fluid version of his. Beneath the Praise-Singer's exhortations the women dirge 'Ale le le, awo mi lo'.*]

Praise-Singer: Elesin Alafin, can you hear my voice?
Elesin: Faintly, my friend, faintly.
Praise-Singer: Elesin Alafin, can you hear my call?
Elesin: Faintly my king, faintly.
Praise-Singer: Is your memory sound Elesin?
Shall my voice be a blade of grass and
Tickle the armpit of the past?
Elesin: My memory needs no prodding but
What do you wish to say to me?
Praise-Singer: Only what has been spoken. Only what concerns
The dying wish of the father of all.
Elesin: It is buried like seed-yam in my mind
This is the season of quick rains, the harvest
Is this moment due for gathering.
Praise-Singer: If you cannot come, I said, swear
You'll tell my favourite horse. I shall
Ride on through the gates alone.
Elesin: Elesin's message will be read
Only when his loyal heart no longer beats.
Praise-Singer: If you cannot come Elesin, tell my dog.
I cannot stay the keeper too long
At the gate.
Elesin: A dog does not outrun the hand
That feeds it meat. A horse that throws its rider
Slows down to a stop. Elesin Alafin
Trusts no beasts with messages between
A king and his companion.
Praise-Singer: If you get lost my dog will track
The hidden path to me.
Elesin: The seven-way crossroads confuses
Only the stranger. The Horseman of the King
Was born in the recesses of the house.
Praise-Singer: I know the wickedness of men. If there is
Weight on the loose end of your sash, such weight
As no mere man can shift; if your sash is earthed
By evil minds who mean to part us at the last . . .

Elesin: My sash is of the deep purple *alari;*
It is no tethering-rope. The elephant
Trails no tethering-rope; that king
Is not yet crowned who will peg an elephant—
Not even you my friend and King.

Praise-Singer: And yet this fear will not depart from me
The darkness of this new abode is deep—
Will your human eyes suffice?

Elesin: In a night which falls before our eyes
However deep, we do not miss our way.

Praise-Singer: Shall I now not acknowledge I have stood
Where wonders met their end? The elephant deserves
Better than that we say "I have caught
A glimpse of something". If we see the tamer
Of the forest let us say plainly, we have seen
An elephant.

Elesin [*his voice is drowsy*]:
I have freed myself of earth and now
It's getting dark. Strange voices guide my feet.

Praise-Singer: The river is never so high that the eyes
Of a fish are covered. The night is not so dark
That the albino fails to find his way. A child
Returning homewards craves no leading by the hand.
Gracefully does the mask regain his grove at the end of day . . .
Gracefully. Gracefully does the mask dance
Homeward at the end of day, gracefully . . .

[Elesin's trance appears to be deepening, his steps heavier.]

Iyaloja: It is the death of war that kills the valiant,
Death of water is how the swimmer goes
It is the death of markets that kills the trader
And death of indecision takes the idle away
The trade of the cutlass blunts its edge
And the beautiful die the death of beauty.
It takes an Elesin to die the death of death . . .
Only Elesin . . . dies the unknowable death of death . . .
Gracefully, gracefully does the horseman regain
The stables at the end of day, gracefully . . .

Praise-Singer: How shall I tell what my eyes have seen? The Horseman gallops on before the courier, how shall I tell what my eyes have seen? He says a dog may be confused by new scents of beings he never dreamt of, so he must precede the dog to heaven. He says a horse may stumble on strange boulders and be lamed, so he races on before the horse to heaven. It is best, he says, to trust no messenger who may falter at the outer gate; oh how shall I tell what my ears have heard? But do you hear me still Elesin, do you hear your faithful one?

[Elesin in his motions appears to feel for a direction of sound, subtly, but he only sinks deeper into his trance-dance.]

Elesin Alafin, I no longer sense your flesh. The drums are changing now but you have gone far ahead of the world. It is not yet noon in heaven; let those who claim it is begin their own journey home. So why must you rush like an impatient bride: why do you race to desert your Olohun-iyo?

[Elesin is now sunk fully deep in his trance, there is no longer sign of any awareness of his surroundings.]

Does the deep voice of *gbedu*[10] cover you then, like the passage of royal elephants? Those drums that brook no rivals, have they blocked the passage to your ears that my voice passes into wind, a mere leaf floating in the night? Is your flesh lightened Elesin, is that lump of earth I slid between your slippers to keep you longer slowly sifting from your feet? Are the drums on the other side now tuning skin to skin with ours in *osugbo*[11]? Are there sounds there I cannot hear, do footsteps surround you which pound the earth like *gbedu*, roll like thunder round the dome of the world? Is the darkness gathering in your head Elesin? Is there now a streak of light at the end of the passage, a light I dare not look upon? Does it reveal whose voices we often heard, whose touches we often felt, whose wisdoms come suddenly into the mind when the wisest have shaken their heads and murmured; It cannot be done? Elesin Alafin, don't think I do not know why your lips are heavy, why your limbs are drowsy as palm oil in the cold of harmattan. I would call you back but when the elephant heads for the jungle, the tail is too small a handhold for the hunter that would pull him back. The sun that heads for the sea no longer heeds the prayers of the farmer. When the river begins to taste the salt of the ocean, we no longer know what deity to call on, the river-god or Olokun. No arrow flies back to the string, the child does not return through the same passage that gave it birth. Elesin Oba, can you hear me at all? Your eyelids are glazed like a courtesan's, is it that you see the dark groom and master of life? And will you see my father? Will you tell him that I stayed with you to the last? Will my voice ring in your ears awhile, will you remember Olohun-iyo even if the music on the other side surpasses his mortal craft? But will they know you over there? Have they eyes to gauge your worth, have they the heart to love you, will they know what thoroughbred prances towards them in caparisons of honour? If they do not Elesin, if any there cuts your yam with a small knife, or pours you wine in a small calabash, turn back and return to welcoming hands. If the world were not greater than the wishes of Olohun-iyo, I would not let you go . . .

[He appears to break down. Elesin dances on, completely in a trance. The dirge wells up louder and stronger. Elesin's dance does not lose its elasticity but his gestures become, if possible, even more weighty. Lights fade slowly on the scene.]

[10]*gbedu:* A ritual drum.

[11]*osugbo:* Wise men and women of the Yoruba society whose role is to judge the passage.

4

A Masque.[12] *The front side of the stage is part of a wide corridor around the great hall of the Residency extending beyond vision into the rear and wings. It is redolent of the tawdry decadence of a far-flung but key imperial frontier. The couples in a variety of fancy-dress are ranged around the walls, gazing in the same direction. The guest-of-honour is about to make an appearance. A portion of the local police brass band with its white conductor is just visible. At last, the entrance of Royalty. The band plays 'Rule Britannia', badly, beginning long before he is visible. The couples bow and curtsey as he passes by them. Both he and his companions are dressed in seventeenth century European costume. Following behind are the Resident and his partner similarly attired. As they gain the end of the hall where the orchestra dais begins the music comes to an end. The Prince bows to the guests. The band strikes up a Viennese waltz and the Prince formally opens the floor. Several bars later the Resident and his companion follow suit. Others follow in appropriate pecking order. The orchestra's waltz rendition is not of the highest musical standard.*

Some time later the Prince dances again into view and is settled into a corner by the Resident who then proceeds to select couples as they dance past for introduction, sometimes threading his way through the dancers to tap the lucky couple on the shoulder. Desperate efforts from many to ensure that they are recognised in spite of, perhaps, their costume. The ritual of introductions soon takes in Pilkings and his wife. The Prince is quite fascinated by their costume and they demonstrate the adaptations they have made to it, pulling down the mask to demonstrate how the egungun *normally appears, then showing the various press-button controls they have innovated for the face flaps, the sleeves, etc. They demonstrate the dance steps and the guttural sounds made by the* egungun, *harrass other dancers in the hall, Mrs Pilkings playing the "restrainer" to Pilkings' manic darts. Everyone is highly entertained, the Royal Party especially who lead the applause.*

At this point a liveried footman comes in with a note on a salver and is intercepted almost absent-mindedly by the Resident who takes the note and reads it. After polite coughs he succeeds in excusing the Pilkingses from the Prince and takes them aside. The Prince considerately offers the Resident's wife his hand and dancing is resumed.

On their way out the Resident gives an order to his Aide-de-Camp. They come into the side corridor where the Resident hands the note to Pilkings.

Resident: As you see it says "emergency" on the outside. I took the liberty of opening it because His Highness was obviously enjoying the entertainment. I didn't want to interrupt unless really necessary.

Pilkings: Yes, yes of course sir.

Resident: Is it really as bad as it says? What's it all about?

Pilkings: Some strange custom they have sir. It seems because the King is dead some important chief has to commit suicide.

Resident: The King? Isn't it the same one who died nearly a month ago?

[12]*Masque:* A masquerade ball.

Pilkings: Yes sir.

Resident: Haven't they buried him yet?

Pilkings: They take their time about these things sir. The pre-burial ceremonies last nearly thirty days. It seems tonight is the final night.

Resident: But what has it got to do with the market women? Why are they rioting? We've waived that troublesome tax haven't we?

Pilkings: We don't quite know that they are exactly rioting yet sir. Sergeant Amusa is sometimes prone to exaggerations.

Resident: He sounds desperate enough. That comes out even in his rather quaint grammar. Where is the man anyway? I asked my aide-de-camp to bring him here.

Pilkings: They are probably looking in the wrong verandah. I'll fetch him myself.

Resident: No no you stay here. Let your wife go and look for them. Do you mind my dear . . . ?

Jane: Certainly not, your Excellency. [*Goes.*]

Resident: You should have kept me informed Pilkings. You realise how disastrous it would have been if things had erupted while His Highness was here.

Pilkings: I wasn't aware of the whole business until tonight sir.

Resident: Nose to the ground Pilkings, nose to the ground. If we all let these little things slip past us where would the empire be eh? Tell me that. Where would we all be?

Pilkings [*low voice*]: Sleeping peacefully at home I bet.

Resident: What did you say Pilkings?

Pilkings: It won't happen again sir.

Resident: It mustn't Pilkings. It musn't. Where is that damned sergeant? I ought to get back to His Highness as quickly as possible and offer him some plausible explanation for my rather abrupt conduct. Can you think of one Pilkings?

Pilkings: You could tell him the truth sir.

Resident: I could? No no no no Pilkings, that would never do. What! Go and tell him there is a riot just two miles away from him? This is supposed to be a secure colony of His Majesty, Pilkings.

Pilkings: Yes sir.

Resident: Ah, there they are. No, these are not our native police. Are these the ring-leaders of the riot?

Pilkings: Sir, these are my police officers.

Resident: Oh, I beg your pardon officers. You do look a little . . . I say, isn't there something missing in their uniform? I think they used to have some rather colourful sashes. If I remember rightly I recommended them myself in my young days in the service. A bit of colour always appeals to the natives, yes, I remember putting that in my report. Well well well, where are we? Make your report man.

Pilkings [*moves close to Amusa, between his teeth*]: And let's have no more superstitious nonsense from you Amusa or I'll throw you in the guardroom for a month and feed you pork!

Resident: What's that? What has pork to do with it?

Pilkings: Sir, I was just warning him to be brief. I'm sure you are most anxious to hear his report.

Resident: Yes yes yes of course. Come on man, speak up. Hey, didn't we give them some colourful fez hats with all those wavy things, yes, pink tassels . . .

Pilkings: Sir, I think if he was permitted to make his report we might find that he lost his hat in the riot.

Resident: Ah yes indeed. I'd better tell His Highness that. Lost his hat in the riot, ha ha. He'll probably say well, as long as he didn't lose his head. [*Chuckles to himself.*] Don't forget to send me a report first thing in the morning young Pilkings.

Pilkings: No sir.

Resident: And whatever you do, don't let things get out of hand. Keep a cool head and—nose to the ground Pilkings. [*Wanders off in the general direction of the hall.*]

Pilkings: Yes sir.

Aide-de-Camp: Would you be needing me sir?

Pilkings: No thanks Bob. I think His Excellency's need of you is greater than ours.

Aide-de-Camp: We have a detachment of soldiers from the capital sir. They accompanied His Highness up here.

Pilkings: I doubt if it will come to that but, thanks, I'll bear it in mind. Oh, could you send an orderly with my cloak.

Aide-de-Camp: Very good sir. [*Goes.*]

Pilkings: Now Sergeant.

Amusa: Sir . . . [*Makes an effort, stops dead. Eyes to the ceiling.*]

Pilkings: Oh, not again.

Amusa: I cannot against death to dead cult. This dress get power of dead.

Pilkings: Alright, let's go. You are relieved of all further duty Amusa. Report to me first thing in the morning.

Jane: Shall I come Simon?

Pilkings: No, there's no need for that. If I can get back later I will. Otherwise get Bob to bring you home.

Jane: Be careful Simon . . . I mean, be clever.

Pilkings: Sure I will. You two, come with me. [*As he turns to go, the clock in the Residency begins to chime. Pilkings looks at his watch then turns, horror-stricken, to stare at his wife. The same thought clearly occurs to her. He swallows hard. An orderly brings his cloak.*] It's midnight. I had no idea it was that late.

Jane: But surely . . . they don't count the hours the way we do. The moon, or something . . .

Pilkings: I am . . . not so sure.

[He turns and breaks into a sudden run. The two constables follow, also at a run. Amusa, who has kept his eyes on the ceiling throughout, waits until the last of the footsteps has faded out of hearing. He salutes suddenly, but without once looking in the direction of the woman.]

Amusa: Goodnight madam.

Jane: Oh. [*She hesitates.*] Amusa . . . [*He goes off without seeming to have heard.*] Poor Simon . . . [*A figure emerges from the shadows, a young black man dressed in a sober western suit. He peeps into the hall, trying to make out the figures of the dancers.*]

Who is that?

Olunde [*emerging into the light*]: I didn't mean to startle you madam. I am looking for the District Officer.

Jane: Wait a minute . . . don't I know you? Yes, you are Olunde, the young man who . . .

Olunde: Mrs Pilkings! How fortunate. I came here to look for your husband.

Jane: Olunde! Let's look at you. What a fine young man you've become. Grand but solemn. Good God, when did you return? Simon never said a word. But you do look well Olunde. Really!

Olunde: You are . . . well, you look quite well yourself Mrs Pilkings. From what little I can see of you.

Jane: Oh, this. It's caused quite a stir I assure you, and not all of it very pleasant. You are not shocked I hope?

Olunde: Why should I be? But don't you find it rather hot in there? Your skin must find it difficult to breathe.

Jane: Well, it is a little hot I must confess, but it's all in a good cause.

Olunde: What cause Mrs Pilkings?

Jane: All this. The ball. And His Highness being here in person and all that.

Olunde [*mildly*]: And that is the good cause for which you desecrate an ancestral mask?

Jane: Oh, so you are shocked after all. How disappointing.

Olunde: No I am not shocked Mrs Pilkings. You forget that I have now spent four years among your people. I discovered that you have no respect for what you do not understand.

Jane: Oh. So you've returned with a chip on your shoulder. That's a pity Olunde. I am sorry.

[*An uncomfortable silence follows.*]

I take it then that you did not find your stay in England altogether edifying.

Olunde: I don't say that. I found your people quite admirable in many ways, their conduct and courage in this war for instance.

Jane: Ah yes the war. Here of course it is all rather remote. From time to time we have a black-out drill just to remind us that there is a war on. And the rare convoy passes through on its way somewhere or on manoeuvres. Mind you there is the occasional bit of excitement like that ship that was blown up in the harbour.

Olunde: Here? Do you mean through enemy action?

Jane: Oh no, the war hasn't come that close. The captain did it himself. I don't quite understand it really. Simon tried to explain. The ship had to be blown up because it had become dangerous to the other ships, even to the city itself. Hundreds of the coastal population would have died.

Olunde: Maybe it was loaded with ammunition and had caught fire. Or some of those lethal gases they've been experimenting on.

Jane: Something like that. The captain blew himself up with it. Deliberately. Simon said someone had to remain on board to light the fuse.

Olunde: It must have been a very short fuse.

Jane [*shrugs*]: I don't know much about it. Only that there was no other way to save lives. No time to devise anything else. The captain took the decision and carried it out.

Olunde: Yes . . . I quite believe it. I met men like that in England.

Jane: Oh just look at me! Fancy welcoming you back with such morbid news. Stale too. It was at least six months ago.

Olunde: I don't find it morbid at all. I find it rather inspiring. It is an affirmative commentary on life.

Jane: What is?

Olunde: That captain's self-sacrifice.

Jane: Nonsense. Life should never be thrown deliberately away.

Olunde: And the innocent people round the harbour?

Jane: Oh, how does one know? The whole thing was probably exaggerated anyway.

Olunde: That was a risk the captain couldn't take. But please Mrs Pilkings, do you think you could find your husband for me? I have to talk to him.

Jane: Simon? Oh. [*As she recollects for the first time the full significance of Olunde's presence.*] Simon is . . . there is a little problem in town. He was sent for. But . . . When did you arrive? Does Simon know you're here?

Olunde [*suddenly earnest*]: I need your help Mrs Pilkings. I've always found you somewhat more understanding than your husband. Please find him for me and when you do, you must help me talk to him.

Jane: I'm afraid I don't quite . . . follow you. Have you seen my husband already?

Olunde: I went to your house. Your houseboy told me you were here. [*He smiles.*] He even told me how I would recognise you and Mr Pilkings.

Jane: Then you must know what my husband is trying to do for you.

Olunde: For me?

Jane: For you. For your people. And to think he didn't even know you were coming back! But how do you happen to be here? Only this evening we were talking about you. We thought you were still four thousand miles away.

Olunde: I was sent a cable.

Jane: A cable? Who did? Simon? The business of your father didn't begin till tonight.

Olunde: A relation sent it weeks ago, and it said nothing about my father. All it said was, Our King is dead. But I knew I had to return home at once so as to bury my father. I understood that.

Jane: Well, thank God you don't have to go through that agony. Simon is going to stop it.

Olunde: That's why I want to see him. He's wasting his time. And since he has been so helpful to me I don't want him to incur the enmity of our people. Especially over nothing.

Jane [*sits down open-mouthed*]: You . . . you Olunde!

Olunde: Mrs Pilkings, I came home to bury my father. As soon as I heard the news I booked my passage home. In fact we were fortunate. We travelled in the same convoy as your Prince, so we had excellent protection.

Jane: But you don't think your father is also entitled to whatever protection is available to him?

Olunde: How can I make you understand? He *has* protection. No one can undertake what he does tonight without the deepest protection the mind can conceive. What can you offer him in place of his peace of mind, in place of the honour and veneration of his own people? What would you think of your Prince if he had refused to accept the risk of losing his life on this voyage? This . . . showing-the-flag tour of colonial possessions.

Jane: I see. So it isn't just medicine you studied in England.

Olunde: Yet another error into which your people fall. You believe that everything which appears to make sense was learnt from you.

Jane: Not so fast Olunde. You have learnt to argue I can tell that, but I never said you made sense. However cleverly you try to put it, it is still a barbaric custom. It is even worse—it's feudal! The king dies and a chieftain must be buried with him. How feudalistic can you get!

Olunde [*waves his hand towards the background. The Prince is dancing past again—to a different step—and all the guests are bowing and curtseying as he passes*]: And this? Even in the midst of a devastating war, look at that. What name would you give to that?

Jane: Therapy, British style. The preservation of sanity in the midst of chaos.

Olunde: Others would call it decadence. However, it doesn't really interest me. You white races know how to survive; I've seen proof of that. By all logical and natural laws this war should end with all the white races wiping out one another, wiping out their so-called civilisation for all time and reverting to a state of primitivism the like of which has so far only existed in your imagination when you thought of us. I thought all that at the beginning. Then I slowly realised that your greatest art is the art of survival. But at least have the humility to let others survive in their own way.

Jane: Through ritual suicide?

Olunde: Is that worse than mass suicide? Mrs Pilkings, what do you call what those young men are sent to do by their generals in this war? Of course you have also mastered the art of calling things by names which don't remotely describe them.

Jane: You talk! You people with your long-winded, roundabout way of making conversation.

Olunde: Mrs Pilkings, whatever we do, we never suggest that a thing is the opposite of what it really is. In your newsreels I heard defeats, thorough, murderous defeats described as strategic victories. No wait, it wasn't just on your newsreels. Don't forget I was attached to hospitals all the time.

Hordes of your wounded passed through those wards. I spoke to them. I spent long evenings by their bedside while they spoke terrible truths of the realities of that war. I know now how history is made.

Jane: But surely, in a war of this nature, for the morale of the nation you must expect . . .

Olunde: That a disaster beyond human reckoning be spoken of as a triumph? No. I mean, is there no mourning in the home of the bereaved that such blasphemy is permitted?

Jane [*after a moment's pause*]: Perhaps I can understand you now. The time we picked for you was not really one for seeing us at our best.

Olunde: Don't think it was just the war. Before that even started I had plenty of time to study your people. I saw nothing, finally, that gave you the right to pass judgement on other peoples and their ways. Nothing at all.

Jane [*hesitantly*]: Was it the . . . colour thing? I know there is some discrimination.

Olunde: Don't make it so simple, Mrs Pilkings. You make it sound as if when I left, I took nothing at all with me.

Jane: Yes . . . and to tell the truth, only this evening, Simon and I agreed that we never really knew what you left with.

Olunde: Neither did I. But I found out over there. I am grateful to your country for that. And I will never give it up.

Jane: Olunde, please . . . promise me something. Whatever you do, don't throw away what you have started to do. You want to be a doctor. My husband and I believe you will make an excellent one, sympathetic and competent. Don't let anything make you throw away your training.

Olunde [*genuinely surprised*]: Of course not. What a strange idea. I intend to return and complete my training. Once the burial of my father is over.

Jane: Oh, please . . . !

Olunde: Listen! Come outside. You can't hear anything against that music.

Jane: What is it?

Olunde: The drums. Can you hear the change? Listen.

[The drums come over, still distant but more distinct. There is a change of rhythm, it rises to a crescendo and then, suddenly, it is cut off. After a silence, a new beat begins, slow and resonant.]

There. It's all over.

Jane: You mean he's . . .

Olunde: Yes Mrs Pilkings, my father is dead. His will-power has always been enormous; I know he is dead.

Jane [*screams*]: How can you be so callous! So unfeeling! You announce your father's own death like a surgeon looking down on some strange . . . stranger's body! You're just a savage like all the rest.

Aide-de-Camp [*rushing out*]: Mrs Pilkings. Mrs Pilkings.[*She breaks down, sobbing.*] Are you alright, Mrs Pilkings?

Olunde: She'll be alright. [*Turns to go.*]

Aide-de-Camp: Who are you? And who the hell asked your opinion?

Olunde: You're quite right, nobody. [*Going.*]

Aide-de-Camp: What the hell! Did you hear me ask you who you were?

Olunde: I have business to attend to.

Aide-de-Camp: I'll give you business in a moment you impudent nigger. Answer my question!

Olunde: I have a funeral to arrange. Excuse me. [*Going.*]

Aide-de-Camp: I said stop! Orderly!

Jane: No no, don't do that. I'm alright. And for heaven's sake don't act so foolishly. He's a family friend.

Aide-de-Camp: Well he'd better learn to answer civil questions when he's asked them. These natives put a suit on and they get high opinions of themselves.

Olunde: Can I go now?

Jane: No no don't go. I must talk to you. I'm sorry about what I said.

Olunde: It's nothing Mrs Pilkings. And I'm really anxious to go. I couldn't see my father before, it's forbidden for me, his heir and successor to set eyes on him from the moment of the king's death. But now . . . I would like to touch his body while it is still warm.

Jane: You will. I promise I shan't keep you long. Only, I couldn't possibly let you go like that. Bob, please excuse us.

Aide-de-Camp: If you're sure . . .

Jane: Of course I'm sure. Something happened to upset me just then, but I'm alright now. Really.

[The Aide-de-Camp goes, somewhat reluctantly.]

Olunde: I mustn't stay long.

Jane: Please, I promise not to keep you. It's just that . . . oh you saw yourself what happens to one in this place. The Resident's man thought he was being helpful, that's the way we all react. But I can't go in among that crowd just now and if I stay by myself somebody will come looking for me. Please, just say something for a few moments and then you can go. Just so I can recover myself.

Olunde: What do you want me to say?

Jane: Your calm acceptance for instance, can you explain that? It was so unnatural. I don't understand that at all. I feel a need to understand all I can.

Olunde: But you explained it yourself. My medical training perhaps. I have seen death too often. And the soldiers who returned from the front, they died on our hands all the time.

Jane: No. It has to be more than that. I feel it has to do with the many things we don't really grasp about your people. At least you can explain.

Olunde: All these things are part of it. And anyway, my father has been dead in my mind for nearly a month. Ever since I learnt of the King's death. I've lived with my bereavement so long now that I cannot think of him alive. On that journey on the boat, I kept my mind on my duties as the one who must perform the rites over his body. I went through it all again and again in my mind as he himself had taught me. I didn't want to do anything wrong, something which might jeopardise the welfare of my people.

Jane: But he had disowned you. When you left he swore publicly you were no longer his son.

Olunde: I told you, he was a man of tremendous will. Sometimes that's another way of saying stubborn. But among our people, you don't disown a child just like that. Even if I had died before him I would still be buried like his eldest son. But it's time for me to go.

Jane: Thank you. I feel calmer. Don't let me keep you from your duties.

Olunde: Goodnight Mrs Pilkings.

Jane: Welcome home. [*She holds out her hand. As he takes it footsteps are heard approaching the drive. A short while later a woman's sobbing is also heard.*]

Pilkings [*off*]: Keep them here till I get back. [*He strides into view, reacts at the sight of Olunde but turns to his wife.*] Thank goodness you're still here.

Jane: Simon, what happened?

Pilkings: Later Jane, please. Is Bob still here?

Jane: Yes, I think so. I'm sure he must be.

Pilkings: Try and get him out here as quietly as you can. Tell him it's urgent.

Jane: Of course. Oh Simon, you remember . . .

Pilkings: Yes yes. I can see who it is. Get Bob out here. [*She runs off.*] At first I thought I was seeing a ghost.

Olunde: Mr Pilkings, I appreciate what you tried to do. I want you to believe that. I can only tell you it would have been a terrible calamity if you'd succeeded.

Pilkings [*opens his mouth several times, shuts it*]: You . . . said what?

Olunde: A calamity for us, the entire people.

Pilkings [*sighs*]: I see. Hm.

Olunde: And now I must go. I must see him before he turns cold.

Pilkings: Oh ah . . . em . . . but this is a shock to see you. I mean er thinking all this while you were in England and thanking God for that.

Olunde: I came on the mail boat. We travelled in the Prince's convoy.

Pilkings: Ah yes, a-ah, hm . . . er well . . .

Olunde: Goodnight I can see you are shocked by the whole business. But you must know by now there are things you cannot understand—or help.

Pilkings: Yes. Just a minute. There are armed policemen that way and they have instructions to let no one pass. I suggest you wait a little. I'll er . . . yes, I'll give you an escort.

Olunde: That's very kind of you. But do you think it could be quickly arranged.

Pilkings: Of course. In fact, yes, what I'll do is send Bob over with some men to the er . . . place. You can go with them. Here he comes now. Excuse me a minute.

Aide-de-Camp: Anything wrong sir?

Pilkings [*takes him to one side*]: Listen Bob, that cellar in the disused annexe of the Residency, you know, where the slaves were stored before being taken down to the coast . . .

Aide-de-Camp: Oh yes, we use it as a storeroom for broken furniture.

Pilkings: But it's still got the bars on it?

Aide-de-Camp: Oh yes, they are quite intact.

Pilkings: Get the keys please. I'll explain later. And I want a strong guard over the Residency tonight.

Aide-de-Camp: We have that already. The detachment from the coast . . .

Pilkings: No, I don't want them at the gates of the Residency. I want you to deploy them at the bottom of the hill, a long way from the main hall so they can deal with any situation long before the sound carries to the house.

Aide-de-Camp: Yes of course.

Pilkings: I don't want His Highness alarmed.

Aide-de-Camp: You think the riot will spread here?

Pilkings: It's unlikely but I don't want to take a chance. I made them believe I was going to lock the man up in my house, which was what I had planned to do in the first place. They are probably assailing it by now. I took a roundabout route here so I don't think there is any danger at all. At least not before dawn. Nobody is to leave the premises of course—the native employees I mean. They'll soon smell something is up and they can't keep their mouths shut.

Aide-de-Camp: I'll give instructions at once.

Pilkings: I'll take the prisoner down myself. Two policemen will stay with him throughout the night. Inside the cell.

Aide-de-Camp: Right sir. [*Salutes and goes off at the double.*]

Pilkings: Jane. Bob is coming back in a moment with a detachment. Until he gets back please stay with Olunde. [*He makes an extra warning gesture with his eyes.*]

Olunde: Please Mr Pilkings . . .

Pilkings: I hate to be stuffy old son, but we have a crisis on our hands. It has to do with your father's affair if you must know. And it happens also at a time when we have His Highness here. I am responsible for security so you'll simply have to do as I say. I hope that's understood. [*Marches off quickly, in the direction from which he made his first appearance.*]

Olunde: What's going on? All this can't be just because he failed to stop my father killing himself.

Jane: I honestly don't know. Could it have sparked off a riot?

Olunde: No. If he'd succeeded that would be more likely to start the riot. Perhaps there were other factors involved. Was there a chieftancy dispute?

Jane: None that I know of.

Elesin [*an animal bellow from off*]: Leave me alone! Is it not enough that you have covered me in shame! White man, take your hand from my body!

[*Olunde stands frozen on the spot. Jane understanding at last, tries to move him.*]

Jane: Let's go in. It's getting chilly out here.

Pilkings [*off*]: Carry him.

Elesin: Give me back the name you have taken away from me you ghost from the land of the nameless!

Pilkings: Carry him! I can't have a disturbance here. Quickly! stuff up his mouth.

Jane: Oh God! Let's go in. Please Olunde. [*Olunde does not move.*]
Elesin: Take your albino's hand from me you . . .

[Sounds of a struggle. His voice chokes as he is gagged.]

Olunde [*quietly*]: That was my father's voice.
Jane: Oh you poor orphan, what have you come home to?

[There is a sudden explosion of rage from off-stage and powerful steps come running up the drive.]

Pilkings: You bloody fools, after him!

[Immediately Elesin, in handcuffs, comes pounding in the direction of Jane and Olunde, followed some moments afterwards by Pilkings and the constables. Elesin confronted by the seeming statue of his son, stops dead. Olunde stares above his head into the distance. The constables try to grab him. Jane screams at them.]

Jane: Leave him alone! Simon, tell them to leave him alone.
Pilkings: All right, stand aside you. [*Shrugs.*] Maybe just as well. It might help to calm him down.

[For several moments they hold the same position. Elesin moves a few steps forward, almost as if he's still in doubt.]

Elesin: Olunde? [*He moves his head, inspecting him from side to side.*] Olunde! [*He collapses slowly at Olunde's feet.*] Oh son, don't let the sight of your father turn you blind!
Olunde [*he moves for the first time since he heard his voice, brings his head slowly down to look on him*]: I have no father, eater of left-overs.

[He walks slowly down the way his father had run. Light fades out on Elesin, sobbing into the ground.]

5

A wide iron-barred gate stretches almost the whole width of the cell in which Elesin is imprisoned. His wrists are encased in thick iron bracelets, chained together; he stands against the bars, looking out. Seated on the ground to one side on the outside is his recent bride, her eyes bent perpetually to the ground. Figures of the two guards can be seen deeper inside the cell, alert to every movement Elesin makes. Pilkings now in a police officer's uniform enters noiselessly, observes him for a while. Then he coughs ostentatiously and approaches. Leans against the bars near a corner, his back to Elesin. He is obviously trying to fall in mood with him. Some moments' silence.

Pilkings: You seem fascinated by the moon.
Elesin [*after a pause*]: Yes, ghostly one. Your twin-brother up there engages my thoughts.
Pilkings: It is a beautiful night.

Elesin: Is that so?

Pilkings: The light on the leaves, the peace of the night . . .

Elesin: The night is not at peace, District Officer.

Pilkings: No? I would have said it was. You know, quiet . . .

Elesin: And does quiet mean peace for you?

Pilkings: Well, nearly the same thing. Naturally there is a subtle difference . . .

Elesin: The night is not at peace ghostly one. The world is not at peace. You have shattered the peace of the world for ever. There is no sleep in the world tonight.

Pilkings: It is still a good bargain if the world should lose one night's sleep as the price of saving a man's life.

Elesin: You did not save my life District Officer. You destroyed it.

Pilkings: Now come on . . .

Elesin: And not merely my life but the lives of many. The end of the night's work is not over. Neither this year nor the next will see it. If I wished you well, I would pray that you do not stay long enough on our land to see the disaster you have brought upon us.

Pilkings: Well, I did my duty as I saw it. I have no regrets.

Elesin: No. The regrets of life always come later.

[Some moments' pause.]

You are waiting for dawn white man. I hear you saying to yourself: only so many hours until dawn and then the danger is over. All I must do is keep him alive tonight. You don't quite understand it all but you know that tonight is when what ought to be must be brought about. I shall ease your mind even more, ghostly one. It is not an entire night but a moment of the night, and that moment is past. The moon was my messenger and guide. When it reached a certain gateway in the sky, it touched that moment for which my whole life has been spent in blessings. Even I do not know the gateway. I have stood here and scanned the sky for a glimpse of that door but, I cannot see it. Human eyes are useless for a search of this nature. But in the house of *osugbo*, those who keep watch through the spirit recognised the moment, they sent word to me through the voice of our sacred drums to prepare myself. I heard them and I shed all thoughts of earth. I began to follow the moon to the abode of gods . . . servant of the white king, that was when you entered my chosen place of departure on feet of desecration.

Pilkings: I'm sorry, but we all see our duty differently.

Elesin: I no longer blame you. You stole from me my firstborn, sent him to your country so you could turn him into something in your own image. Did you plan it all beforehand? There are moments when it seems part of a larger plan. He who must follow my footsteps is taken from me, sent across the ocean. Then, in my turn, I am stopped from fulfilling my destiny. Did you think it all out before, this plan to push our world from its course and sever the cord that links us to the great origin?

Pilkings: You don't really believe that. Anyway, if that was my intention with your son, I appear to have failed.

Elesin: You did not fail in the main thing ghostly one. We know the roof covers the rafters, the cloth covers blemishes; who would have known that the white skin covered our future, preventing us from seeing the death our enemies had prepared for us. The world is set adrift and its inhabitants are lost. Around them, there is nothing but emptiness.

Pilkings: Your son does not take so gloomy a view.

Elesin: Are you dreaming now white man? Were you not present at my reunion of shame? Did you not see when the world reversed itself and the father fell before his son, asking forgiveness?

Pilkings: That was in the heat of the moment. I spoke to him and . . . if you want to know, he wishes he could cut out his tongue for uttering the words he did.

Elesin: No. What he said must never be unsaid. The contempt of my own son rescued something of my shame at your hands. You may have stopped me in my duty but I know now that I did give birth to a son. Once I mistrusted him for seeking the companionship of those my spirit knew as enemies of our race. Now I understand. One should seek to obtain the secrets of his enemies. He will avenge my shame, white one. His spirit will destroy you and yours.

Pilkings: That kind of talk is hardly called for. If you don't want my consolation . . .

Elesin: No white man, I do not want your consolation.

Pilkings: As you wish. Your son anyway, sends his consolation. He asks your forgiveness. When I asked him not to despise you his reply was: I cannot judge him, and if I cannot judge him, I cannot despise him. He wants to come to you to say goodbye and to receive your blessing.

Elesin: Goodbye? Is he returning to your land?

Pilkings: Don't you think that's the most sensible thing for him to do? I advised him to leave at once, before dawn, and he agrees that is the right course of action.

Elesin: Yes, it is best. And even if I did not think so, I have lost the father's place of honour. My voice is broken.

Pilkings: Your son honours you. If he didn't he would not ask your blessing.

Elesin: No. Even a thoroughbred is not without pity for the turf he strikes with his hoof. When is he coming?

Pilkings: As soon as the town is a little quieter. I advised it.

Elesin: Yes white man, I am sure you advised it. You advise all our lives although on the authority of what gods, I do not know.

Pilkings [*opens his mouth to reply, then appears to change his mind. Turns to go. Hesitates and stops again*]: Before I leave you, may I ask just one thing of you?

Elesin: I am listening.

Pilkings: I wish to ask you to search the quiet of your heart and tell me—do you not find great contradictions in the wisdom of your own race?

Elesin: Make yourself clear, white one.

Pilkings: I have lived among you long enough to learn a saying or two. One came to my mind tonight when I stepped into the market and saw what was going on. You were surrounded by those who egged you on with song and praises. I thought, are these not the same people who say: the elder grimly approaches heaven and you ask him to bear your greetings yonder; do you really think he makes the journey willingly? After that, I did not hesitate.

[A pause. Elesin sighs. Before he can speak a sound of running feet is heard.]

Jane [*off*]: Simon! Simon!
Pilkings: What on earth . . . ! [*Runs off.*]

[Elesin turns to his new wife, gazes on her for some moments.]

Elesin: My young bride, did you hear the ghostly one? You sit and sob in your silent heart but say nothing to all this. First I blamed the white man, then I blamed my gods for deserting me. Now I feel I want to blame you for the mystery of the sapping of my will. But blame is a strange peace offering for a man to bring a world he has deeply wronged, and to its innocent dwellers. Oh little mother, I have taken countless women in my life but you were more than a desire of the flesh. I needed you as the abyss across which my body must be drawn, I filled it with earth and dropped my seed in it at the moment of preparedness for my crossing. You were the final gift of the living to their emissary to the land of the ancestors, and perhaps your warmth and youth brought new insights of this world to me and turned my feet leaden on this side of the abyss. For I confess to you, daughter, my weakness came not merely from the abomination of the white man who came violently into my fading presence, there was also a weight of longing on my earth-held limbs. I would have shaken it off, already my foot had begun to lift but then, the white ghost entered and all was defiled.

[Approaching voices of Pilkings and his wife.]

Jane: Oh Simon, you will let her in won't you?
Pilkings: I really wish you'd stop interfering.

[They come in view. Jane is in a dressing-gown. Pilkings is holding a note to which he refers from time to time.]

Jane: Good gracious, I didn't initiate this. I was sleeping quietly, or trying to anyway, when the servant brought it. It's not my fault if one can't sleep undisturbed even in the Residency.
Pilkings: He'd have done the same if we were sleeping at home so don't sidetrack the issue. He knows he can get round you or he wouldn't send you the petition in the first place.
Jane: Be fair Simon. After all he was thinking of your own interests. He is grateful you know, you seem to forget that. He feels he owes you something.
Pilkings: I just wish they'd leave this man alone tonight, that's all.

Jane: Trust him Simon. He's pledged his word it will all go peacefully.

Pilkings: Yes, and that's the other thing. I don't like being threatened.

Jane: Threatened? [*Takes the note.*] I didn't spot any threat.

Pilkings: It's there. Veiled, but it's there. The only way to prevent serious rioting tomorrow—what a cheek!

Jane: I don't think he's threatening you Simon.

Pilkings: He's picked up the idiom alright. Wouldn't surprise me if he's been mixing with commies or anarchists over there. The phrasing sounds too good to be true. Damn! If only the Prince hadn't picked this time for his visit.

Jane: Well, even so Simon, what have you got to lose? You don't want a riot on your hands, not with the Prince here.

Pilkings [*going up to Elesin*]: Let's see what he has to say. Chief Elesin, there is yet another person who wants to see you. As she is not a next-of-kin I don't really feel obliged to let her in. But your son sent a note with her, so it's up to you.

Elesin: I know who that must be. So she found out your hiding-place. Well, it was not difficult. My stench of shame is so strong, it requires no hunter's dog to follow it.

Pilkings: If you don't want to see her, just say so and I'll send her packing.

Elesin: Why should I not want to see her? Let her come. I have no more holes in my rag of shame. All is laid bare.

Pilkings: I'll bring her in. [*Goes off.*]

Jane [*hesitates, then goes to Elesin*]: Please, try and understand. Everything my husband did was for the best.

Elesin [*he gives her a long strange stare, as if he is trying to understand who she is*]: You are the wife of the District Officer?

Jane: Yes. My name is Jane.

Elesin: That is my wife sitting down there. You notice how still and silent she sits? My business is with your husband.

[Pilkings returns with Iyaloja.]

Pilkings: Here she is. Now first I want your word of honour that you will try nothing foolish.

Elesin: Honour? White one, did you say you wanted my word of honour?

Pilkings: I know you to be an honourable man. Give me your word of honour you will receive nothing from her.

Elesin: But I am sure you have searched her clothing as you would never dare touch your own mother. And there are these two lizards of yours who roll their eyes even when I scratch.

Pilkings: And I shall be sitting on that tree trunk watching even how you blink. Just the same I want your word that you will not let her pass anything to you.

Elesin: You have my honour already. It is locked up in that desk in which you will put away your report of this night's events. Even the honour of my people you have taken already; it is tied together with those papers of treachery which make you masters in this land.

Pilkings: Alright. I am trying to make things easy but if you must bring in politics we'll have to do it the hard way. Madam, I want you to remain along this line and move no nearer to that cell door. Guards! [*They spring to attention.*] If she moves beyond this point, blow your whistle. Come on Jane. [*They go off.*]

Iyaloja: How boldly the lizard struts before the pigeon when it was the eagle itself he promised us he would confront.

Elesin: I don't ask you to take pity on me Iyaloja. You have a message for me or you would not have come. Even if it is the curses of the world, I shall listen.

Iyaloja: You made so bold with the servant of the white king who took your side against death. I must tell your brother chiefs when I return how bravely you waged war against him. Especially with words.

Elesin: I more than deserve your scorn.

Iyaloja [*with sudden anger*]: I warned you, if you must leave a seed behind, be sure it is not tainted with the curses of the world. Who are you to open a new life when you dared not open the door to a new existence? I say who are you to make so bold? [*The Bride sobs and Iyaloja notices her. Her contempt noticeably increases as she turns back to Elesin.*] Oh you self-vaunted stem of the plantain, how hollow it all proves. The pith is gone in the parent stem, so how will it prove with the new shoot? How will it go with that earth that bears it? Who are you to bring this abomination on us!

Elesin: My powers deserted me. My charms, my spells, even my voice lacked strength when I made to summon the powers that would lead me over the last measure of earth into the land of the fleshless. You saw it, Iyaloja. You saw me struggle to retrieve my will from the power of the stranger whose shadow fell across the doorway and left me floundering and blundering in a maze I had never before encountered. My senses were numbed when the touch of cold iron came upon my wrists. I could do nothing to save myself.

Iyaloja: You have betrayed us. We fed your sweetmeats such as we hoped awaited you on the other side. But you said No, I must eat the world's left-overs. We said you were the hunter who brought the quarry down; to you belonged the vital portions of the game. No, you said, I am the hunter's dog and I shall eat the entrails of the game and the faeces of the hunter. We said you were the hunter returning home in triumph, a slain buffalo pressing down on his neck; you said wait, I first must turn up this cricket hole with my toes. We said yours was the doorway at which we first spy the tapper when he comes down from the tree, yours was the blessing of the twilight wine, the purl that brings night spirits out of doors to steal their portion before the light of day. We said yours was the body of wine whose burden shakes the tapper like a sudden gust on his perch. You said, No, I am content to lick the dregs from each calabash when the drinkers are done. We said, the dew on earth's surface was for you to wash your feet along the slopes of honour. You said No, I shall step in the vomit of cats and the droppings of mice; I shall fight them for the left-overs of the world.

Elesin: Enough Iyaloja, enough.
Iyaloja: We called you leader and oh, how you led us on. What we have no intention of eating should not be held to the nose.
Elesin: Enough, enough. My shame is heavy enough.
Iyaloja: Wait. I came with a burden.
Elesin: You have more than discharged it.
Iyaloja: I wish I could pity you.
Elesin: I need neither your pity nor the pity of the world. I need understanding. Even I need to understand. You were present at my defeat. You were part of the beginnings. You brought about the renewal of my tie to earth, you helped in the binding of the cord.
Iyaloja: I gave you warning. The river which fills up before our eyes does not sweep us away in its flood.
Elesin: What were warnings beside the moist contact of living earth between my fingers? What were warnings beside the renewal of famished embers lodged eternally in the heart of man. But even that, even if it overwhelmed one with a thousandfold temptations to linger a little while, a man could overcome it. It is when the alien hand pollutes the source of will, when a stranger force of violence shatters the mind's calm resolution, this is when a man is made to commit the awful treachery of relief, commit in his thought the unspeakable blasphemy of seeing the hand of the gods in this alien rupture of his world. I know it was this thought that killed me, sapped my powers and turned me into an infant in the hands of unnamable strangers. I made to utter my spells anew but my tongue merely rattled in my mouth. I fingered hidden charms and the contact was damp; there was no spark left to sever the life-strings that should stretch from every fingertip. My will was squelched in the spittle of an alien race, and all because I had committed this blasphemy of thought—that there might be the hand of the gods in a stranger's intervention.
Iyaloja: Explain it how you will, I hope it brings you peace of mind. The bush-rat fled his rightful cause, reached the market and set up a lamentation. "Please save me!"— are these fitting words to hear from an ancestral mask? "There's a wild beast at my heels" is not becoming language from a hunter.
Elesin: May the world forgive me.
Iyaloja: I came with a burden I said. It approaches the gates which are so well guarded by those jackals whose spittle will from this day on be your food and drink. But first, tell me, you who were once Elesin Oba, tell me, you who know so well the cycle of the plantain: is it the parent shoot which withers to give sap to the younger or, does your wisdom see it running the other way?
Elesin: I don't see your meaning Iyaloja?
Iyaloja: Did I ask you for a meaning? I asked a question. Whose trunk withers to give sap to the other? The parent shoot or the younger?
Elesin: The parent.
Iyaloja: Ah. So you do know that. There are sights in this world which say different Elesin. There are some who choose to reverse this cycle of our

being. Oh you emptied bark that the world once saluted for a pith-laden being, shall I tell you what the gods have claimed of you?

[In her agitation she steps beyond the line indicated by Pilkings and the air is rent by piercing whistles. The two Guards also leap forward and place safe-guarding hands on Elesin. Iyaloja stops, astonished. Pilkings comes racing in, followed by Jane.]

Pilkings: What is it? Did they try something?

Guard: She stepped beyond the line.

Elesin [*in a broken voice*]: Let her alone. She meant no harm.

Iyaloja: Oh Elesin, see what you've become. Once you had no need to open your mouth in explanation because evil-smelling goats, itchy of hand and foot had lost their senses. And it was a brave man indeed who dared lay hands on you because Iyaloja stepped from one side of the earth onto another. Now look at the spectacle of your life. I grieve for you.

Pilkings: I think you'd better leave. I doubt you have done him much good by coming here. I shall make sure you are not allowed to see him again. In any case we are moving him to a different place before dawn, so don't bother to come back.

Iyaloja: We foresaw that. Hence the burden I trudged here to lay beside your gates.

Pilkings: What was that you said?

Iyaloja: Didn't our son explain? Ask that one. He knows what it is. At least we hope the man we once knew as Elesin remembers the lesser oaths he need not break.

Pilkings: Do you know what she is talking about?

Elesin: Go to the gates, ghostly one. Whatever you find there, bring it to me.

Iyaloja: Not yet. It drags behind me on the slow, weary feet of women. Slow as it is Elesin, it has long overtaken you. It rides ahead of your laggard will.

Pilkings: What is she saying now? Christ! Must your people forever speak in riddles?

Elesin: It will come white man, it will come. Tell your men at the gates to let it through.

Pilkings [*dubiously*]: I'll have to see what it is.

Iyaloja: You will. [*Passionately.*] But this is one oath he cannot shirk. White one, you have a king here, a visitor from your land. We know of his presence here. Tell me, were he to die would you leave his spirit roaming restlessly on the surface of earth? Would you bury him here among those you consider less than human? In your land have you no ceremonies of the dead?

Pilkings: Yes. But we don't make our chiefs commit suicide to keep him company.

Iyaloja: Child, I have not come to help your understanding. [*Points to Elesin.*] This is the man whose weakened understanding holds us in bondage to you. But ask him if you wish. He knows the meaning of a king's passage; he was not born yesterday. He knows the peril to the race when our dead father, who goes as intermediary, waits and waits and knows he is betrayed. He knows when the narrow gate was opened and he knows it will not stay for laggards who drag their feet in dung and vomit, whose lips are reeking of the left-overs of lesser men. He knows he has condemned our king to wander in the void of evil with beings who are enemies of life.

Pilkings: Yes er . . . but look here . . .

Iyaloja: What we ask is little enough. Let him release our King so he can ride on homewards alone. The messenger is on his way on the backs of women. Let him send word through the heart that is folded up within the bolt. It is the least of all his oaths, it is the easiest fulfilled.

[The Aide-de-Camp runs in.]

Pilkings: Bob?

Aide-de-Camp: Sir, there's a group of women chanting up the hill.

Pilkings [*rounding on Iyaloja*]: If you people want trouble . . .

Jane: Simon, I think that's what Olunde referred to in his letter.

Pilkings: He knows damned well I can't have a crowd here! Damn it, I explained the delicacy of my position to him. I think it's about time I got him out of town. Bob, send a car and two or three soldiers to bring him in. I think the sooner he takes his leave of his father and gets out the better.

Iyaloja: Save your labour white one. If it is the father of your prisoner you want, Olunde, he who until this night we knew as Elesin's son, he comes soon himself to take his leave. He has sent the women ahead, so let them in.

[Pilkings remains undecided.]

Aide-de-Camp: What do we do about the invasion? We can still stop them far from here.

Pilkings: What do they look like?

Aide-de-Camp: They're not many. And they seem quite peaceful.

Pilkings: No men?

Aide-de-Camp: Mm, two or three at the most.

Jane: Honestly, Simon, I'd trust Olunde. I don't think he'll deceive you about their intentions.

Pilkings: He'd better not. Alright, let them in Bob. Warn them to control themselves. Then hurry Olunde here. Make sure he brings his baggage because I'm not returning him into town.

Aide-de-Camp: Very good sir. [*Goes.*]

Pilkings (*to Iyaloja*): I hope you understand that if anything goes wrong it will be on your head. My men have orders to shoot at the first sign of trouble.

Iyaloja: To prevent one death you will actually make other deaths? Ah, great is the wisdom of the white race. But have no fear. Your Prince will sleep peacefully. So at long last will ours. We will disturb you no further, servant of the white king. Just let Elesin fulfil his oath and we will retire home and pay homage to our King.

Jane: I believe her Simon, don't you?

Pilkings: Maybe.

Elesin: Have no fear ghostly one. I have a message to send my King and then you have nothing more to fear.

Iyaloja: Olunde would have done it. The chiefs asked him to speak the words but he said no, not while you lived.

Elesin: Even from the depths to which my spirit has sunk, I find some joy that this little has been left to me.

[The women enter, intoning the dirge 'Alẹ lẹ lẹ' and swaying from side to side. On their shoulders is borne a longish object roughly like a cylindrical bolt, covered in cloth. They set it down on the spot where Iyaloja had stood earlier, and form a semi-circle round it. The Praise-Singer and Drummer stand on the inside of the semi-circle but the drum is not used at all. The Drummer intones under the Praise-Singer's invocations.]

Pilkings [*as they enter*]: What is *that*?

Iyaloja: The burden you have made white one, but we bring it in peace.

Pilkings: I said *what* is it?

Elesin: White man, you must let me out. I have a duty to perform.

Pilkings: I most certainly will not.

Elesin: There lies the courier of my King. Let me out so I can perform what is demanded of me.

Pilkings: You'll do what you need to do from inside there or not at all. I've gone as far as I intend to with this business.

Elesin: The worshipper who lights a candle in your church to bear a message to his god bows his head and speaks in a whisper to the flame. Have I not seen it ghostly one? His voice does not ring out to the world. Mine are no words for anyone's ears. They are not words even for the bearers of this load. They are words I must speak secretly, even as my father whispered them in my ears and I in the ears of my first-born. I cannot shout them to the wind and the open night-sky.

Jane: Simon . . .

Pilkings: Don't interfere. Please!

Iyaloja: They have slain the favourite horse of the king and slain his dog. They have borne them from pulse to pulse centre of the land receiving prayers for their king. But the rider has chosen to stay behind. Is it too much to ask that he speak his heart to heart of the waiting courier? [*Pilkings turns his back on her.*] So be it. Elesin Oba, you see how even the mere leavings are denied you. [*She gestures to the Praise-Singer.*]

Praise-Singer: Elesin Oba! I call you by that name only this last time. Remember when I said, if you cannot come, tell my horse. [*Pause.*] What? I cannot hear you? I said, if you cannot come, whisper in the ears of my horse. Is your tongue severed from the roots Elesin? I can hear no response. I said, if there are boulders you cannot climb, mount my horse's back, this spotless black stallion, he'll bring you over them [*Pauses.*] Elesin Oba, once you had a tongue that darted like a drummer's stick. I said, if you get lost my dog will track a path to me. My memory fails me but I think you replied: My feet have found the path, Alafin.

[The dirge rises and falls.]

I said at the last, if evil hands hold you back, just tell my horse there is weight on the hem of your smock. I dare not wait too long.

[The dirge rises and falls.]

There lies the swiftest ever messenger of a king, so set me free with the errand of your heart. There lie the head and heart of the favourite of the gods, whisper in his ears. Oh my companion, if you had followed when you should, we would not say that the horse preceded its rider. If you had followed when it was time, we would not say the dog has raced beyond and left his master behind. If you had raised your will to cut the thread of life at the summons of the drums, we would not say your mere shadow fell across the gateway and took its owner's place at the banquet. But the hunter, laden with a slain buffalo, stayed to root in the cricket's hole with his toes. What now is left? If there is a dearth of bats, the pigeon must serve us for the offering. Speak the words over your shadow which must now serve in your place.

Elesin: I cannot approach. Take off the cloth. I shall speak my message from heart to heart of silence.

Iyaloja [*moves forward and removes the covering*]: Your courier Elesin, cast your eyes on the favoured companion of the King.

[Rolled up in the mat, his head and feet showing at either end is the body of Olunde.]

There lies the honour of your household and of our race. Because he could not bear to let honour fly out of doors, he stopped it with his life. The son has proved the father Elesin, and there is nothing left in your mouth to gnash but infant gums.

Praise-Singer: Elesin, we placed the reins of the world in your hands yet you watched it plunge over the edge of the bitter precipice. You sat with folded arms while evil strangers tilted the world from its course and crashed it beyond the edge of emptiness—you muttered, there is little that one man can do, you left us floundering in a blind future. Your heir has taken the burden on himself. What the end will be, we are not gods to tell. But this young shoot has poured its sap into the parent stalk, and we know this is not the way of life. Our world is tumbling in the void of strangers, Elesin.

[Elesin has stood rock-still, his knuckles taut on the bars, his eyes glued to the body of his son. The stillness seizes and paralyses everyone, including Pilkings who has turned to look. Suddenly Elesin flings one arm round his neck, once, and with the loop of the chain, strangles himself in a swift, decisive pull. The guards rush forward to stop him but they are only in time to let his body down. Pilkings has leapt to the door at the same time and struggles with the lock. He rushes within, fumbles with the handcuffs and unlocks them, raises the body to a sitting position while he tries to give resuscitation. The women continue their dirge, unmoved by the sudden event.]

Iyaloja: Why do you strain yourself? Why do you labour at tasks for which no one, not even the man lying there would give you thanks? He is gone at last into the passage but oh, how late it all is. His son will feast on the meat and throw him bones. The passage is clogged with droppings from the King's stallion; he will arrive all stained in dung.

Pilkings [*in a tired voice*]: Was this what you wanted?

Iyaloja: No child, it is what you brought to be, you who play with strangers' lives, who even usurp the vestments of our dead, yet believe that the stain of death will not cling to you. The gods demanded only the old expired plantain but you cut down the sap-laden shoot to feed your pride. There is your board, filled to overflowing. Feast on it. [*She screams at him suddenly, seeing that Pilkings is about to close Elesin's staring eyes.*] Let him alone! However sunk he was in debt he is no pauper's carrion abandoned on the road. Since when have strangers donned clothes of indigo before the bereaved cries out his loss?

[She turns to the Bride who has remained motionless throughout.]

Child.

[The girl takes up a little earth, walks calmly into the cell and closes Elesin's eyes. She then pours some earth over each eyelid and comes out again.]

Now forget the dead, forget even the living. Turn your mind only to the unborn.

[She goes off, accompanied by the Bride. The dirge rises in volume and the women continue their sway. Lights fade to a black-out.]

The End

(1975)

Questions for Discussion and Writing

Close Reading

1. Why is Elesin reluctant to perform his "duty" of committing suicide after the king's death? Is this reluctance a strength or a flaw in this play?
2. What does Pilkings believe is his duty with regard to Elesin's suicide? Where does he derive his sense of duty and his authority?
3. What is the role of Iyaloja in interpreting the events that take place? Where does she derive her power?
4. Why doesn't Olunde's suicide substitute for Elesin's failure to commit suicide?

Critical and Creative Reading

5. Who is primarily responsible for the fact that Elesin fails to complete his duty: Olunde for wanting to break the ties to his father, Pilkings for his interference, or Elesin for his love of life or fear of death?
6. Critics have noted that there is a three-way tension in Soyinka's play between the living, the dead, and the yet-to-be-born. If Elesin is a transitional figure

between these three forces, where is the primary hope for his culture: in the past, the present, or the future?

7. Do you sympathize with Elesin because he, like most people, does not want to die, or do you feel that he should have done his duty according to custom and that he was a weak man? After all, he always knew what would be expected of him.

CONNECTIONS TO OTHER READINGS

8. Compare Soyinka's and Wilfred Owen's attitude toward sacrificing oneself for one's country. From what angle do they approach this question? Do they arrive at the same conclusion?
9. In Shirley Jackson's "The Lottery" a character is sacrificed according to ritual. Does ritual in Jackson's story (the meaning of which is never explained) have a different value than it does in *Death and the King's Horseman*?
10. In William Dean Howells's story "Editha," the character George also resists sacrificing himself for a cause, yet unlike Elesin in *Death and the King's Horseman*, George enlists for the war and dies as a result. Use the opposite fates of these men to discuss the notion of duty and obedience to custom along with the desire to live one's life.

Essays

Henry David Thoreau

Civil Disobedience

One of the most passionate, original American thinkers, Thoreau (1817–1862) is remembered as a writer with deep convictions, a wide-ranging understanding of human thought, and a commitment to truth and simplicity. Thoreau is associated with a group of writers and thinkers known as the New England Transcendentalists that included Ralph Waldo Emerson and Margaret Fuller and that greatly influenced American thought and literature throughout the nineteenth century. He is best known for his rich prose work *Walden,* which describes his life of self-reliance for two years near Walden Pond in Concord, Massachusetts. Thoreau sought to look deeply into the human condition, and two years of solitude communing with nature provided the perfect circumstances for this meditation. The following essay, "Civil Disobedience" (also titled "Resistance to Civil Government"), also has Thoreau searching for insight, but his vision of human nature here was gained not in nature but in that most human of institutions, the prison.

I heartily accept the motto,—"That government is best which governs least"; and I should like to see it acted up to more rapidly and systematically. Carried out, it finally amounts to this, which also I believe,—"That government is best which governs not at all"; and when men are prepared for it, that will be the kind of government which they will have. Government is at best but an expedient; but most governments are usually, and all governments are sometimes, inexpedient. The objections which have been brought against a standing army, and they are many and weighty, and deserve to prevail, may also at last be brought against a standing government. The standing army is only an arm of the standing government. The government itself, which is only the mode which the people have chosen to execute their will, is equally liable to be abused and perverted before the people can act through it. Witness the present Mexican war,[1] the work of comparatively a few individuals using the standing government as their tool; for, in the outset, the people would not have consented to this measure.

This American government,—what is it but a tradition, though a recent one, endeavoring to transmit itself unimpaired to posterity, but each instant losing some of its integrity? It has not the vitality and force of a single living man; for a single man can bend it to his will. It is a sort of wooden gun to the people themselves. But it is not the less necessary for this; for the people must have some complicated machinery or other, and hear its din, to satisfy that idea of government which they have. Governments show thus how successfully men can be imposed on, even impose on themselves, for their own advantage. It is excellent, we must all allow. Yet this government never of itself furthered any enterprise, but by the alacrity with which it got out of its way. *It* does not keep the country free. *It* does not settle the West. *It* does not educate. The character inherent in the American people has done all that has been accomplished; and it would have done somewhat more, if the government had not sometimes got in its way. For government is an expedient by which men would fain succeed in letting one another alone; and, as has been said, when it is most expedient, the governed are most let alone by it. Trade and commerce, if they were not made of India-rubber, would never manage to bounce over the obstacles which legislators are continually putting in their way; and, if one were to judge these men wholly by the effects of their actions and not partly by their intentions, they would deserve to be classed and punished with those mischievous persons who put obstructions on the railroads.

But, to speak practically and as a citizen, unlike those who call themselves no-government men, I ask for, not at once no government, but *at once* a better government. Let every man make known what kind of government would command his respect, and that will be one step toward obtaining it.

After all, the practical reason why, when the power is once in the hands of the people, a majority are permitted, and for a long period continue, to rule, is

[1]*Mexican war:* The war between Mexico and the United States that was fought from 1846 to 1848. It resulted in a decisive U.S. victory that caused Mexico to lose half of its territory and that established the United States as the dominant North American power.

not because they are most likely to be in the right, nor because this seems fairest to the minority, but because they are physically the strongest. But a government in which the majority rule in all cases cannot be based on justice, even as far as men understand it. Can there not be a government in which majorities do not virtually decide right and wrong, but conscience?—in which majorities decide only those questions to which the rule of expediency is applicable? Must the citizen ever for a moment, or in the least degree, resign his conscience to the legislator? Why has every man a conscience, then? I think that we should be men first, and subjects afterward. It is not desirable to cultivate a respect for the law, so much as for the right. The only obligation which I have a right to assume, is to do at any time what I think right. It is truly enough said, that a corporation has no conscience; but a corporation of conscientious men is a corporation *with* a conscience. Law never made men a whit more just; and, by means of their respect for it, even the well-disposed are daily made the agents of injustice. A common and natural result of an undue respect for law is, that you may see a file of soldiers, colonel, captain, corporal, privates, powder-monkeys, and all, marching in admirable order over hill and dale to the wars, against their wills, ay, against their common sense and consciences, which makes it very steep marching indeed, and produces a palpitation of the heart. They have no doubt that it is a damnable business in which they are concerned; they are all peaceably inclined. Now, what are they? Men at all? or small movable forts and magazines, at the service of some unscrupulous man in power? Visit the Navy-Yard, and behold a marine, such a man as an American government can make, or such as it can make a man with its black arts,—a mere shadow and reminiscence of humanity, a man laid out alive and standing, and already, as one may say, buried under arms with funeral accompaniments, though it may be,—

"Not a drum was heard, not a funeral note,
As his corse[2] to the rampart we hurried;
Not a soldier discharged his farewell shot
O'er the grave where our hero we buried."

5 The mass of men serve the state thus, not as men mainly, but as machines, with their bodies. They are the standing army, and the militia, jailers, constables, posse comitatus,[3] &c. In most cases there is no free exercise whatever of the judgment or of the moral sense; but they put themselves on a level with wood and earth and stones; and wooden men can perhaps be manufactured that will serve the purpose as well. Such command no more respect than men of straw or a lump of dirt. They have the same sort of worth only as horses and dogs. Yet such as these even are commonly esteemed good citizens. Others,—as most legislators, politicians, lawyers, ministers, and office-holders,—serve the state chiefly with their heads; and, as they rarely make any moral distinctions, they are

[2]*corse:* A corpse.

[3]*posse comitatus:* Power of the county (Latin). Commonly refers to vigilante groups of citizens who aid the local authority.

as likely to serve the Devil, without *intending* it, as God. A very few, as heroes, patriots, martyrs, reformers in the great sense, and *men*, serve the state with their consciences also, and so necessarily resist it for the most part; and they are commonly treated as enemies by it. A wise man will only be useful as a man, and will not submit to be "clay," and "stop a hole to keep the wind away," but leave that office to his dust at least:—

> "I am too high-born to be propertied
> To be a secondary at control,
> Or useful serving-man and instrument
> To any sovereign state throughout the world."

He who gives himself entirely to his fellow-men appears to them useless and selfish; but he who gives himself partially to them is pronounced a benefactor and philanthropist.

How does it become a man to behave toward this American government to-day? I answer, that he cannot without disgrace be associated with it. I cannot for an instant recognize that political organization as *my* government which is the *slave's* government also.

All men recognize the right of revolution; that is, the right to refuse allegiance to, and to resist, the government, when its tyranny or its inefficiency are great and unendurable. But almost all say that such is not the case now. But such was the case, they think, in the Revolution of '75. If one were to tell me that this was a bad government because it taxed certain foreign commodities brought to its ports, it is most probable that I should not make an ado about it, for I can do without them. All machines have their friction; and possibly this does enough good to counterbalance the evil. At any rate, it is a great evil to make a stir about it. But when the friction comes to have its machine, and oppression and robbery are organized, I say, let us not have such a machine any longer. In other words, when a sixth of the population of a nation which has undertaken to be the refuge of liberty are slaves, and a whole country is unjustly overrun and conquered by a foreign army, and subjected to military law, I think that it is not too soon for honest men to rebel and revolutionize. What makes this duty the more urgent is the fact, that the country so overrun is not our own, but ours is the invading army.

Paley,[4] common authority with many on moral questions, in his chapter on the "Duty of Submission to Civil Government," resolves all civil obligation into expediency; and he proceeds to say, "that so long as the interest of the whole society requires it, that is, so long as the established government cannot be resisted or changed without public inconveniency, it is the will of God that the established government be obeyed, and no longer. . . . This principle being admitted, the justice of every particular case of resistance is reduced to a computation of the quantity of the danger and grievance on the one side, and of the probability

[4]*Paley:* William Paley, eighteenth-century English theologian and philosopher.

and expense of redressing it on the other." Of this, he says, every man shall judge for himself. But Paley appears never to have contemplated those cases to which the rule of expediency does not apply, in which a people, as well as an individual, must do justice, cost what it may. If I have unjustly wrested a plank from a drowning man, I must restore it to him though I drown myself. This, according to Paley, would be inconvenient. But he that would save his life, in such a case, shall lose it. This people must cease to hold slaves, and to make war on Mexico, though it cost them their existence as a people.

In their practice, nations agree with Paley; but does any one think that Massachusetts does exactly what is right at the present crisis?

"A drab of state, a cloth-o'-silver slut,
To have her train borne up, and her soul trail in the dirt."

Practically speaking, the opponents to a reform in Massachusetts are not a hundred thousand politicians at the South, but a hundred thousand merchants and farmers here, who are more interested in commerce and agriculture than they are in humanity, and are not prepared to do justice to the slave and to Mexico, *cost what it may*. I quarrel not with far-off foes, but with those who, near at home, co-operate with, and do the bidding of, those far away, and without whom the latter would be harmless. We are accustomed to say, that the mass of men are unprepared; but improvement is slow, because the few are not materially wiser or better than the many. It is not so important that many should be as good as you, as that there be some absolute goodness somewhere; for that will leaven the whole lump. There are thousands who are *in opinion* opposed to slavery and to the war, who yet in effect do nothing to put an end to them; who, esteeming themselves children of Washington and Franklin, sit down with their hands in their pockets, and say that they know not what to do, and do nothing; who even postpone the question of freedom to the question of free-trade, and quietly read the prices-current along with the latest advices from Mexico, after dinner, and, it may be, fall asleep over them both. What is the price-current of an honest man and patriot to-day? They hesitate, and they regret, and sometimes they petition; but they do nothing in earnest and with effect. They will wait, well disposed, for others to remedy the evil, that they may no longer have it to regret. At most, they give only a cheap vote, and a feeble countenance and God-speed, to the right, as it goes by them. There are nine hundred and ninety-nine patrons of virtue to one virtuous man. But it is easier to deal with the real possessor of a thing than with the temporary guardian of it.

All voting is a sort of gaming, like checkers or backgammon, with a slight moral tinge to it, a playing with right and wrong, with moral questions; and betting naturally accompanies it. The character of the voters is not staked. I cast my vote, perchance, as I think right; but I am not vitally concerned that that right should prevail. I am willing to leave it to the majority. Its obligation, therefore, never exceeds that of expediency. Even voting *for the right* is *doing* nothing for it. It is only expressing to men feebly your desire that it should prevail. A wise man will not leave the right to the mercy of chance, nor wish it to prevail through the power of the majority. There is but little virtue in the action of masses of men. When the majority shall at length vote for the abolition of slavery, it will be because they are indifferent to slavery, or because there is but little slavery left to be abolished by their vote. *They* will then be the only slaves. Only *his* vote can hasten the abolition of slavery who asserts his own freedom by his vote.

I hear of a convention to be held at Baltimore, or elsewhere, for the selection of a candidate for the Presidency, made up chiefly of editors, and men who are politicians by profession; but I think, what is it to any independent, intelligent, and respectable man what decision they may come to? Shall we not have the advantage of his wisdom and honesty, nevertheless? Can we not count upon some independent votes? Are there not many individuals in the country who do not attend conventions? But no: I find that the respectable man, so called, has immediately drifted from his position, and despairs of his country, when his country has more reason to despair of him. He forthwith adopts one of the candidates thus selected as the only *available* one, thus proving that he is himself *available* for any purposes of the demagogue. His vote is of no more worth than that of any unprincipled foreigner or hireling native, who may have been bought. O for a man who is a *man*, and, as my neighbor says, has a bone in his back which you cannot pass your hand through! Our statistics are at fault: the population has been returned too large. How many *men* are there to a square thousand miles in this country? Hardly one. Does not America offer any inducement for men to settle here? The American has dwindled into an Odd Fellow,[5]—one who may be known by the development of his organ of gregariousness, and a manifest lack of intellect and cheerful self-reliance; whose first and chief concern, on coming into the world, is to see that the Almshouses are in good repair; and, before yet he has lawfully donned the virile garb, to collect a fund for the support of the widows and orphans that may be; who, in short, ventures to live only by the aid of the Mutual Insurance company, which has promised to bury him decently.

It is not a man's duty, as a matter of course, to devote himself to the eradication of any, even the most enormous wrong; he may still properly have other concerns to engage him; but it is his duty, at least, to wash his hands of it, and, if he gives it no thought longer, not to give it practically his support. If I devote myself to other pursuits and contemplations, I must first see, at least, that I do not pursue them sitting upon another man's shoulders. I must get off him first, that he may pursue his contemplations too. See what gross inconsistency is tolerated. I have heard some of my townsmen say, "I should like to have them order me out to help put down an insurrection of the slaves, or to march to Mexico;—see if I would go"; and yet these very men have each, directly by their allegiance, and so indirectly, at least, by their money, furnished a substitute. The soldier is applauded who refuses to serve in an unjust war by those who do not refuse to sustain the unjust government which makes the war; is applauded by those whose own act and authority he disregards and sets at naught; as if the State were

[5] *Odd Fellow:* A member of a fraternal organization originally founded in England in the seventeenth century. The group is a benevolent, helpful, charitable society but was not (Thoreau implies) politically effective or intellectually engaged.

penitent to that degree that it hired one to scourge it while it sinned, but not to that degree that it left off sinning for a moment. Thus, under the name of Order and Civil Government, we are all made at last to pay homage to and support our own meanness. After the first blush of sin comes its indifference; and from immoral it becomes, as it were, *un*moral, and not quite unnecessary to that life which we have made.

The broadest and most prevalent error requires the most disinterested virtue to sustain it. The slight reproach to which the virtue of patriotism is commonly liable, the noble are most likely to incur. Those who, while they disapprove of the character and measures of a government, yield to it their allegiance and support, are undoubtedly its most conscientious supporters, and so frequently the most serious obstacles to reform. Some are petitioning the State to dissolve the Union, to disregard the requisitions of the President. Why do they not dissolve it themselves,—the union between themselves and the State,—and refuse to pay their quota into its treasury? Do not they stand in the same relation to the State, that the State does to the Union? And have not the same reasons prevented the State from resisting the Union, which have prevented them from resisting the State?

How can a man be satisfied to entertain an opinion merely, and enjoy *it?* Is 15
there any enjoyment in it, if his opinion is that he is aggrieved? If you are cheated out of a single dollar by your neighbor, you do not rest satisfied with knowing that you are cheated, or with saying that you are cheated, or even with petitioning him to pay you your due; but you take effectual steps at once to obtain the full amount, and see that you are never cheated again. Action from principle, the perception and the performance of right, changes things and relations; it is essentially revolutionary, and does not consist wholly with anything which was. It not only divides states and churches, it divides families; ay, it divides the *individual*, separating the diabolical in him from the divine.

Unjust laws exist: shall we be content to obey them, or shall we endeavor to amend them, and obey them until we have succeeded, or shall we transgress them at once? Men generally, under such a government as this, think that they ought to wait until they have persuaded the majority to alter them. They think that, if they should resist, the remedy would be worse than the evil. But it is the fault of the government itself that the remedy *is* worse than the evil. *It* makes it worse. Why is it not more apt to anticipate and provide for reform? Why does it not cherish its wise minority? Why does it cry and resist before it is hurt? Why does it not encourage its citizens to be on the alert to point out its faults, and *do* better than it would have them? Why does it always crucify Christ, and excommunicate Copernicus and Luther,[6] and pronounce Washington and Franklin rebels?

One would think, that a deliberate and practical denial of its authority was the only offence never contemplated by government; else, why has it not

[6]*Copernicus and Luther:* Both Nicolaus Copernicus (1473–1543), who popularized the scientific belief that the earth revolves around the sun, and Martin Luther (1483–1546), who set in motion the beliefs that split Roman Catholicism from northern European Protestantism, were excommunicated from the Catholic Church.

assigned its definite, its suitable and proportionate penalty? If a man who has no property refuses but once to earn nine shillings for the State, he is put in prison for a period unlimited by any law that I know, and determined only by the discretion of those who placed him there; but if he should steal ninety times nine shillings from the State, he is soon permitted to go at large again.

If the injustice is part of the necessary friction of the machine of government, let it go, let it go: perchance it will wear smooth,—certainly the machine will wear out. If the injustice has a spring, or a pulley, or a rope, or a crank, exclusively for itself, then perhaps you may consider whether the remedy will not be worse than the evil; but if it is of such a nature that it requires you to be the agent of injustice to another, then, I say, break the law. Let your life be a counter friction to stop the machine. What I have to do is to see, at any rate, that I do not lend myself to the wrong which I condemn.

As for adopting the ways which the State has provided for remedying the evil, I know not of such ways. They take too much time, and a man's life will be gone. I have other affairs to attend to. I came into this world, not chiefly to make this a good place to live in, but to live in it, be it good or bad. A man has not everything to do, but something; and because he cannot do *everything*, it is not necessary that he should do *something* wrong. It is not my business to be petitioning the Governor or the Legislature any more than it is theirs to petition me; and, if they should not hear my petition, what should I do then? But in this case the State has provided no way: its very Constitution is the evil. This may seem to be harsh and stubborn and unconciliatory; but it is to treat with the utmost kindness and consideration the only spirit that can appreciate or deserves it. So is all change for the better, like birth and death, which convulse the body.

I do not hesitate to say, that those who call themselves Abolitionists should 20
at once effectually withdraw their support, both in person and property, from the government of Massachusetts, and not wait till they constitute a majority of one, before they suffer the right to prevail through them. I think that it is enough if they have God on their side, without waiting for that other one. Moreover, any man more right than his neighbors constitutes a majority of one already.

I meet this American government, or its representative, the State government, directly, and face to face, once a year—no more—in the person of its tax-gatherer; this is the only mode in which a man situated as I am necessarily meets it; and it then says distinctly, Recognize me; and the simplest, the most effectual, and, in the present posture of affairs, the indispensablest mode of treating with it on this head, of expressing your little satisfaction with and love for it, is to deny it then. My civil neighbor, the tax-gatherer, is the very man I have to deal with,—for it is, after all, with men and not with parchment that I quarrel,—and he has voluntarily chosen to be an agent of the government. How shall he ever know well what he is and does as an officer of the government, or as a man, until he is obliged to consider whether he shall treat me, his neighbor, for whom he has respect, as a neighbor and well-disposed man, or as a maniac and disturber of the peace, and see if he can get over this obstruction to his neighborliness without a ruder and more impetuous thought or speech corresponding with his action. I know this well, that if one thousand, if one hundred, if ten men whom I could name,—if ten *honest* men only,—ay, if *one* HONEST man, in this State of Massachusetts, *ceasing to hold slaves*, were actually to withdraw from this copartnership, and be locked up in the county jail therefor, it would be the abolition of slavery in America. For it matters not how small the beginning may seem to be: what is once well done is done forever. But we love better to talk about it: that we say is our mission. Reform keeps many scores of newspapers in its service, but not one man. If my esteemed neighbor, the State's ambassador, who will devote his days to the settlement of the question of human rights in the Council Chamber, instead of being threatened with the prisons of Carolina, were to sit down the prisoner of Massachusetts, that State which is so anxious to foist the sin of slavery upon her sister,—though at present she can discover only an act of inhospitality to be the ground of a quarrel with her,—the Legislature would not wholly waive the subject the following winter.

Under a government which imprisons any unjustly, the true place for a just man is also a prison. The proper place to-day, the only place which Massachusetts has provided for her freer and less desponding spirits, is in her prisons, to be put out and locked out of the State by her own act, as they have already put themselves out by their principles. It is there that the fugitive slave, and the Mexican prisoner on parole, and the Indian come to plead the wrongs of his race, should find them; on that separate, but more free and honorable ground, where the State places those who are not *with* her, but *against* her,—the only house in a slave State in which a free man can abide with honor. If any think that their influence would be lost there, and their voices no longer afflict the ear of the State, that they would not be as an enemy within its walls, they do not know by how much truth is stronger than error, nor how much more eloquently and effectively he can combat injustice who has experienced a little in his own person. Cast your whole vote, not a strip of paper merely, but your whole influence. A minority is powerless while it conforms to the majority; it is not even a minority then; but it is irresistible when it clogs by its whole weight. If the alternative is to keep all just men in prison, or give up war and slavery, the State will not hesitate which to choose. If a thousand men were not to pay their tax-bills this year, that would not be a violent and bloody measure, as it would be to pay them, and enable the State to commit violence and shed innocent blood. This is, in fact, the definition of a peaceable revolution, if any such is possible. If the tax-gatherer, or any other public officer, asks me, as one has done, "But what shall I do?" my answer is, "If you really wish to do anything, resign your office." When the subject has refused allegiance, and the officer has resigned his office, then the revolution is accomplished. But even suppose blood should flow. Is there not a sort of blood shed when the conscience is wounded? Through this wound a man's real manhood and immortality flow out, and he bleeds to an everlasting death. I see this blood flowing now.

I have contemplated the imprisonment of the offender, rather than the seizure of his goods,—though both will serve the same purpose,—because they who assert the purest right, and consequently are most dangerous to a corrupt State, commonly have not spent much time in accumulating property. To such the State renders comparatively small service, and a slight tax is wont to appear exorbitant, particularly if they are obliged to earn it by special labor with their hands. If there were one who lived wholly without the use of money, the State itself would hesitate to demand it of him. But the rich man,—not to make any invidious comparison,—is always sold to the institution which makes him rich. Absolutely speaking, the more money, the less virtue; for money comes between a man and his objects, and obtains them for him; and it was certainly no great virtue to obtain it. It puts to rest many questions which he would otherwise be taxed to answer; while the only new question which it puts is the hard but superfluous one, how to spend it. Thus his moral ground is taken from under his feet. The opportunities of living are diminished in proportion as what are called the "means" are increased. The best thing a man can do for his culture when he is rich is to endeavor to carry out those schemes which he entertained when he was poor. Christ answered the Herodians according to their condition. "Show me the tribute-money," said he;—and one took a penny out of his pocket;—if you use money which has the image of Cæsar on it, and which he has made current and valuable, that is, *if you are men of the State*, and gladly enjoy the advantages of Cæsar's government, then pay him back some of his own when he demands it; "Render therefore to Cæsar that which is Cæsar's, and to God those things which are God's,"—leaving them no wiser than before as to which was which; for they did not wish to know.

When I converse with the freest of my neighbors, I perceive that, whatever they may say about the magnitude and seriousness of the question, and their regard for the public tranquillity, the long and the short of the matter is, that they cannot spare the protection of the existing government, and they dread the consequences to their property and families of disobedience to it. For my own part, I should not like to think that I ever rely on the protection of the State. But, if I deny the authority of the State when it presents its tax-bill, it will soon take and waste all my property, and so harass me and my children without end. This is hard. This makes it impossible for a man to live honestly, and at the same time comfortably, in outward respects. It will not be worth the while to accumulate property; that would be sure to go again. You must hire or squat somewhere, and raise but a small crop, and eat that soon. You must live within yourself, and depend upon yourself always tucked up and ready for a start, and not have many affairs. A man may grow rich in Turkey even, if he will be in all respects a good subject of the Turkish government. Confucius said: "If a state is governed by the principles of reason, poverty and misery are subjects of shame; if a state is not governed by the principles of reason, riches and honors are the subjects of shame." No: until I want the protection of Massachusetts to be extended to me in some distant Southern port, where my liberty is endangered, or until I am bent solely on building up an estate at home by peaceful enterprise, I can afford to refuse allegiance to Massachusetts, and her right to my property and life. It costs me less in every sense to incur the penalty of disobedience to the State, than it would to obey. I should feel as if I were worth less in that case.

25 Some years ago, the State met me in behalf of the Church, and commanded me to pay a certain sum toward the support of a clergyman whose preaching my father attended, but never I myself. "Pay," it said, "or be locked up in the jail."

I declined to pay. But, unfortunately, another man saw fit to pay it. I did not see why the schoolmaster should be taxed to support the priest, and not the priest the schoolmaster; for I was not the State's schoolmaster, but I supported myself by voluntary subscription. I did not see why the lyceum[7] should not present its tax-bill, and have the State to back its demand, as well as the Church. However, at the request of the selectmen, I condescended to make some such statement as this in writing:—"Know all men by these presents, that I, Henry Thoreau, do not wish to be regarded as a member of any incorporated society which I have not joined." This I gave to the town clerk; and he has it. The State, having thus learned that I did not wish to be regarded as a member of that church, has never made a like demand on me since; though it said that it must adhere to its original presumption that time. If I had known how to name them, I should then have signed off in detail from all the societies which I never signed on to; but I did not know where to find a complete list.

I have paid no poll-tax for six years. I was put into a jail once on this account, for one night; and, as I stood considering the walls of solid stone, two or three feet thick, the door of wood and iron, a foot thick, and the iron grating which strained the light, I could not help being struck with the foolishness of that institution which treated me as if I were mere flesh and blood and bones, to be locked up. I wondered that it should have concluded at length that this was the best use it could put me to, and had never thought to avail itself of my services in some way. I saw that, if there was a wall of stone between me and my townsmen, there was a still more difficult one to climb or break through, before they could get to be as free as I was. I did not for a moment feel confined, and the walls seemed a great waste of stone and mortar. I felt as if I alone of all my townsmen had paid my tax. They plainly did not know how to treat me, but behaved like persons who are underbred. In every threat and in every compliment there was a blunder; for they thought that my chief desire was to stand the other side of that stone wall. I could not but smile to see how industriously they locked the door on my meditations, which followed them out again without let or hindrance, and *they* were really all that was dangerous. As they could not reach me, they had resolved to punish my body; just as boys, if they cannot come at some person against whom they have a spite, will abuse his dog. I saw that the State was half-witted, that it was timid as a lone woman with her silver spoons, and that it did not know its friends from its foes, and I lost all my remaining respect for it, and pitied it.

Thus the State never intentionally confronts a man's sense, intellectual or moral, but only his body, his senses. It is not armed with superior wit or honesty, but with superior physical strength. I was not born to be forced. I will breathe after my own fashion. Let us see who is the strongest. What force has a multitude? They only can force me who obey a higher law than I. They force me to become like themselves. I do not hear of *men* being *forced* to live this way or that by masses of men. What sort of life were that to live? When I meet a government

[7]*lyceum:* A public lecture hall. In nineteenth-century New England, thinkers like Thoreau disseminated their beliefs through public lectures at lyceums.

which says to me, "Your money or your life," why should I be in haste to give it my money? It may be in a great strait, and not know what to do: I cannot help that. It must help itself; do as I do. It is not worth the while to snivel about it. I am not responsible for the successful working of the machinery of society. I am not the son of the engineer. I perceive that, when an acorn and a chestnut fall side by side, the one does not remain inert to make way for the other, but both obey their own laws, and spring and grow and flourish as best they can, till one, perchance, overshadows and destroys the other. If a plant cannot live according to its nature, it dies; and so a man.

The night in prison was novel and interesting enough. The prisoners in their shirt-sleeves were enjoying a chat and the evening air in the doorway, when I entered. But the jailer said, "Come, boys, it is time to lock up"; and so they dispersed, and I heard the sound of their steps returning into the hollow apartments. My room-mate was introduced to me by the jailer, as "a first-rate fellow and a clever man." When the door was locked, he showed me where to hang my hat, and how he managed matters there. The rooms were whitewashed once a month; and this one, at least, was the whitest, most simply furnished, and probably the neatest apartment in the town. He naturally wanted to know where I came from, and what brought me there; and, when I had told him, I asked him in my turn how he came there, presuming him to be an honest man, of course; and, as the world goes, I believe he was. "Why," said he, "they accuse me of burning a barn; but I never did it." As near as I could discover, he had probably gone to bed in a barn when drunk, and smoked his pipe there; and so a barn was burnt. He had the reputation of being a clever man, had been there some three months waiting for his trial to come on, and would have to wait as much longer; but he was quite domesticated and contented, since he got his board for nothing, and thought that he was well treated.

He occupied one window, and I the other; and I saw, that, if one stayed there long, his principal business would be to look out the window. I had soon read all the tracts that were left there, and examined where former prisoners had broken out, and where a grate had been sawed off, and heard the history of the various occupants of that room; for I found that even here there was a history and a gossip which never circulated beyond the walls of the jail. Probably this is the only house in the town where verses are composed, which are afterward printed in a circular form, but not published. I was shown quite a long list of verses which were composed by some young men who had been detected in an attempt to escape, who avenged themselves by singing them.

I pumped my fellow-prisoner as dry as I could, for fear I should never see him again; but at length he showed me which was my bed, and left me to blow out the lamp.

It was like travelling into a far country, such as I had never expected to behold, to lie there for one night. It seemed to me that I never had heard the town-clock strike before, nor the evening sounds of the village; for we slept with the windows open, which were inside the grating. It was to see my native village in the light of the Middle Ages, and our Concord was turned into a Rhine stream, and visions of knights and castles passed before me. They were the voices of old burghers that I heard in the streets. I was an involuntary spectator and auditor of whatever was done and said in the kitchen of the adjacent village-inn,—a wholly new and rare experience to me. It was a closer view of my native town. I was fairly inside of it. I never had seen its institutions before. This is one of its peculiar institutions; for it is a shire town. I began to comprehend what its inhabitants were about.

In the morning, our breakfasts were put through the hole in the door, in small oblong-square tin pans, made to fit, and holding a pint of chocolate, with brown bread, and an iron spoon. When they called for the vessels again, I was green enough to return what bread I had left; but my comrade seized it, and said that I should lay that up for lunch or dinner. Soon after he was let out to work at haying in a neighboring field, whither he went every day, and would not be back till noon; so he bade me good-day, saying that he doubted if he should see me again.

When I came out of prison,—for some one interfered, and paid that tax,—I did not perceive that great changes had taken place on the common, such as he observed who went in a youth, and emerged a tottering and gray-headed man; and yet a change had to my eyes come over the scene,—the town, and State, and country,—greater than any that mere time could effect. I saw yet more distinctly the State in which I lived. I saw to what extent the people among whom I lived could be trusted as good neighbors and friends; that their friendship was for summer weather only; that they did not greatly propose to do right; that they were a distinct race from me by their prejudices and superstitions, as the Chinamen and Malays are; that, in their sacrifices to humanity, they ran no risks, not even to their property; that, after all, they were not so noble but they treated the thief as he had treated them, and hoped, by a certain outward observance and a few prayers, and by walking in a particular straight though useless path from time to time, to save their souls. This may be to judge my neighbors harshly; for I believe that many of them are not aware that they have such an institution as the jail in their village.

It was formerly the custom in our village, when a poor debtor came out of jail, for his acquaintances to salute him, looking through their fingers, which were crossed to represent the grating of a jail window, "How do ye do?" My neighbors did not thus salute me, but first looked at me, and then at one another, as if I had returned from a long journey. I was put into jail as I was going to the shoemaker's to get a shoe which was mended. When I was let out the next morning, I proceeded to finish my errand, and having put on my mended shoe, joined a huckleberry party, who were impatient to put themselves under my conduct; and in half an hour,—for the horse was soon tackled,—was in the midst of a huckleberry field, on one of our highest hills, two miles off, and then the State was nowhere to be seen.

This is the whole history of "My Prisons."

I have never declined paying the highway tax, because I am as desirous of being a good neighbor as I am of being a bad subject; and, as for supporting schools, I am doing my part to educate my fellow-countrymen now. It is for no particular item in the tax-bill that I refuse to pay it. I simply wish to refuse allegiance to the State, to withdraw and stand aloof from it effectually. I do not care to trace the course of my dollar, if I could, till it buys a man or a musket to shoot one with,—the dollar is innocent,—but I am concerned to trace the effects of my allegiance. In fact, I quietly declare war with the State, after my fashion, though I will still make what use and get what advantage of her I can, as is usual in such cases.

If others pay the tax which is demanded of me, from a sympathy with the State, they do but what they have already done in their own case, or rather they abet injustice to a greater extent than the State requires. If they pay the tax from a mistaken interest in the individual taxed, to save his property, or prevent his going to jail, it is because they have not considered wisely how far they let their private feelings interfere with the public good.

30 This, then, is my position at present. But one cannot be too much on his guard in such a case, lest his action be biased by obstinacy, or an undue regard for the opinions of men. Let him see that he does only what belongs to himself and to the hour.

I think sometimes, Why, this people mean well; they are only ignorant; they would do better if they knew how: why give your neighbors this pain to treat you as they are not inclined to? But I think again, this is no reason why I should do as they do, or permit others to suffer much greater pain of a different kind. Again, I sometimes say to myself, When many millions of men, without heat, without ill will, without personal feeling of any kind, demand of you a few shillings only, without the possibility, such is their constitution, of retracting or altering their present demand, and without the possibility, on your side, of appeal to any other millions, why expose yourself to this overwhelming brute force? You do not resist cold and hunger, the winds and the waves, thus obstinately; you quietly submit to a thousand similar necessities. You do not put your head into the fire. But just in proportion as I regard this as not wholly a brute force, but partly a human force, and consider that I have relations to those millions as to so many millions of men, and not of mere brute or inanimate things, I see that appeal is possible, first and instantaneously, from them to the Maker of them, and, secondly, from them to themselves. But, if I put my head deliberately into the fire, there is no appeal to fire or to the Maker of fire, and I have only myself to blame. If I could convince myself that I have any right to be satisfied with men as they are, and to treat them accordingly, and not according, in some respects, to my requisitions and expectations of what they and I ought to be, then, like a good Mussulman[8] and fatalist, I should endeavor to be satisfied with things as they are, and say it is the will of God. And, above all, there is this difference between resisting this and a purely brute or natural force, that I can resist this with some effect; but I cannot expect, like Orpheus,[9] to change the nature of the rocks and trees and beasts.

I do not wish to quarrel with any man or nation. I do not wish to split hairs, to make fine distinctions, or set myself up as better than my neighbors. I seek

[8]*Mussulman:* A Muslim.

[9]*Orpheus:* The legendary Greek figure associated with the transformative power of the arts, especially music. In Ovid's *Metamorphoses*, Dionysus's followers throw sticks and stones at Orpheus, but his music is so beautiful that the missiles do not hit him.

rather, I may say, even an excuse for conforming to the laws of the land. I am but too ready to conform to them. Indeed, I have reason to suspect myself on this head; and each year, as the tax-gatherer comes round, I find myself disposed to review the acts and position of the general and State governments, and the spirit of the people, to discover a pretext for conformity.

"We must affect our country as our parents;
And if at any time we alienate
Our love or industry from doing it honor,
We must respect effects and teach the soul
Matter of conscience and religion,
And not desire of rule or benefit."

I believe that the State will soon be able to take all my work of this sort out of my hands, and then I shall be no better a patriot than my fellow-countrymen. Seen from a lower point of view, the Constitution, with all its faults, is very good; the law and the courts are very respectable; even this State and this American government are, in many respects, very admirable and rare things, to be thankful for, such as a great many have described them; but seen from a point of view a little higher, they are what I have described them; seen from a higher still, and the highest, who shall say what they are, or that they are worth looking at or thinking of at all?

However, the government does not concern me much, and I shall bestow the fewest possible thoughts on it. It is not many moments that I live under a government, even in this world. If a man is thought-free, fancy-free, imagination-free, that which *is not* never for a long time appearing *to be* to him, unwise rulers or reformers cannot fatally interrupt him.

I know that most men think differently from myself; but those whose lives are by profession devoted to the study of these or kindred subjects, content me as little as any. Statesmen and legislators, standing so completely within the institution, never distinctly and nakedly behold it. They speak of moving society, but have no resting-place without it. They may be men of a certain experience and discrimination, and have no doubt invented ingenious and even useful systems, for which we sincerely thank them; but all their wit and usefulness lie within certain not very wide limits. They are wont to forget that the world is not governed by policy and expediency. Webster never goes behind government, and so cannot speak with authority about it. His words are wisdom to those legislators who contemplate no essential reform in the existing government; but for thinkers, and those who legislate for all time, he never once glances at the subject. I know of those whose serene and wise speculations on this theme would soon reveal the limits of his mind's range and hospitality. Yet, compared with the cheap professions of most reformers, and the still cheaper wisdom and eloquence of politicians in general, his are almost the only sensible and valuable words; and we thank Heaven for him. Comparatively, he is always strong, original, and, above all, practical. Still his quality is not wisdom, but prudence. The lawyer's truth is not Truth, but consistency, or a consistent expediency. Truth is always in harmony with herself, and is not concerned chiefly to reveal the justice that may consist with wrong-doing. He well deserves to be called, as he has been called, the Defender of the Constitution. There are really no blows to be given by him but defensive ones. He is not a leader, but a follower. His leaders are the men of '87. "I have never made an effort," he says, "and never propose to make an effort; I have never countenanced an effort, and never mean to countenance an effort, to disturb the arrangement as originally made, by which the various States came into the Union." Still thinking of the sanction which the Constitution gives to slavery, he says, "Because it was a part of the original compact,—let it stand." Notwithstanding his special acuteness and ability, he is unable to take a fact out of its merely political relations, and behold it as it lies absolutely to be disposed of by the intellect,—what, for instance, it behooves a man to do here in America to-day with regard to slavery,—but ventures, or is driven, to make some such desperate answer as the following, while professing to speak absolutely, and as a private man,—from which what new and singular code of social duties might be inferred? "The manner," says he, "in which the governments of those States where slavery exists are to regulate it, is for their own consideration, under their responsibility to their constituents, to the general laws of propriety, humanity, and justice, and to God. Associations formed elsewhere, springing from a feeling of humanity, or any other cause, have nothing whatever to do with it. They have never received any encouragement from me, and they never will."*

They who know of no purer sources of truth, who have traced up its stream 35
no higher, stand, and wisely stand, by the Bible and the Constitution, and drink at it there with reverence and humility; but they who behold where it comes trickling into this lake or that pool, gird up their loins once more, and continue their pilgrimage toward its fountain-head.

No man with a genius for legislation has appeared in America. They are rare in the history of the world. There are orators, politicians, and eloquent men, by the thousand; but the speaker has not yet opened his mouth to speak, who is capable of settling the much-vexed questions of the day. We love eloquence for its own sake, and not for any truth which it may utter, or any heroism it may inspire. Our legislators have not yet learned the comparative value of free-trade and of freedom, of union, and of rectitude, to a nation. They have no genius or talent for comparatively humble questions of taxation and finance, commerce and manufactures and agriculture. If we were left solely to the wordy wit of legislators in Congress for our guidance, uncorrected by the seasonable experience and the effectual complaints of the people, America would not long retain her rank among the nations. For eighteen hundred years, though perchance I have no right to say it, the New Testament has been written; yet where is the legislator who has wisdom and practical talent enough to avail himself of the light which it sheds on the science of legislation?

The authority of government, even such as I am willing to submit to,—for I will cheerfully obey those who know and can do better than I, and in many things even those who neither know nor can do so well,—is still an impure

*These extracts have been inserted since the Lecture was read.

one: to be strictly just, it must have the sanction and consent of the governed. It can have no pure right over my person and property but what I concede to it. The progress from an absolute to a limited monarchy, from a limited monarchy to a democracy, is a progress toward a true respect for the individual. Even the Chinese philosopher was wise enough to regard the individual as the basis of the empire. Is a democracy, such as we know it, the last improvement possible in government? Is it not possible to take a step further towards recognizing and organizing the rights of man? There will never be a really free and enlightened State, until the State comes to recognize the individual as a higher and independent power, from which all its own power and authority are derived, and treats him accordingly. I please myself with imagining a State at last which can afford to be just to all men, and to treat the individual with respect as a neighbor; which even would not think it inconsistent with its own repose, if a few were to live aloof from it, not meddling with it, nor embraced by it, who fulfilled all the duties of neighbors and fellow-men. A State which bore this kind of fruit, and suffered it to drop off as fast as it ripened, would prepare the way for a still more perfect and glorious State, which also I have imagined, but not yet anywhere seen.

(1850)

Questions for Discussion and Writing

Close Reading

1. Carefully summarize Thoreau's critique of his government.
2. Thoreau's account of his experience in prison is somewhat mystical, unlike most of the essay. Look closely at this section again; what kind of insight does he achieve in prison?
3. Find examples of Thoreau's playfulness with language, such as his ability to redefine words for his own purpose. How does this ability support the themes of the essay?

Critical and Creative Reading

4. Should citizens have the right to pay taxes based on what they think is important rather than paying a certain amount of money that the government allocates to causes that it finds important?
5. Although Thoreau's essay predates the Civil War by only a decade, in some ways he anticipates this war. What are the implications of his contention "if *one* HONEST man, in this State of Massachusetts, *ceasing to hold slaves*, were actually to withdraw from this copartnership [of paying taxes to the government], and be locked up in the county jail therefor, it would be the abolition of slavery in America"? Is Thoreau suggesting that armed revolution is not necessary to right social wrongs?
6. If you had to describe Thoreau in one word based on your reading of this essay, would you choose *idealistic*, *cynical*, *radical*, *anti-authoritarian*, or something else? Support your choice with an interpretation of his essay.

CONNECTIONS TO OTHER READINGS

7. What would Henry David Thoreau have done if he were a character living in the world of Shirley Jackson's short story "The Lottery"? Would his actions have changed the practice of the lottery?
8. Compare the view of war in "Civil Disobedience" to the view of war in Wilfred Owen's poem "Dulce et Decorum Est," Alfred, Lord Tennyson's poem "The Charge of the Light Brigade," and/or William Dean Howells's short story "Editha."
9. Compare Thoreau's rebellious actions against his government to the behavior of either Daru in Albert Camus' "The Guest" or George Orwell in his essay "Shooting an Elephant" as a way of answering this question: what are the moral responsibilities of someone to whom society has given authority?

George Orwell

Shooting an Elephant

Eric Arthur Blair (1903–1950), who wrote under the pseudonym George Orwell, was one of the most prolific British writers of his time. Orwell spent considerable time in foreign countries–including India, where he was born, and Burma (now Myanmar), where the following essay takes place–and these experiences undoubtedly shaped both his politics and his literary imagination; much of Orwell's writing is sociopolitical, reflecting his strong humanist values. Although Orwell is perhaps best known for his satirical, antitotalitarian novels *Animal Farm* and *1984,* many critics claim that his essays are especially worthy of attention. Orwell typically uses clear, plain language and a straightforward tone in his essays, even while his content is highly personal. As you read, notice Orwell's tone and style, which sometimes borders on detached or clinical.

In Moulmein, in lower Burma,[1] I was hated by large numbers of people—the only time in my life that I have been important enough for this to happen to me. I was subdivisional police officer of the town, and in an aimless, petty kind of way anti-European feeling was very bitter. No one had the guts to raise a riot, but if a European woman went through the bazaars alone somebody would probably spit betel juice over her dress. As a police officer I was an obvious target and was baited whenever it seemed safe to do so. When a nimble Burman tripped me up on the football field and the referee (another Burman) looked the other way, the crowd yelled with hideous laughter. This happened

[1]*Lower Burma:* A British colony until 1948. Today this Southeast Asian country is called Myanmar.

more than once. In the end the sneering yellow faces of young men that met me everywhere, the insults hooted after me when I was at a safe distance, got badly on my nerves. The young Buddhist priests were the worst of all. There were several thousands of them in the town and none of them seemed to have anything to do except stand on street corners and jeer at Europeans.

All this was perplexing and upsetting. For at that time I had already made up my mind that imperialism was an evil thing and the sooner I chucked up my job and got out of it the better. Theoretically—and secretly, of course—I was all for the Burmese and all against their oppressors, the British. As for the job I was doing, I hated it more bitterly than I can perhaps make clear. In a job like that you see the dirty work of Empire at close quarters. The wretched prisoners huddling in the stinking cages of the lock-ups, the gray, cowed faces of the long-term convicts, the scarred buttocks of the men who had been flogged with bamboos—all these oppressed me with an intolerable sense of guilt. But I could get nothing into perspective. I was young and ill educated and I had had to think out my problems in the utter silence that is imposed on every Englishman in the East. I did not even know that the British Empire is dying, still less did I know that it is a great deal better than the younger empires that are going to supplant it. All I knew was that I was stuck between my hatred of the empire I served and my rage against the evil-spirited little beasts who tried to make my job impossible. With one part of my mind I thought of the British Raj[2] as an unbreakable tyranny, as something clamped down, *in saecula saeculorum*,[3] upon the will of prostrate peoples; with another part I thought that the greatest joy in the world would be to drive a bayonet into a Buddhist priest's guts. Feelings like these are the normal by-products of imperialism; ask any Anglo-Indian official, if you can catch him off duty.

One day something happened which in a roundabout way was enlightening. It was a tiny incident in itself; but it gave me a better glimpse than I had had before of the real nature of imperialism—the real motives for which despotic governments act. Early one morning the sub-inspector at a police station the other end of town rang me up on the 'phone and said that an elephant was ravaging the bazaar. Would I please come and do something about it? I did not know what I could do, but I wanted to see what was happening and I got on to a pony and started out. I took my rifle, an old .44 Winchester and much too small to kill an elephant, but I thought the noise might be useful *in terrorem*. Various Burmans stopped me on the way and told me about the elephant's doings. It was not, of course, a wild elephant, but a tame one which had gone "must." It had been chained up, as tame elephants always are when their attack of "must" is due, but on the previous night it had broken its chain and escaped. Its mahout, the only person who could manage it when it was in that state, had set out in pursuit, but had taken the wrong direction and was now twelve hours' journey away, and in the morning the elephant had suddenly reappeared in the town. The Burmese population had no weapons and were quite helpless against it. It had already destroyed somebody's bamboo hut, killed a cow and raided some fruit-stalls and devoured the stock; also it had met the

[2]*British Raj:* The British rule of the Indian subcontinent (India, Pakistan, Bangladesh, and Burma/Myanmar) from the nineteenth century through 1948.

[3]*in saecula saeculorum:* For ages of ages (Latin); forever.

municipal rubbish van and, when the driver jumped out and took to his heels, had turned the van over and inflicted violences upon it.

The Burmese sub-inspector and some Indian constables were waiting for me in the quarter where the elephant had been seen. It was a very poor quarter, a labyrinth of squalid bamboo huts, thatched with palm-leaf, winding all over a steep hillside. I remember that it was a cloudy, stuffy morning at the beginning of the rains. We began questioning the people as to where the elephant had gone and, as usual, failed to get any definite information. That is invariably the case in the East; a story always sounds clear enough at a distance, but the nearer you get to the scene of events the vaguer it becomes. Some of the people said that the elephant had gone in one direction, some said that he had gone in another, some professed not even to have heard of any elephant. I had almost made up my mind that the whole story was a pack of lies, when we heard yells a little distance away. There was a loud, scandalized cry of "Go away, child! Go away this instant!" and an old woman with a switch in her hand came round the corner of a hut, violently shooing away a crowd of naked children. Some more women followed, clicking their tongues and exclaiming; evidently there was something that the children ought not to have seen. I rounded the hut and saw a man's dead body sprawling in the mud. He was an Indian, a black Dravidian coolie,[4] almost naked, and he could not have been dead many minutes. The people said that the elephant had come suddenly upon him round the corner of the hut, caught him with its trunk, put its foot on his back and ground him into the earth. This was the rainy season and the ground was soft, and his face had scored a trench a foot deep and a couple of yards long. He was lying on his belly with arms crucified and head sharply twisted to one side. His face was coated with mud, the eyes wide open, the teeth bared and grinning with an expression of unendurable agony. (Never tell me, by the way, that the dead look peaceful. Most of the corpses I have seen looked devilish.) The friction of the great beast's foot had stripped the skin from his back as neatly as one skins a rabbit. As soon as I saw the dead man I sent an orderly to a friend's house nearby to borrow an elephant rifle. I had already sent back the pony, not wanting it to go mad with fright and throw me if it smelt the elephant.

5 The orderly came back in a few minutes with a rifle and five cartridges, and meanwhile some Burmans had arrived and told us that the elephant was in the paddy fields below, only a few hundred yards away. As I started forward practically the whole population of the quarter flocked out of the houses and followed me. They had seen the rifle and were all shouting excitedly that I was going to shoot the elephant. They had not shown much interest in the elephant when he was merely ravaging their homes, but it was different now that he was going to be shot. It was a bit of fun to them, and it would be to an English crowd; besides they wanted the meat. It made me vaguely uneasy. I had no intention of shooting the elephant—I had merely sent for the rifle to defend myself if necessary—and it is always unnerving to have a crowd following you. I marched down the hill, looking and feeling a fool, with the rifle over my shoulder and an ever-growing

[4]*Dravidian coolie: Dravidian* refers to people who speak the Dravidian languages (such as Tamil) in southern India and Sri Lanka. A *coolie* is a manual laborer, usually from a British colony: the term in its current usage is derogatory.

army of people jostling at my heels. At the bottom, when you got away from the huts, there was a metalled road and beyond that a miry waste of paddy fields a thousand yards across, not yet ploughed but soggy from the first rains and dotted with coarse grass. The elephant was standing eight yards from the road, his left side toward us. He took not the slightest notice of the crowd's approach. He was tearing up bunches of grass, beating them against his knees to clean them, and stuffing them into his mouth.

I had halted on the road. As soon as I saw the elephant I knew with perfect certainty that I ought not to shoot him. It is a serious matter to shoot a working elephant—it is comparable to destroying a huge and costly piece of machinery—and obviously one ought not to do it if it can possibly be avoided. And at that distance, peacefully eating, the elephant looked no more dangerous than a cow. I thought then and I think now that his attack of "must" was already passing off; in which case he would merely wander harmlessly about until the mahout came back and caught him. Moreover, I did not in the least want to shoot him. I decided that I would watch him for a little while to make sure that he did not turn savage again, and then go home.

But at that moment I glanced round at the crowd that had followed me. It was an immense crowd, two thousand at the least and growing every minute. It blocked the road for a long distance on either side. I looked at the sea of yellow faces above the garish clothes—faces all happy and excited over this bit of fun, all certain that the elephant was going to be shot. They were watching me as they would watch a conjurer about to perform a trick. They did not like me, but with the magical rifle in my hands I was momentarily worth watching. And suddenly I realized that I should have to shoot the elephant after all. The people expected it of me and I had got to do it; I could feel their two thousand wills pressing me forward, irresistibly. And it was at this moment, as I stood there with the rifle in my hands, that I first grasped the hollowness, the futility of the white man's dominion in the East. Here was I, the white man with his gun, standing in front of the unarmed native crowd—seemingly the leading actor of the piece; but in reality I was only an absurd puppet pushed to and fro by the will of those yellow faces behind. I perceived in this moment that when the white man turns tyrant it is his own freedom that he destroys. He becomes a sort of hollow, posing dummy, the conventionalized figure of a sahib.[5] For it is the condition of his rule that he shall spend his life in trying to impress the "natives," and so in every crisis he has got to do what the "natives" expect of him. He wears a mask, and his face grows to fit it. I had got to shoot the elephant. I had committed myself to doing it when I sent for the rifle. A sahib has got to act like a sahib; he has got to appear resolute, to know his own mind and do definite things. To come all that way, rifle in hand, with two thousand people marching at my heels, and then to trail feebly away, having done nothing—no, that was impossible. The crowd would laugh at me. And my whole life, every white man's life in the East, was one long struggle not to be laughed at.

But I did not want to shoot the elephant. I watched him beating his bunch of grass against his knees with that preoccupied grandmotherly air that elephants

[5]*sahib:* A native leader, ruler, or aristocrat.

have. It seemed to me that it would be murder to shoot him. At that age I was not squeamish about killing animals, but I had never shot an elephant and never wanted to. (Somehow it always seems worse to kill a *large* animal.) Besides, there was the beast's owner to be considered. Alive, the elephant was worth at least a hundred pounds; dead, he would only be worth the value of his tusks, five pounds, possibly. But I had got to act quickly. I turned to some experienced-looking Burmans who had been there when we arrived, and asked them how the elephant had been behaving. They all said the same thing: he took no notice of you if you left him alone, but he might charge if you went too close to him.

It was perfectly clear to me what I ought to do. I ought to walk up to within, say, twenty-five yards of the elephant and test his behavior. If he charged, I could shoot; if he took no notice of me, it would be safe to leave him until the mahout came back. But also I knew that I was going to do no such thing. I was a poor shot with a rifle and the ground was soft mud into which one would sink at every step. If the elephant charged and I missed him, I should have about as much chance as a toad under a steam-roller. But even then I was not thinking particularly of my own skin, only of the watchful yellow faces behind. For at that moment, with the crowd watching me, I was not afraid in the ordinary sense, as I would have been if I had been alone. A white man mustn't be frightened in front of "natives"; and so, in general, he isn't frightened. The sole thought in my mind was that if anything went wrong those two thousand Burmans would see me pursued, caught, trampled on, and reduced to a grinning corpse like that Indian up the hill. And if that happened it was quite probable that some of them would laugh. That would never do. There was only one alternative. I shoved the cartridges into the magazine and lay down on the road to get a better aim.

The crowd grew very still, and a deep, low, happy sigh, as of people who see the 10
theater curtain go up at last, breathed from innumerable throats. They were going to have their bit of fun after all. The rifle was a beautiful German thing with cross-hair sights. I did not then know that in shooting an elephant one would shoot to cut an imaginary bar running from ear-hole to ear-hole. I ought, therefore, as the elephant was sideways on, to have aimed straight at his ear-hole; actually I aimed several inches in front of this, thinking the brain would be further forward.

When I pulled the trigger I did not hear the bang or feel the kick—one never does when a shot goes home—but I heard the devilish roar of glee that went up from the crowd. In that instant, in too short a time, one would have thought, even for the bullet to get there, a mysterious, terrible change had come over the elephant. He neither stirred, nor fell, but every line of his body had altered. He looked suddenly stricken, shrunken, immensely old, as though the frightful impact of the bullet had paralyzed him without knocking him down. At last, after what seemed a long time—it might have been five seconds, I dare say—he sagged flabbily to his knees. His mouth slobbered. An enormous senility seemed to have settled upon him. One could have imagined him thousands of years old. I fired again into the same spot. At the second shot he did not collapse but climbed with desperate slowness to his feet and stood weakly upright, with legs sagging and head drooping. I fired a third time. That was the shot that did for him. You could see the agony of it jolt his whole body and knock the last remnant of strength from his legs. But in falling he seemed for a moment to rise, for as his hind legs collapsed beneath him he seemed to tower upward like a huge rock toppling, his trunk reaching skyward like a tree. He trumpeted, for the first and only time. And then down he came, his belly toward me, with a crash that seemed to shake the ground even where I lay.

I got up. The Burmans were already racing past me across the mud. It was obvious that the elephant would never rise again, but he was not dead. He was breathing very rhythmically with long rattling gasps, his great mound of a side painfully rising and falling. His mouth was wide open—I could see far down into caverns of pale pink throat. I waited a long time for him to die, but his breathing did not weaken. Finally I fired my two remaining shots into the spot where I thought his heart must be. The thick blood welled out of him like red velvet, but still he did not die. His body did not even jerk when the shots hit him, the tortured breathing continued without a pause. He was dying, very slowly and in great agony, but in some world remote from me where not even a bullet could damage him further. I felt that I had got to put an end to that dreadful noise. It seemed dreadful to see the great beast lying there, powerless to move and yet powerless to die, and not even to be able to finish him. I sent back for my small rifle and poured shot after shot into his heart and down his throat. They seemed to make no impression. The tortured gasps continued as steadily as the ticking of a clock.

In the end I could not stand it any longer and went away. I heard later that it took him half an hour to die. Burmans were bringing dahs and baskets even before I left, and I was told they had stripped his body almost to the bones by the afternoon.

Afterward, of course, there were endless discussions about the shooting of the elephant. The owner was furious, but he was only an Indian and could do nothing. Besides, legally I had done the right thing, for a mad elephant has to be killed, like a mad dog, if its owner fails to control it. Among the Europeans opinion was divided. The older men said I was right, the younger men said it was a damn shame to shoot an elephant for killing a coolie, because an elephant was worth more than any damn Coringhee coolie. And afterward I was very glad that the coolie had been killed; it put me legally in the right and it gave me a sufficient pretext for shooting the elephant. I often wondered whether any of the others grasped that I had done it solely to avoid looking a fool.

(1936)

Questions for Discussion and Writing

Close Reading

1. How does Orwell feel toward the Burmese people, and what accounts for these feelings?
2. Orwell says his shooting of the elephant gave him "a better glimpse than I had had before of the real nature of imperialism—the real motives for which despotic governments act." What does he mean?
3. Discuss Orwell's use of dramatic imagery—"leading actor," "absurd puppet," "mask," "theatre curtain"—toward the center of the essay.

CRITICAL AND CREATIVE READING

4. The elephant in this essay has already killed one man before Orwell meets it, and the threat exists that it will kill more. Should Orwell shoot it or not? What is the nature of his dilemma?
5. In the essay's final paragraph Orwell discusses the different motivations that people might use to justify his shooting of the elephant: legally, he was in the right, but he admits that he shot the elephant "to avoid looking a fool." Think of other situations in which these two forces are competing with one another.
6. Is there any difference between Orwell's title "Shooting an Elephant" and the other title he might have chosen, "Killing an Elephant"?

CONNECTIONS TO OTHER READINGS

7. Like Pilkings in Wole Soyinka's play *Death and the King's Horseman*, Orwell in this essay is an Englishman living in a British colony who feels he has a certain duty to uphold. Discuss how the tension between the colonial officer and the indigenous people plays out in both of these works. How are Orwell's and Pilkings's sense of duty affected by their response to "the natives"?
8. Discuss the nature of "choice" in this essay and in William Dean Howells's story "Editha." Who or what affects Editha's, George Gearson's, and George Orwell's choices? What are the most powerful forces outside oneself that affect one's choices?
9. Sammy in John Updike's story "A & P" refuses to conform to the expectations of his community. Discuss his nonconformity in conjunction with Orwell's behavior in this essay.

Sarah Vowell

Take the Cannoli

Many of Sarah Vowell's written essays derive from radio pieces she originally read on National Public Radio, especially the program *This American Life*. Vowell (b. 1969) tends to derive insight by reflecting on experiences and observations. Although her work is humorous, it is not afraid to delve into important questions of existence and identity formation in contemporary America. Perhaps better known for her voice than her writing, Vowell has published four books and has written for a number of newspapers, magazines, and journals. How do you hear her "voice" in this essay? Put differently, does this seem like an essay that was originally meant to be heard or to be read?

There comes a time halfway through any halfway decent liberal arts major's college career when she no longer has any idea what she believes. She flies violently through air polluted by conflicting ideas and theories, never stopping at one system of thought long enough to feel at home. All those books, all that talk, and, oh, the self-reflection. Am I an existentialist? A Taoist? A transcendentalist? A modernist, a postmodernist? A relativist-positivist-historicist-dadaist-deconstructionist? Was I Apollonian? Was I Dionysian (or just drunk)? Which was right and which was wrong, *im*pressionism or *ex*pressionism? And while we're at it, is there such a thing as right and wrong?

Until I figured out that the flight between questions is itself a workable system, I craved answers, rules. A code. So by my junior year, I was spending part of every week, sometimes every day, watching *The Godfather* on videotape.

The Godfather was an addiction. And like all self-respecting addicts, I did not want anyone to find out about my habit. Which was difficult considering that I shared a house with my boyfriend and two other roommates, all of whom probably thought my profound interest in their class schedules had to do with love and friendship. But I needed to know when the house would be empty so I could watch snippets of the film. Sometimes it took weeks to get through the whole thing. If I had a free hour between earth science lab and my work-study job, I'd sneak home and get through the scene where Sonny Corleone is gunned down at the toll booth, his shirt polka-dotted with bullet holes. Or, if I finished writing a paper analyzing American mediocrity according to Alexis de Tocqueville,[1] I'd reward myself with a few minutes of Michael Corleone doing an excellent job of firing a pistol into a police captain's face. But if the phone rang while I was watching, I turned off the sound so that the caller wouldn't guess what I was up to. I thought that if anyone knew how much time I was spending with the Corleones, they would think it was some desperate cry for help. I always pictured the moment I was found out as a scene from a movie, a movie considerably less epic than *The Godfather:* My concerned boyfriend would eject the tape from the VCR with a flourish and flush it down the toilet like so much cocaine. Then my parents would ship me off to some treatment center where I'd be put in group therapy with a bunch of Trekkies.[2]

I would sit on my couch with the blinds drawn, stare at the TV screen, and imagine myself inside it. I wanted to cower in the dark brown rooms of Don Corleone, kiss his hand on his daughter's wedding day, explain what my troubles were, and let him tell me he'll make everything all right. Of course, I was prepared to accept this gift knowing that someday—and that day may never come—I may be called upon to do a service. But, he would tell me, "Until that day, accept this justice as a gift on my daughter's wedding day."

"*Grazie*, Godfather." It was as simple as that. 5

Looking back, I wonder why a gangster movie kidnapped my life. *The Godfather* had nothing to do with me. I was a feminist, not Italian, and I went to school at Montana State. I had never set foot in New York, thought ravioli came

[1]*Alexis de Tocqueville:* A nineteenth-century French thinker whose most famous work was *Democracy in America* (1835).

[2]*Trekkies:* Fans of the television show *Star Trek*, who are known for their obsession and identification with the show.

only in a can, and wasn't blind to the fact that all the women in the film were either virgins, mothers, whores, or Diane Keaton.

I fell for those made-up, sexist, East Coast thugs anyway. Partly it was the clothes; fashionwise, there is nothing less glamorous than snow-blown, backpacking college life in the Rocky Mountain states. But the thing that really attracted me to the film was that it offered a three-hour peep into a world with clear and definable moral guidelines; where you know where you stand and you know who you love; where honor was everything; and the greatest sin wasn't murder but betrayal.

My favorite scene in the film takes place on a deserted highway with the Statue of Liberty off in the distance. The don's henchman Clemenza is on the road with two of his men. He's under orders that only one of them is supposed to make the ride back. Clemenza tells the driver to pull over. "I gotta take a leak," he says. As Clemenza empties his bladder, the man in the backseat empties his gun into the driver's skull. There are three shots. The grisly, back-of-the-head murder of a rat fink associate is all in a day's work. But Clemenza's overriding responsibility is to his family. He takes a moment out of his routine madness to remember that he had promised his wife he would bring dessert home. His instruction to his partner in crime is an entire moral manifesto in six little words: "Leave the gun. Take the cannoli."

I loved Clemenza's command because of its total lack of ambiguity. I yearned for certainty. I'd been born into rock-solid Christianity, and every year that went by, my faith eroded a little more, so that by the time I got to college I was a recent, and therefore shaky, atheist. Like a lot of once devout people who have lost religion, I had holes the size of heaven and hell in my head and my heart. Once, I had had a god, commandments, faith, the promise of redemption, and a bible, The Bible, which offered an explanation of everything from creation on through to the end of the world. I had slowly but surely replaced the old-fashioned exclamation points of hallelujahs with the question marks of modern life. God was dead and I had whacked him.

Don Corleone, the Godfather, was not unlike God the father—loving and 10
indulgent one minute, wrathful and judgmental the next. But the only "thou shalt" in the don's dogma was to honor thy family. He dances with his wife, weeps over his son's corpse, dies playing in the garden with his grandson, and preaches that "a man who doesn't spend time with his family can never be a real man."

Don Corleone would not have paid actual money to sit in fluorescent-lit rooms listening to frat boys from Spokane babble on about Descartes, boys in baseball caps whose most sacred philosophical motto could be summarized as "I drink therefore I am." Don Corleone had no time for mind games and conjecture. I, on the other hand, had nothing but time for such things, probably because I'm a frivolous female: "I spend my life trying not to be careless," the don tells his son Michael. "Women and children can be careless but not men."

The Godfather is a film crammed with rules for living. Don't bow down to big shots. It's good when people owe you. This drug business is dangerous. Is vengeance going to bring your son back to you or my boy to me? And then there is the grandeur, the finality, the conviction of the mantra "Never tell anybody outside the family what you're thinking again."

That last one was a rule I myself could follow. Not only did I not tell anyone outside my family what I was thinking, I was pretty tight-lipped with family too. If I was confused about the books I was reading in school, I was equally tormented by my seemingly tranquil life. At twenty-one, I was squandering my youth on hard work and contentment. I had two jobs, got straight A's. I lived with my boyfriend of three years, a perfectly nice person. We were well suited to the point of boredom, enjoying the same movies, the same music, the same friends. We didn't argue, which meant we didn't flirt. I'd always dreamed of *The Taming of the Shrew*[3] and I was living in—well, they don't write dramas about young girls who settle for the adventure that is mutual respect, unless you count *thirtysomething*,[4] and I already had the same haircut as the wifely actress who smiled politely waiting for her husband to come home to their comfortable house. Thanks largely to the boyfriend's decency and patience, my parents and I were getting along better than ever. My sister was my best friend. We all lived within ten blocks of each other, one big happy family, frequently convening for get-togethers and meals. Friends clamored for dinner invitations to my parents' home, acquaintances told the boyfriend and me that we renewed their faith in love, and every time I turned in an essay exam my professors' eyes lit up. I was a good daughter, a good sister, a good girlfriend, a good student, a good citizen, a responsible employee. I was also antsy, resentful, overworked, and hemmed in.

Just as I did not divulge my secret rendezvous with *The Godfather*, I didn't talk about my claustrophobia. I didn't tell anyone that maybe I didn't want to be known only as my sister's sister or my parents' daughter or my boyfriend's girlfriend, that maybe I'd lived in that town too long and I wanted to go someplace where I could leave the house for ten minutes without running into my seventh-grade math teacher. So I told them all I wanted to study abroad to better my chances of getting into graduate school, which sounds a lot better than telling the people who love you that you'd love to get away from them.

I have a few weeks after Christmas before I have to report to Holland for a 15
semester of art history. I fly to Vienna. I get on a train there and another one in Berlin, and another after that, and one thing leads to another and I find myself in Italy. How did that happen? Oh well, as long as I'm in Florence, perhaps I should pop down and give Sicily a look-see.

The fact is, my little freedom flight isn't working out as well as I'd hoped. I swing between the giddiness of my newfound solitude and the loneliness of same. I make a lot of panicked phone calls to my boyfriend from museums that begin with descriptions of Brueghel paintings and end with me sobbing, "What am I going to do?" I am homesick, and since I can't go home, I might as well go to the next closest thing—Sicily. I *know* Sicily. And I love the part of *The Godfather* when Michael's hiding out, traipsing around his ancestral hills, walking the streets of his father's birthplace, Corleone.

I take a night train from Rome down the boot and wake up in the Sicilian capital, Palermo. I feel ridiculous. I thought of myself as a serious person and it

[3]*The Taming of the Shrew:* A comic play by William Shakespeare that is characterized by the contentious relationship of its male and female protagonists.

[4]*thirtysomething:* A bland television drama popular in the 1980s.

didn't seem like serious people travel hundreds of miles out of their way to walk in the footsteps of Al Pacino.

I don't feel so silly, however, that I'm above tracking down a bakery and buying a cannoli, my first. I walk down to the sea and eat it. It's sweeter than I thought it would be, more dense. The filling is flecked with chocolate and candied orange. Clemenza was right: Leave that gun! Take that cannoli!

The town of Corleone really exists and can be reached by bus. I checked. Every day I go to the travel office in Palermo to buy a ticket to the Godfather's hometown. And every morning, when I stand before the ticket agent, I can never quite bring myself to say the word "Corleone" out loud to a real live Sicilian. Because you know they know. Idiot Americans and their idiot films. I have my dignity.

20 So each morning when the ticket agent asks, "Where to?", one of two things happens: I say nothing and just walk off and spend the day in Palermo reading John Irving novels on a bench by the sea, or I utter the name of a proper, art-historically significant town instead. As if the clerk will hear me say, "Agrigento," and say to himself, "Oh, she's going to see the Doric temple. Impressive. Wonder if she's free for a cannoli later?"

On my final day in Sicily—my last chance at Corleone—I walk to the ticket counter, look the clerk in the eye, and ask for a round-trip ticket to Corle— . . . Cefalù. Yeah, Cefalù, that's it, to see a Byzantine mosaic I remember liking in one of my schoolbooks.

Cefalù might as well have been Corleone. It had the same steep cobblestone streets and blanched little buildings that I remembered from the movie. *Lovely*, I thought, as I started walking up the hill to its tiny, twelfth-century cathedral. *Freak*, everyone in the town apparently thought as I marched past them. An entire class of schoolchildren stopped cold to gawk at me. Six-year-old girls pointed at my shoes and laughed. Hunched old men glared, as if the sight of me was a vicious insult. I felt like a living, breathing faux pas.

At least no one was inside the church. The only gaze upon me there came from the looming, sad-eyed Messiah. The Jesus in this mosaic is huge, three times larger than any other figure inside the church. And there's something menacing in the way he holds that tablet with the word of God on it. But his face is compassionate. With that contradictory mix of stern judgment and heart, he may as well have been wearing a tuxedo and stroking a cat and saying something like "What have I ever done to make you treat me so disrespectfully?"

I leave the church and go for lunch. I am the only patron in a tiny family restaurant operated by Mama, Papa, Son 1, and Son 2. They glare at me as if I glow in the dark. Soon they'll wish I glowed in the dark. The power keeps going on and off because of a thunderstorm. The sky outside is nearly black. The Muzak version of "A Whiter Shade of Pale" is playing and it flickers, too, so that every few seconds it's dark and silent. Which is a relief, considering that the rest of the time it's loud and the entire family have seated themselves across from me and gape without smiling. The eggplant on my plate is wonderful, but such is my desire to escape their stares that I have never chewed so fast in my life.

25 How had it never hit me before? The whole point of *The Godfather* is not to trust anyone outside your family. And whatever I may have thought while sitting in front of my VCR, I am not actually Sicilian. I bear no resemblance to

Clemenza, Tessio, or any of the heads of the Five Families. If I were a character in the film at all, I'd be one of those pain-in-the-ass innocent bystanders in the restaurant where Michael murders Sollozzo. I'm the tuba player in Moe Green's casino. I'm that kid who rides his bike past Michael and Kay on Kay's street in New Hampshire who yells hello and neither Michael nor Kay says hello back.

I got sucked in by *The Godfather*'s moral certainty, never quite recognizing that the other side of moral certainty is staying at home and keeping your mouth shut. Given the choice, I prefer chaos and confusion. Why live by those old-world rules? I was enamored of the movie's family ethos without realizing that in order to make a life for myself, I needed to go off on my own. Why not tell people outside the family what you're thinking? As I would later find out, it's a living.

(2000)

Questions for Discussion and Writing

Close Reading

1. What motivates Vowell to leave the comfort of her hometown for a solitary trip through Europe?
2. How do Vowell's experiences in college compare with her experiences traveling through Europe?
3. How do Vowell's consistent allusions to the movie *The Godfather* (from the title on) unite the essay?

Critical and Creative Reading

4. What are the implications of the fact that Sarah Vowell rejects the clear-cut moral standards of Christianity that she learns during youth in favor of the clear-cut but often criminal standards represented in *The Godfather* movies?
5. The most obvious lesson of *The Godfather* movies is that you will survive and flourish if you live according to the code established by the Italian Mafia. How does that lesson apply to Sarah Vowell's life choices?
6. Discuss the balance of humor and seriousness in this essay, or the balance of popular culture allusions and references to classical thinkers.

Connections to Other Readings

7. Use Vowell's observation that "the other side of moral certainty is staying at home and keeping your mouth shut" to analyze her essay and Shirley Jackson's story "The Lottery."
8. Discuss the notion of public ridicule in Orwell's essay "Shooting an Elephant" and Vowell's essay.
9. Is the metaphor of "forbidden fruit" in the poem "Goblin Market" by Christina Rossetti comparable to the metaphor of the cannoli as exotic food in Vowell's essay?

Considering Art: Obedience and Rebellion

The discussion below references art reproduced on color insert pages 1 and 2.

Modern artists from the mid-nineteenth century to the present have identified with people and social groups who oppose those in power. These modern artists often question authority in their subject matter, "heroize" revolutionary political or cultural figures, and challenge or violate "the norm" in established artistic practices. In 1825, utopian philosopher Henri de Saint-Simon adopted the military term ***avant-garde*** to express this idea that a bold, advance guard of artists, scientists, and industrialists could lead society forward to a better place. Many people see modern art as having this active role in imagining social change and making it happen.

***Rosa Parks* (see color insert p. 1).** Residing in the National Portrait Gallery in Washington, D.C., Marshall D. Rumbaugh's carved and painted wooden sculpture *Rosa Parks* (1983) portrays the civil rights activist who played such a significant role in social change in the 1960s. Although this work is three dimensional, we get the best vantage point when we view its three figures from the front. Each stands at about half of life size. Working in a style known as **primitivism**, the artist distorts and simplifies the figures and applies colors in simplified, solid blocks. He achieves an **expressive** effect by manipulating and exaggerating the figures' features and forms to convey meaning and emotion.

***Punk* (see color insert p. 2).** Color and form are similarly simplified in Norwegian artist Wilfred Hildonen's painting *Punk* (2005). Hildonen (b. 1953) is a largely self-taught artist who has worked as an illustrator and cartoonist since the 1970s. While living a bohemian lifestyle and hitchhiking around Europe in 1978, he discovered antiestablishment punk rock and new wave music as it was emerging from London bands like the Clash and the Sex Pistols. On Hildonen's website (http://www.whildonen.net/cv.html), his artist's statement encourages us to read his work as that of an outsider to convention and authority. In *Punk*, he has created not a portrait but an image of a type of performer or persona—a rebellious, energized punk rocker whose orange Mohawk hairdo radiates from his head like the spiky crown on the Statue of Liberty. Hildonen's color **palette** is dominated by warm, pure colors of red and orange, broken only by a few cool green touches. We can imagine that the red cloud pulsating around the figure is a visual equivalent of loud music. The artist seems to suppress details such as clothing, environment, and even gender to simplify the **composition.**

***Voice of the People* (see color insert p. 2).** In *Voice of the People* (1899), French painter Jules Adler (1865–1952) depicts striking miners from a northern French industrial town. Men, women, and children sing as they march together to protest their low wages and inhuman working conditions. Adler produced many large-scale paintings on the subject of work for the Salon—the official public exhibition of the Acadèmie des Beaux Arts in Paris. He painted and publicly displayed *Voice of the People* at an anxious time of growing social unrest, when the government feared that class warfare might erupt from such seemingly peaceful demonstrations. Paintings accepted for the Salon typically drew their subject matter from ancient history, Biblical or mythological tales, or nostalgic images of peasants and rural life, so this painting depicting modern labor relationships was somewhat unusual. Adler's style is much more **naturalistic** and less distorted than the approach used by Rumbaugh or Hildonen. His figures are treated with a high level of individualizing detail and seem to have been observed and drawn from life, although none of the figures are direct portraits. Here, color is also used strategically: the tricolor flags of the French Republic are unfurled in such a way that their red bands are prominent. Note the way that the vertical flags set up a rhythm with the factory smokestacks in the town behind them.

Questions about the Art

1. In the sculpture *Rosa Parks*, compare the way that Rumbaugh depicts attitude, expression, and personality in Rosa Parks to the way that he depicts the figures of authority that constrain her.
2. How does Hildonen's *Punk* convey emotion? What sort of emotions?
3. What is the mood of the people in Adler's *Voice of the People?* Does it seem to be tending toward or away from violence and how is the crowd's mood and its potential expressed?

Connecting Art and Literature

1. Consider the notion of governmental power as it is depicted in this sculptural image of Rosa Parks alongside the essays "Shooting an Elephant" by George Orwell and "Civil Disobedience" by Henry David Thoreau. What do the three works say about the relative power of the individual?
2. Would you describe the speaker of Gregory Corso's poem "Marriage" as a "punk" in the same way that you would describe the subject of Hildonen's *Punk*?
3. Discuss the tension between crowds and individuals in the painting *Voice of the People* and in Shirley Jackson's story "The Lottery." Do the two works convey the same mood?

Common Characters

Icarus

The ancient Greek myth of Icarus and Daedalus (pronounced "Dedalus")—the foolish, ambitious son and the wise father who designed a labyrinth—has been a favorite subject of writers and artists for centuries. At the heart of the story is the simple act of one youth's rebellion against his father's wishes: Daedalus fashions wings for his son so that they can escape from Crete but warns him not to fly too high. Despite this warning, Icarus flies so high that the sun melts his wings and he falls to his death.

Jacob Peter Gowy, *The Fall of Icarus* (1636 or 1637), after a painting by Peter Paul Rubens.

If you consider rebellion "acting against the wishes of an authority figure," you might call Icarus a rebel, and if you believe that a rebel must have a cause or a higher purpose, you might think him merely disobedient. You might also say that his flaw is pride for thinking that he could handle the high flight his father warned him against, or it might be greed for wanting more freedom than he had. Children often defy their parents' advice regardless of the danger to their personal safety. However, think about Icarus. With wings he could fly: in some versions of the story people on the ground thought that he was a god. Given a taste of that kind of freedom, one would naturally forget about the rules.

The story is somewhat complex, as the following readings show. Daedalus, after all, created the labyrinth from which he later wanted to escape. (Think of the labyrinth of rules a parent creates for a child.) Daedalus also created the wings and strapped them on his son. He must be held at least partially accountable for the death of his son, who was only doing what many young boys want to do: redrawing the boundaries that were set for him.

The readings and paintings that follow represent some possible rethinkings of the Icarus story. The collection begins with three ancient Greek versions of the story. Those are followed by three poems, a song lyric by the folk-rock musician Joni Mitchell, and two paintings.

Robert Graves *(1845–1985)*

From The Greek Myths

It was not easy, however, to escape from Crete, since Minos kept all his ships under military guard, and now offered a large reward for his apprehension. But Daedalus made a pair of wings for himself, and another for Icarus, the quill feathers of which were threaded together, but the smaller ones held in place by wax. Having tied on Icarus's pair for him, he said with tears in his eyes: "My son, be warned! Neither soar too high, lest the sun melt the wax; nor swoop too low, lest the feathers be wetted by the sea." Then he slipped his arms into his own pair of wings and they flew off. "Follow me closely," he cried, "do not set your own course!"

As they sped away from the island in a north-easterly direction, flapping their wings, the fishermen, shepherds, and ploughmen who gazed upward mistook them for gods.

They had left Naxos, Delos, and Paros behind them on the left hand, and were leaving Lebynthos and Calymne behind on the right, when Icarus disobeyed his father's instructions and began soaring towards the sun, rejoiced by the lift of his great sweeping wings. Presently, when Daedalus looked over his shoulder, he could no longer see Icarus; but scattered feathers floated on the waves below. The heat of the sun had melted the wax, and Icarus had fallen into the sea and drowned. Daedalus circled around, until the corpse rose to the surface, and then carried it to the nearby island now called Icaria, where he buried it. . . .

(1955)

Ovid *(43 BCE–17 BCE)*

Translated by Rolfe Humphries

From Metamorphoses

Homesick for homeland, Daedalus hated Crete
And his long exile there, but the sea held him.
"Though Minos blocks escape by land or water,"
Daedalus said, "surely the sky is open,
And that's the way we'll go. Minos' dominion
Does not include the air." He turned his thinking
Toward unknown arts, changing the laws of nature.
He laid out feathers in order, first the smallest,
A little larger next it, and so continued,
The way that pan-pipes rise in gradual sequence.
He fastened them with twine and wax, at middle,
At bottom, so, and bent them, gently curving,
So that they looked like wings of birds, most surely.
And Icarus, his son, stood by and watched him,
Not knowing he was dealing with his downfall,
Stood by and watched, and raised his shiny face
To let a feather, light as down, fall on it,
Or stuck his thumb into the yellow wax,
Fooling around, the way a boy will, always,
Whenever a father tries to get some work done.
Still, it was done at last, and the father hovered,
Poised, in the moving air, and taught his son:
"I warn you, Icarus, fly a middle course:
Don't go too low, or water will weigh the wings down;
Don't go too high, or the sun's fire will burn them.
Keep to the middle way. And one more thing,
No fancy steering by star or constellation,
Follow my lead!" That was the flying lesson,
And now to fit the wings to the boy's shoulders.
Between the work and warning the father found
His cheeks were wet with tears, and his hands trembled.
He kissed his son (*Good-bye*, if he had known it),
Rose on his wings, flew on ahead, as fearful
As any bird launching the little nestlings
Out of high nest into thin air. *Keep on,*
Keep on, he signals, *follow me!* He guides him
In flight—O fatal art!—and the wings move
And the father looks back to see the son's wings moving.
Far off, far down, some fisherman is watching
As the rod dips and trembles over the water,

Some shepherd rests his weight upon his crook,
Some ploughman on the handles of the ploughshare,
And all look up, in absolute amazement,
At those air-borne above. They must be gods!
They were over Samos, Juno's sacred island,
Delos and Paros toward the left, Lebinthus
Visible to the right, and another island,
Calymne, rich in honey. And the boy
Thought *This is wonderful!* and left his father,
Soared higher, higher, drawn to the vast heaven,
Nearer the sun, and the wax that held the wings
Melted in that fierce heat, and the bare arms
Beat up and down in air, and lacking oarage
Took hold of nothing. *Father!* he cried, and *Father!*
Until the blue sea hushed him, the dark water
Men call the Icarian now. And Daedalus,
Father no more, called "Icarus, where are you!
Where are you, Icarus? Tell me where to find you!"
And saw the wings on the waves, and cursed his talents,
Buried the body in a tomb, and the land
Was named for Icarus.
    During the burial
A noisy partridge, from a muddy ditch,
Looked out, drummed with her wings in loud approval.
No other bird, those days, was like the partridge,
Newcomer to the ranks of birds; the story
Reflects no credit on Daedalus. His sister,
Ignorant of the fates, had sent her son
To Daedalus as apprentice, only a youngster,
Hardly much more than twelve years old, but clever,
With an inventive turn of mind. For instance,
Studying a fish's backbone for a model,
He had notched a row of teeth in a strip of iron,
Thus making the first saw, and he had bound
Two arms of iron together with a joint
To keep them both together and apart,
One standing still, the other traversing
In a circle, so men came to have the compass.
And Daedalus, in envy, hurled the boy
Headlong from the high temple of Minerva,
And lied about it, saying he had fallen
Through accident, but Minerva, kind protectress
Of all inventive wits, stayed him in air,
Clothed him with plumage; he still retained his aptness
In feet and wings, and kept his old name, Perdix,
But in the new bird-form, Perdix, the partridge,
Never flies high, nor nests in trees, but flutters

Close to the ground, and the eggs are laid in hedgerows.
The bird, it seems, remembers, and is fearful
Of all high places.

(translation 1955)

Edith Hamilton *(1867–1963)*

A Great Adventure

Daedalus was the architect who had contrived the Labyrinth for the Minotaur in Crete, and who showed Ariadne how Theseus could escape from it. When King Minos learned that the Athenians had found their way out, he was convinced that they could have done so only if Daedalus had helped them. Accordingly he imprisoned him and his son Icarus in the Labyrinth, certainly a proof that it was excellently devised since not even the maker of it could discover the exit without a clue. But the great inventor was not at a loss. He told his son,

> Escape may be checked by water and land, but the air and the sky are free,

and he made two pairs of wings for them. They put them on and just before they took flight Daedalus warned Icarus to keep a middle course over the sea. If he flew too high the sun might melt the glue and the wings drop off. However, as stories so often show, what elders say youth disregards. As the two flew lightly and without effort away from Crete the delight of this new and wonderful power went to the boy's head. He soared exultingly up and up, paying no heed to his father's anguished commands. Then he fell. The wings had come off. He dropped into the sea and the waters closed over him. The afflicted father flew safely to Sicily, where he was received kindly by the King.

Minos was enraged at his escape and determined to find him. He made a cunning plan. He had it proclaimed everywhere that a great reward would be given to whoever could pass a thread through an intricately spiraled shell. Daedalus told the Sicilian king that he could do it. He bored a small hole in the closed end of the shell, fastened a thread to an ant, introduced the ant into the hole, and then closed it. When the ant finally came out at the other end, the thread, of course, was running clear through all the twists and turns. "Only Daedalus would think of that," Minos said, and he came to Sicily to seize him. But the King refused to surrender him, and in the contest Minos was slain.

(1940)

W. H. Auden *(1907–1973)*

Musée des Beaux Arts

About suffering they were never wrong,
The Old Masters: how well they understood

Its human position; how it takes place
While someone else is eating or opening a window or just walking dully along;
How, when the aged are reverently, passionately waiting
For the miraculous birth, there always must be
Children who did not specially want it to happen, skating
On a pond at the edge of the wood:
They never forgot
That even the dreadful martyrdom must run its course
Anyhow in a corner, some untidy spot
Where the dogs go on with their doggy life and the torturer's horse
Scratches its innocent behind on a tree.

In Brueghel's *Icarus*, for instance: how everything turns away
Quite leisurely from the disaster; the ploughman may
Have heard the splash, the forsaken cry,
But for him it was not an important failure; the sun shone
As it had to on the white legs disappearing into the green
Water; and the expensive delicate ship that must have seen
Something amazing, a boy falling out of the sky,
Had somewhere to get to and sailed calmly on.

(1940)

Joni Mitchell *(b. 1943)*

Amelia (song lyric from *Hejira*)

I was driving across the burning desert
When I spotted six jet planes
Leaving six white vapor trails across the bleak terrain
It was the hexagram of the heavens
it was the strings of my guitar
Amelia, it was just a false alarm

The drone of flying engines
Is a song so wild and blue
It scrambles time and seasons if it gets through to you
Then your life becomes a travelogue
Of picture-post-card-charms
Amelia, it was just a false alarm

People will tell you where they've gone
They'll tell you where to go
But till you get there yourself you never really know
Where some have found their paradise

Amelia Earhart.

Others just come to harm
Oh Amelia, it was just a false alarm

I wish that he was here tonight
It's so hard to obey
His sad request of me to kindly stay away
So this is how I hide the hurt
As the road leads cursed and charmed
I tell Amelia, it was just a false alarm

A ghost of aviation
She was swallowed by the sky
Or by the sea, like me she had a dream to fly
Like Icarus ascending
On beautiful foolish arms
Amelia, it was just a false alarm

Maybe I've never really loved
I guess that is the truth
I've spent my whole life in clouds at icy altitude
And looking down on everything

I crashed into his arms
Amelia, it was just a false alarm

I pulled into the Cactus Tree Motel
To shower off the dust
And I slept on the strange pillows of my wanderlust
I dreamed of 747s
Over geometric farms
Dreams, Amelia, dreams and false alarms

(1976)

Reginald Shepard *(b. 1963)*

Icarus on Fire Island

Two loves I have, each one
too fair for me to be completed
in his eyes, summer open with Mediterranean blue
where care is left aside, the most
of available light. The Sunday beach with you,
spangled with tan men, their perfect skin
reproach and visible reward (until the sun abandons
them and they withdraw into the inked-in sky
to shine unseen for those who don't concern themselves
with light). I searched the air dazzled with kites
for them. I couldn't want them less. *Since shunning pain*
I ease can never find. I'll score the sky
with string, and there incise my name,
until the gusts decline.
   I have dispersed
the clouds with one small wisp of breath,
his hand commands a paper dragon
through an insurgent breeze. The painted silk
is stolen by flight, the line snaps or he
lets go of the line, playing it out
against a sudden updraft. That was my future
life, lost track of all a summer
afternoon: a black point in a northeast corner of blue
descending, a mote across an open eye of sky
where light drains away.

(1998)

Jack Gilbert *(b. 1925)*

Failing and Flying

Everyone forgets that Icarus also flew.
It's the same when love comes to an end,
or the marriage fails and people say
they knew it was a mistake, that everybody
said it would never work. That she was
old enough to know better. But anything
worth doing is worth doing badly.
Like being there by that summer ocean
on the other side of the island while
love was fading out of her, the stars
burning so extravagantly those nights that
anyone could tell you they would never last.
Every morning she was asleep in my bed
like a visitation, the gentleness in her
like antelope standing in the dawn mist.
Each afternoon I watched her coming back
through the hot stony field after swimming,
the sea light behind her and the huge sky
on the other side of that. Listened to her
while we ate lunch. How can they say
the marriage failed? Like the people who
came back from Provence (when it was Provence)
and said it was pretty but the food was greasy.
I believe Icarus was not failing as he fell,
but just coming to the end of his triumph.

(2005)

ICARUS: QUESTIONS FOR DISCUSSION AND WRITING

1. How do the three versions of the Icarus story from ancient Greek sources differ from one another in emphasis?
2. Use a number of the readings to answer this question: Is flight a miracle or something that people were not meant to do?
3. Compare the speaker's distance from Icarus in the poems by W. H. Auden and Reginald Shephard. How does the difference between this distance affect the theme of each poem?

Considering Art: Icarus

The discussion below references art reproduced on color insert pages 3 and 4.

The mythological Flight of Icarus has long been interpreted as a metaphoric fall from grace. Centuries of moralists have seen in Icarus's downward plummet a parable expressing the idea that pride or vanity comes before a fall and as a warning against *hubris*—thinking too highly of oneself and one's powers. In a still image, however, whether a figure is falling or flying is often left up to the viewer to determine, using the visual cues provided. As Douglas Adams writes in *Life, the Universe and Everything*, "*The Hitch Hiker's Guide to the Galaxy* has this to say on the subject of flying. There is an art, it says, or rather a knack to flying. The knack lies in learning how to throw yourself at the ground and miss."

***The Fall of Icarus* (color insert p. 3).** In the sixteenth century, Flemish artist Pieter the Elder Brueghel (1525–1569) (working in what is today Belgium) visualizes the mythological figure of Icarus falling to earth as if it were a contemporary event happening in a Flemish village. At the narrative moment that Bruegel depicts, Icarus meets his foolish and insignificant end in the ocean. Brueghel's attention to detail is the hallmark of Northern Renaissance oil painting of the fifteenth and sixteenth centuries. We see this detailed style especially in the figures of the plowman, shepherd, and fishermen, who are present as Icarus falls. Brueghel depicts the landscape with a great degree of detail as well, from the hypnotically wavy lines plowed into the field in the foreground to the dramatic rock outcropping in the far distance. Typical of landscape imagery from Northern Europe at this time, the painting provides the viewer with a moral lesson as he or she makes an imaginary journey or pilgrimage through the theatrical and highly detailed space of the image.

***Flight to Freedom* (color insert p. 3).** Canadian painter Patricia A. Schwimmer's *Flight to Freedom* (1994) puts a twist on the Icarus myth in an image that is colorful, playful, and magical at first glance. Schwimmer (b. 1953) has a naïve style that consists of decorative, simplified shapes that are painted in flat tempera paint and arranged in patterns that evoke children's storybook illustrations. Its apparent cheerfulness suggests that we are looking at the world of a dream or fantasy. A manically grinning female figure departs from a window in a stone building and meets in midair several things and creatures that fly and an animal that jumps.

***Icara lands safely, only slightly singed* (color insert p. 4).** Jeanie Tomanek (b. 1949) in *Icara lands safely, only slightly singed* (2002) translates the Icarus myth into an imaginary feminine archetype who survives her flight to the sun and returns to earth somewhat burned or altered by experience but essentially unharmed. By inventing the name "Icara," the artist appropriates the myth to use as a personal metaphor. The wings of the figure are no longer brilliant or snowy white but instead resemble a tattered cape, and her brown tinge hints at the toll that survival takes. The paint surface is bumpy and encrusted. Tomanek applies layers of multiple mediums (such as oils, acrylic, pencil, and thin glazes of paint) and then scratches through them, writes on them, and paints over them in a process of excavating and revealing the image. We can barely make out ghostly traces of text that, along with the mysterious symbols around the figure, suggest many layers of reference. In her artist's statement (at http://www.jeanietomanek.com), Tomanek explains that her working process also contributes to the work's meaning: "In reclaiming and reconstructing areas of the canvas, the process of painting becomes analogous to having a second chance at your life, this time a little closer to the heart's desire."

Questions about the Art

1. How do artists Brueghel, Schwimmer, and Tomanek use painted details in these three visual works to tell their stories?
2. How do Brueghel's details guide our understanding of the Icarus tale? What seems to be the moral of his story?
3. How can we tell if Schwimmer's *Flight to Freedom* is a fantasy of flying, a suicidal leap, a foolish flight, or an act to be morally applauded or condemned? To what does the "freedom" in the title refer?
4. How is Icara's posture and presentation a reversal of the Icarus myth? Why do you think an artist would change the details of the story?
5. Discuss the way *perspective* alters the way artists render the story of Daedalus and Icarus.

Connecting Art and Literature

1. How does Auden's discussion of the way the Old Masters understood suffering apply to the depictions of Icarus other than Brueghel's?
2. Auden's poem "Musée des Beaux Arts" alludes to the painting by Brueghel. Explain how Brueghel's painting inspires Auden's poem. Consider especially the description and feeling in Auden's language.
3. Joni Mitchell's lyrics use the image of Icarus to describe a woman, Amelia Earhart. How is feminine power as depicted in Tomanek's painting useful in understanding the subject of Mitchell's lyrics?
4. Which of the paintings is most useful in capturing the tension in Jack Gilbert's poem between "Failing and Flying"?
5. All of these artistic interpretations of the myth are variations on the original; in what way are they true to the spirit of the retellings of the story at the beginning of the "Common Characters" section? Do they violate the spirit of the myth in any way?

Chapter 13

Love and Lust

Love may be the most common subject of literature. Writers focus on mysteries, and, along with death, love is the greatest of human mysteries. What force inspires us to feel so strongly about one another? How does this force affect the way we conduct our everyday lives, and why is it powerful enough to make us change the direction of our lives? Because there are no easy or cheap answers to these questions, they make fertile ground for the literary imagination.

And then there is lust, love's poor relation. Defined as base, common, sexual desire, or even animal passion, lust is often considered a sin by strict moralists. Preachers condemn it, censors filter it, and parents shudder to think of it. And yet: could romantic love get its foot in the door without lust? There is probably a closer relationship between these terms than anyone would care to admit. Love may be the most common subject of literature, but lust is high up on the list. Serious writers from well before the premodern times of Geoffrey Chaucer, perhaps motivated to explore the human condition honestly, have not put lust in some unopened closet marked "pornography." Like its noble cousin love, lust is also fertile ground for the literary imagination, partly because it has been rendered mysterious by a widespread unwillingness to discuss it.

Lust and love both grow out of desires, maybe out of the same desire: the basic need to be with another person. Yet lust and love are both more specific than simply "companionship." They involve intangible motivations, and they are not easy to define. We might begin with the assumption that lust stems from the body while love stems from the mind or the soul, but how easily can we separate the body from the mind or the soul? Part of the challenge you will face as you work through this chapter is to define lust and love both separately and together, to find a dividing line between the two or perhaps to admit that such a line cannot be drawn.

The fiction in this chapter begins with two early-twentieth-century authors from two different countries: James Joyce from Ireland and Ryunosuke Akutagawa from Japan. They are markedly modern in their skepticism and willingness to dig for truth. The next story, by John Updike, takes place in the 1960s, a period that saw widespread challenges to the solidity of American marriage. The final two works of fiction in this chapter, by American authors Bharati Mukherjee and Susan Minot, feature liberated female characters who desire more than merely sexual liberation.

Pablo Picasso, *The Rendez-vous* (c. 1900).

Poetry on love and lust is not hard to find. We have selected poems that alternate between ideal and realistic definitions of love, such as the famous exchange between a shepherd and a nymph in two poems by Christopher Marlowe and Sir Walter Raleigh. The English Renaissance is rich with poems on this subject, and Marlowe and Raleigh are joined by other famous poets from this era: Thomas Carew, Andrew Marvell, and William Shakespeare. The eighteenth century in England saw a renewed consideration of these subjects, and Aphra Behn addresses the expectations, misconceptions, and unfulfilled longings that often exist between genders. Romantic poet John Keats uses the metaphor of "a doll dressed up" to describe love. Women poets of the late nineteenth and early twentieth centuries such as Emily Dickinson, Elizabeth Barrett Browning, and Edna St. Vincent Millay explore the formerly taboo subject of women's sensual pleasure in verse. The twentieth-century poets represented here—Octavio Paz, Sharon Olds, and Rita Dove—deal frankly with sexual pleasure and the emotions that attend it.

The work of drama in this chapter is *Cat on a Hot Tin Roof* by Tennessee Williams. You probably recognize the title of this twentieth-century American play even if you have not read it. Like Williams's other great plays (such as *The*

Glass Menagerie and *A Streetcar Named Desire*) it exposes the painful truth underneath the superficial exteriors of polite conversation. This kind of exposure, one of the most common themes of twentieth-century drama, is treated with special bitterness and anger in Williams's play. The central battle between Brick and Margaret over their sex life connects *Cat on a Hot Tin Roof* to the other works in this chapter, as well as to works in Chapter 14 ("Honesty and Deception") or Chapter 17 ("Greed, Gluttony, and Generosity").

The essays by nineteenth-century writers Stendhal and Robert Louis Stevenson are at once hopeful about the prospects of long-term love and realistic about the frequency of its occurrence.

The portfolio at the end of the chapter focuses on the figure of Don Juan, the legendary Spanish lover. Don Juan's promiscuity might be seen as a vice—indeed, psychologists have described insatiable lovers who are unable to commit to a single partner as having "Don Juan syndrome"—but Don Juan clearly enjoys himself. Those who have been loved and left by Don Juan might be able to get over their regret, and, as the speaker of Dorothy Parker's poem "The Little Old Lady in Lavender Silk" says, "There was nothing more fun than a man!"

Fiction

James Joyce

The Dead

Irish author James Joyce (1882–1941) is considered one of the greatest twentieth-century English writers. He is especially praised for his stylistic innovation. His first novel, *A Portrait of the Artist as a Young Man,* is the story of Stephen Dedalus and his search for identity that ends in exile from his native land. Though fairly easy to read, the novel uses classical allusions and a style known as stream-of-consciousness, which attempts to mirror the flow of thoughts as they occur in the mind. This technique is taken to greater extremes in two later novels, *Ulysses* and *Finnegans Wake.* Joyce's extraordinary 1922 novel *Ulysses,* based loosely on Homer's *Odyssey,* uses the Greek myth to narrate one day in the life of Leopold Bloom, a kind of "everyman" from Dublin. Its stream-of-consciousness, as well as its puns in several languages, makes for hard reading. Because of these same qualities, many critics deemed Joyce's final novel, *Finnegans Wake,* too difficult for any but the most dedicated scholars. However, the story presented here, "The Dead," is the last story from Joyce's first major work of fiction, a collection entitled *Dubliners.* As it relates an evening in the life of Gabriel Conroy, this narrative addresses many of Joyce's themes with grace, subtlety, and undeniable beauty.

Lily, the caretaker's daughter, was literally run off her feet. Hardly had she brought one gentleman into the little pantry behind the office on the ground floor and helped him off with his overcoat than the wheezy hall-door bell clanged again and she had to scamper along the bare hallway to let in another guest. It was well for her she had not to attend to the ladies also. But Miss Kate and Miss Julia had thought of that and had converted the bathroom upstairs into a ladies' dressing-room. Miss Kate and Miss Julia were there, gossiping and laughing and fussing, walking after each other to the head of the stairs, peering down over the banisters and calling down to Lily to ask her who had come.

It was always a great affair, the Misses Morkan's annual dance. Everybody who knew them came to it, members of the family, old friends of the family, the members of Julia's choir, any of Kate's pupils that were grown up enough and even some of Mary Jane's pupils too. Never once had it fallen flat. For years and years it had gone off in splendid style as long as anyone could remember; ever since Kate and Julia, after the death of their brother Pat, had left the house in Stoney Batter and taken Mary Jane, their only niece, to live with them in the dark gaunt house on Usher's Island, the upper part of which they had rented from Mr Fulham, the cornfactor on the ground floor. That was a good thirty years ago if it was a day. Mary Jane, who was then a little girl in short clothes, was now the main prop of the household for she had the organ in Haddington Road. She had been through the Academy and gave a pupils' concert every year in the upper room of the Antient Concert Rooms.[1] Many of her pupils belonged to better-class families on the Kingstown and Dalkey line. Old as they were, her aunts also did their share. Julia, though she was quite grey, was still the leading soprano in Adam and Eve's, and Kate, being too feeble to go about much, gave music lessons to beginners on the old square piano in the back room. Lily, the caretaker's daughter, did housemaid's work for them. Though their life was modest they believed in eating well; the best of everything: diamond-bone sirloins, three-shilling tea and the best bottled stout. But Lily seldom made a mistake in the orders so that she got on well with her three mistresses. They were fussy, that was all. But the only thing they would not stand was back answers.

Of course they had good reason to be fussy on such a night. And then it was long after ten o'clock and yet there was no sign of Gabriel and his wife. Besides they were dreadfully afraid that Freddy Malins might turn up screwed. They would not wish for worlds that any of Mary Jane's pupils should see him under the influence; and when he was like that it was sometimes very hard to manage him. Freddy Malins always came late but they wondered what could be keeping Gabriel: and that was what brought them every two minutes to the banisters to ask Lily had Gabriel or Freddy come.

—O, Mr Conroy, said Lily to Gabriel when she opened the door for him, Miss Kate and Miss Julia thought you were never coming. Good-night, Mrs Conroy.

[1]*Antient Concert Rooms:* Dublin Concert Hall.

—I'll engage they did, said Gabriel, but they forget that my wife here takes three mortal hours to dress herself.

He stood on the mat, scraping the snow from his goloshes, while Lily led his wife to the foot of the stairs and called out:

—Miss Kate, here's Mrs Conroy.

Kate and Julia came toddling down the dark stairs at once. Both of them kissed Gabriel's wife, said she must be perished alive and asked was Gabriel with her.

—Here I am as right as the mail, Aunt Kate! Go on up. I'll follow, called out Gabriel from the dark.

He continued scraping his feet vigorously while the three women went upstairs, laughing, to the ladies' dressing-room. A light fringe of snow lay like a cape on the shoulders of his overcoat and like toecaps on the toes of his goloshes; and, as the buttons of his overcoat slipped with a squeaking noise through the snow-stiffened frieze, a cold fragrant air from out-of-doors escaped from crevices and folds.

—Is it snowing again, Mr Conroy? asked Lily.

She had preceded him into the pantry to help him off with his overcoat. Gabriel smiled at the three syllables she had given his surname and glanced at her. She was a slim, growing girl, pale in complexion and with hay-coloured hair. The gas in the pantry made her look still paler. Gabriel had known her when she was a child and used to sit on the lowest step nursing a rag doll.

—Yes, Lily, he answered, and I think we're in for a night of it.

He looked up at the pantry ceiling, which was shaking with the stamping and shuffling of feet on the floor above, listened for a moment to the piano and then glanced at the girl, who was folding his overcoat carefully at the end of a shelf.

—Tell me, Lily, he said in a friendly tone, do you still go to school?

—O no, sir, she answered. I'm done schooling this year and more.

—O, then, and Gabriel gaily, I suppose we'll be going to your wedding one of these fine days with your young man, eh?

The girl glanced back at him over her shoulder and said with great bitterness:

—The men that is now is only all palaver and what they can get out of you.

Gabriel coloured as if he felt he had made a mistake and, without looking at her, kicked off his goloshes and flicked actively with his muffler at his patent-leather shoes.

He was a stout tallish young man. The high colour of his cheeks pushed upwards even to his forehead where it scattered itself in a few formless patches of pale red; and on his hairless face there scintillated restlessly the polished lenses and the bright gilt rims of the glasses which screened his delicate and restless eyes. His glossy black hair was parted in the middle and brushed in a long curve behind his ears where it curled slightly beneath the groove left by his hat.

When he had flicked lustre into his shoes he stood up and pulled his waistcoat down more tightly on his plump body. Then he took a coin rapidly from his pocket.

—O Lily, he said, thrusting it into her hands, it's Christmas-time, isn't it? Just . . . here's a little. . . .

He walked rapidly towards the door.

—O no, sir! cried the girl, following him. Really, sir, I wouldn't take it.

—Christmas-time! Christmas-time! said Gabriel, almost trotting to the stairs and waving his hand to her in deprecation.

The girl, seeing that he had gained the stairs, called out after him:

—Well, thank you, sir.

He waited outside the drawing-room door until the waltz should finish, listening to the skirts that swept against it and to the shuffling of feet. He was still discomposed by the girl's bitter and sudden retort. It had cast a gloom over him which he tried to dispel by arranging his cuffs and the bows of his tie. Then he took from his waistcoat pocket a little paper and glanced at the headings he had made for his speech. He was undecided about the lines from Robert Browning for he feared they would be above the heads of his hearers. Some quotation that they could recognise from Shakespeare or from the Melodies would be better. The indelicate clacking of the men's heels and the shuffling of their soles reminded him that their grade of culture differed from his. He would only make himself ridiculous by quoting poetry to them which they could not understand. They would think that he was airing his superior education. He would fail with them just as he had failed with the girl in the pantry. He had taken up a wrong tone. His whole speech was a mistake from first to last, an utter failure.

Just then his aunts and his wife came out of the ladies' dressing-room. His aunts were two small plainly dressed old women. Aunt Julia was an inch or so taller. Her hair, drawn low over the tops of her ears, was grey; and grey also, with darker shadows, was her large flaccid face. Though she was stout in build and stood erect her slow eyes and parted lips gave her the appearance of a woman who did not know where she was or where she was going. Aunt Kate was more vivacious. Her face, healthier than her sister's, was all puckers and creases, like a shriveled red apple, and her hair, braided in the same old-fashioned way, had not lost its ripe nut colour.

They both kissed Gabriel frankly. He was their favourite nephew, the son of their dead elder sister, Ellen, who had married T. J. Conroy of the Port and Docks.

—Gretta tells me you're not going to take a cab back to Monkstown tonight, Gabriel, said Aunt Kate.

—No, said Gabriel, turning to his wife, we had quite enough of that last year, hadn't we? Don't you remember, Aunt Kate, what a cold Gretta got out of it? Cab windows rattling all the way, and the east wind blowing in after we passed Merrion. Very jolly it was. Gretta caught a dreadful cold.

Aunt Kate frowned severely and nodded her head at every word.

—Quite right, Gabriel, quite right, she said. You can't be too careful.

—But as for Gretta there, said Gabriel, she'd walk home in the snow if she were let.

Mrs Conroy laughed.

—Don't mind him, Aunt Kate, she said. He's really an awful bother, what with green shades for Tom's eyes at night and making him do the dumb-bells, and forcing Eva to eat the stirabout.[2] The poor child! And she simply hates the sight of it! . . . O, but you'll never guess what he makes me wear now!

She broke out into a peal of laughter and glanced at her husband, whose admiring and happy eyes had been wandering from her dress to her face and hair. The two aunts laughed heartily too, for Gabriel's solicitude was a standing joke with them.

—Goloshes! said Mrs Conroy. That's the latest. Whenever it's wet underfoot I must put on my goloshes. To-night even he wanted me to put them on, but I wouldn't. The next thing he'll buy me will be a diving suit.

Gabriel laughed nervously and patted his tie reassuringly while Aunt Kate nearly doubled herself, so heartily did she enjoy the joke. The smile soon faded from Aunt Julia's face and her mirthless eyes were directed towards her nephew's face. After a pause she asked:

—And what are goloshes, Gabriel?

—Goloshes, Julia! exclaimed her sister. Goodness me, don't you know what goloshes are? You wear them over your . . . over your boots, Gretta, isn't it?

—Yes, said Mrs Conroy. Guttapercha things. We both have a pair now. Gabriel says everyone wears them on the continent.

—O, on the continent, murmured Aunt Julia, nodding her head slowly.

Gabriel knitted his brows and said, as if he were slightly angered:

—It's nothing very wonderful but Gretta thinks it very funny because she says the word reminds her of Christy Minstrels.[3]

—But tell me, Gabriel, said Aunt Kate, with brisk tact. Of course, you've seen about the room. Gretta was saying . . .

—O, the room is all right, replied Gabriel. I've taken one in the Gresham.

—To be sure, said Aunt Kate, by far the best thing to do. And the children, Gretta, you're not anxious about them?

—O, for one night, said Mrs Conroy. Besides, Bessie will look after them.

—To be sure, said Aunt Kate again. What a comfort it is to have a girl like that, one you can depend on! There's that Lily, I'm sure I don't know what has come over her lately. She's not the girl she was at all.

Gabriel was about to ask his aunt some questions on this point but she broke off suddenly to gaze after her sister who had wandered down the stairs and was craning her neck over the banisters.

—Now, I ask you, she said, almost testily, where is Julia going? Julia! Julia! Where are you going?

Julia, who had gone halfway down one flight, came back and announced blandly:

—Here's Freddy.

At the same moment a clapping of hands and a final flourish of the pianist told that the waltz had ended. The drawing-room door was opened from within and some couples came out. Aunt Kate drew Gabriel aside hurriedly and whispered into his ear:

[2]*stirabout:* Oatmeal.

[3]*Christy Minstrels:* Entertainers in blackface.

—Slip down, Gabriel, like a good fellow and see if he's all right, and don't let him up if he's screwed. I'm sure he's screwed. I'm sure he is.

Gabriel went to the stairs and listened over the banisters. He could hear two persons talking in the pantry. Then he recognised Freddy Malins' laugh. He went down the stairs noisily.

—It's such a relief, said Aunt Kate to Mrs Conroy, that Gabriel is here. I always feel easier in my mind when he's here. . . . Julia, there's Miss Daly and Miss Power will take some refreshment. Thanks for your beautiful waltz, Miss Daly. It made lovely time.

A tall wizen-faced man, with a stiff grizzled moustache and swarthy skin, who was passing out with his partner said:

—And may we have some refreshment, too, Miss Morkan?

—Julia, said Aunt Kate summarily, and here's Mr Browne and Miss Furlong. Take them in, Julia, with Miss Daly and Miss Power.

—I'm the man for the ladies, said Mr Browne, pursing his lips until his moustache bristled and smiling in all his wrinkles. You know, Miss Morkan, the reason they are so fond of me is—

He did not finish his sentence, but, seeing that Aunt Kate was out of earshot, at once led the three young ladies into the back room. The middle of the room was occupied by two square tables placed end to end, and on these Aunt Julia and the caretaker were straightening and smoothing a large cloth. On the sideboard were arrayed dishes and plates, and glasses and bundles of knives and forks and spoons. The top of the closed square piano served also as a sideboard for viands and sweets. At a smaller sideboard in one corner two young men were standing, drinking hop-bitters.

Mr Browne led his charges thither and invited them all, in jest, to some ladies' punch, hot, strong and sweet. As they said they never took anything strong he opened three bottles of lemonade for them. Then he asked one of the young men to move aside, and, taking hold of the decanter, filled out for himself a goodly measure of whisky. The young men eyed him respectfully while he took a trial sip.

—God help me, he said, smiling, it's the doctor's orders.

His wizened face broke into a broader smile, and the three young ladies laughed in musical echo to his pleasantry, swaying their bodies to and fro, with nervous jerks of their shoulders. The boldest said:

—O, now, Mr Browne, I'm sure the doctor never ordered anything of the kind.

Mr Browne took another sip of his whisky and said, with sidling mimicry:

—Well, you see, I'm like the famous Mrs Cassidy, who is reported to have said: *Now, Mary Grimes, if I don't take it, make me take it, for I feel I want it.*

His hot face had leaned forward a little too confidentially and he had assumed a very low Dublin accent so that the young ladies, with one instinct, received his speech in silence. Miss Furlong, who was one of Mary Jane's pupils, asked Miss Daly what was the name of the pretty waltz she had played; and Mr Browne, seeing that he was ignored, turned promptly to the two young men who were more appreciative.

A red-faced young woman, dressed in pansy, came into the room, excitedly clapping her hands and crying:

—Quadrilles! Quadrilles!

Close on her heels came Aunt Kate, crying:

—Two gentlemen and three ladies, Mary Jane!

—O, here's Mr Bergin and Mr Kerrigan, said Mary Jane. Mr Kerrigan, will you take Miss Power? Miss Furlong, may I get you a partner, Mr Bergin. O, that'll just do now.

—Three ladies, Mary Jane, said Aunt Kate.

The two young gentlemen asked the ladies if they might have the pleasure, and Mary Jane turned to Miss Daly.

—O, Miss Daly, you're really awfully good, after playing for the last two dances, but really we're so short of ladies to-night.

—I don't mind in the least, Miss Morkan.

—But I've a nice partner for you, Mr Bartell D'Arcy, the tenor. I'll get him to sing later on. All Dublin is raving about him.

—Lovely voice, lovely voice! said Aunt Kate.

As the piano had twice begun the prelude to the first figure Mary Jane led her recruits quickly from the room. They had hardly gone when Aunt Julia wandered slowly into the room, looking behind her at something.

—What is the matter, Julia? asked Aunt Kate anxiously. Who is it?

Julia, who was carrying in a column of table-napkins, turned to her sister and said, simply, as if the question had surprised her:

—It's only Freddy, Kate, and Gabriel with him.

In fact right behind her Gabriel could be seen piloting Freddy Malins across the landing. The latter, a young man of about forty, was of Gabriel's size and build, with very round shoulders. His face was fleshy and pallid, touched with colour only at the thick hanging lobes of his ears and at the wide wings of his nose. He had coarse features, a blunt nose, a convex and receding brow, tumid and protruded lips. His heavy-lidded eyes and the disorder of his scanty hair made him look sleepy. He was laughing heartily in a high key at a story which he had been telling Gabriel on the stairs and at the same time rubbing the knuckles of his left fist backwards and forwards into his left eye.

—Good-evening, Freddy, said Aunt Julia.

Freddy Malins bade the Misses Morkan good-evening in what seemed an offhand fashion by reason of the habitual catch in his voice and then, seeing that Mr Browne was grinning at him from the sideboard, crossed the room on rather shaky legs and began to repeat in an undertone the story he had just told to Gabriel.

—He's not so bad, is he? said Aunt Kate to Gabriel.

Gabriel's brows were dark but he raised them quickly and answered:

—O no, hardly noticeable.

—Now, isn't he a terrible fellow! she said. And his poor mother made him take the pledge on New Year's Eve. But come on, Gabriel, into the drawing-room.

Before leaving the room with Gabriel she signalled to Mr Browne by frowning and shaking her forefinger in warning to and fro. Mr Browne nodded in answer and, when she had gone, said to Freddy Malins:

—Now, then, Teddy, I'm going to fill you out a good glass of lemonade just to buck you up.

Freddy Malins, who was nearing the climax of his story, waved the offer aside impatiently but Mr Browne, having first called Freddy Malins' attention to a disarray in his dress, filled out and handed him a full glass of lemonade. Freddy Malins' left hand accepted the glass mechanically, his right hand being engaged in the mechanical readjustment of his dress. Mr Browne, whose face was once more wrinkling with mirth, poured out for himself a glass of whisky while Freddy Malins exploded, before he had well reached the climax of his story, in a kink of high-pitched bronchitic laughter and, setting down his untasted and overflowing glass, began to rub the knuckles of his left fist backwards and forwards into his left eye, repeating words of his last phrase as well as his fit of laughter would allow him.

Gabriel could not listen while Mary Jane was playing her Academy piece, full of runs and difficult passages, to the hushed drawing-room. He liked music but the piece she was playing had no melody for him and he doubted whether it had any melody for the other listeners, though they had begged Mary Jane to play something. Four young men, who had come from the refreshment-room to stand in the door-way at the sound of the piano, had gone away quietly in couples after a few minutes. The only persons who seemed to follow the music were Mary Jane herself, her hands racing along the key-board or lifted from it at the pauses like those of a priestess in momentary imprecation, and Aunt Kate standing at her elbow to turn the page.

Gabriel's eyes, irritated by the floor, which glittered with beeswax under the heavy chandelier, wandered to the wall above the piano. A picture of the balcony scene in *Romeo and Juliet* hung there and beside it was a picture of the two murdered princes in the Tower[4] which Aunt Julia had worked in red, blue and brown wools when she was a girl. Probably in the school they had gone to as girls that kind of work had been taught, for one year his mother had worked for him as a birthday present a waistcoat of purple tabinet, with little foxes' heads upon it, lined with brown satin and having round mulberry buttons. It was strange that his mother had had no musical talent though Aunt Kate used to call her the brains carrier of the Morkan family. Both she and Julia had always seemed a little proud of their serious and matronly sister. Her photograph stood before the pierglass. She held an open book on her knees and was pointing out something in it to Constantine who, dressed in a man-o'-war suit, lay at her feet. It was she who had chosen the names for her sons for she was very sensible of the dignity of family life. Thanks to her, Constantine was now senior curate in Balbriggan and, thanks to her, Gabriel himself had taken his degree in the Royal University.

[4] *princes in the Tower:* The nephews of Edward II, who, according to Shakespeare's play, were murdered by their uncle.

A shadow passed over his face as he remembered her sullen opposition to his marriage. Some slighting phrases she had used still rankled in his memory; she had once spoken of Gretta as being country cute and that was not true of Gretta at all. It was Gretta who had nursed her during all her last long illness in their house at Monkstown.

He knew that Mary Jane must be near the end of her piece for she was playing again the opening melody with runs of scales after every bar and while he waited for the end the resentment died down in his heart. The piece ended with a trill of octaves in the treble and a final deep octave in the bass. Great applause greeted Mary Jane as, blushing and rolling up her music nervously, she escaped from the room. The most vigorous clapping came from the four young men in the doorway who had gone away to the refreshment-room at the beginning of the piece but had come back when the piano had stopped.

Lancers were arranged. Gabriel found himself partnered with Miss Ivors. She was a frank-mannered talkative young lady, with a freckled face and prominent brown eyes. She did not wear a low-cut bodice and the large brooch which was fixed in the front of her collar bore on it an Irish device.

When they had taken their places she said abruptly:

—I have a crow to pluck with you.

—With me? said Gabriel.

She nodded her head gravely.

—What is it? asked Gabriel, smiling at her solemn manner.

—Who is G. C.? answered Miss Ivors, turning her eyes upon him.

Gabriel coloured and was about to knit his brows, as if he did not understand, when she said bluntly:

—O, innocent Amy! I have found out that you write for *The Daily Express*. Now, aren't you ashamed of yourself?

—Why should I be ashamed of myself? asked Gabriel, blinking his eyes and trying to smile.

—Well, I'm ashamed of you, said Miss Ivors frankly. To say you'd write for a rag like that. I didn't think you were a West Briton.[5]

A look of perplexity appeared on Gabriel's face. It was true that he wrote a literary column every Wednesday in *The Daily Express*, for which he was paid fifteen shillings. But that did not make him a West Briton surely. The books he received for review were almost more welcome than the paltry cheque. He loved to feel the covers and turn over the pages of newly printed books. Nearly every day when his teaching in the college was ended he used to wander down the quays to the second-hand booksellers, to Hickey's on Bachelor's Walk, to Webb's, or Massey's on Aston's Quay, or to O'Clohissey's in the by-street. He did not know how to meet her charge. He wanted to say that literature was above politics. But they were friends of many years' standing and their careers had been parallel, first at the University and then as teachers: he could not risk a grandiose phrase with her. He continued blinking his eyes and trying to smile and murmured lamely that he saw nothing political in writing reviews of books.

[5] *West Briton:* A person who sees Ireland as part of England, one who opposes Irish independence.

When their turn to cross had come he was still perplexed and inattentive. Miss Ivors promptly took his hand in a warm grasp and said in a soft friendly tone:

—Of course, I was only joking. Come, we cross now.

When they were together again she spoke of the University question and Gabriel felt more at ease. A friend of hers had shown her his review of Browning's poems. That was how she had found out the secret: but she liked the review immensely. Then she said suddenly:

—O, Mr Conroy, will you come for an excursion to the Aran Isles this summer? We're going to stay there a whole month. It will be splendid out in the Atlantic. You ought to come. Mr Clancy is coming, and Mr Kilkelly and Kathleen Kearney. It would be splendid for Gretta too if she'd come. She's from Connacht,[6] isn't she?

—Her people are, said Gabriel shortly.

—But you will come, won't you? said Miss Ivors, laying her warm hand eagerly on his arm.

—The fact is, said Gabriel, I have already arranged to go—

—Go where? asked Miss Ivors.

—Well, you know, every year I go for a cycling tour with some fellows and so—

—But where? asked Miss Ivors.

—Well, we usually go to France or Belgium or perhaps Germany, said Gabriel awkwardly.

—And why do you go to France and Belgium, said Miss Ivors, instead of visiting your own land?

—Well, said Gabriel, it's partly to keep in touch with the languages and partly for a change.

—And haven't you your own language to keep in touch with—Irish? asked Miss Ivors.

—Well, said Gabriel, if it comes to that, you know, Irish is not my language.

Their neighbours had turned to listen to the cross-examination. Gabriel glanced right and left nervously and tried to keep his good humour under the ordeal which was making a blush invade his forehead.

—And haven't you your own land to visit, continued Miss Ivors, that you know nothing of, your own people, and your own country?

—O, to tell you the truth, retorted Gabriel suddenly, I'm sick of my own country, sick of it!

—Why? asked Miss Ivors.

Gabriel did not answer for his retort had heated him.

—Why? repeated Miss Ivors.

They had to go visiting together and, as he had not answered her, Miss Ivors said warmly:

—Of course, you've no answer.

[6]*Connacht:* A part of western Ireland.

Gabriel tried to cover his agitation by taking part in the dance with great energy. He avoided her eyes for he had seen a sour expression on her face. But when they met in the long chain he was surprised to feel his hand firmly pressed. She looked at him from under her brows for a moment quizzically until he smiled. Then, just as the chain was about to start again, she stood on tiptoe and whispered into his ear:

—West Briton!

When the lancers were over Gabriel went away to a remote corner of the room where Freddy Malins' mother was sitting. She was a stout feeble old woman with white hair. Her voice had a catch in it like her son's and she stuttered slightly. She had been told that Freddy had come and that he was nearly all right. Gabriel asked her whether she had had a good crossing. She lived with her married daughter in Glasgow and came to Dublin on a visit once a year. She answered placidly that she had had a beautiful crossing and that the captain had been most attentive to her. She spoke also of the beautiful house her daughter kept in Glasgow, and of all the nice friends they had there. While her tongue rambled on Gabriel tried to banish from his mind all memory of the unpleasant incident with Miss Ivors. Of course the girl or woman, or whatever she was, was an enthusiast but there was a time for all things. Perhaps he ought not to have answered her like that. But she had no right to call him a West Briton before people, even in joke. She had tried to make him ridiculous before people, heckling him and staring at him with her rabbit's eyes.

He saw his wife making her way towards him through the waltzing couples. When she reached him she said into his ear:

—Gabriel, Aunt Kate wants to know won't you carve the goose as usual. Miss Daly will carve the ham and I'll do the pudding.

—All right, said Gabriel.

—She's sending in the younger ones first as soon as this waltz is over so that we'll have the table to ourselves.

—Were you dancing? asked Gabriel.

—Of course I was. Didn't you see me? What words had you with Molly Ivors?

—No words. Why? Did she say so?

—Something like that. I'm trying to get that Mr D'Arcy to sing. He's full of conceit, I think.

—There were no words, said Gabriel moodily, only she wanted me to go for a trip to the west of Ireland and I said I wouldn't.

His wife clasped her hands excitedly and gave a little jump.

—O, do go, Gabriel, she cried. I'd love to see Galway again.

—You can go if you like, said Gabriel coldly.

She looked at him for a moment, then turned to Mrs Malins and said:

—There's a nice husband for you, Mrs Malins.

While she was threading her way back across the room Mrs Malins, without adverting to the interruption, went on to tell Gabriel what beautiful places there were in Scotland and beautiful scenery. Her son-in-law brought them every year to the lakes and they used to go fishing. Her son-in-law was a splendid fisher.

One day he caught a fish, a beautiful big big fish, and the man in the hotel boiled it for their dinner.

Gabriel hardly heard what she said. Now that supper was coming near he began to think again about his speech and about the quotation. When he saw Freddy Malins coming across the room to visit his mother Gabriel left the chair free for him and retired into the embrasure of the window. The room had already cleared and from the back room came the clatter of plates and knives. Those who still remained in the drawing-room seemed tired of dancing and were conversing quietly in little groups. Gabriel's warm trembling fingers tapped the cold pane of the window. How cool it must be outside! How pleasant it would be to walk out alone, first along by the river and then through the park! The snow would be lying on the branches of the trees and forming a bright cap on the top of the Wellington Monument.[7] How much more pleasant it would be there than at the supper-table!

He ran over the headings of his speech: Irish hospitality, sad memories, the Three Graces,[8] Paris, the quotation from Browning. He repeated to himself a phrase he had written in his review: *One feels that one is listening to a thought-tormented music.* Miss Ivors had praised the review. Was she sincere? Had she really any life her own behind all her propagandism? There had never been any ill-feeling between them until that night. It unnerved him to think that she would be at the supper-table, looking up at him while he spoke with her critical quizzing eyes. Perhaps she would not be sorry to see him fail in his speech. An idea came into his mind and gave him courage. He would say, alluding to Aunt Kate and Aunt Julia: *Ladies and Gentlemen, the generation which is now on the wane among us may have had its faults but for my part I think it had certain qualities of hospitality, of humour, of humanity, which the new and very serious and hypereducated generation that is growing up around us seems to me to lack.* Very good: that was one for Miss Ivors. What did he care that his aunts were only two ignorant old women?

A murmur in the room attracted his attention. Mr Browne was advancing from the door, gallantly escorting Aunt Julia, who leaned upon his arm, smiling and hanging her head. An irregular musketry of applause escorted her also as far as the piano and then, as Mary Jane seated herself on the stool, and Aunt Julia, no longer smiling, half turned so as to pitch her voice fairly into the room, gradually ceased. Gabriel recognised the prelude. It was that of an old song of Aunt Julia's—*Arrayed for the Bridal.* Her voice, strong and clear in tone, attacked with great spirit the runs which embellish the air and though she sang very rapidly she did not miss even the smallest of the grace notes. To follow the voice, without looking at the singer's face, was to feel and share the excitement of swift and secure flight. Gabriel applauded loudly with all the others at the close of the song and loud applause was borne in from the invisible supper-table. It sounded so genuine that a little colour struggled into Aunt Julia's face

[7] *Wellington Monument:* A monument in Dublin that commemorates the Duke of Wellington, who was born in Dublin.

[8] *Three Graces:* Goddesses in Greek mythology that represented joy, charm, and beauty.

as she bent to replace in the music-stand the old leather-bound songbook that had her initials on the cover. Freddy Malins, who had listened with his head perched sideways to hear her better, was still applauding when everyone else had ceased and talking animatedly to his mother who nodded her head gravely and slowly in acquiescence. At last, when he could clap no more, he stood up suddenly and hurried across the room to Aunt Julia whose hand he seized and held in both his hands, shaking it when words failed him or the catch in his voice proved too much for him.

—I was just telling my mother, he said, I never heard you sing so well, never. No, I never heard your voice so good as it is to-night. Now! Would you believe that now? That's the truth. Upon my word and honour that's the truth I never heard your voice sound so fresh and so . . . so clear and fresh, never.

Aunt Julia smiled broadly and murmured something about compliments as 155
she released her hand from his grasp. Mr Browne extended his open hand towards her and said to those who were near him in the manner of a showman introducing a prodigy to an audience:

—Miss Julia Morkan, my latest discovery!

He was laughing very heartily at this himself when Freddy Malins turned to him and said:

—Well, Browne, if you're serious you might make a worse discovery. All I can say is I never heard her sing half so well as long as I am coming here. And that's the honest truth.

—Neither did I, said Mr Browne. I think her voice has greatly improved.

Aunt Julia shrugged her shoulders and said with meek pride:

—Thirty years ago I hadn't a bad voice as voices go. 160

—I often told Julia, said Aunt Kate emphatically, that she was simply thrown away in that choir. But she never would be said by me.

She turned as if to appeal to the good sense of the others against a refractory child while Aunt Julia gazed in front of her, a vague smile of reminiscence playing on her face.

—No, continued Aunt Kate, she wouldn't be said or led by anyone, slaving there in that choir night and day, night and day. Six o'clock on Christmas morning! And all for what?

—Well, isn't it for the honour of God, Aunt Kate? asked Mary Jane, twisting round on the piano-stool and smiling.

Aunt Kate turned fiercely on her niece and said: 165

—I know all about the honour of God, Mary Jane, but I think it's not at all honourable for the pope to turn out the women out of the choirs that have slaved there all their lives and put little whipper-snappers of boys over their heads. I suppose it is for the good of the Church if the pope does it. But it's not just, Mary Jane, and it's not right.

She had worked herself into a passion and would have continued in defence of her sister for it was a sore subject with her but Mary Jane, seeing that all the dancers had come back, intervened pacifically:

—Now, Aunt Kate, you're giving scandal to Mr Browne who is of the other persuasion.

Aunt Kate turned to Mr Browne, who was grinning at this allusion to his religion, and said hastily:

—O, I don't question the pope's being right. I'm only a stupid old woman and I wouldn't presume to do such a thing. But there's such a thing as common everyday politeness and gratitude. And if I were in Julia's place I'd tell that Father Healy straight up to his face . . .

—And besides, Aunt Kate, said Mary Jane, we really are all hungry and when we are hungry we are all very quarrelsome.

—And when we are thirsty we are also quarrelsome, added Mr Browne.

—So that we had better go to supper, said Mary Jane, and finish the discussion afterwards.

On the landing outside the drawing-room Gabriel found his wife and Mary Jane trying to persuade Miss Ivors to stay for supper. But Miss Ivors, who had put on her hat and was buttoning her cloak, would not stay. She did not feel in the least hungry and she had already overstayed her time.

—But only for ten minutes, Molly, said Mrs Conroy. That won't delay you.

—To take a pick itself, said Mary Jane, after all your dancing.

—I really couldn't, said Miss Ivors.

—I am afraid you didn't enjoy yourself at all, said Mary Jane hopelessly.

—Ever so much, I assure you, said Miss Ivors, but you really must let me run off now.

—But how can you get home? asked Mrs Conroy.

—O, it's only two steps up the quay.

Gabriel hesitated a moment and said:

—If you will allow me, Miss Ivors, I'll see you home if you really are obliged to go.

But Miss Ivors broke away from them.

—I won't hear of it, she cried. For goodness sake go in to your suppers and don't mind me. I'm quite well able to take care of myself.

—Well, you're the comical girl, Molly, said Mrs Conroy frankly.

—*Beannacht libh*,[9] cried Miss Ivors, with a laugh, as she ran down the staircase.

Mary Jane gazed after her, a moody puzzled expression on her face, while Mrs Conroy leaned over the banisters to listen for the hall-door. Gabriel asked himself was he the cause of her abrupt departure. But she did not seem to be in ill humour: she had gone away laughing. He stared blankly down the staircase.

At that moment Aunt Kate came toddling out of the supper-room, almost wringing her hands in despair.

—Where is Gabriel? she cried. Where on earth is Gabriel? There's everyone waiting in there, stage to let, and nobody to carve the goose!

—Here I am, Aunt Kate! cried Gabriel, with sudden animation, ready to carve a flock of geese, if necessary.

A fat brown goose lay at one end of the table and at the other end, on a bed of creased paper strewn with sprigs of parsley, lay a great ham, stripped of its outer skin and peppered over with crust crumbs, a neat paper frill round its shin

[9]*Beannacht libh:* Goodbye (Gaelic).

and beside this was a round of spiced beef. Between these rival ends ran parallel lines of side-dishes: two little minsters of jelly, red and yellow; a shallow dish full of blocks of blancmange and red jam, a large green leaf-shaped dish with a stalk-shaped handle, on which lay bunches of purple raisins and peeled almonds, a companion dish on which lay a solid rectangle of Smyrna figs, a dish of custard topped with grated nutmeg, a small bowl full of chocolates and sweets wrapped in gold and silver papers and a glass vase in which stood some tall celery stalks. In the centre of the table there stood, as sentries to a fruit-stand which upheld a pyramid of oranges and American apples, two squat old-fashioned decanters of cut glass, one containing port and the other dark sherry. On the closed square piano a pudding in a huge yellow dish lay in waiting and behind it were three squads of bottles of stout and ale and minerals, drawn up according to the colours of their uniforms, the first two black, with brown and red labels, the third and smallest squad white, with transverse green sashes.

Gabriel took his seat boldly at the head of the table and, having looked to the edge of the carver, plunged his fork firmly into the goose. He felt quite at ease now for he was an expert carver and liked nothing better than to find himself at the head of a well-laden table.

—Miss Furlong, what shall I send you? he asked. A wing or a slice of the breast?

—Just a small slice of the breast.

—Miss Higgins, what for you?

—O, anything at all, Mr Conroy.

While Gabriel and Miss Daly exchanged plates of goose and plates of ham and spiced beef Lily went from guest to guest with a dish of hot floury potatoes wrapped in a white napkin. This was Mary Jane's idea and she had also suggested apple sauce for the goose but Aunt Kate had said that plain roast goose without apple sauce had always been good enough for her and she hoped she might never eat worse. Mary Jane waited on her pupils and saw that they got the best slices and Aunt Kate and Aunt Julia opened and carried across from the piano bottles of stout and ale for the gentlemen and bottles of minerals for the ladies. There was a great deal of confusion and laughter and noise, the noise of orders and counter-orders, of knives and forks, of corks and glass-stoppers. Gabriel began to carve second helpings as soon as he had finished the first round without serving himself. Everyone protested loudly so that he compromised by taking a long draught of stout for he had found the carving hot work. Mary Jane settled down quietly to her supper but Aunt Kate and Aunt Julia were still toddling round the table, walking on each other's heels, getting in each other's way and giving each other unheeded orders. Mr Browne begged of them to sit down and eat their suppers and so did Gabriel but they said there was time enough so that, at last, Freddy Malins stood up and, capturing Aunt Kate, plumped her down on her chair amid general laughter.

When everyone had been well served Gabriel said, smiling:

—Now, if anyone wants a little more of what vulgar people call stuffing let him or her speak.

A chorus of voices invited him to begin his own supper and Lily came forward with three potatoes which she had reserved for him.

—Very well, said Gabriel amiably, as he took another preparatory draught, kindly forget my existence, ladies and gentlemen, for a few minutes.

He set to his supper and took no part in the conversation with which the table covered Lily's removal of the plates. The subject of talk was the opera company which was then at the Theatre Royal. Mr Bartell D'Arcy, the tenor, a dark-complexioned young man with a smart moustache, praised very highly the leading contralto of the company but Miss Furlong thought she had a rather vulgar style of production. Freddy Malins said there was a negro chieftain singing in the second part of the Gaiety pantomime who had one of the finest tenor voices he had ever heard.

—Have you heard him? he asked Mr Bartell D'Arcy across the table.

—No, answered Mr Bartell D'Arcy carelessly.

—Because, Freddy Malins explained, now I'd be curious to hear your opinion of him. I think he has a grand voice.

—It takes Teddy to find out the really good things, said Mr Browne familiarly to the table.

—And why couldn't he have a voice too? asked Freddy Malins sharply. Is it because he's only a black?

Nobody answered this question and Mary Jane led the table back to the legitimate opera. One of her pupils had given her a pass for *Mignon.* Of course it was very fine, she said, but it made her think of poor Georgina Burns. Mr Browne could go back farther still, to the old Italian companies that used to come to Dublin—Tietjens, Ilma de Murzka, Campanini, the great Trebelli, Giuglini, Ravelli, Aramburo. Those were the days, he said, when there was something like singing to be heard in Dublin. He told too of how the top gallery of the old Royal used to be packed night after night, of how one night an Italian tenor had sung five encores to *Let Me Like a Soldier Fall,* introducing a high C every time, and of how the gallery boys would sometimes in their enthusiasm unyoke the horses from the carriage of some great *prima donna* and pull her themselves through the streets to her hotel. Why did they never play the grand old operas now, he asked, *Dinorah, Lucrezia Borgia?* Because they could not get the voices to sing them: that was why.

—O, well, said Mr Bartell D'Arcy, I presume there are as good singers today as there were then.

—Where are they? asked Mr Browne defiantly.

—In London, Paris, Milan, said Mr Bartell d'Arcy warmly. I suppose Caruso, for example, is quite as good, if not better than any of the men you have mentioned.

—Maybe so, said Mr Browne. But I may tell you I doubt it strongly.

—O, I'd give anything to hear Caruso sing, said Mary Jane.

—For me, said Aunt Kate, who had been picking a bone, there was only one tenor. To please me, I mean. But I suppose none of you ever heard of him.

—Who was he, Miss Morkan? asked Mr Bartell D'Arcy politely.

—His name, said Aunt Kate, was Parkinson. I heard him when he was in his prime and I think he had then the purest tenor voice that was ever put into a man's throat.

—Strange, said Mr Bartell d'Arcy. I never even heard of him.

—Yes, yes, Miss Morkan is right, said Mr Browne. I remember hearing of old Parkinson but he's too far back for me.

—A beautiful pure sweet mellow English tenor, said Aunt Kate with enthusiasm.

Gabriel having finished, the huge pudding was transferred to the table. The clatter of forks and spoons began again. Gabriel's wife served out spoonfuls of the pudding and passed the plates down the table. Midway down they were held up by Mary Jane, who replenished them with raspberry or orange jelly or with blancmange and jam. The pudding was of Aunt Julia's making and she received praises for it from all quarters. She herself said that it was not quite brown enough.

—Well, I hope, Miss Morkan, said Mr Browne, that I'm brown enough for you because, you know, I'm all brown.

All the gentlemen, except Gabriel, ate some of the pudding out of compliment to Aunt Julia. As Gabriel never ate sweets the celery had been left for him. Freddy Malins also took a stalk of celery and ate it with his pudding. He had been told that celery was a capital thing for the blood and he was just then under doctor's care. Mrs Malins, who had been silent all through the supper, said that her son was going down to Mount Melleray in a week or so. The table then spoke of Mount Melleray, how bracing the air was down there, how hospitable the monks were and how they never asked for a penny-piece from their guests.

—And do you mean to say, asked Mr Browne incredulously, that a chap can go down there and put up there as if it were a hotel and live on the fat of the land and then come away without paying a farthing?

—O, most people give some donation to the monastery when they leave, said Mary Jane.

—I wish we had an institution like that in our Church, said Mr Browne candidly.

He was astonished to hear that the monks never spoke, got up at two in the morning and slept in their coffins. He asked what they did it for.

—That's the rule of the order, said Aunt Kate firmly.

—Yes, but why? asked Mr Browne.

Aunt Kate repeated that it was the rule, that was all. Mr Browne still seemed not to understand. Freddy Malins explained to him, as best he could, that the monks were trying to make up for the sins committed by all the sinners in the outside world. The explanation was not very clear for Mr Browne grinned and said:

—I like that idea very much but wouldn't a comfortable spring bed do them as well as a coffin?

—The coffin, said Mary Jane, is to remind them of their last end.

As the subject had grown lugubrious it was buried in a silence of the table during which Mrs Malins could be heard saying to her neighbour in an indistinct undertone:

—They are very good men, the monks, very pious men.

The raisins and almonds and figs and apples and oranges and chocolates and 235
sweets were now passed about the table and Aunt Julia invited all the guests to have either port or sherry. At first Mr Bartell D'Arcy refused to take either but one of his neighbours nudged him and whispered something to him upon which he allowed his glass to be filled. Gradually as the last glasses were being filled the conversation ceased. A pause followed, broken only by the noise of the wine and by unsettlings of chairs. The Misses Morkan, all three, looked down at the tablecloth. Someone coughed once or twice and then a few gentlemen patted the table gently as a signal for silence. The silence came and Gabriel pushed back his chair and stood up.

The patting at once grew louder in encouragement and then ceased altogether. Gabriel leaned his ten trembling fingers on the tablecloth and smiled nervously at the company. Meeting a row of upturned faces he raised his eyes to the chandelier. The piano was playing a waltz tune and he could hear the skirts sweeping against the drawing-room door. People, perhaps, were standing in the snow on the quay outside, gazing up at the lighted windows and listening to the waltz music. The air was pure there. In the distance lay the park where the trees were weighted with snow. The Wellington Monument wore a gleaming cap of snow that flashed westward over the white field of Fifteen Acres.

He began:

—Ladies and Gentlemen.

—It has fallen to my lot this evening, as in years past, to perform a very pleasing task but a task for which I am afraid my poor powers as a speaker are all too inadequate.

—No, no! said Mr Browne. 240

—But, however that may be, I can only ask you to-night to take the will for the deed and to lend me your attention for a few moments while I endeavour to express to you in words what my feelings are on this occasion.

—Ladies and Gentlemen. It is not the first time that we have gathered together under this hospitable roof, around this hospitable board. It is not the first time that we have been the recipients—or perhaps, I had better say, the victims—of the hospitality of certain good ladies.

He made a circle in the air with his arm and paused. Everyone laughed or smiled at Aunt Kate and Aunt Julia and Mary Jane who all turned crimson with pleasure. Gabriel went on more boldly:

—I feel more strongly with every recurring year that our country has no tradition which does it so much honour and which it should guard so jealously as that of its hospitality. It is a tradition that is unique as far as my experience goes (and I have visited not a few places abroad) among the modern nations. Some would say, perhaps, that with us it is rather a failing than anything to be boasted of. But granted even that, it is, to my mind, a princely failing, and one that I trust will long be cultivated among us. Of one thing, at least, I am sure. As long as this one roof shelters the good ladies aforesaid—and I wish from my heart it may do so for many and many a long year to come—the tradition of genuine warm-hearted courteous Irish hospitality, which our forefathers have handed down to us and which we in turn must hand down to our descendants, is still alive among us.

A hearty murmur of assent ran round the table. It shot through Gabriel's 245
mind that Miss Ivors was not there and that she had gone away discourteously: and he said with confidence in himself:

—Ladies and Gentlemen.

—A new generation is growing up in our midst, a generation actuated by new ideas and new principles. It is serious and enthusiastic for these new ideas and its enthusiasm, even when it is misdirected, is, I believe, in the main sincere. But we are living in a sceptical and, if I may use the phrase, a thought-tormented age: and sometimes I fear that this new generation, educated or hypereducated as it is, will lack those qualities of humanity, of hospitality, of kindly humour which belonged to an older day. Listening to-night to the names of all those great singers of the past it seemed to me, I must confess, that we were living in a less spacious age. Those days might, without exaggeration, be called spacious days: and if they are gone beyond recall let us hope, at least, that in gatherings such as this we shall still speak of them with pride and affection, still cherish in our hearts the memory of those dead and gone great ones whose fame the world will not willingly let die.

—Hear, hear! said Mr Browne loudly.

—But yet, continued Gabriel, his voice falling into a softer inflection, there are always in gatherings such as this sadder thoughts that will recur to our minds: thoughts of the past, of youth, of changes, of absent faces that we miss here to-night. Our path through life is strewn with many such sad memories: and were we to brood upon them always we could not find the heart to go on bravely with our work among the living. We have all of us living duties and living affections which claim, and rightly claim, our strenuous endeavours.

—Therefore, I will not linger on the past. I will not let any gloomy moralis- 250
ing intrude upon us here to-night. Here we are gathered together for a brief moment from the bustle and rush of our everyday routine. We are met here as friends, in the spirit of good-fellowship, as colleagues, also to a certain extent, in the true spirit of *camaraderie*, and as the guests of—what shall I call them?—the Three Graces of the Dublin musical world.

The table burst into applause and laughter at this sally. Aunt Julia vainly asked each of her neighbours in turn to tell her what Gabriel had said.

—He says we are the Three Graces, Aunt Julia, said Mary Jane.

Aunt Julia did not understand but she looked up, smiling, at Gabriel, who continued in the same vein:

—Ladies and Gentlemen.

—I will not attempt to play to-night the part that Paris played on another 255
occasion. I will not attempt to choose between them. The task would be an invidious one and one beyond my poor powers. For when I view them in turn, whether it be our chief hostess herself, whose good heart, whose too good heart, has become a byword with all who know her, or her sister, who seems to be gifted with perennial youth and whose singing must have been a surprise and a revelation to us all to-night, or, last but not least, when I consider our youngest hostess, talented, cheerful, hard-working and the best of nieces, I confess, Ladies and Gentlemen, that I do not know to which of them I should award the prize.

Gabriel glanced down at his aunts and, seeing the large smile on Aunt Julia's face and the tears which had risen to Aunt Kate's eyes, hastened to his close. He raised his glass of port gallantly, while every member of the company fingered a glass expectantly, and said loudly:

—Let us toast them all three together. Let us drink to their health, wealth, long life, happiness and prosperity and may they long continue to hold the proud and self-won position which they hold in their profession and the position of honour and affection which they hold in our hearts.

All the guests stood up, glass in hand, and, turning towards the three seated ladies, sang in unison, with Mr Browne as leader:

For they are jolly gay fellows,
For they are jolly gay fellows,
For they are jolly gay fellows,
Which nobody can deny.

Aunt Kate was making frank use of her handkerchief and even Aunt Julia seemed moved. Freddy Malins beat time with his pudding-fork and the singers turned towards one another, as if in melodious conference, while they sang, with emphasis:

Unless he tells a lie,
Unless he tells a lie.

Then, turning once more towards their hostesses, they sang:

For they are jolly gay fellows,
For they are jolly gay fellows,
For they are jolly gay fellows,
Which nobody can deny.

The acclamation which followed was taken up beyond the door of the supper-room by many of the other guests and renewed time after time, Freddy Malins acting as officer with his fork on high.

The piercing morning air came into the hall where they were standing so that Aunt Kate said:

—Close the door, somebody. Mrs Malins will get her death of cold.

—Browne is out there, Aunt Kate, said Mary Jane.

—Browne is everywhere, said Aunt Kate, lowering her voice.

Mary Jane laughed at her tone.

—Really, she said archly, he is very attentive.

—He has been laid on here like the gas, said Aunt Kate in the same tone, all during the Christmas.

She laughed herself this time good-humouredly and then added quickly:

—But tell him to come in, Mary Jane, and close the door. I hope to goodness he didn't hear me.

At that moment the hall-door was opened and Mr Browne came in from the doorstep, laughing as if his heart would break. He was dressed in a long green overcoat with mock astrakhan cuffs and collar and wore on his head an oval fur cap. He pointed down the snow-covered quay from where the sound of shrill prolonged whistling was borne in.

—Teddy will have all the cabs in Dublin out, he said.

Gabriel advanced from the little pantry behind the office, struggling into his overcoat and, looking round the hall, said:

—Gretta not down yet?

—She's getting on her things, Gabriel, said Aunt Kate.

—Who's playing up there? asked Gabriel.

—Nobody. They're all gone.

—O no, Aunt Kate, said Mary Jane. Bartell D'Arcy and Miss O'Callaghan aren't gone yet.

—Someone is strumming at the piano, anyhow, said Gabriel.

Mary Jane glanced at Gabriel and Mr Browne and said with a shiver:

—It makes me feel cold to look at you two gentlemen muffled up like that. I wouldn't like to face your journey home at this hour.

—I'd like nothing better this minute, said Mr Browne stoutly, than a rattling fine walk in the country or a fast drive with a good spanking goer between the shafts.

—We used to have a very good horse and trap at home, said Aunt Julia sadly.

—The never-to-be-forgotten Johnny, said Mary Jane, laughing.

Aunt Kate and Gabriel laughed too.

—Why, what was wonderful about Johnny? asked Mr Browne.

—The late lamented Patrick Morkan, our grandfather, that is, explained Gabriel, commonly known in his later years as the old gentleman, was a glue-boiler.

—O, now, Gabriel, said Aunt Kate, laughing, he had a starch mill.

—Well, glue or starch, said Gabriel, the old gentleman had a horse by the name of Johnny. And Johnny used to work in the old gentleman's mill, walking round and round in order to drive the mill. That was all very well; but now comes the tragic part about Johnny. One fine day the old gentleman thought he'd like to drive out with the quality to a military review in the park.

—The Lord have mercy on his soul, said Aunt Kate compassionately.

—Amen, said Gabriel. So the old gentleman, as I said, harnessed Johnny and put on his very best tall hat and his very best stock collar and drive out in grand style from his ancestral mansion somewhere near Back Lane, I think.

Everyone laughed, even Mrs Malins, at Gabriel's manner and Aunt Kate said:

—O now, Gabriel, he didn't live in Back Lane, really. Only the mill was there.

—Out from the mansion of his forefathers, continued Gabriel, he drove with Johnny. And everything went on beautifully until Johnny came in sight of King Billy's statue: and whether he fell in love with the horse King Billy sits on or whether he thought he was back again in the mill, anyhow he began to walk round the statue.

Gabriel paced in a circle round the hall in his goloshes amid the laughter of the others.

—Round and round he went, said Gabriel, and the old gentleman, who was a very pompous old gentleman, was highly indignant. *Go on, sir! What do you mean, sir? Johnny! Johnny! Most extraordinary conduct! Can't understand the horse!*

The peals of laughter which followed Gabriel's imitation of the incident were 295
interrupted by a resounding knock at the hall-door. Mary Jane ran to open it and let in Freddy Malins. Freddy Malins, with his hat well back on his head and his shoulders humped with cold, was puffing and steaming after his exertions.

—I could only get one cab, he said.

—O, we'll find another along the quay, said Gabriel.

—Yes, said Aunt Kate. Better not keep Mrs Malins standing in the draught.

Mrs Malins was helped down the front steps by her son and Mr Browne and, after many manœuvres, hoisted into the cab. Freddy Malins clambered in after her and spent a long time settling her on the seat, Mr Browne helping him with advice. At last she was settling comfortably and Freddy Malins invited Mr Browne into the cab. There was a good deal of confused talk, and then Mr Browne got into the cab. The cabman settled his rug over his knees, and bent down for the address. The confusion grew greater and the cabman was directed differently by Freddy Malins and Mr Browne, each of whom had his head out through a window of the cab. The difficulty was to know where to drop Mr Browne along the route and Aunt Kate, Aunt Julia and Mary Jane helped the discussion from the doorstep with cross-directions and contradictions and abundance of laughter. As for Freddy Malins he was speechless with laughter. He popped his head in and out of the window every moment, to the great danger of his hat, and told his mother how the discussion was progressing till at last Mr Browne shouted to the bewildered cabman above the din of everybody's laughter:

—Do you know Trinity College? 300

—Yes, sir, said the cabman.

—Well, drive bang up against Trinity College gates, said Mr Browne, and then we'll tell you where to go. You understand now?

—Yes, sir, said the cabman.

—Make like a bird for Trinity College.

—Right, sir, cried the cabman. 305

The horse was whipped up and the cab rattled off along the quay amid a chorus of laughter and adieus.

Gabriel had not gone to the door with the others. He was in a dark part of the hall gazing up the staircase. A woman was standing near the top of the first flight, in the shadow also. He could not see her face but he could see the terracotta and salmonpink panels of her skirt which the shadow made appear black and white. It was his wife. She was leaning on the banisters, listening to something. Gabriel was surprised at her stillness and strained his ear to listen also. But he could hear little save the noise of laughter and dispute on the front steps, a few chords struck on the piano and a few notes of a man's voice singing.

He stood still in the gloom of the hall, trying to catch the air that the voice was singing and gazing up at his wife. There was grace and mystery in her attitude as if she were a symbol of something. He asked himself what is a woman standing on the stairs in the shadow, listening to distant music, a symbol of. If he were a painter he would paint her in that attitude. Her blue felt hat would show off the bronze of her hair against the darkness and the dark panels of her skirt would show off the light ones. *Distant Music* he would call the picture if he were a painter.

The hall-door was closed; and Aunt Kate, Aunt Julia and Mary Jane came down the hall, still laughing.

—Well, isn't Freddy terrible? said Mary Jane. He's really terrible.

Gabriel said nothing but pointed up the stairs towards where his wife was standing. Now that the hall-door was closed the voice and the piano could be heard more clearly. Gabriel held up his hand for them to be silent. The song seemed to be in the old Irish tonality and the singer seemed uncertain both of his words and of his voice. The voice, made plaintive by distance and by the singer's hoarseness, faintly illuminated the cadence of the air with words expressing grief:

O, the rain falls on my heavy locks
And the dew wets my skin,
My babe lies cold . . .

—O, exclaimed Mary Jane. It's Bartell D'Arcy singing and he wouldn't sing all the night. O, I'll get him to sing a song before he goes.

—O do, Mary Jane, said Aunt Kate.

Mary Jane brushed past the others and ran to the staircase but before she reached it the singing stopped and the piano was closed abruptly.

—O, what a pity! she cried. Is he coming down, Gretta?

Gabriel heard his wife answer yes and saw her come down towards them. A few steps behind her were Mr Bartell D'Arcy and Miss O'Callaghan.

—O, Mr D'Arcy, cried Mary Jane, it's downright mean of you to break off like that when we were all in raptures listening to you.

—I have been at him all the evening, said Miss O'Callaghan, and Mrs Conroy too and he told us he had a dreadful cold and couldn't sing.

—O, Mr D'Arcy, said Aunt Kate, now that was a great fib to tell.

—Can't you see that I'm as hoarse as a crow? said Mr D'Arcy roughly.

He went into the pantry hastily and put on his overcoat. The others, taken aback by his rude speech, could find nothing to say. Aunt Kate wrinkled her brows and made signs to the others to drop the subject. Mr D'Arcy stood swathing his neck carefully and frowning.

—It's the weather, said Aunt Julia, after a pause.

—Yes, everybody has colds, said Aunt Kate readily, everybody.

—They say, said Mary Jane, we haven't had snow like it for thirty years; and I read this morning in the newspapers that the snow is general all over Ireland.

—I love the look of snow, said Aunt Julia sadly.

—So do I, said Miss O'Callaghan. I think Christmas is never really Christmas unless we have the snow on the ground.

—But poor Mr D'Arcy doesn't like the snow, said Aunt Kate, smiling.

Mr D'Arcy came from the pantry, full swathed and buttoned, and in a repentant tone told them the history of his cold. Everyone gave him advice and said it was a great pity and urged him to be very careful of his throat in the night air. Gabriel watched his wife who did not join in the conversation. She was standing right under the dusty fanlight and the flame of the gas lit up the rich bronze of her hair which he had seen her drying at the fire a few days before. She was in the same attitude and seemed unaware of the talk about her. At last she turned towards them and Gabriel saw that there was colour on her cheeks and that her eyes were shining. A sudden tide of joy went leaping out of his heart.

—Mr D'Arcy, she said, what is the name of that song you were singing?

—It's called *The Lass of Aughrim*,[10] said Mr D'Arcy, but I couldn't remember it properly. Why? Do you know it?

—*The Lass of Aughrim*, she repeated. I couldn't think of the name.

—It's a very nice air, said Mary Jane. I'm sorry you were not in voice tonight.

—Now, Mary Jane, said Aunt Kate, don't annoy Mr D'Arcy. I won't have him annoyed.

Seeing that all were ready to start she shepherded them to the door where good-night was said:

—Well, good-night, Aunt Kate, and thanks for the pleasant evening.

—Good-night, Gabriel. Good-night, Gretta!

—Good-night, Aunt Kate, and thanks ever so much. Good-night, Aunt Julia.

—O, good-night, Gretta, I didn't see you.

—Good-night, Mr D'Arcy. Good-night, Miss O'Callaghan.

—Good-night, Miss Morkan.

—Good-night, again.

—Good-night, all. Safe home.

—Good-night. Good-night.

The morning was still dark. A dull yellow light brooded over the houses and the river; and the sky seemed to be descending. It was slushy underfoot; and only streaks and patches of snow lay on the roofs, on the parapets of the quay and on the area railings. The lamps were still burning redly in the murky air and, across the river, the palace of the Four Courts stood out menacingly against the heavy sky.

She was walking on before him with Mr Bartell D'Arcy, her shoes in a brown parcel tucked under one arm and her hands holding her skirt up from the slush. She had no longer any grace of attitude but Gabriel's eyes were still bright with happiness. The blood went bounding along his veins; and the thoughts went rioting through his brain, proud, joyful, tender, valorous.

She was walking on before him so lightly and so erect that he longed to run after her noiselessly, catch her by the shoulders and say something foolish and affectionate into her ear. She seemed to him so frail that he longed to defend her against something and then to be alone with her. Moments of their secret life together burst like stars upon his memory. A heliotrope envelope was lying beside his breakfast-cup and he was caressing it with his hand. Birds were twittering in the ivy and the sunny web of the curtain was shimmering along the

[10]*The Lass of Aughrim:* An Irish ballad about a tragic love affair.

floor: he could not eat for happiness. They were standing on the crowded platform and he was placing a ticket inside the warm palm of her glove. He was standing with her in the cold, looking in through a grated window at a man making bottles in a roaring furnace. It was very cold. Her face, fragrant in the cold air, was quite close to his; and suddenly she called out to the man at the furnace:

—Is the fire hot, sir?

But the man could not hear her with the noise of the furnace. It was just as well. He might have answered rudely.

A wave of yet more tender joy escaped from his heart and went coursing in warm flood along his arteries. Like the tender fires of stars moments of their life together, that no one knew of or would ever know of, broke upon and illumined his memory. He longed to recall to her those moments, to make her forget the years of their dull existence together and remember only their moments of ecstasy. For the years, he felt, had not quenched his soul or hers. Their children, his writing, her household cares had not quenched all their souls' tender fire. In one letter that he had written to her then he had said: *Why is it that words like these seem to me so dull and cold? Is it because there is no word tender enough to be your name?*

Like distant music these words that he had written years before were borne towards him from the past. He longed to be alone with her. When the others had gone away, when he and she were in their room in the hotel, then they would be alone together. He would call her softly:

—Gretta!

Perhaps she would not hear at once: she would be undressing. Then something in his voice would strike her. She would turn and look at him. . . .

At the corner of Winetavern Street they met a cab. He was glad of its rattling noise as it saved him from conversation. She was looking out of the window and seemed tired. The others spoke only a few words, pointing out some building or street. The horse galloped along wearily under the murky morning sky, dragging his old rattling box after his heels, and Gabriel was again in a cab with her, galloping to catch the boat, galloping to their honeymoon.

As the cab drove across O'Connell Bridge Miss O'Callaghan said:

—They say you never cross O'Connell Bridge without seeing a white horse.

—I see a white man this time, said Gabriel.

—Where? asked Mr Bartell D'Arcy.

Gabriel pointed to the statue, on which lay patches of snow. Then he nodded familiarly to it and waved his hand.

—Good-night, Dan, he said gaily.

When the cab drew up before the hotel Gabriel jumped out and, in spite of Mr Bartell D'Arcy's protest, paid the driver. He gave the man a shilling over his fare. The man saluted and said:

—A prosperous New Year to you, sir.

—The same to you, said Gabriel cordially.

She leaned for a moment on his arm in getting out of the cab and while standing at the curbstone, bidding the others good-night. She leaned lightly on his arm, as lightly as when she had danced with him a few hours before. He had felt proud and happy then, happy that she was his, proud of her grace and wifely carriage. But now, after the kindling again of so many memories, the first touch of her body, musical and strange and perfumed, sent through him a keen pang of lust. Under cover of her silence he pressed her arm closely to his side; and, as they stood at the hotel door, he felt that they had escaped from their lives and duties, escaped from home and friends and run away together with wild and radiant hearts to a new adventure.

An old man was dozing in a great hooded chair in the hall. He lit a candle in the office and went before them to the stairs. They followed him in silence, their feet falling in soft thuds on the thickly carpeted stairs. She mounted the stairs behind the porter, her head bowed in the ascent, her frail shoulders curved as with a burden, her skirt girt tightly about her. He could have flung his arms about her hips and held her still for his arms were trembling with desire to seize her and only the stress of his nails against the palms of his hands held the wild impulse of his body in check. The porter halted on the stairs to settle his guttering candle. They halted too on the steps below him. In the silence Gabriel could hear the falling of the molten wax into the tray and the thumping of his own heart against his ribs.

The porter led them along a corridor and opened a door. Then he set his unstable candle down on a toilet-table and asked at what hour they were to be called in the morning.

—Eight, said Gabriel.

The porter pointed to the tap of the electric-light and began a muttered apology but Gabriel cut him short.

—We don't want any light. We have light enough from the street. And I say, he added, pointing to the candle, you might remove that handsome article, like a good man.

The porter took up his candle again, but slowly for he was surprised by such a novel idea. Then he mumbled good-night and went out. Gabriel shot the lock to.

A ghostly light from the street lamp lay in a long shaft from one window to the door. Gabriel threw his overcoat and hat on a couch and crossed the room towards the window. He looked down into the street in order that his emotion might calm a little. Then he turned and leaned against a chest of drawers with his back to the light. She had taken off her hat and cloak and was standing before a large swinging mirror, unhooking her waist. Gabriel paused for a few moments, watching her, and then said:

—Gretta!

She turned away from the mirror slowly and walked along the shaft of light towards him. Her face looked so serious and weary that the words would not pass Gabriel's lips. No, it was not the moment yet.

—You looked tired, he said.

—I am a little, she answered.

—You don't feel ill or weak?

—No, tired: that's all.

She went on to the window and stood there, looking out. Gabriel waited again and then, fearing that diffidence was about to conquer him, he said abruptly:

—By the way, Gretta!

—What is it?

—You know that poor fellow Malins? he said quickly.

—Yes. What about him?

—Well, poor fellow, he's a decent sort of chap after all, continued Gabriel in a false voice. He gave me back that sovereign I lent him and I didn't expect it really. It's a pity he wouldn't keep away from that Browne, because he's not a bad fellow at heart.

He was trembling now with annoyance. Why did she seem so abstracted? He did not know how he could begin. Was she annoyed, too, about something? If she would only turn to him or come to him of her own accord! To take her as she was would be brutal. No, he must see some ardour in her eyes first. He longed to be master of her strange mood.

—When did you lend him the pound? she asked, after a pause.

Gabriel strove to restrain himself from breaking out into brutal language about the sottish Malins and his pound. He longed to cry to her from his soul, to crush her body against his, to overmaster her. But he said:

—O, at Christmas, when he opened that little Christmas-card shop in Henry Street.

He was in such a fever of rage and desire that he did not hear her come from the window. She stood before him for an instant, looking at him strangely. Then, suddenly raising herself on tiptoe and resting her hands lightly on his shoulders, she kissed him.

—You are a very generous person, Gabriel, she said.

Gabriel, trembling with delight at her sudden kiss and at the quaintness of her phrase, put his hands on her hair and began smoothing it back, scarcely touching it with his fingers. The washing had made it fine and brilliant. His heart was brimming over with happiness. Just when he was wishing for it she had come to him of her own accord. Perhaps her thoughts had been running with his. Perhaps she had felt the impetuous desire that was in him and then the yielding mood had come upon her. Now that she had fallen to him so easily he wondered why he had been so diffident.

He stood, holding her head between his hands. Then, slipping one arm swiftly about her body and drawing her towards him, he said softly:

—Gretta dear, what are you thinking about?

She did not answer nor yield wholly to his arm. He said again, softly:

—Tell me what it is, Gretta. I think I know what is the matter. Do I know?

She did not answer at once. Then she said in an outburst of tears:

—O, I am thinking about that song, *The Lass of Aughrim*.

She broke loose from him and ran to the bed and, throwing her arms across the bed-rail, hid her face. Gabriel stood stock-still for a moment in astonishment and then followed her. As he passed in the way of the cheval-glass he caught sight of himself in full length, his broad, well-filled shirt-front, the face whose expression always puzzled him when he saw it in a mirror and his glimmering gilt-rimmed eyeglasses. He halted a few paces from her and said:

—What about the song? Why does that make you cry?

She raised her head from her arms and dried her eyes with the back of her hand like a child. A kinder note than he had intended went into his voice.

—Why, Gretta? he asked.

—I am thinking about a person long ago who used to sing that song.

—And who was the person long ago? asked Gabriel, smiling.

—It was a person I used to know in Galway when I was living with my grandmother, she said.

The smile passed away from Gabriel's face. A dull anger began to gather again at the back of his mind and the dull fires of his lust began to glow angrily in his veins.

—Someone you were in love with? he asked ironically.

—It was a young boy I used to know, she answered, named Michael Furey. He used to sing that song, *The Lass of Aughrim*. He was very delicate.

Gabriel was silent. He did not wish her to think that he was interested in this delicate boy.

—I can see him so plainly, she said after a moment. Such eyes as he had: big dark eyes! And such an expression in them—an expression!

—O then, you were in love with him? said Gabriel.

—I used to go out walking with him, she said, when I was in Galway.

A thought flew across Gabriel's mind.

—Perhaps that was why you wanted to go to Galway with that Ivors girl? he said coldly.

She looked at him and asked in surprise:

—What for?

Her eyes made Gabriel feel awkward. He shrugged his shoulders and said:

—How do I know! To see him perhaps.

She looked away from him along the shaft of light towards the window in silence.

—He is dead, she said at length. He died when he was only seventeen. Isn't it a terrible thing to die so young as that?

—What was he? asked Gabriel, still ironically.

—He was in the gasworks, she said.

Gabriel felt humiliated by the failure of his irony and by the evocation of this figure from the dead, a boy in the gasworks. While he had been full of memories of their secret life together, full of tenderness and joy and desire, she had been comparing him in her mind with another. A shameful consciousness of his own person assailed him. He saw himself as a ludicrous figure, acting as a pennyboy for his aunts, a nervous well-meaning sentimentalist, orating to vulgarians and idealising his own clownish lusts, the pitiable fatuous fellow he had caught a glimpse of in the mirror. Instinctively he turned his back more to the light lest she might see the shame that burned upon his forehead.

He tried to keep up his tone of cold interrogation but his voice when he spoke was humble and indifferent.

—I suppose you were in love with this Michael Furey, Gretta, he said.

—I was great with him at that time, she said.

Her voice was veiled and sad. Gabriel, feeling now how vain it would be to try to lead her whither he had purposed, caressed one of her hands and said, also sadly:

—And what did he die of so young, Gretta? Consumption, was it?

—I think he died for me, she answered.

A vague terror seized Gabriel at this answer as if, at that hour when he had hoped to triumph, some impalpable and vindictive being was coming against him, gathering forces against him in its vague world. But he shook himself free of it with an effort of reason and continued to caress her hand. He did not question her again for he felt that she would tell him of herself. Her hand was warm and moist: it did not respond to his touch but he continued to caress it just as he had caressed her first letter to him that spring morning.

—It was in the winter, she said, about the beginning of the winter when I was going to leave my grandmother's and come up here to the convent. And he was ill at the time in his lodgings in Galway and wouldn't be let out and his people in Oughterard were written to. He was in decline, they said, or something like that. I never knew rightly.

She paused for a moment and sighed.

—Poor fellow, she said. He was very fond of me and he was such a gentle boy. We used to go out together, walking, you know, Gabriel, like the way they do in the country. He was going to study singing only for his health. He had a very good voice, poor Michael Furey.

—Well; and then? asked Gabriel.

—And then when it came to the time for me to leave Galway and come up to the convent he was much worse and I wouldn't be let see him so I wrote a letter saying I was going up to Dublin and would be back in the summer and hoping he would be better then.

She paused for a moment to get her voice under control and then went on:

—Then the night before I left I was in my grandmother's house in Nuns' Island, packing up, and I heard gravel thrown up against the window. The window was so wet I couldn't see so I ran downstairs as I was and slipped out the back into the garden and there was the poor fellow at the end of the garden, shivering.

—And did you not tell him to go back? asked Gabriel.

—I implored him to go home at once and told him he would get his death in the rain. But he said he did not want to live. I can see his eyes as well as well! He was standing at the end of the wall where there was a tree.

—And did he go home? asked Gabriel.

—Yes, he went home. And when I was only a week in the convent he died and he was buried in Oughterard where his people came from. O, the day I heard that, that he was dead!

She stopped, choking with sobs, and overcome by emotion, flung herself face downward on the bed, sobbing in the quilt. Gabriel held her hand for a moment longer, irresolutely, and then, shy of intruding on her grief, let it fall gently and walked quietly to the window.

She was fast asleep.

Gabriel, leaning on his elbow, looked for a few moments unresentfully on 440
her tangled hair and half-open mouth, listening to her deep-drawn breath. So she had had that romance in her life: a man had died for her sake. It hardly pained him now to think how poor a part he, her husband, had played in her life. He watched her while she slept as though he and she had never lived together as man and wife. His curious eyes rested long upon her face and on her hair: and, as he thought of what she must have been then, in that time of her first girlish beauty, a strange friendly pity for her entered his soul. He did not like to say even to himself that her face was no longer beautiful but he knew that it was no longer the face for which Michael Furey had braved death.

Perhaps she had not told him all the story. His eyes moved to the chair over which she had thrown some of her clothes. A petticoat string dangled to the floor. One boot stood upright, its limp upper fallen down: the fellow of it lay upon its side. He wondered at his riot of emotions of an hour before. From what had it proceeded? From his aunt's supper, from his own foolish speech, from the wine and dancing, the merry-making when saying good-night in the hall, the pleasure of the walk along the river in the snow. Poor Aunt Julia! She, too, would soon be a shade with the shade of Patrick Morkan and his horse. He had caught that haggard look upon her face for a moment when she was singing *Arrayed for the Bridal.* Soon, perhaps, he would be sitting in that same drawing-room, dressed in black, his silk hat on his knees. The blinds would be drawn down and Aunt Kate would be sitting beside him, crying and blowing her nose and telling him how Julia had died. He would cast about in his mind for some words that might console her, and would find only lame and useless ones. Yes, yes: that would happen very soon.

The air of the room chilled his shoulders. He stretched himself cautiously along under the sheets and lay down beside his wife. One by one they were all becoming shades. Better pass boldly into that other world, in the full glory of some passion, than fade and wither dismally with age. He thought of how she who lay beside him had locked in her heart for so many years that image of her lover's eyes when he had told her that he did not wish to live.

Generous tears filled Gabriel's eyes. He had never felt like that himself towards any woman but he knew that such a feeling must be love. The tears gathered more thickly in his eyes and in the partial darkness he imagined he saw the form of a young man standing under a dripping tree. Other forms were near. His soul had approached that region where dwell the vast hosts of the dead. He was conscious of, but could not apprehend, their wayward and flickering existence. His own identity was fading out into a grey impalpable world: the solid world itself which these dead had one time reared and lived in was dissolving and dwindling.

A few light taps upon the pane made him turn to the window. It had begun to snow again. He watched sleepily the flakes, silver and dark, falling obliquely against the lamplight. The time had come for him to set out on his journey westward. Yes, the newspapers were right: snow was general all over Ireland. It was falling on every part of the dark central plain, on the treeless hills, falling softly upon the Bog of Allen and, farther westward, softly falling into the dark mutinous Shannon waves. It was falling, too, upon every part of the lonely churchyard on the hill where Michael Furey lay buried. It lay thickly drifted on the crooked crosses and headstones, on the spears of the little gate, on the barren thorns. His soul swooned slowly as he heard the snow falling faintly through the universe and faintly falling, like the descent of their last end, upon all the living and the dead.

(1914)

Questions for Discussion and Writing

Close Reading

1. Note the moments in the story in which Gabriel speaks directly to another character. What is noteworthy about each of these attempts at communication and about all of them together?
2. What is significant about the argument between Gabriel and Miss Eileen Ivors about Irish culture?
3. How does music frame the story's themes?
4. How does Gabriel's speech connect to the final scenes in the hotel room with his wife Gretta, if at all?

Critical and Creative Reading

5. Is it possible that Gretta Conroy loves both her husband and her former lover Michael Furey? How does Gabriel regard this possibility?
6. Gabriel's feelings toward his wife at the end of the story are clearly lustful ("He longed to . . . crush her body against his, to overmaster her"; "his own clownish lusts"). How do these feelings complicate his revelations about the nature of love in the final scenes? Is there evidence that he loves Gretta?
7. Can you ever know with certainty that one human being loves another, or is love built entirely on a kind of faith? In other words, to experience love, do we always have to take someone's word for it? Illustrate your opinion with evidence from "The Dead."

Connections to Other Readings

8. Discuss the connection between privacy, communication, and love in "The Dead" and in Aphra Behn's "The Disappointment."
9. At the end of the story, is Gabriel merely experiencing "doubt" as described in Stendhal's essay "The Birth of Love"? If so, is that experience potentially positive in terms of his marriage?
10. Compare the jealousy Gabriel experiences in "The Dead" to the jealousy Morito experiences in Akutagawa's story "Kesa and Morito." Is jealousy in any way productive in either story? Is jealousy ever productive?

Ryunosuke Akutagawa

Kesa and Morito

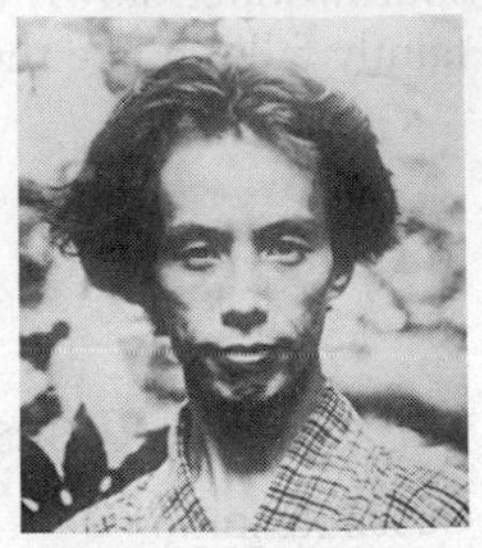

The tragedy of this Japanese author's life is difficult to overlook: Ryunosuke Akutagawa (1892–1927) took his own life after a period of depression. His mother had gone insane when he was young, and his father had given him to relatives for adoption. Yet he was blessed with literary brilliance and managed in his short life to complete over a hundred stories and to gain an international reputation especially through his novella "Rashomon," which was made into a film by legendary director Akira Kurosawa. Akutagawa did not fit comfortably into the literary circles of his time: class-conscious writers and critics dismissed him as dilettantish. However, his imagery is striking, and the distance between his narrative perspective and his characters' lives allows him to be precise. In the following story we see two perspectives, those of the title characters Kesa and Morito. Is one given any privilege over the other?

Part I

Looking at the moon in a pensive mood, Morito walks on the fallen leaves outside the fence of his house.

Morito's Monologue

The moon is rising now. I usually wait for moonrise impatiently. But tonight the bright moonrise shocks me with horror. I shudder to think that tonight will destroy my present self and turn me into a wretched murderer. Imagine when these hands will have turned crimson with blood! What a cursed being I shall seem to myself then! My heart would not be so wrung with pain if I were to kill an enemy I hate, but tonight I have to kill a man whom I do not hate.

I have known him a long time. Though it is only lately that I have learned his name, Wataru Saemon-no-jo, I have known his handsome face ever since I can remember. When I found that he was Kesa's husband, it is true that I burned with jealousy for a while. But now my jealousy has already faded, leaving no trace in my mind or heart. So for my rival in love, I have neither hatred nor spite. Rather, I think kindly of him. When my aunt, Koromogawa, told me how he spared no pain or effort to win Kesa's heart, I felt sympathetic toward him. I understood that out of his whole-hearted desire to win her for his wife, he even took the trouble to learn to write poetry. I cannot imagine that simple and prosaic man writing love poems, and a smile comes to my lips in spite of myself.

Kesa and Morito (1885).

This is not a smile of scorn; I am touched by the tenderness of a man who goes to such extremes to win a woman. It is even possible that his passionate love which makes him idolize my beloved Kesa gives me some satisfaction.

But do I really love Kesa? Our love affair may be separated into two stages, the past and the present. I loved her before she married Wataru, or I thought I did. But now that I look into my heart, I find there were many motives. What did I want from her? She was the kind of woman for whom I felt fleshly desire even in the days when I was chaste. If an overstatement is allowed, my love toward her was nothing more than a sentimental embellishment of the motive that drove Adam to Eve. This is evident from my doubts about my continuing to love her if my desire had been fulfilled. Though I kept her in my mind for the three years after the break in our association, I can not surely say I love her. In my later attachment to her, my greatest regret was that I had not known her intimately. Tortured with discontent, I fell into the present relationship, which terrified me, and yet which I knew must come. Now I ask myself anew, "Do I really love her?"

When I met her again after three years at the celebration of the completion 5 of the Watanabe Bridge, I resorted to all sorts of means to get a chance to meet her secretly. Finally I succeeded. Not only did I succeed in meeting her, but I took her body just as I had been dreaming of. At that time the regret that I had not known her physically was not all that obsessed me. When I sat close to her in the matted room of Koromogawa's house, I noticed that much of my regret had already faded. Probably my desire was weakened by the fact that I was not chaste. But the basic cause was that she was not what I expected her to be. When I sat face to face with her, I found that she was not the image of statuesque beauty I had imagined for the past three years. She was far from the idol I had idealized in my heart. Her face, thickly coated with leaden powder, had lost much of its bloom and smooth charm. Darkish rings had formed beneath her eyes. What remained unchanged in her was her clear, full, dark eyes. When I saw her in this new light, I was shocked, and in spite of myself I could not help turning my eyes away.

Then how is it that I had intercourse with a woman to whom I felt so little attachment? First I was moved by a strange wish to conquer my former heart's desire. Sitting face to face, she gave me a deliberately exaggerated story of her love for her husband. It left nothing but an empty ringing in my ears. "She has a vainglorious idea of her husband," I thought. I also suspected this may be motivated by her wish not to inflame my desire. At the same time my desire to expose her falsehood worked more and more strongly upon me. Why did I consider it a falsehood? If you tell me, dear reader, that my own conceit had led me to suspect the falsehood of her statement, I cannot deny your charge. Nevertheless, then I believed and still now do I believe that it was a lie.

But the desire to conquer was not all that obsessed me at that moment. I blush to mention it—I was dominated by lust. It was not merely my regret that I had not known her body. It was a base lust for lust's sake which did not require that the other party be that woman. Probably no man who hired a woman in a brothel would have been baser than I was then.

Anyway, out of such various motives, I had relations with Kesa. Or, rather, I dishonored her. To return to the first question that I put forth, I need not ask myself now if I loved her. When it was over, I raised her up forcibly in my arms—this woman who had thrown herself down crying. Then she looked more ignominious than I. Her ruffled hair and sweating flesh, everything indicated the ugliness of her mind and body. It would not be wrong to say that I have had a new hatred for her in my heart since that day. And tonight I am going to murder a man I do not hate, for the sake of a woman I do not love.

"Let's kill Wataru," I whispered into her ear. Mad indeed I must have been to have made such a brazen proposal. Distractedly I breathed into her ear my past desire to challenge Wataru to a fight and win her love. Anyway, "Let's kill Wataru," I whispered, and very surely did I whisper clenching my teeth, in spite of myself. Looking back now, I cannot tell what prompted me to do such a rash thing. All I can think of to explain it is that I wanted to patch up the affair for the present, and that the more I despised and hated her, the more impatient I became to bring some disgrace upon her. Nothing could be more suitable for these purposes than to kill the husband she professed to love, and to wring her consent from her willy-nilly. So, like a man in a nightmare, I must have prevailed upon her to commit between ourselves the murder which I do not wish. If that does not suffice to explain my motive for proposing to murder Wataru, no other explanation can be attempted, except that a power unknown to mortals (maybe a devil or demon) led me into an evil course. Persistently and repeatedly I whispered the same thing into her ear.

Finally she raised her face and said, "Yes, you must kill Wataru." Not only was her ready consent a surprise to me, but I saw a mysterious sparkle in her eye which I had not noticed before. An adulteress—that was the impression she gave me then. Instantly disappointment and horror—and yes, contempt—flashed through my feverish brain. I would have canceled my promise on the spot if it had been possible. Then I could have branded her an adulteress, and my conscience could have taken refuge in righteous indignation. But I was unable to do so. I confess that I readily saw its utter impossibility the moment she suddenly gazed at me. Her attitude changed, as though she had seen through my heart. I fell into the sad plight of making an appointment to murder her husband because of my fear that she would take revenge on me if I failed to carry out my part of the bargain. Now this fear has a firm and persistent vise-like grip on me. Laugh, if you wish, at my cowardice. This is the action of one who did not know how base his paramour could be. "If I don't kill her husband, she will kill me one way or another. I must kill him else she will kill me," I thought desperately, looking into her tearless but crying eyes. After I made the vow, did I not detect a smile on her mouth and a dimple forming on her pale cheek? Oh, because of this cursed pledge, I am going to add the crime of a heinous murder to the blackest heart imaginable. If I were to break this impending appointment which is to be fulfilled tonight. . . . No, my vow forbids it. This is more than I can bear. For another thing, I am afraid of her revenge. This is quite true. But there is something else that prompts me to the action. What is this? What is that great power which impels me, this coward '*me*,' to murder an innocent man? I cannot tell. I cannot tell. But possibly. . . . No, it cannot be. I despise her. I fear her. I hate her. And yet, and yet, it may be because I love her.

Morito, continuing to pace, says no more. The singing of a ballad comes out of the night.

The human mind is in the dark.
With not a light to shine upon.
It burns a fire of worldly cares
To go and fade in but a span.

Part II

At night under a lamp, Kesa, lost in thought, biting her sleeve, stands with her back toward the light.

Kesa's Monologue

Is he coming or isn't he, I wonder. It's highly unlikely that he isn't. The moon is already sinking, but not a footstep can be heard, so he may have changed his mind. If he should not come. . . . I shall have to live in shame day after day, like a prostitute. How can I be so lost to shame and evil? For I shall be no better than a dead body tossed by the roadside. I shall be dishonored and trampled on, with my shame brought to light. And yet I shall have to be silent as if dumb. In that case I shall carry my regret beyond the grave. I'm sure he will come. From the moment I looked into his eyes when we parted the other day, that has been my conviction. He is afraid of me. He hates and despises me, and yet he is afraid of me. Indeed, if I were to rely only on myself, I couldn't be sure of him. But I rely on him. I rely on his selfishness. I rely on the vile fear that selfishness inspires in him.

But now that I can no longer rely on myself, what a wretched being I am! Until three years ago I had confidence in myself, and above all, in my beauty! It would be more true to say "until that day" than "three years ago." That day when I met him in the room of my aunt's home, a glance into his eyes showed me my ugliness mirrored in his mind. He spoke loving and comforting words to me, looking as if there were nothing the matter. But how can a woman's heart ever be comforted once it has known the ugliness of her own person? I was mortified, horrified, grieved. How much better was the lurid uneasiness of the eclipse of the moon which I saw as a child in my nurse's arms, compared to the ghostly despair that darkened my mind at that moment! All the visions and dreams I had in my heart vanished. The loneliness of a rainy dawn enshrouded me quietly. Shuddering with loneliness, I finally gave up my body, which was as good as dead, into the arms of a man I did not love—into the arms of a lascivious man who hates and despises me. Could I not endure my loneliness since my ugliness was vividly shown to me? Did I try to bury everything in that delirious moment of putting my face on his chest? Or was I moved by mere shameful desire as he was? The mere thought of it overwhelms me with shame! shame! shame! Especially when I took myself from his arms, how ashamed I was.

Vexation and loneliness brought endless tears to my eyes despite my effort not to weep. I was not only grieved because I had been dishonored, I was tortured and pained above all because I was despised like a leprous dog which is hated and tortured. What have I done since then? I have only the vaguest memory of it as if it were a thing of the distant past. I only remember his low voice whispering, "Let's kill Wataru," and his mustache touched my ear as I was sobbing. The instant I heard these words, I felt strangely enlivened. Yes, I felt lively and bright as pale moonlight, if moonlight can be said to be bright. After all, was I not comforted by these words? Oh, am I not—is not a woman a being that feels joy in being loved by a man even if she has to kill her own husband?

I continued to weep for some time with a lonely and lively feeling like moonlight. When did I ever promise to give a helping hand in this murder of my husband?

Not until then had my husband entered my mind. I honestly say "not until then." Until that time my mind was wholly occupied with myself and my dishonor. Then I saw the image of my husband's smiling face. Probably the moment I remembered his face, the plan flashed across my mind. At that time I was already determined to die, and I was glad of my decision. But when I stopped crying, raised my face, and looked up into his own to find my ugliness mirrored in it, I felt as though all my joy had faded out. It reminded me of the darkness of the eclipse of the moon I saw with my nurse. That, as it were, set free at once all the evil spirits lurking under cover of my joy. Is it really because of my love for my husband that I am going to die for him? No, it is merely that under such reasonable pretext, I want to atone for my sin of having slept with another. Having no courage to commit suicide, I have the mean desire to make a good impression on the public. This meanness of mine can perhaps be condoned. Under the pretext of dying for my husband, was I not planning to revenge myself on my lover's hatred of me, his contempt of me, and his wicked lust? This is verified by the fact that a glance into his face put out the mysterious spark of life which is like pale moonlight, and froze my heart with grief. I am going to die not for my husband but for myself. I am going to die to punish my lover's having hurt my heart and for my grudge at his having sullied my body. Oh, not only am I unworthy of living but unworthy of dying.

But now, how much better it is to die even an ignominious death, than to live. Smiling a forced smile, I repeatedly promised to kill my husband with him. Since he is quick-witted, he must have sensed from my words what the consequences would be if he broke his promise. So it seems impossible that after making such a promise he should fall back on it. Is that the sound of the wind? When I think that my afflictions from that day are at last coming to an end tonight, I feel at ease. Tomorrow will not fail to shed its cold light on my headless body. If my husband sees it, he will . . . no I won't think of him. My husband loves me. But I have no strength to return his love. I can love only one man. And that very man is coming to kill me tonight. Even this rushlight is too bright for me, tortured by my lover as I am.

Kesa blows out the light. Soon the faint sound of the opening of a shutter is heard, and pale moonlight floods in.

(1918)

Questions for Discussion and Writing

Close Reading

1. How do the moon and moonlight function in the story, in the setting, and as a symbol?
2. What are the "various motives" Morito details to explain why he had "relations" with Kesa? Which is most convincing, or do they all work together?
3. How does Morito explain the logic behind his suggestion to kill Wataru, Kesa's husband?
4. How does Kesa describe her reasons for having an affair with Morito?

Critical and Creative Reading

5. In his monologue Morito tries to determine whether he truly loves Kesa. He says, "If an overstatement is allowed, my love toward her was nothing more than a sentimental embellishment of the motive that drove Adam to Eve." What does this mean, and how does it challenge your definition of "love"?
6. In some romantic narratives, the willingness to kill a lover's spouse is seen as a sign of commitment, or a form of love. What should we think of the will to murder in this story? How does it differ from other forms of "love"?
7. Both characters use the word *love.* Is there any love in this story?

Connections to Other Readings

8. Compare the status of lust in this story and in Susan Minot's story "Lust." Is lust an equally destructive force in both stories?
9. Consider the relationship between lust, rage, jealousy, and infidelity in this story and in James Joyce's "The Dead."
10. How does the use of the first-person monologue in this story differ from the way John Updike employs it in "Wife-Wooing"?

John Updike

Wife-Wooing

One of the most famous living American authors, John Updike (b. 1932) is the author of over fifty books. (See also page 243 for Updike's story "A & P" and a photo of the author.) Although he has written a considerable amount of poetry and literary reviews, Updike is best known for his fiction, especially the "Rabbit novels," a series of four novels covering the life of antihero Harry "Rabbit" Angstrom during Cold War America. Updike has gained a reputation as an elaborate stylist and a writer not afraid to write about sex. Both of these traits are evident in one of his early stories, "Wife-Wooing." The narrator is undeniably clever and desperate for his wife's attention. What else is he?

Oh my love. Yes. Here we sit, on warm broad floorboards, before a fire, the children between us, in a crescent, eating. The girl and I share one half-pint of French-fried potatoes; you and the boy share another; and in the center, sharing nothing, making simple reflections within himself like a jewel, the baby, mounted in an Easybaby, sucks at his bottle with frowning mastery, his selfish, contemplative eyes stealing glitter from the center of the flames. And you. You. You allow your skirt, the same black skirt in which this morning you with woman's soft bravery mounted a bicycle and sallied forth to play hymns in difficult keys on the Sunday school's old piano—you allow this black skirt to slide off your raised knees down your thighs, slide *up* your thighs in your body's absolute geography, so the parallel whiteness of their undersides is exposed to the fire's warmth and to my sight. Oh. There is a line of Joyce. I try to recover it from the legendary, imperfectly explored grottoes of *Ulysses:* a garter snapped, to please Blazes Boylan, in a deep Dublin den. What? Smackwarm.[1] That was the crucial word. Smacked smackwarm on her smackable warm woman's thigh. Something like that. A splendid man, to feel that. Smackwarm woman's. Splendid also to feel the curious and potent, inexplicable and irrefutably magical life language leads within itself. What soul took thought and knew that adding "wo" to man would make a woman? The difference exactly. The wide w, the receptive o. Womb. In our crescent the children for all their size seem to come out of you toward me, wet fingers and eyes, tinted bronze. Three children, five persons, seven years. Seven years since I wed wide warm woman, white-thighed. Wooed and wed. Wife. A knife of a word that for all its final bite did not end the wooing. To my wonderment.

We eat meat, meat I wrested warm from the raw hands of the hamburger girl in the diner a mile away, a ferocious place, slick with savagery, wild with chrome; young predators snarling dirty jokes menaced me, old men reached for me with coffee-warmed paws; I wielded my wallet, and won my way back. The fat brown bag of buns was warm beside me in the cold car; the smaller bag holding the two tiny cartons of French-fries emitted an even more urgent heat. Back through the black winter air to the fire, the intimate cave, where halloos and hurrahs greeted me, the deer, mouth agape and its cotton throat gushing, stretched dead across my shoulders. And now you, beside the white O of the plate upon which the children discarded with squeals of disgust the rings of translucent onion that came squeezed in the hamburgers—you push your toes an inch closer to the blaze, and the ashy white of the inside of your deep thigh is lazily laid bare, and the eternally elastic garter snaps smackwarm against my hidden heart.

Who would have thought, wide wife, back there in the white tremble of the ceremony (in the corner of my eye I held, despite the distracting hail of ominous vows, the vibration of the cluster of stephanotis clutched against your waist), that seven years would bring us no distance, through all those warm beds, to the same trembling point, of beginning? The cells change every seven years, and down in the atom, apparently, there is a strange discontinuity; as if God wills the universe anew every instant. (Ah God, dear God, tall friend of my childhood, I will never forget you, though they say dreadful things. They say rose windows in cathedrals are vaginal symbols.) Your legs, exposed as fully as by a bathing suit, yearn deeper into the amber wash of heat. Well: begin. A green jet of flame spits out sideways from a pocket of resin in a log, crying, and the orange shadows on the ceiling sway with fresh life. Begin.

"Remember, on our honeymoon, how the top of the kerosene heater made a great big rose window on the ceiling?"

[1] *Ulysses . . . Blazes Boylan. . . . Smackwarm*: *Ulysses* is a novel by James Joyce, published in 1922. *Blazes Boylan* is a character in the novel, the protagonist's wife's lover. *Smackwarm* is an example of Joyce's playful, inventive use of language in the novel.

"Vnn." Your chin goes to your knees, your shins draw in, all is retracted. Not much to remember, perhaps, for you; blood badly spilled, clumsiness of all sorts. "It was cold for June."

"Mommy, what was cold? What did you say?" the girl asks, enunciating angrily, determined not to let language slip on her tongue and tumble her so that we laugh.

"A house where Daddy and I stayed one time."

"I don't like dat," the boy says, and throws a half bun painted with chartreuse mustard onto the floor.

You pick it up and with beautiful sombre musing ask, "Isn't that funny? Did any of the others have mustard on them?"

"I *hate* dat," the boy insists; he is two. Language is to him thick vague handles swirling by; he grabs what he can.

"Here. He can have mine. Give me his." I pass my hamburger over, you take it, he takes it from you, there is nowhere a ripple of gratitude. There is no more praise of my heroism in fetching Sunday supper, saving you labor. Cunning, you sense, and sense that I sense your knowledge, that I had hoped to hoard your energy toward a more ecstatic spending. We sense everything between us, every ripple, existent and nonexistent; it is tiring. Courting a wife takes tenfold the strength of winning an ignorant girl. The fire shifts, shattering fragments of newspaper that carry in lighter gray the ghost of the ink of their message. You huddle your legs and bring the skirt back over them. With a sizzling noise like the sighs of the exhausted logs, the baby sucks the last from his bottle, drops it to the floor with its distasteful hoax of vacant suds, and begins to cry. His egotist's mouth opens; the delicate membrane of his satisfaction tears. You pick him up and stand. You love the baby more than me.

Who would have thought, blood once spilled, that no barrier would be broken, that you would be each time healed into a virgin again? Tall, fair, obscure, remote, and courteous.

We put the children to bed, one by one, in reverse order of birth. I am limitlessly patient, paternal, good. Yet you know. We watch the paper bags and cartons ignite on the breathing pillow of embers, read, watch television, eat crackers, it does not matter. Eleven comes. For a tingling moment you stand on the bedroom rug in your underpants, untangling your nightie; oh, fat white sweet fat fatness. In bed you read. About Richard Nixon. He fascinates you; you hate him. You know how he defeated Jerry Voorhis,[2] martyred Mrs. Douglas, how he played poker in the Navy despite being a Quaker, every fiendish trick, every low adaptation. Oh my Lord. Let's let the poor man go to bed. We're none of us perfect. "Hey let's turn out the light."

"Wait. He's just about to get Hiss[3] convicted. It's very strange. It says he acted honorably."

"I'm sure he did." I reach for the switch.

[2]*Jerry Voorhis:* Democratic politician from California, defeated by Richard Nixon for reelection to Congress in 1946.

[3]*Hiss:* Alger Hiss, a U.S. State Department official who was accused of being a Soviet spy in 1948. The highly publicized case was controversial, but Hiss was convicted of perjury in 1950 and served forty-four months in prison.

"No. Wait. Just till I finish this chapter. I'm sure there'll be something at the end."

"Honey, Hiss was guilty. We're all guilty. Conceived in concupiscence, we die unrepentant." Once my ornate words wooed you.

I lie against your filmy convex back. You read sideways, a sleepy trick. I see the page through the fringe of your hair, sharp and white as a wedge of crystal. Suddenly it slips. The book has slipped from your hand. You are asleep. Oh cunning trick, cunning. In the darkness I consider. Cunning. The headlights of cars accidentally slide fanning slits of light around our walls and ceiling. The great rose window was projected upward through the petal-shaped perforations in the top of the black kerosene stove, which we stood in the center of the floor. As the flame on the circular wick flickered, the wide soft star of interlocked penumbrae moved and waved as if it were printed on a silk cloth being gently tugged or slowly blown. Its color soft blurred blood. We pay dear in blood for our peaceful homes.

In the morning, to my relief, you are ugly. Monday's wan breakfast light bleaches you blotchily, drains the goodness from your thickness, makes the bathrobe a limp stained tube flapping, disconsolately, exposing sallow décolletage. The skin between your breasts a sad yellow. I feast with the coffee on your drabness. Every wrinkle and sickly tint a relief and a revenge. The children yammer. The toaster sticks. Seven years have worn this woman.

The man, he arrows off to work, jousting for right-of-way, veering on the thin 20
hard edge of the legal speed limit. Out of domestic muddle, softness, pallor, flaccidity: into the city. Stone is his province. The winning of coin. The maneuvering of abstractions. Making heartless things run. Oh the inanimate, adamant joys of job!

I return with my head enmeshed in a machine. A technicality it would take weeks to explain to you snags my brain; I fiddle with phrases and numbers all the blind evening. You serve me supper as a waitress—as less than a waitress, for I have known you. The children touch me timidly, as they would a steep girder bolted into a framework whose height they don't understand. They drift into sleep securely. We survive their passing in calm parallelity. My thoughts rework in chronic right angles the same snagging circuits on the same professional grid. You rustle the book about Nixon; vanish upstairs into the plumbing; the bathtub pipes cry. In my head I seem to have found the stuck switch at last: I push at it; it jams; I push; it is jammed. I grow dizzy, churning with cigarettes. I circle the room aimlessly.

So I am taken by surprise at a turning when at the meaningful hour of ten you come with a kiss of toothpaste to me moist and girlish and quick; the momentous moral of this story being, An expected gift is not worth giving.

(1960)

Questions for Discussion and Writing

Close Reading

1. The story emphasizes alliteration, especially words beginning with *w*. What is the effect of this alliteration?

2. Discuss the imagery of the rose window. (A rose window is a large, round, stained-glass window at the rear of a cathedral.)
3. Why does the narrator pronounce his wife "ugly," and why is he relieved that she is?
4. What is the nature of the narrator's work, and how does that work relate to the story's themes?

Critical and Creative Reading

5. Do seduction rituals change after marriage? Use Updike's story to substantiate your argument.
6. Write a short story called "Husband-Wooing" from the point of view of the wife. Try to keep the same basic plot as in "Wife-Wooing."
7. What effect do children have on romantic love?

Connections to Other Readings

8. In his essay "On Marriage," Robert Louis Stevenson writes, "Times are changed with him who marries; there are no more by-path meadows, where you may innocently linger, but the road lies long and straight and dusty to the grave." Discuss the differences between premarriage and marriage in Stevenson's essay and in "Wife-Wooing." Is the view of Updike's narrator more or less cynical than Stevenson's?
9. Discuss the idea of marital lust and communication in this story and in James Joyce's "The Dead."

Bharati Mukherjee

The Tenant

Bharati Mukherjee (b. 1940) was born into an upper-middle-class Brahmin family in India and emigrated first to Canada, then to the United States. In addition to writing fiction, she teaches at the University of California at Berkeley. The author of a dozen books—primarily novels and short stories—Mukherjee writes about immigrant characters who have difficulty assimilating into American or Canadian society. Mukherjee wants her characters to be regarded as she wants herself to be regarded: as individuals, not as representatives of an ethnic minority. Even so, you will undoubtedly notice a tension in the following story between Maya's individual identity and the pull of her ethnic heritage.

Maya Sanyal has been in Cedar Falls, Iowa, less than two weeks. She's come, books and clothes and one armchair rattling in the smallest truck that U-Haul would rent her, from New Jersey. Before that she was in North Carolina. Before that, Calcutta, India. Every place has something to give. She is sitting at the kitchen table with Fran drinking bourbon for the first time in her life. Fran Johnson found her the furnished apartment and helped her settle in. Now she's brought a bottle of bourbon which gives her the right to stay and talk for a bit. She's breaking up with someone named Vern, a pharmacist. Vern's father is also a pharmacist and owns a drugstore. Maya has seen Vern's father on TV twice already. The first time was on the local news when he spoke out against the selling of painkillers like Advil and Nuprin in supermarkets and gas stations. In the matter of painkillers, Maya is a universalist. The other time he was in a barbershop quartet. Vern gets along all right with his father. He likes the pharmacy business, as business goes, but he wants to go back to graduate school and learn to make films. Maya is drinking her first bourbon tonight because Vern left today for San Francisco State.

"I understand totally," Fran says. She teaches Utopian Fiction and a course in Women's Studies and worked hard to get Maya hired. Maya has a Ph.D. in Comparative Literature and will introduce writers like R. K. Narayan and Chinua Achebe[1] to three sections of sophomores at the University of Northern Iowa. "A person has to leave home. Try out his wings."

Fran has to use the bathroom. "I don't feel abandoned." She pushes her chair away from the table. "Anyway, it was a sex thing totally. We were good together. It'd be different if I'd loved him."

Maya tries to remember what's in the refrigerator. They need food. She hasn't been to the supermarket in over a week. She doesn't have a car yet and so she relies on a corner store—a longish walk—for milk, cereal, and frozen dinners. Someday these exigencies will show up as bad skin and collapsed muscle tone. No folly is ever lost. Maya pictures history as a net, the kind of safety net travelling trapeze artists of her childhood fell into when they were inattentive, or clumsy. Going to circuses in Calcutta with her father is what she remembers vividly. It is a banal memory, for her father, the owner of a steel company, is a complicated man.

5 Fran is out in the kitchen long enough for Maya to worry. They need food. Her mother believed in food. What is love, anger, inner peace, etc., her mother used to say, but the brain's biochemistry. Maya doesn't want to get into that, but she is glad she has enough stuff in the refrigerator to make an omelette. She realizes Indian women are supposed to be inventive with food, whip up exotic delights to tickle an American's palate, and she knows she should be meeting Fran's generosity and candor with some sort of bizarre and effortless countermove. If there's an exotic spice store in Cedar Falls or in neighboring Waterloo, she hasn't found it. She's looked in the phone book for common Indian names, especially Bengali, but hasn't yet struck up culinary intimacies. That will come—it always does. There's a six-pack in the fridge that her landlord, Ted Suminski, had put in because she'd be thirsty after unpacking. She was thirsty,

[1]*R. K. Narayan and Chinua Achebe:* Twentieth-century novelists from India and Nigeria, respectively. Narayan lived from 1906 to 2001. Achebe was born in 1930.

but she doesn't drink beer. She probably should have asked him to come up and drink the beer. Except for Fran she hasn't had anyone over. Fran is more friendly and helpful than anyone Maya has known in the States since she came to North Carolina ten years ago, at nineteen. Fran is a Swede, and she is tall, with blue eyes. Her hair, however, is a dull, darkish brown.

"I don't think I can handle anything that heavy-duty," Fran says when she comes back to the room. She means the omelette. "I have to go home in any case." She lives with her mother and her aunt, two women in their mid-seventies, in a drafty farmhouse. The farmhouse now has a computer store catty-corner from it. Maya's been to the farm. She's been shown photographs of the way the corner used to be. If land values ever rebound, Fran will be worth millions.

Before Fran leaves she says, "Has Rab Chatterji called you yet?"

"No." She remembers the name, a good, reliable Bengali name, from the first night's study of the phone book. Dr. Rabindra Chatterji teaches Physics.

"He called the English office just before I left." She takes car keys out of her pocketbook. She reknots her scarf. "I bet Indian men are more sensitive than Americans. Rab's a Brahmin, that's what people say."

A Chatterji has to be a Bengali Brahmin[2]—last names give ancestral secrets 10
away—but Brahminness seems to mean more to Fran than it does to Maya. She was born in 1954, six full years after India became independent. Her India was Nehru's India: a charged, progressive place.

"All Indian men are wife beaters," Maya says. She means it and doesn't mean it. "That's why I married an American." Fran knows about the divorce, but nothing else. Fran is on the Hiring, Tenure, and Reappointment Committee.

Maya sees Fran down the stairs and to the car which is parked in the back in the spot reserved for Maya's car, if she had owned one. It will take her several months to save enough to buy one. She always pays cash, never borrows. She tells herself she's still recovering from the U-Haul drive halfway across the country. Ted Suminski is in his kitchen watching the women. Maya waves to him because waving to him, acknowledging him in that way, makes him seem less creepy. He seems to live alone though a sign, THE SUMINSKIS, hangs from a metal horse's head in the front yard. Maya hasn't seen Mrs. Suminski. She hasn't seen any children either. Ted always looks lonely. When she comes back from campus, he's nearly always in the back, throwing darts or shooting baskets.

"What's he like?" Fran gestures with her head as she starts up her car. "You hear these stories."

Maya doesn't want to know the stories. She has signed a year's lease. She doesn't want complications. "He's all right. I keep out of his way."

"You know what I'm thinking? Of all the people in Cedar Falls, you're the 15
one who could understand Vern best. His wanting to try out his wings, run away, stuff like that."

"Not really." Maya is not being modest. Fran is being impulsively democratic, lumping her wayward lover and Indian friend together as headstrong adventurers. For Fran, a utopian and feminist, borders don't count. Maya's taken

[2]*Brahmin*: A member of the upper caste of Indian Hindu society.

some big risks, made a break with her parents' ways. She's done things a woman from Ballygunge Park Road doesn't do, even in fantasies. She's not yet shared stories with Fran, apart from the divorce. She's told her nothing of men she picks up, the reputation she'd gained, before Cedar Falls, for "indiscretions." She has a job, equity, three friends she can count on for emergencies. She is an American citizen. But.

Fran's Brahmin calls her two nights later. On the phone he presents himself as Dr. Chatterji, not Rabindra or Rab. An old-fashioned Indian, she assumes. Her father still calls his closest friend, "Colonel." Dr. Chatterji asks her to tea on Sunday. She means to say no but hears herself saying, "Sunday? Fiveish? I'm not doing anything special this Sunday."

Outside, Ted Suminski is throwing darts into his garage door. The door has painted-on rings: orange, purple, pink. The bull's-eye is gray. He has to be fifty at least. He is a big, thick, lonely man about whom people tell stories. Maya pulls the phone cord as far as it'll go so she can look down more directly on her landlord's large, bald head. He has his back to her as he lines up a dart. He's in black running shoes, red shorts, he's naked to the waist. He hunches his right shoulder, he pulls the arm back; a big, lonely man shouldn't have so much grace. The dart is ready to cut through the September evening. But Ted Suminski doesn't let go. He swings on worn rubber soles, catches her eye in the window (she has to have imagined this), takes aim at her shadow. Could she have imagined the noise of the dart's metal tip on her windowpane?

Dr. Chatterji is still on the phone. "You are not having any mode of transportation, is that right?"

20 Ted Suminski has lost interest in her. Perhaps it isn't interest, at all; perhaps it's aggression. "I don't drive," she lies, knowing it sounds less shameful than not owning a car. She has said this so often she can get in the right degree of apology and Asian upper-class helplessness. "It's an awful nuisance."

"Not to worry, please." Then, "It is a great honor to be meeting Dr. Sanyal's daughter. In Calcutta business circles he is a legend."

On Sunday she is ready by four-thirty. She doesn't know what the afternoon holds; there are surely no places for "high tea"—a colonial tradition—in Cedar Falls, Iowa. If he takes her back to his place, it will mean he has invited other guests. From his voice she can tell Dr. Chatterji likes to do things correctly. She has dressed herself in a peach-colored nylon georgette sari, jade drop-earrings and a necklace. The color is good on dark skin. She is not pretty, but she does her best. Working at it is a part of self-respect. In the mid-seventies, when American women felt rather strongly about such things, Maya had been in trouble with her women's group at Duke. She was too feminine. She had tried to explain the world she came out of. Her grandmother had been married off at the age of five in a village now in Bangladesh. Her great-aunt had been burned to death over a dowry problem. She herself had been trained to speak softly, arrange flowers, sing, be pliant. If she were to seduce Ted Suminski, she thinks as she waits in the front yard for Dr. Chatterji, it would be minor heroism. She has broken with the past. But.

Dr. Chatterji drives up for her at about five ten. He is a hesitant driver. The car stalls, jumps ahead, finally slams to a stop. Maya has to tell him to back off a foot or so; it's hard to leap over two sacks of pruned branches in a sari. Ted Suminski is an obsessive pruner and gardener.

"My sincerest apologies, Mrs. Sanyal," Dr. Chatterji says. He leans across the wide front seat of his noisy, very old, very used car and unlocks the door for her. "I am late. But then, I am sure you're remembering that Indian Standard Time is not at all the same as time in the States." He laughs. He could be nervous—she often had that effect on Indian men. Or he could just be chatty. "These Americans are all the time rushing and rushing but where it gets them?" He moves his head laterally once, twice. It's the gesture made famous by Peter Sellers.[3] When Peter Sellers did it, it had seemed hilarious. Now it suggests that Maya and Dr. Chatterji have three thousand years plus civilization, sophistication, moral virtue, over people born on this continent. Like her, Dr. Chatterji is a naturalized American.

"Call me Maya," she says. She fusses with the seat belt. She does it because she needs time to look him over. He seems quite harmless. She takes in the prominent teeth, the eyebrows that run together. He's in a blue shirt and a beige cardigan with the K-Mart logo that buttons tightly over the waist. It's hard to guess his age because he has dyed his hair and his moustache. Late thirties, early forties. Older than she had expected. "Not Mrs. Sanyal."

This isn't the time to tell about ex-husbands. She doesn't know where John is these days. He should have kept up at least. John had come into her life as a graduate student at Duke, and she, mistaking the brief breathlessness of sex for love, had married him. They had stayed together two years, maybe a little less. The pain that John had inflicted all those years ago by leaving her had subsided into a cozy feeling of loss. This isn't the time, but then she doesn't want to be a legend's daughter all evening. She's not necessarily on Dr. Chatterji's side is what she wants to get across early; she's not against America and Americans. She makes the story—of marriage outside the Brahminic pale, the divorce—quick, dull. Her unsentimentality seems to shock him. His stomach sags inside the cardigan.

"We've each had our several griefs," the physicist says. "We're each required to pay our karmic debts."

"Where are we headed?"

"Mrs. Chatterji has made some Indian snacks. She is waiting to meet you because she is knowing your cousin-sister who studied in Scottish Church College. My home is okay, no?"

Fran would get a kick out of this. Maya has slept with married men, with nameless men, with men little more than boys, but never with an Indian man. Never.

The Chatterjis live in a small blue house on a gravelly street. There are at least five or six other houses on the street; the same size but in different colors

[3]*Peter Sellers:* Comic British screen actor (1925–1980).

and with different front yard treatments. More houses are going up. This is the cutting edge of suburbia.

Mrs. Chatterji stands in the driveway. She is throwing a large plastic ball to a child. The child looks about four, and is Korean or Cambodian. The child is not hers because she tells it, "Chung-Hee, ta-ta, bye-bye. Now I play with guest," as Maya gets out of the car.

Maya hasn't seen this part of town. The early September light softens the construction pits. In that light the houses too close together, the stout woman in a striped cotton sari, the child hugging a pink ball, the two plastic lawn chairs by a tender young tree, the sheets and saris on the clothesline in the back, all seem miraculously incandescent.

"Go home now, Chung-Hee. I am busy." Mrs. Chatterji points the child homeward, then turns to Maya, who has folded her hands in traditional Bengali greeting. "It is an honor. We feel very privileged." She leads Maya indoors to a front room that smells of moisture and paint.

In her new, deliquescent mood, Maya allows herself to be backed into the best armchair—a low-backed, boxy Goodwill item draped over with a Rajasthani bedspread—and asks after the cousin Mrs. Chatterji knows. She doesn't want to let go of Mrs. Chatterji. She doesn't want husband and wife to get into whispered conferences about their guest's misadventures in America, as they make tea in the kitchen.

The coffee table is already laid with platters of mutton croquettes, fish chops, onion pakoras, ghugni with puris, samosas, chutneys.[4] Mrs. Chatterji has gone to too much trouble. Maya counts four kinds of sweetmeats in Corning casseroles on an end table. She looks into a see-through lid; spongy, white dumplings float in rosewater syrup. Planets contained, mysteries made visible.

"What are you waiting for, Santana?" Dr. Chatterji becomes imperious, though not unaffectionate. He pulls a dining chair up close to the coffee table. "Make some tea." He speaks in Bengali to his wife, in English to Maya. To Maya he says, grandly, "We are having real Indian Green Label Lipton. A nephew is bringing it just one month back."

His wife ignores him. "The kettle's already on," she says. She wants to know about the Sanyal family. Is it true her great-grandfather was a member of the Star Chamber in England?

Nothing in Calcutta is ever lost. Just as her story is known to Bengalis all over America, so are the scandals of her family, the grandfather hauled up for tax evasion, the aunt who left her husband to act in films. This woman brings up the Star Chamber, the glories of the Sanyal family, her father's philanthropies, but it's a way of saying, *I know the dirt.*

The bedrooms are upstairs. In one of those bedrooms an unseen, tormented presence—Maya pictures it as a clumsy ghost that strains to shake off the body's shell—drops things on the floor. The things are heavy and they make the front room's chandelier shake. Light bulbs, shaped like tiny candle flames, flicker. The Chatterjis have said nothing about children. There are no tricycles in the

[4]*croquettes . . . chutneys:* Traditional Indian appetizers.

hallway, no small sandals behind the doors. Maya is too polite to ask about the noise, and the Chatterjis don't explain. They talk just a little louder. They flip the embroidered cover off the stereo. What would Maya like to hear? Hemanta Kumar? Manna Dey? Oh, that young chap, Manna Dey! What sincerity, what tenderness he can convey!

Upstairs the ghost doesn't hear the music of nostalgia. The ghost throws and thumps. The ghost makes its own vehement music. Maya hears in its voice madness, self-hate.

Finally the water in the kettle comes to a boil. The whistle cuts through all fantasy and pretense. Dr. Chatterji says, "I'll see to it," and rushes out of the room. But he doesn't go to the kitchen. He shouts up the stairwell. "Poltoo, kindly stop this nonsense straightaway! We're having a brilliant and cultured lady-guest and you're creating earthquakes?" The kettle is hysterical.

Mrs. Chatterji wipes her face. The face that had seemed plump and cheery at the start of the evening now is flabby. "My sister's boy," the woman says.

So this is the nephew who has brought with him the cartons of Green Label tea, one of which will be given to Maya.

Mrs. Chatterji speaks to Maya in English as though only the alien language can keep emotions in check. "Such an intelligent boy! His father is government servant. Very highly placed."

Maya is meant to visualize a smart, clean-cut young man from south Calcutta, but all she can see is a crazy, thwarted, lost graduate student. Intelligence, proper family guarantee nothing. Even Brahmins can do self-destructive things, feel unsavory urges. Maya herself had been an excellent student.

"He was First Class First in B. Sc. from Presidency College," the woman says. "Now he's getting Master's in Ag. Science at Iowa State."

The kitchen is silent. Dr. Chatterji comes back into the room with a tray. The teapot is under a tea cozy, a Kashmiri one embroidered with the usual chinar leaves, loops, and chains. "*Her* nephew," he says. The dyed hair and dyed moustache are no longer signs of a man wishing to fight the odds. He is a vain man, anxious to cut losses. "Very unfortunate business."

The nephew's story comes but slowly, over fish chops and mutton croquettes. He is in love with a student from Ghana.

"Everything was A-Okay until the Christmas break. Grades, assistantship for next semester, everything."

"I blame the college. The office for foreign students arranged a Christmas party. And now, *baapre baap*![5] Our poor Poltoo wants to marry a Negro Muslim."

Maya is known for her nasty, ironic one-liners. It has taken her friends weeks to overlook her malicious, un-American pleasure in others' misfortunes. Maya would like to finish Dr. Chatterji off quickly. He is pompous; he is reactionary; he wants to live and work in America but give back nothing except taxes. The confused world of the immigrant—the lostness that Maya and Poltoo feel—that's what Dr. Chatterji wants to avoid. She hates him. But.

[5] *baapre baap:* "For heaven's sake."

Dr. Chatterji's horror is real. A good Brahmin boy in Iowa is in love with an African Muslim. It shouldn't be a big deal. But the more she watches the physicist, the more she realizes that "Brahmin" isn't a caste; it's a metaphor. You break one small rule, and the constellation collapses. She thinks suddenly that John Cheever—she is teaching him as a "world writer" in her classes, cheek-by-jowl with Africans and West Indians—would have understood Dr. Chatterji's dread. Cheever had been on her mind, ever since the late afternoon light slanted over Mrs. Chatterji's drying saris. She remembers now how full of a soft, Cheeverian light Durham had been the summer she had slept with John Hadwen; and how after that, her tidy graduate-student world became monstrous, lawless. All men became John Hadwen; John became all men. Outwardly, she retained her poise, her Brahminical breeding. She treated her crisis as a literary event; she lost her moral sense, her judgment, her power to distinguish. Her parents had behaved magnanimously. They had cabled from Calcutta: WHAT'S DONE IS DONE WE ARE CONFIDENT YOU WILL HANDLE NEW SITUATIONS WELL, ALL LOVE. But she knows more than do her parents. Love is anarchy.

Poltoo is Mrs. Chatterji's favorite nephew. She looks as though it is her fault that the Sunday has turned unpleasant. She stacks the empty platters methodically. To Maya she says, "It is the goddess who pulls the strings. We are puppets. I know the goddess will fix it. Poltoo will not marry that African woman." Then she goes to the coat closet in the hall and staggers back with a harmonium, the kind sold in music stores in Calcutta, and sets it down on the carpeted floor. "We're nothing but puppets," she says again. She sits at Maya's feet, her pudgy hands on the harmonium's shiny, black bellows. She sings, beautifully, in a virgin's high voice, "Come, goddess, come, muse, come to us hapless peoples' rescue."

Maya is astonished. She has taken singing lessons at Dakshini Academy in Calcutta. She plays the sitar and the tanpur,[6] well enough to please Bengalis, to astonish Americans. But stout Mrs. Chatterji is a devotee, talking to God.

A little after eight, Dr. Chatterji drops her off. It's been an odd evening and they are both subdued.

"I want to say one thing," he says. He stops her from undoing her seat belt. The plastic sacks of pruned branches are still at the corner.

"You don't have to get out," she says.

"Please. Give me one more minute of your time."

"Sure."

"Maya is my favorite name."

She says nothing. She turns away from him without making her embarrassment obvious.

"Truly speaking, it is my favorite. You are sometimes lonely, no? But you are lucky. Divorced women can date, they can go to bars and discos. They can see mens, many mens. But inside marriage there is so much loneliness." A groan, low, horrible, comes out of him.

[6]*sitar and the tanpur*: Indian stringed instruments.

She turns back toward him, to unlatch the seat belt and run out of the car. She sees that Dr. Chatterji's pants are unzipped. One hand works hard under his Jockey shorts; the other rests, limp, penitential, on the steering wheel.

"Dr. Chatterji—*really!*" she cries.

The next day, Monday, instead of getting a ride home with Fran—Fran says she *likes* to give rides, she needs the chance to talk, and she won't share gas expenses, absolutely not—Maya goes to the periodicals room of the library. There are newspapers from everywhere, even from Madagascar and New Caledonia. She thinks of the periodicals room as an asylum for homesick aliens. There are two aliens already in the room, both Orientals, both absorbed in the politics and gossip of their far off homes.

She goes straight to the newspapers from India. She bunches her raincoat like a bolster to make herself more comfortable. There's so much to catch up on. A village headman, a known Congress-Indira party worker, has been shot at by scooter-riding snipers. An Indian pugilist has won an international medal—in Nepal. A child drawing well water—the reporter calls the child "a neo-Buddhist, a convert from the now-outlawed untouchable caste"—has been stoned. An editorial explains that the story about stoning is not a story about caste but about failed idealism; a story about promises of green fields and clean, potable water broken, a story about bribes paid and wells not dug. But no, thinks Maya, it's about caste.

Out here, in the heartland of the new world, the India of serious newspapers unsettles. Maya longs again to feel what she had felt in the Chatterjis' living room: virtues made physical. It is a familiar feeling, a longing. Had a suitable man presented himself in the reading room at that instant, she would have seduced him. She goes on to the stack of *India Abroads*, reads through matrimonial columns, and steals an issue to take home.

Indian men want Indian brides. Married Indian men want Indian mistresses. All over America, "handsome, tall, fair" engineers, doctors, data processors—the new pioneers—cry their eerie love calls.

Maya runs a finger down the first column; her fingertip, dark with newsprint, stops at random.

> Hello! Hi! Yes, you *are* the one I'm looking for. You are the new emancipated Indo-American woman. You have a zest for life. You are at ease in USA and yet your ethics are rooted in Indian tradition. The man of your dreams has come. Yours truly is handsome, ear-nose-throat specialist, well-settled in Connecticut. Age is 41 but never married, physically fit, sportsmanly, and strong. I adore idealism, poetry, beauty. I abhor smugness, passivity, caste system. Write with recent photo. Better still, call!!!.

Maya calls. Hullo, hullo, hullo! She hears immigrant lovers cry in crowded shopping malls. Yes, you who are at ease in both worlds, you are the one. She feels she has a fair chance.

A man answers. "Ashoke Mehta speaking."

She speaks quickly into the bright-red mouthpiece of her telephone. He will be in Chicago, in transit, passing through O'Hare. United counter, Saturday, two P.M. As easy as that.

"Good," Ashoke Mehta says. "For these encounters I, too, prefer a neutral zone."

On Saturday at exactly two o'clock the man of Maya's dreams floats toward 75
her as lovers used to in shampoo commercials. The United counter is a loud, harrassed place but passengers and piled-up luggage fall away from him. Full-cheeked and fleshy-lipped, he is handsome. He hasn't lied. He is serene, assured, a Hindu god touching down in Illinois.

She can't move. She feels ugly and unworthy. Her adult life no longer seems miraculously rebellious; it is grim, it is perverse. She has accomplished nothing. She has changed her citizenship but she hasn't broken through into the light, the vigor, the *bustle* of the New World. She is stuck in dead space.

"Hullo, Hullo!" Their fingers touch.

Oh, the excitement! Ashoke Mehta's palm feels so right in the small of her back. Hullo, hullo, hullo. He pushes her out of the reach of anti-Khomeini Iranians, Hare Krishnas, American Fascists,[7] men with fierce wants, and guides her to an empty gate. They have less than an hour.

"What would you like, Maya?"

She knows he can read her mind, she knows her thoughts are open to him. 80
You, she's almost giddy with the thought, with simple desire. "From the snack bar," he says, as though to clarify. "I'm afraid I'm starved."

Below them, where the light is strong and hurtful, a Boeing is being serviced. "Nothing," she says.

He leans forward. She can feel the nap of his scarf—she recognizes the Cambridge colors—she can smell the wool of his Icelandic sweater. She runs her hand along the scarf, then against the flesh of his neck. "Only the impulsive ones call," he says.

The immigrant courtship proceeds. It's easy, he's good with facts. He knows how to come across to a stranger who may end up a lover, a spouse. He makes over a hundred thousand. He owns a house in Hartford, and two income properties in Newark. He plays the market but he's cautious. He's good at badminton but plays handball to keep in shape. He watches all the sports on television. Last August he visited Copenhagen, Helsinki and Leningrad. Once upon a time he collected stamps but now he doesn't have hobbies, except for reading. He counts himself an intellectual, he spends too much on books. Ludlum, Forsyth, MacInnes; other names she doesn't catch. She suppresses a smile, she's told him only she's a graduate student. He's not without his vices. He's a spender, not a saver. He's a sensualist: good food—all foods, but easy on the Indian—good wine. Some temptations he doesn't try to resist.

And I, she wants to ask, do I tempt?

"Now tell me about yourself, Maya." He makes it easy for her. "Have you 85
ever been in love?"

"No."

[7]*anti-Khomeini Iranians, Hare Krishnas*: Fringe political or religious groups who would attempt to gain support in public places like airports.

"But many have loved you, I can see that." He says it not unkindly. It is the fate of women like her, and men like him. Their karmic duty, to be loved. It is expected, not judged. She feels he can see them all, the sad parade of need and demand. This isn't the time to reveal all.

And so the courtship enters a second phase.

When she gets back to Cedar Falls, Ted Suminski is standing on the front porch. It's late at night, chilly. He is wearing a down vest. She's never seen him on the porch. In fact there's no chair to sit on. He looks chilled through. He's waited around a while.

"Hi." She has her keys ready. This isn't the night to offer the six-pack in the fridge. He looks expectant, ready to pounce.

"Hi." He looks like a man who might have aimed the dart at her. What has he done to his wife, his kids? Why isn't there at least a dog? "Say, I left a note upstairs."

The note is written in Magic Marker and thumb-tacked to her apartment door, DUE TO PERSONAL REASONS, NAMELY REMARRIAGE, I REQUEST THAT YOU VACATE MY PLACE AT THE END OF THE SEMESTER.

Maya takes the note down and retacks it to the kitchen wall. The whole wall is like a bulletin board, made of some new, crumbly building-material. Her kitchen, Ted Suminski had told her, was once a child's bedroom. Suminski in love: the idea stuns her. She has misread her landlord. The dart at her window speaks of no twisted fantasy. The landlord wants the tenant out.

She gets a glass out of the kitchen cabinet, gets out a tray of ice, pours herself a shot of Fran's bourbon. She is happy for Ted Suminski. She is. She wants to tell someone how moved she'd been by Mrs. Chatterji's singing. How she'd felt in O'Hare, even about Dr. Rab Chatterji in the car. But Fran is not the person. No one she's ever met is the person. She can't talk about the dead space she lives in. She wishes Ashoke Mehta would call. Right now.

Weeks pass. Then two months. She finds a new room, signs another lease. Her new landlord calls himself Fred. He has no arms, but he helps her move her things. He drives between Ted Suminski's place and his twice in his station wagon. He uses his toes the way Maya uses her fingers. He likes to do things. He pushes garbage sacks full of Maya's clothes up the stairs.

"It's all right to stare," Fred says. "Hell, I would."

That first afternoon in Fred's rooming house, they share a Chianti. Fred wants to cook her pork chops but he's a little shy about Indians and meat. Is it beef, or pork? Or any meat? She says it's okay, any meat, but not tonight. He has an ex-wife in Des Moines, two kids in Portland, Oregon. The kids are both normal; he's the only freak in the family. But he's self-reliant. He shops in the supermarket like anyone else, he carries out the garbage, shovels the snow off the sidewalk. He needs Maya's help with one thing. Just one thing. The box of Tide is a bit too heavy to manage. Could she get him the giant size every so often and leave it in the basement?

The dead space need not suffocate. Over the months, Fred and she will settle into companionship. She has never slept with a man without arms. Two wounded people, he will joke during their nightly contortions. It will shock her, this assumed equivalence with a man so strikingly deficient. She knows she is strange, and lonely, but being Indian is not the same, she would have thought, as being a freak.

One night in spring Fred's phone rings. "Ashoke Mehta speaking." None of this "do you remember me?" nonsense. The god has tracked her down. He hasn't forgotten. "Hullo," he says, in their special way. And because she doesn't answer back, "Hullo, hullo, hullo." She is aware of Fred in the back of the room. He is lighting a cigarette with his toes.

"Yes," she says, "I remember."

"I had to take care of a problem," Ashoke Mehta says. "You know that I have my vices. That time at O'Hare I was honest with you."

She is breathless.

"Who is it, May?" asks Fred.

"You also have a problem," says the voice. His laugh echoes. "You will come to Hartford, I know."

When she moves out, she tells herself, it will not be the end of Fred's world.

(1988)

Questions for Discussion and Writing

Close Reading

1. What subjects do Fran and Maya teach at the University of Northern Iowa? How do these subjects comment on their divergent personalities?
2. When Maya visits the Chatterjis, she looks at some snacks in a container with a see-through lid. The narrator describes these as "mysteries made visible." What mysteries are left invisible in the story? Who makes them invisible, and what is the motivation for doing so?
3. Three paragraphs end with the same one-word sentence: "But." What does that word mean as it is used repeatedly here?

Critical and Creative Reading

4. Consider how the three relationships in this story parallel one another: tenant-landlord, immigrant-citizen, lover-spouse.
5. Based on this story, define *love* and consider whether it is a realistic goal or not.
6. Both Fran and Maya discuss the difference between sex and love in their past relationships. Are they being honest, or are they trying to cover up their feelings of loss, abandonment, regret, or frustration? If a relationship does not develop into a lifelong union, is it a failure? Use this story to illustrate your opinion.

Connections to Other Readings

7. Do the phases of courtship described in "The Tenant" parallel the progression of love in Stendhal's "The Birth of Love"?

8. Compare Maya to the narrator of Susan Minot's story "Lust" in terms of self-respect.
9. Consider the themes of communication and isolation in marriage in this story and in James Joyce's "The Dead," John Updike's "Wife-Wooing," or Tennessee Williams's play *Cat on a Hot Tin Roof*.

Susan Minot

Lust

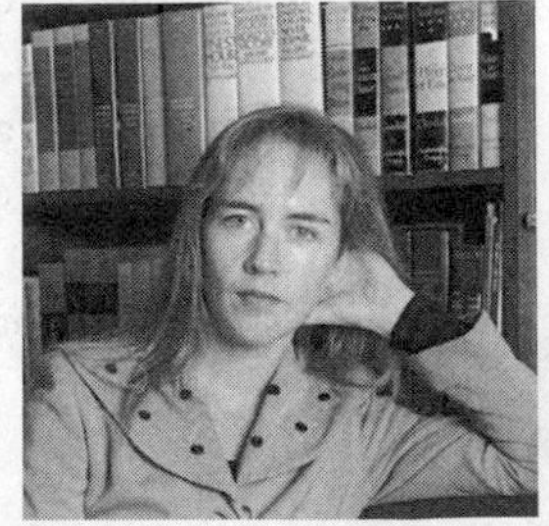

Susan Minot (b. 1956) was born in Boston and studied writing at Brown University and Columbia University. Her novel *Monkeys* was published to great acclaim in 1986, and she has won many awards for her short fiction. She also collaborated with the classic Italian filmmaker Bernardo Bertolucci on his screenplay for the film *Stealing Beauty*. "Lust" is one of her most frequently anthologized stories. It originally appeared in her book *Lust and Other Stories*, a collection that focuses on the difficulty of relationships between men and women.

Leo was from a long time ago, the first one I ever saw nude. In the spring before the Hellmans filled their pool, we'd go down there in the deep end, with baby oil, and like that. I met him the first month away at boarding school. He had a halo from the campus light behind him. I flipped.

Roger was fast. In his illegal car, we drove to the reservoir, the radio blaring, talking fast, fast, fast. He was always going for my zipper. He got kicked out sophomore year.

By the time the band got around to playing "Wild Horses," I had tasted Bruce's tongue. We were clicking in the shadows on the other side of the amplifier, out of Mrs. Donovan's line of vision. It tasted like salt, with my neck bent back, because we had been dancing so hard before.

Tim's line: "I'd like to see you in a bathing suit." I knew it was his line when he said the exact same thing to Annie Hines.

5 You'd go on walks to get off campus. It was raining like hell, my sweater as sopped as a wet sheep. Tim pinned me to a tree, the woods light brown and dark brown, a white house half-hidden with the lights already on. The water was as loud as a crowd hissing. He made certain comments about my forehead, about my cheeks.

We started off sitting at one end of the couch and then our feet were squished against the armrest and then he went over to turn off the TV and came back after he had taken off his shirt and then we slid onto the floor and he got up again to close the door, then came back to me, a body waiting on the rug.

You'd try to wipe off the table or to do the dishes and Willie would untuck your shirt and get his hands up under in front, standing behind you, making puffy noises in your ear.

He likes it when I wash my hair. He covers his face with it and if I start to say something, he goes, "Shush."

For a long time, I had Philip on the brain. The less they noticed you, the more you got them on the brain.

My parents had no idea. Parents never really know what's going on, espe- 10
cially when you're away at school most of the time. If she met them, my mother might say, "Oliver seems nice" or "I like that one" without much of an opinion. If she didn't like them, "He's a funny fellow, isn't he?" or "Johnny's perfectly nice but a drink of water." My father was too shy to talk to them at all, unless they played sports and he'd ask them about that.

The sand was almost cold underneath because the sun was long gone. Eben piled a mound over my feet, patting around my ankles, the ghostly surf rumbling behind him in the dark. He was the first person I ever knew who died, later that summer, in a car crash. I thought about it for a long time.

"Come here," he says on the porch.

I go over to the hammock and he takes my wrist with two fingers.

"What?"

He kisses my palm then directs my hand to his fly.

Songs went with whichever boy it was. "Sugar Magnolia" was Tim, with the 15
line "Rolling in the rushes/down by the riverside." With "Darkness, Darkness," I'd picture Philip with his long hair. Hearing "Under My Thumb" there'd be the smell of Jamie's suede jacket.[1]

We hid in the listening rooms during study hall. With a record cover over the door's window, the teacher on duty couldn't look in. I came out flushed and heady and back at the dorm was surprised how red my lips were in the mirror.

One weekend at Simon's brother's, we stayed inside all day with the shades down, in bed, then went out to Store 24 to get some ice cream. He stood at the

[1] *"Sugar Magnolia". . . . "Darkness, Darkness". . . . "Under My Thumb"*: Rock songs by the Grateful Dead, Led Zeppelin, and the Rolling Stones.

magazine rack and read through MAD[2] while I got butterscotch sauce, craving something sweet.

I could do some things well. Some things I was good at, like math or painting or even sports, but the second a boy put his arm around me, I forgot about wanting to do anything else, which felt like a relief at first until it became like sinking into a muck.

It was different for a girl.

When we were little, the brothers next door tied up our ankles. They held the door of the goat house and wouldn't let us out till we showed them our underpants. Then they'd forget about being after us and when we played whiffleball, I'd be just as good as them.

Then it got to be different. Just because you have on a short skirt, they yell from the cars, slowing down for a while and if you don't look, they screech off and call you a bitch.

"What's the matter with me?" they say, point-blank.

Or else, "Why won't you go out with me? I'm not asking you to get married," about to get mad.

Or it'd be, trying to be reasonable, in a regular voice, "Listen, I just want to have a good time."

So I'd go because I couldn't think of something to say back that wouldn't be obvious, and if you go out with them, you sort of have to do something.

I sat between Mack and Eddie in the front seat of the pickup. They were having a fight about something. I've a feeling about me.

Certain nights you'd feel a certain surrender, maybe if you'd had wine. The surrender would be forgetting yourself and you'd put your nose to his neck and feel like a squirrel, safe, at rest, in a restful dream. But then you'd start to slip from that and the dark would come in and there'd be a cave. You make out the dim shape of the windows and feel yourself become a cave, filled absolutely with air, or with a sadness that wouldn't stop.

Teenage years. You know just what you're doing and don't see the things that start to get in the way.

Lots of boys, but never two at the same time. One was plenty to keep you in a state. You'd start to see a boy and something would rush over you like a fast storm cloud and you couldn't possibly think of anyone else. Boys took it differently. Their eyes perked up at any little number that walked by. You'd act like you weren't noticing.

[2]*MAD:* Comic magazine that satirizes popular culture; popular with teenagers.

The joke was that the school doctor gave out the pill like aspirin. He didn't ask you anything. I was fifteen. We had a picture of him in assembly, holding up an IUD[3] shaped like a T. Most girls were on the pill, if anything, because they couldn't handle a diaphragm. I kept the dial in my top drawer like my mother and thought of her each time I tipped out the yellow tablets in the morning before chapel.

If they were too shy, I'd be more so. Andrew was nervous. We stayed up with his family album, sharing a pack of Old Golds. Before it got light, we turned on the TV. A man was explaining how to plant seedlings. His mouth jerked to the side in a tic. Andrew thought it was a riot and kept imitating him. I laughed to be polite. When we finally dozed off, he dared to put his arm around me but that was it.

You wait till they come to you. With half fright, half swagger, they stand one step down. They dare to touch the button on your coat then lose their nerve and quickly drop their hand so you—you'd do anything for them. You touch their cheek.

The girls sit around in the common room and talk about boys, smoking their heads off.

"What are you complaining about?" says Jill to me when we talk about problems.

"Yeah," says Giddy. "You always have a boyfriend."

I look at them and think, As if.

I thought the worst thing anyone could call you was a cock-teaser. So, if you flirted, you had to be prepared to go through with it. Sleeping with someone was perfectly normal once you had done it. You didn't really worry about it. But there were other problems. The problems had to do with something else entirely.

Mack was during the hottest summer ever recorded. We were renting a house on an island with all sorts of other people. No one slept during the heat wave, walking around the house with nothing on which we were used to because of the nude beach. In the living room, Eddie lay on top of a coffee table to cool off. Mack and I, with the bedroom door open for air, sweated and sweated all night.

"I can't take this," he said at 3 a.m. "I'm going for a swim." He and some guys down the hall went to the beach. The heat put me on edge. I sat on a cracked chest by the open window and smoked and smoked till I felt even worse, waiting for something—I guess for him to get back.

One was on a camping trip in Colorado. We zipped our sleeping bags together, the coyotes' hysterical chatter far away. Other couples murmured in other tents.

[3]*IUD:* "Intrauterine device," a method of birth control.

Paul was up before sunrise, starting a fire for breakfast. He wasn't much of a talker in the daytime. At night, his hand leafed about in the hair at my neck.

There'd be times when you overdid it. You'd get carried away. All the next day, you'd be in a total fog, delirious, absent-minded, crossing the street and nearly getting run over.

The more girls a boy has, the better. He has a bright look, having reaped fruits, blooming. He stalks around, sure-shouldered, and you have the feeling he's got more in him, a fatter heart, more stories to tell. For a girl, with each boy it's like a petal gets plucked each time.

Then you start to get tired. You begin to feel diluted, like watered-down stew.

Oliver came skiing with us. We lolled by the fire after everyone had gone to bed. Each creak you'd think was someone coming downstairs. The silver-loop bracelet he gave me had been a present from his girlfriend before.

On vacations, we went skiing, or you'd go south if someone invited you. Some people had apartments in New York that their families hardly ever used. Or summer houses, or older sisters. We always managed to find some place to go.

We made the plan at coffee hour. Simon snuck out and met me at Main Gate after lights-out. We crept to the chapel and spent the night in the balcony. He tasted like onions from a submarine sandwich.

The boys are one of two ways: either they can't sit still or they don't move. In front of the TV, they won't budge. On weekends they play touch football while we sit on the sidelines, picking blades of grass to chew on, and watch. We're always watching them run around. We shiver in the stands, knocking our boots together to keep our toes warm and they whizz across the ice, chopping their sticks around the puck. When they're in the rink, they refuse to look at you, only eyeing each other beneath low helmets. You cheer for them but they don't look up, even if it's a face-off when nothing's happening, even if they're doing drills before any game has started at all.

Dancing under the pink tent, he bent down and whispered in my ear. We slipped away to the lawn on the other side of the hedge. Much later, as he was leaving the buffet with two plates of eggs and sausage, I saw the grass stains on the knees of his white pants.

Tim's was shaped like a banana, with a graceful curve to it. They're all different. Willie's like a bunch of walnuts when nothing was happening, another's as thin as a thin hot dog. But it's like faces; you're never really surprised.

Still, you're not sure what to expect.

I look into his face and he looks back. I look into his eyes and they look back at mine. Then they look down at my mouth so I look at his mouth, then back to his eyes then, backing up, at his whole face. I think, Who? Who are you? His head tilts to one side.

I say, "Who are you?"

"What do you mean?"

"Nothing."

I look at his eyes again, deeper. Can't tell who he is, what he thinks.

"What?" he says. I look at his mouth.

"I'm just wondering," I say and go wandering across his face. Study the chin line. It's shaped like a persimmon.

"Who are you? What are you thinking?"

He says, "What the hell are you talking about?"

Then they get mad after when you say enough is enough. After, when it's easier to explain that you don't want to. You wouldn't dream of saying that maybe you weren't really ready to in the first place.

Gentle Eddie. We waded into the sea, the waves round and plowing in, buffalo-headed, slapping our thighs. I put my arms around his freckled shoulders and he held me up, buoyed by the water, and rocked me like a sea shell.

I had no idea whose party it was, the apartment jam-packed, stepping over people in the hallway. The room with the music was practically empty, the bare floor, me in red shoes. This fellow slides onto one knee and takes me around the waist and we rock to jazzy tunes, with my toes pointing heavenward, and waltz and spin and dip to "Smoke Gets in Your Eyes" or "I'll Love You Just for Now." He puts his head to my chest, runs a sweeping hand down my inside thigh and we go loose-limbed and sultry and as smooth as silk and I stamp my red heels and he takes me into a swoon. I never saw him again after that but I thought, I could have loved that one.

You wonder how long you can keep it up. You begin to feel like you're showing through, like a bathroom window that only lets in grey light, the kind you can't see out of.

They keep coming around. Johnny drives up at Easter vacation from Baltimore and I let him in the kitchen with everyone sound asleep. He has friends waiting in the car.

"What are you crazy? It's pouring out there," I say.

"It's okay," he says. "They understand."

So he gets some long kisses from me, against the refrigerator, before he goes because I hate those girls who push away a boy's face as if she were made out of Ivory soap, as if she's that much greater than he is.

The note on my cubby told me to see the headmaster. I had no idea for what. He had received complaints about my amorous displays on the town green. It was Willie that spring. The headmaster told me he didn't care what I did but that Casey Academy had a reputation to uphold in the town. He lowered his glasses on his nose. "We've got twenty acres of woods on this campus," he said. "Smooch with your boyfriend there."

Everybody'd get weekend permissions for different places then we'd all go to someone's house whose parents were away. Usually there'd be more boys than girls. We raided the liquor closet and smoked pot at the kitchen table and you'd never know who would end up where, or with whom. There were always disasters. Ceci got bombed and cracked her head open on the bannister and needed stitches. Then there was the time Wendel Blair walked through the picture window at the Lowe's and got slashed to ribbons.

He scared me. In bed, I didn't dare look at him. I lay back with my eyes 70
closed, luxuriating because he knew all sorts of expert angles, his hands never fumbling, going over my whole body, pressing the hair up and off the back of my head, giving an extra hip shove, as if to say *There.* I parted my eyes slightly, keeping the screen of my lashes low because it was too much to look at him, his mouth loose and pink and parted, his eyes looking through my forehead, or kneeling up, looking through my throat. I was ashamed but couldn't look him in the eye.

You wonder about things feeling a little off-kilter. You begin to feel like a piece of pounded veal.

At boarding school, everyone gets depressed. We go in and see the housemother, Mrs. Gunther. She got married when she was eighteen. Mr. Gunther was her high-school sweetheart, the only boyfriend she ever had.

"And you knew you wanted to marry him right off?" we ask her.

She smiles and says, "Yes."

"They always want something from you" says Jill, complaining about her 75
boyfriend.

"Yeah," says Giddy. "You always feel like you have to deliver something."

"You do," says Mrs. Gunther. "Babies."

After sex, you curl up like a shrimp, something deep inside you ruined, slammed in a place that sickens at slamming, and slowly you fill up with an overwhelming sadness, an elusive gaping worry. You don't try to explain it, filled with the knowledge that it's nothing after all, everything filling up finally and absolutely with death. After the briskness of loving, loving stops. And you roll over with death stretched out alongside you like a feather boa, or a snake, light as air, and you . . . you don't even ask for anything or try to say something to him because it's obviously your own damn fault. You haven't been able to—to what? To open your heart. You open your legs but can't, or don't dare anymore, to open your heart.

It starts this way:

You stare into their eyes. They flash like all the stars are out. They look at 80
you seriously, their eyes at a low burn and their hands no matter what starting off

shy and with such a gentle touch that the only thing you can do is take that tenderness and let yourself be swept away. When, with one attentive finger they tuck the hair behind your ear, you—

You do everything they want.

Then comes after. After when they don't look at you. They scratch their balls, stare at the ceiling. Or if they do turn, their gaze is altogether changed. They are surprised. They turn casually to look at you, distracted, and get a mild distracted surprise. You're gone. Their black look tells you that the girl they were fucking is not there anymore. You seem to have disappeared.

(1989)

QUESTIONS FOR DISCUSSION AND WRITING

CLOSE READING

1. Early in the story the narrator states, "It was different for a girl." What specific differences between boys and girls does she describe? What do these generalizations tell you that they might not tell her?
2. At one point the narrator describes herself with a simile: "You begin to feel like you're showing through, like a bathroom window that only lets in grey light, the kind you can't see out of." How does this simile function? Apply it to the story as a whole.
3. The story seems like a catalog of the narrator's sexual escapades. Find the sections that are *not* part of this catalog. Is there a pattern? A progression?

CRITICAL AND CREATIVE READING

4. Is "Lust" about a character who has not yet learned how to love, a character who cannot love, or a character for whom love does not matter?
5. Record your initial response to the narrator of this story (such as pity, or hatred, or indifference). Then connect that response to her method of narration, not simply to her actions and descriptions.
6. Can two people who are attracted enough to one another to have a sexual encounter eventually fall in love? Put differently, can lust be a steppingstone to love? If so, what circumstances must exist for love to develop?

CONNECTIONS TO OTHER READINGS

7. Compare the narrator's attitudes toward men in this story to the narrator's attitudes toward women in John Updike's "Wife-Wooing." Do the stories say more about gender or about the personality of the individual narrators?
8. Discuss the way stereotypes about the opposite sex and public perceptions of one's "reputation" play out in "Lust" and in Bharati Mukherjee's story "The Tenant."
9. Use the description of the progression of love in Stendhal's essay "The Birth of Love" to analyze the narrator's experiences in "Lust."

Poetry

Christopher Marlowe

The Passionate Shepherd to His Love

Christopher Marlowe (1564–1593) was the son of a shoemaker who attended college on scholarship. Instead of taking religious vows, as his education had prepared him to do, he became a playwright and–possibly–a spy for Queen Elizabeth. His successful plays include *Tamburlaine, Dr. Faustus,* and *The Jew of Malta,* and his poetry includes the erotic "Hero and Leander." His short life was marked by intrigue and violence. He was murdered at the age of twenty-nine, allegedly in a tavern brawl, though evidence suggests his death was due to his connections to London spies. The pastoral world of "The Passionate Shepherd to His Love" could not be farther from the world of London intrigue. Many readers have memorized the poem's opening invitation in which the speaker invites his mistress to "live with me and be my love," though almost as many have spoofed its naive assumptions about love. Does the life offered by the shepherd appeal to you?

Come live with me and be my love,
And we will all the pleasures prove
That valleys, groves, hills, and fields,
Woods, or steepy mountain yields.

And we will sit upon the rocks,
Seeing the shepherds feed their flocks,
By shallow rivers to whose falls
Melodious birds sing madrigals.

And I will make thee beds of roses
And a thousand fragrant posies,
A cap of flowers, and a kirtle[1]
Embroidered all with leaves of myrtle;

A gown made of the finest wool
Which from our pretty lambs we pull;
Fair linéd slippers for the cold,
With buckles of the purest gold;

[1] *kirtle:* A bodice, girdle.

A belt of straw and ivy buds,
With coral clasps and amber studs:
And if these pleasures may thee move,
Come live with me, and be my love.

The shepherd swains shall dance and sing
For thy delight each May morning:
If these delights thy mind may move,
Then live with me and be my love.

(1599)

Questions for Discussion and Writing

Close Reading

1. Instead of the traditional offerings of wealth (jewels, prestige), what gifts does the shepherd offer to his love? What do they tell us about his values?
2. What kind of life will the shepherd and his love lead? How will they pass their time?
3. How is nature depicted in this poem? What will be the relationship between these lovers and the natural world if the speaker has his way?
4. Why is the repetition of the line "live with me and be my love" significant?

Critical and Creative Reading

5. This poem makes no reference to lust, physical attraction, or sex of any kind. Do we have any sense of what attracts the shepherd to his love? Do we have any sense of her or what she might want?
6. Does this poem depict an ideal relationship to you? If so, what makes it appealing? If not, what is missing?
7. Although the pastoral world depicted in Renaissance literature never existed, it appealed to people's imaginations. What is the equivalent ideal world today? Does the countryside still have an idealized place in our minds? If you were to update this poem, what would your speaker offer his love?

Connections to Other Readings

8. Sir Walter Raleigh's "The Nymph's Reply to the Shepherd" offers a string of reasons why the shepherd's plan will not work out. Which vision of love is more in line with your views?
9. Compare Marlowe's picture of ideal love to Elizabeth Barrett Browning's in her "Sonnet 43" from *Sonnets from the Portuguese*.

Sir Walter Raleigh

The Nymph's Reply to the Shepherd

Sir Walter Raleigh (1552?–1618) was the quintessential Renaissance man: a courtier, a soldier, an explorer, a poet, and a lover. He lost the favor of Elizabeth I after seducing and then marrying one of her ladies-in-waiting. He was imprisoned in the Tower of London by the queen's successor James I under false charges of treason. While in prison he began a *History of the World,* which was unfinished when he was executed for treason thirteen years after first being imprisoned. "The Nymph's Reply to the Shepherd"—an answer to Christopher Marlowe's "The Passionate Shepherd to His Love"—is one of his most famous poems. (See also his poem "The Lie" in Chapter 14.)

If all the world and love were young,
And truth in every shepherd's tongue,
These pretty pleasures might me move
To live with thee and be thy love.

Time drives the flocks from field to fold,
When rivers rage, and rocks grow cold,
And Philomel[1] becometh dumb;
The rest complain of cares to come.

The flowers do fade, and wanton fields
To wayward winter reckoning yields;
A honey tongue, a heart of gall,
Is fancy's spring, but sorrow's fall.

Thy gowns, thy shoes, thy beds of roses,
Thy cap, thy kirtle,[2] and thy posies
Soon break, soon wither, soon forgotten—
In folly ripe, in reason rotten.

Thy belt of straw and ivy buds,
Thy coral clasps and amber studs,
All these in me no means can move
To come to thee and be thy love.

[1]*Philomel:* In Greek mythology, an Athenian princess who is raped by her brother-in-law, avenged by her sister, and later turned into a nightingale.

[2]*kirtle:* A bodice, girdle.

But could youth last, and love still breed,
Had joys no date, nor age no need,
Then these delights my mind might move
To live with thee and be thy love.

(1600)

Questions for Discussion and Writing

Close Reading

1. What are the nymph's objections to the shepherd's offer? What does she point out about the passage of time? Does this strike you as a valid objection?
2. How does Raleigh's poem parallel Marlowe's in content and form?
3. Describe the poem's tone. Is it light and playful, or more dark and serious? Which words in the poem support your interpretation?

Critical and Creative Reading

4. How does the tone shift in the last stanza? Does the shepherd stand a chance with this woman?
5. What kind of person is the nymph? Is she a cynic or a realist?
6. Write a response to the "Nymph's Reply" (either in prose or in verse) from the point of view of the shepherd. Does he give up?

Connections to Other Readings

7. Compare and contrast the importance of the passage of time in this poem and in Andrew Marvell's "To His Coy Mistress." Do you think Raleigh's nymph is likely to be more persuaded by Marvell's argument than she is by Marlowe's?
8. Compare the nymph's attitude toward romantic love to that of John Keats in "And what is love? It is a doll dressed up." Do you think the nymph would agree with Keats's definition of love?

William Shakespeare

My mistress' eyes are nothing like the sun (Sonnet 130)
My love is a fever longing still (Sonnet 147)

Although William Shakespeare (1564–1615) was married with children, he seems to have spent most of his adult life away from his family as a playwright, actor, and poet in London. The following two poems are part of a series known as his "Dark Lady Sonnets." Scholars have debated the actual identity of this powerful mistress. Unlike many Renaissance poets, Shakespeare never identifies the subjects of his poems. All that is certain is that her relationship with Shakespeare was intensely sexual and emotionally painful. His feelings for her range from desire, to jealousy, to resentment. As you read the following sonnets, ask yourself if the speaker is in love. Are love and lust mutually exclusive for him? (For more on William Shakespeare, see the introduction to *I Henry IV* along with his portrait in Chapter 16, and the introduction to his Sonnet 138 in Chapter 14.)

Sonnet 130

My mistress' eyes are nothing like the sun;
Coral is far more red than her lips' red;
If snow be white, why then her breasts are dun;
If hairs be wires, black wires grow on her head.
I have seen roses damasked,[1] red and white,
But no such roses see I in her cheeks;
And in some perfumes is there more delight
Than in the breath that from my mistress reeks.
I love to hear her speak, yet well I know
That music hath a far more pleasing sound;
I grant I never saw a goddess go;
My mistress, when she walks, treads on the ground.
And yet, by heaven, I think my love as rare
As any she belied with false compare.

(1609)

[1]*damasked*: Decorated or woven with rich patterns.

Sonnet 147

My love is as a fever, longing still
For that which longer nurseth the disease,
Feeding on that which doth preserve the ill,
Th' uncertain sickly appetite to please.
My reason, the physician to my love,
Angry that his prescriptions are not kept,
Hath left me, and I desperate now approve
Desire is death, which physic[1] did except.
Past cure I am, now reason is past care,
And frantic mad with evermore unrest;
My thoughts and my discourse as mad men's are,
At random from the truth vainly expressed;
For I have sworn thee fair, and thought thee bright,
Who art as black as hell, as dark as night.

(1609)

[1]*physic*: A cathartic drug.

Questions for Writing and Discussion

Close Reading

1. "My mistress' eyes" is as much about the exaggerated claims of other poets as about the speaker's mistress. How is Shakespeare critiquing conventional love poetry?
2. Does the speaker seem to love his mistress in spite of or because of the fact that she "treads on the ground"—in other words, that she is a human being, not a goddess?
3. In "My love is as a fever," the speaker compares love to an illness. Why is "reason" an ineffective physician? What does this say about the power of love (or lust)?
4. What do you make of the symbols of light and dark in both poems? Assuming the mistress is as dark-haired and dark-complexioned as the speaker claims, how does he use that detail to suggest his lover's less tangible qualities? What are the common associations of light and darkness?
5. Consider how both poems address how people in love deceive themselves about their lovers. In which poem does the speaker seem to have a more realistic picture of his lover?

Critical and Creative Reading

6. What evidence in the two poems suggests that the relationship between the speaker and his mistress is a loving one? What evidence suggests that it is mostly a sexual relationship? How are the two connected for the speaker?
7. Shakespeare claims that "love is like a fever." Brainstorm other things to which you have heard love and lust compared. Which of these seems most apt to you? Can you think of any metaphors to add to this list?

Connections to Other Readings

8. Contrast Shakespeare's depictions of love and lust to Christopher Marlowe's in "The Passionate Shepherd to His Love."
9. How does the speaker's lust in these poems compare to that of the narrator of Updike's "Wife-Wooing"?
10. Discuss the role of guilt in these Shakespeare poems and in Aphra Behn's "The Disappointment."

Thomas Carew

A Rapture

In addition to writing love poems, Thomas Carew (1595–1640; his name is pronounced "Carey") wrote political verse and criticism. He also worked as a

lawyer, a diplomat, and a soldier under Charles I. In "A Rapture," Carew compares sex to a voyage that will not be impeded by a giant called "Honour" who seeks to prevent the lovers' happy passage to the land of Elysium, a place where the only sin is *not* to follow one's desires. The speaker compares foreplay and intercourse to exploring an undiscovered land. The allusions are explicit, and the poem is Carew's most erotic, describing a Utopian world of unimpeded passion. Not surprisingly, this description of an invented fantasy world contains no mention of the disease that eventually killed Carew: syphilis.

I will enjoy thee now, my Celia, come,
And fly with me to Love's Elysium.[1]
The giant, Honour, that keeps cowards out,
Is but a masquer, and the servile rout
Of baser subjects only bend in vain
To the vast idol, whilst the nobler train
Of valiant lovers daily sail between
The huge Colossus'[2] legs, and pass unseen
Unto the blissful shore. Be bold and wise,
And we shall enter: the grim Swiss denies
Only to tame fools a passage, that not know
He is but form and only frights in show
The duller eyes that look from far; draw near
And thou shalt scorn what we were wont to fear.
We shall see how the stalking pageant goes
With borrow'd legs, a heavy load to those
That made and bear him—not as we once thought
The seed of gods, but a weak model wrought
By greedy men, that seek to enclose the common,
And within private arms empale free woman.
   Come then, and mounted on the wings of love
We'll cut the flitting air and soar above
The monster's head, and in the noblest seats
Of those blessed shades, quench and renew our heats.
There shall the Queens of Love and Innocence,
Beauty, and Nature banish all offence
From our close ivy twines, there I'll behold
Thy bared snow and thy unbraided gold.
There my enfranchised hand on every side
Shall o'er thy naked polish'd ivory slide.
No curtain there, though of transparent lawn,

[1]*Elysium*: Heaven.

[2]*Colossus*: A huge statue of the Greek god Apollo—one of the seven wonders of the ancient world.

Shall be before thy virgin treasure drawn,
But the rich mine to the enquiring eye
Exposed, shall ready still for mintage lie,
And we will coin young Cupids. There a bed
Of roses and fresh myrtles shall be spread
Under the cooler shade of cypress groves;
Our pillows, of the down of Venus'[3] doves,
Whereon our panting limbs we'll gently lay,
In the faint respites of our active play,
That so our slumbers may in dreams have leisure
To tell the nimble fancy our past pleasure,
And so our souls that cannot be embraced,
Shall the embraces of our bodies taste.
Meanwhile the bubbling stream shall court the shore,
Th' enamour'd chirping wood-choir shall adore
In varied tunes the Deity of Love;
The gentle blasts of western winds shall move
The trembling leaves, and through their close boughs breathe
Still music, whilst we rest ourselves beneath
Their dancing shade; till a soft murmur, sent
From souls entranced in amorous languishment
Rouse us, and shoot into our veins fresh fire,
Till we in their sweet ecstasy expire.
　Then, as the empty bee, that lately bore
Into the common treasure all her store,
Flies 'bout the painted field with nimble wing,
Deflow'ring the fresh virgins of the spring,
So will I rifle all the sweets that dwell
In my delicious paradise, and swell
My bag with honey, drawn forth by the power
Of fervent kisses from each spicy flower.
I'll seize the rose buds in their perfumed bed,
The violet knots, like curious mazes spread
O'er all the garden, taste the ripen'd cherry,
The warm, firm apple, tipp'd with coral berry.
Then will I visit with a wand'ring kiss
The vale of lilies and the bower of bliss,
And where the beauteous region both divide
Into two milky ways, my lips shall slide
Down those smooth alleys, wearing as I go
A track for lovers on the printed snow.
Thence climbing o'er the swelling Apennine,[4]
Retire into thy grove of eglantine,[5]

[3] *Venus*: The Roman goddess of love.

[4] *Apennine*: An Italian mountain range.

[5] *eglantine*: Sweetbrier, a wild rose.

Where I will all those ravish'd sweets distill
Through Love's alembic, and with chemic skill
From the mix'd mass one sovereign balm derive,
Then bring that great elixir to thy hive.
    Now in more subtle wreaths I will entwine
My sinewy thighs, my legs and arms with thine;
Thou like a sea of milk shalt lie display'd,
Whilst I the smooth, calm ocean invade
With such a tempest as when Jove of old
Fell down on Danaë[6] in a storm of gold.
Yet my tall pine shall in the Cyprian strait
Ride safe at anchor and unlade[7] her freight;
My rudder with thy bold hand like a tried
And skillful pilot, thou shalt steer, and guide
My bark into love's channel, where it shall
Dance as the bounding waves do rise or fall.
Then shall thy circling arms embrace and clip
My naked body, and thy balmy lip
Bathe me in juice of kisses, whose perfume
Like a religious incense shall consume,
And send up holy vapors to those powers
That bless our loves and crown our sportful hours,
That with such halcyon[8] calmness fix our souls
In steadfast peace, as no affright controls.
There no rude sounds shake us with sudden starts,
No jealous ears, when we unrip our hearts,
Suck our discourse in, no observing spies
This blush, that glance traduce; no envious eyes
Watch our close meetings, nor are we betray'd
To rivals by the bribed chambermaid.
No wedlock bonds unwreathe our twisted loves,
We seek no midnight arbor, no dark groves
To hide our kisses; there, the hated name
Of husband, wife, lust, modest, chaste, or shame,
Are vain and empty words, whose very sound
Was never heard in the Elysian ground.
All things are lawful there that may delight
Nature or unrestrained appetite.
Like and enjoy, to will and act is one;

[6]*Jove . . . Danaë:* According to ancient mythology, Danaë was impregnated by the Roman god Jove when he appeared to her as a shower of gold.

[7]*unlade:* To unload (nautical).

[8]*halcyon:* Peaceful, tranquil, and prosperous.

We only sin when love's rites are not done.
  The Roman Lucrece[9] there reads the divine
Lectures of love's great master, Aretine,[10]
And knows as well as Lais[11] how to move
Her pliant body in the act of love.
To quench the burning ravisher, she hurls
Her limbs into a thousand winding curls,
And studies artful postures, such as be
Carved on the bark of every neighbouring tree
By learned hands, that so adorn'd the rind
Of those fair plants, which, as they lay entwined
Have fann'd their glowing fires. The Grecian dame,
That in her endless web toil'd for a name
As fruitless as her work doth there display
Herself before the youth of Ithaca,
And th' amorous sport of gamesome nights prefer
Before dull dreams of the lost traveller.
Daphne hath broke her bark, and that swift foot
Which th' angry gods had fasten'd with a root
To the fix'd earth, doth now unfetter'd run
To meet th' embraces of the youthful sun.
She hangs upon him like his Delphic lyre,[12]
Her kisses blow the old and breathe new fire;
Full of her god, she sings inspired lays,
Sweet odes of love, such as deserve the bays
Which she herself was. Next her, Laura lies
In Petrarch's[13] learned arms, drying those eyes
That did in such sweet smooth-paced numbers flow,
As made the world enamour'd of his woe.
These and ten thousand beauties more, that died
Slave to the tyrant, now enlarged, deride
His cancell'd laws, and for their time misspent
Pay into Love's exchequer double rent.
  Come then, my Celia, we'll no more forbear
To taste our joys, struck with a panic fear,
But will depose from his imperious sway

[9]*Lucrece:* According to the Roman poet, Ovid, Lucrece was raped by the king of Rome and committed suicide. Shakespeare retold this story in his poem "The Rape of Lucrece."

[10]*Aretine:* A wealthy Italian satirist who was known for his licentious lifestyle and literary attacks on his enemies.

[11]*Lais:* A Greek courtesan.

[12]*Delphic lyre:* An instrument played by the Greek god Apollo.

[13]*Laura . . . Petrarch's:* The fourteenth-century Italian poet Petrarch dedicated his love sonnets to Laura.

This proud usurper and walk as free as they,
With necks unyoked; nor is it just that he
Should fetter your soft sex with chastity,
Which Nature made unapt for abstinence;
When yet this false impostor can dispense
With human justice and with sacred right,
And maugre both their laws, command me fight
With rivals or with emulous[14] loves, that dare
Equal with thine their mistress' eyes or hair.
If thou complain of wrong, and call my sword
To carve out thy revenge, upon that word
He bids me fight and kill, or else he brands
With marks of infamy my coward hands.
And yet religion bids from bloodshed fly,
And damns me for that act. Then tell me why
  This goblin Honour which the world adores
  Should make men atheists, and not women whores.

(1640)

Questions for Discussion and Writing

Close Reading

1. The poem is long but not difficult to follow if you take notes. As you go through the poem, trace Carew's metaphors. Here are only a few images to investigate: a giant, the queens of love and innocence, bared snow and unbridled gold, a bee. How many ways does Carew describe sex without mentioning it directly? Why might he choose to write an erotic poem in which sexuality is only alluded to?
2. Carew makes several references to "Nature." How does the speaker view "Nature"? How does this perception of Nature support his attempts to seduce Celia?
3. According to the speaker, why don't the lovers need to hide their lovemaking? Why does "wedlock" and other "hated names" have no power over them?

Critical and Creative Reading

4. What, according to Carew, is wrong with Honour, for both men and women? How is "Honour" personified? Is this argument persuasive?
5. Carew condemns the sexual double standard to which women are held, though he does so in an attempt to "conquer" his lover as an explorer might conquer "virgin" wilderness. How might a feminist critic respond to this poem?
6. What function do the references to famous lovers of the past serve? How might invoking these other lovers convince Celia to join him in "Elysium"? What famous lover would you add to the list?

[14]*emulous*: Competitive.

7. The speaker frequently mentions his "love" for Celia. What is the relationship between love and sex in this work?
8. Write a prose piece or a poem in which you write "Celia's reply" to the speaker. How might a young woman refute the arguments against "Honour"? What are the risks of traveling with the speaker to Elysium?

Connections to Other Readings

9. Compare this poem to Christopher Marlowe's "The Passionate Shepherd to His Love" and Andrew Marvell's "To His Coy Mistress." What common tactics do the speakers use in their attempt to woo a lover? How do their arguments differ? Which one is the most convincing? Which is the most far-fetched?
10. Compare the attitude of the speaker in this poem to the narrator in John Updike's "Wife-Wooing." How does seducing a lover differ from seducing a wife?

Andrew Marvell

To His Coy Mistress

With "To His Coy Mistress," Andrew Marvell (1621–1678) wrote perhaps the most famous *carpe diem* (Latin for "seize the day") poem in the English language. His argument moves from romantic idealizations of his lover to appalling images of the physical effects of death on the body. His juxtaposition of sex and death is meant to shock and convey a sense of urgency. For more information on Andrew Marvell, see the introduction to "The Mower's Song" in Chapter 15.

Had we but world enough, and time,
This coyness, lady, were no crime.
We would sit down, and think which way
To walk, and pass our long love's day.
Thou by the Indian Ganges'[1] side
Shouldst rubies find; I by the tide
Of Humber[2] would complain. I would
Love you ten years before the Flood,
And you should, if you please, refuse
Till the conversion of the Jews.[3]
My vegetable love should grow
Vaster than empires, and more slow;

[1] *Ganges:* A river in India.

[2] *Humber:* An English river.

[3] *conversion of the Jews:* In Christian tradition, said to be a sign of the end of the world.

An hundred years should go to praise
Thine eyes, and on thy forehead gaze;
Two hundred to adore each breast,
But thirty thousand to the rest.
An age at least to every part,
And the last age should show your heart.
For, lady, you deserve this state,
Nor would I love at lower rate.

But at my back I always hear
Time's wingéd chariot hurrying near;
And yonder all before us lie
Deserts of vast eternity.
Thy beauty shall no more be found,
Nor, in thy marble vault, shall sound
My echoing song; then worms shall try
That long preserv'd virginity,
And your quaint honour turn to dust,
And into ashes all my lust.
The grave's a fine and private place,
But none, I think, do there embrace.

Now therefore, while the youthful hue
Sits on thy skin like morning dew,
And while thy willing soul transpires
At every pore with instant fires,
Now let us sport us while we may,
And now, like am'rous birds of prey,
Rather at once our time devour,
Than languish in his slow-chapp'd power.
Let us roll all our strength, and all
Our sweetness, up into one ball,
And tear our pleasures with rough strife
Thorough the iron gates of life:
Thus, though we cannot make our sun
Stand still, yet we will make him run.

(1681)

Questions for Discussion and Writing

Close Reading

1. The first stanza supposes a hypothetical situation: *if* the speaker and his mistress had "world enough, and time" *then* they could prolong their sexual union indefinitely. How does this stanza, in which Marvell praises his mistress, set up his argument? What does his choice of ways to praise his mistress reveal about his feelings for her?

2. Trace the references to time and the passage of time throughout the poem. How might consummation of their relationship make their sun "run"? Why is this desirable?
3. How does Marvell contrast the images of "vast eternity" with images of immediacy and action? Which images are more powerful to you?

CRITICAL AND CREATIVE READING

4. How would you characterize the poem's tone? Are you more compelled by the morbid images of death and decay or by playful understatements like "The grave's a fine and private place, / But none, I think, do there embrace"?
5. How does the speaker attempt to convince his mistress that he is interested in more than sex? Are you convinced?

CONNECTIONS TO OTHER READINGS

6. Although the tone, argument, and style of this poem contrast with the tone, argument, and style of the narrator of Updike's story "Wife-Wooing," the purpose of both men is the same. Who is probably the more effective seducer?
7. Compare and contrast the attitudes toward "honour" in this poem and in Thomas Carew's "A Rapture." What do these speakers think of honor?
8. Compare and contrast this poem to the *carpe diem* poem featured in Chapter 9: Robert Herrick's "To the Virgins, to Make Much of Time." What connections can you find between the two works? What differences do you see?
9. Discuss the passage of time and encroachment of death in this poem and in Tennessee Williams's play *Cat on a Hot Tin Roof*. How do these motifs complicate the chapter's main theme of love and lust?

Aphra Behn

The Disappointment

What we know about the life of Aphra Behn (1640?–1689) suggests a remarkable woman, as interesting as any of her literary creations. While she may have lived in Surinam as a child, scholars can only speculate about her place of birth, the identity of her parents, and the identity and fate of the husband who was out of the picture by the time she began her writing career. We do know that she worked as a spy for Charles II in his war against the Dutch, but the British crown was slow to pay her and she was imprisoned for debt on her return to London. "Forced to write for bread," as she put it, she began writing plays, stories, and poems in the 1670s and went on to enjoy a successful career with plays like the wildly popular *The Rover* and works of prose like *Oroonoko,* a novella about a slave rebellion in Surinam. Alternately praised for her talent and vilified for her immodesty throughout her life, Behn was buried in Westminster Abbey after her death, a fitting tribute to the first woman in English to earn her living through writing. "The Disappointment" frankly acknowledges the complicated relationship between love, desire, and shame as the "amorous Lysander" finds himself unable to consummate his passionate encounter with the "fair Cloris."

I

One day the amorous Lysander,
By an impatient passion swayed,
Surprised fair Cloris, that loved maid,
Who could defend herself no longer.
All things did with his love conspire;
The gilded planet[1] of the day,
In his gay chariot drawn by fire,
Was now descending to the sea,
And left no light to guide the world,
But what from Cloris' brighter eyes was hurled.

II

In a lone thicket made for love,
Silent as a yielding maid's consent,
She with a charming languishment,
Permits his force, yet gently strove;
Her hands his bosom softly meet,
But not to put him back designed,
Rather to draw him on inclined;
Whilst he lay trembling at her feet,
Resistance 'tis in vain to show;
She wants the power to say—*Ah! What d'ye do?*

III

Her bright eyes sweet, and yet severe,
Where love and shame confusedly strive,
Fresh vigour to Lysander give;
And breathing faintly in his ear,
She cried—*Cease, cease—your vain desire,*
Or I'll call out—what would you do?
My dearer honour even to you
I cannot, must not give—Retire,
Or take this life, whose chiefest part
I gave you with the conquest of my heart.

[1]*gilded planet*: The sun.

IV

But he as much unused to fear,
As he was capable of love,
The blessed minutes to improve,
Kisses her mouth, her neck, her hair;
Each touch her new desire alarms,
His burning trembling hand he pressed
Upon her swelling snowy breast,
While she lay panting in his arms.
All her unguarded beauties lie
The spoils and trophies of the enemy.

V

And now without respect or fear,
He seeks the object of his vows,
(His love no modesty allows)
By swift degrees advancing—where
His daring hand that altar seized,
Where gods of love do sacrifice:
That awful throne, that paradise
Where rage is calmed, and anger pleased;
That fountain where delight still flows,
And gives the universal world repose.

VI

Her balmy lips encountering his,
Their bodies, as their souls, are joined;
Where both in transports unconfined
Extend themselves upon the moss.
Cloris half dead and breathless lay;
Her soft eyes cast a humid light,
Such as divides the day and night;
Or falling stars, whose fires decay:
And now no signs of life she shows,
But what in short-breathed sighs returns and goes.

VII

He saw how at her length she lay;
He saw her rising bosom bare;
Her loose thin robes, through which appear
A shape designed for love and play;
Abandoned by her pride and shame
She does her softest joys dispense,
Offering her virgin innocence
A victim to love's sacred flame;
While the o'er-ravished shepherd lies
Unable to perform the sacrifice.

VIII

Ready to taste a thousand joys,
The too transported hapless swain[2]
Found the vast pleasure turned to pain;
Pleasure which too much love destroys:
The willing garments by he laid,
And Heaven all opened to his view,
Mad to possess, himself he threw
On the defenceless lovely maid.
But Oh what envious god conspires
To snatch his power, yet leave him the desire!

IX

Nature's support (without whose aid
She can no human being give)
Itself now wants the art to live;
Faintness its slackened nerves invade;
In vain th'enraged youth essayed
To call its fleeting vigour back,
No motion 'twill from motion take;
Excess of love his love betrayed;
In vain he toils, in vain commands;
The insensible fell weeping in his hand.

X

In this so amorous cruel strife,
Where love and fate were too severe,
The poor Lysander in despair
Renounced his reason with his life:
Now all the brisk and active fire
That should the nobler part inflame,
Served to increase his rage and shame,
And left no spark of new desire:
Not all her naked charms could move
Or calm that rage that had debauched his love.

XI

Cloris returning from the trance
Which love and soft desire had bred,
Her timorous hand she gently laid
(Or guided by design or chance)
Upon that fabulous Priapus,[3]

[2]*swain:* A country youth.

[3]*Priapus*: A phallus, from the Greek god of male sexual power.

That potent god, as poets feign;
But never did young shepherdess,
Gathering of fern upon the plain,
More nimbly draw her fingers back,
Finding beneath the verdant leaves a snake.

XII

Then Cloris her fair hand withdrew,
Finding that god of her desires
Disarmed of all his awful fires,
And cold as flowers bathed in morning dew.
Who can the nymph's confusion guess?
The blood forsook the hinder place,
And strewed with blushes all her face,
Which both disdain and shame expressed:
And from Lysander's arms she fled,
Leaving him fainting on the gloomy bed.

XIII

Like lightning through the grove she hies,
Or Daphne[4] from the Delphic god,
No print upon the grassy road
She leaves, t'instruct pursuing eyes.
The wind that wantoned in her hair,
And with her ruffled garments played,
Discovered in the flying maid
All that the gods e'er made, if fair.
So Venus,[5] when her love was slain,
With fear and haste flew o'er the fatal plain.

XIV

The nymph's resentments none but I
Can well imagine or condole:
But none can guess Lysander's soul,
But those who swayed his destiny.
His silent griefs swell up to storms,
And not one god his fury spares;
He cursed his birth, his fate, his stars;
But more the shepherdess's charms,
Whose soft bewitching influence
Had damned him to the hell of impotence.

(1680)

[4]*Daphne*: In Ovid, Daphne was transformed into a laurel tree to escape the sexual pursuit of the god Apollo, "the Delphic god."

[5]*Venus*: The Roman goddess of love.

Questions for Discussion and Writing

Close Reading

1. How vigorously does Cloris try to "defend herself"? Why does she resist Lysander when her desires seem as strong as his?
2. How does Behn compare the seduction of Cloris to a religious sacrifice? In what ways is Cloris's submission a sacrifice? A religious experience? In what ways is Behn being ironic? How does the religious imagery reinforce the poem's tone?
3. We are told that Lysander's "rage . . . debauched his love." Why is he enraged? To what does he attribute his failure? What does this tell you about his character?

Critical and Creative Reading

4. Throughout the narrative poem, Cloris's behavior is a mass of contradictions. She struggles against Lysander even as she designs to "draw him on." Then, when she finds he is impotent, she runs away in "shame" and "resentment." How realistic is this reaction to her situation? What does her behavior suggest about her attitude toward sexuality? Does it reflect an attitude still present today?
5. In the last stanza, we are rather jarred by the intrusion of a first-person narrator who claims she is the only one who can understand Cloris's feelings. Why might Behn have added this narrator to the poem? How does this new point of view change our perception of this story as a fictional pastoral? What does the narrator reveal about herself?
6. Do you think Cloris and Lysander are typical young lovers? Are they in love? Write a paragraph in which you imagine their behavior the next time they meet one another. Do you see a future for these two?

Connections to Other Readings

7. Compare and contrast this seventeenth-century poem to a more recent treatment of female sexuality and desire, Susan Minot's story "Lust." What is the relationship between shame and desire in these works? What differences do you see?
8. This poem is a "pastoral," as is Christopher Marlowe's "The Passionate Shepherd to His Love." They both depict an unrealistic country world of shepherds and shepherdesses falling in love, free from the corrupt city life of the court. How do these works depict a more "innocent" world than the one shown in the fiction in this chapter?

John Keats

And what is Love? It is a doll dressed up

John Keats (1795–1821) was the son of a stable-keeper who married his master's daughter. He grew up in London and was orphaned at the age of fourteen, left financially unstable by his mother's death. Keats trained as a

surgeon but soon gave up medicine to devote himself to poetry. His first collection of verse, entitled *Poems,* was published in 1817 and received mixed and often condescending praise. He was branded the "cockney poet" for his working-class background. Keats continued to write and publish poetry, although his career was sadly cut short when he died of consumption at the age of twenty-six. The ephemeral nature of love and its relationship to art was of enduring fascination to him. In his poem "And what is Love?" he comically points out that we cannot all be Romeo and Juliet.

And what is love? It is a doll dressed up
For idleness to cosset, nurse, and dandle;[1]
A thing of soft misnomers, so divine
That silly youth doth think to make itself
Divine by loving, and so goes on
Yawning and doting a whole summer long,
Till Miss's comb is made a pearl tiara,
And common Wellingtons turn Romeo boots;
Till Cleopatra lives at number seven,
And Antony[2] resides in Brunswick Square.
Fools! if some passions high have warmed the world,
If queens and soldiers have played deep for hearts,
It is no reason why such agonies
Should be more common than the growth of weeds.
Fools! make me whole again that weighty pearl
The queen of Egypt melted, and I'll say
That ye may love in spite of beaver hats.

(1820)

Questions for Discussion and Writing

Close Reading

1. In what ways do people "cosset, nurse, and dandle" with love? (You might look up these terms in a dictionary that gives different definitions of words over time, like the *Oxford English Dictionary*.)
2. How does Keats juxtapose "high" and "low" culture (the heroic and the mundane) in this poem?

[1]*cosset, nurse, and dandle:* To pamper and play with like a child.

[2]*Cleopatra . . . and Antony:* An Egyptian queen and her Roman lover, made famous by writers from Shakespeare to Dryden.

3. Twice Keats refers to "Fools!" Who are these fools, and what is the speaker's relationship with these lovers?
4. What do you make of the last line? Why might the speaker deny the experience of love to those who wear "beaver hats"?

Critical and Creative Reading

5. Let's assume you agree with Keats that love is "a doll dressed up," that people imitate great love stories just as children imitate parenting with their dolls. What is the problem with living out such a pretense? Why does it seem to be a problem for the speaker?
6. Keats suggests that real passion is rare and not found in everyday life. Do you agree that the legendary passions of queens and soldiers are not part of most people's lives?

Connections to Other Readings

7. Is it possible to reconcile Shakespeare's claim that love is a fever (Sonnet 147) with Keats's claim that it is a doll dressed up?
8. How does the behavior of Margaret in Williams's *Cat on a Hot Tin Roof* comment on Keats's theme?
9. Compare how this poem and Shakespeare's sonnet "My Mistress' Eyes Are Nothing Like the Sun" comment on traditional expectations of love.

Elizabeth Barrett Browning

Sonnet 43 from *Sonnets from the Portuguese*

Elizabeth Barrett Browning (1806–1861) was born to a wealthy family and grew up in a country manor house. She had early ambitions to become a great poet, but an illness at fifteen that left her an invalid, combined with financial troubles that forced her family's move to London, left the young woman a recluse. She combated her illness and a number of personal losses by writing and publishing poetry. By the 1840s, her reputation as one of England's leading poets was secure. In 1846, she eloped with the then-obscure poet Robert Browning, and they moved to Italy, where her health improved and her writing career flourished. In 1856, Barrett Browning published her masterpiece, *Aurora Leigh,* a verse novel about a woman writer. Her series of poems, *Sonnets from the Portuguese,* were written for her husband: "Portuguese" was Robert Browning's nickname for Elizabeth.

How do I love thee? Let me count the ways.
I love thee to the depth and breadth and height
My soul can reach, when feeling out of sight

For the ends of Being and ideal Grace.
I love thee to the level of everyday's
Most quiet need, by sun and candlelight.
I love thee freely, as men strive for Right;
I love thee purely, as they turn from Praise.
I love thee with the passion put to use
In my old griefs, and with my childhood's faith.
I love thee with a love I seemed to lose
With my lost saints—I love thee with the breath,
Smiles, tears, of all my life!—and, if God choose,
I shall but love thee better after death.

(1850)

Questions for Discussion and Writing

Close Reading

1. Explain the connection between the speaker's earthly love and religious faith.
2. How does the speaker contrast greatness and the ordinary to emphasize her feelings?
3. The speaker promises to "count" the ways. How many are there? Does any one way stand out from the others?

Critical and Creative Reading

4. You are probably familiar with this poem, or at least with its first line. It is one of the most famous love poems ever written. Why do you think this is? What definition of love is Browning offering here, and what is its appeal?
5. Is the version of love presented here realistic or exaggerated? (If exaggerated, for what purpose?)
6. Pretend that you are the "thee" in this poem and write a sonnet back to the poet in which you try to convince her (or him) that you are every bit as much in love, if not more so.

Connections to Other Readings

7. Browning's "counting the ways" echoes Andrew Marvell's praise of his lover in "To His Coy Mistress." Compare the way these two writers praise their lovers and demonstrate the depth of their love.
8. How might the speaker of Shakespeare's "Dark Lady Sonnets" included in this chapter respond to Browning's poem? How is Shakespeare's speaker's conception of love as a fever in opposition to Browning's definition?
9. Whose proclamation of love is more convincing or sincere: the speaker of this poem or the speaker of Marlowe's "The Passionate Shepherd to His Love"?

Emily Dickinson

Wild Nights—Wild Nights! (249)

Arguably the most important and most original American lyric poet, Emily Dickinson (1830–1886) was the author of over 1,700 poems, most published posthumously (10 were published during her lifetime). Her unique style with its trademark dashes and linguistic slippages presents compact poems that are dense with meaning. Associated with New England austerity, in reality Dickinson was not afraid of subjects such as sex, and many of her poems reveal her distaste for "genteel" people who avoid these subjects. (See also Dickinson's poems "Much Madness is divinest Sense" in Chapter 12 [along with her photo], "Tell all the Truth, but tell it slant" in Chapter 14, and "Mine Enemy is growing old" in Chapter 15.)

Wild Nights—Wild Nights!
Were I with thee
Wild Nights should be
Our luxury!

Futile—the Winds—
To a Heart in port—
Done with the Compass—
Done with the Chart!

Rowing in Eden—
Ah, the Sea!
Might I but moor—Tonight—
In Thee!

(c. 1861)

Questions for Discussion and Writing

Close Reading

1. Record all the sailing imagery in the poem and discuss how it operates metaphorically.
2. Look up the word *luxury* in an etymological dictionary like the *Oxford English Dictionary*. Which meanings might be useful in interpreting this poem?
3. Is the "thee" in the first stanza the same as the "Thee" in the final stanza? Whom or what does it refer to?

Critical and Creative Reading

4. This poem is not explicitly about love or lust, the themes of this chapter. Which of the two does it more closely represent?

5. Discuss Dickinson's use of dashes and exclamation points. Could she have conveyed a similar sense if she had not used these punctuation marks this way?
6. This short poem contains a great deal of repetition; what is repeated, and for what purpose?

CONNECTIONS TO OTHER READINGS

7. Consider the use of metaphor in this poem and in Octavio Paz's "Two Bodies." Despite the different metaphors, do the poems reach for a common idea?
8. Discuss the use of alliteration (especially of the letter *w*) in this poem and in John Updike's story "Wife-Wooing." Why this sound? Do the pieces have anything else in common?
9. Discuss the concept of passion in this poem and in Thomas Carew's "A Rapture" and/or Christopher Marlowe's "The Passionate Shepherd to His Love." How do these speakers attempt to convey their passion to their lovers through language?

Edna St. Vincent Millay

What Lips My Lips Have Kissed

Edna St. Vincent Millay (1892–1950) was born in Rockland, Maine, and attended Vassar College before moving to Greenwich Village in New York City, one of the centers of the "Jazz Age" of the 1920s. Millay fit in well with the Bohemian crowd because her poetry was sensuous and honest. Her later poetry was more political in nature, opposing European fascism. The following poem, published in 1923, is representative of her early career.

What lips my lips have kissed, and where, and why,
I have forgotten, and what arms have lain
Under my head till morning; but the rain
Is full of ghosts tonight, that tap and sigh
Upon the glass and listen for reply,
And in my heart there stirs a quiet pain
For unremembered lads that not again
Will turn to me at midnight with a cry.
Thus in the winter stands the lonely tree,
Nor knows what birds have vanished one by one,
Yet knows its boughs more silent than before:
I cannot say what loves have come and gone,
I only know that summer sang in me
A little while, that in me sings no more.

(1923)

Questions for Discussion and Writing

Close Reading

1. Plot the poem's rhyme scheme and discuss its effect on the theme.
2. How does the "lonely tree" in winter act as a metaphor for the speaker's state of mind?
3. Why has the speaker forgotten the "unremembered lads" she has loved, and why does summer no longer "sing" in her?

Critical and Creative Reading

4. The speaker claims to have forgotten not only *what* lips she has kissed but *why* she kissed them. Is there any point in analyzing why one acts on one's romantic or sexual desires?
5. Is the sonnet an appropriate form for expressing the deep pain of loss and loneliness that this speaker feels? Why or why not? (See the discussion of the sonnet in Chapter 5.)
6. Does this poem simply endorse the idea that lust may be exciting but only long-term love relationships are fulfilling, or are its themes and sentiments more complex? Use evidence from the poem in your analysis.

Connections to Other Readings

7. Compare this speaker to the character Gretta Conroy in James Joyce's story "The Dead." Is there evidence that Gretta feels this same kind of loss?
8. Describe the feeling produced by romantic affairs in this poem and in Susan Minot's story "Lust." Do the works share a similar tone?
9. The central portion of Andrew Marvell's "To His Coy Mistress" (beginning with the line "But at my back I always hear / Time's winged chariot hurrying near . . .") connects seduction with the passage of time and with death. Compare Marvell's treatment of this theme to Millay's.

Octavio Paz

Two Bodies

Mexican author Octavio Paz (b. 1914) is a poet and essayist who won the Nobel Prize for literature in 1990. Often concerned with the plight of the indigenous people of Latin America, Paz has lived in Asia, Spain, and the United States and has held diplomatic positions in his native Mexico. Most of his poetry has been translated into English and is available in *The Collected Poems 1957–1987*.

Two bodies face to face
are at times two waves
and night is an ocean.

Two bodies face to face
are at times two stones
and night a desert.

Two bodies face to face
are at times two roots
laced into night.

Two bodies face to face
are at times two knives
and night strikes sparks.

Two bodies face to face
are two stars falling
in an empty sky.

(1984)

Questions for Discussion and Writing

Close Reading

1. The second line of each stanza begins with the phrase "are at times," except in the final stanza. What are the purpose and the effect of this change in the final stanza?
2. Which of the five metaphors (represented by the five stanzas) is unlike the others?
3. How does "night" figure in each of the metaphors?

Critical and Creative Reading

4. Are we meant to read the "two bodies" as the *same* two bodies in each stanza? Are you given any clues on how to respond to that question? What difference does it make whether they are the same two bodies or ten different bodies?
5. Do these two bodies ever become one in any of the metaphors? Is this a poem about separation or union?
6. What are the different connotations of "bodies" and "face to face"? What effect does Paz achieve by repeatedly juxtaposing this word and this phrase?

Connections to Other Readings

7. Consider the use of metaphor in this poem and in Emily Dickinson's "Wild Nights—Wild Nights!"
8. How does the theme of separation work in this poem and in James Joyce's "The Dead"?

9. Which of Paz's metaphors is the most appropriate to describe the narrator of Susan Minot's "Lust"?

Sharon Olds

Sex without Love

Sharon Olds (b. 1942) earned a Ph.D. in English from Columbia University prior to publishing eight collections of poetry. She vowed on the steps of the Columbia library that she would become a poet even if it meant sacrificing everything she learned during her graduate education. Her poetry has won many awards, including the National Book Critics' Award, and is represented in dozens of literature anthologies, testimony that she has developed a valuable poetic voice. Before reading this poem, consider whether you think its title is a paradox or a far too common occurrence.

How do they do it, the ones who make love
without love? Beautiful as dancers,
gliding over each other like ice-skaters
over the ice, fingers hooked
inside each other's bodies, faces
red as steak, wine, wet as the
children at birth whose mothers are going to
give them away. How do they come to the
come to the come to the God come to the
still waters, and not love
the one who came there with them, light
rising slowly as steam off their joined
skin? These are the true religious,
the purists, the pros, the ones who will not
accept a false Messiah, love the
priest instead of the God. They do not
mistake the lover for their own pleasure,
they are like great runners: they know they are alone
with the road surface, the cold, the wind,
the fit of their shoes, their over-all cardiovascular health—just factors, like the partner
in the bed, and not the truth, which is the
single body alone in the universe
against its own best time.

(1984)

Questions for Discussion and Writing

Close Reading

1. What is the difference between the word "sex" in the title and the phrase "make love" in the first line? Why isn't the poet consistent about her use of this word? Why does she refrain from using the word "sex" in her poem?
2. What are the meaning and the effect of the repeated phrase in lines 8 and 9?
3. Summarize and interpret the metaphor of lovers as runners.

Critical and Creative Reading

4. Is there any real wonder or awe in the question the speaker asks in the first two lines? Consider the whole poem in your response.
5. What is the connection between love and truth, in general and in this poem?
6. Can "making love" (a euphemism for sex) lead to love? Does the speaker of this poem consider that possibility?

Connections to Other Readings

7. What other poem in this chapter contains a metaphor that is similar to a lover as a runner?
8. Interpret and summarize the theme of this poem and use that idea to interpret Susan Minot's story "Lust."
9. Discuss the relationship between selfishness and love in this poem and in Christopher Marlowe's "The Passionate Shepherd to His Love," Octavio Paz's "Two Bodies," or John Updike's "Wife-Wooing."
10. Discuss the final scene of Williams's play *Cat on a Hot Tin Roof* in conjunction with the themes of Olds's poem.

Rita Dove

Courtship

Rita Dove (b. 1952) was poet laureate of the United States from 1993 to 1995. Dove was born and raised in Ohio and earned a master's of fine arts degree from the renowned University of Iowa Writer's Workshop in 1977. Her collection *Thomas and Beulah,* from which the following poem is taken, won the Pulitzer Prize in 1987. It is a sequence about her grandparents' courtship, and according to the book's epigraph these poems "tell two sides of a story." Consider how these two sides structure the poem.

1

Fine evening may I have
the pleasure . . .
up and down the block
waiting—for what? A
magnolia breeze, someone
to trot out the stars?

But she won't set a foot
in his turtledove Nash,
it wasn't proper.
Her pleated skirt fans
softly, a circlet of arrows.

King of the Crawfish
in his yellow scarf,
mandolin belly pressed tight
to his hounds-tooth vest—
his wrist flicks for the pleats
all in a row, sighing . . .

2

. . . so he wraps the yellow silk
still warm from his throat
around her shoulders. (He made
good money; he could buy another.)
A gnat flies
in his eye and she thinks
he's crying.

Then the parlor festooned
like a ship and Thomas
twirling his hat in his hands
wondering how did I get here.
China pugs guarding a fringed settee
where a father, half-Cherokee,
smokes and frowns.
I'll give her a good life—
what was he doing,
selling all for a song?
His heart fluttering shut
then slowly opening.

(1987)

Questions for Discussion and Writing

Close Reading

1. How and where does the perspective shift between the two characters (known throughout the collection as Thomas and Beulah)?
2. How do the values of the outside world influence the courtship of these two individuals?
3. How does clothing imagery function in the poem?

Critical and Creative Reading

4. Does this poem describe how love might develop out of physical attraction? If so, is it an unusual courtship or a typical one?
5. Is the male character's doubt about what he's doing in the second section of the poem a healthy component of any love relationship or an indication that their love is doomed?
6. Why are notions of what is "proper" so often rituals of courtship? In other words, why does society care how any two individual lovers behave?

Connections to Other Readings

7. Discuss the behavior of "the heart" in this poem and in Emily Dickinson's "Wild Nights!" Are these two hearts potentially the same? Are any two hearts?
8. Do the two characters in this poem represent any of the descriptions of "two bodies" in Octavio Paz's poem? Which do they represent most closely?
9. Discuss the rituals of courtship in this poem and in John Updike's story "Wife-Wooing."

Drama

Tennessee Williams

Cat on a Hot Tin Roof

Tennessee Williams (1911–1983) is considered one of the most important and enduring American playwrights of the twentieth century. As with the other great playwrights of his time–Eugene O'Neill, Arthur Miller, and Edward Albee–Williams's drama is full of passionate characters whose identity is compromised by a society that resists individuality. Williams's famous plays include *The Glass Menagerie* and *A Streetcar Named Desire,* but he was a prolific playwright who wrote more than two dozen full-length plays as well as many one-act plays. *Cat on a Hot Tin Roof* was first produced in 1955 and won the Pulitzer Prize for drama that year. As in Williams's other works,

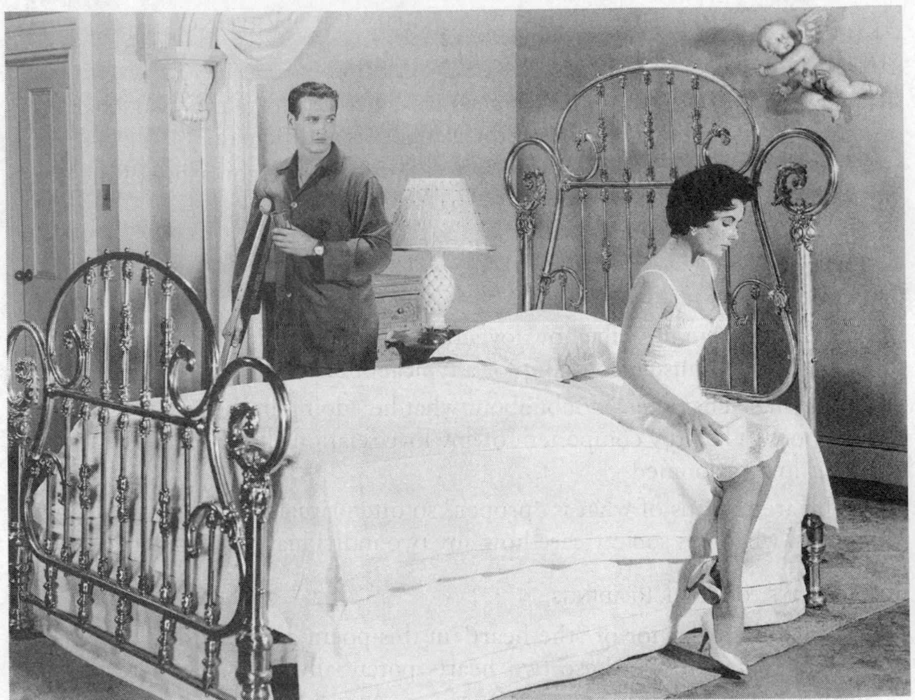

Paul Newman and Elizabeth Taylor in the film version of Tennessee Williams's *Cat on a Hot Tin Roof* (1958)

overbearing characters like Big Daddy and Margaret and fragile, vulnerable characters like Brick are at odds with one another, yet also dependent on one another. This ambiguous relationship fuels the drama. The backdrop is the American South, where Williams was born. This setting is important in Williams's work because it represents a tension between nostalgia for a prosperous, though tainted, past and progress into an unknown future.

And you, my father, there on the sad height,
Curse, bless, me now with your fierce tears, I pray.
Do not go gentle into that good night.
Rage, rage against the dying of the light!

—DYLAN THOMAS

CHARACTERS OF THE PLAY

Margaret
Brick
Mae, sometimes called Sister Woman
Big Mama

Dixie, a little girl
Big Daddy
Reverend Tooker
Gooper, sometimes called Brother Man
Doctor Baugh, pronounced "Baw"
Lacey, a Negro servant
Sookey, another
Children

Cat on a Hot Tin Roof *was originally presented at the Morosco Theatre in New York on March 24, 1955. On July 10, 1974, it was restaged by the American Shakespeare Theatre in Stratford, Connecticut, with the third act completely rewritten, along with other substantial revisions. The play reopened in New York on September 24 at the ANTA Theatre. Both 1974 productions were directed by Michael Kahn; the stage settings were designed by John Conklin, the lighting by Marc B. Weiss, and the costumes by Jane Greenwood. The cast was as follows:*

Margaret	*Elizabeth Ashley*
Brick	*Keir Dullea*
Dixie	*Deborah Grove*
Mae	*Joan Pape*
Gooper	*Charles Siebert*
Big Mama	*Kate Reid*
Sookey	*Saraellen*
Big Daddy	*Fred Gwynne*
Reverend Tooker	*Wyman Pendleton*
Doctor Baugh	*William Larsen*
*Lacey**	*Thomas Anderson*
*Children**	*Jeb Brown, Chris Browning, Betsy Spivak, Susannah Brown*

NOTES FOR THE DESIGNER

The set is the bed-sitting-room of a plantation home in the Mississippi Delta. It is along an upstairs gallery which probably runs around the entire house; it has two pairs of very wide doors opening onto the gallery, showing white balustrades against a fair summer sky that fades into dusk and night during the course of the play, which occupies precisely the time of its performance, excepting, of course, the fifteen minutes of intermission.

Perhaps the style of the room is not what you would expect in the home of the Delta's biggest cotton-planter. It is Victorian with a touch of the Far East. It hasn't changed much since it was occupied by the original owners of the place, Jack Straw and Peter Ochello, a pair of old bachelors who shared this room all their lives together. In other words, the room must evoke some ghosts; it is gently and poetically haunted by a relationship that must have involved a tenderness which

*In the New York production, the part of Lacey was not included, and the number of children was reduced to three, played by Jeb Brown, Sukie Brown, and Amy Borress.

was uncommon. This may be irrelevant or unnecessary, but I once saw a reproduction of a faded photograph of the verandah of Robert Louis Stevenson's home on that Samoan Island where he spent his last years, and there was a quality of tender light on weathered wood, such as porch furniture made of bamboo and wicker, exposed to tropical suns and tropical rains, which came to mind when I thought about the set for this play, bringing also to mind the grace and comfort of light, the reassurance it gives, on a late and fair afternoon in summer, the way that no matter what, even dread of death, is gently touched and soothed by it. For the set is the background for a play that deals with human extremities of emotion, and it needs that softness behind it.

The bathroom door, showing only pale-blue tile and silver towel racks, is in one side wall; the hall door in the opposite wall. Two articles of furniture need mention: a big double bed which staging should make a functional part of the set as often as suitable, the surface of which should be slightly raked to make figures on it seen more easily; and against the wall space between the two huge double doors upstage: a monumental monstrosity peculiar to our times, a huge *console combination of radio-phonograph (hi-fi with three speakers) TV set* and *liquor cabinet, bearing and containing many glasses and bottles, all in one piece, which is a composition of muted silver tones, and the opalescent tones of reflecting glass, a chromatic link, this thing, between the sepia (tawny gold) tones of the interior and the cool (white and blue) tones of the gallery and sky. This piece of furniture (?!), this monument, is a very complete and compact little shrine to virtually all the comforts and illusions behind which we hide from such things as the characters in the play are faced with. . . .*

The set should be far less realistic than I have so far implied in this description of it. I think the walls below the ceiling should dissolve mysteriously into air; the set should be roofed by the sky; stars and moon suggested by traces of milky pallor, as if they were observed through a telescope lens out of focus.

Anything else I can think of? Oh, yes, fanlights (transoms shaped like an open glass fan) above all the doors in the set, with panes of blue and amber, and above all, the designer should take as many pains to give the actors room to move about freely (to show their restlessness, their passion for breaking out) as if it were a set for a ballet.

An evening in summer. The action is continuous, with two intermissions.

ACT ONE

At the rise of the curtain someone is taking a shower in the bathroom, the door of which is half open. A pretty young woman, with anxious lines in her face, enters the bedroom and crosses to the bathroom door.

Margaret [*shouting above roar of water*]: One of those no-neck monsters hit me with a hot buttered biscuit so I have t' change!

[*Margaret's voice is both rapid and drawling. In her long speeches she has the vocal tricks of a priest delivering a liturgical chant, the lines are almost sung, always continuing a little beyond her breath so she has to gasp for another. Sometimes she intersperses the lines with a little wordless singing, such as "Da-da-daaaa!"*

Water turns off and Brick calls out to her, but is still unseen. A tone of politely feigned interest, masking indifference, or worse, is characteristic of his speech with Margaret.]

Brick: Wha'd you say, Maggie? Water was on s' loud I couldn't hearya. . . .

Margaret: Well, I!—just remarked that!—one of th' no-neck monsters messed up m' lovely lace dress so I got t'—cha-a-ange. . . .

[She opens and kicks shut drawers of the dresser.]

Brick: Why d'ya call Gooper's kiddies no-neck monsters?

Margaret: Because they've got no necks! Isn't that a good enough reason?

Brick: Don't they have any necks?

Margaret: None visible. Their fat little heads are set on their fat little bodies without a bit of connection.

Brick: That's too bad.

Margaret: Yes, it's too bad because you can't wring their necks if they've got no necks to wring! Isn't that right, honey?

Paul Newman and Elizabeth Taylor in the film version of Tennessee Williams's *Cat on a Hot Tin Roof* (1958).

[She steps out of her dress, stands in a slip of ivory satin and lace.]

Yep, they're no-neck monsters, all no-neck people are monsters . . .

[Children shriek downstairs.]

Hear them? Hear them screaming? I don't know where their voice boxes are located since they don't have necks. I tell you I got so nervous at that table tonight I thought I would throw back my head and utter a scream you could hear across the Arkansas border an' parts of Louisiana an' Tennessee. I said to your charming sister-in-law, Mae, honey, couldn't you feed those precious little things at a separate table with an oilcloth cover? They make such a mess an' the lace cloth looks *so* pretty! She made enormous eyes at me and said, "Ohhh, noooooo! On Big Daddy's birthday? Why, he would never forgive me!" Well, I want you to know, Big Daddy hadn't been at the table two minutes with those five no-neck monsters slobbering and drooling over their food before he threw down his fork an' shouted, "Fo' God's sake, Gooper, why don't you put them pigs at a trough in th' kitchen?"—Well, I swear, I simply could have di-ieed!

Think of it, Brick, they've got five of them and number six is coming. They've brought the whole bunch down here like animals to display at a county fair. Why, they have those children doin' tricks all the time! "Junior, show Big Daddy how you do this, show Big Daddy how you do that, say your little piece fo' Big Daddy, Sister. Show your dimples, Sugar. Brother, show Big Daddy how you stand on your head!"—It goes on all the time, along with constant little remarks and innuendos about the fact that you and I have not produced any children, are totally childless and therefore totally useless!—Of course it's comical but it's also disgusting since it's so obvious what they're up to!

Brick [*without interest*]: What are they up to, Maggie?

Margaret: Why, you know what they're up to!

Brick [*appearing*]: No, I don't know what they're up to.

[He stands there in the bathroom doorway drying his hair with a towel and hanging onto the towel rack because one ankle is broken, plastered and bound. He is still slim and firm as a boy. His liquor hasn't started tearing him down outside. He has the additional charm of that cool air of detachment that people have who have given up the struggle. But now and then, when disturbed, something flashes behind it, like lightning in a fair sky, which shows that at some deeper level he is far from peaceful. Perhaps in a stronger light he would show some signs of deliquescence, but the fading, still warm, light from the gallery treats him gently.]

Margaret: I'll tell you what they're up to, boy of mine!—They're up to cutting you out of your father's estate, and—

[She freezes momentarily before her next remark. Her voice drops as if it were somehow a personally embarrassing admission.]

—Now we know that Big Daddy's dyin' of—*cancer*. . . .

[There are voices on the lawn below: long-drawn calls across distance. Margaret raises her lovely bare arms and powders her armpits with a light sigh.

[She adjusts the angle of a magnifying mirror to straighten an eyelash, then rises fretfully saying:]

There's so much light in the room it—

Brick [*softly but sharply*]: Do we?

Margaret: Do we what?

Brick: Know Big Daddy's dyin' of cancer?

Margaret: Got the report today.

Brick: Oh . . .

Margaret [*letting down bamboo blinds which cast long, gold-fretted shadows over the room*]: Yep, got th' report just now . . . it didn't surprise me, Baby. . . .

[Her voice has range, and music; sometimes it drops low as a boy's and you have a sudden image of her playing boy's games as a child.]

I recognized the symptoms soon's we got here last spring and I'm willin' to bet you that Brother Man and his wife were pretty sure of it, too. That more than likely explains why their usual summer migration to the coolness of the Great Smokies was passed up this summer in favor of—hustlin' down here ev'ry whipstitch with their whole screamin' tribe! And why so many allusions have been made to Rainbow Hill lately. You know what Rainbow Hill is? Place that's famous for treatin' alcoholics and dope fiends in the movies!

Brick: I'm not in the movies.

Margaret: No, and you don't take dope. Otherwise you're a perfect candidate for Rainbow Hill, Baby, and that's where they aim to ship you—over my dead body! Yep, over my dead body they'll ship you there, but nothing would please them better. Then Brother Man could get a-hold of the purse strings and dole out remittances to us, maybe get power of attorney and sign checks for us and cut off our credit wherever, whenever he wanted! Son-of-a-bitch!—How'd you like that, Baby?—Well, you've been doin' just about ev'rything in your power to bring it about, you've just been doin' ev'rything you can think of to aid and abet them in this scheme of theirs! Quittin' work, devoting yourself to the occupation of drinkin'!—Breakin' your ankle last night on the high school athletic field: doin' what? Jumpin' hurdles? At two or three in the morning? Just fantastic! Got in the paper. *Clarksdale Register* carried a nice little item about it, human interest story about a well-known former athlete stagin' a one-man track meet on the Glorious Hill High School athletic field last night, but was slightly out of condition and didn't clear the first hurdle! Brother Man Gooper claims he exercised his influence t' keep it from goin' out over AP or UP or every goddam "P."

But, Brick? You still have one big advantage!

[During the above swift flood of words, Brick has reclined with contrapuntal leisure on the snowy surface of the bed and has rolled over carefully on his side or belly.]

Brick [*wryly*]: Did you *say* something, Maggie?

Margaret: Big Daddy dotes on you, honey. And he can't stand Brother Man and Brother Man's wife, that monster of fertility, Mae. Know how I know? By little expressions that flicker over his face when that woman is holding fo'th on one of her choice topics such as—how she refused twilight sleep!—when the twins were delivered! Because she feels motherhood's an experience that a woman ought to experience fully!—in order to fully appreciate the wonder and beauty of it! HAH!—and how she made Brother Man come in an' stand beside her in the delivery room so he would not miss out on the "wonder and beauty" of it either!—producin' those no-neck monsters. . . .

[A speech of this kind would be antipathetic from almost anybody but Margaret; she makes it oddly funny, because her eyes constantly twinkle and her voice shakes with laughter which is basically indulgent.]

—Big Daddy shares my attitude toward those two! As for me, well—I give him a laugh now and then and he tolerates me. In fact!—I sometimes suspect that Big Daddy harbors a little unconscious "lech" fo' me. . . .

Brick: What makes you think that Big Daddy has a lech for you, Maggie?

Margaret: Way he always drops his eyes down my body when I'm talkin' to him, drops his eyes to my boobs an' licks his old chops! Ha ha!

Brick: That kind of talk is disgusting.

Margaret: Did anyone ever tell you that you're an ass-aching Puritan, Brick?

I think it's mighty fine that that ole fellow, on the doorstep of death, still takes in my shape with what I think is deserved appreciation!

And you wanta know something else? Big Daddy didn't know how many little Maes and Goopers had been produced! "How many kids have you got?" he asked at the table, just like Brother Man and his wife were new acquaintances to him! Big Mama said he was jokin', but that ole boy wasn't jokin', Lord, no!

And when they infawmed him that they had five already and were turning out number six!—the news seemed to come as a sort of unpleasant surprise. . . .

[Children yell below.]

Scream, monsters!

[Turns to Brick with a sudden, gay, charming smile which fades as she notices that he is not looking at her but into fading gold space with a troubled expression. It is constant rejection that makes her humor "bitchy."]

Yes, you should of been at that supper-table, Baby.

[Whenever she calls him "baby" the word is a soft caress.]

Y'know, Big Daddy, bless his ole sweet soul, he's the dearest ole thing in the world, but he does hunch over his food as if he preferred not to notice anything else. Well, Mae an' Gooper were side by side at the table, direckly across from Big Daddy, watchin' his face like hawks while they jawed an' jabbered about the cuteness an' brillance of th' no-neck monsters!

[She giggles with a hand fluttering at her throat and her breast and her long throat arched.

She comes downstage and recreates the scene with voice and gesture.]

And the no-neck monsters were ranged around the table, some in high chairs and some on th' *Books of Knowledge*, all in fancy little paper caps in honor of Big Daddy's birthday, and all through dinner, well, I want you to know that Brother Man an' his partner never once, for one moment, stopped exchanging pokes an' pinches an' kicks an' signs an' signals!—Why, they were like a couple of cardsharps fleecing a sucker.—Even Big Mama, bless her ole sweet soul, she isn't th' quickest an' brightest thing in the world, she finally noticed, at last, an' said to Gooper, "Gooper, what are you an' Mae makin' all these signs at each other about?"—I swear t' goodness, I nearly choked on my chicken!

[Margaret, back at the dressing table, still doesn't see Brick. He is watching her with a look that is not quite definable —Amused? shocked? contemptuous?—part of those and part of something else.]

Y'know—your brother Gooper still cherishes the illusion he took a giant step up on the social ladder when he married Miss Mae Flynn of the Memphis Flynns.

But I have a piece of Spanish news for Gooper. The Flynns never had a thing in this world but money and they lost that, they were nothing at all but fairly successful climbers. Of course, Mae Flynn came out in Memphis eight years before I made my debut in Nashville, but I had friends at Ward-Belmont who came from Memphis and they used to come to see me and I used to go to see them for Christmas and spring vacations, and so I know who rates an' who doesn't rate in Memphis society. Why, y'know ole Papa Flynn, he barely escaped doing time in the Federal pen for shady manipulations on th' stock market when his chain stores crashed, and as for Mae having been a cotton carnival queen, as they remind us so often, lest we forget, well, that's one honor that I don't envy her for!—Sit on a brass throne on a tacky float an' ride down Main Street, smilin', bowin', and blowin' kisses to all the trash on the street—

[She picks out a pair of jeweled sandals and rushes to the dressing table.]

Why, year before last, when Susan McPheeters was singled out fo' that honor, y' know what happened to her? Y'know what happened to poor little Susie McPheeters?

Brick [*absently*]*:* No. What happened to little Susie McPheeters?

Margaret: Somebody spit tobacco juice in her face.

Brick [*dreamily*]: Somebody spit tobacco juice in her face?

Margaret: That's right, some old drunk leaned out of a window in the Hotel Gayoso and yelled, "Hey, Queen, hey, hey, there, Queenie!" Poor Susie looked up and flashed him a radiant smile and he shot out a squirt of tobacco juice right in poor Susie's face.

Brick: Well, what d'you know about that.
Margaret [gaily]: What do I know about it? I was there, I saw it!
Brick [absently]: Must have been kind of funny.
Margaret: Susie didn't think so. Had hysterics. Screamed like a banshee. They had to stop th' parade an' remove her from her throne an' go on with—

[She catches sight of him in the mirror, gasps slightly, wheels about to face him. Count ten.]

—Why are you looking at me like that?

Brick [whistling softly, now]: Like what, Maggie?
Margaret [intensely, fearfully]: The way y' were lookin' at me just now, befo' I caught your eye in the mirror and you started t' whistle! I don't know how t' describe it but it froze my blood!—I've caught you lookin' at me like that so often lately. What are you thinkin' of when you look at me like that?
Brick: I wasn't conscious of lookin' at you, Maggie.
Margaret: Well, I was conscious of it! What were you thinkin'?
Brick: I don't remember thinking of anything, Maggie.
Margaret: Don't you think I know that—? Don't you—?—Think I know that—?
Brick [coolly]: Know *what*, Maggie?
Margaret [struggling for expression]: That I've gone through this—*hideous!*—*transformation*, become—*hard! Frantic!*

[Then she adds, almost tenderly:]

—cruel!!

That's what you've been observing in me lately. How could y' help but observe it? That's all right. I'm not—thin-skinned any more, can't afford t' be thin-skinned any more.

[She is now recovering her power.]

—But Brick? Brick?

Brick: Did you say something?
Margaret: I was *goin'* t' say something: that I get—lonely. Very!
Brick: Ev'rybody gets that . . .
Margaret: Living with someone you love can be lonelier—than living entirely *alone!*—if the one that y' love doesn't love you . . . .

[There is a pause. Brick hobbles downstage and asks, without looking at her:]

Brick: Would you like to live alone, Maggie?

[Another pause: then—after she has caught a quick, hurt breath:]

Margaret: No!—God!—I wouldn't!

[Another gasping breath. She forcibly controls what must have been an impulse to cry out. We see her deliberately, very forcibly, going all the way back to the world in which you can talk about ordinary matters.]

Did you have a nice shower?

Brick: Uh-huh.
Margaret: Was the water cool?
Brick: No.
Margaret: But it made y' feel fresh, huh?
Brick: Fresher. . . .
Margaret: I know something would make y' feel *much* fresher!
Brick: What?
Margaret: An alcohol rub. Or cologne, a rub with cologne!
Brick: That's good after a workout but I haven't been workin' out, Maggie.
Margaret: You've kept in good shape, though.
Brick [*indifferently*]: You think so, Maggie?
Margaret: I always thought drinkin' men lost their looks, but I was plainly mistaken.
Brick [*wryly*]: Why, thanks, Maggie.
Margaret: You're the only drinkin' man I know that it never seems t' put fat on.
Brick: I'm gettin' softer, Maggie.
Margaret: Well, sooner or later it's bound to soften you up. It was just beginning to soften up Skipper when—

[She stops short.]

I'm sorry. I never could keep my fingers off a sore—I wish you *would* lose your looks. If you did it would make the martyrdom of Saint Maggie a little more bearable. But no such goddam luck. I actually believe you've gotten better looking since you've gone on the bottle. Yeah, a person who didn't know you would think you'd never had a tense nerve in your body or a strained muscle.

[There are sounds of croquet on the lawn below: the click of mallets, light voices, near and distant.]

Of course, you always had that detached quality as if you were playing a game without much concern over whether you won or lost, and now that you've lost the game, not lost but just quit playing, you have that rare sort of charm that usually only happens in very old or hopelessly sick people, the charm of the defeated.—You look so cool, so cool, so enviably cool.

Reverend Tooker [*off stage right*]: Now looka here, boy, lemme show you how to get outa that!
Margaret: They're playing croquet. The moon has appeared and it's white, just beginning to turn a little bit yellow. . . .

You were a wonderful lover. . . .

Such a wonderful person to go to bed with, and I think mostly because you were really indifferent to it. Isn't that right? Never had any anxiety about it, did it naturally, easily, slowly, with absolute confidence and perfect calm, more like opening a door for a lady or seating her at a table than giving expression to any longing for her. Your indifference made you wonderful at lovemaking—*strange?*—but true. . . .

Reverend Tooker: Oh! That's a beauty.
Doctor Baugh: Yeah. I got you boxed.
Margaret: You know, if I thought you would never, never, *never* make love to me again—I would go downstairs to the kitchen and pick out the longest and sharpest knife I could find and stick it straight into my heart, I swear that I would!
Reverend Tooker: Watch out, you're gonna miss it.
Doctor Baugh: You just don't know me, boy!
Margaret: But one thing I don't have is the charm of the defeated, my hat is still in the ring, and I am determined to win!

[There is the sound of croquet mallets hitting croquet balls.]

Reverend Tooker: Mmm—You're too slippery for me.
Margaret: —What is the victory of a cat on a hot tin roof?—I wish I knew. . . .
Just staying on it, I guess, as long as she can. . . .
Doctor Baugh: Jus' like an eel, boy, jus' like an eel!

[More croquet sounds.]

Margaret: Later tonight I'm going to tell you I love you an' maybe by that time you'll be drunk enough to believe me. Yes, they're playing croquet. . . .

Big Daddy is dying of cancer. . . .

What were you thinking of when I caught you looking at me like that? Were you thinking of Skipper?

[Brick takes up his crutch, rises.]

Oh, excuse me, forgive me, but laws of silence don't work! No, laws of silence don't work. . . .

[Brick crosses to the bar, takes a quick drink, and rubs his head with a towel.]

Laws of silence don't work. . . .

When something is festering in your memory or your imagination, laws of silence don't work, it's just like shutting a door and locking it on a house on fire in hope of forgetting that the house is burning. But not facing a fire doesn't put it out. Silence about a thing just magnifies it. It grows and festers in silence, becomes malignant. . . .

[He drops his crutch.]

Brick: Give me my crutch.

[He has stopped rubbing his hair dry but still stands hanging onto the towel rack in a white towel-cloth robe.]

Margaret: Lean on me.
Brick: No, just give me my crutch.
Margaret: Lean on my shoulder.
Brick: *I don't want to lean on your shoulder, I want my crutch!*

[This is spoken like sudden lightning.]

Are you going to give me my crutch or do I have to get down on my knees on the floor and—

Margaret: Here, here, take it, take it!

[She has thrust the crutch at him.]

Brick [*hobbling out*]: Thank . . .

Margaret: We mustn't scream at each other, the walls in this house have ears. . . .

[He hobbles directly to liquor cabinet to get a new drink.]

—but that's the first time I've heard you raise your voice in a long time, Brick. A crack in the wall?—Of composure?

—I think that's a good sign. . . .

A sign of nerves in a player on the defensive!

[Brick turns and smiles at her coolly over his fresh drink.]

Brick: It just hasn't happened yet, Maggie.

Margaret: What?

Brick: The click I get in my head when I've had enough of this stuff to make me peaceful. . . .

Will you do me a favor?

Margaret: Maybe I will. What favor?

Brick: Just, just keep your voice down!

Margaret [*in a hoarse whisper*]: I'll do you that favor, I'll speak in a whisper, if not shut up completely, if *you* will do *me* a favor and make that drink your last one till after the party.

Brick: What party?

Margaret: Big Daddy's birthday party.

Brick: Is this Big Daddy's birthday?

Margaret: You know this is Big Daddy's birthday!

Brick: No, I don't, I forgot it.

Margaret: Well, I remembered it for you. . . .

[They are both speaking as breathlessly as a pair of kids after a fight, drawing deep exhausted breaths and looking at each other with faraway eyes, shaking and panting together as if they had broken apart from a violent struggle.]

Brick: Good for you, Maggie.

Margaret: You just have to scribble a few lines on this card.

Brick: You scribble something, Maggie.

Margaret: It's got to be your handwriting; it's your present, I've given him my present; it's got to be your handwriting!

[The tension between them is building again, the voices becoming shrill once more]

Brick: I didn't get him a present.

Margaret: I got one for you.

Brick: All right. You write the card, then.

Margaret: And have him know you didn't remember his birthday?

Brick: I didn't remember his birthday.
Margaret: You don't have to prove you didn't!
Brick: I don't want to fool him about it.
Margaret: Just write "Love, Brick!" for God's—
Brick: No.
Margaret: You've *got* to!
Brick: I don't have to do anything I don't want to do. You keep forgetting the conditions on which I agreed to stay on living with you.
Margaret [*out before she knows it*]: I'm not living with you. We occupy the same cage.
Brick: You've got to remember the conditions agreed on.
Sonny [*off stage*]: Mommy, give it to me. I had it first.
Mae: Hush.
Margaret: They're impossible conditions!
Brick: Then why don't you—?
Sonny: I want it, I want it!
Mae: Get away!
Margaret: Hush! Who is out there? Is somebody at the door?

[There are footsteps in hall.]

Mae [*outside*]: May I enter a moment?
Margaret: Oh, *you!* Sure. Come in, Mae.

[Mae enters bearing aloft the bow of a young lady's archery set.]

Mae: Brick, is this thing yours?
Margaret: Why, Sister Woman—that's my Diana Trophy. Won it at the intercollegiate archery contest on the Ole Miss campus.
Mae: It's a mighty dangerous thing to leave exposed round a house full of nawmal rid-blooded children attracted t'weapons.
Margaret: "Nawmal rid-blooded children attracted t'weapons" ought t'be taught to keep their hands off things that don't belong to them.
Mae: Maggie, honey, if you had children of your own you'd know how funny that is. Will you please lock this up and put the key out of reach?
Margaret: Sister Woman, nobody is plotting the destruction of your kiddies.—Brick and I still have our special archers' license. We're goin' deer-huntin' on Moon Lake as soon as the season starts. I love to run with dogs through chilly woods, run, run leap over obstructions—

[She goes into the closet carrying the bow.]

Mae: How's the injured ankle, Brick?
Brick: Doesn't hurt. Just itches.
Mae: Oh, my! Brick—Brick, you should've been downstairs after supper! Kiddies put on a show. Polly played the piano, Buster an' Sonny drums, an' then they turned out the lights an' Dixie an' Trixie puhfawmed a toe dance in fairy costume with *spahkluhs!* Big Daddy just beamed! He just beamed!

Margaret [*from the closet with a sharp laugh*]: Oh, I bet. It breaks my heart that we missed it!

[She reenters.]

But Mae? Why did y'give dawgs' names to all your kiddies?

Mae: Dogs' names?

Margaret [*sweetly*]: Dixie, Trixie, Buster, Sonny, Polly!—Sounds like four dogs and a parrot . . .

Mae: Maggie?

[Margaret turns with a smile.]

Why are you so catty?

Margaret: Cause I'm a cat! But why can't *you* take a joke, Sister Woman?

Mae: Nothin' pleases me more than a joke that's funny. You know the real names of our kiddies. Buster's real name is Robert. Sonny's real name is Saunders. Trixie's real name is Marlene and Dixie's—

[Gooper downstairs calls for her. "Hey, Mae! Sister Woman, intermission is over!" —She rushes to door, saying:]

Intermission is over! See ya later!

Margaret: I wonder what Dixie's real name is?

Brick: Maggie, being catty doesn't help things any . . .

Margaret: I know! *WHY!*—Am I so catty?—Cause I'm consumed with envy an' eaten up with longing?—Brick, I'm going to lay out your beautiful Shantung silk suit from Rome and one of your monogrammed silk shirts. I'll put your cuff links in it, those lovely star sapphires I get you to wear so rarely. . . .

Brick: I can't get trousers on over this plaster cast.

Margaret: Yes, you can, I'll help you.

Brick: I'm not going to get dressed, Maggie.

Margaret: Will you just put on a pair of white silk pajamas?

Brick: Yes, I'll do that, Maggie.

Margaret: Thank you, thank you so *much!*

Brick: Don't mention it.

Margaret: Oh, Brick! How long does it have t' go on? This punishment? Haven't I done time enough, haven't I served my term, can't I apply for a—pardon?

Brick: Maggie, you're spoiling my liquor. Lately your voice always sounds like you'd been running upstairs to warn somebody that the house was on fire!

Margaret: Well, no wonder, no wonder. Y'know what I feel like, Brick?

I feel all the time like a cat on a hot tin roof!

Brick: Then jump off the roof, jump off it, cats can jump off roofs and land on their four feet uninjured!

Margaret: Oh, yes!

Brick: Do it!—fo' God's sake, do it . . .

Margaret: Do what?

Brick: Take a lover!

Margaret: I can't see a man but you! Even with my eyes closed, I just see you! Why don't you get ugly, Brick, why don't you please get fat or ugly or something so I could stand it?

[She rushes to hall door, opens it, listens.]

The concert is still going on! Bravo, no-necks, bravo!

[She slams and locks door fiercely.]

Brick: What did you lock the door for?

Margaret: To give us a little privacy for a while.

Brick: You know better, Maggie.

Margaret: No, I don't know better. . . .

[She rushes to gallery doors, draws the rose-silk drapes across them.]

Brick: Don't make a fool of yourself.

Margaret: I don't mind makin' a fool of myself over you!

Brick: I mind, Maggie. I feel embarrassed for you.

Margaret: Feel embarrassed! But don't continue my torture. I can't live on and on under these circumstances.

Brick: You agreed to—

Margaret: I know but—

Brick: —Accept that condition!

Margaret: *I CAN'T! CAN'T! CAN'T!*

[She seizes his shoulder.]

Brick: Let go!

[He breaks away from her and seizes the small boudoir chair and raises it like a lion-tamer facing a big circus cat.

Count five. She stares at him with her fist pressed to her mouth, then bursts into shrill, almost hysterical laughter. He remains grave for a moment, then grins and puts the chair down. Big Mama calls through closed door.]

Big Mama: Son? Son? Son?

Brick: What is it, Big Mama?

Big Mama [*outside*]: Oh, son! We got the most wonderful news about Big Daddy. I just had t' run up an' tell you right this—

[She rattles the knob.]

—What's this door doin', locked, faw? You all think there's robbers in the house?

Margaret: Big Mama, Brick is dressin', he's not dressed yet.

Big Mama: That's all right, it won't be the first time I've seen Brick not dressed. Come on, open this door!

[Margaret, with a grimace, goes to unlock and open the hall door, as Brick hobbles rapidly to the bathroom and kicks the door shut. Big Mama has disappeared from the hall.]

Margaret: Big Mama?

[Big Mama appears through the opposite gallery doors behind Margaret, huffing and puffing like an old bulldog. She is a short, stout woman; her sixty years and 170 pounds have left her somewhat breathless most of the time; she's always tensed like a boxer, or rather, a Japanese wrestler. Her "family" was maybe a little superior to Big Daddy's, but not much. She wears a black or silver lace dress and at least half a million in flashy gems. She is very sincere.]

Big Mama [*loudly, startling Margaret*]: Here—I come through Gooper's and Mae's gall'ry door. Where's Brick? *Brick*—Hurry on out of there, son, I just have a second and want to give you the news about Big Daddy. —I hate locked doors in a house. . . .

Margaret [*with affected lightness*]: I've noticed you do, Big Mama, but people have got to have *some* moments of privacy, don't they?

Big Mama: No, ma'am, not in *my* house. [*without pause*] Whacha took off you' dress faw? I thought that little lace dress was so sweet on yuh, honey.

Margaret: I thought it looked sweet on me, too but one of m' cute little table-partners used it for a napkin so—!

Big Mama [*picking up stockings on floor*]: What?

Margaret: You know, Big Mama, Mae and Gooper's so touchy about those children—thanks, Big Mama . . .

[Big Mama has thrust the picked-up stockings in Margaret's hand with a grunt.]

—that you just don't dare to suggest there's any room for improvement in their—

Big Mama: Brick, hurry out!—Shoot, Maggie, you just don't like children.

Margaret: I do SO like children! Adore them!—well brought up!

Big Mama [*gentle—loving*]: Well, why don't you have some and bring them up well, then, instead of all the time pickin' on Gooper's an' Mae's?

Gooper [*shouting up the stairs*]: Hey, hey, Big Mama, Betsy an' Hugh got to go, waitin' t' tell yuh g'by!

Big Mama: Tell 'em to hold their hawses, I'll be right down in a jiffy!

Gooper: Yes ma'am!

[She turns to the bathroom door and calls out.]

Big Mama: Son? Can you hear me in there?

[There is a muffled answer.]

We just got the full report from the laboratory at the Ochsner Clinic, completely negative, son, ev'rything negative, right on down the line! Nothin' a-tall's wrong with him but some little functional thing called a spastic colon. Can you hear me, son?

Margaret: He can hear you, Big Mama.

Big Mama: Then why don't he say something? God Almighty, a piece of news like that should make him shout. It made *me* shout, I can tell you. I shouted and sobbed and fell right down on my knees!—Look!

[She pulls up her skirt.]

See the bruises where I hit my kneecaps? Took both doctors to haul me back on my feet!

[She laughs—she always laughs like hell at herself.]

Big Daddy was furious with me! But ain't that wonderful news?

[Facing bathroom again, she continues:]

After all the anxiety we been through to git a report like that on Big Daddy's birthday? Big Daddy tried to hide how much of a load that news took off his mind, but didn't fool *me*. He was mighty close to crying about it *himself!*

[Goodbyes are shouted downstairs, and she rushes to door.]

Gooper: Big Mama!
Big Mama: *Hold those people down there, don't let them go!*—Now, git dressed, we're all comin' up to this room fo' Big Daddy's birthday party because of your ankle.—How's his ankle, Maggie?
Margaret: Well, he broke it, Big Mama.
Big Mama: I know he broke it.

[A phone is ringing in hall. A Negro voice answers: "Mistuh Polly's res'dence."]

I mean does it hurt him much still.
Margaret: I'm afraid I can't give you that information, Big Mama. You'll have to ask Brick if it hurts much still or not.
Sookey [*in the hall*]: It's Memphis, Mizz Polly, it's Miss Sally in Memphis.
Big Mama: Awright, Sookey.

[Big Mama rushes into the hall and is heard shouting on the phone:]

Hello, Miss Sally. How are you, Miss Sally?—Yes, well, I was just gonna call you about it. *Shoot!*—
Margaret: Brick, don't!

[Big Mama raises her voice to a bellow.]

Big Mama: *Miss Sally? Don't ever call me from the Gayoso Lobby, too much talk goes on in that hotel lobby, no wonder you can't hear me!* Now listen, Miss Sally. They's nothin' serious wrong with Big Daddy. We got the report just now, they's nothin' wrong but a thing called a—spastic! *SPASTIC!*—colon . . .

[She appears at the hall door and calls to Margaret.]

—Maggie, come out here and talk to that fool on the phone. I'm shouted breathless!

Margaret [*goes out and is heard sweetly at phone*]: Miss Sally? This is Brick's wife, Maggie. So nice to hear your voice. Can you hear *mine?* Well, *good!*—Big Mama just wanted you to know that they've got the report from the Ochsner Clinic and what Big Daddy has is a spastic colon. Yes. Spastic colon, Miss Sally. That's right, spastic colon. *G'bye, Miss Sally, hope I'll see you real soon!*

[Hangs up a little before Miss Sally was probably ready to terminate the talk. She returns through the hall door.]

She heard me perfectly. I've discovered with deaf people the thing to do is not shout at them but just enunciate clearly. My rich old Aunt Cornelia was deaf as the dead but I could make her hear me just by sayin' each word slowly, distinctly, close to her ear. I read her the *Commercial Appeal* ev'ry night, read her the classified ads in it, even, she never missed a word of it. But was she a mean ole thing! Know what I got when she died? Her unexpired subscriptions to five magazines and the Book-of-the-Month Club and a LIBRARY full of ev'ry dull book ever written! All else went to her hellcat of a sister . . . meaner than she was, even!

[Big Mama has been straightening things up in the room during this speech.]

Big Mama [*closing closet door on discarded clothes*]: *Miss Sally sure is a case!* Big Daddy says she's always got her hand out fo' something. He's not mistaken. That poor ole thing always has her hand out fo' somethin'. I don't think Big Daddy gives her as much as he should.

Gooper: Big Mama! Come on now! Betsy and Hugh can't wait no longer!

Big Mama [*shouting*]: I'm comin'!

[She starts out. At the hall door, turns and jerks a forefinger, first toward the bathroom door, then toward the liquor cabinet, meaning: "Has Brick been drinking?" Margaret pretends not to understand, cocks her head and raises her brows as if the pantomimic performance was completely mystifying to her.

Big Mama rushes back to Margaret:]

Shoot! Stop playin' so dumb!—I mean has he been drinkin' that stuff much yet?

Margaret [*with a little laugh*]: Oh! I think he had a highball after supper.

Big Mama: Don't laugh about it!—Some single men stop drinkin' when they git married and others start! Brick never touched liquor before he—!

Margaret [*crying out*]: *THAT'S NOT FAIR!*

Big Mama: Fair or not fair I want to ask you a question, one question: D'you make Brick happy in bed?

Margaret: Why don't you ask if he makes *me* happy in bed?

Big Mama: Because I know that—

Margaret: It works both ways!

Big Mama: Something's not right! You're childless and my son drinks!

Gooper: Come on, Big Mama!

[Gooper has called her downstairs and she has rushed to the door on the line above. She turns at the door and points at the bed.]

—When a marriage goes on the rocks, the rocks are *there*, right *there!*
Margaret: That's—

[Big Mama has swept out of the room and slammed the door.]

—not—*fair* . . .

[Margaret is alone, completely alone, and she feels it. She draws in, hunches her shoulders, raises her arms with fists clenched, shuts her eyes tight as a child about to be stabbed with a vaccination needle. When she opens her eyes again, what she sees is the long oval mirror and she rushes straight to it, stares into it with a grimace and says: "Who are you?"—Then she crouches a little and answers herself in a different voice which is high, thin, mocking: "I am Maggie the Cat!"—Straightens quickly as bathroom door opens a little and Bricks calls out to her.]

Brick: Has Big Mama gone?
Margaret: She's gone.

[He opens the bathroom door and hobbles out, with his liquor glass now empty, straight to the liquor cabinet. He is whistling softly. Margaret's head pivots on her long, slender throat to watch him.

She raises a hand uncertainly to the base of her throat, as if it was difficult for her to swallow, before she speaks:]

You know, our sex life didn't just peter out in the usual way, it was cut off short, long before the natural time for it to, and it's going to revive again, just as sudden as that. I'm confident of it. That's what I'm keeping myself attractive for. For the time when you'll see me again like other men see me. Yes, like other men see me. They still see me, Brick, and they like what they see. Uh-huh. Some of them would give their—

Look, Brick!

[She stands before the long oval mirror, touches her breast and then her hips with her two hands.]

How high my body stays on me!—Nothing has fallen on me—not a fraction. . . .

[Her voice is soft and trembling: a pleading child's. At this moment as he turns to glance at her—a look which is like a player passing a ball to another player, third down and goal to go—she has to capture the audience in a grip so tight that she can hold it till the first intermission without any lapse of attention.]

Other men still want me. My face looks strained, sometimes, but I've kept my figure as well as you've kept yours, and men admire it. I still turn heads on the street. Why, last week in Memphis everywhere that I went men's eyes burned holes in my clothes, at the country club and in restaurants and department stores, there wasn't a man I met or walked by that didn't just eat me up with his eyes and turn around when I passed him and look back at me. Why, at Alice's party for her New York cousins, the best-lookin' man in the crowd—followed me upstairs and tried to force his way in the powder room with me, followed me to the door and tried to force his way in!

Brick: Why didn't you let him, Maggie?

Margaret: Because I'm not that common, for one thing. Not that I wasn't almost tempted to. You like to know who it was? It was Sonny Boy Maxwell, that's who!

Brick: Oh, yeah, Sonny Boy Maxwell, he was a good end-runner but had a little injury to his back and had to quit.

Margaret: He has no injury now and has no wife and still has a lech for me!

Brick: I see no reason to lock him out of a powder room in that case.

Margaret: And have someone catch me at it? I'm not that stupid. Oh, I might sometime cheat on you with someone, since you're so insultingly eager to have me do it!—But if I do, you can be damned sure it will be in a place and a time where no one but me and the man could possibly know. Because I'm not going to give you any excuse to divorce me for being unfaithful or anything else. . . .

Brick: Maggie, I wouldn't divorce you for being unfaithful or anything else. Don't you know that? Hell. I'd be relieved to know that you'd found yourself a lover.

Margaret: Well, I'm taking no chances. No, I'd rather stay on this hot tin roof.

Brick: A hot tin roof's 'n uncomfo'table place t' stay on. . . .

[He starts to whistle softly.]

Margaret [*through his whistle*]: Yeah, but I can stay on it just as long as I have to.

Brick: You could leave me, Maggie.

[He resumes whistle. She wheels about to glare at him.]

Margaret: Don't want to and will not! Besides if I did, you don't have a cent to pay for it but what you get from Big Daddy and he's dying of cancer!

[For the first time a realization of Big Daddy's doom seems to penetrate to Brick's consciousness, visibly, and he looks at Margaret.]

Brick: Big Mama just said he *wasn't*, that the report was okay.

Margaret: That's what she thinks because she got the same story that they gave Big Daddy. And was just as taken in by it as he was, poor ole things. . . .

But tonight they're going to tell her the truth about it. When Big Daddy goes to bed, they're going to tell her that he is dying of cancer.

[She slams the dresser drawer.]

—It's malignant and it's terminal.

Brick: Does Big Daddy know it?

Margaret: Hell, do they *ever* know it? Nobody says, "You're dying." You have to fool them. They have to fool *themselves.*

Brick: Why?

Margaret: Why? Because human beings dream of life everlasting, that's the reason! But most of them want it on earth and not in heaven.

[He gives a short, hard laugh at her touch of humor.]

Well. . . . [*She touches up her mascara.*] That's how it is, anyhow. . . . [*She looks about.*] Where did I put down my cigarette? Don't want to burn up the home-place, at least not with Mae and Gooper and their five monsters in it!

[She has found it and sucks at it greedily. Blows out smoke and continues.]

So this is Big Daddy's last birthday. And Mae and Gooper, they know it, oh, *they* know it, all right. They got the first information from the Ochsner Clinic. That's why they rushed down here with their no-neck monsters. Because. Do you know something? Big Daddy's made no will? Big Daddy's never made out any will in his life, and so this campaign's afoot to impress him, forcibly as possible, with the fact that you drink and I've borne no children!

[He continues to stare at her a moment, then mutters something sharp but not audible and hobbles rather rapidly out onto the long gallery in the fading, much faded, gold light.]

Margaret [*continuing her liturgical chant*]: Y'know, I'm *fond* of Big Daddy, I am genuinely fond of that old man, I really *am*, you know. . . .

Brick [*faintly, vaguely*]: Yes, I know you are. . . .

Margaret: I've always sort of admired him in spite of his coarseness, his four-letter words and so forth. Because Big Daddy *is* what he *is*, and he makes no bones about it. He hasn't turned gentleman farmer, he's still a Mississippi redneck, as much of a redneck as he must have been when he was just overseer here on the old Jack Straw and Peter Ochello place. But he got hold of it an' built it into th' biggest an' finest plantation in the Delta.—I've always *liked* Big Daddy. . . .
[She crosses to the proscenium.]

Well, this is Big Daddy's last birthday. I'm sorry about it. But I'm facing the facts. It takes money to take care of a drinker and that's the office that I've been elected to lately.

Brick: You don't have to take care of me.

Margaret: Yes, I do. Two people in the same boat have got to take care of each other. At least you want money to buy more Echo Spring when this supply is exhausted, or will you be satisfied with a ten-cent beer?

Mae an' Gooper are plannin' to freeze us out of Big Daddy's estate because you drink and I'm childless. But we can defeat that plan. We're *going* to defeat that plan!

Brick, y'know, I've been so God damn disgustingly poor all my life!—That's the *truth*, Brick!

Brick: I'm not sayin' it isn't.

Margaret: Always had to suck up to people I couldn't stand because they had money and I was poor as Job's turkey. You don't know what that's like. Well, I'll tell you, it's like you would feel a thousand miles away from Echo Spring!—And had to get back to it on that broken ankle . . . without a crutch!

That's how it feels to be as poor as Job's turkey and have to suck up to relatives that you hated because they had money and all you had was a bunch of hand-me-down clothes and a few old moldly three-per-cent government bonds. My daddy loved his liquor, he fell in love with his liquor the way you've fallen in love with Echo Spring!—And my poor Mama, having to maintain some semblance of social position, to keep appearances up, on an income of one hundred and fifty dollars a month on those old government bonds!

When I came out, the year that I made my debut, I had just two evening dresses! One Mother made me from a pattern in *Vogue*, the other a hand-me-down from a snotty rich cousin I hated!

—The dress that I married you in was my grandmother's weddin'gown. . . .

So that's why I'm like a cat on a hot tin roof!

[Brick is still on the gallery. Someone below calls up to him in a warm Negro voice, "Hiya, Mistuh Brick, how yuh feelin'?" Brick raises his liquor glass as if that answered the question.]

Margaret: You can be young without money, but you can't be old without it. You've got to be old *with* money because to be old without it is just too awful, you've got to be one or the other, either *young* or *with money*, you can't be old and *without* it.—That's the *truth*, Brick. . . .

[Brick whistles softly, vaguely.]

Well, now I'm dressed, I'm all dressed, there's nothing else for me to do.

[Forlornly, almost fearfully.]

I'm dressed, all dressed, nothing else for me to do. . . .

[She moves about restlessly, aimlessly, and speaks, as if to herself.]

What am I—? Oh!—my bracelets. . . .

[She starts working a collection of bracelets over her hands onto her wrists, about six on each, as she talks.]

I've thought a whole lot about it and now I know when I made my mistake. Yes, I made my mistake when I told you the truth about that thing with Skipper. Never should have confessed it, a fatal error, tellin' you about that thing with Skipper.

Brick: Maggie, shut up about Skipper. I mean it, Maggie; you got to shut up about Skipper.

Margaret: You ought to understand that Skipper and I—

Brick: You don't think I'm serious, Maggie? You're fooled by the fact that I am saying this quiet? Look, Maggie. What you're doing is a dangerous thing to do. You're—you're—you're—foolin' with something that—nobody ought to fool with.

Margaret: This time I'm going to finish what I have to say to you. Skipper and I made love, if love you could call it, because it made both of us feel a little bit closer to you. You see, you son of a bitch, you asked too much of people, of me, of him, of all the unlucky poor damned sons of bitches that happen to love you, and there was a whole pack of them, yes, there was a pack of them besides me and Skipper, you asked too goddam much of people that loved you, you—superior creature!—you godlike being!—And so we made love to each other to dream it was you, both of us! Yes, yes, yes! Truth, truth! What's so awful about it? I like it, I think the truth is—yeah! I shouldn't have told you. . . .

Brick [*holding his head unnaturally still and uptilted a bit*]: It was Skipper that told me about it. Not you, Maggie.

Margaret: I told you!

Brick: After he told me!

Margaret: What does it matter who—?

Dixie: I got your mallet, I got your mallet.

Trixie: Give it to me, give it to me. It's mine.

[Brick turns suddenly out upon the gallery and calls:]

Brick: Little girl! Hey, little girl!

Little Girl [*at a distance*]: What, Uncle Brick?

Brick: Tell the folks to come up!—Bring everybody upstairs!

Trixie: It's mine, it's mine.

Margaret: I can't stop myself! I'd go on telling you this in front of them all, if I had to!

Brick: Little girl! Go on, go on, will you? Do what I told you, call them!

Dixie: Okay.

Margaret: Because it's got to be told and you, you!—you never let me!

[She sobs, then controls herself, and continues almost calmly.]

It was one of those beautiful, ideal things they tell about in the Greek legends, it couldn't be anything else, you being you, and that's what made it so sad, that's what made it so awful, because it was love that never could be carried through to anything satisfying or even talked about plainly.

Brick: Maggie, you gotta stop this.

Margaret: Brick, I tell you, you got to believe me, Brick, I *do* understand all about it! I—I think it was—*noble!* Can't you tell I'm sincere when I say I respect it? My only point, the only point that I'm making, is life has got to be allowed to continue even after the *dream* of life is—all—over. . . .

[Brick is without his crutch. Leaning on furniture, he crosses to pick it up as she continues as if possessed by a will outside herself:]

Why I remember when we double-dated at college, Gladys Fitzgerald and I and you and Skipper, it was more like a date between you and Skipper. Gladys and I were just sort of tagging along as if it was necessary to chaperone you!—to make a good public impression—

Brick [*turns to face her, half lifting his crutch*]: Maggie, you want me to hit you with this crutch? Don't you know I could kill you with this crutch?

Margaret: Good Lord, man, d' you think I'd care if you did?

Brick: One man has one great good true thing in his life. One great good thing which is true!—I had friendship with Skipper.—You are naming it dirty!

Margaret: I'm not naming it dirty! I am naming it clean.

Brick: Not love with you, Maggie, but friendship with Skipper was that one great true thing, and you are naming it dirty!

Margaret: Then you haven't been listenin', not understood what I'm saying! I'm naming it so damn clean that it killed poor Skipper!—You two had something that had to be kept on ice, yes, incorruptible, yes!—and death was the only icebox where you could keep it. . . .

Brick: I married you, Maggie. Why would I marry you, Maggie, if I was—?

Margaret: Brick, let me finish!—I know, believe me I know, that it was only Skipper that harbored even any *unconscious* desire for anything not perfectly pure between you two!—Now let me skip a little. You married me early that summer we graduated out of Ole Miss, and we were happy, weren't we, we were blissful, yes, hit heaven together ev'ry time that we loved! But that fall you an' Skipper turned down wonderful offers of jobs in order to keep on bein' football heroes—pro-football heroes. You organized the Dixie Stars that fall, so you could keep on bein' teammates forever! But somethin' was not right with it!—*Me included!*—between you. Skipper began hittin' the bottle . . . you got a spinal injury—couldn't play the Thanksgivin' game in Chicago, watched it on TV from a traction bed in Toledo. I joined Skipper. The Dixie Stars lost because poor Skipper was drunk. We drank together that night all night in the bar of the Blackstone and when cold day was comin' up over the Lake an' we were comin' out drunk to take a dizzy look at it, I said, "SKIPPER! STOP LOVIN' MY HUSBAND OR TELL HIM HE'S GOT TO LET YOU ADMIT IT TO HIM!"—one way or another!

HE SLAPPED ME HARD ON THE MOUTH!—then turned and ran without stopping once, I am sure, all the way back into his room at the Blackstone. . . .

—When I came to his room that night, with a little scratch like a shy little mouse at his door, he made that pitiful, ineffectual little attempt to prove that what I had said wasn't true. . . .

[Brick strikes at her with crutch, a blow that shatters the gemlike lamp on the table.]

—In this way, I destroyed him, by telling him truth that he and his world which he was born and raised in, yours and his world, had told him could not be told?

—From then on Skipper was nothing at all but a receptacle for liquor and drugs. . . .

—Who shot cock robin? I with my—

[She throws back her head with tight shut eyes.]

—merciful arrow!

[Brick strikes at her; misses.]

Missed me!—Sorry,—I'm not tryin' to whitewash my behavior, Christ, no! Brick, I'm not good. I don't know why people have to pretend to be good, nobody's good. The rich or the well-to-do can afford to respect moral patterns, conventional moral patterns, but I could never afford to, yeah, but—I'm honest! Give me credit for just that, will you *please?*—Born poor, raised poor, expect to die poor unless I manage to get us something out of what Big Daddy leaves when he dies of cancer! But Brick?!—*Skipper is dead! I'm alive!* Maggie the cat is—

[Brick hops awkwardly forward and strikes at her again with his crutch.]

—alive! I am alive, alive! I am . . .

[He hurls the crutch at her, across the bed she took refuge behind, and pitches forward on the floor as she completes her speech.]

—alive!

[A little girl, Dixie, bursts into the room, wearing an Indian war bonnet and firing a cap pistol at Margaret and shouting: "Bang, bang, bang!"
Laughter downstairs floats through the open hall door. Margaret had crouched gasping to bed at child's entrance. She now rises and says with cool fury:]

Little girl, your mother or someone should teach you—[*gasping*]—to knock at a door before you come into a room. Otherwise people might think that you—lack—good breeding. . . .

Dixie: Yanh, yanh, yanh, what is Uncle Brick doin' on th' floor?

Brick: I tried to kill your Aunt Maggie, but I failed—and I fell. Little girl, give me my crutch so I can get up off th' floor.

Margaret: Yes, give your uncle his crutch, he's a cripple, honey, he broke his ankle last night jumping hurdles on the high school athletic field!

Dixie: What were you jumping hurdles for, Uncle Brick?

Brick: Because I used to jump them, and people like to do what they used to do, even after they've stopped being able to do it. . . .

Margaret: That's right, that's your answer, now go away, little girl.

[Dixie fires cap pistol at Margaret three times.]

Stop, you stop that, monster! You little no-neck monster!

[She seizes the cap pistol and hurls it through gallery doors.]

Dixie [*with a precocious instinct for the cruelest thing*]: You're *jealous!*—You're just jealous because you can't have babies!

[She sticks out her tongue at Margaret as she sashays past her with her stomach stuck out, to the gallery. Margaret slams the gallery doors and leans panting against them. There is a pause. Brick has replaced his spilt drink and sits, faraway, on the great four-poster bed.]

Margaret: You see?—they gloat over us being childless, even in front of their five little no-neck monsters!

[Pause. Voices approach on the stairs.]

Brick?—I've been to a doctor in Memphis, a—a gynecologist. . .

I've been completely examined, and there is no reason why we can't have a child whenever we want one. And this is my time by the calendar to conceive. Are you listening to me? Are you? Are you LISTENING TO ME!

Brick: Yes. I hear you, Maggie.

[His attention returns to her inflamed face.]

—But how in hell on earth do you imagine—that you're going to have a child by a man that can't stand you?

Margaret: That's a problem that I will have to work out.

[She wheels about to face the hall door.]

Mae [*off stage left*]: Come on, Big Daddy. We're all goin' up to Brick's room.

[From off stage left, voices: Reverend Tooker, Doctor Baugh, Mae.]

Margaret: Here they come!

[The lights dim.]

CURTAIN

ACT TWO

There is no lapse of time. Margaret and Brick are in the same positions they held at the end of Act I.

Margaret [*at door*]: *Here they come!*

[Big Daddy appears first, a tall man with a fierce, anxious look, moving carefully not to betray his weakness even, or especially, to himself.]

Gooper: I read in the *Register* that you're getting a new memorial window.

[Some of the people are approaching through the hall, others along the gallery: voices from both directions. Gooper and Reverend Tooker become visible outside gallery doors, and their voices come in clearly.

They pause outside as Gooper lights a cigar.]

Reverend Tooker [*vivaciously*]: Oh, but St. Paul's in Grenada has three memorial windows, and the latest one is a Tiffany stained-glass window that cost twenty-five hundred dollars, a picture of Christ the Good Shepherd with a Lamb in His arms.

Margaret: Big Daddy.

Big Daddy: Well, Brick.

Brick: Hello Big Daddy.—Congratulations!

Big Daddy: —Crap. . . .

Gooper: Who give that window, Preach?

Reverend Tooker: Clyde Fletcher's widow. Also presented St. Paul's with a baptismal font.

Gooper: Y'know what somebody ought t' give your church is a *coolin'* system, Preach.

Mae [*almost religiously*]: —Let's see now, they've had their *tyyy*-phoid shots, and their tetanus shots, their diphtheria shots and their hepatitis shots and their polio shots, they got *those* shots every month from May through September, and—Gooper? Hey! Gooper! —What all have the kiddies been shot faw?

Reverend Tooker: Yes, siree, Bob! And y'know what Gus Hamma's family gave in his memory to the church at Two Rivers? A complete new stone parish-house with a basketball court in the basement and a—

Big Daddy [*uttering a loud barking laugh which is far from truly mirthful*]: Hey, Preach! What's all this talk about memorials, Preach? Y' think somebody's about t' kick off around here? 'S that it?

[Startled by this interjection, Reverend Tokier decides to laugh at the question almost as loud as he can.

How he would answer the question we'll never know, as he's spared that embarrassment by the voice of Cooper's wife, Mae, rising high and clear as she appears with "Doc" Baugh, the family doctor, through the hall door.]

Margaret [*overlapping a bit*]: Turn on the hi-fi, Brick! Let's have some music t' start off th' party with!

Brick: You turn it on, Maggie.

[The talk becomes so general that the room sounds like a great aviary of chattering birds. Only Brick remains unengaged, leaning upon the liquor cabinet with his faraway smile, an ice cube in a paper napkin with which he now and then rubs his forehead. He doesn't respond to Margaret's command. She bounds forward and stoops over the instrument panel of the console.]

Gooper: We gave 'em that thing for a third anniversary present, got three speakers in it.

[The room is suddenly blasted by the climax of a Wagnerian opera or a Beethoven symphony.]

Big Daddy: Turn that damn thing off!

[Almost instant silence, almost instantly broken by the shouting charge of Big Mama, entering through hall door like a charging rhino.]

Big Mama: Wha's my Brick, wha's mah precious baby!!

Big Daddy: Sorry! Turn it back on!

[Everyone laughs very loud. Big Daddy is famous for his jokes at Big Mama's expense, and nobody laughs louder at these jokes than Big Mama herself, though sometimes they're pretty cruel and Big Mama has to pick up or fuss with something to cover the hurt that the loud laugh doesn't quite cover.

On this occasion, a happy occasion because the dread in her heart has also been lifted by the false report on Big Daddy's condition, she giggles, grotesquely, coyly, in Big Daddy's direction and bears down upon Brick, all very quick and alive.]

Big Mama: Here he is, here's my precious baby! What's that you've got in your hand? You put that liquor down, son, your hand was made fo' holdin' somethin' better than that!

Gooper: Look at Brick put it down!

[Brick has obeyed Big Mama by draining the glass and handing it to her. Again everyone laughs, some high, some low.]

Big Mama: Oh, you bad boy, you, you're my bad little boy. Give Big Mama a kiss, you bad boy, you!—Look at him shy away, will you? Brick never liked bein' kissed or made a fuss over, I guess because he's always had too much of it!

Son, you turn that thing off!

[Brick has switched on the TV set.]

I can't stand TV, radio was bad enough but TV has gone it one better, I mean—*[plops wheezing in chair]*—one worse, ha ha! Now what'm I sittin' down here faw? I want t' sit next to my sweetheart on the sofa, hold hands with him and love him up a little!

[Big Mama has on a black and white figured chiffon. The large irregular patterns, like the markings of some massive animal, the luster of her great diamonds and many pearls, the brilliants set in the silver frames of her glasses, her riotous voice, booming laugh, have dominated the room since she entered. Big Daddy has been regarding her with a steady grimace of chronic annoyance.]

Big Mama [*still louder*]: Preacher, Preacher, hey, Preach! Give me you' hand an' help me up from this chair!

Reverend Tooker: None of your tricks, Big Mama!

Big Mama: What tricks? You give me you' hand so I can get up an'—

[Reverend Tooker extends her his hand. She grabs it and pulls him into her lap with a shrill laugh that spans an octave in two notes.]

Ever seen a preacher in a fat lady's lap? Hey, hey, folks! Ever seen a preacher in a fat lady's lap?

[Big Mama is notorious throughout the Delta for this sort of inelegant horseplay, Margaret looks on with indulgent humor, sipping Dubonnet "on the rocks" and watching Brick, but Mae and Gooper exchange signs of humorless anxiety over these antics, the sort of behavior which Mae thinks may account for their failure to quite get in with the smartest young married set in Memphis, despite all. One of the Negroes, Lacy or Sookey, peeks in, cackling. They are waiting for a sign to bring in the cake and champagne. But Big Daddy's not amused. He doesn't understand why, in spite of the infinite mental relief he's received from the doctor's report, he still has these same old fox teeth in his guts. "This spastic condition is something else," he says to himself, but aloud he roars at Big Mama:]

Big Daddy: BIG MAMA, WILL YOU QUIT HORSIN'?—You're too old an' too fat fo' that sort of crazy kid stuff an' besides a woman with your blood pressure—she had two hundred last spring!—is riskin' a stroke when you mess around like that. . . .

[Mae blows on a pitch pipe.]

Big Mama: Here comes Big Daddy's birthday!

[Negroes in white jackets enter with an enormous birthday cake ablaze with candles and carrying buckets of champagne with satin ribbons about the bottle necks.

Mae and Gooper strike up song, and everybody, including the Negroes and children, joins in. Only Brick remains aloof.]

Everyone: Happy birthday to you.
Happy birthday to you.
Happy birthday, Big Daddy—

[Some sing: "Dear, Big Daddy!"]

Happy birthday to you.

[Some sing: "How old are you?"]

[Mae has come down center and is organizing her children like a chorus. She gives them a barely audible: "One, two, three!" and they are off in the new tune.]

Children: Skinamarinka—dinka—dink
Skinamarinka—do
We love you.
Skinamarinka—dinka—dink
Skinamarinka—do.

[All together, they turn to Big Daddy.]

Big Daddy, you!

[They turn back front, like a musical comedy chorus.]

We love you in the morning;
We love you in the night.
We love you when we're with you,
And we love you out of sight.
Skinamarinka—dinka—dink
Skinamarinka—do.

[Mae turns to Big Mama.]

Big Mama, too!

[Big Mama bursts into tears. The Negroes leave.]

Big Daddy: Now Ida, what the hell is the matter with you?
Mae: She's just so happy.
Big Mama: I'm just so happy, Big Daddy, I have to cry or something.

[Sudden and loud in the hush:]

Brick, do you know the wonderful news that Doc Baugh got from the clinic about Big Daddy? Big Daddy's one hundred per cent!

Margaret: Isn't that wonderful?

Big Mama: He's just one hundred per cent. Passed the examination with flying colors. Now that we know there's nothing wrong with Big Daddy but a spastic colon, I can tell you something. I was worried sick, half out of my mind, for fear that Big Daddy might have a thing like—

[Margaret cuts through this speech, jumping up and exclaiming shrilly:]

Margaret: Brick, honey, aren't you going to give Big Daddy his birthday present?

[Passing by him, she snatches his liquor glass from him.
[She picks up a fancily wrapped package.]

Here it is, Big Daddy, this is from Brick!

Big Mama: This is the biggest birthday Big Daddy's ever had, a hundred presents and bushels of telegrams from—

Mae [at same time]: What is it, Brick?

Gooper: I bet 500 to 50 that Brick don't *know* what it is.

Big Mama: The fun of presents is not knowing what they are till you open the package. Open your present, Big Daddy.

Big Daddy: Open it you'self. I want to ask Brick somethin! Come here, Brick.

Margaret: Big Daddy's callin' you, Brick.

[She is opening the package.]

Brick: Tell Big Daddy I'm crippled.

Big Daddy: I see you're crippled. I want to know how you got crippled.

Margaret [making diversionary tactics]: Oh, look, oh, look, why, it's a cashmere robe!

[She holds the robe up for all to see.]

Mae: You sound surprised, Maggie.

Margaret: I never saw one before.

Mae: That's funny.—*Hah!*

Margaret [turning on her fiercely, with a brilliant smile]: Why is it funny? All my family ever had was family—and luxuries such as cashmere robes still surprise me!

Big Daddy [ominously]: Quiet!

Mae [heedless in her fury]: I don't see how you could be so surprised when you bought it yourself at Loewenstein's in Memphis last Saturday. You know how I know?

Big Daddy: I said, Quiet!

Mae: —I know because the salesgirl that sold it to you waited on me and said, Oh, Mrs. Pollitt, your sister-in-law just bought a cashmere robe for your husband's father!

Margaret: Sister Woman! Your talents are wasted as a housewife and mother, you really ought to be with the FBI or—

Big Daddy: QUIET!

[Reverend Tooker's reflexes are slower than the others'. He finishes a sentence after the bellow.]

Reverend Tooker [*to Doc Bough*]: —the Stork and the Reaper are running neck and neck!

[He starts to laugh gaily when he notices the silence and Big Daddy's glare. His laugh dies falsely.]

Big Daddy: Preacher, I hope I'm not butting in on more talk about memorial stained-glass windows, am I, Preacher?

[Reverend Tooker laughs feebly, then coughs dryly in the embarrassed silence.]

Preacher?

Big Mama: Now, Big Daddy, don't you pick on Preacher!

Big Daddy [*raising his voice*]: You ever hear that expression all hawk and no spit? You bring that expression to mind with that little dry cough of yours, all hawk an' no spit. . . .

[The pause is broken only by a short startled laugh from Margaret, the only one there who is conscious of and amused by the grotesque.]

Mae [*raising her arms and jangling her bracelets*]: I wonder if the mosquitoes are active tonight?

Big Daddy: What's that, Little Mama? Did you make some remark?

Mae: Yes, I said I wondered if the mosquitoes would eat us alive if we went out on the gallery for a while.

Big Daddy: Well, if they do, I'll have your bones pulverized for fertilizer!

Big Mama [*quickly*]: Last week we had an airplane spraying the place and I think it done some good, at least I haven't had a—

Big Daddy [*cutting her speech*]: Brick, they tell me, if what they tell me is true, that you done some jumping last night on the high school athletic field?

Big Mama: Brick, Big Daddy is talking to you, son.

Brick [*smiling vaguely over his drink*]: What was that, Big Daddy?

Big Daddy: They said you done some jumping on the high school track field last night.

Brick: That's what they told me, too.

Big Daddy: Was it jumping or humping that you were doing out there? What were doing out there at three A.M., layin' a woman on that cinder track?

Big Mama: Big Daddy, you are off the sick-list, now, and I'm not going to excuse you for talkin' so—

Big Daddy: Quiet!

Big Mama: —*nasty* in front of Preacher and—

Big Daddy: *QUIET!*—I ast you, Brick, if you was cuttin' you'self a piece o' poon-tang last night on that cinder track? I thought maybe you were chasin' poon-tang on that track an' tripped over something in the heat of the chase—'sthat it?

[Gooper laughs, loud and false, others nervously following suit. Big Mama stamps her foot, and purses her lips, crossing to Mae and whispering something to her as Brick meets his father's hard, intent, grinning stare with a slow, vague smile that he offers all situations from behind the screen of his liquor.]

Brick: No, sir, I don't think so. . . .

Mae [*at the same time, sweetly*]: Reverend Tooker, let's you and I take a stroll on the widow's walk.

[She and the preacher go out on the gallery as Big Daddy says:]

Big Daddy: Then what the hell were you doing out there at three o'clock in the morning?

Brick: Jumping the hurdles, Big Daddy, runnin' and jumpin' the hurdles, but those high hurdles have gotten too high for me, now.

Big Daddy: Cause you was drunk?

Brick [*his vague smile fading a little*]: Sober I wouldn't have tried to jump the *low* ones. . . .

Big Mama [*quickly*]: Big Daddy, blow out the candles on your birthday cake!

Margaret [*at the same time*]: I want to propose a toast to Big Daddy Pollitt on his sixty-fifth birthday, the biggest cotton planter in—

Big Daddy [*bellowing with fury and disgust*]: *I told you to stop it, now stop it, quit this—!*

Big Mama [*coming in front of Big Daddy with the cake*]: Big Daddy, I will not allow you to talk that way, not even on your birthday, I—

Big Daddy: I'll talk like I want to on my birthday, Ida, or any other goddam day of the year and anybody here that don't like it knows what they can do!

Big Mama: You don't mean that!

Big Daddy: What makes you think I don't mean it?

[Meanwhile various discreet signals have been exchanged and Gooper has also gone out on the gallery.]

Big Mama: I just know you don't mean it.

Big Daddy: You don't know a goddam thing and you never did!

Big Mama: Big Daddy, you don't mean that.

Big Daddy: Oh, yes, I do, oh, yes, I do, I mean it! I put up with a whole lot of crap around here because I thought I was dying. And you thought I was dying and you started taking over, well, you can stop taking over now, Ida, because I'm not gonna die, you can just stop now this business of taking over because you're not taking over because I'm not dying, I went through the laboratory and the goddam exploratory operation and there's nothing wrong with me but a spastic colon. And I'm not dying of cancer which you thought I was dying of. Ain't that so? Didn't you think that I was dying of cancer, Ida?

[Almost everybody is out on the gallery but the two old people glaring at each other across the blazing cake.

Big Mama's chest heaves and she presses a fat fist to her mouth.

Big Daddy continues, hoarsely:]

Ain't that so, Ida? Didn't you have an idea I was dying of cancer and now you could take control of this place and everything on it? I got that impression, I seemed to get that impression. Your loud voice everywhere, your fat old body butting in here and there!

Big Mama: Hush! The Preacher!

Big Daddy: Fuck the goddam preacher!

[Big Mama gasps loudly and sits down on the sofa which is almost too small for her.]

Did you hear what I said? I said fuck the goddam preacher!

[Somebody closes the gallery doors from outside just as there is a burst of fireworks and excited cries from the children.]

Big Mama: I never seen you act like this before and I can't think what's got in you!

Big Daddy: I went through all that laboratory and operation and all just so I would know if you or me was boss here! Well, now it turns out that I am and you ain't—and that's my birthday present—and my cake and champagne!—because for three years now you been gradually taking over. Bossing. Talking. Sashaying your fat old body around the place I made! I made this place! I was overseer on it! I was the overseer on the old Straw and Ochello plantation. I quit school at ten! I quit school at ten years old and went to work like a nigger in the fields. And I rose to be overseer of the Straw and Ochello plantation. And old Straw died and I was Ochello's partner and the place got bigger and bigger and bigger and bigger and bigger! I did all that myself with no goddam help from you, and now you think you're just about to take over. Well, I am just about to tell you that you are not just about to take over, you are not just about to take over a goddamn thing. Is that clear to you, Ida? Is that very plain to you, now? Is that understood completely? I been through the laboratory from A to Z. I've had the goddam exploratory operation, and nothing is wrong with me but a spastic colon—made spastic, I guess, by *disgust!* By all the goddam lies and liars that I have had to put up with, and all the goddam hypocrisy that I lived with all these forty years that we been livin' together!

Hey! Ida!! Blow out the candles on the birthday cake! Purse up your lips and draw a deep breath and blow out the goddam candles on the cake!

Big Mama: Oh, Big Daddy, oh, oh, oh, Big Daddy!

Big Daddy: What's the matter with you?

Big Mama: In all these years you never believed that I loved you??

Big Daddy: Huh?

Big Mama: And I did, I did so much, I did love you!—I even loved your hate and your hardness, Big Daddy!

[She sobs and rushes awkwardly out onto the gallery.]

Big Daddy [*to himself*]: *Wouldn't it be funny if that was true. . . .*

[A pause is followed by a burst of light in the sky from the fireworks.]

BRICK! HEY, BRICK!

[He stands over his blazing birthday cake.
After some moments, Brick hobbles in on his crutch, holding his glass.
Margaret follows him with a bright, anxious smile.]

I didn't call you, Maggie. I called Brick.
Margaret: I'm just delivering him to you.

[She kisses Brick on the mouth which he immediately wipes with the back of his hand. She flies girlishly back out. Brick and his father are alone.]

Big Daddy: Why did you do that?
Brick: Do what, Big Daddy?
Big Daddy: Wipe her kiss off your mouth like she'd spit on you.
Brick: I don't know. I wasn't conscious of it.
Big Daddy: That woman of yours has a better shape on her than Gooper's but somehow or other they got the same look about them.
Brick: What sort of look is that, Big Daddy?
Big Daddy: I don't know how to describe it but it's the same look.
Brick: They don't look peaceful, do they?
Big Daddy: No, they sure in hell don't.
Brick: They look nervous as cats?
Big Daddy: That's right, they look nervous as cats.
Brick: Nervous as a couple of cats on a hot tin roof?
Big Daddy: That's right, boy, they look like a couple of cats on a hot tin roof. It's funny that you and Gooper being so different would pick out the same type of woman.
Brick: Both of us married into society, Big Daddy.
Big Daddy: Crap . . . I wonder what gives them both that look?
Brick: Well. They're sittin' in the middle of a big piece of land, Big Daddy, twenty-eight thousand acres is a pretty big piece of land and so they're squaring off on it, each determined to knock off a bigger piece of it than the other whenever you let it go.
Big Daddy: I got a surprise for those women. I'm not gonna let it go for a long time yet if that's what they're waiting for.
Brick: That's right, Big Daddy. You just sit tight and let them scratch each other's eyes out. . . .
Big Daddy: You bet your life I'm going to sit tight on it and let those sons of bitches scratch their eyes out, ha ha ha. . . .
But Gooper's wife's a good breeder, you got to admit she's fertile. Hell, at supper tonight she had them all at the table and they had to put a couple of extra leafs in the table to make room for them, she's got five head of them, now, and another one's comin'.

Brick: Yep, number six is comin'. . . .
Big Daddy: Six hell, she'll probably drop a litter next time. Brick, you know, I swear to God, I don't know the way it happens?
Brick: The way what happens, Big Daddy?
Big Daddy: You git you a piece of land, by hook or crook, an' things start growin' on it, things accumulate on it, and the first thing you know it's completely out of hand, completely out of hand!
Brick: Well, they say nature hates a vacuum, Big Daddy.
Big Daddy: That's what they say, but sometimes I think that a vacuum is a hell of a lot better than some of the stuff that nature replaces it with.
Is someone out there by that door?
Gooper: Hey Mae.
Brick: Yep.
Big Daddy: Who?

[He has lowered his voice.]

Brick: Someone int'rested in what we say to each other.
Big Daddy: Gooper?———*GOOPER!*

[After a discreet pause, Mae appears in the gallery door.]

Mae: Did you call Gooper, Big Daddy?
Big Daddy: Aw, it was you.
Mae: Do you want Gooper, Big Daddy?
Big Daddy: No, and I don't want you. I want some privacy here, while I'm having a confidential talk with my son Brick. Now it's too hot in here to close them doors, but if I have to close those fuckin' doors in order to have a private talk with my son Brick, just let me know and I'll close 'em. Because I hate eavesdroppers, I don't like any kind of sneakin' an' spyin'.
Mae: Why, Big Daddy—
Big Daddy: You stood on the wrong side of the moon, it threw your shadow!
Mae: I was just—
Big Daddy: You was just nothing but *spyin'* an' you *know* it!
Mae [*begins to sniff and sob*]: Oh, Big Daddy, you're so unkind for some reason to those that really love you!
Big Daddy: Shut up, shut up, shut up! I'm going to move you and Gooper out of that room next to this! It's none of your goddam business what goes on in here at night between Brick an' Maggie. You listen at night like a couple of rutten peekhole spies and go and give a report on what you hear to Big Mama an' she comes to me and says they say such and such and so and so about what they heard goin' on between Brick an' Maggie, and Jesus, it makes me sick. I'm goin' to move you an' Gooper out of that room, I can't stand sneakin' an' spyin', it makes me puke. . . .

[Mae throws back her head and rolls her eyes heavenward and extends her arms as if invoking God's pity for this unjust martyrdom; then she presses a handkerchief to her nose and flies from the room with a loud swish of skirts.]

Brick [*now at the liquor cabinet*]: They listen, do they?

Big Daddy: Yeah. They listen and give reports to Big Mama on what goes on in here between you and Maggie. They say that—

[He stops as if embarrassed.]

—You won't sleep with her, that you sleep on the sofa. Is that true or not true? If you don't like Maggie, get rid of Maggie!—What are you doin' there now?

Brick: Fresh'nin' up my drink.

Big Daddy: Son, you know you got a real liquor problem?

Brick: Yes, sir, yes, I know.

Big Daddy: Is that why you quit sports-announcing, because of this liquor problem?

Brick: Yes, sir, yes, sir, I guess so.

[He smiles vaguely and amiably at his father across his replenished drink.]

Big Daddy: Son, don't guess about it, it's too important.

Brick [*vaguely*]: Yes, sir.

Big Daddy: And listen to me, don't look at the damn chandelier. . . .

[Pause. Big Daddy's voice is husky.]

—Somethin' else we picked up at th' big fire sale in Europe.

[Another pause.]

Life is important. There's nothing else to hold onto. A man that drinks is throwing his life away. Don't do it, hold onto your life. There's nothing else to hold onto. . . .

Sit down over here so we don't have to raise our voices, the walls have ears in this place.

Brick [*hobbling over to sit on the sofa beside him*]: All right, Big Daddy.

Big Daddy: Quit!—how'd that come about? Some disappointment?

Brick: I don't know. Do you?

Big Daddy: I'm askin' you, God damn it! How in hell would I know if you don't?

Brick: I just got out there and found that I had a mouth full of cotton. I was always two or three beats behind what was goin' on on the field and so I—

Big Daddy: Quit!

Brick [*amiably*]: Yes, quit.

Big Daddy: Son?

Brick: Huh?

Big Daddy [*inhales loudly and deeply from his cigar; then bends suddenly a little forward, exhaling loudly and raising a hand to his forehead*]: —Whew!—ha ha!—I took in too much smoke, it made me a little lightheaded. . . .

[The mantel clock chimes.]

Why is it so damn hard for people to talk?
Brick: Yeah. . . .

[The clock goes on sweetly chiming till it has completed the stroke of ten.]

—Nice peaceful-soundin' clock, I like to hear it all night. . . .

[He slides low and comfortable on the sofa; Big Daddy sits up straight and rigid with some unspoken anxiety. All his gestures are tense and jerky as he talks. He wheezes and pants and sniffs through his nervous speech, glancing quickly, shyly, from time to time, at his son.]

Big Daddy: We got that clock the summer we wint to Europe, me an' Big Mama on that damn Cook's Tour, never had such an awful time in my life, I'm tellin' you, son, those gooks over there, they gouge your eyeballs out in their grand hotels. And Big Mama bought more stuff than you could haul in a couple of boxcars, that's no crap. Everywhere she wint on this whirlwind tour, she bought, bought, bought. Why, half that stuff she bought is still crated up in the cellar, under water last spring!

[He laughs.]

That Europe is nothin' on earth but a great big auction, that's all it is, that bunch of old worn-out places, it's just a big fire-sale, the whole fuckin' thing, an' Big Mama wint wild in it, why, you couldn't hold that woman with a mule's harness! Bought, bought, bought!—lucky I'm a rich man, yes siree, Bob, an' half that stuff is mildewin' in th' basement. It's lucky I'm a rich man, it sure is lucky, well, I'm a rich man, Brick, yep, I'm a mighty rich man.

[His eyes light up for a moment.]

Y'know how much I'm worth? Guess, Brick! Guess how much I'm worth!

[Brick smiles vaguely over his drink.]

Close on ten million in cash an' blue-chip stocks, outside, mind you, of twenty-eight thousand acres of the richest land this side of the valley Nile!

But a man can't buy his life with it, he can't buy back his life with it when his life has been spent, that's one thing not offered in the Europe fire-sale or in the American markets or any markets on earth, a man can't buy his life with it, he can't buy back his life when his life is finished. . . .

That's a sobering thought, a very sobering thought, and that's a thought that I was turning over in my head, over and over and over—until today. . . .

I'm wiser and sadder, Brick, for this experience which I just gone through. They's one thing else that I remember in Europe.

Brick: What is that, Big Daddy?

Big Daddy: The hills around Barcelona in the country of Spain and the children running over those bare hills in their bare skins beggin' like starvin' dogs with howls and screeches, and how fat the priests are on the streets of Barcelona, so many of them and so fat and so pleasant, ha ha!—Y'know I could feed that country? I got money enough to feed that goddam country, but the human animal is a selfish beast and I don't reckon the money I passed out there to those howling children in the hills around Barcelona would more than upholster the chairs in this room, I mean pay to put a new cover on this chair!

Hell, I threw them money like you'd scatter feed corn for chickens, I threw money at them just to get rid of them long enough to climb back into th' car and—drive away. . . .

And then in Morocco, them Arabs, why, I remember one day in Marrakech, that old walled Arab city, I set on a broken-down wall to have a cigar, it was fearful hot there and this Arab woman stood in the road and looked at me till I was embarrassed, she stood stock still in the dusty hot road and looked at me till I was embarrassed. But listen to this. She had a naked child with her, a little naked girl with her, barely able to toddle, and after a while she set this child on the ground and give her a push and whispered something to her.

This child come toward me, barely able t' walk, come toddling up to me and—

Jesus, it makes you sick t' remember a thing like this!

It stuck out its hand and tried to unbutton my trousers!

That child was not yet five! Can you believe me? Or do you think that I am making this up? I wint back to the hotel and said to Big Mama, Git packed! We're clearing out of this country. . . .

Brick: Big Daddy, you're on a talkin' jag tonight

Big Daddy [*ignoring this remark*]: Yes, sir, that's how it is, the human animal is a beast that dies but the fact that he's dying don't give him pity for others, no sir, it—

—Did you say something?

Brick: Yes.

Big Daddy: What?

Brick: Hand me over that crutch so I can get up.

Big Daddy: Where you goin'?

Brick: I'm takin' a little short trip to Echo Spring.

Big Daddy: To where?

Brick: Liquor cabinet. . . .

Big Daddy: Yes, sir, boy—

[He hands Brick the crutch.]

—the human animal is a beast that dies and if he's got money he buys and buys and buys and I think the reason he buys everything he can buy is that in the back of his mind he has the crazy hope that one of his purchases will be life everlasting!—Which it never can be. . . . The human animal is a beast that—

Brick [*at the liquor cabinet*]: Big Daddy, you sure are shootin' th' breeze here tonight.

[There is a pause and voices are heard outside.]

Big Daddy: I been quiet here lately, spoke not a word, just sat and stared into space. I had something heavy weighing on my mind but tonight that load was took off me. That's why I'm talking.—The sky looks diff'rent to me. . . .

Brick: You know what I like to hear most?

Big Daddy: What?

Brick: Solid quiet. Perfect unbroken quiet.

Big Daddy: Why?

Brick: Because it's more peaceful.

Big Daddy: Man, you'll hear a lot of that in the grave.

[He chuckles agreeably.]

Brick: Are you through talkin' to me?

Big Daddy: Why are you so anxious to shut me up?

Brick: Well, sir, ever so often you say to me, Brick, I want to have a talk with you, but when we talk, it never materializes. Nothing is said. You sit in a chair and gas about this and that and I look like I listen. I try to look like I listen, but I don't listen, not much. Communication is—awful hard between people an'—somehow between you and me, it just don't—happen.

Big Daddy: Have you ever been scared? I mean have you ever felt downright terror of something?

[He gets up.]

Just one moment.

[He looks off as if he were going to tell an important secret.]

Big Daddy: Brick?

Brick: What?

Big Daddy: Son, I thought I had it!

Brick: Had what? Had what, Big Daddy?

Big Daddy: Cancer!

Brick: Oh . . .

Big Daddy: I thought the old man made out of bones had laid his cold and heavy hand on my shoulder!

Brick: Well, Big Daddy, you kept a tight mouth about it.

Big Daddy: A pig squeals. A man keeps a tight mouth about it, in spite of a man not having a pig's advantage.

Brick: What advantage is that?

Big Daddy: Ignorance—of mortality—is a comfort. A man don't have that comfort, he's the only living thing that conceives of death, that knows what it is. The others go without knowing which is the way that anything living should go, go without knowing, without any knowledge of it, and yet a pig squeals, but a man sometimes, he can keep a tight mouth about it. Sometimes he—

[There is a deep, smoldering ferocity in the old man.]

—can keep a tight mouth about it. I wonder if—

Brick: What, Big Daddy?

Big Daddy: A whiskey highball would injure this spastic condition?

Brick: No, sir, it might do it good.

Big Daddy [*grins suddenly, wolfishly*]: *Jesus, I can't tell you! The sky is open! Christ, it's open again! It's open, boy, it's open!*

[Brick looks down at his drink.]

Brick: You feel better, Big Daddy?

Big Daddy: Better? Hell! I can breathe!—All of my life I been like a doubled up fist. . . .

[He pours a drink.]

—Poundin', smashin', drivin'!—now I'm going to loosen these doubled-up hands and touch things *easy* with them. . . .

[He spreads his hands as if caressing the air.]

You know what I'm contemplating?

Brick [*vaguely*]: No, sir. What are you contemplating?

Big Daddy: Ha ha!—*Pleasure!*—pleasure with *women!*

[Brick's smile fades a little but lingers.]

—Yes, boy. I'll tell you something that you might not guess. I still have desire for women and this is my sixty-fifth birthday.

Brick: I think that's mighty remarkable, Big Daddy.

Big Daddy: Remarkable?

Brick: *Admirable*, Big Daddy.

Big Daddy: You're damn right it is, remarkable and admirable both. I realize now that I never had me enough. I let many chances slip by because of scruples about it, scruples, convention—crap. . . . All that stuff is bull, bull, bull!—It took the shadow of death to make me see it. Now that shadow's lifted, I'm going to cut loose and have, what is it they call it, have me a—ball!

Brick: A ball, huh?

Big Daddy: That's right, a ball, a ball! Hell!—I slept with Big Mama till, let's see, five years ago, till I was sixty and she was fifty-eight, and never even liked her, never did!

[The phone has been ringing down the hall. Big Mama enters, exclaiming:]

Big Mama: Don't you men hear that phone ring? I heard it way out on the gall'ry.

Big Daddy: There's five rooms off this front gall'ry that you could go through. Why do you go through this one?

[Big Mama makes a playful face as she bustles out the hall door.]

Hunh!—Why, when Big Mama goes out of a room, I can't remember what that woman looks like—

Big Mama: Hello.
Big Daddy: —But when Big Mama comes back into the room, boy, then I see what she looks like, and I wish I didn't!

[Bends over laughing at this joke till it hurts his guts and he straightens with a grimace. The laugh subsides to a chuckle as he puts the liquor glass a little distrustfully down the table.]

Big Mama: Hello, Miss Sally.

[Brick has risen and hobbled to the gallery doors.]

Big Daddy: Hey! Where you goin'?
Brick: Out for a breather.
Big Daddy: Not yet you ain't. Stay here till this talk is finished, young fellow.
Brick: I thought it was finished, Big Daddy.
Big Daddy: It ain't even begun.
Brick: My mistake. Excuse me. I just wanted to feel that river breeze.
Big Daddy: Set back down in that chair.

[Big Mama's voice rises, carrying down the hall.]

Big Mama: Miss Sally, you're a case! You're a caution, Miss Sally.
Big Daddy: Jesus, she's talking to my old maid sister again.
Big Mama: Why didn't you give me a chance to explain it to you?
Big Daddy: Brick, this stuff burns me.
Big Mama: Well, goodbye, now, Miss Sally. You come down real soon. Big Daddy's dying to see you.
Big Daddy: Crap!
Big Mama: Yaiss, goodbye, Miss Sally. . . .

[She hangs up and bellows with mirth. Big Daddy groans and covers his ears as she approaches.
Bursting in:]

Big Daddy, that was Miss Sally callin' from Memphis again! You know what she done, Big Daddy? She called her doctor in Memphis to git him to tell her what that spastic thing is! Ha-*HAAAA!*—And called back to tell me how relieved she was that—Hey! Let me in!

[Big Daddy has been holding the door half closed against her.]

Big Daddy: Naw I ain't. I told you not to come and go through this room. You just back out and go through those five other rooms.
Big Mama: Big Daddy? Big Daddy? Oh, big Daddy!—You didn't mean those things you said to me, did you?

[He shuts door firmly against her but she still calls.]

Sweetheart? Sweetheart? Big Daddy? You didn't mean those awful things you said to me?—I know you didn't. I know you didn't mean those things in your heart. . . .

[The childlike voice fades with a sob and her heavy footsteps retreat down the hall. Brick has risen once more on his crutches and starts for the gallery again.]

Big Daddy: All I ask of that woman is that she leave me alone. But she can't admit to herself that she makes me sick. That comes of having slept with her too many years. Should of quit much sooner but that old woman she never got enough of it—and I was good in bed . . . I never should of wasted so much of it on her. . . . They say you got just so many and each one is numbered. Well, I got a few left in me, a few, and I'm going to pick me a good one to spend 'em on! I'm going to pick me a choice one, I don't care how much she costs, I'll smother her in—minks! Ha ha! I'll strip her naked and smother her in minks and choke her with diamonds! Ha ha! I'll strip her naked and choke her with diamonds and smother her with minks and hump her from hell to breakfast. *Ha aha ha ha ha!*

Mae [*gaily at door*]: Who's that laughin' in there?

Gooper: Is Big Daddy laughin' in there?

Big Daddy: Crap!—them two—*drips*. . . .

[He goes over and touches Brick's shoulder.]

Yes, son. Brick, boy.—I'm—*happy!* I'm happy, son, I'm happy!

[He chokes a little and bites his under lip, pressing his head quickly, shyly against his son's head and then, coughing with embarrassment, goes uncertainly back to the table where he set down the glass. He drinks and makes a grimace as it burns his guts. Brick sighs and rises with effort.]

What makes you so restless? Have you got ants in your britches?

Brick: Yes, sir . . .

Big Daddy: Why?

Brick: —Something—hasn't—happened. . . .

Big Daddy: Yeah? What is that!

Brick [*sadly*]: —the click. . . .

Big Daddy: Did you say click?

Brick: Yes, click.

Big Daddy: What click?

Brick: A click that I get in my head that makes me peaceful.

Big Daddy: I sure in hell don't know what you're talking about, but it disturbs me.

Brick: It's just a mechanical thing.

Big Daddy: What is a mechanical thing?

Brick: This click that I get in my head that makes me peaceful. I got to drink till I get it. It's just a mechanical thing, something like a—like a—like a—

Big Daddy: Like a—

Brick: Switch clicking off in my head, turning the hot light off and the cool night on and—

[He looks up, smiling sadly.]

—all of a sudden there's—peace!

Big Daddy [*whistles long and soft with astonishment; he goes back to Brick and clasps his son's two shoulders*]: Jesus! I didn't know it had gotten that bad with you. Why, boy, you're—*alcoholic!*

Brick: That's the truth, Big Daddy. I'm alcoholic.

Big Daddy: This shows how I—let things go!

Brick: I have to hear that little click in my head that makes me peaceful. Usually I hear it sooner than this, sometimes as early as—noon, but—

—Today it's—dilatory. . . .

—I just haven't got the right level of alcohol in my bloodstream yet!

[This last statement is made with energy as he freshens his drink.]

Big Daddy: Uh—huh. Expecting death made me blind. I didn't have no idea that a son of mine was turning into a drunkard under my nose.

Brick [*gently*]: Well, now you do, Big Daddy, the news has penetrated.

Big Daddy: Uh-huh, yes, now I do, the news has—penetrated. . . .

Brick: And so if you'll excuse me—

Big Daddy: No, I won't excuse you.

Brick: —I'd better sit by myself till I hear that click in my head, it's just a mechanical thing but it don't happen except when I'm alone or talking to no one. . . .

Big Daddy: You got a long, long time to sit still, boy, and talk to no one, but now you're talkin' to me. At least I'm talking to you. And you set there and listen until I tell you the conversation is over!

Brick: But this talk is like all the others we've ever had together in our lives! It's nowhere, nowhere!—it's—it's *painful*, Big Daddy. . . .

Big Daddy: All right, then let it be painful, but don't you move from that chair!—I'm going to remove that crutch. . . .

[He seizes the crutch and tosses it across room.]

Brick: I can hop on one foot, and if I fall, I can crawl!

Big Daddy: If you ain't careful you're gonna crawl off this plantation and then, by Jesus, you'll have to hustle your drinks along Skid Row!

Brick: That'll come, Big Daddy.

Big Daddy: Naw, it won't. You're my son and I'm going to straighten you out; now that *I'm* straightened out, I'm going to straighten out you!

Brick: Yeah?

Big Daddy: Today the report come in from Ochsner Clinic. Y'know what they told me?

[His face glows with triumph.]

The only thing that they could detect with all the instruments of science in that great hospital is a little spastic condition of the colon! And nerves torn to pieces by all that worry about it.

[A little girl bursts into room with a sparkler clutched in each fist, hops and shrieks like a monkey gone mad and rushes back out again as Big Daddy strikes at her.

[Silence. The two men stare at each other. A woman laughs gaily outside.]

I want you to know I breathed a sigh of relief almost as powerful as the Vicksburg tornado!

[There is laughter outside, running footsteps, the soft, plushy sound and light of exploding rockets.

Brick stares at him soberly for a long moment; then makes a sort of startled sound in his nostrils and springs up on one foot and hops across the room to grab his crutch, swinging on the furniture for support. He gets the crutch and flees as if in horror for the gallery. His father seizes him by the sleeve of his white silk pajamas.]

Stay here, you son of a bitch!—till I say go!

Brick: I can't.

Big Daddy: You sure in hell will, God damn it!

Brick: No, I can't. We talk, you talk, in—circles! We get no where, no where! It's always the same, you say you want to talk to me and don't have a fuckin' thing to say to me!

Big Daddy: Nothin' to say when I'm tellin' you I'm going to live when I thought I was dying?!

Brick: Oh—*that!*—Is that what you have to say to me?

Big Daddy: Why, you son of a bitch! Ain't that, ain't that—*important?!*

Brick: Well, you said that, that's said, and now I—

Big Daddy: Now you set back down.

Brick: You're all balled up, you—

Big Daddy: I ain't balled up!

Brick: You are, you're all balled up!

Big Daddy: Don't tell me what I am, you drunken whelp! I'm going to tear this coat sleeve off if you don't set down!

Brick: Big Daddy—

Big Daddy: Do what I tell you! I'm the boss here, now! I want you to know I'm back in the driver's seat now!

[Big Mama rushes in, clutching her great heaving bosom.]

Big Mama: Big Daddy!

Big Daddy: What in hell do you want in here, Big Mama?

Big Mama: Oh, Big Daddy! Why are you shouting like that? I just cain't *stainnnnnnnd*—it. . . .

Big Daddy [*raising the back of his hand above his head*]: *GIT!*—outa here.

[She rushes back out, sobbing.]

Brick [*softly, sadly*]: *Christ. . . .*

Big Daddy [*fiercely*]: Yeah! Christ!—is right . . .

[Brick breaks loose and hobbles toward the gallery.

Big Daddy jerks his crutch from under Brick so he steps with the injured ankle. He utters a hissing cry of anguish, clutches a chair and pulls it over on top of him on the floor.]

Son of a—tub of—hog fat. . . .

Brick: Big Daddy! Give me my crutch.

[Big Daddy throws the crutch out of reach.]

Give me that crutch, Big Daddy.

Big Daddy: Why do you drink?

Brick: Don't know, give me my crutch!

Big Daddy: You better think why you drink or give up drinking!

Brick: Will you please give me my crutch so I can get up off this floor?

Big Daddy: First you answer my question. Why do you drink? Why are you throwing your life away, boy, like somethin' disgusting you picked up on the street?

Brick [*getting onto his knees*]: Big Daddy, I'm in pain, I stepped on that foot.

Big Daddy: Good! I'm glad you're not too numb with the liquor in you to feel some pain!

Brick: You—spilled my—drink . . .

Big Daddy: I'll make a bargain with you. You tell me why you drink and I'll hand you one. I'll pour you the liquor myself and hand it to you.

Brick: Why do I drink?

Big Daddy: Yea! Why?

Brick: Give me a drink and I'll tell you.

Big Daddy: Tell me first!

Brick: I'll tell you in one word.

Big Daddy: What word?

Brick: DISGUST!

[The clock chimes softly, sweetly. Big Daddy gives it a short, outraged glance.]

Now how about that drink?

Big Daddy: What are you disgusted with? You got to tell me that, first. Otherwise being disgusted don't make no sense!

Brick: Give me my crutch.

Big Daddy: You heard me, you got to tell me what I asked you first.

Brick: I told you, I said to kill my disgust!

Big Daddy: DISGUST WITH WHAT!

Brick: You strike a hard bargain.

Big Daddy: What are you disgusted with?—an' I'll pass you the liquor.

Brick: I can hop on one foot, and if I fall, I can crawl.

Big Daddy: You want liquor that bad?

Brick [*dragging himself up, clinging to bedstead*]: Yeah, I want it that bad.

Big Daddy: If I give you a drink, will you tell me what it is you're disgusted with, Brick?

Brick: Yes, sir, I will try to.

[The old man pours him a drink and solemnly passes it to him. There is silence as Brick drinks.]

Have you ever heard the word "mendacity"?

Big Daddy: Sure. Mendacity is one of them five dollar words that cheap politicians throw back and forth at each other.
Brick: You know what it means?
Big Daddy: Don't it mean lying and liars?
Brick: Yes, sir, lying and liars.
Big Daddy: Has someone been lying to you?
Children [*chanting in chorus offstage*]: We want Big Dad-dee! We want Big Dad-dee!

[Gooper appears in the gallery door.]

Gooper: Big Daddy, the kiddies are shouting for you out there.
Big Daddy [*fiercely*]: Keep out, Gooper!
Gooper: 'Scuse *me!*

[Big Daddy slams the doors after Gooper.]

Big Daddy: Who's been lying to you, has Margaret been lying to you, has your wife been lying to you about something, Brick?
Brick: Not her. That wouldn't matter.
Big Daddy: Then who's been lying to you, and what about?
Brick: No one single person and no one lie. . . .
Big Daddy: Then what, what then, for Christ's sake?
Brick: —The whole, the whole—thing. . . .
Big Daddy: Why are you rubbing your head? You got a headache?
Brick: No, I'm tryin' to—
Big Daddy: —Concentrate, but you can't because your brain's all soaked with liquor, is that the trouble? Wet brain!

[He snatches the glass from Brick's hand.]

What do you know about this mendacity thing? Hell! I could write a book on it! Don't you know that? I could write a book on it and still not cover the subject? Well, I could, I could write a goddam book on it and still not cover the subject anywhere near enough!!—Think of all the lies I got to put up with!—Pretenses! Ain't that mendacity? Having to pretend stuff you don't think or feel or have any idea of? Having for instance to act like I care for Big Mama!—I haven't been able to stand the sight, sound, or smell of that woman for forty years now!—even when I *laid* her!—regular as a piston. . . .

Pretend to love that son of a bitch of a Gooper and his wife Mae and those five same screechers out there like parrots in a jungle? Jesus! Can't stand to look at 'em!

Church!—it bores the bejesus out of me but I go!—I go an' sit there and listen to the fool preacher!

Clubs!—Elks! Masons! Rotary!—*crap!*

[A spasm of pain makes him clutch his belly. He sinks into a chair and his voice is softer and hoarser.]

You I *do* like for some reason, did always have some kind of real feeling for—affection—respect—yes, always. . . .

You and being a success as a planter is all I ever had any devotion to in my whole life!—and that's the truth. . . .

I don't know why, but it is!

I've lived with mendacity!—Why can't *you* live with it? Hell, you *got* to live with it, there's nothing *else* to *live* with except mendacity, is there?

Brick: Yes, sir. Yes, sir, there is something else that you can live with!

Big Daddy: What?

Brick [*lifting his glass*]: This!—Liquor. . . .

Big Daddy: That's not living, that's dodging away from life.

Brick: I want to dodge away from it.

Big Daddy: Then why don't you kill yourself, man?

Brick: I like to drink. . . .

Big Daddy: Oh, God, I can't talk to you. . . .

Brick: I'm sorry, Big Daddy.

Big Daddy: Not as sorry as I am. I'll tell you something. A little while back when I thought my number was up—

[This speech should have torrential pace and fury.]

—before I found out it was just this—spastic—colon. I thought about you. Should I or should I not, if the jig was up, give you this place when I go—since I hate Gooper an' Mae an' know that they hate me, and since all five same monkeys are little Maes an' Goopers.—And I thought, No!—Then I thought, Yes!—I couldn't make up my mind. I hate Gooper and his five same monkeys and that bitch Mae! Why should I turn over twenty-eight thousand acres of the richest land this side of the valley Nile to not my kind?—But why in hell, on the other hand, Brick—should I subsidize a goddam fool on the bottle?—Liked or not liked, well, maybe even—*loved!*—Why should I do that?—Subsidize worthless behavior? Rot? Corruption?

Brick [*smiling*]: I understand.

Big Daddy: Well, if you do, you're smarter than I am, God damn it, because I don't understand. And this I will tell you frankly. I didn't make up my mind at all on that question and still to this day I ain't made out no will!—Well, now I don't *have* to. The pressure is gone. I can just wait and see if you pull yourself together or if you don't.

Brick: That's right, Big Daddy.

Big Daddy: You sound like you thought I was kidding.

Brick [*rising*]: No, sir, I know you're not kidding.

Big Daddy: But you don't care—?

Brick [*hobbling toward the gallery door*]: No, sir, I don't care. . . .

[He stands in the gallery doorway as the night sky turns pink and green and gold with successive flashes of light.]

Big Daddy: WAIT!—Brick. . . .

[His voice drops. Suddenly there is something shy, almost tender, in his restraining gesture.]

Don't let's—leave it like this, like them other talks we've had, we've always—talked around things, we've—just talked around things for some fuckin' reason, I don't know what, it's always like something was left not spoken, something avoided because neither of us was honest enough with the—other. . . .

Brick: I never lied to you, Big Daddy.

Big Daddy: Did I ever to *you?*

Brick: No, sir. . . .

Big Daddy: Then there is at least two people that never lied to each other.

Brick: But we've never *talked* to each other.

Big Daddy: We can *now.*

Brick: Big Daddy, there don't seem to be anything much to say.

Big Daddy: You say that you drink to kill your disgust with lying.

Brick: You said to give you a reason.

Big Daddy: Is liquor the only thing that'll kill this disgust?

Brick: Now. Yes.

Big Daddy: But not once, huh?

Brick: Not when I was still young an' believing. A drinking man's someone who wants to forget he isn't still young an' believing.

Big Daddy: Believing what?

Brick: Believing. . . .

Big Daddy: Believing *what?*

Brick [*stubbornly evasive*]: Believing. . . .

Big Daddy: I don't know what the hell you mean by believing and I don't think you know what you mean by believing, but if you still got sports in your blood, go back to sports announcing and—

Brick: Sit in a glass box watching games I can't play? Describing what I can't do while players do it? Sweating out their disgust and confusion in contests I'm not fit for? Drinkin' a coke, half bourbon, so I can stand it? That's no goddam good any more, no help—time just outran me, Big Daddy—got there first . . .

Big Daddy: I think you're passing the buck.

Brick: You know many drinkin' men?

Big Daddy [*with a slight, charming smile*]: I have known a fair number of that species.

Brick: Could any of them tell you why he drank?

Big Daddy: Yep, you're passin' the buck to things like time and disgust with "mendacity" and—crap!—if you got to use that kind of language about a thing, it's ninety-proof bull, and I'm not buying any.

Brick: I had to give you a reason to get a drink!

Big Daddy: You started drinkin' when your friend Skipper died.

[Silence for five beats. Then Brick makes a startled movement, reaching for his crutch.]

Brick: What are you suggesting?
Big Daddy: I'm suggesting nothing.

[The shuffle and clop of Brick's rapid hobble away from his father's steady, grave attention.]

—But Gooper an' Mae suggested that there was something not right exactly in your—

Brick [*stopping short downstage as if backed to a wall*]: "Not right"?
Big Daddy: Not, well, exactly *normal* in your friendship with—
Brick: They suggested that, too? I thought that was Maggie's suggestion.

[Brick's detachment is at last broken through. His heart is accelerated; his forehead sweat-beaded; his breath becomes more rapid and his voice hoarse. The thing they're discussing, timidly and painfully on the side of Big Daddy, fiercely, violently on Brick's side, is the inadmissible thing that Skipper died to disavow between them. The fact that if it existed it had to be disavowed to "keep face" in the world they lived in, may be at the heart of the "mendacity" that Brick drinks to kill his disgust with. It may be the root of his collapse. Or maybe it is only a single manifestation of it, not even the most important. The bird that I hope to catch in the net of this play is not the solution of one man's psychological problem. I'm trying to catch the true quality of experience in a group of people, that cloudy, flickering, evanescent—fiercely charged!—interplay of live human beings in the thundercloud of a common crisis. Some mystery should be left in the revelation of character in a play, just as a great deal of mystery is always left in the revelation of character in life, even in one's own character to himself. This does not absolve the playwright of his duty to observe and probe as clearly and deeply as he legitimately *can: but it should steer him away from "pat" conclusions, facile definitions which make a play just a play, not a snare for the truth of human experience.*

The following scene should be played with great concentration, with most of the power leashed but palpable in what is left unspoken.]

Who else's suggestion is it, is it *yours?* How many others thought that Skipper and I were—

Big Daddy [*gently*]: Now, hold on, hold on a minute, son.—I knocked around in my time.
Brick: What's that got to do with—
Big Daddy: I said "Hold on!"—I bummed, I bummed this country till I was—
Brick: Whose suggestion, who else's suggestion is it?
Big Daddy: Slept in hobo jungles and railroad Y's and flophouses in all cities before I—
Brick: Oh, *you* think so, too, you call me your son and a queer. Oh! Maybe that's why you put Maggie and me in this room that was Jack Straw's and Peter Ochello's, in which that pair of old sisters slept in a double bed where both of 'em died!
Big Daddy: Now just don't go throwing rocks at—

[Suddenly Reverend Tooker appears in the gallery doors, his head slightly, playfully, fatuously cocked, with a practiced clergyman's smile, sincere as a bird call blown on a hunter's whistle, the living embodiment of the pious, conventional lie.

[Big Daddy gasps a little at this perfectly timed, but incongruous, apparition.]

—What're you lookin' for, Preacher?

Reverend Tooker: The gentleman's lavatory, ha ha!—heh, heh . . .

Big Daddy [*with strained courtesy*]:—Go back out and walk down to the other end of the gallery, Reverend Tooker, and use the bathroom connected with my bedroom, and if you can't find it, ask them where it is!

Reverend Tooker: Ah, thanks.

[He goes out with a deprecatory chuckle.]

Big Daddy: It's hard to talk in this place . . .

Brick: Son of a—!

Big Daddy [*leaving a lot unspoken*]:—I seen all things and understood a lot of them, till 1910. Christ, the year that—I had worn my shoes through, hocked my—I hopped off a yellow dog freight car half a mile down the road, slept in a wagon of cotton outside the gin—Jack Straw an' Peter Ochello took me in. Hired me to manage this place which grew into this one.—When Jack Straw died—why, old Peter Ochello quit eatin' like a dog does when its master's dead, and died, too!

Brick: Christ!

Big Daddy: I'm just saying I understand such—

Brick [*violently*]: Skipper is dead. I have not quit eating!

Big Daddy: No, but you started drinking.

[Brick wheels on his crutch and hurls his glass across the room shouting.]

Brick: YOU THINK SO, TOO?

[Footsteps run on the gallery. There are women's calls.
Big Daddy goes toward the door.
Brick is transformed, as if a quiet mountain blew suddenly up in volcanic flame.]

Brick: You think so, too? You think so, too? You think me an' Skipper did, did, did!—*sodomy!*—together?

Big Daddy: Hold—!

Brick: That what you—

Big Daddy: —*ON*—a minute!

Brick: You think we did dirty things between us, Skipper an'—

Big Daddy: Why are you shouting like that? Why are you—

Brick: —Me, is that what you think of Skipper, is that—

Big Daddy: —so excited? I don't think nothing. I don't know nothing. I'm simply telling you what—

Brick: You think that Skipper and me were a pair of dirty old men?

Big Daddy: Now that's—

Brick: Straw? Ochello? A couple of—

Big Daddy: Now just—

Brick: —fucking sissies? Queers? Is that what you—

Big Daddy: Shhh.

Brick: —think?

[He loses his balance and pitches to his knees without noticing the pain. He grabs the bed and drags himself up.]

Big Daddy: Jesus!—Whew. . . . Grab my hand!
Brick: Naw, I don't want your hand. . . .
Big Daddy: Well, I want yours. Git up!

[He draws him up, keeps an arm about him with concern and affection.]

You broken out in a sweat! You're panting like you'd run a race with—
Brick [*freeing himself from his father's hold*]: Big Daddy, you shock me, Big Daddy, you, you—*shock* me! Talkin' so—

[He turns away from his father.]

—casually!—about a—thing like that . . .

—Don't you know how people *feel* about things like that? How, how *disgusted* they are by things like that? Why, at Ole Miss when it was discovered a pledge to our fraternity, Skipper's and mine, did a, *attempted* to do a, unnatural thing with—

We not only dropped him like a hot rock!—We told him to git off the campus, and he did, he got!—All the way to—

[He halts, breathless.]

Big Daddy: —Where?
Brick: —North Africa, last I heard!
Big Daddy: Well, I have come back from further away than that, I have just now returned from the other side of the moon, death's country, son, and I'm not easy to shock by anything here.

[He comes downstage and faces out.]

Always, anyhow, lived with too much space around me to be infected by ideas of other people. One thing you can grow on a big place more important than cotton!—is *tolerance!*—I grown it.

[He returns toward Brick.]

Brick: Why can't exceptional friendship, *real, real, deep, deep friendship!* between two men be respected as something clean and decent without being thought of as—
Big Daddy: It can, it is, for God's sake.
Brick: —*Fairies. . . .*

[In his utterance of this word, we gauge the wide and profound reach of the conventional mores he got from the world that crowned him with early laurel.]

Big Daddy: I told Mae an' Gooper—

Brick: Frig Mae and Gooper, frig all dirty lies and liars!—Skipper and me had a clean, true thing between us!—had a clean friendship, practically all our lives, till Maggie got the idea you're talking about. Normal? No!—It was too rare to be normal, any true thing between two people is too rare to be normal. Oh, once in a while he put his hand on my shoulder or I'd put mine on his, oh, maybe even, when we were touring the country in pro-football an' shared hotel-rooms we'd reach across the space between the two beds and shake hands to say goodnight, yeah, one or two times we—

Big Daddy: Brick, nobody thinks that that's not normal!

Brick: Well, they're mistaken, it was! It was a pure an' true thing an' that's not normal.

Mae [*off stage*]: Big Daddy, they're startin' the fireworks.

[They both stare straight at each other for a long moment. The tension breaks and both turn away as if tired.]

Big Daddy: Yeah, it's—hard t'—talk. . . .

Brick: All right, then, let's—let it go. . . .

Big Daddy: Why did Skipper crack up? Why have you?

[Brick looks back at his father again. He has already decided, without knowing that he has made this decision, that he is going to tell his father that he is dying of cancer. Only this could even the score between them: one inadmissible thing in return for another.]

Brick [*ominously*]: All right. You're asking for it, Big Daddy. We're finally going to have that real true talk you wanted. It's too late to stop it, now, we got to carry it through and cover every subject.

[He hobbles back to the liquor cabinet.]

Uh-huh.

[He opens the ice bucket and picks up the silver tongs with slow admiration of their frosty brightness.]

Maggie declares that Skipper and I went into pro-football after we left "Ole Miss" because we were scared to grow up . . .

[He moves downstage with the shuffle and clop of a cripple on a crutch. As Margaret did when her speech became "recitative," he looks out into the house, commanding its attention by his direct, concentrated gaze—a broken, "tragically elegant" figure telling simply as much as he knows of "the Truth":]

—Wanted to—keep on tossing—those long, long!—high, high!—passes that—couldn't be intercepted except by time, the aerial attack that made us famous! And so we did, we did, we kept it up for one season, that aerial attack, we held it high!—Yeah, but—

—that summer, Maggie, she laid the law down to me, said, Now or never, and so I married Maggie. . . .

Big Daddy: How was Maggie in bed?

Brick [*wryly*]: Great! the greatest!

[Big Daddy nods as if he thought so.]

She went on the road that fall with the Dixie Stars. Oh, she made a great show of being the world's best sport. She wore a—wore a—tall bearskin cap! A shako, they call it, a dyed moleskin coat, a moleskin coat dyed red!—Cut up crazy! Rented hotel ballrooms for victory celebrations, wouldn't cancel them when it—turned out—defeat. . . .

MAGGIE THE CAT! Ha ha!

[Big Daddy nods.]

—But Skipper, he had some fever which came back on him which doctors couldn't explain and I got that injury—turned out to be just a shadow on the X-ray plate—and a touch of bursitis. . . .

I lay in a hospital bed, watched our games on TV, saw Maggie on the bench next to Skipper when he was hauled out of a game for stumbles, fumbles!—Burned me up the way she hung on his arm!—Y'know, I think that Maggie had always felt sort of left out because she and me never got any closer together than two people just get in bed, which is not much closer than two cats on a—fence humping. . . .

So! She took this time to work on poor dumb Skipper. He was a less than average student at Ole Miss, you know that, don't you?!—Poured in his mind the dirty, false idea that what we were, him and me, was a frustrated case of that ole pair of sisters that lived in this room, Jack Straw and Peter Ochello!—He, poor Skipper, went to bed with Maggie to prove it wasn't true, and when it didn't work out, he thought it *was* true!—Skipper broke in two like a rotten stick—nobody ever turned so fast to a lush—or died of it so quick. . . .

—Now are you satisfied?

[Big Daddy has listened to this story, dividing the grain from the chaff. Now he looks at his son.]

Big Daddy: Are *you* satisfied?

Brick: With what?

Big Daddy: That half-ass story!

Brick: What's half-ass about it?

Big Daddy: Something's left out of that story. What did you leave out?

[The phone has started ringing in the hall.]

Gooper [*off stage*]: Hello.

[As if it reminded him of something, Brick glances suddenly toward the sound and says:]

Brick: Yes!—I left out a long-distance call which I had from Skipper—

Gooper: Speaking, go ahead.
Brick: —In which he made a drunken confession to me and on which I hung up!
Gooper: No.
Brick: —Last time we spoke to each other in our lives . . .
Gooper: No, sir.
Big Daddy: You musta said something to him before you hung up.
Brick: What could I say to him?
Big Daddy: Anything. Something.
Brick: Nothing.
Big Daddy: Just hung up?
Brick: Just hung up.
Big Daddy: Uh-huh. Anyhow now!—we have tracked down the lie with which you're disgusted and which you are drinking to kill your disgust with, Brick. You been passing the buck. This disgust with mendacity is disgust with yourself.

You!—dug the grave of your friend and kicked him in it!—before you'd face truth with him!

Brick: His truth, not *mine!*
Big Daddy: His truth, okay! But you wouldn't face it with him!
Brick: Who *can* face truth? Can *you?*
Big Daddy: Now don't start passin' the rotten buck again, boy!
Brick: How about these birthday congratulations, these many, many happy returns of the day, when ev'rybody knows there won't be any except you!

[Gooper, who has answered the hall phone, lets out a high, shrill laugh; the voice becomes audible saying: "No, no, you got it all wrong! Upside down! Are you crazy?"

Brick suddenly catches his breath as he realized that he has made a shocking disclosure. He hobbles a few paces, then freezes, and without looking at his father's shocked face, says:]

Let's, let's—go out, now, and—watch the fireworks. Come on, Big Daddy.

[Big Daddy moves suddenly forward and grabs hold of the boy's crutch like it was a weapon for which they were fighting for possession.]

Big Daddy: Oh, no, no! No one's going out! What did you start to say?
Brick: I don't remember.
Big Daddy: "Many happy returns when they know there won't be any"?
Brick: Aw, hell, Big Daddy, forget it. Come on out on the gallery and look at the fireworks they're shooting off for your birthday. . . .
Big Daddy: First you finish that remark you were makin' before you cut off. "Many happy returns when they know there won't be any"?—Ain't that what you just said?
Brick: Look, now. I can get around without that crutch if I have to but it would be a lot easier on the furniture an' glassware if I didn' have to go swinging along like Tarzan of th'—
Big Daddy: FINISH! WHAT YOU WAS SAYIN'!

[An eerie green glow shows in sky behind him.]

Brick [*sucking the ice in his glass, speech becoming thick*]: Leave th' place to Gooper and Mae an' their five little same little monkeys. All I want is—

Big Daddy: "LEAVE TH' PLACE," did you say?

Brick [*vaguely*]: All twenty-eight thousand acres of the richest land this side of the valley Nile.

Big Daddy: Who said I was "leaving the place" to Gooper or anybody? This is my sixty-fifth birthday! I got fifteen years or twenty years left in me! I'll outlive *you!* I'll bury you an' have to pay for your coffin!

Brick: Sure. Many happy returns. Now let's go watch the fireworks, come on, let's

Big Daddy: Lying, have they been lying? About the report from th'—clinic? Did they, did they—find something?—*Cancer.* Maybe?

Brick: Mendacity is a system that we live in. Liquor is one way out an' death's the other. . . .

[He takes the crutch from Big Daddy's loose grip and swings out on the gallery leaving the doors open.

A song, "Pick a Bale of Cotton," is heard.]

Mae [*appearing in door*]: *Oh, Big Daddy, the field hands are singin' fo' you!*

Brick: I'm sorry, Big Daddy. My head don't work any more and it's hard for me to understand how anybody could care if he lived or died or was dying or cared about anything but whether or not there was liquor left in the bottle and so I said what I said without thinking. In some ways I'm no better than the others, in some ways worse because I'm less alive. Maybe it's being alive that makes them lie, and being almost *not* alive makes me sort of accidentally truthful—I don't know but—anyway—we've been friends . . .

—And being friends is telling each other the truth. . . .

[There is a pause.]

You told *me!* I told *you!*

Big Daddy [*slowly and passionately*]: CHRIST—DAMN—

Gooper [*off stage*]: Let her go!

[Fireworks off stage right.]

Big Daddy: —ALL—LYING SONS OF—LYING BITCHES!

[He straightens at last and crosses to the inside door. At the door he turns and looks back as if he had some desperate question he couldn't put into words. Then he nods reflectively and says in a hoarse voice:]

Yes, all liars, all liars, all lying dying liars!

[This is said slowly, slowly, with a fierce revulsion. He goes on out.]

—Lying! Dying! Liars!

[Brick remains motionless as the lights dim out and the curtain falls.]

CURTAIN

ACT THREE

There is no lapse of time. Big Daddy is seen leaving as at the end of ACT II.

Big Daddy: ALL LYIN'—DYIN'!—LIARS! LIARS!—LIARS!

[Margaret enters.]

Margaret: Brick, what in the name of God was goin' on in this room?

[Dixie and Trixie enter through the doors and circle around Margaret shouting. Mae enters from the lower gallery window.]

Mae: Dixie, Trixie, you quit that!

[Gooper enters through the doors.]

Gooper, will y' please get these kiddies to bed right now!

Gooper: Mae, you seen Big Mama?

Mae: Not yet.

[Gooper and kids exit through the doors. Reverend Tooker enters through the windows.]

Reverend Tooker: Those kiddies are so full of vitality. I think I'll have to be starting back to town.

Mae: Not yet, Preacher. You know we regard you as a member of this family, one of our closest an' dearest, so you just got t' be with us when Doc Baugh gives Big Mama th' actual truth about th' report from the clinic.

Margaret: Where do you think you're going?

Brick: Out for some air.

Margaret: Why'd Big Daddy shout "Liars"?

Mae: Has Big Daddy gone to bed, Brick?

Gooper [*entering*]: Now where is that old lady?

Reverend Tooker: I'll look for her.

[He exits to the gallery.]

Mae: Cain'tcha find her, Gooper?

Gooper: She's avoidin' this talk.

Mae: I think she senses somethin'.

Margaret [*going out on the gallery to Brick*]: Brick, they're goin' to tell Big Mama the truth about Big Daddy and she's goin' to need you.

Doctor Baugh: This is going to be painful.

Mae: Painful things caint always be avoided.

Reverend Tooker: I see Big Mama.

Gooper: Hey, Big Mama, come here.

Mae: Hush, Gooper, don't holler.

Big Mama [*entering*]: Too much smell of burnt fireworks makes me feel a little bit sick at my stomach.—Where is Big Daddy?

Mae: That's what I want to know, where has Big Daddy gone?

Big Mama: He must have turned in, I reckon he went to baid . . .
Gooper: Well, then, now we can talk.
Big Mama: What *is* this talk, *what* talk?

[Margaret appears on the gallery, talking to Doctor Baugh.]

Margaret [*musically*]: My family freed their slaves ten years before abolition. My great-great-grandfather gave his slaves their freedom five years before the War between the States started!
Mae: Oh, for God's sake! Maggie's climbed back up in her family tree!
Margaret [*sweetly*]: What, Mae?

[The pace must be very quick: great Southern animation.]

Big Mama [*addressing them all*]: I think Big Daddy was just worn out. He loves his family, he loves to have them around him, but it's a strain on his nerves. He wasn't himself tonight, Big Daddy wasn't himself, I could tell he was all worked up.
Reverend Tooker: I think he's remarkable.
Big Mama: Yaisss! Just remarkable. Did you all notice the food he ate at that table? Did you all notice the supper he put away? Why he ate like a hawss!
Gooper: I hope he doesn't regret it.
Big Mama: What? Why that man—ate a huge piece of cawn bread with molasses on it! Helped himself twice to hoppin' John.
Margaret: Big Daddy loves hoppin' John.—We had a real country dinner.
Big Mama [*overlapping Margaret*]: Yaiss, he simply adores it! an' candied yams? Son? That man put away enough food at that table to stuff a *field* hand!
Gooper [*with grim relish*]: I hope he don't have to pay for it later on . . .
Big Mama [*fiercely*]: What's *that*, Gooper?
Mae: Gooper says he hopes Big Daddy doesn't suffer tonight.
Big Mama: Oh, shoot, Gooper says, Gooper says! Why should Big Daddy suffer for satisfying a normal appetite? There's nothin' wrong with that man but nerves, he's sound as a dollar! And now he knows he is an' that's why he ate such a supper. He had a big load off his mind, knowin' he wasn't doomed t'—what he thought he was doomed to . . .
Margaret [*sadly and sweetly*]: Bless his old sweet soul . . .
Big Mama [*vaguely*]: Yais, bless his heart, where's Brick?
Mae: Outside.
Gooper: —Drinkin' . . .
Big Mama: I know he's drinkin'. Cain't I see he's drinkin' without you continually tellin' me that boy's drinkin'?
Margaret: Good for you, Big Mama!

[She applauds.]

Big Mama: Other people *drink* and *have* drunk an' will *drink*, as long as they make that stuff an' put it in bottles.
Margaret: That's the truth. I never trusted a man that didn't drink.

Big Mama: Brick? Brick!

Margaret: He's still on the gall'ry. I'll go bring him in so we can talk.

Big Mama [*Worriedly*]: I don't know what this mysterious family conference is about.

[Awkward silence. Big Mama looks from face to face, then belches slightly and mutters, "Excuse me . . ." She opens an ornamental fan suspended about her throat. A black lace fan to go with her black lace gown, and fans her wilting corsage, sniffing nervously and looking from face to face in the uncomfortable silence as Margaret calls "Brick?" and Brick sings to the moon on the gallery.]

Margaret: Brick, they're gonna tell Big Mama the truth an' she's gonna need you.

Big Mama: I don't know what's wrong here, you all have such long faces! Open that door on the hall and let some air circulate through here, will you please, Gooper?

Mae: I think we'd better leave that door closed, Big Mama, till after the talk.

Margaret: Brick!

Big Mama: Reveren' Tooker, will *you* please open that door?

Reverend Tooker: I sure will, Big Mama.

Mae: I just didn't think we ought t' take any chance of Big Daddy hearin' a word of this discussion.

Big Mama: I swear! Nothing's going to be said in Big Daddy's house that he caint hear if he want to!

Gooper: Well, Big Mama, it's—

[Mae gives him a quick, hard poke to shut him up. He glares at her fiercely as she circles before him like a burlesque ballerina, raising her skinny bare arms over her head, jangling her bracelets, exclaiming:]

Mae: A breeze! A breeze!

Reverend Tooker: I think this house is the coolest house in the Delta.—Did you all know that Halsey Banks's widow put air-conditioning units in the church and rectory at Friar's Point in memory of Halsey?

[General conversation has resumed; everybody is chatting so that the stage sounds like a bird cage.]

Gooper: Too bad nobody cools your church off for you. I bet you sweat in that pulpit these hot Sundays, Reverend Tooker.

Reverend Tooker: Yes, my vestments are drenched. Last Sunday the gold in my chasuble faded into the purple.

Gooper: Reveren', you musta been preachin' hell's fire last Sunday.

Mae [*at the same time to Doctor Baugh*]: You reckon those vitamin B12 injections are what they're cracked up t' be, Doc Baugh?

Doctor Baugh: Well, if you want to be stuck with something I guess they're as good to be stuck with as anything else.

Big Mama [*at the gallery door*]: *Maggie, Maggie, aren't you comin' with Brick?*

Mae [*suddenly and loudly, creating a silence*]: *I have a strange feeling, I have a peculiar feeling!*

Big Mama [*turning from the gallery*]: What feeling?
Mae: That Brick said somethin' he shouldn't of said t' Big Daddy.
Big Mama: Now what on earth could Brick of said t' Big Daddy that he shouldn't say?
Gooper: Big Mama, there's somethin'—
Mae: NOW, WAIT!

[She rushes up to Big Mama and gives her a quick hug and kiss. Big Mama pushes her impatiently off.]

Doctor Baugh: In my day they had what they call the Keeley cure for heavy drinkers.
Big Mama: Shoot!
Doctor Baugh: But now I understand they just take some kind of tablets.
Gooper: They call them "Annie Bust" tablets.
Big Mama: *Brick* don't need to take *nothing'*.

[Brick and Margaret appear in gallery doors, Big Mama—unaware of his presence behind her.]

That boy is just broken up over Skipper's death. You know how poor Skipper died. They gave him a big, big dose of that sodium amytal stuff at his home and then they called the ambulance and give him another big, big dose of it at the hospital and that and all of the alcohol in his system fo' months an' months just proved too much for his heart . . . I'm scared of needles! I'm more scared of a needle than the knife . . . I think more people have been needled out of this world than—

[She stops short and wheels about.]

Oh—here's Brick! My precious baby—

[She turns upon Brick with short, fat arms extended, at the same time uttering a loud, short sob, which is both comic and touching. Brick smiles and bows slightly, making a burlesque gesture of gallantry for Margaret to pass before him into the room. Then he hobbles on his crutch directly to the liquor cabinet and there is absolute silence, with everybody looking at Brick as everybody has always looked at Brick when he spoke or moved or appeared. One by one he drops ice cubes in his glass, then suddenly, but not quickly, looks back over his shoulder with a wry, charming smile, and says:]

Brick: I'm sorry! Anyone else?
Big Mama [*sadly*]: No, son. I *wish* you wouldn't!
Brick: I wish I didn't have to, Big Mama, but I'm still waiting for that click in my head which makes it all smooth out!
Big Mama: Ow, Brick, you—BREAK MY HEART!
Margaret [*at same time*]: *Brick, go sit with Big Mama!*
Big Mama: I just cain't staiiiiii-nnnnnnnd-it . . .

[She sobs.]

Mae: Now that we're all assembled—

Gooper: We kin talk . . .
Big Mama: Breaks my heart . . .
Margaret: Sit with Big Mama, Brick, and hold her hand.

[Big Mama sniffs very loudly three times, almost like three drumbeats in the pocket of silence.]

Brick: You do that, Maggie. I'm a restless cripple. I got to stay on my crutch.

[Brick hobbles to the gallery door; leans there as if waiting.

Mae sits beside Big Mama, while Gooper moves in front and sits on the end of the couch, facing her. Reverend Tooker moves nervously into the space between them; on the other side, Doctor Baugh stands looking at nothing in particular and lights a cigar. Margaret turns away.]

Big Mama: Why're you all *surroundin'* me—like this? Why're you all starin' at me like this an' makin' signs at each other?

[Reverend Tooker steps back startled.]

Mae: Calm yourself, Big Mama.
Big Mama: Calm you'self, *you'self,* Sister Woman. How could I calm myself with everyone starin' at me as if big drops of blood had broken out on m'face? What's this all about, annh! What?

[Gooper coughs and takes a center position.]

Gooper: Now, Doc Baugh.
Mae: Doc Baugh?
Gooper: Big Mama wants to know the complete truth about the report we got from the Ochsner Clinic.
Mae [*eagerly*]: —on Big Daddy's condition!
Gooper: Yais, on Big Daddy's condition, we got to face it.
Doctor Baugh: Well . . .
Big Mama [*terrified, rising*]: Is there? Something? Something that I? Don't—know?

[In these few words, this startled, very soft, question, Big Mama reviews the history of her forty-five years with Big Daddy, her great, almost embarrassingly true-hearted and simple-minded devotion to Big Daddy, who must have had something Brick has, who made himself loved so much by the "simple expedient" of not loving enough to disturb his charming detachment, also once coupled, like Brick, with virile beauty.

Big Mama has a dignity at this moment; she almost stops being fat.]

Doctor Baugh [*after a pause, uncomfortably*]: Yes?—Well—
Big Mama: I!!!—want to—*knowwwwww* . . .

[Immediately she thrusts her fist to her mouth as if to deny that statement. Then for some curious reason, she snatches the withered corsage from her breast and hurls it on the floor and steps on it with her short, fat feet.]

Somebody must be lyin'!—I want to know!

Mae: Sit down, Big Mama, sit down on this sofa.
Margaret: Brick, go sit with Big Mama.
Big Mama: What is it, what is it?
Doctor Baugh: I never have seen a more thorough examination than Big Daddy Pollitt was given in all my experience with the Ochsner Clinic.
Gooper: It's one of the best in the country.
Mae: It's THE best in the country—bar *none!*

[For some reason she gives Gooper a violent poke as she goes past him. He slaps at her hand without removing his eyes from his mother's face.]

Doctor Baugh: Of course they were ninety-nine and nine-tenths per cent sure before they even started.
Big Mama: Sure of what, sure of what, sure of—*what?—what?*

[She catches her breath in a startled sob. Mae kisses her quickly. She thrusts Mae fiercely away from her, staring at the Doctor.]

Mae: Mommy, be a brave girl!
Brick [*in the doorway, softly*]: "By the light, by the light, Of the sil-ve-ry mo-oo-n . . ."
Gooper: Shut up!—Brick.
Brick: Sorry . . .

[He wanders out on the gallery.]

Doctor Baugh: But now, you see, Big Mama, they cut a piece off this growth, a specimen of the tissue and—
Big Mama: Growth? You told Big Daddy—
Doctor Baugh: Now wait.
Big Mama [fiercely]: You told me and Big Daddy there wasn't a thing wrong with him but—
Mae: Big Mama, they always—
Gooper: Let Doc Baugh talk, will yuh?
Big Mama: —little spastic condition of—

[Her breath gives out in a sob.]

Doctor Baugh: Yes, that's what we told Big Daddy. But we had this bit of tissue run through the laboratory and I'm sorry to say the test was positive on it. It's—well—malignant . . .

[Pause]

Big Mama: —Cancer?! Cancer?!

[Doctor Baugh nods gravely. Big Mama gives a long gasping cry.]

Mae and Gooper: Now, now, now, Big Mama, you had to know . . .
Big Mama: WHY DIDN'T THEY CUT IT OUT OF HIM? HANH? HANH?
Doctor Baugh: Involved too much, Big Mama, too many organs affected.

Mae: Big Mama, the liver's affected and so's the kidneys, both! It's gone way past what they call a—

Gooper: A surgical risk.

Mae: —Uh-huh . . .

[Big Mama draws a breath like a dying gasp.]

Reverend Tooker: Tch, tch, tch, tch, tch!

Doctor Baugh: Yes it's gone past the knife.

Mae: That's why he's turned yellow, Mommy!

Big Mama: Git away from me, git away from me, Mae!

[She rises abruptly.]

I want Brick! Where's Brick? Where is my only son?

Mae: Mama! Did she say "*only* son"?

Gooper: What does that make *me*?

Mae: A sober responsible man with five precious children!—*Six!*

Big Mama: I want Brick to tell me! Brick! Brick!

Margaret [*rising from her reflections in a corner*]: Brick was so upset he went back out.

Big Mama: Brick!

Margaret: Mama, let *me* tell you!

Big Mama: No, no, leave me alone, you're not my blood!

Gooper: Mama, I'm your son! Listen to *me!*

Mae: Gooper's your son, he's your first-born!

Big Mama: Gooper never liked Daddy.

Mae [*as if terribly shocked*]: *That's not TRUE!*

[There is a pause. The minister coughs and rises.]

Reverend Tooker [*to Mae*]: I think I'd better slip away at this point.

[Discreetly]

Good night, good night, everybody, and God bless you all . . . on this place . . .

[He slips out.]

[Mae coughs and points at Big Mama.]

Gooper: Well, Big Mama . . .

[He sighs.]

Big Mama: It's all a mistake, I know it's just a bad dream.

Doctor Baugh: We're gonna keep Big Daddy as comfortable as we can.

Big Mama: Yes, it's just a bad dream, that's all it is, it's just an awful dream.

Gooper: In my opinion Big Daddy is having some pain but won't admit that he has it.

Big Mama: Just a dream, a bad dream.

Doctor Baugh: That's what lots of them do, they think if they don't admit they're having the pain they can sort of escape the fact of it.

Gooper [*with relish*]: Yes, they get sly about it, they get real sly about it.
Mae: Gooper and I think—
Gooper: Shut up, Mae! Big Mama, I think—Big Daddy ought to be started on morphine.
Big Mama: Nobody's going to give Big Daddy morphine.
Doctor Baugh: Now, Big Mama, when that pain strikes it's going to strike mighty hard and Big Daddy's going to need the needle to bear it.
Big Mama: I tell you, nobody's going to give him morphine.
Mae: Big Mama, you don't want to see Big Daddy suffer, you know you—

[Gooper, standing beside her, gives her a savage poke.]

Doctor Baugh [*placing a package on the table*]: I'm leaving this stuff here, so if there's a sudden attack you all won't have to send out for it.
Mae: I know how to give a hypo.
Big Mama: Nobody's gonna give Big Daddy morphine.
Gooper: Mae took a course in nursing during the war.
Margaret: Somehow I don't think Big Daddy would want Mae to give him a hypo.
Mae: You think he'd want *you* to do it?
Doctor Baugh: Well . . .

[Doctor Baugh rises.]

Gooper: Doctor Baugh is goin'.
Doctor Baugh: Yes, I got to be goin'. Well, keep your chin up, Big Mama.
Gooper [with jocularity]: She's gonna keep *both* chins up, aren't you, Big Mama?

[Big Mama sobs.]

Now stop that, Big Mama.
Gooper [*at the door with Doctor Baugh*]: Well, Doc, we sure do appreciate all you done. I'm telling you, we're surely obligated to you for—

[Doctor Baugh has gone out without a glance at him.]

—I guess that doctor has got a lot on his mind but it wouldn't hurt him to act a little more human . . .

[Big Mama sobs.]

Now be a brave girl, Mommy.
Big Mama: It's not true, I know that it's just not true!
Gooper: Mama, those tests are infallible!
Big Mama: Why are you so determined to see your father daid?
Mae: Big Mama!
Margaret [*gently*]: I know what Big Mama means.
Mae [*fiercely*]: Oh, do you?
Margaret [*quietly and very sadly*]: Yes, I think I do.
Mae: For a newcomer in the family you sure do show a lot of understanding.
Margaret: Understanding is needed on this place.

Mae: I guess you must have needed a lot of it in your family, Maggie, with your father's liquor problem and now you've got Brick with his!

Margaret: Brick does not have a liquor problem at all. Brick is devoted to Big Daddy. This thing is a terrible strain on him.

Big Mama: Brick is Big Daddy's boy, but he drinks too much and it worries me and Big Daddy, and, Margaret, you've got to co-operate with us, you've got to co-operate with Big Daddy and me in getting Brick straightened out. Because it will break Big Daddy's heart if Brick don't pull himself together and take hold of things.

Mae: Take hold of *what* things, Big Mama?

Big Mama: The place.

[There is a quick violent look between Mae and Gooper.]

Gooper: Big Mama, you've had a shock.

Mae: Yais, we've all had a shock, but . . .

Gooper: Let's be realistic—

Mae: —Big Daddy would never, would *never*, be foolish enough to—

Gooper: —put this place in irresponsible hands!

Big Mama: Big Daddy ain't going to leave the place in anybody's hands; Big Daddy is *not* going to die. I want you to get that in your heads, all of you!

Mae: Mommy, Mommy, Big Mama, we're just as hopeful an' optimistic as you are about Big Daddy's prospects, we have faith in *prayer*—but nevertheless there are certain matters that have to be discussed an' dealt with, because otherwise—

Gooper: Eventualities have to be considered and now's the time . . . Mae, will you please get my brief case out of our room?

Mae: Yes, honey.

[She rises and goes out through the hall door.]

Gooper [*standing over Big Mama*]: Now, Big Mom. What you said just now was not at all true and you know it. I've always loved Big Daddy in my own quiet way. I never made a show of it, and I know that Big Daddy has always been fond of me in a quiet way, too, and he never made a show of it neither.

[Mae returns with Gooper's brief case.]

Mae: Here's your brief case, Gooper, honey.

Gooper [*handing the brief case back to her*]: Thank you . . . Of cou'se, my relationship with Big Daddy is different from Brick's.

Mae: You're eight years older'n Brick an' always had t' carry a bigger load of th' responsibilities than Brick ever had t' carry. He never carried a thing in his life but a football or a highball.

Gooper: Mae, will y' let me talk, please?

Mae: Yes, honey.

Gooper: Now, a twenty-eight-thousand-acre plantation's a mighty big thing t' run.

Mae: Almost singlehanded.

[Margaret has gone out onto the gallery and can be heard calling softly to Brick.]

Big Mama: You never had to run this place! What are you talking about? As if Big Daddy was dead and in his grave, you had to run it? Why, you just helped him out with a few business details and had your law practice at the same time in Memphis!

Mae: Oh, Mommy, Mommy, Big Mommy! Let's be fair!

Margaret: Brick!

Mae: Why, Gooper has given himself body and soul to keeping this place up for the past five years since Big Daddy's health started failing.

Margaret: Brick!

Mae: Gooper won't say it, Gooper never thought of it as a duty, he just did it. And what did Brick do? Brick kept living in his past glory at college! Still a football player at twenty-seven!

Margaret [*returning alone*]: Who are you talking about now? Brick? A football player? He isn't a football player and you know it. Brick is a sports announcer on T.V. and one of the best-known ones in the country!

Mae: I'm talking about what he was.

Margaret: Well, I wish you would just stop talking about my husband.

Gooper: I've got a right to discuss my brother with other members of MY OWN family, which don't include *you.* Why don't you go out there and drink with Brick?

Margaret: I've never seen such malice toward a brother.

Gooper: How about his for me? Why, he can't stand to be in the same room with me!

Margaret: This is a deliberate campaign of vilification for the most disgusting and sordid reason on earth, and I know what it is! It's *avarice, avarice, greed, greed!*

Big Mama: Oh, I'll scream! I will scream in a moment unless this stops!

[Gooper has stalked up to Margaret with clenched fists at his sides as if he would strike her. Mae distorts her face again into a hideous grimace behind Margaret's back.]

Big Mama [*sobs*]: Margaret. Child. Come here. Sit next to Big Mama.

Margaret: Precious Mommy. I'm sorry, I'm sorry, I—!

[She bends her long graceful neck to press her forehead to Big Mama's bulging shoulder under its black chiffon.]

Mae: How beautiful, how touching, this display of devotion! Do you know why she's childless? She's childless because that big beautiful athlete husband of hers won't go to bed with her!

Gooper: You jest won't let me do this in a nice way, will yah? Aw right—I don't give a goddam if Big Daddy likes me or don't like me or did or never did or will or will never! I'm just appealing to a sense of common decency and fair play. I'll tell you the truth. I've resented Big Daddy's partiality to Brick ever since Brick was born, and the way I've been treated like I was just barely good enough to spit on and sometimes not even good enough for that. Big Daddy is dying of cancer, and it's spread all through him and it's attacked all his vital organs including the kidneys and right now he is sinking into uremia, and you all know what uremia is, it's poisoning of the whole system due to the failure of the body to eliminate its poisons.

Margaret [*to herself, downstage, hissingly*]: *Poisons, poisons! Venomous thoughts and words! In hearts and minds!—That's poisons!*

Gooper [*overlapping her*]: I am asking for a square deal, and, by God, I expect to get one. But if I don't get one, if there's any peculiar shenanigans going on around here behind my back, well, I'm not a corporation lawyer for nothing, I know how to protect my own interests.

[Brick enters from the gallery with a tranquil, blurred smile, carrying an empty glass with him.]

Brick: Storm coming up.

Gooper: Oh! A late arrival!

Mae: Behold the conquering hero comes!

Gooper: The fabulous Brick Pollitt! Remember him?—Who could forget him!

Mae: He looks like he's been injured in a game!

Gooper: Yep, I'm afraid you'll have to warm the bench at the Sugar Bowl this year, Brick!

[Mae laughs shrilly.]

Or was it the Rose Bowl that he made that famous run in?—

[Thunder]

Mae: The punch bowl, honey. It was in the punch bowl, the cut-glass punch bowl!

Gooper: Oh, that's right, I'm getting the bowls mixed up!

Margaret: Why don't you stop venting your malice and envy on a sick boy?

Big Mama: Now you two hush, I mean it, hush, all of you, hush!

Daisy, Sookey: Storm! Storm comin'! Storm! Storm!

Lacey: Brightie, close them shutters.

Gooper: Lacey, put the top up on my Cadillac, will yuh?

Lacey: Yes, suh, Mistah Pollitt!

Gooper [*at the same time*]: Big Mama, you know it's necessary for me t' go back to Memphis in th' mornin' t' represent the Parker estate in a lawsuit.

[Mae sits on the bed and arranges papers she has taken from the brief case.]

Big Mama: Is it, Gooper?

Mae: Yaiss.

Gooper: That's why I'm forced to—to bring up a problem that—

Mae: Something' that's too important t' be put off!

Gooper: If Brick was sober, he ought to be in on this.

Margaret: Brick is present; we're present.

Gooper: Well, good. I will now give you this outline my partner, Tom Bullitt, an' me have drawn up—a sort of dummy—trusteeship.

Margaret: Oh, that's it! You'll be in charge an' dole out remittances, will you?

Gooper: This we did as soon as we got the report on Big Daddy from th' Ochsner Laboratories. We did this thing, I mean we drew up this dummy outline with the advice and assistance of the Chairman of the Boa'd of Directors of th' Southern Plantahs Bank and Trust Company in Memphis, C. C. Bellowes, a man who handles estates for all th' prominent fam'lies in West Tennessee and th' Delta.

Big Mama: Gooper?

Gooper [crouching in front of Big Mama]: Now this is not—not final, or anything like it. This is just a preliminary outline. But it does provide a basis—a design—a—possible, feasible—*plan!*

Margaret: Yes, I'll bet it's a plan.

[Thunder]

Mae: It's a plan to protect the biggest estate in the Delta from irresponsibility an'—

Big Mama: Now you listen to me, all of you, you listen here! They's not goin' to be any more catty talk in my house! And Gooper, you put that away before I grab it out of your hand and tear it right up! I don't know what the hell's in it, and I don't want to know what the hell's in it. I'm talkin' in Big Daddy's language now; I'm his *wife*, not his *widow*, I'm still his *wife!* And I'm talkin' to you in his language an'—

Gooper: Big Mama, what I have here is—

Mae [at the same time]: Gooper explained that it's just a plan . . .

Big Mama: I don't care what you got there. Just put it back where it came from, an' don't let me see it again, not even the outside of the envelope of it! Is that understood? Basis! Plan! Preliminary! Design! I say—what is it Big Daddy always says when he's disgusted?

Brick [from the bar]: Big Daddy says "crap" when he's disgusted.

Big Mama [rising]: That's right—CRAP! I say CRAP too, like Big Daddy!

[Thunder]

Mae: Coarse language doesn't seem called for in this—

Gooper: Somethin' in me is *deeply outraged* by hearin' you talk like this.

Big Mama: Nobody's goin' to take nothin'! —till Big Daddy lets go of it—maybe, just possibly, not—not even then! No, not even then!

[Thunder]

Mae: Sookey, hurry up an' git that po'ch furniture covahed; want th' paint to come off?

Gooper: Lacey, put mah car away!

Lacey: Caint, Mistah Pollitt, you got the keys!

Gooper: Naw, you got 'em, man. Where th' keys to th' car, honey?

Mae: You got 'em in your pocket!

Brick: "You can always hear me singin' this song, Show me the way to go home."

[Thunder distantly]

Big Mama: Brick! Come here, Brick, I need you. Tonight Brick looks like he used to look when he was a little boy, just like he did when he played wild games and used to come home when I hollered myself hoarse for him, all sweaty and pink cheeked and sleepy, with his—red curls shining . . .

[Brick draws aside as he does from all physical contact and continues the song in a whisper, opening the ice bucket and dropping in the ice cubes one by one as if he were mixing some important chemical formula.
Distant thunder.]

Time goes by so fast. Nothin' can outrun it. Death commences too early—almost before you're half acquainted with life—you meet the other . . . Oh, you know we just got to love each other an' stay together, all of us, just as close as we can, especially now that such a *black* thing has come and moved into this place without invitation.

[Awkwardly embracing Brick, she presses her head to his shoulder.
A dog howls off stage.]

Oh, Brick, son of Big Daddy, Big Daddy does so love you. Y'know what would be his fondest dream come true? If before he passed on, if Big Daddy has to pass on . . .

[A dog howls.]

. . . you give him a child of yours, a grandson as much like his son as his son is like Big Daddy . . .

Margaret: I know that's Big Daddy's dream.

Big Mama: That's his dream.

Mae: Such a pity that Maggie and Brick can't oblige.

Big Daddy [*off down stage right on the gallery*]: Looks like the wind was takin' liberties with this place.

Servant [*off stage*]: Yes, sir, Mr. Pollitt.

Margaret [*crossing to the right door*]: Big Daddy's on the gall'ry.

[Big Mama has turned toward the hall door at the sound of Big Daddy's voice on the gallery.]

Big Mama: I can't stay here. He'll see somethin' in my eyes.

[Big Daddy enters the room from up stage right.]

Big Daddy: Can I come in?

[He puts his cigar in an ash tray.]

Margaret: Did the storm wake you up, Big Daddy?

Big Daddy: Which stawm are you talkin' about—th' one outside or th' hullballoo in here?

[Gooper squeezes past Big Daddy.]

Gooper: 'Scuse me.

[Mae tries to squeeze past Big Daddy to join Gooper, but Big Daddy puts his arm firmly around her.]

Big Daddy: I heard some mighty loud talk. Sounded like somethin' important was bein' discussed. What was the powwow about?

Mae [*flustered*]: Why—nothin', Big Daddy . . .

Big Daddy [*crossing to extreme left center, taking Mae with him*]: What is that pregnant-lookin' envelope you're puttin' back in your brief case, Gooper?

Gooper [*at the foot of the bed, caught, as he stuffs papers into envelope*]: That? Nothin,' suh—nothin' much of anythin' at all . . .

Big Daddy: Nothin'? It looks like a whole lot of nothin'!

[He turns up stage to the group.]

You all know th' story about th' young married couple—

Gooper: Yes, sir!

Big Daddy: Hello, Brick—

Brick: Hello, Big Daddy.

[The group is arranged in a semicircle above Big Daddy, Margaret at the extreme right, then Mae and Gooper, then Big Mama, with Brick at the left.]

Big Daddy: Young married couple took Junior out to th' zoo one Sunday, inspected all of God's creatures in their cages, with satisfaction.

Gooper: Satisfaction.

Big Daddy [*crossing to up stage center, facing front*]: This afternoon was a warm afternoon in spring an' that ole elephant had somethin' else on his mind which was bigger'n peanuts. You know this story, Brick?

[Gooper nods.]

Brick: No, sir, I don't know it.

Big Daddy: Y'see, in th' cage adjoinin' they was a young female elephant in heat!

Big Mama [*at Big Daddy's shoulder*]: Oh, Big Daddy!

Big Daddy: What's the matter, preacher's gone, ain't he? All right. That female elephant in the next cage was permeatin' the atmosphere about her with a powerful and excitin' odor of female fertility! Huh! Ain't that a nice way to put it, Brick?

Brick: Yes, sir, nothin' wrong with it.

Big Daddy: Brick says th's nothin' wrong with it!

Big Mama: Oh, Big Daddy!

Big Daddy [*crossing to down stage center*]: So this ole bull elephant still had a couple of fornications left in him. He reared back his trunk an' got a whiff of that elephant lady next door!—began to paw at the dirt in his cage an' butt his head against the separatin' partition and, first thing y'know, there was a conspicuous change in his *profile*—very *conspicuous!* Ain't I tellin' this story in decent language, Brick?

Brick: Yes, sir, too fuckin' decent!

Big Daddy: So, the little boy pointed at it and said, "What's that?" His mama said, "Oh, that's—nothin'!"—His papa said, "She's spoiled!"

[Big Daddy crosses to Brick at left.]

You didn't laugh at that story, Brick.

[Big Mama crosses to down stage right crying. Margaret goes to her. Mae and Gooper hold up stage right center.]

Brick: No, sir, I didn't laugh at that story.

Big Daddy: What is the smell in this room? Don't you notice it, Brick? Don't you notice a powerful and obnoxious odor of mendacity in this room?

Brick: Yes, sir, I think I do, sir.

Gooper: Mae, Mae . . .

Big Daddy: There is nothing more powerful. Is there, Brick?

Brick: No, sir. No, sir, there isn't, an' nothin' more obnoxious.

Big Daddy: Brick agrees with me. The odor of mendacity is a powerful and obnoxious odor an' the stawm hasn't blown it away from this room yet. You notice it, Gooper?

Gooper: What, sir?

Big Daddy: How about you, Sister Woman? You notice the unpleasant odor of mendacity in this room?

Mae: Why, Big Daddy, I don't even know what that is.

Big Daddy: You can smell it. Hell it smells like death!

[Big Mama sobs. Big Daddy looks toward her.]

What's wrong with that fat woman over there, loaded with diamonds? Hey, what's-you-name, what's the matter with you?

Margaret [*crossing toward Big Daddy*]: She had a slight dizzy spell, Big Daddy.

Big Daddy: You better watch that, Big Mama. A stroke is a bad way to go.

Margaret [*crossing to Big Daddy at center*]: Oh, Brick, Big Daddy has on your birthday present to him, Brick, he has on your cashmere robe, the softest material I have ever felt.

Big Daddy: Yeah, this is my soft birthday, Maggie . . . Not my gold or my silver birthday, but my soft birthday, everything's got to be soft for Big Daddy on this soft birthday.

[Maggie kneels before Big Daddy at center.]

Margaret: Big Daddy's got on his Chinese slippers that I gave him, Brick. Big Daddy, I haven't given you my big present yet, but now I will, now's the time for me to present it to you! I have an announcement to make!

Mae: What? What kind of announcement?

Gooper: A sports announcement, Maggie?

Margaret: Announcement of life beginning! A child is coming, sired by Brick, and out of Maggie the Cat! I have Brick's child in my body, an' that's my birthday present to Big Daddy on this birthday!

[Big Daddy looks at Brick who crosses behind Big Daddy to down stage portal, left.]

Big Daddy: Get up, girl, get up off your knees, girl.

[Big Daddy helps Margaret to rise. He crosses above her, to her right, bites off the end of a fresh cigar, taken from his bathrobe pocket, as he studies Margaret.]

Uh-huh, this girl has life in her body, that's no lie!

Big Mama: BIG DADDY'S DREAM COME TRUE!

Brick: JESUS!

Big Daddy [*crossing right below wicker stand*]: Gooper, I want my lawyer in the mornin'.

Brick: Where are you goin', Big Daddy?

Big Daddy: Son, I'm goin' up on the roof, to the belvedere on th' roof to look over my kingdom before I give up my kingdom—twenty-eight thousand acres of th' richest land this side of the valley Nile!

[He exits through right doors, and down right on the gallery.]

Big Mama [*following*]: Sweetheart, sweetheart, sweetheart—can I come with you?

[She exits down stage right.

Margaret is down stage center in the mirror area. Mae has joined Gooper and she gives him a fierce poke, making a low hissing sound and a grimace of fury.]

Gooper [*pushing her aside*]: Brick, could you possibly spare me one small shot of that liquor?

Brick: Why, help yourself, Gooper boy.

Gooper: I will.

Mae [*shrilly*]: Of course we know that this is—a lie.

Gooper: *Be still, Mae.*

Mae: I won't be still! I know she's made this up!

Gooper: Goddam it, I said shut up!

Margaret: Gracious! I didn't know that my little announcement was going to provoke such a storm!

Mae: That woman isn't *pregnant!*

Gooper: Who said she was?

Mae: She did.

Gooper: The doctor didn't. Doc Baugh didn't.

Margaret: I haven't gone to Doc Baugh.

Gooper: Then who'd you go to, Maggie?

Margaret: One of the best gynecologists in the South.

Gooper: Uh huh, uh huh!—I see . . .

[He takes out a pencil and notebook.]

—May we have his name, please?

Margaret: No, you may not, Mister Prosecuting Attorney!

Mae: He doesn't have any name, he doesn't exist!

Margaret: Oh, he exists all right, and so does my child, Brick's baby!

Mae: You can't conceive a child by a man that won't sleep with you unless you think you're—

[Brick has turned on the phonograph. A scat song cuts Mae's speech.]

Gooper: Turn that off!
Mae: We know it's a lie because we hear you in here; he won't sleep with you, we hear you! So don't imagine you're going to put a trick over on us, to fool a dying man with a—

[A long drawn cry of agony and rage fills the house. Margaret turns the phonograph down to a whisper. The cry is repeated.]

Mae: Did you hear that, Gooper, did you hear that?
Gooper: Sounds like the pain has struck.
Gooper: Come along and leave these lovebirds together in their nest!

[He goes out first. Mae follows but turns at the door, contorting her face and hissing at Margaret.]

Mae: Liar!

[She slams the door.
Margaret exhales with relief and moves a little unsteadily to catch hold of Brick's arm.]

Margaret: Thank you for—keeping still . . .
Brick: O.K., Maggie.
Margaret: It was gallant of you to save my face!

[He now pours down three shots in quick succession and stands waiting, silent. All at once he turns with a smile and says:]

Brick: There!
Margaret: What?
Brick: The *click* . . .

[His gratitude seems almost infinite as he hobbles out on the gallery with a drink. We hear his crutch as he swings out of sight. Then, at some distance, he begins singing to himself a peaceful song. Margaret holds the big pillow forlornly as if it were her only companion, for a few moments, then throws it on the bed. She rushes to the liquor cabinet, gathers all the bottles in her arms, turns about undecidedly, then runs out of the room with them, leaving the door ajar on the dim yellow hall. Brick is heard hobbling back along the gallery, singing his peaceful song. He comes back in, sees the pillow on the bed, laughs lightly, sadly, picks it up. He has it under his arm as Margaret returns to the room. Margaret softly shuts the door and leans against it, smiling softly at Brick.]

Margaret: Brick, I used to think that you were stronger than me and I didn't want to be overpowered by you. But now, since you've taken to liquor—you know what?—I guess it's bad, but now I'm stronger than you and I can love you more truly! Don't move that pillow. I'll move it right back if you do!—Brick?

[She turns out all the lamps but a single rose-silk-shaded one by the bed.]

I really have been to a doctor and I know what to do and—Brick?—this is my time by the calendar to conceive.

Brick: Yes, I understand, Maggie. But how are you going to conceive a child by a man in love with his liquor?

Margaret: By locking his liquor up and making him satisfy my desire before I unlock it!

Brick: Is that what you've done, Maggie?

Margaret: Look and see. That cabinet's mighty empty compared to before!

Brick: Well, I'll be a son of a—

[He reaches for his crutch but she beats him to it and rushes out on the gallery, hurls the crutch over the rail and comes back in, panting.]

Margaret: And so tonight we're going to make the lie true, and when that's done, I'll bring the liquor back here and we'll get drunk together, here, tonight, in this place that death has come into . . . —What do you say?

Brick: I don't say anything. I guess there's nothing to say.

Margaret: Oh, you weak people, you weak, beautiful people!—who give up with such grace. What you want is someone to—

[She turns out the rose-silk lamp.]

—take hold of you.—Gently, gently with love hand your life back to you, like somethin' gold you let go of. I *do* love you, Brick, I *do*!

Brick [*smiling with charming sadness*]: Wouldn't it be funny if that was true?

THE END

(1955)

QUESTIONS FOR DISCUSSION AND WRITING

CLOSE READING

1. Find the phrase "cat on a hot tin roof" throughout the play; how does its metaphorical meaning change or develop?
2. What are the various explanations for Margaret's contempt for Brick's family?
3. How are children presented throughout the play? (Think not only of Gooper's "no-neck monsters" but also of Brick as a kind of child and of the child Margaret wants to conceive.)

CRITICAL AND CREATIVE READING

4. How differently do Margaret and Brick act when they are alone and when they are together? If you were to view the play in terms of the need for privacy, how might you interpret its theme?
5. Characters are conscious of Big Daddy's crude language; how does that language function with the play's themes?
6. There is more than a hint of a homoerotic relationship between Brick and his deceased friend Skipper. The subject of homosexuality was taboo in the 1950s when Williams wrote the play, and this content had to be played down

in the Hollywood version of the film because of a restrictive "code" imposed by the guild of producers. How central is that motif to the play's themes?

7. In one of the stage directions of Act II, Williams adds a critical interpretation of his own play when he talks about "the bird [he hopes] to catch in the net of this play" and how he wants the play to act as "a snare for the truth of human experience." Use the author's words here to interpret the play: you might react to his metaphor, test his aims against his art, or even consider whether an author should comment this way on his own art.

Connections to Other Readings

8. Discuss the tension between marital love and lust in *Cat on a Hot Tin Roof* and in James Joyce's story "The Dead."
9. Williams included an epigraph from Dylan Thomas's poem "Do Not Go Gentle into That Good Night" (Chapter 12) in the published version of this play; discuss whether you feel that poem fits with the play.
10. Based on his essay "On Marriage," how would Robert Louis Stevenson react to Williams's play? (Think of all three marriages represented in the play.)

Essays

Marie-Henri Beyle de Stendhal

The Birth of Love

The author known popularly as Stendhal (1783–1842) was born Marie-Henri Beyle in Grenoble in France and adopted the name Stendhal after Napoleon's fall. Stendhal traveled extensively throughout the great cities of Europe and lived in Paris and Milan, among other cities. He aspired to become a great comic satirist and is best known today for his novel *The Charterhouse of Parma.* In 1818 in Milan he met and fell deeply in love with Métilde Viscontini Dembowski, and her cool reception inspired him to write the work *On Love,* from which the following essay is taken. The remainder of the book, which Stendhal considered to be his most important, expounds on the themes and images he puts forth here.

This is what goes on in the mind:

1. Admiration.
2. One says to one's self: "How delightful to kiss her, to be kissed in return," etc.
3. Hope.

One studies her perfections. It is at this moment that a woman should surrender herself, to get the greatest possible sensual pleasure. The eyes of even the most modest women light up the moment hope is born; passion is so strong and pleasure is so acute that they betray themselves in the most obvious manner.

4. Love is born.

To love is to derive pleasure from seeing, touching and feeling through all one's senses and as closely as possible, a lovable person who loves us.

5. The first crystallization begins.

We take a joy in attributing a thousand perfections to a woman of whose love we are sure; we analyze all our happiness with intense satisfaction. This reduces itself to giving ourselves an exaggerated idea of a magnificent possession which has just fallen to us from Heaven in some way we do not understand, and the continued possession of which is assured to us.

This is what you will find if you let a lover turn things over in his mind for twenty-four hours.

In the salt mines of Salzburg a bough stripped of its leaves by winter is thrown into the depths of the disused workings; two or three months later it is pulled out again, covered with brilliant crystals: even the tiniest twigs, no bigger than a tomtit's[1] claw, are spangled with a vast number of shimmering, glittering diamonds, so that the original bough is no longer recognizable.

I call crystallization that process of the mind which discovers fresh perfections in its beloved at every turn of events.

For instance, should a traveller speak of the coolness of Genoese orange groves by the seashore on a scorching summer day, you immediately think how delightful it would be to enjoy this coolness in her company!

One of your friends breaks his arm out hunting: how sweet, you think, to be nursed by a woman you love! To be with her always and to revel in her constant love would almost make your pain blessèd; and you leave your friend's broken arm still more firmly convinced of the angelic sweetness of your mistress. In short, it is sufficient to think of a perfection in order to see it in the person you love.

This phenomenon which I have allowed myself to call *crystallization*, arises from the promptings of Nature which urge us to enjoy ourselves and drive the blood to our brains, from the feeling that our delight increases with the perfections of the beloved, and from the thought: "She is mine." The savage has no time to get beyond the first step. He grasps his pleasures, but his brain is concentrated on following the buck fleeing from him through the forest, and with whose flesh he must repair his own strength as quickly as possible, at the risk of falling beneath the hatchet of his enemy.

At the other extreme of civilization, I have no doubt that a sensitive woman arrives at the point of experiencing no sensual pleasure except with the man

[1] *tomtit:* A small bird.

she loves.[2] This is in direct opposition to the savage. But, amongst civilized communities woman has plenty of leisure, whilst the savage lives so close to essentials that he is obliged to treat his female as a beast of burden. If the females of many animals have an easier lot, it is only because the subsistence of the males is more assured.

But let us leave the forests and return to Paris. A passionate man sees nothing but perfection in the woman he loves; and yet his affections may still wander, for the spirit wearies of monotony, even in the case of the most perfect happiness.[3]

So what happens to rivet his attention is this:

6. Doubt is born.

When his hopes have first of all been raised and then confirmed by ten or a dozen glances, or a whole series of other actions which may be compressed into a moment or spread over several days, the lover, recovering from his first amazement and growing used to his happiness, or perhaps merely guided by theory which, based always on his most frequent experiences, is really only correct in the case of light women, the lover, I say, demands more positive proofs of love and wants to advance the moment of his happiness.

If he takes too much for granted he will be met with indifference,[4] coldness or even anger: in France there will be a suggestion of irony which seems to say: "You think you have made more progress than you really have." A woman behaves in this way either because she is recovering from a moment of intoxication and obeys the behests of modesty, which she is alarmed at having transgressed, or merely from prudence or coquettishness.

The lover begins to be less sure of the happiness which he has promised himself; he begins to criticize the reasons he gave himself for hoping.

He tries to fall back on the other pleasures of life. *He finds they no longer exist.* He is seized with a dread of appalling misery, and his attention becomes concentrated.

7. Second crystallization.

Now begins the second crystallization, producing as its diamonds various confirmations of the following idea:

"She loves me."

[2]If this peculiarity is not found in man, it is because he never has for one moment any modesty to sacrifice. —Stendhal's note.

[3]That is to say that each shade of experience only gives one instant of perfect happiness, by the signs of passion in a man change ten times a day. —Stendhal's note.

[4]What the seventeenth century romances called *love at first sight,* which decides once for all the destiny of the hero and his mistress, is an emotion of the heart which, in spite of having been abused by a vast number of scribblers, nonetheless exists in Nature; it arises from any such defensive manœuvre becoming impossible. The woman who is in love finds too much happiness in the emotions she experiences to be able to succeed in dissembling; tired of prudence, she throws caution to the winds, and gives herself up blindly to the joy of loving. Caution makes love at first sight impossible. —Stendhal's note.

Every quarter of an hour, during the night following the birth of doubt, after a moment of terrible misery, the lover says to himself: "Yes, she loves me"; and crystallization sets to work to discover fresh charms; then gaunt-eyed doubt grips him again and pulls him up with a jerk. His heart misses a beat; he says to himself: "But, does she love me?" Through all these harrowing and delicious alternations the poor lover feels acutely: "With her I would experience joys which she alone in the world could give me."

It is the clearness of this truth and the path he treads between an appalling abyss and the most perfect happiness, that make the second crystallization appear to be so very much more important than the first.

The lover hovers incessantly amongst these three ideas:

1. She is perfect in every way.
2. She loves me.
3. How can I get the strongest possible proof of her love for me?

The most heartrending moment in love that is still young is when it finds that it has been wrong in its chain of reasoning and must destroy a whole agglomeration of crystals.

Even the fact of crystallization itself begins to appear doubtful.

(1820)

Questions for Discussion and Writing

Close Reading

1. Summarize in your own words Stendhal's conception of "crystallization."
2. What distinction does Stendhal make between "the savage" and "civilized communities," and why is this distinction important to his argument?
3. What is the role of doubt in establishing love?

Critical and Creative Reading

4. Is doubt a necessary step in the progression of love, or the enemy of love? Put another way, could love ever develop *without* doubt? Do you agree with Stendhal on this point?
5. Why does Stendhal move so quickly through steps 1–4 of the birth of love? Are these steps, in your opinion, akin to lust, or are they something else?
6. Can one ever be fully secure that one's lover or spouse returns one's love equally? How?

Connections to Other Readings

7. Use Stendhal's description of the birth of love to analyze why love never develops for the narrator of Susan Minot's story "Lust."
8. Discuss where you think Gabriel Conroy—the protagonist of James Joyce's "The Dead"—is in terms of Stendhal's scheme.

Robert Louis Stevenson

On Marriage

Born in Edinburgh, Scotland, Robert Louis Stevenson (1850–1894) became a seasoned world traveler and writer of international renown. He published accounts of many of his voyages, acquiring a reputation as an adventurer. Although his travel accounts and prose works were well received in his lifetime, he is best known today for such classic novels as *Treasure Island* (1883), *The Strange Case of Dr. Jekyll and Mr. Hyde* (1886), and *Kidnapped* (1886). The following essay, "On Marriage," is challenging because of its tone: note places where either the tone or your perception of the tone shifts.

Hope, they say, deserts us at no period of our existence. From first to last, and in the face of smarting disillusions, we continue to expect good fortune, better health, and better conduct; and that so confidently, that we judge it needless to deserve them. I think it improbable that I shall ever write like Shakespeare, conduct an army like Hannibal, or distinguish myself like Marcus Aurelius in the paths of virtue; and yet I have my by-days, hope prompting, when I am very ready to believe that I shall combine all these various excellences in my own person, and go marching down to posterity with divine honors. There is nothing so monstrous but we can believe it of ourselves. About ourselves, about our aspirations and delinquencies, we have dwelt by choice in a delicious vagueness from our boyhood up. No one will have forgotten Tom Sawyer's aspiration: "Ah, if he could only die *temporarily!*" Or, perhaps, better still, the inward resolution of the two pirates, that "so long as they remained in that business, their piracies should not again be sullied with the crime of stealing." Here we recognize the thoughts of our boyhood; and our boyhood ceased—well, when?—not, I think, at twenty; nor, perhaps, altogether at twenty-five; nor yet at thirty; and possibly, to be quite frank, we are still in the thick of that Arcadian period. For as the race of man, after centuries of civilization, still keeps some traits of their barbarian fathers, so man the individual is not altogether quit of youth, when he is already old and honored, and Lord Chancellor of England. We advance in years somewhat in the manner of an invading army in a barren land; the age that we have reached, as the phrase goes, we but hold with an outpost, and still keep open our communications with the extreme rear and first beginnings of the march. There is our true base; that is not only the beginning, but the perennial spring of our faculties; and grandfather William can retire upon occasion into the green enchanted forest of his boyhood.

The unfading boyishness of hope and its vigorous irrationality are nowhere better displayed than in questions of conduct. There is a character in the *Pilgrim's Progress,* one Mr. *Linger-after-Lust,* with whom I fancy we are all on speaking terms; one famous among the famous for ingenuity of hope up to and beyond the moment of defeat; one who, after eighty years of contrary experience, will believe it possible to continue in the business of piracy and yet avoid the guilt of theft. Every sin is our last: every 1st of January a remarkable turning-point in our career. Any overt act, above all, is felt to be alchemic in its power to change. A drunkard takes the pledge; it will be strange if that does not help him. For how many years did Mr. Pepys continue to make and break his little vows? And yet I have not heard that he was discouraged in the end. By such steps we think to fix a momentary resolution; as a timid fellow hies him to the dentist's while the tooth is stinging.

But, alas, by planting a stake at the top of flood, you can neither prevent nor delay the inevitable ebb. There is no hocus-pocus in morality; and even the "sanctimonious ceremony" of marriage leaves the man unchanged. This is a hard saying, and has an air of paradox. For there is something in marriage so natural and inviting, that the step has an air of great simplicity and ease; it offers to bury forever many aching preoccupations; it is to afford us unfailing and familiar company through life; it opens up a smiling prospect of the blest and passive kind of love, rather than the blessing and active; it is approached not only through the delights of courtship, but by a public performance and repeated legal signatures. A man naturally thinks it will go hard with him if he cannot be good and fortunate and happy within such august circumvallations.

And yet there is probably no other act in a man's life so hot-headed and foolhardy as this one of marriage. For years, let us suppose, you have been making the most indifferent business of your career. Your experience has not, we may dare to say, been more encouraging than Paul's or Horace's; like them, you have seen and desired the good that you were not able to accomplish; like them, you have done the evil that you loathed. You have waked at night in a hot or a cold sweat, according to your habit of body, remembering, with dismal surprise, your own unpardonable acts and sayings. You have been sometimes tempted to withdraw entirely from this game of life; as a man who makes nothing but misses withdraws from that less dangerous one of billiards. You have fallen back upon the thought that you yourself most sharply smarted for your misdemeanors, or, in the old, plaintive phrase, that you were nobody's enemy but your own. And then you have been made aware of what was beautiful and amiable, wise and kind, in the other part of your behavior; and it seemed as if nothing could reconcile the contradiction, as indeed nothing can. If you are a man, you have shut your mouth hard and said nothing; and if you are only a man in the making, you have recognized that yours was quite a special case, and you yourself not guilty of your own pestiferous career.

5 Granted, and with all my heart. Let us accept these apologies; let us agree that you are nobody's enemy but your own; let us agree that you are a sort of moral cripple, impotent for good; and let us regard you with the unmingled pity due to such a fate. But there is one thing to which, on these terms, we can never

agree:—we can never agree to have you marry. What! you have had one life to manage, and have failed so strangely, and now can see nothing wiser than to conjoin with it the management of some one else's? Because you have been unfaithful in a very little, you propose yourself to be a ruler over ten cities. You strip yourself by such a step of all remaining consolations and excuses. You are no longer content to be your own enemy; you must be your wife's also. You have been hitherto in a mere subaltern attitude; dealing cruel blows about you in life, yet only half responsible, since you came there by no choice or movement of your own. Now, it appears, you must take things on your own authority: God made you, but you marry yourself; and for all that your wife suffers, no one is responsible but you. A man must be very certain of his knowledge ere he undertake to guide a ticket-of-leave man through a dangerous pass; you have eternally missed your way in life, with consequences that you still deplore, and yet you masterfully seize your wife's hand, and, blindfold, drag her after you to ruin. And it is your wife, you observe, whom you select. She, whose happiness you most desire, you choose to be your victim. You would earnestly warn her from a tottering bridge or bad investment. If she were to marry some one else, how you would tremble for her fate! If she were only your sister, and you thought half as much of her, how doubtfully would you entrust her future to a man no better than yourself!

Times are changed with him who marries; there are no more by-path meadows, where you may innocently linger, but the road lies long and straight and dusty to the grave. Idleness, which is often becoming and even wise in the bachelor, begins to wear a different aspect when you have a wife to support. Suppose, after you are married, one of those little slips were to befall you. What happened last November might surely happen February next. They may have annoyed you at the time, because they were not what you had meant; but how will they annoy you in the future, and how will they shake the fabric of your wife's confidence and peace! A thousand things unpleasing went on in the *chiaroscuro* of a life that you shrank from too particularly realizing; you did not care, in those days, to make a fetish of your conscience; you would recognize your failures with a nod, and so, good-day. But the time for these reserves is over. You have wilfully introduced a witness into your life, the scene of these defeats, and can no longer close the mind's eye upon uncomely passages, but must stand up straight and put a name upon your actions. And your witness is not only the judge, but the victim of your sins; not only can she condemn you to the sharpest penalties, but she must herself share feelingly in their endurance. And observe, once more, with what temerity you have chosen precisely *her* to be your spy, whose esteem you value highest, and whom you have already taught to think you better than you are. You may think you had a conscience, and believed in God; but what is a conscience to a wife? Wise men of yore erected statues of their deities, and consciously performed their part in life before those marble eyes. A god watched them at the board, and stood by their bedside in the morning when they woke; and all about their ancient cities, where they bought and sold, or where they piped and wrestled, there would stand some symbol of the things that are outside of man. These were lessons, delivered in the quiet dialect of art, which told their story faithfully, but gently. It is the same lesson, if you will—but how harrowingly taught!—when the woman you respect shall weep from your unkindness or blush with shame at your misconduct. Poor girls in Italy turn their painted Madonnas to the wall: you cannot set aside your wife. To marry is to domesticate the Recording Angel. Once you are married, there is nothing left for you, not even suicide, but to be good.

And goodness in marriage is a more intricate problem than mere single virtue; for in marriage there are two ideals to be realized. A girl, it is true, has always lived in a glass house among reproving relatives, whose word was law; she has been bred up to sacrifice her judgments and take the key submissively from dear papa; and it is wonderful how swiftly she can change her tune into the husband's. Her morality has been, too often, an affair of precept and conformity. But in the case of a bachelor who has enjoyed some measure both of privacy and freedom, his moral judgments have been passed in some accordance with his nature. His sins were always sins in his own sight; he could then only sin when he did some act against his clear conviction; the light that he walked by was obscure, but it was single. Now, when two people of any grit and spirit put their fortunes into one, there succeeds to this comparative certainty a huge welter of competing jurisdictions. It no longer matters so much how life appears to one; one must consult another: one, who may be strong, must not offend the other, who is weak. The only weak brother I am willing to consider is (to make a bull for once) my wife. For her, and for her only, I must waive my righteous judgments, and go crookedly about my life. How, then, in such an atmosphere of compromise, to keep honor bright and abstain from base capitulations? How are you to put aside love's pleadings? How are you, the apostle of laxity, to turn suddenly about into the rabbi of precision; and after these years of ragged practice, pose for a hero to the lackey who has found you out? In this temptation to mutual indulgence lies the particular peril to morality in married life. Daily they drop a little lower from the first ideal, and for awhile continue to accept these changelings with a gross complacency. At last Love wakes and looks about him; finds his hero sunk into a stout old brute, intent on brandy pawnee; finds his heroine divested of her angel brightness; and in the flash of that first disenchantment, flees forever.

Again, the husband, in these unions, is usually a man, and the wife commonly enough a woman; and when this is the case, although it makes the firmer marriage, a thick additional veil of misconception hangs above the doubtful business. Women, I believe, are somewhat rarer than men; but then, if I were a woman myself, I dare say I should hold the reverse; and at least we all enter more or less wholly into one or other of these camps. A man who delights women by his feminine perceptions will often scatter his admirers by a chance explosion of the under side of man; and the most masculine and direct of women will some day, to your dire surprise, draw out like a telescope into successive lengths of personation. Alas! for the man, knowing her to be at heart more candid than himself, who shall flounder, panting, through these mazes in the quest for truth.

The proper qualities of each sex are, indeed, eternally surprising to the other. Between the Latin and the Teuton races there are similar divergences, not to be bridged by the most liberal sympathy. And in the good, plain, cut-and-dry explanations of this life, which pass current among us as the wisdom of the elders, this difficulty has been turned with the aid of pious lies. Thus, when a young lady has angelic features, eats nothing to speak of, plays all day long on the piano, and sings ravishingly in church, it requires a rough infidelity, falsely called cynicism, to believe that she may be a little devil after all. Yet so it is: she may be a tale-bearer, a liar, and a thief; she may have a taste for brandy, and no heart. My compliments to George Eliot for her Rosamond Vincy; the ugly work of satire she has transmuted to the ends of art, by the companion figure of Lydgate; and the satire was much wanted for the education of young men. That doctrine of the excellence of women, however chivalrous, is cowardly as well as false. It is better to face the fact, and know, when you marry, that you take into your life a creature of equal, if of unlike, frailties; whose weak human heart beats no more tunefully than yours.

But it is the object of a liberal education not only to obscure the knowledge of one sex by another, but to magnify the natural differences between the two. Man is a creature who lives not upon bread alone, but principally by catchwords; and the little rift between the sexes is astonishingly widened by simply teaching one set of catchwords to the girls and another to the boys. To the first, there is shown but a very small field of experience, and taught a very trenchant principle for judgment and action; to the other, the world of life is more largely displayed, and their rule of conduct is proportionately widened. They are taught to follow different virtues, to hate different vices, to place their ideal, even for each other, different achievements. What should be the result of such a course? When a horse has run away, and the two flustered people in the gig have each possessed themselves of a rein, we know the end of that conveyance will be in the ditch. So, when I see a raw youth and a green girl, fluted and fiddled in a dancing measure into that most serious contract, and setting out upon life's journey with ideas so monstrously divergent, I am not surprised that some make shipwreck, but that any come to port. What the boy does almost proudly, as a manly peccadillo, the girl will shudder at as a debasing vice; what is to her the mere common-sense of tactics, he will spit out of his mouth as shameful. Through such a sea of contrarieties must this green couple steer their way; and contrive to love each other; and to respect, forsooth; and be ready, when the time arrives, to educate the little men and women who shall succeed to their places and perplexities.

And yet, when all has been said, the man who should hold back from mar- 10
riage is in the same case with him who runs away from battle. To avoid an occasion for our virtues is a worse degree of failure than to push forward pluckily and make a fall. It is lawful to pray God that we be not led into temptation; but not lawful to skulk from those that come to us. The noblest passage in one of the noblest books of this century, is where the old pope glories in the trial, nay, in the partial fall and but imperfect triumph, of the younger hero. Without

some such manly note, it were perhaps better to have no conscience at all. But there is a vast difference between teaching flight, and showing points of peril that a man may march the more warily. And the true conclusion of this paper is to turn our back on apprehensions, and embrace that shining and courageous virtue, Faith. Hope is the boy, a blind, headlong, pleasant fellow, good to chase swallows with the salt; Faith is the grave, experienced, yet smiling man. Hope lives on ignorance; open-eyed Faith is built upon a knowledge of our life, of the tyranny of circumstance and the frailty of human resolution. Hope looks for unqualified success; but Faith counts certainly on failure, and takes honorable defeat to be a form of victory. Hopc is a kind old pagan; but Faith grew up in Christian days, and early learned humility. In the one temper, a man is indignant that he cannot spring up in a clap to heights of elegance and virtue; in the other, out of a sense of his infirmities, he is filled with confidence because a year has come and gone, and he has still preserved some rags of honor. In the first, he expects an angel for a wife; in the last, he knows that she is like himself—erring, thoughtless, and untrue; but like himself also, filled with a struggling radiancy of better things, and adorned with ineffective qualities. You may safely go to school with hope; but ere you marry, should have learned the mingled lesson of the world: that dolls are stuffed with sawdust, and yet are excellent playthings; that hope and love address themselves to a perfection never realized, and yet, firmly held, become the salt and staff of life; that you yourself are compacted of infirmities, perfect, you might say, in imperfection, and yet you have a something in you lovable and worth preserving; and that, while the mass of mankind lies under this scurvy condemnation, you will scarce find one but, by some generous reading, will become to you a lesson, a model, and a noble spouse through life. So thinking, you will constantly support your own unworthiness, and easily forgive the failings of your friend. Nay, you will be wisely glad that you retain the sense of blemishes; for the faults of married people continually spur up each of them, hour by hour, to do better and to meet and love upon a higher ground. And ever, between the failures, there will come glimpses of kind virtues to encourage and console.

(1881)

Questions for Discussion and Writing

Close Reading

1. Summarize the crucial distinction Stevenson draws between the concepts of "hope" and "faith" toward the end of his essay. What do they have to do with love and marriage?
2. Explain Stevenson's assertion that "there is probably no other act in a man's life so hot-headed and foolhardy as this one of marriage." Why is that concept important to his essay?
3. What metaphors does Stevenson use to explain his concept of love and marriage? How do they function?

CRITICAL AND CREATIVE READING

4. Would you describe this essay as optimistic or pessimistic about the institution of marriage? Or is neither of these terms appropriate to describe the essay?
5. To what degree is marriage (or a similar lifelong commitment) a matter of choice? Stevenson writes, "God made you, but you marry yourself; and for all that your wife suffers, no one is responsible but you." Does this degree of choice or responsibility challenge the popular assumption that everyone has a single "soul mate" whom they cannot truly choose but merely find (or fail to find)?
6. If Stevenson is associating marriage with maturity, is he right to do so? Can't love and marriage (or some similar lifelong commitment) also exist for the very young?

CONNECTIONS TO OTHER READINGS

7. Discuss Stevenson's conceptions of faith and hope as they pertain to James Joyce's story "The Dead."
8. Consider the difference between idealized and realistic love in Stevenson's essay and in Marlowe's "The Passionate Shepherd to His Love" and Raleigh's "The Nymph's Reply to the Shepherd."
9. Margaret and Brick in *Cat on a Hot Tin Roof* discuss the possibility of her having an extramarital affair in Act I. How would Stevenson respond to this discussion?
10. How would Stevenson analyze the narrator of John Updike's story "Wife-Wooing"?

Considering Art: Love and Lust

The discussion below references art reproduced on color insert pages 5, 6, 7, and 8.

Whenever figures are present in a visual image, a suggested narrative or interaction is almost inevitably implied. Sometimes the relationship between the people depicted is fraught with emotional and sexual tension.

***The Young Menage* (see color insert p. 5).** British painter Harold Harvey (1874–1941) in *The Young Menage* (1932) exploits this potential in a scenario involving three figures. The son of a bank manager, Harvey studied art in Paris as a young man and, later in life, became a painter of upper-class interiors. This seated couple's wealth is hinted at in details such as the objects on and above the mantle, the sumptuous **still life** of imported fruits in the foreground, and the full corner dish cupboard that frames the lady of the house. Harvey suggests that this household has not cut back on material or sensual comforts, despite the Great Depression, a time of widespread economic hardship and deprivation. Social class and economic security are articulated in the color and cut of the outfits that the women wear. The seated wife in fashionable black stands out from the surrounding room, whereas the working maid's white uniform seems to be a part of the domestic interior.

***What Freedom!* (see color insert p. 6).** Ukranian artist Ilya Efimovich Repin (1844–1930) in the oil painting *What Freedom!* (1903) depicts a couple seemingly swept away by the forces of nature. Repin at this point in his career was an established painter known for his historical scenes from Russian history. In his letters, however, he often noted that he felt constrained by the expectations of the public and the limitations that the royal art institutions in Russia put on the creative freedom of artists. Like many late nineteenth-century artists, Repin sought symbolic equivalents of strong emotions, looking to the energy and beauty of nature as a force of salvation and liberation.

***The Lovers* (see color insert p. 6).** Belgian **Surrealist** René Magritte (1898–1967) in *The Lovers* (1928) paints human bodies as if they were objects. Using a deadpan, **illusionistic** manner, he creates images that are implausible, irrational, and unsettling. This technique likely came from his early employment as a commercial sign painter. Like many European surrealists of his generation, Magritte was fascinated by Sigmund Freud's *Interpretation of Dreams* (published in 1900) and was hopeful that the release of repressed desires could be a socially transformative energy.

***Blind Date* (see color insert p. 7).** Without making physical contact between figures, Iain Faulkner's (b. 1973) recent painting *Blind Date* (2005) economically sets up formal tensions of inside and outside, male and female, the person who is watching and the person who is being watched or displayed. Strong horizontal and vertical blocks of light and shadow pick up the gray of the man's coat, the black of the woman's chic dress, the interiority of her world, and the public space of the street from which he will enter.

Questions about the Art

1. In Harvey's painting *The Young Menage*, what do the gazes of his figures tell us about this domestic relationship? How are the female figures made different from one another?
2. What sort of freedoms do you imagine that Repin's couple in *What Freedom!* may have found in the ocean waves?
3. The veils that hide the faces in Magritte's *The Lovers* are enigmatic. What kind of power relationship does he imply between these two individuals, and what is our relationship to them? Are they captives? Are they playing a game? Is their relationship ominous or sensual? Is the unknown lover more desirable than the person behind the veil?
4. How do the details that Faulkner includes in *Blind Date* contribute to the sense of tension and uncertainty in the image? From these details, what outcome to the date do you expect and why? What effect does the window's lettering have on our interpretation? What do the two roses suggest? How are the figures "framed" by the window and what might this imply?

Connecting Art and Literature

1. Discuss the painting *The Young Menage* in conjunction with James Joyce's story "The Dead" in their depictions of seemingly happy young couples and their servants.
2. How does the concept of exuberance help you to interpret the painting *What Freedom!* and Dickinson's poem "Wild Nights"? What does love have to do with the forces of nature?
3. Is the mood evoked by the painting *Blind Date* more optimistic, less optimistic, or the same as the mood evoked by one of two stories about lovers who are nearly strangers in this chapter—"Lust" by Susan Minot or "The Tenant" by Bharati Mukherjee?
4. Discuss the idea of bodily contact and love in the painting *Two Lovers* by Magritte and in two poems—"Two Bodies" by Octavio Paz and "What Lips My Lips Have Kissed by Edna St. Vincent Millay."

Common Characters

Don Juan

Although we do not know whether there was an actual person named Don Juan Tenorio, the legend of Don Juan has existed in literature for nearly four centuries. It all began with a Spanish play in 1630 called *El Burlador de Sevilla,* written by a monk under the pen name Tirso de Molina. This early version of the legend set the precedent for the six hundred or more renditions that followed: Don Juan repeatedly attempts to seduce young women by disguising himself as their true lovers. He kills one spouse along the way and is dragged off to hell after the spouse's effigy (a statue) invites him to dinner in a chapel. Don Juan is a proud, swashbuckling lover who refuses to repent his actions.

Well, why would he? In the eyes of a devout monk in sixteenth-century Spain, the answer is clear: Don Juan's behavior is sinful in God's eyes. What Don Juan is doing, according to Catholic morality, is upsetting the order of society,

George Gordon, Lord Byron.

John Barrymore and Jane Winton, *Don Juan* (1926).

acting dishonestly, and robbing young women of their virtue. Don Juan's servant Catalinón is a kind of foil: unlike his master, he knows the value of repentance.

However, legends do not remain the same over time. The cautionary tale of Don Juan in seventeenth-century Spain was revived in Mozart's opera *Don Giovanni*, one of the legend's most famous popular treatments. Although the moral of the Don Juan story is still the same in Mozart's opera, audiences are likely to be amused or even charmed by Don Juan's ability to deceive and his boisterous sense of adventure. Don Juan finally becomes heroic as well as comic in the epic poem by Romantic poet George Gordon, Lord Byron: *Don Juan* (second name pronounced JEW-wan, in this case), excerpted here. Not everyone fears or despises a man whose lusts govern his behavior. Is he a legendary lover who loves life or a lustful lout who lures ladies from lasting love? You decide.

George Gordon, Lord Byron *(1788–1824)*

Excerpts from *Don Juan*, Canto I

1

I want a hero: an uncommon want,
When every year and month sends forth a new one,
Till, after cloying the gazettes with cant,
The age discovers he is not the true one,

Scene from the opera *Don Giovanni* by Wolfgang Amadeus Mozart.

Of such as these I should not care to vaunt,
I'll therefore take our ancient friend Don Juan,
We all have seen him in the pantomime
Sent to the devil, somewhat ere his time.

***

5

Brave men were living before Agamemnon[1]
And since, exceeding valorous and sage,
A good deal like him too, though quite the same none;
But then they shone not on the poet's page,
And so have been forgotten: —I condemn none,
But can't find any in the present age
Fit for my poem (that is, for my new one);
So, as I said, I'll take my friend Don Juan.

[1]*Agamemnon*: A powerful king of ancient Greece.

6

Most epic poets plunge in "medias res,"[2]
(Horace[3] makes this the heroic turnpike road)
And then your hero tells, whene'er you please,
What went before—by way of episode,
While seated after dinner at his ease,
Beside his mistress in some soft abode,
Palace, or garden, paradise, or cavern,
Which serves the happy couple for a tavern.

7

That is the usual method, but not mine—
My way is to begin with the beginning;
The regularity of my design
Forbids all wandering as the worst of sinning,
And therefore I shall open with a line
(Although it cost me half an hour in spinning)
Narrating somewhat of Don Juan's father,
And also of his mother, if you'd rather.

***

49

Young Juan wax'd in goodliness and grace;
At six a charming child, and at eleven
With all the promise of as fine a face
As e'er to man's maturer growth was given:
He studied steadily, and grew apace,
And seem'd, at least, in the right road to heaven,
For half his days were pass'd at church, the other
Between his tutors, confessor, and mother.

50

At six, I said, he was a charming child,
At twelve he was a fine, but quiet boy;
Although in infancy a little wild,
They tamed him down amongst them; to destroy
His natural spirit not in vain they toil'd,
At least it seem'd so; and his mother's joy
Was to declare how sage, and still, and steady,
Her young philosopher was grown already.

[2]*in 'medias res'*: In the middle (Latin).

[3]*Horace*: A Roman literary critic.

51

I had my doubts, perhaps I have them still,
But what I say is neither here nor there:
I knew his father well, and have some skill
In character—but it would not be fair
From sire to son to augur good or ill:
He and his wife were an ill-sorted pair—
But scandal's my aversion—I protest
Against all evil speaking, even in jest.

52

For my part I say nothing—nothing—but
This I will say—my reasons are my own—
That if I had an only son to put
To school (as God be praised that I have none)
'Tis not with Donna Inez I would shut
Him up to learn his catechism alone,
No—no—I'd send him out betimes to college,
For there it was I pick'd up my own knowledge.

53

For there one learns—'tis not for me to boast,
Though I acquired—but I pass over *that*,
As well as all the Greek I since have lost:
I say that there's the place—but "*Verbum sat*,"[4]
I think I pick'd up too, as well as most,
Knowledge of matters—but no matter *what*—
I never married—but, I think, I know
That sons should not be educated so.

54

Young Juan now was sixteen years of age,
Tall, handsome, slender, but well knit; he seem'd
Active, though not so sprightly, as a page;
And every body but his mother deem'd
Him almost man; but she flew in a rage,
And bit her lips (for else she might have scream'd),
If any said so, for to be precocious
Was in her eyes a thing the most atrocious.

55

Amongst her numerous acquaintance, all
Selected for discretion and devotion,

[4]*verbum sat*: A shortened form of *verbum sat sapienti* (Latin), "A word is sufficient for a wise man." Byron is implying that Donna Inez's knowledge of Latin is superficial.

There was the Donna Julia, whom to call
    Pretty were but to give a feeble notion
Of many charms in her as natural
    As sweetness to the flower, or salt to ocean,
Her zone to Venus, or his bow to Cupid,
(But this last simile is trite and stupid).

56

The darkness of her oriental eye
    Accorded with her Moorish origin;
(Her blood was not all Spanish, by the by:
    In Spain, you know, this is a sort of sin).
When proud Grenada fell, and, forced to fly,
    Boabdil wept, of Donna Julia's kin
Some went to Africa, some staid in Spain,
Her great great grandmamma chose to remain.

57

She married (I forget the pedigree)
    With an Hidalgo, who transmitted down
His blood less noble than such blood should be;
    At such alliances his sires would frown,
In that point so precise in each degree
    That they bred *in and in*, as might be shown,
Marrying their cousins—nay, their aunts, and nieces,
Which always spoils the breed, if it increases.

58

This heathenish cross restored the breed again,
    Ruin'd its blood, but much improved its flesh;
For, from a root the ugliest in Old Spain
    Sprung up a branch as beautiful as fresh;
The sons no more were short, the daughters plain:
    But there's a rumour which I fain would hush,
'Tis said that Donna Julia's grandmamma
Produced her Don more heirs at love than law.

59

However this might be, the race went on
    Improving still through every generation,
Until it centr'd in an only son,
    Who left an only daughter; my narration
May have suggested that this single one
    Could be but Julia (whom on this occasion
I shall have much to speak about), and she
Was married, charming, chaste, and twenty-three.

60

Her eye (I'm very fond of handsome eyes)
  Was large and dark, suppressing half its fire
Until she spoke, then through its soft disguise
  Flash'd an expression more of pride than ire,
And love than either; and there would arise
  A something in them which was not desire,
But would have been, perhaps, but for the soul
Which struggled through and chasten'd down the whole.

61

Her glossy hair was cluster'd o'er a brow
  Bright with intelligence, and fair and smooth;
Her eyebrow's shape was like the aerial bow,
  Her cheek all purple with the beam of youth,
Mounting, at times, to a transparent glow,
  As if her veins ran lightning; she, in sooth,
Possess'd an air and grace by no means common:
Her stature tall—I hate a dumpy woman.

62

Wedded she was some years, and to a man
  Of fifty, and such husbands are in plenty;
And yet, I think, instead of such a ONE
  'Twere better to have TWO of five and twenty,
Especially in countries near the sun:
  And now I think on't, "*mi vien in mente,*"
Ladies even of the most uneasy virtue
Prefer a spouse whose age is short of thirty.

63

'Tis a sad thing, I cannot choose but say,
  And all the fault of that indecent sun,
Who cannot leave alone our helpless clay,
  But will keep baking, broiling, burning on,
That howsoever people fast and pray
  The flesh is frail, and so the soul undone:
What men call gallantry, and gods adultery,
Is much more common where the climate's sultry.

64

Happy the nations of the moral north!
  Where all is virtue, and the winter season
Sends sin, without a rag on, shivering forth;
  ('Twas snow that brought St Anthony to reason);

Where juries cast up what a wife is worth
    By laying whate'er sum, in mulct they please on
The lover, who must pay a handsome price,
Because it is a marketable vice.

65

Alfonso was the name of Julia's lord,
    A man well looking for his years, and who
Was neither much beloved, nor yet abhorr'd;
    They lived together as most people do,
Suffering each other's foibles by accord,
    And not exactly either *one* or *two;*
Yet he was jealous, though he did not show it,
For jealousy dislikes the world to know it.

66

Julia was—yet I never could see why—
    With Donna Inez quite a favourite friend;
Between their tastes there was small sympathy,
    For not a line had Julia ever penn'd:
Some people whisper (but, no doubt, they lie,
    For malice still imputes some private end)
That Inez had, ere Don Alfonso's marriage,
Forgot with him her very prudent carriage;

67

And that still keeping up the old connection,
    Which time had lately render'd much more chaste,
She took his lady also in affection,
    And certainly this course was much the best:
She flatter'd Julia with her sage protection,
    And complimented Don Alfonso's taste;
And if she could not (who can?) silence scandal,
At least she left it a more slender handle.

68

I can't tell whether Julia saw the affair
    With other people's eyes, or if her own
Discoveries made, but none could be aware
    Of this, at least no symptom e'er was shown;
Perhaps she did not know, or did not care,
    Indifferent from the first, or callous grown:
I'm really puzzled what to think or say,
She kept her counsel in so close a way.

69

Juan she saw, and, as a pretty child,
Caress'd him often, such a thing might be
Quite innocently done, and harmless styled,
When she had twenty years, and thirteen he;
But I am not so sure I should have smiled
When he was sixteen, Julia twenty-three,
These few short years make wondrous alterations,
Particularly amongst sun-burnt nations.

70

Whate'er the cause might be, they had become
Changed; for the dame grew distant, the youth shy,
Their looks cast down, their greetings almost dumb,
And much embarrassment in either eye;
There surely will be little doubt with some
That Donna Julia knew the reason why,
But as for Juan, he had no more notion
Than he who never saw the sea of ocean.

71

Yet Julia's very coldness still was kind,
And tremulously gentle her small hand
Withdrew itself from his, but left behind
A little pressure, thrilling, and so bland
And slight, so very slight, that to the mind
'Twas but a doubt; but ne'er magician's wand
Wrought change with all Armida's fairy art
Like what this light touch left on Juan's heart.

72

And if she met him, though she smiled no more,
She look'd a sadness sweeter than her smile,
As if her heart had deeper thoughts in store
She must not own, but cherish'd more the while,
For that compression in its burning core;
Even innocence itself has many a wile,
And will not dare to trust itself with truth,
And love is taught hypocrisy from youth.

73

But passion most dissembles yet betrays
Even by its darkness; as the blackest sky
Foretells the heaviest tempest, it displays
Its workings through the vainly guarded eye,

And in whatever aspect it arrays
Itself, 'tis still the same hypocrisy;
Coldness or anger, even disdain or hate,
Are masks it often wears, and still too late.

74

Then there were sighs, the deeper for suppression,
And stolen glances, sweeter for the theft,
And burning blushes, though for no transgression,
Tremblings when met, and restlessness when left;
All these are little preludes to possession,
Of which young Passion cannot be bereft,
And merely tend to show how greatly Love is
Embarrassed at first starting with a novice.

75

Poor Julia's heart was in an awkward state;
She felt it going, and resolved to make
The noblest efforts for herself and mate,
For honour's, pride's, religion's, virtue's sake;
Her resolutions were most truly great,
And almost might have made a Tarquin quake;
She pray'd the Virgin Mary for her grace,
As being the best judge of a lady's case.

76

She vow'd she never would see Juan more,
And next day paid a visit to his mother,
And look'd extremely at the opening door,
Which, by the Virgin's grace, let in another;
Grateful she was, and yet a little sore—
Again it opens, it can be no other,
'Tis surely Juan now—No! I'm afraid
That night the Virgin was no further pray'd.

77

She now determined that a virtuous woman
Should rather face and overcome temptation,
That flight was base and dastardly, and no man
Should ever give her heart the least sensation;
That is to say, a thought beyond the common
Preference, that we must feel upon occasion,
For people who are pleasanter than others,
But then they only seem so many brothers.

78

And even if by chance—and who can tell?
  The devil's so very sly—she should discover
That all within was not so very well,
  And, if still free, that such or such a lover
Might please perhaps, a virtuous wife can quell
  Such thoughts, and be the better when they're over;
And if the man should ask, 'tis but denial:
I recommend young ladies to make trial.

79

And then there are such things as love divine,
  Bright and immaculate, unmix'd and pure,
Such as the angels think so very fine,
  And matrons, who would be no less secure,
Platonic, perfect, "just such love as mine":
  Thus Julia said—and thought so, to be sure,
And so I'd have her think, were I the man
On whom her reveries celestial ran.

80

Such love is innocent, and may exist
  Between young persons without any danger,
A hand may first, and then a lip be kist;
  For my part, to such doings I'm a stranger,
But *hear* these freedoms form the utmost list
  Of all o'er which such love may be a ranger:
If people go beyond, 'tis quite a crime,
But not my fault—I tell them all in time.

81

Love, then, but love within its proper limits,
  Was Julia's innocent determination
In young Don Juan's favour, and to him its
  Exertion might be useful on occasion;
And, lighted at too pure a shrine to dim its
  Etherial lustre, with what sweet persuasion
He might be taught, by love and her together—
I really don't know what, nor Julia either.

82

Fraught with this fine intention, and well fenced
  In mail of proof—her purity of soul,
She, for the future of her strength convinced,
  And that her honour was a rock, or mole,

Exceeding sagely from that hour dispensed
    With any kind of troublesome control;
But whether Julia to the task was equal
Is that which must be mentioned in the sequel.

83

Her plan she deem'd both innocent and feasible,
    And, surely, with a stripling of sixteen
Not scandal's fangs could fix on much that's seizable,
    Or if they did so, satisfied to mean
Nothing but what was good, her breast was peaceable—
    A quiet conscience makes one so serene!
Christians have burnt each other, quite persuaded
That all the Apostles would have done as they did.

84

And if in the mean time her husband died,
    But heaven forbid that such a thought should cross
Her brain, though in a dream! (and then she sigh'd)
    Never could she survive that common loss;
But just suppose that moment should betide,
    I only say suppose *it—inter nos*—[5]
(This should be *entre nous*, for Julia thought
In French, but then the rhyme would go for nought).

85

I only say suppose this supposition:
    Juan being then grown up to man's estate
Would fully suit a widow of condition,
    Even seven years hence it would not be too late;
And in the interim (to pursue this vision)
    The mischief, after all, could not be great,
For he would learn the rudiments of love,
I mean the seraph way of those above.

86

So much for Julia. Now we'll turn to Juan,
    Poor little fellow! he had no idea
Of his own case, and never hit the true one;
    In feelings quick as Ovid's Miss Medea,
He puzzled over what he found a new one,
    But not as yet imagined it could be a
Thing quite in course, and not at all alarming,
Which, with a little patience, might grow charming.

[5]*inter nos . . . entre nous:* Between us (Latin and French).

87

Silent and pensive, idle, restless, slow,
His home deserted for the lonely wood,
Tormented with a wound he could not know,
His, like all deep grief, plunged in solitude:
I'm fond myself of solitude or so,
But then, I beg it may be understood,
By solitude I mean a sultan's, not
A hermit's, with a haram for a grot.

88

"Oh Love! in such a wilderness as this,
Where transport and security entwine,
Here is the empire of thy perfect bliss,
And here thou art a god indeed divine."
The bard I quote from does not sing amiss,
With the exception of the second line,
For that same twining "transport and security"
Are twisted to a phrase of some obscurity.

89

The poet meant, no doubt, and thus appeals
To the good sense and senses of mankind,
The very thing which every body feels,
As all have found on trial, or may find,
That no one likes to be disturb'd at meals
Or love.—I won't say more about "entwined"
Or "transport," as we knew all that before,
But beg "Security" will bolt the door.

90

Young Juan wander'd by the glassy brooks
Thinking unutterable things; he threw
Himself at length within the leafy nooks
Where the wild branch of the cork forest grew;
There poets find materials for their books,
And every now and then we read them through,
So that their plan and prosody are eligible,
Unless, like Wordsworth, they prove unintelligible.

91

He, Juan, (and not Wordsworth) so pursued
His self-communion with his own high soul,
Until his mighty heart, in its great mood,
Had mitigated part, though not the whole

Of its disease; he did the best he could
    With things not very subject to control,
And turn'd, without perceiving his condition,
Like Coleridge,[6] into a metaphysician.

92

He thought about himself, and the whole earth,
    Of man the wonderful, and of the stars,
And how the deuce they ever could have birth;
    And then he thought of earthquakes, and of wars,
How many miles the moon might have in girth,
    Of air-balloons, and of the many bars
To perfect knowledge of the boundless skies;
And then he thought of Donna Julia's eyes.

93

In thoughts like these true wisdom may discern
    Longings sublime, and aspirations high,
Which some are born with, but the most part learn
    To plague themselves withal, they know not why:
'Twas strange that one so young should thus concern
    His brain about the action of the sky;
If *you* think 'twas philosophy that this did,
I can't help thinking puberty assisted.

***

97

Those lonely walks, and lengthening reveries,
    Could not escape the gentle Julia's eyes;
She saw that Juan was not at his ease;
    But that which chiefly may, and must surprise,
Is, that the Donna Inez did not tease
    Her only son with question or surmise;
Whether it was she did not see, or would not,
Or, like all very clever people, could not.

98

This may seem strange, but yet 'tis very common;
    For instance—gentlemen, whose ladies take
Leave to o'erstep the written rights of woman,
    And break the——Which commandment is't they break?

[6]*Wordsworth . . . Coleridge:* William Wordsworth (1770–1850) and Samuel Coleridge (1772–1834) were Romantic poets who praised the transcendent power of nature.

(I have forgot the number, and think no man
  Should rashly quote, for fear of a mistake)
I say, when these same gentlemen are jealous,
They make some blunder, which their ladies tell us.

99

A real husband always is suspicious,
  But still no less suspects in the wrong place,
Jealous of some one who had no such wishes,
  Or pandering blindly to his own disgrace
By harbouring some dear friend extremely vicious;
  The last indeed's infallibly the case:
And when the spouse and friend are gone off wholly,
He wonders at their vice, and not his folly.

***

101

But Inez was so anxious, and so clear
  Of sight, that I must think, on this occasion,
She had some other motive much more near
  For leaving Juan to this new temptation;
But what that motive was, I shan't say here;
  Perhaps to finish Juan's education,
Perhaps to open Don Alfonso's eyes,
In case he thought his wife too great a prize.

102

It was upon a day, a summer's day;—
  Summer's indeed a very dangerous season,
And so is spring about the end of May;
  The sun, no doubt, is the prevailing reason;
But whatsoe'er the cause is, one may say,
  And stand convicted of more truth than treason,
That there are months which nature grows more merry in,
March has its hares, and May must have its heroine.

103

'Twas on a summer's day—the sixth of June:—
  I like to be particular in dates,
Not only of the age, and year, but moon;
  They are a sort of post-house, where the Fates
Change horses, making history change its tune,
  Then spur away o'er empires and o'er states;
Leaving at last not much besides chronology,
Excepting the post-obits of theology.

104

'Twas on the sixth of June, about the hour
  Of half-past six—perhaps still nearer seven,
When Julia sate within as pretty a bower
  As e'er held houri in that heathenish heaven
Described by Mahomet, and Anacreon Moore,[7]
  To whom the lyre and laurels have been given,
With all the trophies of triumphant song—
He won them well, and may he wear them long!

105

She sate, but not alone; I know not well
  How this same interview had taken place,
And even if I knew, I should not tell—
  People should hold their tongues in any case;
No matter how or why the thing befell,
  But there were she and Juan, face to face—
When two such faces are so, 'twould be wise,
But very difficult, to shut their eyes.

106

How beautiful she look'd! her conscious heart
  Glow'd in her cheek, and yet she felt no wrong.
Oh Love! how perfect is thy mystic art,
  Strengthening the weak, and trampling on the strong,
How self-deceitful is the sagest part
  Of mortals whom thy lure hath led along—
The precipice she stood on was immense,
So was her creed in her own innocence.

107

She thought of her own strength, and Juan's youth,
  And of the folly of all prudish fears,
Victorious virtue, and domestic truth,
  And then of Don Alfonso's fifty years;
I wish these last had not occurr'd, in sooth,
  Because that number rarely much endears,
And through all climes, the snowy and the sunny,
Sounds ill in love, whate'er it may in money.

108

When people say, "I've told you *fifty* times,"
  They mean to scold, and very often do;

[7]*Anacreon Moore:* Thomas Moore (1779–1852), whose poetry resembled the Greek poet Anacreon.

When poets say, "I've written *fifty* rhymes,"
  They make you dread that they'll recite them too;
In gangs of *fifty*, thieves commit their crimes;
  At *fifty* love for love is rare, 'tis true,
But then, no doubt, it equally as true is,
A good deal may be bought for *fifty* Louis.

109

Julia had honour, virtue, truth, and love,
  For Don Alfonso; and she inly swore,
By all the vows below to powers above,
  She never would disgrace the ring she wore,
Nor leave a wish which wisdom might reprove;
  And while she ponder'd this, besides much more,
One hand on Juan's carelessly was thrown,
Quite by mistake—she thought it was her own;

110

Unconsciously she lean'd upon the other,
  Which play'd within the tangles of her hair;
And to contend with thoughts she could not smother,
  She seem'd by the distraction of her air.
'Twas surely very wrong in Juan's mother
  To leave together this imprudent pair,
She who for many years had watch'd her son so
I'm very certain *mine* would not have done so.

111

The hand which still held Juan's, by degrees
  Gently, but palpably confirm'd its grasp,
As if it said "detain me, if you please";
  Yet there's no doubt she only meant to clasp
His fingers with a pure Platonic[8] squeeze;
  She would have shrunk as from a toad, or asp,
Had she imagined such a thing could rouse
A feeling dangerous to a prudent spouse.

112

I cannot know what Juan thought of this,
  But what he did, is much what you would do;
His young lip thank'd it with a grateful kiss,
  And then, abash'd at its own joy, withdrew
In deep despair, lest he had done amiss,
  Love is so very timid when 'tis new:
She blush'd, and frown'd not, but she strove to speak,
And held her tongue, her voice was grown so weak.

[8]*Platonic:* Nonsexual, as idealized in Plato's *The Republic*.

113

The sun set, and up rose the yellow moon:
  The devil's in the moon for mischief; they
Who call'd her CHASTE, methinks, began too soon
  Their nomenclature; there is not a day,
The longest, not the twenty-first of June,
  Sees half the business in a wicked way
On which three single hours of moonshine smile—
And then she looks so modest all the while.

114

There is a dangerous silence in that hour,
  A stillness, which leaves room for the full soul
To open all itself, without the power
  Of calling wholly back its self-control;
The silver light which, hallowing tree and tower
  Sheds beauty and deep softness o'er the whole,
Breathes also to the heart, and o'er it throws
A loving languor, which is not repose.

115

And Julia sate with Juan, half embraced
  And half retiring from the glowing arm,
Which trembled like the bosom where 'twas placed;
  Yet still she must have thought there was no harm,
Or else 'twere easy to withdraw her waist;
  But then the situation had its charm,
And then——God knows what next—I can't go on;
I'm almost sorry that I e'er begun.

116

Oh Plato! Plato! you have paved the way,
  With your confounded fantasies, to more
Immoral conduct by the fancied sway
  Your system feigns o'er the controlless core
Of human hearts, than all the long array
  Of poets and romancers:—You're a bore,
A charlatan, a coxcomb—and have been,
At best, no better than a go-between.

117

And Julia's voice was lost, except in sighs,
  Until too late for useful conversation;
The tears were gushing from her gentle eyes,
  I wish, indeed, they had not had occasion,

But who, alas! can love, and then be wise?
Not that remorse did not oppose temptation,
A little still she strove, and much repented,
And whispering 'I will ne'er consent'—consented.

***

134

What then?—I do not know, no more do you—
And so good night.—Return we to our story:
'Twas in November, when fine days are few,
And the far mountains wax a little hoary,
And clap a white cape on their mantles blue;
And the sea dashes round the promontory,
And the loud breaker boils against the rock,
And sober suns must set at five o'clock.

135

'Twas, as the watchmen say, a cloudy night;
No moon, no stars, the wind was low or loud
By gusts, and many a sparkling hearth was bright
With the piled wood, round which the family crowd;
There's something cheerful in that sort of light,
Even as a summer sky's without a cloud:
I'm fond of fire, and crickets, and all that,
A lobster-salad, and champaigne, and chat.

136

'Twas midnight—Donna Julia was in bed,
Sleeping, most probably,—when at her door
Arose a clatter might awake the dead,
If they had never been awoke before,
And that they have been so we all have read,
And are to be so, at the least, once more—
The door was fasten'd, but with voice and Fist
First knocks were heard, then "Madam—Madam—hist!"

137

"For God's sake, Madam—Madam—here's my master,
With more than half the city at his back—
Was ever heard of such a curst disaster!
'Tis not my fault—I kept good watch—Alack!
Do, pray undo the bolt a little faster—
They're on the stair just now, and in a crack
Will all be here; perhaps he yet may fly—
Surely the window's not so *very* high!"

138

By this time Don Alfonso was arrived,
  With torches, friends, and servants in great number;
The major part of them had long been wived,
  And therefore paused not to disturb the slumber
Of any wicked woman, who contrived
  By stealth her husband's temples to encumber:
Examples of this kind are so contagious,
Were *one* not punish'd, *all* would be outrageous.

139

I can't tell how, or why, or what suspicion
  Could enter into Don Alfonso's head;
But for a cavalier of his condition
  It surely was exceedingly ill-bred,
Without a word of previous admonition,
  To hold a levee round his lady's bed,
And summon lackeys, arm'd with fire and sword,
To prove himself the thing he most abhorr'd.

140

Poor Donna Julia! starting as from sleep,
  (Mind—that I do not say—she had not slept)
Began at once to scream, and yawn, and weep;
  Her maid Antonia, who was an adept,
Contrived to fling the bed-clothes in a heap,
  As if she had just now from out them crept:
I can't tell why she should take all this trouble
To prove her mistress had been sleeping double.

141

But Julia mistress, and Antonia maid,
  Appear'd like two poor harmless women, who
Of goblins, but still more of men afraid,
  Had thought one man might be deterr'd by two,
And therefore side by side were gently laid,
  Until the hours of absence should run through,
And truant husband should return, and say,
"My dear, I was the first who came away."

142

Now Julia found at length a voice, and cried,
  "In heaven's name, Don Alfonso, what d'ye mean?
Has madness seized you? would that I had died,
  Ere such a monster's victim I had been!

What may this midnight violence betide,
  A sudden fit of drunkenness or spleen?
Dare you suspect me, whom the thought would kill?
Search, then, the room!"—Alfonso said, "I will."

143

He search'd, *they* search'd, and rummaged every where,
  Closet and clothes'-press, chest and window-seat,
And found much linen, lace, and several pair
  Of stockings, slippers, brushes, combs, complete,
With other articles of ladies fair,
  To keep them beautiful, or leave them neat:
Arras they prick'd and curtains with their swords,
And wounded several shutters, and some boards.

144

Under the bed they search'd, and there they found—
  No matter what—it was not that they sought;
They open'd windows, gazing if the ground
  Had signs or footmarks, but the earth said nought;
And then they stared each other's faces round:
  'Tis odd, not one of all these seekers thought,
And seems to me almost a sort of blunder,
Of looking *in* the bed as well as under.

145

During this inquisition Julia's tongue
  Was not asleep—"Yes, search and search," she cried,
"Insult on insult heap, and wrong on wrong!
  It was for this that I became a bride!
For this in silence I have suffer'd long
  A husband like Alfonso at my side;
But now I'll bear no more, nor here remain,
If there be law, or lawyers, in all Spain.

146

"Yes, Don Alfonso! husband now no more,
  If ever you indeed deserved the name,
Is't worthy of your years?—you have threescore,
  Fifty, or sixty—it is all the same—
Is't wise or fitting causeless to explore
  For facts against a virtuous woman's fame?
Ungrateful, perjured, barbarous Don Alfonso,
How dare you think your lady would go on so?

147

"Is it for this I have disdain'd to hold
The common privileges of my sex?
That I have chosen a confessor so old
And deaf, that any other it would vex,
And never once he has had cause to scold,
But found my very innocence perplex
So much, he always doubted I was married—
How sorry you will be when I've miscarried!

***

150

"Have I not had two bishops at my feet?
The Duke of Ichãr, and Don Fernan Nunez,
And is it thus a faithful wife you treat?
I wonder in what quarter now the moon is:
I praise your vast forbearance not to beat
Me also, since the time so opportune is—
Oh, valiant man! with sword drawn and cock'd trigger,
Now, tell me, don't you cut a pretty figure?

151

"Was it for this you took your sudden journey,
Under pretence of business indispensible
With that sublime of rascals your attorney,
Whom I see standing there, and looking sensible
Of having play'd the fool? though both I spurn, he
Deserves the worst, his conduct's less defensible,
Because, no doubt, 'twas for his dirty fee,
And not from any love to you nor me.

152

"If he comes here to take a deposition,
By all means let the gentleman proceed;
You've made the apartment in a fit condition:—
There's pen and ink for you, sir, when you need—
Let every thing be noted with precision,
I would not you for nothing should be fee'd—
But, as my maid's undrest, pray turn your spies out."
"Oh!" sobb'd Antonia, "I could tear their eyes out."

153

"There is the closet, there the toilet, there
The ante-chamber—search them under, over:

There is the sofa, there the great arm-chair,
The chimney—which would really hold a lover.
I wish to sleep, and beg you will take care
And make no further noise, till you discover
The secret cavern of this lurking treasure—
And when 'tis found, let me, too, have that pleasure.

154

"And now, Hidalgo! now that you have thrown
Doubt upon me, confusion over all,
Pray have the courtesy to make it known
Who is the man you search for? how d'ye call
Him? what's his lineage? let him but be shown—
I hope he's young and handsome—is he tall?
Tell me—and be assured, that since you stain
My honour thus, it shall not be in vain.

155

"At least, perhaps, he has not sixty years,
At that age he would be too old for slaughter,
Or for so young a husband's jealous fears—
(Antonia! let me have a glass of water)
I am ashamed of having shed these tears,
They are unworthy of my father's daughter;
My mother dream'd not in my natal hour
That I should fall into a monster's power.

156

"Perhaps 'tis of Antonia you are jealous,
You saw that she was sleeping by my side
When you broke in upon us with your fellows:
Look where you please—we've nothing, sir, to hide;
Only another time, I trust, you'll tell us,
Or for the sake of decency abide
A moment at the door, that we may be
Drest to receive so much good company.

157

"And now, sir, I have done, and say no more;
The little I have said may serve to show
The guileless heart in silence may grieve o'er
The wrongs to whose exposure it is slow:—
I leave you to your conscience as before,
'Twill one day ask you *why* you used me so?

God grant you feel not then the bitterest grief!
Antonia! Where's my pocket-handkerchief?"

158

She ceased, and turn'd upon her pillow; pale
She lay, her dark eyes flashing through their tears,
Like skies that rain and lighten; as a veil,
Waved and o'ershading her wan cheek, appears
Her streaming hair; the black curls strive, but fail,
To hide the glossy shoulder, which uprears
Its snow through all;—her soft lips lie apart,
And louder than her breathing beats her heart.

159

The Senhor Don Alfonso stood confused;
Antonia bustled round the ransack'd room,
And, turning up her nose, with looks abused
Her master, and his myrmidons, of whom
Not one, except the attorney, was amused;
He, like Achates, faithful to the tomb,
So there were quarrels, cared not for the cause,
Knowing they must be settled by the laws.

160

With prying snub-nose, and small eyes, he stood,
Following Antonia's motions here and there,
With much suspicion in his attitude;
For reputations he had little care;
So that a suit or action were made good,
Small pity had he for the young and fair,
And ne'er believed in negatives, till these
Were proved by competent false witnesses.

161

But Don Alfonso stood with downcast looks,
And, truth to say, he made a foolish figure;
When, after searching in five hundred nooks,
And treating a young wife with so much rigour,
He gain'd no point, except some self-rebukes,
Added to those his lady with such vigour
Had pour'd upon him for the last half-hour,
Quick, thick, and heavy—as a thunder-shower.

162

At first he tried to hammer an excuse,
To which the sole reply were tears, and sobs,
And indications of hysterics, whose
Prologue is always certain throes, and throbs,
Gasps, and whatever else the owners choose:—
Alfonso saw his wife, and thought of Job's;
He saw too, in perspective, her relations,
And then he tried to muster all his patience.

163

He stood in act to speak, or rather stammer,
But sage Antonia cut him short before
The anvil of his speech received the hammer,
With "Pray sir, leave the room, and say no more,
Or madam dies."—Alfonso mutter'd "D—n her,"
But nothing else, the time of words was o'er;
He cast a rueful look or two, and did,
He knew not wherefore, that which he was bid.

164

With him retired his "*posse comitatus*,"[9]
The attorney last, who linger'd near the door,
Reluctantly, still tarrying there as late as
Antonia let him—not a little sore
At this most strange and unexplain'd "*hiatus*"
In Don Alfonso's facts, which just now wore
An awkward look; as he revolved the case
The door was fasten'd in his legal face.

165

No sooner was it bolted, than—Oh shame!
Oh sin! Oh sorrow! and Oh womankind!
How can you do such things and keep your fame,
Unless this world, and t'other too, be blind?
Nothing so dear as an unfilch'd good name!
But to proceed—for there is more behind:
With much heart-felt reluctance be it said,
Young Juan slipp'd, half-smother'd, from the bed.

[9]*posse comitatus:* The power of the county (Latin).

166

He had been hid—I don't pretend to say
  How, nor can I indeed describe the where—
Young, slender, and pack'd easily, he lay,
  No doubt, in little compass, round or square;
But pity him I neither must nor may
  His suffocation by that pretty pair;
'Twere better, sure, to die so, than be shut
With maudlin Clarence in his Malmsey butt.

167

And, secondly, I pity not, because
  He had no business to commit a sin,
Forbid by heavenly, fined by human laws,
  At least 'twas rather early to begin;
But at sixteen the conscience rarely gnaws
  So much as when we call our old debts in
At sixty years, and draw the accompts of evil,
And find a deuced balance with the devil.

***

170

He turn'd his lip to hers, and with his hand
  Call'd back the tangles of her wandering hair;
Even then their love they could not all command,
  And half forgot their danger and despair:
Antonia's patience now was at a stand—
  "Come, come, 'tis no time now for fooling there,"
She whisper'd, in great wrath—"I must deposit
This pretty gentleman within the closet."

171

"Pray, keep your nonsense for some luckier night—
  Who can have put my master in this mood?
What will become on't?—I'm in such a fright,
  The devil's in the urchin, and no good—
Is this a time for giggling? this a plight?
  Why, don't you know that it may end in blood?
You'll lose your life, and I shall lose my place,
My mistress, all, for that half-girlish face.

***

176

Julia, in fact, had tolerable grounds,
  Alfonso's loves with Inez were well known;

But whether 'twas that one's own guilt confounds,
  But that can't be, as has been often shown,
A lady with apologies abounds;
  It might be that her silence sprang alone
From delicacy to Don Juan's ear,
To whom she knew his mother's fame was dear.

177

There might be one more motive, which makes two;
  Alfonso ne'er to Juan had alluded,
Mention'd his jealousy, but never who
  Had been the happy lover, he concluded,
Conceal'd amongst his premises; 'tis true,
  His mind the more o'er this its mystery brooded;
To speak of Inez now were, one may say,
Like throwing Juan in Alfonso's way.

178

A hint, in tender cases, is enough;
  Silence is best, besides there is a *tact*
(That modern phrase appears to me sad stuff,
  But it will serve to keep my verse compact)
Which keeps, when push'd by questions rather rough,
  A lady always distant from the fact—
The charming creatures lie with such a grace,
There's nothing so becoming to the face.

179

They blush, and we believe them; at least I
  Have always done so; 'tis of no great use,
In any case, attempting a reply,
  For then their eloquence grows quite profuse;
And when at length they're out of breath, they sigh,
  And cast their languid eyes down, and let loose
A tear or two, and then we make it up;
And then—and then—and then—sit down and sup.

180

Alfonso closed his speech, and begg'd her pardon,
  Which Julia half withheld, and then half granted,
And laid conditions, he thought, very hard on,
  Denying several little things he wanted:
He stood like Adam lingering near his garden,
  With useless penitence perplex'd and haunted,
Beseeching she no further would refuse,
When lo! he stumbled o'er a pair of shoes.

181

A pair of shoes!—what then? not much, if they
  Are such a fit with lady's feet, but these
(No one can tell how much I grieve to say)
  Were masculine; to see them, and to seize,
Was but a moment's act.—Ah! Well-a-day!
  My teeth begin to chatter, my veins freeze—
Alfonso first examined well their fashion,
And then flew out into another passion.

182

He left the room for his relinquish'd sword,
  And Julia instant to the closet flew.
"Fly, Juan, fly! for heaven's sake—not a word—
  The door is open—you may yet slip through
The passage you so often have explored—
  Here is the garden-key—Fly—fly—Adieu!
Haste—haste!—I hear Alfonso's hurrying feet—
Day has not broke—there's no one in the street."

183

None can say that this was not good advice,
  The only mischief was, it came too late;
Of all experience 'tis the usual price,
  A sort of income-tax laid on by fate:
Juan had reach'd the room-door in a trice,
  And might have done so by the garden-gate,
But met Alfonso in his dressing-gown,
Who threaten'd death—so Juan knock'd him down.

184

Dire was the scuffle, and out went the light,
  Antonia cried out "Rape!" and Julia "Fire!"
But not a servant stirr'd to aid the fight.
  Alfonso, pommell'd to his heart's desire,
Swore lustily he'd be revenged this night;
  And Juan, too, blasphemed an octave higher,
His blood was up; though young, he was a Tartar,
And not at all disposed to prove a martyr.

185

Alfonso's sword had dropp'd ere he could draw it,
  And they continued battling hand to hand,
For Juan very luckily ne'er saw it;
  His temper not being under great command,

If at that moment he had chanced to claw it,
Alfonso's days had not been in the land
Much longer.—Think of husbands', lovers' lives!
And how ye may be doubly widows—wives!

186

Alfonso grappled to detain the foe,
And Juan throttled him to get away,
And blood ('twas from the nose) began to flow;
At last, as they more faintly wrestling lay,
Juan contrived to give an awkward blow,
And then his only garment quite gave way;
He fled, like Joseph, leaving it; but there,
I doubt, all likeness ends between the pair.

187

Lights came at length, and men, and maids, who found
An awkward spectacle their eyes before;
Antonia in hysterics, Julia swoon'd,
Alfonso leaning, breathless, by the door;
Some half-torn drapery scatter'd on the ground,
Some blood, and several footsteps, but no more:
Juan the gate gain'd, turn'd the key about,
And liking not the inside, lock'd the out.

188

Here ends this canto.—Need I sing, or say,
How Juan, naked, favour'd by the night,
Who favours what she should not, found his way,
And reach'd his home in an unseemly plight?
The pleasant scandal which arose next day,
The nine days' wonder which was brought to light,
And how Alfonso sued for a divorce,
Were in the English newspapers, of course.

189

If you would like to see the whole proceedings,
The depositions, and the cause at full,
The names of all the witnesses, the pleadings
Of counsel to nonsuit, or to annul,
There's more than one edition, and the readings
Are various, but they none of them are dull,
The best is that in shorthand ta'en by Gurney,
Who to Madrid on purpose made a journey.

190

But Donna Inez, to divert the train
  Of one of the most circulating scandals
That had for centuries been known in Spain,
  Since Roderic's[10] Goths, or older Genseric's[11] Vandals,
First vow'd (and never had she vow'd in vain)
  To Virgin Mary several pounds of candles;
And then, by the advice of some old ladies,
She sent her son to be embark'd at Cadiz.

191

She had resolved that he should travel through
  All European climes, by land or sea,
To mend his former morals, or get new,
  Especially in France and Italy,
(At least this is the thing most people do).
  Julia was sent into a nunnery,
And there, perhaps, her feelings may be better
Shown in the following copy of her letter:

192

"They tell me 'tis decided; you depart:
  'Tis wise—'tis well, but not the less a pain;
I have no further claim on your young heart,
  Mine was the victim, and would be again;
To love too much has been the only art
  I used;—I write in haste, and if a stain
Be on this sheet, 'tis not what it appears,
My eyeballs burn and throb, but have no tears.

193

"I loved, I love you, for that love have lost
  State, station, heaven, mankind's, my own esteem,
And yet can not regret what it hath cost,
  So dear is still the memory of that dream;
Yet, if I name my guilt, 'tis not to boast,
  None can deem harshlier of me than I deem:
I trace this scrawl because I cannot rest—
I've nothing to reproach, nor to request.

[10]*Roderic:* The last king of the Visigoths, who lived in the eighth century and ruled from Toledo, Spain.

[11]*Genseric:* The fifth-century king of the Vandals, who moved from southern Spain to conquer northern Africa and eventually other Mediterranean lands.

194

"Man's love is of his life a thing apart,
'Tis woman's whole existence; man may range
The court, camp, church, the vessel, and the mart,
Sword, gown, gain, glory, offer in exchange
Pride, fame, ambition, to fill up his heart,
And few there are whom these can not estrange;
Man has all these resources, we but one,
To love again, and be again undone.

195

"My breast has been all weakness, is so yet;
I struggle, but cannot collect my mind;
My blood still rushes where my spirit's set,
As roll the waves before the settled wind;
My brain is feminine, nor can forget—
To all, except your image, madly blind;
As turns the needle trembling to the pole
It ne'er can reach, so turns to you, my soul.

196

"You will proceed in beauty, and in pride,
Beloved and loving many; all is o'er
For me on earth, except some years to hide
My shame and sorrow deep in my heart's core;
These I could bear, but cannot cast aside
The passion which still rends it as before,
And so farewell—forgive me, love me—No,
That word is idle now—but let it go.

197

"I have no more to say, but linger still,
And dare not set my seal upon this sheet,
And yet I may as well the task fulfil,
My misery can scarce be more complete:
I had not lived till now, could sorrow kill;
Death flies the wretch who fain the blow would meet,
And I must even survive this last adieu,
And bear with life, to love and pray for you!"

198

This note was written upon gilt-edged paper
With a neat crow-quill, rather hard, but new;
Her small white fingers scarce could reach the taper,
But trembled as magnetic needles do,

And yet she did not let one tear escape her;
  The seal a sunflower; "*Elle vous suit partout*,"[12]
The motto, cut upon a white cornelian;
The wax was superfine, its hue vermilion.

(1820)

[12]*Elle vous suit partout*: She follows you everywhere (French).

Gustave Flaubert *(1821–1880)*

Passion and Virtue

A Philosophical Tale

Can you speak of what you do not feel at all?
—SHAKESPEARE, *Romeo and Juliet*, ACT 3, SCENE 5

One

She had already seen him twice, I believe. The first time was at a ball at the Minister's house, and the second was at the Théâtre-Français. And although he had neither superior attributes nor good looks, she frequently thought of him in the evenings after extinguishing her lamp. She often lingered for a few thoughtful moments with her hair scattered over her naked breasts and her head turned toward the window where the night cast a dull light, with her arms hanging out of her bed and her soul floating between vague and hideous emotions—like those confused sounds that rise in the fields on autumn evenings.

Far from being the kind of exceptional soul one finds in books and plays, he was dispassionate, equitable, and above all a chemist. But he was also a master of the theory, principles, and rules of seduction. To use the true but crude expression, he had the knack of a skillful man for getting what he wanted.

We're not talking about a pastoral method in the style of Louis XIV, where the first lesson begins with sighs, the second with love notes, and it continues that way until the conclusion. That's the technique outlined so well by Faublas, by second-rate comedies, and by the *Moral Tales* of Marmontel.[1] But nowadays a man approaches a woman, eyes her with his lorgnette, finds her acceptable, and makes a bet with his friends. If she's married, the farce will be all the better.

Then he gets his foot in her door, lends her books, takes her to the theater, and makes sure to do something remarkable and ridiculous to catch her attention. Day after day he takes greater liberties in going to her house. He becomes a friend of the family, of her husband, her children, and her servants. Finally, she notices the trap and wants to drive him away like a lackey. But in response he

[1]*Marmontel*: A popular eighteenth-century author of novels and moral tales for children.

becomes indignant, threatens to publish a brief letter that he interprets in a scandalous way, no matter for whom it was intended. To her husband, he will repeat a random word that was perhaps uttered in a moment of vanity, flirting, or desire. That's the cruelty of an anatomist, but science progresses, and there are people who dissect a heart the way they do a cadaver.

Then that poor, distracted woman cries and begs. But there is no pardon for her, for her children, husband, or mother. Being a man, he is unbending and can expend his strength and violence; he can bruit it about that she is his mistress and can publish it in the newspapers, detail it in a memoir, and prove it, if need be.

Half dead, she surrenders to him. Then he can even parade her in front of his lackeys, who sneer among themselves behind their elegant trappings when they see her return to their master's house in the early morning. And when he has abased and broken her, leaving her to her regrets and thoughts about the past and her deceit, abandoned to her misfortune, he goes away and scarcely recognizes her. At times he even hates her, but he did win his bet, and he is a lucky man.

So he is no Lovelace, as he would have been called sixty years ago, but rather a Don Juan, which is more attractive.

The man who possesses such knowledge in depth, who knows the hidden ins and outs, is not rare these days. Indeed, when you have no soul or sympathy in your heart, it's so easy to seduce a woman who loves you and then leave her there with all the other ones! There are so many ways to get them to love you, either through jealousy, vanity, merit, talents, pride, horror, and even fear or else through your fatuous manners, the stylish casualness of wearing your tie, the pretense of being in despair, sometimes through the cut of your clothes or the elegance of your boots! After all, how many people have owed their conquests only to the competence of their tailor or bootmaker?

Ernest had noticed that Mazza returned his glances with a smile. He pursued her everywhere. For instance, she got bored if he didn't attend the ball. And don't believe that he was such a novice as to praise the whiteness of her hand or the beauty of her rings, as a schoolboy might have done to practice his rhetoric. In her presence he tore down all the other women who were dancing since he knew the strangest and most unheard-of adventures about each one of them. All of that made her laugh and secretly flattered her when she thought that there were no stories to tell about her. Standing right at the brink of the precipice, she firmly resolved to abandon him and never see him again—but a smile on a lover's mouth makes virtue evaporate quickly.

He had noticed that she loved poetry, the sea, the theater, Byron; summing up all these observations into a single one, he said, "She's foolish and I'll have her." When she watched him leave and the door of the salon closed quickly on his departure, she too often said, "Oh, how I love you!"

In addition, consider that Ernest made her believe in phrenology and magnetism, that Mazza was thirty years old, and that her purity had always kept her completely faithful to her husband, turning away from all the desires that arose each day in her soul only to die the next day; consider that she was married to a banker and that, in the arms of this man, passion was nothing less than a duty for her, like watching over her staff and dressing her children.

Two

She was content for a long time with that state of amorous and half-mystical duty. She enjoyed the novelty of gratification, and for a long time played with that love, longer than with the others, and finally became quite smitten, at first by habit and then by need. Laughing and playing with your heart is dangerous, for passion is a firearm that can go off and kill you when you don't believe yourself at risk.

One day Ernest arrived early at Madame Willer's. Since her husband was at the Stock Exchange and her children had gone out, he found himself alone with her. He stayed at her house all day, and when he left around five o'clock in the afternoon, Mazza became so dreamy and sad that she didn't sleep all night.

They conversed for many hours, declaring their love, speaking of poetry, rehearsing the sort of strong and expansive love one reads about in Byron, and then complaining about the social constraints that drew them together and kept them apart for life. They had voiced the trials of their hearts, of life and death, of nature, and of the ocean, which roared nightly. Understanding the world and their passion, their expressions had spoken even more than their lips, which touched often.

It was on one of those long, dreary, and morose March days that imbue your soul with a vague bitterness. Their words had been sad, and Mazza's especially had a harmonious melancholy. Each time Ernest was about to say that he loved her for life, each time he smiled at her, looked at her, or protested his love, Mazza didn't answer. With her mouth open and her brow pale, her large black eyes stared at him in silence.

On that day she felt oppressed, as if an invisible hand were weighing on her chest. She was afraid without knowing why, content to remain in that fear mixed with a strange sensation of love, revery, and mysticism. Once she drew her chair back, frightened by the wild and fearful bestiality of Ernest's smile. But he moved closer to her, took her hands and brought them to his lips. She blushed and said in a tone of affected calm;

"Would you like to court me?"

"To court you, Mazza! You?"

That answer said it all.

"Do you mean that you love me?"

He smiled at her.

"Ernest, you would be wrong."

"Why?"

"My husband! Do you think about him?"

"So what! What does that mean?"

"I'm supposed to love him."

"That's easier said than done. In other words, the law tells you 'You will love him,' and your heart responds like a regiment on maneuvers or an iron bar that you bend with your hands, and if I love you . . ."

"Be quiet, Ernest. Think about what you owe to a woman like me who receives you alone in the morning when her husband is out, subject to your charms."

"Yes, if I love you in turn, it must be because I'm no longer *supposed to,* and nothing more. But is that reasonable and proper?"

"Ah, your logic is marvelous, my dear friend," Mazza said, leaning her head over on her left shoulder and turning her ivory needle case between her fingers. A lock of her hair came undone and fell on her cheeks. She swept it back with a quick but graceful movement of her head. Ernest got up several times, took his hat as if he were going to leave, but then sat down and resumed his conversation.

They often interrupted one another or else looked at each other in silence, barely breathing, heady and satisfied with their glances and sighs. Then they would smile.

Once when Mazza saw Ernest at her feet, sunk down on the carpet of her bedroom, when she saw his head resting on her knees, his hair pulled back, and his eyes drawn close to her breast with his unlined white forehead in front of her mouth, she thought that she was going to take his head into her arms, press it to her heart, and cover it with kisses.

"I'll write you tomorrow," Ernest told her.

"Farewell!"

And he left.

Mazza's mind alternated indecisively from a strange breathlessness to vague foreboding to ineffable daydreams. She awoke at night. Like the eye of a condemned man looking at you, her lamp cast intersecting reflections of trembling circles on the ceiling. She remained that way until daybreak, hearing the hours sound on all the clocks, listening to all the nighttime sounds, the rain falling against the walls, the wind blowing and spinning in the shadows, the windowpanes trembling, the wooden bed groaning with each movement she made when she turned on her mattress, haunted by torturing thoughts and terrible images that completely covered her as she squirmed in her bed sheets.

In such hours of delirious fever, who has not felt those intimate movements of the heart? Who hasn't heard those convulsions of a tormented soul, endlessly twisting under the weight of undefinable thoughts full of both torment and voluptuousness, at first vague and as ill defined as a phantom? Soon that wavering thought stops and comes together, takes on a bodily shape, and becomes an image that makes you weep and tremble. On warm, steamy nights when your skin is seared and insomnia eats at you as you sit at the foot of your bed, who hasn't seen an ashen, dreamy face looking at you sadly? Or else it appears in its gala clothes, if you have seen it dance at a ball, or else wrapped in black veils and crying. And you recall its words, the sound of its voice, the languidness of its eyes.

Poor Mazza! For the first time she felt that she was in love, a love that was going to become a need, then a sentimental delirium and mania. But in her naiveté and ignorance she quickly foresaw a happy future, a tranquil existence where passion would give her joy, and delight would give happiness.

Actually, couldn't she live happily in the arms of the one who loved her and at the same time deceive her husband? "What is all that compared to love?" she wondered. Yet she suffered from that sentimental delirium and sank into it deeper and deeper, like those who get drunk out of pleasure, only to become ravaged by drink. It is true that those palpitations of the heart are poignant and bitter, the anguish of a soul torn between an evanescent world of virtue and a future of real love.

The next day Mazza received a letter written on glazed paper, redolent of roses and musk. It was signed with an E, surrounded by a flourish. I don't know what was in it, but Mazza reread it several times, examining both sheets and their folds, intoxicated by their scent. Then she rolled it into a small wad and threw it in the fire. Consumed by the fire, the letter fluttered, wafted, and then came to rest softly on the andirons like a pleated white veil.

Ernest loves her! He told her so! Oh, how happy she is. The first step has been taken, and the others won't be difficult. Now she will be able to look at him without blushing, and she won't need so many stratagems and the engaging facial expressions women use to make themselves attractive. He comes by himself, gives himself to her, her modesty is controlled, and it's that reserve which women always keep and maintain even in the depths of the most passionate love and most ardent sensuality, like a final sanctuary of love and passion which they use as a veil to hide everything brutal and delicate in them.

A few days later, a veiled woman crossed the Pont des Arts at a fast clip. It was seven o'clock in the morning.

After walking for a long time, she stopped at the service entrance and asked for Ernest. He hadn't gone out, so she went up. The staircase seemed endless to her, and when she got to the third floor she rested on the banister for fear she might faint. She felt everything spinning around her and low muted voices whispering in her ear. Finally, she rang the doorbell with a trembling hand. When she heard its repeated, piercing sound, an echo resounded in her heart, like a galvanic repercussion.

Finally the door opened. It was Ernest himself.

"Oh, is that you, Mazza?"

Drained of color and drenched in sweat, she couldn't answer. Ernest looked at her coldly, twirling the silk cord of his dressing gown. He was afraid of compromising himself.

"Come in," he finally said.

He took her arm and sat her down in an armchair. After a moment of silence, she told him: "Ernest, I have come to tell you something. This is the last time I will speak to you. I must leave you and not see you again."

"Because . . . ?"

"Because you are a burden to me, you overwhelm me, and will be the end of me!"

"I? How is that, Mazza?"

He got up, pulled the curtains, and closed the door.

"What are you doing?" she cried out in horror.

"What am I doing?"

"Yes."

"You are here, Mazza, you came to my apartment. Come on, don't deny it," he said smiling. "I know women."

"Continue," she added angrily.

"Well, Mazza, that's enough."

"And you are so insolent as to tell me that to my face, to a woman you claim to love?"

"Excuse me! Oh, forgive me!"

He knelt and looked at her for a long time.

"Oh, yes, I too love you more than my life. Here, I am giving myself to you."

And right there between the four walls, under the silk curtains, on an armchair, there were more than enough love and kisses, intoxicating embraces, and burning delight to drive you mad or kill you. And after he had sapped, worn out, and thoroughly exhausted her with his embraces, after leaving her spent, broken and gasping, after pressing his chest against hers many times and seeing her faint in his arms, he got up and left her alone.

That evening he had an excellent dinner at Véfour's, where plentiful iced champagne made the rounds and you could hear him raising his voice over dessert, "My good friends, I got another one!"

That other one went home with her soul deeply saddened and her eyes full of tears—not because of her lost honor, for that particular idea did not torture her in the slightest. Having initially asked herself what honor was and finding it to be only a word, she went beyond that. But she thought of the sensations she had experienced and, on reflection, found them only bitter deception, saying to herself, "That's not what I dreamed about!"

For when she left her lover's arms, it seemed to her that something was rumpled within her, just as her clothes had been, something tired and downcast like her eyes. She felt she had fallen far, that love wasn't limited to that. Finally, she wondered if there wasn't a greater voluptuousness beyond the one she had experienced, if there wasn't a greater enjoyment after gratification, for she had an unquenchable thirst for infinite love and unlimited passions. But then she saw that love was only a kiss, a moment of ecstasy where lover and mistress punctuate their caresses with groans, locked in their embrace. And when she realized that it all ends with him getting up, with her leaving, that their convulsive passion needs a bit of flesh for its heady satisfaction, her soul was overcome with a deep weariness, like those starving people whom nothing can nourish.

But she soon gave up her thoughts of the past so as to think only of the smiling present. She closed her eyes to what no longer existed, shook off the fantasy of her former boundless dreams, her vague, ill-defined breathlessness, in order to give herself completely over to a torrent that swept her away. Soon she reached a state of inactivity and nonchalance, of that somnolence when you feel yourself sliding into sleep and intoxication, feel the world slipping far away from you, whereas you remain alone on the skiff that the wave coddles and the ocean sweeps away. She thought no longer of her husband and children, and even less of her reputation, which other women eagerly ripped apart in the salons, while Ernest's young friends sullied and vilified her at will in their cafes and coffeehouses.

But suddenly she heard a melody in nature and in her soul which had remained unknown to her until then. She discovered new worlds in both, immense spaces and limitless horizons. It seemed that everything was born for love, that men were creatures of a superior order, susceptible to passions and feelings, that they were good only for that, and that they should live only for the heart. As for her husband, she still loved him and valued him even more highly. Her children seemed agreeable, but she loved them the way one loves another person's children.

Each day, however, she felt that she loved more than the night before, that her love was becoming needful and necessary for her existence. But that passion which she had initially played with laughingly became serious and terrible. Once it entered her heart, it became a violent love and then mad frenzy. Her passion had so much fiery heat, so many immense desires, such a hunger for ravishment and pleasure coursing through her veins, under her skin, right down to her fingernails, that she became mad and drunkenly disoriented and would have wanted to carry her love beyond the limits of nature. It seemed to her that offering voluptuous caresses, dissipating her life in nights given over to feverish passion, wallowing in everything sublime and wild that passion offers would open up to her a continuous round of ravenous pleasure.

Often, in her raptures she exclaimed that life was only passion, that love was everything for her. With eyes ablaze, hair disheveled, and chest heaving with sobs, she asked her lover if he did not share her desire to live together for centuries in the solitude of a mountain retreat, high atop a rocky pinnacle with waves smashing below. Didn't he also want the two of them to merge with nature and heaven, to blend their sighs with the roar of the storm? And then she looked at him for a long time, asking him again for new kisses and new embraces—and then she fainted silently into his arms.

And when her husband returned in the evening, his inner tranquillity was reflected by his calm exterior as he told her about the day's profits, the good speculation he had made in the morning, how he had bought a farm, sold stock, and that he could add one more servant to their staff and buy two horses for his stable. After these words and these thoughts, he started to kiss her and call her "his love and his life." But fury gripped her soul; she cursed him, and in horror she repelled his caresses and kisses, which were as cold and frightful as those of a monkey.

His love held bitter pain for her, like the dregs of wine, which make it more acidic and harsh.

And when she left her house, family, and staff and found herself seated alone by Ernest's side, she told him that she would like to die by his hand and feel herself smothered in his arms. Then she added that she no longer loved anything, that she despised everything and loved only him. Next she said she had abandoned and sacrificed her love of God for him, was leaving her husband to suffer his humiliation, and was abandoning her children as well. She spit on all of that quite willingly. She ground virtue and religion under her heel, sold her reputation for caresses, and with the greatest delight she made a burnt offering of all that, just to please him. For a single glance or a kiss, she destroyed all her beliefs, illusions, and virtue—in short, everything she loved. And it seemed to her that she would be even more beautiful for having just left his arms and his endless kisses, as faded violets exude the sweetest scent.

Oh, who could possibly know how much sensual frenzy there is beneath the two palpitating breasts of a woman!

Ernest, however, was beginning to love her a bit more than a dancer or an 75
available working girl. He even presented her with poetry he had written for her. Moreover, one day I saw him with reddened eyes, from which you might conclude that he had been crying . . . or had slept badly.

Three

One morning he was thinking of Mazza, seated in a large, comfortable easy chair with his feet propped up on the andirons and his nose buried in the folds of his nightshirt. As he stared at the crackling flames lapping up against the fireplace grill, he was suddenly struck by a surprising thought. He became frightened.

Remembering that he was loved by a woman like Mazza who so lavishly sacrificed her beauty and love, he trembled fearfully at the spectacle of that woman's passion—like children who run far away from the ocean, saying that it is too big. A moral idea came to mind, for that was a habit he had begun to cultivate since he started contributing to the *Journal of Useful Knowledge* and the *Family Gallery*.[2] As I say, he thought it was immoral to seduce a married woman that way and turn her aside from her conjugal duties and maternal love, and that it was wrong to receive all these burnt offerings placed at his feet like a sacrifice. Finally, he was bored and wearied by that woman who took pleasure seriously and could conceive only of a complete and exclusive love, but who could not discuss novels, styles, or the opera.

At first, he wanted to break it off, to leave her there rejected in the middle of society along with other women who had also been used up. Mazza noticed his cool indifference, attributing it to refinement, and loved him all the more. Ernest often avoided and fled from her, but she crossed his path everywhere: at the ball, strolling in public gardens, in museums. She knew how to pick him out of crowds, whisper in his ear, and make him blush in front of all those people who were looking at her.

At other times, it was he who came to her house. He entered with a serious expression and a severe attitude. His young, naive mistress threw her arms around his neck and covered him with kisses. But he coldly repulsed her, saying that they should not make love any more, that it was over between them now that the moment of mad delirium had passed, and that she must respect her husband, adore her children and attend to her family. He added that he had witnessed and studied a great deal, moreover, that Providence was just, that nature was a masterpiece and society an admirable creation, and that, after all, philanthropy was beautiful and one should love mankind.

At that point she cried tears of rage, pride, and love. With a smile on her lips 80
and bitterness in her heart, she asked him if she was no longer beautiful and what she must do to please him. And then she smiled at him, displaying her fair complexion for him, her black hair, her throat and shoulders, and her naked breasts. Ernest was unmoved by such seductiveness because he didn't love her any longer,

[2]*Journal of Useful Knowledge . . . Family Gallery*: Popular and widely distributed publications of the 1830s.

and he left her house with the sort of emotion people feel when they see madmen. And if a trace of passion, or if a slim ray of love kindled his heart, he quickly extinguished it with a bit of logical argument.

How fortunate those people are who can use words to fight against their hearts and use morality to destroy the passion rooted in their souls—a morality that you find pasted only on books, like a bookseller's glaze and the engraver's frontispiece!

One day when she was carried away by delirious rage, Mazza bit his chest and dug her nails into his throat. Seeing blood flow from their lovemaking, Ernest understood that this woman's passion was terribly ferocious, that she was surrounded by a poisoned atmosphere that would choke him and in the end would kill him, that this love was a volcano which always needed something to devour and smash in its convulsions, and that her voluptuous sensuality was a molten lava searing her heart. Therefore, he had to go away and leave her forever—or else throw himself along with her into that whirlwind which pulls you along like vertigo in the immense path of passion, which begins with a smile and ends only at the tomb.

He preferred to leave.

At ten o'clock one night, Mazza received a letter in which she read these words:

"Farewell, Mazza! I will not see you again. The Minister of the Interior has assigned me to a scientific enterprise charged with analyzing the mineral deposits of Mexico. Good-bye! I am leaving from Le Havre. If you wish to be happy, stop loving me. Instead, love virtue and your duties. That's my last advice. Again, adieu! Kisses. *Ernest.*"

She reread it several times, stricken by that word "adieu." She sat still with her eyes fixed on that letter which contained all her misfortune and despair, where she saw all the happiness of her life slip away. She shed no tears and did not cry out. She rang for a servant and told him to order some post-horses and to prepare her post-chaise. Her husband was traveling in Germany, so no one could restrain her will.

She left at midnight, making the horses run at full gallop. She stopped in a town to order a glass of water and resumed her chase, believing that she would see the sea appear at the next turn, over the next hill, at every bend in the road. The ocean was the goal of her desires and her jealousy, since it was going to take away someone dear to her heart. She finally arrived in Le Havre around three o'clock in the afternoon.

As soon as she dismounted, she ran to the end of the jetty and looked out over the sea . . . a white sail was disappearing over the horizon.

Four

He had left! Gone forever! And when she raised her head and peered through her tears, she saw nothing more . . . except the immensity of the ocean.

It was one of those scorching summer days when the earth exhales warm vapors, like the burning air of a furnace. When Mazza got to the end of the jetty, the fresh salt air revived her a bit, for a southerly breeze was swelling the waves, which softly died on the strand and gave their last gasp on the pebbles. To the left, thick black clouds were massing near the setting sun, which shone red on the sea. The clouds seemed on the point of bursting into tears. As it gathered its strength, the ocean struggled against itself, seeming to moan a dirge. When it smashed against the rocks of the jetty, the waves leapt in the air and fell in a silvery dust.

There was a kind of savage harmony in it all. For a long time Mazza listened to it, fascinated by its power. The noise of the waves spoke a special language to her. The sea was as sad and thoroughly anguished as she was. Like her, its waves died as they smashed on the rocks, leaving on the wet sand only a trace of their passage. A patch of grass that grew out of a slit in the rocks bowed its head under the weight of the heavy spray. Each new wave tried to rip it out by the roots, and each time it was detached just a little more. Finally, it disappeared under a whitecap, never again to be seen. And yet it was young and bore flowers! Mazza smiled bitterly. Like her, the flower was borne away by the wave in the freshness of its springtime.

Sailors were returning, lolling in their fishing boats, trailing their nets behind them. Their voices echoed in the distance, along with the cries of night birds who soared and beat their wings above Mazza's head before pouncing all together on debris strewn over the sand by the backwash. She heard a voice calling to her from the depths of an abyss, and leaning her head toward the chasm, she estimated how many minutes and seconds it would take for her agony to end in death. All of nature shared her sadness, and it seemed to her that the waves were sighing and the sea weeping.

I don't know, however, what miserable feeling of existence told her to live. It told her that there was still happiness and love on earth, and one had only to wait and hope in order to eventually discover them. But when night came, the moon appeared in the midst of its dear friends like a sultana appearing in a harem among the women, and you could see only the foaming swells, which shone on the waves like lather on the mouth of a steed—whereas the noise of the town began to recede into the fog. That was the time for Mazza to depart.

Around two o'clock in the morning she opened the coach window and peered outside. They were on an open plain going along a road lined with trees. Moonlight filtering between their branches made their forms resemble gigantic ghosts running in front of Mazza. As they swayed in the gusts of wind, breezes ruffled their foliage like disheveled hair. At one point, the coach stopped in the middle of a field to repair one of its broken harness traces. In the dead of night, all you could hear were the sound of the trees, the breath of the gasping, lathered horses, and the sobs of a lone woman.

Near morning she saw people going toward the nearest city, on their way to market, carrying fruit that was still on the stem and covered with moss to keep it fresh. They were also singing; since the climbing path slowed their steps, she listened to them at length. "At least some people are happy!" she said.

By now it was broad daylight on a Sunday. In a village several hours from Paris, at the time when everybody was filing out of the church into the square, a bright sun was shining on the church's weathervane and making its modest rose window translucent. From inside her coach Mazza could look through the open doors to glimpse the interior of the nave and the candles illuminating the shadowy altar. She examined the blue paint on the wooden vault and the bare old pillars made of whitened stone. Suddenly she saw the benches where the entire population was assembled, dressed in variegated colors. She heard the organ intoning, followed by a swelling mass of people who were stirring about and leaving. Several of them carried bouquets of artificial flowers and wore white stockings. It was a wedding scene, punctuated by rifle volleys in the square to announce the exit of the newlyweds.

The smiling bride wore a white cap and was looking at the two ends of her sash of embroidered lace. The bridegroom kept pace with her, radiating his happiness as he scanned the crowd while he shook hands with various well-wishers. One was the mayor (and hosteler) of the region who that day was giving his daughter's hand to his deputy mayor, the school's headmaster.

A group of women and children stopped in front of Mazza to admire the beautiful open carriage and the red cape hanging from the door latch. They were all smiles and talking in loud voices. After changing horses and starting on her way, she came across the procession as it was entering the town hall. A smile crossed her lips when she saw the lather from the mouths of her horses spray on the newlyweds, as the dust from the hooves covered their white clothes. She leaned forward and gave them a pitiful, envious glance because she had turned from her wretchedness to become spitefully jealous. Then the people showed their hatred for the wealthy. They responded with curses and insults, throwing stones at the luggage compartments of her carriage.

As she continued her long trip, she was lulled by the motion of the carriage suspension and the jingle of the small bells on the harnesses. While a dusty mist discolored her black hair, her thoughts turned to the village wedding and the fiddler at the head of the wedding cortege, the organ sounds, the voices of the children who had stood all around her—all of that beset her ears like the buzzing of a bee or the hiss of a snake.

She was tired from the oppressive heat that penetrated the leather covering of her carriage. The sun struck her in the eyes, causing her to lower her head on the white cushions and fall asleep. She woke up when they arrived at the old gates of Paris.

When you trade the open fields of the country for city streets, daylight recedes into dreariness, as in those theaters at country fairs which are drab and poorly lit. Mazza eagerly plunged into the most tortuous streets, intoxicated by the sounds and rumbling noises that withdrew her from private thoughts and thrust her into the world. Like the shifting projections cast by Chinese lanterns, heads shot past her carriage door. They all seemed cold, impassive, and colorless. For the first time, she was shocked by the misery of those going barefoot along the quays, sporting smiles to hide the hatred in their hearts and the holes in their ragged clothes. She saw the crowds swallowed up by the theaters and cafes, the entire populace of servants and lords that was spread out like a colored cape on parade day.

It all seemed like an immense drama, a vast theater with its stone palaces and brightly lit stores, its elegant outfits, its ridiculous apparel, pasteboard scepters, and queens for a day. Over here the carriage of a ballerina jostles the crowd, while over there a man dies of hunger as he looks at a pile of gold on the other side of a store window. Everywhere there are laughter and tears, wealth and misery, and vice insulting virtue by spitting in its face, like the worn-out shawl of a prostitute brushing against a priest's black cassock as he passes her. Ah, yes! In the heart of a city you find a corrupt, poisonous atmosphere that overcomes you with headiness—something heavy and unhealthy, like those gloomy evening fogs that hover over rooftops.

Mazza filled her lungs with that air of corruption, tasted its aroma, and for the first time she understood the breadth and depth of vice, the sensual voluptuousness of crime.

When she returned home, the great amount of suffering she had undergone in the short span of her intensified life made it seem as if she had been away for a very long time. All night long she wept as she thought of her departure and return. In her mind's eye she saw all the towns she had passed through and the entire road she had traveled. She still seemed to be standing on the jetty, watching the sea and the sail as it disappeared. The wedding with its festive regalia and smiles of happiness also flooded her memory. She recalled the noise of her coach rolling over the paving stones and heard the muffled roar of the waves as they leapt up beneath her. Then she became frightened by the length of time, believing that she had lived for centuries, that she had become old and gray—so much does pain wear you down and misfortune gnaw at you, for certain days age you as if they were years, and some thoughts bring on an abundance of wrinkles.

Smiling with regret, she also remembered her days of happiness, her relaxed 105
vacations on the banks of the Loire when she ran down the shady promenades in the woods, playing with the flowers and crying as she saw beggars pass by. She recalled her first dances, when she waltzed so well and loved the gracious smiles and pleasant chatter. Again she remembered her hours of feverish delight in the arms of her lover, her moments of anger and rapture when she would like each glance to have lasted for centuries, a kiss for eternity. She wondered if all of that was gone and erased forever, like dust along the road or the wake of a ship on the high seas.

Five

She finally returned, but alone! She had no one to sustain her and nothing more to love. What was she to do? Which way could she turn? Well, of course: death and the tomb a hundred times over! Despite the difficulties she had undergone on her trip, she had held little hope in her heart.

What was she waiting for?

She didn't know herself, except that she still had faith in life. She still believed that Ernest loved her, until one day when she received a letter from him. But it was one more disillusionment.

The letter was long, well written, and replete with rich metaphors and impressive words. Ernest told her that she mustn't love him anymore and that she must think of her obligations and of God. In addition, he gave her excellent advice on the family and maternal love, concluding like Monsieur de Bouilly or Madame Cottin with a bit of fine sentiment.[3]

Poor Mazza! So much love, affection, and tenderness offered to such cold 110
and calculating indifference! She declined into lethargy and a feeling of disgust, telling herself one day, "I thought a person could die from a broken heart!" From disgust she fell further into bitterness and envy.

That was when the world's symphony sounded discordant and infernal, when nature seemed like one of God's cruel jokes. She didn't love anything and harbored animosity for everything. As each tender feeling was squeezed from her heart, hatred replaced it so thoroughly that she no longer loved anything on earth, except for one man. Whenever she saw mothers playing with their children in public gardens, smiling at their caresses, and women with their husbands, lovers with mistresses, she both envied and cursed them all for sharing happiness, for smiling and loving life. She wished that she could have crushed them all underfoot. Her lips curled into an ironic smile of pride as she muttered a few scornful words when she passed them in the street.

At other times, despite her raging soul, she smiled when people told her she must be happy in life because of her wealth and position, her good health and sparkling complexion, her apparent contentment, and her every need fulfilled. She exclaimed to herself, "Oh, those imbeciles who see only happiness written in the calm of your face and don't know that torture extracts your laughter."

From that point on, life was a continuous cry of agony. When she saw women adorned with their virtue, others with their love, when she saw happy people who were confident about their faith in God, she tormented them with sneering sarcasm. She made passing priests blush when she gave them a lusty glance and laughed in their ears. As for young virgins, she made them aghast by the love stories and passionate tales she related. People wondered who that haggard woman was, that wandering ghost with the fiery eyes who wore the expression of the damned. If you wanted to come to know her, you would find only a single pain in the depth of her existence, only tears in her actions.

Oh, women, women! It was especially the young and beautiful that she hated from the bottom of her heart. She hated them when they were bathed in candlelight at a ball or in the radiance of chandeliers at the theater, displaying their undulating bosoms and decked in lace and diamonds, with men crowding around to return smile for smile. And when those men flattered and praised them, she wanted to rumple their clothes and their embroidered veils, to spit in those pretty faces, and drag those coldly impassive and haughty faces through the mud. She believed in nothing but misfortune and death.

For her, virtue was only a word, religion an illusion, reputation an impostor's 115
mask like a veil hiding wrinkles. Then she discovered the satisfaction of arrogance, the pleasure of disdain, and she spit on the stoop of churches when she passed by.

[3] *Monsieur de Bouilly . . . Madame Cottin:* A playwright and an author, respectively.

When she thought about Ernest, about his voice, his words, his arms, which had held her so long in trembling surrender to love and which she remembered especially when her husband was kissing her, she was contorted with anguished pain as she struggled against herself, like a man in the midst of his death rattle who cries out a name or weeps for a particular memory. She had children by this man, children who resembled their father, a three-year-old girl and a boy of five, whose playful laughter reached her ears. In the mornings, they came up laughing to kiss away the fresh tears on her cheeks, whereas *she*, their mother, had not any relief all night from her outlandish torments.

When her thoughts turned to Ernest wandering the high seas, perhaps buffeted by a storm that threatened him alone and made him cling to life, and when her mind's eye saw a corpse bobbing in the waves as vulture's prey, her revery was interrupted by joyful cries, the voices of children as they came running up to show her a tree in bloom or the sun making the frost shimmer on the grass. For her, it was like the pain of a man who falls down in the street, only to see the crowd laugh and applaud.

And what was Ernest thinking, so far from her? Sometimes he actually missed her when he had nothing to do, in moments of leisure and idleness, thinking of her, of her wild passion, of her ripe buttocks, her white breasts and long black hair. But he quickly ran for the arms of a slave girl to quench the fire that was kindled in the strongest and most consecrated of loves. Moreover, he made little work of consoling himself for that loss by thinking he had done a good turn as a proper citizen, and that Ben Franklin or Lafayette wouldn't have done better—for at that moment he was standing on the national home ground of patriotism, of slavery, coffee, and temperance: America.

He was one of those people in whom judgment and reason occupy such a large place that they have devoured the heart, like an unwelcome neighbor. An entire world separated them, for on the other hand Mazza was entirely distracted and anguished. While her lover wallowed as much as he wanted to in the arms of Negresses and mulattoes, she was dying of boredom, believing that Ernest too lived only for her and was undergoing an agony that he actually derided with his wild, brutish laugh. He was devoting his efforts to another woman. While that poor woman was crying and cursing God—calling on Hell to aid her and writhing as she wondered why Satan was so long in coming—she passionately kissed a lock of his hair. And perhaps at that same moment, Ernest was strolling across a public square in some city in the United States, attired like a plantation owner in white pants and jacket, on his way to a slave market to trade some gold for a pair of strong and well-muscled black arms, pendulous breasts, and the promise of pleasure.

Besides, he was going about his scientific experiments. He had filled two 120
huge boxes of notes about flint deposits and mineralogical analyses. In addition, the climate suited him very well, and he was thriving in that atmosphere, energized by its scientific academies, railroads, steamboats, sugar cane, and indigo.

What air did Mazza breathe? She lived in a more restricted circle, but it was a world apart which revolved around tears and hopelessness, and which was to become engulfed in the abyss of a crime.

Six

A black cloth hung over the manor's carriage entrance. Its two attached ends looped up to a central point to form a kind of broken ogival arch that allowed you to peer through and see a coffin flanked by two candles. Gusts of wind passing over the black crepe, studded with silver tears, made the flames tremble like the voiced shudder of a dying person. From time to time, the two sextons in charge of the proceedings stood to the side in order to make way for guests who were arriving one after another, all dressed in black with white ties, pressed ascots, and hair freshly done. They doffed their hats when they passed the coffin, and dipped a black-gloved finger in the holy water font.

It was snowing. After the procession left, a young woman in a black cloak came down to the courtyard and walked on tiptoe across the blanket of snow covering the flagstone. Through the slit in her black veil you could see her pallid face as she strained to watch the hearse roll out of sight. Then she extinguished the candles, went back up, undid her coat, warmed her white slippers near the fireplace, and turned her head to look again. But she saw only the black coat of the last funeral employee as he turned the corner.

When she couldn't hear the monotonous clatter of the iron-rimmed wheels of the hearse on the cobblestones, when it was all over—the priests' chants, the funeral cortege—she threw herself on the death bed, twisting her body this way and that, and exclaiming in fits of convulsive joy, "Come, now! It's yours, it's all yours! I am waiting for you, so come on! The pleasures of the nuptial bed are all yours, beloved, yours and yours alone! We'll have a world of love and ecstasy! Come here so that I can stretch out beneath your caresses and feast on your kisses." On the commode she saw a small rosewood box that Ernest had given her one winter day just like this one. When he had arrived, he was wrapped in his coat with snow sprinkled on his hat, which added to the rose scent of his kisses. In the middle of the scented box the initials M and E were entwined. She breathed its fragrance deeply and for a long time remained in dreamy contemplation.

Soon her children were brought to her. They were crying and asking for 125
their father. They sought consolation in Mazza's kisses. She sent them away without so much as a word or a smile.

She was thinking about him, far away from her and never to return.

Seven

She lived that way for several months, as time rolled along, feeling happier and freer each day, while her heart emptied out to make way for love. All the passions, feelings, and sentiments that fill one's heart had fled, like the concerns of childhood. At first there was modesty, followed by religion and virtue, and then their residue, like the fragments of a broken glass. Except for love she no longer had any feminine traits, but it was a terrible, consuming love that inflicted tortures on itself and on others, like Vesuvius ripping itself apart and spilling its molten lava over the flowers in the valley.

She had her children, but they died like their father. Each day they grew increasingly pale and scrawny, awakening each night in a paroxysm of fever, shivering on their bed of agony and saying that a snake was eating away at their chests, for something was incessantly burning and devouring them. Mazza studied their agony, smiling out of anger and vengeance.

Both of them died on the same day. She shed no tears when she watched their coffins being nailed, nor did her heart sigh. Her eyes were cold and dry when she watched them being wrapped in their shrouds. When she was alone at last, her night was happy and sanguine, her soul was calm, and joy filled her heart. She had no regrets or anguished cries, because she was planning to leave France on the following day, after avenging a profaned love and the terrible fate that destiny had given her; after deriding God, men, life, and the fate that had toyed with her for a while; after amusing herself with life and death, tears and grief; and after trading her suffering to heaven in exchange for crimes.

Farewell to European soil, with its mists and glaciers, where souls are as cool 130
as the climate, where love is as slack and soft as its gray clouds. I'll take America and its fiery climes, its hot sun and limpid sky, its beautiful nights in the palm and plain tree groves! Good-bye to the world, and thanks! I'm going on board and leaving. Go, beautiful clipper, run swiftly before your billowing sails! Let your bow split the waves, outrace the storm, ride the bounding main, and should you founder, cast me along with your flotsam on the shore where he breathes!

The night was spent in wild excitement, but it was the frenzy of joyful anticipation. When she thought about him, about kissing and living together forever, she smiled and cried with happiness.

The cemetery ground where her children lay was still freshly damp with holy water.

Eight

The next day she received a letter, mailed seven months earlier. It was from Ernest. She trembled as she broke the seal and eagerly read through it. When she finished, she tried to reread it but was too drained from fright. This is what the letter said:

"Why are your letters so dishonest, madame? Especially the last one. I burned it out of embarrassment that someone else might read it. Couldn't you restrain your passion just a little? Why do you keep after me with your memories, disturbing my work and distracting me from doing my job? What have I done to make you love me so much?

"Once again, madame, I think love should be reasonable. Now that I have 135
left France, you should love your husband and forget me as I have forgotten you. Happiness is found on the beaten path. The paths toward the rocky peaks are strewn with rocks and brambles that soon cut and exhaust you.

"I am now living happily in a small, charming house on a river bank. The river cuts through a field where I hunt for insects and flora. When I return home my Negro servant greets me with a sweeping bow, kissing my feet when he wishes a particular favor. I have shaped a happy, calm, and agreeable existence in the heart of nature and science. Why don't you do as much? Who is stopping you? Where there's a will, there's a way.

"For you and for your very happiness, I advise you to not think of me any more and to stop writing me. What is the point of such an exchange? What good will it do for you to tell me a hundred times that you love me and go on to write as many times in the margins, 'I love you'?

"You must forget all that, madame, and think no more about what we were to each other. Didn't we both get what we wanted?

"I am becoming well established. I am the principal director of the commission on assaying ore, the daughter of the managing director is a charming seventeen-year-old, her father has an income of sixty thousand pounds, and as his only daughter, she is sweet, good, very reasonable, and will have no trouble at all in raising a family and overseeing a household.

"I'm getting married one month from now. You should be pleased if you love me as you always claim, since I am doing it for my happiness.

"Adieu, Madame Willer. Stop thinking about a man who has enough tact to stop loving you, and if you wish to do me one last favor, please send me a pint bottle of prussic acid as soon as possible. The Secretary of the Academy of Sciences is a very competent chemist who will give it to you on my recommendation.

"Farewell. I am counting on you to not forget my acid. *Ernest Vaumont.*"

When Mazza finished the letter she uttered an inarticulate wail, as if someone had burned her with red-hot tongs.

She remained for a long time in a state of surprised consternation. "Oh, that coward!" she finally said. "He seduced and abandoned me for another woman! After giving him everything and having nothing left to give! After throwing everything overboard except for a solitary plank that slips out of your hands while you slip under the waves!"

That poor woman loved him so much! She had sacrificed her virtue for him and offered him all her love. She had renounced God and—far worse!—her husband and children whom she had watched agonize and die, while she smilingly thought of him. What was she going to do? What would become of her? He was telling another woman that he loved her, while he kissed her eyes and breasts, and told her that she was his life and his passion. Another woman! And what about her? Had she had others before him? Hadn't she turned away from her husband in their marriage bed, thinking of him? Hadn't she deceived him with her adulterous lips? Hadn't she poisoned him with her tears of joy?

As her God and her life, he had abandoned her after using her, enjoying her while taking everything from her. And now he is discarding her, throwing her into the bottomless pit of crime and despair!

At other times she couldn't believe her own eyes, as she reread that fateful letter and covered it with her tears.

When her dejection turned to furious anger, she said to herself, "What! What do you mean saying that you're leaving me alone in the world, without any family or relatives? I sacrificed them for you. I am alone, since I sacrificed my honor as a burnt offering to you. I am bereft of reputation because I sacrificed it along with my kisses, in full view of all those who called me your mistress. Your mistress! And now that embarrasses you, coward!

"Where are those who have died?

"Where am I to turn? I had only one thing in my heart, one single idea, and 150
now it's gone. Should I search for you when you send me away like a slave? If I seek out other women, they will abandon me to their laughter, proudly pointing their fingers at me, for they have never loved anyone and don't really know what tears are. So there! Since I still crave love, passion, and life, they will tell me to go wherever pleasure and caresses are sold for a certain price. And in my evenings spent with my companions in luxury, I'll hail passersby from my window. When they come up, I'll have to make sure they get all the pleasure they want, so that when the transaction is completed they will leave satisfied. I won't have any complaints about that good bargain, and I'll laugh at anyone who comes along, for I'll have deserved my fate!

"And just what did I do? I loved you more than any other. Oh, have mercy, Ernest! If you could hear my lament, you might take pity on me, on me who had none for the others. Now I curse myself. I wallow in anguish here, and my clothes are soaked by my tears."

And she ran around madly before falling to the ground and rolling about, as she cursed God, mankind, life itself, everything on earth that lived and thought; she ripped out handfuls of her hair, and her nails were bloody.

"Oh, to be unable to put up with life! To be reduced to throwing myself into the arms of death, as into a mother's arms! And to wonder right up to the last minute whether the tomb holds further suffering, whether oblivion promises more pain! To have no more faith in anything, not even love, the first religion of the heart, and to be unable to rid myself of this continual malaise, like a drunken man who is forced to drink more!

"Why did you invade my solitude to tear me away from my happiness? I was so tranquil and pure, until you came along to love me and I to love you!

"Men are so handsome when they look at you! You offered me the love that 155
you now refuse me, and I nourished it with crimes. And now it kills me too! I was virtuous when you first saw me, and now I am ferociously cruel. I'd like to have something to crush, tear, despoil, and then toss aside, just as was done to me. Ah, I hate everything: men, God, and I hate you too. And yet I still feel that I would give my life for you in return!

"I loved you more and more all the time, like those who drink sea water to quench a thirst that it only increases. And now I am going to die . . . death! The end of everything! Shadows, a tomb, and then . . . the immensity of complete emptiness. Oh, but I still feel that I would like to live and suffer, as I have suffered! Ah, happiness! Where is it? It's just a dream. And virtue? Disappointment. The tomb? What do I know?

"But I will know."

Nine

She got up, dried her tears, and tried to still the heaving sobs that were stifling her lungs. She looked in a mirror to see if her eyes were still red from crying so much, fixed her hair, and went out to accomplish Ernest's last request.

Mazza went to the chemist's home and asked to see him. She was asked to wait in a small sitting room on the second floor, appointed with red and green upholstered furniture, a round mahogany table in the middle, lithographs of Napoleonic battles on the paneled walls, while on the gray marble mantelpiece there was a gold clock with a cupid clinging to the dial as he reclined on his arrows with his other hand. When it chimed two o'clock, the door opened and the chemist entered. He was a small, thin man, with formal manners. He had thin lips, glasses and beady eyes. When Mazza explained the reason for her visit, he began to praise Ernest Vaumont, his traits, character, and attitude. Finally, he produced the vial of acid, led her by the hand to the bottom of the stairs, and even got his shoes damp in the courtyard when he guided her back to the door giving onto the street.

Mazza's head was burning so much she could hardly walk. Several times 160
she thought the blood would burst through the pores of her flushed cheeks. She walked through streets where wretchedness clung to the houses the way fingers of color streak whitened walls. Seeing all that misery, she addressed it, saying, "I'm going to cure myself of your misfortune." Holding the poison with both hands, she passed by the palace of kings and said, "Farewell, existence. I'm going to rid myself of all your cares." When she got home, she glanced backward before closing her door, bidding adieu to the populace she was leaving, and to the city bursting with noise, with commotion and lively voices.

Ten

She opened her writing desk, sealed the bottle of acid, addressed the package, and wrote another note to the main superintendent of police. She rang for a servant and gave it to him.

On a third piece of paper she wrote, "I loved a man. I killed my husband for him, and I killed my children for him. I die without remorse, without hope, but with a few regrets." She placed it on the mantle.

"Just another half-hour," she said. "Soon he'll come to take me to the cemetery."

She took off her clothes, examined her lovely naked body for a few minutes, thinking of all the voluptuousness it had given and the great pleasure she had bestowed on her lover.

The love of that kind of woman is such a treasure! 165

After more tears, she thought about the time that had slipped away from her, about her happiness, dreams, youthful frolics, and then thought about him again for a long time. She wondered what death was like, losing herself in that empty gulf of thought which gnaws and tears at itself out of powerless rage. Then she suddenly arose, as if roused from a dream, poured a few drops of poison in a silver-gilt cup, drank it eagerly, and lay down for the last time on the sofa where she had surrendered so often to the raptures of love in Ernest's arms.

Eleven

When the commissioner entered, Mazza was still in the throes of agony. She writhed on the ground for a while and twisted a few times. All her limbs stiffened, and she uttered a piercing cry.

When he approached her she was dead.

(1877)

Dorothy Parker *(1893–1967)*

The Little Old Lady in Lavender Silk

I was seventy-seven, come August,
  I shall shortly be losing my bloom;
I've experienced zephyr[1] and raw gust
  And (symbolical) flood and simoom.

When you come to this time of abatement,
  To this passing from Summer to Fall,
It is manners to issue a statement
  As to what you got out of it all.

So I'll say, though reflection unnerves me
  And pronouncements I dodge as I can,
That I think (if my memory serves me)
  There was nothing more fun than a man!

In my youth, when the crescent was too wan
  To embarrass with beams from above,
By the aid of some local Don Juan
  I fell into the habit of love.
And I learned how to kiss and be merry—an
  Education left better unsung.
My neglect of the waters Pierian
  Was a scandal, when Grandma was young.

Though the shabby unbalanced the splendid,
  And the bitter outmeasured the sweet,
I should certainly do as I then did,
  Were I given the chance to repeat.

For contrition is hollow and wraithful,
  And regret is no part of my plan,
And I think (if my memory's faithful)
  There was nothing more fun than a man!

(1976)

[1] *zephyr*: A mild breeze.

V. S. Pritchett *(1900–1997)*

A Story of Don Juan

One night of his life Don Juan slept alone. Returning to Seville in the spring, he was held up, some hours' ride from the city, by the floods of the Quadalquivir, a river as dirty as an old lion after the rains, and was obliged to stay at the finca of the Quintero family. The doorway, the walls, the windows of the house were hung with the black and violet draperies of mourning when he arrived there. Quintero's wife was dead. She had been dead a year. The young Quintero took him in and even smiled to see Don Juan spattered and drooping in the rain like a sodden cockerel. There was malice in his smile: Quintero was mad with loneliness and grief. The man who had possessed and discarded all women was received by a man demented because he had lost only one.

"My house is yours," said Quintero, speaking the formula. There was bewilderment in his eyes; those who grieve do not find the world and its people either real or believable. Irony inflects the voices of mourners, and there was malice, too, in Quintero's further greetings; he could receive Don Juan now without that fear, that terror which he brought to the husbands of Seville. It was perfect, Quintero thought, that for once in his life Don Juan should have arrived at an empty house.

There was not even (as Don Juan quickly found out) a maid, for Quintero was served only by a manservant, being unable any longer to bear the sight of women. This servant dried the guest's clothes and in an hour or two brought in a bad dinner, food which stamped up and down in the stomach, like people waiting for a coach in the cold. Quintero was torturing his body as well as his mind, and as the familiar pains arrived they agonised him and set him off about his wife. Grief had also made Quintero an actor. His eyes had the hollow, taper-haunted dusk of the theatre as he spoke of the beautiful girl. He dwelled upon their courtship, on details of her beauty and temperament, and how he had rushed her from the church to the marriage bed like a man racing a tray of diamonds through the streets into the safety of a bank vault. The presence of Don Juan turned every man into an artist when he was telling his own love-story—one had to tantalise and surpass the great seducer—and Quintero, rolling it all off in the grand manner, could not resist telling that his bride had died on her marriage night.

"Man!" cried Don Juan. He started straight off on stories of his own. But Quintero hardly listened; he had returned to the state of exhaustion and emptiness which is natural to grief. As Don Juan talked, the madman followed his own thoughts like an actor preparing and mumbling his next entrance; and the thought he had had, when Don Juan first appeared at the door, returned to him: a man must be a monster to make a man feel triumphant that his own wife was dead. Half-listening, and indigestion aiding, Quintero felt within himself the total hatred of all the husbands of Seville for this diabolical man. And as Quintero brooded upon this it occurred to him that it was probably not by chance that he had a vengeance in his power.

The decision was made. The wine being finished, Quintero called for his manservant and gave orders to change Don Juan's room.

"For," said Quintero dryly, "His Excellency's visit is an honour and I cannot allow one who has slept in the most delicately scented rooms in Spain to pass the night in a chamber which stinks to heaven of goat."

"The closed room?" said the manservant, astonished that the room which still held the great dynastic marriage bed and which had not been used more than half a dozen times by his master since the lady's death was to be given to a stranger.

Yet to this room Quintero led his guest and there parted from him with eyes so sparking with ill-intention that Don Juan, who was sensitive to this kind of point, understood perfectly that the cat was being let into the cage only because the bird had long ago flown out. The humiliation was unpleasant. Don Juan saw the night stretching before him like a desert.

What a bed to lie in: so wide, so unutterably vacant, so malignantly inopportune! He took off his clothes, snuffed the lamp wick. He lay down knowing that on either side of him lay wastes of sheet, draughty and uninhabited except by bugs. A desert. To move an arm one inch to the side, to push out a leg, however cautiously, was to enter desolation. For miles and miles the foot might probe, the fingers or the knee explore a friendless Antarctica. Yet to lie rigid and still was to have a foretaste of the grave. And here, too, he was frustrated; for though the wine kept him yawning, that awful food romped in his stomach, jolting him back from the edge of sleep the moment he got there.

There is an art in sleeping alone in a double bed, but this art was unknown to Don Juan. The difficulty is easily solved. If one cannot sleep on one side of the bed, one moves over and tries the other. Two hours or more must have passed before this occurred to him. Sullen-headed, he advanced into the desert, and the night air lying chill between the sheets flapped and made him shiver. He stretched out his arm and crawled towards the opposite pillow. The coldness, the more than virgin frigidity of linen! He put down his head and, drawing up his knees, he shivered. Soon, he supposed, he would be warm again, but, in the meantime, ice could not have been colder. It was unbelievable.

Ice was the word for that pillow and those sheets. Ice. Was he ill? Had the rain chilled him that his teeth must chatter like this and his legs tremble? Far from getting warmer, he found the cold growing. Now it was on his forehead and his cheeks, like arms of ice on his body, like legs of ice upon his legs. Suddenly in superstition he got up on his hands and stared down at the pillow in the darkness, threw back the bedclothes and looked down upon the sheet; his breath was hot, yet blowing against his cheeks was a breath colder than the grave, his shoulders and body were hot, yet limbs of snow were drawing him down; and just as he would have shouted his appalled suspicion, lips like wet ice unfolded upon his own and he sank down to a kiss, unmistakably a kiss, which froze him like a winter.

In his own room Quintero lay listening. His mad eyes were exalted and his ears were waiting. He was waiting for the scream of horror. He knew the apparition. There would be a scream, a tumble, hands fighting for the light, fists knocking at the door. And Quintero had locked the door. But when no scream came, Quintero lay talking to himself, remembering the night the apparition had first come to him and had made him speechless and left him choked and stiff. It would be even better if there were no scream! Quintero lay awake through the night, building castle after castle of triumphant revenge and receiving, as he did so, the ovations of the husbands of Seville. "The stallion is gelded!" At an early hour Quintero unlocked the door and waited downstairs impatiently. He was a wreck after a night like that.

Don Juan came down at last. He was (Quintero observed) pale. Or was he pale?

"Did you sleep well?" Quintero asked furtively.

"Very well," Don Juan replied.

"I do not sleep well in strange beds myself," Quintero insinuated. Don Juan smiled and replied that he was more used to strange beds than his own. Quintero scowled.

"I reproach myself; the bed was large," he said.

But the large, Don Juan said, were necessarily as familiar to him as the strange. Quintero bit his nails. Some noise had been heard in the night—something like a scream, a disturbance. The manservant had noticed it also. Don Juan answered him that disturbances in the night had indeed bothered him at the beginning of his career, but now he took them in his stride. Quintero dug his nails into the palms of his hands. He brought out the trump.

"I am afraid," Quintero said, 'it was a cold bed. You must have *frozen.*'

"I am never cold for long," Don Juan said, and, unconsciously anticipating the manner of a poem that was to be written in his memory two centuries later, declaimed: "The blood of Don Juan is hot, for the sun is the blood of Don Juan."

Quintero watched. His eyes jumped like flies to every movement of his guest. He watched him drink his coffee. He watched him tighten the stirrups of his horse. He watched Don Juan vault into the saddle. Don Juan was humming, and when he went off was singing, was singing in that intolerable tenor of his which was like a cock-crow in the olive groves.

Quintero went into the house and rubbed his unshaven chin. Then he went out again to the road where the figure of Don Juan was now only a small smoke of dust between the eucalyptus trees. Quintero went up to the room where Don Juan had slept and stared at it with accusations and suspicions. He called the manservant.

"I shall sleep here tonight," Quintero said.

The manservant answered carefully. Quintero was mad again and the moon was still only in its first quarter. The man watched his master during the day looking towards Seville. It was too warm after the rains, the country steamed like a laundry.

And then, when the night came, Quintero laughed at his doubts. He went up to the room and as he undressed he thought of the assurance of those ice-cold lips, those icicle fingers and those icy arms. She had not come last night; oh, what fidelity! To think, he would say in his remorse to the ghost, that malice had so disordered him that he had been base and credulous enough to use the dead for a trick.

Tears were in his eyes as he lay down and for some time he dared not turn on his side and stretch out his hand to touch what, in his disorder, he had been willing to betray. He loathed his heart. He craved—yet how could he hope for it now?—that miracle of recognition and forgiveness. It was this craving which moved him at last. His hands went out. And they were met.

The hands, the arms, the lips moved out of their invisibility and soundlessness towards him. They touched him, they clasped him, they drew him down, but—what was this? He gave a shout, he fought to get away, kicked out and swore; and so the manservant found him wrestling with the sheets, striking out with fists and knees, roaring that he was in hell. Those hands, those lips, those limbs, he screamed, were *burning* him. They were of ice no more. They were of fire.

(1941)

Don Juan: Questions for Discussion and Writing

1. In addition to his way with women, what aspects of Don Juan's personality are evident in several of the renditions of Don Juan included here?
2. Where does Don Juan derive his powers of seduction? Cite one or more of the works in the portfolio.
3. Byron considers Don Juan *heroic*; do any of the other authors or painters?
4. Seduction is sometimes connected with death, as in Marvell's poem "To His Coy Mistress" earlier in this chapter. How do death and seduction function in stories of Don Juan?
5. Early versions of the Don Juan story (in the seventeenth and eighteenth centuries) were strictly moral: Don Juan was meant to be punished for his behavior. Is that true of any of these versions from the nineteenth and twentieth centuries?
6. Another characteristic of early Don Juan stories was the need for Don to repent; discuss the notion of repentance or regret in these more modern versions.
7. Do any of the characters or speakers in earlier selections in this chapter qualify as either Don Juans or victims of Don Juan?
8. Does Don Juan come across in these versions of his story as someone who loves the pleasures of the flesh or someone who cannot control himself?

Considering Art: Don Juan

The discussion below references art reproduced on color insert page 8.

Romanticism in the visual arts, as in literature, is a wide category. The term has been used to describe an eclectic array of styles and subjects taken up internationally by artists in the late eighteenth and early nineteenth centuries. In general, Romantic artists prefer strong emotions and individual experiences to rational or scientific types of knowledge. They exist in a state of rebellion, often feeling misunderstood by the public and opposed to conventions imposed by institutions such as church, state, and the artistic establishment. "Bad boy" characters, including the artistic personas of Lord Byron and the literary persona of Don Juan, appealed to many Romantic artists as subjects or as inspirational figures.

***George Gordon Byron* (see color insert p. 8).** British portraitist Thomas Phillips (1770–1845) painted *George Gordon Byron* (1813) depicting the English Romantic poet and satirist known as Lord Byron. This painting was first publicly shown at the London Royal Academy in 1814, the British parallel to the Paris Salon. During his lifetime, Byron acquired notorious celebrity as a modern-day Don Juan. He scandalized people with his many extravagant love affairs and his flouting of contemporary values and social structures. In a manner of masquerade that is known as "Orientalism," Byron here wears a tribal costume that he had purchased while traveling through southern Albania in 1809. At that time, Albania, like Greece, was part of the Ottoman empire. Byron identified with the people of Albania, who strongly reminded him of the fiercely independent Highlanders of Scotland. The costume he wears consists of a velvet jacket in crimson and gold, a striped shawl worn as a turban, a white shirt closed at the neck by a jeweled brooch, and a sword with a purple hilt. A viewer can read the portrait as a performance by Byron of an alternative "primitive" or non-European persona. This fascination with "the Orient" was common throughout the nineteenth century as an appropriation of what was thought to be a more exotic, authentic, or savage identity. Byron is a national hero in Greece because he fought on the Greek side in the Greek War of Independence (1821–1831). He died of a fever during the Siege of Missolonghi.

***Don Juan in Hell* (see color insert p. 8).** Italian artist Giuseppe Bernardino Bison (1762–1844) paints *Don Juan in Hell* in tempera paint on paper. Bison was surely familiar with the Don Juan legend, which had its origin in seventeenth-century Spain and had appeared in many visual and literary versions. The scene he depicts, of Don Juan's torment in hell, had also been featured in Wolfgang Amadeus Mozart's opera *Don Giovanni* (1787). In this part of the story, after killing the father of a woman he seduced, Don Juan visits the dead man's tomb and mocks his memory by inviting his tomb statue to dine with him. Unfortunately for him, the stone statue comes to life and drags the libertine off to hell. Juan is undone because of his passionate actions and his failure to reflect on the consequences of these actions. Bison shown us the demonic torments that Don Juan suffers in the underworld.

Questions about the Art

1. In Phillips's *George Gordon Byron*, how does Byron's choice to wear this costume for his portrait construct an image of him as an ideal Romantic persona? How does this assumption of an alternate identity tie into Byron's interest in the Spanish character of Don Juan? What do the details of the painting tell us about the sitter's character? How does Byron's case compare

to contemporary artists or writers who use celebrity or controversy to promote their careers?

2. How does the costume of Don Juan in Bison's painting *Don Juan in Hell* compare to that worn by Byron in Phillips's portrait? In Bison's painting, how do contrasts of light and dark lead our eyes through the story? What emotions do we feel when we observe Don Juan in torment in the underworld?

Connecting Art and Literature

1. Does the portrait of Byron connect more readily to the poetic voice in his poem *Don Juan* or to the figure of Don Juan himself as depicted in that poem?
2. Which story is more in line with the version of Don Juan depicted in the painting *Don Juan in Hell*—Flaubert's "Passion and Virtue" or Pritchett's "A Story of Don Juan"?

Chapter 14

Honesty and Deception

You might have heard the expression "Honesty is the best policy." Is it always? While we are taught to be polite, sometimes we cannot be polite and honest at the same time. Imagine sitting down to dinner at a friend's house and saying, "Mrs. Smith, this chicken is horribly overcooked, the sauce is too salty, your haircut is unattractive, and the color of this room is very strange." Although that is honest, it is also rude. We all, on occasion, deviate from the truth, keep secrets, or carefully distribute them in the form of gossip. We hide the truth in the name of politeness or social convention, or we lie to escape blame: would courtroom trials ever take place if everyone told the truth? We naturally protect ourselves and others, often by lying.

At the same time, too much lying can have disastrous results. Even if we are not caught lying, we can become consumed by guilt. The social fabric is built on trust, on "things being as they appear" and on people meaning what they say. Being known as a liar or as untrustworthy ultimately sabotages one's career, friendships, and family life. We do not want to rely on someone who is not trustworthy, and we do not want to be untrustworthy ourselves.

If truth and trust are somewhat abstract and vague concepts, hard to think about in a uniform way, they become even vaguer when the author of a literary work deliberately misleads the reader. Although literature is not always mystery writing, frequently the reader must figure something out, and the speaker, narrator, playwright, or author might be well aware of how much information he or she is providing. At the same time, much literature is involved with telling the "truth," or exposing a kind of reality that might not be generally evident. As a reader, your role might be to take some truth away from literary works by reading and interpreting them carefully, being cautious not to equate the truth with the merely evident. Whether or not honesty is the best policy, *clarity* is a worthwhile goal for the reader of literature.

The works in this chapter look at the way honesty and deception overlap and change meanings in different contexts. One theme that emerges is that we tend to keep secrets from our families: the father in a well-to-do family in India finds a sacred relic and keeps that fact from his family in Salman Rushdie's story "The Prophet's Hair." The male characters in David Long's story "Morphine" and Ann Beattie's story "Weekend" conceal extramarital affairs from their wives, as

Illustration from *The Adventures of Pinocchio* by Carlo Collodi (1883).

well as the deep emotions of their private worlds. Tellingly, at least one secret-keeper in this chapter is also an actor: Natsuo in Mori Yoko's story "Spring Storm." Secret-keepers are subtly different from liars. We do not know whether the protagonist of Charles Chesnutt's story "The Wife of His Youth" believes the story he tells or not, but the speakers of the poems in this chapter by Sir Walter Raleigh, William Shakespeare, Langston Hughes, Emily Dickinson, Paul Laurence Dunbar, and Richard Wilbur and the protagonist of Alifa Rifaat's story are all aware of both the truth and the lies that press against it, and they respond differently to that tension. The essay by Maxine Hong Kingston, "No Name Woman," connects women's experience to lying: Kingston's aunt was shamed for having a baby out of wedlock, and Kingston's family conceals this information from the rest of the world.

This chapter's Common Characters section focuses on the trickster figure, a cunning archetypal character from myth and legend—the prototype of the cartoon figures Bugs Bunny and Roger Rabbit. Like many liars, the trickster is difficult, if not impossible, to pin down: is he a cunning opportunist or a subversive

THECHEQUEISINTHEMAIL
ITWASNTMESHEISONLYAF
RIENDONESIZEFITSALLI
NEVERSAIDTHATITWONTH
URTABITTHATLOOKSGOOD
ONYOUINEVERGOTTHEMES
SAGEIBELIEVEYOUYOUHA
VENTCHANGEDONEBITTHI
SISMYLASTCIGARETTEIL
LPAYYOUBACKIGOTSTUCK
INTRAFFICILLRESPECTY
OUINTHEMORNINGTHEMAN
UALEXPLAINSEVERYTHIN
GITSTHELASTONEINSTOC
KTHEDIETSTARTSTOMORR
OWITHASAMINDOFITSOWN

Tad Lauritzen Wright, *String of Lies* (2005).

rebel? While his motives are usually selfish, his acts often bring benefits to others. The trickster appears to be many things to many people, as suits his purpose. We've all known people like this (many politicians are successful tricksters), and while we may admire their resourcefulness, we often regard them with suspicion.

Oscar Wilde, whose famous comedy *The Importance of Being Earnest* is included in this chapter, once wrote, "No great artist ever sees things as they really are. If he did he would cease to be an artist." If that is true, then all artists are liars. As you explore this chapter, consider how they can be liars who tell the truth.

Fiction

Charles Chesnutt

The Wife of His Youth

Charles Chesnutt (1858–1932) was the son of free blacks who had emigrated from the South to Cleveland, Ohio. After briefly teaching and serving as school principal in his parents' native town, Fayetteville, North Carolina,

Chesnutt returned to Cleveland to fulfill his aspirations as a writer. His famous story, "The Goophered Grapevine," was the first story written by an African American to be published in the *Atlantic Monthly*. Chesnutt went on to excel in the short story form, though he also published three novels and essays. His fiction took on two extremely important issues in post–Civil War America: the difficulties faced by mixed-race Americans and the dangers of romanticizing the South in the era before slavery was abolished. Note the way Chesnutt uses two distinct voices in "The Wife of His Youth," and think about how the stark difference between the voices feeds into the story's theme.

I

Mr. Ryder was going to give a ball. There were several reasons why this was an opportune time for such an event.

Mr. Ryder might aptly be called the dean of the Blue Veins. The original Blue Veins were a little society of colored persons organized in a certain Northern city shortly after the war. Its purpose was to establish and maintain correct social standards among a people whose social condition presented almost unlimited room for improvement. By accident, combined perhaps with some natural affinity, the society consisted of individuals who were, generally speaking, more white than black. Some envious outsider made the suggestion that no one was eligible for membership who was not white enough to show blue veins. The suggestion was readily adopted by those who were not of the favored few, and since that time the society, though possessing a longer and more pretentious name, had been known far and wide as the "Blue Vein Society," and its members as the "Blue Veins."

The Blue Veins did not allow that any such requirement existed for admission to their circle, but, on the contrary, declared that character and culture were the only things considered; and that if most of their members were light-colored, it was because such persons, as a rule, had had better opportunities to qualify themselves for membership. Opinions differed, too, as to the usefulness of the society. There were those who had been known to assail it violently as a glaring example of the very prejudice from which the colored race had suffered most; and later, when such critics had succeeded in getting on the inside, they had been heard to maintain with zeal and earnestness that the society was a lifeboat, an anchor, a bulwark and a shield,—a pillar of cloud by day and of fire by night, to guide their people through the social wilderness. Another alleged prerequisite for Blue Vein membership was that of free birth; and while there was really no such requirement, it is doubtless true that very few of the members would have been unable to meet it if there had been. If there were one or two of the older members who had come up from the South and from slavery, their history presented enough romantic circumstances to rob their servile origin of its grosser aspects.

While there were no such tests of eligibility, it is true that the Blue Veins had their notions on these subjects, and that not all of them were equally liberal in regard to the things they collectively disclaimed. Mr. Ryder was one of the most conservative. Though he had not been among the founders of the society, but had come in some years later, his genius for social leadership was such that he had speedily become its recognized adviser and head, the custodian of its standards, and the preserver of its traditions. He shaped its social policy, was active in providing for its entertainment, and when the interest fell off, as it sometimes did, he fanned the embers until they burst again into a cheerful flame.

There were still other reasons for his popularity. While he was not as white 5
as some of the Blue Veins, his appearance was such as to confer distinction upon them. His features were of a refined type, his hair was almost straight; he was always neatly dressed; his manners were irreproachable, and his morals above suspicion. He had come to Groveland a young man, and obtaining employment in the office of a railroad company as messenger had in time worked himself up to the position of stationery clerk, having charge of the distribution of the office supplies for the whole company. Although the lack of early training had hindered the orderly development of a naturally fine mind, it had not prevented him from doing a great deal of reading or from forming decidedly literary tastes. Poetry was his passion. He could repeat whole pages of the great English poets; and if his pronunciation was sometimes faulty, his eye, his voice, his gestures, would respond to the changing sentiment with a precision that revealed a poetic soul and disarmed criticism. He was economical, and had saved money; he owned and occupied a very comfortable house on a respectable street. His residence was handsomely furnished, containing among other things a good library, especially rich in poetry, a piano, and some choice engravings. He generally shared his house with some young couple, who looked after his wants and were company for him; for Mr. Ryder was a single man. In the early days of his connection with the Blue Veins he had been regarded as quite a catch, and young ladies and their mothers had manœuvred with much ingenuity to capture him. Not, however, until Mrs. Molly Dixon visited Groveland had any woman ever made him wish to change his condition to that of a married man.

Mrs. Dixon had come to Groveland from Washington in the spring, and before the summer was over she had won Mr. Ryder's heart. She possessed many attractive qualities. She was much younger than he; in fact, he was old enough to have been her father, though no one knew exactly how old he was. She was whiter than he, and better educated. She had moved in the best colored society of the country, at Washington, and had taught in the schools of that city. Such a superior person had been eagerly welcomed to the Blue Vein Society, and had taken a leading part in its activities. Mr. Ryder had at first been attracted by her charms of person, for she was very good looking and not over twenty-five; then by her refined manners and the vivacity of her wit. Her husband had been a government clerk, and at his death had left a considerable life insurance. She was visiting friends in Groveland, and, finding the town and the people to her liking, had prolonged her stay indefinitely. She had not seemed displeased at Mr. Ryder's attentions, but on the contrary had given him every proper encouragement; indeed, a younger and less cautious man would long since have spoken. But he had made up his mind, and had only to determine the time when he would ask her to be his wife. He decided to give a ball in her honor, and at some time during the evening of the ball to offer her his heart and hand. He had no special fears about the outcome, but, with a little touch of romance, he wanted the surroundings to be in harmony with his own feelings when he should have received the answer he expected.

Mr. Ryder resolved that this ball should mark an epoch in the social history of Groveland. He knew, of course,—no one could know better,—the entertainments that had taken place in past years, and what must be done to surpass them. His ball must be worthy of the lady in whose honor it was to be given, and must, by the quality of its guests, set an example for the future. He had observed of late a growing liberality, almost a laxity, in social matters, even among members of his own set, and had several times been forced to meet in a social way persons whose complexions and callings in life were hardly up to the standard which he considered proper for the society to maintain. He had a theory of his own.

"I have no race prejudice," he would say, "but we people of mixed blood are ground between the upper and the nether millstone. Our fate lies between absorption by the white race and extinction in the black. The one doesn't want us yet, but may take us in time. The other would welcome us, but it would be for us a backward step. 'With malice towards none, with charity for all,' we must do the best we can for ourselves and those who are to follow us. Self-preservation is the first law of nature."

His ball would serve by its exclusiveness to counteract leveling tendencies, and his marriage with Mrs. Dixon would help to further the upward process of absorption he had been wishing and waiting for.

II

The ball was to take place on Friday night. The house had been put in order, the 10
carpets covered with canvas, the halls and stairs decorated with palms and potted plants; and in the afternoon Mr. Ryder sat on his front porch, which the shade of a vine running up over a wire netting made a cool and pleasant lounging place. He expected to respond to the toast "The Ladies" at the supper, and from a volume of Tennyson[1]—his favorite poet—was fortifying himself with apt quotations. The volume was open at "A Dream of Fair Women." His eyes fell on these lines, and he read them aloud to judge better of their effect:—

"At length I saw a lady within call,
 Stiller than chisell'd marble, standing there;
A daughter of the gods, divinely tall,
 And most divinely fair."

He marked the verse, and turning the page read the stanza beginning,—

"O sweet pale Margaret,
 O rare pale Margaret."

[1]*Tennyson:* Alfred, Lord Tennyson (1809–1892), poet laureate of England from 1850 to 1892. (See his poem "The Charge of the Light Brigade" in Chapter 12.) "O Sweet Pale Margaret" is a quotation from one of his early poems, "Margaret." The next reference is to a poem titled "Sir Lancelot and Queen Guinevere."

He weighed the passage a moment, and decided that it would not do. Mrs. Dixon was the palest lady he expected at the ball, and she was of a rather ruddy complexion, and of lively disposition and buxom build. So he ran over the leaves until his eye rested on the description of Queen Guinevere:—

"She seem'd a part of joyous Spring;
A gown of grass-green silk she wore,
Buckled with golden clasps before;
A light-green tuft of plumes she bore
Closed in a golden ring.

* * * * * *

"She look'd so lovely, as she sway'd
The rein with dainty finger-tips,
A man had given all other bliss,
And all his worldly worth for this,
To waste his whole heart in one kiss
Upon her perfect lips."

As Mr. Ryder murmured these words audibly, with an appreciative thrill, he heard the latch of his gate click, and a light footfall sounding on the steps. He turned his head, and saw a woman standing before his door.

She was a little woman, not five feet tall, and proportioned to her height. Although she stood erect, and looked around her with very bright and restless eyes, she seemed quite old; for her face was crossed and recrossed with a hundred wrinkles, and around the edges of her bonnet could be seen protruding here and there a tuft of short gray wool. She wore a blue calico gown of ancient cut, a little red shawl fastened around her shoulders with an old-fashioned brass brooch, and a large bonnet profusely ornamented with faded red and yellow artificial flowers. And she was very black,—so black that her toothless gums, revealed when she opened her mouth to speak, were not red, but blue. She looked like a bit of the old plantation life, summoned up from the past by the wave of a magician's wand, as the poet's fancy had called into being the gracious shapes of which Mr. Ryder had just been reading.

He rose from his chair and came over to where she stood.

"Good-afternoon, madam," he said.

15 "Good-evenin', suh," she answered, ducking suddenly with a quaint curtsy. Her voice was shrill and piping, but softened somewhat by age. "Is dis yere whar Mistuh Ryduh lib, suh?" she asked, looking around her doubtfully, and glancing into the open windows, through which some of the preparations for the evening were visible.

"Yes," he replied, with an air of kindly patronage, unconsciously flattered by her manner, "I am Mr. Ryder. Did you want to see me?"

"Yas, suh, ef I ain't 'sturbin' of you too much."

"Not at all. Have a seat over here behind the vine, where it is cool. What can I do for you?"

"'Scuse me, suh," she continued, when she had sat down on the edge of a chair, "'scuse me, suh, I 's lookin' for my husban'. I heerd you wuz a big man an' had libbed heah a long time, an' I 'lowed you would n't min' ef I 'd come roun' an' ax you ef you 'd ever heerd of a merlatter man by de name er Sam Taylor 'quirin' roun' in de chu'ches ermongs' de people fer his wife 'Liza Jane?"

Mr. Ryder seemed to think for a moment.

"There used to be many such cases right after the war," he said, "but it has been so long that I have forgotten them. There are very few now. But tell me your story, and it may refresh my memory."

She sat back farther in her chair so as to be more comfortable, and folded her withered hands in her lap.

"My name 's 'Liza," she began, "'Liza Jane. W'en I wuz young I us'ter b'long ter Marse Bob Smif, down in ole Missoura. I wuz bawn down dere. W'en I wuz a gal I wuz married ter a man named Jim. But Jim died, an' after dat I married a merlatter man named Sam Taylor. Sam wuz freebawn, but his mammy and daddy died, an' de w'ite folks 'prenticed him ter my marster fer ter work fer 'im 'tel he wuz growed up. Sam worked in de fiel', an' I wuz de cook. One day Ma'y Ann, ole miss's maid, came rushin' out ter de kitchen, an' says she, ''Liza Jane, ole marse gwine sell yo' Sam down de ribber.'

"'Go way f'm yere,' says I; 'my husban' 's free!'

"'Don' make no diff'ence. I heerd ole marse tell ole miss he wuz gwine take yo' Sam 'way wid 'im ter-morrow, fer he needed money, an' he knowed whar he could git a t'ousan' dollars fer Sam an' no questions axed.'

"W'en Sam come home f'm de fiel' dat night, I tole him 'bout ole marse gwine steal 'im, an' Sam run erway. His time wuz mos' up, an' he swo' dat w'en he wuz twenty-one he would come back an' he'p me run erway, er else save up de money ter buy my freedom. An' I know he 'd 'a' done it, fer he thought a heap er me, Sam did. But w'en he come back he did n' fin' me, fer I wuz n' dere. Ole marse had heerd dat I warned Sam, so he had me whip' an' sol' down de ribber.

"Den de wah broke out, an' w'en it wuz ober de cullud folks wuz scattered. I went back ter de ole home; but Sam wuz n' dere, an' I could n' l'arn nuffin' 'bout 'im. But I knowed he 'd be'n dere to look fer me an' had n' foun' me, an' had gone erway ter hunt fer me.

"I 's be'n lookin' fer 'im eber sence," she added simply, as though twenty-five years were but a couple of weeks, "an' I knows he 's be'n lookin' fer me. Fer he sot a heap er sto' by me, Sam did, an' I know he 's be'n huntin' fer me all dese years,—'less'n he 's be'n sick er sump'n, so he could n' work, er out'n his head, so he could n' 'member his promise. I went back down de ribber, fer I 'lowed he 'd gone down dere lookin' fer me. I 's be'n ter Noo Orleens, an' Atlanty, an' Charleston, an' Richmon'; an' w'en I 'd be'n all ober de Souf I come ter de Norf. Fer I knows I 'll fin' 'im some er dese days," she added softly, "er he 'll fin' me, an' den we 'll bofe be as happy in freedom as we wuz in de ole days befo' de wah." A smile stole over her withered countenance as she paused a moment, and her bright eyes softened into a far-away look.

This was the substance of the old woman's story. She had wandered a little here and there. Mr. Ryder was looking at her curiously when she finished.

"How have you lived all these years?" he asked.

"Cookin', suh. I 's a good cook. Does you know anybody w'at needs a good cook, suh? I 's stoppin' wid a cullud fam'ly roun' de corner yonder 'tel I kin git a place."

"Do you really expect to find your husband? He may be dead long ago."

She shook her head emphatically. "Oh no, he ain' dead. De signs an' de tokens tells me. I dremp three nights runnin' on'y dis las' week dat I foun' him."

"He may have married another woman. Your slave marriage would not have prevented him, for you never lived with him after the war, and without that your marriage does n't count."

"Would n' make no diff'ence wid Sam. He would n' marry no yuther 'ooman 'tel he foun' out 'bout me. I knows it," she added. "Sump'n 's be'n tellin' me all dese years dat I 's gwine fin' Sam 'fo' I dies."

"Perhaps he 's outgrown you, and climbed up in the world where he would n't care to have you find him."

"No, indeed, suh," she replied, "Sam ain' dat kin' er man. He wuz good ter me, Sam wuz, but he wuz n' much good ter nobody e'se, fer he wuz one er de triflin'es' han's on de plantation. I 'spec's ter haf ter suppo't 'im w'en I fin' 'im, fer he nebber would work 'less'n he had ter. But den he wuz free, an' he did n' git no pay fer his work, an' I don' blame 'im much. Mebbe he 's done better sence he run erway, but I ain' 'spectin' much."

"You may have passed him on the street a hundred times during the twenty-five years, and not have known him; time works great changes."

She smiled incredulously. "I 'd know 'im 'mongs' a hund'ed men. Fer dey wuz n' no yuther merlatter man like my man Sam, an' I could n' be mistook. I 's toted his picture roun' wid me twenty-five years."

"May I see it?" asked Mr. Ryder. "It might help me to remember whether I have seen the original."

As she drew a small parcel from her bosom he saw that it was fastened to a string that went around her neck. Removing several wrappers, she brought to light an old-fashioned daguerreotype in a black case. He looked long and intently at the portrait. It was faded with time, but the features were still distinct, and it was easy to see what manner of man it had represented.

He closed the case, and with a slow movement handed it back to her.

"I don't know of any man in town who goes by that name," he said, "nor have I heard of any one making such inquiries. But if you will leave me your address, I will give the matter some attention, and if I find out anything I will let you know."

She gave him the number of a house in the neighborhood, and went away, after thanking him warmly.

He wrote the address on the fly-leaf of the volume of Tennyson, and, when she had gone, rose to his feet and stood looking after her curiously. As she walked down the street with mincing step, he saw several persons whom she passed turn and look back at her with a smile of kindly amusement. When she had turned the corner, he went upstairs to his bedroom, and stood for a long time before the mirror of his dressing-case, gazing thoughtfully at the reflection of his own face.

III

At eight o'clock the ballroom was a blaze of light and the guests had begun to assemble; for there was a literary programme and some routine business of the society to be gone through with before the dancing. A black servant in evening dress waited at the door and directed the guests to the dressing-rooms.

The occasion was long memorable among the colored people of the city; not alone for the dress and display, but for the high average of intelligence and culture that distinguished the gathering as a whole. There were a number of school-teachers, several young doctors, three or four lawyers, some professional singers, an editor, a lieutenant in the United States army spending his furlough in the city, and others in various polite callings; these were colored, though most of them would not have attracted even a casual glance because of any marked difference from white people. Most of the ladies were in evening costume, and dress coats and dancing pumps were the rule among the men. A band of string music, stationed in an alcove behind a row of palms, played popular airs while the guests were gathering.

The dancing began at half past nine. At eleven o'clock supper was served. Mr. Ryder had left the ballroom some little time before the intermission, but reappeared at the supper-table. The spread was worthy of the occasion, and the guests did full justice to it. When the coffee had been served, the toast-master, Mr. Solomon Sadler, rapped for order. He made a brief introductory speech, complimenting host and guests, and then presented in their order the toasts of the evening. They were responded to with a very fair display of after-dinner wit.

"The last toast," said the toast-master, when he reached the end of the list, "is one which must appeal to us all. There is no one of us of the sterner sex who is not at some time dependent upon woman,—in infancy for protection, in manhood for companionship, in old age for care and comforting. Our good host has been trying to live alone, but the fair faces I see around me to-night prove that he too is largely dependent upon the gentler sex for most that makes life worth living,—the society and love of friends,—and rumor is at fault if he does not soon yield entire subjection to one of them. Mr. Ryder will now respond to the toast,—The Ladies."

There was a pensive look in Mr. Ryder's eyes as he took the floor and adjusted his eyeglasses. He began by speaking of woman as the gift of Heaven to man, and after some general observations on the relations of the sexes he said: "But perhaps the quality which most distinguishes woman is her fidelity and devotion to those she loves. History is full of examples, but has recorded none more striking than one which only to-day came under my notice."

He then related, simply but effectively, the story told by his visitor of the afternoon. He gave it in the same soft dialect which came readily to his lips, while the company listened attentively and sympathetically. For the story had awakened a responsive thrill in many hearts. There were some present who had seen, and others who had heard their fathers and grandfathers tell, the wrongs and sufferings of this past generation, and all of them still felt, in their darker moments, the shadow hanging over them. Mr. Ryder went on:—

"Such devotion and confidence are rare even among women. There are many who would have searched a year, some who would have waited five years, a few who might have hoped ten years; but for twenty-five years this woman has retained her affection for and her faith in a man she has not seen or heard of in all that time.

"She came to me to-day in the hope that I might be able to help her find this long-lost husband. And when she was gone I gave my fancy rein, and imagined a case I will put to you.

"Suppose that this husband, soon after his escape, had learned that his wife had been sold away, and that such inquiries as he could make brought no information of her whereabouts. Suppose that he was young, and she much older than he; that he was light, and she was black; that their marriage was a slave marriage, and legally binding only if they chose to make it so after the war. Suppose, too, that he made his way to the North, as some of us have done, and there, where he had larger opportunities, had improved them, and had in the course of all these years grown to be as different from the ignorant boy who ran away from fear of slavery as the day is from the night. Suppose, even, that he had qualified himself, by industry, by thrift, and by study, to win the friendship and be considered worthy the society of such people as these I see around me to-night, gracing my board and filling my heart with gladness; for I am old enough to remember the day when such a gathering would not have been possible in this land. Suppose, too, that, as the years went by, this man's memory of the past grew more and more indistinct, until at last it was rarely, except in his dreams, that any image of this bygone period rose before his mind. And then suppose that accident should bring to his knowledge the fact that the wife of his youth, the wife he had left behind him,—not one who had walked by his side and kept pace with him in his upward struggle, but one upon whom advancing years and a laborious life had set their mark,—was alive and seeking him, but that he was absolutely safe from recognition or discovery, unless he chose to reveal himself. My friends, what would the man do? I will presume that he was one who loved honor, and tried to deal justly with all men. I will even carry the case further, and suppose that perhaps he had set his heart upon another, whom he had hoped to call his own. What would he do, or rather what ought he to do, in such a crisis of a lifetime?

"It seemed to me that he might hesitate, and I imagined that I was an old friend, a near friend, and that he had come to me for advice; and I argued the case with him. I tried to discuss it impartially. After we had looked upon the matter from every point of view, I said to him, in words that we all know: —

'This above all: to thine own self be true,
And it must follow, as the night the day,
Thou canst not then be false to any man.'

Then, finally, I put the question to him, 'Shall you acknowledge her?'

"And now, ladies and gentlemen, friends and companions, I ask you, what should he have done?"

There was something in Mr. Ryder's voice that stirred the hearts of those who sat around him. It suggested more than mere sympathy with an imaginary situation; it seemed rather in the nature of a personal appeal. It was observed, too, that his look rested more especially upon Mrs. Dixon, with a mingled expression of renunciation and inquiry.

She had listened, with parted lips and streaming eyes. She was the first to speak: "He should have acknowledged her."

"Yes," they all echoed, "he should have acknowledged her."

"My friends and companions," responded Mr. Ryder, "I thank you, one and all. It is the answer I expected, for I knew your hearts."

He turned and walked toward the closed door of an adjoining room, while every eye followed him in wondering curiosity. He came back in a moment, leading by the hand his visitor of the afternoon, who stood startled and trembling at the sudden plunge into this scene of brilliant gayety. She was neatly dressed in gray, and wore the white cap of an elderly woman.

"Ladies and gentlemen," he said, "this is the woman, and I am the man, whose story I have told you. Permit me to introduce to you the wife of my youth."

(1898)

Questions for Discussion and Writing

Close Reading

1. Define the "Blue Veins" society. Do we know how the narrator feels about this society, or is he completely neutral about it?
2. Discuss the differences between the passage of poetry Ryder rejects and the passage he chooses (both by Tennyson). Also consider how this declaration of love, couched in poetic language, differs from the declaration of love uttered by "the wife of his youth," couched in southern black dialect.
3. Does anything in the story foreshadow its surprising ending?

Critical and Creative Reading

4. Write the scene that might follow the end of this story if it were to continue.
5. Some say that the tendency to reinvent oneself is a consistent component of American mythology. Consider whether you have reinvented yourself (even as recently as when you began college), and write an essay about whether a reinvented person has any obligations to his or her past.
6. If the wife of his youth had never shown up, do you think Ryder would ever have acknowledged his past? Assess how you feel about his character based on your response.

Connections to Other Readings

7. "Passing" was an important and hotly debated issue in the years following the American Civil War. It involved the willingness of light-skinned African Americans to "pass for white" by affecting the manners, looks, and speech of white Americans. How is that issue treated in "The Wife of His Youth" and in Natasha Trethewey's poem "Letter Home"?

8. Is storytelling a form of power? Consider this story and Maxine Hong Kingston's essay "No Name Woman" in your response.
9. Discuss the connection between the truth and belief in this story and in Oscar Wilde's *The Importance of Being Earnest*.
10. Consider the meaning of this story in terms of a "mask" as defined by Paul Laurence Dunbar in "We Wear the Mask." How would Dunbar react to Ryder?

Salman Rushdie

The Prophet's Hair

Salman Rushdie (b.1947) was born just two months before Pakistan and India separated into two independent states, an event that forms the basis for his award-winning novel *Midnight's Children*. Raised in both countries, Rushdie was educated at the prestigious Rugby school in England from the age of fourteen, and the question of national identity is at the heart of much of his fiction. For Rushdie, the question became infinitely more complicated after the publication of his controversial novel *The Satanic Verses* in 1988. The book was deemed offensive by many fundamentalist Muslims for its depiction of the prophet Muhammad. *The Satanic Verses* was banned in a dozen countries with predominantly Muslim populations, and on February 14, 1989, the Ayatollah Khomieni, the leader of Iran, condemned Rushdie to death and offered a reward for his murder. For more than a decade Rushdie lived in exile under police protection; depending on one's perspective, his case represents the global religious tension of our time, a monumental challenge to free expression, or the ways an artist's duties are divided in a political world. The following story, "The Prophet's Hair," was published in Rushdie's 1994 collection *East, West*. Like much of his fiction, it plays with language and with the convention of stories told within other stories.

Early in the year 19—, when Srinagar was under the spell of a winter so fierce it could crack men's bones as if they were glass, a young man upon whose cold-pinked skin there lay, like a frost, the unmistakable sheen of wealth was to be seen entering the most wretched and disreputable part of the city, where the houses of wood and corrugated iron seemed perpetually on the verge of losing their balance, and asking in low, grave tones where he might go to engage the services of a dependably professional burglar. The young man's name was Atta, and the rogues in that part of town directed him gleefully into ever darker and less public alleys, until in a yard wet with the blood of a slaughtered chicken he was set upon by two men whose faces he never saw, robbed of the substantial bank-roll which he had insanely brought on his solitary excursion, and beaten within an inch of his life.

Night fell. His body was carried by anonymous hands to the edge of the lake, whence it was transported by shikara across the water and deposited, torn and bleeding, on the deserted embankment of the canal which led to the gardens of Shalimar. At dawn the next morning a flower-vendor was rowing his boat through water to which the cold of the night had given the cloudy consistency of wild honey when he saw the prone form of young Atta, who was just beginning to stir and moan, and on whose now deathly pale skin the sheen of wealth could still be made out dimly beneath an actual layer of frost.

The flower-vendor moored his craft and by stooping over the mouth of the injured man was able to learn the poor fellow's address, which was mumbled through lips that could scarcely move; whereupon, hoping for a large tip, the hawker rowed Atta home to a large house on the shores of the lake, where a beautiful but inexplicably bruised young woman and her distraught, but equally handsome mother, neither of whom, it was clear from their eyes, had slept a wink from worrying, screamed at the sight of their Atta—who was the elder brother of the beautiful young woman—lying motionless amidst the funereally stunted winter blooms of the hopeful florist.

The flower-vendor was indeed paid off handsomely, not least to ensure his silence, and plays no further part in our story. Atta himself, suffering terribly from exposure as well as a broken skull, entered a coma which caused the city's finest doctors to shrug helplessly. It was therefore all the more remarkable that on the very next evening the most wretched and disreputable part of the city received a second unexpected visitor. This was Huma, the sister of the unfortunate young man, and her question was the same as her brother's, and asked in the same low, grave tones:

"Where may I hire a thief?"

The story of the rich idiot who had come looking for a burglar was already common knowledge in those insalubrious gullies, but this time the young woman added: "I should say that I am carrying no money, nor am I wearing any jewellery items. My father has disowned me and will pay no ransom if I am kidnapped; and a letter has been lodged with the Deputy Commissioner of Police, my uncle, to be opened in the event of my not being safe at home by morning. In that letter he will find full details of my journey here, and he will move Heaven and Earth to punish my assailants."

Her exceptional beauty, which was visible even through the enormous welts and bruises disfiguring her arms and forehead, coupled with the oddity of her inquiries, had attracted a sizable group of curious onlookers, and because her little speech seemed to them to cover just about everything, no one attempted to injure her in any way, although there were some raucous comments to the effect that it was pretty peculiar for someone who was trying to hire a crook to invoke the protection of a high-up policeman uncle.

She was directed into ever darker and less public alleys until finally in a gully as dark as ink an old woman with eyes which stared so piercingly that Huma instantly understood she was blind motioned her through a doorway from which darkness seemed to be pouring like smoke. Clenching her fists, angrily ordering her heart to behave normally, Huma followed the old woman into the gloom-wrapped house.

The faintest conceivable rivulet of candlelight trickled through the darkness; following this unreliable yellow thread (because she could no longer see the old lady), Huma received a sudden sharp blow to the shins and cried out involuntarily, after which she at once bit her lip, angry at having revealed her mounting terror to whoever or whatever waited before her, shrouded in blackness.

She had, in fact, collided with a low table on which a single candle burned 10
and beyond which a mountainous figure could be made out, sitting cross-legged on the floor. "Sit, sit," said a man's calm, deep voice, and her legs, needing no more flowery invitation, buckled beneath her at the terse command. Clutching her left hand in her right, she forced her voice to respond evenly:

"And you, sir, will be the thief I have been requesting?"

Shifting its weight very slightly, the shadow-mountain informed Huma that all criminal activity originating in this zone was well organised and also centrally controlled, so that all requests for what might be termed freelance work had to be channelled through this room.

He demanded comprehensive details of the crime to be committed, including a precise inventory of items to be acquired, also a clear statement of all financial inducements being offered with no gratuities excluded, plus, for filing purposes only, a summary of the motives for the application.

At this, Huma, as though remembering something, stiffened both in body and resolve and replied loudly that her motives were entirely a matter for herself; that she would discuss details with no one but the thief himself; but that the rewards she proposed could only be described as "lavish."

"All I am willing to disclose to you, sir, since it appears that I am on the 15
premises of some sort of employment agency, is that in return for such lavish rewards I must have the most desperate criminal at your disposal, a man for whom life holds no terrors, not even the fear of God.

"The worst of fellows, I tell you—nothing less will do!"

At this a paraffin storm-lantern was lighted, and Huma saw facing her a grey-haired giant down whose left cheek ran the most sinister of scars, a cicatrice[1] in the shape of the letter *sín* in the Nastaliq[2] script. She was gripped by the insupportably nostalgic notion that the bogeyman of her childhood nursery had risen

[1]*cicatrice:* A scar.

[2]*Nastaliq:* An ornate form of Arabic writing.

up to confront her, because her ayah had always forestalled any incipient acts of disobedience by threatening Huma and Atta: "You don't watch out and I'll send that one to steal you away—that Sheikh Sín, the Thief of Thieves!"

Here, grey-haired but unquestionably scarred, was the notorious criminal himself—and was she out of her mind, were her ears playing tricks, or had he truly just announced that, given the stated circumstances, he himself was the only man for the job?

Struggling hard against the newborn goblins of nostalgia, Huma warned the fearsome volunteer that only a matter of extreme urgency and peril would have brought her unescorted into these ferocious streets.

"Because we can afford no last-minute backings-out," she continued, "I am 20
determined to tell you everything, keeping back no secrets whatsoever. If, after hearing me out, you are still prepared to proceed, then we shall do everything in our power to assist you, and to make you rich."

The old thief shrugged, nodded, spat. Huma began her story.

Six days ago, everything in the household of her father, the wealthy moneylender Hashim, had been as it always was. At breakfast her mother had spooned khichri lovingly on to the moneylender's plate; the conversation had been filled with those expressions of courtesy and solicitude on which the family prided itself.

Hashim was fond of pointing out that while he was not a godly man he set great store by "living honourably in the world." In that spacious lakeside residence, all outsiders were greeted with the same formality and respect, even those unfortunates who came to negotiate for small fragments of Hashim's large fortune, and of whom he naturally asked an interest rate of over seventy per cent, partly, as he told his khichri-spooning wife, "to teach these people the value of money; let them only learn that, and they will be cured of this fever of borrowing borrowing all the time—so you see that if my plans succeed, I shall put myself out of business!"

In their children, Atta and Huma, the moneylender and his wife had successfully sought to inculcate the virtues of thrift, plain dealing and a healthy independence of spirit. On this, too, Hashim was fond of congratulating himself.

Breakfast ended; the family members wished one another a fulfilling day. Within 25
a few hours, however, the glassy contentment of that household, of that life of porcelain delicacy and alabaster sensibilities, was to be shattered beyond all hope of repair.

The moneylender summoned his personal shikara and was on the point of stepping into it when, attracted by a glint of silver, he noticed a small vial floating between the boat and his private quay. On an impulse, he scooped it out of the glutinous water.

It was a cylinder of tinted glass cased in exquisitely wrought silver, and Hashim saw within its walls a silver pendant bearing a single strand of human hair.

Closing his fist around this unique discovery, he muttered to the boatman that he'd changed his plans, and hurried to his sanctum, where, behind closed doors, he feasted his eyes on his find.

There can be no doubt that Hashim the moneylender knew from the first that he was in possession of the famous relic of the Prophet Muhammad, that revered hair whose theft from its shrine at Hazratbal[3] mosque the previous morning had created an unprecedented hue and cry in the valley.

The thieves—no doubt alarmed by the pandemonium, by the procession through the streets of endless ululating crocodiles of lamentation, by the riots, the political ramifications and by the massive police search which was commanded and carried out by men whose entire careers now hung upon the finding of this lost hair—had evidently panicked and hurled the vial into the gelatine bosom of the lake.

Having found it by a stroke of great good fortune, Hashim's duty as a citizen was clear: the hair must be restored to its shrine, and the state to equanimity and peace.

But the moneylender had a different notion.

All around him in his study was the evidence of his collector's mania. There were enormous glass cases full of impaled butterflies from Gulmarg, three dozen scale models in various metals of the legendary cannon Zamzama,[4] innumerable swords, a Naga spear,[5] ninety-four terracotta camels of the sort sold on railway station platforms, many samovars,[6] and a whole zoology of tiny sandalwood animals, which had originally been carved to serve as children's bathtime toys.

"And after all," Hashim told himself, "the Prophet would have disapproved mightily of this relic-worship. He abhorred the idea of being deified! So, by keeping this hair from its distracted devotees, I perform—do I not?—a finer service than I would by returning it! Naturally, I don't want it for its religious value . . . I'm a man of the world, of this world. I see it purely as a secular object of great rarity and blinding beauty. In short, it's the silver vial I desire, more than the hair.

"They say there are American millionaires who purchase stolen art masterpieces and hide them away—they would know how I feel. I must, must have it!"

Every collector must share his treasures with one other human being, and Hashim summoned—and told—his only son Atta, who was deeply perturbed but, having been sworn to secrecy, only spilled the beans when the troubles became too terrible to bear.

[3]*Hazratbal:* This shrine is located in Kashmir and is said to contain a hair of the prophet Muhammad.

[4]*legendary cannon Zamzama:* A cannon in Pakistan made famous by Rudyard Kipling in his book *Kim*.

[5]*Naga spear:* A traditional handmade Indian spear.

[6]*samovars:* Containers for brewing tea.

The youth excused himself and left his father alone in the crowded solitude of his collections. Hashim was sitting erect in a hard, straight-backed chair, gazing intently at the beautiful vial.

It was well known that the moneylender never ate lunch, so it was not until evening that a servant entered the sanctum to summon his master to the dining-table. He found Hashim as Atta had left him. The same, and not the same—for now the moneylender looked swollen, distended. His eyes bulged even more than they always had, they were red-rimmed, and his knuckles were white.

He seemed to be on the point of bursting! As though, under the influence of the misappropriated relic, he had filled up with some spectral fluid which might at any moment ooze uncontrollably from his every bodily opening.

He had to be helped to the table, and then the explosion did indeed take place.

Seemingly careless of the effect of his words on the carefully constructed and fragile constitution of the family's life, Hashim began to gush, to spume long streams of awful truths. In horrified silence, his children heard their father turn upon his wife, and reveal to her that for many years their marriage had been the worst of his afflictions. "An end to politeness!" he thundered. "An end to hypocrisy!"

Next, and in the same spirit, he revealed to his family the existence of a mistress; he informed them also of his regular visits to paid women. He told his wife that, far from being the principal beneficiary of his will, she would receive no more than the eighth portion which was her due under Islamic law. Then he turned upon his children, screaming at Atta for his lack of academic ability —"A dope! I have been cursed with a dope!"—and accusing his daughter of lasciviousness, because she went around the city barefaced, which was unseemly for any good Muslim girl to do. She should, he commanded, enter purdah forthwith.

Hashim left the table without having eaten and fell into the deep sleep of a man who has got many things off his chest, leaving his children stunned, in tears, and the dinner going cold on the sideboard under the gaze of an anticipatory bearer.

At five o'clock the next morning the moneylender forced his family to rise, wash and say their prayers. From then on, he began to pray five times daily for the first time in his life, and his wife and children were obliged to do likewise.

Before breakfast, Huma saw the servants, under her father's direction, constructing a great heap of books in the garden and setting fire to it. The only volume left untouched was the Qur'an,[7] which Hashim wrapped in a silken cloth and placed on a table in the hall. He ordered each member of his family to read passages from this book for at least two hours per day. Visits to the cinema were forbidden. And if Atta invited male friends to the house, Huma was to retire to her room.

[7] *Qur'an:* The sacred text of Islam.

By now, the family had entered a state of shock and dismay; but there was worse to come.

That afternoon, a trembling debtor arrived at the house to confess his inability to pay the latest instalment of interest owed, and made the mistake of reminding Hashim, in somewhat blustering fashion, of the Qur'an's strictures against usury. The moneylender flew into a rage and attacked the fellow with one of his large collection of bullwhips.

By mischance, later the same day a second defaulter came to plead for time, and was seen fleeing Hashim's study with a great gash in his arm, because Huma's father had called him a thief of other men's money and had tried to cut off the wretch's right hand with one of the thirty-eight kukri knives[8] hanging on the study walls.

These breaches of the family's unwritten laws of decorum alarmed Atta and Huma, and when, that evening, their mother attempted to calm Hashim down, he struck her on the face with an open hand. Atta leapt to his mother's defence and he, too, was sent flying.

"From now on," Hashim bellowed, "there's going to be some discipline around here!"

The moneylender's wife began a fit of hysterics which continued throughout that night and the following day, and which so provoked her husband that he threatened her with divorce, at which she fled to her room, locked the door and subsided into a raga of sniffling. Huma now lost her composure, challenged her father openly, and announced (with that same independence of spirit which he had encouraged in her) that she would wear no cloth over her face; apart from anything else, it was bad for the eyes.

On hearing this, her father disowned her on the spot and gave her one week in which to pack her bags and go.

By the fourth day, the fear in the air of the house had become so thick that it was difficult to walk around. Atta told his shock-numbed sister: "We are descending to gutter-level—but I know what must be done."

That afternoon, Hashim left home accompanied by two hired thugs to extract the unpaid dues from his two insolvent clients. Atta went immediately to his father's study. Being the son and heir, he possessed his own key to the moneylender's safe. This he now used, and removing the little vial from its hiding-place, he slipped it into his trouser pocket and re-locked the safe door.

Now he told Huma the secret of what his father had fished out of Lake Dal, and exclaimed: "Maybe I'm crazy—maybe the awful things that are happening have made me cracked—but I am convinced there will be no peace in our house until this hair is out of it."

His sister at once agreed that the hair must be returned, and Atta set off in a hired shikara to Hazratbal mosque. Only when the boat had delivered him into

[8]*kukri knives:* Curved steel knives traditionally used in battle.

the throng of the distraught faithful which was swirling around the desecrated shrine did Atta discover that the relic was no longer in his pocket. There was only a hole, which his mother, usually so attentive to household matters, must have overlooked under the stress of recent events.

Atta's initial surge of chagrin was quickly replaced by a feeling of profound relief.

"Suppose," he imagined, "that I had already announced to the mullahs that the hair was on my person! They would never have believed me now—and this mob would have lynched me! At any rate, it has gone, and that's a load off my mind." Feeling more contented than he had for days, the young man returned home.

Here he found his sister bruised and weeping in the hall; upstairs, in her bedroom, his mother wailed like a brand-new widow. He begged Huma to tell him what had happened, and when she replied that their father, returning from his brutal business trip, had once again noticed a glint of silver between boat and quay, had once again scooped up the errant relic, and was consequently in a rage to end all rages, having beaten the truth out of her—then Atta buried his face in his hands and sobbed out his opinion, which was that the hair was persecuting them, and had come back to finish the job.

It was Huma's turn to think of a way out of their troubles.

While her arms turned black and blue and great stains spread across her forehead, she hugged her brother and whispered to him that she was determined to get rid of the hair *at all costs*—she repeated this last phrase several times.

"The hair," she then declared, "was stolen from the mosque; so it can be stolen from this house. But it must be a genuine robbery, carried out by a bona-fide thief, not by one of us who are under the hair's thrall—by a thief so desperate that he fears neither capture nor curses."

Unfortunately, she added, the theft would be ten times harder to pull off now that their father, knowing that there had already been one attempt on the relic, was certainly on his guard.

"Can you do it?"

Huma, in a room lit by candle and storm-lantern, ended her account with one further question: "What assurances can you give that the job holds no terrors for you still?"

The criminal, spitting, stated that he was not in the habit of providing references, as a cook might, or a gardener, but he was not alarmed so easily, certainly not by any children's djinni of a curse. Huma had to be content with this boast, and proceeded to describe the details of the proposed burglary.

"Since my brother's failure to return the hair to the mosque, my father has taken to sleeping with his precious treasure under his pillow. However, he sleeps alone, and very energetically; only enter his room without waking him, and he will certainly have tossed and turned quite enough to make the theft a simple matter. When you have the vial, come to my room," and here she handed Sheikh

Sín a plan of her home, "and I will hand over all the jewellery owned by my mother and myself. You will find . . . it is worth . . . that is, you will be able to get a fortune for it . . ."

It was evident that her self-control was weakening and that she was on the point of physical collapse.

"Tonight," she burst out finally. "You must come tonight!"

No sooner had she left the room than the old criminal's body was convulsed by 70
a fit of coughing: he spat blood into an old vanaspati can. The great Sheikh, the "Thief of Thieves," had become a sick man, and every day the time drew nearer when some young pretender to his power would stick a dagger in his stomach. A lifelong addiction to gambling had left him almost as poor as he had been when, decades ago, he had started out in this line of work as a mere pickpocket's apprentice; so in the extraordinary commission he had accepted from the moneylender's daughter he saw his opportunity of amassing enough wealth at a stroke to leave the valley for ever, and acquire the luxury of a respectable death which would leave his stomach intact.

As for the Prophet's hair, well, neither he nor his blind wife had ever had much to say for prophets—that was one thing they had in common with the moneylender's thunderstruck clan.

It would not do, however, to reveal the nature of this, his last crime, to his four sons. To his consternation, they had all grown up to be hopelessly devout men, who even spoke of making the pilgrimage to Mecca some day. "Absurd!" their father would laugh at them. "Just tell me how you will go?" For, with a parent's absolutist love, he had made sure they were all provided with a lifelong source of high income by crippling them at birth, so that, as they dragged themselves around the city, they earned excellent money in the begging business.

The children, then, could look after themselves.

He and his wife would be off soon with the jewel-boxes of the moneylender's women. It was a timely chance indeed that had brought the beautiful bruised girl into his corner of the town.

That night, the large house on the shore of the lake lay blindly waiting, with 75
silence lapping at its walls. A burglar's night: clouds in the sky and mists on the winter water. Hashim the moneylender was asleep, the only member of his family to whom sleep had come that night. In another room, his son Atta lay deep in the coils of his coma with a blood-clot forming on his brain, watched over by a mother who had let down her long greying hair to show her grief, a mother who placed warm compresses on his head with gestures redolent of impotence. In a third bedroom Huma waited, fully dressed, amidst the jewel-heavy caskets of her desperation.

At last a bulbul sang softly from the garden below her window and, creeping downstairs, she opened a door to the bird, on whose face there was a scar in the shape of the Nastaliq letter *sín*.

Noiselessly, the bird flew up the stairs behind her. At the head of the staircase they parted, moving in opposite directions along the corridor of their conspiracy without a glance at one another.

Entering the moneylender's room with professional ease, the burglar, Sín, discovered that Huma's predictions had been wholly accurate. Hashim lay sprawled diagonally across his bed, the pillow untenanted by his head, the prize easily accessible. Step by padded step, Sín moved towards the goal.

It was at this point that, in the bedroom next door, young Atta sat bolt upright in his bed, giving his mother a great fright, and without any warning—prompted by goodness knows what pressure of the blood-clot upon his brain—began screaming at the top of his voice:

"Thief! Thief! Thief!" 80

It seems probable that his poor mind had been dwelling, in these last moments, upon his own father; but it is impossible to be certain, because having uttered these three emphatic words the young man fell back upon his pillow and died.

At once his mother set up a screeching and a wailing and a keening and a howling so earsplittingly intense that they completed the work which Atta's cry had begun—that is, her laments penetrated the walls of her husband's bedroom and brought Hashim wide awake.

Sheikh Sín was just deciding whether to dive beneath the bed or brain the moneylender good and proper when Hashim grabbed the tiger-striped swordstick which always stood propped up in a corner beside his bed, and rushed from the room without so much as noticing the burglar who stood on the opposite side of the bed in the darkness. Sín stooped quickly and removed the vial containing the Prophet's hair from its hiding-place.

Meanwhile Hashim had erupted into the corridor, having unsheathed the sword inside his cane. In his right hand he held the weapon and was waving it about dementedly. His left hand was shaking the stick. A shadow came rushing towards him through the midnight darkness of the passageway and, in his somnolent anger, the moneylender thrust his sword fatally through its heart. Turning up the light, he found that he had murdered his daughter, and under the dire influence of this accident he was so overwhelmed by remorse that he turned the sword upon himself, fell upon it and so extinguished his life. His wife, the sole surviving member of the family, was driven mad by the general carnage and had to be committed to an asylum for the insane by her brother, the city's Deputy Commissioner of Police.

Sheikh Sín had quickly understood that the plan had gone awry. 85

Abandoning the dream of the jewel-boxes when he was but a few yards from its fulfilment, he climbed out of Hashim's window and made his escape during the appalling events described above. Reaching home before dawn, he woke his wife and confessed his failure. It would be necessary, he whispered, for him to vanish for a while. Her blind eyes never opened until he had gone.

The noise in the Hashim household had roused their servants and even managed to awaken the night-watchman, who had been fast asleep as usual on his charpoy by the street-gate. They alerted the police, and the Deputy Commissioner himself was informed. When he heard of Huma's death, the mournful officer opened and read the sealed letter which his niece had given him, and instantly led a large detachment of armed men into the light-repellent gullies of the most wretched and disreputable part of the city.

The tongue of a malicious cat-burglar named Huma's fellow-conspirator; the finger of an ambitious bank-robber pointed at the house in which he lay concealed; and although Sín managed to crawl through a hatch in the attic and attempt a roof-top escape, a bullet from the Deputy Commissioner's own rifle penetrated his stomach and brought him crashing messily to the ground at the feet of Huma's enraged uncle.

From the dead thief's pocket rolled a vial of tinted glass, cased in filigree silver.

The recovery of the Prophet's hair was announced at once on All-India Radio. 90
One month later, the valley's holiest men assembled at the Hazratbal mosque and formally authenticated the relic. It sits to this day in a closely guarded vault by the shores of the loveliest of lakes in the heart of the valley which was once closer than any other place on earth to Paradise.

But before our story can properly be concluded, it is necessary to record that when the four sons of the dead Sheikh awoke on the morning of his death, having unwittingly spent a few minutes under the same roof as the famous hair, they found that a miracle had occurred, that they were all sound of limb and strong of wind, as whole as they might have been if their father had not thought to smash their legs in the first hours of their lives. They were, all four of them, very properly furious, because the miracle had reduced their earning powers by 75 per cent, at the most conservative estimate; so they were ruined men.

Only the Sheikh's widow had some reason for feeling grateful, because although her husband was dead she had regained her sight, so that it was possible for her to spend her last days gazing once more upon the beauties of the valley of Kashmir.

(1994)

QUESTIONS FOR DISCUSSION AND WRITING

CLOSE READING

1. This story has an elaborate plot; before discussing it or writing about it, summarize the plot.
2. Consider the parallels in the story between the two "thieves," the burglar Sheikh Sín and the moneylender Hashim.
3. The prophet's hair alters people's behavior; it also performs a series of "miracles." List the alterations in behavior and the miracles it causes; then attempt to classify these actions as negative, positive, or neutral.

Critical and Creative Reading

4. After he finds and possesses the prophet's hair, Hashim, who was once a "worldly" nonreligious man, begins to lead his life according to strict religious principles. He also tells the truth about his life as he sees it. Discuss the story's simultaneous comments on religion and honesty.
5. Consider the way secrecy and the exposure of the truth are connected to this story's theme as you define it.
6. Like many stories, "The Prophet's Hair" is built on a series of extraordinary coincidences, such as the hole in Atta's pocket or the fact that he calls out the word "Thief!" three times just before dying. Is it a story about fate or about the fatal consequences of choice?

Connections to Other Readings

7. Examine how the convention of stories-within-stories operates in "The Prophet's Hair" and in Charles Chesnutt's story "The Wife of His Youth."
8. The belief in the importance of a material object is an important motif in this story and in Alifa Rifaat's "Another Evening at the Club." What do these stories say about human behavior in relation to possessions?
9. Write about the tension between family secrets and public knowledge in this story and in David Long's "Morphine" or Ann Beattie's "Weekend."

David Long

Morphine

Best known for his short fiction, especially that collected in *Blue Spruce* (1995), David Long (b. 1948) has also published a novel, *Falling Boy* (1998), published the same year that the following short story appeared in the *New Yorker*. Long commonly sets his stories in 1950s Montana: indeed, Montana and the year 1959 are stated explicitly as the setting for "Morphine." Note the narrator's cautious distance from the protagonist, a country doctor whose secrets are carefully disguised even in his private journal.

He's a handsome man, lanky, with black sleepy eyes and soft skillful hands: Gerald Wilcox, a doctor in Sperry, Montana, specializing in the ear, nose, and throat. He no longer drinks much now—champagne at a wedding, wine at the table if guests are present. A glass, maybe two. He's not graced with a huge reservoir of will power. You do what you can, and what he's been able to do is rein in the drinking. Not give it dominion.

"It makes you morose, don't you see that? Not to mention the driving around, not to mention people's trust in you. It's too small a town. Why do I have to say these things?"

This is Charlotte talking, his wife of twenty-two years. Born Charlotte Timmins—calls to mind "timid," that's the joke of it—she is a tall, forthright woman, brassy-haired. "Gerald," she tells him, "I am forty-four years old. I never intended to be a woman who wears a girdle, a woman with chins." She pinches the excess flesh, creates a wattle, and exhales with showy contempt. Of their marriage, she has lately said, "This is not a business arrangement, Gerald. This is something else. Do I make myself clear?"

He pretends bafflement. "Darling," he says, "my feelings have not changed one iota—in fact they've grown deeper, more complex."

But, yes, he knows what she's talking about. Blessedly, these complaints are intermittent. Life proceeds, slips from one state to the next; at odd moments, passions reawaken.

Their only child, Jeanette, is plain-faced, secretive, bookish, as lanky as Gerald. She has recently asked that he knock off calling her his Little Bean.

"And what might you prefer," he inquired, "Jeanette, Queen of the Euphrates?"[1]

"Don't be mean," Charlotte told him.

He said he wasn't. "You don't think I'm being mean, do you, honey?" he asked his daughter.

She cut her eyes at him, made them slits. "No, Daddy."

Last year she was reading. *Little Women*,[2] this year—it's 1959—John O'Hara.[3] Wilcox came upon the book among her things while foraging for the stapler. "Well, we don't censor what a person chooses to read in this house," Charlotte said when he showed one passage to her.

Wilcox read aloud: "'He kissed her and put his hand on her breast. Without taking her mouth away from his she unbuttoned the jacket of her suit and he discovered that she was wearing a dickey, not a blouse, and then put his hand down into her brassiere until he was able to cup her breast in the curving palm of his hand.'"

A great arching of Charlotte's brows. She brought her face near his. "Oh *my*," she said. "Would you put your hand down into my brassiere, Gerald? Would you cup my breast?"

He has decided that each of them has a talent for secretiveness. Three secret hearts under one roof.

Nearly every night, he inscribes a few lines in his journal. He notes the ebb and flow of infectious disease. If he and Charlotte have been to a movie, a

[1]*Euphrates:* A river that begins in Turkey, flows through Syria, and in Iraq merges with the Tigris River to empty into the Persian Gulf. One of the four possible sites for what is called the cradle of civilization.

[2]*Little Women:* A nineteenth-century American novel for young adults written by Louisa May Alcott.

[3]*John O'Hara:* A twentieth-century American fiction writer (1905–1970).

synopsis appears, a terse critique. He makes reference to the weather, if noteworthy: *Cheated of summer this year. Such gloom.* Or: *Woke last evening to a lightning storm. Jeanette came into our bed, fearing wildfires . . . explained how remote the possibility.* Or: *Walked uptown over the noon hour. Green fuzz on the trees all along First.*

Now and then, something like: *Saw Mrs. D——this forenoon, had the very disagreeable task of telling her that the tumor has begun to encroach on the esophagus. Where some people get their stoicism is more than I can fathom.*

Flipping back a few years—1952, 1949—he finds the occasional entry he can make no sense of: *That business with the Bagnolds continues to nettle me.*

Not a clue.

Strangely, he seldom rereads what he's written. He's not addicted to it. If pressed, he couldn't say why he goes to the trouble, except it pleases him to keep this accounting. Giving up the journal falls outside the realm of what he can do.

In any case, the daily drinking is history, done with two years now and not much missed. But one night perhaps every six weeks, he takes to his office—it occupies the spacious front parlor of the house at 118 Plympton Street, a house of high ceilings spidered with hairline cracks, endowed with several rooms the Wilcoxes barely use—and injects himself with an ampule of morphine. Then he composes longer entries in his journal.

For instance: *I do not feel invincible. Indeed, I feel so near the great powers that it is no trouble to imagine being crushed by them, ground into powder, yet I do feel very much alive, there is no doubt of that. A pity one cannot feel this way more of the God-damned time.* Having written this, he pauses. *No, disastrous,* he writes, lets the fountain pen dawdle in his hand.

The journal books, black and soft-sided, are kept in the top-right drawer of his desk. It's a locking desk, but the key has long ago vanished, so it's conceivable that Charlotte has inspected them at length. Perhaps even his daughter as well. Once, he went to the trouble of plucking a long hair from his head, licking it, and pasting it unobtrusively across the opening of the drawer, a trick he'd acquired from a mystery story. Then he thought better of it, and had a laugh at himself.

And, too, some incidents fail to appear in the journals. The night, for instance, when he drove his car onto the ice of McCafferty's Slough. A luscious, ludicrous evening. This slough had the shape of an oxbow, nearly a full circle segregated from the river's main channel by a narrow, birch-lined dike. A thin crust of snow lay atop the ice, but in places the wind had blown it clear. He drove from one end to the other, spinning gloriously, dodging the occasional squat black icehouse. It was late winter, the air mild and seductive. How had he come to be there, out on the ice? Drinking, yes, he'd been to a roadhouse called Sammy's, but he wasn't very drunk, only softened, estranged from care.

Driving, he had been telling one of his oldest, lamest jokes—*Hey, you in the field there, I been going up this hill close to two hours, don't it ever end? Oh hell, stranger, there ain't no hill here, you just lost your two hind wheels*—when the hind wheels of his own car cracked through the ice. McCafferty's Slough wasn't deep, seven or eight feet at most. It harbored perch and whitefish. Muskrats burrowed in the mud along its bank. Walking the ice, you'd see them squiggle out and follow beneath your boots, elongated, trailing bubbles. But there were—he *did* know this—springs feeding the slough, which left the ice untrustworthy in spots. And so as he finessed a lovely skidding spin, telling his lame joke, the back end of the Buick dropped through, stopping them short. It was quickly apparent that no amount of clever rocking back and forth would help.

"For shit's sake, Gerry," his companion said.

She was Glenny Parker, a slender girl with a ferocious hook nose, and a belly that was literally concave. A shallow white basin. At work, sometimes, he thought of his hand idling there, making quarter-size circles, which seemed to please her. She hadn't believed him at first, that he was a doctor, thought he was teasing her.

They set out across the ice, she gripping his arm, with his topcoat around her shoulders, her shoes red kidskin with straps like fine red wire. The night's hilarity had leached away. They hiked back up the gravel ramp they'd barrelled down a half hour before. The air seemed less mild now. Wind poured off the foothills, jangling the snowberries and the brittle remains of the cottonwood leaves. Up the way, not far, was a farmhouse with a light burning. As they drew closer, the light went out.

Wilcox squinted at the mailbox, saw the name, "Maki." Old Finn, he thought, starting up the drive. A dog emerged from the blackest patch of shadow and ratcheted off a few congested barks, but made no serious effort to charge him.

A cowled light came on above the door. Glenny Parker didn't know whether to follow or stand back out of sight. She elected to do a little of both.

After a moment, a man in pants and nightshirt came onto the canted slab of concrete that served as a back stoop. Unshaven at this hour, he had a big, fair boy's face gone to thickness.

"Who's there?" he said. "Is someone there?" Then, shielding his eyes, "Dr. Wilcox? Is that you?"

All along, the doctor knew, there'd been the chance he'd be recognized, though, naturally, he'd hoped otherwise. But who was this man? A patient? Husband or son of a patient?

Maki looked beyond him. "Somebody out there with you?"

The doctor hesitated, then, hearing Glenny's feet on the gravel, found himself in the position of saying yes, actually, he did have a friend along.

Maki nodded. "That wouldn'ta been you out on the ice?" he asked.

Wilcox wiped his face, chuckled uneasily. "To be honest with you," he said, "I'm in kind of a jam here."

Maki acknowledged that he was. The girl's hands were plunged up to her elbows in the deep pockets of his coat; she looked tiny, brutally out of place. Maki eyed her without comment.

"Let me get the tractor," he said to the doctor.

Wilcox began to protest. All he really wanted was the use of the telephone, though just who he'd had in mind to call at one in the morning wasn't at all clear.

Maki turned back to the girl. "You better wait inside," he said. Head down, she slipped away from Wilcox, went up the stoop, and passed through the mudroom into the bright-lit kitchen.

Maki secured the door, then the two men made their way back to the slough, Maki a stolid unhurried presence at the wheel of the tractor, and the doctor standing on the back, grasping the back rim of the seat, authentically chilled now. Yet thinking, This could turn out all right.

Maki insisted on doing the work himself, crouching on the ice with his tow chain, grunting out a few words that were lost to the Buick's undercarriage. He hoisted himself back up to the seat of the tractor. A short blast of diesel smoke, a slippage of the tire cleats before they grabbed, and the car bumped from its hole.

Wilcox stood by, rubbing his hands.

Maki got down again to uncouple the chain, dropped it with a clank into the box on the side of the tractor, and climbed back to the seat.

A week later, undressing in their bedroom, Charlotte asked, "You remember Arlette Bledsoe? She said her brother gave you a hand the other day."

Arlette Bledsoe's brother?

"Helped with the car, fixed a flat or some such thing?"

"Oh, that," he said. "Yes."

"You didn't mention it."

"I guess I didn't, no."

"They've had a rotten time of it," Charlotte said. She reminded him that Walter Maki had lost his wife, and that she, Charlotte, had attended the service. At Immanuel Lutheran? In the pouring rain? She was deploying the voice she used for reminding him of things an ordinary person would remember.

He dropped his cufflinks into the wooden tray on his dresser, studying his wife a moment. Nothing accusatory there.

Briefly, he let himself recall the trip back to town with Glenny Parker. Reaching a pint bottle from the glove box, asking if she wanted a little warmup. "Sure, why not?" she said. She took a small mouthful, swished it between her teeth, then bounced the bottle down on the seat between them. She rode with her head against the far window, eyes shut. He drove her into town, back to her apartment on Lancaster Street, but did not go in.

And so tonight, three winters later, Gerald Wilcox is sequestered in his front room, stocking feet on desk, savoring the distant murmur of the furnace, the first swirls of wind brushing the waters of his thoughts. *Morphine, alkaloid derivative of opium . . . from the Greek "morph," the curious shapes seen in dreams.* He can't hear the word in his mind's ear without hearing as well his orotund, long-deceased Grandfather Vail. Each evening, one hand on newel post, the old man would announce he was headed up into the arms of Morpheus, if the seedy bastard would have him. It's an association Wilcox can't shake to this day: morphia and sleep, forgetting. Yet unless he overdoes it, unless the day has drained him, he can bypass the sludgy, soporific effect, and achieve a state he thinks of as *attentiveness.*

Or that's his aim.

His wife is upstairs in bed. She's been soldiering through a life of Michelangelo, so bloated a tome she has to brace it with a pillow. She reads bits aloud, saying, "What that man endured, up on that scaffolding?" She says, "Oh, that Pope, that Julius, what a *monster.*"

He hears her neck crack as she turns to see if he's listening, before she chides him. He says he hasn't missed a word. Secretly, it pleases him that Charlotte still gives a good God damn about matters beyond the Sperry Golf Club, the hospital auxiliary, the preparation of sauces, and that she cares that the life they'd set out to lead together is not entirely extinguished. And, beyond that, isn't there a deep, atavistic pleasure in being read to? She has a whiskey voice, as a mystery writer would put it, though in fact the scratchy timbre results from tiny polyps on her vocal cords. Sometimes she lets the book fall, and asks about his patients: the McVicar sisters, Valen and Isabel, six-footers, retired nurses; the Lomasny girl, whose larynx was crushed by a strand of barbed wire; and so on, the human parade, morning and afternoon. He should keep their infirmities to himself, but instead he tells Charlotte these true stories, and none of it goes beyond her. If she knows of his wandering, there's no sign of it. If she knows it's in the past now, there's no sign of that, either.

But tonight he's downstairs, with the latest journal book in his lap. Charlotte will have doused the light and gone to sleep.

The telephone sounds.

The upstairs phone rests on the bedside table. By the third ring, Charlotte will have reached for it; her free hand will be sweeping the empty sheets in search of him. He fetches the thing quickly into his lap, and says, "Yes?"

"Walter Maki," the caller says.

"What's the trouble, Mr. Maki?"

"I was counting on having you," Maki says. Already there's a note of intransigence.

It's Maki's boy, Leonard. Ear problem.

"He's in a certain amount of pain then?"

"I told him to go back to sleep, there wasn't anything we could do till morning, but he was past that."

Infected mastoid, Wilcox imagines. He asks how old the boy is. He wonders, hearing his words go out, if he sounds drugged. No, certainly not.

Maki says the boy is thirteen.

"All right," the doctor says. "Bring him in to the office."

That pushiness in Maki's voice: "I was thinking of you coming out here."

So Wilcox agrees to a house call. Driving out Lower Valley Road, he thinks, isn't it a wonder he's never before been summoned out on a night he's injected himself. He feels robust—*in the pocket*, as the horn players used to say. He lifts his hands from the wheel and the car careers along, hugging the blacktop's soft-edged runnels, bending neither right nor left. Taking hold again, he drives past the old community hall at Aaberg's Landing, past the low spot choked with cattails that floods each spring. A burst of aspen leaves blows through the splay of headlights, the words "gold leaf" appear in his head, and he thinks then about angels. Imagine the ceiling of the world ruptured, spewing forth angels. He's not a believer—not remotely—but this is how his mind works on these nights. Another few miles and he draws alongside the slough. The water is black, still.

Maki admits him, leads him through the mudroom into the kitchen. The boy is on the sofa in the front room. Maki has the stove cranked. There's a smell, a scent added to the water kettle atop it. Mentholatum. The boy's cheeks are fiery, and the skin of his neck clammy. He lacks Maki's square features. His eyes are tipped and melancholy, his face long and weak-chinned.

The swelling is greater than Wilcox had supposed. He palpates the space behind the ear with a light touch. It's too late in the game for medication alone.

"This has been hurting for a few days, hasn't it, Leonard?" he asks.

The boy offers a constricted nod.

"You can lie back down."

To his son, Maki says, fiercely, "Whyn't you say anything before now?"

"You thought it would take care of itself," the doctor says, "Isn't that right?"

Leonard stares at the two men, blinking, his mouth open in a shallow pant.

"Just human nature," Wilcox says. He goes back to the brightness of the kitchen and Maki follows.

"We should get him into town," Wilcox says.

Again Maki balks. He looks intractable, almost menacing.

"We're not going to tussle over this are we?" Wilcox asks, but immediately he undergoes a change of heart, rises to the challenge. "Never mind," he says. "We can do it here."

Leonard is brought into the kitchen and seated at the enamel-topped table, with his head on a folded towel covered by a sheet. The doctor numbs the skin behind the ear, though this will work only minimally.

"I have a girl," he says to the boy. "She's a little older than you. Jeanette, Queen of the Tigris and Euphrates, I call her."

With one hand he holds the head still, and with the other makes a cut. The boy flinches, but his reaction is remarkably controlled. The incision produces perhaps three tablespoons of pus, viscous green, vile-smelling. "That's it," Wilcox says. "Good." He irrigates the area with antiseptic, bandages it, administers a hefty dose of sulfa, and Leonard is put to bed again in the front room.

"You'll sleep now," Wilcox tells him. The boy stares back, disbelieving, but his eyes already have a glassy, listing look.

"Give you a drink?" Maki says.

"Thanks, no."

"No drink for you?"

"No."

"Can I give you some tea?"

"That's all right," Wilcox says. He has entered the stage where his thoughts wither, when if he were home he might consider a second dose, a touch-up. It's never the right idea. He need only recall the night he lost track and went to his knees, retching in the downstairs lavatory, his heart thready and arrhythmic, his rubbery blue-phantomed skin the skin of a corpse. He was mortified that Charlotte might discover him, horrified that she wouldn't. Nearly three months elapsed before he picked up the needle again. He thought maybe he'd cured himself, but no.

Maki has taken a seat at the table. His palms are turned down upon it, as if to keep it from levitating.

"The boy will be fine," Wilcox says. He's still on his feet, bag in hand.

"Sit down," Maki says.

Wilcox smiles and sits down. "I could stay a minute," he says.

"This evens us out," Maki says.

"Well, now, I wouldn't look at it that way."

"That night on the ice," Maki says. "You were a sorry-looking thing."

Wilcox looks at him, waiting.

"You and that girl."

"Yes, sir."

"So let me ask you," Maki says. "Do you think I ever stepped out on my wife?"

"Mr. Maki, I wouldn't hazard the first thought on that subject," Wilcox says.

So this is a chastising. There are worse things.

"You're sure he's O.K.," Maki says. "He won't lose his hearing?"

"His hearing will be fine," Wilcox says. "Trust me."

"He plays the trumpet."

"Is that so?"

"His mother was musical," Maki says. "She wanted him to have the lessons."

"This shouldn't hurt a thing."

Maki shakes his head. He says, "You're hopped up on something, aren't you?"

"I'm going to have to be going now," Wilcox says, standing again. "I'll leave you this prescription. Be sure he takes all of it." He pulls out the blank and writes, watching the extravagant looping that is his signature. "Let me see him in a few days," he says.

Maki leaves the paper where it lies. "You and that silly girl," he says.

Wilcox's headlights judder on the washboard, the Buick's hindquarters drift as he corners at the section lines. Then, abruptly, he's on blacktop again. He pictures Leonard Maki off in a back room with his trumpet, his embouchure, hopes to Christ the boy possesses a little natural aptitude. The idea of him bleating away in his mother's memory is more than Wilcox can take just now.

He lets himself in the rear door of the house on Plympton Street, hangs his coat on the ivory knob in the hall, listens for symptoms of unrest. He pours himself a short inch of bourbon and carries it to his office. Ten past three. No, that's unfair, he thinks. She was not a silly girl, Glenny—just in the wrong company. She had her talents. For a moment, he recalls her lips creeping into the hollow beneath his ear as he drove, keeping to the back roads, her voice tiny but remorseless, *I know what you'd like, Gerry. Stop the car, can't you?* Yet he only saw her one more time after that night on the frozen slough, and it had not gone well.

He sits for a time. Eventually, he takes up the journal, and writes: *Why do you never get used to the stink of pus? If you could smell that exact hue of green, that's how it would be . . . and yet it's just a broth of white cells, the body's defenses. What purpose is served? Why not the rusty smell of blood, the sweetness of breast milk instead? Was I ever taught this?*

Again he finds himself picturing the ceiling of the world, with white cells clustering like a mob of angels.

He writes: *Why this clamoring for purpose?*

There's a footfall outside his door. He slaps the journal shut and braces himself.

But it proves to be his daughter. "What are you writing?" she asks.

"Oh, you know, these notebooks of mine," he says. "You don't mean you've never poked around in them?"

"I wouldn't do *that*," Jeanette says, aggrieved.

Getting to be quite a capable liar, Wilcox thinks, not unhappily.

"What are you doing up?"

Jeanette shrugs, approaches the desk.

"Not sleeping again?" he asks. "Would you like me to give you something?"

"No."

"I could."

"I know," Jeanette says. "Anyway, it's too *late*."

Wilcox checks the filagreed clock hands again and somehow it's gotten to be five past five. "So it is," he says.

Jeanette is barefoot, wearing a long flannel gown with a tiny satin bow at the collar. Her hair is profuse, like Charlotte's, but not nearly so radiant a yellow, and at the moment it looks sea-wracked. She has a long neck and still no bust to speak of, though she's been menstruating for a good two years. Were it not for her gaze—watchful, not in the least dreamy—she might have been painted by Maxfield Parrish.

"Aren't your feet cold?" he says.

"I suppose."

Wilcox asks if she knows a boy named Leonard Maki.

Jeanette shakes her head.

"He plays the trumpet."

"Don't know him," she says.

"I thought you might. From school."

She stands, arms crossed, shifting her weight, her lungs filling and emptying.

After a moment, he asks, "Anything troubling your soul, dear heart?"

"No."

"You can tell me."

But of course she can't.

"Something's always troubling the soul," Wilcox says. "It's an irritable organ."

He offers a smile, which is not returned.

"I'm all right," she says. "I'm not dis*consolate*."

Wilcox smiles inwardly at this word she's plucked from the ether. "Well, it is the way it is," he says. Then it's her turn to nod, and he supposes they understand one another.

"You hungry?" he asks, standing, putting the journal aside. He touches her on the head, works his fingers into the tumbling snarls, which, briefly, she allows.

She follows him down the dim hallway into the kitchen. He opens the refrigerator and stares in at the lighted shelves and closes the door again.

"Do you know how to make that coffee cake?" he asks his daughter. "With the crumbles?"

"In the brown book," Jeanette says, pointing with her chin. "Fannie Farmer."

Wilcox reaches it down, locates the page, which is grease-spattered to transparency in places, with notations in his wife's dishevelled, back-slanting hand: "Gerald likes."

"No yeast in this one?" he asks.

"No, Daddy."

He gets out what he needs, also the coffee tin. An easy recipe. In a matter of minutes, he slides the baking pan onto the oven rack.

"Better set the timer," Jeanette says, and so he sets the timer.

He collects the bowl and the utensils and runs water on them in the sink. Over his shoulder, he says, "Why don't you go wake your mother?"

"She won't want to get up this early."

"Oh, I know," he says. "But go anyway. Tell her she won't want to miss this." He shakes his hands, dries them under his armpits, looks his daughter in the eye. "Use those exact words. Say, 'He says you won't want to miss this.'"

No further objection from Jeanette. In fact, he detects a twitch of conspiracy about the lips as she leaves the room. After a moment, he notes her tread along the squeaky boards of the upstairs hall.

He goes and stands at the back door, looking out where a thin silver light is falling through the empty chestnut branches. He doesn't feel too damn awful, considering. Has the makings of a headache, where the neck cords meet the skull, but it will pass. Food will help, and caffeine. Later, in the afternoon, the fatigue will hit, the fuzziness he detests. If there's no one in the office, maybe he can sneak upstairs and lie down and shut his eyes. If not, the tiredness, too, will pass. He pictures himself beginning a new page: *18 November. Made Charlotte a coffee cake*. Maybe he'll record what she has to say about this unusual occurrence. Maybe she'll notice him climbing the stairs, and follow, launching salacious suggestions at him in a stage whisper. Maybe later he'll get to write: *C. and I napped before supper.* He watches a black dog cut through the yard, tail switching. After a while, the timer dings; his whole upper body startles, as if he's been seized from behind. Then he remembers to breathe again.

He slides the baking pan from the oven, sniffs the sugary cinnamon, pokes a toothpick into the center the way Charlotte would. It comes out clean and dry. He sets the pan on a wire rack, runs water into the percolator, taps in coffee, sets the flame. He listens for his wife. He pictures her getting to her feet and pulling on her robe, the slippery blue nylon, yanking the sash, then tousling some life into her night-heavy hair. Waiting, alone here in the kitchen, he suddenly wonders what will become of the journals after his death. He's barely given this a thought before. He's not fifty yet—how many more will have accumulated in the drawer by then, the pebbled-leather volumes swollen with his daily commentary, his nagging queries of himself? And how soon will it be before he relaxes his guard and lets the rest come forth—that chill along his inner arm before the needle slips in. The warming flood of ruminations. He pictures the heap of journals pulled into a lap, flopped open and read, one after another. How can it feel like comfort to him that they will be? And then what? Strange to admit, it's not a thought that troubles him.

(1998)

Questions for Discussion and Writing

Close Reading

1. Gerald Wilcox notes at one point that he, his wife, and his daughter all have a "talent for secretiveness." What secrets do the three of them keep from one another?
2. Make two lists: the things Gerald can control and the things he can't control. How does the tension between these two lists fuel the story's conflict?
3. Why does Gerald keep journals? What is the nature of his writings in them?

Critical and Creative Reading

4. This is a story about one man's attempts to keep his private life concealed. Are these attempts doomed to failure? Assume that all his secrets are discovered: what does he suppose will happen as a result?
5. Consider the practice of keeping a journal: is it ever possible for journal-keepers to be completely honest about their deepest secrets, or will their complete honesty always be hampered by the fear that someone will read these journals? Who is the audience of a journal?
6. Is "escape" a healthy practice?

Connections to Other Readings

7. Compare the practice of keeping secrets in this story and in Maxine Hong Kingston's "No Name Woman."
8. Discuss the following statement as it applies to "Morphine" and to Ann Beattie's "Weekend": you cannot claim to love someone from whom you keep secrets.
9. Is the "mask" Gerald Wilcox wears in this story similar to or different from the metaphor of the mask in Paul Laurence Dunbar's poem "We Wear the Mask"?

Alifa Rifaat

Translated by Denys Johnson-Davies

Another Evening at the Club

Alifa Rifaat (b. 1930) is an Egyptian short story writer who focuses on the relationship between men and women in Muslim societies. Rifaat's work, written in Arabic, subtly seeks to heighten awareness of the position of women in these societies and puts the burden of reform on men. Although her work is controversial because it questions the values of a fairly strict society, Rifaat is a devout Muslim. Her best-known work in English is the story collection *Distant View of a Minaret.* As you read "Another Evening at the Club," consider what range of options the protagonist Samia has.

In a state of tension, she awaited the return of her husband. At a loss to predict what would happen between them, she moved herself back and forth in the rocking chair on the wide wooden verandah that ran along the bank and occupied part of the river itself, its supports being fixed in the river bed, while around it grew grasses and reeds. As though to banish her apprehension, she passed her fingers across her hair. The spectres of the eucalyptus trees ranged along the garden fence rocked before her gaze, with white egrets slumbering on their high branches like huge white flowers among the thin leaves.

The crescent moon rose from behind the eastern mountains and the peaks of the gently stirring waves glistened in its feeble rays, intermingled with threads of light leaking from the houses of Manfalout[1] scattered along the opposite bank. The coloured bulbs fixed to the trees in the garden of the club at the far end of the town stood out against the surrounding darkness. Somewhere over there her husband now sat, most likely engrossed in a game of chess.

It was only a few years ago that she had first laid eyes on him at her father's house, meeting his gaze that weighed up her beauty and priced it before offering the dowry. She had noted his eyes ranging over her as she presented him with the coffee in the Japanese cups that were kept safely locked away in the cupboard for important guests. Her mother had herself laid them out on the silver-plated tray with its elaborately embroidered spread. When the two men had taken their coffee, her father had looked up at her with a smile and had told her to sit down, and she had seated herself on the sofa facing them, drawing the end of her dress over her knees and looking through lowered lids at the man who might choose her as his wife. She had been glad to see that he was tall, well-built and clean-shaven except for a thin greying moustache. In particular she noticed the well-cut coat of English tweed and the silk shirt with gold links. She had felt herself blushing as she saw him returning her gaze. Then the man turned to her father and took out a gold case and offered him a cigarette.

"You really shouldn't, my dear sir," said her father, patting his chest with his left hand and extracting a cigarette with trembling fingers. Before he could bring out his box of matches Abboud Bey had produced his lighter.

"No, after you, my dear sir," said her father in embarrassment. Mingled with her sense of excitement at this man who gave out such an air of worldly self-confidence was a guilty shame at her father's inadequacy.

After lighting her father's cigarette Abboud Bey sat back, crossing his legs, and took out a cigarette for himself. He tapped it against the case before putting it in the corner of his mouth and lighting it, then blew out circles of smoke that followed each other across the room.

"It's a great honour for us, my son," said her father, smiling first at Abboud Bey, then at his daughter, at which Abboud Bey looked across at her and asked:

"And the beautiful little girl's still at secondary school?"

She lowered her head modestly and her father had answered:

"As from today she'll be staying at home in readiness for your happy life together, Allah permitting," and at a glance from her father she had hurried off to join her mother in the kitchen.

[1]*Manfalout:* An Egyptian town.

"You're a lucky girl," her mother had told her. "He's a real find. Any girl would be happy to have him. He's an Inspector of Irrigation though he's not yet forty. He earns a big salary and gets a fully furnished government house wherever he's posted, which will save us the expense of setting up a house—and I don't have to tell you what our situation is—and that's besides the house he owns in Alexandria where you'll be spending your holidays."

Samia had wondered to herself how such a splendid suitor had found his way to her door. Who had told him that Mr. Mahmoud Barakat, a mere clerk at the Court of Appeal, had a beautiful daughter of good reputation?

The days were then taken up with going the rounds of Cairo's shops and choosing clothes for the new grand life she would be living. This was made possible by her father borrowing on the security of his government pension. Abboud Bey, on his part, never visited her without bringing a present. For her birthday, just before they were married, he bought her an emerald ring that came in a plush box bearing the name of a well-known jeweller in Kasr el-Nil Street. On her wedding night, as he put a diamond bracelet round her wrist, he had reminded her that she was marrying someone with a brilliant career in front of him and that one of the most important things in life was the opinion of others, particularly one's equals and seniors. Though she was still only a young girl she must try to act with suitable dignity.

"Tell people you're from the well-known Barakat family and that your father was a judge," and he went up to her and gently patted her cheeks in a fatherly, reassuring gesture that he was often to repeat during their times together.

Then, yesterday evening, she had returned from the club somewhat lightheaded from the bottle of beer she had been required to drink on the occasion of someone's birthday. Her husband, noting the state she was in, hurriedly took her back home. She had undressed and put on her nightgown, leaving her jewellery on the dressing-table, and was fast asleep seconds after getting into bed. The following morning, fully recovered, she slept late, then rang the bell as usual and had breakfast brought to her. It was only as she was putting her jewellery away in the wooden and mother-of-pearl box that she realized her emerald ring was missing.

Could it have dropped from her finger at the club? In the car on the way back? No, she distinctly remembered it last thing at night, remembered the usual difficulty she had in getting it off her finger. She stripped the bed of its sheets, turned over the mattress, looked inside the pillow cases, crawled on hands and knees under the bed. The tray of breakfast lying on the small bedside table caught her eye and she remembered the young servant coming in that morning with it, remembered the noise of the tray being put down, the curtains being drawn, the tray then being lifted up again and placed on the bedside table. No one but the servant had entered the room. Should she call her and question her?

Eventually, having taken two aspirins, she decided to do nothing and await the return of her husband from work.

Directly he arrived she told him what had happened and he took her by the arm and seated her down beside him:

"Let's just calm down and go over what happened."

She repeated, this time with further details, the whole story.

"And you've looked for it?"

"Everywhere. Every possible and impossible place in the bedroom and the bathroom. You see, I remember distinctly taking it off last night."

He grimaced at the thought of last night, then said:

"Anybody been in the room since Gazia when she brought in the breakfast?"

"Not a soul. I've even told Gazia not to do the room today."

"And you've not mentioned anything to her?"

"I thought I'd better leave it to you."

"Fine, go and tell her I want to speak to her. There's no point in your saying anything but I think it would be as well if you were present when I talk to her."

Five minutes later Gazia, the young servant girl they had recently employed, entered behind her mistress. Samia took herself to a far corner of the room while Gazia stood in front of Abboud Bey, her hands folded across her chest, her eyes lowered.

"Yes, sir?"

"Where's the ring?"

"What ring are you talking about, sir?"

"Now don't make out you don't know. The one with the green stone. It would be better for you if you hand it over and then nothing more need be said."

"May Allah blind me if I've set eyes on it."

He stood up and gave her a sudden slap on the face. The girl reeled back, put one hand to her cheek, then lowered it again to her chest and made no answer to any of Abboud's questions. Finally he said to her:

"You've got just fifteen seconds to say where you've hidden the ring or else, I swear to you, you're not going to have a good time of it."

As he lifted up his arm to look at his watch the girl flinched slightly but continued in her silence. When he went to the telephone Samia raised her head and saw that the girl's cheeks were wet with tears. Abboud Bey got through to the Superintendent of Police and told him briefly what had occurred.

"Of course I haven't got any actual proof but seeing that no one else entered the room, it's obvious she's pinched it. Anyway I'll leave the matter in your capable hands—I know your people have their ways and means."

He gave a short laugh, then listened for a while and said: "I'm really most grateful to you."

He put down the receiver and turned round to Samia:

"That's it, my dear. There's nothing more to worry about. The Superintendent has promised me we'll get it back. The patrol car's on the way."

The following day, in the late afternoon, she'd been sitting in front of her dressing-table rearranging her jewellery in its box when an earring slipped from her grasp and fell to the floor. As she bent to pick it up she saw the emerald ring stuck between the leg of the table and the wall. Since that moment she had sat in a state of panic awaiting her husband's return from the club. She even felt tempted to walk down to the water's edge and throw it into the river so as to be rid of the unpleasantness that lay ahead.

At the sound of the screech of tires rounding the house to the garage, she slipped the ring onto her finger. As he entered she stood up and raised her hand to show him the ring. Quickly, trying to choose her words but knowing that she was expressing herself clumsily, she explained what an extraordinary thing it was that it should have lodged itself between the dressing-table and the wall, what an extraordinary coincidence she should have dropped the earring and so seen it, how she'd thought of ringing him at the club to tell him the good news but . . .

She stopped in mid-sentence when she saw his frown and added weakly: "I'm sorry. I can't think how it could have happened. What do we do now?"

He shrugged his shoulders as though in surprise. 45

"Are you asking me, my dear lady? Nothing of course."

"But they've been beating up the girl—you yourself said they'd not let her be till she confessed."

Unhurriedly, he sat himself down as though to consider this new aspect of the matter. Taking out his case, he tapped a cigarette against it in his accustomed manner, then moistened his lips, put the cigarette in place and lit it. The smoke rings hovered in the still air as he looked at his watch and said:

"In any case she's not got all that long before they let her go. They can't keep her for more than forty-eight hours without getting any evidence or a confession. It won't kill her to put up with things for a while longer. By now the whole town knows the servant stole the ring—or would you like me to tell everyone: 'Look, folks, the fact is that the wife got a bit tiddly on a couple of sips of beer and the ring took off on its own and hid itself behind the dressing-table.?' What do you think?"

"I know the situation's a bit awkward . . ." 50

"Awkward? It's downright ludicrous. Listen, there's nothing to be done but to give it to me and the next time I go down to Cairo I'll sell it and get something else in its place. We'd be the laughing-stock of the town."

He stretched out his hand and she found herself taking off the ring and placing it in the outstretched palm. She was careful that their eyes should not meet. For a moment she was on the point of protesting and in fact uttered a few words:

"I'd just like to say we could . . ."

Putting the ring away in his pocket, he bent over her and with both hands gently patted her on the cheeks. It was a gesture she had long become used to, a gesture that promised her continued security, that told her that this man who was her husband and the father of her child had also taken the place of her father who, as though assured that he had found her a suitable substitute, had followed up her marriage with his own funeral. The gesture told her more eloquently than any words that he was the man, she the woman, he the one who carried the responsibilities, made the decisions, she the one whose role it was to be beautiful, happy, carefree. Now, though, for the first time in their life together the gesture came like a slap in the face.

55 Directly after he removed his hands her whole body was seized with an uncontrollable trembling. Frightened he would notice, she rose to her feet and walked with deliberate steps towards the large window. She leaned her forehead against the comforting cold surface and closed her eyes tightly for several seconds. When she opened them she noticed that the café lights strung between the trees on the opposite shore had been turned on and that there were men seated under them and a waiter moving among the tables. The dark shape of a boat momentarily blocked out the café scene; in the light from the hurricane lamp hanging from its bow she saw it cutting through several of those floating islands of Nile waterlilies that, rootless, are swept along with the current.

Suddenly she became aware of his presence alongside her.

"Why don't you go and change quickly while I take the car out? It's hot and it would be nice to have supper at the club."

"As you like. Why not?"

By the time she had turned round from the window she was smiling.

(1987)

Questions for Discussion and Writing

Close Reading

1. How do you interpret the title? Could it refer to the night Samia lost her ring after returning from the club, or does it refer to the night just following the story's conclusion?
2. How does Samia feel about the fate of her servant Gazia?
3. Samia makes a connection between her father and her husband; is her behavior consistent when she is with both men?

Critical and Creative Reading

4. What could be behind Samia's smile at the end of this story? When does a smile connote something other than happiness?
5. What would be the consequences if Samia were to tell the truth to the authorities about what happened to the ring?
6. For a moment, Samia considers concealing the truth about the ring from her husband. Imagine that she did so. How would that decision affect the outcome of the story?

Connections to Other Readings

7. Salman Rushdie's story "The Prophet's Hair" is also about theft within a patriarchal Muslim culture. Compare the related themes of theft and honesty in this story and in Rushdie's.
8. Considering the smile at the end of "Another Evening at the Club" as a kind of mask, compare this story to Paul Laurence Dunbar's poem "We Wear the Mask."
9. Compare the notion of honor in this story and in Maxine Hong Kingston's essay "No Name Woman."

Ann Beattie

Weekend

Ann Beattie (b. 1947) was working toward a Ph.D. in English at the University of Connecticut in the early 1970s when she first submitted a short story to the *New Yorker*. Her first acceptance launched a literary carccr that includes an equal number of short story collections and novels and that has given her a solid literary reputation for three decades. She is associated with a movement in American fiction known as "minimalism" that flourished in the 1970s and 1980s. As the name implies, this mode of writing–usually in the form of short stories–is spare. In the mode of Ernest Hemingway, an American writer active in the first part of the twentieth century, minimalist writers such as Beattie allow a story to be told through significant moments, images, and dialogue exchanges rather than through extensive narrative commentary. As you read "Weekend," note the way Beattie intersperses the third-person narrative with dialogue: what significant patterns do you see?

On Saturday morning Lenore is up before the others. She carries her baby into the living room and puts him in George's favorite chair, which tilts because its back legs are missing, and covers him with a blanket. Then she lights a fire in the fireplace, putting fresh logs on a few embers that are still glowing from the night before. She sits down on the floor beside the chair and checks the baby, who has already gone back to sleep—a good thing, because there are guests in the house. George, the man she lives with, is very hospitable and impetuous; he extends invitations whenever old friends call, urging them to come spend the weekend. Most of the callers are his former students—he used to be an English professor—and when they come it seems to make things much worse. It makes *him* much worse, because he falls into smoking too much and drinking and not eating, and then his ulcer bothers him. When the guests leave, when the weekend is over, she has to cook bland food: applesauce, oatmeal, puddings. And his drinking does not taper off easily anymore; in the past he would stop cold when the guests left, but lately he only tapers down from Scotch to wine, and drinks wine well into the week—a lot of wine, perhaps a whole bottle with his meal—until his stomach is much worse. He is hard to live with. Once when a former student, a woman named Ruth, visited them—a lover, she suspected—she overheard George talking to her in his study, where he had taken her to see a photograph of their house before he began repairing it. George had told Ruth that she, Lenore, stayed with him because she was simple. It hurt her badly, made her actually dizzy with surprise and shame, and since then, no matter who the guests are, she never feels quite at ease on the weekends. In the past she enjoyed some of the things she and George did with their guests, but since overhearing what he said to Ruth she feels that all their visitors have been secretly told the same thing about her. To her, though, George is usually kind. But she is sure that is the reason he has not married her, and when he recently remarked on their daughter's intelligence (she is five years old, a girl named Maria) she found that she could no longer respond with simple pride; now she feels spite as well, feels that Maria exists as proof of her own good genes. She has begun to expect perfection of the child. She knows this is wrong, and she has tried hard not to communicate her anxiety to Maria, who is already, as her kindergartern teacher says, "untypical."

At first Lenore loved George because he was untypical, although after she had moved in with him and lived with him for a while she began to see that he was not exceptional but a variation on a type. She is proud of observing that, and she harbors the discovery—her silent response to his low opinion of her. She does not know why he found her attractive—in the beginning he did—because she does not resemble the pretty, articulate young women he likes to invite, with their lovers or girl friends, to their house for the weekend. None of these young women have husbands; when they bring a man with them at all they bring a lover, and they seem happy not to be married. Lenore, too, is happy to be single—not out of conviction that marriage is wrong but because she knows that it would be wrong to be married to George if he thinks she is simple. She thought at first to confront him with what she had overheard, to demand an explanation. But he can weasel out of any corner. At best, she can mildly fluster him, and later he will only blame it on Scotch. Of course she might ask why he has all these women come to visit, why he devotes so little time to her or the children. To that he would say that it was the quality of the time they spent together that mattered, not the quantity. He has already said that, in fact, without being asked. He says things over and over so that she will accept them as truths. And eventually she does. She does not like to think long and hard, and when there is an answer—even his answer—it is usually easier to accept it and go on with things. She goes on with what she has always done: tending the house and the children and George, when he needs her. She likes to bake and she collects art postcards. She is proud of their house, which was bought cheaply and improved by George when he was still interested in that kind of work, and she is happy to have visitors come there, even if she does not admire them or even like them.

Except for teaching a night course in photography at a junior college once a week, George has not worked since he left the university two years ago, after he was denied tenure. She cannot really tell if he is unhappy working so little, because he keeps busy in other ways. He listens to classical music in the morning, slowly sipping herbal teas, and on fair afternoons he lies outdoors in the sun, no matter how cold the day. He takes photographs, and walks alone in the woods. He does errands for her if they need to be done. Sometimes at night he goes to the library or goes to visit friends; he tells her that these people often ask her to come too, but he says she would not like them. This is true—she would not like them. Recently he has done some late-night cooking. He has always kept a journal, and he is a great letter writer. An aunt left him most of her estate, ten thousand dollars, and said in her will that he was the only one who really cared, who took the time, again and again, to write. He had not seen his aunt for five years before she died, but he wrote regularly. Sometimes Lenore finds notes that he has left for her. Once, on the refrigerator, there was a long note suggesting clever Christmas presents for her family that he had thought of while she was out. Last week he Scotch-taped a slip of paper to a casserole dish that contained leftover veal stew, saying: "This was delicious." He does not compliment her verbally, but he likes to let her know that he is pleased.

A few nights ago—the same night they got a call from Julie and Sarah, saying they were coming for a visit—she told him that she wished he would talk more, that he would confide in her.

"Confide what?" he said.

"You always take that attitude," she said. "You pretend that you have no thoughts. Why does there have to be so much silence?"

"I'm not a professor anymore," he said. "I don't have to spend every minute *thinking*."

But he loves to talk to the young women. He will talk to them on the phone for as much as an hour; he walks with them through the woods for most of the day when they visit. The lovers the young women bring with them always seem to fall behind; they give up and return to the house to sit and talk to her, or to help with the preparation of the meal, or to play with the children. The young woman and George come back refreshed, ready for another round of conversation at dinner.

A few weeks ago one of the young men said to her, "Why do you let it go on?" They had been talking lightly before that—about the weather, the children—and then, in the kitchen, where he was sitting shelling peas, he put his head on the table and said, barely audibly, "Why do you let it go on?" He did not raise his head, and she stared at him, thinking that she must have imagined his speaking. She was surprised—surprised to have heard it, and surprised that he said nothing after that, which made her doubt that he had spoken.

"Why do I let what go on?" she said.

There was a long silence. "Whatever this sick game is, I don't want to get involved in it," he said at last. "It was none of my business to ask. I understand that you don't want to talk about it."

"But it's really cold out there," she said. "What could happen when it's freezing out?"

He shook his head, the way George did, to indicate that she was beyond understanding. But she wasn't stupid, and she knew what might be going on. She had said the right thing, had been on the right track, but she had to say what she felt, which was that nothing very serious could be happening at that moment because they were walking in the woods. There wasn't even a barn on the property. She knew perfectly well that they were talking.

When George and the young woman had come back, he fixed hot apple juice, into which he trickled rum. Lenore was pleasant, because she was sure of what had not happened; the young man was not, because he did not think as she did. Still at the kitchen table, he ran his thumb across a pea pod as though it were a knife.

This weekend Sarah and Julie are visiting. They came on Friday evening. Sarah was one of George's students—the one who led the fight to have him rehired.

She does not look like a troublemaker; she is pale and pretty, with freckles on her cheeks. She talks too much about the past, and this upsets him, disrupts the peace he has made with himself. She tells him that they fired him because he was "in touch" with everything, that they were afraid of him because he was so in touch. The more she tells him the more he remembers, and then it is necessary for Sarah to say the same things again and again; once she reminds him, he seems to need reassurance—needs to have her voice, to hear her bitterness against the members of the tenure committee. By evening they will both be drunk. Sarah will seem both agitating and consoling, Lenore and Julie and the children will be upstairs, in bed. Lenore suspects that she will not be the only one awake listening to them. She thinks that in spite of Julie's glazed look she is really very attentive. The night before, when they were all sitting around the fireplace talking, Sarah made a gesture and almost upset her wineglass, but Julie reached for it and stopped it from toppling over. George and Sarah were talking so energetically that they did not notice. Lenore's eyes met Julie's as Julie's hand shot out. Lenore feels that she is like Julie: Julie's face doesn't betray emotion, even when she is interested, even when she cares deeply. Being the same kind of person, Lenore can recognize this.

Before Sarah and Julie arrived Friday evening, Lenore asked George if Sarah was his lover.

"Don't be ridiculous," he said. "You think every student is my lover? Is Julie my lover?"

She said, "That wasn't what I said."

"Well, if you're going to be preposterous, go ahead and say that," he said. "If you think about it long enough, it would make a lot of sense, wouldn't it?"

He would not answer her question about Sarah. He kept throwing Julie's 20
name into it. Some other woman might then think that he was protesting too strongly—that Julie really was his lover. She thought no such thing. She also stopped suspecting Sarah, because he wanted that, and it was her habit to oblige him.

He is twenty-one years older than Lenore. On his last birthday he was fifty-five. His daughter from his first marriage (his *only* marriage; she keeps reminding herself that they are not married, because it often seems that they might as well be) sent him an Irish country hat. The present made him irritable. He kept putting it on and putting it down hard on his head. "She wants to make me a laughable old man," he said. "She wants me to put this on and go around like a fool." He wore the hat all morning, complaining about it, frightening the children. Eventually, to calm him, she said, "She intended *nothing.*" She said it with finality, her tone so insistent that he listened to her. But having lost his reason for bitterness, he said, "Just because you don't think doesn't mean others don't think." Is he getting old? She does not want to think of him getting old. In spite of his ulcer, his body is hard. He is tall and handsome, with a thick mustache and a thin black goatee, and there is very little gray in his kinky black hair. He dresses in tight-fitting blue jeans and black turtleneck sweaters in the winter, and old white shirts with the sleeves rolled up in the summer. He pretends not to care about his looks, but he does. He shaves carefully, scraping slowly down each side of his goatee. He orders his soft leather shoes from a store in California. After taking one of his long walks—even if he does it twice a day—he invariably takes a shower. He always looks refreshed, and very rarely admits any insecurity. A few times, at night in bed, he has asked, "Am I still the man of your dreams?" And when she says yes he always laughs, turning it into a joke, as if he didn't care. She knows he does. He pretends to have no feeling for clothing, but actually he cares so strongly about his turtlenecks and shirts (a few are Italian silk) and shoes that he will have no others. She has noticed that the young women who visit are always vain. When Sarah arrived, she was wearing a beautiful silk scarf, pale as conch shells.

Sitting on the floor on Saturday morning, Lenore watches the fire she has just lit. The baby, tucked in George's chair, smiles in his sleep, and Lenore thinks what a good companion he would be if only he were an adult. She gets up and goes into the kitchen and tears open a package of yeast and dissolves it, with sugar and salt, in hot water, slushing her fingers through it and shivering because it is so cold in the kitchen. She will bake bread for dinner—there is always a big meal in the early evening when they have guests. But what will she do for the rest of the day? George told the girls the night before that on Saturday they would walk in the woods, but she does not really enjoy hiking, and George will be irritated because of the discussion the night before, and she does not want to aggravate him. "You are unwilling to challenge anyone," her brother wrote her in a letter that came a few days ago. He has written her for years—all the years she has been with George—asking when she is going to end the relationship. She rarely writes back because she knows that her answers sound too simple. She has a comfortable house. She cooks. She keeps busy and she loves her two children. "It seems unkind to say *but*," her brother writes, "but . . ." It is true; she likes simple things. Her brother, who is a lawyer in Cambridge, cannot understand that.

Lenore rubs her hand down the side of her face and says good morning to Julie and Sarah, who have come downstairs. Sarah does not want orange juice; she already looks refreshed and ready for the day. Lenore pours a glass for Julie. George calls from the hallway, "Ready to roll?" Lenore is surprised that he wants to leave so early. She goes into the living room. George is wearing a denim jacket, his hands in the pockets.

"Morning," he says to Lenore. "You're not up for a hike, are you?"

Lenore looks at him, but does not answer. As she stands there, Sarah walks around her and joins George in the hallway and he holds the door open for her. "Let's walk to the store and get Hershey bars to give us energy for a long hike," George says to Sarah. They are gone. Lenore finds Julie still in the kitchen, waiting for the water to boil. Julie says that she had a bad night and she is happy not to be going with George and Sarah. Lenore fixes tea for them. Maria sits next to her on the sofa, sipping orange juice. The baby likes company, but Maria is a very private child; she would rather that she and her mother were always alone. She has given up being possessive about her father. Now she gets out a cardboard box and takes out her mother's collection of postcards, which she arranges on the floor in careful groups, Whenever she looks up, Julie smiles nervously at her; Maria does not smile, and Lenore doesn't prod her. Lenore goes into the kitchen to punch down the bread, and Maria follows. Maria has recently gotten over chicken pox, and there is a small new scar in the center of her forehead. Instead of looking at Maria's blue eyes, Lenore lately has found herself focusing on the imperfection.

As Lenore is stretching the loaves onto the cornmeal-covered baking sheet, she hears the rain start. It hits hard on the garage roof.

After a few minutes Julie comes into the kitchen. "They're caught in this downpour," Julie says. "If Sarah had left the car keys, I could go get them."

"Take my car and pick them up," Lenore says, pointing with her elbow to the keys hanging on a nail near the door.

"But I don't know where the store is."

"You must have passed it driving to our house last night. Just go out of the driveway and turn right. It's along the main road."

Julie gets her purple sweater and takes the car keys. "I'll be right back," she says.

Lenore can sense that she is glad to escape from the house, that she is happy the rain began.

In the living room Lenore turns the pages of a magazine, and Maria mutters a refrain of "Blue, blue, dark blue, green blue," noticing the color every time it appears. Lenore sips her tea. She puts a Michael Hurley record on George's stereo. Michael Hurley is good rainy-day music. George has hundreds of records. His students used to love to paw through them. Cleverly, he has never made any attempt to keep up with what is currently popular. Everything is jazz or eclectic: Michael Hurley, Keith Jarrett, Ry Cooder.

Julie comes back. "I couldn't find them," she says. She looks as if she expects to be punished.

Lenore is surprised. She is about to say something like "You certainly didn't look very hard, did you?" but she catches Julie's eye. She looks young and afraid, and perhaps even a little crazy.

"Well, we tried," Lenore says.

Julie stands in front of the fire, with her back to Lenore. Lenore knows she is thinking that she is dense—that she does not recognize the implications.

"They might have walked through the woods instead of along the road," Lenore says. "That's possible."

"But they would have gone out to the road to thumb when the rain began, wouldn't they?"

Perhaps she misunderstood what Julie was thinking. Perhaps it has never occurred to Julie until now what might be going on.

"Maybe they got lost," Julie says. "Maybe something happened to them."

"Nothing happened to them," Lenore says. Julie turns around and Lenore catches that small point of light in her eye again. "Maybe they took shelter under a tree," she says. "Maybe they're screwing. How should I know?"

It is not a word Lenore often uses. She usually tries not to think about that at all, but she can sense that Julie is very upset.

"Really?" Julie says. "Don't you care, Mrs. Anderson?"

Lenore is amused. There's a switch. All the students call her husband George and her Lenore; now one of them wants to think there's a real adult here to explain all this to her.

"What am I going to do?" Lenore says. She shrugs.

Julie does not answer.

"Would you like me to pour you tea?" Lenore asks.

"Yes," Julie says. "Please."

George and Sarah return in the middle of the afternoon. George says that they decided to go on a spree to the big city—it is really a small town he is talking about, but calling it the big city gives him an opportunity to speak ironically. They sat in a restaurant bar, waiting for the rain to stop, George says, and then they thumbed a ride home. "But I'm completely sober," George says, turning for the first time to Sarah. "What about you?" He is all smiles. Sarah lets him down. She looks embarrassed. Her eyes meet Lenore's quickly, and jump to Julie. The two girls stare at each other, and Lenore, left with only George to look at, looks at the fire and then gets up to pile on another log.

Gradually it becomes clear that they are trapped together by the rain. Maria undresses her paper doll and deliberately rips a feather off its hat. Then she takes the pieces to Lenore, almost in tears. The baby cries, and Lenore takes him off the sofa, where he has been sleeping under his yellow blanket, and props him in the space between her legs as she leans back on her elbows to watch the fire. It's her fire, and she has the excuse of presiding over it.

"How's my boy?" George says. The baby looks, and looks away.

It gets dark early, because of the rain. At four-thirty George uncorks a bottle of Beaujolais and brings it into the living room, with four glasses pressed against his chest with his free arm. Julie rises nervously to extract the glasses, thanking him too profusely for the wine. She gives a glass to Sarah without looking at her.

They sit in a semicircle in front of the fire and drink the wine. Julie leafs through magazines—*New Times*, *National Geographic*—and Sarah holds a small white dish painted with gray-green leaves that she has taken from the coffee table; the dish contains a few shells and some acorn caps, a polished stone or two, and Sarah lets these objects run through her fingers. There are several such dishes in the house, assembled by George. He and Lenore gathered the shells long ago, the first time they went away together, at a beach in North Carolina. But the acorn caps, the shiny turquoise and amethyst stones—those are there, she knows, because George likes the effect they have on visitors; it is an expected unconventionality, really. He has also acquired a few small framed pictures, which he points out to guests who are more important than worshipful students—tiny oil paintings of fruit, prints with small details from the unicorn tapestries. He pretends to like small, elegant things. Actually, when they visit museums in New York he goes first to El Grecos and big Mark Rothko[1] canvases. She could never get him to admit that what he said or did was sometimes false. Once, long ago, when he asked if he was still the man of her dreams, she said,

[1] *El Grecos . . . Mark Rothko*: El Greco (1541–1614) was born as Domenicos Theotokopoulas in Crete of Greek parentage and painted in Toledo, Spain, for most of his career. His paintings often show figures that are expressively elongated. Rothko (1903–1970) was an abstract expressionist painter who was born in Latvia and moved to the United States in 1913; his best-known canvases show large stacked rectangles of color.

"We don't get along well anymore." "Don't talk about it," he said—no denial, no protest. At best, she could say things and get away with them; she could never get him to continue such a conversation.

At the dinner table, lit with white candles burning in empty wine bottles, they eat 55
off his grandmother's small flowery plates. Lenore looks out a window and sees, very faintly in the dark, their huge oak tree. The rain has stopped. A few stars have come out, and there are glints on the wet branches. The oak tree grows very close to the window. George loved it when her brother once suggested that some of the bushes and trees should be pruned away from the house so it would not always be so dark inside; it gave him a chance to rave about the beauty of nature, to say that he would never tamper with it. "It's like a tomb in here all day," her brother had said. Since moving here, George has learned the names of almost all the things that are growing on the land: he can point out abelia bushes, spirea, laurels. He subscribes to *National Geographic* (although she rarely sees him looking at it). He is at last in touch, he says, being in the country puts him in touch. He is saying it now to Sarah, who has put down her ivory-handled fork to listen to him. He gets up to change the record. Side two of the Telemann record begins softly.

Sarah is still very much on guard with Lenore; she makes polite conversation with her quickly when George is out of the room. "You people are so wonderful," she says. "I wish my parents could be like you."

"George would be pleased to hear that," Lenore says, lifting a small piece of pasta to her lips.

When George is seated again, Sarah, anxious to please, tells him, "If only my father could be like you."

"Your father," George says. "I won't have that analogy." He says it pleasantly, but barely disguises his dismay at the comparison.

"I mean, he cares about nothing but business," the girl stumbles on. 60

The music, in contrast, grows lovelier.

Lenore goes into the kitchen to get the salad and hears George say, "I simply won't let you girls leave. Nobody leaves on a Saturday."

There are polite protests, there are compliments to Lenore on the meal—there is too much talk. Lenore has trouble caring about what's going on. The food is warm and delicious. She pours more wine and lets them talk.

"Godard, yes, I know . . . panning that row of honking cars *so* slowly, that long line of cars stretching on and on."

She has picked up the end of George's conversation. His arm slowly waves 65
out over the table, indicating the line of motionless cars in the movie.

"That's a lovely plant," Julie says to Lenore.

"It's Peruvian ivy," Lenore says. She smiles. She is supposed to smile. She will not offer to hack shoots off her plant for these girls.

Sarah asks for a Dylan record when the Telemann[2] finishes playing. White wax drips onto the wood table. George waits for it to solidify slightly, then

[2]*Dylan . . . Telemann:* Bob Dylan (b. 1941) is a prominent American folk-rock songwriter and performer. Georg Telemann (1681–1767) was a German composer of classical Baroque music.

scrapes up the little circles and with thumb and index finger flicks them gently toward Sarah. He explains (although she asked for no particular Dylan record) that he has only Dylan before he went electric. And *Planet Waves*—"because it's so romantic. That's silly of me, but true." Sarah smiles at him. Julie smiles at Lenore. Julie is being polite, taking her cues from Sarah, really not understanding what's going on. Lenore does not smile back. She has done enough to put them at ease. She is tired now, brought down by the music, a full stomach, and again the sounds of rain outside. For dessert there is homemade vanilla ice cream, made by George, with small black vanilla-bean flecks in it. He is still drinking wine, though; another bottle has been opened. He sips wine and then taps his spoon on his ice cream, looking at Sarah. Sarah smiles, letting them all see the smile, then sucks the ice cream off her spoon. Julie is missing more and more of what's going on. Lenore watches as Julie strokes her hand absently on her napkin. She is wearing a thin silver choker and—Lenore notices for the first time—a thin silver ring on the third finger of her right hand.

"It's just terrible about Anna," George says, finishing his wine, his ice cream melting, looking at no one in particular, although Sarah was the one who brought up Anna the night before, when they had been in the house only a short time—Anna dead, hit by a car, hardly an accident at all. Anna was also a student of his. The driver of the car was drunk, but for some reason charges were not pressed. (Sarah and George have talked about this before, but Lenore blocks it out. What can she do about it? She met Anna once: a beautiful girl, with tiny, childlike hands, her hair thin and curly—wary, as beautiful people are wary.) Now the driver has been flipping out, Julie says, and calling Anna's parents, wanting to talk to them to find out why it has happened.

The baby begins to cry. Lenore goes upstairs, pulls up more covers, talks to him for a minute. He settles for this. She goes downstairs. The wine must have affected her more than she realizes; otherwise, why is she counting the number of steps?

In the candlelit dining room, Julie sits alone at the table. The girl has been left alone again; George and Sarah took the umbrellas, decided to go for a walk in the rain.

It is eight o'clock. Since helping Lenore load the dishes into the dishwasher, when she said what a beautiful house Lenore had, Julie has said very little. Lenore is tired, and does not want to make conversation. They sit in the living room and drink wine.

"Sarah is my best friend," Julie says. She seems apologetic about it. "I was so out of it when I came back to college. I was in Italy, with my husband, and suddenly I was back in the States. I couldn't make friends. But Sarah wasn't like the other people. She cared enough to be nice to me."

"How long have you been friends?"

"For two years. She's really the best friend I've ever had. We understand things—we don't always have to talk about them."

"Like her relationship with George," Lenore says.

Too direct. Too unexpected. Julie has no answer.

"You act as if you're to blame," Lenore says.

"I feel strange because you're such a nice lady."

80 A nice lady! What an odd way to speak. Has she been reading Henry James? Lenore has never known what to think of herself, but she certainly thinks of herself as being more complicated than a "lady."

"Why do you look that way?" Julie asks. "You *are* nice. I think you've been very nice to us. You've given up your whole weekend."

"I always give up my weekends. Weekends are the only time we socialize, really. In a way, it's good to have something to do."

"But to have it turn out like this . . ." Julie says. "I think I feel so strange because when my own marriage broke up I didn't even suspect. I mean, I couldn't act the way you do, anyway, but I—"

"For all I know, nothing's going on," Lenore says. "For all I know, your friend is flattering herself, and George is trying to make me jealous." She puts two more logs on the fire. When these are gone, she will either have to walk to the woodshed or give up and go to bed. "Is there something . . . *major* going on?" she asks.

85 Julie is sitting on the rug, by the fire, twirling her hair with her finger. "I didn't know it when I came out here," she says. "Sarah's put me in a very awkward position."

"But do you know how far it has gone?" Lenore asks, genuinely curious now.

"No," Julie says.

No way to know if she's telling the truth. Would Julie speak the truth to a lady? Probably not.

"Anyway," Lenore says with a shrug, "I don't want to think about it all the time."

90 "I'd never have the courage to live with a man and not marry," Julie says. "I mean, I wish I had, that we hadn't gotten married, but I just don't have that kind of . . . I'm not secure enough."

"You have to live somewhere," Lenore says.

Julie is looking at her as if she does not believe that she is sincere. Am I? Lenore wonders. She has lived with George for six years, and sometimes she thinks she has caught his way of playing games, along with his colds, his bad moods.

"I'll show you something," Lenore says. She gets up, and Julie follows. Lenore puts on the light in George's study, and they walk through it to a bathroom he has converted to a darkroom. Under a table, in a box behind another box, there is a stack of pictures. Lenore takes them out and hands them to Julie. They are pictures that Lenore found in his darkroom last summer; they were left out by mistake, no doubt, and she found them when she went in with some contact prints he had left in their bedroom. They are high-contrast photographs of George's face. In all of them he looks very serious and very sad; in some of them his eyes seem to be narrowed in pain. In one, his mouth is open. It is an excellent photograph of a man in agony, a man about to scream.

"What are they?" Julie whispers.

95 "Pictures he took of himself," Lenore says. She shrugs. "So I stay," she says.

Julie nods. Lenore nods, taking the pictures back. Lenore has not thought until this minute that this may be why she stays. In fact, it is not the only reason. It is just a very demonstrable, impressive reason. When she first saw the pictures, her own face had become as distorted as George's. She had simply not known what to do. She had been frightened and ashamed. Finally she put them in an empty box, and put the box behind another box. She did not even want him to see the horrible pictures again. She does not know if he has ever found them, pushed back against the wall in that other box. As George says, there can be too much communication between people.

Later, Sarah and George come back to the house. It is still raining. It turns out that they took a bottle of brandy with them, and they are both drenched and drunk. He holds Sarah's finger with one of his. Sarah, seeing Lenore, lets his finger go. But then he turns—they have not even said hello yet—and grabs her up, spins her around, stumbling into the living room, and says, "I am in love."

Julie and Lenore watch them in silence.

"See no evil," George says, gesturing with the empty brandy bottle to Julie. "Hear no evil," George says, pointing to Lenore. He hugs Sarah closer. "I speak no evil. I speak the truth. I am in love!"

Sarah squirms away from him, runs from the room and up the stairs in the dark.

George looks blankly after her, then sinks to the floor and smiles. He is going to pass it off as a joke. Julie looks at him in horror, and from upstairs Sarah can be heard sobbing. Her crying awakens the baby.

"Excuse me," Lenore says. She climbs the stairs and goes into her son's room, and picks him up. She talks gently to him, soothing him with lies. He is too sleepy to be alarmed for long. In a few minutes he is asleep again, and she puts him back in his crib. In the next room Sarah is crying more quietly now. Her crying is so awful that Lenore almost joins in, but instead she pats her son. She stands in the dark by the crib and then at last goes out and down the hallway to her bedroom. She takes off her clothes and gets into the cold bed. She concentrates on breathing normally. With the door closed and Sarah's door closed, she can hardly hear her. Someone taps lightly on her door.

"Mrs. Anderson," Julie whispers. "Is this your room?"

"Yes," Lenore says. She does not ask her in.

"We're going to leave. I'm going to get Sarah and leave. I didn't want to just walk out without saying anything."

Lenore just cannot think how to respond. It was really very kind of Julie to say something. She is very close to tears, so she says nothing.

"Okay," Julie says, to reassure herself. "Good night. We're going."

There is no more crying. Footsteps. Miraculously, the baby does not wake up again, and Maria has slept through all of it. She has always slept well. Lenore herself sleeps worse and worse, and she knows that George walks much of the night, most nights. She hasn't said anything about it. If he thinks she's simple, what good would her simple wisdom do him?

The oak tree scrapes against the window in the wind and rain. Here on the second floor, under the roof, the tinny tapping is very loud. If Sarah and Julie say anything to George before they leave, she doesn't hear them. She hears the car start, then die out. It starts again—she is praying for the car to go—and after conking out once more it rolls slowly away, crunching gravel. The bed is no warmer; she shivers. She tries hard to fall asleep. The effort keeps her awake. She squints her eyes in concentration instead of closing them. The only sound in the house is the electric clock, humming by her bed. It is not even midnight.

She gets up, and without turning on the light, walks downstairs. George is 110
still in the living room. The fire is nothing but ashes and glowing bits of wood. It is as cold there as it was in the bed.

"That damn bitch," George says. "I should have known she was a stupid little girl."

"You went too far," Lenore says. "I'm the only one you can go too far with."

"Damn it," he says, and pokes the fire. A few sparks shoot up. "Damn it," he repeats under his breath.

His sweater is still wet. His shoes are muddy and ruined. Sitting on the floor by the fire, his hair matted down on his head, he looks ugly, older, unfamiliar.

She thinks of another time, when it was warm. They were walking on the 115
beach together, shortly after they met, gathering shells. Little waves were rolling in. The sun went behind the clouds and there was a momentary illusion that the clouds were still and the sun was racing ahead of them. "Catch me," he said, breaking away from her. They had been talking quietly, gathering shells. She was so surprised at him for breaking away that she ran with all her energy and did catch him, putting her hand out and taking hold of the band of his swimming trunks as he veered into the water. If she hadn't stopped him, would he really have run far out into the water, until she couldn't follow anymore? He turned on her, just as abruptly as he had run away, and grabbed her and hugged her hard, lifted her high. She had clung to him, held him close. He had tried the same thing when he came back from the walk with Sarah, and it hadn't worked.

"I wouldn't care if their car went off the road," he says bitterly.

"Don't say that," she says.

They sit in silence, listening to the rain. She slides over closer to him, puts her hand on his shoulder and leans her head there, as if he could protect her from the awful things he has wished into being.

(1976)

QUESTIONS FOR DISCUSSION AND WRITING

CLOSE READING

1. Why won't George marry Lenore?
2. Lenore reflects on a letter she has received from her brother; what does the letter tell us about Lenore's personality? Is her brother's assessment accurate?
3. Why do the photographs George took of himself explain why Lenore stays with him?

Critical and Creative Reading

4. The narrator of "Weekend" observes that George "says things over and over so that [Lenore] will accept them as truths." Do lies become more believable when they are repeated?
5. Toward the end of the story Lenore recalls a phrase that George uses: "there can be too much communication between people." What is your opinion of that statement, especially as it applies to spouses or romantic partners?
6. When Sarah wakes up the baby with her crying, Lenore "talks gently to him, soothing him with lies." Discuss the notion that a lie can be "soothing." If that's true, is lying a form of love?

Connections to Other Readings

7. Discuss the theme of self-deception in "Weekend" and in Mark Halperin's poem, "The Escape."
8. The men in this story and in David Long's "Morphine" both carry on affairs; do you judge the two men similarly? If not, how does that difference relate to the way the stories are told?
9. What do you think Algernon, from *The Importance of Being Earnest*, would think of Beattie's story? How would he judge these characters?

Raymond Carver

Jerry and Molly and Sam

Disgruntled, angry, alcoholic, working poor characters populate the stories of Raymond Carver (1938–1988). Like Ann Beattie, whose story "Weekend" precedes this one, he is associated with "minimalism," which showcases emotionally charged scenes in spare language. Carver wrote an impressive number of essays, poems, and especially short stories before his death of lung cancer at the age of fifty, though he never turned his attention to the novel form. As you read the following story, look carefully for the names in the title, which do not refer to the story's main characters.

As Al saw it, there was only one solution. He had to get rid of the dog without Betty or the kids finding out about it. At night. It would have to be done at night. He would simply drive Suzy—well, someplace, later he'd decide where—open the door, push her out, drive away. The sooner the better. He felt relieved making the decision. Any action was better than no action at all, he was becoming convinced.

It was Sunday. He got up from the kitchen table where he had been eating a late breakfast by himself and stood by the sink, hands in his pockets. Nothing was going right lately. He had enough to contend with without having to worry about a stinking dog. They were laying off at Aerojet when they should be hiring. The middle of the summer, defense contracts let all over the country and Aerojet was talking of cutting back. *Was* cutting back, in fact, a little more every day. He was no safer than anyone else even though he'd been there two years going on three. He got along with the right people, all right, but seniority or friendship, either one, didn't mean a damn these days. If your number was up, that was that—and there was nothing anybody could do. They got ready to lay off, they laid off. Fifty, a hundred men at a time.

No one was safe, from the foreman and supers right on down to the man on the line. And three months ago, just before all the layoffs began, he'd let Betty talk him into moving into this cushy two-hundred-a-month place. Lease, with an option to buy. Shit!

Al hadn't really wanted to leave the other place. He had been comfortable enough. Who could know that two weeks after he'd move they'd start laying off? But who could know anything these days? For example, there was Jill. Jill worked in bookkeeping at Weinstock's. She was a nice girl, said she loved Al. She was just lonely, that's what she told him the first night. She didn't make it a habit, letting herself be picked up by married men, she also told him the first night. He'd met Jill about three months ago, when he was feeling depressed and jittery with all the talk of layoffs just beginning. He met her at the Town and Country, a bar not too far from his new place. They danced a little and he drove her home and they necked in the car in front of her apartment. He had not gone upstairs with her that night, though he was sure he could have. He went upstairs with her the next night.

5 Now he was having an *affair*, for Christ's sake, and he didn't know what to do about it. He did not want it to go on, and he did not want to break it off: you don't throw everything overboard in a storm. Al was drifting, and he knew he was drifting, and where it was all going to end he could not guess at. But he was beginning to feel he was losing control over everything. Everything. Recently, too, he had caught himself thinking about old age after he'd been constipated a few days—an affliction he had always associated with the elderly. Then there was the matter of the tiny bald spot and of his having just begun to wonder how he would comb his hair a different way. What was he going to do with his life? he wanted to know.

He was thirty-one.

All these things to contend with and then *Sandy*, his wife's younger sister, giving the kids, Alex and Mary, that mongrel dog about four months ago. He wished he'd never seen that dog. Or Sandy, either, for that matter. That bitch! She was always turning up with some shit or other that wound up costing him money, some little flimflam that went haywire after a day or two and *had* to be repaired, something the kids could scream over and fight over and beat the shit out of each other about. God! And then turning right around to touch him, through *Betty*, for twenty-five bucks. The mere thought of all the twenty-five- or fifty-buck checks, and the one just a few months ago for eighty-five to make her car payment—her *car* payment, for God's sake, when he didn't even know if he was going to have a roof over his head—made him want to *kill* the goddamn dog.

Sandy! Betty and Alex and Mary! Jill! And Suzy the goddamn dog!

This was Al.

He had to start someplace—setting things in order, sorting all this out. It 10
was time to *do* something, time for some straight thinking for a change. And he intended to start tonight.

He would coax the dog into the car undetected and, on some pretext or another, go out. Yet he hated to think of the way Betty would lower her eyes as she watched him dress, and then, later, just before he went out the door, ask him where, how long, etc., in a resigned voice that made him feel all the worse. He could never get used to the lying. Besides, he hated to use what little reserve he might have left with Betty by telling her a lie for something different from what she suspected. A wasted lie, so to speak. But he could not tell her the truth, could not say he was *not* going drinking, was *not* going calling on somebody, was instead going to do away with the goddamn dog and thus take the first step toward setting his house in order.

He ran his hand over his face, tried to put it all out of his mind for a minute. He took out a cold half quart of Lucky from the fridge and popped the aluminum top. His life had become a maze, one lie overlaid upon another until he was not sure he could untangle them if he had to.

"The goddamn dog," he said out loud.

"She doesn't have good sense!" was how Al put it. She was a sneak, besides. The moment the back door was left open and everyone gone, she'd pry open the screen, come through to the living room, and urinate on the carpet. There were at least a half dozen map-shaped stains on it right now. But her favorite place was the utility room, where she could root in the dirty clothes, so that all of the shorts and panties now had crotch or seat chewed away. And she chewed through the antenna wires on the outside of the house, and once Al pulled into the drive and found her lying in the front yard with one of his Florsheims in her mouth.

"She's crazy," he'd say. "And she's driving me crazy. I can't make it fast 15
enough to replace it. The sonofabitch, I'm going to kill her one of these days!"

Betty tolerated the dog at greater durations, would go along apparently unruffled for a time, but suddenly she would come upon it, with fists clenched, call it a bastard, a bitch, shriek at the kids about keeping it out of their room, the living room, etc. Betty was that way with the children, too. She could go along with them just so far, let them get away with just so much, and then she would turn on them savagely and slap their faces, screaming, "Stop it! Stop it! I can't stand any more of it!"

But then Betty would say, "It's their first dog. You remember how fond you must have been of your first dog."

"My dog had brains," he would say. "It was an Irish setter!"

The afternoon passed. Betty and the kids returned from someplace or another in the car, and they all had sandwiches and potato chips on the patio. He fell asleep on the grass, and when he woke it was nearly evening.

He showered, shaved, put on slacks and a clean shirt. He felt rested but slug- 20
gish. He dressed and he thought of Jill. He thought of Betty and Alex and Mary and Sandy and Suzy. He felt drugged.

"We'll have supper pretty soon," Betty said, coming to the bathroom door and staring at him.

"That's all right. I'm not hungry. Too hot to eat," he said fiddling with his shirt collar. "I might drive over to Carl's, shoot a few games of pool, have a couple of beers."

She said, "I see."

He said, "Jesus!"

She said, "Go ahead, I don't care." 25

He said, "I won't be gone long."

She said, "Go ahead, I said. I said I don't care."

In the garage, he said, "Goddamn you all!" and kicked the rake across the cement floor. Then he lit a cigaret and tried to get hold of himself. He picked up the rake and put it away where it belonged. He was muttering to himself, saying, "Order, order," when the dog came up to the garage, sniffed around the door, and looked in.

"Here. Come here, Suzy. Here, girl," he called.

The dog wagged her tail but stayed where she was. 30

He went over to the cupboard above the lawn mower and took down one, then two, and finally three cans of food.

"All you want tonight, Suzy, old girl. All you can eat," he coaxed, opening up both ends of the first can and sliding the mess into the dog's dish.

He drove around for nearly an hour, not able to decide on a place. If he dropped her off in just any neighborhood and the pound were called, the dog would be back at the house in a day or two. The county pound was the first place Betty would call. He remembered reading stories about lost dogs finding their way hundreds of miles back home again. He remembered crime programs where someone saw a license number, and the thought made his heart jump. Held up to public view, without all the facts being in, it'd be a shameful thing to be caught abandoning a dog. He would have to find the right place.

He drove over near the American River. The dog needed to get out more anyway, get the feel of the wind on its back, be able to swim and wade in the river when it wanted; it was a pity to keep a dog fenced in all the time. But the fields near the levee seemed too desolate, no houses around at all. After all, he did want the dog to be found and cared for. A large old two-story house was what he had in mind, with happy, well-behaved reasonable children who needed a dog, who desperately needed a dog. But there were no old two-story houses here, not a one.

He drove back onto the highway. He had not been able to look at the dog 35
since he'd managed to get her into the car. She lay quietly on the back seat now. But when he pulled off the road and stopped the car, she sat up and whined, looking around.

He stopped at a bar, rolled all the car windows down before he went inside. He stayed nearly an hour, drinking beer and playing the shuffleboard. He kept wondering if he should have left all the doors ajar too. When he went back outside, Suzy sat up in the seat and rolled her lips back, showing her teeth.

He got in and started off again.

Then he thought of the place. The neighborhood where they used to live, swarming with kids and just across the line in Yolo County, that would be just the right place. If the dog were picked up, it would be taken to the Woodland Pound, not the pound in Sacramento. Just drive onto one of the streets in the old neighborhood, stop, throw out a handful of the shit she ate, open the door, a little assistance in the way of a push, and out she'd go while he took off. Done! It would be done.

He stepped on it getting out there.

There were porch lights on and at three or four houses he saw men and women sitting on the front steps as he drove by. He cruised along, and when he came to his old house he slowed down almost to a stop and stared at the front door, the porch, the lighted windows. He felt even more insubstantial, looking at the house. He had lived there—how long? A year, sixteen months? Before that, Chico, Red Bluff, Tacoma, Portland—where he'd met Betty—Yakima . . . Toppenish, where he was born and went to high school. Not since he was a kid, it seemed to him, had he known what it was to be free from worry and worse. He thought of summers fishing and camping in the Cascades, autumns when he'd hunt pheasants behind Sam, the setter's flashing red coat a beacon through cornfields and alfalfa meadows where the boy that he was and the dog that he had would both run like mad. He wished he could keep driving and driving tonight until he was driving onto the old bricked main street of Toppenish, turning left at the first light, then left again, stopping when he came to where his mother lived, and never, never, for any reason ever, ever leave again.

He came to the darkened end of the street. There was a large empty field straight ahead and the street turned to the right, skirting it. For almost a block there were no houses on the side nearer the field and only one house, completely dark, on the other side. He stopped the car and, without thinking any longer about what he was doing, scooped a handful of dog food up, leaned over the seat, opened the back door nearer the field, threw the stuff out, and said, "Go on, Suzy." He pushed her until she jumped down reluctantly. He leaned over farther, pulled the door shut, and drove off, slowly. Then he drove faster and faster.

He stopped at Dupee's, the first bar he came to on the way back to Sacramento. He was jumpy and perspiring. He didn't feel exactly unburdened or relieved, as he had thought he would feel. But he kept assuring himself it was a step in the right direction, that the good feeling would settle on him tomorrow. The thing to do was to wait it out.

After four beers a girl in a turtleneck sweater and sandals and carrying a suitcase sat down beside him. She set the suitcase between the stools. She seemed to know the bartender, and the bartender had something to say to her whenever he came by, once or twice stopping briefly to talk. She told Al her name was Molly, but she wouldn't let him buy her a beer. Instead, she offered to eat half a pizza.

He smiled at her, and she smiled back. He took out his cigarets and his lighter and put them on the bar.

45 "Pizza it is!" he said.

Later, he said, "Can I give you a lift somewhere?"

"No, thanks. I'm waiting for someone," she said.

He said, "Where you heading for?"

She said, "No place. Oh," she said, touching the suitcase with her toe, "you mean that?" laughing. "I live here in West Sac. I'm not going anyplace. It's just a washing-machine motor inside belongs to my mother. Jerry—that's the bartender—he's good at fixing things. Jerry said he'd fix it for nothing."

50 Al got up. He weaved a little as he leaned over her. He said, "Well, goodbye, honey. I'll see you around."

"You bet!" she said. "And thanks for the pizza. Hadn't eaten since lunch. Been trying to take some of this off." She raised her sweater, gathered a handful of flesh at the waist.

"Sure I can't give you a lift someplace?" he said.

The woman shook her head.

In the car again, driving, he reached for his cigarets and then, frantically, for his lighter, remembering leaving everything on the bar. The hell with it, he thought, let her have it. Let her put the lighter and the cigarets in the suitcase along with the washing machine. He chalked it up against the dog, one more expense. But the last, by God! It angered him now, now that he was getting things in order, that the girl hadn't been more friendly. If he'd been in a different frame of mind, he could have picked her up. But when you're depressed, it shows all over you, even the way you light a cigaret.

55 He decided to go see Jill. He stopped at a liquor store and bought a pint of whiskey and climbed the stairs to her apartment and he stopped at the landing to catch his breath and to clean his teeth with his tongue. He could still taste the mushrooms from the pizza, and his mouth and throat were seared from the whiskey. He realized that what he wanted to do was to go right to Jill's bathroom and use her toothbrush.

He knocked. "It's me, Al," he whispered. "Al," he said louder. He heard her feet hit the floor. She threw the lock and then tried to undo the chain as he leaned heavily against the door.

"Just a minute, honey. Al, you'll have to quit pushing—I can't unhook it. There," she said and opened the door, scanning his face as she took him by the hand.

They embraced clumsily, and he kissed her on the cheek.

"Sit down, honey. Here." She switched on a lamp and helped him to the couch. Then she touched her fingers to her curlers and said, "I'll put on some lipstick. What would you like in the meantime? Coffee? Juice? A beer? I think I have some beer. What do you have there . . . whiskey? What would you like, honey?" She stroked his hair with one hand and leaned over him, gazing into his eyes. "Poor baby, what would you like?" she said.

"Just want you hold me," he said. "Here. Sit down. No lipstick," he said, 60
pulling her onto his lap. "Hold. I'm falling," he said.

She put an arm around his shoulders. She said, "You come on over to the bed, baby, I'll give you what you like."

"Tell you, Jill," he said, "skating on thin ice. Crash through any minute . . . I don't know." He stared at her with a fixed, puffy expression that he could feel but not correct. "Serious," he said.

She nodded. "Don't think about anything, baby. Just relax," she said. She pulled his face to hers and kissed him on the forehead and then the lips. She turned slightly on his lap and said, "No, don't move, Al," the fingers of both hands suddenly slipping around the back of his neck and gripping his face at the same time. His eyes wobbled around the room an instant, then tried to focus on what she was doing. She held his head in place in her strong fingers. With her thumbnails she was squeezing out a blackhead to the side of his nose.

"Sit still!" she said.

"No," he said. "Don't! Stop! Not in the mood for that." 65

"I almost have it. Sit still, I said! . . . There, look at that. What do you think of that? Didn't know that was there, did you? Now just one more, a big one, baby. The last one," she said.

"Bathroom," he said, forcing her off, freeing his way.

At home it was all tears, confusion. Mary ran out to the car, crying, before he could get parked.

"Suzy's gone," she sobbed. "Suzy's gone. She's never coming back, Daddy, I know it. She's gone!"

My God, heart lurching. *What have I done?* 70

"Now don't worry, sweetheart. She's probably just off running around somewhere. She'll be back," he said.

"She isn't, Daddy, I know she isn't. Mama said we may have to get another dog."

"Wouldn't that be all right, honey?" he said. "Another dog, if Suzy doesn't come back? We'll go to the pet store—"

"I don't want another dog!" the child cried, holding onto his leg.

"Can we have a monkey, Daddy, instead of a dog?" Alex asked. "If we go to 75
the pet store to look for a dog, can we have a monkey instead?"

"I don't want a monkey!" Mary cried. "I want Suzy."

"Everybody let go now, let Daddy in the house. Daddy has a terrible, terrible headache," he said.

Betty lifted a casserole dish from the oven. She looked tired, irritable . . . older. She didn't look at him. "The kids tell you? Suzy's gone? I've combed the neighborhood. Everywhere, I swear."

"That dog'll turn up," he said. "Probably just running around somewhere. That dog'll come back," he said.

"Seriously," she said, turning to him with her hands on her hips, "I think it's 80
something else. I think she might have got hit by a car. I want you to drive around. The kids called her last night, and she was gone then. That's the last's been seen of her. I called the pound and described her to them, but they said all their trucks aren't in yet. I'm supposed to call again in the morning."

He went into the bathroom and could hear her still going on. He began to run the water in the sink, wondering, with a fluttery sensation in his stomach, how grave exactly was his mistake. When he turned off the faucets, he could still hear her. He kept staring at the sink.

"Did you hear me?" she called. "I want you to drive around and look for her after supper. The kids can go with you and look too . . . Al?"

"Yes, yes," he answered.

"What?" she said. "What'd you say?"

"I said yes. Yes! All right. Anything! Just let me wash up first, will you?" 85

She looked through from the kitchen. "Well, what in the hell is eating you? I didn't ask you to get drunk last night, did I? I've had enough of it, I can tell you! I've had a hell of a day, if you want to know. Alex waking me up at five this morning getting in with me, telling me his daddy was snoring so loud that . . . that you *scared* him! *I* saw you out there with your clothes on passed out and the room smelling to high heaven. I tell you, I've had enough of it!" She looked around the kitchen quickly, as if to seize something.

He kicked the door shut. Everything was going to hell. While he was shaving, he stopped once and held the razor in his hand and looked at himself in the mirror: his face doughy, characterless—*immoral*, that was the word. He laid the razor down. *I believe I have made the gravest mistake this time. I believe I have made the gravest mistake of all.* He brought the razor up to his throat and finished.

He did not shower, did not change clothes. "Put my supper in the oven for me," he said. "Or in the refrigerator. I'm going out. Right now," he said.

"You can wait till after supper. The kids can go with you."

"No, the hell with that. Let the kids eat supper, look around here if they 90
want. I'm not hungry, and it'll be dark soon."

"Is everybody going crazy?" she said. "I don't know what's going to happen to us. I'm ready for a nervous breakdown. I'm ready to lose my mind. What's going to happen to the kids if I lose my mind?" She slumped against the draining board, her face crumpled, tears rolling off her cheeks. "You don't love them, anyway! You never have. It isn't the dog I'm worried about. It's us! It's us! I know you don't love me any more—goddamn you!—but you don't even love the kids!"

"Betty, Betty!" he said. "My God!" he said. "Everything's going to be all right. I promise you," he said. "Don't worry," he said. "I promise you, things'll be all right. I'll find the dog and then things will be all right," he said.

He bounded out of the house, ducked into the bushes as he heard his children coming: the girl crying, saying, "Suzy, Suzy"; the boy saying maybe a train ran over her. When they were inside the house, he made a break for the car.

He fretted at all the lights he had to wait for, bitterly resented the time lost when he stopped for gas. The sun was low and heavy, just over the squat range of hills at the far end of the valley. At best, he had an hour of daylight.

He saw his whole life a ruin from here on in. If he lived another fifty years— 95
hardly likely—he felt he'd never get over it, abandoning the dog. He felt he was

finished if he didn't find the dog. A man who would get rid of a little dog wasn't worth a damn. That kind of man would do anything, would stop at nothing.

He squirmed in the seat, kept staring into the swollen face of the sun as it moved lower into the hills. He knew the situation was all out of proportion now, but he couldn't help it. He knew he must somehow retrieve the dog, as the night before he had known he must lose it.

"I'm the one going crazy," he said and then nodded his head in agreement.

He came in the other way this time, by the field where he had let her off, alert for any sign of movement.

"Let her be there," he said.

He stopped the car and searched the field. Then he drove on, slowly. A station wagon with the motor idling was parked in the drive of the lone house, and he saw a well-dressed woman in heels come out the front door with a little girl. They stared at him as he passed. Farther on he turned left, his eyes taking in the street and the yards on each side as far down as he could see. Nothing. Two kids with bicycles a block away stood beside a parked car.

"Hi," he said to the two boys as he pulled up alongside. "You fellows see anything of a little white dog around today? A kind of white shaggy dog? I lost one."

One boy just gazed at him. The other said, "I saw a lot of little kids playing with a dog over there this afternoon. The street the other side of this one. I don't know what kind of dog it was. It was white maybe. There was a lot of kids."

"Okay, good. Thanks," Al said. "Thank you very very much," he said.

He turned right at the end of the street. He concentrated on the street ahead. The sun had gone down now. It was nearly dark. Houses pitched side by side, trees, lawns, telephone poles, parked cars, it struck him as serene, untroubled. He could hear a man calling his children; he saw a woman in an apron step to the lighted door of her house.

"Is there still a chance for me?" Al said. He felt tears spring to his eyes. He was amazed. He couldn't help but grin at himself and shake his head as he got out his handkerchief. Then he saw a group of children coming down the street. He waved to get their attention.

"You kids see anything of a little white dog?" Al said to them.

"Oh sure," one boy said. "Is it your dog?"

Al nodded.

"We were just playing with him about a minute ago down the street. In Terry's yard." The boy pointed. "Down the street."

"You got kids?" one of the little girls spoke up.

"I do," Al said.

"Terry said he's going to keep him. He don't have a dog," the boy said.

"I don't know," Al said. "I don't think my kids would like that. It belongs to them. It's just lost," Al said.

He drove on down the street. It was dark now, hard to see, and he began to panic again, cursing silently. He swore at what a weathervane he was, changing this way and that, one moment this, the next moment that.

He saw the dog then. He understood he had been looking at it for a time. 115
The dog moved slowly, nosing the grass along a fence. Al got out of the car, started across the lawn, crouching forward as he walked, calling, "Suzy, Suzy, Suzy."

The dog stopped when she saw him. She raised her head. He sat down on his heels, reached out his arm, waiting. They looked at each other. She moved her tail in greeting. She lay down with her head between her front legs and regarded him. He waited. She got up. She went around the fence and out of sight.

He sat there. He thought he didn't feel so bad, all things considered. The world was full of dogs. There were dogs and there were dogs. Some dogs you just couldn't do anything with.

(1976)

Questions for Discussion and Writing

Close Reading

1. Who are Jerry and Molly and Sam? How does Carver's choice of a title (as opposed to something like "Jill and Betty and Suzy") feed into the story's themes?
2. Why does Al deem himself "immoral"?
3. How does the background of the story—the situation at Al's work at Aerojet—serve as a context for Al's behavior?

Critical and Creative Reading

4. Al clearly regrets his decision to "lose" the family dog; does he ever regret his affair? If not, what would it take to get him to do so? What do the dog and the affair have to do with one another?
5. Would you feel differently about Al if he were wealthier?
6. Does Al's finding the dog after some effort redeem him in any way? (The broader version of this question is: can one make up for deception through positive actions?)

Connections to Other Readings

7. The main characters of "Jerry and Molly and Sam" and of David Long's "Morphine" are both men who cheat on their wives. Compare the two characters to discover which one earns more of your sympathy (even if neither earns much of your sympathy).
8. Ryder in Chesnutt's "The Wife of His Youth" comes clean about his past. Should Al in "Jerry and Molly and Sam" do the same thing? What would be gained through such honesty following a lifetime of deception?
9. Gauge your level of empathy for Betty in this story and Lenore in Ann Beattie's "Weekend," two women whose partners are cheating on them. To what degree is your reaction controlled by the level of attention paid to those women by the stories' narrators?

Mori Yoko

Translated by Makoto Ueda

Spring Storm

Mori Yoko (1940–1993) wrote short fiction dealing mainly with the lifestyles of young people in contemporary Japan. Her short stories often have urban settings and reflect the growing pains of a culture in which men's and women's traditional roles are changing. Consider the story's title before you read it: what associations do you have with a spring storm (as opposed to a storm in another season)?

The small orange light on the lobby wall showed the elevator was still at the seventh floor. Natsuo's eyes were fixed on it.

From time to time her heart pounded furiously, so furiously that it seemed to begin skipping beats. For some time now she had been wild with excitement.

Intense joy is somewhat like pain, she thought. Or like a dizzy spell. Strangely, it was not unlike grief. The suffocating feeling in her chest was almost unbearable.

The elevator still had not moved from the seventh floor.

The emergency stairway was located alongside the outer walls of the build- 5
ing, completely exposed to the elements. Unfortunately for Natsuo, it was raining outside. There was a wind, too.

A spring storm. The words, perhaps romantic, well described the heavy, slanting rain, driven by a wind that had retained the rawness of winter. If Natsuo were to climb the stairs to the sixth floor, she would be soaked to the skin.

She took a cigarette from her handbag and lit it.

This is unusual for me, she thought. She had never smoked while waiting for the elevator. Indeed, she had not smoked anywhere while standing up.

Exhaling the smoke from the depths of her throat, she fell to thinking. I'll be experiencing all kinds of new things from now on, I've just come a big step up the ladder. No, not just one, I've jumped as many as ten steps in one leap. There were thirty-four rivals, and I beat them all.

All thirty-four people were well-experienced performers. There was a 10
dancer with considerably more skill than she. Physically also the odds were against her: there were a sizable number of women with long, stylish legs and tight, shapely waists. One Eurasian woman had such alluring looks that everyone admired her. There were professional actresses currently active on the stage, too.

In spite of everything, Natsuo was the one selected for the role.

When the agency called to tell her the news, she at first thought she was being teased.

"You must be kidding me," she said, a little irritated. She had indeed taken it for a bad joke. "You can't trick me like this. I don't believe you."

"Let me ask you a question, then," responded the man who had been acting as her manager. In a teasing voice, he continued, "Were you just kidding when you auditioned for that musical?"

"Of course not!" she retorted. She had been quite serious and, although she would not admit it, she had wanted the role desperately. At the audition, she had done her very best.

"But I'm sure I didn't make it," she said to her manager. "At the interview, I blushed terribly."

Whenever she tried to express herself in front of other people, blood would rush to her face, turning it scarlet.

"You're a bashful person, aren't you?" one of her examiners had commented to her at the interview. His tone carried an objective observation rather than sympathetic inquiry.

"Do you think you're an introvert?" another examiner asked.

"I'm probably on the shy side," Natsuo answered, painfully aware that her earlobes had turned embarrassingly red and her palms were moist.

"The heroine of this drama," added the third examiner, "is a spirited woman with strong willpower. Do you know that?"

Natsuo had sensed the skepticism that was running through the panel of examiners. Without doubt she was going to fail the test, unless she did something right now. She looked up.

"It's true that I'm not very good at expressing myself, or speaking up for myself, in front of other people. But playing a dramatic role is something different. It's very different." She was getting desperate. "I'm very bashful about myself. But I'm perfectly all right when I play someone else."

If I am to express someone else's emotion, I have no reason to be shy, she confirmed to herself. I can calmly go about doing the job.

"Well, then, would you please play someone else?" the chief examiner said, with a nod toward the stage.

Natsuo retired to the wings of the stage and tried to calm herself. When she trotted out onto the stage and confidently faced them, she was no longer a timid, blushing woman.

It was impossible to guess, though, how the examiners appraised her performance. They showed little, if any, emotion. When the test was over there was a chorus of murmured "Thank yous." That was all.

Her manager was still speaking on the phone. "I don't know about the third-raters. But I can tell you that most good actors and actresses are introverted, naive, and always feeling nervous inside."

He then added, "If you don't believe me, why don't you go to the office of that production company and find out for yourself?"

Natsuo decided to do just that.

At the end of a dimly lit hallway, a small group of men and women were looking at a large blackboard. Most of the board was powdered with half-obliterated previous scribblings, but at the top was written the cast of the new musical, with the names of the actors and actresses selected for the roles.

Natsuo's name was second from the top. It was scrawled in a large, carefree hand. The name at the top was her co-star, a well-known actor in musicals.

Natsuo stood immobile for ten seconds or so, staring at her name on the blackboard. It was her own name, but she felt as if it belonged to someone else. Her eyes still fixed on the name, she moved a few steps backwards. Then she turned around and hurried out of the building. It never occurred to her to stop by the office and thank the staff.

Sheer joy hit her a little later.

It was raining, and there was wind, too. She had an umbrella with her, but she walked without opening it. Finally realizing the fact, she stopped to unfold the umbrella.

"I did it!" she cried aloud. That was the moment. An incomparable joy began to rise up inside her, like the bubbles crowding to exit from a champagne bottle; and not just joy, pain as well, accompanied by the flow and ebb of some new irritation. That was how she experienced her moment of victory.

When she came to, she found herself standing in the lobby of her apartment building. The first person she wanted to tell the news to was, naturally, her husband, Yūsuke.

The elevator seemed to be out of order. It was not moving at all. How long had she been waiting there? Ten minutes? A couple of minutes? Natsuo had no idea. Her senses had been numbed. A round clock on the wall showed 9:25. Natsuo gave up and walked away.

The emergency stairway that zigzagged upwards was quite steep and barely wide enough for one person, so Natsuo could not open her umbrella. She climbed up the stairs at a dash.

By the time she reached the sixth floor, her hair was dripping wet and, with no raincoat on, her dress, too, was heavy with rain.

But Natsuo was smiling. Drenched and panting, she was still beaming with an excess of happiness when she pushed the intercom buzzer of their apartment.

"Why are you grinning? You make me nervous," Yūsuke said as he let her in. "You're soaking wet, too."

"The elevator never came."

"Who would have considered using the emergency stairs in this rain!"

"This apartment is no good, with a stairway like that," Natsuo said with a grin. "Let's move to a better place."

"You talk as if that were something very simple." Yūsuke laughed wryly and tossed a terry robe to her.

"But it is simple."

"Where would we find the money?"

"Just be patient. We'll get the money very soon," Natsuo said cheerfully, taking off her wet clothes.

"You passed the audition, didn't you?" Yūsuke asked, staring intently at her face. "Didn't you?"

Natsuo stared back at him. He looked nervous, holding his breath and waiting for her answer.

"Natsuo, did you pass the audition?" As he asked again, his face collapsed, his shoulders fell. He looked utterly forlorn.

"How . . . ," she answered impulsively, "how could I have passed? I was just kidding."

Yūsuke frowned. "You failed?"

"I was competing with professionals, you know—actresses with real stage experience. How could I have beaten them?" Natsuo named several contending actresses.

"You didn't pass?" Yūsuke repeated, his frown deepening. "Answer me clearly, please. You still haven't told me whether you passed."

"What a mean person you are!" Natsuo stuttered. "You must have guessed by now, but you're forcing me to spell it out." Her eyes met his for a moment. "I didn't make it," she said, averting her eyes. "I failed with flying colors."

There was silence. Wiping her wet hair with a towel, Natsuo was aghast and mystified at her lie.

"No kidding?" said Yūsuke, starting to walk toward the kitchen. "I was in a state of shock for a minute, really."

"How come? Were you so sure I wouldn't make it?" Natsuo spoke to him from behind, her tone a test of his sincerity.

"You were competing with professionals." There was not a trace of consolation in his voice. "It couldn't be helped. You'll have another chance."

Although Yūsuke was showing sympathy, happiness hung in the air about him.

"You sound as if you were pleased to see me fail and lose my chance."

Combing her hair, Natsuo inspected her facial expression in the small mirror on the wall. You're a liar, she told her image. How are you going to unravel this mess you've got yourself into?

"How could I be happy to see you fail?" Yūsuke responded, placing a kettle on the gas range. His words carried with them the tarnish of guilt. "But, you know, it's not that great for you to get chosen for a major role all of a sudden."

"Why not?"

"Because you'd be a star. A big new star."

"You are being a bit too dramatic." Natsuo's voice sank low.

"When that happens, your husband would become like a Mr. Judy Garland. Asai Yūsuke would disappear completely, and in his place there would be just the husband of Midori Natsuo. I wouldn't like that."

"You're inventing problems for yourself," she said. "You are what you are. You are a script writer named Asai Yūsuke."

"A script writer who might soon be forced to write a musical."

"But hasn't that been your dream, to write a musical?" Natsuo's voice was tender. "Suppose, just suppose, that I make a successful debut as an actress in a musical. As soon as I become influential enough and people begin to listen to what I say, I'll let you write a script for a musical."

"Let you write, huh?" Yūsuke picked on Natsuo's phrasing. "If you talk like that even when you're making it up, I wonder how it'd be for real."

The kettle began to erupt steam. Yūsuke flicked off the flame, dropped instant coffee into two cups, and splashed in the hot water.

"Did you hear that story about Ingrid Bergman?[1]" Yūsuke asked, his eyes looking into the distance. "Her third husband was a famous theatrical producer. A talented producer, too." Passing one of the cups to Natsuo, he continued. "One day Bergman asked her producer-husband, 'Why don't you ever try to get me a good play to act in?' He answered, 'Because you're a goose that lays golden eggs. Any play that features you is going to be a success. It will be a sellout for sure. For me, that's too easy.'" Yūsuke sipped the coffee slowly. Then, across the rising steam, he added, "I perfectly understand how he felt."

"Does this mean that I'll have to be a minor actress all my life?" Natsuo mused.

"Who knows? I may become famous one of these days," Yūsuke sighed. "Or maybe you first."

"And what would you do in the latter case?"

"Well," Yūsuke stared at the coffee. "If that happens, we'll get a divorce. That will be the best solution. Then, neither of us will be bothered by all the petty problems."

Natsuo walked toward the window. "Are you serious?" she asked.

"Yes." Yūsuke came and stood next to her. "That's the only way to handle the situation. That way, I'll be able to feel happy for you from the bottom of my heart."

"Can't a husband be happy for his wife's success?"

"Ingrid Bergman's second husband was Roberto Rossellini.[2] Do you know the last words he said to her? He said, 'I'm tired of living as Mr. Ingrid Bergman.' Even Rossellini felt that way."

"You are not a Rossellini, nor I a Bergman."

"Our situation would be even worse."

From time to time, gusts of rain slapped at the window.

"When this spring storm is over, I expect the cherry blossoms will suddenly be bursting out," Yūsuke whispered.

"There'll be another storm in no time. The blossoms will be gone, and summer will be here." Brushing back her still-moist hair with her fingers, Natsuo turned and looked over the apartment she knew so well.

"You've been standing all this time. Aren't you getting tired?" her husband asked in a gentle voice. She shook her head.

"You're looking over the apartment as though it were for the first time." Yūsuke said, gazing at his wife's profile. "Or, is it for the last time?"

Startled by his last words, Natsuo impulsively reached into her handbag for a cigarette and put it in her mouth. Yūsuke produced a lighter from his pocket and lit it for her.

"Aren't you going to continue with your work this evening?" she asked.

"No. No more work tonight."

"What's the matter?"

"I can't concentrate when someone else is in the apartment. You know that, don't you?"

[1] *Ingrid Bergman:* Swedish film actress (1915–1982).

[2] *Roberto Rossellini:* Italian film director (1906–1977).

Natsuo nodded.

"Won't you sit down?" Yūsuke said.

"Why?"

"I have an uneasy feeling when you stand there and smoke like that."

Natsuo cast her eyes on the cigarette held between her fingers. "This is the second time today I've been smoking without sitting down." The words seemed to flow from her mouth at their own volition. His back towards her, Yūsuke was collecting some sheets of writing paper scattered on his desk.

"You passed the audition. Right?" he said. His voice was so low that the last word was almost inaudible.

"How did you know?"

"I knew it from the beginning."

"From the beginning?"

"From the moment you came in. You were shouting with your whole body—'I've made it, I'm the winner!' You were trembling like a drenched cat, but your face was lit up like a Christmas tree."

Natsuo did not respond.

"The clearest evidence is the way you're smoking right now."

"Did you notice it?"

"Yes."

"Me, too. It first happened when I was waiting for the elevator down in the lobby. I was so impatient, I smoked a cigarette while standing. I've got the strangest feeling about myself."

"You feel like a celebrity?"

"I feel I've outreached myself."

"But the way you look now, it's not you."

"No, it's not me."

"You'd better not smoke standing up."

"Right. I won't do it again."

There was silence.

"You don't at all feel like congratulating me?" Natsuo asked.

Yūsuke did not answer.

"Somehow I knew it might be like this," Yūsuke continued. "I knew this moment was coming."

Now she knew why her joy had felt like pain, a pain almost indistinguishable from grief. Now she knew the source of the suffocating presence in her chest.

"That Rossellini, you know . . ." Yūsuke began again.

"Can't we drop the topic?"

"Please listen to me, dear. Rossellini was a jealous person and didn't want to see his wife working for any director other than himself. He would say to her, 'Don't get yourself involved in that play. It'll be a disaster.' One time, Bergman ignored the warning and took a part in a play. It was a big success. Rossellini was watching the stage from the wings. At the curtain call, Bergman glanced at him while bowing to the audience. Their eyes met. That instant, they both knew their love was over, with the thundering applause of the audience ringing in their ears . . ." Yūsuke paused, and then added, "I'll go and see your musical on the opening day."

Natsuo contemplated her husband's face from the wings of the room. He looked across.

Their eyes met.

(1984)

Questions for Discussion and Writing

Close Reading

1. Natsuo observes early in the story that "intense joy is somewhat like pain." How does the story illustrate that idea?
2. Why is Natsuo initially convinced that she did not pass the audition?
3. At what point does Yūsuke know for sure that Natsuo is lying about the results of the audition?

Critical and Creative Reading

4. Why does Natsuo lie to Yūsuke? Do their careers as actress and writer interfere with their marriage?
5. Are actors inherently untrustworthy? Are they less trustworthy than anyone else, or are they just better at deceiving others?
6. Do spouses or life partners have to be completely honest with one another at all times for the relationship to succeed, or is the opposite true: that partners must deceive one another from time to time?

Connections to Other Readings

7. In Ann Beattie's story "Weekend" Lenore knows that George is deceiving her. Compare the way she "reads" evidence in her husband's behavior to the way Yūsuke "reads" Natsuo in "Spring Storm." Is deception clearer in language or in gestures?
8. Natsuo's lie is a kind of game here: she will eventually tell Yūsuke the truth. In this sense it is similar to the situation in Richard Wilbur's poem "Lying." Consider lying as a form of entertainment in these works.

Poetry

Sir Walter Raleigh

The Lie

One of Elizabeth I's "favorites," or privileged courtiers, Sir Walter Raleigh (1552?–1618) had the reputation of a reckless, swashbuckling explorer as well as a poet and prose writer. Legend says that he fell out of favor with the queen by seducing one of her maids of honor. He managed to be reinstated to the queen's court in the last years of her reign, but her successor King

James I brought charges of treason against Raleigh, who was imprisoned in the Tower of London for thirteen years. He was released on the promise that he would discover gold in South America, but he attacked a Spanish settlement on his voyage and on returning to England was condemned and put to death. The following poem, "The Lie," was composed while Raleigh sat in the Tower of London awaiting his execution. Note: to "give the lie" means to accuse someone, publicly and directly, of lying. It is considered an insult; as Raleigh suggests in the final stanza, it might provoke the accused to violence. (See also Raleigh's "The Nymph's Reply to the Shepherd" and an image of the author in Chapter 13.)

Go, soul, the body's guest,
Upon a thankless errand;
Fear not to touch the best;
The truth shall be thy warrant.
Go, since I needs must die,
And give the world the lie.

Say to the court, it glows
And shines like rotten wood;
Say to the church, it shows
What's good, and doth no good.
If church and court reply,
Then give them both the lie.

Tell potentates,[1] they live
Acting by others' action;
Not loved unless they give,
Not strong but by a faction.
If potentates reply,
Give potentates[1] the lie.

Tell men of high condition,
That manage the estate,
Their purpose is ambition,
Their practice only hate.
And if they once reply,
Then give them all the lie.

Tell them that brave it most,
They beg for more by spending,
Who, in their greatest cost,
Seek nothing but commending.
And if they make reply,
Then give them all the lie.

[1]*potentates*: Those who have power and rule over others.

Tell zeal it wants devotion;
Tell love it is but lust;
Tell time it is but motion;
Tell flesh it is but dust.
And wish them not reply,
For thou must give the lie.

Tell age it daily wasteth;
Tell honor how it alters;
Tell beauty how she blasteth;
Tell favor how it falters.
And as they shall reply,
Give every one the lie.

Tell wit how much it wrangles
In tickle[2] points of niceness;
Tell wisdom she entangles
Herself in overwiseness.
And when they do reply,
Straight give them both the lie.

Tell physic of her boldness;
Tell skill it is pretension;
Tell charity of coldness;
Tell law it is contention.
And as they do reply,
So give them still the lie.

Tell fortune of her blindness;
Tell nature of decay;
Tell friendship of unkindness;
Tell justice of delay.
And if they will reply,
Then give them all the lie.

Tell arts they have no soundness,
But vary by esteeming;
Tell schools they want profoundness,
And stand too much on seeming.
If arts and schools reply,
Give arts and schools the lie.

Tell faith it's fled the city;
Tell how the country erreth;
Tell manhood shakes off pity;
Tell virtue least preferreth.

[2] *tickle*: Sensitive.

And if they do reply,
Spare not to give the lie.

So when thou hast, as I
Commanded thee, done blabbing—
Although to give the lie
Deserves no less than stabbing—
Stab at thee he that will,
No stab the soul can kill.

(ca. 1592)

QUESTIONS FOR DISCUSSION AND WRITING

CLOSE READING

1. What is the relationship between the soul and the body as Raleigh imagines it?
2. What worldly institutions does Raleigh attack, and what is his gripe with each of them?
3. What human traits does Raleigh attack? Are these attacks specific to his time and place, or do they apply to human nature in general?

CRITICAL AND CREATIVE READING

4. Raleigh does not spare any of the institutions and human traits that appear in his poem. What institutions or traits do not appear in his poem and thus are not part of his satire?
5. Write a version of the poem for contemporary times. What institutions and human traits would you address? Is it easy or difficult to preserve this poem's structure, meter, and rhyme scheme while substituting contemporary references?
6. What are the consequences of accusing people or institutions of falsehood? If you tried to "give the lie" to some person or institution today, what resistance would you meet? How would you be expected to defend your charges? What would be the most effective forum for your accusations (if not in a poem)?

CONNECTIONS TO OTHER READINGS

7. If Emily Dickinson's poem "Tell all the Truth, but tell it slant" is about the role of the poet, how would she react to Raleigh's speaker in "The Lie"? Is "The Lie" told "straight" or with a "slant"?
8. Compare notions of the truth in this poem to notions of the truth in Langston Hughes's "Theme for English B" and/or Paul Laurence Dunbar's "We Wear the Mask."
9. Think about Raleigh's notion that the *soul* must be the part of human experience that accuses human institutions and human behavior of falsehood. How could this concept be used to elucidate the theme of Salman Rushdie's story "The Prophet's Hair"?

William Shakespeare

When my love swears that she is made of truth (Sonnet 138)

Although Shakespeare is most familiar as a dramatist, his collection of 154 sonnets earned him a reputation as one of the most accomplished lyric poets of his time. Sonnet sequences were common among poets of the English Renaissance; most focused on the way a male lover idealized a single woman. Shakespeare's sonnets departed from this model. Critics point to three distinct sections in his sequence: an early section devoted to the growth and beauty of a young man, a long second section concerned with the destructive power of time and the redemptive power of art, and a third section (in which the following poem occurs) concentrating on a "dark lady," a seductive but potentially dangerous object of desire. Shakespeare was so influential that this type of sonnet, or fourteen-line poem, is often called the "Shakespearean sonnet." Each line is precise iambic pentameter (ten syllables following a unstressed/stressed pattern), and the poem has three quatrains (alternating rhymed pairs) with a couplet at the end (two consecutive rhymed lines). (See Chapter 5 for a more detailed discussion of these conventions.) How might this structure actually liberate a poet? (See also Chapter 13 for more examples of Shakespeare's sonnets and Chapter 16 for his play *I Henry IV* as well as his portrait.)

When my love swears that she is made of truth,
I do believe her, though I know she lies.
That she might think me some untutored youth,
Unlearnèd in the world's false subtleties.
Thus vainly thinking that she thinks me young,
Although she knows my days are past the best,
Simply I credit her false-speaking tongue:
On both sides thus is simple truth suppressed.
But wherefore says she not she is unjust?
And wherefore say not I that I am old?
Oh, love's best habit[1] is in seeming trust,
And age in love loves not to have years told.
Therefore I lie with her and she with me,
And in our faults by lies we flattered be.

(1609)

[1]*habit*: A customary practice; also means clothing.

QUESTIONS FOR DISCUSSION AND WRITING

CLOSE READING

1. How can the speaker both "believe" his lover and "know she lies" (line 2)?
2. List the words that Shakespeare repeats (or varies) in the poem; what is the effect of this repetition?
3. In the final quatrain (lines 9–12) the poet uses the word "not" three times; why does he express these ideas in the negative?

CRITICAL AND CREATIVE READING

4. Write a sonnet from the point of view of the speaker's lover. Assume that she, like the speaker, knows that she is being deceived, specifically about his age.
5. Is lying a form of power? If so, is that power diminished if each person knows that the other is lying (even if they don't let on that they know)? Use Sonnet 138 to illustrate your response.
6. What are the "world's false subtleties" the speaker alludes to in line 4?

CONNECTIONS TO OTHER READINGS

7. Use the idea expressed in line 11 ("Oh, love's best habit is in seeming trust") to analyze both this poem and Raymond Carver's "Jerry and Molly and Sam."
8. Compare this poem to Sir Walter Raleigh's poem "The Lie," published shortly before Sonnet 138. What accounts for the ways the two speakers approach the truth? Why wouldn't the speaker of Shakespeare's poem "give his lover the lie" (accuse her of lying)?
9. Based on *The Importance of Being Earnest*, how would Oscar Wilde respond to Shakespeare's speaker and his attitude toward lying and the truth?

Emily Dickinson

Tell all the Truth, but tell it slant (1129)

A woman known in her lifetime as a mysterious recluse, Emily Dickinson (1830–1886) is now considered one of the greatest lyric poets in American literature, if not the greatest. Raised in one of the most prominent families in picturesque Amherst, Massachusetts, Dickinson received an above-average education for a woman at that time and read widely, especially in the British literature of her era. Her quirky poetry with its trademark dashes and brilliant slippages was largely unpublished in her lifetime: following an early, strong desire to see her verse in print, Dickinson closed herself off from the publishing world and the world in general. Her more than 1,700 poems, published posthumously, continue to intrigue students and critics. (See also "Much Madness is divinest Sense" and her portrait in Chapter 12.)

Tell all the Truth but tell it slant—
Success in Circuit lies
Too bright for our infirm Delight
The Truth's superb surprise
As Lightning to the Children eased
With explanation kind
The Truth must dazzle gradually
Or every man be blind—

(c. 1868, 1945)

Questions for Discussion and Writing

Close Reading

1. What is Dickinson's definition of "success"? What are the possible meanings of "Success in Circuit" (line 2)?
2. The punctuation in this poem is unconventional, to say the least. Punctuate it as you see fit: how does your punctuation affect the meaning of the poem? Where does it place emphasis?
3. How does "Lightning" operate metaphorically, both as something to be explained and as something witnessed?

Critical and Creative Reading

4. Assume this poem can be applied to literature; what are some of the ways writers "Tell all the Truth but tell it slant"?
5. What would be an example of the truth dazzling too quickly? What effect would it have on its witness (the metaphorical "blindness" in Dickinson's formula)?
6. "Truth" is repeated three times in this short poem and capitalized each time. Is "truth" something unified and superior, as you see it? Put differently, is there one "Truth" or are there many "truths"?

Connections to Other Readings

7. Consider the situation in the stories by David Long ("Morphine") and Ann Beattie ("Weekend"). Could you say that the two men in these stories who cheat on their wives are "telling the truth slant," or are they simply concealing the truth?
8. What is the difference between "telling the truth slant" and lying? Compare Dickinson's poem to the poems by Raleigh, Shakespeare, and/or Wilbur in this section.
9. In what way does the speaker of this poem resemble the trickster figure, as featured in this chapter's Common Characters section?

Paul Laurence Dunbar

We Wear the Mask

Born to former slaves in the immediate aftermath of the American Civil War, Paul Laurence Dunbar (1872–1906) was influenced by the stories of his parents' experiences during that conflict. Although Dunbar achieved early critical success for his poetry, he fell out of favor with some early-twentieth-century critics for his reliance on dialect, the attempt to preserve authentic African American speech in verse. In addition to an impressive body of poetry, he managed to publish essays and multiple short story collections before his death of tuberculosis at an early age. The following poem, "We Wear the Mask," remains his most famous; it is often read as an example of what the African American critic W. E. B. Du Bois described as "double-consciousness," a mode of perception that causes black people to see themselves as filtered through the eyes of whites who might harbor racist stereotypes.

We wear the mask that grins and lies,
It hides our cheeks and shades our eyes,—
This debt we pay to human guile;
With torn and bleeding hearts we smile,
And mouth with myriad subtleties.

Why should the world be over-wise,
In counting all our tears and sighs?
Nay, let them only see us, while
  We wear the mask.

We smile, but, O great Christ, our cries
To thee from tortured souls arise.
We sing, but oh the clay is vile
Beneath our feet, and long the mile;
But let the world dream otherwise,
  We wear the mask!

(1913)

QUESTIONS FOR DISCUSSION AND WRITING

CLOSE READING

1. Compare the rhyme scheme and the length of the three stanzas; why might Dunbar have organized the poem this way?

2. Is there a pattern to the placement of the phrase "we wear the mask" within the poem?
3. Usually, "they" is the rhetorical opposite of "we"; what is the opposite of "we" in this poem, and how is it defined?

CRITICAL AND CREATIVE READING

4. Is "the mask" in this poem a positive or negative force?
5. Do people ever wear "masks" that do something besides grin and lie and hide their cheeks and shade their eyes? Do masks ever frown? When?
6. The headnote suggests that this poem is based on the black American experience in the tormented decades following the Civil War. If you remove that historical context, what other situations could this poem apply to?

CONNECTIONS TO OTHER READINGS

7. Use Dunbar's poem to analyze Oscar Wilde's play *The Importance of Being Earnest*. How is "bunburying" a version of "wearing the mask"?
8. Does the concept of the "mask" operate the same way here and in Mori Yoko's story "Spring Storm"?
9. What kinds of "masks" exist in Shakespeare's Sonnet 138? Are masks regarded the same way in these two poems?

Thomas Hardy

At Tea

British author Thomas Hardy (1840–1928) is known primarily as a novelist: *Tess of the D'Urbervilles, Jude the Obscure,* and *Far from the Madding Crowd* are still frequently read and taught in high school and college classrooms. Hardy marks the transition from the repression of the Victorian era to the depression of the modern era. About halfway through his career, in 1896, Hardy stopped writing novels and turned his attention to poetry (see also "The Ruined Maid" in the Common Characters section in Chapter 16). Certain themes unite the two halves of his career and the two genres that define them: a heavy emphasis on fate as the force that determines the outcome of human lives and pessimism about the ability of humankind to improve its condition.

The kettle descants in a cosy drone,
And the young wife looks in her husband's face,
And then at her guest's, and shows in her own
Her sense that she fills an envied place;
And the visiting lady is all abloom,
And says there was never so sweet a room.

And the happy young housewife does not know
That the woman beside her was first his choice,
Till the fates ordained it could not be so. . . .
Betraying nothing in look or voice
The guest sits smiling and sips her tea,
And he throws her a stray glance yearningly.

(1911)

QUESTIONS FOR DISCUSSION AND WRITING

CLOSE READING

1. Half of the lines in this short poem—six out of twelve—begin with the word "and." What is the effect of that repetition?
2. The poem depicts a scene that is full of visual details yet is largely silent. What sounds are described in the poem? How important are they to the poem's overall effect?
3. List as many differences between the first and second stanzas as you can; then discuss how the two stanzas work together.

CRITICAL AND CREATIVE READING

4. Why does the poet refrain from telling us exactly why the husband and the lady visitor did not marry, saying only "the fates ordained it could not be so. . . ."? What might the reason be? How would the poem read if the speaker had told us outright?
5. The title seems understated given the poem's agonizing subject; why do you think Hardy chose to name it "At Tea" as opposed to something like "Betrayal" or "A Stray Glance"?
6. Rewrite the poem using one of its three characters as the speaker.

CONNECTIONS TO OTHER READINGS

7. Compare the marital deception described in this poem to the marital deception described in one or more of the following three stories: David Long's "Morphine," Ann Beattie's "Weekend," and Raymond Carver's "Jerry and Molly and Sam."
8. Consider the way formal "polite" society creates deception in "At Tea" and in Edith Wharton's story "Roman Fever" (Chapter 15).
9. Based on this poem and Richard Wilbur's "Lying," discuss whether you think a little deception should be expected in marriage.

Langston Hughes

Theme for English B

Langston Hughes (1902–1967) is the most prominent writer associated with the literary period known as the Harlem Renaissance in America. Also called the New Negro Renaissance, this era, beginning in the 1920s, gave rise to a new set of traditions in African American literature and the arts. The development of jazz music coincided with the development of new ways of writing; like jazz, the writings of Langston Hughes and others were challenging and accessible. Hughes is a deceptively simple writer. His poems are expansive, a trait that reflects his development from someone born into humble circumstances in Missouri to a world traveler and international spokesman who wrote about large themes for a broad audience. How does the following poem connect the personal with more general themes?

The instructor said,

Go home and write
a page tonight.
And let that page come out of you—
Then, it will be true.

I wonder if it's that simple?
I am twenty-two, colored, born in Winston-Salem.
I went to school there, then Durham,[1] then here
to this college on the hill above Harlem.
I am the only colored student in my class.
The steps from the hill lead down into Harlem,
through a park, then I cross St. Nicholas,
Eighth Avenue, Seventh, and I come to the Y,
the Harlem Branch Y,[2] where I take the elevator
up to my room, sit down and write this page:

It's not easy to know what is true for you or me
at twenty-two, my age. But I guess I'm what
I feel and see and hear, Harlem, I hear you:
hear you, hear me—we two—you, me, talk on this page.
(I hear New York, too) Me—who?

[1]*Winston-Salem . . . Durham*: Cities in North Carolina.

[2]*Harlem Branch Y*: In Manhattan, the YMCA is a place for cultural events like readings and performances.

Well, I like to eat, sleep, drink, and be in love.
I like to work, read, learn, and understand life.
I like a pipe for a Christmas present,
or records—Bessie,[3] bop, or Bach.
I guess being colored doesn't make me *not* like
the same things other folks like who are other races.
So will my page be colored that I write?
Being me, it will not be white.
But it will be
a part of you, instructor.
You are white—
yet a part of me, as I am a part of you.
That's American.
Sometimes perhaps you don't want to be a part of me.
Nor do I often want to be a part of you.
But we are, that's true!
As I learn from you,
I guess you learn from me—
although you're older—and white—
and somewhat more free.

This is my page for English B.

(1949)

[3]*Bessie, bop, or Bach*: Bessie Smith (1892–1937) was an early blues singer. Bop was a style of jazz from the mid-twentieth century. Johann Sebastian Bach (1665–1750) was a German composer in the Baroque period.

QUESTIONS FOR DISCUSSION AND WRITING

CLOSE READING

1. Where does the speaker address the instructor directly? Where do we fit in as a general audience?
2. Take note of the end rhyme in this poem; is there a pattern?
3. Other than end rhyme, what poetic conventions does Hughes employ and to what effect?

CRITICAL AND CREATIVE READING

4. Why does the speaker question the statement "And let that page come out of you— / Then, it will be true"? Does true writing involve more than simply letting something "come out of you"?
5. How does the relationship between any writer and reader act as a metaphor for race relations in this poem? Would the poem be less effective if it were not based on a racial dichotomy (I'm black, you're white)?
6. Try writing a response to the "instructor's" assignment, a page that comes out of you. Is it "true"?

CONNECTIONS TO OTHER READINGS

7. Compare notions of the truth in Hughes's poem and in Sir Walter Raleigh's "The Lie." Do the speakers have similar goals in mind? Do they use similar methods?
8. Read Hughes's poem alongside Paul Laurence Dunbar's "We Wear the Mask." Is the speaker's response to his instructor's assignment a mask or an attempt to remove a mask?
9. Is there a danger to revealing too much about yourself? Consider Hughes's poem along with Emily Dickinson's "Tell all the Truth, but tell it slant."

Louise Glück

The Mountain

Louise Glück (b. 1943) was the U.S. poet laureate from 2003 to 2004, and her numerous awards include the Pulitzer Prize. Although she was raised and educated in New York, she is associated with Vermont, where she served as state poet, and with northwestern Massachusetts, where she has taught for over two decades at Williams College. Most famous for her short works, she has also produced long, lush poems. Uniting all of her poetry is an intense focus on emotion: she is clearly influenced by the confessional school of poetry, whose early representatives include Robert Lowell, Sylvia Plath, and Anne Sexton. All these writers create poetry that is deeply personal, honest, and autobiographical.

My students look at me expectantly.
I explain to them that the life of art is a life
of endless labor. Their expressions
hardly change; they need to know
a little more about endless labor.
So I tell them the story of Sisyphus,[1]
how he was doomed to push
a rock up a mountain, knowing nothing
would come of this effort
but that he would repeat it

[1]*Sisyphus:* In Greek mythology, Sisyphus angered the gods and was doomed to a punishment that involved rolling a boulder up a mountain, watching it roll back down, and rolling it back up again for eternity.

indefinitely. I tell them
there is joy in this, in the artist's life,
that one eludes
judgment, and as I speak
I am secretly pushing a rock myself,
slyly pushing it up the steep
face of a mountain. Why do I lie
to these children? They aren't listening,
they aren't deceived, their fingers
tapping at the wooden desks—
So I retract
the myth; I tell them it occurs
in hell, and that the artist lies
because he is obsessed with attainment,
that he perceives the summit
as that place where he will live forever,
a place about to be
transformed by his burden: with every breath,
I am standing at the top of the mountain.
Both my hands are free. And the rock has added
height to the mountain.

(1985)

QUESTIONS FOR DISCUSSION AND WRITING

CLOSE READING

1. What is the "lie" the speaker tells her students in lines 17 and 18?
2. Explain the metaphor of the mountain in this poem. (It may signify more than one thing.)
3. What is the difference between the story of Sisyphus and the speaker's life?

CRITICAL AND CREATIVE READING

4. Why would a teacher "deceive" his or her students, deliberately or not?
5. Is it ethical for an artist to lie "because he is obsessed with attainment"? Shouldn't artists tell the truth?
6. Why do you suppose the poem emphasizes the "wooden desks" of her students as the only physical detail in the poem?

CONNECTIONS TO OTHER READINGS

7. Compare the teacher-student relationship in this poem with that in Langston Hughes's "Theme for English B."
8. Discuss whether the role of art in Emily Dickinson's "Tell all the Truth, but tell it slant" is fundamentally similar to the role of art in "The Mountain."
9. Discuss the use of allusion in "The Mountain" and in Richard Wilbur's "Lying."

Richard Wilbur

Lying

Richard Wilbur (b. 1921) was the second poet laureate of the United States (after Robert Penn Warren) from 1987 to 1988. Educated at Amherst College and Harvard University, Wilbur served in the army during World War II and returned to publish a number of collections that received great acclaim during the 1950s, the decade in which his fame reached its apex. His poetry, a comprehensive collection of which was published in 2004, is characterized by precise observation of the details of the familiar world. His wife, on first reading the following poem, described it as "incomprehensible from beginning to end," then grew to like it on later readings. You might have a similar experience.

To claim, at a dead party, to have spotted a grackle[1]
When in fact you haven't of late, can do no harm.
Your reputation for saying things of interest
Will not be marred, if you hasten to other topics,
Nor will the delicate web of human trust
Be ruptured by that airy fabrication.
Later, however, talking with toxic zest
Of golf, or taxes, or the rest of it
Where the beaked ladle plies the chuckling ice,
You may enjoy a chill of severance, hearing
Above your head the shrug of unreal wings.
Not that the world is tiresome in itself:
We know what boredom is: it is a dull
Impatience or a fierce velleity,[2]
A champing wish, stalled by our lassitude,
To make or do. In the strict sense, of course,
We invent nothing, merely bearing witness
To what each morning brings again to light:
Gold crosses, cornices, astonishment
Of panes, the turbine-vent which natural law
Spins on the grill-end of the diner's roof,
Then grass and grackles or, at the end of town
In sheen-swept pastureland, the horse's neck
Clothed with its usual thunder, and the stones

[1]*grackle*: A crowlike bird.
[2]*velleity*: A low-level wish.

Beginning now to tug their shadows in
And track the air with glitter. All these things
Are there before us; there before we look
Or fail to look; there to be seen or not
By us, as by the bee's twelve thousand eyes,
According to our means and purposes.
So too with strangeness not to be ignored,
Total eclipse or snow upon the rose,
And so with that most rare conception, nothing.
What is it, after all, but something missed?
It is the water of a dried-up well
Gone to assail the cliffs of Labrador.[3]
There is what galled the arch-negator, sprung
From Hell to probe with intellectual sight
The cells and heavens of a given world
Which he could take but as another prison:
Small wonder that, pretending not to be,
He drifted through the bar-like boles of Eden
In a *black mist low creeping*, dragging down
And darkening with moody self-absorption
What, when he left it, lifted and, if seen
From the sun's vantage, seethed with vaulting hues.
Closer to making than the deftest fraud
Is seeing how the catbird's tail was made
To counterpoise, on the mock-orange spray,
Its light, up-tilted spine; or, lighter still,
How the shucked tunic of an onion, brushed
To one side on a backlit chopping-board
And rocked by trifling currents, prints and prints
Its bright, ribbed shadow like a flapping sail.
Odd that a thing is most itself when likened:
The eye mists over, basil hints of clove,
The river glazes toward the dam and spills
To the drubbed rocks below its crashing cullet,
And in the barnyard near the sawdust-pile
Some great thing is tormented. Either it is
A tarp torn loose and in the groaning wind
Now puffed, now flattened, or a hip-shot beast
Which tries again, and once again, to rise.
What, though for pain there is no other word,
Finds pleasure in the cruellest simile?
It is something in us like the catbird's song
From neighbor bushes in the grey of morning

[3]*cliffs of Labrador*: In Newfoundland, Canada. Its cliffs were visited by Norse seamen in the tenth century.

That, harsh or sweet, and of its own accord,
Proclaims its many kin. It is a chant
Of the first springs, and it is tributary
To the great lies told with the eyes half-shut
That have the truth in view: the tale of Chiron[4]
Who, with sage head, wild heart, and planted hoof
Instructed brute Achilles[5] in the lyre,
Or of the garden where we first mislaid
Simplicity of wish and will, forgetting
Out of what cognate splendor all things came
To take their scattering names; and nonetheless
That matter of a baggage-train surprised
By a few Gascons[6] in the Pyrenees
Which, having worked three centuries and more
In the dark caves of France, poured out at last
The blood of Roland,[7] who to Charles his king
And to the dove that hatched the dove-tailed world
Was faithful unto death, and shamed the Devil.

(1989)

Questions for Discussion and Writing

Close Reading

1. What is the speaker saying about his wife's idle lie at a party and the nature of reality?
2. What is the role of the devil ("arch-negator") in this poem?
3. The speaker says, "Odd that a thing is most itself when likened." What does he mean, and how is that idea illustrated in the poem?

Critical and Creative Reading

4. The poet goes from a glib, ordinary observation of his wife to, among other subjects, Greek mythology, French history, and biblical legend. How does he get to these other subjects? What is the relationship in literature between ordinary observation and allusion to things outside our experience?
5. What are "the great lies told with the eyes half-shut / That have the truth in view"?
6. Do you agree or disagree with the poet's assertion "In the strict sense, of course, / We invent nothing"? Consider the whole poem in your response.

[4]*Chiron:* According to Greek legend, the tutor of Achilles and Hercules and a centaur: half-man, half-horse.

[5]*Achilles:* A Greek hero from the *Iliad*.

[6]*Gascons:* People from the Basque region.

[7]*Roland:* A medieval French hero who was the nephew of Charlemagne and defender of Christianity. He was killed in an eighth-century battle.

CONNECTIONS TO OTHER READINGS

7. What is the value of the truth in this poem and in Oscar Wilde's play *The Importance of Being Earnest?*
8. How does lying act as a form of entertainment in this poem and in the story "Spring Storm" by Mori Yoko? Is it the same kind of entertainment in both cases?
9. Compare the relationship described in this poem to the relationship described in Shakespeare's Sonnet 138.

Mark Halperin

The Escape

Mark Halperin (b. 1938) is the author of four volumes of poetry, with a fifth, *Falling Through the Music* due out soon. Although Halperin's early college training was in physics, he earned an M.F.A in poetry and teaches poetry at Central Washington University. In addition to his poetry collections, Halperin is the coauthor of *Accent on Meter*, a guide for reading poetry. The recipient of multiple Fulbright fellowships, he has also taught abroad in Japan, Estonia, and repeatedly in Russia. His interest in Russia has also led him to translate Russian authors, especially Viktor Sosnora. The following poem is from his 2002 collection *Time as Distance*.

Amused when she asks, *is your wife Jewish?* and,
because it's easier, because I don't
want to think, I answer *yes*. It's the first time.
Later, a pushy man wants to know my
son's birthday. Confused, I make him younger
and the shift of dates feels so natural

I let it stand. Then it's happening with family
names, with where I work, how long, with
whom—minor changes in my *vita*, small alterations,
other lives, one variant for this person,
another for that, as though I were picking out
ballpoint pens or books, rummaging for

keep-sakes to give away, a different self to
each, each time. Months pass before I

catch on too and admit I've done what I did out of
caution, an attempt to screen the self,
erase the scent, obscure the trail with a series
of dead-ends until no one could thread

a way ahead through those dense thickets back to
me, reeking of fear, what did I think I
had worth hiding and who was I trying to deceive?
Tell me: surrounded by those casual lies
fabricating with disarming aplomb, why didn't I ask
whose escape I imagined I was fashioning?

(2002)

Questions for Discussion and Writing

Close Reading

1. What is the difference between the speaker's first explanation of his reason for lying and his second?
2. He compares his acts of lying to "picking out / ballpoint pens or books" (lines 11–12): how does the comparison work?
3. What is the effect of addressing the reader directly in line 22 ("Tell me:")?

Critical and Creative Reading

4. Is the speaker of "The Escape" revealing something crucial about his personality in the final two stanzas of the poem?
5. Is the speaker like most people in his tendency to make "minor changes" to the details of his life when people ask him questions? Does everyone lie? If so, are this speaker's explanations for his own behavior useful in analyzing human nature in general?
6. What do you think the speaker is trying to hide? Explain by writing a brief monologue from the point of view of the speaker.

Connections to Other Readings

7. The speaker of Richard Wilbur's "Lying" notices that his wife tells meaningless little lies, not much different from the ones the speaker of "The Escape" tells. Why do the poems go in different directions?
8. To what degree is the speaker of "The Escape" following (or not following) Emily Dickinson's poetic advice to "Tell all the Truth, but tell it slant"?
9. Discuss the notions of deception and escape in this poem and in Oscar Wilde's play *The Importance of Being Ernest*.

Jessica Greenbaum

Sonnets for the Autobiographical Urban Dweller

Jessica Greenbaum (b. 1957) was born in Brooklyn, New York City, and earned her M.A. in creative writing at the University of Houston. Her first poetry collection, *Inventing Difficulty* (2000), received the Gerald Cable Book Award, and she has also received the P.E.N. Emerging Writer award. Her poems, criticism, and personal essays have appeared in the *New Yorker*, the *Gettysburg Review*, *Ploughshares*, *Kenyon Review*, *Partisan Review*, *The Nation*, *Salamander*, and elsewhere. She lives in Brooklyn with her husband and two daughters.

This little room fills up with light. It's big
when you consider all the ways to re-
configure books, or how the walls bow, rigged
to hold whole lives, which, often, neighbors see
and hear. The urge to frame one's tale takes hold,
then, mirrored, gives you pause. This window's wide,
but honesty as policy? Truth told:
to share shared stories we both show *and* hide,
or coat our private parts of speech, because
regardless of our tender subjects we
tilt, bare, toward sunlit panes, parlaying flaws
to blushed, polite applause. It's our *esprit.*[1]
Dark days I tend the window box—looks good—
then pull the shades down on our neighborhood.

(2004)

Questions for Writing and Discussion

Close Reading

1. The poem begins with an observation of a light day and concludes with an observation of a dark day: how does this transition frame the poem's themes?
2. Consider and discuss the relationship between windows and stories in this poem.
3. How does the room that is the setting for this poem act as a metaphor?

[1]*esprit*: Spirit (French).

Critical and Creative Reading

4. The introduction to this chapter questioned the cliché "Honesty is the best policy." Discuss how that cliché is addressed in this poem and in your own experience. What does the word "policy" imply?
5. Write a sonnet with your room as its subject.
6. How do books and language figure in this poem?

Connections to Other Readings

7. Compare this poem as a sonnet to Shakespeare's Sonnet 138 in this chapter. How does Greenbaum depart from the sonnet form? Does she build an "argument" the same way Shakespeare does? (You might consult the definition of a sonnet in Chapter 5: "Reading and Writing about Poetry.")
8. Discuss the notion of "truth-telling" in this poem and in Dickinson's "Tell all the Truth but tell it slant."
9. Compare the theme of this poem to the theme of Paul Laurence Dunbar's "We Wear the Mask."

Melissa Kwasny

Deception

Melissa Kwasny (b. 1954), a native of Indiana, has become associated with the state of Montana. After graduating from the University of Montana she moved to San Francisco, where she taught in the Poets in the Schools program, but she has since returned to rural Montana. She is the author of a collection of poems (*Archival Birds*) and of two unconventional novels. She is also the editor of *Toward the Open Field: Poets on the Art of Poetry 1800–1950*. In "Deception," the title should be read as the first word of the poem.

Has a glow to it, distant and round at the end of the mine
shaft, a yellow malignant light.

Once seen, it loses power, becomes tarnished and dull
as river stones, lifted from their affair with water.

Money that has lain too long in the vault no longer has value.
The currencies we so believed in have changed.

To build the secret cell ultimately will involve torture.
One forgets where one has come from, one's companions.

Announces itself with the loud cacophony of trapped birds,
intercepted en route to their illegal sale.

There is a truth in it, which is suffocating, buried somewhere
alive. There is the dress left un-hemmed, drain field sinking.

One wants to believe in a strong voice, the snare
the earth caves into, the stinking pool of rotting timbers, sod.

The din is the din of I did not choose this.
Though one is left fingering the beads of deception in the dark.

Deception holds us sweetly while it carves with a dull knife.
Then the dreams begin so even sleep is unsafe for us.

Deception has a partner, sometimes a twin, whose face
turns away from us. Whose hair is an unnatural shade of red.

They are experts in erasure, transforming words into a story
we all want to believe: one that isn't anyone else's business.

Deception swallows all other points of view, and hence,
there are no lies. Blind-side. Hoodwink. Always a catch.

All that we banked on slid into the stream during the rains.
Silt, that solidity a deception. A lover turns an ugly face toward us.

And the deceived? She is losing her feathers. She has eaten
her foot. She exists with the ghost-letters, the forgotten language.

(2005)

QUESTIONS FOR DISCUSSION AND WRITING

CLOSE READING

1. Trace all the metaphors and similes Kwasny uses in her contemplation of deception: is there a pattern to them?
2. Discuss the imagery of capture and torture throughout the poem.
3. How does the poem's concluding stanza resolve the imagery of the rest of the poem?

CRITICAL AND CREATIVE READING

4. In line 19, the speaker claims that "Deception has a partner," then goes on to describe that partner. How would you describe deception's partner in nonmetaphorical language?

5. Write an essay about the usefulness of the following lines that begin the twelfth stanza: "Deception swallows all other points of view, and hence, / there are no lies."
6. Retype the poem, omitting its title, the word "deception" from the beginning of stanzas 9, 10, and 12, and the word "deceived" from the final stanza. (Leave blank spaces where these words had been.) Then give the revised version to others who have not read the poem and ask them to figure out its title and the omitted words. Were they able to come up with the word "deception"? If so, how did they figure it out? If not, how does the word they came up with compare to "deception"?

CONNECTIONS TO OTHER READINGS

7. Use Kwasny's interpretation of deception to comment on David Long's story "Morphine."
8. Discuss the importance of metaphor in this poem and in Glück's "The Mountain," Dunbar's "We Wear the Mask," and Greenbaum's "Sonnets for the Autobiographical Urban Dweller."
9. The themes of this chapter can be treated lightly (as in Wilbur's poem "Lying," Oscar Wilde's play, *The Importance of Being Earnest*, or some of the stories of trickster figures in the Common Characters section) or seriously (as in Ann Beattie's story "Weekend," Dunbar's poem "We Wear the Mask," or this poem by Kwasny). Using these examples or others from this chapter, consider whether light or serious treatments of honesty and deception reveal more insight into human nature.

Natasha Trethewey

Letter Home

Natasha Trethewey (b. 1966) was born in Mississippi and earned her M.F.A. in poetry from the University of Massachusetts. The author of three collections of poetry, Trethewey is the recipient of numerous awards and fellowships. She was selected by Rita Dove as the inaugural recipient of the Cave Canem poetry prize for the best collection of poetry by an African American author. The following poem, "Letter Home," has as its background the history of "passing"– the attempt by certain light-skinned black Americans in post–Civil War America to "pass as white" by affecting the manner, dress, and speech of white people. (See also Charles Chesnutt's story "The Wife of His Youth" in this chapter.)

New Orleans, November 1910

Four weeks have passed since I left, and still
I must write to you of no work. I've worn down
the soles and walked through the tightness
of my new shoes calling upon the merchants,
their offices bustling. All the while I kept thinking
my plain English and good writing would secure
for me some modest position. Though I dress each day
in my best, hands covered with the lace gloves
you crocheted—no one needs a *girl*. How flat
the word sounds, and heavy. My purse thins,
I spend foolishly to make an appearance of quiet
industry, to mask the desperation that tightens
my throat. I sit watching—

though I pretend not to notice—the dark maids
ambling by with their white charges. Do I deceive
anyone? Were they to see my hands, brown
as your dear face, they'd know I'm not quite
what I pretend to be. I walk these streets
a white woman, or so I think, until I catch the eyes
of some stranger upon me, and I must lower mine,
a *negress* again. There are enough things here
to remind me who I am. Mules lumbering through
the crowded streets send me into reverie, their footfall
the sound of a pointer and chalk hitting the blackboard
at school, only louder. Then there are women, clicking
their tongues in conversation, carrying their loads
on their heads. Their husky voices, the wash pots
and irons of the laundresses call to me.

I thought not to do the work I once did, back bending
and domestic; my schooling a gift—even those half days
at picking time, listening to Miss J—. How
I'd come to know words, the recitations I practiced
to sound like her, lilting, my sentences curling up
or trailing off at the ends. I read my books until
I nearly broke their spines, and in the cotton field,
I repeated whole sections I'd learned by heart,
spelling each word in my head to make a picture
I could see, as well as a weight I could feel
in my mouth. So now, even as I write this
and think of you at home, *Goodbye*

is the waving map of your palm, is
a stone on my tongue.

(2002)

Questions for Discussion and Writing

Close Reading

1. What are the various ways the speaker is "not quite / what [she] pretend[s] to be" (lines 17–18)?
2. How is the setting ("New Orleans, November 1910") significant?
3. The speaker explicitly discusses language: what is she emphasizing by doing so?

Critical and Creative Reading

4. The poem is entitled "Letter Home." Does the speaker's language sound more like that of a letter or of a poem? What is the difference?
5. How are work and education tied up with racial identity in this poem?
6. Explain the significance of the two metaphorical interpretations of the word "Goodbye" in the final stanza of the poem.

Connections to Other Readings

7. Discuss the implications of "passing for white" in "Letter Home" and in Charles Chesnutt's story "The Wife of His Youth."
8. Use the metaphor of the "mask" from Paul Laurence Dunbar's poem "We Wear the Mask" as a way of discussing Trethewey's poem.
9. In Langston Hughes's poem "Theme for English B" the speaker wonders if an essay that comes from him with a specific audience (his instructor) can be "true." Write an essay based on Hughes's poem and on "Letter Home" discussing the relationship between truth and writing.

Drama

Oscar Wilde

The Importance of Being Earnest

A Trivial Comedy for Serious People

Oscar Wilde was born in 1854 in Ireland. After studying on a scholarship at Trinity College in Dublin, Wilde received another scholarship to study at Oxford, where he was influenced by the prominent critics John Ruskin and Walter Pater. Having excelled in Greek at Trinity College, Wilde developed into an aesthete at Oxford, someone who idealized art and beauty. He became associated with the phrase "art for art's sake" and was a proponent of the pursuit of beauty in all things. He made a sensation by dressing in flamboyant clothing, a habit that caused him to stand out in the genteel, conservative London of the late nineteenth century. Wilde made his living initially through selling poetry, writing plays, and lecturing in Paris and the United States as well as England. He married Constance Mary Lloyd in 1884, and the couple had two children. Wilde's career flourished in the 1890s, a decade that saw the publication of his only novel (*The Picture of Dorian Gray*, 1891) and the majority of his plays, including his masterpiece *The Importance of Being Earnest* (1895), reprinted here. The last five years of Wilde's life were marked by scandal and tragedy. Following an affair with a young man, he was found guilty of gross indecency and sentenced to two years of hard labor in prison. Constance moved to Switzerland, taking their children with her. Following his release from jail, Wilde spent the last three years of his life largely alone and ostracized; he died from complications following a recurrent ear infection in 1900. The themes of this chapter—honesty, deception, secrets, and masks—are evident in this play.

FIRST ACT

Scene: Morning-room in Algernon's flat in Half Moon Street. The room is luxuriously and artistically furnished. The sound of a piano is heard in the adjoining room.

[Lane is arranging afternoon tea on the table, and after the music has ceased, Algernon enters.]

Algernon: Did you hear what I was playing, Lane?
Lane: I didn't think it polite to listen, sir.
Algernon: I'm sorry for that, for your sake. I don't play accurately—anyone can play accurately—but I play with wonderful expression. As far as the piano is concerned, sentiment is my forte. I keep science for Life.
Lane: Yes, sir.
Algernon: And, speaking of the science of Life, have you got the cucumber sandwiches cut for Lady Bracknell?
Lane: Yes, sir. [*Hands them on a salver.*]
Algernon [*inspects them, takes two, and sits down on the sofa*]: Oh! . . . by the way, Lane, I see from your book[1] that on Thursday night, when Lord Shoreham and Mr Worthing were dining with me, eight bottles of champagne are entered as having been consumed.
Lane: Yes, sir; eight bottles and a pint.
Algernon: Why is it that at a bachelor's establishment the servants invariably drink the champagne? I ask merely for information.
Lane: I attribute it to the superior quality of the wine, sir. I have often observed that in married households the champagne is rarely of a first-rate brand.
Algernon: Good Heavens! Is marriage so demoralizing as that?

[1]*your book*: A volume in which wines purchased and consumed were recorded.

Scene from a stage version of *The Importance of Being Earnest* by Oscar Wilde.

Lane: I believe it *is* a very pleasant state, sir. I have had very little experience of it myself up to the present. I have only been married once. That was in consequence of a misunderstanding between myself and a young person.

Algernon [*languidly*]: I don't know that I am much interested in your family life, Lane.

Lane: No, sir; it is not a very interesting subject. I never think of it myself.

Algernon: Very natural, I am sure. That will do, Lane, thank you.

Lane: Thank you, sir. [*Lane goes out.*]

Algernon: Lane's views on marriage seem somewhat lax. Really, if the lower orders don't set us a good example, what on earth is the use of them? They seem, as a class, to have absolutely no sense of moral responsibility.

[Enter Lane.]

Lane: Mr Ernest Worthing.

[Enter Jack. Lane goes out.]

Algernon: How are you, my dear Ernest? What brings you up to town?

Jack: Oh, pleasure, pleasure! What else should bring one anywhere? Eating as usual, I see, Algy!

Algernon [*stiffly*]: I believe it is customary in good society to take some slight refreshment at five o'clock. Where have you been since last Thursday?

Jack [*sitting down on the sofa*]: In the country.

Algernon: What on earth do you do there?

Jack [*pulling off his gloves*]: When one is in town one amuses oneself. When one is in the country one amuses other people. It is excessively boring.

Algernon: And who are the people you amuse?

Jack [*airily*]: Oh, neighbours, neighbours.

Algernon: Got nice neighbours in your part of Shropshire?

Jack: Perfectly horrid! Never speak to one of them.

Algernon: How immensely you must amuse them! [*Goes over and takes sandwich.*] By the way, Shropshire is your county, is it not?

Jack: Eh? Shropshire? Yes, of course. Hallo! Why all these cups? Why cucumber sandwiches? Why such reckless extravagance in one so young? Who is coming to tea?

Algernon: Oh! merely Aunt Augusta and Gwendolen.

Jack: How perfectly delightful!

Algernon: Yes, that is all very well; but I am afraid Aunt Augusta won't quite approve of your being here.

Jack: May I ask why?

Algernon: My dear fellow, the way you flirt with Gwendolen is perfectly disgraceful. It is almost as bad as the way Gwendolen flirts with you.

Jack: I am in love with Gwendolen. I have come up to town expressly to propose to her.

Algernon: I thought you had come up for pleasure? . . . I call that business.

Jack: How utterly unromantic you are!

Algernon: I really don't see anything romantic in proposing. It is very romantic to be in love. But there is nothing romantic about a definite proposal. Why, one may be accepted. One usually is, I believe. Then the excitement is all over. The very essence of romance is uncertainty. If I ever get married, I'll certainly try to forget the fact.

Jack: I have no doubt about that, dear Algy. The Divorce Court was specially invented for people whose memories are so curiously constituted.

Algernon: Oh! there is no use speculating on that subject. Divorces are made in Heaven—[*Jack puts out his hand to take a sandwich. Algernon at once interferes.*] Please don't touch the cucumber sandwiches. They are ordered specially for Aunt Augusta. [*Takes one and eats it.*]

Jack: Well, you have been eating them all the time.

Algernon: That is quite a different matter. She is my aunt. [*Takes plate from below.*] Have some bread and butter. The bread and butter is for Gwendolen. Gwendolen is devoted to bread and butter.

Jack [*advancing to table and helping himself*]: And very good bread and butter it is too.

Algernon: Well, my dear fellow, you need not eat as if you were going to eat it all. You behave as if you were married to her already. You are not married to her already, and I don't think you ever will be.

Jack: Why on earth do you say that?

Algernon: Well, in the first place girls never marry the men they flirt with. Girls don't think it right.

Jack: Oh, that is nonsense!

Algernon: It isn't. It is a great truth. It accounts for the extraordinary number of bachelors that one sees all over the place. In the second place, I don't give my consent.

Jack: Your consent!

Algernon: My dear fellow, Gwendolen is my first cousin. And before I allow you to marry her, you will have to clear up the whole question of Cecily. [*Rings bell.*]

Jack: Cecily! What on earth do you mean? What do you mean, Algy, by Cecily? I don't know anyone of the name of Cecily.

[Enter Lane.]

Algernon: Bring me that cigarette case Mr Worthing left in the smoking-room the last time he dined here.

Lane: Yes, sir. [*Lane goes out.*]

Jack: Do you mean to say you have had my cigarette case all this time? I wish to goodness you had let me know. I have been writing frantic letters to Scotland Yard about it. I was very nearly offering a large reward.

Algernon: Well, I wish you would offer one. I happen to be more than usually hard up.

Jack: There is no good offering a large reward now that the thing is found.

[Enter Lane with the cigarette case on a salver. Algernon takes it at once. Lane goes out.]

Algernon: I think that is rather mean of you, Ernest, I must say. [*Opens case and examines it.*] However, it makes no matter, for, now that I look at the inscription inside, I find that the thing isn't yours after all.

Jack: Of course it's mine. [*Moving to him.*] You have seen me with it a hundred times, and you have no right whatsoever to read what is written inside. It is a very ungentlemanly thing to read a private cigarette case.

Algernon: Oh! it is absurd to have a hard-and-fast rule about what one should read and what one shouldn't. More than half of modern culture depends on what one shouldn't read.

Jack: I am quite aware of the fact, and I don't propose to discuss modern culture. It isn't the sort of thing one should talk of in private. I simply want my cigarette case back.

Algernon: Yes; but this isn't your cigarette case. This cigarette case is a present from someone of the name of Cecily, and you said you didn't know anyone of that name.

Jack: Well, if you want to know, Cecily happens to be my aunt.

Algernon: Your aunt!

Jack: Yes. Charming old lady she is, too. Lives at Tunbridge Wells.[2] Just give it back to me, Algy.

[2]*Tunbridge Wells:* A resort town outside London.

Algernon [*retreating to back of sofa*]: But why does she call herself little Cecily if she is your aunt and lives at Tunbridge Wells? [*Reading.*] "From little Cecily with her fondest love."

Jack [*moving to sofa and kneeling upon it*]: My dear fellow, what on earth is there in that? Some aunts are tall, some aunts are not tall. That is a matter that surely an aunt may be allowed to decide for herself. You seem to think that every aunt should be exactly like your aunt! That is absurd! For Heaven's sake give me back my cigarette case. [*Follows Algernon round the room.*]

Algernon: Yes. But why does your aunt call you her uncle? "From little Cecily, with her fondest love to her dear Uncle Jack." There is no objection, I admit, to an aunt being a small aunt, but why an aunt, no matter what her size may be, should call her own nephew her uncle, I can't quite make out. Besides, your name isn't Jack at all; it is Ernest.

Jack: It isn't Ernest; it's Jack.

Algernon: You have always told me it was Ernest. I have introduced you to everyone as Ernest. You answer to the name of Ernest. You look as if your name was Ernest. You are the most earnest looking person I ever saw in my life. It is perfectly absurd your saying that your name isn't Ernest. It's on your cards. Here is one of them. [*Taking it from case.*] "Mr Ernest Worthing, B. 4, The Albany.[3]" I'll keep this as a proof that your name is Ernest if ever you attempt to deny it to me, or to Gwendolen, or to anyone else. [*Puts the card in his pocket.*]

Jack: Well, my name is Ernest in town and Jack in the country, and the cigarette case was given to me in the country.

Algernon: Yes, but that does not account for the fact that your small Aunt Cecily, who lives at Tunbridge Wells, calls you her dear uncle. Come, old boy, you had much better have the thing out at once.

Jack: My dear Algy, you talk exactly as if you were a dentist. It is very vulgar to talk like a dentist when one isn't a dentist. It produces a false impression.

Algernon: Well, that is exactly what dentists always do. Now, go on! Tell me the whole thing. I may mention that I have always suspected you of being a confirmed and secret Bunburyist, and I am quite sure of it now.

Jack: Bunburyist? What on earth do you mean by a Bunburyist?

Algernon: I'll reveal to you the meaning of that incomparable expression as soon as you are kind enough to inform me why you are Ernest in town and Jack in the country.

Jack: Well, produce my cigarette case first.

Algernon: Here it is. [*Hands cigarette case.*] Now produce your explanation, and pray make it improbable. [*Sits on sofa.*]

Jack: My dear fellow, there is nothing improbable about my explanation at all. In fact it's perfectly ordinary. Old Mr Thomas Cardew, who adopted me when I was a little boy, made me in his will guardian to his granddaughter, Miss Cecily Cardew. Cecily who addresses me as her uncle from motives of

[3]*The Albany*: A fashionable apartment building.

respect that you could not possibly appreciate, lives at my place in the country under the charge of her admirable governess, Miss Prism.

Algernon: Where is that place in the country, by the way?

Jack: That is nothing to you, dear boy. You are not going to be invited. . . . I may tell you candidly that the place is not in Shropshire.

Algernon: I suspected that, my dear fellow! I have Bunburyed all over Shropshire on two separate occasions. Now, go on. Why are you Ernest in town and Jack in the country?

Jack: My dear Algy, I don't know whether you will be able to understand my real motives. You are hardly serious enough. When one is placed in the position of guardian, one has to adopt a very high moral tone on all subjects. It's one's duty to do so. And as a high moral tone can hardly be said to conduce very much to either one's health or one's happiness, in order to get up to town I have always pretended to have a younger brother of the name of Ernest, who lives in the Albany, and gets into the most dreadful scrapes. That, my dear Algy, is the whole truth pure and simple.

Algernon: The truth is rarely pure and never simple. Modern life would be very tedious if it were either, and modern literature a complete impossibility!

Jack: That wouldn't be at all a bad thing.

Algernon: Literary criticism is not your forte, my dear fellow. Don't try it. You should leave that to people who haven't been at a University. They do it so well in the daily papers. What you really are is a Bunburyist. I was quite right in saying you were a Bunburyist. You are one of the most advanced Bunburyists I know.

Jack: What on earth do you mean?

Algernon: You have invented a very useful younger brother called Ernest, in order that you may be able to come up to town as often as you like. I have invented an invaluable permanent invalid called Bunbury, in order that I may be able to go down into the country whenever I choose. Bunbury is perfectly invaluable. If it wasn't for Bunbury's extraordinary bad health, for instance, I wouldn't be able to dine with you at Willis's tonight, for I have been really engaged to Aunt Augusta for more than a week.

Jack: I haven't asked you to dine with me anywhere tonight.

Algernon: I know. You are absurdly careless about sending out invitations. It is very foolish of you. Nothing annoys people so much as not receiving invitations.

Jack: You had much better dine with your Aunt Augusta.

Algernon: I haven't the smallest intention of doing anything of the kind. To begin with, I dined there on Monday, and once a week is quite enough to dine with one's own relations. In the second place, whenever I do dine there I am always treated as a member of the family, and sent down with either no woman at all, or two. In the third place, I know perfectly well whom she will place me next to, tonight. She will place me next Mary Farquhar, who always flirts with her own husband across the dinner-table. That is not very pleasant. Indeed, it is not even decent . . . and that sort of thing is enormously on the increase. The amount of women in London who flirt with their own husbands is perfectly scandalous. It looks so bad. It is simply washing one's clean linen in public. Besides, now that I know you to be a confirmed Bunburyist I naturally want to talk to you about Bunburying. I want to tell you the rules.

Jack: I'm not a Bunburyist at all. If Gwendolen accepts me, I am going to kill my brother, indeed I think I'll kill him in any case. Cecily is a little too much interested in him. It is rather a bore. So I am going to get rid of Ernest. And I strongly advise you to do the same with Mr . . . with your invalid friend who has the absurd name.

Algernon: Nothing will induce me to part with Bunbury, and if you ever get married, which seems to me extremely problematic, you will be very glad to know Bunbury. A man who marries without knowing Bunbury has a very tedious time of it.

Jack: That is nonsense. If I marry a charming girl like Gwendolen, and she is the only girl I ever saw in my life that I would marry, I certainly won't want to know Bunbury.

Algernon: Then your wife will. You don't seem to realize, that in married life three is company and two is none.

Jack [*sententiously*]: That, my dear young friend, is the theory that the corrupt French Drama has been propounding for the last fifty years.

Algernon: Yes; and that the happy English home has proved in half the time.

Jack: For heaven's sake, don't try to be cynical. It's perfectly easy to be cynical.

Algernon: My dear fellow, it isn't easy to be anything nowadays. There's such a lot of beastly competition about. [*The sound of an electric bell is heard.*] Ah! that must be Aunt Augusta. Only relatives, or creditors, ever ring in that Wagnerian manner.[4] Now, if I get her out of the way for ten minutes, so that you can have an opportunity for proposing to Gwendolen, may I dine with you tonight at Willis's?

Jack: I suppose so, if you want to.

Algernon: Yes, but you must be serious about it. I hate people who are not serious about meals. It is so shallow of them.

[Enter Lane.]

Lane: Lady Bracknell and Miss Fairfax.

[Algernon goes forward to meet them. Enter Lady Bracknell and Gwendolen.]

Lady Bracknell: Good afternoon, dear Algernon, I hope you are behaving very well.

Algernon: I'm feeling very well, Aunt Augusta.

Lady Bracknell: That's not quite the same thing. In fact the two things rarely go together. [*Sees Jack and bows to him with icy coldness.*]

Algernon [*to Gwendolen*]: Dear me, you are smart!

Gwendolen: I am always smart! Aren't I, Mr Worthing?

[4]*Wagnerian manner*: In the style of the German composer Richard Wagner (1813–1883)—that is, loud and insistent.

Jack: You're quite perfect, Miss Fairfax.

Gwendolen: Oh! I hope I am not that. It would leave no room for developments, and I intend to develop in many directions. [*Gwendolen and Jack sit down together in the corner.*]

Lady Bracknell: I'm sorry if we are a little late, Algernon, but I was obliged to call on dear Lady Harbury. I hadn't been there since her poor husband's death. I never saw a woman so altered; she looks quite twenty years younger. And now I'll have a cup of tea, and one of those nice cucumber sandwiches you promised me.

Algernon: Certainly, Aunt Augusta. [*Goes over to tea-table.*]

Lady Bracknell: Won't you come and sit here, Gwendolen?

Gwendolen: Thanks, mamma, I'm quite comfortable where I am.

Algernon [*picking up empty plate in horror*]: Good heavens! Lane! Why are there no cucumber sandwiches? I ordered them specially.

Lane [*gravely*]: There were no cucumbers in the market this morning, sir. I went down twice.

Algernon: No cucumbers!

Lane: No, sir. Not even for ready money.

Algernon: That will do, Lane, thank you.

Lane: Thank you, sir. [*Goes out.*]

Algernon: I am greatly distressed, Aunt Augusta, about there being no cucumbers, not even for ready money.

Lady Bracknell: It really makes no matter, Algernon. I had some crumpets with Lady Harbury, who seems to me to be living entirely for pleasure now.

Algernon: I hear her hair has turned quite gold from grief.

Lady Bracknell: It certainly has changed its colour. From what cause I, of course, cannot say. [*Algernon crosses and hands tea.*] Thank you. I've quite a treat for you tonight, Algernon. I am going to send you down with Mary Farquhar. She is such a nice woman, and so attentive to her husband. It's delightful to watch them.

Algernon: I am afraid, Aunt Augusta, I shall have to give up the pleasure of dining with you tonight after all.

Lady Bracknell [*frowning*]: I hope not, Algernon. It would put my table completely out. Your uncle would have to dine upstairs. Fortunately he is accustomed to that.

Algernon: It is a great bore, and, I need hardly say, a terrible disappointment to me, but the fact is I have just had a telegram to say that my poor friend Bunbury is very ill again. [*Exchanges glances with Jack.*] They seem to think I should be with him.

Lady Bracknell: It is very strange. This Mr Bunbury seems to suffer from curiously bad health.

Algernon: Yes; poor Bunbury is a dreadful invalid.

Lady Bracknell: Well, I must say, Algernon, that I think it is high time that Mr Bunbury made up his mind whether he was going to live or to die. This shillyshallying with the question is absurd. Nor do I in any way approve of the modern sympathy with invalids. I consider it morbid. Illness of any kind is hardly a thing to be encouraged in others. Health is the primary duty of life. I am always telling that to your poor uncle, but he never seems to take much notice . . . as far as any improvement in his ailments goes. I should be much obliged if you would ask Mr Bunbury, from me, to be kind enough not to have a relapse on Saturday, for I rely on you to arrange my music for me. It is my last reception, and one wants something that will encourage conversation, particularly at the end of the season when everyone has practically said whatever they had to say, which, in most cases, was probably not much.

Algernon: I'll speak to Bunbury, Aunt Augusta, if he is still conscious, and I think I can promise you he'll be all right by Saturday. Of course the music is a great difficulty. You see, if one plays good music, people don't listen, and if one plays bad music people don't talk. But I'll run over the programme I've drawn out, if you will kindly come into the next room for a moment.

Lady Bracknell: Thank you, Algernon. It is very thoughtful of you. [*Rising, and following Algernon.*] I'm sure the programme will be delightful, after a few expurgations. French songs I cannot possibly allow. People always seem to think that they are improper, and either look shocked, which is vulgar, or laugh, which is worse. But German sounds a thoroughly respectable language, and indeed, I believe is so. Gwendolen, you will accompany me.

Gwendolen: Certainly, mamma.

[Lady Bracknell and Algernon go into the music-room, Gwendolen remains behind.]

Jack: Charming day it has been, Miss Fairfax.

Gwendolen: Pray don't talk to me about the weather, Mr Worthing. Whenever people talk to me about the weather, I always feel quite certain that they mean something else. And that makes me so nervous.

Jack: I do mean something else.

Gwendolen: I thought so. In fact, I am never wrong.

Jack: And I would like to be allowed to take advantage of Lady Bracknell's temporary absence . . .

Gwendolen: I would certainly advise you to do so. Mamma has a way of coming back suddenly into a room that I have often had to speak to her about.

Jack [*nervously*]: Miss Fairfax, ever since I met you I have admired you more than any girl . . . I have ever met since . . . I met you.

Gwendolen: Yes, I am quite aware of the fact. And I often wish that in public, at any rate, you had been more demonstrative. For me you have always had an irresistible fascination. Even before I met you I was far from indifferent to you. [*Jack looks at her in amazement.*] We live, as I hope you know, Mr Worthing, in an age of ideals. The fact is constantly mentioned in the more expensive monthly magazines, and has reached the provincial pulpits I am told: and my ideal has always been to love some one of the name of Ernest. There is something in that name that inspires absolute confidence. The moment Algernon first mentioned to me that he had a friend called Ernest, I knew I was destined to love you.

Jack: You really love me, Gwendolen?
Gwendolen: Passionately!
Jack: Darling! You don't know how happy you've made me.
Gwendolen: My own Ernest!
Jack: But you don't really mean to say that you couldn't love me if my name wasn't Ernest?
Gwendolen: But your name is Ernest.
Jack: Yes, I know it is. But supposing it was something else? Do you mean to say you couldn't love me then?
Gwendolen [*glibly*]: Ah! that is clearly a metaphysical speculation, and like most metaphysical speculations has very little reference at all to the actual facts of real life, as we know them.
Jack: Personally, darling, to speak quite candidly, I don't much care about the name of Ernest . . . I don't think the name suits me at all.
Gwendolen: It suits you perfectly. It is a divine name. It has a music of its own. It produces vibrations.
Jack: Well, really, Gwendolen, I must say that I think there are lots of other much nicer names. I think Jack, for instance, a charming name.
Gwendolen: Jack? . . . No, there is very little music in the name Jack, if any at all, indeed. It does not thrill. It produces absolutely no vibrations . . . I have known several Jacks, and they all, without exception, were more than usually plain. Besides, Jack is a notorious domesticity for John! And I pity any woman who is married to a man called John. She would probably never be allowed to know the entrancing pleasure of a single moment's solitude. The only really safe name is Ernest.
Jack: Gwendolen, I must get christened at once—I mean we must get married at once. There is no time to be lost.
Gwendolen: Married, Mr Worthing?
Jack [*astounded*]: Well . . . surely. You know that I love you, and you led me to believe, Miss Fairfax, that you were not absolutely indifferent to me.
Gwendolen: I adore you. But you haven't proposed to me yet. Nothing has been said at all about marriage. The subject has not even been touched on.
Jack: Well . . . may I propose to you now?
Gwendolen: I think it would be an admirable opportunity. And to spare you any possible disappointment, Mr Worthing, I think it only fair to tell you quite frankly beforehand that I am fully determined to accept you.
Jack: Gwendolen!
Gwendolen: Yes, Mr Worthing, what have you got to say to me?
Jack: You know what I have got to say to you.
Gwendolen: Yes, but you don't say it.
Jack: Gwendolen, will you marry me? [*Goes on his knees.*]
Gwendolen: Of course I will, darling. How long you have been about it! I am afraid you have had very little experience in how to propose.
Jack: My own one, I have never loved anyone in the world but you.
Gwendolen: Yes, but men often propose for practice. I know my brother Gerald does. All my girl-friends tell me so. What wonderfully blue eyes you have,

Ernest! They are quite, quite, blue. I hope you will always look at me just like that, especially when there are other people present.

[Enter Lady Bracknell.]

Lady Bracknell: Mr Worthing! Rise, sir, from this semi-recumbent posture. It is most indecorous.

Gwendolen: Mamma! [*He tries to rise; she restrains him.*] I must beg you to retire. This is no place for you. Besides, Mr Worthing has not quite finished yet.

Lady Bracknell: Finished what, may I ask?

Gwendolen: I am engaged to Mr Worthing, mamma. [*They rise together.*]

Lady Bracknell: Pardon me, you are not engaged to anyone. When you do become engaged to some one, I, or your father, should his health permit him, will inform you of the fact. An engagement should come on a young girl as a surprise, pleasant or unpleasant, as the case may be. It is hardly a matter that she could be allowed to arrange for herself. . . . And now I have a few questions to put to you, Mr Worthing. While I am making these inquiries, you, Gwendolen, will wait for me below in the carriage.

Gwendolen [*reproachfully*]: Mamma!

Lady Bracknell: In the carriage, Gwendolen! [*Gwendolen goes to the door. She and Jack blow kisses to each other behind Lady Bracknell's back. Lady Bracknell looks vaguely about as if she could not understand what the noise was. Finally turns round.*] Gwendolen, the carriage!

Gwendolen: Yes, mamma. [*Goes out, looking back at Jack.*]

Lady Bracknell [*sitting down*]: You can take a seat, Mr Worthing.

[Looking in her pocket for note-book and pencil.]

Jack: Thank you, Lady Bracknell, I prefer standing.

Lady Bracknell [*pencil and note-book in hand*]: I feel bound to tell you that you are not down on my list of eligible young men, although I have the same list as the dear Duchess of Bolton has. We work together, in fact. However, I am quite ready to enter your name, should your answers be what a really affectionate mother requires. Do you smoke?

Jack: Well, yes, I must admit I smoke.

Lady Bracknell: I am glad to hear it. A man should always have an occupation of some kind. There are far too many idle men in London as it is. How old are you?

Jack: Twenty-nine.

Lady Bracknell: A very good age to be married at. I have always been of opinion that a man who desires to get married should know either everything or nothing. Which do you know?

Jack [*after some hesitation*]: I know nothing, Lady Bracknell.

Lady Bracknell: I am pleased to hear it. I do not approve of anything that tampers with natural ignorance. Ignorance is like a delicate exotic fruit; touch it and the bloom is gone. The whole theory of modern education is radically unsound. Fortunately in England, at any rate, education produces no effect whatsoever. If it did, it would prove a serious danger to the upper classes, and probably lead to acts of violence in Grosvenor Square.[5] What is your income?

Jack: Between seven and eight thousand a year.

Lady Bracknell [*makes a note in her book*]: In land, or in investments?

Jack: In investments, chiefly.

Lady Bracknell: That is satisfactory. What between the duties expected of one during one's lifetime, and the duties exacted from one after one's death, land has ceased to be either a profit or a pleasure. It gives one position, and prevents one from keeping it up. That's all that can be said about land.

Jack: I have a country house with some land, of course, attached to it, about fifteen hundred acres, I believe; but I don't depend on that for my real income. In fact, as far as I can make out, the poachers are the only people who make anything out of it.

Lady Bracknell: A country house! How many bedrooms? Well, that point can be cleared up afterwards. You have a town house, I hope? A girl with a simple, unspoiled nature, like Gwendolen, could hardly be expected to reside in the country.

Jack: Well, I own a house in Belgrave Square,[6] but it is let by the year to Lady Bloxham. Of course, I can get it back whenever I like, at six months' notice.

Lady Bracknell: Lady Bloxham? I don't know her.

Jack: Oh, she goes about very little. She is a lady considerably advanced in years.

Lady Bracknell: Ah, nowadays that is no guarantee of respectability of character. What number in Belgrave Square?

Jack: 149.

Lady Bracknell [*shaking her head*]: The unfashionable side. I thought there was something. However, that could easily be altered.

Jack: Do you mean the fashion, or the side?

Lady Bracknell [*sternly*]: Both, if necessary, I presume. What are your politics?

Jack: Well, I am afraid I really have none. I am a Liberal Unionist.

Lady Bracknell: Oh, they count as Tories. They dine with us. Or come in the evening, at any rate. Now to minor matters. Are your parents living?

Jack: I have lost both my parents.

Lady Bracknell: Both? To lose one parent may be regarded as a misfortune—to lose *both* seems like carelessness. Who was your father? He was evidently a man of some wealth. Was he born in what the Radical papers call the purple of commerce, or did he rise from the ranks of the aristocracy[7]?

Jack: I am afraid I really don't know. The fact is, Lady Bracknell, I said I had lost my parents. It would be nearer the truth to say that my parents seem to

[5] *Grosvenor Square:* A fashionable neighborhood in West London.

[6] *Belgrave Square:* A nearby fashionable neighborhood.

[7] *rise from the ranks of aristocracy:* The joke here is that, given the social changes of the nineteenth century, aristocrats would not be expected to be wealthy. It is in "the purple ranks of commerce" that Gwendolen could expect to find a wealthy husband.

have lost me . . . I don't actually know who I am by birth. I was. . . well, I was found.

Lady Bracknell: Found!

Jack: The late Mr Thomas Cardew, an old gentleman of a very charitable and kindly disposition, found me, and gave me the name of Worthing, because he happened to have a first-class ticket for Worthing in his pocket at the time. Worthing is a place in Sussex. It is a seaside resort.

Lady Bracknell: Where did the charitable gentleman who had a first-class ticket for this seaside resort find you?

Jack [*gravely*]: In a hand-bag.

Lady Bracknell: A hand-bag?

Jack [*very seriously*]: Yes, Lady Bracknell. I was in a hand-bag—a somewhat large, black leather hand-bag, with handles to it—an ordinary hand-bag in fact.

Lady Bracknell: In what locality did this Mr James, or Thomas, Cardew come across this ordinary hand-bag?

Jack: In the cloak-room at Victoria Station.[8] It was given to him in mistake for his own.

Lady Bracknell: The cloak-room at Victoria Station?

Jack: Yes. The Brighton line.

Lady Bracknell: The line is immaterial. Mr Worthing, I confess I feel somewhat bewildered by what you have just told me. To be born, or at any rate bred, in a hand-bag, whether it had handles or not, seems to me to display a contempt for the ordinary decencies of family life that reminds one of the worst excesses of the French Revolution.[9] And I presume you know what that unfortunate movement led to? As for the particular locality in which the hand-bag was found, a cloak-room at a railway station might serve to conceal a social indiscretion—has probably, indeed, been used for that purpose before now—but it could hardly be regarded as an assured basis for a recognized position in good society.

Jack: May I ask you then what you would advise me to do? I need hardly say I would do anything in the world to ensure Gwendolen's happiness.

Lady Bracknell: I would strongly advise you, Mr Worthing, to try and acquire some relations as soon as possible, and to make a definite effort to produce at any rate one parent, of either sex, before the season is quite over.

Jack: Well, I don't see how I could possibly manage to do that. I can produce the hand-bag at any moment. It is in my dressing-room at home. I really think that should satisfy you, Lady Bracknell.

Lady Bracknell: Me, sir! What has it to do with me? You can hardly imagine that I and Lord Bracknell would dream of allowing our only daughter—a girl brought up with the utmost care—to marry into a cloak-room, and form an alliance with a parcel? Good morning, Mr Worthing!

[Lady Bracknell sweeps out in majestic indignation.]

[8]*Victoria Station:* A national rail station located in central London.

[9]*worst excesses of the French Revolution*: The beheading of thousands of aristocrats, including Louis XVI and Marie Antoinette. Lady Bracknell lives in constant fear of revolution and class warfare.

Jack: Good morning! [*Algernon, from the other room, strikes up the Wedding March. Jack looks perfectly furious, and goes to the door.*] For goodness' sake don't play that ghastly tune, Algy! How idiotic you are!

[The music stops, and Algernon enters cheerily.]

Algernon: Didn't it go off all right, old boy? You don't mean to say Gwendolen refused you? I know it is a way she has. She is always refusing people. I think it is most ill-natured of her.

Jack: Oh, Gwendolen is as right as a trivet. As far as she is concerned, we are engaged. Her mother is perfectly unbearable. Never met such a Gorgon[10] . . . I don't really know what a Gorgon is like, but I am quite sure that Lady Bracknell is one. In any case, she is a monster, without being a myth, which is rather unfair . . . I beg your pardon, Algy, I suppose I shouldn't talk about your own aunt in that way before you.

Algernon: My dear boy, I love hearing my relations abused. It is the only thing that makes me put up with them at all. Relations are simply a tedious pack of people, who haven't got the remotest knowledge of how to live, nor the smallest instinct about when to die.

Jack: Oh, that is nonsense!

Algernon: It isn't!

Jack: Well, I won't argue about the matter. You always want to argue about things.

Algernon: That is exactly what things were originally made for.

Jack: Upon my word, if I thought that, I'd shoot myself . . . [*A pause.*] You don't think there is any chance of Gwendolen becoming like her mother in about a hundred and fifty years, do you Algy?

Algernon: All women become like their mothers. That is their tragedy. No man does. That's his.

Jack: Is that clever?

Algernon: It is perfectly phrased! and quite as true as any observation in civilized life should be.

Jack: I am sick to death of cleverness. Everybody is clever nowadays. You can't go anywhere without meeting clever people. The thing has become an absolute public nuisance. I wish to goodness we had a few fools left.

Algernon: We have.

Jack: I should extremely like to meet them. What do they talk about?

Algernon: The fools? Oh! about the clever people, of course.

Jack: What fools!

Algernon: By the way, did you tell Gwendolen the truth about your being Ernest in town, and Jack in the country?

Jack [*in a very patronizing manner*]: My dear fellow, the truth isn't quite the sort of thing one tells to a nice sweet refined girl. What extraordinary ideas you have about the way to behave to a woman!

[10]*Gorgon*: A Greek mythological monster whose face would turn people to stone.

Algernon: The only way to behave to a woman is to make love to her, if she is pretty, and to someone else if she is plain.

Jack: Oh, that is nonsense.

Algernon: What about your brother? What about the profligate Ernest?

Jack: Oh, before the end of the week I shall have got rid of him. I'll say he died in Paris of apoplexy.[11] Lots of people die of apoplexy, quite suddenly, don't they?

Algernon: Yes, but it's hereditary, my dear fellow. It's a sort of thing that runs in families. You had much better say a severe chill.

Jack: You are sure a severe chill isn't hereditary, or anything of that kind?

Algernon: Of course it isn't!

Jack: Very well, then. My poor brother Ernest is carried off suddenly in Paris, by a severe chill. That gets rid of him.

Algernon: But I thought you said that . . . Miss Cardew was a little too much interested in your poor brother Ernest? Won't she feel his loss a good deal?

Jack: Oh, that is all right. Cecily is not a silly romantic girl, I am glad to say. She has got a capital appetite, goes long walks, and pays no attention at all to her lessons.

Algernon: I would rather like to see Cecily.

Jack: I will take very good care you never do. She is excessively pretty, and she is only just eighteen.

Algernon: Have you told Gwendolen yet that you have an excessively pretty ward who is only just eighteen?

Jack: Oh! one doesn't blurt these things out to people. Cecily and Gwendolen are perfectly certain to be extremely great friends. I'll bet you anything you like that half an hour after they have met, they will be calling each other sister.

Algernon: Women only do that when they have called each other a lot of other things first. Now, my dear boy, if we want to get a good table at Willis's, we really must go and dress. Do you know it is nearly seven?

Jack [*irritably*]: Oh! it always is nearly seven.

Algernon: Well, I'm hungry.

Jack: I never knew you when you weren't. . . .

Algernon: What shall we do after dinner? Go to a theatre?

Jack: Oh no! I loathe listening.

Algernon: Well, let us go to the Club?

Jack: Oh, no! I hate talking.

Algernon: Well, we might trot round to the Empire[12] at ten?

Jack: Oh, no! I can't bear looking at things. It is so silly.

Algernon: Well, what shall we do?

Jack: Nothing!

Algernon: It is awfully hard work doing nothing. However, I don't mind hard work where there is no definite object of any kind.

[11]*apoplexy*: A common Victorian term for a stroke.

[12]*Empire*: A London music hall.

[Enter Lane.]

Lane: Miss Fairfax.

[Enter Gwendolen. Lane goes out.]

Algernon: Gwendolen, upon my word!
Gwendolen: Algy, kindly turn your back. I have something very particular to say to Mr Worthing.
Algernon: Really, Gwendolen, I don't think I can allow this at all.
Gwendolen: Algy, you always adopt a strictly immoral attitude towards life. You are not quite old enough to do that.

[Algernon retires to the fireplace.]

Jack: My own darling!
Gwendolen: Ernest, we may never be married. From the expression on mamma's face I fear we never shall. Few parents nowadays pay any regard to what their children say to them. The old-fashioned respect for the young is fast dying out. Whatever influence I ever had over mamma, I lost at the age of three. But although she may prevent us from becoming man and wife, and I may marry someone else, and marry often, nothing that she can possibly do can alter my eternal devotion to you.
Jack: Dear Gwendolen!
Gwendolen: The story of your romantic origin, as related to me by mamma, with unpleasing comments, has naturally stirred the deeper fibres of my nature. Your Christian name has an irresistible fascination. The simplicity of your character makes you exquisitely incomprehensible to me. Your town address at the Albany I have. What is your address in the country?
Jack: The Manor House, Woolton, Hertfordshire.

[Algernon, who has been carefully listening, smiles to himself, and writes the address on his shirt-cuff. Then picks up the Railway Guide.]

Gwendolen: There is a good postal service, I suppose? It may be necessary to do something desperate. That of course will require serious consideration. I will communicate with you daily.
Jack: My own one!
Gwendolen: How long do you remain in town?
Jack: Till Monday.
Gwendolen: Good! Algy, you may turn round now.
Algernon: Thanks, I've turned round already.
Gwendolen: You may also ring the bell.
Jack: You will let me see you to your carriage, my own darling?
Gwendolen: Certainly.
Jack [*to Lane, who now enters*]: I will see Miss Fairfax out.
Lane: Yes, sir. [*Jack and Gwendolen go off.*]

[Lane presents several letters on a salver to Algernon. It is to be surmised that they are bills, as Algernon, after looking at the envelopes, tears them up.]

Algernon: A glass of sherry, Lane.
Lane: Yes, sir.
Algernon: Tomorrow, Lane, I'm going Bunburying.
Lane: Yes, sir.
Algernon: I shall probably not be back till Monday. You can put up my dress clothes, my smoking jacket,[13] and all the Bunbury suits . . .
Lane: Yes, sir. [*Handing sherry.*]
Algernon: I hope tomorrow will be a fine day, Lane.
Lane: It never is, sir.
Algernon: Lane, you're a perfect pessimist.
Lane: I do my best to give satisfaction, sir.

[Enter Jack. Lane goes off.]

Jack: There's a sensible, intellectual girl! the only girl I ever cared for in my life. [*Algernon is laughing immoderately.*] What on earth are you so amused at?
Algernon: Oh, I'm a little anxious about poor Bunbury, that is all.
Jack: If you don't take care, your friend Bunbury will get you into a serious scrape some day.
Algernon: I love scrapes. They are the only things that are never serious.
Jack: Oh, that's nonsense, Algy. You never talk anything but nonsense.
Algernon: Nobody ever does.

[*Jack looks indignantly at him, and leaves the room. Algernon lights a cigarette, reads his shirt-cuff, and smiles.*]

ACT DROP

SECOND ACT

Scene: Garden at the Manor House. A flight of gray stone steps leads up to the house. The garden, an old-fashioned one, full of roses. Time of year, July. Basket chairs, and a table covered with books, are set under a large yew tree.

[Miss Prism discovered seated at the table. Cecily is at the back watering flowers.]

Miss Prism [*calling*]: Cecily, Cecily! Surely such a utilitarian occupation as the watering of flowers is rather Moulton's duty than yours? Especially at a moment when intellectual pleasures await you. Your German grammar is on the table. Pray open it at page fifteen. We will repeat yesterday's lesson.
Cecily [*coming over very slowly*]: But I don't like German. It isn't at all a becoming language. I know perfectly well that I look quite plain after my German lesson.

[13]*smoking jacket*: A jacket worn by men to cover their clothing when smoking cigars.

Miss Prism: Child, you know how anxious your guardian is that you should improve yourself in every way. He laid particular stress on your German, as he was leaving for town yesterday. Indeed, he always lays stress on your German when he is leaving for town.

Cecily: Dear Uncle Jack is so very serious! Sometimes he is so serious that I think he cannot be quite well.

Miss Prism [*drawing herself up*]: Your guardian enjoys the best of health, and his gravity of demeanour is especially to be commended in one so comparatively young as he is. I know no one who has a higher sense of duty and responsibility.

Cecily: I suppose that is why he often looks a little bored when we three are together.

Miss Prism: Cecily! I am surprised at you. Mr Worthing has many troubles in his life. Idle merriment and triviality would be out of place in his conversation. You must remember his constant anxiety about that unfortunate young man his brother.

Cecily: I wish Uncle Jack would allow that unfortunate young man, his brother, to come down here sometimes. We might have a good influence over him, Miss Prism. I am sure you certainly would. You know German, and geology, and things of that kind influence a man very much. [*Cecily begins to write in her diary.*]

Miss Prism [*shaking her head*]: I do not think that even I could produce any effect on a character that according to his own brother's admission is irretrievably weak and vacillating. Indeed I am not sure that I would desire to reclaim him. I am not in favour of this modern mania for turning bad people into good people at a moment's notice. As a man sows so let him reap. You must put away your diary, Cecily. I really don't see why you should keep a diary at all.

Cecily: I keep a diary in order to enter the wonderful secrets of my life. If I didn't write them down I should probably forget all about them.

Miss Prism: Memory, my dear Cecily, is the diary that we all carry about with us.

Cecily: Yes, but it usually chronicles the things that have never happened, and couldn't possibly have happened. I believe that Memory is responsible for nearly all the three-volume novels that Mudie[14] sends us.

Miss Prism: Do not speak slightly of the three-volume novel, Cecily. I wrote one myself in earlier days.

Cecily: Did you really, Miss Prism? How wonderfully clever you are! I hope it did not end happily? I don't like novels that end happily. They depress me so much.

Miss Prism: The good ended happily, and the bad unhappily. That is what Fiction means.

[14]*Mudie:* A library through which popular books circulated among subscribers. Its books typically conformed to Victorian notions of respectability.

Cecily: I suppose so. But it seems very unfair. And was your novel ever published?

Miss Prism: Alas! no. The manuscript unfortunately was abandoned. I use the word in the sense of lost or mislaid. To your work, child, these speculations are profitless.

Cecily [*smiling*]: But I see dear Dr Chasuble[15] coming up through the garden.

Miss Prism [*rising and advancing*]: Dr Chasuble! This is indeed a pleasure.

[Enter Canon Chasuble.]

Chasuble: And how are we this morning? Miss Prism, you are, I trust, well?

Cecily: Miss Prism has just been complaining of a slight headache. I think it would do her so much good to have a short stroll with you in the Park, Dr Chasuble.

Miss Prism: Cecily, I have not mentioned anything about a headache.

Cecily: No, dear Miss Prism, I know that, but I felt instinctively that you had a headache. Indeed I was thinking about that, and not about my German lesson, when the Rector came in.

Chasuble: I hope Cecily, you are not inattentive.

Cecily: Oh, I am afraid I am.

Chasuble: That is strange. Were I fortunate enough to be Miss Prism's pupil, I would hang upon her lips. [*Miss Prism glares.*] I spoke metaphorically.—My metaphor was drawn from bees. Ahem! Mr Worthing I suppose, has not returned from town yet?

Miss Prism: We do not expect him till Monday afternoon.

Chasuble: Ah yes, he usually likes to spend his Sunday in London. He is not one of those whose sole aim is enjoyment, as, by all accounts, that unfortunate young man his brother seems to be. But I must not disturb Egeria[16] and her pupil any longer.

Miss Prism: Egeria? My name is Laetitia,[17] Doctor.

Chasuble [*bowing*]: A classical allusion merely, drawn from the Pagan authors. I shall see you both no doubt at Evensong?[18]

Miss Prism: I think, dear Doctor, I will have a stroll with you. I find I have a headache after all, and a walk might do it good.

Chasuble: With pleasure, Miss Prism, with pleasure. We might go as far as the schools and back.

Miss Prism: That would be delightful. Cecily, you will read your Political Economy in my absence. The chapter on the Fall of the Rupee you may omit. It is somewhat too sensational. Even these metallic problems have their melodramatic side.

[Goes down the garden with Dr Chasuble.]

[15]*Chasuble:* A liturgical garment worn by priests for celebrating the Eucharist.

[16]*Egeria:* A Roman queen known for giving counsel.

[17]*Laetitia:* A Roman goddess of fertility. The name also means "joy."

[18]*Evensong:* Evening church services.

Cecily [*picks up books and throws them back on table*]: Horrid Political Economy! Horrid Geography! Horrid, horrid German!

[Enter Merriman with a card on a salver.]

Merriman: Mr Ernest Worthing has just driven over from the station. He has brought his luggage with him.

Cecily [*takes the card and reads it*]: "Mr Ernest Worthing, B.4 The Albany, W." Uncle Jack's brother! Did you tell him Mr Worthing was not in town?

Merriman: Yes, Miss. He seemed very much disappointed. I mentioned that you and Miss Prism were in the garden. He said he was anxious to speak to you privately for a moment.

Cecily: Ask Mr Ernest Worthing to come here. I suppose you had better talk to the housekeeper about a room for him.

Merriman: Yes, Miss. [*Merriman goes off.*]

Cecily: I have never met any really wicked person before. I feel rather frightened. I am so afraid he will look just like everyone else.

[Enter Algernon, very gay and debonair.]

He does!

Algernon [*raising his hat*]: You are my little cousin Cecily, I'm sure.

Cecily: You are under some strange mistake. I am not little. In fact, I believe I am more than usually tall for my age. [*Algernon is rather taken aback.*] But I am your cousin Cecily. You, I see from your card, are Uncle Jack's brother, my cousin Ernest, my wicked cousin Ernest.

Algernon: Oh! I am not really wicked at all, cousin Cecily. You mustn't think that I am wicked.

Cecily: If you are not, then you have certainly been deceiving us all in a very inexcusable manner. I hope you have not been leading a double life, pretending to be wicked and being really good all the time. That would be hypocrisy.

Algernon [*looks at her in amazement*]: Oh! Of course I have been rather reckless.

Cecily: I am glad to hear it.

Algernon: In fact, now you mention the subject, I have been very bad in my own small way.

Cecily: I don't think you should be so proud of that, although I am sure it must have been very pleasant.

Algernon: It is much pleasanter being here with you.

Cecily: I can't understand how you are here at all. Uncle Jack won't be back till Monday afternoon.

Algernon: That is a great disappointment. I am obliged to go up by the first train on Monday morning. I have a business appointment that I am anxious . . . to miss.

Cecily: Couldn't you miss it anywhere but in London?

Algernon: No: the appointment is in London.

Cecily: Well, I know, of course, how important it is not to keep a business engagement, if one wants to retain any sense of the beauty of life, but still I think you had better wait till Uncle Jack arrives. I know he wants to speak to you about your emigrating.

Algernon: About my what?

Cecily: Your emigrating. He has gone up to buy your outfit.

Algernon: I certainly wouldn't let Jack buy my outfit. He has no taste in neckties at all.

Cecily: I don't think you will require neckties. Uncle Jack is sending you to Australia.

Algernon: Australia! I'd sooner die.

Cecily: Well, he said at dinner on Wednesday night, that you would have to choose between this world, the next world, and Australia.

Algernon: Oh, well! The accounts I have received of Australia and the next world, are not particularly encouraging. This world is good enough for me, cousin Cecily.

Cecily: Yes, but are you good enough for it?

Algernon: I'm afraid I'm not that. That is why I want you to reform me. You might make that your mission, if you don't mind, cousin Cecily.

Cecily: I'm afraid I've no time, this afternoon.

Algernon: Well, would you mind my reforming myself this afternoon?

Cecily: It is rather Quixotic of you. But I think you should try.

Algernon: I will. I feel better already.

Cecily: You are looking a little worse.

Algernon: That is because I am hungry.

Cecily: How thoughtless of me. I should have remembered that when one is going to lead an entirely new life, one requires regular and wholesome meals. Won't you come in?

Algernon: Thank you. Might I have a buttonhole first? I never have any appetite unless I have a buttonhole first.

Cecily: A Maréchal Niel?[19] [*Picks up scissors.*]

Algernon: No, I'd sooner have a pink rose.

Cecily: Why? [*Cuts a flower.*]

Algernon: Because you are like a pink rose, Cousin Cecily.

Cecily: I don't think it can be right for you to talk to me like that. Miss Prism never says such things to me.

Algernon: Then Miss Prism is a short-sighted old lady. [*Cecily puts the rose in his buttonhole.*] You are the prettiest girl I ever saw.

Cecily: Miss Prism says that all good looks are a snare.

Algernon: They are a snare that every sensible man would like to be caught in.

Cecily: Oh! I don't think I would care to catch a sensible man. I shouldn't know what to talk to him about.

[They pass into the house. Miss Prism and Dr Chasuble return.]

Miss Prism: You are too much alone, dear Dr Chasuble. You should get married. A misanthrope I can understand—a womanthrope, never!

[19]*Maréchal Niel:* A yellow variety of rose.

Chasuble [*with a scholar's shudder*]: Believe me, I do not deserve so neologistic a phrase. The precept as well as the practice of the Primitive Church was distinctly against matrimony.

Miss Prism [*sententiously*]: That is obviously the reason why the Primitive Church has not lasted up to the present day. And you do not seem to realize, dear Doctor, that by persistently remaining single, a man converts himself into a permanent public temptation. Men should be more careful; this very celibacy leads weaker vessels astray.

Chasuble: But is a man not equally attractive when married?

Miss Prism: No married man is ever attractive except to his wife.

Chasuble: And often, I've been told, not even to her.

Miss Prism: That depends on the intellectual sympathies of the woman. Maturity can always be depended on. Ripeness can be trusted. Young women are green. [*Dr Chasuble starts.*] I spoke horticulturally. My metaphor was drawn from fruits. But where is Cecily?

Chasuble: Perhaps she followed us to the schools.

[Enter Jack slowly from the back of the garden. He is dressed in the deepest mourning, with crape hat-band and black gloves.]

Miss Prism: Mr Worthing!

Chasuble: Mr Worthing?

Miss Prism: This is indeed a surprise. We did not look for you till Monday afternoon.

Jack [*shakes Miss Prism's hand in a tragic manner*]: I have returned sooner than I expected. Dr Chasuble, I hope you are well?

Chasuble: Dear Mr Worthing, I trust this garb of woe does not betoken some terrible calamity?

Jack: My brother.

Miss Prism: More shameful debts and extravagance?

Chasuble: Still leading his life of pleasure?

Jack [*shaking his head*]: Dead!

Chasuble: Your brother Ernest dead?

Jack: Quite dead.

Miss Prism: What a lesson for him! I trust he will profit by it.

Chasuble: Mr Worthing, I offer you my sincere condolence. You have at least the consolation of knowing that you were always the most generous and forgiving of brothers.

Jack: Poor Ernest! He had many faults, but it is a sad, sad blow.

Chasuble: Very sad indeed. Were you with him at the end?

Jack: No. He died abroad; in Paris, in fact. I had a telegram last night from the manager of the Grand Hotel.

Chasuble: Was the cause of death mentioned?

Jack: A severe chill, it seems.

Miss Prism: As a man sows, so shall he reap.

Chasuble [*raising his hand*]: Charity, dear Miss Prism, charity! None of us are perfect. I myself am peculiarly susceptible to draughts. Will the interment take place here?

Jack: No. He seemed to have expressed a desire to be buried in Paris.

Chasuble: In Paris! [*Shakes his head.*] I fear that hardly points to any very serious state of mind at the last. You would no doubt wish me to make some slight allusion to this tragic domestic affliction next Sunday. [*Jack presses his hand convulsively.*] My sermon on the meaning of the manna in the wilderness can be adapted to almost any occasion, joyful, or, as in the present case, distressing. [*All sigh.*] I have preached it at harvest celebrations, christenings, confirmations, on days of humiliation and festal days. The last time I delivered it was in the Cathedral, as a charity sermon on behalf of the Society for the Prevention of Discontent among the Upper Orders. The Bishop, who was present, was much struck by some of the analogies I drew.

Jack: Ah! that reminds me, you mentioned christenings[20] I think, Dr Chasuble? I suppose you know how to christen all right? [*Dr Chasuble looks astounded.*] I mean, of course, you are continually christening, aren't you?

Miss Prism: It is, I regret to say, one of the Rector's most constant duties in this parish. I have often spoken to the poorer classes on the subject. But they don't seem to know what thrift is.

Chasuble: But is there any particular infant in whom you are interested, Mr Worthing? Your brother was, I believe, unmarried, was he not?

Jack: Oh, yes.

Miss Prism [*bitterly*]: People who live entirely for pleasure usually are.

Jack: But it is not for any child, dear Doctor. I am very fond of children. No! the fact is, I would like to be christened myself, this afternoon, if you have nothing better to do.

Chasuble: But surely, Mr Worthing, you have been christened already?

Jack: I don't remember anything about it.

Chasuble: But have you any grave doubts on the subject?

Jack: I certainly intend to have. Of course I don't know if the thing would bother you in any way, or if you think I am a little too old now.

Chasuble: Not at all. The sprinkling, and, indeed, the immersion of adults is a perfectly canonical practice.

Jack: Immersion!

Chasuble: You need have no apprehensions. Sprinkling is all that is necessary, or indeed I think advisable. Our weather is so changeable. At what hour would you wish the ceremony performed?

Jack: Oh, I might trot round about five if that would suit you.

Chasuble: Perfectly, perfectly! In fact I have two similar ceremonies to perform at that time. A case of twins that occurred recently in one of the outlying cottages on your own estate. Poor Jenkins the carter, a most hard-working man.

Jack: Oh! I don't see much fun in being christened along with other babies. It would be childish. Would half-past five do?

Chasuble: Admirably! Admirably! [*Takes out watch.*] And now, dear Mr Worthing, I will not intrude any longer into a house of sorrow. I would

[20]*christenings*: Jack seeks this sacrament not out of a desire to join the Church of England but because the sacrament would be accompanied by a new name—in this case, Ernest.

merely beg you not to be too much bowed down by grief. What seem to us bitter trials are often blessings in disguise.

Miss Prism: This seems to me a blessing of an extremely obvious kind.

[Enter Cecily from the house.]

Cecily: Uncle Jack! Oh, I am pleased to see you back. But what horrid clothes you have got on! Do go and change them.

Miss Prism: Cecily!

Chasuble: My child! my child!

[Cecily goes towards Jack; he kisses her brow in a melancholy manner.]

Cecily: What is the matter, Uncle Jack? Do look happy! You look as if you had toothache, and I have got such a surprise for you. Who do you think is in the dining-room? Your brother!

Jack: Who?

Cecily: Your brother Ernest. He arrived about half an hour ago.

Jack: What nonsense! I haven't got a brother.

Cecily: Oh, don't say that. However badly he may have behaved to you in the past he is still your brother. You couldn't be so heartless as to disown him. I'll tell him to come out. And you will shake hands with him, won't you, Uncle Jack? [*Runs back into the house.*]

Chasuble: These are very joyful tidings.

Miss Prism: After we had all been resigned to his loss, his sudden return seems to me peculiarly distressing.

Jack: My brother is in the dining-room? I don't know what it all means. I think it is perfectly absurd.

[Enter Algernon and Cecily hand in hand. They come slowly up to Jack.]

Jack: Good heavens! [*Motions Algernon away.*]

Algernon: Brother John, I have come down from town to tell you that I am very sorry for all the trouble I have given you, and that I intend to lead a better life in the future.

[Jack glares at him and does not take his hand.]

Cecily: Uncle Jack, you are not going to refuse your own brother's hand?

Jack: Nothing will induce me to take his hand. I think his coming down here disgraceful. He knows perfectly well why.

Cecily: Uncle Jack, do be nice. There is some good in everyone. Ernest has just been telling me about his poor invalid friend Mr Bunbury whom he goes to visit so often. And surely there must be much good in one who is kind to an invalid, and leaves the pleasures of London to sit by a bed of pain.

Jack: Oh! he has been talking about Bunbury has he?

Cecily: Yes, he has told me all about poor Mr Bunbury, and his terrible state of health.

Jack: Bunbury! Well, I won't have him talk to you about Bunbury or about anything else. It is enough to drive one perfectly frantic.

Algernon: Of course I admit that the faults were all on my side. But I must say that I think that Brother John's coldness to me is peculiarly painful. I expected a more enthusiastic welcome, especially considering it is the first time I have come here.

Cecily: Uncle Jack, if you don't shake hands with Ernest I will never forgive you.

Jack: Never forgive me?

Cecily: Never, never, never!

Jack: Well, this is the last time I shall ever do it. [*Shakes hands with Algernon and glares.*]

Chasuble: It's pleasant, is it not, to see so perfect a reconciliation? I think we might leave the two brothers together.

Miss Prism: Cecily, you will come with us.

Cecily: Certainly, Miss Prism. My little task of reconciliation is over.

Chasuble: You have done a beautiful action today, dear child.

Miss Prism: We must not be premature in our judgments.

Cecily: I feel very happy. [*They all go off.*]

Jack: You young scoundrel, Algy, you must get out of this place as soon as possible. I don't allow any Bunburying here.

[Enter Merriman.]

Merriman: I have put Mr Ernest's things in the room next to yours, sir. I suppose that is all right?

Jack: What?

Merriman: Mr Ernest's luggage, sir. I have unpacked it and put it in the room next to your own.

Jack: His luggage?

Merriman: Yes, sir. Three portmanteaus, a dressing-case, two hat-boxes, and a large luncheon-basket.

Algernon: I am afraid I can't stay more than a week this time.

Jack: Merriman, order the dog-cart at once. Mr Ernest has been suddenly called back to town.

Merriman: Yes, sir. [*Goes back into the house.*]

Algernon: What a fearful liar you are, Jack. I have not been called back to town at all.

Jack: Yes, you have.

Algernon: I haven't heard anyone call me.

Jack: Your duty as a gentleman calls you back.

Algernon: My duty as a gentleman has never interfered with my pleasures in the smallest degree.

Jack: I can quite understand that.

Algernon: Well, Cecily is a darling.

Jack: You are not to talk of Miss Cardew like that. I don't like it.

Algernon: Well, I don't like your clothes. You look perfectly ridiculous in them. Why on earth don't you go up and change? It is perfectly childish to be in deep mourning for a man who is actually staying for a whole week with you in your house as a guest. I call it grotesque.

Jack: You are certainly not staying with me for a whole week as a guest or anything else. You have got to leave . . . by the four-five train.

Algernon: I certainly won't leave you so long as you are in mourning. It would be most unfriendly. If I were in mourning you would stay with me, I suppose. I should think it very unkind if you didn't.

Jack: Well, will you go if I change my clothes?

Algernon: Yes, if you are not too long. I never saw anybody take so long to dress, and with such little result.

Jack: Well, at any rate, that is better than being always over-dressed as you are.

Algernon: If I am occasionally a little over-dressed, I make up for it by being always immensely over-educated.

Jack: Your vanity is ridiculous, your conduct an outrage, and your presence in my garden utterly absurd. However, you have got to catch the four-five, and I hope you will have a pleasant journey back to town. This Bunburying, as you call it, has not been a great success for you. [*Goes into the house.*]

Algernon: I think it has been a great success. I'm in love with Cecily, and that is everything.

[Enter Cecily at the back of the garden. She picks up the can and begins to water the flowers.]

But I must see her before I go, and make arrangements for another Bunbury.

Ah, there she is.

Cecily: Oh, I merely came back to water the roses. I thought you were with Uncle Jack.

Algernon: He's gone to order the dog-cart for me.

Cecily: Oh, is he going to take you for a nice drive?

Algernon: He's going to send me away.

Cecily: Then have we got to part?

Algernon: I am afraid so. It's a painful parting.

Cecily: It is always painful to part from people whom one has known for a very brief space of time. The absence of old friends one can endure with equanimity. But even a momentary separation from anyone to whom one has just been introduced is almost unbearable.

Algernon: Thank you.

[Enter Merriman.]

Merriman: The dog-cart is at the door, sir.

[Algernon looks appealingly at Cecily.]

Cecily: It can wait, Merriman . . . for . . . five minutes.

Merriman: Yes, Miss. [*Exit Merriman.*]

Algernon: I hope, Cecily, I shall not offend you if I state quite frankly and openly that you seem to me to be in every way the visible personification of absolute perfection.

Cecily: I think your frankness does you great credit, Ernest. If you will allow me I will copy your remarks into my diary. [*Goes over to table and begins writing in diary.*]

Algernon: Do you really keep a diary? I'd give anything to look at it. May I?

Cecily: Oh no. [*Puts her hand over it.*] You see, it is simply a very young girl's record of her own thoughts and impressions, and consequently meant for publication. When it appears in volume form I hope you will order a copy. But pray, Ernest, don't stop. I delight in taking down from dictation. I have reached "absolute perfection." You can go on. I am quite ready for more.

Algernon [*somewhat taken aback*]: Ahem! Ahem!

Cecily: Oh, don't cough, Ernest. When one is dictating one should speak fluently and not cough. Besides, I don't know how to spell a cough. [*Writes as Algernon speaks.*]

Algernon [*speaking very rapidly*]: Cecily, ever since I first looked upon your wonderful and incomparable beauty, I have dared to love you wildly, passionately, devotedly, hopelessly.

Cecily: I don't think that you should tell me that you love me wildly, passionately, devotedly, hopelessly. Hopelessly doesn't seem to make much sense, does it?

Algernon: Cecily!

[Enter Merriman.]

Merriman: The dog-cart is waiting, sir.

Algernon: Tell it to come round next week, at the same hour.

Merriman [*looks at Cecily, who makes no sign*]: Yes, sir. [*Merriman retires.*]

Cecily: Uncle Jack would be very much annoyed if he knew you were staying on till next week, at the same hour.

Algernon: Oh, I don't care about Jack. I don't care for anybody in the whole world but you. I love you, Cecily. You will marry me, won't you?

Cecily: You silly boy! Of course. Why, we have been engaged for the last three months.

Algernon: For the last three months?

Cecily: Yes, it will be exactly three months on Thursday.

Algernon: But how did we become engaged?

Cecily: Well, ever since dear Uncle Jack first confessed to us that he had a younger brother who was very wicked and bad, you of course have formed the chief topic of conversation between myself and Miss Prism. And of course a man who is much talked about is always very attractive. One feels there must be something in him after all. I daresay it was foolish of me, but I fell in love with you, Ernest.

Algernon: Darling! And when was the engagement actually settled?

Cecily: On the 14th of February last. Worn out by your entire ignorance of my existence, I determined to end the matter one way or the other, and after a long struggle with myself I accepted you under this dear old tree here. The next day I bought this little ring in your name, and this is the little bangle with the true lovers' knot I promised you always to wear.

Algernon: Did I give you this? It's very pretty, isn't it?

Cecily: Yes, you've wonderfully good taste, Ernest. It's the excuse I've always given for your leading such a bad life. And this is the box in which I keep all your dear letters. [*Kneels at table, opens box, and produces letters tied up with blue ribbon.*]

Algernon: My letters! But my own sweet Cecily, I have never written you any letters.

Cecily: You need hardly remind me of that, Ernest. I remember only too well that I was forced to write your letters for you. I wrote always three times a week, and sometimes oftener.

Algernon: Oh, do let me read them, Cecily?

Cecily: Oh, I couldn't possibly. They would make you far too conceited. [*Replaces box.*] The three you wrote me after I had broken off the engagement are so beautiful, and so badly spelled, that even now I can hardly read them without crying a little.

Algernon: But was our engagement ever broken off?

Cecily: Of course it was. On the 22nd of last March. You can see the entry if you like. [*Shows diary.*] "Today I broke off my engagement with Ernest. I feel it is better to do so. The weather still continues charming."

Algernon: But why on earth did you break it off? What had I done? I had done nothing at all. Cecily, I am very much hurt indeed to hear you broke it off. Particularly when the weather was so charming.

Cecily: It would hardly have been a really serious engagement if it hadn't been broken off at least once. But I forgave you before the week was out.

Algernon [*crossing to her, and kneeling*]: What a perfect angel you are, Cecily.

Cecily: You dear romantic boy. [*He kisses her, she puts her fingers through his hair.*] I hope your hair curls naturally, does it?

Algernon: Yes, darling, with a little help from others.

Cecily: I am so glad.

Algernon: You'll never break off our engagement again, Cecily?

Cecily: I don't think I could break it off now that I have actually met you. Besides, of course, there is the question of your name.

Algernon: Yes, of course. [*Nervously.*]

Cecily: You must not laugh at me, darling, but it had always been a girlish dream of mine to love some one whose name was Ernest. [*Algernon rises, Cecily also.*] There is something in that name that seems to inspire absolute confidence. I pity any poor married woman whose husband is not called Ernest.

Algernon: But, my dear child, do you mean to say you could not love me if I had some other name?

Cecily: But what name?

Algernon: Oh, any name you like—Algernon—for instance . . .

Cecily: But I don't like the name of Algernon.

Algernon: Well, my own dear, sweet, loving little darling, I really can't see why you should object to the name of Algernon. It is not at all a bad name. In fact, it is rather an aristocratic name. Half of the chaps who get into the Bankruptcy Court are called Algernon. But seriously, Cecily . . . [*moving to her*] . . . if my name was Algy, couldn't you love me?

Cecily [*rising*]: I might respect you, Ernest, I might admire your character, but I fear that I should not be able to give you my undivided attention.

Algernon: Ahem! Cecily! [*Picking up hat.*] Your Rector here is, I suppose, thoroughly experienced in the practice of all the rites and ceremonials of the Church?

Cecily: Oh yes. Dr Chasuble is a most learned man. He has never written a single book, so you can imagine how much he knows.

Algernon: I must see him at once on a most important christening—I mean on most important business.

Cecily: Oh!

Algernon: I shan't be away more than half an hour.

Cecily: Considering that we have been engaged since February the 14th, and that I only met you today for the first time, I think it is rather hard that you should leave me for so long a period as half an hour. Couldn't you make it twenty minutes?

Algernon: I'll be back in no time. [*Kisses her and rushes down the garden.*]

Cecily: What an impetuous boy he is! I like his hair so much. I must enter his proposal in my diary.

[Enter Merriman.]

Merriman: A Miss Fairfax has just called to see Mr Worthing. On very important business Miss Fairfax states.

Cecily: Isn't Mr Worthing in his library?

Merriman: Mr Worthing went over in the direction of the Rectory some time ago.

Cecily: Pray ask the lady to come out here; Mr Worthing is sure to be back soon. And you can bring tea.

Merriman: Yes, Miss. [*Goes out.*]

Cecily: Miss Fairfax! I suppose one of the many good elderly women who are associated with Uncle Jack in some of his philanthropic work in London. I don't quite like women who are interested in philanthropic work. I think it is so forward of them.

[Enter Merriman.]

Merriman: Miss Fairfax.

[Enter Gwendolen. Exit Merriman.]

Cecily [*advancing to meet her*]: Pray let me introduce myself to you. My name is Cecily Cardew.

Gwendolen: Cecily Cardew? [*Moving to her and shaking hands.*] What a very sweet name! Something tells me that we are going to be great friends. I like you already more than I can say. My first impressions of people are never wrong.

Cecily: How nice of you to like me so much after we have known each other such a comparatively short time. Pray sit down.

Gwendolen [*still standing up*]: I may call you Cecily, may I not?

Cecily: With pleasure!
Gwendolen: And you will always call me Gwendolen, won't you.
Cecily: If you wish.
Gwendolen: Then that is all quite settled, is it not?
Cecily: I hope so.

[A pause. They both sit down together.]

Gwendolen: Perhaps this might be a favourable opportunity for my mentioning who I am. My father is Lord Bracknell. You have never heard of papa, I suppose?
Cecily: I don't think so.
Gwendolen: Outside the family circle, papa, I am glad to say, is entirely unknown. I think that is quite as it should be. The home seems to me to be the proper sphere for the man. And certainly once a man begins to neglect his domestic duties he becomes painfully effeminate, does he not? And I don't like that. It makes men so very attractive. Cecily, mamma, whose views on education are remarkably strict, has brought me up to be extremely short-sighted; it is part of her system; so do you mind my looking at you through my glasses?
Cecily: Oh! not at all, Gwendolen. I am very fond of being looked at.
Gwendolen [*after examining Cecily carefully through a lorgnette*]:[21] You are here on a short visit I suppose.
Cecily: Oh no! I live here.
Gwendolen: [*severely*] Really? Your mother, no doubt, or some female relative of advanced years, resides here also?
Cecily: Oh no! I have no mother, nor, in fact, any relations.
Gwendolen: Indeed?
Cecily: My dear guardian, with the assistance of Miss Prism, has the arduous task of looking after me.
Gwendolen: Your guardian?
Cecily: Yes, I am Mr Worthing's ward.
Gwendolen: Oh! It is strange he never mentioned to me that he had a ward. How secretive of him! He grows more interesting hourly. I am not sure, however, that the news inspires me with feelings of unmixed delight. [*Rising and going to her.*] I am very fond of you, Cecily; I have liked you ever since I met you! But I am bound to state that now that I know that you are Mr Worthing's ward, I cannot help expressing a wish you were—well just a little older than you seem to be—and not quite so very alluring in appearance. In fact, if I may speak candidly—
Cecily: Pray do! I think that whenever one has anything unpleasant to say, one should always be quite candid.
Gwendolen: Well, to speak with perfect candour, Cecily, I wish that you were fully forty-two, and more than usually plain for your age. Ernest has a strong upright nature. He is the very soul of truth and honour. Disloyalty would be as impossible to him as deception. But even men of the noblest

[21]*lorgnette*: Opera glasses.

possible moral character are extremely susceptible to the influence of the physical charms of others. Modern, no less than Ancient History, supplies us with many most painful examples of what I refer to. If it were not so, indeed, History would be quite unreadable.

Cecily: I beg your pardon, Gwendolen, did you say Ernest?

Gwendolen: Yes.

Cecily: Oh, but it is not Mr Ernest Worthing who is my guardian. It is his brother—his elder brother.

Gwendolen [*sitting down again*]: Ernest never mentioned to me that he had a brother.

Cecily: I am sorry to say they have not been on good terms for a long time.

Gwendolen: Ah! that accounts for it. And now that I think of it I have never heard any man mention his brother. The subject seems distasteful to most men. Cecily, you have lifted a load from my mind. I was growing almost anxious. It would have been terrible if any cloud had come across a friendship like ours, would it not? Of course you are quite, quite sure that it is not Mr Ernest Worthing who is your guardian?

Cecily: Quite sure. [*A pause.*] In fact, I am going to be his.

Gwendolen [*enquiringly*]: I beg your pardon?

Cecily [*rather shy and confidingly*]: Dearest Gwendolen, there is no reason why I should make a secret of it to you. Our little county newspaper is sure to chronicle the fact next week. Mr Ernest Worthing and I are engaged to be married.

Gwendolen [*quite politely, rising*]: My darling Cecily, I think there must be some slight error. Mr Ernest Worthing is engaged to me. The announcement will appear in the "Morning Post" on Saturday at the latest.

Cecily [*very politely, rising*]: I am afraid you must be under some misconception. Ernest proposed to me exactly ten minutes ago. [*Shows diary.*]

Gwendolen [*examines diary through her lorgnette carefully*]: It is certainly very curious, for he asked me to be his wife yesterday afternoon at 5.30. If you would care to verify the incident, pray do so. [*Produces diary of her own.*] I never travel without my diary. One should always have something sensational to read in the train. I am so sorry, dear Cecily, if it is any disappointment to you, but I am afraid I have the prior claim.

Cecily: It would distress me more than I can tell you, dear Gwendolen, if it caused you any mental or physical anguish, but I feel bound to point out that since Ernest proposed to you he clearly has changed his mind.

Gwendolen [*meditatively*]: If the poor fellow has been entrapped into any foolish promise I shall consider it my duty to rescue him at once, and with a firm hand.

Cecily [*thoughtfully and sadly*]: Whatever unfortunate entanglement my dear boy may have got into, I will never reproach him with it after we are married.

Gwendolen: Do you allude to me, Miss Cardew, as an entanglement? You are presumptuous. On an occasion of this kind it becomes more than a moral duty to speak one's mind. It becomes a pleasure.

Cecily: Do you suggest, Miss Fairfax, that I entrapped Ernest into an engagement? How dare you? This is no time for wearing the shallow mask of manners. When I see a spade I call it a spade.

Gwendolen [*satirically*]: I am glad to say that I have never seen a spade. It is obvious that our social spheres have been widely different.

[Enter Merriman, followed by the footman. He carries a salver, table cloth, and plate stand. Cecily is about to retort. The presence of the servants exercises a restraining influence, under which both girls chafe.]

Merriman: Shall I lay tea here as usual, Miss?

Cecily [*sternly, in a calm voice*]: Yes, as usual.

[Merriman begins to clear table and lay cloth. A long pause. Cecily and Gwendolen glare at each other.]

Gwendolen: Are there many interesting walks in the vicinity, Miss Cardew?

Cecily: Oh! yes! a great many. From the top of one of the hills quite close one can see five counties.

Gwendolen: Five counties! I don't think I should like that. I hate crowds.

Cecily [*sweetly*]: I suppose that is why you live in town?

[Gwendolen bites her lip, and beats her foot nervously with her parasol.]

Gwendolen [*looking round*]: Quite a well-kept garden this is, Miss Cardew.

Cecily: So glad you like it, Miss Fairfax.

Gwendolen: I had no idea there were any flowers in the country.

Cecily: Oh, flowers are as common here, Miss Fairfax, as people are in London.

Gwendolen: Personally, I cannot understand how anybody manages to exist in the country, if anybody who is anybody does. The country always bores me to death.

Cecily: Ah! This is what the newspapers call agricultural depression, is it not? I believe the aristocracy are suffering very much from it just at present. It is almost an epidemic amongst them, I have been told. May I offer you some tea, Miss Fairfax?

Gwendolen [*with elaborate politeness*]: Thank you. [*Aside.*] Detestable girl! But I require tea!

Cecily [*sweetly*]: Sugar?

Gwendolen [*superciliously*]: No, thank you. Sugar is not fashionable any more.

[Cecily looks angrily at her, takes up the tongs and puts four lumps of sugar into the cup.]

Cecily [*severely*]: Cake or bread and butter?

Gwendolen [*in a bored manner*]: Bread and butter, please. Cake is rarely seen at the best houses nowadays.

Cecily [*cuts a very large slice of cake, and puts it on the tray*]: Hand that to Miss Fairfax.

[Merriman does so, and goes out with footman. Gwendolen drinks the tea and makes a grimace. Puts down cup at once, reaches out her hand to the bread and butter, looks at it, and finds it is cake. Rises in indignation.]

Gwendolen: You have filled my tea with lumps of sugar, and though I asked most distinctly for bread and butter, you have given me cake. I am known for the gentleness of my disposition, and the extraordinary sweetness of my nature, but I warn you, Miss Cardew, you may go too far.

Cecily [*rising*]: To save my poor, innocent, trusting boy from the machinations of any other girl there are no lengths to which I would not go.

Gwendolen: From the moment I saw you I distrusted you. I felt that you were false and deceitful. I am never deceived in such matters. My first impressions of people are invariably right.

Cecily: It seems to me, Miss Fairfax, that I am trespassing on your valuable time. No doubt you have many other calls of a similar character to make in the neighbourhood.

[Enter Jack.]

Gwendolen [*catching sight of him*]: Ernest! My own Ernest!

Jack: Gwendolen! Darling! [*Offers to kiss her.*]

Gwendolen [*drawing back*]: A moment! May I ask if you are engaged to be married to this young lady? [*Points to Cecily.*]

Jack [*laughing*]: To dear little Cecily! Of course not! What could have put such an idea into your pretty little head?

Gwendolen: Thank you. You may! [*Offers her cheek.*]

Cecily [*very sweetly*]: I knew there must be some misunderstanding, Miss Fairfax. The gentleman whose arm is at present round your waist is my dear guardian, Mr John Worthing.

Gwendolen: I beg your pardon?

Cecily: This is Uncle Jack.

Gwendolen [*receding*]: Jack! Oh!

[Enter Algernon.]

Cecily: Here is Ernest.

Algernon [*goes straight over to Cecily without noticing anyone else*]: My own love!

[Offers to kiss her.]

Cecily [*drawing back*]: A moment, Ernest! May I ask you—are you engaged to be married to this young lady?

Algernon [*looking round*]: To what young lady? Good heavens! Gwendolen!

Cecily: Yes, to good heavens, Gwendolen, I mean to Gwendolen.

Algernon [*laughing*]: Of course not! What could have put such an idea into your pretty little head?

Cecily: Thank you. [*Presenting her cheek to be kissed.*] You may.

[Algernon kisses her.]

Gwendolen: I felt there was some slight error, Miss Cardew. The gentleman who is now embracing you is my cousin, Mr Algernon Moncrieff.

Cecily [*breaking away from Algernon*]: Algernon Moncrieff! Oh!

[The two girls move towards each other and put their arms round each other's waists as if for protection.]

Cecily: Are you called Algernon?
Algernon: I cannot deny it.
Cecily: Oh!
Gwendolen: Is your name really John?
Jack [*standing rather proudly*]: I could deny it if I liked. I could deny anything if I liked. But my name certainly is John. It has been John for years.
Cecily [*to Gwendolen*]: A gross deception has been practised on both of us.
Gwendolen: My poor wounded Cecily!
Cecily: My sweet wronged Gwendolen!
Gwendolen [*slowly and seriously*]: You will call me sister, will you not?

[They embrace. Jack and Algernon groan and walk up and down.]

Cecily [*rather brightly*]: There is just one question I would like to be allowed to ask my guardian.
Gwendolen: An admirable idea! Mr Worthing, there is just one question I would like to be permitted to put to you. Where is your brother Ernest? We are both engaged to be married to your brother Ernest, so it is a matter of some importance to us to know where your brother Ernest is at present.
Jack [*slowly and hesitatingly*]: Gwendolen—Cecily—It is very painful for me to be forced to speak the truth. It is the first time in my life that I have ever been reduced to such a painful position, and I am really quite inexperienced in doing anything of the kind. However I will tell you quite frankly that I have no brother Ernest. I have no brother at all. I never had a brother in my life, and I certainly have not the smallest intention of ever having one in the future.
Cecily [*surprised*]: No brother at all?
Jack [*cheerily*]: None!
Gwendolen [*severely*]: Had you never a brother of any kind?
Jack [*pleasantly*]: Never. Not even of any kind.
Gwendolen: I am afraid it is quite clear, Cecily, that neither of us is engaged to be married to anyone.
Cecily: It is not a very pleasant position for a young girl suddenly to find herself in. Is it?
Gwendolen: Let us go into the house. They will hardly venture to come after us there.
Cecily: No, men are so cowardly, aren't they?

[They retire into the house with scornful looks.]

Jack: This ghastly state of things is what you call Bunburying, I suppose?
Algernon: Yes, and a perfectly wonderful Bunbury it is. The most wonderful Bunbury I have ever had in my life.
Jack: Well, you've no right whatsoever to Bunbury here.
Algernon: That is absurd. One has a right to Bunbury anywhere one chooses. Every serious Bunburyist knows that.

Jack: Serious Bunburyist! Good heavens!

Algernon: Well, one must be serious about something, if one wants to have any amusement in life. I happen to be serious about Bunburying. What on earth you are serious about I haven't got the remotest idea. About everything, I should fancy. You have such an absolutely trivial nature.

Jack: Well, the only small satisfaction I have in the whole of this wretched business is that your friend Bunbury is quite exploded. You won't be able to run down to the country quite so often as you used to do, dear Algy. And a very good thing too.

Algernon: Your brother is a little off colour, isn't he, dear Jack? You won't be able to disappear to London quite so frequently as your wicked custom was. And not a bad thing either.

Jack: As for your conduct towards Miss Cardew, I must say that your taking in a sweet, simple, innocent girl like that is quite inexcusable. To say nothing of the fact that she is my ward.

Algernon: I can see no possible defence at all for your deceiving a brilliant, clever, thoroughly experienced young lady like Miss Fairfax. To say nothing of the fact that she is my cousin.

Jack: I wanted to be engaged to Gwendolen, that is all. I love her.

Algernon: Well, I simply wanted to be engaged to Cecily. I adore her.

Jack: There is certainly no chance of your marrying Miss Cardew.

Algernon: I don't think there is much likelihood, Jack, of you and Miss Fairfax being united.

Jack: Well, that is no business of yours.

Algernon: If it was my business, I wouldn't talk about it. [*Begins to eat muffins.*] It is very vulgar to talk about one's business. Only people like stockbrokers do that, and then merely at dinner parties.

Jack: How you can sit there, calmly eating muffins when we are in this horrible trouble, I can't make out. You seem to me to be perfectly heartless.

Algernon: Well, I can't eat muffins in an agitated manner. The butter would probably get on my cuffs. One should always eat muffins quite calmly. It is the only way to eat them.

Jack: I say it's perfectly heartless your eating muffins at all, under the circumstances.

Algernon: When I am in trouble, eating is the only thing that consoles me. Indeed, when I am in really great trouble, as anyone who knows me intimately will tell you, I refuse everything except food and drink. At the present moment I am eating muffins because I am unhappy. Besides, I am particularly fond of muffins. [*Rising.*]

Jack [*rising*]: Well, that is no reason why you should eat them all in that greedy way. [*Takes muffins from Algernon.*]

Algernon [*offering tea-cake*]: I wish you would have tea-cake instead. I don't like tea-cake.

Jack: Good heavens! I suppose a man may eat his own muffins in his own garden.

Algernon: But you have just said it was perfectly heartless to eat muffins.

Jack: I said it was perfectly heartless of you, under the circumstances. That is a very different thing.

Algernon: That may be. But the muffins are the same. [*He seizes the muffin-dish from Jack.*]

Jack: Algy, I wish to goodness you would go.

Algernon: You can't possibly ask me to go without having some dinner. It's absurd. I never go without my dinner. No one ever does, except vegetarians and people like that. Besides I have just made arrangements with Dr Chasuble to be christened at a quarter to six under the name of Ernest.

Jack: My dear fellow, the sooner you give up that nonsense the better. I made arrangements this morning with Dr Chasuble to be christened myself at 5.30, and I naturally will take the name of Ernest. Gwendolen would wish it. We can't both be christened Ernest. It's absurd. Besides, I have a perfect right to be christened if I like. There is no evidence at all that I ever have been christened by anybody. I should think it extremely probable I never was, and so does Dr Chasuble. It is entirely different in your case. You have been christened already.

Algernon: Yes, but I have not been christened for years.

Jack: Yes, but you have been christened. That is the important thing.

Algernon: Quite so. So I know my constitution can stand it. If you are not quite sure about your ever having been christened, I must say I think it rather dangerous your venturing on it now. It might make you very unwell. You can hardly have forgotten that someone very closely connected with you was very nearly carried off this week in Paris by a severe chill.

Jack: Yes, but you said yourself that a severe chill was not hereditary.

Algernon: It usen't to be, I know—but I daresay it is now. Science is always making wonderful improvements in things.

Jack [*picking up the muffin-dish*]: Oh, that is nonsense; you are always talking nonsense.

Algernon: Jack, you are at the muffins again! I wish you wouldn't. There are only two left. [*Takes them.*] I told you I was particularly fond of muffins.

Jack: But I hate tea-cake.

Algernon: Why on earth then do you allow tea-cake to be served up for your guests? What ideas you have of hospitality!

Jack: Algernon! I have already told you to go. I don't want you here. Why don't you go!

Algernon: I haven't quite finished my tea yet! and there is still one muffin left.

[*Jack groans, and sinks into a chair. Algernon still continues eating.*]

ACT DROP

THIRD ACT

Scene: Morning-room[22] *at the Manor House.*

[*Gwendolen and Cecily are at the window, looking out into the garden.*]

[22]*Morning-room:* An informal room that was used for receiving morning visitors.

Gwendolen: The fact that they did not follow us at once in the house, as anyone else would have done, seems to me to show that they have some sense of shame left.

Cecily: They have been eating muffins. That looks like repentance.

Gwendolen [*after a pause*]: They don't seem to notice us at all. Couldn't you cough?

Cecily: But I haven't got a cough.

Gwendolen: They're looking at us. What effrontery!

Cecily: They're approaching. That's very forward of them.

Gwendolen: Let us preserve a dignified silence.

Cecily: Certainly. It's the only thing to do now.

[Enter Jack followed by Algernon. They whistle some dreadful popular air from a British Opera.]

Gwendolen: This dignified silence seems to produce an unpleasant effect.

Cecily: A most distasteful one.

Gwendolen: But we will not be the first to speak.

Cecily: Certainly not.

Gwendolen: Mr Worthing, I have something very particular to ask you. Much depends on your reply.

Cecily: Gwendolen, your common sense is invaluable. Mr Moncrieff, kindly answer me the following question. Why did you pretend to be my guardian's brother?

Algernon: In order that I might have an opportunity of meeting you.

Cecily [*to Gwendolen*]: That certainly seems a satisfactory explanation, does it not?

Gwendolen: Yes, dear, if you can believe him.

Cecily: I don't. But that does not affect the wonderful beauty of his answer.

Gwendolen: True. In matters of grave importance, style, not sincerity is the vital thing. Mr Worthing, what explanation can you offer to me for pretending to have a brother? Was it in order that you might have an opportunity of coming up to town to see me as often as possible?

Jack: Can you doubt it, Miss Fairfax?

Gwendolen: I have the gravest doubts upon the subject. But I intend to crush them. This is not the moment for German scepticism. [*Moving to Cecily.*] Their explanations appear to be quite satisfactory, especially Mr Worthing's. That seems to me to have the stamp of truth upon it.

Cecily: I am more than content with what Mr Moncrieff said. His voice alone inspires one with absolute credulity.

Gwendolen: Then you think we should forgive them?

Cecily: Yes. I mean no.

Gwendolen: True! I had forgotten. There are principles at stake that one cannot surrender. Which of us should tell them? The task is not a pleasant one.

Cecily: Could we not both speak at the same time?

Gwendolen: An excellent idea! I nearly always speak at the same time as other people. Will you take the time from me?

Cecily: Certainly.

[Gwendolen beats time with uplifted finger.]

Gwendolen and Cecily [*speaking together*]: Your Christian names[23] are still an insuperable barrier. That is all!

Jack and Algernon [*speaking together*]: Our Christian names! Is that all? But we are going to be christened this afternoon.

Gwendolen [*to Jack*]: For my sake you are prepared to do this terrible thing?

Jack: I am.

Cecily [*to Algernon*]: To please me you are ready to face this fearful ordeal?

Algernon: I am!

Gwendolen: How absurd to talk of the equality of the sexes! Where questions of self-sacrifice are concerned, men are infinitely beyond us.

Jack: We are. [*Clasps hands with Algernon.*]

Cecily: They have moments of physical courage of which we women know absolutely nothing.

Gwendolen [*to Jack*]: Darling!

Algernon [*to Cecily*]: Darling! [*They fall into each other's arms.*]

[Enter Merriman. When he enters he coughs loudly, seeing the situation.]

Merriman: Ahem! Ahem! Lady Bracknell!

Jack: Good heavens!

[Enter Lady Bracknell. The couples separate in alarm.] [Exit Merriman.]

Lady Bracknell: Gwendolen! What does this mean?

Gwendolen: Merely that I am engaged to be married to Mr Worthing, mamma.

Lady Bracknell: Come here. Sit down. Sit down immediately. Hesitation of any kind is a sign of mental decay in the young, of physical weakness in the old. [*Turns to Jack.*] Apprised, sir, of my daughter's sudden flight by her trusty maid, whose confidence I purchased by means of a small coin, I followed her at once by a luggage train. Her unhappy father is, I am glad to say, under the impression that she is attending a more than usually lengthy lecture by the University Extension Scheme on the Influence of a permanent income on Thought. I do not propose to undeceive him. Indeed I have never undeceived him on any question. I would consider it wrong. But of course, you will clearly understand that all communication between yourself and my daughter must cease immediately from this moment. On this point, as indeed on all points, I am firm.

Jack: I am engaged to be married to Gwendolen, Lady Bracknell!

Lady Bracknell: You are nothing of the kind, sir. And now, as regards Algernon! . . . Algernon!

Algernon: Yes, Aunt Augusta.

Lady Bracknell: May I ask if it is in this house that your invalid friend Mr Bunbury resides?

Algernon [*stammering*]: Oh! No! Bunbury doesn't live here. Bunbury is somewhere else at present. In fact, Bunbury is dead.

[23]*Christian names*: First names, the names that people are christened with.

Lady Bracknell: Dead! When did Mr Bunbury die? His death must have been extremely sudden.

Algernon [*airily*]: Oh! I killed Bunbury this afternoon. I mean poor Bunbury died this afternoon.

Lady Bracknell: What did he die of?

Algernon: Bunbury? Oh, he was quite exploded.

Lady Bracknell: Exploded! Was he the victim of a revolutionary outrage? I was not aware that Mr Bunbury was interested in social legislation. If so, he is well punished for his morbidity.

Algernon: My dear Aunt Augusta, I mean he was found out! The doctors found out that Bunbury could not live, that is what I mean—so Bunbury died.

Lady Bracknell: He seems to have had great confidence in the opinion of his physicians. I am glad, however, that he made up his mind at the last to some definite course of action, and acted under proper medical advice. And now that we have finally got rid of this Mr Bunbury, may I ask, Mr Worthing, who is that young person whose hand my nephew Algernon is now holding in what seems to me a peculiarly unnecessary manner?

Jack: That lady is Miss Cecily Cardew, my ward.

[Lady Bracknell bows coldly to Cecily.]

Algernon: I am engaged to be married to Cecily, Aunt Augusta.

Lady Bracknell: I beg your pardon?

Cecily: Mr Moncrieff and I are engaged to be married, Lady Bracknell.

Lady Bracknell [*with a shiver, crossing to the sofa and sitting down*]: I do not know whether there is anything peculiarly exciting in the air of this particular part of Hertfordshire, but the number of engagements that go on seems to me considerably above the proper average that statistics have laid down for our guidance. I think some preliminary enquiry on my part would not be out of place. Mr Worthing, is Miss Cardew at all connected with any of the larger railway stations in London? I merely desire information. Until yesterday I had no idea that there were any families or persons whose origins was a Terminus.

[Jack looks perfectly furious, but restrains himself.]

Jack [*in a clear, cold voice*]: Miss Cardew is the granddaughter of the late Mr Thomas Cardew of 149, Belgrave Square, S.W.; Gervase Park, Dorking, Surrey; and the Sporran, Fifeshire, N.B.

Lady Bracknell: That sounds not unsatisfactory. Three addresses always inspire confidence, even in tradesmen. But what proof have I of their authenticity?

Jack: I have carefully preserved the Court Guides[24] of the period. They are open to your inspection, Lady Bracknell.

Lady Bracknell [*grimly*]: I have known strange errors in that publication.

Jack: Miss Cardew's family solicitors are Messrs Markby, Markby, and Markby.

Lady Bracknell: Markby, Markby, and Markby? A firm of the very highest position in their profession. Indeed I am told that one of the Mr Markbys is occasionally to be seen at dinner parties. So far I am satisfied.

[24]*Court Guides*: Directories.

Jack [*very irritably*]: How extremely kind of you, Lady Bracknell! I have also in my possession, you will be pleased to hear, certificates of Miss Cardew's birth, baptism, whooping cough, registration, vaccination, confirmation, and the measles; both the German and the English variety.

Lady Bracknell: Ah! A life crowded with incident, I see; though perhaps somewhat too exciting for a young girl. I am not myself in favour of premature experiences. [*Rises, looks at her watch.*] Gwendolen! the time approaches for our departure. We have not a moment to lose. As a matter of form, Mr Worthing, I had better ask you if Miss Cardew has any little fortune?

Jack: Oh! about a hundred and thirty thousand pounds in the Funds. That is all. Goodbye, Lady Bracknell. So pleased to have seen you.

Lady Bracknell [*sitting down again*]: A moment, Mr Worthing. A hundred and thirty thousand pounds! And in the Funds! Miss Cardew seems to me a most attractive young lady, now that I look at her. Few girls of the present day have any really solid qualities, any of the qualities that last, and improve with time. We live, I regret to say, in an age of surfaces. [*To Cecily.*] Come over here, dear. [*Cecily goes across.*] Pretty child! your dress is sadly simple, and your hair seems almost as Nature might have left it. But we can soon alter all that. A thoroughly experienced French maid produces a really marvellous result in a very brief space of time. I remember recommending one to young Lady Lancing, and after three months her own husband did not know her.

Jack [*aside*]: And after six months nobody knew her.

Lady Bracknell [*glares at Jack for a few moments. Then bends, with a practised smile, to Cecily.*]: Kindly turn round, sweet child. [*Cecily turns completely round.*] No, the side view is what I want. [*Cecily presents her profile.*] Yes, quite as I expected. There are distinct social possibilities in your profile. The two weak points in our age are its want of principle and its want of profile. The chin a little higher, dear. Style largely depends on the way the chin is worn. They are worn very high, just at present. Algernon!

Algernon: Yes, Aunt Augusta!

Lady Bracknell: There are distinct social possibilities in Miss Cardew's profile.

Algernon: Cecily is the sweetest, dearest, prettiest girl in the whole world. And I don't care twopence about social possibilities.

Lady Bracknell: Never speak disrespectfully of Society, Algernon. Only people who can't get into it do that. [*To Cecily.*] Dear child, of course you know that Algernon has nothing but his debts to depend upon. But I do not approve of mercenary marriages. When I married Lord Bracknell I had no fortune of any kind. But I never dreamed for a moment of allowing that to stand in my way. Well, I suppose I must give my consent.

Algernon: Thank you, Aunt Augusta.

Lady Bracknell: Cecily, you may kiss me!

Cecily [*kisses her*]: Thank you, Lady Bracknell.

Lady Bracknell: You may also address me as Aunt Augusta for the future.

Cecily: Thank you, Aunt Augusta.

Lady Bracknell: The marriage, I think, had better take place quite soon.

Algernon: Thank you, Aunt Augusta.

Cecily: Thank you, Aunt Augusta.

Lady Bracknell: To speak frankly, I am not in favour of long engagements. They give people the opportunity of finding out each other's character before marriage, which I think is never advisable.

Jack: I beg your pardon for interrupting you, Lady Bracknell, but this engagement is quite out of the question. I am Miss Cardew's guardian, and she cannot marry without my consent until she comes of age. That consent I absolutely decline to give.

Lady Bracknell: Upon what grounds may I ask? Algernon is an extremely, I may almost say an ostentatiously, eligible young man. He has nothing, but he looks everything. What more can one desire?

Jack: It pains me very much to have to speak frankly to you, Lady Bracknell, about your nephew, but the fact is that I do not approve at all of his moral character. I suspect him of being untruthful.

[Algernon and Cecily look at him in indignant amazement.]

Lady Bracknell: Untruthful! My nephew Algernon? Impossible! He is an Oxonian.

Jack: I fear there can be no possible doubt about the matter. This afternoon, during my temporary absence in London on an important question of romance, he obtained admission to my house by means of the false pretence of being my brother. Under an assumed name he drank, I've just been informed by my butler, an entire pint bottle of my Perrier-Jouet, Brut, '89; a wine I was specially reserving for myself. Continuing his disgraceful deception, he succeeded in the course of the afternoon in alienating the affections of my only ward. He subsequently stayed to tea, and devoured every single muffin. And what makes his conduct all the more heartless is, that he was perfectly well aware from the first that I have no brother, that I never had a brother, and that I don't intend to have a brother, not even of any kind. I distinctly told him so myself yesterday afternoon.

Lady Bracknell: Ahem! Mr Worthing, after careful consideration I have decided entirely to overlook my nephew's conduct to you.

Jack: That is very generous of you, Lady Bracknell. My own decision, however, is unalterable. I decline to give my consent.

Lady Bracknell [*to Cecily*]: Come here, sweet child. [*Cecily goes over.*] How old are you, dear?

Cecily: Well, I am really only eighteen, but I always admit to twenty when I go to evening parties.

Lady Bracknell: You are perfectly right in making some slight alteration. Indeed, no woman should ever be quite accurate about her age. It looks so calculating. . . . [*In a meditative manner.*] Eighteen, but admitting to twenty at evening parties. Well, it will not be very long before you are of age and free from the restraints of tutelage. So I don't think your guardian's consent is, after all, a matter of any importance.

Jack: Pray excuse me, Lady Bracknell, for interrupting you again, but it is only fair to tell you that according to the terms of her grandfather's will Miss Cardew does not come legally of age till she is thirty-five.

Lady Bracknell: That does not seem to me to be a grave objection. Thirty-five is a very attractive age. London society is full of women of the very highest birth who have, of their own free choice, remained thirty-five for years. Lady Dumbleton is an instance in point. To my own knowledge she has been thirty-five ever since she arrived at the age of forty, which was many years ago now. I see no reason why our dear Cecily should not be even still more attractive at the age you mention than she is at present. There will be a large accumulation of property.

Cecily: Algy, could you wait for me till I was thirty-five?

Algernon: Of course I could, Cecily. You know I could.

Cecily: Yes, I felt it instinctively, but I couldn't wait all that time. I hate waiting even five minutes for anybody. It always makes me rather cross. I am not punctual myself, I know, but I do like punctuality in others, and waiting, even to be married, is quite out of the question.

Algernon: Then what is to be done, Cecily?

Cecily: I don't know, Mr Moncrieff.

Lady Bracknell: My dear Mr Worthing, as Miss Cardew states positively that she cannot wait till she is thirty-five—a remark which I am bound to say seems to me to show a somewhat impatient nature—I would beg of you to reconsider your decision.

Jack: But my dear Lady Bracknell, the matter is entirely in your own hands. The moment you consent to my marriage with Gwendolen, I will most gladly allow your nephew to form an alliance with my ward.

Lady Bracknell [*rising and drawing herself up*]: You must be quite aware that what you propose is out of the question.

Jack: Then a passionate celibacy is all that any of us can look forward to.

Lady Bracknell: That is not the destiny I propose for Gwendolen. Algernon, of course, can choose for himself. [*Pulls out her watch.*] Come, dear; [*Gwendolen rises.*] we have already missed five, if not six, trains. To miss any more might expose us to comment on the platform.

[Enter Dr Chasuble.]

Chasuble: Everything is quite ready for the christenings.

Lady Bracknell: The christenings, sir! Is not that somewhat premature?

Chasuble [*looking rather puzzled, and pointing to Jack and Algernon*]: Both these gentlemen have expressed a desire for immediate baptism.

Lady Bracknell: At their age? The idea is grotesque and irreligious! Algernon, I forbid you to be baptized. I will not hear of such excesses. Lord Bracknell would be highly displeased if he learned that that was the way in which you wasted your time and money.

Chasuble: Am I to understand then that there are to be no christenings at all this afternoon?

Jack: I don't think that, as things are now, it would be of much practical value to either of us, Dr Chasuble.

Chasuble: I am grieved to hear such sentiments from you, Mr Worthing. They savour of the heretical views of the Anabaptists,[25] views that I have completely refuted in four of my unpublished sermons. However, as your present mood seems to be one peculiarly secular, I will return to the church at once. Indeed, I have just been informed by the pew-opener that for the last hour and a half Miss Prism has been waiting for me in the vestry.

Lady Bracknell [*starting*]: Miss Prism! Did I hear you mention a Miss Prism?

Chasuble: Yes, Lady Bracknell. I am on my way to join her.

Lady Bracknell: Pray allow me to detain you for a moment. This matter may prove to be one of vital importance to Lord Bracknell and myself. Is this Miss Prism a female of repellent aspect, remotely connected with education?

Chasuble [*somewhat indignantly*]: She is the most cultivated of ladies, and the very picture of respectability.

Lady Bracknell: It is obviously the same person. May I ask what position she holds in your household?

Chasuble [*severely*]: I am a celibate, madam.

Jack [*interposing*]: Miss Prism, Lady Bracknell, has been for the last three years Miss Cardew's esteemed governess and valued companion.

Lady Bracknell: In spite of what I hear of her, I must see her at once. Let her be sent for.

Chasuble [*looking off*]: She approaches; she is nigh.

[Enter Miss Prism hurriedly.]

Miss Prism: I was told you expected me in the vestry, dear Canon. I have been waiting for you there for an hour and three quarters. [*Catches sight of Lady Bracknell who has fixed her with a stony glare. Miss Prism grows pale and quails. She looks anxiously round as if desirous to escape.*]

Lady Bracknell [*in a severe, judicial voice*]: Prism! [Miss *Prism bows her head in shame.*] Come here, Prism! [*Miss Prism approaches in a humble manner.*] Prism! Where is that baby? [*General consternation. The Canon starts back in horror. Algernon and Jack pretend to be anxious to shield Cecily and Gwendolen from hearing the details of a terrible public scandal.*] Twenty-eight years ago, Prism, you left Lord Bracknell's house, Number 104, Upper Grosvenor Street, in charge of a perambulator[26] that contained a baby, of the male sex. You never returned. A few weeks later, through the elaborate investigations of the Metropolitan police, the perambulator was discovered at midnight, standing by itself in a remote comer of Bayswater.[27] It contained the manuscript of a three-volume novel of more than usually revolting sentimentality. [*Miss Prism starts in involuntary indignation.*] But the baby was not there! [*Everyone looks at Miss Prism.*] Prism! Where is that baby? [*A pause.*]

[25]*Anabaptists:* Members of a Protestant denomination that does not practice infant baptism.

[26]*perambulator:* A baby carriage.

[27]*Bayswater:* A district in West London.

Miss Prism: Lady Bracknell, I admit with shame that I do not know. I only wish I did. The plain facts of the case are these. On the morning of the day you mention, a day that is for ever branded on my memory, I prepared as usual to take the baby out in its perambulator. I had also with me a somewhat old, but capacious hand-bag in which I had intended to place the manuscript of a work of fiction that I had written during my few unoccupied hours. In a moment of mental abstraction, for which I never can forgive myself, I deposited the manuscript in the bassinette, and placed the baby in the hand-bag.

Jack [*who has been listening attentively*]: But where did you deposit the hand-bag?

Miss Prism: Do not ask me, Mr Worthing.

Jack: Miss Prism, this is a matter of no small importance to me. I insist on knowing where you deposited the hand-bag that contained that infant.

Miss Prism: I left it in the cloak-room of one of the larger railway stations in London.

Jack: What railway station?

Miss Prism [*quite crushed*]: Victoria. The Brighton line. [*Sinks into a chair.*]

Jack: I must retire to my room for a moment. Gwendolen, wait here for me.

Gwendolen: If you are not too long, I will wait here for you all my life. [*Exit Jack in great excitement.*]

Chasuble: What do you think this means, Lady Bracknell?

Lady Bracknell: I dare not even suspect, Dr Chasuble. I need hardly tell you that in families of high position strange coincidences are not supposed to occur. They are hardly considered the thing.

[Noises heard overhead as if someone was throwing trunks about. Everyone looks up.]

Cecily: Uncle Jack seems strangely agitated.

Chasuble: Your guardian has a very emotional nature.

Lady Bracknell: This noise is extremely unpleasant. It sounds as if he was having an argument. I dislike arguments of any kind. They are always vulgar, and often convincing.

Chasuble [*looking up*]: It has stopped now. [*The noise is redoubled.*]

Lady Bracknell: I wish he would arrive at some conclusion.

Gwendolen. This suspense is terrible. I hope it will last.

[Enter Jack with a hand-bag of black leather in his hand.]

Jack [*rushing over to Miss Prism*]: Is this the hand-bag, Miss Prism? Examine it carefully before you speak. The happiness of more than one life depends on your answer.

Miss Prism [*calmly*]: It seems to be mine. Yes, here is the injury it received through the upsetting of a Gower Street omnibus in younger and happier days. Here is the stain on the lining caused by the explosion of a temperance beverage, an incident that occurred at Leamington. And here, on the lock, are my initials. I had forgotten that in an extravagant mood I had had them placed there. The bag is undoubtedly mine. I am delighted to have it so unexpectedly restored to me. It has been a great inconvenience being without it all these years.

Jack [*in a pathetic voice*]: Miss Prism, more is restored to you than this hand-bag. I was the baby you placed in it.

Miss Prism [*amazed*]: You?

Jack [*embracing her*]: Yes . . . mother!

Miss Prism [*recoiling in indignant astonishment*]: Mr Worthing! I am unmarried!

Jack: Unmarried! I do not deny that is a serious blow. But after all, who has the right to cast a stone against one who has suffered? Cannot repentance wipe out an act of folly? Why should there be one law for men, and another for women? Mother, I forgive you. [*Tries to embrace her again.*]

Miss Prism [*still more indignant*]: Mr Worthing, there is some error. [*Pointing to Lady Bracknell.*] There is the lady who can tell you who you really are.

Jack [*after a pause*]: Lady Bracknell, I hate to seem inquisitive, but would you kindly inform me who I am?

Lady Bracknell: I am afraid that the news I have to give you will not altogether please you. You are the son of my poor sister, Mrs Moncrieff, and consequently Algernon's elder brother.

Jack: Algy's elder brother! Then I have a brother after all. I knew I had a brother! I always said I had a brother! Cecily—how could you have ever doubted that I had a brother. [*Seizes hold of Algernon.*] Dr Chasuble, my unfortunate brother. Miss Prism, my unfortunate brother. Gwendolen, my unfortunate brother. Algy, you young scoundrel, you will have to treat me with more respect in the future. You have never behaved to me like a brother in all your life.

Algernon: Well, not till today, old boy, I admit. I did my best, however, though I was out of practice. [*Shakes hands.*]

Gwendolen [*to Jack*]: My own! But what own are you? What is your Christian name, now that you have become someone else?

Jack: Good heavens! . . . I had quite forgotten that point. Your decision on the subject of my name is irrevocable, I suppose?

Gwendolen: I never change, except in my affections.

Cecily: What a noble nature you have, Gwendolen!

Jack: Then the question had better be cleared up at once. Aunt Augusta, a moment. At the time when Miss Prism left me in the hand-bag, had I been christened already?

Lady Bracknell: Every luxury that money could buy, including christening, had been lavished on you by your fond and doting parents.

Jack: Then I was christened! That is settled. Now, what name was I given? Let me know the worst.

Lady Bracknell: Being the eldest son you were naturally christened after your father.

Jack [*irritably*]: Yes, but what was my father's Christian name?

Lady Bracknell [*meditatively*]: I cannot at the present moment recall what the General's Christian name was. But I have no doubt he had one. He was eccentric, I admit. But only in later years. And that was the result of the Indian climate, and marriage, and indigestion, and other things of that kind.

Jack: Algy! Can't you recollect what our father's Christian name was?

Algernon: My dear boy, we were never even on speaking terms. He died before I was a year old.

Jack: His name would appear in the Army Lists of the period, I suppose, Aunt Augusta?

Lady Bracknell: The General was essentially a man of peace, except in his domestic life. But I have no doubt his name would appear in any military directory.

Jack: The Army Lists of the last forty years are here. These delightful records should have been my constant study. [*Rushes to bookcase and tears the books out.*] M. Generals . . . Mallam, Maxbohm, Magley, what ghastly names they have—Markby, Migsby, Mobbs, Moncrieff! Lieutenant 1840, Captain, Lieutenant-Colonel, Colonel, General 1869, Christian names, Ernest John. [*Puts book very quietly down and speaks quite calmly.*] I always told you, Gwendolen, my name was Ernest, didn't I? Well, it is Ernest after all. I mean it naturally is Ernest.

Lady Bracknell: Yes, I remember now that the General was called Ernest. I knew I had some particular reason for disliking the name.

Gwendolen: Ernest! My own Ernest! I felt from the first that you could have no other name!

Jack: Gwendolen, it is a terrible thing for a man to find out suddenly that all his life he has been speaking nothing but the truth. Can you forgive me?

Gwendolen: I can. For I feel that you are sure to change.

Jack: My own one!

Chasuble [*to Miss Prism*]: Laetitia! [*Embraces her.*]

Miss Prism [*enthusiastically*]: Frederick! At last!

Algernon: Cecily! [*Embraces her.*] At last!

Jack: Gwendolen! [*Embraces her.*] At last!

Lady Bracknell: My nephew, you seem to be displaying signs of triviality.

Jack: On the contrary, Aunt Augusta, I've now realized for the first time in my life the vital Importance of Being Earnest.

CURTAIN TABLEAU

(1894, performed 1895; 1899)

QUESTIONS FOR DISCUSSION AND WRITING

CLOSE READING

1. What is "bunburying"? Why does Algernon think "bunburying" is a particularly necessary habit for married men?
2. Discuss the play on the word "earnest." What, if anything, are these characters earnest about?
3. On what grounds does Lady Bracknell object to Jack's marriage with her daughter? What do these objections reveal about her values?

CRITICAL AND CREATIVE READING

4. The play reverses several traditional hierarchies, including gender roles, social class, and youth and age. Choose one of these categories and examine how Wilde questions these traditional hierarchies in his play.
5. Who do you think is the most honest character in this play? Is honesty necessarily a positive trait in this play?
6. What is the significance of the fact that Cecily lies in her diary? To what degree is there any "truth" in what she writes? What comments might Wilde be making about the way we deceive ourselves?

CONNECTIONS TO OTHER READINGS

7. Based on your reading of this chapter's Common Characters section, is Algernon a trickster figure? What qualities does he share with that common folk character?
8. How do the lovers in *The Importance of Being Earnest* follow Emily Dickinson's advice to "Tell all the Truth but tell it slant"?
9. How do the relationships of the romantic couples resemble those in the more serious stories in this chapter? Can you extract serious themes from this play?

Essays

Maxine Hong Kingston

No Name Woman

Maxine Hong Kingston (b. 1940) is one of the most prominent Asian American writers active today. She has earned her reputation through patient literary output; although she is not prolific, critics have looked forward to each of her books following the extraordinary critical and popular success of *The Woman Warrior* (1975), a book of memoirs that imaginatively incorporates legend and fiction into Kingston's life story. Although her subject matter varies, two prominent motifs in Kingston's work are the sometimes difficult merging of Chinese and American identity and the weight of past wisdom on present generations. Both of these themes are evident in the following essay, "No Name Woman." Kingston has also focused much attention on raising consciousness about the rights of women and the ongoing struggle for world peace.

“You must not tell anyone,” my mother said, “what I am about to tell you. In China your father had a sister who killed herself. She jumped into the family well. We say that your father has all brothers because it is as if she had never been born.

“In 1924 just a few days after our village celebrated seventeen hurry-up weddings—to make sure that every young man who went ‘out on the road’ would responsibly come home—your father and his brothers and your grandfather and his brothers and your aunt’s new husband sailed for America, the Gold Mountain. It was your grandfather’s last trip. Those lucky enough to get contracts waved good-bye from the decks. They fed and guarded the stowaways and helped them off in Cuba, New York, Bali, Hawaii. ‘We’ll meet in California next year,’ they said. All of them sent money home.

“I remember looking at your aunt one day when she and I were dressing; I had not noticed before that she had such a protruding melon of a stomach. But I did not think, ‘She’s pregnant,’ until she began to look like other pregnant women, her shirt pulling and the white tops of her black pants showing. She could not have been pregnant, you see, because her husband had been gone for years. No one said anything. We did not discuss it. In early summer she was ready to have the child, long after the time when it could have been possible.

“The village had also been counting. On the night the baby was to be born the villagers raided our house. Some were crying. Like a great saw, teeth strung with lights, files of people walked zigzag across our land, tearing the rice. Their lanterns doubled in the disturbed black water, which drained away through the broken bunds. As the villagers closed in, we could see that some of them, probably men and women we knew well, wore white masks. The people with long hair hung it over their faces. Women with short hair made it stand up on end. Some had tied white bands around their foreheads, arms, and legs.

“At first they threw mud and rocks at the house. Then they threw eggs and 5
began slaughtering our stock. We could hear the animals scream their deaths—the roosters, the pigs, a last great roar from the ox. Familiar wild heads flared in our night windows; the villagers encircled us. Some of the faces stopped to peer at us, their eyes rushing like searchlights. The hands flattened against the panes, framed heads, and left red prints.

“The villagers broke in the front and the back doors at the same time, even though we had not locked the doors against them. Their knives dripped with the blood of our animals. They smeared blood on the doors and walls. One woman swung a chicken, whose throat she had slit, splattering blood in red arcs about her. We stood together in the middle of our house, in the family hall with the pictures and tables of the ancestors around us, and looked straight ahead.

“At that time the house had only two wings. When the men came back, we would build two more to enclose our courtyard and a third one to begin a second courtyard. The villagers pushed through both wings, even your grandparents’ rooms, to find your aunt’s, which was also mine until the men returned. From this room a new wing for one of the younger families would grow. They ripped up her clothes and shoes and broke her combs, grinding them underfoot. They tore her work from the loom. They scattered the cooking fire and rolled the new weaving in it. We could hear them in the kitchen breaking our bowls and banging the pots. They overturned the great waist-high earthenware jugs; duck eggs, pickled fruits, vegetables burst out and mixed in acrid torrents. The old woman from the next field swept a broom through the air and loosed the spirits-of-the-broom over our heads. 'Pig.' 'Ghost.' 'Pig,' they sobbed and scolded while they ruined our house.

"When they left, they took sugar and oranges to bless themselves. They cut pieces from the dead animals. Some of them took bowls that were not broken and clothes that were not torn. Afterward we swept up the rice and sewed it back up into sacks. But the smells from the spilled preserves lasted. Your aunt gave birth in the pigsty that night. The next morning when I went for the water, I found her and the baby plugging up the family well.

"Don't let your father know that I told you. He denies her. Now that you have started to menstruate, what happened to her could happen to you. Don't humiliate us. You wouldn't like to be forgotten as if you had never been born. The villagers are watchful."

10 Whenever she had to warn us about life, my mother told stories that ran like this one, a story to grow up on. She tested our strength to establish realities. Those in the emigrant generations who could not reassert brute survival died young and far from home. Those of us in the first American generations have had to figure out how the invisible world the emigrants built around our childhoods fit in solid America.

The emigrants confused the gods by diverting their curses, misleading them with crooked streets and false names. They must try to confuse their offspring as well, who, I suppose, threaten them in similar ways—always trying to get things straight, always trying to name the unspeakable. The Chinese I know hide their names; sojourners take new names when their lives change and guard their real names with silence.

Chinese-Americans, when you try to understand what things in you are Chinese, how do you separate what is peculiar to childhood, to poverty, insanities, one family, your mother who marked your growing with stories, from what is Chinese? What is Chinese tradition and what is the movies?

If I want to learn what clothes my aunt wore, whether flashy or ordinary, I would have to begin, "Remember Father's drowned-in-the-well sister?" I cannot ask that. My mother has told me once and for all the useful parts. She will add nothing unless powered by Necessity, a riverbank that guides her life. She plants vegetable gardens rather than lawns; she carries the odd-shaped tomatoes home from the fields and eats food left for the gods.

Whenever we did frivolous things, we used up energy; we flew high kites. We children came up off the ground over the melting cones our parents brought home from work and the American movie on New Year's Day—*Oh, You Beautiful Doll* with Betty Grable one year, and *She Wore a Yellow Ribbon* with John Wayne another year. After the one carnival ride each, we paid in guilt; our tired father counted his change on the dark walk home.

15 Adultery is extravagance. Could people who hatch their own chicks and eat the embryos and the heads for delicacies and boil the feet in vinegar for party

food, leaving only the gravel, eating even the gizzard lining—could such people engender a prodigal aunt? To be a woman, to have a daughter in starvation time was a waste enough. My aunt could not have been the lone romantic who gave up everything for sex. Women in the old China did not choose. Some man had commanded her to lie with him and be his secret evil. I wonder whether he masked himself when he joined the raid on her family.

Perhaps she encountered him in the fields or on the mountain where the daughters-in-law collected fuel. Or perhaps he first noticed her in the marketplace. He was not a stranger because the village housed no strangers. She had to have dealings with him other than sex. Perhaps he worked an adjoining field, or he sold her the cloth for the dress she sewed and wore. His demand must have surprised, then terrified her. She obeyed him; she always did as she was told.

When the family found a young man in the next village to be her husband, she stood tractably beside the best rooster, his proxy, and promised before they met that she would be his forever. She was lucky that he was her age and she would be the first wife, an advantage secure now. The night she first saw him, he had sex with her. Then he left for America. She had almost forgotten what he looked like. When she tried to envision him, she only saw the black and white face in the group photograph the men had had taken before leaving.

The other man was not, after all, much different from her husband. They both gave orders: she followed. "If you tell your family, I'll beat you. I'll kill you. Be here again next week." No one talked sex, ever. And she might have separated the rapes from the rest of living if only she did not have to buy her oil from him or gather wood in the same forest. I want her fear to have lasted just as long as rape lasted so that the fear could have been contained. No drawn-out fear. But women at sex hazarded birth and hence lifetimes. The fear did not stop but permeated everywhere. She told the man, "I think I'm pregnant." He organized the raid against her.

On nights when my mother and father talked about their life back home, sometimes they mentioned an "outcast table" whose business they still seemed to be settling, their voices tight. In a commensal tradition, where food is precious, the powerful older people made wrongdoers eat alone. Instead of letting them start separate new lives like the Japanese, who could become samurais and geishas, the Chinese family, faces averted but eyes glowering sideways, hung on to the offenders and fed them leftovers. My aunt must have lived in the same house as my parents and eaten at an outcast table. My mother spoke about the raid as if she had seen it, when she and my aunt, a daughter-in-law to a different household, should not have been living together at all. Daughters-in-law lived with their husbands' parents, not their own; a synonym for marriage in Chinese is "taking a daughter-in-law." Her husband's parents could have sold her, mortgaged her, stoned her. But they had sent her back to her own mother and father, a mysterious act hinting at disgraces not told me. Perhaps they had thrown her out to deflect the avengers.

She was the only daughter; her four brothers went with her father, husband, 20
and uncles "out on the road" and for some years became western men. When the goods were divided among the family, three of the brothers took land, and the youngest, my father, chose an education. After my grandparents gave their daughter away to her husband's family, they had dispensed all the adventure and

all the property. They expected her alone to keep the traditional ways, which her brothers, now among the barbarians, could fumble without detection. The heavy, deep-rooted women were to maintain the past against the flood, safe for returning. But the rare urge west had fixed upon our family, and so my aunt crossed boundaries not delineated in space.

The work of preservation demands that the feelings playing about in one's guts not be turned into action. Just watch their passing like cherry blossoms. But perhaps my aunt, my forerunner, caught in a slow life, let dreams grow and fade and after some months or years went toward what persisted. Fear at the enormities of the forbidden kept her desires delicate, wire and bone. She looked at a man because she liked the way the hair was tucked behind his ears, or she liked the question-mark line of a long torso curving at the shoulder and straight at the hip. For warm eyes or a soft voice or a slow walk—that's all—a few hairs, a line, a brightness, a sound, a pace, she gave up family. She offered us up for a charm that vanished with tiredness, a pigtail that didn't toss when the wind died. Why, the wrong lighting could erase the dearest thing about him.

It could very well have been, however, that my aunt did not take subtle enjoyment of her friend, but, a wild woman, kept rollicking company. Imagining her free with sex doesn't fit, though. I don't know any women like that, or men either. Unless I see her life branching into mine, she gives me no ancestral help.

To sustain her being in love, she often worked at herself in the mirror, guessing at the colors and shapes that would interest him, changing them frequently in order to hit on the right combination. She wanted him to look back.

On a farm near the sea, a woman who tended her appearance reaped a reputation for eccentricity. All the married women blunt-cut their hair in flaps about their ears or pulled it back in tight buns. No nonsense. Neither style blew easily into heart-catching tangles. And at their weddings they displayed themselves in their long hair for the last time. "It brushed the backs of my knees," my mother tells me. "It was braided, and even so, it brushed the backs of my knees."

At the mirror my aunt combed individuality into her bob. A bun could have 25
been contrived to escape into black streamers blowing in the wind or in quiet wisps about her face, but only the older women in our picture album wear buns. She brushed her hair back from her forehead, tucking the flaps behind her ears. She looped a piece of thread, knotted into a circle between her index fingers and thumbs and ran the double strand across her forehead. When she closed her fingers as if she were making a pair of shadow geese bite, the string twisted together catching the little hairs. Then she pulled the thread away from her skin, ripping the hairs out neatly, her eyes watering from the needles of pain. Opening her fingers, she cleaned the thread, then rolled it along her hairline and the tops of her eyebrows. My mother did the same to me and my sisters and herself. I used to believe that the expression "caught by the short hairs" meant a captive held with a depilatory string.[1] It especially hurt at the temples, but my mother said we were lucky we didn't have to have our feet bound when we were seven. Sisters used to sit on their beds and cry together, she said, as their mothers or their slaves removed the bandages for a few minutes each night and let the blood gush back

[1] *depilatory string:* Two strings were used to grasp and remove tiny hairs near eyebrows.

into their veins. I hope that the man my aunt loved appreciated a smooth brow, that he wasn't just a tits-and-ass man.

Once my aunt found a freckle on her chin, at a spot that the almanac said predestined her for unhappiness. She dug it out with a hot needle and washed the wound with peroxide. More attention to her looks than these pullings of hairs and pickings at spots would have caused gossip among the villagers. They owned work clothes and good clothes, and they wore good clothes for feasting the new seasons. But since a woman combing her hair hexes beginnings, my aunt rarely found an occasion to look her best. Women looked like great sea snails—the corded wood, babies, and laundry they carried were the whorls on their backs. The Chinese did not admire a bent back, goddesses and warriors stood straight. Still there must have been a marvelous freeing of beauty when a worker laid down her burden and stretched and arched.

Such commonplace loveliness, however, was not enough for my aunt. She dreamed of a lover for the fifteen days of New Year's, the time for families to exchange visits, money, and food. She plied her secret comb. And sure enough she cursed the year, the family, the village, and herself.

Even as her hair lured her imminent lover, many other men looked at her. Uncles, cousins, nephews, brothers would have looked, too, had they been home between journeys. Perhaps they had already been restraining their curiosity, and they left, fearful that their glances, like a field of nesting birds, might be startled and caught. Poverty hurt, and that was their first reason for leaving. But another, final reason for leaving the crowded house was the never-said.

She may have been unusually beloved, the precious only daughter, spoiled and mirror gazing because of the affection the family lavished on her. When her husband left, they welcomed the chance to take her back from the in-laws; she could live like the little daughter for just a while longer. There are stories that my grandfather was different from other people, "crazy ever since the little Jap bayoneted him in the head." He used to put his naked penis on the dinner table, laughing. And one day he brought home a baby girl, wrapped up inside his brown western-style greatcoat. He had traded one of his sons, probably my father, the youngest, for her. My grandmother made him trade back. When he finally got a daughter of his own, he doted on her. They must have all loved her, except perhaps my father, the only brother who never went back to China, having once been traded for a girl.

Brothers and sisters, newly men and women, had to efface their sexual color 30
and present plain miens. Disturbing hair and eyes, a smile like no other threatened the ideal of five generations living under one roof. To focus blurs, people shouted face to face and yelled from room to room. The immigrants I know have loud voices, unmodulated to American tones even after years away from the village where they called their friendships out across the fields. I have not been able to stop my mother's screams in public libraries or over telephones. Walking erect (knees straight, toes pointed forward, not pigeon-toed, which is Chinese-feminine) and speaking in an inaudible voice, I have tried to turn myself American-feminine. Chinese communication was loud, public. Only sick people had to whisper. But at the dinner table, where the family members came nearest one

another, no one could talk, not the outcasts nor any eaters. Every word that falls from the mouth is a coin lost. Silently they gave and accepted food with both hands. A preoccupied child who took his bowl with one hand got a sideways glare. A complete moment of total attention is due everyone alike. Children and lovers have no singularity here, but my aunt used a secret voice, a separate attentiveness.

She kept the man's name to herself throughout her labor and dying; she did not accuse him that he be punished with her. To save her inseminator's name she gave silent birth.

He may have been somebody in her own household, but intercourse with a man outside the family would have been no less abhorrent. All the village were kinsmen, and the titles shouted in loud country voices never let kinship be forgotten. Any man within visiting distance would have been neutralized as a lover—"brother," "younger brother," "older brother"—one hundred and fifteen relationship titles. Parents researched birth charts probably not so much to assure good fortune as to circumvent incest in a population that has but one hundred surnames. Everybody has eight million relatives. How useless then sexual mannerisms, how dangerous.

As if it came from an atavism deeper than fear, I used to add "brother" silently to boys' names. It hexed the boys, who would or would not ask me to dance, and made them less scary and as familiar and deserving of benevolence as girls.

But, of course, I hexed myself also—no dates. I should have stood up, both arms waving, and shouted out across libraries, "Hey, you! Love me back." I had no idea, though, how to make attraction selective, how to control its direction and magnitude. If I made myself American-pretty so that the five or six Chinese boys in the class fell in love with me, everyone else—the Caucasian, Negro, and Japanese boys—would too. Sisterliness, dignified and honorable, made much more sense.

Attraction eludes control so stubbornly that whole societies designed to 35
organize relationships among people cannot keep order, not even when they bind people to one another from childhood and raise them together. Among the very poor and the wealthy, brothers married their adopted sisters, like doves. Our family allowed some romance, paying adult brides' prices and providing dowries so that their sons and daughters could marry strangers. Marriage promises to turn strangers into friendly relatives—a nation of siblings.

In the village structure, spirits shimmered among the live creatures, balanced and held in equilibrium by time and land. But one human being flaring up into violence could open up a black hole, a maelstrom that pulled in the sky. The frightened villagers, who depended on one another to maintain the real, went to my aunt to show her a personal, physical representation of the break she had made in the "roundness." Misallying couples snapped off the future, which was to be embodied in true offspring. The villagers punished her for acting as if she could have a private life, secret and apart from them. If my aunt had betrayed the family at a time of large grain yields and peace, when many boys were born, and wings were being built on many houses, perhaps she might have escaped such severe punishment. But the men—hungry, greedy, tired of planting in dry soil, cuckolded—had had to leave the village in order to send food-money home. There were ghost plagues, bandit plagues, wars with the Japanese, floods. My Chinese brother and sister had died of an unknown sickness. Adultery, perhaps only a mistake during good times, became a crime when the village needed food.

The round moon cakes and round doorways, the round tables of graduated size that fit one roundness inside another, round windows and rice bowls—these talismen had lost their power to warn this family of the law: a family must be whole, faithfully keeping the descent line by having sons to feed the old and the dead, who in turn look after the family. The villagers came to show my aunt and her lover-in-hiding a broken house. The villagers were speeding up the circling of events because she was too shortsighted to see that her infidelity had already harmed the village, that waves of consequences would return unpredictably, sometimes in disguise, as now, to hurt her. This roundness had to be made coin-sized so that she would see its circumference: punish her at the birth of her baby. Awaken her to the inexorable. People who refused fatalism because they could invent small resources insisted on culpability. Deny accidents and wrest fault from the stars.

After the villagers left, their lanterns now scattering in various directions toward home, the family broke their silence and cursed her. "Aiaa, we're going to die. Death is coming. Death is coming. Look what you've done. You've killed us. Ghost! Dead ghost! Ghost! You've never been born." She ran out into the fields, far enough from the house so that she could no longer hear their voices, and pressed herself against the earth, her own land no more. When she felt the birth coming, she thought that she had been hurt. Her body seized together. "They've hurt me too much," she thought. "This is gall, and it will kill me." Her forehead and knees against the earth, her body convulsed and then released her onto her back. The black well of sky and stars went out and out and out forever; her body and her complexity seemed to disappear. She was one of the stars, a bright dot in blackness, without home, without a companion, in eternal cold and silence. An agoraphobia rose in her, speeding higher and higher, bigger and bigger; she would not be able to contain it; there would be no end to fear.

Flayed, unprotected against space, she felt pain return, focusing her body. This pain chilled her—a cold, steady kind of surface pain. Inside, spasmodically, the other pain, the pain of the child, heated her. For hours she lay on the ground, alternately body and space. Sometimes a vision of normal comfort obliterated reality: she saw the family in the evening gambling at the dinner table, the young people massaging their elders' backs. She saw them congratulating one another, high joy on the mornings the rice shoots came up. When these pictures burst, the stars drew yet further apart. Black space opened.

She got to her feet to fight better and remembered that old-fashioned 40
women gave birth in their pigsties to fool the jealous, pain-dealing gods, who do not snatch piglets. Before the next spasms could stop her, she ran to the pigsty, each step a rushing out into emptiness. She climbed over the fence and knelt in the dirt. It was good to have a fence enclosing her, a tribal person alone.

Laboring, this woman who had carried her child as a foreign growth that sickened her every day, expelled it at last. She reached down to touch the hot, wet, moving mass, surely smaller than anything human, and could feel that it was human after all—fingers, toes, nails, nose. She pulled it up on to her belly, and it lay curled there, butt in the air, feet precisely tucked one under the other. She opened her loose shirt and buttoned the child inside. After resting, it squirmed and thrashed and she pushed it up to her breast. It turned its head this way and that until it found her nipple. There, it made little snuffling noises. She clenched her teeth at its preciousness, lovely as a young calf, a piglet, a little dog.

She may have gone to the pigsty as a last act of responsibility: she would protect this child as she had protected its father. It would look after her soul, leaving supplies on her grave. But how would this tiny child without family find her grave when there would be no marker for her anywhere, neither in the earth nor the family hall? No one would give her a family hall name. She had taken the child with her into the wastes. At its birth the two of them had felt the same raw pain of separation, a wound that only the family pressing tight could close. A child with no descent line would not soften her life but only trail after her, ghostlike, begging her to give it purpose. At dawn the villagers on their way to the fields would stand around the fence and look.

Full of milk, the little ghost slept. When it awoke, she hardened her breasts against the milk that crying loosens. Toward morning she picked up the baby and walked to the well.

Carrying the baby to the well shows loving. Otherwise abandon it. Turn its face into the mud. Mothers who love their children take them along. It was probably a girl; there is some hope of forgiveness for boys.

"Don't tell anyone you had an aunt. Your father does not want to hear her 45
name. She has never been born." I have believed that sex was unspeakable and words so strong and fathers so frail that "aunt" would do my father mysterious harm. I have thought that my family, having settled among immigrants who had also been their neighbors in the ancestral land, needed to clean their name, and a wrong word would incite the kinspeople even here. But there is more to this silence: they want me to participate in her punishment. And I have.

In the twenty years since I heard this story I have not asked for details nor said my aunt's name; I do not know it. People who can comfort the dead can also chase after them to hurt them further—a reverse ancestor worship. The real punishment was not the raid swiftly inflicted by the villagers, but the family's deliberately forgetting her. Her betrayal so maddened them, they saw to it that she would suffer forever, even after death. Always hungry, always needing, she would have to beg food from other ghosts, snatch and steal it from those whose living descendants give them gifts. She would have to fight the ghosts massed at crossroads for the buns a few thoughtful citizens leave to decoy her away from village and home so that the ancestral spirits could feast unharassed. At peace, they could act like gods, not ghosts, their descent lines providing them with paper suits and dresses, spirit money, paper houses, paper automobiles, chicken, meat, and rice into eternity—essences delivered up in smoke and flames, steam and incense rising from each rice bowl. In an attempt to make the Chinese care for people outside the family, Chairman Mao encourages us now to give our paper replicas to the spirits of outstanding soldiers and workers, no matter whose ancestors they may be. My aunt remains forever hungry. Goods are not distributed evenly among the dead.

My aunt haunts me—her ghost drawn to me because now, after fifty years of neglect, I alone devote pages of paper to her, though not origamied into houses and clothes. I do not think she always means me well. I am telling on her, and she was a spite suicide, drowning herself in the drinking water. The Chinese are always very frightened of the drowned one, whose weeping ghost, wet hair hanging and skin bloated, waits silently by the water to pull down a substitute.

(1975)

Questions for Discussion and Writing

Close Reading

1. What are the connotations of the word "ghost" in this essay?
2. Why does Kingston's mother tell her the story of her aunt at this particular time? What effect does her mother hope it will have, and what effect does it actually have?
3. Given only the outline of her aunt's story, Kingston is compelled to imagine her aunt's experience further. How is this creative imagining of her aunt's life an attempt to make her aunt's story meaningful to her own experience? In other words, what lesson does she learn by telling her version of her aunt's story?

Critical and Creative Reading

4. Consider the importance of the audience of Kingston's essay. Recall that the essay begins with her mother's warning: "You must not tell anyone . . . what I am about to tell you."
5. What does the essay say about the forces of conformity and the need for individuality? How does the tension between those forces affect the theme of this chapter (honesty and deception)?
6. According to Kingston's essay, what is the best way for living people to regard their deceased ancestors?

Connections to Other Readings

7. What is the connection between "keeping a secret" and "punishing someone" in this essay and in Alifa Rifaat's story "Another Evening at the Club"?
8. Consider what this essay says about differences between male and female experiences with regard to secrecy and honesty, and compare it to Ann Beattie's story "Weekend."
9. Write about family honor as it is represented in this essay and in the stories "Morphine" by David Long and "The Prophet's Hair" by Salman Rushdie.

Considering Art: Honesty and Deception

The discussion below references art reproduced on color insert pages 9 and 10.

All visual images are inherently deceptive or secretive to some degree. The artist creates an illusion, inviting the viewer into the world of the artistically created reality. The painting sets up questions in the viewer's mind, such as "What is true about it? What can be known or not known about what is going on? What is going on out of view, outside the frame? What does the painting reveal, and what does it hide? Why? As in literature and life, this indeterminate quality in art captures our attention, inspires our curiosity, and draws us in, with wonderment.

***A Great Secret* (see color insert p. 9).** In *A Great Secret* (n. d.) Haynes King (1831–1904) depicts two young women in a domestic interior. Such Victorian paintings of interiors are known as *genre scenes*, and they are frequently packed with ordinary, everyday details that the viewer must interpret to arrive at a moral judgment. King's setting is a small, perhaps one-room, rural home, where the kitchen cupboard lies beside the bed. Both women have put aside their domestic labor of cooking and cleaning to share a secret. The red-haired woman pauses, a colander of apples in her lap, as the dark-haired woman, her outer skirt tied back for work, puts down her broom to whisper into her friend's ear. We observe a spreading smile as the secret passes from one to the other.

***Many Masks* (see color insert p. 9).** Patricia A. Schwimmer's (b. 1953) tempera painting *Many Masks* (1995) depicts a single figure standing against a golden background. Flat fields of pattern on the figure's garment confuse a sense of three-dimensional space. We are not sure where the body, clothes, or masks begin or end. She holds at least three masks, and each expresses a different emotion. On her face (which may itself be masked), tears weep from one eye, and snakes fall from the other. Because this work is not a portrait of any specific individual or a narrative of a moment in time, we can read the image as a metaphor for states of mind as they are expressed on the face. Wearing colorful masks is part of the yearly pre-Lent carnival traditions of many countries, such as Italy and Brazil. The practice of masquerade gives the wearer anonymity to release pent up emotions in ritual festive events during which everyday social rules are suspended: almost anything goes. Masquerade offers both the privacy of living out secret fantasies and the sinister potential of deception.

***Trust Me* (see color insert p. 10).** *Trust Me* (ca. 1862) by John Everett Millais (1829–1896) is a Victorian "problem picture." It seems to present a story of a moral dilemma without giving enough information to infer the dilemma's conclusion or solution. Millais, along with a group of young painters who called themselves the Pre-Raphaelite Brotherhood, dedicated their artistic careers to the careful study of the world around them. They made art that they hoped would mirror reality. Here, in the interior of a wealthy home, an older man in stark profile faces a young woman (whose expression is hard to read). The artist clearly delineates the anxious space between them, suggesting their emotional distance. We may infer that a power struggle being waged between middle-aged father and adolescent daughter, between worldly authority and budding independence. Although the relationship is not entirely clear, the emphasis on the figures' hands and gestures and on the letter that the woman holds behind her back clearly refer to a dramatic conclusion to this story that is forever suspended in the image. Art historian Paul Barlow, in *Time Present and Time Past: The Art of John Everett Millais*, compares the narrative theme of this painting to the serialized novels that were a new form of popular culture at just this time.

Questions about the Art

1. How does color move our eye through King's painting *A Great Secret?* What is the focal point? What sort of secret do you suppose they are sharing? Why is she smiling?
2. Which mask seems to be the most important or sincere in Schwimmer's painting, *Many Masks?*
3. In Millais's painting *Trust Me*, who is asking to be trusted? How does changing the speaker of this phrase change the way we interpret the image? What, if anything, can we see or know that is hidden from the figures depicted?
4. Comparing the King and Millais paintings, does there seem to be a moral to the story about the keeping of secrets or the sorts of people who engage in secrecy and deception? What can we assume is being hidden?

Connecting Art and Literature

1. How would the speaker of Paul Laurence Dunbar's poem "We Wear the Mask" respond to the painting *Many Masks?* Does he feel we wear multiple masks or just one?
2. Consider the relationship between the characters in the story and the reader in David Long's story "Morphine" and the relationship between the characters in John Everett Millais's painting *Trust Me* and the viewer. Are you invited to feel a part of the secret or distant from it? Do you have the impulse to reveal the secret or to spill it?
3. A secret seems to hold intimacy and power in King's painting *A Great Secret*. The listener seems delighted to be receiving a secret. Does secrecy have that same status in any of the literary works you have read in this chapter, or is it always somewhat sinister?

Common Characters

The Trickster Figure

"Fee Fi Fo Fum. I smell the blood of an Englishman!" And the giant discovered Jack hiding in his kitchen and ate him up! We all know that the story doesn't end that way. Jack is a trickster figure, a common character type in myth, folk tales, and fiction who outwits his enemies despite being smaller and less powerful. The trickster figure has its origins in Native American and African myths where characters such as coyote, rabbit, spider, and other cunning animals use their wits to overcome difficult situations. Traditionally, the trickster was a god or supernatural character who often conferred benefits on mankind; however, this generosity was usually a side effect rather than a deliberate goal.

Although tricksters can be clever, they occasionally are too clever and find themselves on the receiving end of their own tricks. Consider the serpent in the Garden of Eden: "More subtle than any beast in the field," according to Genesis. He uses his cunning to bring about the fall of mankind, essentially undoing the work of God and His angels in one short conversation. Yet while the serpent triumphs over Adam and Eve, he is punished for his transgression.

The trickster figure is an ambiguous character. He is a shapeshifter, able to transform himself from animal to human, male to female, old to young. In this

Jack and the Beanstalk.

Gustare Dore, *The Disguised Wolf in Bed* (1862)

collection, the Native American figure Manabozho, or "The Great Hare," shifts from a living thing to a dead thing and back again. An amoral figure, the trickster is out for himself—to get out of trouble, to secure a meal, to exact revenge. Robert Browning's poem, "The Pied Piper of Hamelin," is a disturbing retelling of the legend of the Pied Piper in which an angry piper, who had saved the town of Hamelin from rats, later exacts revenge on its ungrateful residents by luring their children away permanently.

Literature, television, and film have given us a number of human trickster figures, from folk characters like Hansel and Gretel to Tom Sawyer (whose famous scheme for avoiding chores is included here). Bart Simpson is a modern-day trickster who outwits all the adults in his life, frequently avoiding trouble by thinking on his feet. Harry Potter, the orphaned wizard of Hogwarts, uses his invisibility cloak to move easily between the worlds of good and evil. Captain Jack Sparrow, a central character in the Pirates of the Caribbean movies, is another example. His irrepressibly mischievous behavior sets him apart from both proper society and other pirates.

While the trickster is represented in various ways today, we can still locate him in his animal form. Bugs Bunny's "What's Up Doc?" is one of the most famous lines in the English language, a line delivered as Bugs once again avoids the trap or the gun of Elmer Fudd. (Tweety Bird and the Road Runner are different versions of the same type.) Bugs Bunny is a descendant of Brer (or Brother or "Buh") Rabbit, a popular character in African American folk tales. Brer Rabbit's many victories over his enemies, particularly Brer Fox, made him a folk hero among African American slaves. Two Brer Rabbit stories are included here: in both, the trickster is himself tricked but ultimately gets away. The story of "Little Girl and Buh Rabby" features two tricksters: not only Buh Rabby, but also Little Girl, who uses her wits to trick Buh Rabby into a trap.

Though sexually ambiguous, the trickster is typically male, but not always. In addition to Little Girl, folk tales feature female tricksters like Little Red Riding Hood, who, in one version of the tale, escapes from the wolf's clutches by pretending she has to go to the bathroom. Molly Whuppie, in the story in this collection, is a female version of Jack from "Jack in the Beanstalk." As you read tales of female tricksters, you might consider any differences between the male and female forms of this type. Above all, the trickster figure is a survivor, and while we may alternate between condemning his deception and admiring his audacity, we cannot help but be entertained by his resourcefulness and energy.

Algonquin Folk Tale

Manabozho, The Great Hare

Once while the Buzzard was soaring away through the air he saw Manabozho walking along. He flew a little toward the ground, with his wings outspread, and heard Manabozho say to him, "Buzzard, you must be very happy up there where you can soar through the air and see what is transpiring in the world beneath. Take me on your back so that I may ascend with you and see how it appears down here from where you live." The Buzzard came down, and said, "Manabozho, get on my back and I will take you up into the sky to let you see how the world appears from my abode." Manabozho approached the Buzzard, but seeing how smooth his back appeared said, "Buzzard, I am afraid you will let me slide from your back, so you must be careful not to sweep around too rapidly, that I may retain my place upon your back." The Buzzard told Manabozho that he would be careful, although the bird was determined to play a trick on him if possible. Manabozho mounted the Buzzard and held on to his feathers as well as he could. The Buzzard took a short run, leaped from the ground, spread his wings and rose into the air. Manabozho felt rather timid as the Buzzard swept through the air, and as he circled around his body leaned so much that Manabozho could scarcely retain his position, and he was afraid of slipping off. Presently, as Manabozho was looking down upon the broad earth below, the Buzzard made a sharp curve to one side so that his body leaned more than ever. Manabozho, losing his grasp, slipped off and dropped to earth like an arrow. He struck the ground with such force as to knock him senseless. The Buzzard returned to his place in the sky, but hovered around to see what would become of Manabozho.

Manabozho lay a long time like one dead. When he recovered he saw something close to and apparently staring him in the face. He could not at first recognize it, but when he put his hands against the object he found that it was his own buttocks, because he had been all doubled up. He arose and prepared to go on his way, when he espied the Buzzard above him, laughing at his own trickery.

Manabozho then said, "Buzzard, you have played a trick on me by letting me fall, but as I am more powerful than you I shall revenge myself." The Buzzard then replied, "No, Manabozho, you will not do anything of the kind, because you cannot deceive me. I shall watch you."

Manabozho kept on, and the Buzzard, not noticing anything peculiar in the movements of Manabozho, flew on his way through the air. Manabozho then decided to transform himself into a dead deer, because he knew the Buzzard had chosen to subsist on dead animals and fish. Manabozho then went to a place visible from a great distance and from many directions, where he laid himself down and changed himself into the carcass of a deer. Soon the various birds and beasts and crawling things that subsist on such food began to congregate about the dead deer. The Buzzard saw the birds flying toward the place where the body lay, and joined them. He flew around several times to see if it was Manabozho trying to deceive him, then thought to himself, "No, that is not Manabozho; it is truly a dead deer." He then approached the body and began to pick a hole into the fleshy part of the thigh. Deeper and deeper into the flesh the Buzzard picked until his head and neck was buried each time he reached in to pluck the fat from the intestines. Without warning, while the Buzzard had his head completely hidden in the carcass of the deer, the deer jumped up and pinched together his flesh, thus firmly grasping the head and neck of the Buzzard. Then Manabozho said, "Aha! Buzzard, I did catch you after all, as I told you I would. Now pull out your head." The Buzzard with great difficulty withdrew his head from the cavity in which it had been inclosed, but the feathers were all pulled off, leaving his scalp and neck covered with nothing but red skin. Then Manabozho said to the bird, "Thus do I punish you for your deceitfulness; henceforth you will go through the world without feathers on your head and neck, and you shall always stink because of the food you will be obliged to eat." That is why the buzzard is such a bad-smelling fellow, and why his head and neck are featherless.

Joseph Jacobs *(1854–1916)*

Molly Whuppie

Once upon a time there was a man and a wife who had too many children, and they could not get meat for them, so they took the three youngest and left them in a wood. They travelled and travelled and could never see a house. It began to be dark, and they were hungry. At last they saw a light and made for it; it turned out to be a house. They knocked at the door, and a woman came to it, who said: "What do you want?" They said: "Please let us in and give us something to eat." The woman said: "I can't do that, as my man is a giant, and he would kill you if he comes home." They begged hard. "Let us stop for a little while," said they, "and we will go away before he comes." So she took them in, and set them down before the fire, and gave them milk and bread; but just as they had begun to eat, a great knock came to the door, and a dreadful voice said:

Fee, fie, fo, fum,
I smell the blood of some earthly one.

"Who have you there, wife?" "Eh," said the wife, "it's three poor lassies cold and hungry, and they will go away. Ye won't touch, 'em, man." He said nothing, but ate up a big supper, and ordered them to stay all night. Now he had three lassies of his own, and they were to sleep in the same bed with the three strangers. The youngest of the three strange lassies was called Molly Whuppie, and she was very clever. She noticed that before they went to bed the giant put straw ropes round her neck and her sisters', and round his own lassies' necks, he put gold chains. So Molly took care and did not fall asleep, but waited till she was sure everyone was sleeping sound. Then she slipped out of bed, and took the straw ropes off her own and her sisters' necks, and took the gold chains off the giant's lassies. She then put the straw ropes on the giant's lassies and the gold on herself and her sisters, and lay down. And in the middle of the night up rose the giant, armed with a great club, and felt for the necks with the straw. It was dark. He took his own lassies out of the bed on to the floor, and battered them until they were dead, and then lay down again, thinking he had managed finely. Molly thought it time she and her sisters were off and away, so she wakened them and told them to be quiet, and they slipped out of the house. They all got out safe, and they ran and ran, and never stopped until morning, when they saw a grand house before them. It turned out to be a king's house: so Molly went in, and told her story to the king.

He said: "Well, Molly, you are a clever girl, and you have managed well; but, if you would manage better, and go back, and steal the giant's sword that hangs on the back of his bed, I would give your eldest sister my eldest son to marry." Molly said she would try. So she went back, and managed to slip into the giant's house, and crept in below the bed. The giant came home, and ate up a great supper, and went to bed. Molly waited until he was snoring, and she crept out, and reached over the giant and got down the sword; but just as she got it out over the bed it gave a rattle, and up jumped the giant, and Molly ran out at the door and the sword with her; and she ran, and he ran, till they came to the "Bridge of one hair"; and she got over, but he couldn't and he says, "Woe worth ye, Molly Whuppie! never ye come again." And she says: "Twice yet," quoth she, "I'll come to Spain." So Molly took the sword to the king, and her sister was married to his son.

Well, the king he says: "Ye've managed well, Molly; but if ye would manage better, and steal the purse that lies below the giant's pillow, I would marry your second sister to my second son." And Molly said she would try. So she set out for the giant's house, and slipped in, and hid again below the bed, and waited till the giant had eaten his supper, and was snoring sound asleep. She slipped out and slipped her hand below the pillow, and got out the purse; but just as she was going out the giant wakened, and ran after her; and she ran, and he ran, till they came to the "Bridge of one hair", and she got over, but he couldn't, and he said, "Woe worth ye, Molly Whuppie! never you come again." "Once yet," quoth she, "I'll come to Spain." So Molly took the purse to the king, and her second sister was married to the king's second son.

After that the king says to Molly: "Molly, you are a clever girl, but if you would do better yet, and steal the giant's ring that he wears on his finger, I will give you my youngest son for yourself." Molly said she would try. So back she goes to the giant's house, and hides herself below the bed. The giant wasn't long ere he came home, and, after he had eaten a great big supper, he went to his bed, and shortly was snoring loud. Molly crept out and reached over the bed, and got hold of the giant's hand, and she pulled and she pulled until she got off the ring; but just as she got it off the giant got up, and gripped her by the hand and he says: "Now I have caught you, Molly Whuppie, and, if I done as much ill to you as ye have done to me, what would ye do to me?"

Molly says: "I would put you into a sack, and I'd put the cat inside wi' you, and the dog aside you, and a needle and thread and shears, and I'd hang you up upon the wall, and I'd go to the wood, and choose the thickest stick I could get, and I would come home, and take you down, and bang you till you were dead."

"Well, Molly," says the giant, "I'll just do that to you."

So he gets a sack, and puts Molly into it, and the cat and the dog beside her, and a needle and thread and shears, and hangs her up upon the wall, and goes to the wood to choose a stick.

Molly she sings out: "Oh, if ye saw what I see."

"Oh,' says the giant's wife, 'what do you see, Molly?"

But Molly never said a word but, "Oh, if ye saw what I see!"

The giant's wife begged that Molly would take her up into the sack till she would see what Molly saw. So Molly took the shears and cut a hole in the sack, and took out the needle and thread with her, and jumped down and helped the giant's wife up into the sack, and sewed up the hole.

The giant's wife saw nothing, and began to ask to get down again; but Molly never minded, but hid herself at the back of the door. Home came the giant, and a great big tree in his hand, and he took down the sack, and began to batter it. His wife cried, "It's me, man"; but the dog barked and the cat mewed, and he did not know his wife's voice. But Molly came out from the back of the door, and the giant saw her and he ran after her; and he ran, and she ran, till they came to the "Bridge of one hair," and she got over but he couldn't; and he said, "Woe worth you, Molly Whuppie! never you come again." "Never more," quoth she, "will I come again to Spain."

So Molly took the ring to the king, and she was married to his youngest son, and she never saw the giant again.

Virginia Hamilton *(1936–2002)*

Little Girl and Buh Rabby

Little Girl was always home. Her mama had her go down, pick some peas in the garden. "Now I must go to market, take my vegetables every day," Mama told her. "Today, you mind the house and garden. Couple days from now, you can come along."

"I'll mind everything, I will," says Little Girl. But soon as Mama was gone, Buh Rabby comes by. Big, stand-up ears, white puff tail.

Says the rabbit, "Little Girl, I see you are picking peas."

"I sure am," says Little Girl. "Mama told me to."

"I saw your mama going out, and she greeted me," said Buh Rabby. "Says to me, 'Tell Little Girl to let you in for some peas.'"

"All right, if Mama said so," Little Girl said. She opened the gate and let Buh Rabby in.

Buh Rabby ate a whole row of sweet, tender peas in a minute. Him, stand-up ears, tail, big ole feet. Says, "Let me out now."

So she did.

Mama came home from market, asked Little Girl how she was doing.

"I let Buh Rabby in like you told him to tell me to," Little Girl said to her mama.

"Well, I never saw him to tell, and I never said anything to that pesty Buh Rabby," her mama told her. "If he comes back tomorrow, you let him in the garden, but don't let him out. When your daddy comes home, he'll help you take care of Buh Rabby."

Next day, Buh Rabby hopped on over. "Hey, there, Little Girl," he said, "I come for to visit the garden."

Little Girl stayed quiet, but she opened the gate, and Buh Rabby hopped inside. White puff tail, big feet, flippity-flop he goes.

Little Girl locked the gate behind Buh Rabby. Puff tail, up and down the sweet-pea row, ears just waving.

Buh Rabby stayed all day. Then, way late, he dragged his full-belly self to the gate. It was almost time for Little Girl's daddy to come home from his labor, too. But that rabbit didn't know a thing.

Buh Rabby called Little Girl, hollered at her: "Girl! Turn me loose now. I am all finished here."

Little Girl told him, "I am busy, Buh Rabby. I hasn't no time right now to turn you loose."

So Buh Rabby sat down to wait. He didn't like waiting, but what was he going to do? After a while, he says, real polite, "Little Girl, I must leave right now. Let me out. Please."

She tells him, "Buh Rabby, can't you see I am fixing these sweet peas for my mama? I can't be bothered with you!"

Little Girl's daddy came home right then. He saw what was in the garden besides Little Girl. Buh Rabby, that's what. All ears, puff tail, and big feet.

"What are you doing in there?" asked the daddy.

Buh Rabby tells him, "Little Girl let me in here, sir."

"Commere, I got something for you better than them pea pods," Daddy told Buh Rabby.

Buh Rabby hopped to the gate, flippity-flop. Little Girl and her daddy grabbed him by the ears. They stuffed him in a gunnysack and hung him in the wild honey locust. Up and down its trunk and branches, that tree had thorns as long as a man's finger.

"Ole Buh Rabby is high-strung and prickled!" Little Girl told her mama. Her daddy went away in the woods to cut some switches; going to smart Buh Rabby for sure.

But Wolf came along, heard Buh Rabby coughing in the gunnysack. Said, "That you, Rabby? What you doing in there?"

"Oh," said Buh Rabby, thinking fast. "I'm on my way to Heaven for Little Girl. You want to come along?"

"Yes, indeed!" said the wolf.

"Then open my sack and come on in," Buh Rabby told him.

So big ole Wolf did it, he jumped in. Buh Rabby jumped out, tied the wolf in the gunnysack. "Hey!" hollered Wolf. But Buh Rabby was gone, even before he started, fast as he could get.

Little Girl and her daddy came back. She gave the sack a once-over, said, "You're no rabbit in there. Wolf, what you doing?"

"I'm a-go to Heaven for you, Little Girl, like Buh Rabby say I do if I go in here."

Little Girl giggled, and her daddy smiled. "Now I'm a-going to finish this," Daddy said. "And it won't be Heaven you will get." With that, he switched Wolf's hide about ten-sting times.

"Ow-ow-ow!" Wolf hollered.

Daddy said, "When you see a gunnysack again, Wolf, you better take care!"

Little Girl told Wolf, "And you make sure Buh Rabby won't hide a trick in it, too!"

Anybody see that Little Girl at the market, tell her:

I go around the bend.
I see a fence to mend.
On it is hung my story end.

S. E. Schlosser (*b. 1968*)

Brer Rabbit Meets a Tar Baby

Well now, that rascal Brer Fox hated Brer Rabbit on account of he was always cutting capers and bossing everyone around. So Brer Fox decided to capture and kill Brer Rabbit if it was the last thing he ever did! He thought and he thought until he came up with a plan. He would make a tar baby! Brer Fox went and got some tar and he mixed it with some turpentine and he sculpted it into the figure of a cute little baby. Then he stuck a hat on the Tar Baby and sat her in the middle of the road.

Brer Fox hid himself in the bushes near the road and he waited and waited for Brer Rabbit to come along. At long last, he heard someone whistling and chuckling to himself, and he knew that Brer Rabbit was coming up over the hill. As he reached the top, Brer Rabbit spotted the cute little Tar Baby. Brer Rabbit

Brer Rabbit chatting with little rabbit children.

was surprised. He stopped and stared at this strange creature. He had never seen anything like it before!

"Good Morning," said Brer Rabbit, doffing his hat. "Nice weather we're having."

The Tar Baby said nothing. Brer Fox laid low and grinned an evil grin.

Brer Rabbit tried again. "And how are you feeling this fine day?" 5

The Tar Baby, she said nothing. Brer Fox grinned an evil grin and lay low in the bushes.

Brer Rabbit frowned. This strange creature was not very polite. It was beginning to make him mad.

"Ahem!" said Brer Rabbit loudly, wondering if the Tar Baby were deaf. "I said 'HOW ARE YOU THIS MORNING?'"

The Tar Baby said nothing. Brer Fox curled up into a ball to hide his laughter. His plan was working perfectly!

"Are you deaf or just rude?" demanded Brer Rabbit, losing his temper. "I can't stand folks that are stuck up! You take off that hat and say 'Howdy-do' or I'm going to give you such a lickin'!"

The Tar Baby just sat in the middle of the road looking as cute as a button and saying nothing at all. Brer Fox rolled over and over under the bushes, fit to bust because he didn't dare laugh out loud.

"I'll learn ya!" Brer Rabbit yelled. He took a swing at the cute little Tar Baby and his paw got stuck in the tar.

"Lemme go or I'll hit you again," shouted Brer Rabbit. The Tar Baby, she said nothing.

"Fine! Be that way," said Brer Rabbit, swinging at the Tar Baby with his free paw. Now both his paws were stuck in the tar, and Brer Fox danced with glee behind the bushes.

"I'm gonna kick the stuffin' out of you," Brer Rabbit said and pounced on the Tar Baby with both feet. They sank deep into the Tar Baby. Brer Rabbit was so furious he head-butted the cute little creature until he was completely covered with tar and unable to move.

Brer Fox leapt out of the bushes and strolled over to Brer Rabbit. "Well, well, what have we here?" he asked, grinning an evil grin.

Brer Rabbit gulped. He was stuck fast. He did some fast thinking while Brer Fox rolled about on the road, laughing himself sick over Brer Rabbit's dilemma.

"I've got you this time, Brer Rabbit," said Brer Fox, jumping up and shaking off the dust. "You've sassed me for the very last time. Now I wonder what I should do with you?"

Brer Rabbit's eyes got very large. "Oh please Brer Fox, whatever you do, please don't throw me into the briar patch."

"Maybe I should roast you over a fire and eat you," mused Brer Fox. "No, that's too much trouble. Maybe I'll hang you instead."

"Roast me! Hang me! Do whatever you please," said Brer Rabbit "Only please, Brer Fox, please don't throw me into the briar patch."

"If I'm going to hang you, I'll need some string," said Brer Fox. "And I don't have any string handy. But the stream's not far away, so maybe I'll drown you instead."

"Drown me! Roast me! Hang me! Do whatever you please," said Brer Rabbit. "Only please, Brer Fox, please don't throw me into the briar patch."

"The briar patch, eh?" said Brer Fox. "What a wonderful idea! You'll be torn into little pieces!"

Grabbing up the tar-covered rabbit, Brer Fox swung him around and around and then flung him head over heels into the briar patch. Brer Rabbit let out such a scream as he fell that all of Brer Fox's fur stood straight up. Brer Rabbit fell into the briar bushes with a crash and a mighty thump. Then there was silence.

Brer Fox cocked one ear toward the briar patch, listening for whimpers of pain. But he heard nothing. Brer Fox cocked the other ear toward the briar patch, listening for Brer Rabbit's death rattle. He heard nothing.

Then Brer Fox heard someone calling his name. He turned around and looked up the hill. Brer Rabbit was sitting on a log combing the tar out of his fur with a wood chip and looking smug.

"I was bred and born in the briar patch, Brer Fox," he called. "Born and bred in the briar patch."

And Brer Rabbit skipped away as merry as a cricket while Brer Fox ground his teeth in rage and went home.

(2005)

Robert Browning *(1812–1889)*

The Pied Piper of Hamelin

Hamelin Town's in Brunswick
By famous Hanover city;
The river Weser, deep and wide,
Washes its wall on the southern side;
A pleasanter spot you never spied;
But, when begins my ditty,
Almost five hundred years ago,
To see the townsfolk suffer so
From vermin was a pity.

Rats!
They fought the dogs, and killed the cats,
And bit the babies in the cradles,
And ate the cheeses out of the vats,
And licked the soup from the cook's own ladles,
Split open the kegs of salted sprats,
Made nests inside men's Sunday hats,
And even spoiled the women's chats,
By drowning their speaking
With shrieking and squeaking
In fifty different sharps and flats.

At last the people in a body
To the Town Hall came flocking:
"'Tis clear," cried they, "our Mayor's a noddy;
And as for our Corporation—shocking
To think that we buy gowns lined with ermine
For dolts that can't or won't determine
What's best to rid us of our vermin!
You hope, because you're old and obese,
To find in the furry civic robe ease?

Rouse up, sirs! Give your brain a racking
To find the remedy we're lacking,
Or, sure as fate, we'll send you packing!"
At this the Mayor and Corporation
Quaked with a mighty consternation.

An hour they sat in council,
At length the Mayor broke silence:
"For a guilder I'd my ermine gown sell;
I wish I were a mile hence!
It's easy to bid one rack one's brain—
I'm sure my poor head aches again
I've scratched it so, and all in vain,
Oh for a trap, a trap, a trap!"
Just as he said this, what should hap
At the chamber door but a gentle tap?
"Bless us," cried the Mayor, "what's that?"
(With the Corporation as he sat,
Looking little though wondrous fat;
Nor brighter was his eye, nor moister,
Than a too-long-opened oyster,
Save when at noon his paunch grew mutinous
For a plate of turtle green and glutinous),
"Only a scraping of shoes on the mat?
Anything like the sound of a rat
Makes my heart go pit-a-pat!"

"Come in!"—the Mayor cried, looking bigger:
And in did come the strangest figure.
His queer long coat from heel to head
Was half of yellow and half of red;
And he himself was tall and thin,
With sharp blue eyes, each like a pin,
And light loose hair, yet swarthy skin,
No tuft on cheek nor beard on chin,
But lips where smiles went out and in—
There was no guessing his kith and kin!
And nobody could enough admire
The tall man and his quaint attire.
Quoth one: "It's as my great grandsire,
Starting up at the Trump of Doom's tone,
Had walked this way from his painted tombstone."

He advanced to the council-table:
And, "Please, your honours," said he, "I'm able,
By means of a secret charm, to draw

All creatures living beneath the sun,
That creep, or swim, or fly, or run,
After me so as you never saw!
And I chiefly use my charm
On creatures that do people harm,
The mole, and toad, and newt, and viper;
And people call me the Pied Piper."
(And here they noticed round his neck
A scarf of red and yellow stripe,
To match with his coat of the selfsame cheque;
And at the scarf's end hung a pipe;
And his fingers, they noticed, were ever straying
As if impatient to be playing
Upon this pipe, as low it dangled
Over his vesture so old-fangled.)
"Yet," said he, "poor piper as I am,
In Tartary I freed the Cham,
Last June, from his huge swarms of gnats;
I eased in Asia the Nizam
Of a monstrous brood of vampire bats:
And, as for what your brain bewilders,
If I can rid your town of rats
Will you give me a thousand guilders?"
"One? fifty thousand!"—was the exclamation
Of the astonished Mayor and Corporation.

Into the street the Piper stept,
Smiling first a little smile,
As if he knew what magic slept
In his quiet pipe the while;
Then, like a musical adept,
To blow the pipe his lips he wrinkled,
And green and blue his sharp eyes twinkled
Like a candle-flame where salt is sprinkled;
And ere three shrill notes the pipe uttered,
You heard as if an army muttered;
And the muttering grew to a grumbling;
And the grumbling grew to a mighty rumbling;
And out of the house the rats came tumbling.
Great rats, small rats, lean rats, brawny rats,
Brown rats, black rats, gray rats, tawny rats,
Grave old plodders, gay young friskers,
Fathers, mothers, uncles, cousins,
Cocking tails and pricking whiskers,
Families by tens and dozens,
Brothers, sisters, husbands, wives—

Followed the Piper for their lives.
From street to street he piped advancing,
And step by step they followed dancing,
Until they came to the river Weser
Wherein all plunged and perished
—Save one, who, stout as Julius Caesar,
Swam across and lived to carry
(As he the manuscript he cherished)
To Rat-land home his commentary,
Which was, "At the first shrill notes of the pipe,
I heard a sound as of scraping tripe,
And putting apples, wondrous ripe,
Into a cider press's gripe;
And a moving away of pickle-tub boards,
And a drawing the corks of train-oil flasks,
And a breaking the hoops of butter casks;
And it seemed as if a voice
(Sweeter far than by harp or by psaltery
Is breathed) called out, Oh, rats! rejoice!
The world is grown to one vast drysaltery!
To munch on, crunch on, take your nuncheon,
Breakfast, supper, dinner, luncheon!
And just as a bulky sugar puncheon,
All ready staved, like a great sun shone
Glorious scarce an inch before me,
Just as methought it said, come, bore me!
—I found the Weser rolling o'er me."

You should have heard the Hamelin people
Ringing the bells till they rocked the steeple.
  "Go," cried the Mayor, "and get long poles!
  Poke out the nests and block up the holes!
  Consult with carpenters and builders,
  And leave in our town not even a trace
  Of the rats!"—when suddenly up the face
  Of the Piper perked in the market-place,
With a, "First, if you please, my thousand guilders!"

A thousand guilders! The Mayor looked blue;
So did the Corporation too.
For council dinners made rare havoc
With Claret, Moselle, Vin-de-Grave, Hock;
And half the money would replenish
Their cellar's biggest butt with Rhenish.
To pay this sum to a wandering fellow
With a gipsy coat of red and yellow!

"Beside," quoth the Mayor, with a knowing wink,
"Our business was done at the river's brink;
We saw with our eyes the vermin sink,
And what's dead can't come to life, I think.
So, friend, we're not the folks to shrink
From the duty of giving you something to drink,
And a matter of money to put in your poke,
But, as for the guilders, what we spoke
Of them, as you very well know, was in joke.
Besides, our losses have made us thrifty;
A thousand guilders! Come, take fifty!"

The piper's face fell, and he cried,
"No trifling! I can't wait, beside!
I've promised to visit by dinnertime
Bagdad, and accepted the prime
Of the Head Cook's pottage, all he's rich in,
For having left the Caliph's kitchen,
Of a nest of scorpions no survivor—
With him I proved no bargain-driver,
With you, don't think I'll bate a stiver!
And folks who put me in a passion
May find me pipe to another fashion."

"How?" cried the Mayor, "d'ye think I'll brook
Being worse treated than a Cook?
Insulted by a lazy ribald
With idle pipe and vesture piebald?
You threaten us, fellow? Do your worst,
Blow your pipe there till you burst!"

Once more he stept into the street;
  And to his lips again
Laid his long pipe of smooth straight cane;
  And ere he blew three notes (such sweet
Soft notes as yet musicians cunning
  Never gave the enraptured air),
There was a rustling, that seemed like a bustling
Of merry crowds justling, at pitching and hustling,
Small feet were pattering, wooden shoes clattering,
Little hands clapping, and little tongues, chattering,
And, like fowls in a farmyard when barley is scattering,
Out came the children running.
All the little boys and girls,
With rosy cheeks and flaxen curls,
And sparkling eyes and teeth like pearls,

Tripping and skipping, ran merrily after
The wonderful music with shouting and laughter.

The Mayor was dumb, and the Council stood
As if they were changed into blocks of wood,
Unable to move a step, or cry
To the children merrily skipping by—
And could only follow with the eye
That joyous crowd at the Piper's back.
But how the Mayor was on the rack,
And the wretched Council's bosoms beat,
As the piper turned from the High Street
To where the Weser rolled its waters
Right in the way of their sons and daughters!
However, he turned from South to West,
And to Koppelberg Hill his steps addressed,
And after him the children pressed;
Great was the joy in every breast.
"He never can cross that mighty top!
He's forced to let the piping drop
And we shall see our children stop!"
When lo! As they reached the mountain's side,
A wondrous portal opened wide,
As if a cavern was suddenly hollowed;
And the Piper advanced and the children followed,
And when all were in to the very last,
The door in the mountain-side shut fast.
Did I say all? No! one was lame,
And could not dance the whole of the way;
And in after years, if you would blame
His sadness, he was used to say:
"It's dull in our town since my playmates left;
I can't forget that I'm bereft
Of all the pleasant sights they see,
Which the Piper also promised me;
For he led us, he said, to a joyous land,
Joining the town and just at hand,
Where waters gushed and fruit trees grew,
And flowers put forth a fairer hue,
And everything was strange and new.
The sparrows were brighter than peacocks here,
And their dogs outran our fallow deer,
And honey-bees had lost their stings;
And horses were born with eagle's wings;
And just as I became assured
My lame foot would be speedily cured,

The music stopped, and I stood still,
And found myself outside the Hill,
Left alone against my will,
To go now limping as before,
And never hear of that country more!!"

Alas, alas for Hamelin!
  There came into many a burger's pate
  A text which says, that Heaven's Gate
Opes to the Rich at as easy rate
As the needle's eye takes a camel in!
The Mayor sent East, West, North and South,
To offer the Piper by word of mouth,
  Wherever it was men's lot to find him,
Silver and gold to his heart's content,
If he'd only return the way he went,
  And bring the children all behind him.
But when they saw 'twas a lost endeavour,
And Piper and dancers were gone forever
They made a decree that lawyers never
  Should think their records dated duly
If, after the day of the month and year,
These words did not as well appear,
  "And so long after what happened here
  On the twenty-second of July,
  Thirteen hundred and seventy-six:"
And the better in memory to fix
The place of the Children's last retreat,
They called it, the Pied Piper's street—
Where anyone playing on pipe or tabor,
Was sure for the future to lose his labour.
Nor suffered they hostelry or tavern
To shock with mirth a street so solemn;
But opposite the place of the cavern
  They wrote the story on a column,
And on the great church window painted
The same, to make the world acquainted
How their children were stolen away;
And there it stands to this very day.
And I must not omit to say
That in Transylvania there's a tribe
Of alien people that ascribe
The outlandish ways and dress,
On which their neighbours lay such stress,
To their fathers and mothers having risen
Out of some subterraneous prison,

Into which they were trepanned
Long time ago in a mighty band
Out of Hamelin town in Brunswick land,
But how or why they don't understand.

(1842)

Mark Twain *(1835–1910)*

From The Adventures of Tom Sawyer

Chapter 2

Saturday morning was come, and all the summer world was bright and fresh, and brimming with life. There was a song in every heart; and if the heart was young the music issued at the lips. There was cheer in every face, and a spring in every step. The locust trees were in bloom, and the fragrance of the blossoms filled the air.

Cardiff Hill, beyond the village and above it, was green with vegetation, and it lay just far enough away to seem a Delectable Land, dreamy, reposeful, and inviting.

Tom appeared on the side-walk with a bucket of whitewash and a long-handled brush. He surveyed the fence, and the gladness went out of nature, and a deep melancholy settled down upon his spirit. Thirty yards of board fence nine feet high! It seemed to him that life was hollow, and existence but a burden. Sighing he dipped his brush and passed it along the topmost plank; repeated the operation; did it again; compared the insignificant whitewashed streak with the far-reaching continent of unwhitewashed fence, and sat down on a tree-box discouraged. Jim came skipping out at the gate with a tin pail, and singing *Buffalo Gals*. Bringing water from the town pump had always been hateful work in Tom's eyes before, but now it did not strike him so. He remembered that there was company at the pump. White, mulatto, and Negro boys and girls were always there waiting their turns, resting, trading playthings, quarrelling, fighting, skylarking. And he remembered that although the pump was only a hundred and fifty yards off Jim never got back with a bucket of water under an hour; and even then somebody generally had to go after him. Tom said:

"Say, Jim; I'll fetch the water if you'll whitewash some."

Jim shook his head, and said: 5

"Can't, Mar's Tom. Ole missis she tole me I got to go an' git dis water an' not stop foolin' 'roun' wid anybody. She say she spec' Ma'rs Tom gwyne to ax me to whitewash, an' so she tole me go 'long an' 'tend to my own business—she 'lowed *she'd* 'tend to de whitewashin'."

"Oh, never you mind what she said, Jim. That's the way she always talks. Gimme the bucket—I won't be gone only a minute. *She* won't ever know."

"Oh, I dasn't, Ma'rs Tom. Ole missis she'd take an' tar de head off'n me. 'Deed she would."

"*She!* she never licks anybody—whacks 'em over the head with her thimble, and who cares for that, I'd like to know? She talks awful, but talk don't hurt—anyways, it don't if she don't cry. Jim, I'll give you a marble. I'll give you a white alley!"

Illustration from *The Adventures of Tom Sawyer* by Mark Twain.

Jim began to waver.

"White alley, Jim; and it's a bully tow."

"My; dat's a mighty gay marvel, *I* tell you. But, Ma'rs Tom, I's powerful 'fraid ole missis."

But Jim was only human—this attention was too much for him. He put down his pail, took the white alley. In another minute he was flying down the street with his pail and a tingling rear, Tom was whitewashing with vigour, and Aunt Polly was retiring from the field with a slipper in her hand and triumph in her eye.

But Tom's energy did not last. He began to think of the fun he had planned for this day, and his sorrows multiplied. Soon the free boys would come tripping along on all sorts of delicious expeditions, and they would make a world of fun of him for having to work—the very thought of it burnt him like fire. He got out his worldly wealth and examined it—bits of toys, marbles, and trash; enough to buy an exchange of work maybe, but not enough to buy so much as half an hour of pure freedom. So he returned his straitened means to his pocket, and gave up the idea of trying to buy the boys. At this dark and hopeless moment an inspiration burst upon him. Nothing less than a great, magnificent inspiration. He took up his brush and went tranquilly to work. Ben Rogers hove in sight presently; the very boy of all boys whose ridicule he had been dreading. Ben's gait was the hop, skip, and jump—proof enough that his heart was light and his anticipations high. He was eating an apple, and giving a long melodious whoop at intervals, followed by a deep-toned ding dong dong, ding dong dong, for he was personating a steamboat! As he drew near he slackened speed, took the middle of the street, leaned far over to starboard, and rounded-to ponderously, and with laborious pomp and circumstance, for he was personating the *Big Missouri*, and considered himself to be drawing nine feet of water. He was boat, and captain, and engine-bells combined, so he had to imagine himself standing on his own hurricane-deck giving the orders and executing them.

"Stop her, sir! Ling-a-ling-ling." The headway ran almost out, and he drew up slowly towards the side-walk. "Ship up to back! Ling-a-ling-ling!" His arms straightened and stiffened down his sides. "Set her back on the stabboard! Ling-a-ling-ling! Chow! ch-chow-wow-chow!" his right hand meantime describing stately circles, for it was representing a forty-foot wheel. "Let her go back on the labboard! Ling-a-ling-ling! Chow-ch-chow-chow!" The left hand began to describe circles.

"Stop the stabboard! Ling-a-ling-ling! Stop the labboard! Come ahead on the stabboard! Stop her! Let your outside turn over slow! Ling-a-ling-ling! Chow-ow-ow! Get out that head-line! Lively, now! Come—out with your spring-line—what're you about there? Take a turn round that stump with the bight of it! Stand by that stage now—let her go! Done with the engines, sir! Ling-a-ling-ling!"

"Sht! s'sht! sht!" (Trying the gauge-cocks.)

Tom went on whitewashing—paid no attention to the steamer. Ben stared a moment, and then said:

"Hi-yi! You're up a stump, ain't you!"

No answer. Tom surveyed his last touch with the eye of an artist; then he gave his brush another gentle sweep, and surveyed the result as before. Ben ranged up alongside of him. Tom's mouth watered for the apple, but he stuck to his work. Ben said:

"Hello, old chap; you got to work, hey?"

"Why, it's you, Ben! I warn't noticing."

"Say, I'm going in a swimming, I am. Don't you wish you could? But of course, you'd druther work, wouldn't you? 'Course you would!"

Tom contemplated the boy a bit, and said:

"What do you call work?"

"Why, ain't that work?"

Tom resumed his whitewashing, and answered carelessly:

"Well, maybe it is, and maybe it ain't. All I know is, it suits Tom Sawyer."

"Oh, come now, you don't mean to let on that you like it?"

The brush continued to move.

"Like it? Well, I don't see why I oughtn't to like it. Does a boy get a chance to whitewash a fence every day?"

That put the thing in a new light. Ben stopped nibbling his apple. Tom swept his brush daintily back and forth—stepped back to note the effect—added a touch here and there—criticized the effect again, Ben watching every move, and getting more and more interested, more and more absorbed. Presently he said:

"Say, Tom, let me whitewash a little."

Tom considered; was about to consent; but he altered his mind: "No, no; I reckon it wouldn't hardly do, Ben. You see, Aunt Polly's awful particular about this fence—right here on the street, you know—but if it was the back fence I wouldn't mind, and she wouldn't. Yes, she's awful particular about this fence; it's got to be done very careful; I reckon there ain't one boy in a thousand, maybe two thousand, that can do it the way it's got to be done."

"No—is that so? Oh, come now; lemme just try, only just a little. I'd let you, if you was me, Tom."

"Ben, I'd like to, honest injun; but Aunt Polly—well, Jim wanted to do it, but she wouldn't let him. Sid wanted to do it, but she wouldn't let Sid. Now, don't you see how I am fixed? If you was to tackle this fence, and anything was to happen to it—"

"Oh, shucks; I'll be just as careful. Now lemme try. Say I'll give you the core of my apple."

"Well, here. No, Ben; now don't; I'm afeard—"

"I'll give you all of it!"

Tom gave up the brush with reluctance in his face, but alacrity in his heart. And while the late steamer *Big Missouri* worked and sweated in the sun, the retired artist sat on a barrel in the shade close by, dangled his legs, munched his apple, and planned the slaughter of more innocents. There was no lack of material; boys happened along every little while; they came to jeer, but remained to whitewash. By the time Ben was fagged out, Tom had traded the next chance to Billy Fisher for a kite in good repair; and when he played out, Johnny Miller bought in for a dead rat and a string to swing it with; and so on, and so on, hour after hour. And when the middle of the afternoon came, from being a poor poverty-stricken boy in the morning Tom was literally rolling in wealth. He had, besides the things I have mentioned, twelve marbles, part of a jew's harp, a piece of blue bottle-glass to look through, a spool-cannon, a key that wouldn't unlock anything, a fragment of chalk, a glass stopper of a decanter, a tin soldier, a couple of tadpoles, six fire-crackers, a kitten with only one eye, a brass door-knob, a dog-collar—but no dog—the handle of a knife, four pieces of orange-peel, and a dilapidated old window-sash. He had had a nice, good, idle time all the while—plenty of company—and the fence had three coats of whitewash on it! If he hadn't run out of whitewash he would have bankrupted every boy in the village.

Tom said to himself that it was not such a hollow world after all. He had discovered a great law of human action, without knowing it, namely, that, in order to make a man or a boy covet a thing, it is only necessary to make the thing difficult to attain. If he had been a great and wise philosopher, like the writer of this book, he would now have comprehended that work consists of whatever a body is obliged to do, and that play consists of whatever a body is not obliged to do. And this would help him to understand why constructing artificial flowers, or performing on a tread-mill, is work, whilst rolling nine-pins or climbing Mont Blanc is only amusement. There are wealthy gentlemen in England who drive four-horse passenger-coaches twenty or thirty miles on a daily line, in the summer, because the privilege costs them considerable money; but if they were offered wages for the service that would turn it into work, then they would resign.

(1876)

Questions for Discussion and Writing

1. How does Manabozho manage to deceive the buzzard, even though the buzzard is on the lookout for his tricks?
2. Manabozho, Buh Rabby, and Brer Rabbit all get themselves into difficult situations. What character trait gets them into trouble? Does the same trait get them out of trouble?
3. The giant's wife in "Molly Whuppie" suffers a painful beating. What, if anything, did she do to deserve being on the receiving end of Molly's tricks?
4. Do you think the people of Hamelin got what they deserved? How about some of the trickster figure's victims in other stories? To what degree is the trickster an effective dispenser of justice?
5. Think of people you know (or public figures that come to mind) that share qualities with the literary trickster figure. What are the best and worst qualities of these people? How drawn are you to them?
6. Who is the better trickster figure, Little Girl or Buh Rabby? Why?
7. Tom Sawyer discovers that "in order to make a man or boy covet a thing, it is only necessary to make the thing difficult to attain." How does Algernon use this principle to woo Cecily in Wilde's play *The Importance of Being Earnest?*
8. Does Tom lie to his friends, or does he tell the truth "slant," as Emily Dickinson recommends to her readers? What is the difference?
9. In what ways is Montressor, the narrator of Edgar Allan Poe's "The Cask of Amontillado" (in Chapter 15), a trickster figure? How does he deviate from the traditional trickster character?

Considering Art: The Trickster

The discussion below references art reproduced on color insert pages 11 and 12.

Many tales of deception can be read as metaphors for creation, knowledge, and creativity. Similarly, Trickster characters in Native American tales, Caribbean and West African fables, Greek myths, and Viking or Norse folklore are credited with both deceptive and inventive qualities. Because these rascals believe themselves to be outside the confines of any authority, they often are able to transcend conventional patterns of thought.

***Loki with His Fishing Net* (see color insert p. 11).** In Norse mythology, Loki, the god of mischief, enrages the other gods by his destructive and deceitful tricks and so goes into hiding in the mountains. During daylight hours, he changes shape into a salmon, swimming in the mountain streams and hiding in a waterfall. Obsessively fearful of being caught by the other gods, he invents the method of his capture. He fashions the first fish net made by twisting string. He tries to find a way out of it should it ever be used against him, but he cannot. When the other gods are approaching his hideout, Loki burns the net in a fire so that it cannot be used against him. Its ashes give his invention away, and a net is made that captures him. The outsmarted trickster is quite literally snared in his own net. This image of Loki, dressed in a jester's outfit and holding a fishnet, comes from an eighteenth-century Icelandic manuscript.

***The Pied Piper Leading Away the Children of Hamelin* (see color insert p. 11).** *The Pied Piper Leading Away the Children of Hamelin* (c. 1899) is a book illustration to the centuries-old cautionary folk tale of deception. Historians have speculated on the origins of this story, relating it to various social crises, from the thirteenth-century plague that devastated Europe to a particular historical abduction of 130 children from the German town of Hamelin after the residents refused to pay a wily itinerant rat catcher. The latter explanation is elaborated in several versions of the fairy tale, such as that of Jacob and Wilhelm Grimm. Like many fairy tales, this story has the cautionary message, reminding us that evil opportunists may exploit the naïve trust of children. The same enchanting tones of the piper's flute that led the rats from town will lure the unsuspecting village children of the villagers who dared deny his fee. In this image, the piper wears the outfit of a jester. His cape swirls ominously, its dark shadows in stark contrast to the smiling faces of the surrounding children.

***Eden, the First Exodus* (see color insert p. 12).** Judeo-Christian traditions name the serpent in the Garden of Eden as the first trickster. Scottish painter Celia Washington's painting, *Eden, The First Exodus* (1989) is a contemporary take on this Biblical tale. Rather than directly depicting the tale of Adam and Eve and their fall from grace into knowledge, Washington uses the garden as a modern, poetic, and personal metaphor. This dream-world garden seems at once familiar and strangely grey, somber, and overcast. Menacingly, the snake winds around and through one of the many apple trees that spring from the earth's spiny vegetation. The woman who enters the composition from the right, suitcase in hand, may not yet be aware of the dangers lurking in this garden. The path she travels in the foreground leads past the serpent and so implies an inevitable contact with him.

Questions about the Art

1. In the Scandinavian image of Loki, what attributes is he given that may mark him as deceptive? What moment in the tale is depicted?

2. Do you suppose that the woman in Washington's *Eden, The First Exodus* is running away from or toward something? How can the image be read as a metaphor for passing from one time of life to another? What do you suppose her baggage might hold?
3. In *The Pied Piper*, what kind of conclusion could we make about the power of music, or art for that matter, over reason or rational thought?

Connecting Art and Literature

1. What attributes do the figure of Loki and the animal tricksters in "Manabozho, the Great Hare" or "Br'er Rabbit Meets a Tar Baby" have in common?
2. Does the tone of Browning's poem "The Pied Piper of Hamelin" match the general mood evoked in the visual image of the Pied Piper?
3. The serpent in Washington's *Eden, The First Exodus* seems imposing and powerful; would any of the tricksters discussed in this section be depicted the same way if they were the subject of visual art?

Chapter 15

Vengeance and Forgiveness

"I'll get you my pretty. And your little dog too!" In the classic film *The Wizard of Oz*, the Wicked Witch of the West promises vengeance after Dorothy's house falls from the sky onto the witch's sister. With her cackle, her green face, and her monomaniacal pursuit of Dorothy, the witch will have her revenge or die trying. *The Wizard of Oz* illustrates a familiar lesson: good people forgive their enemies; wicked people pursue revenge.

The Bible teaches its readers to "turn the other cheek," and in the parable of the prodigal son, the father is willing to do that. (See the Common Characters section of this chapter, page 982.) However, forgiveness is not always easy. In the prodigal son parable, the dutiful brother is angry that his father welcomes his wasteful, dissipated brother back to the family. Can you relate to his feelings? To the father's? While parental forgiveness is a part of human nature, so too is a desire to "get back" at our enemies, to take justice into our own hands.

Children often say, "It's not fair." Parents usually answer, "Well, life isn't fair," as if those words will make us feel better. They don't. Life isn't fair: "bad" people sometimes get away with cheating, lying, and killing, while "good" people sometimes lose everything through no fault of their own. We can usually accept that fact and forgive those who wrong us. However, sometimes we want to have revenge to restore a feeling of justice. After all, another well-known biblical phrase is "an eye for an eye and a tooth for a tooth."

Consider the popularity of Mafia movies and television shows. Although we would never behave like Michael Corleone or Tony Soprano, we watch those driven by the dark code of justice in horrified admiration. Thankfully, most forms of revenge are less sinister than the violent mob hits presented in the media. A betrayed friend might spill a rival's secrets; a disgruntled employee might slack off or call in sick at a busy time; an annoyed driver may not let another driver into the flow of traffic; a child might break a vase and place the blame on a favored sibling; and an offended person may ostracize the offending person by not calling, writing, or responding to any peace overtures. A few years ago, a group of Internet users exacted revenge on a notorious spammer, Alan Ralsky, by inundating the bulk e-mailer with hundreds of mass mailings delivered to his

Al Pacino in the film *The Godfather* (1972).

home—ads, catalogs, magazines, campaign brochures, and so on. Was their action appropriate, giving Ralsky a taste of his own medicine? Or should they have turned the other cheek?

Writing has often served as a means of revenge. When the Romantic poet Lord Byron ended his scandalous affair with the married Lady Caroline Lamb, she published a scathing novel, *Glenarvon*, in which the villain is a thinly disguised portrait of her former lover. For his part, Byron attacked his rivals, critics, and lovers in his poems throughout his career whenever he perceived even the slightest injury. In 1819, after his wife left him because of his reported madness, incest, and abuse, Byron retaliated by satirizing her as Donna Inez in his epic poem *Don Juan* (see Chapter 13).

The readings in this chapter explore the difficulties of forgiving and the satisfaction that often accompanies revenge. They also explore the redemption that comes with forgiveness, as well as the guilt that accompanies many acts of revenge. In the *New Yorker* cartoon pictured here, one relaxed, well-dressed man says to another, "Forget living well. The best revenge is revenge." This cartoon turns the tables on the well-known saying "The best revenge is living well," which encourages injured people to move on with their lives and to torment their enemies by remaining happy and successful. This chapter features poetry, stories, plays, and essays that both affirm and challenge these ideas. Is revenge wicked, or is it justice? Does the answer depend on circumstances?

"Forget living well. The best revenge is revenge."

© The New Yorker Collection 1988 William Hamilton from cartoonbank.com.

Fiction

Edgar Allan Poe

The Cask of Amontillado

Edgar Allan Poe (1809–1849) was born in Baltimore, Maryland, and was raised by a wealthy family after the death of his mother, an actress. Unlike many of the transcendentalist authors who were his contemporaries, Poe never completed college. He attended the University of Virginia and West Point but dropped out of both for financial and personal reasons. He married his thirteen-year-old cousin and worked as a writer, critic, and editor for a variety of literary journals. Poe is considered the father of the American detective story and was a proponent of the "art for art's sake" school of criticism. While some critics feel that much of his writing is overly sentimental or morbid, none would deny the power of his classic texts: his poem "The Raven" and stories like "The Tell-tale Heart," "The Purloined Letter," and "Mask of the Red Death." One of Poe's favorite fictional subjects was revenge, and his interest in the topic was more than academic. Poe had a knack for making enemies and once engaged in a public war of words with the writer Thomas Dunn English. His hatred for English and his feelings of superiority are said to have inspired "The Cask of Amontillado" (1846), possibly the most famous tale of vengeance in American literature. Poe's narrator never tells us what his enemy has done to deserve his terrible fate; his emphasis is on committing the perfect act of revenge.

The thousand injuries of Fortunato I had borne as I best could, but when he ventured upon insult, I vowed revenge. You, who so well know the nature of my soul, will not suppose, however, that I gave utterance to a threat. *At length* I would be avenged; this was a point definitely settled—but the very definitiveness with which it was resolved, precluded the idea of risk. I must not only punish, but punish with impunity. A wrong is unredressed when retribution overtakes its redresser. It is equally unredressed when the avenger fails to make himself felt as such to him who has done the wrong.

It must be understood that neither by word nor deed had I given Fortunato cause to doubt my good will. I continued as was my wont, to smile in his face, and he did not perceive that my smile *now* was at the thought of his immolation.

He had a weak point—this Fortunato—although in other regards he was a man to be respected and even feared. He prided himself on his connoisseurship in wine. Few Italians have the true virtuoso spirit. For the most part their enthusiasm is adapted to suit the time and opportunity—to practice imposture upon the British and Austrian *millionaires*. In painting and gemmary[1] Fortunato, like his country men, was a quack—but in the matter of old wines he was sincere. In this respect I did not differ from him materially: I was skilful in the Italian vintages myself, and bought largely whenever I could.

It was about dusk, one evening during the supreme madness of the carnival season, that I encountered my friend. He accosted me with excessive warmth, for he had been drinking much. The man wore motley. He had on a tight-fitting parti-striped dress, and his head was surmounted by the conical cap and bells. I was so pleased to see him, that I thought I should never have done wringing his hand.

I said to him: "My dear Fortunato, you are luckily met. How remarkably 5
well you are looking to-day! But I have received a pipe of what passes for Amontillado,[2] and I have my doubts."

[1]*gemmary:* Of or pertaining to precious gems or minerals.

[2]*Amontillado:* A type of sherry or fortified wine. It is named after the Montilla region of southern Spain. When Fortunato claims that Luchresi cannot tell the difference between Amontillado and sherry, he is referring to common, everyday sherry.

"How?" said he. "Amontillado? A pipe? Impossible! And in the middle of the carnival!"

"I have my doubts," I replied; "and I was silly enough to pay the full Amontillado price without consulting you in the matter. You were not to be found, and I was fearful of losing a bargain."

"Amontillado!"

"I have my doubts."

"Amontillado!"

"And I must satisfy them."

"Amontillado!"

"As you are engaged, I am on my way to Luchresi. If any one has a critical turn, it is he. He will tell me—"

"Luchresi cannot tell Amontillado from Sherry."

"And yet some fools will have it that his taste is a match for your own."

"Come, let us go."

"Whither?"

"To your vaults."

"My friend, no; I will not impose upon your good nature. I perceive you have an engagement. Luchresi——"

"I have no engagement;—come."

"My friend, no. It is not the engagement, but the severe cold with which I perceive you are afflicted. The vaults are insufferably damp. They are encrusted with nitre."

"Let us go, nevertheless. The cold is merely nothing. Amontillado! You have been imposed upon. And as for Luchresi, he cannot distinguish Sherry from Amontillado."

Thus speaking, Fortunato possessed himself of my arm. Putting on a mask of black silk, and drawing a *roquelaire*[3] closely about my person, I suffered him to hurry me to my palazzo.

There were no attendants at home; they had absconded to make merry in honor of the time. I had told them that I should not return until the morning, and had given them explicit orders not to stir from the house. These orders were sufficient, I well knew, to insure their immediate disappearance, one and all, as soon as my back was turned.

I took from their sconces two flambeaux, and giving one to Fortunato, bowed him through several suites of rooms to the archway that led into the vaults. I passed down a long and winding staircase, requesting him to be cautious as he followed. We came at length to the foot of the descent, and stood together on the damp ground of the catacombs of the Montresors.

The gait of my friend was unsteady, and the bells upon his cap jingled as he strode.

"The pipe?" said he.

"It is farther on," said I; "but observe the white web-work which gleams from these cavern walls."

[3]*roquelaire:* A cloak.

He turned toward me, and looked into my eyes with two filmy orbs that distilled the rheum of intoxication.

"Nitre?" he asked, at length.

"Nitre," I replied. "How long have you had that cough?"

"Ugh! ugh! ugh!—ugh! ugh! ugh!—ugh! ugh! ugh!—ugh! ugh! ugh!—ugh! ugh! ugh!"

My poor friend found it impossible to reply for many minutes.

"It is nothing," he said, at last.

"Come," I said, with decision, "we will go back; your health is precious. You are rich, respected, admired, beloved; you are happy, as once I was. You are a man to be missed. For me it is no matter. We will go back; you will be ill, and I cannot be responsible. Besides, there is Luchresi——"

"Enough," he said; "the cough is a mere nothing; it will not kill me. I shall not die of a cough."

"True—true," I replied; "and, indeed, I had no intention of alarming you unnecessarily—but you should use all proper caution. A draught of this Medoc[4] will defend us from the damps."

Here I knocked off the neck of a bottle which I drew from a long row of its fellows that lay upon the mould.

"Drink," I said, presenting him the wine.

He raised it to his lips with a leer. He paused and nodded to me familiarly, while his bells jingled.

"I drink," he said, "to the buried that repose around us."

"And I to your long life."

He again took my arm, and we proceeded.

"These vaults," he said, "are extensive."

"The Montresors," I replied, "were a great and numerous family."

"I forget your arms."

"A huge human foot d'or, in a field azure; the foot crushes a serpent rampant whose fangs are imbedded in the heel."

"And the motto?"

"*Nemo me impune lacessit.*"[5]

"Good!" he said.

The wine sparkled in his eyes and the bells jingled. My own fancy grew warm with the Medoc. We had passed through walls of piled bones, with casks and puncheons intermingling, into the inmost recesses of the catacombs. I paused again, and this time I made bold to seize Fortunato by an arm above the elbow.

"The nitre!" I said; "see, it increases. It hangs like moss upon the vaults. We are below the river's bed. The drops of moisture trickle among the bones. Come, we will go back ere it is too late. Your cough——"

"It is nothing," he said; "let us go on. But first, another draught of the Medoc."

[4]*Medoc:* A rare red wine that comes from the Médoc region in France.

[5]*Nemo me impune lacessit:* No one wounds me with impunity (Latin). Montressor is giving Fortunato another hint about his fate.

I broke and reached him a flagon of De Grave.[6] He emptied it at a breath. His eyes flashed with a fierce light. He laughed and threw the bottle upward with a gesticulation I did not understand.

I looked at him in surprise. He repeated the movement—a grotesque one.

"You do not comprehend?" he said.

"Not I," I replied.

"Then you are not of the brotherhood."

"How?"

"You are not of the masons."[7]

"Yes, yes," I said; "yes, yes."

"You? Impossible! A mason?"

"A mason," I replied.

"A sign," he said.

"It is this," I answered, producing a trowel from beneath the folds of my *roquelaire*.

"You jest," he exclaimed, recoiling a few paces. "But let us proceed to the Amontillado."

"Be it so," I said, replacing the tool beneath the cloak, and again offering my arm. He leaned upon it heavily. We continued our route in search of the Amontillado. We passed through a range of low arches, descended, passed on, and descending again, arrived at a deep crypt, in which the foulness of the air caused our flambeaux rather to glow than flame.

At the most remote end of the crypt there appeared another less spacious. Its walls had been lined with human remains, piled to the vault overhead, in the fashion of the great catacombs of Paris. Three sides of this interior crypt were still ornamented in this manner. From the fourth the bones had been thrown down, and lay promiscuously upon the earth, forming at one point a mount of some size. Within the wall thus exposed by the displacing of the bones, we perceived a still interior recess, in depth about four feet, in width three, in height six or seven. It seemed to have been constructed for no especial use within itself, but formed merely the interval between two of the colossal supports of the roof of the catacombs, and was backed by one of their circumscribing walls of solid granite.

It was in vain that Fortunato, uplifting his dull torch, endeavored to pry into the depth of the recess. Its termination the feeble light did not enable us to see.

"Proceed," I said; "herein is the Amontillado. As for Luchresi——"

"He is an ignoramus," interrupted my friend, as he stepped unsteadily forward, while I followed immediately at his heels. In an instant he had reached the extremity of the niche, and finding his progress arrested by the rock, stood stupidly bewildered. A moment more and I had fettered him to the granite. In its

[6]*De Grave:* A wine from the Graves region in France. The name is also a pun on the word *grave*.

[7]*masons:* A reference to the Freemasons, a fraternal society that dates back to the early eighteenth century. Montressor puns on the word to refer to the trade of masonry. Although Fortunato gets the joke, he fails to question why Montressor would need a trowel in the catacombs.

surface were two iron staples, distant from each other about two feet, horizontally. From one of these depended a short chain, from the other a padlock. Throwing the links about his waist, it was but the work of a few seconds to secure it. He was too much astounded to resist. Withdrawing the key I stepped back from the recess.

"Pass your hand," I said, "over the wall; you cannot help feeling the nitre. Indeed it is *very* damp. Once more let me *implore* you to return. No? Then I must positively leave you. But I must first render you all the little attentions in my power."

"The Amontillado!" ejaculated my friend, not yet recovered from his astonishment.

"True," I replied; "the Amontillado."

As I said these words I busied myself among the pile of bones of which I have 75
before spoken. Throwing them aside, I soon uncovered a quantity of building stone and mortar. With these materials and with the aid of my trowel, I began vigorously to wall up the entrance of the niche.

I had scarcely laid the first tier of the masonry when I discovered that the intoxication of Fortunato had in a great measure worn off. The earliest indication I had of this was a low moaning cry from the depth of the recess. It was *not* the cry of a drunken man. There was then a long and obstinate silence. I laid the second tier, and the third, and the fourth; and then I heard the furious vibrations of the chain. The noise lasted for several minutes, during which, that I might hearken to it with the more satisfaction, I ceased my labors and sat down upon the bones. When at last the clanking subsided, I resumed the trowel, and finished without interruption the fifth, the sixth, and the seventh tier. The wall was now nearly upon a level with my breast. I again paused, and holding the flambeaux over the mason-work, threw a few feeble rays upon the figure within.

A succession of loud and shrill screams, bursting suddenly from the throat of the chained form, seemed to thrust me violently back. For a brief moment I hesitated—I trembled. Unsheathing my rapier, I began to grope with it about the recess; but the thought of an instant reassured me. I placed my hand upon the solid fabric of the catacombs, and felt satisfied. I reapproached the wall. I replied to the yells of him who clamored. I re-echoed—I aided—I surpassed them in volume and in strength. I did this, and the clamorer grew still.

It was now midnight, and my task was drawing to a close. I had completed the eighth, the ninth, and the tenth tier. I had finished a portion of the last and the eleventh; there remained but a single stone to be fitted and plastered in. I struggled with its weight; I placed it partially in its destined position. But now there came from out the niche a low laugh that erected the hairs upon my head. It was succeeded by a sad voice, which I had difficulty in recognizing as that of the noble Fortunato. The voice said—

"Ha! ha! ha!—he! he!—a very good joke indeed—an excellent jest. We will have many a rich laugh about it at the palazzo—he! he! he!—over our wine—he! he! he!"

"The Amontillado!" I said. 80

"He! he! he!—he! he! he!—yes, the Amontillado. But is it not getting late? Will not they be awaiting us at the palazzo, the Lady Fortunato and the rest? Let us be gone."

"Yes," I said, "let us be gone."

"For the love of God, Montresor!"

"Yes," I said, "for the love of God!"

But to these words I hearkened in vain for a reply. I grew impatient. I called 85
aloud;

"Fortunato!"

No answer. I called again;

"Fortunato!"

No answer still. I thrust a torch through the remaining aperture and let it fall within. There came forth in return only a jingling of the bells. My heart grew sick—on account of the dampness of the catacombs. I hastened to make an end of my labor. I forced the last stone into its position; I plastered it up. Against the new masonry I re-erected the old rampart of bones. For the half of a century no mortal has disturbed them. *In pace requiescat!*[8]

(1846)

QUESTIONS FOR DISCUSSION AND WRITING

CLOSE READING

1. In paragraph 1, Montressor articulates his "rules" for revenge. What, in his opinion, constitutes successful vengeance? Does his scheme ultimately conform to his definition?
2. Name three things we know about Fortunato based on Montressor's description of him. Is he a sympathetic or unsympathetic character? Are he and Montressor alike or different?
3. Describe the setting and atmosphere. How does the contrast between the dark, nitrous catacombs below and the festive carnival above contribute to the story's tone?

CRITICAL AND CREATIVE READING

4. Montressor frequently discusses his ancestors, among whose remains the story takes place. Consider what we know about his family: they are "great and numerous" and their motto translates as "no one insults me with impunity." Is Montressor exacting revenge in the name of his family or himself? Is it fitting or ironic that Fortunato's remains will mingle with those of Montressor's ancestors and—eventually—with his murderer?
5. Why is Montressor telling this story now, fifty years later, and to whom? He addresses his listener as one who "knows the nature of [his] soul." Who

[8]*In pace requiescat:* May he rest in peace (Latin).

might this listener be? Write a brief paragraph from the point of view of two of the following potential listeners to Montressor's tale: yourself, God, a lawyer, the ghost of Fortunato, the ghost of a Montressor.

6. Fortunato follows Montressor to sample a rare bottle of Amontillado. Montressor tells us that his victim had been drinking, and Fortunato continues to drink as he descends into the catacombs. Do you think Fortunato contributes to his own death by his weakness for alcohol? How important is his drunkenness to the story?

CONNECTIONS TO OTHER READINGS

7. Compare and contrast Montressor with the father in Andre Dubus's story "Killings." Which character is stronger? Which is more justified in their revenge? Besides revenge, do the two characters have anything in common?
8. Compare Montressor's attempts to justify his behavior with those of the women in Edith Wharton's "Roman Fever." Why do these characters insist on being understood? How successfully do they explain themselves?
9. Choose another work in this chapter (like "Babylon Revisited," "On the Antler," "Roman Fever," or "The Rime of the Ancient Mariner") and consider how the setting contributes to the work's impact.

Edith Wharton

Roman Fever

Edith Wharton (1862–1937) was born to a wealthy New York family and raised with the expectation that she would grow up to be a prominent figure in the New York social scene, playing the role of gracious wife and hostess (much like her character Mrs. Slade in the following story). Her parents discouraged her writing ambitions, and her husband Edward Wharton (whom she divorced in 1912) also did little to encourage them. Nonetheless, she was publishing fiction by 1899, and her first novel, *The House of Mirth,* appeared in 1905. She wrote prolifically for the rest of her life, earning a Pulitzer Prize for her 1920 novel *The Age of Innocence*. Following her divorce, Wharton lived in France and became a member of the Legion of Honor for her relief work during World War I. Although the pivotal action in "Roman Fever" takes place over twenty years before the opening scene, the revenge lies not so much in what happened but in the women's decision to reveal the secrets of the past.

I

From the table at which they had been lunching two American ladies of ripe but well-cared-for middle age moved across the lofty terrace of the Roman restaurant and, leaning on its parapet, looked first at each other, and then down on the outspread glories of the Palatine and the Forum,[1] with the same expression of vague but benevolent approval.

As they leaned there a girlish voice echoed up gaily from the stairs leading to the court below. "Well, come along, then," it cried, not to them but to an invisible companion, "and let's leave the young things to their knitting"; and a voice as fresh laughed back: "Oh, look here, Babs, not actually *knitting*—" "Well, I mean figuratively," rejoined the first. "After all, we haven't left our poor parents much else to do . . ." and at that point the turn of the stairs engulfed the dialogue.

The two ladies looked at each other again, this time with a tinge of smiling embarrassment, and the smaller and paler one shook her head and colored slightly.

"Barbara!" she murmured, sending an unheard rebuke after the mocking voice in the stairway.

The other lady, who was fuller, and higher in color, with a small determined 5
nose supported by vigorous black eyebrows, gave a good-humored laugh. "That's what our daughters think of us!"

Her companion replied by a deprecating gesture. "Not of us individually. We must remember that. It's just the collective modern idea of Mothers. And you see—" Half-guiltily she drew from her handsomely mounted black handbag a twist of crimson silk run through by two fine knitting needles. "One never knows," she murmured. "The new system has certainly given us a good deal of time to kill; and sometimes I get tired just looking—even at this." Her gesture was now addressed to the stupendous scene at their feet.

The dark lady laughed again, and they both relapsed upon the view, contemplating it in silence, with a sort of diffused serenity which might have been borrowed from the spring effulgence of the Roman skies. The luncheon hour was long past, and the two had their end of the vast terrace to themselves. At its opposite extremity a few groups, detained by a lingering look at the outspread city, were gathering up guidebooks and fumbling for tips. The last of them scattered, and the two ladies were alone on the air-washed height.

"Well, I don't see why we shouldn't just stay here," said Mrs. Slade, the lady of the high color and energetic brows. Two derelict basket chairs stood near, and she pushed them into the angle of the parapet, and settled herself in one, her gaze upon the Palatine. "After all, it's still the most beautiful view in the world."

"It always will be, to me," assented her friend Mrs. Ansley, with so slight a stress on the "me" that Mrs. Slade, though she noticed it, wondered if it were not merely accidental, like the random underlinings of old-fashioned letter writers.

"Grace Ansley was always old-fashioned," she thought; and added aloud, with a 10
retrospective smile: "It's a view we've both been familiar with for a good many years. When we first met here we were younger than our girls are now. You remember?"

[1]*Palatine . . . Forum:* The Palatine Hill is one of the seven hills of Rome. The Roman Forum was the center of political activity during Rome's Republic.

"Oh, yes, I remember," murmured Mrs. Ansley, with the same undefinable stress. "There's that headwaiter wondering," she interpolated. She was evidently far less sure than her companion of herself and of her rights in the world.

"I'll cure him of wondering," said Mrs. Slade, stretching her hand toward a bag as discreetly opulent-looking as Mrs. Ansley's. Signing to the headwaiter, she explained that she and her friend were old lovers of Rome, and would like to spend the end of the afternoon looking down on the view—that is, if it did not disturb the service? The headwaiter, bowing over her gratuity, assured her that the ladies were most welcome, and would be still more so if they would condescend to remain for dinner. A full-moon night, they would remember. . . .

Mrs. Slade's black brows drew together, as though references to the moon were out of place and even unwelcome. But she smiled away her frown as the headwaiter retreated. "Well, why not? We might do worse. There's no knowing, I suppose, when the girls will be back. Do you even know back from *where?* I don't!"

Mrs. Ansley again colored slightly. "I think those young Italian aviators we met at the Embassy invited them to fly to Tarquinia[2] for tea. I suppose they'll want to wait and fly back by moonlight."

"Moonlight—moonlight! What a part it still plays. Do you suppose they're as sentimental as we were?"

"I've come to the conclusion that I don't in the least know what they are," said Mrs. Ansley. "And perhaps we didn't know much more about each other."

"No; perhaps we didn't."

Her friend gave her a shy glance. "I never should have supposed you were sentimental, Alida."

"Well, perhaps I wasn't." Mrs. Slade drew her lids together in retrospect; and for a few moments the two ladies, who had been intimate since childhood, reflected how little they knew each other. Each one, of course, had a label ready to attach to the other's name; Mrs. Delphin Slade, for instance, would have told herself, or anyone who asked her, that Mrs. Horace Ansley, twenty-five years ago, had been exquisitely lovely—no, you wouldn't believe it, would you? . . . though, of course, still charming, distinguished. . . . Well, as a girl she had been exquisite; far more beautiful than her daughter Barbara, though certainly Babs, according to the new standards at any rate, was more effective—had more *edge*, as they say. Funny where she got it, with those two nullities as parents. Yes; Horace Ansley was—well, just the duplicate of his wife. Museum specimens of old New York. Good-looking, irreproachable, exemplary. Mrs. Slade and Mrs. Ansley had lived opposite each other—actually as well as figuratively—for years. When the drawing-room curtains in No. 20 East 73rd Street were renewed, No. 23, across the way, was always aware of it. And of all the movings, buyings, travels, anniversaries, illnesses—the tame chronicle of an estimable pair. Little of it escaped Mrs. Slade. But she had grown bored with it by the time her husband made his big *coup* in Wall Street, and when they bought in upper Park Avenue had already begun to think: "I'd rather live opposite a speakeasy for a change; at least one might see it raided." The idea of seeing Grace raided was so amusing

[2]*Tarquinia:* An ancient Etruscan city.

that (before the move) she launched it at a woman's lunch. It made a hit, and went the rounds—she sometimes wondered if it had crossed the street, and reached Mrs. Ansley. She hoped not, but didn't much mind. Those were the days when respectability was at a discount, and it did the irreproachable no harm to laugh at them a little.

20 A few years later, and not many months apart, both ladies lost their husbands. There was an appropriate exchange of wreaths and condolences, and a brief renewal of intimacy in the half-shadow of their mourning; and now, after another interval, they had run across each other in Rome, at the same hotel, each of them the modest appendage of a salient daughter. The similarity of their lot had again drawn them together, lending itself to mild jokes, and the mutual confession that, if in old days it must have been tiring to "keep up" with daughters, it was now, at times, a little dull not to.

No doubt, Mrs. Slade reflected, she felt her unemployment more than poor Grace ever would. It was a big drop from being the wife of Delphin Slade to being his widow. She had always regarded herself (with a certain conjugal pride) as his equal in social gifts, as contributing her full share to the making of the exceptional couple they were: but the difference after his death was irremediable. As the wife of the famous corporation lawyer, always with an international case or two on hand, every day brought its exciting and unexpected obligation: the impromptu entertaining of eminent colleagues from abroad, the hurried dashes on legal business to London, Paris or Rome, where the entertaining was so handsomely reciprocated; the amusement of hearing in her wake: "What, that handsome woman with the good clothes and the eyes is Mrs. Slade—*the* Slade's wife? Really? Generally the wives of celebrities are such frumps."

Yes; being *the* Slade's widow was a dullish business after that. In living up to such a husband all her faculties had been engaged; now she had only her daughter to live up to, for the son who seemed to have inherited his father's gifts had died suddenly in boyhood. She had fought through that agony because her husband was there, to be helped and to help; now, after the father's death, the thought of the boy had become unbearable. There was nothing left but to mother her daughter; and dear Jenny was such a perfect daughter that she needed no excessive mothering. "Now with Babs Ansley I don't know that I *should* be so quiet," Mrs. Slade sometimes half-enviously reflected; but Jenny, who was younger than her brilliant friend, was that rare accident, an extremely pretty girl who somehow made youth and prettiness seem as safe as their absence. It was all perplexing—and to Mrs. Slade a little boring. She wished that Jenny would fall in love—with the wrong man, even; that she might have to be watched, out-maneuvered, rescued. And instead, it was Jenny who watched her mother, kept her out of drafts, made sure that she had taken her tonic. . . .

Mrs. Ansley was much less articulate than her friend, and her mental portrait of Mrs. Slade was slighter, and drawn with fainter touches. "Alida Slade's awfully brilliant; but not as brilliant as she thinks," would have summed it up; though she would have added, for the enlightenment of strangers, that Mrs. Slade had been an extremely dashing girl; much more so than her daughter, who was pretty, of course, and clever in a way, but had none of her mother's—well, "vividness," someone had once called it. Mrs. Ansley would take up current words like this, and cite them in quotation marks, as unheard-of audacities. No; Jenny was not like her mother. Sometimes Mrs. Ansley thought Alida Slade was disappointed; on the whole she had had a sad life. Full of failures and mistakes; Mrs. Ansley had always been rather sorry for her. . . .

So these two ladies visualized each other, each through the wrong end of her little telescope.

II

For a long time they continued to sit side by side without speaking. It seemed as though, to both, there was a relief in laying down their somewhat futile activities in the presence of the vast Memento Mori which faced them. Mrs. Slade sat quite still, her eyes fixed on the golden slope of the Palace of the Caesars, and after a while Mrs. Ansley ceased to fidget with her bag, and she too sank into meditation. Like many intimate friends, the two ladies had never before had occasion to be silent together, and Mrs. Ansley was slightly embarrassed by what seemed, after so many years, a new stage in their intimacy, and one with which she did not yet know how to deal.

Suddenly the air was full of that deep clangor of bells which periodically covers Rome with a roof of silver. Mrs. Slade glanced at her wristwatch. "Five o'clock already," she said, as though surprised.

Mrs. Ansley suggested interrogatively: "There's bridge at the Embassy at five." For a long time Mrs. Slade did not answer. She appeared to be lost in contemplation, and Mrs. Ansley thought the remark had escaped her. But after a while she said, as if speaking out of a dream: "Bridge, did you say? Not unless you want to. . . . But I don't think I will, you know."

"Oh, no," Mrs. Ansley hastened to assure her. "I don't care to at all. It's so lovely here; and so full of old memories, as you say." She settled herself in her chair, and almost furtively drew forth her knitting. Mrs. Slade took sideway note of this activity, but her own beautifully cared-for hands remained motionless on her knee.

"I was just thinking," she said slowly, "what different things Rome stands for to each generation of travelers. To our grandmothers, Roman fever;[3] to our mothers, sentimental dangers—how we used to be guarded!—to our daughters, no more dangers than the middle of Main Street. They don't know it—but how much they're missing!"

The long golden light was beginning to pale, and Mrs. Ansley lifted her knitting a little closer to her eyes. "Yes; how we were guarded!"

"I always used to think," Mrs. Slade continued, "that our mothers had a much more difficult job than our grandmothers. When Roman fever stalked the streets it must have been comparatively easy to gather in the girls at the danger hour; but when you and I were young, with such beauty calling us, and

[3] *Roman fever:* A dangerous form of malaria that was believed to be contracted at night.

the spice of disobedience thrown in, and no worse risk than catching cold during the cool hour after sunset, the mothers used to be put to it to keep us in—didn't they?"

She turned again toward Mrs. Ansley, but the latter had reached a delicate point in her knitting. "One, two, three—slip two; yes, they must have been," she assented, without looking up.

Mrs. Slade's eyes rested on her with a deepened attention. "She can knit—in the face of *this!* How like her. . . ."

Mrs. Slade leaned back, brooding, her eyes ranging from the ruins which faced her to the long green hollow of the Forum, the fading flow of the church fronts beyond it, and the outlying immensity of the Colosseum. Suddenly she thought: It's all very well to say that our girls have done away with sentiment and moonlight. But if Babs Ansley isn't out to catch that young aviator—the one who's a Marchese—then I don't know anything. And Jenny has no chance beside her. I know that too. I wonder if that's why Grace Ansley likes the two girls to go everywhere together? My poor Jenny as a foil—!" Mrs. Slade gave a hardly audible laugh, and at the sound Mrs. Ansley dropped her knitting.

"Yes—?"

"I—oh, nothing. I was only thinking how your Babs carries everything before her. That Campolieri boy is one of the best matches in Rome. Don't look so innocent, my dear—you know he is. And I was wondering, ever so respectfully, you understand . . . wondering how two such exemplary characters as you and Horace had managed to produce anything quite so dynamic." Mrs. Slade laughed again, with a touch of asperity.

Mrs. Ansley's hands lay inert across her needles. She looked straight out at the great accumulated wreckage of passion and splendor at her feet. But her small profile was almost expressionless. At length she said: "I think you overrate Babs, my dear."

Mrs. Slade's tone grew easier. "No; I don't. I appreciate her. And perhaps envy you. Oh, my girl's perfect; if I were a chronic invalid I'd—well, I think I'd rather be in Jenny's hands. There must be times . . . but there! I always wanted a brilliant daughter . . . and never quite understood why I got an angel instead."

Mrs. Ansley echoed her laugh in a faint murmur. "Babs is an angel too."

"Of course—of course! But she's got rainbow wings. Well, they're wandering by the sea with their young men; and here we sit . . . and it all brings back the past a little too acutely."

Mrs. Ansley had resumed her knitting. One might almost have imagined (if one had known her less well, Mrs. Slade reflected) that, for her also, too many memories rose from the lengthening shadows of those august ruins. But no; she was simply absorbed in her work. What was there for her to worry about? She knew that Babs would almost certainly come back engaged to the extremely eligible Campolieri. "And she'll sell the New York house, and settle down near them in Rome, and never be in their way . . . she's much too tactful. But she'll have an excellent cook, and just the right people in for bridge and cocktails . . . and a perfectly peaceful old age among her grandchildren."

Mrs. Slade broke off this prophetic flight with a recoil of self-disgust. There was no one of whom she had less right to think unkindly than of Grace Ansley. Would she never cure herself of envying her? Perhaps she had begun too long ago.

She stood up and leaned against the parapet, filling her troubled eyes with the tranquilizing magic of the hour. But instead of tranquilizing her the sight seemed to increase her exasperation. Her gaze turned toward the Colosseum.[4] Already its golden flank was downed in purple shadow, and above it the sky curved crystal clear, without light or color. It was the moment when afternoon and evening hang balanced in midheaven.

Mrs. Slade turned back and laid her hand on her friend's arm. The gesture was so abrupt that Mrs. Ansley looked up, startled.

"The sun's set. You're not afraid, my dear?"

"Afraid—?"

"Of Roman fever or pneumonia? I remember how ill you were that winter. As a girl you had a very delicate throat, hadn't you?"

"Oh, we're all right up here. Down below, in the Forum, it does get deathly cold, all of a sudden . . . but not here."

"Ah, of course you know because you had to be so careful." Mrs. Slade turned back to the parapet. She thought: "I must make one more effort not to hate her." Aloud she said: "Whenever I look at the Forum from up here, I remember that story about a great-aunt of yours, wasn't she? A dreadfully wicked great-aunt?"

"Oh, yes; great-aunt Harriet. The one who was supposed to have sent her young sister out to the Forum after sunset to gather a nightblooming flower for her album. All our great-aunts and grandmothers used to have albums of dried flowers."

Mrs. Slade nodded. "But she really sent her because they were in love with the same man—"

"Well, that was the family tradition. They said Aunt Harriet confessed it years afterward. At any rate, the poor little sister caught the fever and died. Mother used to frighten us with the story when we were children."

"And you frightened *me* with it, that winter when you and I were here as girls. The winter I was engaged to Delphin."

Mrs. Ansley gave a faint laugh. "Oh, did I? Really frightened you? I don't believe you're easily frightened."

"Not often; but I was then. I was easily frightened because I was too happy. I wonder if you know what that means?"

"I—yes . . ." Mrs. Ansley faltered.

"Well, I suppose that was why the story of your wicked aunt made such an impression on me. And I thought: 'There's no more Roman fever, but the Forum is deathly cold after sunset—especially after a hot day. And the Colosseum's even colder and damper.'"

[4]*Colosseum:* A first-century Roman amphitheater that was used for gladiator fights and other spectacles.

"The Colosseum—?"

"Yes. It wasn't easy to get in, after the gates were locked for the night. Far from easy. Still, in those days it could be managed; it *was* managed, often. Lovers met there who couldn't meet elsewhere. You knew that?"

"I—I dare say. I don't remember."

"You don't remember? You don't remember going to visit some ruins or other one evening, just after dark, and catching a bad chill? You were supposed to have gone to see the moon rise. People always said that expedition was what caused your illness."

There was a moment's silence; then Mrs. Ansley rejoined: "Did they? It was all so long ago."

"Yes. And you got well again—so it didn't matter. But I suppose it struck your friends—the reason given for your illness, I mean—because everybody knew you were so prudent on account of your throat, and your mother took such care of you. . . . You *had* been out late sight-seeing, hadn't you, that night?"

"Perhaps I had. The most prudent girls aren't always prudent. What made you think of it now?"

Mrs. Slade seemed to have no answer ready. But after a moment she broke out: "Because I simply can't bear it any longer—!"

Mrs. Ansley lifted her head quickly. Her eyes were wide and very pale. "Can't bear what?"

"Why—your not knowing that I've always known why you went."

"Why I went—?"

"Yes. You think I'm bluffing, don't you? Well, you went to meet the man I was engaged to—and I can repeat every word of the letter that took you there."

While Mrs. Slade spoke Mrs. Ansley had risen unsteadily to her feet. Her bag, her knitting and gloves, slid in a panic-stricken heap to the ground. She looked at Mrs. Slade as though she were looking at a ghost.

"No, no—don't," she faltered out.

"Why not? Listen, if you don't believe me. 'My one darling, things can't go on like this. I must see you alone. Come to the Colosseum immediately after dark tomorrow. There will be somebody to let you in. No one whom you need fear will suspect'—but perhaps you've forgotten what the letter said?"

Mrs. Ansley met the challenge with an unexpected composure. Steadying herself against the chair she looked at her friend, and replied: "No; I know it by heart too."

"And the signature? 'Only *your* D.S.' Was that it? I'm right, am I? That was the letter that took you out that evening after dark?"

Mrs. Ansley was still looking at her. It seemed to Mrs. Slade that a slow struggle was going on behind the voluntarily controlled mask of her small quiet face. "I shouldn't have thought she had herself so well in hand," Mrs. Slade reflected, almost resentfully. But at this moment Mrs. Ansley spoke. "I don't know how you knew. I burnt the letter at once."

"Yes; you would, naturally—you're so prudent!" The sneer was open now. "And if you burnt the letter you're wondering how on earth I know what was in it. That's it, isn't it?"

Mrs. Slade waited, but Mrs. Ansley did not speak.

"Well, my dear, I know what was in that letter because I wrote it!"

"You wrote it?"

"Yes."

The two women stood for a minute staring at each other in the last golden light. Then Mrs. Ansley dropped back into her chair. "Oh," she murmured, and covered her face with her hands.

Mrs. Slade waited nervously for another word or movement. None came, and at length she broke out: "I horrify you."

Mrs. Ansley's hands dropped to her knee. The face they uncovered was streaked with tears. "I wasn't thinking of you. I was thinking—it was the only letter I ever had from him!"

"And I wrote it. Yes; I wrote it! But I was the girl he was engaged to. Did you happen to remember that?"

Mrs. Ansley's head drooped again. "I'm not trying to excuse myself . . . I remembered. . . ."

"And still you went?"

"Still I went."

Mrs. Slade stood looking down on the small bowed figure at her side. The flame of her wrath had already sunk, and she wondered why she had ever thought there would be any satisfaction in inflicting so purposeless a wound on her friend. But she had to justify herself.

"You do understand? I'd found out—and I hated you, hated you. I knew you were in love with Delphin—and I was afraid; afraid of you, of your quiet ways, your sweetness . . . your . . . well, I wanted you out of the way, that's all. Just for a few weeks; just till I was sure of him. So in a blind fury I wrote that letter . . . I don't know why I'm telling you now."

"I suppose," said Mrs. Ansley slowly, "it's because you've always gone on hating me."

"Perhaps. Or because I wanted to get the whole thing off my mind." She paused. "I'm glad you destroyed the letter. Of course I never thought you'd die."

Mrs. Ansley relapsed into silence, and Mrs. Slade, leaning above her, was conscious of a strange sense of isolation, of being cut off from the warm current of human communion. "You think me a monster!"

"I don't know. . . . It was the only letter I had, and you say he didn't write it?"

"Ah, how you care for him still!"

"I cared for that memory," said Mrs. Ansley.

Mrs. Slade continued to look down on her. She seemed physically reduced by the blow—as if, when she got up, the wind might scatter her like a puff of dust. Mrs. Slade's jealousy suddenly leapt up again at the sight. All these years the woman had been living on that letter. How she must have loved him, to treasure the mere memory of its ashes! The letter of the man her friend was engaged to. Wasn't it she who was the monster?

"You tried your best to get him away from me, didn't you? But you failed; and I kept him. That's all."

"Yes. That's all."

"I wish now I hadn't told you. I'd no idea you'd feel about it as you do; I thought you'd be amused. It all happened so long ago, as you say; and you must do me the justice to remember that I had no reason to think you'd ever taken it seriously. How could I, when you were married to Horace Ansley two months afterward? As soon as you could get out of bed your mother rushed you off to Florence and married you. People were rather surprised—they wondered at its being done so quickly; but I thought I knew. I had an idea you did it out of *pique*—to be able to say you'd got ahead of Delphin and me. Girls have such silly reasons for doing the most serious things. And your marrying so soon convinced me that you'd never really cared."

"Yes. I suppose it would," Mrs. Ansley assented. 100

The clear heaven overhead was emptied of all its gold. Dusk spread over it, abruptly darkening the Seven Hills. Here and there lights began to twinkle through the foliage at their feet. Steps were coming and going on the deserted terrace—waiters looking out of the doorway at the head of the stairs, then reappearing with trays and napkins and flasks of wine. Tables were moved, chairs straightened. A feeble string of electric lights flickered out. Some vases of faded flowers were carried away, and brought back replenished. A stout lady in a dust coat suddenly appeared, asking in broken Italian if anyone had seen the elastic band which held together her tattered Baedeker. She poked with her stick under the table at which she had lunched, the waiters assisting.

The corner where Mrs. Slade and Mrs. Ansley sat was still shadowy and deserted. For a long time neither of them spoke. At length Mrs. Slade began again: "I suppose I did it as a sort of joke—"

"A joke?"

"Well, girls are ferocious sometimes, you know. Girls in love especially. And I remember laughing to myself all that evening at the idea that you were waiting around there in the dark, dodging out of sight, listening for every sound, trying to get in—Of course I was upset when I heard you were so ill afterward."

Mrs. Ansley had not moved for a long time. But now she turned slowly 105
toward her companion. "But I didn't wait. He'd arranged everything. He was there. We were let in at once," she said.

Mrs. Slade sprang up from her leaning position. "Delphin there? They let you in?—Ah, now you're lying!" she burst out with violence.

Mrs. Ansley's voice grew clearer, and full of surprise. "But of course he was there. Naturally he came—"

"Came? How did he know he'd find you there? You must be raving!"

Mrs. Ansley hesitated, as though reflecting. "But I answered the letter. I told him I'd be there. So he came."

Mrs. Slade flung her hands up to her face. "Oh, God—you answered! I never 110
thought of your answering. . . ."

"It's odd you never thought of it, if you wrote the letter."

"Yes. I was blind with rage."

Mrs. Ansley rose, and drew her fur scarf about her. "It is cold here. We'd better go . . . I'm sorry for you," she said, as she clasped the fur about her throat.

The unexpected words sent a pang through Mrs. Slade. "Yes; we'd better go." She gathered up her bag and cloak. "I don't know why you should be sorry for me," she muttered.

Mrs. Ansley stood looking away from her toward the dusky secret mass of the Colosseum. "Well—because I didn't have to wait that night."

Mrs. Slade gave an unquiet laugh. "Yes; I was beaten there. But I oughtn't to begrudge it to you, I suppose. At the end of all these years. After all, I had everything; I had him for twenty-five years. And you had nothing but that one letter that he didn't write."

Mrs. Ansley was again silent. At length she turned toward the door of the terrace. She took a step, and turned back, facing her companion.

"I had Barbara," she said, and began to move ahead of Mrs. Slade toward the stairway.

(1911)

Questions for Discussion and Writing

Close Reading

1. Although the opening scene appears to show two middle-aged women enjoying a leisurely afternoon in Rome, Wharton suggests a relationship fraught with competitiveness, distrust, and misunderstanding. What details in the women's words and actions alert us to this undercurrent?
2. How do the two generations of women view one another?
3. How would you characterize the Slade marriage? What do you infer about the marriage from Mrs. Slade's thought that "it was a big drop from being the wife of Delphin Slade to being his widow"?
4. While "Roman fever" is another name for the disease malaria, Wharton is clearly intending other connotations of the term as well. How else does the title resonate in the story?

Critical and Creative Reading

5. What provokes Mrs. Slade to confess to having written "Delphin's" letter after so many years? Does she get satisfaction from this confession?
6. Wharton's narrator writes that "these two ladies visualized each other, each through the wrong end of her little telescope." How does each woman view the other? What do they understand about one another, and what don't they understand? Does one woman seem to have a more accurate understanding of the other than her "friend" does?
7. Although Mrs. Ansley had sex with her friend's fiancé and lied about it for years, many people find her a more sympathetic character than Mrs. Slade. Do you share that view? Why or why not? If so, how does Wharton align your sympathies with her?

CONNECTIONS TO OTHER READINGS

8. Both this story and "Babylon Revisited" involve people unable to forgive and forget events in the distant past. Examine the reasons the past has such a hold on Mrs. Slade and Marion. Why are they unable to let go of their hatred?
9. Compare Mrs. Slade and Mrs. Ansley to the narrator in "Inspector Remorse." How much remorse do any of these women feel? Are their actions justified or at least understandable?

Zora Neale Hurston

Sweat

Zora Neale Hurston (1891–1960) attended Howard University and Barnard College, where she earned a degree in anthropology. Active in the period of African American artistic outpouring known as the Harlem Renaissance, Hurston published works of folklore, essays, novels, and short stories, including *Jonah's Gourd Vine* (1934) and *Their Eyes Were Watching God* (1937). Although her work fell out of favor during her lifetime and she died in obscurity, her literary reputation has experienced a revival partly through the efforts of Alice Walker. "Sweat," like many revenge stories, details the battle of the sexes. Its characters speak in the African American dialect of Hurston's childhood community of Eatonville, Florida.

It was eleven o'clock of a Spring night in Florida. It was Sunday. Any other night, Delia Jones would have been in bed for two hours by this time. But she was a washwoman, and Monday morning meant a great deal to her. So she collected the soiled clothes on Saturday when she returned the clean things. Sunday night after church, she sorted and put the white things to soak. It saved her almost a half-day's start. A great hamper in the bedroom held the clothes that she brought home. It was so much neater than a number of bundles lying around.

She squatted on the kitchen floor beside the great pile of clothes, sorting them into small heaps according to color, and humming a song in a mournful key, but wondering through it all where Sykes, her husband, had gone with her horse and buckboard.

Just then something long, round, limp and black fell upon her shoulders and slithered to the floor beside her. A great terror took hold of her. It softened her knees and dried her mouth so that it was a full minute before she could cry out or move. Then she saw that it was the big bull whip her husband liked to carry when he drove.

She lifted her eyes to the door and saw him standing there bent over with laughter at her fright. She screamed at him.

5 "Sykes, what you throw dat whip on me like dat? You know it would skeer me—looks just like a snake, an' you knows how skeered Ah is of snakes."

"Course Ah knowed it! That's how come Ah done it." He slapped his leg with his hand and almost rolled on the ground in his mirth. "If you such a big fool dat you got to have a fit over a earth worm or a string, Ah don't keer how bad Ah skeer you."

"You ain't got no business doing it. Gawd knows it's a sin. Some day Ah'm gointuh drop dead from some of yo' foolishness. 'Nother thing, where you been wid mah rig? Ah feeds dat pony. He ain't fuh you to be drivin' wid no bull whip."

"You sho' is one aggravatin' nigger woman!" he declared and stepped into the room. She resumed her work and did not answer him at once. "Ah done tole you time and again to keep them white folks' clothes outa dis house."

He picked up the whip and glared at her. Delia went on with her work. She went out into the yard and returned with a galvanized tub and set it on the wash-bench. She saw that Sykes had kicked all of the clothes together again, and now stood in her way truculently, his whole manner hoping, *praying*, for an argument. But she walked calmly around him and commenced to re-sort the things.

10 "Next time, Ah'm gointer kick 'em outdoors," he threatened as he struck a match along the leg of his corduroy breeches.

Delia never looked up from her work, and her thin, stooped shoulders sagged further.

"Ah ain't for no fuss t'night Sykes. Ah just come from taking sacrament at the church house."

He snorted scornfully. "Yeah, you just come from de church house on a Sunday night, but heah you is gone to work on them clothes. You ain't nothing but a hypocrite. One of them amen-corner Christians—sing, whoop, and shout, then come home and wash white folks' clothes on the Sabbath."

He stepped roughly upon the whitest pile of things, kicking them helter-skelter as he crossed the room. His wife gave a little scream of dismay, and quickly gathered them together again.

15 "Sykes, you quit grindin' dirt into these clothes! How can Ah git through by Sat'day if Ah don't start on Sunday?"

"Ah don't keer if you never git through. Anyhow, Ah done promised Gawd and a couple of other men, Ah ain't gointer have it in mah house. Don't gimme no lip neither, else Ah'll throw 'em out and put mah fist up side yo' head to boot."

Delia's habitual meekness seemed to slip from her shoulders like a blown scarf. She was on her feet; her poor little body, her bare knuckly hands bravely defying the strapping hulk before her.

"Looka heah, Sykes, you done gone too fur. Ah been married to you fur fifteen years, and Ah been takin' in washin' fur fifteen years. Sweat, sweat, sweat! Work and sweat, cry and sweat, pray and sweat!"

"What's that got to do with me?" he asked brutally.

20 "What's it got to do with you, Sykes? Mah tub of suds is filled yo' belly with vittles more times than yo' hands is filled it. Mah sweat is done paid for this house and Ah reckon Ah kin keep on sweatin' in it."

She seized the iron skillet from the stove and struck a defensive pose, which act surprised him greatly, coming from her. It cowed him and he did not strike her as he usually did.

"Naw you won't," she panted, "that ole snaggle-toothed black woman you runnin' with ain't comin' heah to pile up on *mah* sweat and blood. You ain't paid for nothin' on this place, and Ah'm gointer stay right heah till Ah'm toted out foot foremost."

"Well, you better quit gittin' me riled up, else they'll be totin' you out sooner than you expect. Ah'm so tired of you Ah don't know whut to do. Gawd! How Ah hates skinny wimmen!"

A little awed by this new Delia, he sidled out of the door and slammed the back gate after him. He did not say where he had gone, but she knew too well. She knew very well that he would not return until nearly daybreak also. Her work over, she went on to bed but not to sleep at once. Things had come to a pretty pass!

25 She lay awake, gazing upon the debris that cluttered their matrimonial trail. Not an image left standing along the way. Anything like flowers had long ago been drowned in the salty stream that had been pressed from her heart. Her tears, her sweat, her blood. She had brought love to the union and he had brought a longing after the flesh. Two months after the wedding, he had given her the first brutal beating. She had the memory of his numerous trips to Orlando with all of his wages when he had returned to her penniless, even before the first year had passed. She was young and soft then, but now she thought of her knotty, muscled limbs, her harsh knuckly hands, and drew herself up into an unhappy little ball in the middle of the big feather bed. Too late now to hope for love, even if it were not Bertha it would be someone else. This case differed from the others only in that she was bolder than the others. Too late for everything except her little home. She had built it for her old days, and planted one by one the trees and flowers there. It was lovely to her, lovely.

Somehow, before sleep came, she found herself saying aloud: "Oh well, whatever goes over the Devil's back, is got to come under his belly. Sometime or ruther, Sykes, like everybody else, is gointer reap his sowing." After that she was able to build a spiritual earthworks against her husband. His shells could no longer reach her. AMEN. She went to sleep and slept until he announced his presence in bed by kicking her feet and rudely snatching the covers away.

"Gimme some kivah heah, an' git yo' damn foots over on yo' own side! Ah oughter mash you in yo' mouf fuh drawing dat skillet on me."

Delia went clear to the rail without answering him. A triumphant indifference to all that he was or did.

II

The week was as full of work for Delia as all other weeks, and Saturday found her behind her little pony, collecting and delivering clothes.

30 It was a hot, hot day near the end of July. The village men on Joe Clarke's porch even chewed cane listlessly. They did not hurl the cane-knots as usual.

They let them dribble over the edge of the porch. Even conversation had collapsed under the heat.

"Heah come Delia Jones," Jim Merchant said, as the shaggy pony came 'round the bend of the road toward them. The rusty buckboard was heaped with baskets of crisp, clean laundry.

"Yep," Joe Lindsay agreed. "Hot or col', rain or shine, jes'ez reg'lar ez de weeks roll roun' Delia carries 'em an' fetches 'em on Sat'day."

"She better if she wanter eat," said Moss. "Syke Jones ain't wuth de shot an' powder hit would tek tuh kill 'em. Not to *huh* he ain't."

"He sho' ain't," Walter Thomas chimed in. "It's too bad, too, cause she wuz a right pretty li'l trick when he got huh. Ah'd uh mah'ied huh mahself if he hadnter beat me to it."

Delia nodded briefly at the men as she drove past. 35

"Too much knockin' will ruin *any* 'oman. He done beat huh 'nough tuh kill three women, let 'lone change they looks," said Elijah Moseley. "How Syke kin stommuck dat big black greasy Mogul he's layin' roun' wid, gits me. Ah swear dat eight-rock couldn't kiss a sardine can Ah done thowed out de back do' 'way las' yeah."

"Aw, she's fat, thass how come. He's allus been crazy 'bout fat women," put in Merchant. "He'd a' been tied up wid one long time ago if he could a' found one tuh have him. Did Ah tell yuh 'bout him come sidlin' roun' *mah* wife—bringin' her a basket uh peecans outa his yard fuh a present? Yessir, mah wife! She tol' him tuh take 'em right straight back home, 'cause Delia works so hard ovah dat washtub she reckon everything on de place taste lak sweat an' soapsuds. Ah jus' wisht Ah'd a' caught 'im 'roun' dere! Ah'd a' made his hips ketch on fiah down dat shell road."

"Ah know he done it, too. Ah sees 'im grinnin' at every 'oman dat passes," Walter Thomas said. "But even so, he useter eat some mighty big hunks uh humble pie tuh git dat li'l 'oman he got. She wuz ez pritty ez a speckled pup! Dat wuz fifteen years ago. He useter be so skeered uh losin' huh, she could make him do some parts of a husband's duty. Dey never wuz de same in de mind."

"There oughter be a law about him," said Lindsay. "He ain't fit tuh carry guts tuh a bear."

Clarke spoke for the first time. "Tain't no law on earth dat kin make a man 40
be decent if it ain't in 'im. There's plenty men dat takes a wife lak dey do a joint uh sugar-cane. It's round, juicy an' sweet when dey gits it. But dey squeeze an' grind, squeeze an' grind an' wring tell dey wring every drop uh pleasure dat's in 'em out. When dey's satisfied dat dey is wrung dry, dey treats 'em jes' lak dey do a cane-chew. Dey thows 'em away. Dey knows whut dey is doin' while dey is at it, an' hates theirselves fuh it but they keeps on hangin' after huh tell she's empty. Den dey hates huh fuh bein' a cane-chew an' in de way."

"We oughter take Syke an' dat stray 'oman uh his'n down in Lake Howell swamp an' lay on de rawhide till they cain't say Lawd a' mussy. He allus wuz uh ovahbearin niggah, but since dat white 'oman from up north done teached 'im how to run a automobile, he done got too beggety to live—an' we oughter kill 'im," Old Man Anderson advised.

A grunt of approval went around the porch. But the heat was melting their civic virtue and Elijah Moseley began to bait Joe Clarke.

"Come on, Joe, git a melon outa dere an' slice it up for yo' customers. We'se all sufferin' wid de heat. De bear's done got *me*!"

"Thass right, Joe, a watermelon is jes' whut Ah needs tuh cure de eppizudicks," Walter Thomas joined forces with Moseley. "Come on dere, Joe. We all is steady customers an' you ain't set us up in a long time. Ah chooses dat long, bowlegged Floridy favorite."

"A god, an' be dough. You all gimme twenty cents and slice away," Clarke 45
retorted. "Ah needs a col' slice m'self. Heah, everybody chip in. Ah'll lend y'all mah meat knife."

The money was all quickly subscribed and the huge melon brought forth. At that moment, Sykes and Bertha arrived. A determined silence fell on the porch and the melon was put away again.

Merchant snapped down the blade of his jackknife and moved toward the store door.

"Come on in, Joe, an' gimme a slab uh sow belly an' uh pound uh coffee—almost fuhgot 'twas Sat'day. Got to git on home." Most of the men left also.

Just then Delia drove past on her way home, as Sykes was ordering magnificently for Bertha. It pleased him for Delia to see.

"Git whutsoever yo' heart desires, Honey. Wait a minute, Joe. Give huh two 50
bottles uh strawberry soda-water, uh quart parched ground-peas, an' a block uh chewin' gum."

With all this they left the store, with Sykes reminding Bertha that this was his town and she could have it if she wanted it.

The men returned soon after they left, and held their watermelon feast.

"Where did Syke Jones git da 'oman from nohow?" Lindsay asked.

"Ovah Apopka.[1] Guess dey musta been cleanin' out de town when she lef'. She don't look lak a thing but a hunk uh liver wid hair on it."

"Well, she sho' kin squall," Dave Carter contributed. "When she gits ready 55
tuh laff, she jes' opens huh mouf an' latches it back tuh de las' notch. No ole granpa alligator down in Lake Bell ain't got nothin' on huh."

III

Bertha had been in town three months now. Sykes was still paying her room-rent at Delia Lewis'—the only house in town that would have taken her in. Sykes took her frequently to Winter Park to "stomps." He still assured her that he was the swellest man in the state.

"Sho' you kin have dat li'l ole house soon's Ah git dat 'oman outa dere. Everything b'longs tuh me an' you sho' kin have it. Ah sho' 'bominates uh skinny 'oman. Lawdy, you sho' is got one portly shape on you! You kin git *anything* you wants. Dis is *mah* town an' you sho' kin have it."

[1]*Apopka:* A city in Florida about ten miles from Orlando.

Delia's work-worn knees crawled over the earth in Gethsemane and up the rocks of Calvary many, many times during these months. She avoided the villagers and meeting places in her efforts to be blind and deaf. But Bertha nullified this to a degree, by coming to Delia's house to call Sykes out to her at the gate.

Delia and Sykes fought all the time now with no peaceful interludes. They slept and ate in silence. Two or three times Delia had attempted a timid friendliness, but she was repulsed each time. It was plain that the breaches must remain agape.

The sun had burned July to August. The heat streamed down like a million 60
hot arrows, smiting all things living upon the earth. Grass withered, leaves browned, snakes went blind in shedding and men and dogs went mad. Dog days!

Delia came home one day and found Sykes there before her. She wondered, but started to go on into the house without speaking, even though he was standing in the kitchen door and she must either stoop under his arm or ask him to move. He made no room for her. She noticed a soap box beside the steps, but paid no particular attention to it, knowing that he must have brought it there. As she was stooping to pass under his outstretched arm, he suddenly pushed her backward, laughingly.

"Look in de box dere Delia, Ah done brung yuh somethin'!"

She nearly fell upon the box in her stumbling, and when she saw what it held, she all but fainted outright.

"Syke! Syke, mah Gawd! You take dat rattlesnake 'way from heah! You *gottuh*. Oh, Jesus, have mussy!"

"Ah ain't got tuh do nuthin' uh de kin'—fact is Ah ain't got tuh do nothin' 65
but die. Tain't no use uh you puttin' on airs makin' out lak you skeered uh dat snake—he's gointer stay right heah tell he die. He wouldn't bite me cause Ah knows how tuh handle 'im. Nohow he wouldn't risk breakin' out his fangs 'gin *yo* skinny laigs."

"Naw, now Syke, don't keep dat thing 'round tryin' tuh skeer me tuh death. You knows Ah'm even feared uh earth worms. Thass de biggest snake Ah evah did see. Kill 'im Syke, please."

"Doan ast me tuh do nothin' fuh yuh. Goin' 'round tryin' tuh be so damn asterperious. Naw, Ah ain't gonna kill it. Ah think uh damn sight mo' uh him dan you! Dat's a nice snake an' anybody doan lak 'im kin jes' hit de grit."

The village soon heard that Sykes had the snake, and came to see and ask questions.

"How de hen-fire did you ketch dat six-foot rattler, Syke?" Thomas asked.

"He's full uh frogs so he cain't hardly move, thass how Ah eased up on 'm. 70
But Ah'm a snake charmer an' knows how tuh handle 'em. Shux, dat ain't nothin'. Ah could ketch one eve'y day if Ah so wanted tuh."

"Whut he needs is a heavy hick'ry club leaned real heavy on his head. Dat's de bes' way tuh charm a rattlesnake."

"Naw, Walt, y'all jes' don't understand dese diamon' backs lak Ah do," said Sykes in a superior tone of voice.

The village agreed with Walter, but the snake stayed on. His box remained by the kitchen door with its screen wire covering. Two or three days later it had digested its meal of frogs and literally came to life. It rattled at every movement in the kitchen or the yard. One day as Delia came down the kitchen steps she saw his chalky-white fangs curved like scimitars hung in the wire meshes. This time she did not run away with averted eyes as usual. She stood for a long time in the doorway in a red fury that grew bloodier for every second that she regarded the creature that was her torment.

That night she broached the subject as soon as Sykes sat down to the table.

75 "Syke, Ah wants you tuh take dat snake 'way fum heah. You done starved me an' Ah put up widcher, you done beat me an Ah took dat, but you done kilt all mah insides bringin' dat varmint heah."

Sykes poured out a saucer full of coffee and drank it deliberately before he answered her.

"A whole lot Ah keer 'bout how you feels inside uh out. Dat snake ain't goin' no damn wheah till Ah gits ready fuh 'im tuh go. So fur as beatin' is concerned, yuh ain't took near all dat you gointer take ef yuh stay 'round *me*."

Delia pushed back her plate and got up from the table. "Ah hates you, Sykes," she said calmly. "Ah hates you tuh de same degree dat Ah useter love yuh. Ah done took an' took till mah belly is full up tuh mah neck. Dat's de reason Ah got mah letter fum de church an' moved mah membership tuh Woodbridge—so Ah don't haftuh take no sacrament wid yuh. Ah don't wantuh see yuh 'round me atall. Lay 'round wid dat 'oman all yuh wants tuh, but gwan 'way fum me an' mah house. Ah hates yuh lak uh suck-egg dog."

Sykes almost let the huge wad of corn bread and collard greens he was chewing fall out of his mouth in amazement. He had a hard time whipping himself up to the proper fury to try to answer Delia.

80 "Well, Ah'm glad you does hate me. Ah'm sho' tiahed uh you hangin' ontuh me. Ah don't want yuh. Look at yuh stringey ole neck! Yo' rawbony laigs an' arms is enough tuh cut uh man tuh death. You looks jes' lak de devvul's doll-baby tuh *me*. You cain't hate me no worse dan Ah hates you. Ah been hatin' *you* fuh years."

"Yo' ole black hide don't look lak nothin' tuh me, but uh passle uh wrinkled up rubber, wid yo' big ole yeahs flappin' on each side lak uh paih uh buzzard wings. Don't think Ah'm gointuh be run 'way fum mah house neither. Ah'm goin' tuh de white folks 'bout *you*, mah young man, de very nex' time you lay yo' han's on me. Mah cup is done run ovah." Delia said this with no signs of fear and Sykes departed from the house, threatening her, but made not the slightest move to carry out any of them.

That night he did not return at all, and the next day being Sunday, Delia was glad she did not have to quarrel before she hitched up her pony and drove the four miles to Woodbridge.

She stayed to the night service—"love feast"—which was very warm and full of spirit. In the emotional winds her domestic trials were borne far and wide so that she sang as she drove homeward,

Jurden water, black an' col
Chills de body, not de soul
An' Ah wantah cross Jurden in uh calm time.

She came from the barn to the kitchen door and stopped.

"Whut's de mattah, ol' Satan, you ain't kickin' up yo' racket?" She addressed the snake's box. Complete silence. She went on into the house with a new hope in its birth struggles. Perhaps her threat to go to the white folks had frightened Sykes! Perhaps he was sorry! Fifteen years of misery and suppression had brought Delia to the place where she would hope *anything* that looked towards a way over or through her wall of inhibitions.

She felt in the match-safe behind the stove at once for a match. There was only one there.

"Dat niggah wouldn't fetch nothin' heah tuh save his rotten neck, but he kin run thew whut Ah brings quick enough. Now he done toted off nigh on tuh haff uh box uh matches. He done had dat 'oman heah in mah house, too."

Nobody but a woman could tell how she knew this even before she struck the match. But she did and it put her into a new fury.

Presently she brought in the tubs to put the white things to soak. This time she decided she need not bring the hamper out of the bedroom; she would go in there and do the sorting. She picked up the pot-bellied lamp and went in. The room was small and the hamper stood hard by the foot of the white iron bed. She could sit and reach through the bedposts—resting as she worked.

"*Ah wantah cross Jurden in uh calm time.*" She was singing again. The mood of the 'love feast' had returned. She threw back the lid of the basket almost gaily. Then, moved by both horror and terror, she sprang back toward the door. *There lay the snake in the basket!* He moved sluggishly at first, but even as she turned round and round, jumped up and down in an insanity of fear, he began to stir vigorously. She saw him pouring his awful beauty from the basket upon the bed, then she seized the lamp and ran as fast as she could to the kitchen. The wind from the open door blew out the light and the darkness added to her terror. She sped to the darkness of the yard, slamming the door after her before she thought to set down the lamp. She did not feel safe even on the ground, so she climbed up in the hay barn.

There for an hour or more she lay sprawled upon the hay a gibbering wreck.

Finally she grew quiet, and after that came coherent thought. With this stalked through her a cold, bloody rage. Hours of this. A period of introspection, a space of retrospection, then a mixture of both. Out of this an awful calm.

"Well, Ah done de bes' Ah could. If things ain't right, Gawd knows tain't mah fault."

She went to sleep—a twitch sleep—and woke up to a faint gray sky. There was a loud hollow sound below. She peered out. Sykes was at the wood-pile, demolishing a wire-covered box.

He hurried to the kitchen door, but hung outside there some minutes before he entered, and stood some minutes more inside before he closed it after him.

The gray in the sky was spreading. Delia descended without fear now, and crouched beneath the low bedroom window. The drawn shade shut out the dawn, shut in the night. But the thin walls held back no sound.

"Dat ol' scratch is woke up now!" She mused at the tremendous whirr inside, which every woodsman knows, is one of the sound illusions. The rattler is a ventriloquist. His whirr sounds to the right, to the left, straight ahead, behind, close under foot—everywhere but where it is. Woe to him who guesses wrong unless he is prepared to hold up his end of the argument! Sometimes he strikes without rattling at all.

Inside, Sykes heard nothing until he knocked a pot lid off the stove while trying to reach the match-safe in the dark. He had emptied his pockets at Bertha's.

The snake seemed to wake up under the stove and Sykes made a quick leap into the bedroom. In spite of the gin he had had, his head was clearing now.

"Mah Gawd!" he chattered, "ef Ah could on'y strack uh light!"

The rattling ceased for a moment as he stood paralyzed. He waited. It seemed that the snake waited also.

"Oh, fuh de light! Ah thought he'd be too sick"—Sykes was muttering to himself when the whirr began again, closer, right underfoot this time. Long before this, Sykes' ability to think had been flattened down to primitive instinct and he leaped—onto the bed.

Outside Delia heard a cry that might have come from a maddened chimpanzee, a stricken gorilla. All the terror, all the horror, all the rage that man possibly could express, without a recognizable human sound.

A tremendous stir inside there, another series of animal screams, the intermittent whirr of the reptile. The shade torn violently down from the window, letting in the red dawn, a huge brown hand seizing the window stick, great dull blows upon the wooden floor punctuating the gibberish of sound long after the rattle of the snake had abruptly subsided. All this Delia could see and hear from her place beneath the window, and it made her ill. She crept over to the four-o'clocks and stretched herself on the cool earth to recover.

She lay there. "Delia, Delia!" She could hear Sykes calling in a most despairing tone as one who expected no answer. The sun crept on up, and he called. Delia could not move—her legs had gone flabby. She never moved, he called, and the sun kept rising.

"Mah Gawd!" She heard him moan, "Mah Gawd fum Heben!" She heard him stumbling about and got up from her flower-bed. The sun was growing warm. As she approached the door she heard him call out hopefully, "Delia, is dat you Ah heah?"

She saw him on his hands and knees as soon as she reached the door. He crept an inch or two toward her—all that he was able, and she saw his horribly swollen neck and his one open eye shining with hope. A surge of pity too strong to support bore her away from that eye that must, could not, fail to see the tubs. He would see the lamp. Orlando with its doctors was too far. She could scarcely reach the chinaberry tree, where she waited in the growing heat while inside she knew the cold river was creeping up and up to extinguish that eye which must know by now that she knew.

(1926)

Questions for Discussion and Writing

Close Reading

1. What details does Hurston use in the first two paragraphs to align your sympathies with Delia?
2. Discuss the significance of Sykes's throwing a whip at Delia to simulate a coiled snake. What does this simple "joke" tell us about his character? How is it ironic in light of later events?
3. Sykes is condemned by the men of the town as well as by his wife. Why is this important? What do they say about him?
4. Why is Delia's home so important to her? What does it represent?

Critical and Creative Reading

5. At the end of the story, the narrator tells us that Delia feels for Sykes "pity too strong to support." What do you make of this pity? Is pity related to forgiveness? Do you share her pity for the dying Sykes?
6. What is Sykes's objection to Delia's work? Why do you think the story's title emphasizes the "sweat" of her life? Why, for example, might Hurston have chosen this title over "The Rattlesnake" or "Vengeance"?
7. How important is the character of Bertha to the outcome of this story? Since Delia no longer loves her husband, why is his relationship with Bertha a problem for her?
8. The last paragraph tells us that Sykes "know[s] by now that she knew." Write a paragraph from Sykes's point of view in which you articulate his understanding of Delia's knowledge. Does he regret his treatment of her in his dying moments? Is he angry? Does he want forgiveness or revenge?

Connections to Other Readings

9. Delia's revenge is a passive one. Since Sykes planted the rattlesnake in Delia's washing basket, he dies by his own hand. Sykes seems to be receiving some kind of cosmic revenge, though not through Delia's actions. Could the same be said of the narrator in "Inspector Remorse"? Why or why not?
10. Listening to their foes die, both Montressor in "The Cask of Amontillado" and Delia stand by. Compare this moment in both stories. Are the emotions and thoughts of the characters similar or different? How do you think it would feel to know you are getting what you want in such a horrible way?

F. Scott Fitzgerald

Babylon Revisited

F. Scott Fitzgerald (1896–1940) grew up in St. Paul, Minnesota, and began writing while in his teens. He briefly attended Princeton University and later joined the army, but World War I ended before he was sent overseas. He

published his first novel, *This Side of Paradise,* in 1920 and married Zelda Sayre (1900–1948) the following week. Their tumultuous marriage, including frequent stints abroad, was both an inspiration for his writing and a drain on it. Zelda was diagnosed with schizophrenia in 1930 and afterward spent much time in mental institutions. Fitzgerald continued to publish short stories and novels, including his masterpiece, *The Great Gatsby* (1925). Charlie and Helen's relationship in "Babylon Revisited" resembles Fitzgerald's own relationship with his wife. By the 1930s, Fitzgerald was deeply in debt and moved to Hollywood to write for the screen. He died of a heart attack. Fitzgerald was a master of mixing the comic with the tragic. Are both elements present in this story?

I

"And where's Mr. Campbell?" Charlie asked.

"Gone to Switzerland. Mr. Campbell's a pretty sick man, Mr. Wales."

"I'm sorry to hear that. And George Hardt?" Charlie inquired.

"Back in America, gone to work."

"And where is the Snow Bird?" 5

"He was in here last week. Anyway, his friend, Mr. Schaeffer, is in Paris." Two familiar names from the long list of a year and a half ago. Charlie scribbled an address in his notebook and tore out the page.

"If you see Mr. Schaeffer, give him this," he said. "It's my brother-in-law's address. I haven't settled on a hotel yet."

He was not really disappointed to find Paris was so empty. But the stillness in the Ritz bar was strange and portentous. It was not an American bar any more—he felt polite in it, and not as if he owned it. It had gone back into France. He felt the stillness from the moment he got out of the taxi and saw the doorman, usually in a frenzy of activity at this hour, gossiping with a *chasseur* by the servants' entrance.

Passing through the corridor, he heard only a single, bored voice in the 10
once-clamorous women's room. When he turned into the bar he travelled the twenty feet of green carpet with his eyes fixed straight ahead by old habit; and then, with his foot firmly on the rail, he turned and surveyed the room, encountering only a single pair of eyes that fluttered up from a newspaper in the corner. Charlie asked for the head barman, Paul, who in the latter days of the bull market had come to work in his own custom-built car—disembarking, however, with due nicety at the nearest corner. But Paul was at his country house today and Alix giving him information.

"No, no more," Charlie said, "I'm going slow these days."

Alix congratulated him: "You were going pretty strong a couple of years ago."

"I'll stick to it all right," Charlie assured him. "I've stuck to it for over a year and a half now."

"How do you find conditions in America?"

"I haven't been to America for months. I'm in business in Prague, representing a couple of concerns there. They don't know about me down there."

Alix smiled.

"Remember the night of George Hardt's bachelor dinner here?" said Charlie. "By the way, what's become of Claude Fessenden?"

Alix lowered his voice confidentially: "He's in Paris, but he doesn't come here any more. Paul doesn't allow it. He ran up a bill of thirty thousand francs, charging all his drinks and his lunches, and usually his dinner, for more than a year. And when Paul finally told him he had to pay, he gave him a bad check."

Alix shook his head sadly.

"I don't understand it, such a dandy fellow. Now he's all bloated up—" He made a plump apple of his hands.

Charlie watched a group of strident queens installing themselves in a corner.

"Nothing affects them," he thought. "Stocks rise and fall, people loaf or work, but they go on forever." The place oppressed him. He called for the dice and shook with Alix for the drink.

"Here for long, Mr. Wales?"

"I'm here for four or five days to see my little girl."

"Oh-h! You have a little girl?"

Outside, the fire-red, gas-blue, ghost-green signs shone smokily through the tranquil rain. It was late afternoon and the streets were in movement; the *bistros* gleamed. At the corner of the Boulevard des Capucines[1] he took a taxi. The Place de la Concorde moved by in pink majesty; they crossed the logical Seine,[2] and Charlie felt the sudden provincial quality of the Left Bank.

Charlie directed his taxi to the Avenue de l'Opera, which was out of his way. But he wanted to see the blue hour spread over the magnificent façade, and imagine that the cab horns, playing endlessly the first few bars of *La Plus que Lent*, were the trumpets of the Second Empire. They were closing the iron grill in front of Brentano's Book-store, and people were already at dinner behind the trim little bourgeois hedge of Duval's. He had never eaten at a really cheap restaurant in Paris. Five-course dinner, four francs fifty, eighteen cents, wine included. For some odd reason he wished that he had.

As they rolled on to the Left Bank and he felt its sudden provincialism, he thought, "I spoiled this city for myself. I didn't realize it, but the days came along one after another, and then two years were gone, and everything was gone, and I was gone."

He was thirty-five, and good to look at. The Irish mobility of his face was sobered by a deep wrinkle between his eyes. As he rang his brother-in-law's bell in the Rue Palatine, the wrinkle deepened till it pulled down his brows; he felt a cramping sensation in his belly. From behind the maid who opened the door darted

[1] *Boulevard des Capucines:* A fashionable street in Paris. Charlie's travels take him across town and back again several times. The next few paragraphs describe areas in Paris that Charlie would have visited in years' past.

[2] *Seine:* The river that runs through Paris, dividing the city into the Left and Right Banks.

a lovely little girl of nine who shrieked "Daddy!" and flew up, struggling like a fish, into his arms. She pulled his head around by one ear and set her cheek against his.

"My old pie," he said.

"Oh, daddy, daddy, daddy, daddy, dads, dads, dads!"

She drew him into the salon, where the family waited, a boy and girl his daughter's age, his sister-in-law and her husband. He greeted Marion with his voice pitched carefully to avoid either feigned enthusiasm or dislike, but her response was more frankly tepid, though she minimized her expression of unalterable distrust by directing her regard toward his child. The two men clasped hands in a friendly way and Lincoln Peters rested his for a moment on Charlie's shoulder.

The room was warm and comfortably American. The three children moved intimately about, playing through the yellow oblongs that led to other rooms; the cheer of six o'clock spoke in the eager smacks of the fire and the sounds of French activity in the kitchen. But Charlie did not relax; his heart sat up rigidly in his body and he drew confidence from his daughter, who from time to time came close to him, holding in her arms the doll he had brought.

"Really extremely well," he declared in answer to Lincoln's question. "There's a lot of business there that isn't moving at all, but we're doing even better than ever. In fact, damn well. I'm bringing my sister over from America next month to keep house for me. My income last year was bigger than it was when I had money. You see, the Czechs—"

His boasting was for a specific purpose; but after a moment, seeing a faint restiveness in Lincoln's eye, he changed the subject:

"Those are fine children of yours, well brought up, good manners."

"We think Honoria's a great little girl too."

Marion Peters came back from the kitchen. She was a tall woman with worried eyes, who had once possessed a fresh American loveliness. Charlie had never been sensitive to it and was always surprised when people spoke of how pretty she had been. From the first there had been an instinctive antipathy between them.

"Well, how do you find Honoria?" she asked.

"Wonderful. I was astonished how much she's grown in ten months. All the children are looking well."

"We haven't had a doctor for a year. How do you like being back in Paris?"

"It seems very funny to see so few Americans around."

"I'm delighted," Marion said vehemently. "Now at least you can go into a store without their assuming you're a millionaire. We've suffered like everybody, but on the whole it's a good deal pleasanter."

"But it was nice while it lasted," Charlie said. "We were a sort of royalty, almost infallible, with a sort of magic around us. In the bar this afternoon"—he stumbled, seeing his mistake—"there wasn't a man I knew."

She looked at him keenly. "I should think you'd have had enough of bars."

"I only stayed a minute. I take one drink every afternoon, and no more."

"Don't you want a cocktail before dinner?" Lincoln asked.

"I take only one drink every afternoon, and I've had that."

"I hope you keep to it," said Marion.

50 Her dislike was evident in the coldness with which she spoke, but Charlie only smiled; he had larger plans. Her very aggressiveness gave him an advantage, and he knew enough to wait. He wanted them to initiate the discussion of what they knew had brought him to Paris.

At dinner he couldn't decide whether Honoria was most like him or her mother. Fortunate if she didn't combine the traits of both that had brought them to disaster. A great wave of protectiveness went over him. He thought he knew what to do for her. He believed in character; he wanted to jump back a whole generation and trust in character again as the eternally valuable element. Everything wore out.

He left soon after dinner, but not to go home. He was curious to see Paris by night with clearer and more judicious eyes than those of other days. He bought a *strapontin*[3] for the Casino and watched Josephine Baker[4] go through her chocolate arabesques.

After an hour he left and strolled toward Montmartre, up the Rue Pigalle into the Place Blanche. The rain had stopped and there were a few people in evening clothes disembarking from taxis in front of cabarets, and *cocottes* prowling singly or in pairs, and many Negroes. He passed a lighted door from which issued music, and stopped with the sense of familiarity; it was Bricktop's, where he had parted with so many hours and so much money. A few doors farther on he found another ancient rendezvous and incautiously put his head inside. Immediately an eager orchestra burst into sound, a pair of professional dancers leaped to their feet and a maître d'hôtel swooped toward him, crying, "Crowd just arriving, sir!" But he withdrew quickly.

"You have to be damn drunk," he thought.

55 Zelli's was closed, the bleak and sinister cheap hotels surrounding it were dark; up in the Rue Blanche there was more light and a local, colloquial French crowd. The Poet's Cave had disappeared, but the two great mouths of the Café of Heaven and the Café of Hell still yawned—even devoured, as he watched, the meager contents of a tourist bus—a German, a Japanese, and an American couple who glanced at him with frightened eyes.

So much for the effort and ingenuity of Montmartre. All the catering to vice and waste was on an utterly childish scale, and he suddenly realized the meaning of the word "dissipate"—to dissipate into thin air; to make nothing out of something. In the little hours of the night every move from place to place was an enormous human jump, an increase of paying for the privilege of slower and slower motion.

He remembered thousand-franc notes given to an orchestra for playing a single number, hundred-franc notes tossed to a doorman for calling a cab.

But it hadn't been given for nothing.

It had been given, even the most wildly squandered sum, as an offering to destiny that he might not remember the things most worth remembering, the

[3]*strapontin:* A seat or folding chair.

[4]*Josephine Baker:* Josephine Baker (1906–1975) was an American jazz singer and dancer who performed in Paris during the 1920s and early 1930s. In Paris, she was able to achieve a level of celebrity as a black performer that was impossible in the United States.

things that now he would always remember—his child taken from his control, his wife escaped to a grave in Vermont.

In the glare of a *brasserie* a woman spoke to him. He bought her some eggs 60
and coffee, and then, eluding her encouraging stare, gave her a twenty-franc note and took a taxi to his hotel.

II

He woke upon a fine fall day—football weather. The depression of yesterday was gone and he liked the people on the streets. At noon he sat opposite Honoria at Le Grand Vatel, the only restaurant he could think of not reminiscent of champagne dinners and long luncheons that began at two and ended in a blurred and vague twilight.

"Now, how about vegetables? Oughtn't you to have some vegetables?"

"Well, yes."

"Here's *épinards* and *chou-fleur* and carrots and *haricots*."

"I'd like *chou-fleur*." 65

"Wouldn't you like to have two vegetables?"

"I usually only have one at lunch."

The waiter was pretending to be inordinately fond of children. *"Qu'elle est mignonne la petite? Elle parle exactement comme une Française."*

"How about dessert? Shall we wait and see?"

The waiter disappeared. Honoria looked at her father expectantly. 70

"What are we going to do?"

"First, we're going to that toy store in the Rue Saint-Honoré and buy you anything you like. And then we're going to the vaudeville at the Empire."

She hesitated. "I like it about the vaudeville, but not the toy store."

"Why not?"

"Well, you brought me this doll." She had it with her. "And I've got lots of 75
things. And we're not rich any more, are we?"

"We never were. But today you are to have anything you want."

"All right," she agreed resignedly.

When there had been her mother and a French nurse he had been inclined to be strict; now he extended himself, reached out for a new tolerance; he must be both parents to her and not shut any of her out of communication.

"I want to get to know you," he said gravely. "First let me introduce myself. My name is Charles J. Wales, of Prague."

"Oh, daddy!" her voice cracked with laughter. 80

"And who are you, please?" he persisted, and she accepted a role immediately: "Honoria Wales, Rue Palatine, Paris."

"Married or single?"

"No, not married. Single."

He indicated the doll. "But I see you have a child, madame."

Unwilling to disinherit it, she took it to her heart and thought quickly: "Yes, 85
I've been married, but I'm not married now. My husband is dead."

He went on quickly, "And the child's name?"

"Simone. That's after my best friend at school."

"I'm very pleased that you're doing so well at school."

"I'm third this month," she boasted. "Elsie"—that was her cousin—"is only about eighteenth, and Richard is about at the bottom."

"You like Richard and Elsie, don't you?"

"Oh, yes. I like Richard quite well and I like her all right."

Cautiously and casually he asked: "And Aunt Marion and Uncle Lincoln—which do you like best?"

"Oh, Uncle Lincoln, I guess."

He was increasingly aware of her presence. As they came in, a murmur of ". . . adorable" followed them, and now the people at the next table bent all their silences upon her, staring as if she were something no more conscious than a flower.

"Why don't I live with you?" she asked suddenly. "Because mamma's dead?"

"You must stay here and learn more French. It would have been hard for daddy to take care of you so well."

"I don't really need much taking care of any more. I do everything for myself."

Going out of the restaurant, a man and a woman unexpectedly hailed him.

"Well, the old Wales!"

"Hello there, Lorraine. . . . Dunc."

Sudden ghosts out of the past: Duncan Schaeffer, a friend from college. Lorraine Quarrles, a lovely, pale blonde of thirty; one of a crowd who had helped them make months into days in the lavish times of three years ago.

"My husband couldn't come this year," she said, in answer to his question. "We're poor as hell. So he gave me two hundred a month and told me I could do my worst on that. . . . This your little girl?"

"What about coming back and sitting down?" Duncan asked.

"Can't do it." He was glad for an excuse. As always, he felt Lorraine's passionate, provocative attraction, but his own rhythm was different now.

"Well, how about dinner?" she asked.

"I'm not free. Give me your address and let me call you."

"Charlie, I believe you're sober," she said judicially. "I honestly believe he's sober, Dunc. Pinch him and see if he's sober."

Charlie indicated Honoria with his head. They both laughed.

"What's your address?" said Duncan sceptically.

He hesitated, unwilling to give the name of his hotel.

"I'm not settled yet. I'd better call you. We're going to see the vaudeville at the Empire."

"There! That's what I want to do," Lorraine said. "I want to see some clowns and acrobats and jugglers. That's just what we'll do, Dunc."

"We've got to do an errand first," said Charlie. "Perhaps we'll see you there."

"All right, you snob. . . . Good-by, beautiful little girl."

"Good-by."

Honoria bobbed politely.

Somehow, an unwelcome encounter. They liked him because he was functioning, because he was serious; they wanted to see him, because he was stronger than they were now, because they wanted to draw a certain sustenance from his strength.

At the Empire, Honoria proudly refused to sit upon her father's folded coat. She was already an individual with a code of her own, and Charlie was more and more absorbed by the desire of putting a little of himself into her before she crystallized utterly. It was hopeless to try to know her in so short a time.

Between the acts they came upon Duncan and Lorraine in the lobby where the band was playing.

"Have a drink?"

"All right, but not up at the bar. We'll take a table."

"The perfect father."

Listening abstractedly to Lorraine, Charlie watched Honoria's eyes leave their table, and he followed them wistfully about the room, wondering what they saw. He met her glance and she smiled.

"I liked that lemonade," she said.

What had she said? What had he expected? Going home in a taxi afterward, he pulled her over until her head rested against his chest.

"Darling, do you ever think about your mother?"

"Yes, sometimes," she answered vaguely.

"I don't want you to forget her. Have you got a picture of her?"

"Yes, I think so. Anyhow, Aunt Marion has. Why don't you want me to forget her?"

"She loved you very much."

"I loved her too."

They were silent for a moment.

"Daddy, I want to come and live with you," she said suddenly.

His heart leaped; he had wanted it to come like this.

"Aren't you perfectly happy?"

"Yes, but I love you better than anybody. And you love me better than anybody, don't you, now that mummy's dead?"

"Of course I do. But you won't always like me best, honey. You'll grow up and meet somebody your own age and go marry him and forget you ever had a daddy."

"Yes, that's true," she agreed tranquilly.

He didn't go in. He was coming back at nine o'clock and he wanted to keep himself fresh and new for the thing he must say then.

"When you're safe inside, just show yourself in that window."

"All right. Good-by, dads, dads, dads, dads."

He waited in the dark street until she appeared, all warm and glowing, in the window above and kissed her fingers out into the night.

III

They were waiting. Marion sat behind the coffee service in a dignified black dinner dress that just faintly suggested mourning. Lincoln was walking up and down with the animation of one who had already been talking. They were as anxious as he was to get into the question. He opened it almost immediately:

"I suppose you know what I want to see you about—why I really came to Paris."

Marion played with the black stars on her necklace and frowned. 145

"I'm awfully anxious to have a home," he continued. "And I'm awfully anxious to have Honoria in it. I appreciate your taking in Honoria for her mother's sake, but things have changed now"—he hesitated and then continued more forcibly—"changed radically with me, and I want to ask you to reconsider the matter. It would be silly for me to deny that about three years ago I was acting badly—"

Marion looked up at him with hard eyes.

"—but all that's over. As I told you, I haven't had more than a drink a day for over a year, and I take that drink deliberately, so that the idea of alcohol won't get too big in my imagination. You see the idea?"

"No," said Marion succinctly.

"It's a sort of stunt I set myself. It keeps the matter in proportion." 150

"I get you," said Lincoln. "You don't want to admit it's got any attraction for you."

"Something like that. Sometimes I forget and don't take it. But I try to take it. Anyhow, I couldn't afford to drink in my position. The people I represent are more than satisfied with what I've done, and I'm bringing my sister over from Burlington to keep house for me, and I want awfully to have Honoria too. You know that even when her mother and I weren't getting along well we never let anything that happened touch Honoria. I know she's fond of me and I know I'm able to take care of her and—well, there you are. How do you feel about it?"

He knew that now he would have to take a beating. It would last an hour or two hours, and it would be difficult, but if he modulated his inevitable resentment to the chastened attitude of the reformed sinner, he might win his point in the end.

Keep your temper, he told himself. You don't want to be justified. You want Honoria.

Lincoln spoke first: "We've been talking it over ever since we got your letter 155
last month. We're happy to have Honoria here. She's a dear little thing, and we're glad to be able to help her, but of course that isn't the question—"

Marion interrupted suddenly. "How long are you going to stay sober, Charlie?" she asked.

"Permanently, I hope."

"How can anybody count on that?"

"You know I never did drink heavily until I gave up business and came over here with nothing to do. Then Helen and I began to run around with—"

"Please leave Helen out of it. I can't bear to hear you talk about her like that." 160

He stared at her grimly; he had never been certain how fond of each other the sisters were in life.

"My drinking only lasted about a year and a half—from the time we came over until I—collapsed."

"It was time enough."

"It was time enough," he agreed.

"My duty is entirely to Helen," she said. "I try to think what she would have wanted me to do. Frankly, from the night you did that terrible thing you haven't really existed for me. I can't help that. She was my sister."

"Yes."

"When she was dying she asked me to look out for Honoria. If you hadn't been in a sanitarium then, it might have helped matters."

He had no answer.

"I'll never in my life be able to forget the morning when Helen knocked at my door, soaked to the skin and shivering, and said you'd locked her out."

Charlie gripped the sides of the chair. This was more difficult than he expected; he wanted to launch out into a long expostulation and explanation, but he only said: "The night I locked her out—" and she interrupted, "I don't feel up to going over that again."

After a moment's silence Lincoln said: "We're getting off the subject. You want Marion to set aside her legal guardianship and give you Honoria. I think the main point for her is whether she has confidence in you or not."

"I don't blame Marion," Charlie said slowly, "but I think she can have entire confidence in me. I had a good record up to three years ago. Of course, it's within human possibilities I might go wrong any time. But if we wait much longer I'll lose Honoria's childhood and my chance for a home." He shook his head, "I'll simply lose her, don't you see?"

"Yes, I see," said Lincoln.

"Why didn't you think of all this before?" Marion asked.

"I suppose I did, from time to time, but Helen and I were getting along badly. When I consented to the guardianship, I was flat on my back in a sanitarium and the market had cleaned me out. I knew I'd acted badly, and I thought if it would bring any peace to Helen, I'd agree to anything. But now it's different. I'm functioning, I'm behaving damn well, so far as—"

"Please don't swear at me," Marion said.

He looked at her, startled. With each remark the force of her dislike became more and more apparent. She had built up all her fear of life into one wall and faced it toward him. This trivial reproof was possibly the result of some trouble with the cook several hours before. Charlie became increasingly alarmed at leaving Honoria in this atmosphere of hostility against himself; sooner or later it would come out, in a word here, a shake of the head there, and some of that distrust would be irrevocably implanted in Honoria. But he pulled his temper down out of his face and shut it up inside him; he had won a point, for Lincoln realized the absurdity of Marion's remark and asked her lightly since when she had objected to the word "damn."

"Another thing," Charlie said: "I'm able to give her certain advantages now. I'm going to take a French governess to Prague with me. I've got a lease on a new apartment—"

He stopped, realizing that he was blundering. They couldn't be expected to accept with equanimity the fact that his income was again twice as large as their own.

"I suppose you can give her more luxuries than we can," said Marion. "When you were throwing away money we were living along watching every ten francs. . . . I suppose you'll start doing it again."

"Oh, no," he said. "I've learned. I worked hard for ten years, you know—until I got lucky in the market, like so many people. Terribly lucky. It didn't seem any use working any more, so I quit. It won't happen again."

There was a long silence. All of them felt their nerves straining, and for the first time in a year Charlie wanted a drink. He was sure now that Lincoln Peters wanted him to have his child.

Marion shuddered suddenly; part of her saw that Charlie's feet were planted on the earth now, and her own maternal feeling recognized the naturalness of his desire; but she had lived for a long time with a prejudice—a prejudice founded on a curious disbelief in her sister's happiness, and which, in the shock of one terrible night, had turned to hatred for him. It had all happened at a point in her life where the discouragement of ill health and adverse circumstances made it necessary for her to believe in tangible villainy and a tangible villain.

"I can't help what I think!" she cried out suddenly. "How much you were responsible for Helen's death, I don't know. It's something you'll have to square with your own conscience."

An electric current of agony surged through him; for a moment he was almost on his feet, an unuttered sound echoing in his throat. He hung on to himself for a moment, another moment.

"Hold on there," said Lincoln uncomfortably. "I never thought you were responsible for that."

"Helen died of heart trouble," Charlie said dully.

"Yes, heart trouble." Marion spoke as if the phrase had another meaning for her. Then, in the flatness that followed her outburst, she saw him plainly and she knew he had somehow arrived at control over the situation. Glancing at her husband, she found no help from him, and as abruptly as if it were a matter of no importance, she threw up the sponge.

"Do what you like!" she cried, springing up from her chair. "She's your child. I'm not the person to stand in your way. I think if it were my child I'd rather see her—" She managed to check herself. "You two decide it. I can't stand this. I'm sick. I'm going to bed."

She hurried from the room; after a moment Lincoln said:

"This has been a hard day for her. You know how strongly she feels—" His voice was almost apologetic: "When a woman gets an idea in her head."

"Of course."

"It's going to be all right. I think she sees now that you—can provide for the child, and so we can't very well stand in your way or Honoria's way."

"Thank you, Lincoln."

"I'd better go along and see how she is."

"I'm going."

He was still trembling when he reached the street, but a walk down the Rue Bonaparte to the quais set him up, and as he crossed the Seine, fresh and new by the quai lamps, he felt exultant. But back in his room he couldn't sleep. The image of Helen haunted him. Helen whom he had loved so until they had senselessly begun to abuse each other's love, tear it into shreds. On that terrible February night that Marion remembered so vividly, a slow quarrel had gone on for hours. There was a scene at the Florida, and then he attempted to take her home, and then she kissed young Webb at a table; after that there was what she had hysterically said. When he arrived home alone he turned the key in the lock in wild anger. How could he know she would arrive an hour later alone, that there would be a snowstorm in which she wandered about in slippers, too confused to find a taxi? Then the aftermath, her escaping pneumonia by a miracle, and all the attendant horror. They were "reconciled," but that was the beginning of the end, and Marion, who had seen with her own eyes and who imagined it to be one of many scenes from her sister's martyrdom, never forgot.

Going over it again brought Helen nearer, and in the white, soft light that steals upon half sleep near morning he found himself talking to her again. She said that he was perfectly right about Honoria and that she wanted Honoria to be with him. She said she was glad he was being good and doing better. She said a lot of other things—very friendly things—but she was in a swing in a white dress, and swinging faster and faster all the time, so that at the end he could not hear clearly all that she said.

IV

He woke up feeling happy. The door of the world was open again. He made plans, vistas, futures for Honoria and himself, but suddenly he grew sad, remembering all the plans he and Helen had made. She had not planned to die. The present was the thing—work to do and someone to love. But not to love too much, for he knew the injury that a father can do to a daughter or a mother to a son by attaching them too closely: afterward, out in the world, the child would seek in the marriage partner the same blind tenderness and, failing probably to find it, turn against love and life.

It was another bright, crisp day. He called Lincoln Peters at the bank where he worked and asked if he could count on taking Honoria when he left for Prague. Lincoln agreed that there was no reason for delay. One thing—the legal guardianship. Marion wanted to retain that a while longer. She was upset by the whole matter, and it would oil things if she felt that the situation was still in her control for another year. Charlie agreed, wanting only the tangible, visible child.

Then the question of a governess. Charlie sat in a gloomy agency and talked to a cross Béarnaise and to a buxom Breton peasant, neither of whom he could have endured. There were others whom he would see tomorrow.

He lunched with Lincoln Peters at Griffons,[5] trying to keep down his exultation. "There's nothing quite like your own child," Lincoln said. "But you understand how Marion feels too."

[5]*Griffons:* A hotel in Paris.

"She's forgotten how hard I worked for seven years there," Charlie said. "She just remembers one night."

"There's another thing." Lincoln hesitated. "While you and Helen were tearing around Europe throwing money away, we were just getting along. I didn't touch any of the prosperity because I never got ahead enough to carry anything but my insurance. I think Marion felt there was some kind of injustice in it—you not even working toward the end, and getting richer and richer."

"It went just as quick as it came," said Charlie. 205

"Yes, a lot of it stayed in the hands of *chasseurs* and saxophone players and maîtres d'hôtel—well, the big party's over now. I just said that to explain Marion's feeling about those crazy years. If you drop in about six o'clock tonight before Marion's too tired, we'll settle the details on the spot."

Back at his hotel, Charlie found a *pneumatique* that had been redirected from the Ritz bar where Charlie had left his address for the purpose of finding a certain man.

> Dear Charlie:
>
> You were so strange when we saw you the other day that I wondered if I did something to offend you. If so, I'm not conscious of it. In fact, I have thought about you too much for the last year, and it's always been in the back of my mind that I might see you if I came over here. We *did* have such good times that crazy spring, like the night you and I stole the butcher's tricycle, and the time we tried to call on the president and you had the old derby rim and the wire cane. Everybody seems so old lately, but I don't feel old a bit. Couldn't we get together some time today for old time's sake? I've got a vile hang-over for the moment, but will be feeling better this afternoon and will look for you about five in the sweat-shop at the Ritz.
>
> Always devotedly,
> Lorraine.

His first feeling was one of awe that he had actually, in his mature years, stolen a tricycle and pedalled Lorraine all over the Étoile between the small hours and dawn. In retrospect it was a nightmare. Locking out Helen didn't fit in with any other act of his life, but the tricycle incident did—it was one of many. How many weeks or months of dissipation to arrive at that condition of utter irresponsibility?

He tried to picture how Lorraine had appeared to him then—very attractive; Helen was unhappy about it, though she said nothing. Yesterday, in the restaurant, Lorraine had seemed trite, blurred, worn away. He emphatically did not want to see her, and he was glad Alix had not given away his hotel address. It was a relief to think, instead, of Honoria, to think of Sundays spent with her and of saying good morning to her and of knowing she was there in his house at night, drawing her breath in the darkness.

At five he took a taxi and bought presents for all the Peters—a piquant cloth doll, a box of Roman soldiers, flowers for Marion, big linen handkerchiefs for Lincoln.

He saw, when he arrived in the apartment, that Marion had accepted the 210
inevitable. She greeted him now as though he were a recalcitrant member of the family, rather than a menacing outsider. Honoria had been told she was going; Charlie was glad to see that her tact made her conceal her excessive happiness. Only on his lap did she whisper her delight and the question "When?" before she slipped away with the other children. He and Marion were alone for a minute in the room, and on an impulse he spoke out boldly:

"Family quarrels are bitter things. They don't go according to any rules. They're not like aches or wounds; they're more like splits in the skin that won't heal because there's not enough material. I wish you and I could be on better terms."

"Some things are hard to forget," she answered. "It's a question of confidence." There was no answer to this and presently she asked, "When do you propose to take her?"

"As soon as I can get a governess. I hoped the day after tomorrow."

"That's impossible. I've got to get her things in shape. Not before Saturday."

He yielded. Coming back into the room, Lincoln offered him a drink. 215

"I'll take my daily whisky," he said.

It was warm here, it was a home, people together by a fire. The children felt very safe and important; the mother and father were serious, watchful. They had things to do for the children more important than his visit here. A spoonful of medicine was, after all, more important than the strained relations between Marion and himself. They were not dull people, but they were very much in the grip of life and circumstances. He wondered if he couldn't do something to get Lincoln out of his rut at the bank.

A long peal at the door-bell; the *bonne à tout faire* passed through and went down the corridor. The door opened upon another long ring, and then voices, and the three in the salon looked up expectantly; Lincoln moved to bring the corridor within his range of vision, and Marion rose. Then the maid came back along the corridor, closely followed by the voices, which developed under the light into Duncan Schaeffer and Lorraine Quarrles.

They were gay, they were hilarious, they were roaring with laughter. For a moment Charlie was astounded; unable to understand how they ferreted out the Peters' address.

"Ah-h-h!" Duncan wagged his finger roguishly at Charlie. "Ah-h-h!" 220

They both slid down another cascade of laughter. Anxious and at a loss, Charlie shook hands with them quickly and presented them to Lincoln and Marion. Marion nodded, scarcely speaking. She had drawn back a step toward the fire; her little girl stood beside her, and Marion put an arm about her shoulder.

With growing annoyance at the intrusion, Charlie waited for them to explain themselves. After some concentration Duncan said:

"We came to invite you out to dinner. Lorraine and I insist that all this shishi, cagy business 'bout your address got to stop."

Charlie came closer to them, as if to force them backward down the corridor.

"Sorry, but I can't. Tell me where you'll be and I'll phone you in half an hour."

This made no impression. Lorraine sat down suddenly on the side of a chair, and focussing her eyes on Richard, cried, "Oh, what a nice little boy! Come here, little boy." Richard glanced at his mother, but did not move. With a perceptible shrug of her shoulders, Lorraine turned back to Charlie:

"Come and dine. Sure your cousins won' mine. See you so sel'om. Or solemn."

"I can't," said Charlie sharply. "You two have dinner and I'll phone you."

Her voice became suddenly unpleasant. "All right, we'll go. But I remember once when you hammered on my door at four A.M. I was enough of a good sport to give you a drink. Come on, Dunc."

Still in slow motion, with blurred, angry faces, with uncertain feet, they retired along the corridor.

"Good night," Charlie said.

"Good night!" responded Lorraine emphatically.

When he went back into the salon Marion had not moved, only now her son was standing in the circle of her other arm. Lincoln was still swinging Honoria back and forth like a pendulum from side to side.

"What an outrage!" Charlie broke out. "What an absolute outrage!" Neither of them answered. Charlie dropped into an armchair, picked up his drink, set it down again and said:

"People I haven't seen for two years having the colossal nerve—"

He broke off. Marion had made the sound "Oh!" in one swift, furious breath, turned her body from him with a jerk and left the room.

Lincoln set down Honoria carefully.

"You children go in and start your soup," he said, and when they obeyed, he said to Charlie:

"Marion's not well and she can't stand shocks. That kind of people make her really physically sick."

"I didn't tell them to come here. They wormed your name out of somebody. They deliberately—"

"Well, it's too bad. It doesn't help matters. Excuse me a minute."

Left alone, Charlie sat tense in his chair. In the next room he could hear the children eating, talking in monosyllables, already oblivious to the scene between their elders. He heard a murmur of conversation from a farther room and then the ticking bell of a telephone receiver picked up, and in a panic he moved to the other side of the room and out of earshot.

In a minute Lincoln came back. "Look here, Charlie. I think we'd better call off dinner for tonight. Marion's in bad shape."

"Is she angry with me?"

"Sort of," he said, almost roughly. "She's not strong and—"

"You mean she's changed her mind about Honoria?"

"She's pretty bitter right now. I don't know. You phone me at the bank tomorrow."

"I wish you'd explain to her I never dreamed these people would come here. I'm just as sore as you are."

"I couldn't explain anything to her now."

Charlie got up. He took his coat and hat and started down the corridor. Then he opened the door of the dining room and said in a strange voice, "Good night, children." Honoria rose and ran around the table to hug him.

"Good night, sweetheart," he said vaguely, and then trying to make his voice more tender, trying to conciliate something, "Good night, dear children."

V

Charlie went directly to the Ritz bar with the furious idea of finding Lorraine and Duncan, but they were not there, and he realized that in any case there was nothing he could do. He had not touched his drink at the Peters', and now he ordered a whisky-and-soda. Paul came over to say hello.

"It's a great change," he said sadly. "We do about half the business we did. So many fellows I hear about back in the States lost everything, maybe not in the first crash, but then in the second. Your friend George Hardt lost every cent, I hear. Are you back in the States?"

"No, I'm in business in Prague."

"I heard that you lost a lot in the crash."

"I did," and he added grimly, "but I lost everything I wanted in the boom."

"Selling short."

"Something like that."

Again the memory of those days swept over him like a nightmare—the people they had met travelling; then people who couldn't add a row of figures or speak a coherent sentence. The little man Helen had consented to dance with at the ship's party, who had insulted her ten feet from the table; the women and girls carried screaming with drink or drugs out of public places—

—The men who locked their wives out in the snow, because the snow of twenty-nine wasn't real snow. If you didn't want it to be snow, you just paid some money.

He went to the phone and called the Peters' apartment; Lincoln answered.

"I called up because this thing is on my mind. Has Marion said anything definite?"

"Marion's sick," Lincoln answered shortly. "I know this thing isn't altogether your fault, but I can't have her go to pieces about it. I'm afraid we'll have to let it slide for six months; I can't take the chance of working her up to this state again."

"I see."

"I'm sorry, Charlie."

He went back to his table. His whisky glass was empty, but he shook his head when Alix looked at it questioningly. There wasn't much he could do now except send Honoria some things; he would send her a lot of things tomorrow. He thought rather angrily that this was just money—he had given so many people money. . . .

"No, no more," he said to another waiter. "What do I owe you?"

He would come back some day; they couldn't make him pay forever. But he wanted his child, and nothing was much good now, beside that fact. He wasn't young any more, with a lot of nice thoughts and dreams to have by himself. He was absolutely sure Helen wouldn't have wanted him to be so alone.

(1931)

Questions for Discussion and Writing

Close Reading

1. Contrast the Paris of the story's setting with the one Charlie had left a year and a half before.
2. Charlie's troubles partly stem from his relationship with his dead wife, Helen, a character we never meet. What do we know about Helen? What was Charlie and Helen's marriage like?
3. Why does Marion react the way she does to the visit by Lorraine and Duncan? Do you think her reaction is justified?

Critical and Creative Reading

4. Although Charlie is a sympathetic character, even he questions his ability to remain sober indefinitely. Is Honoria better off living with him or with her aunt and uncle? If you were a judge assigning custody, how would you rule?
5. In his conversations with Lincoln and Marion, Charlie expresses contrition and asks to be forgiven. However, the story's point of view (third-person limited) allows us to see that he is deeply resentful of Marion, that he is adopting "the chastened attitude of the reformed sinner" so that he can "win his point in the end." How sincere is Charlie? Cite evidence from the text to support your opinion.
6. At the end of the story, Charlie thinks, "they couldn't make him pay forever." But in fact, they can. Do you think Charlie will "pay" for his treatment of his wife by losing his daughter altogether? Where do you see Charlie, Honoria, and Marion a year after the story's close? Ten years? Is Marion capable of forgiving Charlie?

Connections to Other Readings

7. Compare Charlie to the mariner in Samuel Taylor Coleridge's "The Rime of the Ancient Mariner." How are they defined by their guilt? How are they similar and different in the way they respond to their guilt?
8. Compare Charlie as a "prodigal father" to the prodigal son in this chapter's Common Characters section. Is one more deserving of a second chance than the other?

Sembene Ousmane

Her Three Days

Sembene Ousmane (b. 1923) was born in Senegal, a former French colony, and moved to France after World War II. (He is also referred to as "Ousmane Sembene"; the difference has to do with French literary conventions.) He became a dockworker in Marseilles, a union leader, and a member of the French Communist Party. His first novel, *Le Docker Noir* (1956), reflects his experiences in Marseilles. "Her Three Days" is about a Muslim woman's feelings of rejection when her husband takes another wife. The three days refers to the time every month that a Muslim wife in Mali is entitled to spend with her husband. The protagonist's "revenge" is subtle but potentially revolutionary.

She raised her haggard face, and her far-away look ranged beyond the muddle of roofs, some tiled, others of thatch or galvanized-iron; the wide fronds of the twin coconut-palms were swaying slowly in the breeze, and in her mind she could hear their faint rustling. Noumbe was thinking of "her three days." Three days for her alone, when she would have her husband Mustapha to herself . . . It was a long time since she had felt such emotion. To have Mustapha! The thought comforted her. She had heart trouble and still felt some pain, but she had been dosing herself for the past two days, taking more medicine than was prescribed. It was a nice syrup that just slipped down, and she felt the beneficial effects at once. She blinked; her eyes were like two worn buttonholes, with lashes that were like frayed thread, in little clusters of fives and threes; the whites were the colour of old ivory.

"What's the matter, Noumbe?" asked Aida, her next-door neighbour, who was sitting at the door of her room.

"Nothing," she answered, and went on cutting up the slice of raw meat, helped by her youngest daughter.

"Ah, it's your three days," exclaimed Aida, whose words held a meaning that she could not elaborate on while the little girl was present. She went on: "You're looking fine enough to prevent a holy man from saying his prayers properly!"

"Aida, be careful what you say," she protested, a little annoyed. 5

But it was true; Noumbe had plaited her hair and put henna[1] on her hands and feet. And that morning she had got the children up early to give her room a thorough clean. She was not old, but one pregnancy after another—and she had five children—and her heart trouble had aged her before her time.

[1] *henna:* A plant used cosmetically, especially in northern Africa and the Middle East, to dye skin.

"Go and ask Laity to give you five francs' worth of salt and twenty francs' worth of oil," Noumbe said to the girl. "Tell him I sent you. I'll pay for them as soon as your father is here, at midday." She looked disapprovingly at the cut-up meat in the bottom of the bowl.

The child went off with the empty bottle and Noumbe got to her feet. She was thin and of average height. She went into her one-room shack, which was sparsely furnished; there was a bed with a white cover, and in one corner stood a table with pieces of china on display. The walls were covered with enlargements and photos of friends and strangers framed in passe-partout.

When she came out again she took the Moorish stove and set about lighting it.

Her daughter had returned from her errand.

"He gave them to you?" asked Noumbe.

"Yes, mother."

A woman came across the compound to her. "Noumbe, I can see that you're preparing a delicious dish."

"Yes," she replied. "It's my three days. I want to revive the feasts of the old days, so that his palate will retain the taste of the dish for many moons, and he'll forget the cooking of his other wives."

"Ah-ha! So that his palate is eager for dishes to come," said the woman, who was having a good look at the ingredients.

"I'm feeling in good form," said Noumbe, with some pride in her voice. She grasped the woman's hand and passed it over her loins.

"*Thieh, souya dome!* I hope you can say the same tomorrow morning . . ."

The woman clapped her hands; as if it were a signal or an invitation, other women came across, one with a metal jar, another with a saucepan, which they beat while the woman sang:

Sope dousa rafetail,
Sopa nala dousa rafetail
Sa yahi n'diguela.
(Worship of you is not for your beauty,
I worship you not for your beauty
But for your backbone.)

In a few moments, they improvised a wild dance to this chorus. At the end, panting and perspiring, they burst out laughing. Then one of them stepped into Noumbe's room and called the others.

"Let's take away the bed! Because tonight they'll wreck it!"

"She's right. Tomorrow this room will be . . ."

Each woman contributed an earthy comment which set them all laughing hilariously. Then they remembered they had work to do, and brought their amusement to an end; each went back to her family occupations.

Noumbe had joined in the laughter; she knew this boisterous "ragging" was the custom in the compound. No one escaped it. Besides, she was an exceptional case, as they all knew. She had a heart condition and her husband had quite openly neglected her. Mustapha had not been to see her for a fortnight. All this time she had been hoping that he would come, if only for a moment. When she went to the clinic for mothers and children she compelled her youngest daughter to stay at home, so that—thus did her mind work—if her husband turned up the child could detain him until she returned. She ought to have gone to the clinic again this day, but she had spent what little money she possessed on preparing for Mustapha. She did not want her husband to esteem her less than his other wives, or to think her meaner. She did not neglect her duty as a mother, but her wifely duty came first—at certain times.

She imagined what the next three days would be like; already her "three days" filled her whole horizon. She forgot her illness and her baby's ailments. She had thought about these three days in a thousand different ways. Mustapha would not leave before the Monday morning. In her mind she could see Mustapha and his henchmen crowding into her room, and could hear their suggestive jokes. "If she had been a perfect wife . . ." She laughed to herself. "Why shouldn't it always be like that for every woman—to have a husband of one's own?" She wondered why not.

The morning passed at its usual pace, the shadows of the coconut-palms and the people growing steadily shorter. As midday approached, the housewives busied themselves with the meal. In the compound each one stood near her door, ready to welcome her man. The kids were playing around, and their mothers' calls to them crossed in the air. Noumbe gave her children a quick meal and sent them out again. She sat waiting for Mustapha to arrive at any moment . . . he wouldn't be much longer now.

An hour passed, and the men began going back to work. Soon the compound was empty of the male element; the women, after a long siesta, joined one another under the coconut-palms and the sounds of their gossiping gradually increased.

Noumbe, weary of waiting, had finally given up keeping a lookout. Dressed in her mauve velvet, she had been on the watch since before midday. She had eaten no solid food, consoling herself with the thought that Mustapha would appear at any moment. Now she fought back the pangs of hunger by telling herself that in the past Mustapha had a habit of arriving late. In those days, this lateness was pleasant. Without admitting it to herself, those moments (which had hung terribly heavy) had been very sweet; they prolonged the sensual pleasure of anticipation. Although those minutes had been sometimes shot through with doubts and fears (often, very often, the thought of her coming disgrace had assailed her; for Mustapha, who had taken two wives before her, had just married another), they had not been too hard to bear. She realized that those demanding minutes were the price she had to pay for Mustapha's presence. Then she began to reckon up the score, in small ways, against the *veudieux*, the other wives. One washed his *boubous*[2] when it was another wife's turn, or kept him long into the night; another sometimes held him in her embrace a whole day, knowing quite well that she was preventing Mustapha from carrying out his marital duty elsewhere.

[2] *boubous:* A long gown with intricate designs.

She sulked as she waited; Mustapha had not been near her for a fortnight. All these bitter thoughts brought her up against reality: four months ago Mustapha had married a younger woman. This sudden realization of the facts sent a pain to her heart, a pain of anguish. The additional pain did not prevent her heart from functioning normally, rather was it like a sick person whose sleep banishes pain but who once awake again finds his suffering is as bad as ever, and pays for the relief by a redoubling of pain.

She took three spoonfuls of her medicine instead of the two prescribed, and felt a little better in herself.

She called her youngest daughter. "Tell Mactar I want him."

The girl ran off and soon returned with her eldest brother.

"Go and fetch your father," Noumbe told him.

"Where, mother?"

"Where? Oh, on the main square or at one of your other mothers'."

"But I've been to the main square already, and he wasn't there."

"Well, go and have another look. Perhaps he's there now."

The boy looked up at his mother, then dropped his head again and reluctantly turned to go.

"When your father has finished eating, I'll give you what's left. It's meat. Now be quick, Mactar."

It was scorching hot and the clouds were riding high. Mactar was back after an hour. He had not found his father. Noumbe went and joined the group of women. They were chattering about this and that; one of them asked (just for the sake of asking), "Noumbe, has your uncle (darling) arrived?" "Not yet," she replied, then hastened to add, "Oh, he won't be long now. He knows it's my three days." She deliberately changed the conversation in order to avoid a long discussion about the other three wives. But all the time she was longing to go and find Mustapha. She was being robbed of her three days. And the other wives knew it. Her hours alone with Mustapha were being snatched from her. The thought of his being with one of the other wives, who was feeding him and opening his waistcloth when she ought to be doing all that, who was enjoying those hours which were hers by right, so numbed Noumbe that it was impossible for her to react. The idea that Mustapha might have been admitted to hospital or taken to a police station never entered her head.

She knew how to make tasty little dishes for Mustapha which cost him nothing. She never asked him for money. Indeed, hadn't she got herself into debt so that he would be more comfortable and have better meals at her place? And in the past, when Mustapha sometimes arrived unexpectedly—this was soon after he had married her—hadn't she hastened to make succulent dishes for him? All her friends knew this.

A comforting thought coursed through her and sent these aggressive and vindictive reflections to sleep. She told herself that Mustapha was bound to come to her this evening. The certainty of his presence stripped her mind of the too cruel thought that the time of her disfavour was approaching; this thought had been as much a burden to her as a heavy weight dragging a drowning man to the bottom. When all the bad, unfavourable thoughts besetting her had been dispersed, like piles of rubbish on waste land swept by a flood, the future seemed brighter, and she joined in the conversation of the women with childish enthusiasm, unable to hide her pleasure and her hopes. It was like something in a parcel; questioning eyes wondered what was inside, but she alone knew and enjoyed the secret, drawing an agreeable strength from it. She took an active part in the talking and brought her wit into play. All this vivacity sprang from the joyful conviction that Mustapha would arrive this evening very hungry and be hers alone.

In the far distance, high above the tree-tops, a long trail of dark-grey clouds tinged with red was hiding the sun. The time for the *tacousane,* the afternoon prayer, was drawing near. One by one, the women withdrew to their rooms, and the shadows of the trees grew longer, wider and darker.

Night fell; a dark, starry night.

Noumbe cooked some rice for the children. They clamoured in vain for some of the meat. Noumbe was stern and unyielding: "The meat is for your father. He didn't eat at midday." When she had fed the children, she washed herself again to get rid of the smell of cooking and touched up her toilette, rubbing oil on her hands, feet and legs to make the henna more brilliant. She intended to remain by her door, and sat down on the bench; the incense smelt strongly, filling the whole room. She was facing the entrance to the compound and could see the other women's husbands coming in.

But for her there was no one. 45

She began to feel tired again. Her heart was troubling her, and she had a fit of coughing. Her inside seemed to be on fire. Knowing that she would not be going to the dispensary during her "three days," in order to economize, she went and got some wood-ash which she mixed with water and drank. It did not taste very nice, but it would make the medicine last longer, and the drink checked and soothed the burning within her for a while. She was tormenting herself with the thoughts passing through her mind. Where can he be? With the first wife? No, she's quite old. The second then? Everyone knew that she was out of favour with Mustapha. The third wife was herself. So he must be with the fourth. There were puckers of uncertainty and doubt in the answers she gave herself. She kept putting back the time to go to bed, like a lover who does not give up waiting when the time of the rendezvous is long past, but with an absurd and stupid hope waits still longer, self-torture and the heavy minutes chaining him to the spot. At each step Noumbe took, she stopped and mentally explored the town, prying into each house inhabited by one of the other wives. Eventually she went indoors.

So that she would not be caught unawares by Mustapha nor lose the advantages which her make-up and good clothes gave her, she lay down on the bed fully dressed and alert. She had turned down the lamp as far as possible, so the room was dimly lit. But she fell asleep despite exerting great strength of mind to remain awake and saying repeatedly to herself, "I shall wait for him." To make sure that she would be standing there expectantly when he crossed the threshold, she had bolted the door. Thus she would be the devoted wife, always ready to serve her husband, having got up at once and appearing as elegant as if it were broad daylight. She had even thought of making a gesture as she stood there, of passing her hands casually over her hips so that Mustapha would hear the clinking of the beads she had strung round her waist and be incited to look at her from head to foot.

Morning came, but there was no Mustapha.

When the children awoke they asked if their father had come. The oldest of them, Mactar, a promising lad, was quick to spot that his mother had not made the bed, that the bowl containing the stew was still in the same place, by a dish of rice, and the loaf of bread on the table was untouched. The children got a taste of their mother's anger. The youngest, Amadou, took a long time over dressing. Noumbe hurried them up and sent the youngest girl to Laity's to buy five francs' worth of ground coffee. The children's breakfast was warmed-up rice with a meagre sprinkling of gravy from the previous day's stew. Then she gave them their wings, as the saying goes, letting them all out except the youngest daughter. Noumbe inspected the bottle of medicine and saw that she had taken a lot of it; there were only three spoonfuls left. She gave herself half a spoonful and made up for the rest with her mixture of ashes and water. After that she felt calmer.

"Why, Noumbe, you must have got up bright and early this morning, to be so dressed up. Are you going off on a long journey?"

It was Aida, her next-door neighbour, who was surprised to see her dressed in such a manner, especially for a woman who was having "her three days." Then Aida realized what had happened and tried to rectify her mistake.

"Oh, I see he hasn't come yet. They're all the same, these men!"

"He'll be here this morning, Aida." Noumbe bridled, ready to defend her man. But it was rather her own worth she was defending, wanting to conceal what an awful time she had spent. It had been a broken night's sleep, listening to harmless sounds which she had taken for Mustapha's footsteps, and this had left its mark on her already haggard face.

"I'm sure he will! I'm sure he will!" exclaimed Aida, well aware of this comedy that all the women played in turn.

"Mustapha is such a kind man, and so noble in his attitude," added another woman, rubbing it in.

"If he weren't, he wouldn't be my master," said Noumbe, feeling flattered by this description of Mustapha.

The news soon spread round the compound that Mustapha had slept elsewhere during Noumbe's three days. The other women pitied her. It was against all the rules for Mustapha to spend a night elsewhere. Polygamy had its laws, which should be respected. A sense of decency and common dignity restrained a wife from keeping the husband day and night when his whole person and everything connected with him belonged to another wife during "her three days." The game, however, was not without its underhand tricks that one wife played on another; for instance, to wear out the man and hand him over when he was incapable of performing his conjugal duties. When women criticized the practice of polygamy they always found that the wives were to blame, especially those who openly dared to play a dirty trick. The man was whitewashed. He was a weakling who always ended by falling into the enticing traps set for him by woman. Satisfied with this conclusion, Noumbe's neighbours made common cause with her and turned to abusing Mustapha's fourth wife.

Noumbe made some coffee—she never had any herself, because of her heart. She consoled herself with the thought that Mustapha would find more things at her place. The bread had gone stale; she would buy some more when he arrived.

The hours dragged by again, long hours of waiting which became harder to bear as the day progressed. She wished she knew where he was . . . The thought obsessed her, and her eyes became glazed and searching. Every time she heard a man's voice she straightened up quickly. Her heart was paining her more and more, but the physical pain was separate from the mental one; they never came together, alternating in a way that reminded her of the acrobatic feat of a man riding two speeding horses.

At about four o'clock Noumbe was surprised to see Mustapha's second wife appear at the door. She had come to see if Mustapha was there, knowing that it was Noumbe's three days. She did not tell Noumbe the reason for her wishing to see Mustapha, despite being pressed. So Noumbe concluded that it was largely due to jealousy, and was pleased that the other wife could see how clean and tidy her room was, and what a display of fine things she had, all of which could hardly fail to make the other think that Mustapha had been (and still was) very generous to her, Noumbe. During the rambling conversation her heart thumped ominously, but she bore up and held off taking any medicine.

Noumbe remembered only too well that when she was newly married she had usurped the second wife's three days. At that time she had been the youngest wife. Mustapha had not let a day pass without coming to see her. Although not completely certain, she believed she had conceived her third child during this wife's three days. The latter's presence now and remarks that she let drop made Noumbe realize that she was no longer the favourite. This revelation, and the polite, amiable tone and her visitor's eagerness to inquire after her children's health and her own, to praise her superior choice of household utensils, her taste in clothes, the cleanliness of the room and the lingering fragrance of the incense, all this was like a stab in cold blood, a cruel reminder of the perfidy of words and the hypocrisy of rivals; and all part of the world of women. This observation did not get her anywhere, except to arouse a desire to escape from the circle of polygamy and to cause her to ask herself—it was a moment of mental aberration really—"Why do we allow ourselves to be men's playthings?"

The other wife complimented her and insisted that Noumbe's children should go and spend a few days with her own children (in this she was sincere). By accepting in principle, Noumbe was weaving her own waist-cloth of hypocrisy. It was all to make the most of herself, to set tongues wagging so that she would lose none of her respectability and rank. The other wife casually added—before she forgot, as she said—that she wanted to see Mustapha, and if mischief-makers told Noumbe that "their" husband had been to see her during Noumbe's three days, Noumbe shouldn't think ill of her, and she would rather have seen him here to tell him what she had to say. To save face, Noumbe dared not ask her when she had last seen Mustapha. The other would have replied with a smile, "The last morning of my three days, of course. I've only come here because it's urgent." And Noumbe would have looked embarrassed and put on an air of innocence. "No, that isn't what I meant. I just wondered if you had happened to meet him by chance."

Neither of them would have lost face. It was all that remained to them. They were not lying, to their way of thinking. Each had been desired and spoilt for a time; then the man, like a gorged vulture, had left them on one side and the venom of chagrin at having been mere playthings had entered their hearts. They quite understood, it was all quite clear to them, that they could sink no lower; so they clung to what was left to them, that is to say, to saving what dignity remained to them by false words and gaining advantages at the expense of the other. They did not indulge in this game for the sake of it. This falseness contained all that remained of the flame of dignity. No one was taken in, certainly not themselves. Each knew that the other was lying, but neither could bring herself to further humiliation, for it would be the final crushing blow.

The other wife left. Noumbe almost propelled her to the door, then stood there thoughtful for a few moments. Noumbe understood the reason for the other's visit. She had come to get her own back. Noumbe felt absolutely sure that Mustapha was with his latest wife. The visit meant in fact: "You stole those days from me because I am older than you. Now a younger woman than you is avenging me. Try as you might to make everything nice and pleasant for him, you have to toe the line with the rest of us now, you old carcass. He's slept with someone else—and he will again."

The second day passed like the first, but was more dreadful. She ate no proper food, just enough to stave off the pangs of hunger.

It was Sunday morning and all the men were at home; they nosed about in one room and another, some of them cradling their youngest in their arms, others playing with the older children. The draught-players had gathered in one place, the card-players in another. There was a friendly atmosphere in the compound, with bursts of happy laughter and sounds of guttural voices, while the women busied themselves with the housework.

Aida went to see Noumbe to console her, and said without much conviction, "He'll probably come today. Men always seem to have something to do at the last minute. It's Sunday today, so he'll be here."

"Aida, Mustapha doesn't work," Noumbe pointed out, hard-eyed. She gave a cough. "I've been waiting for him now for two days and nights! When it's my three days I think the least he could do is to be here—at night, anyway. I might die. . . ."

"Do you want me to go and look for him?"

"No."

She had thought "yes." It was the way in which Aida had made the offer that embarrassed her. Of course she would like her to! Last night, when everyone had gone to bed, she had started out and covered quite some distance before turning back. The flame of her dignity had been fanned on the way. She did not want to abase herself still further by going to claim a man who seemed to have no desire to see her. She had lain awake until dawn, thinking it all over and telling herself that her marriage to Mustapha was at an end, that she would divorce him. But this morning there was a tiny flicker of hope in her heart: "Mustapha will come, all the same. This is my last night."

She borrowed a thousand francs from Aida, who readily lent her the money. And she followed the advice to send the children off again, to Mustapha's fourth wife.

"Tell him that I must see him at once, I'm not well!"

She hurried off to the little market near by and bought a chicken and several other things. Her eyes were feverishly, joyfully bright as she carefully added seasoning to the dish she prepared. The appetizing smell of her cooking was wafted out to the compound and its Sunday atmosphere. She swept the room again, shut the door and windows, but the heady scent of the incense escaped through the cracks between the planks.

The children returned from their errand.

"Is he ill?" she asked them.

"No, mother. He's going to come. We found him with some of his friends at Voulimata's (the fourth wife). He asked about you."

"And that's all he said?"

"Yes, mother."

"Don't come indoors. Here's ten francs. Go and play somewhere else."

A delicious warm feeling spread over her. "He was going to come." Ever since Friday she had been harbouring spiteful words to throw in his face. He would beat her, of course. . . . But never mind. Now she found it would be useless to utter those words. Instead she would do everything possible to make up for the lost days. She was happy, much too happy to bear a grudge against him, now that she knew he was coming—he might even be on the way with his henchmen. The only means of getting her own back was to cook a big meal . . . then he would stay in bed.

She finished preparing the meal, had a bath and went on to the rest of her toilette. She did her hair again, put antimony on her lower lip, eyebrows and lashes, then dressed in a white starched blouse and a hand-woven waist-cloth, and inspected her hands and feet. She was quite satisfied with her appearance.

But the waiting became prolonged.

No one in the compound spoke to her for fear of hurting her feelings. She had sat down outside the door, facing the entrance to the compound, and the other inhabitants avoided meeting her sorrowful gaze. Her tears overflowed the brim of her eyes like a swollen river its banks; she tried to hold them back, but in vain. She was eating her heart out.

The sound of a distant tom-tom was being carried on the wind. Time passed over her, like the seasons over monuments. Twilight came and darkness fell.

On the table were three plates in a row, one for each day.

"I've come to keep you company," declared Aida as she entered the room. Noumbe was sitting on the foot of the bed—she had fled from the silence of the others. "You mustn't get worked up about it," went on Aida. "Every woman goes through it. Of course it's not nice! But I don't think he'll be long now."

Noumbe raised a moist face and bit her lips nervously. Aida saw that she had made up her mind not to say anything.

Everything was shrouded in darkness; no light came from her room. After supper, the children had refrained from playing their noisy games.

Just when adults were beginning to feel sleepy and going to bed, into the compound walked Mustapha, escorted by two of his lieutenants. He was clad entirely in white. He greeted the people still about in an oily manner, then invited his companions into Noumbe's hut.

She had not stirred.

"Wife, where's the lamp?"

"Where you left it this morning when you went out."

"How are you?" inquired Mustapha when he had lit the lamp. He went and sat down on the bed, and motioned to the two men to take the bench.

"God be praised," Noumbe replied to his polite inquiry. Her thin face seemed relaxed and the angry lines had disappeared.

"And the children?"

"They're well, praise be to God."

"Our wife isn't very talkative this evening," put in one of the men.

"I'm quite well, though."

"Your heart isn't playing you up now?" asked Mustapha, not unkindly.

"No, it's quite steady," she answered.

"God be praised! Mustapha, we'll be off," said the man, uncomfortable at Noumbe's cold manner.

"Wait," said Mustapha, and turned to Noumbe. "Wife, are we eating tonight or tomorrow?"

"Did you leave me something when you went out this morning?"

"What? That's not the way to answer."

"No, uncle (darling). I'm just asking . . . Isn't it right?"

Mustapha realized that Noumbe was mocking him and trying to humiliate him in front of his men.

"You do like your little joke. Don't you know it's your three days?"

"Oh, uncle, I'm sorry, I'd quite forgotten. What an unworthy wife I am!" she exclaimed, looking straight at Mustapha.

"You're making fun of me!"

"Oh, uncle, I shouldn't dare! What, I? And who would help me into Paradise, if not my worthy husband? Oh, I would never poke fun at you, neither in this world nor the next."

"Anyone would think so."

"Who?" she asked.

"You might have stood up when I came in, to begin with . . ."

"Oh, uncle, forgive me. I'm out of my mind with joy at seeing you again. But whose fault is that, uncle?"

"And just what are these three plates for?" said Mustapha with annoyance.

"These three plates?" She looked at him, a malicious smile on her lips. "Nothing. Or rather, my three days. Nothing that would interest you. Is there anything here that interests you . . . uncle?"

As if moved by a common impulse, the three men stood up.

Noumbe deliberately knocked over one of the plates. "Oh, uncle, forgive me . . ." Then she broke the other two plates. Her eyes had gone red; suddenly a pain stabbed at her heart, she bent double, and as she fell to the floor gave a loud groan which roused the whole compound.

Some women came hurrying in. "What's the matter with her?"

"Nothing . . . only her heart. Look what she's done, the silly woman. One of these days her jealousy will suffocate her. I haven't been to see her—only two days, and she cries her eyes out. Give her some ash and she'll be all right," gabbled Mustapha, and went off.

"Now these hussies have got their associations, they think they're going to run the country," said one of his men.

"Have you heard that at Bamako[3] they passed a resolution condemning polygamy?" added the other. "Heaven preserve us from having only one wife."

"They can go out to work then," pronounced Mustapha as he left the compound.

Aida and some of the women lifted Noumbe on to the bed. She was groaning. They got her to take some of her mixture of ash and water . . .

(1974)

QUESTIONS FOR DISCUSSION AND WRITING

CLOSE READING

1. How does Noumbe's attitude toward her marriage change over the course of the story? How does Ousmane illustrate these changes?
2. Describe the wary relationship between the women in "Her Three Days." Are they allies or competitors?
3. Given her fading looks, how does Noumbe plan to win her husband back to her? What do these choices say about her husband? About her?
4. How does Mustapha react to Noumbe's reception of him?

CRITICAL AND CREATIVE READING

5. What effect on Noumbe does the visit by Mustapha's second wife have? How does this visit change the way she thinks about her marriage?
6. Noumbe admits that she once cheated Mustapha's second wife out of her three days and once gloated over her favored position. Do you see Mustapha's rejection of her as justice? Is Noumbe right to view the second wife's visit as her way of "getting her own back"?
7. What do you think the relationship between Noumbe and Mustapha will be like after these three days? In challenging Mustapha, is Noumbe rejecting outright the terms of her marriage? What options does she have now?

[3]*Bamako:* The capital of Mali, a country in western Africa near Senegal. It was the site of a number of human rights and environmental summits involving multiple African nations.

CONNECTIONS TO OTHER READINGS

8. Discuss the competition between women in this story and in "Inspector Remorse." How are Noumbe and the narrator in Weldon's story guilty of perpetuating this competition?
9. Compare the attitudes about aging in this story and in Emily Dickinson's "Mine Enemy is growing old." How is aging seen as a form of retribution?

E. Annie Proulx

On the Antler

E. Annie Proulx (b. 1935) was born in Norwich, Connecticut. Her second novel, *The Shipping News,* won the National Book Award and the Pulitzer Prize and was made into a film. Since the publication of *The Shipping News*, set in the Canadian Maritimes, many of Proulx's stories have been set in the American West, including "Brokeback Mountain," a story made into an Academy Award–nominated film in 2005. "On the Antler" tells the story of a life consumed by hatred and petty vengeances. As you read, consider why Hawkheel and Stong have perpetuated their enmity for so long.

Hawkheel's face was as finely wrinkled as grass-dried linen, his thin back bent like a branch weighted with snow. He still spent most of his time in the field and on the streams, sweeter days than when he was that half-wild boy who ran panting up the muddy logging road, smashing branches to mute the receding roar of the school bus. Then he had hated books, had despised everything except the woods.

But in the insomnia of old age he read half the night, the patinated words gliding under his eyes like a river coursing over polished stones: books on wild geese, nymph patterns for brook trout, wolves fanning across the snow. He went through his catalogues, putting red stars against the few books he could buy and black crosses like tiny grave markers against the rarities he would never be able to afford—Halford's *Floating Flies and How to Dress Them*, Lanman's *Haw-Ho-Noo,* Phillips' A *Natural History of the Ducks* with color plates as fine as if the wild waterfowl had been pressed like flowers between the pages.

His trailer was on the north bank of the Feather River in the shadow of Antler Mountain.[1] These few narrow acres were all that was left of the home place. He'd sold it off little by little since Josepha had left him, until he was down to the trailer, ten spongy acres of river bottom and his social security checks.

[1]*Antler Mountain:* Although there is a Feather River in northern California, the setting of Proulx's story appears to be a northwestern Rocky Mountain state, most likely Montana, and the place names are her invention.

Yet he thought this was the best part of his life. It was as if he'd come into flat water after half a century and more of running the rapids. He was glad to put the paddle down and float the rest of the way.

He had his secret places hidden all through Chopping County and he visited them like stations of the cross; in order, in reverence and in expectation of results. In late May he followed the trout up the narrow, sun-warmed streams, his rod thrusting skillfully through the alders, crushing underfoot ferns whose broken stems released an elusive bitter scent. In October, mists came down on him as he waded through drenched goldenrod meadows, alert for grouse. And in the numb silence of November Hawkheel was a deer hunter up on the shoulder of Antler Mountain, his back against a beech while frozen threads of ice formed on the rifle's blue metal.

The deer hunt was the end and summit of his year: the irrevocable shot, the thin, ringing silence that followed, the buck down and still, the sky like clouded marble from which sifted snow finer than dust, and the sense of a completed cycle as the cooling blood ran into the dead leaves.

Bill Stong couldn't leave things alone. All through their lives there had been sparks and brushfires of hatred between Hawkheel and him, never quite quenched, but smoldering until some wind fanned up the flames.

In school Hawkheel had been The Lone Woodsman, a moody, insubordinate figure prowling the backcountry. Stong was a wiseacre with a streak of meanness. He hunted with his father and brothers and shot his first buck when he was eleven. How could he miss, thought woman-raised Hawkheel bitterly, how, when he sat in a big pine right over a deer trail and his old man whispered, "Now! Shoot now!" at the moment?

Stong's father farmed a little, ran a feed store and got a small salary to play town constable. He broke up Saturday-night dance fights, shot dogs that ran sheep and sometimes acted as the truant officer. His big, pebbled face was waiting for Hawkheel one school morning when he slid down the rocks to a trout pool.

"Plannin' to cut school again? Well, since your old man's not in a position to do it for you, I'm going to give you a lesson you'll remember." He flailed Hawkheel with a trimmed ash sapling and then drove him to school.

"You don't skip no more school, buddy, or I'll come get you again."

In the classroom Bill Stong's sliding eyes told Hawkheel he had been set up. "I'll fix him," Hawkheel told his sister, Urna, at noon. "I'll think up something. He won't know what hit him when I'm done." The game began, and the thread of rage endured like a footnote to their lives.

In late October, on the Sunday before Stong's fifteenth birthday, an event that exposed his mother's slovenly housekeeping ways took his family away.

Chopping County farmers soaked their seed corn in strychnine to kill the swaggering crows that gorged on the germinating kernels. One of the Stongs, no one knew which one, had mixed the deadly solution in a big roasting pan. The seed was sown and the unwashed pan shoved beneath the blackened iron griddles on the pantry floor where it stayed until autumn hog butchering.

The day was cold and windy, the last of summer thrown up into the sky by turbulent air. Stong's mother pulled out the pan and loaded it with a pork roast big enough to feed the Sunday gathering of family. The pork killed them all except Bill Stong, who was rolling around in Willard Iron's hayloft on a first shameful adventure. The equation of sex and death tainted his adolescent years.

As Stong grew older, he let the farm go down. He sat in the feed store year after year listening in on the party line. His sharp-tongued gossip rasped at the shells of others' lives until the quick was exposed. At the weekend dances Stong showed up alone, never dancing himself, but watching the women gallop past, their print blouses damp with sweat under the arms, their skirts sticking to their hot legs. At night he walked through town seeing which ones left the window shades up. He went uninvited to church suppers and card parties, winked out juicy tales and stained the absent with mean innuendo. Often his razor tongue stropped itself on the faults and flaws of his dead parents as though he had come fresh from a rancorous argument with them, and at other times he called them saints in a tearful voice.

Stong caught Hawkheel with petty tricks again and again. After Hawkheel started farming, once or twice a year he found the mailbox knocked over, water in the tractor's gas tank or the gate opened so the cows got onto the highway. He knew who'd done it.

Still, he kept on buying grain at the feed store until Stong told him about Josepha. Stong's eyes shone like those of a greedy barn cat who has learned to fry mice in butter.

"Hell, everybody in town knows she's doin' it but you," he whispered. He ate Hawkheel up with his eyes, sucked all the juice out of his sad condition.

It was cold in the store and the windows were coated with grain dust. Hawkheel felt the fine powder between his fingers and in his dry mouth. They stared at each other, then Stong scurried out through the chilly passageway that led to the house.

"He's got something coming now," said Hawkheel to Urna. "I could wire him up out in the woods and leave him for the dogs. I could do something real bad to him any time, but I want to see how far he goes."

Stong had sour tricks for everybody. Trade dropped away at the feed store, and there were some, like Hawkheel, who spat when they saw the black pickup heading out of town, Stong's big head turning from side to side to get his fill of the sights before the woods closed in.

For a long time Urna made excuses for Stong, saying that his parents' death had "turned" him, as though he were a bowl of milk gone sour in thundery weather. But when Stong told the game warden there was a summer doe in her cellar she got on the phone and burned Hawkheel's ear.

"Leverd, what kind of a man turns in his neighbor over some deer meat he likes to eat just as good as anybody?"

Hawkheel had an answer, but he didn't give it.

A few years after Josepha left, Hawkheel began to slide deep into the books. He was at Mosely's auction hoping the shotguns would come up early so he could get out of the crowd and take off. But it dragged on, hundreds of the old lady's doilies and quilts going one by one to the summer people. Hawkheel poked through the boxes on the back porch, away from the noise. A book called

Further Adventures of the One-Eyed Poacher sounded good and he dipped into it like a swallow picking mosquitoes off the water, keeping one ear on the auctioneer's patter. He sat on the broken porch glider and read until the auctioneer, pulling the crowd behind him like a train, came around to the back and shouted "Who'll give me five dollars for them boxes a books!"

Surrounded in his trailer by those books and the hundreds he'd added to them over the decades, Hawkheel enjoyed his solitude.

Stong, too, was more and more alone up at the store. As he got older, his trade dwindled to a few hard-pressed farmers who still bought feed from him because they always had and because Stong carried them until their milk checks came in. Listening in on the phone wasn't enough now; he interrupted conversations, shouting "Get off the line! I got a emergency."

"You ask me," said Urna to Hawkheel, "he's funny in the head. The only emergency he's got is himself. You watch, they'll find him laying on the kitchen floor some day as stiff as a January barn nail."

"When I get through with him," said Hawkheel, "he'll be stiff, all right."

Stong might have fallen to the cold kitchen linoleum with an iron ringing sound, but in his sixties his hair turned a fine platinum white and his face thinned to show good bones. It was a time when people were coming into the country, buying up the old farmhouses and fields and making the sugarhouses into guest cottages.

"Bill, you look like a character out of a Rupert Frost[2] poem," said the woman who'd bought Potter's farm and planted a thousand weedy birches on prime pasture. The new people said Stong was a character. They liked his stories, they read morals into his rambling lies and encouraged him by standing around the feed store playing farmer—buying salt blocks for the deer, sunflower seeds for the bluejays and laying mash for the pet chickens they had to give away each fall.

Stong set his tattered sails to catch this changing wind. In late life he found himself admired and popular for the first time, and he was grateful. He saw what the summer people liked, and to please them he carried armloads of canning jars, books, tools and other family goods down from the house to the store. He arranged generations of his family's possessions on the shelves beside the work gloves and udder balm. He filled the dusty window with pieces of old harness, wooden canes and chipped china.

In autumn he laid in ammunition for the summer men who came back for their week of deer hunting. The sign in his window read GUNS BLUE SEAL FEED WINE ANTIQUES, a small part of what he offered, for all his family's interests and enterprises were tangled together on the shelves as if he had drawn a rake through their lives and piled the debris in the store.

"They say," said Urna, "that he's cleaned out everything from kettles to cobwebs and put a price tag on it. You know, don't you, that he's selling all them old books his grandfather used to have. He's got them out there in the barn, higgledy-piggledy where the mice can gnaw on them."

[2]*Rupert Frost:* The woman is referring to Robert Frost.

"Has he," said Hawkheel.

"I suppose you're going up there to look at them."

"Well," said Hawkheel, "I might."

The Stong place was high on a bluff, a mile upstream from Hawkheel's trailer as the crow flew. To Hawkheel, every turn of the road was like the bite of an auger into the past. He did not remember his adult journeys up Stong's driveway, but recalled with vivid clarity sitting in the dust-colored passenger seat of their old Ford while his father drove over a sodden mat of leaves. The car window had been cranked down, and far below, the hissing river, heavy with rain, cracked boulders along its bottom. His father drove jerkily, lips moving in whispered conversation with invisible imps. Hawkheel had kept his hand on the door handle in case the old man steered for the edge and he had to jump. It was one of the last memories he had of his father.

The Stong place, he saw now, had run down. The real-estate agents would 40
get it pretty soon. The sagging clapboard house tapered away into a long ell and the barn. The store was still in the ell, but Hawkheel took the old shortcut around back, driving through the stinging nettles and just catching a glimpse through the store window of Stong's white head bobbing over a handful of papers.

The barn was filled with dim, brown light shot through like Indian silk with brilliant threads of sunlight. There was a faint smell of apples. On the other side of the wall a rooster beat his wings. Hawkheel looked around and saw, behind the grain sacks, hundreds of books, some in boxes, some stacked on shelves and windowsills. The first one he took up was a perfect copy of Thad Norris's 1865 *The American Angler's Book.* He'd seen it listed in his catalogue at home at $85. Stong wanted one dollar.

Hawkheel went at the boxes. He turned out Judge Nutting's nice little book on grouse, *The History of One Day Out of Seventeen Thousand.* A box of stained magazines was hiding a rare 1886 copy of Halford's *Floating Flies*, the slipcase deeply marked with Stong's penciled price of $1.50.

"Oh god," said Hawkheel, "I got him now."

He disguised the valuable books by mixing them with dull-jacketed works on potatoes and surveying, and carried the stack into the feed store. Stong sat at the counter, working his adding machine. Hawkheel noticed he had taken to wearing overalls, and a bandana knotted around his big neck. He looked to see if there was a straw hat on a nail.

"Good to see you, Leverd," said Stong in a creamy voice. He gossiped and 45
joked as if Hawkheel were one of the summer people, winked and said, "Don't spend your whole social security check on books, Leverd. Save a little out for a good time. You seen the new Ruger shotguns?" A mellowed and ripened Stong, improved by admiration, thought Hawkheel.

The books had belonged to Stong's grandfather, a hero of the waters whose name had once been in the Boston papers for his record trout. The stuffed and mounted trout still hung on the store wall beside the old man's enlarged photograph showing his tilted face and milky eyes behind the oval curve of glass.

"Bill, what will you take for your grandpa today?" cried the summer people who jammed the store on Saturdays, and Stong always answered, "Take what I can get," making a country virtue out of avarice.

Stong was ready to jump into his grandfather stories with a turn of the listener's eye. "The old fool was so slack-brained he got hisself killed with crow bait."

Hawkheel, coming in from the barn with book dust on him, saw that Stong still lied as easily as he breathed. The summer people stood around him like grinning dogs waiting for the warm hearts and livers of slain hares.

Stong's best customers were the autumn hunters. They reopened their sum- 50
mer camps, free now from wives and children, burned the wood they had bought in August from Bucky Pincoke and let the bottle of bourbon stand out on the kitchen table with the deck of cards.

"Roughin' it, are you?" Stong would cry jovially to Mr. Rose, splendid in his new red L.L. Bean suspenders. The hunters bought Stong's knives and ammunition and went away with rusted traps, worn horseshoes and bent pokers pulled from the bins labeled "Collector's Items." In their game pockets were bottles of Stong's cheap Spanish wine, faded orange from standing in the sun. Stong filled their ears to overflowing with his inventions.

"Yes," he would say, "that's what Antler Mountain is named for, not because there's any big bucks up there, which there is *not*"—with a half wink for Hawkheel who stood in the doorway holding rare books like hot bricks—"but because this couple named Antler, Jane and Anton Antler, lived up there years ago. Kind of simple, like some old families hereabouts get."

A sly look. Did he mean Hawkheel's father, who was carted away with wet chin and shaking hands to the state asylum believing pitchfork handles were adders?

"Yes, they had a little cabin up there. Lived off raccoons and weeds. Then old Jane had this baby, only one they ever had. Thought a lot of it, couldn't do enough for it, but it didn't survive their care and when it was only a few months old it died."

Stong, like a petulant tenor, turned away then and arranged the dimes 55
in the cash register. The hunters rubbed their soft hands along the counter and begged for the rest of the story. Hawkheel himself wondered how it would come out.

"Well, sir, they couldn't bear to lay that baby away in the ground, so they put it in a five-gallon jar of pure alcohol. My own grandfather—used to stand right here behind the counter where I'm standing now—sold 'em the jar. We used to carry them big jars. Can't get 'em any more. They set that jar with the baby on a stump in front of their cabin the way we might set out a plaster duck on the lawn." He would pause a moment for good effect, then say, *"The stump's still there."*

They asked him to draw maps on the back of paper bags and went up onto the Antler to stare at the stump as if the impression of the jar had been burned into it by holy fire. Stong, with a laugh like a broken cream separator, told Hawkheel that every stick from that cut maple was in his woodshed. For each lie he heard, Hawkheel took three extra books.

All winter long Hawkheel kept digging away at the book mine in the barn, putting good ones at the bottom of the deepest pile so no one else would find them, cautiously buying only a few each week.

"Why, you're getting to be my best customer, Leverd," said Stong, looking through the narrow, handmade Dutch pages of John Beever's *Practical Fly-fishing*, which Hawkheel guessed was worth $200 on the collector's market, but for which Stong wanted only fifty cents. Hawkheel was afraid Stong would feel the quality of paper, notice that it was a numbered copy, somehow sense its rarity and value. He tried a diversion.

"Bill! You'll be interested that last week I seen the heaviest buck I seen in many years. He was pawing through the leaves about thirty yards from My Place."

In Chopping County "My Place" meant the speaker's private deer stand. It was a county of still hunting, and good stands were passed from father to son. Hawkheel's Place on the Antler regularly gave him big deer, usually the biggest deer in Feather River. Stong's old Place in the comfortable pine was useless, discovered by weekend hunters from out of state who shot his bucks and left beer cans under the tree while he tended the store. They brought the deer to be weighed on Stong's reporting scales, bragging, not knowing they'd usurped his stand, while he smiled and nodded. Stong had not even had a small doe in five years.

"Your Place up on the Antler, Leverd?" said Stong, letting the cover of the Beever fall closed. "Wasn't that over on the south slope?"

"No, it's in that beech stand on the shoulder. Too steep for flat landers to climb so I do pretty good there. A big buck. I'd say he'd run close to one-eighty, dressed."

Stong raked the two quarters toward him and commenced a long lie about a herd of white deer that used to live in the swamp in the old days, but his eyes went back to the book in Hawkheel's hands.

The long fine fishing days began a few weeks later, and Hawkheel decided to walk the high northeast corner of the county looking for new water. In late summer he found it.

At the head of a rough mountain pass a waterfall poured into a large trout pool like champagne into a wine glass. Images of clouds and leaves lay on the slowly revolving surface. Dew, like crystal insect eggs, shone in the untrodden moss along the stream. The kingfisher screamed and clattered his wings as Hawkheel played a heavy rainbow into the shallows. In a few weeks he came to think that since the time of the St. Francis Indians,[3] only he had ever found the way there.

As August waned Hawkheel grew possessive of the pool and arranged stones and twigs when he could not come for several days, searching later for signs of their disarray from trespassing feet. Nothing was ever changed, except when a cloudburst washed his twigs into a huddle.

One afternoon the wind came up too strong to cast from below the pool, and Hawkheel took off his shoes and stockings and crept cautiously onto the steep rock slab above the waterfall. He gripped his bare white toes into the granite

[3]*St. Francis Indians:* The Abenaki Indians of Quebec migrated to a village called St. Francoise in the late seventeenth and early eighteenth centuries. They were characterized by constant violent conflict with French and English settlers and, like other indigenous North Americans, were driven westward.

fissures, climbing the rough face. The wind blew his hair up the wrong way and he felt he must look like the kingfisher.

From above the pool he could see the trout swimming smoothly in the direction of the current. The whole perspective of the place was new; it was as if he were seeing it for the first time. There was the back of the dead spruce and the kingfisher's hidden entrance revealed. There, too, swinging from an invisible length of line wound around a branch stub, was a faded red and white plastic bobber that the Indians had not left.

"Isn't anything safe any more?" shouted Hawkheel, coming across the rock 70
too fast. He went down hard and heard his knee crack. He cursed the trout, the spruce, the rock, the invader of his private peace, and made a bad trip home leaning on a forked stick.

Urna brought over hot suppers until he could get around and do for himself again. The inside of the trailer was packed with books and furniture and the cramped space made him listless. He got in the habit of cooking only every three or four days, making up big pots of venison stew or pea soup and picking at it until it was used up or went bad.

He saw in the mirror that he looked old. He glared at his reflection and asked, "Where's your medicine bottle and sweater?" He thought of his mother who sat for years in the rocker, her thick, ginger-shellacked cane hooked over the arm, and fled into his books, reading until his eyes stung and his favorites were too familiar to open. The heavy autumnal rain hammered on the trailer and stripped the leaves from the trees. Not until the day before deer season was he well enough to drive up to Stong's feed store for more books.

He went through the familiar stacks gloomily, keeping his weight off the bad leg and hoping to find something he'd overlooked among the stacks of fine-printed agricultural reports and ink-stained geographies.

He picked up a big dark album that he'd passed over a dozen times. The old-fashioned leather cover was stamped with a design of flowing feathers in gold, and tortured gothic letters spelled "Family Album." Inside he saw photographs, snapshots, ocher newspaper clippings whose paste had disintegrated, postcards, prize ribbons. The snapshots showed scores of curd-faced Stongs squinting into the sun, Stong children with fat knees holding wooden pull-along ducks, and a black and white dog Hawkheel dimly remembered.

He looked closer at one snapshot, drawn by something familiar. A heavy boy 75
stood on a slab of rock, grinning up into the sky. In his hand a fishing rod pointed at the upper branches of a spruce where a bobber was hopelessly entangled in the dark needles. A blur of moving water rushed past the boy into a black pool.

"You bastard," said Hawkheel, closing the album on the picture of Stong, Bill Stong of years ago, trespassing at Hawkheel's secret pool.

He pushed the album up under the back of his shirt so it lay against his skin. It felt the size of a Sears' catalogue and made him throw out his shoulders stiffly. He took a musty book at random—*The Boy's Companion*—and went out to the treacherous Stong.

"Haven't seen you for quite a while, Leverd. Hear you been laid up," said Stong.

"Bruised my knee." Hawkheel put the book on the counter.

"Got to expect to be laid up now and then at our age," said Stong. "I had trouble with my hip off and on since April. I got something here that'll fix you up." He took a squat, foreign bottle out from under the counter.

"Mr. Rose give me this for checking his place last winter. Apple brandy, and about as strong as anything you ever tasted. Too strong for me, Leverd. I get dizzy just smelling the cork." He poured a little into a paper cup and pushed it at Hawkheel.

The fragrance of apple wood and autumn spread out as Hawkheel tasted the Calvados. A column of fire rose in the chimney of his throat with a bitter aftertaste like old cigar smoke.

"I suppose you're all ready for opening day, Leverd. Where you going for deer this year?"

"Same place I always go—*My Place* up on the Antler."

"You been up there lately?"

"No, not since spring." Hawkheel felt the album's feathered design transferring to his back.

"Well, Leverd," said Stong in a mournful voice, "there's no deer up there now. Got some people bought land up there this summer, think the end of the world is coming so they built a cement cabin, got in a ton of dried apricots and pinto beans. They got some terrible weapons to keep the crowds away. Shot up half the trees on the Antler testing their machine guns. Surprised you didn't hear it. No deer within ten miles of the Antler now. You might want to try someplace else. They say it's good over to Slab City."

Hawkheel knew one of Stong's lies when he heard it and wondered what it meant. He wanted to get home with the album and examine the proof of Stong's trespass at the secret pool, but Stong poured from the bottle again and Hawkheel knocked it back.

"Where does your fancy friend get this stuff?" he asked, feeling electrical impulses sweep through his fingers as though they itched to play the piano.

"Frawnce," said Stong in an elegant tone. "He goes there every year to talk about books at some college." His hard eyes glittered with malice. "He's a liberian." Stong's thick forefinger opened the cover of *The Boy's Companion,* exposing a red-bordered label Hawkheel had missed; it was marked $55.

"He says I been getting skinned over my books, Leverd."

"Must of been quite a shock to you," said Hawkheel, thinking he didn't like the taste of apple brandy, didn't like librarian Rose. He left the inflated *Boy's Companion* on the counter and hobbled out to the truck, the photograph album between his shoulder blades giving him a ramrod dignity. In the rearview mirror he saw Stong at the door staring after him.

Clouds like grey waterweed under the ice choked the sky and a gusting wind banged the door against the trailer. Inside, Hawkheel worked the album out from under his shirt and laid it on the table while he built up the fire and put on some leftover pea soup to heat. "'Liberian!'" he said once and snorted. After supper he felt queasy and went to bed early thinking the pea soup might have stood too long.

In the morning Hawkheel's bowels beat with urgent tides of distress and there was a foul taste in his mouth. When he came back from the bathroom he gripped the edge of the table which bent and surged in his hands, then gave up and took to his bed. He could hear sounds like distant popcorn and thought it was knotty wood in the stove until he remembered it was the first day of deer season. "Goddammit," he cried, "I already been stuck here six weeks and now I'm doing it again."

A sound woke him in late afternoon. He was thirsty enough to drink tepid water from the spout of the teakettle. There was another shot on the Antler and he peered out the window at the shoulder of the mountain. He thought he could see specks of brightness in the dull grey smear of hardwood and brush, and he shuffled over to the gun rack to get his .30-.30, clinging to the backs of the chairs for balance. He rested the barrel on the breadbox and looked through the scope, scanning the slope for his deer stand, and at once caught the flash of orange.

He could see two of them kneeling beside the bark-colored curve of a dead deer at his Place. He could make out the bandana at the big one's neck, see a knife gleam briefly like falling water. He watched them drag the buck down toward the logging road until the light faded and their orange vests turned black under the trees.

"Made sure I couldn't go out with your goddamned poison brandy, didn't you?" said Hawkheel.

He sat by the stove with the old red Indian blanket pulled around him, feeling like he'd stared at a light bulb too long. Urna called after supper. Her metallic voice rang in his ear.

"I suppose you heard all about it."

"Only thing I heard was the shots, but I seen him through the scope from the window. What'd it weigh out at?"

"I heard two-thirty, dressed out, so live weight must of been towards three hundred. Warden said it's probably the biggest buck ever took in the county, a sixteen-pointer, too, and probably a state record. I didn't know you could see onto the Antler from your window."

"Oh, I can see good, but not good enough to see who was with him."

"He's the one bought Willard Iron's place and put a tennis court onto the garden," said Urna scornfully. "Rose. They say he was worse than Bill, jumping around and screaming for them to take pictures."

"Did they?"

"Course they did. Then they all went up to Mr. Tennis Court's to have a party. Stick your head out the door and you'll hear them on the wind."

Hawkheel did not stick his head out the door, but opened the album to look at the Stongs, their big, rocklike faces bent over wedding cakes and infants. Many of the photographs were captioned in a spiky, antique hand: "Cousin Mattie with her new skates," "Pa on the porch swing," simple statements of what was already clear as though the writer feared the images would someday dissolve into blankness, leaving the happiness of the Stongs unknown.

He glared, seeing Stong at the secret pool, the familiar sly eyes, the fatuous gaping mouth unchanged. He turned the pages to a stiff portrait of Stong's parents, the grandfather standing behind them holding what Hawkheel thought was a cat until he recognized the stuffed trout. On the funeral page the same portraits were reduced in size and joined by a flowing black ribbon that bent and curled in ornate flourishes. The obituary from the *Rutland Herald* was headlined "A Farm Tragedy."

"Too bad Bill missed that dinner," said Hawkheel.

He saw that on many pages there were empty places where photographs had been wrenched away. He found them, mutilated and torn, at the end of the album. Stong was in every photograph. In the high school graduation picture, surrounded by clouds of organdy and stiff new suits, Stong's face was inked out and black blood ran from the bottoms of his trousers. Here was another, Stong on a fat-tired white bicycle with a dozen arrows drawn piercing his body. A self-composed obituary, written in a hand like infernal corrosive lace that scorched the page, told how this miserable boy, "too bad to live" and "hated by everybody" had met his various ends. Over and over Stong had killed his photographic images. He listed every member of his family as a survivor.

Hawkheel was up and about the next morning, a little unsteady but with a 110
clear head. At first light the shots had begun on the Antler, hunters trying for a buck to match the giant that Stong had brought down. The Antler, thought Hawkheel, was as good as bulldozed.

By afternoon he felt well enough for a few chores, stacking hay bales around the trailer foundation and covering the windows over with plastic. He took two trout out of the freezer and fried them for supper. He was washing the frying pan when Urna called.

"They was on T.V. with the deer," she said. "They showed the game commissioner looking up the record in some book and saying this one beat it. I been half expecting to hear from you all day, wondering what you're going to do."

"Don't you worry," said Hawkheel. "Bill's got it comin' from me. There's a hundred things I could do."

"Well," said Urna, "he's got it coming."

It took Hawkheel forty minutes to pack the boxes and load them into the 115
pickup. The truck started hard after sitting in the cold blowing rain for two days, but by the time he got it onto the main road it ran smooth and steady, the headlights opening a sharp yellow path through the night.

At the top of Stong's drive he switched the lights off and coasted along in neutral. A half-full moon, ragged with rushing clouds, floated in the sky. Another storm breeder, thought Hawkheel.

The buck hung from a gambrel in the big maple, swaying slowly in the gusting wind. The body cavity gaped black in the moonlight. "Big," said Hawkheel, seeing the glint of light on the hooves scraping an arc in the leaves, "damn big." He got out of the truck and leaned his forehead against the cold metal for a minute.

From a box in the back of the truck he took one of his books and opened it. It was *Haw-Ho-Noo*. He leaned over a page as if he could read the faint print in the moonlight, then gripped it and tore it out. One after another he seized the books, ripped the pages and cracked their spines. He hurled them at the black, swaying deer and they fell to the bloodied ground beneath it.

"Fool with me, will you?" shouted Hawkheel, tearing soft paper with both hands, tossing books up at the moon, and his blaring sob rose over the sound of the boulders cracking in the river below.

(1983)

Questions for Discussion and Writing

Close Reading

1. Why does Hawkheel determine that his old age constitutes "the best part of his life"?
2. Hawkheel frequently threatens revenge against Stong but rarely acts on these threats. Why?
3. When Hawkheel realizes that Stong is selling books at lower than market value, he declares, "Oh god. I got him now." What does Hawkheel plan to do to "get" Stong? In what way is his plan ironic?

Critical and Creative Reading

4. Are Hawkheel and Stong more alike or different?
5. Consider the nature of Hawkheel's final actions, ripping up the books that could earn him thousands of dollars. In exacting his revenge, he is clearly hurting himself, yet there is a certain triumph in his lines "Fool with me, will you?" How might the destruction of these books be seen as an act against Stong? What do you think Stong's response will be?
6. Why does Hawkheel steal the Stong photo album? Do you think Stong meant for him to find it? If so, why? What does he learn about Stong from that album? Do the contents of the album make you more sympathetic to Stong?

Connections to Other Readings

7. In Poe's story "The Cask of Amontillado," Montressor declares that a perfect act of revenge never "overtakes the redresser." Consider "On the Antler" and one other in this chapter in which you think the revenge has overtaken the redresser. In this kind of case, was it worth it?
8. Consider the importance of setting in "On the Antler," Andre Dubus's story "Killings," and Zora Neale Hurston's story "Sweat." How important is our environment in shaping our reactions to the people around us? Might the outcomes for these characters have been different in different locations?

Andre Dubus

Killings

Andre Dubus (1936–1999) was born in Louisiana and in 1966 moved to Massachusetts, where he spent the majority of his career as a teacher and writer of stories and essays. His short stories earned him a Guggenheim fellowship and a MacArthur "Genius" grant. *Dancing after Hours,* his final collection of stories, was a finalist for the National Book Award. Dubus's life was changed forever when he was hit by a car in 1986; he lost one leg and the use of his other. His struggle to overcome the physical and spiritual pain of that loss is chronicled in his collection of essays, *Broken Vessels* (1990). The film *In the Bedroom* (2001), starring Sissy Spacek, is based on his story "Killings," a tragedy in which one act of vengeance begets another.

On the August morning when Matt Fowler buried his youngest son, Frank, who had lived for twenty-one years, eight months, and four days, Matt's older son, Steve, turned to him as the family left the grave and walked between their friends, and said: "I should kill him." He was twenty-eight, his brown hair starting to thin in front where he used to have a cowlick. He bit his lower lip, wiped his eyes, then said it again. Ruth's arm, linked with Matt's, tightened; he looked at her. Beneath her eyes there was swelling from the three days she had suffered. At the limousine Matt stopped and looked back at the grave, the casket, and the Congregationalist minister who he thought had probably had a difficult job with the eulogy though he hadn't seemed to, and the old funeral director who was saying something to the six young pallbearers. The grave was on a hill and overlooked the Merrimack,[1] which he could not see from where he stood; he looked at the opposite bank, at the apple orchard with its symmetrically planted trees going up a hill.

Next day Steve drove with his wife back to Baltimore where he managed the branch office of a bank, and Cathleen, the middle child, drove with her husband back to Syracuse. They had left the grandchildren with friends. A month after the funeral Matt played poker at Willis Trottier's because Ruth, who knew this was the second time he had been invited, told him to go, he couldn't sit home with her for the rest of her life, she was all right. After the game Willis went outside to tell everyone goodnight and, when the others had driven away, he walked with Matt to his car. Willis was a short, silver-haired man who had opened a diner after World War II, his trade then mostly very early breakfast, which he cooked, and then lunch for the men who worked at the leather and shoe factories. He now owned a large restaurant.

"He walks the Goddamn streets," Matt said.

[1]*Merrimack:* A river near the border of Massachusetts and New Hampshire.

"I know. He was in my place last night, at the bar. With a girl."

"I don't see him. I'm in the store all the time. Ruth sees him. She sees him too much. She was at Sunnyhurst today getting cigarettes and aspirin, and there he was. She can't even go out for cigarettes and aspirin. It's killing her."

"Come back in for a drink."

Matt looked at his watch. Ruth would be asleep. He walked with Willis back into the house, pausing at the steps to look at the starlit sky. It was a cool summer night; he thought vaguely of the Red Sox, did not even know if they were at home tonight; since it happened he had not been able to think about any of the small pleasures he believed he had earned, as he had earned also what was shattered now forever: the quietly harried and quietly pleasurable days of fatherhood. They went inside. Willis's wife, Martha, had gone to bed hours ago, in the rear of the large house which was rigged with burglar and fire alarms. They went downstairs to the game room: the television set suspended from the ceiling, the pool table, the poker table with beer cans, cards, chips, filled ashtrays, and the six chairs where Matt and his friends had sat, the friends picking up the old banter as though he had only been away on vacation; but he could see the affection and courtesy in their eyes. Willis went behind the bar and mixed them each a Scotch and soda; he stayed behind the bar and looked at Matt sitting on the stool.

"How often have you thought about it?" Willis said.

"Every day since he got out. I didn't think about bail. I thought I wouldn't have to worry about him for years. She sees him all the time. It makes her cry."

"He was in my place a long time last night. He'll be back."

"Maybe he won't."

"The band. He likes the band."

"What's he doing now?"

"He's tending bar up to Hampton Beach. For a friend. Ever notice even the worst bastard always has friends? He couldn't get work in town. It's just tourists and kids up to Hampton. Nobody knows him. If they do, they don't care. They drink what he mixes."

"Nobody tells me about him."

"I hate him, Matt. My boys went to school with him. He was the same then. Know what he'll do? Five at the most. Remember that woman about seven years ago? Shot her husband and dropped him off the bridge in the Merrimack with a hundred pound sack of cement and said all the way through it that nobody helped her. Know where she is now? She's in Lawrence now, a secretary. And whoever helped her, where the hell is he?"

"I've got a .38 I've had for years. I take it to the store now. I tell Ruth it's for the night deposits. I tell her things have changed: we got junkies here now too. Lots of people without jobs. She knows though."

"What does she know?"

"She knows I started carrying it after the first time she saw him in town. She knows it's in case I see him, and there's some kind of a situation—"

He stopped, looked at Willis, and finished his drink. Willis mixed him another.

"What kind of a situation?"

"Where he did something to me. Where I could get away with it."

“How does Ruth feel about that?”

“She doesn’t know.”

“You said she does, she’s got it figured out.”

He thought of her that afternoon: when she went into Sunnyhurst, Strout was waiting at the counter while the clerk bagged the things he had bought; she turned down an aisle and looked at soup cans until he left.

“Ruth would shoot him herself, if she thought she could hit him.”

“You got a permit?”

“No.”

“I do. You could get a year for that.”

“Maybe I’ll get one. Or maybe I won’t. Maybe I’ll just stop bringing it to the store.”

Richard Strout was twenty-six years old, a high school athlete, football scholarship to the University of Massachusetts where he lasted for almost two semesters before quitting in advance of the final grades that would have forced him not to return. People then said: Dickie can do the work; he just doesn’t want to. He came home and did construction work for his father but refused his father’s offer to learn the business; his two older brothers had learned it, so that Strout and Sons trucks going about town, and signs on construction sites, now slashed wounds into Matt Fowler’s life. Then Richard married a young girl and became a bartender, his salary and tips augmented and perhaps sometimes matched by his father, who also posted his bond. So his friends, his enemies (he had those: fist fights or, more often, boys and then young men who had not fought him when they thought they should have), and those who simply knew him by face and name, had a series of images of him which they recalled when they heard of the killing: the high school running back, the young drunk in bars, the oblivious hard-hatted young man eating lunch at a counter, the bartender who could perhaps be called courteous but not more than that: as he tended bar, his dark eyes and dark, wide-jawed face appeared less sullen, near blank.

One night he beat Frank. Frank was living at home and waiting for September, for graduate school in economics, and working as a lifeguard at Salisbury Beach, where he met Mary Ann Strout, in her first month of separation. She spent most days at the beach with her two sons. Before ten o’clock one night Frank came home; he had driven to the hospital first, and he walked into the living room with stitches over his right eye and both lips bright and swollen.

“I’m all right,” he said, when Matt and Ruth stood up, and Matt turned off the television, letting Ruth get to him first: the tall, muscled but slender suntanned boy. Frank tried to smile at them but couldn’t because of his lips.

“It was her husband, wasn’t it?” Ruth said.

“Ex,” Frank said. “He dropped in.”

Matt gently held Frank’s jaw and turned his face to the light, looked at the stitches, the blood under the white of the eye, the bruised flesh.

“Press charges,” Matt said.

“No.”

“What’s to stop him from doing it again? Did you hit him at all? Enough so he won’t want to next time?”

"I don't think I touched him."

"So what are you going to do?"

"Take karate," Frank said, and tried again to smile.

"That's not the problem," Ruth said.

"You know you like her," Frank said.

"I like a lot of people. What about the boys? Did they see it?"

"They were asleep."

"Did you leave her alone with him?"

"He left first. She was yelling at him. I believe she had a skillet in her hand."

"Oh for God's sake," Ruth said.

Matt had been dealing with that too: at the dinner table on evenings when Frank wasn't home, was eating with Mary Ann; or, on the other nights—and Frank was with her every night—he talked with Ruth while they watched television, or lay in bed with the windows open and he smelled the night air and imagined, with both pride and muted sorrow, Frank in Mary Ann's arms. Ruth didn't like it because Mary Ann was in the process of divorce, because she had two children, because she was four years older than Frank, and finally—she told this in bed, where she had during all of their marriage told him of her deepest feelings: of love, of passion, of fears about one of the children, of pain Matt had caused her or she had caused him—she was against it because of what she had heard: that the marriage had gone bad early, and for most of it Richard and Mary Ann had both played around.

"That can't be true," Matt said. "Strout wouldn't have stood for it."

"Maybe he loves her."

"He's too hot-tempered. He couldn't have taken that."

But Matt knew Strout had taken it, for he had heard the stories too. He wondered who had told them to Ruth; and he felt vaguely annoyed and isolated: living with her for thirty-one years and still not knowing what she talked about with her friends. On these summer nights he did not so much argue with her as try to comfort her, but finally there was no difference between the two: she had concrete objections, which he tried to overcome. And in his attempt to do this, he neglected his own objections, which were the same as hers, so that as he spoke to her he felt as disembodied as he sometimes did in the store when he helped a man choose a blouse or dress or piece of costume jewelry for his wife.

"The divorce doesn't mean anything," he said. "She was young and maybe she liked his looks and then after a while she realized she was living with a bastard. I see it as a positive thing."

"She's not divorced yet."

"It's the same thing. Massachusetts has crazy laws, that's all. Her age is no problem. What's it matter when she was born? And that other business: even if it's true, which it probably isn't, it's got nothing to do with Frank, it's in the past. And the kids are no problem. She's been married six years; she ought to have kids. Frank likes them. He plays with them. And he's not going to marry her anyway, so it's not a problem of money."

"Then what's he doing with her?"

"She probably loves him, Ruth. Girls always have. Why can't we just leave it at that?"

"He got home at six o'clock Tuesday morning."

"I didn't know you knew. I've already talked to him about it."

Which he had: since he believed almost nothing he told Ruth, he went to Frank with what he believed. The night before, he had followed Frank to the car after dinner.

"You wouldn't make much of a burglar," he said.

"How's that?"

Matt was looking up at him; Frank was six feet tall, an inch and a half taller than Matt, who had been proud when Frank at seventeen outgrew him; he had only felt uncomfortable when he had to reprimand or caution him. He touched Frank's bicep, thought of the young taut passionate body, believed he could sense the desire, and again he felt the pride and sorrow and envy too, not knowing whether he was envious of Frank or Mary Ann.

"When you came in yesterday morning, I woke up. One of these mornings your mother will. And I'm the one who'll have to talk to her. She won't interfere with you. Okay? I know it means—" But he stopped, thinking: I know it means getting up and leaving that suntanned girl and going sleepy to the car, I know—

"Okay," Frank said, and touched Matt's shoulder and got into the car.

There had been other talks, but the only long one was their first one: a night driving to Fenway Park, Matt having ordered the tickets so they could talk, and knowing when Frank said yes, he would go, that he knew the talk was coming too. It took them forty minutes to get to Boston, and they talked about Mary Ann until they joined the city traffic along the Charles River, blue in the late sun. Frank told him all the things that Matt would later pretend to believe when he told them to Ruth.

"It seems like a lot for a young guy to take on," Matt finally said.

"Sometimes it is. But she's worth it."

"Are you thinking about getting married?"

"We haven't talked about it. She can't for over a year. I've got school."

"I *do* like her," Matt said.

He did. Some evenings, when the long summer sun was still low in the sky, Frank brought her home; they came into the house smelling of suntan lotion and the sea, and Matt gave them gin and tonics and started the charcoal in the backyard, and looked at Mary Ann in the lawn chair: long and very light brown hair (Matt thinking that twenty years ago she would have dyed it blonde), and the long brown legs he loved to look at; her face was pretty; she had probably never in her adult life gone unnoticed into a public place. It was in her wide brown eyes that she looked older than Frank; after a few drinks Matt thought what he saw in her eyes was something erotic, testament to the rumors about her; but he knew it wasn't that, or all that: she had, very young, been through a sort of pain that his children, and he and Ruth, had been spared. In the moments of his recognizing that pain, he wanted to tenderly touch her hair, wanted with some gesture to give her solace and hope. And he would glance at Frank, and hope they would love each other, hope Frank would soothe that pain in her heart, take it from her eyes; and her divorce, her age, and her children did not matter at all. On the first two evenings she did not bring her boys, and then Ruth asked her to bring them next time. In bed that night Ruth said, "She hasn't brought them because she's embarrassed. She shouldn't feel embarrassed."

Richard Strout shot Frank in front of the boys. They were sitting on the living 75
room floor watching television, Frank sitting on the couch, and Mary Ann just returning from the kitchen with a tray of sandwiches. Strout came in the front door and shot Frank twice in the chest and once in the face with a 9 mm. automatic. Then he looked at the boys and Mary Ann, and went home to wait for the police.

It seemed to Matt that from the time Mary Ann called weeping to tell him until now, a Saturday night in September, sitting in the car with Willis, parked beside Strout's car, waiting for the bar to close, that he had not so much moved through his life as wandered through it, his spirit like a dazed body bumping into furniture and corners. He had always been a fearful father: when his children were young, at the start of each summer he thought of them drowning in a pond or the sea, and he was relieved when he came home in the evenings and they were there; usually that relief was his only acknowledgment of his fear, which he never spoke of, and which he controlled within his heart. As he had when they were very young and all of them in turn, Cathleen too, were drawn to the high oak in the backyard, and had to climb it. Smiling, he watched them, imagining the fall: and he was poised to catch the small body before it hit the earth. Or his legs were poised; his hands were in his pockets or his arms were folded and, for the child looking down, he appeared relaxed and confident while his heart beat with the two words he wanted to call out but did not: *Don't fall.* In winter he was less afraid: he made sure the ice would hold him before they skated, and he brought or sent them to places where they could sled without ending in the street. So he and his children had survived their childhood, and he only worried about them when he knew they were driving a long distance, and then he lost Frank in a way no father expected to lose his son, and he felt that all the fears he had borne while they were growing up, and all the grief he had been afraid of, had backed up like a huge wave and struck him on the beach and swept him out to sea. Each day he felt the same and when he was able to forget how he felt, when he was able to force himself not to feel that way, the eyes of his clerks and customers defeated him. He wished those eyes were oblivious, even cold; he felt he was withering in their tenderness. And beneath his listless wandering, every day in his soul he shot Richard Strout in the face; while Ruth, going about town on errands, kept seeing him. And at nights in bed she would hold Matt and cry, or sometimes she was silent and Matt would touch her tightening arm, her clenched fist.

As his own right fist was now, squeezing the butt of the revolver, the last of the drinkers having left the bar, talking to each other, going to their separate cars which were in the lot in front of the bar, out of Matt's vision. He heard their voices, their cars, and then the ocean again, across the street. The tide was in and sometimes it smacked the sea wall. Through the windshield he looked at the dark red side wall of the bar, and then to his left, past Willis, at Strout's car, and through its windows he could see the now-emptied parking lot, the road, the sea wall. He could smell the sea.

The front door of the bar opened and closed again and Willis looked at Matt then at the corner of the building; when Strout came around it alone Matt got out of the car, giving up the hope he had kept all night (and for the past week) that Strout would come out with friends, and Willis would simply drive away; thinking: *All right then. All right;* and he went around the front of Willis's car, and at Strout's he stopped and aimed over the hood at Strout's blue shirt ten feet away. Willis was aiming too, crouched on Matt's left, his elbow resting on the hood.

"Mr. Fowler," Strout said. He looked at each of them, and at the guns. "Mr. Trottier."

Then Matt, watching the parking lot and the road, walked quickly between the car and the building and stood behind Strout. He took one leather glove from his pocket and put it on his left hand.

"Don't talk. Unlock the front and back and get in."

Strout unlocked the front door, reached in and unlocked the back, then got in, and Matt slid into the back seat, closed the door with his gloved hand, and touched Strout's head once with the muzzle.

"It's cocked. Drive to your house."

When Strout looked over his shoulder to back the car, Matt aimed at his temple and did not look at his eyes.

"Drive slowly," he said. "Don't try to get stopped."

They drove across the empty front lot and onto the road, Willis's headlights shining into the car; then back through town, the sea wall on the left hiding the beach, though far out Matt could see the ocean; he uncocked the revolver; on the right were the places, most with their neon signs off, that did so much business in summer: the lounges and cafés and pizza houses, the street itself empty of traffic, the way he and Willis had known it would be when they decided to take Strout at the bar rather than knock on his door at two o'clock one morning and risk that one insomniac neighbor. Matt had not told Willis he was afraid he could not be alone with Strout for very long, smell his smells, feel the presence of his flesh, hear his voice, and then shoot him. They left the beach town and then were on the high bridge over the channel: to the left the smacking curling white at the breakwater and beyond that the dark sea and the full moon, and down to his right the small fishing boats bobbing at anchor in the cove. When they left the bridge, the sea was blocked by abandoned beach cottages, and Matt's left hand was sweating in the glove. Out here in the dark in the car he believed Ruth knew. Willis had come to his house at eleven and asked if he wanted a nightcap; Matt went to the bedroom for his wallet, put the gloves in one trouser pocket and the .38 in the other and went back to the living room, his hand in his pocket covering the bulge of the cool cylinder pressed against his fingers, the butt against his palm. When Ruth said goodnight she looked at his face, and he felt she could see in his eyes the gun, and the night he was going to. But he knew he couldn't trust what he saw. Willis's wife had taken her sleeping pill, which gave her eight hours—the reason, Willis had told Matt, he had the alarms installed, for nights when he was late at the restaurant—and when it was all done and Willis got home he would leave ice and a trace of Scotch and soda in two glasses in the game room and tell Martha in the morning that he had left the restaurant early and brought Matt home for a drink.

"He was making it with my wife." Strout's voice was careful, not pleading.

Matt pressed the muzzle against Strout's head, pressed it harder than he wanted to, feeling through the gun Strout's head flinching and moving forward; then he lowered the gun to his lap.

"Don't talk," he said.

Strout did not speak again. They turned west, drove past the Dairy Queen 90
closed until spring, and the two lobster restaurants that faced each other and were crowded all summer and were now also closed, onto the short bridge crossing the tidal stream, and over the engine Matt could hear through his open window the water rushing inland under the bridge; looking to his left he saw its swift moonlit current going back into the marsh which, leaving the bridge, they entered: the salt marsh stretching out on both sides, the grass tall in patches but mostly low and leaning earthward as though windblown, a large dark rock sitting as though it rested on nothing but itself, and shallow pools reflecting the bright moon.

Beyond the marsh they drove through woods, Matt thinking now of the hole he and Willis had dug last Sunday afternoon after telling their wives they were going to Fenway Park. They listened to the game on a transistor radio, but heard none of it as they dug into the soft earth on the knoll they had chosen because elms and maples sheltered it. Already some leaves had fallen. When the hole was deep enough they covered it and the piled earth with dead branches, then cleaned their shoes and pants and went to a restaurant farther up in New Hampshire where they ate sandwiches and drank beer and watched the rest of the game on television. Looking at the back of Strout's head he thought of Frank's grave; he had not been back to it; but he would go before winter, and its second burial of snow.

He thought of Frank sitting on the couch and perhaps talking to the children as they watched television, imagined him feeling young and strong, still warmed from the sun at the beach, and feeling loved, hearing Mary Ann moving about in the kitchen, hearing her walking into the living room; maybe he looked up at her and maybe she said something, looking at him over the tray of sandwiches, smiling at him, saying something the way women do when they offer food as a gift, then the front door opening and this son of a bitch coming in and Frank seeing that he meant the gun in his hand, this son of a bitch and his gun the last person and thing Frank saw on earth.

When they drove into town the streets were nearly empty: a few slow cars, a policeman walking his beat past the darkened fronts of stores. Strout and Matt both glanced at him as they drove by. They were on the main street, and all the stoplights were blinking yellow. Willis and Matt had talked about that too: the lights changed at midnight, so there would be no place Strout had to stop and where he might try to run. Strout turned down the block where he lived and Willis's headlights were no longer with Matt in the back seat. They had planned that too, had decided it was best for just the one car to go to the house, and again Matt had said nothing about his fear of being alone with Strout, especially in his house: a duplex, dark as all the houses on the street were, the street itself lit at the corner of each block. As Strout turned into the driveway Matt thought of the one insomniac neighbor, thought of some man or woman sitting alone in the dark living room, watching the all-night channel from Boston. When Strout stopped the car near the front of the house, Matt said: "Drive it to the back."

He touched Strout's head with the muzzle.

"You wouldn't have it cocked, would you? For when I put on the brakes."

Matt cocked it, and said: "It is now."

Strout waited a moment; then he eased the car forward, the engine doing little more than idling, and as they approached the garage he gently braked. Matt opened the door, then took off the glove and put it in his pocket. He stepped out and shut the door with his hip and said: "All right."

Strout looked at the gun, then got out, and Matt followed him across the grass, and as Strout unlocked the door Matt looked quickly at the row of small backyards on either side, and scattered tall trees, some evergreens, others not, and he thought of the red and yellow leaves on the trees over the hole, saw them falling soon, probably in two weeks, dropping slowly, covering. Strout stepped into the kitchen.

"Turn on the light."

Strout reached to the wall switch, and in the light Matt looked at his wide back, the dark blue shirt, the white belt, the red plaid pants.

"Where's your suitcase?"

"My suitcase?"

"Where is it."

"In the bedroom closet."

"That's where we're going then. When we get to a door you stop and turn on the light."

They crossed the kitchen, Matt glancing at the sink and stove and refrigerator: no dishes in the sink or even the dish rack beside it, no grease splashings on the stove, the refrigerator door clean and white. He did not want to look at any more but he looked quickly at all he could see: in the living room magazines and newspapers in a wicker basket, clean ashtrays, a record player, the records shelved next to it, then down the hall where, near the bedroom door, hung a color photograph of Mary Ann and the two boys sitting on a lawn—there was no house in the picture—Mary Ann smiling at the camera or Strout or whoever held the camera, smiling as she had on Matt's lawn this summer while he waited for the charcoal and they all talked and he looked at her brown legs and at Frank touching her arm, her shoulder, her hair; he moved down the hall with her smile in his mind, wondering: was that when they were both playing around and she was smiling like that at him and they were happy, even sometimes, making it worth it? He recalled her eyes, the pain in them, and he was conscious of the circles of love he was touching with the hand that held the revolver so tightly now as Strout stopped at the door at the end of the hall.

"There's no wall switch."

"Where's the light?"

"By the bed."

"Let's go."

Matt stayed a pace behind, then Strout leaned over and the room was lighted: the bed, a double one, was neatly made; the ashtray on the bedside table clean, the bureau top dustless, and no photographs; probably so the girl—who *was* she?—would not have to see Mary Ann in the bedroom she believed was theirs. But because Matt was a father and a husband, though never an ex-husband, he knew (and did not want to know) that this bedroom had never been theirs alone. Strout turned around; Matt looked at his lips, his wide jaw, and thought of Frank's doomed and fearful eyes looking up from the couch.

"Where's Mr. Trottier?"

"He's waiting. Pack clothes for warm weather."

"What's going on?"

"You're jumping bail." 115

"Mr. Fowler—"

He pointed the cocked revolver at Strout's face. The barrel trembled but not much, not as much as he had expected. Strout went to the closet and got the suitcase from the floor and opened it on the bed. As he went to the bureau, he said: "He was making it with my wife. I'd go pick up my kids and he'd be there. Sometimes he spent the night. My boys told me."

He did not look at Matt as he spoke. He opened the top drawer and Matt stepped closer so he could see Strout's hands: underwear and socks, the socks rolled, the underwear folded and stacked. He took them back to the bed, arranged them neatly in the suitcase, then from the closet he was taking shirts and trousers and a jacket; he laid them on the bed and Matt followed him to the bathroom and watched from the door while he packed his shaving kit; watched in the bedroom as he folded and packed those things a person accumulated and that became part of him so that at times in the store Matt felt he was selling more than clothes.

"I wanted to try to get together with her again." He was bent over the suitcase. "I couldn't even talk to her. He was always with her. I'm going to jail for it; if I ever get out I'll be an old man. Isn't that enough?"

"You're not going to jail." 120

Strout closed the suitcase and faced Matt, looking at the gun. Matt went to his rear, so Strout was between him and the lighted hall; then using his handkerchief he turned off the lamp and said: "Let's go."

They went down the hall, Matt looking again at the photograph, and through the living room and kitchen, Matt turning off the lights and talking, frightened that he was talking, that he was telling this lie he had not planned: "It's the trial. We can't go through that, my wife and me. So you're leaving. We've got you a ticket, and a job. A friend of Mr. Trottier's. Out west. My wife keeps seeing you. We can't have that anymore."

Matt turned out the kitchen light and put the handkerchief in his pocket, and they went down the two brick steps and across the lawn. Strout put the suitcase on the floor of the back seat, then got into the front seat and Matt got in the back and put on his glove and shut the door.

"They'll catch me. They'll check passenger lists."

"We didn't use your name." 125

"They'll figure that out too. You think I wouldn't have done it myself if it was that easy?"

He backed into the street, Matt looking down the gun barrel but not at the profiled face beyond it.

"You were alone," Matt said. "We've got it worked out."

"There's no planes this time of night, Mr. Fowler."

"Go back through town. Then north on 125." 130

They came to the corner and turned, and now Willis's headlights were in the car with Matt.

"Why north, Mr. Fowler?"

"Somebody's going to keep you for a while. They'll take you to the airport." He uncocked the hammer and lowered the revolver to his lap and said wearily: "No more talking."

As they drove back through town, Matt's body sagged, going limp with his spirit and its new and false bond with Strout, the hope his lie had given Strout. He had grown up in this town whose streets had become places of apprehension and pain for Ruth as she drove and walked, doing what she had to do; and for him too, if only in his mind as he worked and chatted six days a week in his store; he wondered now if his lie would have worked, if sending Strout away would have been enough; but then he knew that just thinking of Strout in Montana or whatever place lay at the end of the lie he had told, thinking of him walking the streets there, loving a girl there (who *was* she?) would be enough to slowly rot the rest of his days. And Ruth's. Again he was certain that she knew, that she was waiting for him.

They were in New Hampshire now, on the narrow highway, passing the 135 shopping center at the state line, and then houses and small stores and sandwich shops. There were few cars on the road. After ten minutes he raised his trembling hand, touched Strout's neck with the gun, and said: "Turn in up here. At the dirt road."

Strout flicked on the indicator and slowed.

"Mr. Fowler?"

"They're waiting here."

Strout turned very slowly, easing his neck away from the gun. In the moonlight the road was light brown, lighter and yellowed where the headlights shone; weeds and a few trees grew on either side of it, and ahead of them were the woods.

"There's nothing back here, Mr; Fowler." 140

"It's for your car. You don't think we'd leave it at the airport, do you?"

He watched Strout's large, big-knuckled hands tighten on the wheel, saw Frank's face that night: not the stitches and bruised eye and swollen lips, but his own hand gently touching Frank's jaw, turning his wounds to the light. They rounded a bend in the road and were out of sight of the highway: tall trees all around them now, hiding the moon. When they reached the abandoned gravel pit on the left, the bare flat earth and steep pale embankment behind it, and the black crowns of trees at its top, Matt said: "Stop here."

Strout stopped but did not turn off the engine. Matt pressed the gun hard against his neck, and he straightened in the seat and looked in the rearview mirror, Matt's eyes meeting his in the glass for an instant before looking at the hair at the end of the gun barrel.

"Turn it off."

Strout did, then held the wheel with two hands, and looked in the mirror. 145

"I'll do twenty years, Mr. Fowler; at least. I'll be forty-six years old."

"That's nine years younger than I am," Matt said, and got out and took off the glove and kicked the door shut. He aimed at Strout's ear and pulled back the hammer. Willis's headlights were off and Matt heard him walking on the soft thin layer of dust, the hard earth beneath it. Strout opened the door, sat for a moment in the interior light, then stepped out onto the road. Now his face was pleading. Matt did not look at his eyes, but he could see it in the lips.

"Just get the suitcase. They're right up the road."

Willis was beside him now, to his left. Strout looked at both guns. Then he opened the back door, leaned in, and with a jerk brought the suitcase out. He was turning to face them when Matt said: "Just walk up the road. Just ahead."

Strout turned to walk, the suitcase in his right hand, and Matt and Willis followed; as Strout cleared the front of his car he dropped the suitcase and, ducking, took one step that was the beginning of a sprint to his right. The gun kicked in Matt's hand, and the explosion of the shot surrounded him, isolated him in a nimbus of sound that cut him off from all his time, all his history, isolated him standing absolutely still on the dirt road with the gun in his hand, looking down at Richard Strout squirming on his belly, kicking one leg behind him, pushing himself forward, toward the woods. Then Matt went to him and shot him once in the back of the head.

Driving south to Boston, wearing both gloves now, staying in the middle lane and looking often in the rearview mirror at Willis's headlights, he relived the suitcase dropping, the quick dip and turn of Strout's back, and the kick of the gun, the sound of the shot. When he walked to Strout, he still existed within the first shot, still trembled and breathed with it. The second shot and the burial seemed to be happening to someone else, someone he was watching. He and Willis each held an arm and pulled Strout face-down off the road and into the woods, his bouncing sliding belt white under the trees where it was so dark that when they stopped at the top of the knoll, panting and sweating, Matt could not see where Strout's blue shirt ended and the earth began. They pulled off the branches then dragged Strout to the edge of the hole and went behind him and lifted his legs and pushed him in. They stood still for a moment. The woods were quiet save for their breathing, and Matt remembered hearing the movements of birds and small animals after the first shot. Or maybe he had not heard them. Willis went down to the road. Matt could see him clearly out on the tan dirt, could see the glint of Strout's car and, beyond the road, the gravel pit. Willis came back up the knoll with the suitcase. He dropped it in the hole and took off his gloves and they went down to his car for the spades. They worked quietly. Sometimes they paused to listen to the woods. When they were finished Willis turned on his flashlight and they covered the earth with leaves and branches and then went down to the spot in front of the car, and while Matt held the light Willis crouched and sprinkled dust on the blood, backing up till he reached the grass and leaves, then he used leaves until they had worked up to the grave again. They did not stop. They walked around the grave and through the woods, using the light on the ground, looking up through the trees to where they ended at the lake. Neither of them spoke above the sounds of their heavy and clumsy strides through low brush and over fallen branches. Then they reached it: wide and dark, lapping softly at the bank, pine needles smooth under Matt's feet, moonlight on the lake, a small island near its middle, with black, tall evergreens. He took out the gun and threw for the island: taking two steps back on the pine needles, striding with the throw and going to one knee as he followed through, looking up to see the dark shapeless object arcing downward, splashing.

They left Strout's car in Boston, in front of an apartment building on Commonwealth Avenue. When they got back to town Willis drove slowly over the bridge and Matt threw the keys into the Merrimack. The sky was turning light. Willis let him out a block from his house, and walking home he listened for sounds from the houses he passed. They were quiet. A light was on in his living room. He turned it off and undressed in there, and went softly toward the bedroom; in the hall he smelled the smoke, and he stood in the bedroom doorway and looked at the orange of her cigarette in the dark. The curtains were closed. He went to the closet and put his shoes on the floor and felt for a hanger.

"Did you do it?" she said.

He went down the hall to the bathroom and in the dark he washed his hands and face. Then he went to her, lay on his back, and pulled the sheet up to his throat.

"Are you all right?" she said.

"I think so."

Now she touched him, lying on her side, her hand on his belly, his thigh.

"Tell me," she said.

He started from the beginning, in the parking lot at the bar; but soon with his eyes closed and Ruth petting him, he spoke of Strout's house: the order, the woman presence, the picture on the wall.

"The way she was smiling," he said.

"What about it?"

"I don't know. Did you ever see Strout's girl? When you saw him in town?"

"No."

"I wonder who she was."

Then he thought: *not was: is. Sleeping now she is his girl.* He opened his eyes, then closed them again. There was more light beyond the curtains. With Ruth now he left Strout's house and told again his lie to Strout, gave him again that hope that Strout must have for a while believed, else he would have to believe only the gun pointed at him for the last two hours of his life. And with Ruth he saw again the dropping suitcase, the darting move to the right: and he told of the first shot, feeling her hand on him but his heart isolated still, beating on the road still in that explosion like thunder. He told her the rest, but the words had no images for him, he did not see himself doing what the words said he had done; he only saw himself on that road.

"We can't tell the other kids," she said. "It'll hurt them, thinking he got away. But we mustn't."

"No."

She was holding him, wanting him, and he wished he could make love with her but he could not. He saw Frank and Mary Ann making love in her bed, their eyes closed, their bodies brown and smelling of the sea; the other girl was faceless, bodiless, but he felt her sleeping now; and he saw Frank and Strout, their faces alive; he saw red and yellow leaves falling to the earth, then snow; falling and freezing and falling; and holding Ruth, his cheek touching her breast, he shuddered with a sob that he kept silent in his heart.

(1979)

QUESTIONS FOR DISCUSSION AND WRITING

CLOSE READING

1. What is Matt's *specific* motive for revenge against Richard Strout? For whose sake is he getting revenge?
2. Describe Matt's relationship with his son Frank. Why does he seem so fascinated with Frank and Mary Ann's sex life?
3. What role does Ruth play as the story unfolds? Do you see her as a primarily strong or weak character? What kind of relationship do she and Matt have?

CRITICAL AND CREATIVE READING

4. Do you think the murder of Richard Strout is an act of vengeance or of justice? Would Matt be less justified if he believed Strout faced a long prison sentence? Do you fault Matt for his actions? If you were serving on a jury, would you vote to send Matt to prison for what he did?
5. What do Ruth's and Matt's concerns about Mary Ann suggest about their values? What do they like about Mary Ann? Why are they wary of her?
6. How does Dubus build suspense during the night of Strout's killing? At what point do you know what Matt is planning?
7. The title of the story is "Killings"—plural. Both of the killings in the story are acts of vengeance. Both are premeditated. Both are justified in the minds of the murderers. How does the point of view affect our reading of this story? Would we feel differently if the story followed Strout's point of view rather than Matt's?

CONNECTIONS TO OTHER READINGS

8. Both Strout and Medea seek revenge against unfaithful spouses. Compare and contrast the two characters in terms of motives, methods of revenge, and their ultimate fates. Is one more or less "guilty" than the other?
9. Has Matt committed the perfect revenge, according to the definition put forth by Montressor in Poe's "The Cask of Amontillado"?

Fay Weldon

Inspector Remorse

Fay Weldon (b. 1936) was born "Franklin Birkenshaw," a masculine name she thinks helped her get accepted to study economics at the University of Scotland. She spent her childhood in New Zealand and moved with her mother to England,where she went on to work successfully as a copywriter for an advertising agency. In 1967 she published her first novel, *The Fat Woman's Joke,* and has published a large number of novels, short stories, and works of nonfiction since then. Her most famous novel is a tale of fantasy and revenge, *The Life and Loves of a She-devil* (1984). As you read "Inspector Remorse," consider both revenge and forgiveness. Which of the two seems uppermost in the narrator's mind?

Sociopaths don't feel remorse. That's how the condition is diagnosed. This does not mean that everyone who fails to feel remorse is a sociopath. In the world of logic that's an error known as the fallacy of the undistributed middle. You could, for example, not feel remorseful not because you were a sociopath but because you had nothing to be remorseful about. You were a saint.

Here I sit, a rather elegant woman of around forty in a neat grey suit in a large empty Victorian church on Easter Friday, between services. I ponder these things, inspecting my soul for remorse, in the hope of finding just a trace of it, but failing. I conclude I am either very good or very bad. One has to be rigorous in this kind of moral inspection, worry away at clues like a detective to make sure one hasn't missed a thing. Saint, sinner or sociopath. Which? A case for Inspector Remorse! Is that a tingling of proper emotion I detect inside? A flicker of anxiety and shame mixed—which I suppose is what remorse is? An internalised wail—'I shouldn't have done that: oh, I'm sorry, I'm sorry: don't do the same to me. Forgive me, I knew not what I did.' No.

Easter Friday, Yom Kippur, Ramadan[1]—all religions have a time for remorse, a ritual for atonement. One belief structure, they told me at school, was much like any other. So I have ended up with a cosy mish-mash of beliefs, a Munchkin religion; God is Good, Death is Not Final, Reincarnation offers Justice. Take the Ten Commandments minus the one about adultery, mix up with Wheel of Life and Tantric Yoga, the Quest for the Inner Child, the Brilliance of the Ineffable.[2] Don't we all?

[1]*Easter Friday, Yom Kippur, Ramadan:* Days of religious fasting in Christianity, Judaism, and Islam, respectively.

[2]*Wheel of Life . . . Brilliance of the Ineffable:* The narrator is selecting tenets of various religions and belief systems, such as the Judeo-Christian, Buddhist, and Hindu.

Everyone I meet believes they're good, does the best he or she can in the circumstances. But if everyone's good why is the world in such a state? And why should I not suffer from the same common delusion, that of my own goodness?

How this place echoes. Just a footstep is enough to make me jump. 5

Bleep, bleep, bleep, there goes my mobile phone. In a church of all places. They ought to be banned. "Hello, hello, oh it's you, Ian. No, I can't speak now. I'm in a church . . . Just sitting, contemplating my navel, considering my sins, if any. It suits me, it suits the day . . . . I won't be here long, the cold is getting into my bones. I must go. Goodbye." Click. Off. Bleep. Beat the breast and smear the ashes.

It would be sensible to leave. I'm not sure why I stay. The cold is easing through the soles of my shoes. Little lace-up pointy boots, built for fashion not for cold stone floors. Is that the sin of vanity? Do I feel remorse for this? No, I have pretty feet, why shouldn't I show them off? Besides, I suffer for it. I pay for my pleasure. Cold feet, fear of being alive.

The cold heart I sometimes show to Ian, who loves me more than I love him, so I have power over him. I abuse it, I make him suffer. He flushes, he creeps, he is eaten up with sexual jealousy. Do I feel remorse for this? No. Ian should know better than to love me: it's his doing, not mine. A wimp, a wimp, Ian is a wimp. He is also a banker, and older than me, and rich.

Prelates flutter by in white gowns; others stride in thick-soled boots. Clump, clump. Easter Friday is a busy day in the Anglican church, just bleak and cold as my heart. An unflowered place, till Sunday.

Bleep, bleep, Ian again. Something he forgot to say. Switch it off. I want my 10
thoughts, not his. Sociopath or saint. Inspector Remorse, still not a sign of you. Lost in a flurry of priests.

My breath begins to show up as mist. I can't believe this church is so cold. Perhaps the chill comes from me, emanates from me. I am aware of sin.

Lucy Brown died because of me. No, that's absurd. Lucy died because she had cold feet: she was afraid to go on living. If you're afraid of life you deserve to die.

Exmoor is a cold, wild, cruel place; all heather and bog and grass that snaps and crackles beneath the feet in winter. It's always winter. Forget the tourists, forget the sweet Exmoor ponies: the devil rides them bareback on stormy nights: listen hard: that's not the howl of the wind: that's the devil shrieking his delight. I have a sweet face, Ian says, lovely lips. If only my breath didn't fog the air so.

I'd never have chosen to live on the edge of Exmoor. But then I'm an art critic not a creative person: what do I know. Hard weather and stone floors, enough to depress anyone. Lucy Brown was certainly depressed: she was married to Terry

Brown. They were artists: he was successful, she was not. Terry won the Rome prize—she won nothing. When I met them I was only twenty-five but already powerful; I had a weekly column in *The Times*, in which I could make or break an up-and-coming painter. I enjoyed the power. I feel no remorse for that. What is power but something to use? If people deserved it I praised them: if they were crap I said so. I still do. And I am right. When and if I turn up at a show the room falls silent. I would rather be feared than loved. It's what I am, how I am.

I have long, long legs, I know how to sit, how to attract, how to repel: I always have. I first met them at Terry's private view. Lucy was a quiet, proud, plain thing: fifteen years older than me, edgy, awkward, hating the publicity, loathing the fuss, wanting to get home to the cottage on Exmoor and the snails which came up the drainpipe into the sink. They had a little daughter, Hilda. Exmoor, Terry, Lucy and Hilda. It sounded so cosy.

"Terry's good enough," I said to Lucy, "but I've seen your work too. You're in the first division. He's just top of the second where all the glitter is." Her eyes lit up. She begged me and Ian to go down and visit. She had paintings to show me: she wanted my advice. That is to say she wanted some recognition and her name in the papers. She was intolerably vain. I asked Ian; he wanted to go; he's a sucker for creative folk. He's like some soft puppy. He likes to please: he's for ever wriggling. I sit still and calm, look beautiful and seldom smile, so people feel the need to placate me. I get the best seat in restaurants, get upgraded at airports; smokers stub out their fags at my approach.

Terry and Lucy's cottage was the usual kind of artist's home. Messy, beautiful, unkempt, crowded, nice pieces of furniture in need of polish. It began to snow. We couldn't leave, we had to stay overnight. That pleased them. When the power lines came down there were candles to hand: they built a wood fire in the grate. They were excited by discomfort: I was horrified. I told Lucy I wouldn't look at her paintings this time around. It was too cold to concentrate. I'd come down again in the summer, I said, take pics and do a proper article when the fuss over Terry was over.

Do I feel remorse for this random spite? No. I was annoyed by her sullen patience. How could she possibly merit the love Terry showed her? Terry was charismatic, tall, talented, good-looking, he could have had anyone, even me. But all he seemed to want was Lucy. And all I had was Ian, a dolt. I have to have someone rich: I have a high standard of living. Art critics don't earn much, apart from a lot of abuse. How can I be remorseful for something which is just a fact? That night, I sat on the floor by the fire in a long diaphanous dress, with bare feet, and my hair flowing and played the flute and sang sweet songs. Men are such suckers they usually fall for it. But Terry just left the room in the middle of my song because he said he heard little Hilda crying.

The next day Lucy really annoyed me. She told me to go and fetch wood for the fire. She already had Ian peeling potatoes. I am not a servant to be ordered about.

I lost my temper with her and heard the Cockney[3] whine of my beginnings in my voice, and hated to hear it.

"You're just jealous," she said, and laughed, "because you're a critic and I'm a painter, and Ian is dull and Terry takes no notice of you. Calm down."

And I managed to smile at her and apologise, but it was unforgivable that she knew so much about me. And later I went upstairs and found Terry sitting by the sleeping Hilda's bed, and brushed my breast past his cheek, which usually works, and it did. He looked at me thereafter in a different way. I don't think he liked me, but what does that matter? It is interesting to see lust and distaste battle it out in a man's eyes, and watch the wife watching too, to see which one wins. Lust won. It usually does. Ian noticed nothing at all. He is not sensitive to atmosphere.

The snow turned to sleet, sleet turned to rain, the power came back on: Ian and I dug the car out of mud and went home to our apartment, thankfully and carefully minimalist.

A couple of days later Terry called me. I was expecting it. He was coming to town: could he see me. It's not up to me to feel remorse for a thing like that. He called me, I didn't call him. He acted, I responded. Besides, the thing was greater than both of us. I told him so and he believed me. It's easy to relieve a man of his guilt. To me that's doing a kindness, not compounding a sin. Who wants to go to heaven anyway: such a boring place: people behaving properly. How white and thick my breath is upon the air.

Bleep, bleep, bleep. Ian, is that you? Yes, just about stopped communing, I'm coming home in a minute. Pour me a drink; make sure the gin is icy cold. I've inspected my life and find no cause for remorse.

I want to celebrate my sainthood now, not wait till Easter Sunday.

Terry joined me in the minimalist flat. Ian was away in Brussels. Sex has a logic of its own. No sociopath feels remorse, but not all who feel no remorse are sociopaths. That figures. Terry asked when he would see me again and I said never, and hid his watch so he forgot to put it back on, and when he had gone I rang Lucy, and said, Oh, Lucy, Terry was here and left his watch, and there was a silence at the end of the phone, and then she put the receiver down. It annoys me the way men expect you to keep their secrets. Not to tell. Why shouldn't I tell? Serve Ian right for being away, even if he did find out, which he didn't.

Later that night, the phone rang and it was Terry saying bitch, bitch, bitch. I wish I could feel remorse, I really do. Perhaps it's too far in the past: fifteen years ago. By the time Terry got home, I heard later, Lucy was in a coma. Whisky and sleeping pills: a note. Terry got her to hospital and they stomach-pumped her, but it was too late. What she did was unforgivable. She did it to spite Terry, because she was jealous of his success, and to harm Hilda because Terry loved

[3]*Cockney:* A British accent suggesting that the speaker is from the working class.

her, and to get back the attention to herself, to get her paintings posthumously recognised, which was what happened, though not through any doing of mine. As for Terry, he never painted anything in particular after that, and he wasn't up to much in the first place. Or that's what I tell myself.

Sergeant Doubt, is that you? Yes. And here comes your friend at last, Inspector Remorse, clump, clump, clumping down the aisle. I see you.

Bleep, bleep. Ian is that you? I have a confession to make. Remember Lucy Brown the one who killed herself? The painter? It was because of me, because of what I did, what I made Terry do. Can you forgive me that, or is it going to be the last straw? What, can't you hear me? Too distorted? The batteries must be going. Forget it, Ian, nothing important. I'm on my way home. People are coming in for the next service. I don't know what I'm doing here anyway. 'Bye.

Gone again, Inspector Remorse, and just as well.

It's warming up in here. I can't see my breath any more. Time to go. Not a saint, not a sinner, just an ordinary sociopath.

No sociopath feels remorse, but not all those who fail to feel remorse are sociopaths. Let us at least get the logic right.

(1998)

Questions for Discussion and Writing

Close Reading

1. As the narrator sits in church contemplating her life, she says, "It would be sensible to leave. I'm not sure why I stay." Does the text suggest a reason why she remains in the church?
2. The narrator frequently makes reference to her cold feet and foggy breath, ultimately attributing both to the chill of the church. What is the significance of this recurrent imagery? Why else might the narrator be feeling cold?
3. Why does the narrator resent Lucy Brown so much? Are her resentments justified?

Critical and Creative Reading

4. Since the story is told in first-person voice, we see all the characters through the eyes of the narrator. How reliable is her information about them? Do you feel you have a sense of the "real" Ian, Lucy, and Terry, or is it difficult to see through the narrator's filter?
5. The story reveals several little acts of revenge, all secondary, perhaps, to the narrator's seduction of Terry. How many things does the narrator have to feel remorseful about? Is she right to place some of the blame on others?

6. How remorseful do you think the narrator is? Look beyond her actual words to her actions and justifications. Is she as confident as she seems? Do you have any pity for her?

CONNECTIONS TO OTHER READINGS

7. Compare the first-person narrators in this story and in "The Cask of Amontillado." Both characters want to both confess to and justify their actions. Look at the language and attitudes of both characters. How are they similar?
8. What role does religion play in this story and in Martin Luther King's essay "Letter from Birmingham Jail"? What kind of relationship do the narrator of this story and the author in King's essay have with religion and with God?

Poetry

Andrew Marvell

The Mower's Song

Andrew Marvell (1621–1678) grew up in Yorkshire, England, and studied at Cambridge University. He worked as a tutor and as a member of Parliament and was appointed by Cromwell as Latin Secretary to the Council of State. He published a few poems during his lifetime. After his death, his housekeeper published his *Miscellaneous Poems* (1681), along with the claim that she had been his wife (a claim that has never been proved). Whether or not she was telling the truth, we can thank her for giving to posterity "To His Coy Mistress" (see Chapter 13 for the poem and a portrait of the author). "The Mower's Song" is one of a series of "Mower" poems. Here, the mower threatens to displace his vengeance against his lover onto the meadows that he tends.

My mind was once the true survey[1]
Of all these meadows fresh and gay,
And in the greenness of the grass
Did see its hopes as in a glass;
When Juliana came, and she
What I do to the grass, does to my thoughts and me.

But these, while I with sorrow pine,
Grew more luxuriant still and fine,
That not one blade of grass you spied,
But had a flower on either side;
When Juliana came, and she
What I do to the grass, does to my thoughts and me.

[1]*survey:* A report on or a map of what has been surveyed.

Unthankful meadows, could you so
A fellowship so true forgo,
And in your gaudy May-games[2] meet,
While I lay trodden under feet?
When Juliana came, and she
What I do to the grass, does to my thoughts and me.

But what you in compassion ought,
Shall now by my revenge be wrought:
And flow'rs, and grass, and I and all,
Will in one common ruin fall.
For Juliana comes, and she
What I do to the grass, does to my thoughts and me.

And thus, ye meadows, which have been
Companions of my thoughts more green,
Shall now the heraldry become
With which I will adorn my tomb;
For Juliana comes, and she
What I do to the grass, does to my thoughts and me.

(1681)

Questions for Discussion and Writing

Close Reading

1. What is the relationship between the meadow and the speaker's mind?
2. Why does the speaker resent that the meadow grew "more luxuriant"?
3. What are the mower's plans for the meadow?
4. How does the speaker personify the meadows? Why might he do so?

Critical and Creative Reading

5. Why doesn't the speaker threaten revenge against Juliana? What does his transference of his vengeance suggest about him?
6. How would you characterize the poem's tone?
7. Is the speaker an ironic figure? How seriously are we supposed to take his threats?

Connections to Other Readings

8. Compare the effectiveness of the speaker's revenge in this poem and in Robert Herrick's "The Bubble: A Song."
9. The speaker takes out his frustrated love on something nonhuman. How common is this tendency? Can you think of another reading from this chapter in which revenge is similarly indirect?

[2]*May-games:* Spring fertility rituals involving the gathering of flowers.

Robert Herrick

The Bubble: A Song

Robert Herrick (1591–1674) was born in London and became an ordained Episcopal minister, chaplain to a country parish in Devonshire. While living in the country, he longed for the sophistication of his literary circle in London. A devoted royalist, he was expelled from his parish under Cromwell's government but returned to Devonshire in 1660 with the restoration of Charles II. His major collection of poems, *Hesperides*, was published in 1648 along with a companion volume, *Noble Numbers*, which took on sacred subjects. Herrick is generally remembered as a Cavalier poet who wrote of drink and young maidens (see "To the Virgins, to Make Much of Time" in Chapter 9). In "The Bubble: A Song," the speaker imagines all his negative thoughts as a bubble floating toward his enemy.

To my revenge, and to her desperate fears,
Fly, thou made bubble of my sighs and tears!
In the wild air, when thou hast roll'd about,
And, like a blasting planet, found her out;
Stoop, mount, pass by to take her eye—then glare
Like to a dreadful comet in the air:
Next, when thou dost perceive her fixed sight
For thy revenge to be most opposite,
Then, like a globe, or ball of wild-fire, fly,
And break thyself in shivers on her eye!

(1648)

QUESTIONS FOR DISCUSSION AND WRITING

CLOSE READING

1. Unlike Emily Dickinson's poem, in which the speaker passively gets revenge by waiting for her enemy to grow old (p. 925), "The Bubble" is full of action. Note the poem's active images. How do the poet's words create the impression of vigorous activity? Why is this impression ironic?
2. "The Bubble" contains a number of metaphors and similes for revenge, in addition to its title image. As revenge is compared to a bubble, a blasting planet, a dreadful comet, a globe, and a ball of wild-fire, how does its meaning shift? What exactly does the speaker want his revenge to be?

3. The bubble of revenge is composed of the speaker's "sighs and tears." What do you think is the speaker's motive for revenge?

CRITICAL AND CREATIVE READING

4. Despite the active words and violent images, the speaker is essentially powerless. Why is his planned revenge so ineffective (even in his imagination)?
5. There is a saying that "revenge is a dish best served cold." We see in Herrick's poem a number of other metaphors for revenge. Write a poem in which you come up with your own metaphor for revenge. If you could compare revenge to something in everyday life, what would it be?

CONNECTIONS TO OTHER READINGS

6. Compare the style and content of this poem to Langston Hughes's "Harlem," another work in which the author uses several metaphors to convey an idea. How do the tone and subject of the poems differ?
7. Compare the attitude of the speakers in this poem and in Dickinson's "Mine Enemy is growing old."

Samuel Taylor Coleridge

The Rime of the Ancient Mariner

Samuel Taylor Coleridge (1772–1834) was born in London and attended a grammar school for the children of the poor. Although he showed early promise, he never finished his university education at Cambridge. As a young man, he and his friend Robert Southey decided to form a utopian community in America. The idea never got off the ground and led to an unhappy marriage that was contracted in the early stages of the plan. Coleridge then turned to writing poetry and, in collaboration with William Wordsworth, published the influential *Lyrical Ballads* (1798). Despite economic and personal setbacks, including a battle against drug addiction, Coleridge wrote poetry and literary criticism throughout his life. His "Rime of the Ancient Mariner" tells the story of an old mariner who stops a wedding guest amidst the celebrations. Plagued by guilt for shooting an albatross, he is compelled to wander the countryside telling his story. As you read, consider the nature of the mariner's "sin."

Argument

How a Ship having passed the Line was driven by storms to the cold Country towards the South Pole; and how from thence she made her course to the tropical Latitude of the Great Pacific Ocean; and of the strange things that befell; and in what manner the Ancient Mariner came back to his own Country.

Epigraph (1817)

(From Thomas Burnet's Archaeologiae Philosophicae *of 1692, in Derek Roper's translation.)*

I can readily believe that in the sum of existing things there are more invisible beings than visible, [and that there are more angels in heaven than there are fishes in the sea.*] 1. But who will explain this great family to us—their ranks, their relationships, their differences, and their respective duties? [What do they do, and where do they live?†] 2. Man's intelligence has always sought knowledge of these matters, but has never attained it. Meanwhile, I do not deny that it pleases me sometimes to contemplate in my mind, as in a picture, the idea of a greater and better world; lest the mind, grown used to dealing with the small matters of everyday life, should dwindle and be wholly submerged in petty thoughts. Nevertheless we should be vigilant of truth and keep a sense of proportion, so that we may discriminate between things certain and things uncertain, daylight and darkness.

PART I

It is an ancient Mariner,
　And he stoppeth one of three.
"By thy long grey beard and glittering eye,
　Now wherefore stopp'st thou me?

The Bridegroom's doors are opened wide
　And I am next of kin;
The guests are met, the feast is set:—
　May'st hear the merry din."

But still he holds the Wedding-Guest—
　"There was a ship," quoth he—
"Nay, if thou'st got a laughsome tale,
　Mariner! come with me."

He holds him with his skinny hand,
　Quoth he, "there was a Ship"—
"Now get thee hence, thou grey-beard loon!
　Or my Staff shall make thee skip."

He holds him with his glittering eye—
　The Wedding-Guest stood still,
And listens like a three years' child:
　The Mariner hath his will.

*Omitted by Coleridge.

†Added by Coleridge.

The Wedding-Guest sat on a stone:
He cannot choose but hear;
And thus spake on that ancient man,
The bright-eyed Mariner.

"The ship was cheered, the harbour cleared,
Merrily did we drop
Below the kirk,[1] below the hill,
Below the lighthouse top.

The Sun came up upon the left,
Out of the sea came he!
And he shone bright, and on the right
Went down into the sea.

Higher and higher every day,
Till over the mast at noon"—
The Wedding-Guest here beat his breast,
For he heard the loud bassoon.

The bride hath paced into the hall,
Red as a rose is she;
Nodding their heads before her goes
The merry minstrelsy.

The Wedding-Guest he beat his breast,
Yet he cannot choose but hear;
And thus spake on that ancient man,
The bright-eyed Mariner.

"Listen, Stranger! Storm and Wind,
A Wind and Tempest strong!
For days and weeks it play'd us freaks—
Like chaff[2] we drove along.

With sloping masts and dipping prow,
As who pursued with yell and blow
Still treads the shadow of his foe,
And forward bends his head,
The ship drove fast, loud roared the blast,
And southward aye we fled.

[1]*kirk:* A church.

[2]*chaff:* The light scales that hold grains in place and that are removed during threshing.

And now there came both mist and snow,
And it grew wondrous cold:
And ice, mast-high, came floating by
As green as emerald.

And through the drifts the snowy clifts
Did send a dismal sheen:
Nor shapes of men nor beasts we ken—
The ice was all between.

The ice was here, the ice was there,
The ice was all around:
It cracked and growled, and roared and howled,
Like noises in a swound!

At length did cross an Albatross,[3]
Thorough the fog it came;
As if it had been a Christian soul,
We hailed it in God's name.

The mariners gave it biscuit-worms,
And round and round it flew.
The ice did split with a thunder-fit;
The helmsman steered us through!

And a good south wind sprung up behind;
The Albatross did follow,
And every day, for food or play,
Came to the mariner's hollo!

In mist or cloud, on mast or shroud,
It perched for vespers nine;
Whiles all the night, through fog-smoke white,
Glimmered the white Moon-shine."

"God save thee, ancient Mariner!
From the fiends, that plague thee thus!—
Why look'st thou so?"—With my cross-bow
I shot the Albatross.

PART II

The Sun came up upon the right,
Out of the sea came he;
And broad as a weft upon the left
Went down into the sea.

[3]*Albatross:* A large seagull-like bird that is common in the Southern Hemisphere.

And the good south wind still blew behind,
But no sweet bird did follow,
Nor any day for food or play
Came to the mariners' hollo!

And I had done a hellish thing,
And it would work 'em woe:
For all averred, I had killed the bird
That made the breeze to blow.
Ah wretch! said they, the bird to slay,
That made the breeze to blow!

Nor dim nor red, like God's own head,
The glorious Sun uprist:
Then all averred, I had killed the bird
That brought the fog and mist.
'Twas right, said they, such birds to slay,
That bring the fog and mist.

The fair breeze blew, the white foam flew,
The furrow followed free;
We were the first that ever burst
Into that silent sea.

Down dropt the breeze, the sails dropt down,
'Twas sad as sad could be;
And we did speak only to break
The silence of the sea!

All in a hot and copper sky,
The bloody Sun, at noon,
Right up above the mast did stand,
No bigger than the Moon.

Day after day, day after day,
We stuck, nor breath nor motion;
As idle as a painted ship
Upon a painted ocean.

Water, water, every where,
And all the boards did shrink;
Water, water, every where,
Nor any drop to drink.

The very deep did rot: O Christ!
That ever this should be!
Yea, slimy things did crawl with legs
Upon the slimy sea.

About, about, in reel and rout
    The death-fires danced at night;
The water, like a witch's oils,
    Burnt green, and blue and white.

And some in dreams assuréd were
    Of the Spirit that plagued us so;
Nine fathom deep he had followed us
    From the land of mist and snow.

And every tongue, through utter drought,
    Was withered at the root;
We could not speak, no more than if
    We had been choked with soot.

Ah! well a-day! what evil looks
    Had I from old and young!
Instead of the cross, the Albatross
    About my neck was hung.

PART III

There passed a weary time. Each throat
    Was parched, and glazed each eye.
A weary time! a weary time!
    How glazed each weary eye,
When looking westward, I beheld
    A something in the sky.

At first it seemed a little speck,
    And then it seemed a mist;
It moved and moved, and took at last
    A certain shape, I wist.[4]

A speck, a mist, a shape, I wist!
    And still it neared and neared:
As if it dodged a water-sprite,
    It plunged and tacked and veered.

With throats unslaked, with black lips baked,
    We could nor laugh nor wail;
Then while through drought all dumb they stood
I bit my arm and sucked the blood
    And cried, A sail! a sail!

[4]*wist:* Understood (archaic).

With throats unslaked, with black lips baked,
Agape they heard me call:
Gramercy! they for joy did grin,
And all at once their breath drew in,
As they were drinking all.

See! see! (I cried) she tacks no more!
Hither to work us weal;
Without a breeze, without a tide,
She steadies with upright keel!

The western wave was all a-flame.
The day was well nigh done!
Almost upon the western wave
Rested the broad bright Sun;
When that strange shape drove suddenly
Betwixt us and the Sun.

And straight the Sun was flecked with bars,
(Heaven's Mother send us grace!)
As if through a dungeon-grate he peered
With broad and burning face.

Alas! (thought I, and my heart beat loud)
How fast she nears and nears!
Are those *her* sails that glance in the Sun,
Like restless gossameres?

Are those *her* ribs through which the Sun
Did peer, as through a grate?
And is that Woman all her crew?
Is that a Death? and are there two?
Is Death that woman's mate ?

This Ship it was a plankless thing,
—A bare Anatomy!
A plankless spectre—and it mov'd
Like a Being of the Sea!
The Woman and a fleshless Man
Therein sate merrily.

His bones were black with many a crack,
All black and bare, I ween;
Jet-black and bare, save where with rust
Of mouldy damps and charnel crust
They're patched with purple and green.

Her lips were red, *her* looks were free,
Her locks were yellow as gold:
Her skin was as white as leprosy,
The Night-mare Life-in-Death was she
Who thicks man's blood with cold.

The naked hulk alongside came,
And the twain were casting dice;
"The game is done! I've won! I've won!"
Quoth she, and whistles thrice.

A gust of wind sterte up behind
And whistled through his bones;
Through the holes of his eyes and the hole of his mouth
Half-whistles and half-groans.

The Sun's rim dips; the stars rush out
At one stride comes the dark;
With far-heard whisper, o'er the sea,
Off shot the spectre-bark.

With far-heard whisper on the main
Off shot the spectre-ship;
And stifled words and groans of pain
Mix'd on each murmuring lip.

We listened and looked sideways up!
Fear at my heart, as at a cup,
My life-blood seemed to sip!
The stars were dim, and thick the night,
The steersman's face by his lamp gleamed white;
From the sails the dews did drip—
Till clomb above the eastern bar
The horned Moon, with one bright star
Within the nether tip.

The Sun's rim dips; the stars rush out:
At one stride comes the dark;
With far-heard whisper, o'er the sea,
Off shot the spectre-bark.

We listened and looked sideways up!
Fear at my heart, as at a cup,
My life-blood seemed to sip!
The stars were dim, and thick the night,
The steersman's face by his lamp gleamed white;

From the sails the dews did drip—
Till clomb above the eastern bar
The horned Moon, with one bright star
Within the nether tip.

One after one, by the star-dogged Moon,
Too quick for groan or sigh,
Each turned his face with a ghastly pang,
And cursed me with his eye.

Four times fifty living men,
(And I heard nor sigh nor groan)
With heavy thump, a lifeless lump,
They dropped down one by one.

The souls did from their bodies fly,—
They fled to bliss or woe!
And every soul, it passed me by,
Like the whizz of my cross-bow!

PART IV

"I fear thee, ancient Mariner!
I fear thy skinny hand!
And thou art long, and lank, and brown,
As is the ribbed sea-sand.

I fear thee and thy glittering eye,
And thy skinny hand, so brown."—
Fear not, fear not, thou Wedding-Guest!
This body dropt not down.

Alone, alone, all, all alone,
Alone on a wide wide sea!
And Christ would take no pity on
My soul in agony.

The many men, so beautiful!
And they all dead did lie:
And a million million slimy things
Lived on; and so did I.

I looked upon the rotting sea,
And drew my eyes away;
I looked upon the rotting deck,
And there the dead men lay.

I looked to heaven, and tried to pray;
  But or ever a prayer had gusht,
A wicked whisper came, and made
  My heart as dry as dust.

I closed my lids, and kept them close,
  And the balls like pulses beat;
For the sky and the sea, and the sea and the sky
Lay like a load on my weary eye,
  And the dead were at my feet.

The cold sweat melted from their limbs,
  Nor rot nor reek did they:
The look with which they looked on me
  Had never passed away.

An orphan's curse would drag to hell
  A spirit from on high;
But oh! more horrible than that
  Is the curse in a dead man's eye!
Seven days, seven nights, I saw that curse,
  And yet I could not die.

The moving Moon went up the sky,
  And no where did abide:
Softly she was going up,
  And a star or two beside—

Her beams bemocked the sultry main,
  Like April hoar-frost spread;
But where the ship's huge shadow lay,
The charméd water burnt alway
  A still and awful red.

Beyond the shadow of the ship,
  I watched the water-snakes:
They moved in tracks of shining white,
And when they reared, the elfish light
  Fell off in hoary flakes.

Within the shadow of the ship
  I watched their rich attire:
Blue, glossy green, and velvet black,
They coiled and swam; and every track
  Was a flash of golden fire.

O happy living things! no tongue
    Their beauty might declare:
A spring of love gushed from my heart,
    And I blessed them unaware:
Sure my kind saint took pity on me,
    And I blessed them unaware.

The self-same moment I could pray;
    And from my neck so free
The Albatross fell off, and sank
    Like lead into the sea.

PART V

Oh sleep! it is a gentle thing,
    Beloved from pole to pole!
To Mary Queen the praise be given!
She sent the gentle sleep from Heaven,
    That slid into my soul.

The silly buckets on the deck,
    That had so long remained,
I dreamt that they were filled with dew;
    And when I awoke, it rained.

My lips were wet, my throat was cold,
    My garments all were dank;
Sure I had drunken in my dreams,
    And still my body drank.

I moved, and could not feel my limbs:
    I was so light—almost
I thought that I had died in sleep,
    And was a blesséd ghost.

And soon I heard a roaring wind:
    It did not come anear;
But with its sound it shook the sails,
    That were so thin and sere.

The upper air burst into life!
    And a hundred fire-flags sheen,
To and fro they were hurried about!
And to and fro, and in and out,
    The wan stars danced between.

And the coming wind did roar more loud,
  And the sails did sigh like sedge;
And the rain poured down from one black cloud;
  The Moon was at its edge.

The thick black cloud was cleft, and still
  The Moon was at its side:
Like waters shot from some high crag,
The lightning fell with never a jag,
  A river steep and wide.

The strong wind reach'd the ship: it roar'd
  And dropp'd down, like a stone!
Beneath the lightning and the Moon
  The dead men gave a groan.

They groaned, they stirred, they all uprose,
  Nor spake, nor moved their eyes;
It had been strange, even in a dream,
  To have seen those dead men rise.

The helmsman steered, the ship moved on;
  Yet never a breeze up-blew;
The mariners all 'gan work the ropes,
  Where they were wont to do;
They raised their limbs like lifeless tools—
  We were a ghastly crew.

The body of my brother's son
  Stood by me, knee to knee:
The body and I pulled at one rope,
  But he said nought to me.
And I quak'd to think of my own voice
  How frightful it would be!

"I fear thee, ancient Mariner!"
  Be calm, thou wedding-guest!
'Twas not those souls, that fled in pain,
Which to their corses came again,
  But a troop of Spirits blest.

For when it dawned—they dropped their arms,
  And clustered round the mast:
Sweet sounds rose slowly through their mouths,
  And from their bodies passed.

Around, around, flew each sweet sound,
  Then darted to the Sun;
Slowly the sounds came back again,
  Now mixed, now one by one.

Sometimes a-dropping from the sky
  I heard the sky-lark sing;
Sometimes all little birds that are,
How they seemed to fill the sea and air
  With their sweet jargoning!

And now 'twas like all instruments,
  Now like a lonely flute;
And now it is an angel's song,
  That makes the heavens be mute.

It ceased; yet still the sails made on
  A pleasant noise till noon,
A noise like of a hidden brook
  In the leafy month of June,
That to the sleeping woods all night
  Singeth a quiet tune.

Listen, O listen, thou Wedding-Guest!
  "Mariner! thou hast thy will:
For that, which comes out of thine eye, doth make
  My body and soul to be still."

Never sadder tale was told
  To a man of woman born:
Sadder and wiser thou Wedding-Guest!
  Thou'lt rise tomorrow morn.

Never sadder tale was heard
  By man of woman born:
The mariners all return'd to work
  As silent as beforne.

The mariners all 'gan pull the ropes,
  But look at me they n'old:
Thought I, I am as thin as air—
  They cannot me behold.

Till noon we quietly sailed on,
  Yet never a breeze did breathe:
Slowly and smoothly went the ship,
  Moved onward from beneath.

Under the keel nine fathom deep,
From the land of mist and snow,
The spirit slid: and it was he
That made the ship to go.
The sails at noon left off their tune,
And the ship stood still also.

The Sun, right up above the mast,
Had fixed her to the ocean:
But in a minute she 'gan stir,
With a short uneasy motion—
Backwards and forwards half her length
With a short uneasy motion.

Then like a pawing horse let go,
She made a sudden bound:
It flung the blood into my head,
And I fell down in a swound.

How long in that same fit I lay,
I have not to declare;
But ere my living life returned,
I heard and in my soul discerned
Two voices in the air.

"Is it he?" quoth one, "Is this the man?
By him who died on cross,
With his cruel bow he laid full low
The harmless Albatross.

The spirit who bideth by himself
In the land of mist and snow,
He loved the bird that loved the man
Who shot him with his bow."

The other was a softer voice,
As soft as honey-dew:
Quoth he, "The man hath penance done,
And penance more will do."

PART VI

First Voice

"But tell me, tell me! speak again,
Thy soft response renewing—
What makes that ship drive on so fast?
What is the ocean doing?"

Second Voice

"Still as a slave before his lord,
The ocean hath no blast;
His great bright eye most silently
Up to the Moon is cast—

If he may know which way to go;
For she guides him smooth or grim.
See brother, see! how graciously
She looketh down on him."

First Voice

"But why drives on that ship so fast,
Without or wave or wind?"

Second Voice

"The air is cut away before,
And closes from behind.

Fly, brother, fly! more high, more high!
Or we shall be belated:
For slow and slow that ship will go,
When the Mariner's trance is abated."

I woke, and we were sailing on
As in a gentle weather:

'Twas night, calm night, the moon was high;
The dead men stood together.

All stood together on the deck,
For a charnel-dungeon[5] fitter:
All fixed on me their stony eyes,
That in the Moon did glitter.

The pang, the curse, with which they died,
Had never passed away:
I could not draw my eyes from theirs,
Nor turn them up to pray.

And now this spell was snapt: once more
I viewed the ocean green,
And looked far forth, yet little saw
Of what had else been seen—

[5]*charnel-dungeon:* A charnel is a repository for the bones of the dead.

Like one, that on a lonesome road
Doth walk in fear and dread,
And having once turned round walks on,
And turns no more his head;
Because he knows, a frightful fiend
Doth close behind him tread.

But soon there breathed a wind on me,
Nor sound nor motion made:
Its path was not upon the sea,
In ripple or in shade.

It raised my hair, it fanned my cheek
Like a meadow-gale of spring—
It mingled strangely with my fears,
Yet it felt like welcoming.

Swiftly, swiftly flew the ship,
Yet she sailed softly too:
Sweetly, sweetly blew the breeze—
On me alone it blew.

Oh! dream of joy! is this indeed
The light-house top I see?
Is this the hill? is this the kirk?
Is this mine own countree?

We drifted o'er the harbour-bar,
And I with sobs did pray—
O let me be awake, my God!
Or let me sleep alway.

The harbour-bay was clear as glass,
So smoothly it was strewn!
And on the bay the moonlight lay,
And the shadow of the Moon.

The moonlight bay was white all o'er,
Till rising from the same,
Full many shapes, that shadows were,
Like as of torches came.

A little distance from the prow
Those dark-red shadows were;
But soon I saw that my own flesh
Was red as in a glare.

I turn'd my head in fear and dread,
  And by the holy rood,
The bodies had advanc'd, and now
  Before the mast they stood.

They lifted up their stiff right arms,
  They held them strait and tight;
And each right-arm burnt like a torch,
  A torch that's borne upright.
Their stony eye-balls glitter' d on
  In the red and smoky light.

I pray'd and turn'd my head away
  Forth looking as before.
There was no breeze upon the bay,
  No wave against the shore.

The rock shone bright, the kirk no less,
  That stands above the rock:
The moonlight steeped in silentness
  The steady weathercock.

And the bay was white with silent light,
  Till rising from the same,
Full many shapes, that shadows were,
  In crimson colours came.

A little distance from the prow
  Those crimson shadows were:
I turned my eyes upon the deck—
  Oh, Christ! what saw I there!

Each corse[6] lay flat, lifeless and flat,
  And, by the holy rood!
A man all light, a seraph-man,[7]
  On every corse there stood.

This seraph-band, each waved his hand:
  It was a heavenly sight!
They stood as signals to the land,
  Each one a lovely light;

[6]*corse:* A corpse (archaic).

[7]*seraph-man:* An angel.

This seraph-band, each waved his hand,
No voice did they impart—
No voice; but oh! the silence sank
Like music on my heart.

But soon I heard the dash of oars,
I heard the Pilot's cheer;
My head was turned perforce away
And I saw a boat appear.

Then vanish'd all the lovely lights;
The bodies rose anew:
With silent pace, each to his place,
Came back the ghastly crew.
The wind, that shade nor motion made,
On me alone it blew.

The Pilot and the Pilot's boy,
I heard them coming fast:
Dear Lord in Heaven! it was a joy
The dead men could not blast.

I saw a third—I heard his voice:
It is the Hermit good!
He singeth loud his godly hymns
That he makes in the wood.
He'll shrieve[8] my soul, he'll wash away
The Albatross's blood.

PART VII

This Hermit good lives in that wood
Which slopes down to the sea.
How loudly his sweet voice he rears!
He loves to talk with marineres
That come from a far countree.

He kneels at morn, and noon, and eve—
He hath a cushion plump:
It is the moss that wholly hides
The rotted old oak-stump.

The skiff-boat neared: I heard them talk,
"Why, this is strange, I trow!
Where are those lights so many and fair,
That signal made but now?"

[8]*shrieve:* To hear one's confession.

"Strange, by my faith!" the Hermit said—
"And they answered not our cheer!
The planks look warped! and see those sails,
How thin they are and sere!
I never saw aught like to them,
Unless perchance it were

Brown skeletons of leaves that lag
My forest-brook along;
When the ivy-tod is heavy with snow,
And the owlet whoops to the wolf below,
That eats the she-wolf's young."

"Dear Lord! it hath a fiendish look—"
(The Pilot made reply)
"I am a-feared"—"Push on, push onl"
Said the Hermit cheerily.

The boat came closer to the ship,
But I nor spake nor stirred;
The boat came close beneath the ship,
And straight a sound was heard.

Under the water it rumbled on,
Still louder and more dread:
It reached the ship, it split the bay;
The ship went down like lead.

Stunned by that loud and dreadful sound,
Which sky and ocean smote,
Like one that hath been seven days drowned
My body lay afloat;
But swift as dreams, myself I found
Within the Pilot's boat.

Upon the whirl, where sank the ship,
The boat spun round and round;
And all was still, save that the hill
Was telling of the sound.

I moved my lips—the Pilot shrieked
And fell down in a fit;
The holy Hermit raised his eyes,
And prayed where he did sit.

I took the oars: the Pilot's boy,
    Who now doth crazy go,
Laughed loud and long, and all the while
    His eyes went to and fro.
"Ha! ha!" quoth he, "full plain I see,
    The Devil knows how to row."

And now all in my own countree,
    I stood on the firm land!
The Hermit stepped forth from the boat,
    And scarcely he could stand.

"O shrieve me, shrieve me, holy man!"
    The Hermit crossed his brow.
"Say quick," quoth he, "I bid thee say—
    What manner of man art thou?"

Forthwith this frame of mine was wrenched
    With a woful agony,
Which forced me to begin my tale;
    And then it left me free.

Since then, at an uncertain hour,
    That agony returns:
And till my ghastly tale is told,
    This heart within me burns.

I pass, like night, from land to land;
    I have strange power of speech;
That moment that his face I see,
I know the man that must hear me:
    To him my tale I teach.

What loud uproar bursts from that door!
    The wedding-guests are there:
But in the garden-bower the bride
    And bride-maids singing are:
And hark the little vesper bell,[9]
    Which biddeth me to prayer!

O Wedding-Guest! this soul hath been
    Alone on a wide wide sea:
So lonely 'twas, that God himself
    Scarce seemèd there to be.

[9]*vesper bell:* A bell that sounds a late-afternoon church service.

O sweeter than the marriage-feast,
'Tis sweeter far to me,
To walk together to the kirk
With a goodly company!—

To walk together to the kirk,
And all together pray,
While each to his great Father bends,
Old men, and babes, and loving friends
And youths and maidens gay!

Farewell, farewell! but this I tell
To thee, thou Wedding-Guest!
He prayeth well, who loveth well
Both man and bird and beast.

He prayeth best, who loveth best
All things both great and small;
For the dear God who loveth us,
He made and loveth all.

The Mariner, whose eye is bright,
Whose beard with age is hoar,
Is gone: and now the Wedding-Guest
Turned from the bridegroom's door.

He went like one that hath been stunned,
And is of sense forlorn:
A sadder and a wiser man,
He rose the morrow morn.

(1798)

Questions for Discussion and Writing

Close Reading

1. The poem is a ballad, a medieval poetic form meant to be sung and dramatizing an episode in narrative form (see Chapter 5). Early ballads tended to include supernatural events, to emphasize physical courage and love, and to center on common people. Coleridge uses archaic spellings to indicate a setting in the distant past. What is the effect of this choice of form and style?
2. Why does the mariner shoot the albatross?
3. Why are the men on the mariner's ship punished along with him?
4. What is the significance of the game of dice between death and death-in-life? (Which punishment would you prefer?)

CRITICAL AND CREATIVE READING

5. How does the mariner's relationship with nature change over the course of the story?
6. What is the role of the supernatural in this poetic story?
7. Why does the albatross finally fall off the mariner? How is that moment a turning point in his fate?
8. Do you think the mariner's punishment fits his crime? Will he ever be "free"?
9. What is the role of the wedding guest in this ballad? Why do you think Coleridge included this frame tale?

CONNECTIONS TO OTHER READINGS

10. The ancient mariner, like Montressor in "The Cask of Amontillado," addresses his story to a specific listener. Discuss the significance of this audience in both works.

Emily Dickinson

Mine Enemy is growing old (1509)

Emily Dickinson (1830–1886) was born in Amherst, Massachusetts, and attended Amherst Academy and Holyoke Female Seminary. Although she wrote poetry throughout most of her adult life, only ten of her poems were published during her lifetime. Most of her nearly 1,800 poems were published after her death, and she is now considered among the greatest of American lyric poets. Although she led a private, even reclusive life, her poetry describes a range of human experiences, from marriage to death, and her experimental style influenced the later generation of modernists. Much of her poetry is deceptively simple. "Mine Enemy is growing old" is a short poem with a controlling metaphor that suggests several layers of meaning. (See also other poems by Emily Dickinson and her portrait in Chapters 12, 13, and 14.)

Mine Enemy is growing old—
I have at last Revenge—
The Palate of the Hate departs—
If any would avenge

Let him be quick—the Viand flits—
It is a faded Meat—
Anger as soon as fed is dead—
'Tis starving makes it fat—

(1868)

Questions for Discussion and Writing

Close Reading

1. What kind of "revenge" does the speaker have over her enemy?
2. The word *palate* has a number of meanings: the roof of the mouth, an artist's palette of paints (spelled differently), and the source of the sense of taste. It can also refer to a liking for something. What does Dickinson mean by the "Palate of the Hate"? Can you apply more than one of these definitions to the poem?
3. Dickinson breaks her poem into two stanzas in the middle of a sentence, making it easy to become confused. Read the last line of the first stanza and part of the first line of the second stanza as one sentence, without a break. What is the effect of separating the two stanzas at that point?

Critical and Creative Reading

4. In addition to the word *palate*, what images of food does the poem offer? How do they work together to convey the impression of revenge as a meal?
5. "Growing old" is something that will happen to all of us (if we are lucky). Why might someone see it as revenge?
6. What is the speaker's tone in this poem? Does she seem satisfied or disappointed that she has revenge?

Connections to Other Readings

7. Dickinson's speaker writes, "Anger as soon as fed is dead." Apply this line to one of the short stories in this chapter (you might consider "On the Antler" or "Killings"). Does Dickinson's claim apply to other literary depictions of revenge?
8. Consider the characters in Edith Wharton's story "Roman Fever," two women who are themselves growing old. How might the sentiments in Dickinson's poem reflect the thoughts of Mrs. Slade and Mrs. Ansley?

Robert Frost

Fire and Ice

Most students have encountered Robert Frost (1874–1963) before college, usually through one of his famous poems like "Stopping by Woods on a Snowy Evening" or "The Road Not Taken." This three-time Pulitzer Prize recipient is one of America's most beloved poets, and the range of his talents is not encompassed by these two familiar poems, which give only glimpses of the depth and darkness of his philosophical vision. The following poem reads like light verse, but it is deadly serious. (See also "The Tuft of Flowers" in Chapter 16.)

Some say the world will end in fire,
Some say in ice.
From what I've tasted of desire
I hold with those who favor fire.
But if it had to perish twice,
I think I know enough of hate
To say that for destruction ice
Is also great
And would suffice.

(1923)

QUESTIONS FOR DISCUSSION AND WRITING

CLOSE READING

1. What is the poem's rhyme scheme? How does it affect your interpretation?
2. How do fire and ice operate metaphorically in this poem?
3. What do hate and desire have to do with fire and ice?

CRITICAL AND CREATIVE READING

4. Think of the implications of this poem on a smaller scale than the end of the world. In what other scenarios could "fire" and "ice" act as metaphors for the end of something?
5. Why is the poem, from its title on, structured with fire first and ice second? Would its meaning change if it were organized the other way around?
6. Take two other destructive scenarios—say, flood and drought—and write a similar poem to Frost's using them as the dominant metaphors. What is your poem about?

CONNECTIONS TO OTHER READINGS

7. Based on Frost's interpretation of these words, is the destructiveness at the end of Wharton's "Roman Fever" *fire* or *ice*?
8. Write about metaphor in this poem and in Robert Herrick's "The Bubble: A Song."

Margaret Walker

Since 1619

Margaret Walker (1915–1998) was educated in church schools in the American South and earned her college degree from Northwestern University and an MA and a PhD from the University of Iowa. Her first poetry collection, *For My People* (1942), from which this poem was taken, won the Yale Series of Younger Poets Award. Her poetry forms a crucial link between the African American writers of the Harlem Renaissance period (such as Langston Hughes, whose poem "Harlem" immediately follows in this chapter) and the later African American writers who wrote more politicized literature appropriate to the civil rights movement of the 1950s and 1960s.

....

How many years since 1619 have I been singing Spirituals?
How long have I been praising God and shouting hallelujahs?
How long have I been hated and hating?
How long have I been living in hell for heaven?

When will I see my brother's face wearing another color?
When will I be ready to die in an honest fight?
When will I be conscious of the struggle—now to do or die?
When will these scales fall away from my eyes?

What will I say when days of wrath descend:
When the money-gods take all my life away;
When the death knell sounds
And peace is a flag of far-flung blood and filth?

When will I understand the cheated and the cheaters;
Their paltry pittances and cold concessions to my pride?
When will I burst from my kennel an angry mongrel,
Lean and hungry and tired of my dry bones and years?

(1942)

Questions for Discussion and Writing

Close Reading

1. What does the speaker mean by "living in hell for heaven" (line 4)?
2. Comment on the way the speaker uses rhetorical phrasing.
3. How does the poem shift between the past and the future? How does this shift connect with the poem's themes?

Critical and Creative Reading

4. If you were to honestly respond to the speaker's questions, what would those responses look like?
5. The speaker refers to "cold concessions to my pride" (line 14). What might some of these concessions be? Why might the speaker reject them?
6. Why 1619? Would the poem have a different meaning if it were titled "Since 1775" or "Since 1860"?

Connections to Other Readings

7. Both Walker and Langston Hughes in his poem "Harlem" allude to a potential explosion between white and black races in the future; which explosion seems more menacing? (Look carefully at the language of both poems.)
8. Compare the speaker of this poem to Delia, the protagonist of Zora Neale Hurston's "Sweat" in terms of capacity for patience.
9. Consider the notion of history in this poem and in Edith Wharton's story "Roman Fever." How do both works demonstrate the way the past impacts the future?

Langston Hughes

Harlem

Langston Hughes (1902–1967) was a poet, novelist, playwright, and journalist who is best known today for being at the center of the arts movement known as the Harlem Renaissance. He grew up in the Midwest, spent a year in Mexico, traveled around the world, including to Paris and Africa, and eventually came to call Harlem his home. His first volume of poetry, *The Weary Blues,* was published in 1926. (See the poem "The Weary Blues" in Chapter 5 as well as "Theme for English B," along with a photo of the author, in Chapter 14.) During World War II he joined the war effort, writing jingles to advertise U.S. bonds. During the 1950s, Hughes sustained his career by renouncing his earlier attraction to communism, and he continued to write, edit, and revise his works throughout his life. He was inducted into the National Institute of Arts and Letters in 1961. His short poem "Harlem" suggests a collective revenge based more on justice than on vengeance.

What happens to a dream deferred?

Does it dry up
like a raisin in the sun?
Or fester like a sore—
And then run?
Does it stink like rotten meat?
Or crust and sugar over—
like a syrupy sweet?

Maybe it just sags
like a heavy load.

Or does it explode?

(1951)

Questions for Discussion and Writing

Close Reading

1. What might be the "dream deferred" that Hughes refers to in his opening question?
2. Note the unpleasant verbs suggested as answers to Hughes's question, like "fester" and "stink." How do these words contribute to the overall effect?
3. Look at each of the metaphors with which Hughes answers his original question. Each suggests a possible response that African Americans might have toward their deferred dreams. How might each of these metaphors translate into actual human responses?
4. Why is the last question italicized?

Critical and Creative Reading

5. Is Hughes making a threat in this poem? A prediction? Who is the implied audience of the poem?
6. Why do you think Hughes talks about a dream "deferred" rather than "denied"? Is this an important distinction?
7. What is the difference between justice and revenge here?

Connections to Other Readings

8. The implied revenge in this poem is not in response to a personal insult (as in "The Cask of Amontillado"). Rather, Hughes implies, any "exploding" to come is a result of years of slavery, Jim Crow laws, and other forms of institutional injustice. Matt, in "Killings," also claims that his killing of Strout is about more than personal vengeance, that he is acting in the interest of justice. What is your response to people taking justice into their own hands?
9. Marilyn Nelson's poem "Minor Miracle" is about a man who apologizes for making a racist comment. Compare or contrast the attitudes about racial progress in the two poems.

Nellie Wong

Mama, Come Back

Nellie Wong (b. 1934) was born in California to Chinese immigrant parents and began publishing poetry while attending San Francisco State University in her mid-thirties. Her first collection of poetry, *Dreams in Harrison Railroad Park,* was published in 1977, and her work has appeared in over two hundred publications. She is an activist for feminist and socialist causes and a frequent speaker on feminist, Third World, and Asian issues. Her poem "Mama, Come Back" centers on a complex mother-daughter relationship. As you read, consider whether the speaker is seeking or offering forgiveness.

Mama, come back.
Why did you leave
now that I am learning you?
The landlady next door
how she apologizes
for my rough brown skin
to her tenant from Hong Kong
as if I were her daughter,
as if she were you.

How do I say I miss you
your scolding
your presence
your roast loin of pork
more succulent, more tender
than any hotel chef's?

The fur coat you wanted
making you look like a polar bear
and the mink-trimmed coat
I once surprised you
on Christmas morning.

Mama, how you said "importment"
for important,
your gold tooth flashing
an insecurity you dared not bare,
wanting recognition
simply as eating noodles
and riding in a motor car
to the supermarket
the movie theater
adorned in your gold and jade
as if all your jewelry
confirmed your identity
a Chinese woman in America.

How you said "you better"
always your last words
glazed through your dark eyes
following me fast as you could

one November evening in New York City
how I thought "Hello, Dolly!"
showed you an America
you never saw.

How your fear of being alone
kept me dutiful in body
resentful in mind.
How my fear of being single
kept me
from moving out.

How I begged your forgiveness
after that one big fight
how I wasn't wrong
but needed you to love me
as warmly as you hugged strangers.

(1986)

Questions for Discussion and Writing

Close Reading

1. What kind of woman was (is?) the speaker's mother?
2. How does the speaker's use of nonstandard English ("learning you," and "the mink-trimmed coat / I once surprised you / on Christmas morning") add to our understanding of her as a character?
3. How many of the speaker's problems with her mother seem to stem from the mother's "wanting recognition"?
4. What does the speaker miss about her mother? How did she feel about her when she was still present?

Critical and Creative Reading

5. The poem details a complicated relationship between a mother and a daughter. Why do you think this relationship is so complicated?
6. Where do you think the mother has gone?
7. At the end of the poem, the speaker claims that she had once "begged for forgiveness" although she "wasn't wrong." What does this statement tell you about the mother and daughter's relationship?
8. Do you think the speaker is seeking forgiveness from her mother or trying to forgive her?

Connections to Other Readings

9. Compare the relationship between the daughter and the mother to the relationships in Alice Walker's "Everyday Use" (in the Common Characters

section), another story about a lack of understanding between two generations of women.

10. Compare the speaker's begging for forgiveness while claiming to be innocent to Charlie's reaction to Marion in F. Scott Fitzgerald's "Babylon Revisited." Do these characters really want forgiveness?

Marilyn Nelson

Minor Miracle

Poet laureate of Connecticut and English professor at the University of Connecticut, Marilyn Nelson (b. 1946) graduated from the University of California, Davis, and received graduate degrees from the University of Pennsylvania and the University of Minnesota. Her poetry has won two Pushcart prizes, two grants from the National Endowment for the Arts, and a Guggenheim fellowship, and several of her books have been finalists for the National Book Award, including *Fields of Praise* (1997), in which "Minor Miracle" was published. Do you agree with the speaker that the apology at the poem's end constitutes a "miracle"?

Which reminds me of another knock-on-wood
memory. I was cycling with a male friend,
through a small midwestern town. We came to a 4-way
stop and stopped, chatting. As we started again,
a rusty old pick-up truck, ignoring the stop sign,
hurricaned past scant inches from our front wheels.
My partner called, "Hey, that was a 4-way stop!"
The truck driver, stringy blond hair a long fringe
under his brand-name beer cap, looked back and yelled,
    "You fucking niggers!"
And sped off.
My friend and I looked at each other and shook our heads.
We remounted our bikes and headed out of town.
We were pedaling through a clear blue afternoon
between two fields of almost-ripened wheat
bordered by cornflowers and Queen Anne's lace
when we heard an unmuffled motor, a honk-honking.
We stopped, closed ranks, made fists.
It was the same truck. It pulled over.
A tall, very much in shape young white guy slid out:
greasy jeans, homemade finger tattoos, probably

a Marine Corps boot-camp footlockerful
of martial arts techniques.

"What did you say back there!" he shouted.
My friend said, "I said it was a 4-way stop.
You went through it."
"And what did I say?" the white guy asked.
"You said: 'You fucking niggers.'"
The afternoon froze.

"Well," said the white guy,
shoving his hands into his pockets
and pushing dirt around with the pointed toe of his boot,
"I just want to say I'm sorry."
He climbed back into his truck
and drove away.

(1997)

Questions for Discussion and Writing

Close Reading

1. The poem begins *in medias res*—in the middle of the action. Why do you think Nelson opens her poem with a dependent clause? How does this beginning affect the relationship between the speaker and her audience?
2. How does the setting contrast to the racist words of the truck driver? What effect does this contrast have on you as a reader?
3. How does Nelson build suspense in her narrative?

Critical and Creative Reading

4. What do the cyclists expect from the driver when he emerges from his truck? What did you expect to happen?
5. Why do you think Nelson ends her poem with the trucker's apology? Why do we not see the cyclists' reaction to these words?
6. Is "I'm sorry" enough to counteract the violent effect of the driver's original taunt? Should he be so easily forgiven for introducing such ugliness into the cyclists' peaceful day?

Connections to Other Readings

7. Compare the relationship between the races in this poem to that in Langston Hughes's "Harlem." Which poem strikes you as more hopeful?
8. Consider the tone of discourse about race in this poem and in Martin Luther King's "Letter from Birmingham Jail."

Galway Kinnell

It All Comes Back

Galway Kinnell (b. 1927) has moved from traditional poetry (in its form and its Christian underpinnings) to more experimental forms over the course of his career. An academic poet who earned his undergraduate degree from Princeton and who has taught abroad and at prestigious American universities, Kinnell has received a number of important awards, including the Pulitzer Prize. He is the author of more than a dozen collections of poetry and has remained an important chronicler of personal stories based on deep mythologies. Consider the relationship between the personal and the universal in the following poem, "It All Comes Back."

We placed the cake, with its four candles
poking out of thick soft frosting, on the seat
of his chair at the head of the table
for just a moment, while we unfolded and spread
Spanish cloth over Vermont maple.

Suddenly he stepped from the group
of schoolmates and parents and family friends
and ran to the table, and just as someone cried
No, no! Don't sit! he sat on his chair and his cake,
and the room broke into groans and guffaws.

Actually it was pretty funny, we all
started yelping our heads off, and actually
it wasn't in the least funny. He ran to me,
and I picked him up but I was still laughing,
and in indignant fury he jabbed his thumbs

into the corners of my mouth, grasped
my cheeks, and yanked—he was so muscled
and so outraged I felt as if he might rip
my whole face off, and then I realized
that was exactly what he was trying to do.

It came to me: I was one of his keepers,
his birth and the birth of his sister
had put me on earth a second time,

with the duty this time to protect them
and to help them to love themselves,

and yet here I was, locked in solidarity
with these adults against my own child,
hee-hawing away, without once wondering
if we weren't, underneath, all of us, striking back,
too late, at our parents for humiliating us.

I gulped down my laughter and held him and
apologized and commiserated and explained and then
things were right again, but to this day it remains
loose, this face, seat of superior smiles,
on the bones, from that hard yanking.

Shall I publish this anecdote from the past
and risk embarrassing him? I like it
that he fought back, but what's the good,
now he's thirty-six, in telling the tale
of his mortification when he was four?

Let him decide—I'll give him three choices.
He can scratch his slapdash checkmark,
whose rakish hook reminds me
of his old high-school hockey stick,
in whichever box applies:

☐ *Tear it up.* ☐ *Don't publish it but give me a copy.*
☐ *O.K., publish it on the chance that*
somewhere someone survives
of those said to die miserably every day
for lack of the small clarifications sometimes found in poems.

(2005)

Questions for Discussion and Writing

Close Reading

1. Each stanza is five lines; yet where do the sentences begin and end? What is the effect of structuring the poem this way?
2. What does the speaker realize about parenthood?
3. Where does the poem address aging? What images does the poet use to indicate the passing of time?

Critical and Creative Reading

4. The poem ends with three boxes to check, a familiar testing motif. What other "choices" might exist besides these three?
5. If your parent had written this poem or one like it that brought up an embarrassing moment from your past, which box would you have checked? (Think of an embarrassing moment before you reply.)
6. Is the son's act of pulling violently on his father's face an act of revenge, in your understanding of that word?
7. How do you understand the speaker's wondering "if we weren't, underneath, all of us, striking back, / too late, at our parents for humiliating us"? How does that realization affect your interpretation of the entire poem?
8. Does the son's evident checking of the third box indicate forgiveness or something else?

Connections to Other Readings

9. Write an essay about the way children forgive or do not forgive their parents using this poem and F. Scott Fitzgerald's story "Babylon Revisited."
10. Discuss forgiveness in families in this poem and in the readings in the Common Characters section at the end of the chapter.

Drama

Euripedes

Translated by E. P. Coleridge

Medea

Euripedes (480–406 BC) was born in Athens and wrote approximately ninety-two plays. Although his work was widely admired, it received little official acclaim because he was a freethinker who questioned his culture's religion and lived most of his life isolated from the Athens theater scene. Many of his liberal friends were executed for their views (including the view that the sun was not a chariot driven across the sky by Apollo but a burning mass), and Euripedes himself was tried for impiety and banished from Athens. His grisly fate rivaled anything he might have imagined for his characters. Having received refuge in Macedonia, he was torn to pieces by the king's dogs in a freak accident. His plays include *The Bacchae* and *Hyppolytus.*

Medea is a story of a terrible revenge in which innocent life is taken to redress a wrong. The story opens as Medea has learned that her husband Jason has left her to marry another woman, the daughter of the king of Corinth. According to Greek legend, Medea was a sorceress who helped Jason save his kingdom in exchange for his promise of eternal love and faithfulness. Now, years later, the middle-aged Jason has lost interest in his wife; to make matters worse, his new father-in-law is banishing Medea from his kingdom because she has threatened to kill his daughter. The play features a chorus, a convention of Greek drama in which a group of actors comment on the events of the play. Medea's crime is unthinkable. How much sympathy do you have for her situation?

DRAMATIS PERSONAE

Nurse of Medea
Attendant on her Children
Medea
Chorus of Corinthian Women
Creon, King of Corinth
Jason
Aegeus, King of Athens
Messenger
The Two Sons of Jason and Medea

SCENE

(Before Medea's house in Corinth, near the palace of Creon. The Nurse enters from the house.)

Nurse: Ah! Would to Heaven the good ship Argo[1] ne'er had sped its course to the Colchian land through the misty blue Symplegades, nor ever in the glens of Pelion the pine been felled to furnish with oars the chieftain's hands, who went to fetch the golden fleece for Pelias; for then would my own mistress Medea never have sailed to the turrets of Iolcos, her soul with love for Jason smitten, nor would she have beguiled the daughters of Pelias to slay their father and come to live here in the land of Corinth with her husband and children, where her exile found favour with the citizens to whose land she had come, and in all things of her own accord was she at one with Jason, the greatest safeguard this when wife and husband do agree; but now their love is all turned to hate, and tenderest ties are weak. For Jason hath betrayed his own children and my mistress dear for the love of a royal bride, for he hath wedded the daughter of Creon, lord of this land. While Medea, his hapless wife, thus scorned, appeals to the oaths he swore, recalls the strong pledge his right hand gave, and bids heaven be witness what requital she is finding from Jason. And here she lies fasting, yielding her body to her grief, wasting away in tears ever since she learnt that she was wronged by her husband, never lifting her eye nor raising her face from off the ground; and she lends as deaf an ear to her friend's warning as if she were a rock or ocean billow, save when she turns her snow-white neck aside and softly to herself bemoans her father dear, her country and her home, which she gave up to come hither with the man who now holds her in dishonour. She, poor lady, hath by sad experience learnt how good a thing it is never to quit one's native land. And she hates her children now and feels no joy at seeing them; I fear she may contrive some untoward scheme; for her mood is dangerous nor will she brook her cruel treatment; full well I know her, and I much do dread that she will plunge the keen sword through their hearts, stealing without a word into the chamber where their marriage couch is spread, or else that she will slay the prince and bridegroom too, and so find some calamity still more grievous than the present; for dreadful is her wrath; verily the man that doth incur her hate will have no easy task to raise o'er her a song of triumph. Lo! where her sons come hither from their childish sports; little they reck of their mother's woes, for the soul of the young is no friend to sorrow.

[The Attendant leads in Medea's children.]

Attendant: Why dost thou, so long my lady's own handmaid, stand here at the gate alone, loudly lamenting to thyself the piteous tale? How comes it that Medea will have thee leave her to herself?

Nurse: Old man, attendant on the sons of Jason, our masters' fortunes when they go awry make good slaves grieve and touch their hearts. Oh!

[1]*Argo:* The ship on which Jason, son of Aeson, sailed to Iolchos to stake his claim to Aeson's kingdom that had been usurped by Pelias.

have come to such a pitch of grief that there stole a yearning wish upon me to come forth hither and proclaim to heaven and earth my mistress's hard fate.

Attendant: What! has not the poor lady ceased yet from her lamentation?

Nurse: Would I were as thou art! The mischief is but now beginning; it has not reached its climax yet.

Attendant: O foolish one, if I may call my mistress such a name; how little she recks of evils yet more recent!

Nurse: What mean'st, old man? Grudge not to tell me.

Attendant: 'Tis naught; I do repent me even of the words I have spoken.

Nurse: Nay, by thy beard I conjure thee, hide it not from thy fellow-slave; I will be silent, if need be, on that text.

Attendant: I heard one say, pretending not to listen as I approached the place where our greybeards sit playing draughts near Pirene's sacred spring,[2] that Creon, the ruler of this land, is bent on driving these children and their mother from the boundaries of Corinth; but I know not whether the news is to be relied upon, and would fain it were not.

Nurse: What! will Jason brook such treatment of his sons, even though he be at variance with their mother?

Attendant: Old ties give way to new; he bears no longer any love to this family.

Nurse: Undone, it seems, are we, if to old woes fresh ones we add, ere we have drained the former to the dregs.

Attendant: Hold thou thy peace, say not a word of this; 'tis no time for our mistress to learn hereof.

Nurse: O children, do ye hear how your father feels towards you? Perdition catch him, but no he is my master still; yet is he proved a very traitor to his nearest and dearest.

Attendant: And who 'mongst men is not? Art learning only now, that every single man cares for himself more than for his neighbour, some from honest motives, others for mere gain's sake? Seeing that to indulge his passion their father has ceased to love these children.

Nurse: Go, children, within the house; all will be well. Do thou keep them as far away as may be, and bring them not near their mother in her evil hour. For ere this have I seen her eyeing them savagely, as though she were minded to do them some hurt, and well I know she will not cease from her fury till she have pounced on some victim. At least may she turn her hand against her foes, and not against her friends.

Medea [*chanting within*]: Ah, me! a wretched suffering woman I! O would that I could die!

Nurse [*chanting*]: 'Tis as I said, my dear children; wild fancies stir your mother's heart, wild fury goads her on. Into the house without delay, come not near her eye, approach her not, beware her savage mood, the fell tempest of her reckless heart. In, in with what speed ye may. For 'tis plain she will soon redouble her fury; that cry is but the herald of the gathering storm-cloud whose lightning soon will flash; what will her proud restless soul, in the anguish of despair, be guilty of?

[2] *Pirene's sacred spring:* A spring born of Pirene's tears.

Fiona Shaw in *Medea.*

[The Attendant takes the children into the house.]

Medea [*chanting within*]: Ah, me! the agony I have suffered, deep enough to call for these laments! Curse you and your father too, ye children damned, sons of a doomed mother! Ruin seize the whole family!

Nurse [*chanting*]: Ah me! ah me! the pity of it! Why, pray, do thy children share their father's crime? Why hatest thou them? Woe is you, poor children, how do I grieve for you lest ye suffer some outrage! Strange are the tempers of princes, and maybe because they seldom have to obey, and mostly lord it over others, change they their moods with difficulty. 'Tis better then to have been trained to live on equal terms. Be it mine to reach old age, not in proud pomp, but in security! Moderation wins the day first as a better word for men to use, and likewise it is far the best course for them to pursue; but greatness that doth o'erreach itself, brings no blessing to mortal men; but pays a penalty of greater ruin whenever fortune is wroth with a family.

[The Chorus enters. The following lines between the Nurse, Chorus, and Medea are sung.]

Chorus: I heard the voice, uplifted loud, of our poor Colchian lady, nor yet is she quiet; speak, aged dame, for as I stood by the house with double gates I heard a voice of weeping from within, and I do grieve, lady, for the sorrows of this house, for it hath won my love.

Nurse: 'Tis a house no more; all that is passed away long since; a royal bride keeps Jason at her side, while our mistress pines away in her bower, finding no comfort for her soul in aught her friends can say.

Medea [*within*]: Oh, oh! Would that Heaven's levin bolt[3] would cleave this head in twain! What gain is life to me? Woe, woe is me! O, to die and win release, quitting this loathed existence!

Chorus: Didst hear, O Zeus,[4] thou earth, and thou, O light, the piteous note of woe the hapless wife is uttering? How shall a yearning for that insatiate resting-place ever hasten for thee, poor reckless one, the end that death alone can bring? Never pray for that. And if thy lord prefers a fresh love, be not angered with him for that; Zeus will judge 'twixt thee and him herein. Then mourn not for thy husband's loss too much, nor waste thyself away.

Medea [*within*]: Great Themis, and husband of Themis,[5] behold what I am suffering now, though I did bind that accursed one, my husband, by strong oaths to me! O, to see him and his bride some day brought to utter destruction, they and their house with them, for that they presume to wrong me thus unprovoked. O my father, my country, that I have left to my shame, after slaying my own brother.

Nurse: Do ye hear her words, how loudly she adjures Themis, oft invoked, and Zeus, whom men regard as keeper of their oaths? On no mere trifle surely will our mistress spend her rage.

Chorus: Would that she would come forth for us to see, and listen to the words of counsel we might give, if haply she might lay aside the fierce fury of her wrath, and her temper stern. Never be my zeal at any rate denied my friends! But go thou and bring her hither outside the house, and tell her this our friendly thought; haste thee ere she do some mischief to those inside the house, for this sorrow of hers is mounting high.

Nurse: This will I do; but I doubt whether I shall persuade my mistress; still willingly will I undertake this trouble for you; albeit, she glares upon her servants with the look of a lioness with cubs, whenso anyone draws nigh to speak to her. Wert thou to call the men of old time rude uncultured boors thou wouldst not err, seeing that they devised their hymns for festive occasions, for banquets, and to grace the board, a pleasure to catch the ear, shed o'er our life, but no man hath found a way to allay hated grief by music and the minstrel's varied strain, whence arise slaughters and fell strokes of fate to o'erthrow the homes of men. And yet this were surely a gain, to heal men's wounds by music's spell, but why tune they their idle song where rich banquets are spread? For of itself doth the rich banquet, set before them, afford to men delight.

Chorus: I heard a bitter cry of lamentation! loudly, bitterly she calls on the traitor of her marriage bed, her perfidious spouse; by grievous wrongs oppressed she invokes Themis, bride of Zeus, witness of oaths, who brought her unto Hellas, the land that fronts the strand of Asia, o'er the sea by night through ocean's boundless gate.

[3]*levin bolt:* A lightning bolt.

[4]*Zeus:* The chief god in Greek mythology. He is also the god of lightning and thunder and is known for his capacity for malicious revenge.

[5]*Themis:* The goddess of order and justice.

[As the Chorus finishes its song, Medea enters from the house.]

Medea: From the house I have come forth, Corinthian ladies, for fear lest you be blaming me; for well I know that amongst men many by showing pride have gotten them an ill name and a reputation for indifference, both those who shun men's gaze and those who move amid the stranger crowd, and likewise they who choose a quiet walk in life. For there is no just discernment in the eyes of men, for they, or ever they have surely learnt their neighbour's heart, loathe him at first sight, though never wronged by him; and so a stranger most of all should adopt a city's views; nor do I commend that citizen, who, in the stubbornness of his heart, from churlishness resents the city's will.

But on me hath fallen this unforeseen disaster, and sapped my life; ruined I am, and long to resign the boon of existence, kind friends, and die. For he who was all the world to me, as well thou knowest, hath turned out the worst of men, my own husband. Of all things that have life and sense we women are the most hapless creatures; first must we buy a husband at a great price, and o'er ourselves a tyrant set which is an evil worse than the first; and herein lies the most important issue, whether our choice be good or bad. For divorce is not honourable to women, nor can we disown our lords. Next must the wife, coming as she does to ways and customs new, since she hath not learnt the lesson in her home, have a diviner's eye to see how best to treat the partner of her life. If haply we perform these tasks with thoroughness and tact, and the husband live with us, without resenting the yoke, our life is a happy one; if not, 'twere best to die. But when a man is vexed with what he finds indoors, he goeth forth and rids his soul of its disgust, betaking him to some friend or comrade of like age; whilst we must needs regard his single self.

And yet they say we live secure at home, while they are at the wars, with their sorry reasoning, for I would gladly take my stand in battle array three times o'er, than once give birth. But enough! this language suits not thee as it does me; thou hast a city here, a father's house, some joy in life, and friends to share thy thoughts, but I am destitute, without a city, and therefore scorned by my husband, a captive I from a foreign shore, with no mother, brother, or kinsman in whom to find a new haven of refuge from this calamity. Wherefore this one boon and only this I wish to win from thee,—thy silence, if haply I can some way or means devise to avenge me on my husband for this cruel treatment, and on the man who gave to him his daughter, and on her who is his wife. For though woman be timorous enough in all else, and as regards courage, a coward at the mere sight of steel, yet in the moment she finds her honour wronged, no heart is filled with deadlier thoughts than hers.

Leader of the Chorus: This will I do; for thou wilt be taking a just vengeance on thy husband, Medea. That thou shouldst mourn thy lot surprises me not. But lo! I see Creon, king of this land coming hither, to announce some new resolve.

[Creon enters, with his retinue.]

Creon: Hark thee, Medea, I bid thee take those sullen looks and angry thoughts against thy husband forth from this land in exile, and with thee take both thy children and that without delay, for I am judge in this sentence, and I will not return unto my house till I banish thee beyond the borders of the land.

Medea: Ah, me! now is utter destruction come upon me, unhappy that I am! For my enemies are bearing down on me full sail, nor have I any landing-place to come at in my trouble. Yet for all my wretched plight I will ask thee, Creon, wherefore dost thou drive me from the land?

Creon: I fear thee,—no longer need I veil my dread 'neath words,—lest thou devise against my child some cureless ill. Many things contribute to this fear of mine; thou art a witch by nature, expert in countless sorceries, and thou art chafing for the loss of thy husband's affection. I hear, too, so they tell me, that thou dost threaten the father of the bride, her husband, and herself with some mischief; wherefore I will take precautions ere our troubles come. For 'tis better for me to incur thy hatred now, lady, than to soften my heart and bitterly repent it hereafter.

Medea: Alas! this is not now the first time, but oft before, O Creon, hath my reputation injured me and caused sore mischief. Wherefore whoso is wise in his generation ought never to have his children taught to be too clever; for besides the reputation they get for idleness, they purchase bitter odium from the citizens. For if thou shouldst import new learning amongst dullards, thou wilt be thought a useless trifler, void of knowledge; while if thy fame in the city o'ertops that of the pretenders to cunning knowledge, thou wilt win their dislike. I too myself share in this ill-luck. Some think me clever and hate me, others say I am too reserved, and some the very reverse; others find me hard to please and not so very clever after all. Be that as it may, thou dost fear me lest I bring on thee something to mar thy harmony. Fear me not, Creon, my position scarce is such that should seek to quarrel with princes. Why should I, for how hast thou injured me? Thou hast betrothed thy daughter where thy fancy prompted thee. No, 'tis my husband I hate, though I doubt not thou hast acted wisely herein. And now I grudge not thy prosperity; betroth thy child, good luck to thee, but let me abide in this land, for though I have been wronged I will be still and yield to my superiors.

Creon: Thy words are soft to hear, but much I dread lest thou art devising some mischief in thy heart, and less than ever do I trust thee now; for cunning woman, and man likewise, is easier to guard against when quick-tempered than when taciturn. Nay, begone at once! speak me no speeches, for this is decreed, nor hast thou any art whereby thou shalt abide amongst us, since thou hatest me.

Medea: O, say not so! by thy knees and by thy daughter newlywed, I do implore!

Creon: Thou wastest words; thou wilt never persuade me.

Medea: What, wilt thou banish me, and to my prayers no pity yield?

Creon: I will, for I love not thee above my own family.

Medea: O my country! what fond memories I have of thee in this hour!

Creon: Yea, for I myself love my city best of all things save my children.

Medea: Ah me! ah me! to mortal man how dread a scourge is love!

Creon: That, I deem, is according to the turn our fortunes take.

Medea: O Zeus! let not the author of these my troubles escape thee.

Creon: Begone, thou silly woman, and free me from my toil.

Medea: The toil is mine, no lack of it.

Creon: Soon wilt thou be thrust out forcibly by the hand of servants.

Medea: Not that, not that, I do entreat thee, Creon.

Creon: Thou wilt cause disturbance yet, it seems.

Medea: I will begone; I ask thee not this boon to grant.

Creon: Why then this violence? Why dost thou not depart?

Medea: Suffer me to abide this single day and devise some plan for the manner of my exile, and means of living for my children, since their father cares not to provide his babes therewith. Then pity them; thou too hast children of thine own; thou needs must have a kindly heart. For my own lot I care naught, though I an exile am, but for those babes I weep, that they should learn what sorrow means.

Creon: Mine is a nature anything but harsh; full oft by showing pity have suffered shipwreck; and now albeit I clearly see my error, yet shalt thou gain this request, lady; but I do forewarn thee, if tomorrow's rising sun shall find thee and thy children within the borders of this land, thou diest; my word is spoken and it will not lie. So now, if abide thou must, stay this one day only, for in it thou canst not do any of the fearful deeds I dread.

[Creon and his retinue go out.]

Chorus [*chanting*]: Ah! poor lady, woe is thee! Alas, for thy sorrows! Whither wilt thou turn? What protection, what home or country to save thee from thy troubles wilt thou find? O Medea, in what a hopeless sea of misery heaven hath plunged thee!

Medea: On all sides sorrow pens me in. Who shall gainsay this? But all is not yet lost! Think not so. Still are there troubles in store for the new bride, and for her bridegroom no light toil. Dost think I would ever have fawned on yonder man, unless to gain some end or form some scheme? Nay, would not so much as have spoken to him or touched him with my hand. But he has in folly so far stepped in that, though he might have checked my plot by banishing me from the land, he hath allowed me to abide this day, in which I will lay low in death three of my enemies—a father and his daughter and my husband too. Now, though I have many ways to compass their death, I am not sure, friends, which I am to try first. Shall I set fire to the bridal mansion, or plunge the whetted sword through their hearts, softly stealing into the chamber where their couch is spread? One thing stands in my way. If I am caught making my way into the chamber, intent on my design, I shall be put to death and cause my foes to mock. 'Twere best to take the shortest way—the way we women are most skilled in—by poison to destroy them. Well, suppose them dead; what city will receive me? What friendly host will give me a shelter in his land, a home secure, and save my soul alive? None. So I will wait yet a little while in case some tower of defence rise up for me; then will I proceed to this bloody deed in crafty silence; but if some unexpected mischance drive me forth, I will with mine own hand seize the sword, e'en though I die for it, and slay them, and go forth on my bold path of daring. By that dread queen whom I revere before all others and have chosen to share my task, by Hecate who dwells within my inmost chamber, not one of them shall wound my heart and rue it not. Bitter and sad will I make their marriage for them; bitter shall be the wooing of it, bitter my exile from the land. Up, then, Medea, spare not the secrets of thy art in plotting and devising; on to the danger. Now comes a struggle needing courage. Dost see what thou art suffering? 'Tis not for thee to be a laughing-stock to the race of Sisyphus[6] by reason of this wedding of Jason, sprung, as thou art, from noble sire, and of the Sun-god's race. Thou hast cunning; and, more than this, we women, though by nature little apt for virtuous deeds, are most expert to fashion any mischief.

Chorus [singing]:

Strophe 1: Back to their source the holy rivers turn their tide. Order and the universe are being reversed. 'Tis men whose counsels are treacherous, whose oath by heaven is no longer sure. Rumour shall bring a change o'er my life, bringing it into good repute. Honour's dawn is breaking for woman's sex; no more shall the foul tongue of slander fix upon us.

Antistrophe 1: The songs of the poets of old shall cease to make our faithlessness their theme. Phoebus, lord of minstrelsy, hath not implanted in our mind the gift of heavenly song, else had I sung an answering strain to the race of males, for time's long chapter affords many a theme on their sex as well as ours.

Strophe 2: With mind distraught didst thou thy father's house desert on thy voyage betwixt ocean's twin rocks, and on a foreign strand thou dwellest thy bed left husbandless, poor lady, and thou an exile from the land, dishonoured, persecuted.

Antistrophe 2: Gone is the grace that oaths once had. Through all the breadth of Hellas honour is found no more; to heaven hath it sped away. For thee no father's house is open, woe is thee! to be a haven from the troublous storm, while o'er thy home is set another queen, the bride that is preferred to thee.

[As the Chorus finishes its song, Jason enters, alone. Medea comes out of the house.]

Jason: It is not now I first remark, but oft ere this, how unruly a pest is a harsh temper. For instance, thou, hadst thou but patiently endured the will of thy superiors, mightest have remained here in this land and house, but now for

[6]*Sisyphus:* Because he angered the gods, Sisyphus was doomed to roll a boulder up a mountain, watch it roll back down, and roll it up again and again for eternity.

thy idle words wilt thou be banished. Thy words are naught to me. Cease not to call Jason basest of men; but for those words thou hast spoken against our rulers, count it all gain that exile is thy only punishment. I ever tried to check the outbursts of the angry monarch, and would have had thee stay, but thou wouldst not forego thy silly rage, always reviling our rulers, and so thou wilt be banished. Yet even after all this I weary not of my goodwill, but am come with thus much forethought, lady, that thou mayst not be destitute nor want for aught, when, with thy sons, thou art cast out. Many an evil doth exile bring in its train with it; for even though thou hatest me, never will I harbour hard thoughts of thee.

Medea: Thou craven villain (for that is the only name my tongue can find for thee, a foul reproach on thy unmanliness), comest thou to me, thou, most hated foe of gods, of me, and of all mankind? 'Tis no proof of courage or hardihood to confront thy friends after injuring them, but that worst of all human diseases-loss of shame. Yet hast thou done well to come; for I shall ease my soul by reviling thee, and thou wilt be vexed at my recital. I will begin at the very beginning. I saved thy life, as every Hellene knows who sailed with thee aboard the good ship Argo, when thou wert sent to tame and yoke fire-breathing bulls, and to sow the deadly tilth. Yea, and I slew the dragon which guarded the golden fleece, keeping sleepless watch o'er it with many a wreathed coil, and I raised for thee a beacon of deliverance. Father and home of my free will I left and came with the to Iolcos, 'neath Pelion's hills, for my love was stronger than my prudence. Next I caused the death of Pelias by a doom most grievous, even by his own children's hand, beguiling them of all their fear. All this have I done for thee, thou traitor! and thou hast cast me over, taking to thyself another wife, though children have been born to us. Hadst thou been childless still, I could have pardoned thy desire for this new union. Gone is now the trust I put in oaths. I cannot even understand whether thou thinkest that the gods of old no longer rule, or that fresh decrees are now in vogue amongst mankind, for thy conscience must tell thee thou hast not kept faith with me. Ah! poor right hand, which thou didst often grasp. These knees thou didst embrace! All in vain, I suffered a traitor to touch me! How short of my hopes I am fallen! But come, I will deal with the as though thou wert my friend. Yet what kindness can I expect from one so base as thee? But yet I will do it, for my questioning will show thee yet more base. Whither can I turn me now? to my father's house, to my own country, which I for thee deserted to come hither? to the hapless daughters of Pelias? A glad welcome, I trow, would they give me in their home, whose father's death I compassed! My case stands even thus: I am become the bitter foe to those of mine own home, and those whom I need ne'er have wronged I have made mine enemies to pleasure thee. Wherefore to reward me for this thou hast made me doubly blest in the eyes of many wife in Hellas; and in thee I own a peerless, trusty lord. O woe is me, if indeed I am to be cast forth an exile from the land, without one friend; one lone woman with her babes forlorn! Yea, a fine reproach to thee in thy bridal hour, that thy children and the wife who saved thy life are beggars and vagabonds! O Zeus! why hast thou granted unto man clear signs to know the sham in gold, while on man's brow no brand is stamped whereby to gauge the villain's heart?

Leader of the Chorus: There is a something terrible and past all cure, when quarrels arise 'twixt those who are near and dear.

Jason: Needs must I now, it seems, turn orator, and, like a good helmsman on a ship with close-reefed sails, weather that wearisome tongue of thine. Now, I believe, since thou wilt exaggerate thy favours, that to Cypri, alone of gods or men I owe the safety of my voyage. Thou hast a subtle wit enough; yet were it a hateful thing for me to say that the Love-god constrained thee by his resistless shaft to save my life. However, I will not reckon this too nicely; 'twas kindly done, however thou didst serve me. Yet for my safety hast thou received more than ever thou gavest, as I will show. First, thou dwellest in Hellas, instead of thy barbarian land, and hast learnt what justice means and how to live by law, not by the dictates of brute force; and all the Hellenes recognize thy cleverness, and thou hast gained a name; whereas, if thou hadst dwelt upon the confines of the earth, no tongue had mentioned thee. Give me no gold within my halls, nor skill to sing a fairer strain than ever Orpheus sang, unless there-with my fame be spread abroad! So much I say to thee about my own toils, for 'twas thou didst challenge me to this retort. As for the taunts thou urgest against my marriage with the princess, I will prove to thee, first, that I am prudent herein, next chastened in my love, and last powerful friend to thee and to thy sons; only hold thy peace. Since I have here withdrawn from Iolcos with many a hopeless trouble at my back, what happier device could I, an exile, frame than marriage with the daughter of the king? 'Tis not because I loathe thee for my wife—the thought that rankles in thy heart; 'tis not because I am smitten with desire for a new bride, nor yet that I am eager to vie with others in begetting many children, for those we have are quite enough, and I do not complain. Nay, 'tis that we—and this is most important—may dwell in comfort, instead of suffering want (for well I know that every whilom friend avoids the poor), and that I might rear my sons as doth befit my house; further, that I might be the father of brothers for the children thou hast borne, and raise these to the same high rank, uniting the family in one,—to my lasting bliss. Thou, indeed, hast no need of more children, but me it profits to help my present family by that which is to be. Have I miscarried here? Not even thou wouldest say so unless a rival's charms rankled in thy bosom. No, but you women have such strange ideas, that you think all is well so long as your married life runs smooth; but if some mischance occur to ruffle your love, all that was good and lovely erst you reckon as your foes. Yea, men should have begotten children from some other source, no female race existing; thus would no evil ever have fallen on mankind.

Leader: This speech, O Jason, hast thou with specious art arranged; but yet I think—albeit in speaking I am indiscreet—that thou hast sinned in thy betrayal of thy wife.

Medea: No doubt I differ from the mass of men on many points; for, to my mind, whoso hath skill to fence with words in an unjust cause, incurs the heaviest penalty; for such an one, confident that he can cast a decent veil of words o'er his injustice, dares to practise it; and yet he is not so very clever after all. So do not thou put forth thy specious pleas and clever words to me now, for one word of mine will lay thee low. Hadst thou not had a villain's heart, thou shouldst have gained my consent, then made this match, instead of hiding it from those who loved thee.

Jason: Thou wouldest have lent me ready aid, no doubt, in this proposal, if had told thee of my marriage, seeing that not even now canst thou restrain thy soul's hot fury.

Medea: This was not what restrained thee; but thine eye was turned towards old age, and a foreign wife began to appear a shame to thee.

Jason: Be well assured of this: 'twas not for the woman's sake I wedded the king's daughter, my present wife; but, as I have already told thee, I wished to insure thy safety and to be the father of royal sons bound by blood to my own children—a bulwark to our house.

Medea: May that prosperity, whose end is woe, ne'er be mine, nor such wealth as would ever sting my heart!

Jason: Change that prayer as I will teach thee, and thou wilt show more wisdom. Never let happiness appear in sorrow's guise, nor, when thy fortune smiles, pretend she frowns!

Medea: Mock on; thou hast a place of refuge; I am alone, an exile soon to be.

Jason: Thy own free choice was this; blame no one else.

Medea: What did I do? Marry, then betray thee?

Jason: Against the king thou didst invoke an impious curse.

Medea: On thy house too maybe I bring the curse.

Jason: Know this, I will no further dispute this point with thee. But, if thou wilt of my fortune somewhat take for the children or thyself to help thy exile, say on; for I am ready to grant it with ungrudging hand, yea and to bend tokens to my friends elsewhere who shall treat thee well. If thou refuse this offer, thou wilt do a foolish deed, but if thou cease from anger the greater will be thy gain.

Medea: I will have naught to do with friends of thine, naught will I receive of thee, offer it not to me; a villain's gifts can bring no blessing.

Jason: At least I call the gods to witness, that I am ready in all things to serve thee and thy children, but thou dost scorn my favours and thrustest thy friends stubbornly away; wherefore thy lot will be more bitter still.

Medea: Away! By love for thy young bride entrapped, too long thou lingerest outside her chamber; go wed, for, if God will, thou shalt have such a marriage as thou wouldst fain refuse.

[Jason goes out.]

Chorus [singing]:

Strophe 1: When in excess and past all limits Love doth come, he brings not glory or repute to man; but if the Cyprian queen in moderate might approach, no goddess is so full of charm as she. Never, O never, lady mine, discharge at me from thy golden bow a shaft invincible, in passion's venom dipped.

Antistrophe 1: On me may chastity, heaven's fairest gift, look with a favouring eye; never may Cypris, goddess dread, fasten on me a temper to dispute, or restless jealousy, smiting my soul with mad desire for unlawful love, but may she hallow peaceful married life and shrewdly decide whom each of us shall wed.

Strophe 2: O my country, O my own dear home! God grant I may never be an outcast from my city, leading that cruel helpless life, whose every day is misery. Ere that may I this life complete and yield to death, ay, death; for there is no misery that doth surpass the loss of fatherland.

Antistrophe 2: I have seen with mine eyes, nor from the lips of others have I the lesson learnt; no city, not one friend doth pity thee in this thine awful woe. May he perish and find no favour, whoso hath not in him honour for his friends, freely unlocking his heart to them. Never shall he be friend of mine.

[Medea has been seated in despair on her door-step during the choral song. Aegeus and his attendants enter.]

Aegeus: All hail, Medea! no man knoweth fairer prelude to the greeting of friends than this.

Medea: All hail to thee likewise, Aegeus, son of wise Pandion. Whence comest thou to this land?

Aegeus: From Phoebus'[7] ancient oracle.

Medea: What took thee on thy travels to the prophetic centre of the earth?

Aegeus: The wish to ask how I might raise up seed unto myself.

Medea: Pray tell me, hast thou till now dragged on a childless life?

Aegeus: I have no child owing to the visitation of some god.

Medea: Hast thou a wife, or hast thou never known the married state?

Aegeus: I have a wife joined to me in wedlock's bond.

Medea: What said Phoebus to thee as to children?

Aegeus: Words too subtle for man to comprehend.

Medea: Surely I may learn the god's answer?

Aegeus: Most assuredly, for it is just thy subtle wit it needs.

Medea: What said the god? speak, if I may hear it.

Aegeus: He bade me "not loose the wineskin's pendent neck."

Medea: Till when? what must thou do first, what country visit?

Aegeus: Till I to my native home return.

Medea: What object hast thou in sailing to this land?

Aegeus: O'er Troezen's realm is Pittheus king.

Medea: Pelops' son, a man devout they say.

Aegeus: To him I fain would impart the oracle of the god.

[7] *Phoebus' ancient oracle:* Phoebus is Apollo, the god of the sun, who also presides over the oracles at Delphi, a sacred precinct on Mount Parnassus where prophecies were made.

Medea: The man is shrewd and versed in such-like lore.
Aegeus: Aye, and to me the dearest of all my warrior friends.
Medea: Good luck to thee! success to all thy wishes!
Aegeus: But why that downcast eye, that wasted cheek?
Medea: O Aegeus, my husband has proved most evil.
Aegeus: What meanest thou? Explain to me clearly the cause of thy despondency.
Medea: Jason is wronging me though I have given him no cause.
Aegeus: What hath he done? Tell me more clearly.
Medea: He is taking another wife to succeed me as mistress of his house.
Aegeus: Can he have brought himself to such a dastard deed?
Medea: Be assured thereof; I, whom he loved of yore, am in dishonour now.
Aegeus: Hath he found a new love? Or does he loathe thy bed?
Medea: Much in love is he! A traitor to his friend is he become.
Aegeus: Enough! If he is a villain as thou sayest.
Medea: The alliance he is so much enamoured of is with a princess.
Aegeus: Who gives his daughter to him? Go on, I pray.
Medea: Creon, who is lord of this land of Corinth.
Aegeus: Lady, I can well pardon thy grief.
Medea: I am undone, and more than that, am banished from the land.
Aegeus: By whom? Fresh woe this word of thine unfolds.
Medea: Creon drives me forth in exile from Corinth.
Aegeus: Doth Jason allow it? This too I blame him for.
Medea: Not in words, but he will not stand out against it. O, I implore thee by this beard and by thy knees, in suppliant posture, pity, O pity my sorrows; do not see me cast forth forlorn, but receive me in thy country, to a seat within thy halls. So may thy wish by heaven's grace be crowned with a full harvest of offspring, and may thy life close in happiness! Thou knowest not the rare good luck thou findest here, for I will make thy childlessness to cease and cause thee to beget fair issue; so potent are the spells I know.
Aegeus: Lady, on many grounds I am most fain to grant thee this thy boon, first for the gods' sake, next for the children whom thou dost promise I shall beget; for in respect of this I am completely lost. 'Tis thus with me; if e'er thou reach my land, I will attempt to champion thee as I am bound to do. Only one warning I do give thee first, lady; I will not from this land bear thee away, yet if of thyself thou reach my halls, there shalt thou bide in safety and I will never yield thee up to any man. But from this land escape without my aid, for I have no wish to incur the blame of my allies as well.
Medea: It shall be even so; but wouldst thou pledge thy word to this, I should in all be well content with thee.
Aegeus: Surely thou dost trust me? Or is there aught that troubles thee?
Medea: Thee I trust; but Pelias' house and Creon are my foes. Wherefore, if thou art bound by an oath, thou wilt not give me up to them when they come to drag me from the land, but, having entered into a compact and sworn by heaven as well, thou wilt become my friend and disregard their overtures. Weak is any aid of mine, whilst they have wealth and a princely house.

Aegeus: Lady, thy words show much foresight, so if this is thy will, I do not, refuse. For I shall feel secure and safe if I have some pretext to offer to thy foes, and thy case too the firmer stands. Now name thy gods.

Medea: Swear by the plain of Earth, by Helios my father's sire, and, in one comprehensive oath, by all the race of gods.

Aegeus: What shall I swear to do, from what refrain? Tell me that.

Medea: Swear that thou wilt never of thyself expel me from thy land, nor, whilst life is thine, permit any other, one of my foes maybe, to hale me thence if so he will.

Aegeus: By Earth I swear, by the Sun-god's holy beam and by all the host of heaven that I will stand fast to the terms I hear thee make.

Medea: 'Tis enough. If thou shouldst break this oath, what curse dost thou invoke upon thyself?

Aegeus: Whate'er betides the impious.

Medea: Go in peace; all is well, and I with what speed I may, will to thy city come, when I have wrought my purpose and obtained my wish.

[Aegeus and his retinue depart.]

Aegeus [*chanting*]: May Maia's princely son go with thee on thy way to bring thee to thy home, and mayest thou attain that on which thy soul is set so firmly, for to my mind thou seemest a generous man, O Aegeus.

Medea: O Zeus, and Justice, child of Zeus, and Sun-god's light, now will triumph o'er my foes, kind friends; on victory's road have I set forth; good hope have I of wreaking vengeance on those I hate. For where we were in most distress this stranger hath appeared, to be a haven in my counsels; to him will we make fast the cables of our ship when we come to the town and citadel of Pallas. But now will I explain to thee my plans in full; do not expect to hear a pleasant tale. A servant of mine will I to Jason send and crave an interview; then when he comes I will address him with soft words, say, "this pleases me," and, "that is well," even the marriage with the princess, which my treacherous lord is celebrating, and add "it suits us both, 'twas well thought out"; then will I entreat that here my children may abide, not that I mean to leave them in a hostile land for foes to flout, but that I may slay the king's daughter by guile. For I will send them with gifts in their hands, carrying them unto the bride to save them from banishment, a robe of finest woof and a chaplet of gold. And if these ornaments she take and put them on, miserably shall she die, and likewise everyone who touches her; with such fell poisons will I smear my gifts. And here I quit this theme; but I shudder at the deed I must do next; for I will slay the children I have borne; there is none shall take them from my toils; and when I have utterly confounded Jason's house I will leave the land, escaping punishment for my dear children's murder, after my most unholy deed. For I cannot endure the taunts of enemies, kind friends; enough! What gain is life to me? I have no country, home, or refuge left. O, I did wrong, that hour I left my father's home, persuaded by that Hellene's words, who now shall pay the penalty, so help me God, Never shall he see again alive the children I bore to him, nor from his new bride shall he beget issue, for she must die a hideous death, slain by my drugs. Let no one deem me a poor weak woman who sits with folded hands, but of another mould, dangerous to foes and well-disposed to friends; for they win the fairest fame who live then, life like me.

Leader of the Chorus: Since thou hast imparted this design to me, I bid thee hold thy hand, both from a wish to serve thee and because I would uphold the laws men make.

Medea: It cannot but be so; thy words I pardon since thou art not in the same sorry plight that I am.

Leader: O lady, wilt thou steel thyself to slay thy children twain?

Medea: I will, for that will stab my husband to the heart.

Leader: It may, but thou wilt be the saddest wife alive.

Medea: No matter; wasted is every word that comes 'twixt now and then. Ho!

[The Nurse enters in answer to her call.]

Thou, go call me Jason hither, for thee I do employ on every mission of trust. No word divulge of all my purpose, as thou art to thy mistress loyal and likewise of my sex.

[The Nurse goes out.]

Chorus [*singing*]:

Strophe 1: Sons of Erechtheus, heroes happy from of yore, children of the blessed gods, fed on wisdom's glorious food in a holy land ne'er pillaged by its foes, ye who move with sprightly step through a climate ever bright and clear, where, as legend tells, the Muses nine, Pieria's holy maids, were brought to birth by Harmonia with the golden hair.

Antistrophe 1: And poets sing how Cypris drawing water from the streams of fair-flowing Cephissus breathes o'er the land a gentle breeze of balmy winds, and ever as she crowns her tresses with a garland of sweet rose-buds sends forth the Loves to sit by wisdom's side, to take part in every excellence.

Strophe 2: How then shall the city of sacred streams, the land that welcomes those it loves, receive thee, the murderess of thy children, thee whose presence with others is a pollution? 'Think on the murder of thy children, consider the bloody deed thou takest on thee. Nay, by thy knees we, one and all, implore thee, slay not thy babes.

Antistrophe 2: Where shall hand or heart find hardihood enough in wreaking such a fearsome deed upon thy sons? How wilt thou look upon thy babes, and still without a tear retain thy bloody purpose? Thou canst not, when they fall at thy feet for mercy, steel thy heart and dip in their blood thy hand.

[Jason enters.]

Jason: I am come at thy bidding, for e'en though thy hate for me is bitter thou shalt not fail in this small boon, but I will hear what new request thou hast to make of me, lady.

Medea: Jason, I crave thy pardon for the words I spoke, and well thou mayest brook my burst of passion, for ere now we twain have shared much love. For I have reasoned with my soul and railed upon me thus, "Ah! poor heart! Why am I thus distraught, why so angered 'gainst all good advice, why have I come to hate the rulers of the land, my husband too, who does the best for me he can, in wedding with a princess and rearing for my children noble brothers? Shall I not cease to fret? What possesses me, when heaven its best doth offer? Have I not my children to consider? Do I forget that we are fugitives, in need of friends?" When I had thought all this I saw how foolish I had been, how senselessly enraged. So now do commend thee and think thee most wise in forming this connection for us; but I was mad, I who should have shared in these designs, helped on thy plans, and lent my aid to bring about the match, only too pleased to wait upon thy bride. But what we are, we are, we women, evil I will not say; wherefore thou shouldst not sink to our sorry level nor with our weapons meet our childishness.

I yield and do confess that I was wrong then, but now have I come to a better mind. Come hither, my children, come, leave the house, step forth, and with me greet and bid farewell to your father, be reconciled from all past bitterness unto your friends, as now your mother is; for we have made a truce and anger is no more.

[The Attendant comes out of the house with the children.]

Take his right hand; ah me! my sad fate! when I reflect, as now, upon the hidden future. O my children, since there awaits you even thus a long, long life, stretch forth the hand to take a fond farewell. Ah me! how new to tears am I, how full of fear! For now that I have at last released me from my quarrel with your father, I let the tear-drops stream adown my tender cheek.

Leader of the Chorus: From my eyes too bursts forth the copious tear; O, may no greater ill than the present e'er befall!

Jason: Lady, I praise this conduct, not that I blame what is past; for it is but natural to the female sex to vent their spleen against a husband when he trafficks in other marriages besides his own. But thy heart is changed to wiser schemes and thou art determined on the better course, late though it be; this is acting like a woman of sober sense. And for you, my sons, hath your father provided with all good heed a sure refuge, by God's grace; for ye, I trow, shall with your brothers share hereafter the foremost rank in this Corinthian realm. Only grow up, for all the rest your sire and whoso of the gods is kind to us is bringing to pass. May I see you reach man's full estate, high o'er the heads of those I hate! But thou, lady, why with fresh tears dost thou thine eyelids wet, turning away thy wan cheek, with no welcome for these my happy tidings?

Medea: 'Tis naught; upon these children my thoughts were turned.

Jason: Then take heart; for I will see that it is well with them.

Medea: I will do so; nor will I doubt thy word; woman is a weak creature, ever given to tears.

Jason: Why prithee, unhappy one, dost moan o'er these children?

Medea: I gave them birth; and when thou didst pray long life for them, pity entered into my soul to think that these things must be. But the reason of thy coming hither to speak with me is partly told, the rest will I now mention. Since it is the pleasure of the rulers of the land to banish me, and well I know 'twere best for me to stand not in the way of thee or of the rulers by dwelling here, enemy as I am thought unto their house, forth from this land in exile am I going, but these children,—that they may know thy fostering hand, beg Creon to remit their banishment.

Jason: I doubt whether I can persuade him, yet must I attempt it.

Medea: At least do thou bid thy wife ask her sire this boon, to remit the exile of the children from this land.

Jason: Yea, that will I; and her methinks I shall persuade, since she is woman like the rest.

Medea: I too will aid thee in this task, for by the children's hand I will send to her gifts that far surpass in beauty, I well know, aught that now is seen 'mongst men, a robe of finest tissue and a chaplet of chased gold. But one of my attendants must haste and bring the ornaments hither.

[A servant goes into the house.]

Happy shall she be not once alone but ten thousand-fold, for in thee she wins the noblest soul to share her love, and gets these gifts as well which on a day my father's sire, the Sun-god, bestowed on his descendants.

[The servant returns and hands the gifts to the children.]

My children, take in your hands these wedding gifts, and bear them as an offering to the royal maid, the happy bride; for verily the gifts she shall receive are not to be scorned.

Jason: But why so rashly rob thyself of these gifts? Dost think a royal palace wants for robes or gold? Keep them, nor give them to another. For well I know that if my lady hold me in esteem, she will set my price above all wealth.

Medea: Say not so; 'tis said that gifts tempt even gods; and o'er men's minds gold holds more potent sway than countless words. Fortune smiles upon thy bride, and heaven now doth swell her triumph; youth is hers and princely power; yet to save my children from exile I would barter life, not dross alone. Children, when we are come to the rich palace, pray your father's new bride, my mistress, with suppliant voice to save you from exile, offering her these ornaments the while; for it is most needful that she receive the gifts in her own hand. Now go and linger not; may ye succeed and to your mother bring back the glad tidings she fain would hear.

[Jason, the Attendant, and the children go out together.]

Chorus [*singing*]:

Strophe 1: Gone, gone is every hope I had that the children yet might live; forth to their doom they now proceed. The hapless bride will take, ay, take the golden crown that is to be her ruin; with her own hand will she lift and place upon her golden locks the garniture of death.

Antistrophe 1: Its grace and sheen divine will tempt her to put on the robe and crown of gold, and in that act will she deck herself to be a bride amid the dead. Such is the snare whereinto she will fall, such is the deadly doom that waits the hapless maid, nor shall she from the curse escape.

Strophe 2: And thou, poor wretch, who to thy sorrow art wedding a king's daughter, little thinkest of the doom thou art bringing on thy children's life, or of the cruel death that waits thy bride. Woe is thee! how art thou fallen from thy high estate!

Antistrophe 2: Next do I bewail thy sorrows, O mother hapless in thy children, thou who wilt slay thy babes because thou hast a rival, the babes thy husband hath deserted impiously to join him to another bride.

[The Attendant enters with the children.]

Attendant: Thy children, lady, are from exile freed, and gladly did the royal bride accept thy gifts in her own hands, and so thy children made their peace with her.

Medea: Ah!

Attendant: Why art so disquieted in thy prosperous hour? Why turnest thou thy cheek away, and hast no welcome for my glad news?

Medea: Ah me!

Attendant: These groans but ill accord with the news I bring.

Medea: Ah me! once more I say.

Attendant: Have I unwittingly announced some evil tidings? Have I erred in thinking my news was good?

Medea: Thy news is as it is; I blame thee not.

Attendant: Then why this downcast eye, these floods of tears?

Medea: Old friend, needs must I weep; for the gods and I with fell intent devised these schemes.

Attendant: Be of good cheer; thou too of a surety shalt by thy sons yet be brought home again.

Medea: Ere that shall I bring others to their home, ah! woe is me.

Attendant: Thou art not the only mother from thy children reft. Bear patiently thy troubles as a mortal must.

Medea: I will obey; go thou within the house and make the day's provision for the children. [*The Attendant enters the house. Medea turns to the children.*] O my babes, my babes, ye have still a city and a home, where far from me and my sad lot you will live your lives, reft of your mother for ever; while I must to another land in banishment, or ever I have had my joy of you, or lived to see you happy, or ever I have graced your marriage couch, your bride, your bridal bower, or lifted high the wedding torch. Ah me! a victim of my own self-will. So it was all in vain I reared you, O my sons; in vain did suffer, racked with anguish, enduring the cruel pangs of childbirth. 'Fore Heaven I once had hope, poor me! High hope of ye that you would nurse me in my age and deck my corpse with loving hands, a boon we mortals covet; but now is my sweet fancy dead and gone; for I must lose you both and in bitterness and sorrow drag through life. And ye shall never with fond eyes see your mother more for o'er your life there comes a change. Ah me! ah me! why do ye look at me so, my children? why smile that last sweet smile? Ah me! what am I to do? My heart gives way when I behold my children's laughing eyes. O, I cannot; farewell to all my former schemes; I will take the children from the land, the babes I bore. Why should I wound their sire by wounding them, and get me a twofold measure of sorrow? No, no, I will not do it. Farewell my scheming! And yet what possesses me? Can I consent to let those foes of mine escape from punishment, and incur their mockery? I must face this deed. Out upon my craven heart! to think that I should even have let the soft words escape my soul. Into the house, children! [*The children go into the house.*] And whoso feels he must not be present at my sacrifice, must see to it himself; I will not spoil my handiwork. Ah! ah! do not, my heart, O do not do this deed! Let the children go, unhappy one, spare the babes! For if they live, they will cheer thee in our exile there. Nay, by the fiends of hell's abyss, never, never will I hand my children over to their foes to mock and flout. Die they must in any case, and since 'tis so, why I, the mother who bore them, will give the fatal blow. In any case their doom is fixed and there is no escape. Already the crown is on her head, the robe is round her, and she is dying, the royal bride; that do I know full well. But now since I have a piteous path to tread, and yet more piteous still the path I send my children on, fain would I say farewell to them. [*The children come out at her call. She takes them in her arms.*] O my babes, my babes, let your mother kiss your hands. Ah! hands I love so well, O lips most dear to me! O noble form and features of my children, I wish ye joy, but in that other land, for here your father robs you of your home. O the sweet embrace, the soft young cheek, the fragrant breath! my children! Go, leave me; I cannot bear to longer look upon ye; my sorrow wins the day. At last I understand the awful deed I am to do; but passion, that cause of direst woes to mortal man, hath triumphed o'er my sober thoughts.

[She goes into the house with the children.]

Chorus [*chanting*]: Oft ere now have I pursued subtler themes and have faced graver issues than woman's sex should seek to probe; but then e'en we aspire to culture, which dwells with us to teach us wisdom; I say not all; for small is the class amongst women—(one maybe shalt thou find 'mid many)—that is not incapable of wisdom. And amongst mortals I do assert that they who are wholly without experience and have never had children far surpass in happiness those who are parents. The childless, because they have never proved whether children grow up to be a blessing or curse to men are removed from all share in many troubles; whilst those who have a sweet race of children growing up in their houses do wear away, as I perceive, their whole life through; first with the thought how they may train them up in virtue, next how they shall leave their sons the means to live; and after all this 'tis far from clear whether on good or bad children they bestow their toil. But one last crowning woe for every mortal man now will name; suppose that they have found sufficient means to live, and seen their children grow to man's estate and walk in virtue's path, still if fortune so befall, comes Death and bears the children's bodies off to Hades. Can it be any profit to the gods to heap upon us mortal men beside our other woes this further grief for children lost, a grief surpassing all?

[Medea comes out of the house.]

Medea: Kind friends, long have I waited expectantly to know how things would at the palace chance. And lo! I see one of Jason's servants coming hither, whose hurried gasps for breath proclaim him the bearer of some fresh tidings.

[A Messenger rushes in.]

Messenger: Fly, fly, Medea! who hast wrought an awful deed, transgressing every law: nor leave behind or sea-borne bark or car that scours the plain.

Medea: Why, what hath chanced that calls for such a flight of mine?

Messenger: The princess is dead, a moment gone, and Creon too, her sire, slain by those drugs of thine.

Medea: Tidings most fair are thine! Henceforth shalt thou be ranked amongst my friends and benefactors.

Messenger: Ha! What? Art sane? Art not distraught, lady, who hearest with joy the outrage to our royal house done, and art not at the horrid tale afraid?

Medea: Somewhat have I, too, to say in answer to thy words. Be not so hasty, friend, but tell the manner of their death, for thou wouldst give me double joy, if so they perished miserably.

Messenger: When the children twain whom thou didst bear came with their father and entered the palace of the bride, right glad were we thralls who had shared thy griefs, for instantly from ear to ear a rumour spread that thou and thy lord had made up your former quarrel. One kissed thy children's hands, another their golden hair, while I for very joy went with them in person to the women's chambers. Our mistress, whom now we do revere in thy room, cast a longing glance at Jason, ere she saw thy children twain; but then she veiled her eyes and turned her blanching cheek away, disgusted at their coming; but thy husband tried to check his young bride's angry humour with these words: "O, be not angered 'gainst thy friends; cease from wrath and turn once more thy face this way, counting as friends whomso thy husband counts, and accept these gifts, and for my sake crave thy sire to remit these children's exile." Soon as she saw the ornaments, no longer she held out, but yielded to her lord in all; and ere the father and his sons were far from the palace gone, she took the broidered robe and put it on, and set the golden crown about her tresses, arranging her hair at her bright mirror, with many a happy smile at her breathless counterfeit. Then rising from her seat she passed across the chamber, tripping lightly on her fair white foot, exulting in the gift, with many a glance at her uplifted ankle. When lo! a scene of awful horror did ensue. In a moment she turned pale, reeled backwards, trembling in every limb, and sinks upon a seat scarce soon enough to save herself from falling to the ground. An aged dame, one of her company, thinking belike it was a fit from Pan or some god sent, raised a cry of prayer, till from her mouth she saw the foam-flakes issue, her eyeballs rolling in their sockets, and all the blood her face desert; then did she raise a loud scream far different from her former cry. Forthwith one handmaid rushed to her father's house, another to her new bridegroom to tell his bride's sad fate, and the whole house echoed with their running to and fro. By this time would a quick walker have made the turn in a course of six plethra and reached the goal, when she with one awful shriek awoke, poor sufferer, from her speechless trance and oped her closed eyes, for against her a twofold anguish was warring. The chaplet of gold about her head was sending forth a wondrous stream of ravening flame, while the fine raiment, thy children's gift, was preying on the hapless maiden's fair white flesh; and she starts from her seat in a blaze and seeks to fly, shaking her hair and head this way and that, to cast the crown therefrom; but the gold held firm to its fastenings, and the flame, as she shook her locks, blazed forth the more with double fury. Then to the earth she sinks, by the cruel blow o'ercome; past all recognition now save to a father's eye; for her eyes had lost their tranquil gaze, her face no more its natural look preserved, and from the crown of her head blood and fire in mingled stream ran down; and from her bones the flesh kept peeling off beneath the gnawing of those secret drugs, e'en as when the pine-tree weeps its tears of pitch, a fearsome sight to see. And all were afraid to touch the corpse, for we were warned by what had chanced. Anon came her hapless father unto the house, all unwitting of her doom, and stumbles o'er the dead, and loud he cried, and folding his arms about her kissed her, with words like these the while, "O my poor, poor child, which of the gods hath destroyed thee thus foully? Who is robbing me of thee, old as I am and ripe for death? O my child, alas! would I could die with thee!" He ceased his sad lament, and would have raised his aged frame, but found himself held fast by the fine-spun robe as ivy that clings to the branches of the bay, and then ensued a fearful struggle. He strove to rise, but she still held him back; and if ever he pulled with all his might, from off his bones his aged flesh he tore. At last he gave it up, and breathed forth his soul in awful suffering; for he could no longer master the pain. So there they lie, daughter and aged sire, dead side by side, a grievous sight that calls for tears. And as for thee, I leave thee out of my consideration, for thyself must discover a means to escape punishment. Not now for the first time I think this human life a shadow; yea, and without shrinking I will say that they amongst men who pretend to wisdom and expend deep thought on words do incur a serious charge of folly; for amongst mortals no man is happy; wealth may pour in and make one luckier than another, but none can happy be.

[The Messenger departs.]

Leader of the Chorus: This day the deity, it seems, will mass on Jason, as he well deserves, heavy load of evils. Woe is thee, daughter of Creon. We pity thy sad fate, gone as thou art to Hades' halls as the price of thy marriage with Jason.

Medea: My friends, I am resolved upon the deed; at once will I slay my children and then leave this land, without delaying long enough to hand them over to some more savage hand to butcher. Needs must they die in any case; and since they must, I will slay them—I, the mother that bore them. O heart of mine, steel thyself! Why do I hesitate to do the awful deed that must be done? Come, take the sword, thou wretched hand of mine! Take it, and advance to the post whence starts thy life of sorrow! Away with cowardice! Give not one thought to thy babes, how dear they are or how thou art their mother. This one brief day forget thy children dear, and after that lament; for though thou wilt slay them yet they were thy darlings still, and I am a lady of sorrows.

[Medea enters the house.]

Chorus [*chanting*]: O earth, O sun whose beam illumines all, look, look upon this lost woman, ere she stretch forth her murderous hand upon her sons for blood; for lo! these are scions of thy own golden seed, and the blood of gods is in danger of being shed by man. O light, from Zeus proceeding, stay her, hold her hand, forth from the house chase this fell bloody fiend by demons led. Vainly wasted were the throes thy children cost thee; vainly hast thou borne, it seems, sweet babes, O thou who hast left behind thee that passage through the blue Symplegades, that strangers justly hate. Ah! hapless one, why doth fierce anger thy soul assail? Why in its place is fell murder growing up? For grievous unto mortal men are pollutions that come of kindred blood poured on the earth, woes to suit each crime hurled from heaven on the murderer's house.

First Son [*within*]: Ah, me; what can I do? Whither fly to escape my mother's blows?

Second Son [*within*]: I know not, sweet brother mine; we are lost.

Chorus [*chanting*]: Didst hear, didst hear the children's cry? O lady, born to sorrow, victim of an evil fate! Shall I enter the house? For the children's sake I am resolved to ward off the murder.

First Son [*within*]: Yea, by heaven I adjure you; help, your aid is needed.

Second Son [*within*]: Even now the toils of the sword are closing round us.

Chorus [*chanting*]: O hapless mother, surely thou hast a heart of stone or steel to slay the offspring of thy womb by such a murderous doom. Of all the wives of yore I know but one who laid her hand upon her children dear, even Ino, whom the gods did madden in the day that the wife of Zeus drove her wandering from her home. But she, poor sufferer, flung herself into the sea because of the foul murder of her children, leaping o'er the wave-beat cliff, and in her death was she united to her children twain. Can there be any deed of horror left to follow this? Woe for the wooing of women fraught with disaster! What sorrows hast thou caused for men ere now!

[Jason and his attendants enter.]

Jason: Ladies, stationed near this house, pray tell me is the author of these hideous deeds, Medea, still within, or hath she fled from hence? For she must hide beneath the earth or soar on wings towards heaven's vault, if she would avoid the vengeance of the royal house. Is she so sure she will escape herself unpunished from this house, when she hath slain the rulers of the land? But enough of this! I am forgetting her children. As for her, those whom she hath wronged will do the like by her; but I am come to save the children's life, lest the victim's kin visit their wrath on me, in vengeance for the murder foul, wrought by my children's mother.

Leader of the Chorus: Unhappy man, thou knowest not the full extent of thy misery, else had thou never said those words.

Jason: How now? Can she want to kill me too?

Leader: Thy sons are dead; slain by their own mother's hand.

Jason: O God! what sayest thou? Woman, thou hast sealed my doom.

Leader: Thy children are no more; be sure of this.

Jason: Where slew she them; within the palace or outside?

Leader: Throw wide the doors and see thy children's murdered corpses.

Jason: Haste, ye slaves, loose the bolts, undo the fastenings, that I may see the sight of twofold woe, my murdered sons and her, whose blood in vengeance I will shed.

[Medea appears above the house, on a chariot drawn by dragons; the children's corpses are beside her.]

Medea: Why shake those doors and attempt to loose their bolts, in quest of the dead and me their murderess? From such toil desist. If thou wouldst aught with me, say on, if so thou wilt; but never shalt thou lay hand on me, so swift the steeds the sun, my father's sire, to me doth give to save me from the hand of my foes.

Jason: Accursed woman! By gods, by me and all mankind abhorred as never woman was, who hadst the heart to stab thy babes, thou their mother, leaving me undone and childless; this hast thou done and still dost gaze upon the sun and earth after this deed most impious. Curses on thee! now perceive what then I missed in the day I brought thee, fraught with doom, from thy home in a barbarian land to dwell in Hellas, traitress to thy sire and to the land that nurtured thee. On me the gods have hurled the curse that dogged thy steps, for thou didst slay thy brother at his hearth ere thou cam'st aboard our fair ship, Argo. Such was the outset of thy life of crime; then didst thou wed with me, and having borne me sons to glut thy passion's lust, thou now hast slain them. Not one amongst the wives of Hellas e'er had dared this deed; yet before them all I chose thee for my wife, wedding a foe to be my doom, no woman, but a lioness fiercer than

Tyrrhene Scylla[8] in nature. But with reproaches heaped thousandfold I cannot wound thee, so brazen is thy nature. Perish, vile sorceress, murderess of thy babes! Whilst I must mourn my luckless fate, for I shall ne'er enjoy my new-found bride, nor shall I have the children, whom I bred and reared, alive to say the last farewell to me; nay, I have lost them.

Medea: To this thy speech I could have made a long reply, but Father Zeus knows well all I have done for thee, and the treatment thou hast given me. Yet thou wert not ordained to scorn my love and lead a life of joy in mockery of me, nor was thy royal bride nor Creon, who gave thee a second wife, to thrust me from this land and rue it not. Wherefore, if thou wilt, call me e'en a lioness, and Scylla, whose home is in the Tyrrhene land; for I in turn have wrung thy heart, as well I might.

Jason: Thou, too, art grieved thyself, and sharest in my sorrow.

Medea: Be well assured I am; but it relieves my pain to know thou canst not mock at me.

Jason: O my children, how vile a mother ye have found!

Medea: My sons, your father's feeble lust has been your ruin!

Jason: 'Twas not my hand, at any rate, that slew them.

Medea: No, but thy foul treatment of me, and thy new marriage.

Jason: Didst think that marriage cause enough to murder them?

Medea: Dost think a woman counts this a trifling injury?

Jason: So she be self-restrained; but in thy eyes all is evil.

Medea: Thy sons are dead and gone. That will stab thy heart.

Jason: They live, methinks, to bring a curse upon thy head.

Medea: The gods know, whoso of them began this troublous coil.

Jason: Indeed, they know that hateful heart of thine.

Medea: Thou art as hateful. I am aweary of thy bitter tongue.

Jason: And I likewise of thine. But parting is easy.

Medea: Say how; what am I to do? For I am fain as thou to go.

Jason: Give up to me those dead, to bury and lament.

Medea: No, never! I will bury them myself, bearing them to Hera's sacred field, who watches o'er the Cape, that none of their foes may insult them by pulling down their tombs; and in this land of Sisyphus I will ordain hereafter a solemn feast and mystic rites to atone for this impious murder. Myself will now to the land of Erechtheus, to dwell with Aegeus, Pandion's son. But thou, as well thou mayst, shalt die a caitiff's death, thy head crushed 'neath a shattered relic of Argo, when thou hast seen the bitter ending of my marriage.

Jason: The curse of our sons' avenging spirit and of justice, that calls for blood, be on thee!

Medea: What god or power divine hears thee, breaker of oaths and every law of hospitality?

Jason: Fie upon thee! Cursed witch! Child-murderess!

Medea: To thy house! Go, bury thy wife.

[8]*Scylla:* A female sea monster that is part fish, part many-headed dog.

Jason: I go, bereft of both my sons.
Medea: Thy grief is yet to come; wait till old age is with thee too.
Jason: O my dear, dear children!
Medea: Dear to their mother, not to thee.
Jason: And yet thou didst slay them?
Medea: Yea, to vex thy heart.
Jason: One last fond kiss, ah me! I fain would on their lips imprint.
Medea: Embraces now, and fond farewells for them; but then a cold repulse!
Jason: By heaven I do adjure thee, let me touch their tender skin.
Medea: No, no! In vain this word has sped its flight.
Jason: O Zeus, dost hear how I am driven hence; dost mark the treatment I receive from this she-lion, fell murderess of her young? Yet so far as I may and can, I raise for them a dirge, and do adjure the gods to witness how thou hast slain my sons, and wilt not suffer me to embrace or bury their dead bodies. Would I had never begotten them to see thee slay them after all!

[The chariot carries Medea away.]

Chorus [*chanting*]: Many a fate doth Zeus dispense, high on his Olympian throne; oft do the gods bring things to pass beyond man's expectation; that, which we thought would be, is not fulfilled, while for the unlooked-for god finds out a way; and such hath been the issue of this matter.
THE END

(431 BCE)

QUESTIONS FOR DISCUSSION AND WRITING

CLOSE READING

1. What early indications suggest to the audience that Medea is capable of terrible vengeance? What do others say about her? How do they respond to her? What does she say about herself?
2. Reread Medea's address to the "Corinthian ladies" in which she laments "we women are the most hapless creatures." What are her complaints about the role of women in her society? Do these complaints seem justified? How many of them might apply to women today?
3. What kind of man is Jason? How does he defend himself against Medea's accusations? Is his defense convincing? As he attempts to console Medea, he tells her, "Change that prayer as I will teach thee, and thou wilt show more wisdom." What does this statement suggest about his character?
4. Why does Creon agree to give Medea one more day in Corinth? Why does he regret this decision even as he's making it?

CRITICAL AND CREATIVE READING

5. As Medea sends her sons to the house of Creon, she declares, "Ah me! a victim of my own self-will." She goes on to discuss how important her children

have always been to her. Do you think she loves her children? In punishing Jason she is also punishing herself. Why does she do this?

6. Does Jason bear any responsibility for his fate and the fate of his children? How sympathetic are you with him in the end?
7. Consider the role of the chorus. They sometimes function as narrators, explaining background information and summarizing events. They also comment on the play's drama, reacting as any common person might to uncommon events. Did the chorus's views and responses reflect your own? How much do you have in common with the Greek "man on the street"?

CONNECTIONS TO OTHER READINGS

8. In his essay "On Revenge," Francis Bacon says that "the most tolerable sort of revenge, is for those wrongs which there is no law to remedy." Does that statement apply to Medea? How would Bacon react to Medea's actions?
9. Both Medea and the ancient mariner are potentially good or even great but are brought down through their own weaknesses or flaws. Both of these characters destroy innocence, and in doing so, harm themselves as well as others. Compare their motivations. Is one character more justified than the other? Who is guiltier, and who (if either) is more innocent?
10. Compare the role of the chorus in this play to the role of the townspeople in Zora Neale Hurston's story "Sweat."

Essays

Sir Francis Bacon

On Revenge

Francis Bacon (1561–1626) was born during the reign of Elizabeth I and was serving in the House of Commons by the age of twenty-three. Under the reign of James I, he was given a baronetcy and rose to become Lord Chancellor of England. After losing his fortune and position in a political power play in which he was found guilty of accepting a bribe, he retired to a life of intellectual pursuits. He is known today for his rejection of the ancient system of learning and arts for a more modern humanism, as well as for introducing the modern essay form into English. He promoted scientific inquiry based on empirical evidence rather than learning based on the Aristotelian model. His thoughts "on revenge" shed light on a number of readings in this chapter.

Revenge is a kind of wild justice; which the more man's nature runs to, the more ought law to weed it out. For as for the first wrong, it doth but offend the law; but the revenge of that wrong, putteth the law out of office. Certainly, in taking revenge, a man is but even with his enemy; but in passing it over, he is superior; for it is a prince's part to pardon. And Solomon,[1] I am sure, saith, *It is the glory of a man, to pass by an offence.* That which is past is gone, and irrevocable; and wise men have enough to do, with things present and to come; therefore they do but trifle with themselves, that labor in past matters. There is no man doth a wrong, for the wrong's sake; but thereby to purchase himself profit, or pleasure, or honor, or the like. Therefore why should I be angry with a man, for loving himself better than me? And if any man should do wrong, merely out of ill-nature, why, yet it is but like the thorn or briar, which prick and scratch, because they can do no other. The most tolerable sort of revenge, is for those wrongs which there is no law to remedy; but then let a man take heed, the revenge be such as there is no law to punish; else a man's enemy is still before hand, and it is two for one. Some, when they take revenge, are desirous, the party should know, whence it cometh. This is the more generous. For the delight seemeth to be, not so much in doing the hurt, as in making the party repent. But base and crafty cowards, are like the arrow that flieth in the dark. Cosmus, duke of Florence, had a desperate saying against perfidious or neglecting friends, as if those wrongs were unpardonable; *You shall read* (saith he) *that we are commanded to forgive our enemies; but you never read, that we are commanded to forgive our friends.* But yet the spirit of Job was in a better tune: *Shall we* (saith he) *take good at God's hands, and not be content to take evil also?* And so of friends in a proportion. This is certain, that a man that studieth revenge, keeps his own wounds green, which otherwise would heal, and do well. Public revenges are for the most part fortunate; as that for the death of Caesar; for the death of Pertinax;[2] for the death of Henry the Third of France;[3] and many more. But in private revenges, it is not so. Nay rather, vindictive persons live the life of witches; who, as they are mischievous, so end they infortunate.

(1625)

QUESTIONS FOR DISCUSSION AND WRITING

CLOSE READING

1. Why does Bacon assert that foregoing revenge makes a person superior to his enemy?
2. According to Bacon, is revenge ever justified?
3. In what way does Bacon suggest that revenge injures the avenger as much as the object of revenge?

[1]*Solomon:* A Hebrew king who was the son of David and was known for his wisdom.

[2]*Pertinax:* A second-century Roman emperor who was assassinated by members of his own guard after ruling for eighty-six days because they felt he had not paid them their due wages.

[3]*Henry the Third of France:* A sixteenth-century French monarch who was assassinated following his suppression of Protestantism and his murder of the popular Duke of Guise.

Critical and Creative Reading

4. Although Bacon seems to condemn revenge, he also admits that it is a form of "wild justice." How does Bacon reconcile the desire for justice with his advice to forego revenge?
5. According to Bacon, people exact revenge for the pleasure of "making the party repent." Do you agree? What other satisfactions do you think people seek in revenge?
6. Do you agree with Bacon that there is a difference between public and private revenge? Why? Can you give examples (either from the readings or from other examples such as current headlines) of public revenge that Bacon might approve of?

Connections to Other Readings

7. According to Bacon, "vindictive persons live the life of witches; who, as they are mischievous, so end they infortunate." Those words could certainly apply to a number of characters in this chapter (Euripedes' Medea comes to mind), but other characters seem to have escaped this fate. Consider Montressor in Edgar Allan Poe's "The Cask of Amontillado," or Matt in Andre Dubus's "Killings," or the narrator in Fay Weldon's "Inspector Remorse." To what degree do these characters "end infortunate"?
8. Bacon says that "the most tolerable sort of revenge" occurs when there is no recourse to law. Consider Delia in Zora Neale Hurston's "Sweat" or Euripedes' Medea in light of his claim. Would he consider the revenge of those characters to be "tolerable"? Why or why not?
9. Edith Wharton's "Roman Fever" and E. Annie Proulx's "On the Antler" feature characters who have kept "their own wounds green" by nursing long-standing grievances. Compare their situations in light of Bacon's essay.

Martin Luther King, Jr.

Letter from Birmingham Jail

Martin Luther King, Jr. (1929–1968), was the most influential figure in the struggle for African American civil rights during the 1950s and 1960s. Though King had national prominence, he worked mostly in the southern United States to redress the unconstitutional and unfair practices of racial segregation. His philosophy of nonviolence grew out of Christianity and was emboldened by Gandhi's nonviolent mass protests in India. Known for his oratorical effectiveness, King drew attention to his cause and gained a vast following; eventually, his efforts led to changes in both racist attitudes and actual legislation. He was awarded the Nobel Prize for Peace in 1964. The

1960s was a decade of violent upheaval, and King was one of its victims: he was assassinated in 1968. King wrote this letter, a masterpiece of rhetorical persuasion, in prison as a response to a published statement by eight white clergymen. Consider how the letter's audience is both narrow and broad.

....

April 16, 1963

My Dear Fellow Clergymen:

While confined here in the Birmingham city jail, I came across your recent statement calling my present activities "unwise and untimely." Seldom do I pause to answer criticism of my work and ideas. If I sought to answer all the criticisms that cross my desk, my secretaries would have little time for anything other than such correspondence in the course of the day, and I would have no time for constructive work. But since I feel that you are men of genuine good will and that your criticisms are sincerely set forth, I want to try to answer your statement in what I hope will be patient and reasonable terms.

Martin Luther King, Jr., in a jail cell in Birmingham, Alabama, 1963

I think I should indicate why I am here in Birmingham, since you have been influenced by the view which argues against "outsiders coming in." I have the honor of serving as president of the Southern Christian Leadership Conference, an organization operating in every southern state, with headquarters in Atlanta, Georgia. We have some eighty-five affiliated organizations across the South, and one of them is the Alabama Christian Movement for Human Rights. Frequently we share staff, educational, and financial resources with our affiliates. Several months ago the affiliate here in Birmingham asked us to be on call to engage in a nonviolent direct-action program if such were deemed necessary. We readily consented, and when the hour came we lived up to our promise. So I, along with several members of my staff, am here because I was invited here. I am here because I have organizational ties here.

But more basically, I am in Birmingham because injustice is here. Just as the prophets of the eighth century B.C. left their villages and carried their "thus saith the Lord" far beyond the boundaries of their home towns, and just as the Apostle Paul[1] left his village of Tarsus and carried the gospel of Jesus Christ to the far corners of the Greco-Roman world, so am I compelled to carry the gospel of freedom beyond my own home town. Like Paul, I must constantly respond to the Macedonian call for aid.

Moreover, I am cognizant of the interrelatedness of all communities and states. I cannot sit idly by in Atlanta and not be concerned about what happens in Birmingham. Injustice anywhere is a threat to justice everywhere. We are caught in an inescapable network of mutuality, tied in a single garment of destiny. Whatever affects one directly, affects all indirectly. Never again can we afford to live with the narrow, provincial, "outside agitator" idea. Anyone who lives inside the United States can never be considered an outsider anywhere within its bounds.

You deplore the demonstrations taking place in Birmingham. But your state- 5
ment, I am sorry to say, fails to express a similar concern for the conditions that brought about the demonstrations. I am sure that none of you would want to rest content with the superficial kind of social analysis that deals merely with effects and does not grapple with underlying causes. It is unfortunate that demonstrations are taking place in Birmingham, but it is even more unfortunate that the city's white power structure left the Negro community with no alternative.

In any nonviolent campaign there are four basic steps: collection of the facts to determine whether injustices exist; negotiation; self-purification; and direct action. We have gone through all these steps in Birmingham. There can be no gainsaying the fact that racial injustice engulfs this community. Birmingham is probably the most thoroughly segregated city in the United States. Its ugly record of brutality is widely known. Negroes have experienced grossly unjust treatment in the courts. There have been more unsolved bombings of Negro homes and churches in Birmingham than in any other city in the nation. There are the hard brutal facts of the case. On the basis of these conditions, Negro

[1]*Paul:* Saint Paul, originally Saul of Tarsus, was a follower of Jesus who went on a mission after seeing a vision that the Macedonian people needed his help. Martin Luther King is also following in Paul's tradition as a writer of inspirational letters.

leaders sought to negotiate with the city fathers. But the latter consistently refused to engage in good-faith negotiation.

Then, last September, came the opportunity to talk with leaders of Birmingham's economic community. In the course of the negotiations, certain promises were made by the merchants—for example, to remove the stores' humiliating racial signs. On the basis of these promises, the Reverend Fred Shuttlesworth[2] and the leaders of the Alabama Christian Movement for Human Rights agreed to a moratorium on all demonstrations. As the weeks and months went by, we realized that we were the victims of a broken promise. A few signs, briefly removed, returned; the others remained.

As in so many past experiences, our hopes had been blasted, and the shadows of deep disappointment settled upon us. We had no alternative except to prepare for direct action, whereby we would present our very bodies as a means of laying our case before the conscience of the local and the national community. Mindful of the difficulties involved, we decided to undertake a process of self-purification. We began a series of workshops on nonviolence, and we repeatedly asked ourselves: "Are you able to accept blows without retaliating?" "Are you able to endure the ordeal of jail?" We decided to schedule our direct-action program for the Easter season, realizing that except for Christmas, this is the main shopping period of the year. Knowing that a strong economic-withdrawal program would be the by-product of direct action, we felt that this would be the best time to bring pressure to bear on the merchants for the needed change.

Then it occurred to us that Birmingham's mayoral election was coming up in March, and we speedily decided to postpone action until after election day. When we discovered that the Commissioner of Public Safety, Eugene "Bull" Connor, had piled up enough votes to be in the run-off, we decided again to postpone action until the day after the run-off so that the demonstrations could not be used to cloud the issues. Like many others, we waited to see Mr. Connor defeated, and to this end we endured postponement after postponement. Having aided in this community need, we felt that our direct-action program could be delayed no longer.

You may well ask, "Why direct action? Why sit-ins, marches, and so forth? 10
Isn't negotiation a better path?" You are quite right in calling for negotiation. Indeed, this is the very purpose of direct action. Nonviolent direct action seeks to create such a crisis and foster such a tension that a community which has constantly refused to negotiate is forced to confront the issue. It seeks so to dramatize the issue that it can no longer be ignored. My citing the creation of tension as part of the work of the nonviolent resister may sound rather shocking. But I must confess that I am not afraid of the word "tension." I have earnestly opposed violent tension, but there is a type of constructive, non-violent tension which is necessary for growth. Just as Socrates felt that it was necessary to create a tension in the mind so that individuals could rise from the bondage of myths and half truths to the unfettered realm of creative analysis and objective appraisal, so must we see the need for nonviolent gadflies to create the kind of tension in society

[2]*Reverend Fred Shuttlesworth:* Fred Shuttlesworth (b. 1922) was a civil rights activist who fought against segregation.

that will help men rise from the dark depths of prejudice and racism to the majestic heights of understanding and brotherhood.

The purpose of our direct-action program is to create a situation so crisis-packed that it will inevitably open the door to negotiation. I therefore concur with you in your call for negotiation. Too long has our beloved Southland been bogged down in a tragic effort to live in monologue rather than dialogue.

One of the basic points in your statement is that the action that I and my associates have taken in Birmingham is untimely. Some have asked: "Why didn't you give the new city administration time to act?" The only answer that I can give to this query is that the new Birmingham administration must be prodded about as much as the outgoing one, before it will act. We are sadly mistaken if we feel that the election of Albert Boutwell as mayor will bring the millennium to Birmingham. While Mr. Boutwell is a much more gentle person than Mr. Connor, they are both segregationists, dedicated to maintenance of the status quo. I have hoped that Mr. Boutwell will be reasonable enough to see the futility of massive resistance to desegregation. But he will not see this without pressure from devotees of civil rights. My friends, I must say to you that we have not made a single gain in civil rights without determined legal and nonviolent pressure. Lamentably, it is an historical fact that privileged groups seldom give up their privileges voluntarily. Individuals may see the moral light and voluntarily give up their unjust posture; but, as Reinhold Niebuhr[3] has reminded us, groups tend to be more immoral than individuals.

We know through painful experience that freedom is never voluntarily given by the oppressor; it must be demanded by the oppressed. Frankly, I have yet to engage in a direct-action campaign that was "well timed" in the view of those who have not suffered unduly from the disease of segregation. For years now I have heard the word "Wait!" It rings in the ear of every Negro with piercing familiarity. This "Wait" has almost always meant "Never." We must come to see, with one of our distinguished jurists, that "justice too long delayed is justice denied."

We have waited for more than 340 years for our constitutional and God-given rights. The nations of Asia and Africa are moving with jet-like speed toward gaining political independence, but we still creep at horse-and-buggy pace toward gaining a cup of coffee at a lunch counter. Perhaps it is easy for those who have never felt the stinging darts of segregation to say, "Wait." But when you have seen vicious mobs lynch your mothers and fathers at will and drown your sisters and brothers at whim; when you have seen hate-filled policemen curse, kick, and even kill your black brothers and sisters; when you see the vast majority of your twenty million Negro brothers smothering in an airtight cage of poverty in the midst of an affluent society; when you suddenly find your tongue twisted and your speech stammering as you seek to explain to your six-year-old daughter why she can't go to the public amusement park that has just been advertised on television, and see tears welling up in her eyes when she is told that Funtown is closed to colored children, and see ominous clouds of

[3]*Reinhold Niebuhr:* Reinhold Niebuhr (1892–1971) was a Protestant theologian and philosopher who attempted to reconcile Christianity and pacifism with the need to fight against injustice.

inferiority beginning to form in her little mental sky, and see her beginning to distort her personality by developing an unconscious bitterness toward white people; when you have to concoct an answer for a five-year-old son who is asking, "Daddy, why do white people treat colored people so mean?"; when you take a cross-country drive and find it necessary to sleep night after night in the uncomfortable corners of your automobile because no motel will accept you; when you are humiliated day in and day out by nagging signs reading "white" and "colored"; when your first name becomes "nigger," your middle name becomes "boy" (however old you are) and your last name becomes "John," and your wife and mother are never given the respected title "Mrs."; when you are harried by day and haunted by night by the fact that you are a Negro, living constantly at tiptoe stance, never quite knowing what to expect next, and are plagued with inner fears and outer resentments; when you are forever fighting a degenerating sense of "nobodiness"—then you will understand why we find it difficult to wait. There comes a time when the cup of endurance runs over, and men are no longer willing to be plunged into the abyss of despair. I hope, sirs, you can understand our legitimate and unavoidable impatience.

You express a great deal of anxiety over our willingness to break laws. This 15
is certainly a legitimate concern. Since we so diligently urge people to obey the Supreme Court's decision of 1954 outlawing segregation in the public schools, at first glance it may seem rather paradoxical for us consciously to break laws. One may well ask: "How can you advocate breaking some laws and obeying others?" The answer lies in the fact that there are two types of laws: just and unjust. I would be the first to advocate obeying just laws. One has not only a legal but a moral responsibility to obey just laws. Conversely, one has a moral responsibility to disobey unjust laws. I would agree with St. Augustine that "an unjust law is no law at all."

Now, what is the difference between the two? How does one determine whether a law is just or unjust? A just law is a man-made code that squares with the moral law or the law of God. An unjust law is a code that is out of harmony with the moral law. To put it in the terms of St. Thomas Aquinas: An unjust law is a human law that is not rooted in eternal law and natural law. Any law that uplifts human personality is just. Any law that degrades human personality is unjust. All segregation statutes are unjust because segregation distorts the soul and damages the personality. It gives the segregator a false sense of superiority and the segregated a false sense of inferiority. Segregation, to use the terminology of the Jewish philosopher Martin Buber, substitues an "I-it" relationship for an "I-thou" relationship and ends up relegating persons to the status of things. Hence segregation is not only politically, economically, and sociologically unsound, it is morally wrong and sinful. Paul Tillich has said that sin is separation. Is not segregation an existential expression of man's tragic separation, his awful estrangement, his terrible sinfullness? Thus it is that I can urge men to obey the 1954 decision of the Supreme Court, for it is morally right; and I can urge them to disobey segregation ordinances, for they are morally wrong.

Let us consider a more concrete example of just and unjust laws. An unjust law is a code that a numerical or power majority group compels a minority group to obey but does not make binding on itself. This is *difference* made legal. By the same token, a just law is a code that a majority compels a minority to follow and that it is willing to follow itself. This is *sameness* made legal.

Let me give another explanation. A law is unjust if it is inflicted on a minority that, as a result of being denied the right to vote, had no part in enacting or devising the law. Who can say that the legislature of Alabama which set up that state's segregation laws was democratically elected? Throughout Alabama all sorts of devious methods are used to prevent Negroes from becoming registered voters, and there are some counties in which, even though Negroes constitute a majority of the population, not a single Negro is registered. Can any law enacted under such circumstances be considered democratically structured?

Sometimes a law is just on its face and unjust in its application. For instance, I have been arrested on a charge of parading without a permit. Now, there is nothing wrong in having an ordinance which requires a permit for a parade. But such an ordinance becomes unjust when it is used to maintain segregation and to deny citizens the First Amendment privilege of peaceful assembly and protest.

20 I hope you are able to see the distinction I am trying to point out. In no sense do I advocate evading or defying the law, as would the rabid segregationist. That would lead to anarchy. One who breaks an unjust law must do so openly, lovingly, and with a willingness to accept the penalty. I submit that an individual who breaks a law that conscience tells him is unjust, and who willingly accepts the penalty of imprisonment in order to arouse the conscience of the community over its injustice, is in reality expressing the highest respect for law.

Of course, there is nothing new about this kind of civil disobedience. It was evidenced sublimely in the refusal of Shadrach, Meshach, and Abednego to obey the laws of Nebuchadnezzar,[4] on the ground that a higher moral law was at stake. It was practiced superbly by the early Christians, who were willing to face hungry lions and the excruciating pain of chopping blocks rather than submit to certain unjust laws of the Roman Empire. To a degree, academic freedom is a reality today because Socrates practiced civil disobedience. In our own nation, the Boston Tea Party represented a massive act of civil disobedience.

We should never forget that everything Adolf Hitler did in Germany was "legal" and everything the Hungarian freedom fighters did in Hungary was "illegal." It was "illegal" to aid and comfort a Jew in Hitler's Germany. Even so, I am sure that, had I lived in Germany at the time, I would have aided and comforted my Jewish brothers. If today I lived in a Communist country where certain principles dear to the Christian faith are suppressed, I would openly advocate disobeying that country's antireligious laws.

I must make two honest confessions to you, my Christian and Jewish brothers. First, I must confess that over the past few years I have been gravely disappointed with the white moderate. I have almost reached the regrettable conclusion that

[4]*Nebuchadnezzar:* A leader of Babylon who helped build his empire through conquests of Jerusalem and Judah. In the Book of Daniel, he ordered Shadrach, Meshach, and Abednego to worship a golden idol, and when they refused, he threw them into a furnace, but they were miraculously unharmed.

the Negro's great stumbling block in his stride toward freedom is not the White Citizen's Counciler or the Ku Klux Klanner, but the white moderate, who is more devoted to "order" than to justice, who prefers a negative peace which is the absence of tension to a positive peace which is the presence of justice; who constantly says, "I agree with you in the goal you seek, but I cannot agree with your methods of direct action"; who paternalistically believes he can set the timetable for another man's freedom; who lives by a mythical concept of time and who constantly advises the Negro to wait for a "more convenient season." Shallow understanding from people of good will is more frustrating than absolute misunderstanding from people of ill will. Lukewarm acceptance is much more bewildering than outright rejection.

I had hoped that the white moderate would understand that law and order exist for the purpose of establishing justice and that when they fail in this purpose they become the dangerously structured dams that block the flow of social progress. I had hoped that the white moderate would understand that the present tension in the South is a necessary phase of the transition from an obnoxious negative peace, in which the Negro passively accepted his unjust plight, to a substantive and positive peace, in which all men will respect the dignity and worth of human personality. Actually, we who engage in nonviolent direct action are not the creators of tension. We merely bring to the surface the hidden tension that is already alive. We bring it out in the open, where it can be seen and dealt with. Like a boil that can never be cured so long as it is covered up but must be opened with all its ugliness to the natural medicines of air and light, injustices must be exposed, with all the tension its exposure creates, to the light of human conscience and the air of national opinion, before it can be cured.

In your statement you assert that our actions, even though peaceful, must be 25
condemned because they precipitate violence. But is this a logical assertion? Isn't this like condemning a robbed man because his possession of money precipitated the evil act of robbery? Isn't this like condemning Socrates because his unswerving commitment to truth and his philosophical inquiries precipitated the act by the misguided populace in which they made him drink hemlock? Isn't this like condemning Jesus because his unique God-consciousness and never-ceasing devotion to God's will precipitated the evil act of crucifixion? We must come to see that, as the federal courts have consistently affirmed, it is wrong to urge an individual to cease his efforts to gain his basic constitutional rights because the quest may precipitate violence. Society must protect the robbed and punish the robber.

I had also hoped that the white moderate would reject the myth concerning time in relation to the struggle for freedom. I have just received a letter from a white brother in Texas. He writes: "All Christians know that the colored people will receive equal rights eventually, but it is possible that you are in too great a religious hurry. It has taken Christianity almost two thousand years to accomplish what it has. The teachings of Christ take time to come to earth." Such an attitude stems from a tragic misconception of time, from the strangely irrational notion that there is something in the very flow of time that will inevitably cure all ills. Actually, time itself is neutral; it can be used either destructively or constructively. More and more I feel that the people of ill will have used time much more effectively than have the people of good will. We will have to repent in this generation not merely for the hateful words and actions of the bad people, but for the appalling silence of the good people. Human progress never rolls in on wheels of inevitability; it comes through the tireless efforts of men willing to be co-workers with God, and without this hard work, time itself becomes an ally of the forces of social stagnation. We must use time creatively, in the knowledge that the time is always ripe to do right. Now is the time to make real the promise of democracy and transform our pending national elegy into a creative psalm of brotherhood. Now is the time to lift our national policy from the quicksand of racial injustice to the solid rock of human dignity.

You speak of our activity in Birmingham as extreme. At first I was rather disappointed that fellow clergymen would see my nonviolent efforts as those of an extremist. I began thinking about the fact that I stand in the middle of two opposing forces in the Negro community. One is a force of complacency made up in part of Negroes who, as a result of long years of oppression, are so drained of self-respect and a sense of "somebodiness" that they have adjusted to segregation; and in part of a few middle-class Negroes who, because of a degree of academic and economic security and because in some ways they profit by segregation, have become insensitive to the problems of the masses. The other force is one of bitterness and hatred, and it comes perilously close to advocating violence. It is expressed in the various black nationalist groups that are springing up across the nation, the largest and best known being Elijah Muhammed's Muslim movement. Nourished by the Negro's frustration over the continued existence of racial discrimination, this movement is made up of people who have lost faith in America, who have absolutely repudiated Christianity, and who have concluded that the white man is an incorrigible "devil."

I have tried to stand between these two forces, saying that we need emulate neither the "do-nothingism" of the complacent nor the hatred and despair of the black nationalist. For there is the more excellent way of love and nonviolent protest. I am grateful to God that, through the influence of the Negro church, the way of nonviolence became an integral part of our struggle.

If this philosophy had not emerged, by now many streets of the South would, I am convinced, be flowing with blood. And I am further convinced that if our white brothers dismiss as "rabble-rousers" and "outside agitators" those of us who employ nonviolent direct action, and if they refuse to support our nonviolent efforts, millions of Negroes will, out of frustration and despair, seek solace and security in black nationalist ideologies—a development that would inevitably lead to a frightening racial nightmare.

Oppressed people cannot remain oppressed forever. The yearning for free- 30
dom eventually manifests itself, and that is what has happened to the American Negro. Something within has reminded him of his birthright of freedom, and something without has reminded him that it can be gained. Consciously or unconsciously, he has been caught up by the Zeitgeist,[5] and with his black brothers of Africa and his brown and yellow brothers of Asia, South America, and the

[5] *Zeitgeist:* Spirit of the times (German).

Caribbean, the United States Negro is moving with a sense of great urgency toward the promised land of racial justice. If one recognizes this vital urge that has engulfed the Negro community, one should readily understand why public demonstrations are taking place. The Negro has many pent-up resentments and latent frustrations, and he must release them. So let him march; let him make prayer pilgrimages to the city hall, let him go on freedom rides—and try to understand why he must do so. If his repressed emotions are not released in nonviolent ways, they will seek expression through violence; this is not a threat but a fact of history. So I have not said to my people, "Get rid of your discontent." Rather, I have tried to say that this normal and healthy discontent can be channeled into the creative outlet of nonviolent direct action. And now this approach is being termed extremist.

But though I was initially disappointed at being categorized as an extremist, as I continued to think about the matter I gradually gained a measure of satisfaction from the label. Was not Jesus an extremist for love: "Love your enemies, bless them that curse you, do good to them that hate you, and pray for them which despitefully use you, and persecute you." Was not Amos an extremist for justice: "Let justice roll down like waters and righteousness like an ever-flowing stream." Was not Paul an extremist for the Christian gospel: "I bear in my body the marks of the Lord Jesus." Was not Martin Luther[6] an extremist: "Here I stand; I cannot do otherwise, so help me God." And John Bunyan:[7] "I will stay in jail to the end of my days before I make a butchery of my conscience." And Abraham Lincoln: "This nation cannot survive half slave and half free." And Thomas Jefferson: "We hold these truths to be self-evident, that all men are created equal. . . ." So the question is not whether we will be extremists, but what kind of extremists we will be. Will we be extremists for hate or for love? Will we be extremists for the preservation of injustice or for the extension of justice? In that dramatic scene on Calvary's hill three men were crucified. We must never forget that all three were crucified for the same crime—the crime of extremism. Two were extremists for immorality, and thus fell below their environment. The other, Jesus Christ, was an extremist for love, truth, and goodness, and thereby rose above his environment. Perhaps the South, the nation, and the world are in dire need of creative extremists.

I had hoped that the white moderate would see this need. Perhaps I was too optimistic; perhaps I expected too much. I suppose I should have realized that few members of the oppressor race can understand the deep groans and passionate yearnings of the oppressed race, and still fewer have the vision to see that injustice must be rooted out by strong, persistent, and determined action. I am thankful, however, that some of our white brothers in the South have grasped the meaning of this social revolution and committed themselves to it. They are still

[6]*Martin Luther:* Martin Luther (1483–1546) was a German monk and religious dissident whose "95 Theses" nailed to a church door in 1517 marked the beginning of the Protestant Reformation in Europe.

[7]*John Bunyan:* John Bunyan (1628–1688) was an English writer and preacher who wrote *Pilgrim's Progress* (published in 1678 and 1684), a highly influential Christian allegory.

all too few in quantity, but they are big in quality. Some—such as Ralph McGill, Lillian Smith, Harry Golden, James McBride Dabbs, Ann Braden, and Sarah Patton Boyle—have written about our struggle in eloquent and prophetic terms. Others have marched with us down nameless streets of the South. They have languished in filthy, roach-infested jails, suffering the abuse and brutality of policemen who view them as "dirty nigger-lovers." Unlike so many of their moderate brothers and sisters, they have recognized the urgency of the moment and sensed the need for powerful "action" antidotes to combat the disease of segregation.

Let me take note of my other major disappointment. I have been so greatly disappointed with the white church and its leadership. Of course, there are some notable exceptions. I am not unmindful of the fact that each of you has taken some significant stands on this issue. I commend you, Reverend Stallings, for your Christian stand on this past Sunday, in welcoming Negroes to your worship service on a non-segregated basis. I commend the Catholic leaders of this state for integrating Spring Hill College[8] several years ago.

But despite these notable exceptions, I must honestly reiterate that I have been disappointed with the church. I do not say this as one of those negative critics who can always find something wrong with the church. I say this as a minister of the gospel, who loves the church; who was nurtured in its bosom; who has been sustained by its spiritual blessings and who will remain true to it as long as the cord of life shall lengthen.

When I was suddenly catapulted into the leadership of the bus protest in 35
Montgomery, Alabama, a few years ago, I felt we would be supported by the white church. I felt that the white ministers, priests, and rabbis of the South would be among our strongest allies. Instead, some have been outright opponents, refusing to understand the freedom movement and misrepresenting its leaders; all too many others have been more cautious than courageous and have remained silent behind the anesthetizing security of stained-glass windows.

In spite of my shattered dreams, I came to Birmingham with the hope that the white religious leadership of this community would see the justice of our cause and, with deep moral concerns, would serve as the channel through which our just grievances could reach the power structure. I had hoped that each of you would understand. But again I have been disappointed. . . .

There was a time when the church was very powerful— in the time when the early Christians rejoiced at being deemed worthy to suffer for what they believed. In those days the church was not merely a thermometer that recorded the ideas and principles of popular opinion; it was a thermostat that transformed the mores of society. Whenever the early Christians entered a town, the people in power became disturbed and immediately sought to convict the Christians for being "disturbers of the peace" and "outside agitators." But the Christians pressed on, in the conviction that they were "a colony of heaven," called to obey

[8]*Spring Hill College:* The first Catholic Jesuit college in the South, Spring Hill College (located in Mobile, Alabama) was desegregated in 1954, just before the United States Supreme Court's landmark decision banning segregation.

God rather than man. Small in number, they were big in commitment. They were too God intoxicated to be "astronomically intimidated." By their effort and example they brought an end to such ancient evils as infanticide and gladiatorial contests.

Things are different now. So often the contemporary church is a weak, ineffectual voice with an uncertain sound. So often it is an archdefender of the status quo. Far from being disturbed by the presence of the church, the power structure of the average community is consoled by the church's silent—and often even vocal—sanction of things as they are.

But the judgment of God is upon the church as never before. If today's church does not recapture the sacrificial spirit of the early church, it will lose its authenticity, forfeit the loyalty of millions, and be dismissed as an irrelevant social club with no meaning for the twentieth century. Every day I meet young people whose disappointment with the church has turned into outright disgust.

40 Perhaps I have once again been too optimistic. Is organized religion too inextricably bound to the status quo to save our nation and the world? Perhaps I must turn my faith to the inner spiritual church, the church within the church, as the true ekklesia and the hope of the world. But again I am thankful to God that some noble souls from the ranks of organized religion have broken loose from the paralyzing chains of conformity and joined us as active partners in the struggle for freedom. They have left their secure congregations and walked the streets of Albany, Georgia, with us. They have gone down the highways of the South on torturous rides for freedom. Yes, they have gone to jail with us. Some have been dismissed from their churches, have lost the support of their bishops and fellow ministers. But they have acted in the faith that right defeated is stronger than evil triumphant. Their witness has been the spiritual salt that has preserved the true meaning of the gospel in these troubled times. They have carved a tunnel of hope through the dark mountain of disappointment.

I hope the church as a whole will meet the challenge of this decisive hour. But even if the church does not come to the aid of justice, I have no despair about the future. I have no fear about the outcome of our struggle in Birmingham, even if our motives are at present misunderstood. We will reach the goal of freedom in Birmingham and all over the nation, because the goal of America is freedom. Abused and scorned though we may be, our destiny is tied up with America's destiny. Before the pilgrims landed at Plymouth, we were here. Before the pen of Jefferson etched the majestic words of the Declaration of Independence across the pages of history, we were here. For more than two centuries our forebears labored in this country without wages; they made cotton king; they built the homes of their masters while suffering gross injustice and shameful humiliation—and yet out of a bottomless vitality they continued to thrive and develop. If the inexpressible cruelties of slavery could not stop us, the opposition we now face will surely fail. We will win our freedom because the sacred heritage of our nation and the eternal will of God are embodied in our echoing demands.

Before closing I feel impelled to mention one other point in your statement that has troubled me profoundly. You warmly commended the Birmingham police force for keeping "order" and "preventing violence." I doubt that you would have so warmly commended the police force if you had seen its dogs sinking their teeth into unarmed, non-violent Negroes. I doubt that you would so quickly commend the policemen if you were to observe their ugly and inhumane treatment of Negroes here in the city jail; if you were to watch them push and curse old Negro women and young Negro girls; if you were to see them slap and kick old Negro men and young boys; if you were to observe them, as they did on two occasions, refuse to give us food because we wanted to sing our grace together. I cannot join you in your praise of the Birmingham police department.

It is true that the police have exercised a degree of discipline in handling the demonstrators. In this sense they have conducted themselves rather "nonviolently" in public. But for what purpose? To preserve the evil system of segregation. Over the past few years I have consistently preached that nonviolence demands that the means we use must be as pure as the ends we seek. I have tried to make clear that it is wrong to use immoral means to attain moral ends. But now I must affirm that it is just as wrong, or perhaps even more so, to use moral means to preserve immoral ends. Perhaps Mr. Connor and his policemen have been rather nonviolent in public, as was Chief Pritchett in Albany, Georgia, but they have used the moral means of nonviolence to maintain the immoral end of racial injustice. As T. S. Eliot has said, "The last temptation is the greatest treason: To do the right deed for the wrong reason."

I wish you had commended the Negro sit-inners and demonstrators of Birmingham for their sublime courage, their willingness to suffer, and their amazing discipline in the midst of great provocation. One day the South will recognize its real heroes. They will be the James Merediths,[9] with the noble sense of purpose that enables them to face jeering and hostile mobs, and with the agonizing loneliness that characterizes the life of the pioneer. They will be old, oppressed, battered Negro women, symbolized in a seventy-two-year-old woman in Montgomery, Alabama, who rose up with a sense of dignity and with her people decided not to ride segregated buses, and who responded with ungrammatical profundity to one who inquired about her weariness: "My feets is tired, but my soul is at rest." They will be the young high school and college students, the young ministers of the gospel and a host of their elders, courageously and nonviolently sitting in at lunch counters and willingly going to jail for conscience' sake. One day the South will know that when these disinherited children of God sat down at lunch counters, they were in reality standing up for what is best in the American dream and for the most sacred values in our Judaeo-Christian heritage, thereby bringing our nation back to those great wells of democracy which were dug deep by the founding fathers in their formulation of the Constitution and the Declaration of Independence.

Never before have I written so long a letter. I'm afraid it is much too long to 45
take your precious time. I can assure you that it would have been much shorter if I had been writing from a comfortable desk, but what else can one do when he is

[9]*James Merediths*: James Meredith (b. 1933) was an African American student whose enrollment in the University of Mississippi in 1962 set off riots at the campus in Oxford, Mississippi.

alone in a narrow jail cell, other than write long letters, think long thoughts, and pray long prayers?

If I have said anything in this letter that overstates the truth and indicates an unreasonable impatience, I beg you to forgive me. If I have said anything that understates the truth and indicates my having a patience that allows me to settle for anything less than brotherhood, I beg God to forgive me.

I hope this letter finds you strong in the faith. I also hope that circumstances will soon make it possible for me to meet each of you, not as an integrationist or a civil rights leader but as a fellow clergyman and a Christian brother. Let us all hope that the dark clouds of racial prejudice will soon pass away and the deep fog of misunderstanding will be lifted from our fear-drenched communities, and in some not too distant tomorrow the radiant stars of love and brotherhood will shine over our great nation with all their scintillating beauty.

Yours in the cause of Peace and Brotherhood,

Martin Luther King, Jr.

(1963)

Questions for Discussion and Writing

Close Reading

1. What does King mean by the statement, "Injustice anywhere is a threat to justice everywhere"? How does it feed into his overall argument?
2. Trace the way King uses the words "just" and "unjust" in his argument.
3. What is the relationship between white moderates, the Christian church, and the Birmingham police in King's argument?

Critical and Creative Reading

4. King states, "Any law that uplifts human personality is just. Any law that degrades human personality is unjust." Think of examples of each. Do any laws fit into neither of these categories?
5. King gradually accepts the label of "extremist," a term that usually has negative connotations. Write an essay about extremism as either a negative or positive force in society.
6. Would you submit yourself to jail time for a cause? If so, what cause? How much jail time?

Connections to Other Readings

7. Consider the concept of forgiveness in King's essay and in Fitzgerald's story "Babylon Revisited."
8. Write an essay that positions racial injustice in the poems "Harlem" by Langston Hughes and "Minor Miracle" by Marilyn Nelson alongside King's "Letter from Birmingham Jail."

9. Is the law a higher force than a personal understanding of right and wrong? Use examples from King's "Letter" and Andre Dubus's story "Killings" in your response.

Considering Art: Vengeance and Forgiveness

The discussion below references art reproduced on color insert pages 13 and 14.

Dorothy, the Scarecrow, and the Wicked Witch of the West from *The Wizard of Oz* (see color insert p. 13). The film *The Wizard of Oz* (1939) was made in Depression-era America and was based on the children's book *The Wonderful Wizard of Oz* (1900), written by L. Frank Baum (1856–1919) and illustrated by W. W. Denslow (1856–1915). The movie has become an enduring classic. It shows good and evil standing in stark opposition and contrasts the world of rural America (filmed in black and white) with the dreamlike, artistic realm of Oz (filmed in magical Technicolor). In this film still, Dorothy encounters the Scarecrow, who is the first of three companions she meets on the yellow brick road to the Emerald City, where all four characters believe they will find what they need most. Here the two are secretly observed by the Wicked Witch of the West, who wants the powerful ruby slippers that Dorothy obtained when she accidentally caused the death of the witch's sister.

***Mary-Magdalen at the House of the Pharisee* (see color insert p. 13).** The biblical figure of Mary Magdalene has long served artists as a model figure of penitence. Many legends, such as her later saintly life as a **hermit** in a cave on the south coast of France, grew up around her life. From the seventeenth century onward, her example was used to illustrate the power of the individual's free will to return to an original state of grace. In the late nineteenth century, however, the image of the "fallen women" rarely offered the possibility of redemption. In his *Mary-Magdalen at the House of the Pharisee* (1891), French painter Jean Béraud (1849–1936) depicts the tale of Christ explaining his forgiveness of the penitent prostitute. Rather than trying to be historically accurate, Béraud imagines this scene as a modern event occurring in a gentlemen's private club in Paris. The figures depicted were recognizable portraits of prominent French citizens. Christ has the features of socialist journalist Albert Duc-Quercy, and Simon the Pharisee is the writer and philosopher Ernest Renan, whose controversial book *The Life of Jesus* (1863) argued for a historical and biographic reading of Christ's life and the spreading of Christianity. This depiction of Mary Magdalene may have been modeled for by a notorious courtesan, and she is dressed in the latest Paris fashions. See Richard Thomson, *The Troubled Republic: Visual Culture and Social Debate in France, 1889–1900* (New Haven: Yale University Press, 2004), 150–52.

***After the Fox?* (see color insert p. 14).** Contemporary painter Mark Copeland (b. 1956) imagines what happens when the tables are turned in *After the Fox?* (1997). In the British sport of fox hunting, described by the playwright Oscar Wilde as "the unspeakable in pursuit of the uneatable," a small red fox is pursued by packs of dogs and hunters mounted on horseback. The pursuit and eventual killing of the fox (which originated as a method of limiting the fox population) entails gallops through woodlands and difficult jumps over hedges and stone walls, with horns blaring and dogs barking. Fox hunting is highly controversial in modern Britain. For the landed gentry and those who wish they were, it is a romanticized ritual. For animal-rights activists, it is an inexcusable cruelty to animals. In this painting, instead of a massively overequipped hunting party in pursuit of one small animal, Copeland reverses the **scale** of his players. The gigantic red fox crouches, ready to pounce on the scattering, minuscule hunting party.

Questions about the Art

1. What does color and body posture tell us about the characters? If there was the possibility of forgiveness for the Witch of the West in Oz or back in Kansas how would the tale change?
2. How does the modern setting affect the way a viewer understands the message of Béraud's painting?
3. What is the effect or message of Copeland's reversal of scale? Who is hunted now? How do the natural and manmade details of the landscape contribute to the narrative?

Connecting Art and Literature

1. Discuss the power of the oppressed in Copeland's painting and in Langston Hughes's poem "Harlem."
2. Consider the idea of persuasiveness in Beraud's painting and in King's "Letter from Birmingham Jail."
3. Compare and contrast the image of the Wicked Witch from *The Wizard of Oz* to Medea, another vengeful female character with harmful powers.

Common Characters

The Prodigal Son

Jesus uses the parable of the prodigal son in Luke's Gospel to illustrate God's love and capacity for forgiveness. The story is well known to Christians and non-Christians alike because the three main characters are recognizably human: the wayward and rebellious son who tires of life on his father's farm and wants to see the world, only to regret his folly; the dutiful brother who remains behind to care for his father and the family property and feels unappreciated; and the grateful and generous father who allows his child to go his own way and welcomes him back with unconditional love and forgiveness. Everyone has experienced repentance and has needed to ask for forgiveness, yet we also know the feeling of resentment when we think someone has "gotten away with" something. The older brother's reaction is not merely petty: while his brother

Albrecht Dürer, *The Prodigal Son* (c. 1500).

was spending his entire inheritance in "wild living," he eased his father's sorrow back at home by working hard and living an upright life. Most people can understand the older brother's desire for justice, yet they hope that when *they* are the ones needing a second chance, they will be welcomed back with open arms.

Luke *(1st century CE)*

The Parable of the Lost Son, *from* Luke 15:11–32

[11]"There was a man who had two sons. [12]The younger one said to his father, 'Father, give me my share of the estate.' So he divided his property between them.

[13]"Not long after that, the younger son got together all he had, set off for a distant country and there squandered his wealth in wild living. [14]After he had spent everything, there was a severe famine in that whole country, and he began to be in need. [15]So he went and hired himself out to a citizen of that country, who sent him to his fields to feed pigs. [16]He longed to fill his stomach with the pods that the pigs were eating, but no one gave him anything.

[17]"When he came to his senses, he said, 'How many of my father's hired men have food to spare, and here I am starving to death! [18]I will set out and go back to my father and say to him: Father, I have sinned against heaven and against you. [19]I am no longer worthy to be called your son; make me like one of your hired men.' [20]So he got up and went to his father.

"But while he was still a long way off, his father saw him and was filled with compassion for him; he ran to his son, threw his arms around him and kissed him.

[21]"The son said to him, 'Father, I have sinned against heaven and against you. I am no longer worthy to be called your son.'

[22]"But the father said to his servants, 'Quick! Bring the best robe and put it on him. Put a ring on his finger and sandals on his feet. [23]Bring the fattened calf and kill it. Let's have a feast and celebrate. [24]For this son of mine was dead and is alive again; he was lost and is found.' So they began to celebrate.

[25]"Meanwhile, the older son was in the field. When he came near the house, he heard music and dancing. [26]So he called one of the servants and asked him what was going on.

[27]'Your brother has come,' he replied, 'and your father has killed the fattened calf because he has him back safe and sound.'

[28]"The older brother became angry and refused to go in. So his father went out and pleaded with him. [29]But he answered his father, 'Look! All these years I've been slaving for you and never disobeyed your orders. Yet you never gave me even a young goat so I could celebrate with my friends. [30]But when this son of yours who has squandered your property with prostitutes comes home, you kill the fattened calf for him!'

31"'My son,' the father said, 'you are always with me, and everything I have 10
is yours. 32But we had to celebrate and be glad, because this brother of yours was dead and is alive again; he was lost and is found.'"

James Baldwin *(1924–1987)*

Sonny's Blues

I read about it in the paper, in the subway, on my way to work. I read it, and I couldn't believe it, and I read it again. Then perhaps I just stared at it, at the newsprint spelling out his name, spelling out the story. I stared at it in the swinging lights of the subway car, and in the faces and bodies of the people, and in my own face, trapped in the darkness which roared outside.

It was not to be believed and I kept telling myself that as I walked from the subway station to the high school. And at the same time I couldn't doubt it. I was scared, scared for Sonny. He became real to me again. A great block of ice got settled in my belly and kept melting there slowly all day long, while I taught my classes algebra. It was a special kind of ice. It kept melting, sending trickles of ice water all up and down my veins, but it never got less. Sometimes it hardened and seemed to expand until I felt my guts were going to come spilling out or that I was going to choke or scream. This would always be at a moment when I was remembering some specific thing Sonny had once said or done.

When he was about as old as the boys in my classes his face had been bright and open, there was a lot of copper in it; and he'd had wonderfully direct brown eyes, and great gentleness and privacy. I wondered what he looked like now. He had been picked up, the evening before, in a raid on an apartment downtown, for peddling and using heroin.

I couldn't believe it: but what I mean by that is that I couldn't find any room for it anywhere inside me. I had kept it outside me for a long time. I hadn't wanted to know. I had had suspicions, but I didn't name them, I kept putting them away. I told myself that Sonny was wild, but he wasn't crazy. And he'd always been a good boy, he hadn't ever turned hard or evil or disrespectful, the way kids can, so quick, so quick, especially in Harlem. I didn't want to believe that I'd ever see my brother going down, coming to nothing, all that light in his face gone out, in the condition I'd already seen so many others. Yet it had happened and here I was, talking about algebra to a lot of boys who might, every one of them for all I knew, be popping off needles every time they went to the head. Maybe it did more for them than algebra could.

I was sure that the first time Sonny had ever had horse,[1] he couldn't have 5
been much older than these boys were now. These boys, now, were living as we'd been living then, they were growing up with a rush and their heads bumped abruptly against the low ceiling of their actual possibilities. They were filled with

[1]*horse:* Heroin.

rage. All they really knew were two darknesses, the darkness of their lives, which was now closing in on them, and the darkness of the movies, which had blinded them to that other darkness, and in which they now, vindictively, dreamed, at once more together than they were at any other time, and more alone.

When the last bell rang, the last class ended, I let out my breath. It seemed I'd been holding it for all that time. My clothes were wet—I may have looked as though I'd been sitting in a steam bath, all dressed up, all afternoon. I sat alone in the classroom a long time. I listened to the boys outside, downstairs, shouting and cursing and laughing. Their laughter struck me for perhaps the first time. It was not the joyous laughter which—God knows why—one associates with children. It was mocking and insular, its intent was to denigrate. It was disenchanted, and in this, also, lay the authority of their curses. Perhaps I was listening to them because I was thinking about my brother and in them I heard my brother. And myself.

One boy was whistling a tune, at once very complicated and very simple, it seemed to be pouring out of him as though he were a bird, and it sounded very cool and moving through all that harsh, bright air, only just holding its own through all those other sounds.

I stood up and walked over to the window and looked down into the courtyard. It was the beginning of the spring and the sap was rising in the boys. A teacher passed through them every now and again, quickly, as though he or she couldn't wait to get out of that courtyard, to get those boys out of their sight and off their minds. I started collecting my stuff. I thought I'd better get home and talk to Isabel.

The courtyard was almost deserted by the time I got downstairs. I saw this boy standing in the shadow of a doorway, looking just like Sonny. I almost called his name. Then I saw that it wasn't Sonny, but somebody we used to know, a boy from around our block. He'd been Sonny's friend. He'd never been mine, having been too young for me, and, anyway, I'd never liked him. And now, even though he was a grown-up man, he still hung around that block, still spent hours on the street corner, was always high and raggy. I used to run into him from time to time and he'd often work around to asking me for a quarter or fifty cents. He always had some real good excuse, too, and I always gave it to him, I don't know why.

10 But now, abruptly, I hated him. I couldn't stand the way he looked at me, partly like a dog, partly like a cunning child. I wanted to ask him what the hell he was doing in the school courtyard.

He sort of shuffled over to me, and he said, "I see you got the papers. So you already know about it."

"You mean about Sonny? Yes, I already know about it. How come they didn't get you?"

He grinned. It made him repulsive and it also brought to mind what he'd looked like as a kid. "I wasn't there. I stay away from them people."

"Good for you." I offered him a cigarette and I watched him through the smoke. "You come all the way down here just to tell me about Sonny?"

15 "That's right." He was sort of shaking his head and his eyes looked strange, as though they were about to cross. The bright sun deadened his damp dark brown skin and it made his eyes look yellow and showed up the dirt in his conked

hair. He smelled funky. I moved a little away from him and I said, "Well, thanks. But I already know about it and I got to get home."

"I'll walk you a little ways," he said. We started walking. There were a couple of kids still loitering in the courtyard and one of them said good night to me and looked strangely at the boy beside me.

"What're you going to do?" he asked me. "I mean, about Sonny?"

"Look. I haven't seen Sonny for over a year, I'm not sure I'm going to do anything. Anyway, what the hell *can* I do?"

"That's right," he said quickly, "ain't nothing you can do. Can't much help old Sonny no more, I guess."

It was what I was thinking and so it seemed to me he had no right to say it. 20

"I'm surprised at Sonny, though," he went on—he had a funny way of talking, he looked straight ahead as though he were talking to himself—"I thought Sonny was a smart boy, I thought he was too smart to get hung."

"I guess he thought so too," I said sharply, "and that's how he got hung. And how about you? You're pretty goddamn smart, I bet."

Then he looked directly at me, just for a minute. "I ain't smart," he said. "If I was smart, I'd have reached for a pistol a long time ago."

"Look. Don't tell *me* your sad story, if it was up to me, I'd give you one." Then I felt guilty—guilty, probably, for never having supposed that the poor bastard *had* a story of his own, much less a sad one, and I asked, quickly, "What's going to happen to him now?"

He didn't answer this. He was off by himself some place. "Funny thing," he 25
said, and from his tone we might have been discussing the quickest way to get to Brooklyn, "when I saw the papers this morning, the first thing I asked myself was if I had anything to do with it. I felt sort of responsible."

I began to listen more carefully. The subway station was on the corner, just before us, and I stopped. He stopped, too. We were in front of a bar and he ducked slightly, peering in, but whoever he was looking for didn't seem to be there. The juke box was blasting away with something black and bouncy and I half watched the barmaid as she danced her way from the juke box to her place behind the bar. And I watched her face as she laughingly responded to something someone said to her, still keeping time to the music. When she smiled one saw the little girl, one sensed the doomed, still-struggling woman beneath the battered face of the semi-whore.

"I never *give* Sonny nothing," the boy said finally, "but a long time ago I come to school high and Sonny asked me how it felt." He paused, I couldn't bear to watch him, I watched the barmaid, and I listened to the music which seemed to be causing the pavement to shake. "I told him it felt great." The music stopped, the barmaid paused and watched the juke box until the music began again. "It did."

All this was carrying me some place I didn't want to go. I certainly didn't want to know how it felt. It filled everything, the people, the houses, the music, the dark, quicksilver barmaid, with menace; and this menace was their reality.

"What's going to happen to him now?" I asked again.

"They'll send him away some place and they'll try to cure him." He shook 30
his head. "Maybe he'll even think he's kicked the habit. Then they'll let him loose"—he gestured, throwing his cigarette into the gutter. "That's all."

"What do you mean, that's *all?*"

But I knew what he meant.

"I *mean,* that's *all.*" He turned his head and looked at me, pulling down the corners of his mouth. "Don't you know what I mean?" he asked softly.

"How the hell *would* I know what you mean?" I almost whispered it, I don't know why.

"That's right," he said to the air, "how would *he* know what I mean?" He 35
turned toward me again, patient and calm, and yet I somehow felt him shaking, shaking as though he were going to fall apart. I felt that ice in my guts again, the dread I'd felt all afternoon; and again I watched the barmaid, moving about the bar, washing glasses, and singing. "Listen. They'll let him out and then it'll just start all over again. That's what I mean."

"You mean—they'll let him out. And then he'll just start working his way back in again. You mean he'll never kick the habit. Is that what you mean?"

"That's right," he said, cheerfully. "*You* see what I mean."

"Tell me," I said at last, "why does he want to die? He must want to die, he's killing himself, why does he want to die?"

He looked at me in surprise. He licked his lips. "He don't want to die. He wants to live. Don't nobody want to die, ever."

Then I wanted to ask him—too many things. He could not have answered, 40
or if he had, I could not have borne the answers. I started walking. "Well, I guess it's none of my business."

"It's going to be rough on old Sonny," he said. We reached the subway station. "This is your station?" he asked. I nodded. I took one step down. "Damn!" he said, suddenly. I looked up at him. He grinned again. "Damn if I didn't leave all my money home. You ain't got a dollar on you, have you? Just for a couple of days, is all."

All at once something inside gave and threatened to come pouring out of me. I didn't hate him any more. I felt that in another moment I'd start crying like a child.

"Sure," I said. "Don't sweat." I looked in my wallet and didn't have a dollar, I only had a five. "Here," I said. "That hold you?"

He didn't look at it—he didn't want to look at it. A terrible, closed look came over his face, as though he were keeping the number on the bill a secret from him and me. "Thanks," he said, and now he was dying to see me go. "Don't worry about Sonny. Maybe I'll write him or something."

"Sure," I said. "You do that. So long." 45

"Be seeing you," he said. I went on down the steps.

And I didn't write Sonny or send him anything for a long time. When I finally did, it was just after my little girl died, he wrote me back a letter which made me feel like a bastard.

Here's what he said:

Dear Brother,

You don't know how much I needed to hear from you. I wanted to write you many a time but I dug how much I must have hurt you and so I didn't write. But now I feel like a man who's been trying to climb up out of some deep, real deep and funky hole and just saw the sun up there, outside. I got to get outside.

I can't tell you much about how I got here. I mean I don't know how to tell you. I guess I was afraid of something or I was trying to escape from something and you know I have never been very strong in the head (smile). I'm glad Mama and Daddy are dead and can't see what's happened to their son and I swear if I'd known what I was doing I would never have hurt you so, you and a lot of other fine people who were nice to me and who believed in me.

I don't want you to think it had anything to do with me being a musician. It's more than that. Or maybe less than that. I can't get anything straight in my head down here and I try not to think about what's going to happen to me when I get outside again. Sometime I think I'm going to flip and *never* get outside and sometime I think I'll come straight back. I tell you one thing, though, I'd rather blow my brains out than go through this again. But that's what they all say, so they tell me. If I tell you when I'm coming to New York and if you could meet me, I sure would appreciate it. Give my love to Isabel and the kids and I was sorry to hear about little Gracie. I wish I could be like Mama and say the Lord's will be done, but I don't know it seems to me that trouble is the one thing that never does get stopped and I don't know what good it does to blame it on the Lord. But maybe it does some good if you believe it.

Your brother,
Sonny

Then I kept in constant touch with him and I sent him whatever I could and I went to meet him when he came back to New York. When I saw him many things I thought I had forgotten came flooding back to me. This was because I had begun, finally, to wonder about Sonny, about the life that Sonny lived inside. This life, whatever it was, had made him older and thinner and it had deepened the distant stillness in which he had always moved. He looked very unlike my baby brother. Yet, when he smiled, when we shook hands, the baby brother I'd never known looked out from the depths of his private life, like an animal waiting to be coaxed into the light.

"How you been keeping?" he asked me.

"All right. And you?"

"Just fine." He was smiling all over his face. "It's good to see you again."

"It's good to see you."

The seven years' difference in our ages lay between us like a chasm: I wondered if these years would ever operate between us as a bridge. I was remembering, and it made it hard to catch my breath, that I had been there when he was born; and I had heard the first words he had ever spoken. When he started to walk, he walked from our mother straight to me. I caught him just before he fell when he took the first steps he ever took in this world.

"How's Isabel?"

"Just fine. She's dying to see you."

"And the boys?"

"They're fine, too. They're anxious to see their uncle."

"Oh, come on. You know they don't remember me."

"Are you kidding? Of course they remember you."

He grinned again. We got into a taxi. We had a lot to say to each other, far too much to know how to begin.

As the taxi began to move, I asked, "You still want to go to India?"

He laughed. "You still remember that. Hell, no. This place is Indian enough for me."

"It used to belong to them," I said.

And he laughed again. "They damn sure knew what they were doing when they got rid of it."

Years ago, when he was around fourteen, he'd been all hipped on the idea of going to India. He read books about people sitting on rocks, naked, in all kinds of weather, but mostly bad, naturally, and walking barefoot through hot coals and arriving at wisdom. I used to say that it sounded to me as though they were getting away from wisdom as fast as they could. I think he sort of looked down on me for that.

"Do you mind," he asked, "if we have the driver drive alongside the park? On the west side—I haven't seen the city in so long."

"Of course not," I said. I was afraid that I might sound as though I were humoring him, but I hoped he wouldn't take it that way.

So we drove along, between the green of the park and the stony, lifeless elegance of hotels and apartment buildings, toward the vivid, killing streets of our childhood. These streets hadn't changed, though housing projects jutted up out of them now like rocks in the middle of a boiling sea. Most of the houses in which we had grown up had vanished, as had the stores from which we had stolen, the basements in which we had first tried sex, the rooftops from which we had hurled tin cans and bricks. But houses exactly like the houses of our past yet dominated the landscape, boys exactly like the boys we once had been found themselves smothering in these houses, came down into the streets for light and air and found themselves encircled by disaster. Some escaped the trap, most didn't. Those who got out always left something of themselves behind, as some animals amputate a leg and leave it in the trap. It might be said, perhaps, that I had escaped, after all, I was a school teacher; or that Sonny had, he hadn't lived in Harlem for years. Yet, as the cab moved uptown through streets which seemed, with a rush, to darken with dark people, and as I covertly studied Sonny's face, it came to me that what we both were seeking through our separate cab windows was that part of ourselves which had been left behind. It's always at the hour of trouble and confrontation that the missing member aches.

We hit 110th Street and started rolling up Lenox Avenue.[2] And I'd known this avenue all my life, but it seemed to me again, as it had seemed on the day I'd first heard about Sonny's trouble, filled with a hidden menace which was its very breath of life.

"We almost there," said Sonny.

"Almost." We were both too nervous to say anything more.

We live in a housing project. It hasn't been up long. A few days after it was up it seemed uninhabitably new, now, of course, it's already run-down. It looks like a parody of the good, clean, faceless life—God knows the people who live in it do their best to make it a parody. The beat-looking grass lying around isn't enough to make their lives green, the hedges will never hold out the streets, and they know it. The big windows fool no one, they aren't big enough to make space out of no space. They don't bother with the windows, they watch the TV screen instead. The playground is most popular with the children who don't play at jacks, or skip rope, or roller skate, or swing, and they can be found in it after dark. We moved in partly because it's not too far from where I teach, and partly for the kids; but it's really just like the houses in which Sonny and I grew up. The same things happen, they'll have the same things to remember. The moment Sonny and I started into the house I had the feeling that I was simply bringing him back into the danger he had almost died trying to escape.

Sonny has never been talkative. So I don't know why I was sure he'd be dying to talk to me when supper was over the first night. Everything went fine, the oldest boy remembered him, and the youngest boy liked him, and Sonny had remembered to bring something for each of them; and Isabel, who is really much nicer than I am, more open and giving, had gone to a lot of trouble about dinner and was genuinely glad to see him. And she's always been able to tease Sonny in a way that I haven't. It was nice to see her face so vivid again and to hear her laugh and watch her make Sonny laugh. She wasn't, or, anyway, she didn't seem to be, at all uneasy or embarrassed. She chatted as though there were no subject which had to be avoided and she got Sonny past his first, faint stiffness. And thank God she was there, for I was filled with that icy dread again. Everything I did seemed awkward to me, and everything I said sounded freighted with hidden meaning. I was trying to remember everything I'd heard about dope addiction and I couldn't help watching Sonny for signs. I wasn't doing it out of malice. I was trying to find out something about my brother. I was dying to hear him tell me he was safe. "Safe!" my father grunted, whenever Mama suggested trying to move to a neighborhood which might be safer for children. "Safe, hell! Ain't no place safe for kids, nor nobody."

He always went on like this, but he wasn't, ever, really as bad as he sounded, not even on weekends, when he got drunk. As a matter of fact, he was always on the lookout for "something a little better," but he died before he found it. He died suddenly, during a drunken weekend in the middle of the war, when Sonny was fifteen. He and Sonny hadn't ever got on too well. And this was partly

[2]*110th Street . . . Lenox Avenue:* Main streets in Harlem, a neighborhood in northern Manhattan that runs from 110th Street to 155th Street. By 1920, the district was populated mostly by African Americans, and by the middle of the twentieth century it was known as a place of poverty and urban blight.

because Sonny was the apple of his father's eye. It was because he loved Sonny so much and was frightened for him, that he was always fighting with him. It doesn't do any good to fight with Sonny. Sonny just moves back, inside himself, where he can't be reached. But the principal reason that they never hit it off is that they were so much alike. Daddy was big and rough and loud-talking, just the opposite of Sonny, but they both had—that same privacy.

Mama tried to tell me something about this, just after Daddy died. I was 75
home on leave from the army.

This was the last time I ever saw my mother alive. Just the same, this picture gets all mixed up in my mind with pictures I had of her when she was younger. The way I always see her is the way she used to be on a Sunday afternoon, say, when the old folks were talking after the big Sunday dinner. I always see her wearing pale blue. She'd be sitting on the sofa. And my father would be sitting in the easy chair, not far from her. And the living room would be full of church folks and relatives. There they sit, in chairs all around the living room, and the night is creeping up outside, but nobody knows it yet. You can see the darkness growing against the window-panes and you hear the street noises every now and again, or maybe the jangling beat of a tambourine from one of the churches close by, but it's real quiet in the room. For a moment nobody's talking, but every face looks darkening, like the sky outside. And my mother rocks a little from the waist, and my father's eyes are closed. Everyone is looking at something a child can't see. For a minute they've forgotten the children. Maybe a kid is lying on the rug half asleep. Maybe somebody's got a kid on his lap and is absent-mindedly stroking the kid's head. Maybe there's a kid, quiet and big-eyed, curled up in a big chair in the corner. The silence, the darkness coming, and the darkness in the faces frightens the child obscurely. He hopes that the hand which strokes his forehead will never stop—will never die. He hopes that there will never come a time when the old folks won't be sitting around the living room, talking about where they've come from, and what they've seen, and what's happened to them and their kinfolk.

But something deep and watchful in the child knows that this is bound to end, is already ending. In a moment someone will get up and turn on the light. Then the old folks will remember the children and they won't talk any more that day. And when light fills the room, the child is filled with darkness. He knows that every time this happens he's moved just a little closer to that darkness outside. The darkness outside is what the old folks have been talking about. It's what they've come from. It's what they endure. The child knows that they won't talk any more because if he knows too much about what's happened to *them*, he'll know too much too soon, about what's going to happen to *him*.

The last time I talked to my mother, I remember I was restless. I wanted to get out and see Isabel. We weren't married then and we had a lot to straighten out between us.

There Mama sat, in black, by the window. She was humming an old church song, *Lord, you brought me from a long ways off.* Sonny was out somewhere. Mama kept watching the streets.

"I don't know," she said, "if I'll ever see you again, after you go off from here. 80
But I hope you'll remember the things I tried to teach you."

"Don't talk like that," I said, and smiled. "You'll be here a long time yet."

She smiled, too, but she said nothing. She was quiet for a long time. And I said, "Mama, don't you worry about nothing. I'll be writing all the time, and you be getting the checks. . . ."

"I want to talk to you about your brother," she said, suddenly. "If anything happens to me he ain't going to have nobody to look out for him."

"Mama," I said, "ain't nothing going to happen to you *or* Sonny. Sonny's all right. He's a good boy and he's got good sense."

"It ain't a question of his being a good boy," Mama said, "nor of his having good sense. It ain't only the bad ones, nor yet the dumb ones that gets sucked under." She stopped, looking at me. "Your Daddy once had a brother," she said, and she smiled in a way that made me feel she was in pain. "You didn't never know that, did you?"

"No," I said, "I never knew that," and I watched her face.

"Oh, yes," she said, "your Daddy had a brother." She looked out of the window again. "I know you never saw your Daddy cry. But *I* did—many a time, through all these years."

I asked her, "What happened to his brother? How come nobody's ever talked about him?"

This was the first time I ever saw my mother look old.

"His brother got killed," she said, "when he was just a little younger than you are now. I knew him. He was a fine boy. He was maybe a little full of the devil, but he didn't mean nobody no harm."

Then she stopped and the room was silent, exactly as it had sometimes been on those Sunday afternoons. Mama kept looking out into the streets.

"He used to have a job in the mill," she said, "and, like all young folks, he just liked to perform on Saturday nights. Saturday nights, him and your father would drift around to different places, go to dances and things like that, or just sit around with people they knew, and your father's brother would sing, he had a fine voice, and play along with himself on his guitar. Well, this particular Saturday night, him and your father was coming home from some place, and they were both a little drunk and there was a moon that night, it was bright like day. Your father's brother was feeling kind of good, and he was whistling to himself, and he had his guitar slung over his shoulder. They was coming down a hill and beneath them was a road that turned off from the highway. Well, your father's brother, being always kind of frisky, decided to run down this hill, and he did, with that guitar banging and clanging behind him, and he ran across the road, and he was making water behind a tree. And your father was sort of amused at him and he was still coming down the hill, kind of slow. Then he heard a car motor and that same minute his brother stepped from behind the tree, into the road, in the moonlight. And he started to cross the road. And your father started to run down the hill, he says he don't know why. This car was full of white men. They was all drunk, and when they seen your father's brother they let out a great whoop and holler and they aimed the car straight at him. They was having fun, they just wanted to scare him, the way they do sometimes, you know. But they was drunk. And I guess the boy, being drunk, too, and scared, kind of lost his head. By the time he jumped it was too late. Your father says he heard his brother scream when the car rolled over him, and he heard the wood of that guitar when it give, and he heard them strings go flying, and he heard them white men shouting, and the car kept on a-going and it ain't stopped till this day. And, time your father got down the hill, his brother weren't nothing but blood and pulp."

Tears were gleaming on my mother's face. There wasn't anything I could say. "He never mentioned it," she said, "because I never let him mention it before you children. Your Daddy was like a crazy man that night and for many a night thereafter. He says he never in his life seen anything as dark as that road after the lights of that car had gone away. Weren't nothing, weren't nobody on that road, just your Daddy and his brother and that busted guitar. Oh, yes. Your Daddy never did really get right again. Till the day he died he weren't sure but that every white man he saw was the man that killed his brother."

She stopped and took out her handkerchief and dried her eyes and looked 95
at me.

"I ain't telling you all this," she said, "to make you scared or bitter or to make you hate nobody. I'm telling you this because you got a brother. And the world ain't changed."

I guess I didn't want to believe this. I guess she saw this in my face. She turned away from me, toward the window again, searching those streets.

"But I praise my Redeemer," she said at last, "that He called your Daddy home before me. I ain't saying it to throw no flowers at myself, but, I declare, it keeps me from feeling too cast down to know I helped your father get safely through this world. Your father always acted like he was the roughest, strongest man on earth. And everybody took him to be like that. But if he hadn't had *me* there—to see his tears!"

She was crying again. Still, I couldn't move. I said, "Lord, Lord, Mama, I didn't know it was like that."

"Oh, honey," she said, "there's a lot that you don't know. But you are going 100
to find it out." She stood up from the window and came over to me. "You got to hold on to your brother," she said, "and don't let him fall, no matter what it looks like is happening to him and no matter how evil you gets with him. You going to be evil with him many a time. But don't you forget what I told you, you hear?"

"I won't forget," I said. "Don't you worry, I won't forget. I won't let nothing happen to Sonny."

My mother smiled as though she were amused at something she saw in my face. Then, "You may not be able to stop nothing from happening. But you got to let him know you's *there*."

Two days later I was married, and then I was gone. And I had a lot of things on my mind and I pretty well forgot my promise to Mama until I got shipped home on a special furlough for her funeral.

And, after the funeral, with just Sonny and me alone in the empty kitchen, I tried to find out something about him.

"What do you want to do?" I asked him. 105

"I'm going to be a musician," he said.

For he had graduated, in the time I had been away, from dancing to the juke box to finding out who was playing what, and what they were doing with it, and he had bought himself a set of drums.

"You mean, you want to be a drummer?" I somehow had the feeling that being a drummer might be all right for other people but not for my brother Sonny.

"I don't think," he said, looking at me very gravely, "that I'll ever be a good drummer. But I think I can play a piano."

I frowned. I'd never played the role of the older brother quite so seriously 110
before, had scarcely ever, in fact, *asked* Sonny a damn thing. I sensed myself in the presence of something I didn't really know how to handle, didn't understand. So I made my frown a little deeper as I asked: "What kind of musician do you want to be?"

He grinned. "How many kinds do you think there are?"

"Be *serious*," I said.

He laughed, throwing his head back, and then looked at me. "I *am* serious."

"Well, then, for Christ's sake, stop kidding around and answer a serious question. I mean, do you want to be a concert pianist, you want to play classical music and all that, or—or what?" Long before I finished he was laughing again. "For Christ's *sake*, Sonny!"

He sobered, but with difficulty. "I'm sorry. But you sound so—*scared!*" and 115
he was off again.

"Well, you may think it's funny now, baby, but it's not going to be so funny when you have to make your living at it, let me tell you *that*." I was furious because I knew he was laughing at me and I didn't know why.

"No," he said, very sober now, and afraid, perhaps, that he'd hurt me, "I don't want to be a classical pianist. That isn't what interests me. I mean"—he paused, looking hard at me, as though his eyes would help me to understand, and then gestured helplessly, as though perhaps his hand would help—"I mean, I'll have a lot of studying to do, and I'll have to study *everything*, but I mean, I want to play *with*—jazz musicians." He stopped. "I want to play jazz," he said.

Well, the word had never before sounded as heavy, as real, as it sounded that afternoon in Sonny's mouth. I just looked at him and I was probably frowning a real frown by this time. I simply couldn't see why on earth he'd want to spend his time hanging around night clubs, clowning around on bandstands, while people pushed each other around a dance floor. It seemed—beneath him, somehow. I had never thought about it before, had never been forced to, but I suppose I had always put jazz musicians in a class with what Daddy called "good-time people."

"Are you *serious?*"

"Hell, *yes*, I'm serious." 120

He looked more helpless than ever, and annoyed, and deeply hurt.

I suggested, helpfully: "You mean—like Louis Armstrong?"

His face closed as though I'd struck him. "No. I'm not talking about none of that old-time, down home crap."

"Well, look, Sonny, I'm sorry, don't get mad. I just don't altogether get it, that's all. Name somebody—you know, a jazz musician you admire."

"Bird.[3]" 125

[3]*Bird:* A reference to Charlie Parker (1920–1955), a saxophone virtuoso associated with the type of jazz known as bop. Parker became addicted to heroin and died young.

"Who?"

"Bird! Charlie Parker! Don't they teach you nothing in the goddamn army?"

I lit a cigarette. I was surprised and then a little amused to discover that I was trembling. "I've been out of touch," I said. "You'll have to be patient with me. Now. Who's this Parker character?"

"He's just one of the greatest jazz musicians alive," said Sonny, sullenly, his hands in his pockets, his back to me. "Maybe *the* greatest," he added, bitterly, "that's probably why *you* never heard of him."

"All right," I said. "I'm ignorant. I'm sorry. I'll go out and buy all the cat's 130
records right away, all right?"

"It don't," said Sonny, with dignity, "make any difference to me. I don't care what you listen to. Don't do me no favors."

I was beginning to realize that I'd never seen him so upset before. With another part of my mind I was thinking that this would probably turn out to be one of those things kids go through and that I shouldn't make it seem important by pushing it too hard. Still, I didn't think it would do any harm to ask: "Doesn't all this take a lot of time? Can you make a living at it?"

He turned back to me and half leaned, half sat, on the kitchen table. "Everything takes time," he said, "and—well, yes, sure, I can make a living at it. But what I don't seem to be able to make you understand is that it's the only thing I want to do."

"Well Sonny," I said, gently, "you know people can't always do exactly what they *want* to do—"

"*No*, I don't know that," said Sonny, surprising me. "I think people *ought* to 135
do what they want to do, what else are they alive for?"

"You getting to be a big boy," I said desperately, "it's time you started thinking about your future."

"I'm thinking about my future," said Sonny, grimly. "I think about it all the time."

I gave up. I decided, if he didn't change his mind, that we could always talk about it later. "In the meantime," I said, "you got to finish school." We had already decided that he'd have to move in with Isabel and her folks. I knew this wasn't the ideal arrangement because Isabel's folks are inclined to be dicty and they hadn't especially wanted Isabel to marry me. But I didn't know what else to do. "And we have to get you fixed up at Isabel's."

There was a long silence. He moved from the kitchen table to the window. "That's a terrible idea. You know it yourself."

"Do you have a *better* idea?" 140

He just walked up and down the kitchen for a minute. He was as tall as I was. He had started to shave. I suddenly had the feeling that I didn't know him at all.

He stopped at the kitchen table and picked up my cigarettes. Looking at me with a kind of mocking, amused defiance, he put one between his lips. "You mind?"

"You smoking already?"

He lit the cigarette and nodded, watching me through the smoke. "I just wanted to see if I'd have the courage to smoke in front of you." He grinned and blew a great cloud of smoke to the ceiling. "It was easy." He looked at my face. "Come on, now. I bet you was smoking at my age, tell the truth."

I didn't say anything but the truth was on my face, and he laughed. But now 145
there was something very strained in his laugh. "Sure. And I bet that ain't all you was doing."

He was frightening me a little. "Cut the crap," I said. "We already decided that you was going to go and live at Isabel's. Now what's got into you all of a sudden?"

"*You* decided it," he pointed out. "*I* didn't decide nothing." He stopped in front of me, leaning against the stove, arms loosely folded. "Look, brother. I don't want to stay in Harlem no more, I really don't." He was very earnest. He looked at me, then over toward the kitchen window. There was something in his eyes I'd never seen before, some thoughtfulness, some worry all his own. He rubbed the muscle of one arm. "It's time I was getting out of here."

"Where do you want to *go*, Sonny?"

"I want to join the army. Or the navy, I don't care. If I say I'm old enough they'll believe me."

Then I got mad. It was because I was so scared. "You must be crazy. You god- 150
damn fool, what the hell do you want to go and join the *army* for?"

"I just told you. To get out of Harlem."

"Sonny, you haven't even finished *school.* And if you really want to be a musician, how do you expect to study if you're in the *army?*"

He looked at me, trapped, and in anguish. "There's ways. I might be able to work out some kind of deal. Anyway, I'll have the G.I. Bill when I come out."

"*If* you come out." We stared at each other. "Sonny, please. Be reasonable. I know the setup is far from perfect. But we got to do the best we can."

"I ain't learning nothing in school," he said. "Even when I go." He turned 155
away from me and opened the window and threw his cigarette out into the narrow alley. I watched his back. "At least, I ain't learning nothing you'd want me to learn." He slammed the window so hard I thought the glass would fly out, and turned back to me. "And I'm sick of the stink of these garbage cans!"

"Sonny," I said, "I know how you feel. But if you don't finish school now, you're going to be sorry later that you didn't." I grabbed him by the shoulders. "And you only got another year. It ain't so bad. And I'll come back and I swear I'll help you do *whatever* you want to do. Just try to put up with it till I come back. Will you please do that? For me?"

He didn't answer and he wouldn't look at me.

"Sonny. You hear me?"

He pulled away. "I hear you. But you never hear anything *I* say."

I didn't know what to say to that. He looked out of the window and then 160
back at me. "OK," he said, and sighed. "I'll try."

Then I said, trying to cheer him up a little, "They got a piano at Isabel's. You can practice on it."

And as a matter of fact, it did cheer him up for a minute. "That's right," he said to himself. "I forgot that." His face relaxed a little. But the worry, the thoughtfulness, played on it still, the way shadows play on a face which is staring into the fire. But I thought I'd never hear the end of that piano. At first, Isabel would write me, saying how nice it was that Sonny was so serious about his music and how, as soon as he came in from school, or wherever he had been when he was supposed to be at school, he went straight to that piano and stayed there until suppertime. And, after supper, he went back to that piano and stayed there until everybody went to bed. He was at the piano all day Saturday and all day Sunday. Then he bought a record player and started playing records. He'd play one record over and over again, all day long sometimes, and he'd improvise along with it on the piano. Or he'd play one section of the record, one chord, one change, one progression, then he'd do it on the piano. Then back to the record. Then back to the piano.

Well, I really don't know how they stood it. Isabel finally confessed that it wasn't like living with a person at all, it was like living with sound. And the sound didn't make any sense to her, didn't make any sense to any of them—naturally. They began, in a way, to be afflicted by this presence that was living in their home. It was as though Sonny were some sort of god, or monster. He moved in an atmosphere which wasn't like theirs at all. They fed him and he ate, he washed himself, he walked in and out of their door; he certainly wasn't nasty or unpleasant or rude, Sonny isn't any of those things; but it was as though he were all wrapped up in some cloud, some fire, some vision all his own; and there wasn't any way to reach him.

At the same time, he wasn't really a man yet, he was still a child, and they had to watch out for him in all kinds of ways. They certainly couldn't throw him out. Neither did they dare to make a great scene about that piano because even they dimly sensed, as I sensed, from so many thousands of miles away, that Sonny was at that piano playing for his life.

But he hadn't been going to school. One day a letter came from the school 165
board and Isabel's mother got it—there had, apparently, been other letters but Sonny had torn them up. This day, when Sonny came in, Isabel's mother showed him the letter and asked where he'd been spending his time. And she finally got it out of him that he'd been down in Greenwich Village, with musicians and other characters, in a white girl's apartment. And this scared her and she started to scream at him and what came up, once she began—though she denies it to this day—was what sacrifices they were making to give Sonny a decent home and how little he appreciated it.

Sonny didn't play the piano that day. By evening, Isabel's mother had calmed down but then there was the old man to deal with, and Isabel herself. Isabel says she did her best to be calm but she broke down and started crying. She says she just watched Sonny's face. She could tell, by watching him, what was happening with him. And what was happening was that they penetrated his cloud, they had reached him. Even if their fingers had been a thousand times more gentle than human fingers ever are, he could hardly help feeling that they had stripped him naked and were spitting on that nakedness. For he also had to see that his presence, that music, which was life or death to him, had been torture for them and that they had endured it, not at all for his sake, but only for mine. And Sonny couldn't take that. He can take it a little better today than he could then but he's still not very good at it and, frankly, I don't know anybody who is.

The silence of the next few days must have been louder than the sound of all the music ever played since time began. One morning, before she went to work, Isabel was in his room for something and she suddenly realized that all of his records were gone. And she knew for certain that he was gone. And he was. He went as far as the navy would carry him. He finally sent me a postcard from some place in Greece and that was the first I knew that Sonny was still alive. I didn't see him any more until we were both back in New York and the war had long been over.

He was a man by then, of course, but I wasn't willing to see it. He came by the house from time to time, but we fought almost every time we met. I didn't like the way he carried himself, loose and dreamlike all the time, and I didn't like his friends, and his music seemed to be merely an excuse for the life he led. It sounded just that weird and disordered.

Then we had a fight, a pretty awful fight, and I didn't see him for months. By and by I looked him up, where he was living, in a furnished room in the Village, and I tried to make it up. But there were lots of other people in the room and Sonny just lay on his bed, and he wouldn't come downstairs with me, and he treated these other people as though they were his family and I weren't. So I got mad and then he got mad, and then I told him that he might just as well be dead as live the way he was living. Then he stood up and he told me not to worry about him any more in life, that he *was* dead as far as I was concerned. Then he pushed me to the door and the other people looked on as though nothing were happening, and he slammed the door behind me. I stood in the hallway, staring at the door. I heard somebody laugh in the room and then the tears came to my eyes. I started down the steps, whistling to keep from crying, I kept whistling to myself, *You going to need me, baby, one of these cold, rainy days.*

I read about Sonny's trouble in the spring. Little Grace died in the fall. She 170
was a beautiful little girl. But she only lived a little over two years. She died of polio and she suffered. She had a slight fever for a couple of days, but it didn't seem like anything and we just kept her in bed. And we would certainly have called the doctor, but the fever dropped, she seemed to be all right. So we thought it had just been a cold. Then, one day, she was up, playing; Isabel was in the kitchen fixing lunch for the two boys when they'd come in from school, and she heard Grace fall down in the living room. When you have a lot of children you don't always start running when one of them falls, unless they start screaming or something. And, this time, Grace was quiet. Yet, Isabel says that when she heard that *thump* and then that silence, something happened in her to make her afraid. And she ran to the living room and there was little Grace on the floor, all twisted up and the reason she hadn't screamed was that she couldn't get her breath. And when she did scream, it was the worst sound, Isabel says, that she'd ever heard in all her life, and she still hears it sometimes in her dreams. Isabel will sometimes wake me up with a low, moaning, strangled sound and I have to be quick to awaken her and hold her to me and where Isabel is weeping against me seems a mortal wound.

I think I may have written Sonny the very day that little Grace was buried. I was sitting in the living room in the dark, by myself, and I suddenly thought of Sonny. My trouble made his real.

One Saturday afternoon, when Sonny had been living with us, or, anyway, been in our house, for nearly two weeks, I found myself wandering aimlessly about the living room, drinking from a can of beer, and trying to work up the courage to search Sonny's room. He was out, he was usually out whenever I was home, and Isabel had taken the children to see their grandparents. Suddenly I was standing still in front of the living room window, watching Seventh Avenue. The idea of searching Sonny's room made me still. I scarcely dared to admit to myself what I'd be searching for. I didn't know what I'd do if I found it. Or if I didn't.

On the sidewalk across from me, near the entrance to a barbecue joint, some people were holding an old-fashioned revival meeting. The barbecue cook, wearing a dirty white apron, his conked hair reddish and metallic in the pale sun and a cigarette between his lips, stood in the doorway, watching them. Kids and older people paused in their errands and stood there, along with some older men and a couple of very tough-looking women who watched everything that happened on the avenue, as though they owned it, or were maybe owned by it. Well, they were watching this, too. The revival was being carried on by three sisters in black, and a brother. All they had were their voices and their Bibles and a tambourine. The brother was testifying and while he testified two of the sisters stood together, seeming to say, Amen, and the third sister walked around with the tambourine outstretched and a couple of people dropped coins into it. Then the brother's testimony ended and the sister who had been taking up the collection dumped the coins into her palm and transferred them to the pocket of her long black robe. Then she raised both hands, striking the tambourine against the air, and then against one hand, and she started to sing. And the two other sisters and the brother joined in.

It was strange, suddenly, to watch, though I had been seeing these street meetings all my life. So, of course, had everybody else down there. Yet, they paused and watched and listened and I stood still at the window. *"Tis the old ship of Zion,"* they sang, and the sister with the tambourine kept a steady, jangling beat, *"It has rescued many a thousand!"* Not a soul under the sound of their voices was hearing this song for the first time, not one of them had been rescued. Nor had they seen much in the way of rescue work being done around them. Neither did they especially believe in the holiness of the three sisters and the brother, they knew too much about them, knew where they lived, and how. The woman with the tambourine, whose voice dominated the air, whose face was bright with joy, was divided by very little from the woman who stood watching her, a cigarette between her heavy, chapped lips, her hair a cuckoo's nest, her face scarred and swollen from many beatings, and her black eyes glittering like coal. Perhaps they both knew this, which was why, when, as rarely, they addressed each other, they addressed each other as Sister. As the singing filled the air the watching, listening faces underwent a change, the eyes focusing on something within; the music seemed to soothe a poison out of them; and time seemed, nearly, to fall away from the sullen, belligerent, battered faces, as though they were fleeing back to their first condition, while dreaming of their last. The barbecue cook half shook his head and smiled, and dropped his cigarette and disappeared into his joint. A man fumbled in his pockets for change and stood holding it in his hand impatiently, as though he had just remembered a pressing appointment further up the avenue. He looked furious. Then I saw Sonny, standing on the edge of the crowd. He was carrying a wide, flat notebook with a green cover, and it made him look, from where I was standing, almost like a schoolboy. The coppery sun brought out the copper in his skin, he was very faintly smiling, standing very still. Then the singing stopped, the tambourine turned into a collection plate again. The furious man dropped in his coins and vanished, so did a couple of the women, and Sonny dropped some change in the plate, looking directly at the woman with a little smile. He started across the avenue, toward the house. He has a slow, loping walk, something like the way Harlem hipsters walk, only he's imposed on this his own halfbeat. I had never really noticed it before.

I stayed at the window, both relieved and apprehensive. As Sonny disap- 175
peared from my sight, they began singing again. And they were still singing when his key turned in the lock.

"Hey," he said.

"Hey, yourself. You want some beer?"

"No. Well, maybe." But he came up to the window and stood beside me, looking out. "What a warm voice," he said.

They were singing *If I could only hear my mother pray again!*

"Yes," I said, "and she can sure beat that tambourine." 180

"But what a terrible song," he said, and laughed. He dropped his notebook on the sofa and disappeared into the kitchen. "Where's Isabel and the kids?"

"I think they went to see their grandparents. You hungry?"

"No." He came back into the living room with his can of beer. "You want to come some place with me tonight?"

I sensed, I don't know how, that I couldn't possibly say No. "Sure. Where?"

He sat down on the sofa and picked up his notebook and started leafing 185
through it. "I'm going to sit in with some fellows in a joint in the Village."

"You mean, you're going to play, tonight?"

"That's right." He took a swallow of his beer and moved back to the window. He gave me a sidelong look. "If you can stand it."

"I'll try," I said.

He smiled to himself and we both watched as the meeting across the way broke up. The three sisters and the brother, heads bowed, were singing *God be with you till we meet again.* The faces around them were very quiet. Then the song ended. The small crowd dispersed. We watched the three women and the lone man walk slowly up the avenue.

"When she was singing before," said Sonny, abruptly, "her voice reminded 190
me for a minute of what heroin feels like sometimes—when it's in your veins. It makes you feel sort of warm and cool at the same time. And distant. And—and sure." He sipped his beer, very deliberately not looking at me. I watched his face. "It makes you feel—in control. Sometimes you've got to have that feeling."

"Do you?" I sat down slowly in the easy chair.

"Sometimes." He went to the sofa and picked up his notebook again. "Some people do."

"In order," I asked, "to play?" And my voice was very ugly, full of contempt and anger.

"Well"—he looked at me with great, troubled eyes, as though, in fact, he hoped his eyes would tell me things he could never otherwise say—"they *think* so. And *if* they think so—"

"And what do *you* think?" I asked. 195

He sat on the sofa and put his can of beer on the floor. "I don't know," he said, and I couldn't be sure if he were answering my question or pursuing his thoughts. His face didn't tell me. "It's not so much to *play*. It's to *stand* it, to be able to make it at all. On any level." He frowned and smiled: "In order to keep from shaking to pieces."

"But these friends of yours," I said, "they seem to shake themselves to pieces pretty goddamn fast."

"Maybe." He played with the notebook. And something told me that I should curb my tongue, that Sonny was doing his best to talk, that I should listen. "But of course you only know the ones that've gone to pieces. Some don't—or at least they haven't *yet* and that's just about all *any* of us can say." He paused. "And then there are some who just live, really, in hell, and they know it and they see what's happening and they go right on. I don't know." He sighed, dropped the notebook, folded his arms. "Some guys, you can tell from the way they play, they on something *all* the time. And you can see that, well, it makes something real for them. But of course," he picked up his beer from the floor and sipped it and put the can down again, "they *want* to, too, you've got to see that. Even some of them that say they don't—*some*, not all."

"And what about you?" I asked—I couldn't help it. "What about you? Do *you* want to?"

He stood up and walked to the window and remained silent for a long time. 200
Then he sighed. "Me," he said. Then: "While I was downstairs before, on my way here, listening to that woman sing, it struck me all of a sudden how much suffering she must have had to go through—to sing like that. It's *repulsive* to think you have to suffer that much."

I said: "But there's no way not to suffer—is there, Sonny?"

"I believe not," he said, and smiled, "but that's never stopped anyone from trying." He looked at me. "Has it?" I realized, with this mocking look, that there stood between us, forever, beyond the power of time or forgiveness, the fact that I had held silence—so long!—when he had needed human speech to help him. He turned back to the window. "No, there's no way not to suffer. But you try all kinds of ways to keep from drowning in it, to keep on top of it, and to make it seem—well, like *you*. Like you did something, all right, and now you're suffering for it. You know?" I said nothing. "Well, you know," he said, impatiently, "why *do* people suffer? Maybe it's better to do something to give it a reason, *any* reason."

"But we just agreed," I said, "that there's no way not to suffer. Isn't it better, then, just to—take it?"

"But nobody just takes it," Sonny cried, "that's what I'm telling you! *Everybody* tries not to. You're just hung up on the *way* some people try—it's not *your* way!"

The hair on my face began to itch, my face felt wet. "That's not true," I said, "that's not true. I don't give a damn what other people do, I don't even care how they suffer. I just care how *you* suffer." And he looked at me. "Please believe me," I said, "I don't want to see you—die—trying not to suffer."

"I won't," he said, flatly, "die trying not to suffer. At least, not any faster than anybody else."

"But there's no need," I said, trying to laugh, "is there? in killing yourself."

I wanted to say more, but I couldn't. I wanted to talk about will power and how life could be—well, beautiful. I wanted to say that it was all within; but was it? Or, rather, wasn't that exactly the trouble? And I wanted to promise that I would never fail him again. But it would all have sounded—empty words and lies.

So I made the promise to myself and prayed that I would keep it.

"It's terrible sometimes, inside," he said, "that's what's the trouble. You walk these streets, black and funky and cold, and there's not really a living ass to talk to, and there's nothing shaking, and there's no way of getting it out—that storm inside. You can't talk it and you can't make love with it, and when you finally try to get with it and play it, you realize *nobody's* listening. So *you've* got to listen. You got to find a way to listen."

And then he walked away from the window and sat on the sofa again, as though all the wind had suddenly been knocked out of him. "Sometimes you'll do *anything* to play, even cut your mother's throat." He laughed and looked at me. "Or your brother's." Then he sobered. "Or your own." Then: "Don't worry. I'm all right now and I think I'll *be* all right. But I can't forget—where I've been. I don't mean just the physical place I've been, I mean where I've *been*. And *what* I've been."

"What have you been, Sonny?" I asked.

He smiled—but sat sideways on the sofa, his elbow resting on the back, his fingers playing with his mouth and chin, not looking at me. "I've been something I didn't recognize, didn't know I could be. Didn't know anybody could be." He stopped, looking inward, looking helplessly young, looking old. "I'm not talking about it now because I feel *guilty* or anything like that—maybe it would be better if I did, I don't know. Anyway, I can't really talk about it. Not to you, not to anybody," and now he turned and faced me. "Sometimes, you know, and it was actually when I was most *out* of the world, I felt that I was in it, and that I was *with* it, really, and I could play or I didn't really have to *play*, it just came out of me, it was there. And I don't know how I played, thinking about it now, but I know I did awful things, those times, sometimes, to people. Or it wasn't that I *did* anything to them—it was that they weren't real." He picked up the beer can; it was empty; he rolled it between his palms: "And other times—well, I needed a fix, I needed to find a place to lean, I needed to clear a space to *listen*—and I couldn't find it, and I—went crazy, I did terrible things to *me*, I was terrible *for* me." He began pressing the beer can between his hands, I watched the metal begin to give. It glittered, as he played with it, like a knife, and I was afraid he would cut himself, but I said nothing. "Oh well. I can never tell you. I was all by myself at the bottom of something, stinking and sweating and crying and shaking, and I smelled it, you know? *My* stink, and I thought I'd die if I couldn't get away from it and yet, all the same, I knew that everything I was doing was just locking me in with it. And I didn't know," he paused, still flattening the beer can, "I didn't know, I still *don't* know, something kept telling me that maybe it was good to smell your own stink, but I didn't think that *that* was what I'd been trying to do—and—who can stand it?" and he abruptly dropped the ruined beer can, looking at me with a small, still smile, and then rose, walking to the window as though it were the lodestone rock. I watched his face, he watched the avenue. "I couldn't tell you when Mama died—but the reason I wanted to leave Harlem so bad was to get away from drugs. And then, when I ran away, that's what I was running from—really. When I came back, nothing had changed, *I* hadn't changed, I was just—older." And he stopped, drumming with his fingers on the windowpane. The sun had vanished, soon darkness would fall. I watched his face. "It can come again," he said, almost as though speaking to himself. Then he turned to me. "It can come again," he repeated. "I just want you to know that."

"All right," I said, at last. "So it can come again. All right."

He smiled, but the smile was sorrowful. "I had to try to tell you," he said.

"Yes," I said. "I understand that."

"You're my brother," he said, looking straight at me, and not smiling at all.

"Yes," I repeated, "yes. I understand that."

He turned back to the window, looking out. "All that hatred down there," he said, "all that hatred and misery and love. It's a wonder it doesn't blow the avenue apart." We went to the only night club on a short, dark street, downtown. We squeezed through the narrow, chattering, jam-packed bar to the entrance of the big room, where the bandstand was. And we stood there for a moment, for the lights were very dim in this room and we couldn't see. Then, "Hello, boy," said a voice and an enormous black man, much older than Sonny or myself, erupted out of all that atmospheric lighting and put an arm around Sonny's shoulder. "I been sitting right here," he said, "waiting for you."

He had a big voice, too, and heads in the darkness turned toward us.

Sonny grinned and pulled a little away, and said, "Creole, this is my brother. I told you about him."

Creole shook my hand. "I'm glad to meet you, son," he said, and it was clear that he was glad to meet me *there*, for Sonny's sake. And he smiled, "You got a real musician in *your* family," and he took his arm from Sonny's shoulder and slapped him, lightly, affectionately, with the back of his hand.

"Well. Now I've heard it all," said a voice behind us. This was another musician, and a friend of Sonny's, a coal-black, cheerful-looking man, built close to the ground. He immediately began confiding to me, at the top of his lungs, the most terrible things about Sonny, his teeth gleaming like a lighthouse and his laugh coming up out of him like the beginning of an earthquake. And it turned out that everyone at the bar knew Sonny, or almost everyone; some were musicians, working there, or nearby, or not working, some were simply hangers-on, and some were there to hear Sonny play. I was introduced to all of them and they were all very polite to me. Yet, it was clear that, for them, I was only Sonny's brother. Here, I was in Sonny's world. Or, rather: his kingdom. Here, it was not even a question that his veins bore royal blood.

They were going to play soon and Creole installed me, by myself, at a table in a dark corner. Then I watched them, Creole, and the little black man, and Sonny, and the others, while they horsed around, standing just below the bandstand. The light from the bandstand spilled just a little short of them and, watching them laughing and gesturing and moving about, I had the feeling that they, nevertheless, were being most careful not to step into that circle of light too suddenly: that if they moved into the light too suddenly, without thinking, they would perish in flame. Then, while I watched, one of them, the small, black man, moved into the light and crossed the bandstand and started fooling around with his drums. Then—being funny and being, also, extremely ceremonious—Creole took Sonny by the arm and led him to the piano. A woman's voice called Sonny's name and a few hands started clapping. And Sonny, also being funny and being ceremonious, and so touched, I think, that he could have cried, but neither hiding it nor showing it, riding it like a man, grinned, and put both hands to his heart and bowed from the waist.

Creole then went to the bass fiddle and a lean, very bright-skinned brown man jumped up on the bandstand and picked up his horn. So there they were, and the atmosphere on the bandstand and in the room began to change and tighten. Someone stepped up to the microphone and announced them. Then there were all kinds of murmurs. Some people at the bar shushed others. The waitress ran around, frantically getting in the last orders, guys and chicks got closer to each other, and the lights on the bandstand, on the quartet, turned to a kind of indigo. Then they all looked different there. Creole looked about him for the last time, as though he were making certain that all his chickens were in the coop, and then he jumped and struck the fiddle. And there they were.

All I know about music is that not many people ever really hear it. And even then, on the rare occasions when something opens within, and the music enters, what we mainly hear, or hear corroborated, are personal, private, vanishing evocations. But the man who creates the music is hearing something else, is dealing with the roar rising from the void and imposing order on it as it hits the air. What is evoked in him, then, is of another order, more terrible because it has no words, and triumphant, too, for that same reason. And his triumph, when he triumphs, is ours. I just watched Sonny's face. His face was troubled, he was working hard, but he wasn't with it. And I had the feeling that, in a way, everyone on the bandstand was waiting for him, both waiting for him and pushing him along. But as I began to watch Creole, I realized that it was Creole who held them all back. He had them on a short rein. Up there, keeping the beat with his whole body, wailing on the fiddle, with his eyes half closed, he was listening to everything, but he was listening to Sonny. He was having a dialogue with Sonny. He wanted Sonny to leave the shore line and strike out for the deep water. He was Sonny's witness that deep water and drowning were not the same thing—he had been there, and he knew. And he wanted Sonny to know. He was waiting for Sonny to do the things on the keys which would let Creole know that Sonny was in the water.

And, while Creole listened, Sonny moved, deep within, exactly like someone in torment. I had never before thought of how awful the relationship must be between the musician and his instrument. He has to fill it, this instrument, with the breath of life, his own. He has to make it do what he wants it to do. And a piano is just a piano. It's made out of so much wood and wires and little hammers and big ones, and ivory. While there's only so much you can do with it, the only way to find this out is to try and make it do everything.

And Sonny hadn't been near a piano for over a year. And he wasn't on much better terms with his life, not the life that stretched before him now. He and the piano stammered, started one way, got scared, stopped; started another way, panicked, marked time, started again; then seemed to have found a direction, panicked again, got stuck. And the face I saw on Sonny I'd never seen before. Everything had been burned out of it, and, at the same time, things usually hidden were being burned in, by the fire and fury of the battle which was occurring in him up there.

Yet, watching Creole's face as they neared the end of the first set, I had the feeling that something had happened, something I hadn't heard. Then they finished, there was scattered applause, and then, without an instant's warning, Creole started into something else, it was almost sardonic, it was *Am I Blue*. And, as though he commanded, Sonny began to play. Something began to happen. And Creole let out the reins. The dry, low, black man said something awful on the drums, Creole answered, and the drums talked back. Then the horn insisted, sweet and high, slightly detached perhaps, and Creole listened, commenting now and then, dry, and driving, beautiful and calm and old. Then they all came together again, and Sonny was part of the family again. I could tell this from his face. He seemed to have found, right there beneath his fingers, a damn brand-new piano. It seemed that he couldn't get over it. Then, for awhile, just being happy with Sonny, they seemed to be agreeing with him that brand-new pianos certainly were a gas.

Then Creole stepped forward to remind them that what they were playing 230
was the blues. He hit something in all of them, he hit something in me, myself, and the music tightened and deepened, apprehension began to beat the air. Creole began to tell us what the blues were all about. They were not about anything very new. He and his boys up there were keeping it new, at the risk of ruin, destruction, madness, and death, in order to find new ways to make us listen. For, while the tale of how we suffer, and how we are delighted, and how we may triumph is never new, it always must be heard. There isn't any other tale to tell, it's the only light we've got in all this darkness.

And this tale, according to that face, that body, those strong hands on those strings, has another aspect in every country, and a new depth in every generation. Listen, Creole seemed to be saying, listen. Now these are Sonny's blues. He made the little black man on the drums know it, and the bright, brown man on the horn. Creole wasn't trying any longer to get Sonny in the water. He was wishing him Godspeed. Then he stepped back, very slowly, filling the air with the immense suggestion that Sonny speak for himself.

Then they all gathered around Sonny and Sonny played. Every now and again one of them seemed to say, Amen. Sonny's fingers filled the air with life, his life. But that life contained so many others. And Sonny went all the way back, he really began with the spare, flat statement of the opening phrase of the song. Then he began to make it his. It was very beautiful because it wasn't hurried and it was no longer a lament. I seemed to hear with what burning he had made it his, with what burning we had yet to make it ours, how we could cease lamenting. Freedom lurked around us and I understood, at last, that he could help us to be free if we would listen, that he would never be free until we did. Yet, there was no battle in his face now. I heard what he had gone through, and would continue to go through until he came to rest in earth. He had made it his: that long line, of which we knew only Mama and Daddy. And he was giving it back, as everything must be given back, so that, passing through death, it can live forever. I saw my mother's face again, and felt, for the first time, how the stones of the road she had walked on must have bruised her feet. I saw the moonlit road where my father's brother died. And it brought something else back to me, and carried me past it, I saw my little girl again and felt Isabel's tears again, and I felt my own tears begin to rise. And I was yet aware that this was only a moment, that the world waited outside, as hungry as a tiger, and that trouble stretched above us, longer than the sky.

Then it was over. Creole and Sonny let out their breath, both soaking wet, and grinning. There was a lot of applause and some of it was real. In the dark, the girl came by and I asked her to take drinks to the bandstand. There was a long pause, while they talked up there in the indigo light and after awhile I saw the girl put a Scotch and milk on top of the piano for Sonny. He didn't seem to notice it, but just before they started playing again, he sipped from it and looked toward me, and nodded. Then he put it back on top of the piano. For me, then, as they began to play again, it glowed and shook above my brother's head like the very cup of trembling.

(1957)

Alice Walker *(b. 1944)*

Everyday Use

For Your Grandmama

I will wait for her in the yard that Maggie and I made so clean and wavy yesterday afternoon. A yard like this is more comfortable than most people know. It is not just a yard. It is like an extended living room. When the hard clay is swept clean as a floor and the fine sand around the edges lined with tiny, irregular grooves, anyone can come and sit and look up into the elm tree and wait for the breezes that never come inside the house.

Maggie will be nervous until after her sister goes: she will stand hopelessly in corners, homely and ashamed of the burn scars down her arms and legs, eying her sister with a mixture of envy and awe. She thinks her sister has held life always in the palm of one hand, that "no" is a word the world never learned to say to her.

You've no doubt seen those TV shows where the child who has "made it" is confronted, as a surprise, by her own mother and father, tottering in weakly from backstage. (A pleasant surprise, of course: What would they do if parent and child came on the show only to curse out and insult each other?) On TV mother and child embrace and smile into each other's faces. Sometimes the mother and father weep, the child wraps them in her arms and leans across the table to tell how she would not have made it without their help. I have seen these programs.

Sometimes I dream a dream in which Dee and I are suddenly brought together on a TV program of this sort. Out of a dark and soft-seated limousine I am ushered into a bright room filled with many people. There I meet a smiling, gray, sporty man like Johnny Carson[1] who shakes my hand and tells me what a fine girl I have. Then we are on the stage and Dee is embracing me with tears in her eyes. She pins on my dress a large orchid, even though she has told me once that she thinks orchids are tacky flowers.

In real life I am a large, big-boned woman with rough, man-working hands. 5
In the winter I wear flannel nightgowns to bed and overalls during the day. I can kill and clean a hog as mercilessly as a man. My fat keeps me hot in zero weather. I can work outside all day, breaking ice to get water for washing; I can eat pork liver cooked over the open fire minutes after it comes steaming from the hog. One winter I knocked a bull calf straight in the brain between the eyes with a sledge hammer and had the meat hung up to chill before nightfall. But of course all this does not show on television. I am the way my daughter would want me to be: a hundred pounds lighter, my skin like an uncooked barley pancake. My hair glistens in the hot bright lights. Johnny Carson has much to do to keep up with my quick and witty tongue.

But that is a mistake. I know even before I wake up. Who ever knew a Johnson with a quick tongue? Who can even imagine me looking a strange white man in the eye? It seems to me I have talked to them always with one foot raised in flight, with my head turned in whichever way is farthest from them. Dee, though. She would always look anyone in the eye. Hesitation was no part of her nature.

"How do I look, Mama?" Maggie says, showing just enough of her thin body enveloped in pink skirt and red blouse for me to know she's there, almost hidden by the door.

"Come out into the yard," I say.

Have you ever seen a lame animal, perhaps a dog run over by some careless person rich enough to own a car, sidle up to someone who is ignorant enough to be kind to him? That is the way my Maggie walks. She has been like this, chin on chest, eyes on ground, feet in shuffle, ever since the fire that burned the other house to the ground.

[1]*Johnny Carson:* Johnny Carson (1925–2005) was the affable late-night talk show host of *The Tonight Show Starring Johnny Carson* from 1962 to 1992.

Dee is lighter than Maggie, with nicer hair and a fuller figure. She's a woman 10 now, though sometimes I forget. How long ago was it that the other house burned? Ten, twelve years? Sometimes I can still hear the flames and feel Maggie's arms sticking to me, her hair smoking and her dress falling off her in little black papery flakes. Her eyes seemed stretched open, blazed open by the flames reflected in them. And Dee. I see her standing off under the sweet gum tree she used to dig gum out of; a look of concentration on her face as she watched the last dingy gray board of the house fall in toward the red-hot brick chimney. Why don't you do a dance around the ashes? I'd want to ask her. She had hated the house that much.

I used to think she hated Maggie, too. But that was before we raised the money, the church and me, to send her to Augusta to school. She used to read to us without pity; forcing words, lies, other folks' habits, whole lives upon us two, sitting trapped and ignorant underneath her voice. She washed us in a river of make-believe, burned us with a lot of knowledge we didn't necessarily need to know. Pressed us to her with the serious way she read, to shove us away at just the moment, like dimwits, we seemed about to understand.

Dee wanted nice things. A yellow organdy dress to wear to her graduation from high school; black pumps to match a green suit she'd made from an old suit somebody gave me. She was determined to stare down any disaster in her efforts. Her eyelids would not flicker for minutes at a time. Often I fought off the temptation to shake her. At sixteen she had a style of her own: and knew what style was.

I never had an education myself. After second grade the school was closed down. Don't ask me why: in 1927 colored asked fewer questions than they do now. Sometimes Maggie reads to me. She stumbles along good-naturedly but can't see well. She knows she is not bright. Like good looks and money, quickness passed her by. She will marry John Thomas (who has mossy teeth in an earnest face) and then I'll be free to sit here and I guess just sing church songs to myself. Although I never was a good singer. Never could carry a tune. I was always better at a man's job. I used to love to milk till I was hooked in the side in '49. Cows are soothing and slow and don't bother you, unless you try to milk them the wrong way.

I have deliberately turned my back on the house. It is three rooms, just like the one that burned, except the roof is tin; they don't make shingle roofs any more. There are no real windows, just some holes cut in the sides, like the portholes in a ship, but not round and not square, with rawhide holding the shutters up on the outside. This house is in a pasture, too, like the other one. No doubt when Dee sees it she will want to tear it down. She wrote me once that no matter where we "choose" to live, she will manage to come see us. But she will never bring her friends. Maggie and I thought about this and Maggie asked me, "Mama, when did Dee ever *have* any friends?"

She had a few. Furtive boys in pink shirts hanging about on washday after 15 school. Nervous girls who never laughed. Impressed with her they worshipped the well-turned phrase, the cute shape, the scalding humor that erupted like bubbles in lye. She read to them.

When she was courting Jimmy T she didn't have much time to pay to us, but turned all her faultfinding power on him. He *flew* to marry a cheap city girl from a family of ignorant flashy people. She hardly had time to recompose herself.

When she comes I will meet—but there they are!

Maggie attempts to make a dash for the house, in her shuffling way, but I stay her with my hand. "Come back here," I say. And she stops and tries to dig a well in the sand with her toe.

It is hard to see them clearly through the strong sun. But even the first glimpse of leg out of the car tells me it is Dee. Her feet were always neat-looking, as if God himself had shaped them with a certain style. From the other side of the car comes a short, stocky man. Hair is all over his head a foot long and hanging from his chin like a kinky mule tail. I hear Maggie suck in her breath. "Uhnnnh," is what it sounds like. Like when you see the wriggling end of a snake just in front of your foot on the road. "Uhnnnh."

Dee next. A dress down to the ground, in this hot weather. A dress so loud it 20
hurts my eyes. There are yellows and oranges enough to throw back the light of the sun. I feel my whole face warming from the heat waves it throws out. Earrings gold, too, and hanging down to her shoulders. Bracelets dangling and making noises when she moves her arm up to shake the folds of the dress out of her armpits. The dress is loose and flows, and as she walks closer, I like it. I hear Maggie go "Uhnnnh" again. It is her sister's hair. It stands straight up like the wool on a sheep. It is black as night and around the edges are two long pigtails that rope about like small lizards disappearing behind her ears.

"Wa-su-zo-Tean-o!" she says, coming on in that gliding way the dress makes her move. The short stocky fellow with the hair to his navel is all grinning and he follows up with "Asalamalakim, my mother and sister!" He moves to hug Maggie but she falls back, right up against the back of my chair. I feel her trembling there and when I look up I see the perspiration falling off her chin.

"Don't get up," says Dee. Since I am stout it takes something of a push. You can see me trying to move a second or two before I make it. She turns, showing white heels through her sandals, and goes back to the car. Out she peeks next with a Polaroid. She stoops down quickly and lines up picture after picture of me sitting there in front of the house with Maggie cowering behind me. She never takes a shot without making sure the house is included. When a cow comes nibbling around the edge of the yard she snaps it and me and Maggie *and* the house. Then she puts the Polaroid in the back seat of the car, and comes up and kisses me on the forehead.

Meanwhile Asalamalakim is going through motions with Maggie's hand. Maggie's hand is as limp as a fish, and probably as cold, despite the sweat, and she keeps trying to pull it back. It looks like Asalamalakim wants to shake hands but wants to do it fancy. Or maybe he don't know how people shake hands. Anyhow, he soon gives up on Maggie.

"Well," I say. "Dee."

"No, Mama," she says. "Not 'Dee,' Wangero Leewanika Kemanjo!" 25

"What happened to 'Dee'?" I wanted to know.

"She's dead," Wangero said. "I couldn't bear it any longer, being named after the people who oppress me."

"You know as well as me you was named after your aunt Dicie," I said. Dicie is my sister. She named Dee. We called her "Big Dee" after Dee was born.

"But who was *she* named after?" asked Wangero.

"I guess after Grandma Dee," I said. 30

"And who was she named after?" asked Wangero.

"Her mother," I said, and saw Wangero was getting tired. "That's about as far back as I can trace it," I said. Though, in fact, I probably could have carried it back beyond the Civil War through the branches.

"Well," said Asalamalakim, "there you are."

"Uhnnnh," I heard Maggie say.

"There I was not," I said, "before 'Dicie' cropped up in our family, so why 35
should I try to trace it that far back?"

He just stood there grinning, looking down on me like somebody inspecting a Model A car. Every once in a while he and Wangero sent eye signals over my head.

"How do you pronounce this name?" I asked.

"You don't have to call me by it if you don't want to," said Wangero. 40

"Why shouldn't I?" I asked. "If that's what you want us to call you, we'll call you."

"I know it might sound awkward at first," said Wangero.

"I'll get used to it," I said. "Ream it out again."

Well, soon we got the name out of the way. Asalamalakim had a name twice as long and three times as hard. After I tripped over it two or three times he told me to just call him Hakim-a-barber. I wanted to ask him was he a barber, but I didn't really think he was, so I didn't ask.

"You must belong to those beef-cattle peoples down the road," I said. They said "Asalamalakim" when they met you, too, but they didn't shake hands. Always too busy: feeding the cattle, fixing the fences, putting up salt-lick shelters, throwing down hay. When the white folks poisoned some of the herd the men stayed up all night with rifles in their hands. I walked a mile and a half just to see the sight.

Hakim-a-barber said, "I accept some of their doctrines, but farming and raising cattle is not my style." (They didn't tell me, and I didn't ask, whether Wangero [Dee] had really gone and married him.)

We sat down to eat and right away he said he didn't eat collards and pork was 45
unclean. Wangero, though, went on through the chitlins and corn bread, the greens and everything else. She talked a blue streak over the sweet potatoes. Everything delighted her. Even the fact that we still used the benches her daddy made for the table when we couldn't afford to buy chairs.

"Oh, Mama!" she cried. Then turned to Hakim-a-barber. "I never knew how lovely these benches are. You can feel the rump prints," she said, running her hands underneath her and long the bench. Then she gave a sigh and her hand closed over Grandma Dee's butter dish. "That's it!" she said. "I knew there was something I wanted to ask you if I could have." She jumped up from the table and went over in the corner where the churn stood, the milk in it clabber by now. She looked at the churn and looked at it.

"This churn top is what I need," she said. "Didn't Uncle Buddy whittle it out of a tree you all used to have?"

"Yes," I said.

"Uh huh," she said happily. "And I want the dasher, too."

"Uncle Buddy whittle that, too?" asked the barber. 50

Dee (Wangero) looked up at me.

"Aunt Dee's first husband whittled the dash," said Maggie so low you almost couldn't hear her. "His name was Henry, but they called him Stash."

"Maggie's brain is like an elephant's," Wangero said, laughing. "I can use the churn top as a centerpiece for the alcove table," she said, sliding a plate over the churn, "and I'll think of something artistic to do with the dasher."

When she finished wrapping the dasher the handle stuck out. I took it for a moment in my hands. You didn't even have to look close to see where hands pushing the dasher up and down to make butter had left a kind of sink in the wood. In fact, there were a lot of small sinks; you could see where thumbs and fingers had sunk into the wood. It was beautiful light yellow wood, from a tree that grew in the yard where Big Dee and Stash had lived.

After dinner Dee (Wangero) went to the trunk at the foot of my bed and 55
started rifling through it. Maggie hung back in the kitchen over the dishpan. Out came Wangero with two quilts. They had been pieced by Grandma Dee and then Big Dee and me had hung them on the quilt frames on the front porch and quilted them. One was in the Lone Star pattern. The other was Walk Around the Mountain. In both of them were scraps of dresses Grandma Dee had worn fifty and more years ago. Bits and pieces of Grandpa Jarrell's Paisley shirts. And one teeny faded blue piece, about the size of a penny matchbox, that was from Great Grandpa Ezra's uniform that he wore in the Civil War.

"Mama," Wangero said sweet as a bird. "Can I have these old quilts?"

I heard something fall in the kitchen, and a minute later the kitchen door slammed.

"Why don't you take one or two of the others?" I asked. "These old things was just done by me and Big Dee from some tops your grandma pieced before she died."

"No," said Wangero. "I don't want those. They are stitched around the borders by machine."

"That'll make them last better," I said. 60

"That's not the point," said Wangero. "These are all pieces of dresses Grandma used to wear. She did all this stitching by hand. Imagine!" She held the quilts securely in her arms, stroking them.

"Some of the pieces, like those lavender ones, come from old clothes her mother handed down to her," I said, moving up to touch the quilts. Dee (Wangero) moved back just enough so that I couldn't reach the quilts. They already belonged to her.

"Imagine!" she breathed again, clutching them closely to her bosom.

"The truth is," I said, "I promised to give them quilts to Maggie, for when she marries John Thomas."

She gasped like a bee had stung her.

"Maggie can't appreciate these quilts!" she said. "She'd probably be backward enough to put them to everyday use."

"I reckon she would," I said. "God knows I been saving 'em for long enough with nobody using 'em. I hope she will!" I didn't want to bring up how I had offered Dee (Wangero) a quilt when she went away to college. Then she had told me they were old-fashioned, out of style.

"But they're *priceless!*" she was saying now, furiously; for she has a temper. "Maggie would put them on the bed and in five years they'd be in rags. Less than that!"

"She can always make some more," I said. "Maggie knows how to quilt."

Dee (Wangero) looked at me with hatred. "You just will not understand. The point is these quilts, *these* quilts!"

"Well," I said, stumped. "What would *you* do with them?"

"Hang them," she said. As if that was the only thing you *could* do with quilts.

Maggie by now was standing in the door. I could almost hear the sound her feet made as they scraped over each other.

"She can have them, Mama," she said, like somebody used to never winning anything, or having anything reserved for her. "I can 'member Grandma Dee without the quilts."

I looked at her hard. She had filled her bottom lip with checkerberry snuff and it gave her face a kind of dopey, hangdog look. It was Grandma Dee and Big Dee who taught her how to quilt herself. She stood there with her scarred hands hidden in the folds of her skirt. She looked at her sister with something like fear but she wasn't mad at her. This was Maggie's portion. This was the way she knew God to work.

When I looked at her like that something hit me in the top of my head and ran down to the soles of my feet. Just like when I'm in church and the spirit of God touches me and I get happy and shout. I did something I never had done before: hugged Maggie to me, then dragged her on into the room, snatched the quilts out of Miss Wangero's hands and dumped them into Maggie's lap. Maggie just sat there on my bed with her mouth open.

"Take one or two of the others," I said to Dee.

But she turned without a word and went out to Hakim-a-barber.

"You just don't understand," she said, as Maggie and I came out to the car.

"What don't I understand?" I wanted to know.

"Your heritage," she said. And then she turned to Maggie, kissed her, and said, "You ought to try to make something of yourself, too, Maggie. It's really a new day for us. But from the way you and Mama still live you'd never know it."

She put on some sunglasses that hid everything above the tip of her nose and her chin. Maggie smiled; maybe at the sunglasses. But a real smile, not scared. After we watched the car dust settle I asked Maggie to bring me a dip of snuff. And then the two of us sat there just enjoying, until it was time to go in the house and go to bed.

(1973)

THE PRODIGAL SON: QUESTIONS FOR DISCUSSION AND WRITING

1. What precipitates the younger son's remorse in Luke's parable? Do you think he would have sought forgiveness if he had not spent his fortune?
2. What does the older brother seem to want from his father? Do you think he is justified in his reaction to his brother's return?
3. Why do you think the father is so ready to forgive his youngest son? Is his reaction realistic?
4. In Alice Walker's "Everyday Use," the returning daughter is not repentant. Do you still see this story as a "prodigal son" tale?
5. How does gender change the effect of "Everyday Use"? As a culture, do we respond differently to males and females who leave their family to seek their own way? Why or why not?
6. Because "Sonny's Blues" does not feature a living father character, the focus is on the relationship between the two brothers. Does the narrator forgive Sonny by the end of the story? Does Sonny want to be forgiven?
7. Rewrite this parable from the perspective of one of the two brothers. What motivates him to leave or to stay? How does he feel about his choice over time? How does your character feel about his brother at the end of the story? What kind of relationship will they have in the future?
8. In an essay, discuss the degree to which you think the parable of the prodigal son is influential in modern life. Do you think our culture reinforces the message of the father's unconditional forgiveness or the brother's desire for life to be fair? You can use Common Characters materials, examples from popular culture, and interviews with people to support your argument.
9. Discuss the importance of apologizing in this parable and in Marilyn Nelson's "Minor Miracle." What is the relationship between apology and forgiveness?
10. Look at the Rembrandt and Wilson paintings. What do they have in common? What is the focus of each painting? How do the expressions and body language of the people in the paintings reveal their emotions? In your opinion, which painting best interprets the parable?

Considering Art: The Prodigal Son

The discussion below references art reproduced on color insert pages 15 and 16.

For many centuries, the theme of the prodigal son has provided a dramatic narrative for visual artists. Although the biblical tale suggests an ancient setting, it has often been translated, imagined, and updated to a variety of social contexts and national identities. Its wide appeal as a metaphor, rather than as an historical anecdote, comes from the moral that the story seems to encompass—the importance of empathy, compassion, and tolerance within families and communities.

***The Return of the Prodigal Son* (see color insert p. 15).** French painter James Tissot (1836–1902) had a successful career in London in the late nineteenth century. Many of his early paintings are genre scenes set in the Middle Ages and are filled with historical details, such as period costume and picturesque architecture. Tissot's parents both worked in the textile and fashion business in his hometown of Nantes, and his paintings show an intimate knowledge of and a fascination with clothing. *The Return of the Prodigal Son* (1862) imagines that the events of this parable are transpiring in a medieval city. Within the space of a courtyard, as if on a stage, the son's bare torso is dramatically highlighted. Every figure in the painting responds to his arrival, bending, leaning, making theatrical gestures that indicate their surprise and skepticism.

***The Prodigal Son in Modern Life: The Return* (see color insert p. 15).** Tissot returns to the same theme twenty years later in *The Prodigal Son in Modern Life: The Return* (1882). This painting is one of a series of four that depicts the son's fall and redemption in a modern setting. The series was reproduced in prints that were marketed internationally to great financial success. In this modern genre scene, the son falls into the vigorous embrace of his father on the wet dock of a busy harbor. Behind him, animals are being unloaded from a ship. This detail reminds the viewer that the formerly wealthy son had sunken to the level of living with pigs in the mud. Behind the father stands the jealous brother and a female companion whose fashionable clothing is a stark contrast to the scruffy son and the dock workers. Although Tissot was a cosmopolitan artist (who lived a somewhat decadent and scandalous life), he spent his childhood in a busy French shipping port and frequently painted scenes on board ships or by the seaside.

***Return of the Prodigal Son* (see color insert p. 16).** African American artist Romare Bearden (1914–1988) was born in North Carolina but grew up surrounded by the literary, musical, and artistic luminaries of the Harlem Renaissance in New York City. Bearden studied mathematics and philosophy in New York and Paris, but as an artist he was primarily self-taught. For many years, he worked abstractly before developing his own individualized and signature approach to collage that is inspired by the improvisation of jazz. In *Return of the Prodigal Son* (1967), Bearden draws on his own experiences of moving from the rural South to New York. The artist has explained that his prodigal son left North Carolina, fell into bad company, and returned home (http://www.albrightknox.org/ArtStart/Bearden.html). Family is represented here by two women who welcome the son as he enters from the left. It is part of a series titled "The Prevalence of Ritual," in which the family is central. Its love, support, and everyday rituals give stability and focus to the individual and to the culture at large.

Questions about the Art

1. In his earlier version of the prodigal son, how does Tissot use details to encourage our eyes to move around the image? As we read from left to right and back again, what do we conclude about the reception of the son?

2. What has the artist done differently in the second version in terms of detail and focus? Is the effect on the viewer different?
3. How does the exclusion of the brother and father from Bearden's version change the meaning of the story for the viewer? How can we compare its attention to detail to that of the Tissot paintings?

Connecting Art and Literature

1. Discuss the role of family acceptance in the stories by Baldwin and Walker and in Bearden's painting.
2. How do the two paintings by Tissot develop the themes advanced in the biblical version of the Prodigal Son?
3. How does a modern setting affect the Prodigal Son themes in the stories by Baldwin and Walker and in Tissot's *The Prodigal Son in Modern Life: The Return* and Beardon's *Return of the Prodigal Son?* How important is setting to this story?

Chapter 16

Industry and Idleness

A great deal of literature is about work. If, as many say, reading literature provides an escape from our daily routines, why would we want to read about work? The truth is that although people complain about work, claim to live for weekends and vacation, or say they just "clock in and out" to get a paycheck, most of us would be lost without work and are fascinated by its complicated relation to our lives.

As literature helps us understand, work can be both a virtue and a vice, with advantages and disadvantages closely intermingled. For many, work provides a sense of identity, a helpful structure, a feeling of connection to other people and to the larger world, and a satisfying feeling of accomplishment, purpose, and direction. Hard work often produces results that society values, such as wealth, innovation, advancements in the arts and sciences, and other tangible accomplishments. It can teach valuable lessons, such as the need for compromise and teamwork, and it can give a person strength, confidence, independence, and self-sufficiency.

At the same time, working too hard can limit our horizons, shorten our lives, make us too money oriented, or depersonalize us into faceless functionaries, "like cogs in a wheel." It can lead to exploitation, corruption, greed, mind-numbing tedium, or physical and mental exhaustion—a kind of death in life. In literature, as in life, no formula regarding work holds true across all situations.

The fiction section of this chapter features a few characters who do not want to work, at least at a certain job. Washington Irving's "Rip Van Winkle" recounts the story of a character who napped for twenty years; Herman Melville's "Bartleby, the Scrivener" presents a character who repeatedly tells his boss that he "would prefer not to" work; and Ruth Prawer Jhabvala's story "The Interview" centers on a character who avoids an interview. Some characters have no choice but to work: the stories by Rebecca Harding Davis and Ann Cummins detail the lives of people who work hard and yet never get ahead. (See also Chapter 11, in which student George Scala uses Davis's story as the basis for his research project.)

The first two poems in this chapter are frequently paired together: the first, Stephen Duck's "The Thresher's Labour," describes the workday of a thresher, or fieldworker; Mary Collier, who wrote "The Woman's Labour," felt that Duck denigrated the accomplishments of women. Joanna Baillie's poem sees work as a collective experience, whereas William Wordsworth's poem sees it as a solitary one. Walt Whitman and Robert Frost look at the beauty that is an offshoot of work; Tennyson's poem "Ulysses" considers work as duty, but Philip Larkin and Philip Levine see it more as a necessity: Larkin uses the metaphor of

Daniel Nevins, *The Dream Tree* (1993).

a toad to understand work. Theodore Roethke and Marge Piercy regard work as potential drudgery in their poems. Seamus Heaney sees deep personal meaning in his poem "Digging" while Elizabeth Alexander's speaker regards herself as "lazy" in the first line of hers, and she is proud of that fact.

The play in this chapter is one of Shakespeare's history plays, the first part of *Henry IV*. Like Tennyson's poem "Ulysses," it focuses on the duties of kings; however, one of the focal characters, Prince Hal (Henry IV's son), is not ready to accept this duty and spends much of his time in the company of tavern-dwellers, especially the drunkard Sir John Falstaff, whose empty boasting provides a counterpart to the accomplishments of the royal characters.

The first essay in this collection is by the British novelist Virginia Woolf, who considers the different expectations and advantages faced by working men and women. The essayist Aristides refuses to complain about work and discusses how one can enjoy it. The "Common Characters" section of this chapter presents different versions of the "rags to riches" story—the story of Cinderella. Ann Sexton uses that story in her poem "Cinderella" ironically; Russell Banks's story "Success Story" is also ironic. In fact, irony also dominates the poems "Richard Cory" and "The Ruined Maid."

Literature seeks to make any seemingly easy formula complex. Because society depends on its members' productivity and contributions, we naturally tend to frown on lazy people and applaud and reward ambitious, hard-working self-starters. At the same time, no child has ever responded to the common question "What do you want to be when you grow up?" by saying, "an overworked drone." No one approaching death has ever wanted his or her gravestone to read, "Workaholic." Those with busy, stressful jobs often discuss the difficulty of striking a balance between work and the rest of life. Those who do not strike this balance and become obsessed with their all-consuming jobs or careers are often told, either to their faces or behind their backs, to "get a life." As you read the following works of literature, representing a range of perspectives, eras, and cultures, consider what light they shed on your own work situation and on our own times.

Fiction

Washington Irving

Rip Van Winkle

A Posthumous Writing of Diedrich Knickerbocker

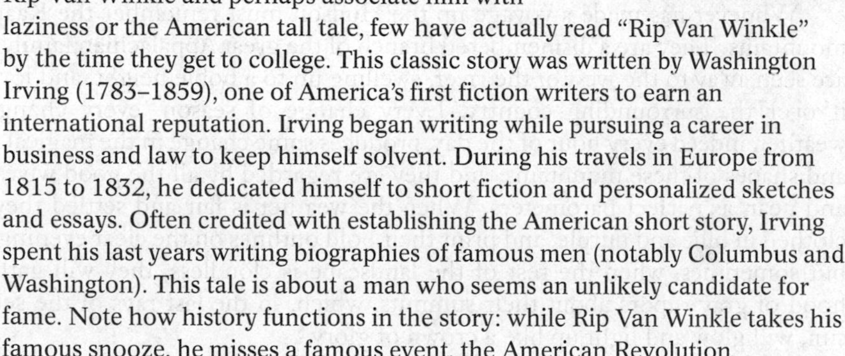

Although most American children know the legend of Rip Van Winkle and perhaps associate him with laziness or the American tall tale, few have actually read "Rip Van Winkle" by the time they get to college. This classic story was written by Washington Irving (1783–1859), one of America's first fiction writers to earn an international reputation. Irving began writing while pursuing a career in business and law to keep himself solvent. During his travels in Europe from 1815 to 1832, he dedicated himself to short fiction and personalized sketches and essays. Often credited with establishing the American short story, Irving spent his last years writing biographies of famous men (notably Columbus and Washington). This tale is about a man who seems an unlikely candidate for fame. Note how history functions in the story: while Rip Van Winkle takes his famous snooze, he misses a famous event, the American Revolution.

By Woden, God of Saxons,
From whence comes Wensday that is Wodensday
Truth is a thing that ever I will keep
Until thylke day in which I creep into
My sepulchre–
–Cartwright[1]

The following tale was found among the papers of the late Diedrich Knickerbocker,[2] *an old gentleman of New York, who was very curious, in the Dutch History of the province, and the manners of the descendants from its primitive settlers. His historical researches, however, did not lie so much among books as among men; for the former are lamentably scanty on his favorite topics; whereas he found the old burghers, and still more, their*

[1] *Cartwright:* William Cartwright, British dramatist (1611–1643).

[2] *Knickerbocker:* An author that Irving invented.

wives, rich in that legendary lore, so invaluable to true history. Whenever, therefore, he happened upon a genuine Dutch family, snugly shut up in its low-roofed farmhouse under a spreading sycamore, he looked upon it as a little clasped volume of black-letter, and studied it with the zeal of a bookworm.*

The result of all these researches was a history of the province during the reign of the Dutch governors, which he published some years since. There have been various opinions as to the literary character of his work, and, to tell the truth, it is not a whit better than it should be. Its chief merit is its scrupulous accuracy, which, indeed, was a little questioned on its first appearance, but has since been completely established; and it is now admitted into all historical collections as a book of unquestionable authority.

The old gentleman died shortly after the publication of his work, and, now that he is dead and gone, it cannot do much harm to his memory to say that his time might have been much better employed in weightier labors. He, however, was apt to ride his hobby his own way; and though it did now and then kick up the dust a little in the eyes of his neighbors, and grieve the spirit of some friends for whom he felt the truest deference and affection, yet his errors and follies are remembered "more in sorrow than in anger," and it begins to be suspected that he never intended to injure or offend. But however his memory may be appreciated by critics, it is still held dear among many folk, whose good opinion is well worth having; particularly by certain biscuit bakers, who have gone so far as to imprint his likeness on their New-Year cakes, and have thus given him a chance for immortality almost equal to the being stamped on a Waterloo medal, or a Queen Anne's farthing.[3]

Whoever has made a voyage up the Hudson must remember the Kaatskill mountains. They are a dismembered branch of the great Appalachian family, and are seen away to the west of the river, swelling up to a noble height, and lording it over the surrounding country. Every change of season, every change of weather, indeed every hour of the day, produces some change in the magical hues and shapes of these mountains; and they are regarded by all the good wives, far and near, as perfect barometers. When the weather is fair and settled they are clothed in blue and purple, and print their bold outlines on the clear evening sky; but sometimes, when the rest of the landscape is cloudless, they will gather a hood of gray vapors about their summits, which, in the last rays of the setting sun, will glow and light up like a crown of glory.

At the foot of these fairy mountains the voyager may have descried the light smoke curling up from a village, whose shingle roofs gleam among the trees just where the blue tints of the upland melt away into the fresh green of the nearer landscape. It is a little village of great antiquity having been founded by some of the Dutch colonists, in the early times of the province, just about the beginning of the government of the good Peter Stuyvesant[4] (may he rest in peace!), and there were some of the houses of the original settlers standing within a few years, built of small yellow bricks brought from Holland, having latticed windows and gable fronts, surmounted with weathercocks.

*Vide the excellent discourse of G. C. Verplanck, Esq., before the New York Historical Society. [Irving's note]

[3]*Queen Anne's Farthing:* A relatively worthless coin: many of these medals were in circulation at the time.

[4]*Stuyvesant:* Peter Stuyvesant (1600–1672) was the Dutch governor of what became New York City when it was still part of the colony of New Netherland.

In that same village, and in one of these very houses (which, to tell the precise truth, was sadly time-worn and weather-beaten), there lived many years since, while the country was yet a province of Great Britain, a simple, good-natured fellow, of the name of Rip Van Winkle. He was a descendant of the Van Winkles who figure so gallantly in the chivalrous days of Peter Stuyvesant and accompanied him to the siege of Fort Christina.[5] He inherited, however, but little of the martial character of his ancestors. I have observed that he was a simple, good-natured man; he was moreover a kind neighbor, and an obedient henpecked husband. Indeed, to the latter circumstance might be owing that meekness of spirit which gained him such universal popularity; for those men are most apt to be obsequious and conciliating abroad who are under the discipline of shrews at home. Their tempers, doubtless, are rendered pliant and malleable in the fiery furnace of domestic tribulation, and a curtain lecture is worth all the sermons in the world for teaching the virtues of patience and long-suffering. A termagant wife may, therefore, in some respects, be considered a tolerable blessing; and, if so, Rip Van Winkle was thrice blessed.

Certain it is that he was a great favorite among all the good wives of the village, who, as usual with the amiable sex, took his part in all family squabbles, and never failed, whenever they talked those matters over in their evening gossipings, to lay all the blame on Dame Van Winkle. The children of the village, too, would shout with joy whenever he approached. He assisted at their sports, made their playthings, taught them to fly kites and shoot marbles, and told them long stories of ghosts, witches, and Indians. Whenever he went dodging about the village, he was surrounded by a troop of them hanging on his skirts, clambering on his back, and playing a thousand tricks on him with impunity; and not a dog would bark at him throughout the neighborhood.

The great error in Rip's composition was an insuperable aversion to all kinds 5
of profitable labor. It could not be from the want of assiduity or perseverance; for he would sit on a wet rock, with a rod as long and heavy as a Tartar's lance, and fish all day without a murmur, even though he should not be encouraged by a single nibble. He would carry a fowling-piece on his shoulder, for hours together, trudging through woods and swamps, and up hill and down dale, to shoot a few squirrels or wild pigeons. He would never refuse to assist a neighbor even in the roughest toil, and was a foremost man at all country frolics for husking Indian corn, or building stone fences. The women of the village, too, used to employ him to run their errands, and to do such little odd jobs as their less obliging husbands would not do for them—in a word, Rip was ready to attend to anybody's business but his own; but as to doing family duty, and keeping his farm in order, he found it impossible.

In fact, he declared it was of no use to work on his farm; it was the most pestilent little piece of ground in the whole country; everything about it went wrong, and would go wrong in spite of him. His fences were continually falling to pieces; his cow would either go astray, or get among the cabbages; weeds were

[5]*Fort Christina:* The principal fort of New Sweden, in present-day Delaware, conquered by Stuyvesant in 1655.

"He looked round for his gun, but in place of the clean well-oiled fowling-piece, he found an old firelock lying by him, the barrel encrusted with rust."

Rip Van Winkle.

sure to grow quicker in his fields than anywhere else; the rain always made a point of setting in just as he had some outdoor work to do; so that, though his patrimonial estate had dwindled away under his management, acre by acre, until there was little more left than a mere patch of Indian corn and potatoes, yet it was the worst conditioned farm in the neighborhood.

His children, too, were as ragged and wild as if they belonged to nobody. His son Rip, an urchin begotten in his own likeness, promised to inherit the habits, with the old clothes of his father. He was generally seen trooping like a colt at his mother's heels, equipped in a pair of his father's cast-off galligaskins, which he had much ado to hold up with one hand, as a fine lady does her train in bad weather.

Rip Van Winkle, however, was one of those happy mortals, of foolish, well-oiled dispositions, who take the world easy, eat white bread or brown, whichever can be got with least thought or trouble, and would rather starve on a penny than work for a pound. If left to himself, he would have whistled life away in perfect contentment; but his wife kept continually dinning in his ears about his idleness, his carelessness, and the ruin he was bringing on his family. Morning, noon, and night, her tongue was incessantly going, and everything he said or did was sure to produce a torrent of household eloquence. Rip had but one way of replying to all lectures of the kind, and that, by frequent use, had grown into a habit. He shrugged his shoulders, shook his head, cast up his eyes, but said nothing. This, however, always provoked a fresh volley from his wife, so that he was fain to draw off his forces, and take to the outside of the house—the only side which, in truth, belongs to a henpecked husband.

Rip's sole domestic adherent was his dog Wolf, who was as much henpecked as his master; for Dame Van Winkle regarded them as companions in idleness, and even looked upon Wolf with an evil eye, as the cause of his master's going so often astray. True it is, in all points of spirit befitting an honorable dog, he was as courageous an animal as ever scoured the woods—but what courage can withstand the ever-during and all-besetting terrors of a woman's tongue? The moment Wolf entered the house, his crest fell, his tail drooped to the ground, or curled between his legs, he sneaked about with a gallows air, casting many a sidelong glance at Dame Van Winkle, and at the least flourish of a broomstick or ladle he would fly to the door with yelping precipitation.

Times grew worse and worse with Rip Van Winkle, as years of matrimony 10
rolled on: a tart temper never mellows with age, and a sharp tongue is the only edge tool that grows keener with constant use. For a long while he used to console himself, when driven from home, by frequenting a kind of perpetual club of the sages, philosophers, and other idle personages of the village, which held its sessions on a bench before a small inn, designated by a rubicund portrait of his Majesty George the Third.[6] Here they used to sit in the shade, of a long lazy summer's day, talking listlessly over village gossip, or telling endless sleepy stories about nothing. But it would have been worth any statesman's money to have heard the profound discussions which sometimes took place, when by chance an old newspaper fell into their hands from some passing traveler. How solemnly they would listen to the contents, as drawled out by Derrick Van Bummel, the schoolmaster, a dapper learned little man, who was not to be daunted by the most gigantic word in the dictionary; and how sagely they would deliberate upon public events some months after they had taken place.

The opinions of this junto were completely controlled by Nicholas Vedder, a patriarch of the village, and landlord of the inn, at the door of which he took his seat from morning till night, just moving sufficiently to avoid the sun, and keep in the shade of a large tree; so that the neighbors could tell the hour by his movements as accurately as by a sun-dial. It is true he was rarely heard to speak, but smoked his pipe incessantly. His adherents, however (for every great man has his adherents), perfectly understood him, and knew how to gather his opinions. When anything that was read or related displeased him, he was observed to smoke his pipe vehemently and to send forth short, frequent, and angry puffs; but when pleased, he would inhale the smoke slowly and tranquilly, and emit it in light and placid clouds, and sometimes taking the pipe from his mouth, and letting the fragrant vapor curl about his nose, would gravely nod his head in token of perfect approbation.

From even this stronghold the unlucky Rip was at length routed by his termagant wife, who would suddenly break in upon the tranquillity of the assemblage, and call the members all to naught; nor was that august personage,

[6]*George the Third:* George III (1783–1820) was the British monarch during the American Revolution.

Nicholas Vedder himself, sacred from the daring tongue of this terrible virago, who charged him outright with encouraging her husband in habits of idleness.

Poor Rip was at last reduced almost to despair, and his only alternative to escape from the labor of the farm and the clamor of his wife was to take gun in hand and stroll away into the woods. Here he would sometimes seat himself at the foot of a tree, and share the contents of his wallet with Wolf, with whom he sympathized as a fellow-sufferer in persecution. "Poor Wolf," he would say, "thy mistress leads thee a dog's life of it; but never mind, my lad, while I live thou shalt never want a friend to stand by thee!" Wolf would wag his tail, look wistfully in his master's face, and if dogs can feel pity, 1 verily believe he reciprocated the sentiment with all his heart.

In a long ramble of the kind, on a fine autumnal day, Rip had unconsciously scrambled to one of the highest parts of the Kaatskill mountains. He was after his favorite sport of squirrel-shooting, and the still solitudes had echoed and reechoed with the reports of his gun. Panting and fatigued, he threw himself, late in the afternoon, on a green knoll covered with mountain herbage that crowned the brow of a precipice. From an opening between the trees, he could overlook all the lower country for many a mile of rich woodland. He saw at a distance the lordly Hudson, far, far below him, moving on its silent but majestic course, with the reflection of a purple cloud, or the sail of a lagging bark, here and there sleeping on its glassy bosom, and at last losing itself in the blue highlands.

On the other side he looked down into a deep mountain glen, wild, lonely, and shagged, the bottom filled with fragments from the impending cliffs, and scarcely lighted by the reflected rays of the setting sun. For some time Rip lay musing on this scene; evening was gradually advancing; the mountains began to throw their long blue shadows over the valleys; he saw that it would be dark long before he could reach the village; and he heaved a heavy sigh when he thought of encountering the terrors of Dame Van Winkle.

As he was about to descend, he heard a voice from a distance, hallooing, "Rip Van Winkle! Rip Van Winkle!" He looked around, but could see nothing but a crow winging its solitary flight across the mountain. He thought his fancy must have deceived him, and turned again to descend, when he heard the same cry ring through the still evening air, "Rip Van Winkle! Rip Van Winkle!"—at the same time Wolf bristled up his back, and giving a low growl, skulked to his master's side, looking fearfully down into the glen. Rip now felt a vague apprehension stealing over him; he looked anxiously in the same direction, and perceived a strange figure slowly toiling up the rocks, and bending under the weight of something he carried on his back. He was surprised to see any human being in this lonely and unfrequented place; but supposing it to be some one of the neighborhood in need of his assistance, he hastened down to yield it.

On nearer approach, he was still more surprised at the singularity of the stranger's appearance. He was a short, square-built old fellow, with thick bushy hair, and a grizzled beard. His dress was of the antique Dutch fashion—a cloth jerkin strapped round the waist—several pair of breeches, the outer one of ample volume, decorated with rows of buttons down the sides, and bunches at the knees. He bore on his shoulders a stout keg, that seemed full of liquor, and made signs for Rip to approach and assist him with the load. Though rather shy and distrustful of this new acquaintance, Rip complied with his usual alacrity, and, mutually relieving each other, they clambered up a narrow gully, apparently the dry bed of a mountain torrent. As they ascended, Rip every now and then heard long rolling peals, like distant thunder, that seemed to issue out of a deep ravine, or rather cleft, between lofty rocks, toward which their rugged path conducted. He paused for an instant, but supposing it to be the muttering of one of those transient thunder-showers which often take place in mountain heights, he proceeded. Passing through the ravine, they came to a hollow, like a small amphitheater, surrounded by perpendicular precipices, over the brinks of which impending trees shot their branches, so that you only caught glimpses of the azure sky and the bright evening cloud. During the whole time, Rip and his companion had labored on in silence; for though the former marveled greatly what could be the object of carrying a keg of liquor up this wild mountain, yet there was something strange and incomprehensible about the unknown that inspired awe and checked familiarity.

On entering the amphitheater, new objects of wonder presented themselves. On a level spot in the center was a company of odd-looking personages playing at nine-pins. They were dressed in a quaint outlandish fashion; some wore short doublets, others jerkins, with long knives in their belts, and most of them had enormous breeches, of similar style with that of the guide's. Their visages, too, were peculiar: one had a large head, broad face, and small piggish eyes; the face of another seemed to consist entirely of nose, and was surmounted by a white sugar-loaf hat, set off with a little red cock's tail. They all had beards, of various shapes and colors. There was one who seemed to be the commander. He was a stout old gentleman, with a weather-beaten countenance; he wore a laced doublet, broad belt and hanger, high-crowned hat and feather, red stockings, and high-heeled shoes, with roses in them. The whole group reminded Rip of the figures in an old Flemish painting, in the parlor of Dominie Van Schaick, the village parson, and which had been brought over from Holland at the time of the settlement.

What seemed particularly odd to Rip was that, though these folks were evidently amusing themselves, yet they maintained the gravest faces, the most mysterious silence, and were, withal, the most melancholy party of pleasure he had ever witnessed. Nothing interrupted the stillness of the scene but the noise of the balls, which, whenever they rolled, echoed along the mountains like rumbling peals of thunder.

As Rip and his companion approached them, they suddenly desisted from 20
their play, and stared at him with such a fixed statue-like gaze, and such strange, uncouth, lackluster countenances, that his heart turned within him, and his knees smote together. His companion now emptied the contents of the keg into large flagons, and made signs to him to wait upon the company. He obeyed with fear and trembling; they quaffed the liquor in profound silence, and then returned to their game.

By degrees Rip's awe and apprehension subsided. He even ventured, when no eye was fixed upon him, to taste the beverage, which he found had much of the flavor of excellent Hollands. He was naturally a thirsty soul, and was soon tempted to repeat the draught. One taste provoked another, and he reiterated his visits to the flagon so often that at length his senses were overpowered, his eyes swam in his head, his head gradually declined, and he fell into a deep sleep.

On waking, he found himself on the green knoll from whence he had first seen the old man of the glen. He rubbed his eyes—it was a bright sunny morning. The birds were hopping and twittering among the bushes, and the eagle was wheeling aloft, and breasting the pure mountain breeze. "Surely," thought Rip, "I have not slept here all night." He recalled the occurrences before he fell asleep. The strange man with the keg of liquor—the mountain ravine—the wild retreat among the rocks—the woe-begone party at nine-pins—the flagon— "Oh! that wicked flagon!" thought Rip—"what excuse shall I make to Dame Van Winkle?"

He looked round for his gun, but in place of the clean, well-oiled fowling-piece, he found an old firelock lying by him, the barrel incrusted with rust, the lock falling off, and the stock worm-eaten. He now suspected that the grave roisterers of the mountain had put a trick upon him, and having dosed him with liquor, had robbed him of his gun. Wolf, too, had disappeared, but he might have strayed away after a squirrel or partridge. He whistled after him, and shouted his name, but all in vain; the echoes repeated his whistle and shout, but no dog was to be seen.

He determined to revisit the scene of the last evening's gambol, and if he met with any of the party, to demand his dog and gun. As he rose to walk, he found himself stiff in the joints, and wanting in his usual activity. "These mountain beds do not agree with me," thought Rip, "and if this frolic should lay me up with a fit of the rheumatism, I shall have a blessed time with Dame Van Winkle." With some difficulty he got down into the glen; he found the gully up which he and his companion had ascended the preceding evening; but to his astonishment a mountain stream was now foaming down it, leaping from rock to rock, and filling the glen with babbling murmurs. He, however, made shift to scramble up its sides, working his toilsome way through thickets of birch, sassafras, and witch-hazel; and sometimes tripped up or entangled by the wild grape-vines that twisted their coils and tendrils from tree to tree, and spread a kind of network in his path.

At length he reached to where the ravine had opened through the cliffs to the amphitheater; but no traces of such opening remained. The rocks presented a high, impenetrable wall, over which the torrent came tumbling in a sheet of feathery foam, and fell into a broad deep basin, black from the shadows of the surrounding forest. Here, then, poor Rip was brought to a stand. He again called and whistled after his dog; he was only answered by the cawing of a flock of idle crows, sporting high in air about a dry tree that overhung a sunny precipice; and who, secure in their elevation, seemed to look down and scoff at the poor man's perplexities. What was to be done? The morning was passing away, and Rip felt famished for want of his breakfast. He grieved to give up his dog and gun; he dreaded to meet his wife; but it would not do to starve among the mountains. He shook his head, shouldered the rusty firelock, and, with a heart full of trouble and anxiety, turned his steps homeward.

As he approached the village, he met a number of people, but none whom he knew, which somewhat surprised him, for he had thought himself acquainted with every one in the country round. Their dress, too, was of a different fashion from that to which he was accustomed. They all stared at him with equal marks of surprise, and whenever they cast eyes upon him, invariably stroked their chins. The constant recurrence of this gesture induced Rip, involuntarily, to do the same, when, to his astonishment, he found his beard had grown a foot long!

He had now entered the skirts of the village. A troop of strange children ran at his heels, hooting after him, and pointing at his gray beard. The dogs, too, not one of which he recognized for an old acquaintance, barked at him as he passed. The very village was altered; it was larger and more populous. There were rows of houses which he had never seen before, and those which had been his familiar haunts had disappeared. Strange names were over the doors—strange faces at the windows—everything was strange. His mind now misgave him; he began to doubt whether both he and the world around him were not bewitched. Surely this was his native village, which he had left but a day before. There stood the Kaatskill mountains—there ran the silver Hudson at a distance—there was every hill and dale precisely as it had always been. Rip was sorely perplexed. "That flagon last night," thought he, "has addled my poor head sadly!"

It was with some difficulty that he found the way to his own house, which he approached with silent awe, expecting every moment to hear the shrill voice of Dame Van Winkle. He found the house gone to decay—the roof fallen in, the windows shattered, and the doors off the hinges. A half-starved dog, that looked like Wolf, was skulking about it. Rip called him by name, but the cur snarled, showed his teeth, and passed on. This was an unkind cut indeed. "My very dog," sighed poor Rip, "has forgotten me!"

He entered the house, which, to tell the truth, Dame Van Winkle had always kept in neat order. It was empty, forlorn, and apparently abandoned. This desolateness overcame all his connubial fears—he called loudly for his wife and children—the lonely chambers rang for a moment with his voice, and then all again was silence.

He now hurried forth, and hastened to his old resort, the village inn—but it too was gone. A large rickety wooden building stood in its place, with great gaping windows, some of them broken, and mended with old hats and petticoats, and over the door was painted, "The Union Hotel, by Jonathan Doolittle." Instead of the great tree that used to shelter the quiet little Dutch inn of yore, there now was reared a tall naked pole, with something on the top that looked like a red nightcap, and from it was fluttering a flag, on which was a singular assemblage of stars and stripes—all this was strange and incomprehensible. He recognized on the sign, however, the ruby face of King George, under which he had smoked so many a peaceful pipe, but even this was singularly metamorphosed. The red coat was changed for one of blue and buff, a sword was held in the hand instead of a scepter, the head was decorated with a cocked hat, and underneath was painted in large characters, GENERAL WASHINGTON.

There was, as usual, a crowd of folk about the door, but none that Rip recollected. The very character of the people seemed changed. There was a busy, bustling, disputatious tone about it, instead of the accustomed phlegm and drowsy tranquillity. He looked in vain for the sage Nicholas Vedder, with his broad face, double chin, and fair long pipe, uttering clouds of tobacco smoke, instead of idle speeches; or Van Bummel, the schoolmaster, doling forth the contents of an ancient newspaper. In place of these, a lean, bilious-looking fellow, with his pockets full of handbills, was haranguing vehemently about rights of citizens—election—members of Congress—liberty—Bunker's hill—heroes of seventy-six—and other words, that were a perfect Babylonish jargon to the bewildered Van Winkle.

The appearance of Rip, with his long, grizzled beard, his rusty fowling-piece, his uncouth dress, and the army of women and children that had gathered at his heels, soon attracted the attention of the tavern politicians. They crowded round him, eying him from head to foot, with great curiosity. The orator bustled up to him, and drawing him partly aside, inquired, "on which side he voted?" Rip stared in vacant stupidity. Another short but busy little fellow pulled him by the arm, and rising on tiptoe, inquired in his ear, "whether he was Federal or Democrat." Rip was equally at a loss to comprehend the question; when a knowing, self-important old gentleman, in a sharp cocked hat, made his way through the crowd, putting them to the right and left with his elbows as he passed, and planting himself before Van Winkle, with one arm akimbo, the other resting on his cane, his keen eyes and sharp hat penetrating, as it were, into his very soul, demanded in an austere tone, "what brought him to the election with a gun on his shoulder, and a mob at his heels, and whether he meant to breed a riot in the village?"—"Alas! gentlemen," cried Rip, somewhat dismayed, "I am a poor, quiet man, a native of the place, and a loyal subject of the King, God bless him!"

Here a general shout burst from the bystanders—"a Tory! a Tory! a spy! a refugee! hustle him! away with him!" It was with great difficulty that the self-important man in the cocked hat restored order; and having assumed a tenfold austerity of brow, demanded again of the unknown culprit, what he came there for, and whom he was seeking. The poor man humbly assured him that he meant no harm, but merely came there in search of some of his neighbors, who used to keep about the tavern.

"Well—who are they?—name them."

Rip bethought himself a moment, and inquired, "Where's Nicholas Vedder?"

There was a silence for a little while, when an old man replied, in a thin, piping voice, "Nicholas Vedder? why, he is dead and gone these eighteen years! There was a wooden tombstone in the churchyard that used to tell all about him, but that's rotten and gone too."

"Where's Brom Dutcher?"

"Oh, he went off to the army in the beginning of the war; some say he was killed at the storming of Stony Point—others say he was drowned in the squall, at the foot of Antony's Nose. I don't know—he never came back again."

"Where's Van Bummel, the schoolmaster?"

"He went off to the wars, too; was a great militia general, and is now in Congress."

Rip's heart died away at hearing of these sad changes in his home and friends, and finding himself thus alone in the world. Every answer puzzled him, too, by treating of such enormous lapses of time, and of matters which he could not understand: war—Congress—Stony Point;—he had no courage to ask after any more friends, but cried out in despair, "Does nobody here know Rip Van Winkle?"

"Oh, Rip Van Winkle!" exclaimed two or three. "Oh, to be sure! that's Rip Van Winkle yonder, leaning against the tree."

Rip looked, and beheld a precise counterpart of himself as he went up the mountain; apparently as lazy, and certainly as ragged. The poor fellow was now completely confounded. He doubted his own identity, and whether he was himself or another man. In the midst of his bewilderment, the man in the cocked hat demanded who he was, and what was his name.

"God knows," exclaimed he, at his wit's end; "I'm not myself—I'm somebody else—that's me yonder—no—that's somebody else, got into my shoes—I was my self last night, but I fell asleep on the mountain, and they've changed my gun, and everything's changed, and I'm changed, and I can't tell what's my name, or who I am!"

The bystanders began now to look at each other, nod, wink significantly, and tap their fingers against their foreheads. There was a whisper, also, about securing the gun, and keeping the old fellow from doing mischief, at the very suggestion of which, the self-important man with the cocked hat retired with some precipitation. At this critical moment a fresh, comely woman passed through the throng to get a peep at the gray-bearded man. She had a chubby child in her arms, which, frightened at his looks, began to cry. "Hush, Rip," cried she, "hush, you little fool; the old man won't hurt you." The name of the child, the air of the mother, the tone of her voice, all awakened a train of recollections in his mind. "What is your name, my good woman?" asked he.

"Judith Gardenier."

"And your father's name?"

"Ah, poor man, Rip Van Winkle was his name, but it's twenty years since he went away from home with his gun, and never has been heard of since—his dog came home without him; but whether he shot himself, or was carried away by the Indians, nobody can tell. I was then but a little girl."

Rip had but one question more to ask; but he put it with a faltering voice: "Where's your mother?"

Oh, she too had died but a short time since: she broke a blood-vessel in a fit of passion at a New England peddler.

There was a drop of comfort, at least, in this intelligence. The honest man could contain himself no longer. He caught his daughter and her child in his arms. "I am your father!" cried he—"young Rip Van Winkle once—old Rip Van Winkle now!—Does nobody know poor Rip Van Winkle?"

All stood amazed, until an old woman, tottering out from among the crowd, put her hand to her brow, and peering under it in his face for a moment, exclaimed, "Sure enough! it is Rip Van Winkle—it is himself! Welcome home again, old neighbor. Why, where have you been these twenty long years?"

Rip's story was soon told, for the whole twenty years had been to him but as one night. The neighbors stared when they heard it; some were seen to wink at each other, and put their tongues in their cheeks; and the self-important man in the cocked hat, who, when the alarm was over, had returned to the field, screwed down the corners of his mouth, and shook his head—upon which there was a general shaking of the head throughout the assemblage.

It was determined, however, to take the opinion of old Peter Vanderdonk, 55
who was seen slowly advancing up the road. He was a descendant of the historian of that name, who wrote one of the earliest accounts of the province. Peter was the most ancient inhabitant of the village, and well versed in all the wonderful events and traditions of the neighborhood. He recollected Rip at once, and corroborated his story in the most satisfactory manner. He assured the company that it was a fact, handed down from his ancestor the historian, that the Kaatskill mountains had always been haunted by strange beings. That it was affirmed that the great Hendrick Hudson, the first discoverer of the river and country, kept a kind of vigil there every twenty years, with his crew of the Half-Moon being permitted in this way to revisit the scenes of his enterprise, and keep a guardian eye upon the river and the great city called by his name. That his father had once seen them in their old Dutch dresses playing at nine-pins in a hollow of the mountain; and that he himself had heard, one summer afternoon, the sound of their balls, like distant peals of thunder.

To make a long story short, the company broke up, and returned to the more important concerns of the election. Rip's daughter took him home to live with her; she had a snug, well-furnished house, and a stout cheery farmer for a husband, whom Rip recollected for one of the urchins that used to climb upon his back. As to Rip's son and heir, who was the ditto of himself, seen leaning against the tree, he was employed to work on the farm; but evinced a hereditary disposition to attend to anything else but his business.

Rip now resumed his old walks and habits; he soon found many of his former cronies, though all rather the worse for the wear and tear of time; and preferred making friends among the rising generation, with whom he soon grew into great favor.

Having nothing to do at home, and being arrived at that happy age when a man can be idle with impunity, he took his place once more on the bench at the inn door, and was reverenced as one of the patriarchs of the village, and a chronicle of the old times "before the war." It was some time before he could get into the regular track of gossip, or could be made to comprehend the strange events that had taken place during his torpor. How that there had been a revolutionary war—that the country had thrown off the yoke of old England,—and that, instead of being a subject of his Majesty George the Third, he was now a free citizen of the United States. Rip, in fact, was no politician; the changes of states and empires made but little impression on him; but there was one species of despotism under which he had long groaned, and that was—petticoat government. Happily that was at an end; he had got his neck out of the yoke of matrimony, and could go in and out whenever he pleased, without dreading the tyranny of Dame Van Winkle. Whenever her name was mentioned, however, he shook his head, shrugged his shoulders, and cast up his eyes; which might pass either for an expression of resignation to his fate, or joy at his deliverance.

He used to tell his story to every stranger that arrived at Mr. Doolittle's hotel. He was observed, at first, to vary on some points every time he told it, which was, doubtless, owing to his having so recently awaked. It at last settled down precisely to the tale I have related, and not a man, woman, or child in the neighborhood but knew it by heart. Some always pretended to doubt the reality of it, and insisted that Rip had been out of his head, and that this was one point on which he always remained flighty. The old Dutch inhabitants, however, almost universally gave it full credit. Even to this day, they never hear a thunderstorm of a summer afternoon about the Kaatskill, but they say Hendrick Hudson and his crew are at their game of nine-pins; and it is a common wish of all henpecked husbands in the neighborhood, when life hangs heavy on their hands, that they might have a quieting draught out of Rip Van Winkle's flagon.

Note

The foregoing Tale, one would suspect, had been suggested to Mr. Knickerbocker by a little German superstition about the Emperor Frederick der Rothbart and the Kypphauser mountain; the subjoined note, however, which he had appended to the tale, shows that it is an absolute fact, narrated with his usual fidelity.

"The story of Rip Van Winkle may seem incredible to many, but nevertheless I give it my full belief, for I know the vicinity of our old Dutch settlements to have been very subject to marvelous events and appearances. Indeed, I have heard many stranger stories than this, in the villages along the Hudson, all of which were too well authenticated to admit of a doubt. I have even talked with Rip Van Winkle myself, who, when last I saw him, was a very venerable old man, and so perfectly rational and consistent on every other point that I think no conscientious person could refuse to take this into the bargain; nay, I have seen a certificate on the subject taken before a country justice and signed with a cross, in the justice's own handwriting. The story, therefore, is beyond the possibility of doubt. —D.K."

Postscript

The following are travel notes from a memorandum-book of Mr. Knickerbocker.

The Kaatsberg, or Catskill Mountains, have always been a region full of fable. The Indians considered them the abode of spirits, who influenced the weather, spreading sunshine or clouds over the landscape, and sending good or bad hunting-seasons. They were ruled by an old squaw spirit, said to be their mother. She dwelt on the highest peak of the Catskills, and had charge of the doors of day and night to open and shut them at the proper hour. She hung up the new moons in the skies, and cut up the old ones into stars. In times of drought, if properly propitiated, she would spin light summer clouds out of cobwebs and morning dew, and send them off from the crest of the mountain, flake after flake, like flakes of carded cotton, to float in the air; until, dissolved by the heat of the sun, they would fall in gentle showers, causing the grass to spring, the fruits to ripen, and the corn to grow an inch an hour. If displeased, however, she would brew up clouds black as ink, sitting in the midst of them like a bottle-bellied spider in the midst of its web; and when these clouds broke, woe betide the valleys!

(1819–1820)

In old times, say the Indian traditions, there was a kind of Manitou or Spirit, who kept about the wildest recesses of the Catskill Mountains, and took a mischievous pleasure in wreaking all kinds of evils and vexations upon the red men. Sometimes he would assume the form of a bear, a panther, or a deer, lead the bewildered hunter a weary chase through tangled forests and among ragged rocks; and then spring off with a loud ho! ho! leaving him aghast on the brink of a beetling precipice or raging torrent.

The favorite abode of this Manitou is still shown. It is a great rock or cliff on the loneliest part of the mountains, and, from the flowering vines which clamber about it, and the wild flowers which abound in its neighborhood, is known by the name of the Garden Rock. Near the foot of it is a small lake, the haunt of the solitary bittern, with water-snakes basking in the sun on the leaves of the pond-lilies which lie on the surface. This place was held in great awe by the Indians, insomuch that the boldest hunter would not pursue his game within its precincts. Once upon a time, however, a hunter who had lost his way, penetrated to the garden rock, where he beheld a number of gourds placed in the crotches of trees. One of these he seized and made off with it, but in the hurry of his retreat he let it fall among the rocks, when a great stream gushed forth, which washed him away and swept him down precipices, where he was dashed to pieces, and the stream made its way to the Hudson, and continues to flow to the present day; being the identical stream known by the name of the Kaaters-kill.

Questions for Discussion and Writing

Close Reading

1. How does the frame tale—the introduction at the beginning and the "note" and "postscript" at the end—highlight themes within the main story?
2. Examine carefully the town before Rip falls asleep and afterwards. What has changed as a result of the American Revolution?
3. How does Rip's relationship with his wife, Dame Van Winkle, figure into the story's themes?

Critical and Creative Reading

4. The narrator states, "The great error in Rip's composition was an insuperable aversion to all kinds of profitable labor." While Rip would often help others, he was reluctant to tend to his own farm. Discuss the notion of "profitable labor" both in the story and in general. Are people who would rather work for others than for themselves flawed?
5. Discuss Rip's basic actions (avoiding work, drinking too much, sleeping too long) in conjunction with the fact that he misses history.
6. Is Rip Van Winkle admirable?

Connections to Other Readings

7. Compare Rip's "aversion to profitable labor" with Bartleby's preference not to work in Herman Melville's story "Bartleby, the Scrivener."
8. Working with the selections from the Common Characters section at the end of this chapter and with "Rip Van Winkle," respond to the following

question: is hard work and its attendant success the best possible path for everyone?

9. Along with Rebecca Harding Davis's story "Life in the Iron-Mills," consider "Rip Van Winkle" in terms of the following question: is it desirable to avoid hard work?

Rebecca Harding Davis

Life in the Iron-Mills

Rebecca Harding Davis (1831–1910) was thirty years old when she published her first story, "Life in the Iron-Mills," in the *Atlantic Monthly*. Although she continued to publish prolifically through her lifetime, she is best remembered for this story. Like the narrator, Davis grew up in the industrial town of Wheeling, West Virginia (then part of Virginia), in a prosperous middle-class family. Also like her narrator, Davis is in a unique position to witness the bleak lives of industrial laborers in the iron-mills and to speak to the educated, relatively wealthy readers of the *Atlantic Monthly*, who (she assumes) have never witnessed such lives before. Pay attention to the narrator's opinions of her readers, especially at the beginning of her tale. (See also Chapter 11, in which George Scala uses Davis's story as the basis for his research paper.)

"Is this the end?
O Life, as futile, then, as frail!
What hope of answer or redress?"

A cloudy day: do you know what that is in a town of iron-works? The sky sank down before dawn, muddy, flat, immovable. The air is thick, clammy with the breath of crowded human beings. It stifles me. I open the window, and, looking out, can scarcely see through the rain the grocer's shop opposite, where a crowd of drunken Irishmen are puffing Lynchburg tobacco in their pipes. I can detect the scent through all the foul smells ranging loose in the air.

The idiosyncrasy of this town is smoke. It rolls sullenly in slow folds from the great chimneys of the iron-foundries, and settles down in black, slimy pools on the muddy streets. Smoke on the wharves, smoke on the dingy boats, on the yellow river,—clinging in a coating of greasy soot to the house-front, the two faded poplars, the faces of the passers-by. The long train of mules, dragging masses of pig-iron through the narrow street, have a foul vapor hanging to their reeking sides. Here, inside, is a little broken figure of an angel pointing upward from the mantel-shelf; but even its wings are covered with smoke, clotted and black. Smoke everywhere! A dirty canary chirps desolately in a cage beside me. Its dream of green fields and sunshine is a very old dream,—almost worn out, I think.

A superintendent checks the work of a young girl spinner, 1908.

From the back-window I can see a narrow brick-yard sloping down to the river-side, strewed with rain-butts and tubs. The river, dull and tawny-colored, *(la belle rivière!)*[1] drags itself sluggishly along, tired of the heavy weight of boats and coal-barges. What wonder? When I was a child, I used to fancy a look of weary, dumb appeal upon the face of the negro-like river slavishly bearing its burden day after day. Something of the same idle notion comes to me to-day, when from the street-window I look on the slow stream of human life creeping past night and morning, to the great mills. Masses of men, with dull, besotted faces bent to the ground, sharpened here and there by pain or cunning; skin and muscle and flesh begrimed with sacks and ashes; stooping all night over boiling caldrons of metal, laired by day in dens of drunkenness and infamy; breathing from infancy to death an air saturated with fog and grease and soot, vileness for soul and body. What do you make of a case like that, amateur psychologist? You call it an altogether serious thing to be alive: to these men it is a drunken jest, a joke,—horrible to angels perhaps, to them commonplace enough. My fancy about the river was an idle one: it is no type of such a life. What if it be stagnant and slimy here? It knows that beyond there waits for it odorous sunlight,—quaint old gardens, dusky with soft, green foliage of apple-trees, and flushing crimson with roses,—air, and fields, and mountains. The future of the Welsh puddler[2] passing just now is not so pleasant. To be stowed away, after his grimy

[1]*la belle rivière:* The pretty river (French).

[2]*puddler*: An ironworker.

Boys work in the spool room of a cotton mill, 1908.

work is done, in a hole in the muddy graveyard, and after that,—*not* air, nor green fields, nor curious roses.

Can you see how foggy the day is? As I stand here, idly tapping the window-pane, and looking out through the rain at the dirty back-yard and the coal-boats below, fragments of an old story float up before me,—a story of this old house into which I happened to come today. You may think it a tiresome story enough, as foggy as the day, sharpened by no sudden flashes of pain or pleasure.—I know: only the outline of a dull life, that long since, with thousands of dull lives like its own, was vainly lived and lost: thousands of them,—massed, vile, slimy lives, like those of the torpid lizards in yonder stagnant water-butt.—Lost? There is a curious point for you to settle, my friend, who study psychology in a lazy, *dilettante* way. Stop a moment. I am going to be honest. This is what I want you to do. I want you to hide your disgust, take no heed to your clean clothes, and come right down with me,—here, into the thickest of the fog and mud and foul effluvia. I want you to hear this story. There is a secret down here, in this nightmare fog, that has lain dumb for centuries: I want to make it a real thing to you. You, Egoist, or Pantheist, or Arminian,[3] busy in making straight paths for your feet on the hills, do not see it clearly,—this terrible question which men here have gone

[3]*Egoist, or Pantheist, or Arminian:* An egoist sees the world centered around the self; a pantheist sees a divine presence in nature. Arminian, in this context, refers to someone who believes that Jesus's martyrdom will redeem humanity.

mad and died trying to answer. I dare not put this secret into words. I told you it was dumb. These men, going by with drunken faces and brains full of unawakened power, do not ask it of Society or of God. Their lives ask it; their deaths ask it. There is no reply. I will tell you plainly that I have a great hope; and I bring it to you to be tested. It is this: that this terrible dumb question is its own reply; that it is not the sentence of death we think it, but, from the very extremity of its darkness, the most solemn prophecy which the world has known of the Hope to come. I dare make my meaning no clearer, but will only tell my story. It will, perhaps, seem to you as foul and dark as this thick vapor about us, and as pregnant with death; but if your eyes are free as mine are to look deeper, no perfume-tinted dawn will be so fair with promise of the day that shall surely come.

My story is very simple,—only what I remember of the life of one of these 5
men,—a furnace-tender in one of Kirby & John's rolling-mills,—Hugh Wolfe. You know the mills? They took the great order for the Lower Virginia railroad there last winter; run usually with about a thousand men. I cannot tell why I choose the half-forgotten story of this Wolfe more than that of myriads of other furnace-hands. Perhaps because there is a secret underlying sympathy between that story and this day with its impure fog and thwarted sunshine,—or perhaps simply for the reason that this house is the one where the Wolfes lived. There were the father and son,—both hands, as I said, in one of Kirby & John's mills for making railroad-iron,—and Deborah, their cousin, a picker in some of the cotton-mills. The house was rented then to half a dozen families. The Wolfes had two of the cellar-rooms. The old man, like many of the puddlers and feeders of the mills, was Welsh,—had spent half of his life in the Cornish[4] tin-mines. You may pick the Welsh emigrants, Cornish miners, out of the throng passing the windows, any day. They are a trifle more filthy; their muscles are not so brawny; they stoop more. When they are drunk, they neither yell, nor shout, nor stagger, but skulk along like beaten hounds. A pure, unmixed blood, I fancy: shows itself in the slight angular bodies and sharply-cut facial lines. It is nearly thirty years since the Wolfes lived here. Their lives were like those of their class: incessant labor, sleeping in kennel-like rooms, eating rank pork and molasses, drinking—God and the distillers only know what; with an occasional night in jail, to atone for some drunken excess. Is that all of their lives?—of the portion given to them and these their duplicates swarming the streets to-day?—nothing beneath?—all? So many a political reformer will tell you,—and many a private reformer, too, who has gone among them with a heart tender with Christ's charity, and come out outraged, hardened.

One rainy night, about eleven o'clock, a crowd of half-clothed women stopped outside of the cellar-door. They were going home from the cotton-mill.

"Good-night, Deb," said one, a mulatto, steadying herself against the gas-post. She needed the post to steady her. So did more than one of them.

"Dah 's a ball to Miss Potts' to-night. Ye 'd best come."

"Inteet, Deb, if hur 'll come, hur 'll hef fun," said a shrill Welsh voice in the crowd.

[4]*Cornish:* From Cornwall, a county in southwest England.

Two or three dirty hands were thrust out to catch the gown of the woman, who was groping for the latch of the door. 10

"No."

"No? Where 's Kit Small, then?"

"Begorra! on the spools. Alleys behint, though we helped her, we dud. An wid ye! Let Deb alone! It's ondacent frettin' a quite body. Be the powers, an' we 'll have a night of it! there 'll be lashin's o' drink—the Vargent be blessed and praised for 't!"

They went on, the mulatto inclining for a moment to show fight, and drag the woman Wolfe off with them; but, being pacified, she staggered away.

Deborah groped her way into the cellar, and, after considerable stumbling, kindled a match, and lighted a tallow dip, that sent a yellow glimmer over the room. It was low, damp,—the earthen floor covered with a green, slimy moss,—a fetid air smothering the breath. Old Wolfe lay asleep on a heap of straw, wrapped in a torn horse-blanket. He was a pale, meek little man, with a white face and red rabbit-eyes. The woman Deborah was like him; only her face was even more ghastly, her lips bluer, her eyes more watery. She wore a faded cotton gown and a slouching bonnet. When she walked, one could see that she was deformed, almost a hunchback. She trod softly, so as not to waken him, and went through into the room beyond. There she found by the half-extinguished fire an iron saucepan filled with cold boiled potatoes, which she put upon a broken chair with a pint-cup of ale. Placing the old candlestick beside this dainty repast, she untied her bonnet, which hung limp and wet over her face, and prepared to eat her supper. It was the first food that had touched her lips since morning. There was enough of it, however: there is not always. She was hungry,—one could see that easily enough,—and not drunk, as most of her companions would have been found at this hour. She did not drink, this woman,—her face told that, too—nothing stronger than ale. Perhaps the weak, flaccid wretch had some stimulant in her pale life to keep her up,—some love or hope, it might be, or urgent need. When that stimulant was gone, she would take to whiskey. Man cannot live by work alone. While she was skinning the potatoes, and munching them, a noise behind her made her stop. 15

"Janey!" she called, lifting the candle and peering into the darkness. "Janey, are you there?"

A heap of ragged coats was heaved up, and the face of a young girl emerged, staring sleepily at the woman.

"Deborah," she said, at last, "I'm here the night."

"Yes, child. Hur's welcome," she said, quietly eating on.

The girl's face was haggard and sickly; her eyes were heavy with sleep and hunger: real Milesian[5] eyes they were, dark, delicate blue, glooming out from black shadows with a pitiful fright. 20

"I was alone," she said, timidly.

[5]*Milesian:* Relating to the mythological invaders of Ireland; the adjective is synonymous with deep Irish ancestry.

"Where's the father?" asked Deborah, holding out a potato, which the girl greedily seized.

"He's beyant,—wid Haley,—in the stone house." (Did you ever hear the word *jail* from an Irish mouth?) "I came here. Hugh told me never to stay me-lone."

"Hugh?"

"Yes."

A vexed frown crossed her face. The girl saw it, and added quickly,—

"I have not seen Hugh the day, Deb. The old man says his watch lasts till the mornin'."

The woman sprang up, and hastily began to arrange some bread and flitch in a tin pail, and to pour her own measure of ale into a bottle. Tying on her bonnet, she blew out the candle.

"Lay ye down, Janey dear," she said, gently, covering her with the old rags. "Hur can eat the potatoes, if hur's hungry."

"Where are ye goin', Deb? The rain's sharp."

"To the mill, with Hugh's supper."

"Let him bide till th' morn. Sit ye down."

"No, no,"—sharply pushing her off. "The boy 'll starve."

She hurried from the cellar, while the child wearily coiled herself up for sleep. The rain was falling heavily, as the woman, pail in hand, emerged from the mouth of the alley, and turned down the narrow street, that stretched out, long and black, miles before her. Here and there a flicker of gas lighted an uncertain space of muddy footwalk and gutter; the long rows of houses, except an occasional lager-bier shop, were closed; now and then she met a band of mill-hands skulking to or from their work.

Not many even of the inhabitants of a manufacturing town know the vast machinery of system by which the bodies of workmen are governed, that goes on unceasingly from year to year. The hands of each mill are divided into watches that relieve each other as regularly as the sentinels of an army. By night and day the work goes on, the unsleeping engines groan and shriek, the fiery pools of metal boil and surge. Only for a day in the week, in half-courtesy to public censure, the fires are partially veiled; but as soon as the clock strikes midnight, the great furnaces break forth with renewed fury, the clamor begins with fresh, breathless vigor, the engines sob and shriek like "gods in pain."

As Deborah hurried down through the heavy rain, the noise of these thousand engines sounded through the sleep and shadow of the city like far-off thunder. The mill to which she was going lay on the river, a mile below the city-limits. It was far, and she was weak, aching from standing twelve hours at the spools. Yet it was her almost nightly walk to take this man his supper, though at every square she sat down to rest, and she knew she should receive small word of thanks.

Perhaps, if she had possessed an artist's eye, the picturesque oddity of the scene might have made her step stagger less, and the path seem shorter; but to her the mills were only "summat deilish to look at by night."

The road leading to the mills had been quarried from the solid rock, which rose abrupt and bare on one side of the cinder-covered road, while the river, sluggish and black, crept past on the other. The mills for rolling iron are simply immense tent-like roofs, covering acres of ground, open on every side. Beneath these roofs Deborah looked in on a city of fires, that burned hot and fiercely in the night. Fire in every horrible form: pits of flame waving in the wind; liquid metal-flames writhing in tortuous streams through the sand; wide caldrons filled with boiling fire, over which bent ghastly wretches stirring the strange brewing; and through all, crowds of half-clad men, looking like revengeful ghosts in the red light, hurried, throwing masses of glittering fire. It was like a street in Hell. Even Deborah muttered, as she crept through, "'T looks like t' Devil's place!" It did,—in more ways than one.

She found the man she was looking for, at last, heaping coal on a furnace. He had not time to eat his supper; so she went behind the furnace, and waited. Only a few men were with him, and they noticed her only by a "Hyur comes t' hunch-back, Wolfe."

Deborah was stupid with sleep; her back pained her sharply; and her teeth chattered with cold, with the rain that soaked her clothes and dripped from her at every step. She stood, however, patiently holding the pail, and waiting.

"Hout, woman! ye look like a drowned cat. Come near to the fire,"—said one of the men, approaching to scrape away the ashes.

She shook her head. Wolfe had forgotten her. He turned, hearing the man, and came closer.

"I did no' think; gi' me my supper, woman."

She watched him eat with a painful eagerness. With a woman's quick instinct, she saw that he was not hungry,—was eating to please her. Her pale, watery eyes began to gather a strange light.

"Is 't good, Hugh? T' ale was a bit sour, I feared."

"No, good enough." He hesitated a moment. "Ye 're tired, poor lass! Bide here till I go. Lay down there on that heap of ash, and go to sleep."

He threw her an old coat for a pillow, and turned to his work. The heap was the refuse of the burnt iron, and was not a hard bed; the half-smothered warmth, too, penetrated her limbs, dulling their pain and cold shiver.

Miserable enough she looked, lying there on the ashes like a limp, dirty rag,—yet not an unfitting figure to crown the scene of hopeless discomfort and veiled crime: more fitting, if one looked deeper into the heart of things,—at her thwarted woman's form, her colorless life, her waking stupor that smothered pain and hunger,—even more fit to be a type of her class. Deeper yet if one could look, was there nothing worth reading in this wet, faded thing, half-covered with ashes? no story of a soul filled with groping passionate love, heroic unselfishness, fierce jealousy? of years of weary trying to please the one human being whom she loved, to gain one look of real heart-kindness from him? If anything like this were hidden beneath the pale, bleared eyes, and dull, washed-out-looking face, no one had ever taken the trouble to read its faint signs: not the half-clothed furnace-tender, Wolfe, certainly. Yet he was kind to her: it was his nature to be kind, even to the very rats that swarmed in the cellar: kind to her in just the same way. She knew that. And it might be that very knowledge had given to her face its apathy and vacancy more than her low, torpid life. One sees that dead, vacant look steal sometimes over the rarest, finest of women's faces,—in the very midst, it may be, of their warmest summer's day; and then one can guess at the secret of intolerable solitude that lies hid beneath the delicate laces and brilliant smile. There was no warmth, no brilliancy, no summer for this woman; so the stupor and vacancy had time to gnaw into her face perpetually. She was young, too, though no one guessed it; so the gnawing was the fiercer.

She lay quiet in the dark corner. Listening, through the monotonous din and uncertain glare of the works, to the dull plash of the rain in the far distance,—shrinking back whenever the man Wolfe happened to look towards her. She knew, in spite of all his kindness, that there was that in her face and form which made him loathe the sight of her. She felt by instinct, although she could not comprehend it, the finer nature of the man, which made him among his fellow-workmen something unique, set apart. She knew, that, down under all the vileness and coarseness of his life, there was a groping passion for whatever was beautiful and pure,—that his soul sickened with disgust at her deformity, even when his words were kindest. Through this dull consciousness, which never left her, came, like a sting, the recollection of the dark blue eyes and lithe figure of the little Irish girl she had left in the cellar. The recollection struck through even her stupid intellect with a vivid glow of beauty and of grace. Little Janey, timid, helpless, clinging to Hugh as her only friend: that was the sharp thought, the bitter thought, that drove into the glazed eyes a fierce light of pain. You laugh at it? Are pain and jealousy less savage realities down here in this place I am taking you to than in your own house or your own heart,—your heart, which they clutch at sometimes? The note is the same, I fancy, be the octave high or low.

If you could go into this mill where Deborah lay, and drag out from the hearts of these men the terrible tragedy of their lives, taking it as a symptom of the disease of their class, no ghost Horror would terrify you more. A reality of soul-starvation, of living death, that meets you every day under the besotted faces on the street,—I can paint nothing of this, only give you the outside outlines of a night, a crisis in the life of one man: whatever muddy depth of soul-history lies beneath you can read according to the eyes God has given you.

Wolfe, while Deborah watched him as a spaniel its master, bent over the furnace with his iron pole, unconscious of her scrutiny, only stopping to receive orders. Physically, Nature had promised the man but little. He had already lost the strength and instinct vigor of a man, his muscles were thin, his nerves weak, his face (a meek, woman's face) haggard, yellow with consumption. In the mill he was known as one of the girl-men: "Molly Wolfe" was his *sobriquet*.[6] He was never seen in the cockpit, did not own a terrier, drank but seldom; when he did, desperately. He fought sometimes, but was always thrashed, pommelled to a jelly. The man was game enough, when his blood was up: but he was no favorite in the mill; he had the taint of school-learning on him,—not to a dangerous extent, only a quarter or so in the free-school in fact, but enough to ruin him as a good hand in a fight.

[6]*sobriquet:* A nickname.

For other reasons, too, he was not popular. Not one of themselves, they felt that, though outwardly as filthy and ash-covered; silent, with foreign thoughts and longings breaking out through his quietness in innumerable curious ways: this one, for instance. In the neighboring furnace-buildings lay great heaps of the refuse from the ore after the pig-metal is run. *Korl* we call it here: a light, porous substance, of a delicate, waxen, flesh-colored tinge. Out of the blocks of this korl, Wolfe, in his off-hours from the furnace, had a habit of chipping and moulding figures,—hideous, fantastic enough, but sometimes strangely beautiful: even the mill-men saw that, while they jeered at him. It was a curious fancy in the man, almost a passion. The few hours for rest he spent hewing and hacking with his blunt knife, never speaking, until his watch came again,—working at one figure for months, and when it was finished, breaking it to pieces perhaps, in a fit of disappointment. A morbid, gloomy man, untaught, unled, left to feed his soul in grossness and crime, and hard, grinding labor.

I want you to come down and look at this Wolfe, standing there among the lowest of his kind, and see him just as he is, that you may judge him justly when you hear the story of this night. I want you to look back, as he does every day, at his birth in vice, his starved infancy; to remember the heavy years he has groped through as boy and man,—the slow, heavy years of constant, hot work. So long ago he began, that he thinks sometimes he has worked there for ages. There is no hope that it will ever end. Think that God put into this man's soul a fierce thirst for beauty,—to know it, to create it; to *be*—something, he knows not what,—other than he is. There are moments when a passing cloud, the sun glinting on the purple thistles, a kindly smile, a child's face, will rouse him to a passion of pain,—when his nature starts up with a mad cry of rage against God, man, whoever it is that has forced this vile, slimy life upon him. With all this groping, this mad desire, a great blind intellect stumbling through wrong, a loving poet's heart, the man was by habit only a coarse, vulgar laborer, familiar with sights and words you would blush to name. Be just: when I tell you about this night, see him as he is. Be just,—not like man's law, which seizes on one isolated fact, but like God's judging angel, whose clear, sad eye saw all the countless cankering days of this man's life, all the countless nights, when, sick with starving, his soul fainted in him, before it judged him for this night, the saddest of all.

I called this night the crisis of his life. If it was, it stole on him unawares. These great turning-days of life cast no shadow before, slip by unconsciously. Only a trifle, a little turn of the rudder, and the ship goes to heaven or hell.

Wolfe, while Deborah watched him, dug into the furnace of melting iron with his pole, dully thinking only how many rails the lump would yield. It was late,—nearly Sunday morning; another hour, and the heavy work would be done,—only the furnaces to replenish and cover for the next day. The workmen were growing more noisy, shouting, as they had to do, to be heard over the deep clamor of the mills. Suddenly they grew less boisterous,—at the far end, entirely silent. Something unusual had happened. After a moment, the silence came nearer; the men stopped their jeers and drunken choruses. Deborah, stupidly lifting up her head, saw the cause of the quiet. A group of five or six men were slowly approaching, stopping to examine each furnace as they came. Visitors often came to see the mills after night: except by growing less noisy, the men took no notice of them. The furnace where Wolfe worked was near the bounds of the works; they halted there hot and tired: a walk over one of these great foundries is no trifling task. The woman, drawing out of sight, turned over to sleep. Wolfe, seeing them stop, suddenly roused from his indifferent stupor, and watched them keenly. He knew some of them: the overseer, Clarke,—a son of Kirby, one of the mill-owners,—and a Doctor May, one of the town-physicians. The other two were strangers. Wolfe came closer. He seized eagerly every chance that brought him into contact with this mysterious class that shone down on him perpetually with the glamour of another order of being. What made the difference between them? That was the mystery of his life. He had a vague notion that perhaps to-night he could find it out. One of the strangers sat down on a pile of bricks, and beckoned young Kirby to his side.

"This *is* hot, with a vengeance. A match, please?"—lighting his cigar. "But the walk is worth the trouble. If it were not that you must have heard it so often, Kirby, I would tell you that your works look like Dante's Inferno."[7]

Kirby laughed.

"Yes. Yonder is Farinata himself in the burning tomb,"[8]—pointing to some figure in the shimmering shadows.

"Judging from some of the faces of your men," said the other, "they bid fair to try the reality of Dante's vision, some day."

Young Kirby looked curiously around, as if seeing the faces of his hands for the first time.

"They're bad enough, that 's true. A desperate set, I fancy. Eh, Clarke?"

The overseer did not hear him. He was talking of net profits just then,—giving, in fact, a schedule of the annual business of the firm to a sharp peering little Yankee, who jotted down notes on a paper laid on the crown of his hat: a reporter for one of the city-papers, getting up a series of reviews of the leading manufactories. The other gentlemen had accompanied them merely for amusement. They were silent until the notes were finished, drying their feet at the furnaces, and sheltering their faces from the intolerable heat. At last the overseer concluded with—

"I believe that is a pretty fair estimate, Captain."

"Here, some of you men!" said Kirby, "bring up those boards. We may as well sit down, gentlemen, until the rain is over. It cannot last much longer at this rate."

"Pig-metal,"—mumbled the reporter,—"um!—coal facilities,—um!—hands employed, twelve hundred,—bitumen,—um!—all right, I believe, Mr. Clarke;—sinking-fund,—what did you say was your sinking-fund?"

"Twelve hundred hands?" said the stranger, the young man who had first spoken. "Do you control their votes, Kirby?"

[7]*Dante's Inferno:* Dante Alighieri (1265–1321) was an Italian poet whose *Divine Comedy* is one of the great works of world literature. The inferno alluded to here is hell. Dante's work sought to explore the Christian cosmos.

[8]*Farinata:* A tormented figure from Dante's *Inferno*.

"Control? No." The young man smiled complacently. "But my father brought seven hundred votes to the polls for his candidate last November. No force-work, you understand,—only a speech or two, a hint to form themselves into a society, and a bit of red and blue bunting to make them a flag. The Invincible Roughs,—I believe that is their name. I forget the motto: 'Our country's hope,' I think."

There was a laugh. The young man talking to Kirby sat with an amused light in his cool gray eye, surveying critically the half-clothed figures of the puddlers, and the slow swing of their brawny muscles. He was a stranger in the city,—spending a couple of months in the borders of a Slave State, to study the institutions of the South,—a brother-in-law of Kirby's,—Mitchell. He was an amateur gymnast,—hence his anatomical eye; a patron, in a *blasé* way, of the prize-ring; a man who sucked the essence out of a science or philosophy in an indifferent, gentlemanly way; who took Kant, Novalis, Humboldt,[9] for what they were worth in his own scales; accepting all, despising nothing, in heaven, earth, or hell, but one-idead men; with a temper yielding and brilliant as summer water, until his Self was touched, when it was ice, though brilliant still. Such men are not rare in the States.

As he knocked the ashes from his cigar, Wolfe caught with a quick pleasure the contour of the white hand, the blood-glow of a red ring he wore. His voice, too, and that of Kirby's, touched him like music,—low, even, with chording cadences. About this man Mitchell hung the impalpable atmosphere belonging to the thorough-bred gentleman. Wolfe, scraping away the ashes beside him, was conscious of it, did obeisance to it with his artist sense, unconscious that he did so.

The rain did not cease. Clarke and the reporter left the mills; the others, comfortably seated near the furnace, lingered, smoking and talking in a desultory way. Greek would not have been more unintelligible to the furnace-tenders, whose presence they soon forgot entirely. Kirby drew out a newspaper from his pocket and read aloud some article, which they discussed eagerly. At every sentence, Wolfe listened more and more like a dumb, hopeless animal, with a duller, more stolid look creeping over his face, glancing now and then at Mitchell, marking acutely every smallest sign of refinement, then back to himself, seeing as in a mirror his filthy body, his more stained soul.

Never! He had no words for such a thought, but he knew now, in all the sharpness of the bitter certainty, that between them there was a great gulf never to be passed. Never!

The bell of the mills rang for midnight. Sunday morning had dawned. Whatever hidden message lay in the tolling bells floated past these men unknown. Yet it was there. Veiled in the solemn music ushering the risen Saviour was a key-note to solve the darkest secrets of a world gone wrong,—even this social riddle which the brain of the grimy puddler grappled with madly to-night.

[9]*Kant, Novalis, Humboldt:* Three German thinkers. Immanuel Kant (1724–1804) was a philosopher, Novalis (1711–1801) was the pseudonym for philosopher Georg Philipp Friedrich Freiherr von Hardenberg, and Friedrich von Humboldt (1769–1859) was a scientist.

The men began to withdraw the metal from the caldrons. The mills were deserted on Sundays, except by the hands who fed the fires, and those who had no lodgings and slept usually on the ash-heaps. The three strangers sat still during the next hour, watching the men cover the furnaces, laughing now and then at some jest of Kirby's.

"Do you know," said Mitchell, "I like this view of the works better than when the glare was fiercest? These heavy shadows and the amphitheatre of smothered fires are ghostly, unreal. One could fancy these red smouldering lights to be the half-shut eyes of wild beasts, and the spectral figures their victims in the den."

Kirby laughed. "You are fanciful. Come, let us get out of the den. The spectral figures, as you call them, are a little too real for me to fancy a close proximity in the darkness,—unarmed, too."

The others rose, buttoning their overcoats, and lighting cigars.

"Raining, still," said Doctor May, "and hard. Where did we leave the coach, Mitchell?"

"At the other side of the works.—Kirby, what's that?"

Mitchell started back, half-frightened, as, suddenly turning a corner, the white figure of a woman faced him in the darkness,—a woman, white, of giant proportions, crouching on the ground, her arms flung out in some wild gesture of warning.

"Stop! Make that fire burn there!" cried Kirby, stopping short.

The flame burst out, flashing the gaunt figure into bold relief.

Mitchell drew a long breath.

"I thought it was alive," he said, going up curiously.

The others followed.

"Not marble, eh?" asked Kirby, touching it.

One of the lower overseers stopped.

"Korl, Sir."

"Who did it?"

"Can't say. Some of the hands; chipped it out in off-hours."

"Chipped to some purpose, I should say. What a flesh-tint the stuff has! Do you see, Mitchell?"

"I see."

He had stepped aside where the light fell boldest on the figure, looking at it in silence. There was not one line of beauty or grace in it: a nude woman's form, muscular, grown coarse with labor, the powerful limbs instinct with some one poignant longing. One idea: there it was in the tense, rigid muscles, the clutching hands, the wild, eager face, like that of a starving wolf's. Kirby and Doctor May walked around it, critical, curious. Mitchell stood aloof, silent. The figure touched him strangely.

"Not badly done," said Doctor May. "Where did the fellow learn that sweep of the muscles in the arm and hand? Look at them! They are groping,—do you see?—clutching: the peculiar action of a man dying of thirst."

"They have ample facilities for studying anatomy," sneered Kirby, glancing at the half-naked figures.

"Look," continued the Doctor, "at this bony wrist, and the strained sinews 95
of the instep! A working-woman,—the very type of her class."

"God forbid!" muttered Mitchell.

"Why?" demanded May. "What does the fellow intend by the figure? I cannot catch the meaning."

"Ask him," said the other, dryly. "There he stands,"—pointing to Wolfe, who stood with a group of men, leaning on his ash-rake.

The Doctor beckoned him with the affable smile which kind-hearted men put on, when talking to these people.

"Mr. Mitchell has picked you out as the man who did this,—I'm sure I don't 100
know why. But what did you mean by it?"

"She be hungry."

Wolfe's eyes answered Mitchell, not the Doctor.

"Oh-h! But what a mistake you have made, my fine fellow! You have given no sign of starvation to the body. It is strong,—terribly strong. It has the mad, half-despairing gesture of drowning."

Wolfe stammered, glanced appealingly at Mitchell, who saw the soul of the thing, he knew. But the cool, probing eyes were turned on himself now,—mocking, cruel, relentless.

"Not hungry for meat," the furnace-tender said at last. 105

"What then? Whiskey?" jeered Kirby, with a coarse laugh.

Wolfe was silent a moment, thinking.

"I dunno," he said, with a bewildered look. "It mebbe. Summat to make her live, I think,—like you. Whiskey ull do it, in a way."

The young man laughed again. Mitchell flashed a look of disgust somewhere,—not at Wolfe.

"May," he broke out impatiently, "are you blind? Look at that woman's face! 110
It asks questions of God, and says, 'I have a right to know.' Good God, how hungry it is!"

They looked a moment; then May turned to the mill-owner:—

"Have you many such hands as this? What are you going to do with them? Keep them at puddling iron?"

Kirby shrugged his shoulders. Mitchell's look had irritated him.

"*Ce n'est pas mon affaire.*[10] I have no fancy for nursing infant geniuses. I suppose there are some stray gleams of mind and soul among these wretches. The Lord will take care of his own; or else they can work out their own salvation. I have heard you call our American system a ladder which any man can scale. Do you doubt it? Or perhaps you want to banish all social ladders, and put us all on a flat table-land,—eh, May?"

The Doctor looked vexed, puzzled. Some terrible problem lay hid in this 115
woman's face, and troubled these men. Kirby waited for an answer, and, receiving none, went on, warming with his subject.

[10]*Ce n'est pas mon affaire:* It is not my business (French).

"I tell you, there's something wrong that no talk of '*Liberté*' or '*Égalité*'[11] will do away. If I had the making of men, these men who do the lowest part of the world's work should be machines,—nothing more,—hands. It would be kindness. God help them! What are taste, reason, to creatures who must live such lives as that?" He pointed to Deborah, sleeping on the ash-heap. "So many nerves to sting them to pain. What if God had put your brain, with all its agony of touch, into your fingers, and bid you work and strike with that?"

"You think you could govern the world better?" laughed the Doctor.

"I do not think at all."

"That is true philosophy. Drift with the stream, because you cannot dive deep enough to find bottom, eh?"

"Exactly," rejoined Kirby. "I do not think. I wash my hands of all social problems,—slavery, caste, white or black. My duty to my operatives has a narrow limit,—the pay-hour on Saturday night. Outside of that, if they cut korl, or cut each other's throats, (the more popular amusement of the two,) I am not responsible."

The Doctor sighed,—a good honest sigh, from the depths of his stomach. "God help us! Who is responsible?"

"Not I, I tell you," said Kirby, testily. "What has the man who pays them money to do with their souls' concerns, more than the grocer or butcher who takes it?"

"And yet," said Mitchell's cynical voice, "look at her! How hungry she is!"

Kirby tapped his boot with his cane. No one spoke. Only the dumb face of the rough image looking into their faces with the awful question, "What shall we do to be saved?" Only Wolfe's face, with its heavy weight of brain, its weak, uncertain mouth, its desperate eyes, out of which looked the soul of his class,—only Wolfe's face turned towards Kirby's. Mitchell laughed,—a cool, musical laugh.

"Money has spoken!" he said, seating himself lightly on a stone with the air of an amused spectator at a play. "Are you answered?"—turning to Wolfe his clear, magnetic face.

Bright and deep and cold as Arctic air, the soul of the man lay tranquil beneath. He looked at the furnace-tender as he had looked at a rare mosaic in the morning; only the man was the more amusing study of the two.

"Are you answered? Why, May, look at him! '*De profundis clamavi.*' Or, to quote in English, 'Hungry and thirsty, his soul faints in him.' And so Money sends back its answer into the depths through you, Kirby! Very clear the answer, too!—I think I remember reading the same words somewhere:—washing your hands in Eau de Cologne, and saying, 'I am innocent of the blood of this man. See ye to it!'"

Kirby flushed angrily.

"You quote Scripture freely."

"Do I not quote correctly? I think I remember another line, which may amend my meaning: 'Inasmuch as ye did it unto one of the least of these, ye did

[11]*Liberté or Égalité: Liberté* (liberty), *fraternité* (brotherhood), and *égalité* (equality) became the tenets of the French Republic during the French Revolution (1789–1795).

it unto me.' Deist?[12] Bless you, man, I was raised on the milk of the Word. Now, Doctor, the pocket of the world having uttered its voice, what has the heart to say? You are a philanthropist, in a small way,—*n 'est ce pas?* Here, boy, this gentleman can show you how to cut korl better,—or your destiny. Go on, May!"

"I think a mocking devil possesses you to-night," rejoined the Doctor, seriously.

He went to Wolfe and put his hand kindly on his arm. Something of a vague idea possessed the Doctor's brain that much good was to be done here by a friendly word or two: a latent genius to be warmed into life by a waited-for sunbeam. Here it was: he had brought it. So he went on complacently:—

"Do you know, boy, you have it in you to be a great sculptor, a great man?—do you understand?" (talking down to the capacity of his hearer: it is a way people have with children, and men like Wolfe,)— "to live a better, stronger life than I, or Mr. Kirby here? A man may make himself anything he chooses. God has given you stronger powers than many men,—me, for instance."

May stopped, heated, glowing with his own magnanimity. And it was mag- 135
nanimous. The puddler had drunk in every word, looking through the Doctor's flurry, and generous heat, and self-approval, into his will, with those slow, absorbing eyes of his.

"Make yourself what you will. It is your right."

"I know," quietly. "Will you help me?"

Mitchell laughed again. The Doctor turned now, in a passion,—

"You know, Mitchell, I have not the means. You know, if I had, it is in my heart to take this boy and educate him for"—

"The glory of God, and the glory of John May." 140

May did not speak for a moment; then, controlled, he said,—

"Why should one be raised, when myriads are left?—I have not the money, boy," to Wolfe, shortly.

"Money?" He said it over slowly, as one repeats the guessed answer to a riddle, doubtfully. "That is it? Money?"

"Yes, money,—that is it," said Mitchell, rising, and drawing his furred coat about him. "You've found the cure for all the world's diseases.—Come, May, find your good-humor, and come home. This damp wind chills my very bones. Come and preach your Saint-Simonian doctrines[13] to-morrow to Kirby's hands. Let them have a clear idea of the rights of the soul, and I'll venture next week they'll strike for higher wages. That will be the end of it."

"Will you send the coach-driver to this side of the mills?" asked Kirby, turn- 145
ing to Wolfe.

He spoke kindly: it was his habit to do so. Deborah, seeing the puddler go, crept after him. The three men waited outside. Doctor May walked up and down, chafed. Suddenly he stopped.

[12]*Deist:* Deists were a group of Enlightenment-era Christians who believed in a rational God that did not get directly involved in human affairs.

[13]*Saint-Simonian doctrines:* Doctrines of the French socialist Comte Claude de Saint-Simeon (1760–1825).

"Go back, Mitchell! You say the pocket and the heart of the world speak without meaning to these people. What has its head to say? Taste, culture, refinement? Go!"

Mitchell was leaning against a brick wall. He turned his head indolently, and looked into the mills. There hung about the place a thick, unclean odor. The slightest motion of his hand marked that he perceived it, and his insufferable disgust. That was all. May said nothing, only quickened his angry tramp.

"Besides," added Mitchell, giving a corollary to his answer, "it would be of no use. I am not one of them."

"You do not mean"——said May, facing him.

"Yes, I mean just that. Reform is born of need, not pity. No vital movement of the people's has worked down, for good or evil; fermented, instead, carried up the heaving, cloggy mass. Think back through history, and you will know it. What will this lowest deep—thieves, Magdalens, negroes—do with the light filtered through ponderous Church creeds, Baconian theories, Goethe schemes?[14] Some day, out of their bitter need will be thrown up their own light-bringer,—their Jean Paul, their Cromwell, their Messiah."

"Bah!" was the Doctor's inward criticism. However, in practice, he adopted the theory; for, when, night and morning, afterwards, he prayed that power might be given these degraded souls to rise, he glowed at heart, recognizing an accomplished duty.

Wolfe and the woman had stood in the shadow of the works as the coach drove off. The Doctor had held out his hand in a frank, generous way, telling him to "take care of himself, and to remember it was his right to rise." Mitchell had simply touched his hat, as to an equal, with a quiet look of thorough recognition. Kirby had thrown Deborah some money, which she found, and clutched eagerly enough. They were gone now, all of them. The man sat down on the cinderroad, looking up into the murky sky.

"'T be late, Hugh. Wunnot hur come?"

He shook his head doggedly, and the woman crouched out of his sight against the wall. Do you remember rare moments when a sudden light flashed over yourself, your world, God? when you stood on a mountain-peak, seeing your life as it might have been, as it is? one quick instant, when custom lost its force and every-day usage? when your friend, wife, brother, stood in a new light? your soul was bared, and the grave,—a foretaste of the nakedness of the Judgment-Day? So it came before him, his life, that night. The slow tides of pain he had borne gathered themselves up and surged against his soul. His squalid daily life, the brutal coarseness eating into his brain, as the ashes into his skin: before, these things had been a dull aching into his consciousness; tonight, they were reality. He griped the filthy red shirt that clung, stiff with soot, about him, and tore it savagely from his arm. The flesh beneath was muddy with grease and ashes,—and the heart beneath that! And the soul? God knows.

[14]*Baconian theories, Goethe schemes:* Christian ideas as revised by English philosopher Francis Bacon (1561–1626) and German thinker Johann Wolfgang von Goethe (1749–1832).

Then flashed before his vivid poetic sense the man who had left him,—the pure face, the delicate, sinewy limbs, in harmony with all he knew of beauty or truth. In his cloudy fancy he had pictured a Something like this. He had found it in this Mitchell, even when he idly scoffed at his pain: a Man all-knowing, all-seeing, crowned by Nature, reigning,—the keen glance of his eye falling like a sceptre on other men. And yet his instinct taught him that he too——He! He looked at himself with sudden loathing, sick, wrung his hands with a cry, and then was silent. With all the phantoms of his heated, ignorant fancy, Wolfe had not been vague in his ambitions. They were practical, slowly built up before him out of his knowledge of what he could do. Through years he had day by day made this hope a real thing to himself,—a clear, projected figure of himself, as he might become.

Able to speak, to know what was best, to raise these men and women working at his side up with him: sometimes he forgot this defined hope in the frantic anguish to escape,—only to escape,—out of the wet, the pain, the ashes, somewhere, anywhere,—only for one moment of free air on a hill-side, to lie down and let his sick soul throb itself out in the sunshine. But to-night he panted for life. The savage strength of his nature was roused; his cry was fierce to God for justice.

"Look at me!" he said to Deborah, with a low, bitter laugh, striking his puny chest savagely. "What am I worth, Deb? Is it my fault that I am no better? My fault? My fault?"

He stopped, stung with a sudden remorse, seeing her hunchback shape writhing with sobs. For Deborah was crying thankless tears, according to the fashion of women.

"God forgi' me, woman! Things go harder wi' you nor me. It 's a worse share."

He got up and helped her to rise; and they went doggedly down the muddy street, side by side.

"It's all wrong," he muttered, slowly,— "all wrong! I dunnot understan'. But it'll end some day."

"Come home, Hugh!" she said, coaxingly; for he had stopped, looking around bewildered.

"Home,—and back to the mill!" He went on saying this over to himself, as if he would mutter down every pain in this dull despair.

She followed him through the fog, her blue lips chattering with cold. They reached the cellar at last. Old Wolfe had been drinking since she went out, and had crept nearer the door. The girl Janey slept heavily in the corner. He went up to her, touching softly the worn white arm with his fingers. Some bitterer thought stung him, as he stood there. He wiped the drops from his forehead, and went into the room beyond, livid, trembling. A hope, trifling, perhaps, but very dear, had died just then out of the poor puddler's life, as he looked at the sleeping, innocent girl,—some plan for the future, in which she had borne a part. He gave it up that moment, then and forever. Only a trifle, perhaps, to us: his face grew a shade paler,—that was all. But, somehow, the man's soul, as God and the angels looked down on it, never was the same afterwards.

Deborah followed him into the inner room. She carried a candle, which she placed on the floor, closing the door after her. She had seen the look on his face, as he turned away: her own grew deadly. Yet, as she came up to him, her eyes glowed. He was seated on an old chest, quiet, holding his face in his hands.

"Hugh!" she said, softly.

He did not speak.

"Hugh, did hur hear what the man said,—him with the clear voice? Did hur hear? Money, money,—that it wud do all?"

He pushed her away,—gently, but he was worn out; her rasping tone fretted him.

"Hugh!"

The candle flared a pale yellow light over the cobwebbed brick walls, and the woman standing there. He looked at her. She was young, in deadly earnest; her faded eyes, and wet, ragged figure caught from their frantic eagerness a power akin to beauty.

"Hugh, it is true! Money ull do it! Oh, Hugh, boy, listen till me! He said it true! It is money!"

"I know. Go back! I do not want you here."

"Hugh, it is t' last time. I'll never worrit hur again."

There were tears in her voice now, but she choked them back.

"Hear till me only to-night! If one of t' witch people wud come, them we heard of t' home, and gif hur all hur wants, what then? Say, Hugh!"

"What do you mean?"

"I mean money."

Her whisper shrilled through his brain.

"If one of t' witch dwarfs wud come from t' lane moors to-night, and gif hur money, to go out,—*out*, I say,—out, lad, where t' sun shines, and t' heath grows, and t' ladies walk in silken gownds, and God stays all t' time,—where t' man lives that talked to us to-night,—Hugh knows,—Hugh could walk there like a king!"

He thought the woman mad, tried to check her, but she went on, fierce in her eager haste.

"If *I* were t' witch dwarf, if I had t' money, wud hur thank me? Wud hur take me out o' this place wid hur and Janey? I wud not come into the gran' house hur wud build, to vex hur wid t' hunch,—only at night, when t' shadows were dark, stand far off to see hur."

Mad? Yes! Are many of us mad in this way?

"Poor Deb! poor Deb!" he said, soothingly.

"It is here," she said, suddenly jerking into his hand a small roll. "I took it! I did it! Me, me!—not hur! I shall be hanged, I shall be burnt in hell, if anybody knows I took it! Out of his pocket, as he leaned against t' bricks. Hur knows?"

She thrust it into his hand, and then, her errand done, began to gather chips together to make a fire, choking down hysteric sobs.

"Has it come to this?"

That was all he said. The Welsh Wolfe blood was honest. The roll was a small green pocket-book containing one or two gold pieces, and a check for an incredible amount, as it seemed to the poor puddler. He laid it down, hiding his face again in his hands.

"Hugh, don't be angry wud me! It's only poor Deb,—hur knows?" 190

He took the long skinny fingers kindly in his.

"Angry? God help me, no! Let me sleep. I am tired."

He threw himself heavily down on the wooden bench, stunned with pain and weariness. She brought some old rags to cover him.

It was late on Sunday evening before he awoke. I tell God's truth, when I say he had then no thought of keeping this money. Deborah had hid it in his pocket. He found it there. She watched him eagerly, as he took it out.

"I must gif it to him," he said, reading her face. 195

"Hur knows," she said with a bitter sigh of disappointment. "But it is hur right to keep it."

His right! The word struck him. Doctor May had used the same. He washed himself, and went out to find this man Mitchell. His right! Why did this chance word cling to him so obstinately? Do you hear the fierce devils whisper in his ear, as he went slowly down the darkening street?

The evening came on, slow and calm. He seated himself at the end of an alley leading into one of the larger streets. His brain was clear to-night, keen, intent, mastering. It would not start back, cowardly, from any hellish temptation, but meet it face to face. Therefore the great temptation of his life came to him veiled by no sophistry, but bold, defiant, owning its own vile name, trusting to one bold blow for victory.

He did not deceive himself. Theft! That was it. At first the word sickened him; then he grappled with it. Sitting there on a broken cart-wheel, the fading day, the noisy groups, the church-bells' tolling passed before him like a panorama, while the sharp struggle went on within. This money! He took it out, and looked at it. If he gave it back, what then? He was going to be cool about it.

People going by to church saw only a sickly mill-boy watching them quietly 200
at the alley's mouth. They did not know that he was mad, or they would not have gone by so quietly: mad with hunger; stretching out his hands to the world, that had given so much to them, for leave to live the life God meant him to live. His soul within him was smothering to death; he wanted so much, thought so much, and *knew*—nothing. There was nothing of which he was certain, except the mill and things there. Of God and heaven he had heard so little, that they were to him what fairy-land is to a child: something real, but not here; very far off. His brain, greedy, dwarfed, full of thwarted energy and unused powers, questioned these men and women going by, coldly, bitterly, that night. Was it not his right to live as they,—a pure life, a good, true-hearted life, full of beauty and kind words? He only wanted to know how to use the strength within him. His heart warmed, as he thought of it. He suffered himself to think of it longer. If he took the money?

Then he saw himself as he might be, strong, helpful, kindly. The night crept on, as this one image slowly evolved itself from the crowd of other thoughts and stood triumphant. He looked at it. As he might be! What wonder, if it blinded him to delirium,—the madness that underlies all revolution, all progress, and all fall?

You laugh at the shallow temptation? You see the error underlying its argument so clearly,—that to him a true life was one of full development rather than self-restraint? that he was deaf to the higher tone in a cry of voluntary suffering for truth's sake than in the fullest flow of spontaneous harmony? I do not plead his cause. I only want to show you the mote in my brother's eye: then you can see clearly to take it out.

The money,—there it lay on his knee, a little blotted slip of paper, nothing in itself; used to raise him out of the pit; something straight from God's hand. A thief! Well, what was it to be a thief? He met the question at last, face to face, wiping the clammy drops of sweat from his forehead. God made this money—the fresh air, too—for his children's use. He never made the difference between poor and rich. The Something who looked down on him that moment through the cool gray sky had a kindly facc, he knew,—loved his children alike. Oh, he knew that!

There were times when the soft floods of color in the crimson and purple flames, or the clear depth of amber in the water below the bridge, had somehow given him a glimpse of another world than this,—of an infinite depth of beauty and of quiet somewhere,—somewhere,—a depth of quiet and rest and love. Looking up now, it became strangely real. The sun had sunk quite below the hills, but his last rays struck upward, touching the zenith. The fog had risen, and the town and river were steeped in its thick, gray damp; but overhead, the sun-touched smoke-clouds opened like a cleft ocean,—shifting, rolling seas of crimson mist, waves of billowy silver veined with blood-scarlet, inner depths unfathomable of glancing light. Wolfe's artist-eye grew drunk with color. The gates of that other world! Fading, flashing before him now! What, in that world of Beauty, Content, and Right, were the petty laws, the mine and thine, of mill-owners and mill-hands?

A consciousness of power stirred within him. He stood up. A man,—he 205
thought, stretching out his hands,—free to work, to live, to love! Free! His right! He folded the scrap of paper in his hand. As his nervous fingers took it in, limp and blotted, so his soul took in the mean temptation, lapped it in fancied rights, in dreams of improved existences, drifting and endless as the cloud-seas of color. Clutching it, as if the tightness of his hold would strengthen his sense of possession, he went aimlessly down the street. It was his watch at the mill. He need not go, need never go again, thank God!—shaking off the thought with unspeakable loathing.

Shall I go over the history of the hours of that night? how the man wandered from one to another of his old haunts, with a half-consciousness of bidding them farewell,—lanes and alleys and back-yards where the mill-hands lodged,—noting, with a new eagerness, the filth and drunkenness, the pig-pens, the ash-heaps covered with potato-skins, the bloated, pimpled women at the doors,—with a new disgust, a new sense of sudden triumph, and, under all, a new, vague dread, unknown before, smothered down, kept under, but still there? It left him but once during the night, when, for the second time in his life, he entered a church. It was a sombre Gothic pile, where the stained light lost itself in far-retreating arches; built to meet the requirements and sympathies of a far other class than Wolfe's. Yet it touched, moved him uncontrollably. The distances, the shadows, the still, marble figures, the mass of silent kneeling worshippers, the mysterious music, thrilled, lifted his soul with a wonderful pain.

Wolfe forgot himself, forgot the new life he was going to live, the mean terror gnawing underneath. The voice of the speaker strengthened the charm; it was clear, feeling, full, strong. An old man, who had lived much, suffered much; whose brain was keenly alive, dominant; whose heart was summer-warm with charity. He taught it to-night. He held up Humanity in its grand total; showed the great world-cancer to his people. Who could show it better? He was a Christian reformer; he had studied the age thoroughly; his outlook at man had been free, world-wide, over all time. His faith stood sublime upon the Rock of Ages; his fiery zeal guided vast schemes by which the gospel was to be preached to all nations. How did he preach it to-night? In burning, light-laden words he painted the incarnate Life, Love, the universal Man: words that became reality in the lives of these people,—that lived again in beautiful words and actions, trifling, but heroic. Sin, as he defined it, was a real foe to them; their trials, temptations, were his. His words passed far over the furnace-tender's grasp, toned to suit another class of culture; they sounded in his ears a very pleasant song in an unknown tongue. He meant to cure this world-cancer with a steady eye that had never glared with hunger, and a hand that neither poverty nor strychnine-whiskey had taught to shake. In this morbid, distorted heart of the Welsh puddler he had failed.

Wolfe rose at last, and turned from the church down the street. He looked up; the night had come on foggy, damp; the golden mists had vanished, and the sky lay dull and ash-colored. He wandered again aimlessly down the street, idly wondering what had become of the cloud-sea of crimson and scarlet. The trial-day of this man's life was over, and he had lost the victory. What followed was mere drifting circumstance,—a quicker walking over the path,—that was all. Do you want to hear the end of it? You wish me to make a tragic story out of it? Why, in the police-reports of the morning paper you can find a dozen such tragedies: hints of shipwrecks unlike any that ever befell on the high seas; hints that here a power was lost to heaven,—that there a soul went down where no tide can ebb or flow. Commonplace enough the hints are,—jocose sometimes, done up in rhyme.

Doctor May, a month after the night I have told you of, was reading to his wife at breakfast from this fourth column of the morning-paper: an unusual thing,—these police-reports not being, in general, choice reading for ladies; but it was only one item he read.

"Oh, my dear! You remember that man I told you of, that we saw at Kirby's mill?—that was arrested for robbing Mitchell? Here he is; just listen:—'Circuit Court. Judge Day. Hugh Wolfe, operative in Kirby & John's Loudon Mills. Charge, grand larceny. Sentence, nineteen years hard labor in penitentiary.'—Scoundrel! Serves him right! After all our kindness that night! Picking Mitchell's pocket at the very time!"

His wife said something about the ingratitude of that kind of people, and then they began to talk of something else.

Nineteen years! How easy that was to read! What a simple word for Judge Day to utter! Nineteen years! Half a lifetime!

Hugh Wolfe sat on the window-ledge of his cell, looking out. His ankles were ironed. Not usual in such cases; but he had made two desperate efforts to escape. "Well," as Haley, the jailer, said, "small blame to him! Nineteen years' imprisonment was not a pleasant thing to look forward to." Haley was very good-natured about it, though Wolfe had fought him savagely.

"When he was first caught," the jailer said afterwards, in telling the story, "before the trial, the fellow was cut down at once,—laid there on that pallet like a dead man, with his hands over his eyes. Never saw a man so cut down in my life. Time of the trial, too, came the queerest dodge of any customer I ever had. Would choose no lawyer. Judge gave him one, of course. Gibson it was. He tried to prove the fellow crazy; but it wouldn't go. Thing was plain as daylight: money found on him. 'Twas a hard sentence,—all the law allows; but it was for 'xample's sake. These millhands are gettin' onbearable. When the sentence was read, he just looked up, and said the money was his by rights, and that all the world had gone wrong. That night, after the trial, a gentleman came to see him here, name of Mitchell,—him as he stole from. Talked to him for an hour. Thought he came for curiosity, like. After he was gone, thought Wolfe was remarkable quiet, and went into his cell. Found him very low; bed all bloody. Doctor said he had been bleeding at the lungs. He was as weak as a cat; yet, if ye 'll b'lieve me, he tried to get a-past me and get out. I just carried him like a baby, and threw him on the pallet. Three days after, he tried it again: that time reached the wall. Lord help you! he fought like a tiger,—giv' some terrible blows. Fightin' for life, you see; for he can't live long, shut up in the stone crib down yonder. Got a death-cough now. 'T took two of us to bring him down that day; so I just put the irons on his feet. There he sits, in there. Goin' to-morrow, with a batch more of 'em. That woman, hunchback, tried with him,—you remember?—she's only got three years. 'Complice. But *she's* a woman, you know. He's been quiet ever since I put on irons: giv' up, I suppose. Looks white, sick-lookin'. It acts different on 'em, bein' sentenced. Most of 'em gets reckless, devilish-like. Some prays awful, and sings them vile songs of the mills, all in a breath. That woman, now, she 's desper't'. Been beggin' to see Hugh, as she calls him, for three days. I'm a-goin' to let her in. She don't go with him. Here she is in this next cell. I'm a-goin' now to let her in."

He let her in. Wolfe did not see her. She crept into a corner of the cell, and stood watching him. He was scratching the iron bars of the window with a piece of tin which he had picked up, with an idle, uncertain, vacant stare, just as a child or idiot would do.

"Tryin' to get out, old boy?" laughed Haley. "Them irons will need a crowbar beside your tin, before you can open 'em."

Wolfe laughed, too, in a senseless way.

"I think I'll get out," he said.

"I believe his brain's touched," said Haley, when he came out.

The puddler scraped away with the tin for half an hour. Still Deborah did not speak. At last she ventured nearer, and touched his arm.

"Blood?" she said, looking at some spots on his coat with a shudder.

He looked up at her. "Why, Deb!" he said, smiling,—such a bright, boyish smile, that it went to poor Deborah's heart directly, and she sobbed and cried out loud.

"Oh, Hugh, lad! Hugh! dunnot look at me, when it wur my fault! To think I brought hur to it! And I loved hur so! Oh, lad, I dud!"

The confession, even in this wretch, came with the woman's blush through the sharp cry.

He did not seem to hear her,—scraping away diligently at the bars with the bit of tin.

Was he going mad? She peered closely into his face. Something she saw there made her draw suddenly back,—something which Haley had not seen, that lay beneath the pinched, vacant look it had caught since the trial, or the curious gray shadow that rested on it. That gray shadow,—yes, she knew what that meant. She had often seen it creeping over women's faces for months, who died at last of slow hunger or consumption. That meant death, distant, lingering: but this——Whatever it was the woman saw, or thought she saw, used as she was to crime and misery, seemed to make her sick with a new horror. Forgetting her fear of him, she caught his shoulders, and looked keenly, steadily, into his eyes.

"Hugh!" she cried, in a desperate whisper,—"oh, boy, not that! for God's sake, not *that!*"

The vacant laugh went off his face, and he answered her in a muttered word or two that drove her away. Yet the words were kindly enough. Sitting there on his pallet, she cried silently a hopeless sort of tears, but did not speak again. The man looked up furtively at her now and then. Whatever his own trouble was, her distress vexed him with a momentary sting.

It was market-day. The narrow window of the jail looked down directly on the carts and wagons drawn up in a long line, where they had unloaded. He could see, too, and hear distinctly the clink of money as it changed hands, the busy crowd of whites and blacks shoving, pushing one another, and the chaffering and swearing at the stalls. Somehow, the sound, more than anything else had done, wakened him up,—made the whole real to him. He was done with the world and the business of it. He let the tin fall, and looked out, pressing his face close to the rusty bars. How they crowded and pushed! And he,—he should never walk that pavement again! There came Neff Sanders, one of the feeders at the mill, with a basket on his arm. Sure enough, Neff was married the other week. He whistled, hoping he would look up; but he did not. He wondered if Neff remembered he was there,—if any of the boys thought of him up there, and thought that he never was to go down that old cinder-road again. Never again! He had not quite understood it before; but now he did. Not for days or years, but never!—that was it.

How clear the light fell on that stall in front of the market! and how like a picture it was, the dark-green heaps of corns, and the crimson beets, and golden melons! There was another with game: how the light flickered on that pheasant's breast, with the purplish blood dripping over the brown feathers! He could see the red shining of the drops, it was so near. In one minute he could be down there. It was just a step. So easy, as it seemed, so natural to go! Yet it could never be—not in all the thousands of years to come—that he should put his foot on that street again! He thought of himself with a sorrowful pity, as of some one else. There was a dog down in the market, walking after his master with such a stately, grave look!—only a dog, yet he could go backwards and forwards just as he pleased: he had good luck! Why, the very vilest cur, yelping there in the gutter, had not lived his life, had been free to act out whatever thought God had put into his brain; while he——No, he would not think of that! He tried to put the thought away, and to listen to a dispute between a countryman and a woman about some meat; but it would come back. He, what had he done to bear this?

Then came the sudden picture of what might have been, and now. He knew what it was to be in the penitentiary,—how it went with men there. He knew how in these long years he should slowly die, but not until soul and body had become corrupt and rotten,—how, when he came out, if he lived to come, even the lowest of the mill-hands would jeer him,—how his hands would be weak, and his brain senseless and stupid. He believed he was almost that now. He put his hand to his head, with a puzzled, weary look. It ached, his head, with thinking. He tried to quiet himself. It was only right, perhaps; he had done wrong. But was there right or wrong for such as he? What was right? And who had ever taught him? He thrust the whole matter away. A dark, cold quiet crept through his brain. It was all wrong; but let it be! It was nothing to him more than the others. Let it be!

The door grated, as Haley opened it.

"Come, my woman! Must lock up for t' night. Come, stir yerself!"

She went up and took Hugh's hand.

"Good-night, Deb," he said, carelessly.

She had not hoped he would say more; but the tired pain on her mouth just then was bitterer than death. She took his passive hand and kissed it.

"Hur 'll never see Deb again!" she ventured, her lips growing colder and more bloodless.

What did she say that for? Did he not know it? Yet he would not be impatient with poor old Deb. She had trouble of her own, as well as he.

"No, never again," he said, trying to be cheerful.

She stood just a moment, looking at him. Do you laugh at her, standing there, with her hunchback, her rags, her bleared, withered face, and the great despised love tugging at her heart?

"Come, you!" called Haley, impatiently.

She did not move.

"Hugh!" she whispered.

It was to be her last word. What was it?

"Hugh, boy, not THAT!"

He did not answer. She wrung her hands, trying to be silent, looking in his face in an agony of entreaty. He smiled again, kindly.

"It is best, Deb. I cannot bear to be hurted any more."

"Hur knows," she said, humbly.

"Tell my father good-bye; and—and kiss little Janey."

She nodded, saying nothing, looked in his face again, and went out of the door. As she went, she staggered.

"Drinkin' to-day?" broke out Haley, pushing her before him. "Where the Devil did you get it? Here, in with ye!" and he shoved her into her cell, next to Wolfe's, and shut the door.

Along the wall of her cell there was a crack low down by the floor, through which she could see the light from Wolfe's. She had discovered it days before. She hurried in now, and, kneeling down by it, listened, hoping to hear some sound. Nothing but the rasping of the tin on the bars. He was at his old amusement again. Something in the noise jarred on her ear, for she shivered as she heard it. Hugh rasped away at the bars. A dull old bit of tin, not fit to cut korl with.

He looked out of the window again. People were leaving the market now. A tall mulatto girl, following her mistress, her basket on her head, crossed the street just below, and looked up. She was laughing; but, when she caught sight of the haggard face peering out through the bars, suddenly grew grave, and hurried by. A free, firm step, a clear-cut olive face, with a scarlet turban tied on one side, dark, shining eyes, and on the head the basket poised, filled with fruit and flowers, under which the scarlet turban and bright eyes looked out half-shadowed. The picture caught his eye. It was good to see a face like that. He would try to-morrow, and cut one like it. *To-morrow!* He threw down the tin, trembling, and covered his face with his hands. When he looked up again, the daylight was gone.

Deborah, crouching near by on the other side of the wall, heard no noise. He sat on the side of the low pallet, thinking. Whatever was the mystery which the woman had seen on his face, it came out now slowly, in the dark there, and became fixed,—a something never seen on his face before. The evening was darkening fast. The market had been over for an hour; the rumbling of the carts over the pavement grew more infrequent: he listened to each, as it passed, because he thought it was to be for the last time. For the same reason, it was, I suppose, that he strained his eyes to catch a glimpse of each passer-by, wondering who they were, what kind of homes they were going to, if they had children,—listening eagerly to every chance word in the street, as if—(God be merciful to the man! what strange fancy was this?)—as if he never should hear human voices again.

It was quite dark at last The street was a lonely one. The last passenger, he thought, was gone. No,—there was a quick step: Joe Hill, lighting the lamps. Joe was a good old chap; never passed a fellow without some joke or other. He remembered once seeing the place where he lived with his wife. "Granny Hill" the boys called her. Bedridden she was; but so kind as Joe was to her! kept the room so clean!—and the old woman, when he was there, was laughing at "some of t' lad's foolishness." The step was far down the street; but he could see him place the ladder, run up, and light the gas. A longing seized him to be spoken to once more.

"Joe!" he called, out of the grating. "Good-bye, Joe!" 255

The old man stopped a moment, listening uncertainly; then hurried on. The prisoner thrust his hand out of the window, and called again, louder; but Joe was too far down the street. It was a little thing; but it hurt him,—this disappointment.

"Good-bye, Joe!" he called, sorrowfully enough.

"Be quiet!" said one of the jailers, passing the door, striking on it with his club.

Oh, that was the last, was it?

There was an inexpressible bitterness on his face, as he lay down on the bed, 260
taking the bit of tin, which he had rasped to a tolerable degree of sharpness, in his hand,—to play with, it may be. He bared his arms, looking intently at their corded veins and sinews. Deborah, listening in the next cell, heard a slight clicking sound, often repeated. She shut her lips tightly, that she might not scream; the cold drops of sweat broke over her, in her dumb agony.

"Hur knows best," she muttered at last, fiercely clutching the boards where she lay.

If she could have seen Wolfe, there was nothing about him to frighten her. He lay quite still, his arms outstretched, looking at the pearly stream of moonlight coming into the window. I think in that one hour that came then he lived back over all the years that had gone before. I think that all the low, vile life, all his wrongs, all his starved hopes, came then, and stung him with a farewell poison that made him sick unto death. He made neither moan nor cry, only turned his worn face now and then to the pure light, that seemed so far off, as one that said, "How long, O Lord? how long?"

The hour was over at last. The moon, passing over her nightly path, slowly came nearer, and threw the light across his bed on his feet. He watched it steadily, as it crept up, inch by inch, slowly. It seemed to him to carry with it a great silence. He had been so hot and tired there always in the mills! The years had been so fierce and cruel! There was coming now quiet and coolness and sleep. His tense limbs relaxed, and settled in a calm languor. The blood ran fainter and slow from his heart. He did not think now with a savage anger of what might be and was not; he was conscious only of deep stillness creeping over him. At first he saw a sea of faces: the mill-men,—women he had known, drunken and bloated,—Janeys timid and pitiful,—poor old Debs: then they floated together like a mist, and faded away, leaving only the dear, pearly moonlight.

Whether, as the pure light crept up the stretched-out figure, it brought with it calm and peace, who shall say? His dumb soul was alone with God in judgment. A Voice may have spoken for it from far-off Calvary,[15] "Father, forgive them, for they know not what they do!" Who dare say? Fainter and fainter the heart rose and fell, slower and slower the moon floated from behind a cloud, until, when at last its full tide of white splendor swept over the cell, it seemed to wrap and fold into a deeper stillness the dead figure that never should move again. Silence deeper than the Night! Nothing that moved, save the black, nauseous stream of blood dripping slowly from the pallet to the floor!

There was outcry and crowd enough in the cell the next day. The coroner 265
and his jury, the local editors, Kirby himself, and boys with their hands thrust knowingly into their pockets and heads on one side, jammed into the corners. Coming and going all day. Only one woman. She came late, and outstayed them all. A Quaker,[16] or Friend, as they call themselves. I think this woman was known

[15]*Calvary:* According to the New Testament in the Bible, the hillside site of Jesus's crucifixion.

[16]*Quaker*: A member of the Society of Friends, a pacifist, Christian religious sect that arose in the eighteenth-century United States and is still active today.

by that name in heaven. A homely body, coarsely dressed in gray and white. Deborah (for Haley had let her in) took notice of her. She watched them all—sitting on the end of the pallet, holding his head in her arms—with the ferocity of a watch-dog, if any of them touched the body. There was no meekness, no sorrow, in her face; the stuff out of which murderers are made, instead. All the time Haley and the woman were laying straight the limbs and cleaning the cell, Deborah sat still, keenly watching the Quaker's face. Of all the crowd there that day, this woman alone had not spoken to her,—only once or twice had put some cordial to her lips. After they all were gone, the woman, in the same still, gentle way, brought a vase of wood-leaves and berries, and placed it by the pallet, then opened the narrow window. The fresh air blew in, and swept the woody fragrance over the dead face. Deborah looked up with a quick wonder.

"Did hur know my boy wud like it? Did hur know Hugh?"

"I know Hugh now."

The white fingers passed in a slow, pitiful way over the dead, worn face. There was a heavy shadow in the quiet eyes.

"Did hur know where they'll bury Hugh?" said Deborah in a shrill tone, catching her arm.

This had been the question hanging on her lips all day.

"In t' town-yard? Under t' mud and ash? T' lad 'll smother, woman! He wur born on t' lane moor, where t' air is frick and strong. Take hur out, for God's sake, take hur out where t' air blows!"

The Quaker hesitated, but only for a moment. She put her strong arm around Deborah and led her to the window.

"Thee sees the hills, friend, over the river? Thee sees how the light lies warm there, and the winds of God blow all the day? I live there,—where the blue smoke is, by the trees. Look at me." She turned Deborah's face to her own, clear and earnest. "Thee will believe me? I will take Hugh and bury him there to-morrow."

Deborah did not doubt her. As the evening wore on, she leaned against the iron bars, looking at the hills that rose far off, through the thick sodden clouds, like a bright, unattainable calm. As she looked, a shadow of their solemn repose fell on her face: its fierce discontent faded into a pitiful, humble quiet. Slow, solemn tears gathered in her eyes: the poor weak eyes turned so hopelessly to the place where Hugh was to rest, the grave heights looking higher and brighter and more solemn than ever before. The Quaker watched her keenly. She came to her at last, and touched her arm.

"When thee comes back," she said, in a low, sorrowful tone, like one who speaks from a strong heart deeply moved with remorse or pity, "thee shall begin thy life again,—there on the hills. I came too late; but not for thee,—by God's help, it may be."

Not too late. Three years after, the Quaker began her work. I end my story here. At evening-time it was light. There is no need to tire you with the long years of sunshine, and fresh air, and slow, patient Christ-love, needed to make healthy and hopeful this impure body and soul. There is a homely pine house, on one of these hills, whose windows overlook broad, wooded slopes and clover-crimsoned meadows,—niched into the very place where the light is warmest, the air freest. It is the Friends' meeting-house. Once a week they sit there, in their grave, earnest way, waiting for the Spirit of Love to speak, opening their simple hearts to receive His words. There is a woman, old, deformed, who takes a humble place among them: waiting like them: in her gray dress, her worn face, pure and meek, turned now and then to the sky. A woman much loved by these silent, restful people; more silent than they, more humble, more loving. Waiting: with her eyes turned to hills higher and purer than these on which she lives,—dim and far off now, but to be reached some day. There may be in her heart some latent hope to meet there the love denied her here,—that she shall find him whom she lost, and that then she will not be all-unworthy. Who blames her? Something is lost in the passage of every soul from one eternity to the other,—something pure and beautiful, which might have been and was not: a hope, a talent, a love, over which the soul mourns, like Esau deprived of his birthright. What blame to the meek Quaker, if she took her lost hope to make the hills of heaven more fair?

Nothing remains to tell that the poor Welsh puddler once lived, but this figure of the mill-woman cut in korl. I have it here in a corner of my library. I keep it hid behind a curtain,—it is such a rough, ungainly thing. Yet there are about it touches, grand sweeps of outline, that show a master's hand. Sometimes,—tonight, for instance,—the curtain is accidentally drawn back, and I see a bare arm stretched out imploringly in the darkness, and an eager, wolfish face watching mine: a wan, woful face, through which the spirit of the dead korl-cutter looks out, with its thwarted life, its mighty hunger, its unfinished work. Its pale, vague lips seem to tremble with a terrible question. "Is this the End?" they say,—"nothing beyond?—no more?" Why, you tell me you have seen that look in the eyes of dumb brutes,—horses dying under the lash. I know.

The deep of the night is passing while I write. The gas-light wakens from the shadows here and there the objects which lie scattered through the room: only faintly, though; for they belong to the open sunlight. As I glance at them, they each recall some task or pleasure of the coming day. A half-moulded child's head; Aphrodite a bough of forest-leaves; music; work; homely fragments, in which lie the secrets of all eternal truth and beauty. Prophetic all! Only this dumb, woful face seems to belong to and end with the night. I turn to look at it. Has the power of its desperate need commanded the darkness away? While the room is yet steeped in heavy shadow, a cool, gray light suddenly touches its head like a blessing hand, and its groping arm points through the broken cloud to the far East, where, in the flickering, nebulous crimson, God has set the promise of the Dawn.

(1861)

Questions for Discussion and Writing

Close Reading

1. Look again at the "social problem" debate between Kirby, Mitchell, and Dr. May. Does any perspective emerge as the most sane or most humane during this discussion? Is any solution posed, or is Davis simply presenting the problem?

2. Reexamine the debate Hugh Wolfe has with himself as he decides what to do with the money. What forces are at war within him?
3. Consider the different versions of English present in this story and the way they operate together. (Consider the narrator's voice alongside the voices of the characters in her story.)

CRITICAL AND CREATIVE READING

4. Can money buy freedom? Think about the question in general terms and also in terms of "Life in the Iron-Mills."
5. What is the function of art for a hard worker like Hugh? Examine closely his response to the questions about his art put to him by Kirby, May, and Mitchell; also look at the descriptions of his art and its effect on its viewers.
6. Most people need to work to survive. Survival is a basic animal instinct. Can it be argued that work dehumanizes people? Illustrate your response with examples from Davis's story.

CONNECTIONS TO OTHER READINGS

7. The narrator of Ann Cummins's story "Where I Work" is also a manual laborer. Discuss the difference between her perspective and the perspective of the narrator of "Life in the Iron-Mills," who knows and observes manual laborers but is not one of them. What difference does narrative perspective make to the expression of theme in these stories?
8. Compare the speaker's attitude toward his readers in Philip Levine's "What Work Is" to the narrator's attitude toward her readers in "Life in the Iron-Mills." In both cases, does reading about workers give you a better sense of "what work is"?
9. Compare the distance between the narrator and the workers in "Life in the Iron-Mills" to the distance between the speaker of Wordsworth's "The Solitary Reaper" and his subject. What are the difficulties and the benefits of being educated and well-to-do when writing about the working class?

Herman Melville

Bartleby, the Scrivener

A Tale of Wall-Street

Perhaps the most famous American short story ever written, "Bartleby, the Scrivener" impresses many readers as a tale of quiet, cryptic rebellion. Like all great fiction, it operates on many levels. Its author Herman Melville (1819–1891) subtitled the story "A Tale of Wall-Street," a qualifier that emphasizes the story's reliance on work. One of the greatest and most profound American writers, Melville is known primarily for his long philosophical novel *Moby-Dick*. Melville tells an entertaining story while leading the reader to consider some of humanity's most perplexing problems. "Bartleby" was first published in 1853. Scriveners performed the task of a present-day photocopying machine by hand: meticulously copying legal documents. Can you think of any work today that is equally tedious?

....

I am a rather elderly man. The nature of my avocations, for the last thirty years, has brought me into more than ordinary contact with what would seem an interesting and somewhat singular set of men, of whom, as yet, nothing, that I know of, has ever been written—I mean, the law-copyists, or scriveners. I have known very many of them, professionally and privately, and, if I pleased, could relate divers histories, at which good-natured gentlemen might smile, and sentimental souls might weep. But I waive the biographies of all other scriveners, for a few passages in the life of Bartleby, who was a scrivener, the strangest I ever saw, or heard of. While, of other law-copyists, I might write the complete life, of Bartleby nothing of that sort can be done. I believe that no materials exist, for a full and satisfactory biography of this man. It is an irreparable loss to literature. Bartleby was one of those beings of whom nothing is ascertainable, except from the original sources, and, in his case, those are very small. What my own astonished eyes saw of Bartleby, *that* is all I know of him, except, indeed, one vague report, which will appear in the sequel.

Ere introducing the scrivener, as he first appeared to me, it is fit I make some mention of myself, my *employés*, my business, my chambers, and general surroundings; because some such description is indispensable to an adequate understanding of the chief character about to be presented.

Imprimis:[1] I am a man who, from his youth upwards, has been filled with a profound conviction that the easiest way of life is the best. Hence, though I belong to a profession proverbially energetic and nervous, even to turbulence, at times, yet nothing of that sort have I ever suffered to invade my peace. I am one of those unambitious lawyers who never address a jury, or in any way draw down public applause; but, in the cool tranquillity of a snug retreat, do a snug business among rich men's bonds, and mortgages, and title-deeds. All who know me, consider me an eminently *safe* man. The late John Jacob Astor,[2] a personage little given to poetic enthusiasm, had no hesitation in pronouncing my first grand point to be prudence; my next, method. I do not speak it in vanity, but simply record the fact, that I was not unemployed in my profession by the late John Jacob Astor; a name which, I admit, I love to repeat; for it hath a rounded and orbicular sound to it, and rings like unto bullion. I will freely add, that I was not insensible to the late John Jacob Astor's good opinion.

[1]*Imprimis:* In the first place (Latin).

[2]*John Jacob Astor:* John Jacob Astor (1763–1848) was the first millionaire in the United States and, at the time of his death, the wealthiest man in the country. He made his fortune from fur trading and, in relation to this story, Manhattan real estate.

Some time prior to the period at which this little history begins, my avocations had been largely increased. The good old office, now extinct in the State of New-York, of a Master in Chancery,[3] had been conferred upon me. It was not a very arduous office, but very pleasantly remunerative. I seldom lose my temper; much more seldom indulge in dangerous indignation at wrongs and outrages; but I must be permitted to be rash here and declare, that I consider the sudden and violent abrogation of the office of Master in Chancery, by the new Constitution, as a—premature act; inasmuch as I had counted upon a life-lease of the profits, whereas I only received those of a few short years. But this is by the way.

5 My chambers were up stairs, at No.——Wall Street. At one end, they looked upon the white wall of the interior of a spacious sky-light shaft, penetrating the building from top to bottom. This view might have been considered rather tame than otherwise, deficient in what landscape painters call "life." But, if so, the view from the other end of my chambers offered, at least, a contrast, if nothing more. In that direction, my windows commanded an unobstructed view of a lofty brick wall, black by age and everlasting shade; which wall required no spy-glass to bring out its lurking beauties, but, for the benefit of all near-sighted spectators, was pushed up to within ten feet of my windowpanes. Owing to the great height of the surrounding buildings, and my chambers being on the second floor, the interval between this wall and mine not a little resembled a huge square cistern.

At the period just preceding the advent of Bartleby, I had two persons as copyists in my employment, and a promising lad as an office-boy. First, Turkey; second, Nippers; third, Ginger Nut. These may seem names, the like of which are not usually found in the Directory. In truth, they were nicknames, mutually conferred upon each other by my three clerks, and were deemed expressive of their respective persons or characters. Turkey was a short, pursy Englishman, of about my own age—that is, somewhere not far from sixty. In the morning, one might say, his face was of a fine florid hue, but after twelve o'clock, meridian—his dinner hour—it blazed like a grate full of Christmas coals; and continued blazing—but, as it were, with a gradual wane—till six o'clock, P.M., or thereabout, after which, I saw no more of the proprietor of the face, which, gaining its meridian with the sun, seemed to set with it, to rise, culminate, and decline the following day, with the like regularity and undiminished glory. There are many singular coincidences I have known in the course of my life, not the least among which was the fact, that, exactly when Turkey displayed his fullest beams from his red and radiant countenance, just then, too, at that critical moment, began the daily period when I considered his business capacities as seriously disturbed for the remainder of the twenty-four hours. Not that he was absolutely idle, or averse to business then; far from it. The difficulty was, he was apt to be altogether too energetic. There was a strange, inflamed, flurried, flighty recklessness of activity about him. He would be incautious in dipping his pen into his inkstand. All his blots upon my documents were dropped there after twelve o'clock, meridian. Indeed, not only would he be reckless, and sadly given to making blots in the afternoon,

[3]*Master in Chancery:* A government-appointed judicial position with largely ceremonial duties.

but, some days, he went further, and was rather noisy. At such times, too, his face flamed with augmented blazonry, as if cannel coal had been heaped on anthracite. He made an unpleasant racket with his chair; spilled his sand-box; in mending his pens, impatiently split them all to pieces, and threw them on the floor in a sudden passion; stood up, and leaned over his table, boxing his papers about in a most indecorous manner, very sad to behold in an elderly man like him. Nevertheless, as he was in many ways a most valuable person to me, and all the time before twelve o'clock, meridian, was the quickest, steadiest creature, too, accomplishing a great deal of work in a style not easily to be matched—for these reasons, I was willing to overlook his eccentricities, though, indeed, occasionally, I remonstrated with him. I did this very gently, however, because, though the civilest, nay, the blandest and most reverential of men in the morning, yet, in the afternoon, he was disposed, upon provocation, to be slightly rash with his tongue—in fact, insolent. Now, valuing his morning services as I did, and resolved not to lose them—yet, at the same time, made uncomfortable by his inflamed ways after twelve o'clock—and being a man of peace, unwilling by my admonitions to call forth unseemly retorts from him, I took upon me, one Saturday noon (he was always worse on Saturdays) to hint to him, very kindly, that, perhaps, now that he was growing old, it might be well to abridge his labors; in short, he need not come to my chambers after twelve o'clock, but, dinner over, had best go home to his lodgings, and rest himself till tea-time. But no; he insisted upon his afternoon devotions. His countenance became intolerably fervid, as he oratorically assured me—gesticulating with a long ruler at the other end of the room—that if his services in the morning were useful, how indispensable, then, in the afternoon?

"With submission, sir," said Turkey, on this occasion, "I consider myself your right-hand man. In the morning I but marshal and deploy my columns; but in the afternoon I put myself at their head, and gallantly charge the foe, thus"—and he made a violent thrust with the ruler.

"But the blots, Turkey," intimated I.

"True,—with submission, sir, behold these hairs! I am getting old. Surely, sir, a blot or two of a warm afternoon is not to be severely urged against gray hairs. Old age—even if it blot the page—is honorable. With submission, sir, we *both* are getting old."

This appeal to my fellow-feeling was hardly to be resisted. At all events, I
saw that go he would not. So, I made up my mind to let him stay, resolving, nev- 10
ertheless, to see to it that, during the afternoon, he had to do with my less important papers.

Nippers, the second on my list, was a whiskered, sallow, and, upon the whole, rather piratical-looking young man, of about five and twenty. I always deemed him the victim of two evil powers—ambition and indigestion. The ambition was evinced by a certain impatience of the duties of a mere copyist, an unwarrantable usurpation of strictly professional affairs, such as the original drawing up of legal documents. The indigestion seemed betokened in an occasional nervous testiness and grinning irritability, causing the teeth to audibly grind together over mistakes committed in copying; unnecessary maledictions, hissed, rather than spoken, in the heat of business; and especially by a continual discontent with the height of the table where he worked. Though of a very ingenious mechanical turn, Nippers could never get this table to suit him. He put chips under it, blocks of various sorts, bits of pasteboard, and at last went so far as to attempt an exquisite adjustment by final pieces of folded blotting-paper. But no invention would answer. If, for the sake of easing his back, he brought the table lid at a sharp angle well up towards his chin, and wrote there like a man using the steep roof of a Dutch house for his desk, then he declared that it stopped the circulation in his arms. If now he lowered the table to his waistbands, and stooped over it in writing, then there was a sore aching in his back. In short, the truth of the matter was, Nippers knew not what he wanted. Or, if he wanted anything, it was to be rid of a scrivener's table altogether. Among the manifestations of his diseased ambition was a fondness he had for receiving visits from certain ambiguous-looking fellows in seedy coats, whom he called his clients. Indeed, I was aware that not only was he, at times, considerable of a ward-politician, but he occasionally did a little business at the Justices' courts, and was not unknown on the steps of the Tombs.[4] I have good reason to believe, however, that one individual who called upon him at my chambers, and who, with a grand air, he insisted was his client, was no other than a dun, and the alleged title deed, a bill. But, with all his failings, and the annoyances he caused me, Nippers, like his compatriot Turkey, was a very useful man to me; wrote a neat, swift hand; and, when he chose, was not deficient in a gentlemanly sort of deportment. Added to this, he always dressed in a gentlemanly sort of way; and so, incidentally, reflected credit upon my chambers. Whereas, with respect to Turkey, I had much ado to keep him from being a reproach to me. His clothes were apt to look oily, and smell of eating houses. He wore his pantaloons very loose and baggy in summer. His coats were execrable; his hat not to be handled. But while the hat was a thing of indifference to me, inasmuch as his natural civility and deference, as a dependent Englishman, always led him to doff it the moment he entered the room, yet his coat was another matter. Concerning his coats, I reasoned with him, but with no effect. The truth was, I suppose, that a man with so small an income could not afford to sport such a lustrous face and a lustrous coat at one and the same time. As Nippers once observed, Turkey's money went chiefly for red ink. One winter day, I presented Turkey with a highly respectable-looking coat of my own—a padded gray coat, of a most comfortable warmth, and which buttoned straight up from the knee to the neck. I thought Turkey would appreciate the favor, and abate his rashness and obstreperousness of afternoons. But no; I verily believe that buttoning himself up in so downy and blanket-like a coat had a pernicious effect upon him—upon the same principle that too much oats are bad for horses. In fact, precisely as a rash, restive horse is said to feel his oats, so Turkey felt his coat. It made him insolent. He was a man whom prosperity harmed.

Though, concerning the self-indulgent habits of Turkey, I had my own private surmises, yet, touching Nippers, I was well persuaded that, whatever might

[4]*the Tombs:* A massive nineteenth-century prison and detention facility in New York City officially known as the Halls of Justice.

be his faults in other respects, he was, at least, a temperate young man. But, indeed, nature herself seemed to have been his vintner, and, at his birth, charged him so thoroughly with an irritable, brandy-like disposition, that all subsequent potations were needless. When I consider how, amid the stillness of my chambers, Nippers would sometimes impatiently rise from his seat, and stooping over his table, spread his arms wide apart, seize the whole desk, and move it, and jerk it, with a grim, grinding motion on the floor, as if the table were a perverse voluntary agent, intent on thwarting and vexing him, I plainly perceive that, for Nippers, brandy-and-water were altogether superfluous.

It was fortunate for me that, owing to its peculiar cause—indigestion—the irritability and consequent nervousness of Nippers were mainly observable in the morning, while in the afternoon he was comparatively mild. So that, Turkey's paroxysms only coming on about twelve o'clock, I never had to do with their eccentricities at one time. Their fits relieved each other, like guards. When Nippers's was on, Turkey's was off; and *vice versa.* This was a good natural arrangement, under the circumstances.

Ginger Nut, the third on my list was a lad some twelve years old. His father was a carman, ambitious of seeing his son on the bench instead of a cart, before he died. So he sent him to my office, as student at law, errand boy, cleaner and sweeper, at the rate of one dollar a week. He had a little desk to himself, but he did not use it much. Upon inspection, the drawer exhibited a great array of the shells of various sorts of nuts. Indeed, to this quick-witted youth, the whole noble science of the law was contained in a nut shell. Not the least among the employments of Ginger Nut, as well as one which he discharged with the most alacrity, was his duty as cake and apple purveyor for Turkey and Nippers. Copying law-papers being proverbially a dry, husky sort of business, my two scriveners were fain to moisten their mouths very often with Spitzenbergs,[5] to be had at the numerous stalls nigh the Custom House and Post Office. Also, they sent Ginger Nut very frequently for that peculiar cake—small, flat, round, and very spicy—after which he had been named by them. Of a cold morning, when business was but dull, Turkey would gobble up scores of these cakes, as if they were mere wafers—indeed, they sell them at the rate of six or eight for a penny—the scrape of his pen blending with the crunching of the crisp particles in his mouth. Of all the fiery afternoon blunders and flurried rashnesses of Turkey, was his once moistening a ginger-cake between his lips, and clapping it on to a mortgage, for a seal. I came within an ace of dismissing him then. But he mollified me by making an oriental bow, and saying:

"With submission, sir, it was generous of me to find you in stationery on my 15
own account."

Now my original business—that of a conveyancer and title hunter, and drawer-up of recondite documents of all sorts—was considerably increased by receiving the Master's office. There was now great work for scriveners. Not only must I push the clerks already with me, but I must have additional help.

[5]*Spitzenbergs:* A type of apple.

In answer to my advertisement, a motionless young man one morning stood upon my office threshold, the door being open, for it was summer. I can see that figure now—pallidly neat, pitiably respectable, incurably forlorn! It was Bartleby.

After a few words touching his qualifications, I engaged him, glad to have among my corps of copyists a man of so singularly sedate an aspect, which I thought might operate beneficially upon the flighty temper of Turkey, and the fiery one of Nippers.

I should have stated before that ground glass folding-doors divided my premises into two parts, one of which was occupied by my scriveners, the other by myself. According to my humor, I threw open these doors, or closed them. I resolved to assign Bartleby a corner by the folding-doors, but on my side of them, so as to have this quiet man within easy call, in case any trifling thing was to be done. I placed his desk close up to a small side-window in that part of the room, a window which originally had afforded a lateral view of certain grimy backyards and bricks, but which, owing to subsequent erections, commanded at present no view at all, though it gave some light. Within three feet of the panes was a wall, and the light came down from far above, between two lofty buildings, as from a very small opening in a dome. Still further to a satisfactory arrangement, I procured a high green folding screen, which might entirely isolate Bartleby from my sight, though not remove him from my voice. And thus, in a manner, privacy and society were conjoined.

At first, Bartleby did an extraordinary quantity of writing. As if long famishing for something to copy, he seemed to gorge himself on my documents. There was no pause for digestion. He ran a day and night line, copying by sun-light and by candle-light. I should have been quite delighted with his application, had he been cheerfully industrious. But he wrote on silently, palely, mechanically.

20 It is, of course, an indispensable part of a scrivener's business to verify the accuracy of his copy, word by word. Where there are two or more scriveners in an office, they assist each other in this examination, one reading from the copy, the other holding the original. It is a very dull, wearisome, and lethargic affair. I can readily imagine that, to some sanguine temperaments, it would be altogether intolerable. For example, I cannot credit that the mettlesome poet Byron would have contentedly sat down with Bartleby to examine a law document of, say five hundred pages, closely written in a crimpy hand.

Now and then, in the haste of business, it had been my habit to assist in comparing some brief document myself, calling Turkey or Nippers for this purpose. One object I had, in placing Bartleby so handy to me behind the screen, was to avail myself of his services on such trivial occasions. It was on the third day, I think, of his being with me, and before any necessity had arisen for having his own writing examined, that, being much hurried to complete a small affair I had in hand, I abruptly called to Bartleby. In my haste and natural expectancy of instant compliance, I sat with my head bent over the original on my desk, and my right hand sideways, and somewhat nervously extended with the copy, so that, immediately upon emerging from his retreat, Bartleby might snatch it and proceed to business without the least delay.

In this very attitude did I sit when I called to him, rapidly stating what it was I wanted him to do—namely, to examine a small paper with me. Imagine my surprise, nay, my consternation, when, without moving from his privacy, Bartleby, in a singularly mild, firm voice, replied, "I would prefer not to."

I sat awhile in perfect silence, rallying my stunned faculties. Immediately it occurred to me that my ears had deceived me, or Bartleby had entirely misunderstood my meaning. I repeated my request in the clearest tone I could assume. But in quite as clear a one came the previous reply, "I would prefer not to."

"Prefer not to," echoed I, rising in high excitement, and crossing the room with a stride. "What do you mean? Are you moon-struck? I want you to help me compare this sheet here—take it," and I thrust it towards him.

"I would prefer not to," said he.

I looked at him steadfastly. His face was leanly composed; his gray eye dimly calm. Not a wrinkle of agitation rippled him. Had there been the least uneasiness, anger, impatience or impertinence in his manner; in other words, had there been anything ordinarily human about him, doubtless I should have violently dismissed him from the premises. But as it was, I should have as soon thought of turning my pale plaster-of-paris bust of Cicero[6] out of doors. I stood gazing at him awhile, as he went on with his own writing, and then reseated myself at my desk. This is very strange, thought I. What had one best do? But my business hurried me. I concluded to forget the matter for the present, reserving it for my future leisure. So calling Nippers from the other room, the paper was speedily examined.

A few days after this, Bartleby concluded four lengthy documents, being quadruplicates of a week's testimony taken before me in my High Court of Chancery. It became necessary to examine them. It was an important suit, and great accuracy was imperative. Having all things arranged, I called Turkey, Nippers and Ginger Nut, from the next room, meaning to place the four copies in the hands of my four clerks, while I should read from the original. Accordingly, Turkey, Nippers, and Ginger Nut had taken their seats in a row, each with his document in his hand, when I called to Bartleby to join this interesting group.

"Bartleby! quick, I am waiting."

I heard a slow scrape of his chair legs on the uncarpeted floor, and soon he appeared standing at the entrance of his hermitage.

"What is wanted?" said he mildly.

"The copies, the copies," said I hurriedly. "We are going to examine them. There"—and I held towards him the fourth quadruplicate.

"I would prefer not to," he said, and gently disappeared behind the screen.

For a few moments I was turned into a pillar of salt, standing at the head of my seated column of clerks. Recovering myself, I advanced towards the screen, and demanded the reason for such extraordinary conduct.

"*Why* do you refuse?"

[6]*Cicero*: Roman statesman, political theorist, and lawyer (106–42 BCE). It is ironic that the narrator has a statue of Cicero, who was a brave public figure and a staunch defender of the Roman Republic.

"I would prefer not to."

With any other man I should have flown outright into a dreadful passion, scorned all further words, and thrust him ignominiously from my presence. But there was something about Bartleby that not only strangely disarmed me, but in a wonderful manner, touched and disconcerted me. I began to reason with him.

"These are your own copies we are about to examine. It is labor saving to you, because one examination will answer for your four papers. It is common usage. Every copyist is bound to help examine his copy. Is it not so? Will you not speak? Answer!"

"I prefer not to," he replied in a flute-like tone. It seemed to me that, while I had been addressing him, he carefully revolved every statement that I made; fully comprehended the meaning; could not gainsay the irresistible conclusion; but, at the same time, some paramount consideration prevailed with him to reply as he did.

"You are decided, then, not to comply with my request—a request made according to common usage and common sense?"

He briefly gave me to understand, that on that point my judgment was sound. Yes: his decision was irreversible.

It is not seldom the case that when a man is browbeaten in some unprecedented and violently unreasonable way, he begins to stagger in his own plainest faith. He begins, as it were, vaguely to surmise that, wonderful as it may be, all the justice and all the reason is on the other side. Accordingly, if any disinterested persons are present, he turns to them for some reinforcement for his own faltering mind.

"Turkey," said I, "what do you think of this? Am I not right?"

"With submission, sir," said Turkey, in his blandest tone, "I think that you are."

"Nippers," said I, "what do *you* think of it?"

"I think I should kick him out of the office."

(The reader of nice perceptions will here perceive that, it being morning, Turkey's answer is couched in polite and tranquil terms, but Nippers replies in ill-tempered ones. Or, to repeat a previous sentence, Nippers's ugly mood was on duty, and Turkey's off.)

"Ginger Nut," said I, willing to enlist the smallest suffrage in my behalf, "what do *you* think of it?"

"I think sir, he's a little *luny*," replied Ginger Nut, with a grin.

"You hear what they say," said I, turning towards the screen, "come forth and do your duty."

But he vouchsafed no reply. I pondered a moment in sore perplexity. But once more business hurried me. I determined again to postpone the consideration of this dilemma to my future leisure. With a little trouble we made out to examine the papers without Bartleby, though at every page or two Turkey deferentially dropped his opinion, that this proceeding was quite out of the common; while Nippers, twitching in his chair with a dyspeptic nervousness, ground out, between his set teeth, occasional hissing maledictions against the stubborn oaf behind the screen. And for his (Nippers's) part, this was the first and the last time he would do another man's business without pay.

Meanwhile Bartleby sat in his hermitage, oblivious to everything but his own peculiar business there.

Some days passed, the scrivener being employed upon another lengthy work. His late remarkable conduct led me to regard his ways narrowly. I observed that he never went to dinner; indeed, that he never went anywhere. As yet I had never, of my personal knowledge, known him to be outside of my office. He was a perpetual sentry in the corner. At about eleven o'clock though, in the morning, I noticed that Ginger Nut would advance toward the opening in Bartleby's screen, as if silently beckoned thither by a gesture invisible to me where I sat. The boy would then leave the office, jingling a few pence, and reappear with a handful of ginger nuts, which he delivered in the hermitage, receiving two of the cakes for his trouble.

He lives, then, on ginger nuts, thought I; never eats a dinner, properly speaking; he must be a vegetarian, then; but no; he never eats even vegetables, he eats nothing but ginger nuts. My mind then ran on in reveries concerning the probable effects upon the human constitution of living entirely on ginger-nuts. Ginger nuts are so called, because they contain ginger as one of their peculiar constituents, and the final flavoring one. Now, what was ginger? A hot, spicy thing. Was Bartleby hot and spicy? Not at all. Ginger, then, had no effect upon Bartleby. Probably he preferred it should have none.

Nothing so aggravates an earnest person as a passive resistance. If the individual so resisted be of a not inhumane temper, and the resisting one perfectly harmless in his passivity, then, in the better moods of the former, he will endeavor charitably to construe to his imagination what proves impossible to be solved by his judgment. Even so, for the most part, I regarded Bartleby and his ways. Poor fellow! thought I, he means no mischief; it is plain he intends no insolence; his aspect sufficiently evinces that his eccentricities are involuntary. He is useful to me. I can get along with him. If I turn him away, the chances are he will fall in with some less indulgent employer, and then he will be rudely treated, and perhaps driven forth miserably to starve. Yes. Here I can cheaply purchase a delicious self-approval. To befriend Bartleby; to humor him in his strange wilfulness, will cost me little or nothing, while I lay up in my soul what will eventually prove a sweet morsel for my conscience. But this mood was not invariable with me. The passiveness of Bartleby sometimes irritated me. I felt strangely goaded on to encounter him in new opposition—to elicit some angry spark from him answerable to my own. But, indeed, I might as well have essayed to strike fire with my knuckles against a bit of Windsor soap. But one afternoon the evil impulse in me mastered me, and the following little scene ensued:

"Bartleby," said I, "when those papers are all copied, I will compare them with you."

"I would prefer not to."

"How? Surely you do not mean to persist in that mulish vagary?"

No answer.

I threw open the folding doors near by, and, turning upon Turkey and Nippers, exclaimed in an excited manner—

"He says, a second time, he won't examine his papers. What do you think of it, Turkey?"

It was afternoon, be it remembered. Turkey sat glowing like a brass boiler; his bald head steaming; his hands reeling among his blotted papers.

"Think of it?" roared Turkey; "I think I'll just step behind his screen, and black his eyes for him!"

So saying, Turkey rose to his feet and threw his arms into a pugilistic position. He was hurrying away to make good his promise, when I detained him, alarmed at the effect of incautiously rousing Turkey's combativeness after dinner.

"Sit down, Turkey," said I, "and hear what Nippers has to say. What do you think of it, Nippers? Would I not be justified in immediately dismissing Bartleby?"

"Excuse me, that is for you to decide, sir. I think his conduct quite unusual, and, indeed, unjust, as regards Turkey and myself. But it may only be a passing whim."

"Ah," exclaimed I, "you have strangely changed your mind, then—you speak very gently of him now."

"All beer," cried Turkey; "gentleness is effects of beer—Nippers and I dined together to-day. You see how gentle *I* am, sir. Shall I go and black his eyes?"

"You refer to Bartleby, I suppose. No, not to-day, Turkey," I replied; "pray, put up your fists."

I closed the doors, and again advanced towards Bartleby. I felt additional incentives tempting me to my fate. I burned to be rebelled against again. I remembered that Bartleby never left the office.

"Bartleby," said I, "Ginger Nut is away; just step around to the Post Office, won't you?" (it was but a three minutes' walk) "and see if there is anything for me."

"I would prefer not to."

"You *will* not?"

"I *prefer* not."

I staggered to my desk, and sat there in a deep study. My blind inveteracy returned. Was there any other thing in which I could procure myself to be ignominiously repulsed by this lean, penniless wight?—my hired clerk? What added thing is there, perfectly reasonable, that he will be sure to refuse to do?

"Bartleby!"

No answer.

"Bartleby," in a louder tone.

No answer.

"Bartleby," I roared.

Like a very ghost, agreeably to the laws of magical invocation, at the third summons, he appeared at the entrance of his hermitage.

"Go to the next room, and tell Nippers to come to me."

"I prefer not to," he respectfully and slowly said, and mildly disappeared.

"Very good, Bartleby," said I, in a quiet sort of serenely severe self-possessed tone, intimating the unalterable purpose of some terrible retribution very close at hand. At the moment I half intended something of the kind. But upon the whole, as it was drawing towards my dinner-hour, I thought it best to put on my hat and walk home for the day, suffering much from perplexity and distress of mind.

Shall I acknowledge it? The conclusion of this whole business was, that it soon became a fixed fact of my chambers, that a pale young scrivener, by the name of

Bartleby, had a desk there; that he copied for me at the usual rate of four cents a folio (one hundred words); but he was permanently exempt from examining the work done by him, that duty being transferred to Turkey and Nippers, out of compliment, doubtless, to their superior acuteness; moreover, said Bartleby was never, on any account, to be dispatched on the most trivial errand of any sort; and that even if entreated to take upon him such a matter, it was generally understood that he would "prefer not to"—in other words, that he would refuse point-blank.

85 As days passed on, I became considerably reconciled to Bartleby. His steadiness, his freedom from all dissipation, his incessant industry (except when he chose to throw himself into a standing revery behind his screen), his great stillness, his unalterableness of demeanor under all circumstances, made him a valuable acquisition. One prime thing was this—*he was always there*—first in the morning, continually through the day, and the last at night. I had a singular confidence in his honesty. I felt my most precious papers perfectly safe in his hands. Sometimes, to be sure, I could not, for the very soul of me, avoid falling into sudden spasmodic passions with him. For it was exceeding difficult to bear in mind all the time those strange peculiarities, privileges, and unheard of exemptions, forming the tacit stipulations on Bartleby's part under which he remained in my office. Now and then, in the eagerness of dispatching pressing business, I would inadvertently summon Bartleby, in a short, rapid tone, to put his finger, say, on the incipient tie of a bit of red tape with which I was about compressing some papers. Of course, from behind the screen the usual answer, "I prefer not to," was sure to come; and then, how could a human creature with the common infirmities of our nature, refrain from bitterly exclaiming upon such perverseness—such unreasonableness. However, every added repulse of this sort which I received only tended to lessen the probability of my repeating the inadvertence.

Here it must be said, that, according to the custom of most legal gentlemen occupying chambers in densely-populated law buildings, there were several keys to my door. One was kept by a woman residing in the attic, which person weekly scrubbed and daily swept and dusted my apartments. Another was kept by Turkey for convenience sake. The third I sometimes carried in my own pocket. The fourth I knew not who had.

Now, one Sunday morning I happened to go to Trinity Church, to hear a celebrated preacher, and finding myself rather early on the ground I thought I would walk round to my chambers for a while. Luckily I had my key with me; but upon applying it to the lock, I found it resisted by something inserted from the inside. Quite surprised, I called out; when to my consternation a key was turned from within; and thrusting his lean visage at me, and holding the door ajar, the apparition of Bartleby appeared, in his shirt-sleeves, and otherwise in a strangely tattered deshabille, saying quietly that he was sorry, but he was deeply engaged just then, and—preferred not admitting me at present. In a brief word or two, he moreover added, that perhaps I had better walk round the block two or three times, and by that time he would probably have concluded his affairs.

Now, the utterly unsurmised appearance of Bartleby, tenanting my law-chambers of a Sunday morning, with his cadaverously gentlemanly *nonchalance*, yet withal firm and self-possessed, had such a strange effect upon me, that incontinently I slunk away from my own door, and did as desired. But not without sundry twinges of impotent rebellion against the mild effrontery of this unaccountable scrivener. Indeed, it was his wonderful mildness chiefly, which not only disarmed me, but unmanned me, as it were. For I consider that one, for the time, is a sort of unmanned when he tranquilly permits his hired clerk to dictate to him, and order him away from his own premises. Furthermore, I was full of uneasiness as to what Bartleby could possibly be doing in my office in his shirt sleeves, and in an otherwise dismantled condition of a Sunday morning. Was anything amiss going on? Nay, that was out of the question. It was not to be thought of for a moment that Bartleby was an immoral person. But what could he be doing there?—copying? Nay again, whatever might be his eccentricities, Bartleby was an eminently decorous person. He would be the last man to sit down to his desk in any state approaching to nudity. Besides, it was Sunday; and there was something about Bartleby that forbade the supposition that he would by any secular occupation violate the proprieties of the day.

Nevertheless, my mind was not pacified; and full of a restless curiosity, at last I returned to the door. Without hindrance I inserted my key, opened it, and entered. Bartleby was not to be seen. I looked round anxiously, peeped behind his screen; but it was very plain that he was gone. Upon more closely examining the place, I surmised that for an indefinite period Bartleby must have ate, dressed, and slept in my office, and that too without plate, mirror, or bed. The cushioned seat of a rickety old sofa in one corner bore the faint impress of a lean, reclining form. Rolled away under his desk, I found a blanket; under the empty grate, a blacking box and brush; on a chair, a tin basin, with soap and a ragged towel; in a newspaper a few crumbs of ginger nuts and a morsel of cheese. Yes, thought I, it is evident enough that Bartleby has been making his home here, keeping bachelor's hall all by himself. Immediately then the thought came sweeping across me, what miserable friendlessness and loneliness are here revealed! His poverty is great; but his solitude, how horrible! Think of it. Of a Sunday, Wall-Street is deserted as Petra;[7] and every night of every day it is an emptiness. This building, too, which of week-days hums with industry and life, at nightfall echoes with sheer vacancy, and all through Sunday is forlorn. And here Bartleby makes his home; sole spectator of a solitude which he has seen all populous—a sort of innocent and transformed Marius brooding among the ruins of Carthage![8]

For the first time in my life a feeling of overpowering stinging melancholy 90
seized me. Before, I had never experienced aught but a not-unpleasing sadness. The bond of a common humanity now drew me irresistibly to gloom. A fraternal melancholy! For both I and Bartleby were sons of Adam. I remembered the bright silks and sparkling faces I had seen that day, in gala trim, swan-like sailing down the Mississippi of Broadway; and I contrasted them with the pallid copyist,

[7]*Petra:* An ancient city in Jordan.

[8]*Marius . . . Carthage:* Carthage was a North African city-state that was destroyed by Rome during the Third Punic War. Gaius Marius (157–86 BCE) was a Roman general who was between eight and eleven years old when Carthage was destroyed.

and thought to myself, Ah, happiness courts the light, so we deem the world is gay; but misery hides aloof, so we deem that misery there is none. These sad fancyings—chimeras, doubtless, of a sick and silly brain—led on to other and more special thoughts, concerning the eccentricities of Bartleby. Presentiments of strange discoveries hovered round me. The scrivener's pale form appeared to me laid out, among uncaring strangers, in its shivering winding sheet.

Suddenly I was attracted by Bartleby's closed desk, the key in open sight left in the lock.

I mean no mischief, seek the gratification of no heartless curiosity, thought I; besides, the desk is mine, and its contents, too, so I will make bold to look within. Everything was methodically arranged, the papers smoothly placed. The pigeon holes were deep, and removing the files of documents, I groped into their recesses. Presently I felt something there, and dragged it out. It was an old bandanna handkerchief, heavy and knotted. I opened it, and saw it was a savings' bank.

I now recalled all the quiet mysteries which I had noted in the man. I remembered that he never spoke but to answer; that though at intervals he had considerable time to himself, yet I had never seen him reading—no, not even a newspaper; that for long periods he would stand looking out, at his pale window behind the screen, upon the dead brick wall; I was quite sure he never visited any refectory or eating house; while his pale face clearly indicated that he never drank beer like Turkey, or tea and coffee even, like other men; that he never went anywhere in particular that I could learn; never went out for a walk, unless indeed, that was the case at present; that he had declined telling who he was, or whence he came, or whether he had any relatives in the world; that though so thin and pale, he never complained of ill-health. And more than all, I remembered a certain unconscious air of pallid—how shall I call it?—of pallid haughtiness, say, or rather an austere reserve about him, which had positively awed me into my tame compliance with his eccentricities, when I had feared to ask him to do the slightest incidental thing for me, even though I might know, from his long-continued motionlessness, that behind his screen he must be standing in one of those dead-wall reveries of his.

Revolving all these things, and coupling them with the recently discovered fact that he made my office his constant abiding place and home, and not forgetful of his morbid moodiness; revolving all these things, a prudential feeling began to steal over me. My first emotions had been those of pure melancholy and sincerest pity; but just in proportion as the forlornness of Bartleby grew and grew to my imagination, did that same melancholy merge into fear, that pity into repulsion. So true it is, and so terrible, too, that up to a certain point the thought or sight of misery enlists our best affections; but, in certain special cases, beyond that point it does not. They err who would assert that invariably this is owing to the inherent selfishness of the human heart. It rather proceeds from a certain hopelessness of remedying excessive and organic ill. To a sensitive being, pity is not seldom pain. And when at last it is perceived that such pity cannot lead to effectual succor, common sense bids the soul be rid of it. What I saw that morning persuaded me that the scrivener was the victim of innate and incurable disorder. I might give alms to his body; but his body did not pain him; it was his soul that suffered, and his soul I could not reach.

I did not accomplish the purpose of going to Trinity Church that morning. 95
Somehow, the things I had seen disqualified me for the time from church-going. I walked homeward, thinking what I would do with Bartleby. Finally, I resolved upon this;—I would put certain calm questions to him the next morning, touching his history, etc., and if he declined to answer them openly and unreservedly (and I supposed he would prefer not), then to give him a twenty dollar bill over and above whatever I might owe him, and tell him his services were no longer required; but that if in any other way I could assist him, I would be happy to do so, especially if he desired to return to his native place, wherever that might be, I would willingly help to defray the expenses. Moreover, if, after reaching home, he found himself at any time in want of aid, a letter from him would be sure of a reply.

The next morning came.

"Bartleby," said I, gently calling to him behind his screen.

No reply.

"Bartleby," said I, in a still gentler tone, "come here; I am not going to ask you to do anything you would prefer not to do—I simply wish to speak to you."

Upon this he noiselessly slid into view. 100

"Will you tell me, Bartleby, where you were born?"

"I would prefer not to."

"Will you tell me *anything* about yourself?"

"I would prefer not to."

"But what reasonable objection can you have to speak to me? I feel friendly 105
towards you."

He did not look at me while I spoke, but kept his glance fixed upon my bust of Cicero, which, as I then sat, was directly behind me, some six inches above my head.

"What is your answer, Bartleby?" said I, after waiting a considerable time for a reply, during which his countenance remained immovable, only there was the faintest conceivable tremor of the white attenuated mouth.

"At present I prefer to give no answer," he said, and retired into his hermitage.

It was rather weak in me I confess, but his manner, on this occasion, nettled me. Not only did there seem to lurk in it a certain calm disdain, but his perverseness seemed ungrateful, considering the undeniable good usage and indulgence he had received from me.

Again I sat ruminating what I should do. Mortified as I was at his behavior, and resolved as I had been to dismiss him when I entered my office, nevertheless 110
I strangely felt something superstitious knocking at my heart, and forbidding me to carry out my purpose, and denouncing me for a villain if I dared to breathe one bitter word against this forlornest of mankind. At last, familiarly drawing my chair behind his screen, I sat down and said: "Bartleby, never mind, then, about revealing your history; but let me entreat you, as a friend, to comply as far as may be with the usages of this office. Say now, you will help to examine papers

to-morrow or next day: in short, say now, that in a day or two you will begin to be a little reasonable:—say so, Bartleby."

"At present I would prefer not to be a little reasonable," was his mildly cadaverous reply.

Just then the folding-doors opened, and Nippers approached. He seemed suffering from an unusually bad night's rest, induced by severer indigestion than common. He overheard those final words of Bartleby.

"*Prefer not*, eh?" gritted Nippers—"I'd *prefer* him, if I were you, sir," addressing me—"I'd *prefer* him; I'd give him preferences, the stubborn mule! What is it, sir, pray, that he *prefers* not to do now?"

Bartleby moved not a limb.

"Mr. Nippers," said I, "I'd prefer that you would withdraw for the present."

Somehow, of late I had got into the way of involuntarily using this word 115
"prefer" upon all sorts of not exactly suitable occasions. And I trembled to think that my contact with the scrivener had already and seriously affected me in a mental way. And what further and deeper aberration might it not yet produce? This apprehension had not been without efficacy in determining me to summary measures.

As Nippers, looking very sour and sulky, was departing, Turkey blandly and deferentially approached.

"With submission, sir," said he, "yesterday I was thinking about Bartleby here, and I think that if he would but prefer to take a quart of good ale every day, it would do much towards mending him, and enabling him to assist in examining his papers."

"So you have got the word, too," said I, slightly excited.

"With submission, what word, sir?" asked Turkey, respectfully crowding himself into the contracted space behind the screen, and by so doing, making me jostle the scrivener. "What word, sir?"

"I would prefer to be left alone here," said Bartleby, as if offended at being 120
mobbed in his privacy.

"*That's* the word, Turkey," said I—"*that's* it."

"Oh, *prefer*? oh yes—queer word. I never use it myself. But, sir, as I was saying, if he would but prefer—"

"Turkey," interrupted I, "you will please withdraw."

"Oh certainly, sir, if you prefer that I should."

As he opened the folding-door to retire, Nippers at his desk caught a 125
glimpse of me, and asked whether I would prefer to have a certain paper copied on blue paper or white. He did not in the least roguishly accent the word "prefer." It was plain that it involuntarily rolled from his tongue. I thought to myself, surely I must get rid of a demented man, who already has in some degree turned the tongues, if not the heads of myself and clerks. But I thought it prudent not to break the dismission at once.

The next day I noticed that Bartleby did nothing but stand at his window in his dead-wall revery. Upon asking him why he did not write, he said that he had decided upon doing no more writing.

"Why, how now? what next?" exclaimed I, "do no more writing?"

"No more."

"And what is the reason?"

"Do you not see the reason for yourself?" he indifferently replied. 130

I looked steadfastly at him, and perceived that his eyes looked dull and glazed. Instantly it occurred to me, that his unexampled diligence in copying by his dim window for the first few weeks of his stay with me might have temporarily impaired his vision.

I was touched. I said something in condolence with him. I hinted that of course he did wisely in abstaining from writing for a while; and urged him to embrace that opportunity of taking wholesome exercise in the open air. This, however, he did not do. A few days after this, my other clerks being absent, and being in a great hurry to dispatch certain letters by the mail, I thought that, having nothing else earthly to do, Bartleby would surely be less inflexible than usual, and carry these letters to the post-office. But he blankly declined. So, much to my inconvenience, I went myself.

Still added days went by. Whether Bartleby's eyes improved or not, I could not say. To all appearance, I thought they did. But when I asked him if they did, he vouchsafed no answer. At all events, he would do no copying. At last, in reply to my urgings, he informed me that he had permanently given up copying.

"What!" exclaimed I; "suppose your eyes should get entirely well—better than ever before—would you not copy then?"

"I have given up copying," he answered, and slid aside. 135

He remained as ever, a fixture in my chamber. Nay—if that were possible—he became still more of a fixture than before. What was to be done? He would do nothing in the office: why should he stay there? In plain fact, he had now become a millstone to me, not only useless as a necklace, but afflictive to bear. Yet I was sorry for him. I speak less than truth when I say that, on his own account, he occasioned me uneasiness. If he would but have named a single relative or friend, I would instantly have written, and urged their taking the poor fellow away to some convenient retreat. But he seemed alone, absolutely alone in the universe. A bit of wreck in the mid Atlantic. At length, necessities connected with my business tyrannized over all other considerations. Decently as I could, I told Bartleby that in six days' time he must unconditionally leave the office. I warned him to take measures, in the interval, for procuring some other abode. I offered to assist him in this endeavor, if he himself would but take the first step towards a removal. "And when you finally quit me, Bartleby," added I, "I shall see that you go not away entirely unprovided. Six days from this hour, remember."

At the expiration of that period, I peeped behind the screen, and lo! Bartleby was there.

I buttoned up my coat, balanced myself; advanced slowly towards him, touched his shoulder, and said, "The time has come; you must quit this place; I am sorry for you; here is money; but you must go."

"I would prefer not," he replied, with his back still towards me.

"You *must*." 140

He remained silent.

Now I had an unbounded confidence in this man's common honesty. He had frequently restored to me sixpences and shillings carelessly dropped upon the floor, for I am apt to be very reckless in such shirt-button affairs. The proceeding, then, which followed will not be deemed extraordinary.

"Bartleby," said I, "I owe you twelve dollars on account; here are thirty-two; the odd twenty are yours.—Will you take it?" and I handed the bills towards him.

But he made no motion.

"I will leave them here, then," putting them under a weight on the table. Then taking my hat and cane and going to the door, I tranquilly turned and added—"After you have removed your things from these offices, Bartleby, you will of course lock the door—since every one is now gone for the day but you—and if you please, slip your key underneath the mat, so that I may have it in the morning. I shall not see you again; so good-bye to you. If, hereafter, in your new place of abode, I can be of any service to you, do not fail to advise me by letter. Good-bye, Bartleby, and fare you well."

But he answered not a word; like the last column of some ruined temple, he remained standing mute and solitary in the middle of the otherwise deserted room.

As I walked home in a pensive mood, my vanity got the better of my pity. I could not but highly plume myself on my masterly management in getting rid of Bartleby. Masterly I call it, and such it must appear to any dispassionate thinker. The beauty of my procedure seemed to consist in its perfect quietness. There was no vulgar bullying, no bravado of any sort, no choleric hectoring, and striding to and fro across the apartment, jerking out vehement commands for Bartleby to bundle himself off with his beggarly traps. Nothing of the kind. Without loudly bidding Bartleby depart—as an inferior genius might have done—I *assumed* the ground that depart he must; and upon that assumption built all I had to say. The more I thought over my procedure, the more I was charmed with it. Nevertheless, next morning, upon awakening, I had my doubts,—I had somehow slept off the fumes of vanity. One of the coolest and wisest hours a man has, is just after he awakes in the morning. My procedure seemed as sagacious as ever—but only in theory. How it would prove in practice—there was the rub. It was truly a beautiful thought to have assumed Bartleby's departure; but, after all, that assumption was simply my own, and none of Bartleby's. The great point was, not whether I had assumed that he would quit me, but whether he would prefer so to do. He was more a man of preferences than assumptions.

After breakfast, I walked down town, arguing the probabilities *pro* and *con*. One moment I thought it would prove a miserable failure, and Bartleby would be found all alive at my office as usual; the next moment it seemed certain that I should find his chair empty. And so I kept veering about. At the corner of Broadway and Canal Street, I saw quite an excited group of people standing in earnest conversation.

"I'll take odds he doesn't," said a voice as I passed.

"Doesn't go?—done!" said I, "put up your money."

I was instinctively putting my hand in my pocket to produce my own, when I remembered that this was an election day. The words I had overheard bore no reference to Bartleby, but to the success or non-success of some candidate for the mayoralty. In my intent frame of mind, I had, as it were, imagined that all Broadway shared in my excitement, and were debating the same question with me. I passed on, very thankful that the uproar of the street screened my momentary absent-mindedness.

As I had intended, I was earlier than usual at my office door. I stood listening for a moment. All was still. He must be gone. I tried the knob. The door was locked. Yes, my procedure had worked to a charm; he indeed must be vanished. Yet a certain melancholy mixed with this: I was almost sorry for my brilliant success. I was fumbling under the door mat for the key, which Bartleby was to have left there for me, when accidentally my knee knocked against a panel, producing a summoning sound, and in response a voice came to me from within—"Not yet; I am occupied."

It was Bartleby.

I was thunderstruck. For an instant I stood like the man who, pipe in mouth, was killed one cloudless afternoon long ago in Virginia, by summer lightning; at his own warm open window he was killed, and remained leaning out there upon the dreamy afternoon, till some one touched him, when he fell.

"Not gone!" I murmured at last. But again obeying that wondrous ascen- 155
dancy which the inscrutable scrivener had over me, and from which ascendancy, for all my chafing, I could not completely escape, I slowly went down stairs and out into the street, and while walking round the block, considered what I should next do in this unheard-of perplexity. Turn the man out by an actual thrusting I could not; to drive him away by calling him hard names would not do; calling in the police was an unpleasant idea; and yet, permit him to enjoy his cadaverous triumph over me,—this, too, I could not think of. What was to be done? or, if nothing could be done, was there anything further that I could *assume* in the matter? Yes, as before I had prospectively assumed that Bartleby would depart, so now I might retrospectively assume that departed he was. In the legitimate carrying out of this assumption, I might enter my office in a great hurry, and pretending not to see Bartleby at all, walk straight against him as if he were air. Such a proceeding would in a singular degree have the appearance of a home-thrust. It was hardly possible that Bartleby could withstand such an application of the doctrine of assumptions. But upon second thoughts the success of the plan seemed rather dubious. I resolved to argue the matter over with him again.

"Bartleby," said I, entering the office, with a quietly severe expression, "I am seriously displeased. I am pained, Bartleby. I had thought better of you. I had imagined you of such a gentlemanly organization, that in any delicate dilemma a slight hint would suffice—in short, an assumption. But it appears I am deceived. Why," I added, unaffectedly starting, "you have not even touched that money yet," pointing to it, just where I had left it the evening previous.

He answered nothing.

"Will you, or will you not, quit me?" I now demanded in a sudden passion, advancing close to him.

"I would prefer *not* to quit you," he replied, gently emphasizing the *not*.

"What earthly right have you to stay here? Do you pay any rent? Do you pay 160
my taxes? Or is this property yours?"

He answered nothing.

"Are you ready to go on and write now? Are your eyes recovered? Could you copy a small paper for me this morning? or help examine a few lines? or step round to the post-office? In a word, will you do anything at all, to give a coloring to your refusal to depart the premises?"

He silently retired into his hermitage.

I was now in such a state of nervous resentment that I thought it but prudent to check myself at present from further demonstrations. Bartleby and I were alone. I remembered the tragedy of the unfortunate Adams and the still more unfortunate Colt[9] in the solitary office of the latter; and how poor Colt, being dreadfully incensed by Adams, and imprudently permitting himself to get wildly excited, was at unawares hurried into his fatal act—an act which certainly no man could possibly deplore more than the actor himself. Often it had occurred to me in my ponderings upon the subject that had that altercation taken place in the public street, or at a private residence, it would not have terminated as it did. It was the circumstance of being alone in a solitary office, up stairs, of a building entirely unhallowed by humanizing domestic associations—an uncarpeted office, doubtless, of a dusty, haggard sort of appearance;—that it must have been, which greatly helped to enhance the irritable desperation of the hapless Colt.

But when this old Adam of resentment rose in me and tempted me concerning Bartleby, I grappled him and threw him. How? Why, simply by recalling the 165
divine injunction: "A new commandment give I unto you, that ye love one another." Yes, this it was that saved me. Aside from higher considerations, charity often operates as a vastly wise and prudent principle—a great safeguard to its possessor. Men have committed murder for jealousy's sake, and anger's sake, and hatred's sake, and selfishness' sake, and spiritual pride's sake; but no man, that ever I heard of, ever committed a diabolical murder for sweet charity's sake. Mere self-interest, then, if no better motive can be enlisted, should, especially with high-tempered men, prompt all beings to charity and philanthropy. At any rate, upon the occasion in question, I strove to drown my exasperated feelings towards the scrivener by benevolently construing his conduct. Poor fellow, poor fellow! thought I, he don't mean any thing; and besides, he has seen hard times, and ought to be indulged.

I endeavored also immediately to occupy myself, and at the same time to comfort my despondency. I tried to fancy, that in the course of the morning, at such time as might prove agreeable to him, Bartleby, of his own free accord, would emerge from his hermitage, and take up some decided line of march in the direction of the door. But no. Half-past twelve o'clock came; Turkey began to

[9]*poor Colt, being dreadfully incensed by Adams:* In 1841, John C. Colt murdered Samuel Adams, who had called at his office because Colt owed him money. The details of the murder were grisly, and the trial created an unprecedented sensation. Colt was kept in the Tombs prison during the trial and committed suicide after being sentenced to death.

glow in the face, overturn his inkstand, and become generally obstreperous; Nippers abated down into quietude and courtesy; Ginger Nut munched his noon apple; and Bartleby remained standing at his window in one of his profoundest dead-wall reveries. Will it be credited? Ought I to acknowledge it? That afternoon I left the office without saying one further word to him.

Some days now passed, during which, at leisure intervals I looked a little into "Edwards on the Will," and "Priestley on Necessity." Under the circumstances, those books induced a salutary feeling. Gradually I slid into the persuasion that these troubles of mine, touching the scrivener, had been all predestinated from eternity, and Bartleby was billeted upon me for some mysterious purpose of an all-wise Providence, which it was not for a mere mortal like me to fathom. Yes, Bartleby, stay there behind your screen, thought I; I shall persecute you no more; you are harmless and noiseless as any of these old chairs; in short, I never feel so private as when I know you are here. At last I see it, I feel it; I penetrate to the predestinated purpose of my life. I am content. Others may have loftier parts to enact; but my mission in this world, Bartleby, is to furnish you with office-room for such period as you may see fit to remain.

I believe that this wise and blessed frame of mind would have continued with me, had it not been for the unsolicited and uncharitable remarks obtruded upon me by my professional friends who visited the rooms. But thus it often is, that the constant friction of illiberal minds wears out at last the best resolves of the more generous. Though to be sure, when I reflected upon it, it was not strange that people entering my office should be struck by the peculiar aspect of the unaccountable Bartleby, and so be tempted to throw out some sinister observations concerning him. Sometimes an attorney having business with me, and calling at my office, and finding no one but the scrivener there, would undertake to obtain some sort of precise information from him touching my whereabouts; but without heeding his idle talk, Bartleby would remain standing immovable in the middle of the room. So after contemplating him in that position for a time, the attorney would depart, no wiser than he came.

Also, when a Reference was going on, and the room full of lawyers and witnesses, and business driving fast, some deeply-occupied legal gentleman present, seeing Bartleby wholly unemployed, would request him to run round to his (the legal gentleman's) office and fetch some papers for him. Thereupon, Bartleby would tranquilly decline, and yet remain idle as before. Then the lawyer would give a great stare, and turn to me. And what could I say? At last I was made aware that all through the circle of my professional acquaintance, a whisper of wonder was running round, having reference to the strange creature I kept at my office. This worried me very much. And as the idea came upon me of his possibly turning out a long-lived man, and keep occupying my chambers, and denying my authority; and perplexing my visitors; and scandalizing my professional reputation; and casting a general gloom over the premises; keeping soul and body together to the last upon his savings (for doubtless he spent but half a dime a day), and in the end perhaps outlive me, and claim possession of my office by right of his perpetual occupancy: as all these dark anticipations crowded upon me more and more, and my friends continually intruded their relentless remarks upon the apparition in my room; a great change was wrought in me. I resolved to gather all my faculties together, and forever rid me of this intolerable incubus.

Ere revolving any complicated project, however, adapted to this end, I first 170
simply suggested to Bartleby the propriety of his permanent departure. In a calm and serious tone, I commended the idea to his careful and mature consideration. But having taken three days to meditate upon it, he apprised me, that his original determination remained the same; in short, that he still preferred to abide with me.

What shall I do? I now said to myself, buttoning up my coat to the last button. What shall I do? what ought I to do? what does conscience say I *should* do with this man, or, rather ghost. Rid myself of him, I must; go, he shall. But how? You will not thrust him, the poor, pale, passive mortal—you will not thrust such a helpless creature out of your door? you will not dishonor yourself by such cruelty? No, I will not, I cannot do that. Rather would I let him live and die here, and then mason up his remains in the wall. What, then, will you do? For all your coaxing, he will not budge. Bribes he leaves under your own paper-weight on your table; in short, it is quite plain that he prefers to cling to you.

Then something severe, something unusual must be done. What! surely you will not have him collared by a constable, and commit his innocent pallor to the common jail? And upon what ground could you procure such a thing to be done?—a vagrant, is he? What! he a vagrant, a wanderer, who refuses to budge? It is because he will *not* be a vagrant, then, that you seek to count him *as* a vagrant. That is too absurd. No visible means of support: there I have him. Wrong again: for indubitably he *does* support himself, and that is the only unanswerable proof that any man can show of his possessing the means so to do. No more, then. Since he will not quit me, I must quit him. I will change my offices; I will move elsewhere; and give him fair notice, that if I find him on my new premises I will then proceed against him as a common trespasser.

Acting accordingly, next day I thus addressed him: "I find these chambers too far from the City Hall; the air is unwholesome. In a word, I propose to remove my offices next week, and shall no longer require your services. I tell you this now, in order that you may seek another place."

He made no reply, and nothing more was said.

On the appointed day I engaged carts and men, proceeded to my chambers, 175
and, having but little furniture, everything was removed in a few hours. Throughout, the scrivener remained standing behind the screen, which I directed to be removed the last thing. It was withdrawn; and, being folded up like a huge folio, left him the motionless occupant of a naked room. I stood in the entry watching him a moment, while something from within me upbraided me.

I re-entered, with my hand in my pocket—and—and my heart in my mouth.

"Good-bye, Bartleby; I am going—good-bye, and God some way bless you; and take that," slipping something in his hand. But it dropped upon the floor, and then,—strange to say—I tore myself from him whom I had so longed to be rid of.

Established in my new quarters, for a day or two I kept the door locked, and started at every footfall in the passages. When I returned to my rooms, after any little absence, I would pause at the threshold for an instant, and attentively listen, ere applying my key. But these fears were needless. Bartleby never came nigh me.

I thought all was going well, when a perturbed-looking stranger visited me, inquiring whether I was the person who had recently occupied rooms at No.——Wall Street.

Full of forebodings, I replied that I was. 180

"Then, sir," said the stranger, who proved a lawyer, "you are responsible for the man you left there. He refuses to do any copying; he refuses to do anything; he says he prefers not to; and he refuses to quit the premises."

"I am very sorry, sir," said I, with assumed tranquillity, but an inward tremor, "but, really, the man you allude to is nothing to me—he is no relation or apprentice of mine, that you should hold me responsible for him."

"In mercy's name, who is he?"

"I certainly cannot inform you. I know nothing about him. Formerly I employed him as a copyist; but he has done nothing for me now for some time past."

"I shall settle him, then—good morning, sir." 185

Several days passed, and I heard nothing more; and, though I often felt a charitable prompting to call at the place and see poor Bartleby, yet a certain squeamishness of I know not what withheld me.

All is over with him, by this time, thought I, at last, when through another week no further intelligence reached me. But, coming to my room the day after, I found several persons waiting at my door in a high state of nervous excitement.

"That's the man—here he comes," cried the foremost one, whom I recognized as the lawyer who had previously called upon me alone.

"You must take him away, sir, at once," cried a portly person among them, advancing upon me, and whom I knew to be the landlord of No. —— Wall-Street "These gentlemen, my tenants, cannot stand it any longer; Mr. B——," pointing to the lawyer, "has turned him out of his room, and he now persists in haunting the building generally, sitting upon the banisters of the stairs by day, and sleeping in the entry by night. Everybody is concerned; clients are leaving the offices; some fears are entertained of a mob; something you must do, and that without delay."

Aghast at this torrent, I fell back before it, and would fain have locked myself 190
in my new quarters. In vain I persisted that Bartleby was nothing to me—no more than to any one else. In vain;—I was the last person known to have anything to do with him, and they held me to the terrible account. Fearful, then, of being exposed in the papers (as one person present obscurely threatened), I considered the matter, and, at length, said, that if the lawyer would give me a confidential interview with the scrivener, in his (the lawyer's) own room, I would, that afternoon, strive my best to rid them of the nuisance they complained of.

Going up stairs to my old haunt, there was Bartleby silently sitting upon the banister at the landing.

"What are you doing here, Bartleby?" said I.

"Sitting upon the banister," he mildly replied.

I motioned him into the lawyer's room, who then left us.

"Bartleby," said I, "are you aware that you are the cause of great tribulation to me, by persisting in occupying the entry after being dismissed from the office?"

No answer.

"Now one of two things must take place. Either you must do something, or something must be done to you. Now what sort of business would you like to engage in? Would you like to re-engage in copying for some one?"

"No; I would prefer not to make any change."

"Would you like a clerkship in a dry-goods store?"

"There is too much confinement about that. No, I would not like a clerkship; but I am not particular."

"Too much confinement," I cried, "why you keep yourself confined all the time!"

"I would prefer not to take a clerkship," he rejoined, as if to settle that little item at once.

"How would a bar-tender's business suit you? There is no trying of the eyesight in that."

"I would not like it at all; though, as I said before, I am not particular."

His unwonted wordiness inspirited me. I returned to the charge.

"Well then, would you like to travel through the country collecting bills for the merchants? That would improve your health."

"No, I would prefer to be doing something else."

"How then would going as a companion to Europe, to entertain some young gentleman with your conversation—how would that suit you?"

"Not at all. It does not strike me that there is anything definite about that. I like to be stationary. But I am not particular."

"Stationary you shall be, then," I cried, now losing all patience, and for the first time in all my exasperating connection with him, fairly flying into a passion. "If you do not go away from these premises before night, I shall feel bound—indeed I *am* bound—to—to—to quit the premises myself!" I rather absurdly concluded, knowing not with what possible threat to try to frighten his immobility into compliance. Despairing of all further efforts, I was precipitately leaving him, when a final thought occurred to me—one which had not been wholly unindulged before.

"Bartleby," said I, in the kindest tone I could assume under such exciting circumstances, "will you go home with me now—not to my office, but my dwelling—and remain there till we can conclude upon some convenient arrangement for you at our leisure? Come, let us start now, right away."

"No: at present I would prefer not to make any change at all."

I answered nothing; but, effectually dodging every one by the suddenness and rapidity of my flight, rushed from the building, ran up Wall-Street towards Broadway, and, jumping into the first omnibus, was soon removed from pursuit. As soon as tranquillity returned, I distinctly perceived that I had now done all that I possibly could, both in respect to the demands of the landlord and his tenants, and with regard to my own desire and sense of duty, to benefit Bartleby, and shield him from rude persecution. I now strove to be entirely care-free and quiescent; and my conscience justified me in the attempt; though indeed, it was not so successful as I could have wished. So fearful was I of being again hunted out by the incensed landlord and his exasperated tenants, that, surrendering my business to Nippers, for a few days I drove about the upper part of the town and through the suburbs, in my rockaway; crossed over to Jersey City and Hoboken, and paid fugitive visits to Manhattanville and Astoria. In fact, I almost lived in my rockaway for the time.

When again I entered my office, lo, a note from the landlord lay upon the desk. I opened it with trembling hands. It informed me that the writer had sent to the police, and had Bartleby removed to the Tombs as a vagrant. Moreover, since I knew more about him than any one else, he wished me to appear at that place, and make a suitable statement of the facts. These tidings had a conflicting effect upon me. At first I was indignant; but at last, almost approved. The landlord's energetic, summary disposition had led him to adopt a procedure which I do not think I would have decided upon myself; and yet, as a last resort, under such peculiar circumstances, it seemed the only plan.

As I afterwards learned, the poor scrivener, when told that he must be con- 215
ducted to the Tombs, offered not the slightest obstacle, but, in his pale unmoving way, silently acquiesced.

Some of the compassionate and curious by-standers joined the party; and headed by one of the constables arm in arm with Bartleby, the silent procession filed its way through all the noise, and heat, and joy of the roaring thoroughfares at noon.

The same day I received the note, I went to the Tombs, or, to speak more properly, the Halls of Justice. Seeking the right officer, I stated the purpose of my call, and was informed that the individual I described was indeed within. I then assured the functionary that Bartleby was a perfectly honest man, and greatly to be compassionated, however unaccountably eccentric. I narrated all I knew, and closed by suggesting the idea of letting him remain in as indulgent confinement as possible, till something less harsh might be done—though, indeed, I hardly knew what. At all events, if nothing else could be decided upon, the alms-house must receive him. I then begged to have an interview.

Being under no disgraceful charge, and quite serene and harmless in all his ways, they had permitted him freely to wander about the prison and especially in the inclosed grass-platted yards thereof. And so I found him there, standing all alone in the quietest of the yards, his face towards a high wall, while all around, from the narrow slits of the jail windows, I thought I saw peering out upon him the eyes of murderers and thieves.

"Bartleby!"

"I know you," he said, without looking round,— "and I want nothing to say 220
to you."

"It was not I that brought you here, Bartleby," said I, keenly pained at his implied suspicion. "And to you, this should not be so vile a place. Nothing reproachful attaches to you by being here. And see, it is not so sad a place as one might think. Look, there is the sky, and here is the grass."

"I know where I am," he replied, but would say nothing more, and so I left him.

As I entered the corridor again, a broad meat-like man, in an apron, accosted me, and, jerking his thumb over his shoulder, said—"Is that your friend?"

"Yes."

"Does he want to starve? If he does, let him live on the prison fare, that's all."

"Who are you?" asked I, not knowing what to make of such an unofficially speaking person in such a place.

"I am the grub-man. Such gentlemen as have friends here, hire me to provide them with something good to eat."

"Is this so?" said I, turning to the turnkey.

He said it was.

"Well, then," said I, slipping some silver into the grub-man's hands (for so they called him). "I want you to give particular attention to my friend there; let him have the best dinner you can get. And you must be as polite to him as possible."

"Introduce me, will you?" said the grub-man, looking at me with an expression which seemed to say he was all impatience for an opportunity to give a specimen of his breeding.

Thinking it would prove of benefit to the scrivener, I acquiesced; and, asking the grub-man his name, went up with him to Bartleby.

"Bartleby, this is Mr Cutlets; you will find him very useful to you."

"Your sarvant, sir, your sarvant," said the grub-man, making a low salutation behind his apron. "Hope you find it pleasant here, sir; spacious grounds—cool apartments—hope you'll stay with us some time—try to make it agreeable. May Mrs Cutlets and I have the pleasure of your company to dinner, sir, in Mrs Cutlets' private room?"

"I prefer not to dine to-day," said Bartleby, turning away. "It would disagree with me; I am unused to dinners." So saying, he slowly moved to the other side of the inclosure, and took up a position fronting the dead-wall.

"How's this?" said the grub-man, addressing me with a stare of astonishment. "He's odd, ain't he?"

"I think he is a little deranged," said I, sadly.

"Deranged? deranged is it? Well, now, upon my word, I thought that friend of yourn was a gentleman forger; they are always pale and genteel-like, them forgers. I can't help pity 'em—can't help it, sir. Did you know Monroe Edwards?" he added touchingly, and paused. Then, laying his hand piteously on my shoulder, sighed, "he died of consumption at Sing-Sing.[10] So you weren't acquainted with Monroe?"

"No, I was never socially acquainted with any forgers. But I cannot stop longer. Look to my friend yonder. You will not lose by it. I will see you again."

Some few days after this, I again obtained admission to the Tombs, and went through the corridors in quest of Bartleby; but without finding him.

[10]*Monroe Edwards . . . Sing-Sing:* Monroe Edwards was a financier convicted of forgery in 1842. Sing-Sing Correctional Facility was a prison in Ossining, New York.

"I saw him coming from his cell not long ago," said a turnkey, "may be he's gone to loiter in the yards."

So I went in that direction.

"Are you looking for the silent man?" said another turnkey, passing me. "Yonder he lies—sleeping in the yard there. 'Tis not twenty minutes since I saw him lie down."

The yard was entirely quiet. It was not accessible to the common prisoners. The surrounding walls, of amazing thickness, kept off all sounds behind them. The Egyptian character of the masonry weighed upon me with its gloom. But a soft imprisoned turf grew under foot. The heart of the eternal pyramids, it seemed, wherein, by some strange magic, through the clefts, grass-seed, dropped by birds, had sprung.

Strangely huddled at the base of the wall, his knees drawn up, and lying on 245
his side, his head touching the cold stones, I saw the wasted Bartleby. But nothing stirred. I paused; then went close up to him; stooped over, and saw that his dim eyes were open; otherwise he seemed profoundly sleeping. Something prompted me to touch him. I felt his hand, when a tingling shiver ran up my arm and down my spine to my feet.

The round face of the grub-man peered upon me now. "His dinner is ready. Won't he dine to-day, either? Or does he live without dining?"

"Lives without dining," said I, and closed the eyes.

"Eh!—He's asleep, ain't he?"

"With kings and counselors,"[11] murmured I.

There would seem little need for proceeding further in this history. Imagi- 250
nation will readily supply the meagre recital of poor Bartleby's interment. But, ere parting with the reader, let me say, that if this little narrative has sufficently interested him, to awaken curiosity as to who Bartleby was, and what manner of life he led prior to the present narrator's making his acquaintance, I can only reply, that in such curiosity I fully share, but am wholly unable to gratify it. Yet here I hardly know whether I should divulge one little item of rumor, which came to my ear a few months after the scrivener's decease. Upon what basis it rested, I could never ascertain; and hence, how true it is I cannot now tell. But, inasmuch as this vague report has not been without a certain suggestive interest to me, however sad, it may prove the same with some others; and so I will briefly mention it. The report was this: that Bartleby had been a subordinate clerk in the Dead Letter Office[12] at Washington, from which he had been suddenly removed by a change in the administration. When I think over this rumor, hardly can I express the emotions which seize me. Dead letters! does it not sound like dead men? Conceive a man by nature and misfortune prone to a pallid hopelessness, can any business seem more fitted to heighten it than that of continually handling these dead letters, and assorting them for the flames? For by the cart-load

[11] *With kings and counselors:* That is, he is dead. The narrator's quotation comes from the Bible, Job: 3:14.

[12] *Dead Letter Office:* The office for the disposal of letters that could not be delivered through the U.S. mail.

they are annually burned. Sometimes from out the folded paper the pale clerk takes a ring:—the finger it was meant for, perhaps, moulders in the grave; a bank-note sent in swiftest charity—he whom it would relieve, nor eats nor hungers any more; pardon for those who died despairing; hope for those who died unhoping; good tidings for those who died stifled by unrelieved calamities. On errands of life, these letters speed to death.

Ah Bartleby! Ah humanity!

(1853)

Questions for Discussion and Writing

Close Reading

1. How does the narrator of the story characterize himself?
2. What is odd about the interaction of the other three workers in the narrator's office (Turkey, Nippers, and Ginger Nut)?
3. How does the information about Bartleby's past—his work at a "dead letter office"—hold one key to unlocking the mysteries of his life?

Critical and Creative Reading

4. Why doesn't the narrator fire Bartleby the first time he refuses to work?
5. Look carefully at the way the narrator describes his chambers. What is significant about this workplace? Is the narrator implicated in any way in Bartleby's behavior?
6. Imagine that a student enters your class for the first time halfway through the semester. This student does not bring a book, has not done the reading, and whenever your instructor asks him to do anything, the student replies, "I prefer not to." What should your instructor do?

Connections to Other Readings

7. Does the behavior of Rip Van Winkle in Washington Irving's story explain Bartleby's behavior in this story, or are they two completely different character types?
8. Consider the attitude of Kirby toward his workers in Davis's "Life in the Iron-Mills" along with the attitude of the narrator toward his workers in "Bartleby, the Scrivener." What duties or obligations does an employer have toward his or her employees? Is an employer obliged to keep workers happy or only to pay them?
9. Think about the distance between the narrator and his workers in "Bartleby, the Scrivener" and the distance between the speakers and workers in the poems "The Solitary Reaper" by William Wordsworth and "Sparkles from the Wheel" by Walt Whitman. Are these narrators limited in their ability to understand the experiences of the workers they describe?

Ruth Prawer Jhabvala

The Interview

Ruth Prawer Jhabvala (b. 1927) was born in Cologne, Germany, moved to England (where she earned a degree in English literature), and moved to India in 1951, where she and her husband raised three daughters. She is the author of a dozen novels and collections of short fiction, one of which (*Heat and Dust*) won the prestigious Booker Prize in England in 1975, yet she is equally famous as a screenwriter who has adapted numerous classic works of fiction for the legendary director/producer duo Ismail Merchant and James Ivory. (Her adaptations of the E. M. Forster novels *A Room with a View* and *Howards End* both won Academy Awards.) Do you see any evidence of her film background in the following story, "The Interview"?

I am always very careful of my appearance, so you could not say that I spent much more time than usual over myself that morning. It is true, I trimmed and oiled my moustache, but then I often do that; I always like it to look very neat, like Raj Kapoor's, the film star's. But I knew my sister-in-law and my wife were watching me. My sister-in-law was smiling, and she had one hand on her hip; my wife only looked anxious. I knew she was anxious. All night she had been whispering to me. She had whispered, "Get this job and take me away to live somewhere alone, only you and I and our children." I had answered, "Yes," because I wanted to go to sleep. I don't know where and why she has taken this notion that we should go and live alone.

When I had finished combing my hair, I sat on the floor and my sister-in-law brought me my food on a tray. It may sound strange that my sister-in-law should serve me, and not my wife, but it is so in our house. It used to be my mother who brought me my food, even after I was married; she would never allow my wife to do this for me, though my wife wanted to very much. Then, when my mother got so old, my sister-in-law began to serve me. I know that my wife feels deeply hurt by this, but she doesn't dare to say anything. My mother doesn't notice many things anymore, otherwise she certainly would not allow my sister-in-law to bring me my food; she has always been very jealous of this privilege herself, though she never cared who served my brother. Now she has become so old that she can hardly see anything, and most of the time she sits in the corner by the family trunks and folds and strokes her pieces of cloth. For years now she has been collecting pieces of cloth. Some of them are very old and dirty, but she doesn't care, she loves them all equally. Nobody is allowed to touch them. Once there was a great quarrel, because my wife had taken one of them to make a dress for our child. My mother shouted at her—it was terrible to hear her: but then, she has never liked my wife—and my wife was very much afraid and cried and tried to excuse herself. I hit her across the face, not very hard and not because I wanted to, but only to satisfy my mother. The old woman kept quiet then and went back to folding and stroking her pieces of cloth.

All the time I was eating, I could feel my sister-in-law looking at me and smiling. It made me uncomfortable. I thought she might be smiling because she knew I wouldn't get the job for which I had to go and be interviewed. I also knew I wouldn't get it, but I didn't like her to smile like that. It was as if she were saying, "You see, you will always have to be dependent on us." It is clearly my brother's duty to keep me and my family until I can get work and contribute my own earnings to the family household. There is no need for her to smile about it. But it is true that I am more dependent on her now than on anyone else. Since my mother has got so old, my sister-in-law has become more and more the most important person in the house, so that she even keeps the keys and the household stores. At first I didn't like this. As long as my mother managed the household, I was sure of getting many extra tidbits. But now I find that my sister-in-law is also very kind to me—much more kind than she is to her husband. It is not for him that she saves the tidbits, nor for her children, but for me; and when she gives them to me, she never says anything and I never say anything, but she smiles and then I feel confused and rather embarrassed. My wife has noticed what she does for me.

I have found that women are usually kind to me. I think they realize that I am a rather sensitive person and that therefore I must be treated very gently. My mother has always treated me very gently. I am her youngest child, and I am fifteen years younger than my brother who is next to me (she did have several children in between us, but they all died). Right from the time when I was a tiny baby, she understood that I needed greater care and tenderness than other children. She always made me sleep close beside her in the night, and in the day I usually sat with her and my grandmother and my widowed aunt, who were also very fond of me. When I got bigger, my father sometimes wanted to take me to help in his stall (he had a little grocer's stall, where he sold lentils and rice and cheap cigarettes and colored drinks in bottles) but my mother and grandmother and aunt never liked to let me go. Once he did take me with him, and he made me pour some lentils out of paper bags into a tin. I rather liked pouring the lentils—they made such a nice noise as they landed in the tin—but suddenly my mother came and was very angry with my father for making me do this work. She took me home at once, and when she told my grandmother and aunt what had happened, they stroked me and kissed me and then they gave me a hot fritter to eat. The fact is, right from childhood I have been a person who needs a lot of peace and rest, and my food too has to be rather more delicate than that of other people. I have often tried to explain this to my wife, but as she is not very intelligent, she doesn't seem to understand.

Now my wife was watching me while I ate. She was squatting on the floor, 5
washing our youngest baby; the baby's head was in her lap, and all one could see of it was the back of its legs and its naked bottom. My wife did not watch me as openly as my sister-in-law did; only from time to time she raised her eyes to me,

I could feel it, and they were very worried and troubled. She too was thinking about the job for which I was going to be interviewed, but she was anxious that I should get it. "We will go and live somewhere alone," she had said. Why did she say it? When she knows that it is not possible and never will be.

And even if it were possible, I would not like it. I can't live away from my mother; and I don't think I would like to live away from my sister-in-law. I often look at her and it makes me happy. Even though she is not young anymore, she is still beautiful. She is tall, with big hips and big breasts and eyes that flash; she often gets angry, and when she is angry, she is the most beautiful of all. Then her eyes are like fire and she shows all her teeth, which are very strong and white, and her head is proud with the black hair flying loose. My wife is not beautiful at all. I was very disappointed in her when they first married me to her. Now I have got used to her and I even like her, because she is so good and quiet and never troubles me at all. I don't think anybody else in our house likes her. My sister-in-law always calls her "that beauty," but she does not mean it; and she makes her do all the most difficult household tasks, and often she shouts at her and even beats her. This is not right; my wife has never done anything to her—on the contrary, she always treats her with respect. But I cannot interfere in their quarrels.

Then I was ready to go, though I didn't want to go. I knew only too well what would happen at the interview. My mother blessed me, and my sister-in-law looked at me over her shoulder and her great eyes flashed with laughter. I didn't look at my wife, who still sat squatting on the floor, but I knew she was pleading with me to get the job like she had pleaded in the night. As I walked down the stairs, the daughter of the carpenter, who lives in one of the rooms on the lower floor, came out of her door and she walked up the stairs as I walked down, and she passed very close beside me, with her eyes lowered but her arm just touching my sleeve. She always waits for me to come out and then she passes me on the stairs. We have never spoken together. She is a very young girl, her breasts are only just forming; her blouse has short sleeves and her arms are beautiful, long and slender. I think soon she is to be married, I have heard my sister-in-law say so. My sister-in-law laughed when she told me, she said, "It is high time" and then she said something coarse. Perhaps she has noticed that the girl waits for me to pass on the stairs.

No, I did not want to go to the interview. I had been to so many during the last few months, and always the same things happened. I know I have to work, in order to earn money and give it to my mother or my sister-in-law for the household, but there is no pleasure for me in the work. Last time I had work, it was in an insurance office and all day they made me sit at a desk and write figures. What pleasure could there be for me in that? I am a very thoughtful person, and I like always to sit and think my own thoughts; but while I thought my own thoughts in the office, I sometimes made mistakes over the figures and then my superiors were very angry with me. I was always afraid of their anger, and I begged their forgiveness and admitted that I was much at fault. When they forgave me, I was no longer afraid and I continued doing my work and thinking my thoughts. But the last time they would not forgive me again, though I begged and begged and cried what a faulty, bad man I was and what good men they were, and how they were my mother and my father and how I looked only to them for my life and the lives of my children. But when they still said I must go, I saw that the work there was really finished and I stopped crying. I went into the washroom and combed my hair and folded my soap in my towel, and then I took my money from the accountant without a word and I left the office with my eyes lowered. But I was no longer afraid, because what is finished is finished, and my brother still had work and probably one day I would get another job.

Ever since then my brother has been trying to get me into government service. He himself is a clerk in government service and enjoys many advantages: every five years he gets an increase of ten rupees[1] in his salary and he has ten days sick leave in the year and when he retires he will get a pension. It would be good for me also to have such a job; but it is difficult to get, because first there is an interview at which important people sit at a desk and ask many questions. I am afraid of them, and I cannot understand properly what they are saying, so I answer what I think they want me to answer. But it seems that my answers are not after all the right ones, because up till now they have not given me a job.

On my way to this interview, I thought how much nicer it would be to go to the cinema instead. If I had had ten annas,[2] perhaps I would have gone; it was just time for the morning show. The young clerks and the students would be collecting in a queue outside the cinema now. They would be standing and not talking much, holding their ten annas and waiting for the box office to open. I enjoy these morning shows, perhaps because the people who come to them are all young men like myself, all silent and rather sad. I am often sad; it would even be right to say that I am sad most of the time. But when the film begins, I am happy. I love to see the beautiful women, dressed in golden clothes with heavy earrings and necklaces and bracelets covering their arms, and their handsome lovers who are all the things I would like to be. And when they sing their love songs, so full of deep feelings, the tears sometimes come into my eyes; but not because I am sad, no, on the contrary, because I am so happy. After the film is over, I never go home straightaway, but I walk around the streets and think about how wonderful life could be.

When I arrived at the place where the interview was, I had to walk down 10
many corridors and ask directions from many peons[3] before I could find the right room. The peons were all rude to me, because they knew what I had come for. They lounged on benches outside the offices, and when I asked them, they looked me up and down before answering, and sometimes they made jokes about me with one another. I was very polite to them, for even though they were only peons, they had uniforms and jobs and belonged here, and they knew the right way whereas I did not. At last I came to the room where I had to wait. Many others were already sitting there, on chairs that were drawn up all around the room against the wall. No one was talking. I also sat on a chair, and after a while an official came in with a list and he asked if anyone else had come. I got

[1]*rupees:* Indian currency unit.

[2]*annas:* Coins worth one-sixteenth of a rupee (not much).

[3]*peons:* Workers in menial positions, or servants.

up and he asked my name, and then he looked down the list and made a tick with a pencil. He said to me very sternly, "Why are you late?" I begged pardon and told him the bus in which I had come had an accident. He said, "When you are called for interview, you have to be here exactly on time, otherwise your name is crossed off the list." I begged pardon again and asked him very humbly please not to cross me off this time. I knew that all the others were listening, though none of them looked at us. He was very stern with me and even scornful, but in the end he said, "Wait here, and when your name is called, you must go in at once."

I did not count the number of people waiting in the room, but there were many. Perhaps there was one job free, perhaps two or three. I knew that all the others were very worried and anxious to get the job, so I became worried and anxious too. The walls of the room were painted green halfway up and white above that and were quite bare. There was a fan turning from the ceiling, but it was not turning fast enough to give much breeze. Behind the big door the interview was going on; one by one we would all be called in behind this closed door.

I began to worry desperately. It always happens like this. When I come to an interview, I don't want the job at all, but when I see all the others waiting and worrying, I want it terribly. Yet at the same time I know that I don't want it. It would only be the same thing over again: writing figures and making mistakes and then being afraid when they found out. And there would be a superior officer to whom I would have to be very deferential, and every time I saw him or heard his voice I would begin to be afraid that he had found out something against me. For weeks and months I would sit and write figures, getting wearier of it and wearier, so that more and more I would be thinking my own thoughts. Then the mistakes would come, and my superior officer would be angry and I afraid.

My brother never makes mistakes. For years he has been sitting in the same office, writing figures and being deferential to his superior officer; he concentrates very hard on his work, and so he doesn't make mistakes. But all the same he is afraid; that is why he concentrates so hard—because he is afraid that he will make a mistake and they will be angry with him and take away his job. He is afraid of this all the time. And he is right: what would become of us all if he also lost his job? It is not the same with me. I think I am afraid to lose my job only because that is a thing of which one is expected to be afraid. When I have actually lost it, I am really relieved. But I am very different from my brother; even in appearance I am very different. It is true, he is fifteen years older than I am, but even when he was my age, he never looked like I do. My appearance has always attracted others, and up to the time I was married, my mother used to stroke my hair and my face and say many tender things to me. Once, when I was walking on my way to school through the bazaar, a man called to me, very softly, and when I came he gave me a ripe mango, and then he took me into a dark passage that led to a disused mosque, and he touched me under my clothes and he said, "You are so nice, so nice." He was very kind to me. I love wearing fine clothes, very thin white muslin kurtas that have been freshly washed and starched and are embroidered at the shoulders. Sometimes I also use scent, a fine khas[4] smell; my hair oil also smells of khas. Some years ago, when the carpenter's daughter was still a small child and did not yet wait for me on the stairs, there was a girl living in the tailor's shop opposite our house and she used to follow me when I went out. But it is my brother who is married to a beautiful wife, and my wife is not beautiful at all. He is not happy with his wife; when she talks to him, she talks in a hard scornful way; and it is not for him that she saves the best food, but for me, even though I have not brought money home for many months.

The big closed door opened and the man who had been in there for interview came out. We all looked at him, but he walked out in a great hurry, with a preoccupied expression on his face; probably he was going over in his mind all that had been said at the interview. I could feel the anxiety in the other men getting stronger, so mine got stronger too. The official with the list came and we all looked at him. He read out another name and the man whose name was called jumped up from his chair; he did not notice that his dhoti[5] had got caught on a nail in the chair and he wondered why he could not go farther. When he realized what had happened, he tried to disentangle himself, but his fingers shook so much that he could not get the dhoti off the nail. The official watched him and said, "Hurry, now, do you think the gentlemen will wait for you for as long as you please?" Then the man also dropped the umbrella he was carrying and now he was trying both to disentangle the dhoti and to pick up the umbrella. When he could not get the dhoti loose, he became so desperate that he tore at the cloth and ripped it free. It was a pity to see the dhoti torn because it was a new one, which he was probably wearing for the first time and had put on specially for the interview. He clasped his umbrella to his chest and walked in a great hurry to the interviewing room, with his dhoti hanging about his legs and his face swollen with embarrassment and confusion.

We all sat and waited. The fan, which seemed to be a very old one, made a 15
creaking noise. One man kept cracking his finger joints—tik, we heard, *tik* (it made my own finger joints long to be cracked too). All the rest of us kept very still. From time to time the official with the list came in, he walked around the room very slowly, tapping his list, and then we all looked down at our feet and the man who had been cracking his finger joints stopped doing it. A faint and muffled sound of voices came from behind the closed door. Sometimes a voice was raised, but even then I could not make out what was being said, though I strained very hard.

The last time I had an interview, it was very unpleasant for me. One of the people who was interviewing took a dislike to me and shouted at me very loudly. He was a large fat man and he wore an English suit; his teeth were quite yellow, and when he became angry and shouted, he showed them all, and even though I was very upset, I couldn't help looking at them and wondering how they had

[4]*khas:* A spice made of poppy seed.

[5]*dhoti:* A sarong-style covering for men that is wrapped around the lower body and knotted at the waist.

become so yellow. I don't know why he was angry. He shouted: "Good God, man, can't you understand what's said to you?" It was true, I could not understand, but I had been trying so hard to answer well. What more did he expect of me? Probably there was something in my appearance that he did not like. It happens that way sometimes—they take a dislike to you, and then of course there is nothing you can do.

When I thought of the man with the yellow teeth, I became more anxious than ever. I need great calm in my life. Whenever anything worries me too much, I have to cast the thought of it off immediately, otherwise there is a danger that I may become very ill. All my limbs were itching so that it was difficult for me to sit still, and I could feel blood rushing into my brain. It was this room that was doing me so much harm: all the other men waiting, anxious and silent, and the noise from the fan and the official with the list walking around, tapping his list or striking it against his thigh, and the big closed door behind which the interview was going on. I felt great need to get up and go away. I didn't *want* the job. I wasn't even thinking about it anymore—I was thinking only about how to avoid having to sit here and wait.

Now the door opened again and the man with the torn new dhoti came out. He was biting his lip and scratching the back of his neck, and he too walked straight out without looking at us at all. The big door was left slightly open for a moment, and I could see a man's arm in a white shirtsleeve and part of the back of his head. His shirt was very white and of good material, and his ears stood away from his head so that one could see how his spectacles fitted into the backs of his ears. I realized at once that this man would be my enemy and that he would make things very difficult for me and perhaps even shout at me. Then I knew it was no use for me to stay there. The official with the list came back and great panic seized me that he would read out my name. I got up quickly, murmuring, "Please excuse me—bathroom," and went out. The official with the list called after me, "Hey mister, where are you going?" so I lowered my head and walked faster. I would have started to run, but that might have caused suspicion, so I just walked as fast as I could, down the long corridors and right out of the building. There at last I was able to stop and take a deep breath, and I felt much better.

I stood still for only a little while, then I moved on, though not in any particular direction. There were many clerks and peons moving around in the street, hurrying from one office building to another and carrying files and papers. Everyone seemed to have something to do. I was glad when I had moved out of this block and on to the open space where people like myself, who had nothing to do, sat under the trees or in any other patch of shade they could find. But I couldn't sit there; it was too close to the office blocks, and any moment someone might come and say to me, "Why did you go away?" So I walked farther. I was feeling quite light-hearted; it was such a relief for me not to have to be interviewed.

I came to a row of eating stalls, and I sat down on a wooden bench outside 20
one of them, which was called the Paris Hotel, and asked for tea. I felt badly in need of tea, and since I intended to walk part of the way home, I was in a

position to pay for it. There were two Sikhs[6] sitting at the end of my bench who were eating with great appetite, dipping their hands very rapidly into brass bowls. In between eating they exchanged remarks with the proprietor of the Paris Hotel, who sat high up inside his stall, stirring in a big brass pot in which he was cooking the day's food. He was chewing a betel leaf, and from time to time he spat out the red betel juice far over the cooking pot and on to the ground between the wooden benches and tables.

I sat quietly at my end of the bench and drank my tea. The food smelled very good, and it made me realize that I was hungry. I decided that if I walked all the way home, I could afford a little cake (I am very fond of sweet things). The cake was not new, but it had a beautiful piece of bright-green peel inside it. On reaching home I would lie down at once to sleep and not wake up again till tomorrow morning. That way no one would be able to ask me any questions. I would not look at my wife at all, so I would be able to avoid her eyes. I would not look at my sister-in-law either; but she would be smiling, that I knew already—leaning against the wall with her hand on her hip, looking at me and smiling. She would know that I had run away, but she would not say anything.

Let her know! What does it matter? It is true I have no job and no immediate prospect of getting one. It is true that I am dependent on my brother. Everyone knows that. There is no shame in it: there are many people without jobs. And she has been so kind to me up till now, there is no reason why she should not continue to be kind to me. Though I know she is not by nature a kind woman; she speaks mostly with a very harsh tongue and her actions also are harsh. Only to me she has been kind.

The Sikhs at the end of the bench had finished eating. They licked their fingers and belched deeply, the way one does after a good meal. They started to laugh and joke with the proprietor. I sat quiet and alone at the end of the bench. Of course they did not laugh and joke with me. They knew that I was superior to them, for whereas they work with their hands, I am a lettered man who does not have to sweat for a living but sits on a chair in an office and writes figures and can speak in English. My brother is very proud of his superiority, and he has great contempt for carpenters and mechanics and such people who work with their hands. I am also proud of being a lettered man, but when I listened to the Sikhs laughing and joking, the thought came to me that perhaps their life was happier than mine. It was a thought that had come to me before. There is the carpenter who lives downstairs in our house, the one whose daughter waits for me on the stairs, and though he is poor, there is always great eating in his house and many people come and I hear them laughing and singing and even dancing. The carpenter is a big strong man and he always looks happy, never anxious and sick with worry the way my brother does. He doesn't wear shoes and clean white clothes like my brother and I do, nor does he speak any English, but all the same he is happy. Even though his work is inferior, I don't think he gets as weary of it as I do of mine, and he has no superior officer to make him afraid.

[6]*Sikhs:* Adherents of Sikhism, a religion widely practiced in the Punjab region of India.

Then I thought again about my sister-in-law and I thought that if I were kind to her, she would continue to be kind to me. I became quite excited when I thought of being kind to her. I would know then how her big breasts felt under the blouse, how warm they were and how soft. And I would know about the inside of her mouth with the big strong teeth. Her tongue and palate are very pink, like the pink satin blouse she wears on festive occasions, and I had often wondered whether they felt as soft as the blouse too. Her eyes would be shut and perhaps there would be tears on the lashes; and she would be making warm animal sounds and her big body too would be warm like an animal's. I became very excited when I thought of it; but when the excitement had passed, I was sad. Because then I thought of my wife, who is thin and not beautiful and there is no excitement in her body. But she does whatever I want and always tries to please me. I remembered her whispering to me in the night, "Take me away, let us go and live somewhere alone, only you and I and our children." That can never be, and so always she will have to be unhappy.

I was very sad when I thought of her being unhappy; because it is not only she who is unhappy but I also and many others. Everywhere there is unhappiness. I thought of the man whose new dhoti had been torn and who would now have to go home and sew it carefully so that the tear would not be seen. I thought of all the other men sitting and waiting to be interviewed, all but one or two of whom would not get the job for which they had come to be interviewed, and so again they would have to go to another interview and another and another, to sit and wait and be anxious. And my brother who has a job, but is frightened that he will lose it; and my mother so old that she can only sit on the floor and stroke her pieces of cloth; and my sister-in-law who does not care for her husband; and the carpenter's daughter who is to be married and perhaps she also will not be happy. Yet life could be so different. When I go to the cinema and hear the beautiful songs they sing, I know how different it could be; and also sometimes when I sit alone and think my thoughts, then I have a feeling that everything could be so beautiful. But now my tea was finished and also my cake, and I wished I had not bought them, because it was a long way to walk home and I was tired.

(1986)

Questions for Discussion and Writing

Close Reading

1. How does the narrator feel about the job for which he is to be interviewed?
2. What factors contribute to the narrator's departure from the interview?
3. Why does the narrator spend so much time discussing his family members? What does his family have to do with his job?

Critical and Creative Reading

4. Summarize the narrator's attitude toward work in general. Is it typical?

5. The narrator shares the attitudes of other nonlabor workers in his culture: they feel "superior" to manual laborers such as the Sikhs that appear toward the end of the story. How does that attitude of superiority function in a story of a man who is unemployed?
6. In a story called "The Interview" that is largely about work, what percentage of the story is actually devoted to other topics? What are these topics, and why do they figure so prominently?

CONNECTIONS TO OTHER READINGS

7. Is this narrator's aversion to work similar to Rip Van Winkle's aversion to work in Washington Irving's story?
8. Which narrator do you trust more: the narrator of "The Interview" or the narrator of "Bartleby, the Scrivener"? Look for moments where each narrator either affirms your trust or jeopardizes it.
9. This narrator claims to find no pleasure in work. Use Aristides's essay "Work and Its Contents" to analyze him.

Ann Cummins

Where I Work

Ann Cummins (b. 1954) writes fiction about working-class people living in the American Southwest. Now a professor in Arizona, she was born in Colorado and raised in a working-class setting. Her fiction has appeared in national magazines such as the *New Yorker* and has been selected repeatedly for inclusion in the *Best American Short Stories* annual volume. Like the narrator of this story, Cummins once worked in a factory that made blue jeans. How does the story reflect authentic experience?

It's piecework that brings in the money. You get four bucks an hour or ten cents a pocket. The old-timers can sew two pockets a minute and make eighteen an hour. They're a whiz. Most get between ten and fifteen. Me, I get four, today maybe five. I'm on my way. You don't worry if you're no good at first. You catch on. You're guaranteed the four bucks no matter if you can't get one pocket on in an hour. This is my third day.

Sam Hunt with the measuring tape comes to my machine and measures the straightness of my stitching. He wears the tan vest, tan creased pants, brown polished shoes, white shirt. He has a perfectly formed nose, neither upturning nor downturning, and when he stands in front of my machine, I can smell a mysterious cologne coming from him. When he comes this close, I can see that the white shirt does not stick to any part of his skin, because he does not sweat.

But the fat women from Galveston sweat like pigs. Turn up the air conditioning! they'll yell. Today at lunch, I sat with the fat women from Galveston, Texas. You can hear them all over the lunchroom talking about the Texas heat, complaining about this rain. They say, My bones never ached like this in Texas. In Galveston, the fat women plopped their rumps on the beach and watched the hurricanes come in. I have never seen a hurricane. When I sit with the Texans, they tell me all about it.

And they say, How's your love life, darling? These women mull things over.

It is my duty to make them laugh. This is a social skill my brother, Michael, 5
taught me. Make them laugh, he said, and you won't get fired.

Make them laugh or compliment them. Don't tell lies. Don't say things like, "I'd like to tear her little twat out"; if you have to say something like this, say it approximately, not exactly, or you'll scare people. He told me I scare people, and that's one reason why I can't hold a job, and because I tell lies. If you have to tell lies, tell little ones, he says. Try not to talk out loud when you're not talking to anybody.

At lunch yesterday, when they asked me about my lover, I said, He has a waterbed on his roof.

A waterbed on his roof? they said. In this rain?

Some laughed, some didn't. It's difficult to say what will make the women around here laugh.

But I admire their industry. They hardly make mistakes. Sam Hunt docks 10
you a pocket for every mistake, and these add up.

Sam Hunt drives a scooter to work, a very little one. I have seen him from the bus window. He drives on the edge of the road, on the white line, and the Sandy Street bus could squash him like a penny. Then who would see to the time cards? It takes a certain kind of man. Serious. Not a drinker, I'd say. Nice fitting suit, gleaming face.

My brother says my face is better than what you usually see. I would marry my brother in an instant, though he's sinister and disrespectful.

My brother drives a taxi and knows the timing of the streetlights by heart. He drives two-fingered with his foot both on and off the gas pedal, never speeding up, never slowing down, through the city neighborhoods. Some nights I sit on the passenger's side, and the customers sit in the back. My brother's taxi smells like fire. Cinder and ash. In the ashtrays, fat men have stuffed cigars.

I wouldn't mind a fat man. A fat man would be somebody you could wrap yourself around and never meet yourself coming or going. If I married a fat man, I'd draw stars on his back every night. I'd say, How many points does this star have? Now pay attention, termite, I'd say. How many points does this star have?

In his taxi, my brother totes around the downtown whores. Some have the 15
names of the months. June, July, and August. Ask them how much they make a night. Depends on how fast your brother drives, they say. Hurry up, baby, time's money, they like to say. And they spend it in Washington Park, just junkies in Washington Park.

Washington Park smells like garbage, those houses around there. In the Washington Park housing project, don't go up to a black woman's door. They don't want you. Don't go up to the men on the steps. Keep your hands at your sides. Walk fast or run. Don't look in the windows of a car slowing down. Walk slow if there're dogs or they'll chase you. Keep your hand on your purse. If somebody approaches you, if he gets within ten feet, say, "I am fully proficient in the use of semi-automatic weapons."

My brother bought me a gun when I moved out on my own, because a woman living alone in this city should be able to defend herself. You go for the knees. We put cardboard circles on a fence post in the country. I can hit them the majority of the time. If you go for the heart or head and murder a person, you could be held liable by the dead man's family, even if he broke into your apartment. This is the justice system in our country, my brother says, and he's right. The justice system in this country treats us like a bunch of stinking fish.

There. A perfect pocket. This is a keeper, so that's one. These are my practice days. They give you a couple of practice days to start out, and after the third day or so, you begin to develop a system. Like one thing is not to stop when you're coming to a corner—not to slow down or speed up, and keep your hands going with your foot on the pedal and just turn the corner without thinking. If you ruin one, put it in your purse—if it's really bad.

Next week, we're moving to a new line. Sam Hunt said when he oriented me that we're moving out of the blue and into the white. We'll have enough blue by the end of the week. How's your eyes? he says. The white stitches on the white material can blind you, so remember to blink often.

There's something wrong with my eyes. I can't cry. I'm just a happy idiot, my 20
brother says, but I say there's something wrong with my eyes. They are deteriorating in my head. I have that condition—you read about it—where the eyes dry out unnaturally. I don't cry.

All of the women at this table wear glasses. And smoke. The lunchroom's like a chimney. And they say, How's your love life, darling?

The reason I'm not married yet is because I haven't found the right man. I don't know who he is, but I'll know him when I see him, and he'll look like something, and he won't whore around. Which, I'd shoot him, any man who whored around on me. Like that man in the laundry room. He was married, because I saw the ring. And he says, How thin are your wrists? Look at how thin your wrists are. See, he says, I can put my fingers around you and not touch any part, a married man said this.

A lot of the good ones are married. He had green eyes and a friendly manner, and he asked me which was my apartment. He lives right above me—him and his wife. Says, come up and watch TV sometime. I may just do that. I would like to see their home and their furnishings.

I will ask him to help me move furniture in. When I get my first check I'm going to buy a lamp, a nice brass one, and when I save enough I'm going to buy a brass bed, too, and one of those checkerboard coffee tables, the kind with different colors of wood in squares, and some rugs, throw rugs, and ask them to dinner, the man and his wife, which, you could never ask anybody to dinner at Michael's house because nobody ever does the dishes, and there's nothing in that house but Bob Marley posters and dirt and screaming fits.

My brother has paid my rent for the last time. If he's got to have such a screaming fit about it.

Outside the window in my new apartment on the east side is a mystery tree. We don't know what it is. I've asked around but nobody knows. On a muggy night, if you don't turn the light on, you can see animals in the tree. Opossum. Eight, nine, ten of them, gliding along the mystery tree and the tree's branches all in a panic. Black like tar, the branches gleam in the moonlight, all the little opossum claws scratching where you can't see or hear. Shall I open the window? my brother said when he came over. Want some pets? Hold on to your hair. They could get into your hair. He says they're rats, but I have seen them up close. On this, he's wrong. He says this because he's jealous.

Who pays your rent? he says. He says, Who the fuck pays your rent?

My brother has paid my rent for the last time if it's such a big deal.

"My brother had a fire in his taxi."

"What?"

"My brother drives a taxi and somebody started a fire in the back seat."

"Ain't that something." She's the nice one. She says, Sit with us, honey, and tells me about the Texas hurricanes. She's someone you can talk to. "Did he have insurance?"

"What's the difference between a tornado and a hurricane?" The woman has bitten her fingernails to the quick. You can see it from here.

"A tornado? You know, I never considered it. Hey, Lynn. What's the difference between a hurricane and a tornado?"

"One's by sea, one's by land."

"One thing I do know. They can both come up on you in a minute."

"Same with a fire. My brother had a fire in his taxi."

"Ain't that something."

"Somebody left a cigar or cigarette burning in the back. It went, just like that."

"Anybody hurt?"

"They're made of straw. That's why the seats can go just like that."

Then you're walking.

So let him walk. See how that feels.

In the Projects a man came up to me. He says, Woman? Woman? He says, Where can I find a pepper grinder? He says for fish, that he was cooking fish and he wanted some fresh ground pepper, and then started laughing and laughed his fool head off.

In the Projects, a person can get shot and nobody's going to look for you. In the Projects, someone has busted out every streetlight, and there's glass in the street, and children playing in it. In the Projects, you can walk down one street, up another, a street without lights so you don't see the dirty yellow walls all alike, street after street, with dogs that'll chase you and black women who don't want you, and it smells like garbage in the Projects. Those people are filthy.

I don't care if it is cheaper there. He says, You don't have to worry. I'm not going to let anything happen to you. Don't make me cry, Michael. Joyce, I'm not going to let anything happen to you, he says. I told him I'd cry, but there's something wrong with my eyes.

Damn! Now that thread's broken. Where's Sam Hunt? Where's that weasel? Run the flag. Got a problem, he says. Pull this little string. I'll see your flag and respond. They can't be having girls run up and down the aisles looking for the weasel. That way if anything's missing or disturbed anyplace in the vicinity, we'll blame it on Betsy Ross's ghost, he says to me, and has equipped every sewing machine in the place with a little flag. If you have to go to the bathroom, raise the flag, take your purse, don't put it on the floor in the stall, because the weasel is not responsible for stolen or lost property.

Somebody should burn that man up.

There are instances where fires occur by spontaneous combustion, and instances where water will not put a fire out. There are oil slicks on the ocean. In dreams, too—there are people burning on the ocean or in impossible places, instances where burning oil floats on water and your clothes are on fire, and your hair is on fire, and in the water the fire goes inward. If it's dirty with oil and muck. Sometimes there's no way to put the fire out.

In such a dream, go into a well. Make it from rocks. The bottom of the well is very smooth, and the rocks are cool. Close your eyes. Put your cheek against a rock. If you're dizzy, reach your arm out. Touch the other side. Twirl in a circle. Put yourself in a blue well, and keep your eyes closed. Turn around and around until the fire stops.

"Joyce? What is it?"

"My thread broke."

"Your thread broke? Do you remember how I showed you to reload your thread? Did you try that? Here. Show me. Remember? Here now, you hook it around this wire first. Remember. Okay, good. That's right. Yes. Down the pole, into the needle. You pull that back or it's going to know when you begin to sew. Good. Very good. See? That wasn't so hard. Was it?

"How you doing? You getting along okay? You getting to know people?"

"Yes."

"Let's see what you've done today. No, now you're holding your material too tightly. That's what'll give you the tangled stitches. Remember how I told you to roll it under the foot—just like it's a rolling pin and you're making pie crusts. Remember? You bake, Joyce? Just roll it under the foot with a nice, steady movement."

"Yes, I bake."

"No, now this one's not going to work. See, you've got the X in the corner. You can't overshoot the pattern or you'll have a little X. See? And here's another one.

"Joyce, where are the rest of them? I counted sixty pockets out for you this morning. Now I count—let's see—where're the rest of them?"

"That's all you gave me."

"No. This morning I counted out sixty, and now there are—they can't just disappear. Let's see. Forty-eight . . .

"This your third day? You're not picking this up, are you? Maybe we should transfer you to pant legs. There aren't as many angles. Come and talk with me when your shift's over."

"I can't. I'll miss my bus."

"Catch the next bus. Come and talk to me. We'll take a look at your file. See what we can do."

I can do this.

This is a cinch. Go forward and backward to lock in the stitch. Be careful not to overshoot the pattern—be careful not to overshoot the pattern because that's when the X occurs. You can't rip it out because the buying customer will see where the ripping occurred. Now that's ruined. Put it in your purse.

Here's the rest of them. These are ruined. I forgot about these in my purse.

Forgetting is not lying. I'll say, I didn't lie. I forgot, and that's the truth.

What's she smiling at? What's so funny about that pocket? That's a hilarious pocket. These women will laugh behind your back. They listen in on every conversation and then they laugh behind your back. Well, fuck them.

I can do this. So let them laugh. You go forward and backward. Every system has its routine. In a house when you live alone, you check the rock by the front door when you come home to see if it's been moved in your absence. If it's been moved, someone has gone into your house. This is just real funny. I'd like to squash her pea brain. Now that's ruined.

Check the rock and you check for broken windows before you unlock the door, and you keep your gun in the drawer by your bed. I'm going to tell him to give me another chance. This wasn't so good today, but tomorrow's a different story. My brain's ruined for this day. That's a sad thing how a woman will just laugh in your face like that. They think they're so hot.

You keep your gun in the drawer by your bed. If, at three in the morning, some person breaks in your house, you take the phone off the hook, dial O. You don't have time to dial 911. You've got your gun and you're kneeling in bed or on the floor, and you say, I'm fully proficient in the use of semi-automatic weapons. I live at One One-Three Four East Holly. You're saying this to the operator who will call the cops.

Say, "I am proficient in the use of semi-automatic weapons—"

"What?"

"What are you looking at?"

"What did you say?"

"I didn't say anything."

"Yes, you did."

"What are you looking at?"

"Hey, don't worry about it. Don't sweat it. Sam's okay. Gets a bee in his lugudimous maximus every now and again, but he's O.K."

"They're going to fire me from this job."

"Nah, they ain't going to fire you."

"He's going to look at my file."

"Listen—"

"They look at your file, and then they look at you."

"You've got to—"

"Don't look at me."

"Now, honey—"

"Don't look at me! Don't look at my face."

Don't look anywhere.

They open your files and then they fire you. Everything is ruined now. So who cares.

These are ruined. I ruined these. Meaning to or not doesn't count. Did you or didn't you? Did you or didn't you? he'll say. He'll call me on the phone. Did you or did you not? Michael will say. I'll say—

When Michael calls—

I'll say, I didn't get to these yet. These were misplaced, I'll say. I'll say, I forgot about these in my purse.

This place is filthy. Somebody ought to clean this place up.

You just do your work. You just pay attention.

I'll leave my coat in the locker. I'll sneak out the back way, and I'll leave my coat in the locker.

I'll say, These are my practice days, Mr. Hunt. I can do this.

I'll sneak out the back way.

I'll catch the Sandy Street bus. If I miss the Sandy Street, I'll catch the Burnside. I won't look at the bums sleeping there. When I walk across the bridge, across the Burnside Bridge—if they ask me for money, I'll look straight ahead.

When Michael calls to ask me how it went—If my brother calls—

I'll say, Not too bad. That's what I'll say.

He'll say, Way to go, Joyce. That's money in the bank.

For dinner, I'll make mashed potatoes or I'll make rice. I'll sit at the table by the kitchen window. I'll watch the sun go down.

I will set my alarm for six so I can catch the Sandy Street bus at seven, because the Burnside bus will get me here too late. Sam Hunt sees to the time cards. Don't be late or you're docked pockets, and these add up.

I will set the alarm for six and I'll go to bed at ten. If I wake up in the night—if a dream or nightmare wakes me. I must not wake up in the night. A working girl needs her sleep.

(1994)

Questions for Discussion and Writing

Close Reading

1. How is the story structured? According to what logic does one paragraph follow another?
2. What is the effect of the narrator repeating the detail that she can't cry because something is wrong with her eyes?
3. How does the character Sam Hunt function in the story? Is he just the boss, or does his presence mean something else?

Critical and Creative Reading

4. The narrator is paid either by piecework—the amount of work she accomplishes—or according to how much time she puts in. Discuss the ethics of paying workers according to time versus according to work accomplished.

5. What kinds of "masks" does the narrator wear at work? How are "masks" necessary to workers? Do we know anything important about the narrator that her coworkers don't know?
6. Would you describe this story as pessimistic, optimistic, or neutral with regard to the narrator's life circumstances and general well-being?

CONNECTIONS TO OTHER READINGS

7. This narrator admits that she sometimes tells lies. Does that admission make her more or less trustworthy than the first-person narrators of the other stories in this chapter?
8. Discuss gender in this story using Virginia Woolf's "Professions for Women" and/or Mary Collier's "The Woman's Labour" as points of comparison.
9. What power relationships exist between bosses and workers? Use "Where I Work" along with Davis's "Life in the Iron-Mills" in your response.

Poetry

Stephen Duck

The Thresher's Labour

Stephen Duck (1705?–1756) did not have the benefit of formal education. He rose from the status of a common laborer to a poet of some renown in eighteenth-century England, when poetry was a serious and often nasty business because legendary satirists like John Dryden and Alexander Pope delighted in making fun of lesser poets. Duck reportedly worked harder than his fellow laborers so that he could buy a book and spend what little spare time he had reading it. He benefited from a system of patronage in which wealthy people sponsored poets and other artists who did not have the time and money to complete their creative work. He became a court poet and was an important public figure, though also the object of some satire by other poets.

The grateful Tribute of these rural Lays,
Which to her Patron's Hand the Muse conveys,
Deign to accept; 'tis just She Tribute bring
To Him whose Bounty gives her Life to sing:
To Him whose generous Favours tune her Voice,
And bid her 'midst her Poverty rejoice.
Inspir'd by These, she dares her self prepare,

To sing the Toils of each revolving Year:
Those endless Toils, which always grow anew,
And the poor *Thresher's* destin'd to pursue;
Ev'n these with pleasure can the Muse rehearse,
When You, and Gratitude, command the Verse.

Soon as the Harvest hath laid bare the Plains,
And Barns well fill'd reward the Farmer's Pains;
What Corn each Sheaf will yield, intent to hear,
And guess from thence the Profits of the Year;
Or else impending Ruin to prevent,
By paying, timely, threat'ning Landlord's Rent,
He calls his Threshers forth: Around we stand,
With deep Attention waiting his Command.
To each our Tasks he readily divides,
And pointing, to our different Stations guides.
As he directs, to different Barns we go;
Here two for Wheat, and there for Barley two.
But first, to shew what he expects to find,
These Words, or Words like these, disclose his Mind:
So dry the Corn was carried from the Field,
So easily 'twill Thresh, so well 'twill Yield;
Sure large Day's Work I well may hope for now;
Come, strip, and try, let's see what you can do.
Divested of our Cloaths, with Flail in Hand,
At a just Distance, Front to Front we stand;
And first the Threshall's gently swung, to prove,
Whether with just Exactness it will move:
That once secure, more quick we whirl them round,
From the strong Planks our Crab-Tree Staves rebound,
And echoing Barns return the rattling Sound.
Now in the Air our knotty Weapons fly;
And now with equal Force descend from high:
Down one, one up, so well they keep the Time,
The *Cyclops*[1] Hammers could not truer chime;
Nor with more heavy Strokes could *Ætna*[2] groan,
When *Vulcan* forg'd the Arms for *Thetis*' Son.[3]
In briny Streams our Sweat descends apace,
Drops from our Locks, or trickles down our Face.
No intermission in our Works we know;
The noisy Threshall must for ever go.

[1]*Cyclops:* A Greek mythological race of giants known for strength and power.
[2]*Aetna:* A volcanic mountain in Sicily.
[3]*Thetis's son:* Achilles. In Greek mythology, the fleet-footed messenger of the gods.

Their Master absent, others safely play;
The sleeping Threshall doth it self betray.
Nor yet the tedious Labour to beguile,
And make the passing Minutes sweetly smile.
Can we, like Shepherds, tell a merry Tale?
The Voice is lost, drown'd by the noisy Flail.
But we may think——Alas! what pleasing thing
Here to the Mind can the dull Fancy bring?
The Eye beholds no pleasant Object here:
No chearful Sound diverts the list'ning Ear.
The Shepherd well may tune his Voice to sing,
Inspir'd by all the Beauties of the Spring:
No Fountains murmur here, no Lambkins play,
No Linets warble, and no Fields look gay;
'Tis all a dull and melancholy Scene,
Fit only to provoke the Muses Spleen.
When sooty Pease we thresh, you scarce can know
Our native Colour, as from Work we go;
The Sweat, and Dust, and suffocating Smoke,
Make us so much like *Ethiopians* look:
We scare our Wives, when Evening brings us home;
And frighted Infants think the Bug-bear come.
Week after Week we this dull Task pursue,
Unless when winnowing Days produce a new;
A new indeed, but frequently a worse,
The Threshall yields but to the Master's Curse:
He counts the Bushels, counts how much a Day,
Then swears we've idled half our Time away.
Why look ye, Rogues! D'ye think that this will do?
Your Neighbours thresh as much again as you.
Now in our Hands we wish our noisy Tools,
To drown the hated Names of Rogues and Fools;
But wanting those, we just like School-boys look,
When th' angry Master views the blotted Book:
They cry their Ink was faulty, and their Pen;
We, The Corn threshes bad, 'twas cut too green.
But now the Winter hides his hoary Head,
And Nature's Face is with new Beauty spread;
The Spring appears, and kind Refreshing Showers
New clothe the Field with Grass, and deck with Flowers.
Next her, the ripening Summer presses on,
And *Sol* begins his longest Stage to run:
Before the Door our welcome Master stands,
And tells us the ripe Grass requires our Hands.
The long much-wish'd Intelligence imparts
Life to our Looks, and Spirit to our Hearts:

We wish the happy Season may be fair,
And joyful, long to breathe in opener Air.
This Change of Labour seems to give much Ease;
And does, at least, Imagination please.
With Thoughts of Happiness our Joy's complete,
There's always Bitter mingled with the Sweet.
When Morn does thro' the Eastern Windows peep,
Strait from our Beds we start, and shake off Sleep;
This new Employ with eager haste to prove,
This new Employ becomes so much our Love:
Alas! that human Joys shou'd change so soon,
Even this may bear another Face at Noon!
The Birds salute us as to Work we go,
And a new Life seems in our Breasts to glow.
A-cross one's Shoulder hangs a Scythe well steel'd,
The Weapon destin'd to unclothe the Field:
T'other supports the Whetstone, Scrip, and Beer;
That for our Scythes, and These ourselves to chear.
And now the Field design'd our Strength to try
Appears, and meets at last our longing Eye;
The Grass and Ground each chearfully surveys,
Willing to see which way th' Advantage lays.
As the best Man, each claims the foremost Place,
And our first Work seems but a sportive Race:
With rapid Force our well-whet Blades we drive,
Strain every Nerve, and Blow for Blow we give:
Tho' but this Eminence the Foremost gains,
Only t' excel the rest in Toil and Pains.
But when the scorching Sun is mounted high,
And no kind Barns with friendly Shades are nigh,
Our weary Scythes entangle in the Grass,
And Streams of Sweat run trickling down a-pace;
Our sportive Labour we too late lament,
And wish that Strength again, we vainly spent.
Thus in the Morn a Courser I have seen,
With headlong Fury scour the level Green,
Or mount the Hills, if Hills are in his way,
As if no Labour could his Fire allay,
'Till the meridian Sun with sultry Heat,
And piercing Beams hath bath'd his Sides in Sweat;
The lengthen'd Chace scarce able to sustain,
He measures back the Hills and Dales with pain.
With Heat and Labour tir'd, our Scythes we quit,
Search out a shady Tree, and down we sit;
From Scrip and Bottle hope new Strength to gain;
But Scrip and Bottle too are try'd in vain.

Down our parch'd Throats we scarce the Bread can get,
And quite o'er-spent with Toil, but faintly eat;
Nor can the Bottle only answer all,
Alas! the Bottle and the Beer's too small.
Our Time slides on, we move from off the Grass,
And each again betakes him to his Place.
Not eager now, as late, our Strength to prove,
But all contented regular to move:
Often we whet, as often view the Sun,
To see how near his tedious Race is run;
At length he vails his radiant Face from sight,
And bids the weary Traveller good-night:
Homewards we move, but so much spent with Toil,
We walk but slow, and rest at every Stile.
Our good expecting Wives, who think we stay,
Got to the Door, soon eye us in the way;
Then from the Pot the Dumpling's catch'd in haste,
And homely by its side the Bacon's plac'd.
Supper and Sleep by Morn new Strength supply,
And out we set again our Works to try:
But not so early quite, nor quite so fast,
As to our Cost we did the Morning past.
Soon as the rising Sun hath drank the Dew,
Another Scene is open'd to our View;
Our Master comes, and at his Heels a Throng
Of prattling Females, arm'd with Rake and Prong:
Prepar'd, whil'st he is here, to make his Hay;
Or, if he turns his Back, prepar'd to play.
But here, or gone, sure of this Comfort still,
Here's Company, so they may chat their fill:
And were their Hands as active as their Tongues,
How nimbly then would move their Rakes and Prongs?
The Grass again is spread upon the Ground,
'Till not a vacant Place is to be found;
And while the piercing Sun-beams on it shine,
The Haymakers have time allow'd to dine:
That soon dispatch'd, they still sit on the Ground,
And the brisk Chat renew'd, a-fresh goes round:
All talk at once, but seeming all to fear,
That all they speak so well, the rest won't hear;
By quick degrees so high their Notes they strain,
That Standers-by can naught distinguish plain:
So loud their Speech, and so confus'd their Noise,
Scarce puzzled Echo can return a Voice;
Yet spite of this, they bravely all go on,
Each scorns to be, or seem to be, outdone:

'Till (unobserv'd before) a low'ring Sky,
Fraught with black Clouds, proclaims a Shower nigh;
The tattling Croud can scarce their Garments gain,
Before descends the thick impetuous Rain:
Their noisy Prattle all at once is done,
And to the Hedge they all for Shelter run.

Thus have I seen on a bright Summer's Day,
On some green Brake a Flock of Sparrows play;
From Twig to Twig, from Bush to Bush they fly,
And with continu'd Chirping fill the Sky;
But on a sudden, if a Storm appears,
Their chirping Noise no longer dins your Ears;
They fly for Shelter to the thickest Bush,
There silent sit, and all at once is hush.
But better Fate succeeds this rainy Day,
And little Labour serves to make the Hay;
Fast as 'tis cut, so kindly shines the Sun,
Turn'd once or twice, the pleasing Work is done:
Next Day the Cocks appear in equal Rows,
Which the glad Master in safe Reeks bestows.

But now the Field we must no longer range,
And yet, hard Fate! still Work for Work we change.
Back to the Barns again in haste we're sent,
Where lately so much Time we pensive spent:
Not pensive now; we bless the friendly Shade,
And to avoid the parching Sun are glad.
But few Days here we're destin'd to remain,
Before our Master calls us forth again:
For Harvest now, says he, yourselves prepare,
The ripen'd Harvest now demands your Care.
Early next Morn I shall disturb your Rest,
Get all things ready, and be quickly drest.
Strict to his Word, scarce the next Dawn appears,
Before his hasty Summons fills our Ears.
Obedient to his Call, strait up we get,
And finding soon our Company complete;
With him, our Guide, we to the Wheat-Field go;
He, to appoint, and we, the Work to do.
Ye Reapers, cast your Eyes around the Field,
And view the Scene its different Beauties yield:
Then look again with a more tender Eye,
To think how soon it must in Ruin lie.
For once set in, where-e'er our Blows we deal,

There's no resisting of the well-whet Steel:
But here or there, where-e'er our Course we bend,
Sure Desolation does our Steps attend.
Thus, when *Arabia*'s Sons, in hopes of Prey,
To some more fertile Country take their way;
How beauteous all things in the Morn appear,
There Villages, and pleasing Cots are here;
So many pleasing Objects meet the Sight,
The ravish'd Eye could willing gaze 'till Night:
But long e'er then, where-e'er their Troops have past,
Those pleasant Prospects lie a gloomy Waste.

The Morning past, we sweat beneath the Sun,
And but uneasily our Work goes on.
Before us we perplexing Thistles find,
And Corn blown adverse with the ruffling Wind:
Behind our Backs the Female Gleaners wait,
Who sometimes stoop, and sometimes hold a Chat.
Each Morn we early rise, go late to Bed,
And lab'ring hard, a painful Life we lead:
For Toils, scarce ever ceasing, press us now,
Rest never does, but on the Sabbath show,
And barely that, our Master will allow.
Nor, when asleep, are we secure from Pain,
We then perform our Labours o'er again:
Our mimic Fancy always restless seems,
And what we act awake, she acts in Dreams.
Hard Fate! Our Labours ev'n in Sleep don't cease,
Scarce *Hercules*[4] e'er felt such Toils as these.
At length in Rows stands up the well-dry'd Corn,
A grateful Scene, and ready for the Barn.
Our well-pleas'd Master views the Sight with joy,
And we for carrying all our Force employ.
Confusion soon o'er all the Field appears,
And stunning Clamours fill the Workmens Ears;
The Bells, and clashing Whips, alternate sound,
And rattling Waggons thunder o'er the Ground.
The Wheat got in, the Pease, and other Grain,
Share the same Fate, and soon leave bare the Plain:
In noisy Triumph the last Load moves on,
And loud Huzza's proclaim the Harvest done.
Our Master joyful at the welcome Sight,
Invites us all to feast with him at Night.

[4]*Hercules:* In Greek mythology, the heroic son of Zeus known for his superhuman strength.

A Table plentifully spread we find,
And Jugs of humming Beer to cheer the Mind;
Which he, too generous, pushes on so fast,
We think no Toils to come, nor mind the past.
But the next Morning soon reveals the Cheat,
When the same Toils we must again repeat:
To the same Barns again must back return,
To labour there for room for next Year's Corn.

Thus, as the Year's revolving Course goes round,
No respite from our Labour can be found:
Like *Sysiphus*,[5] our Work is never done,
Continually rolls back the restless Stone:
Now growing Labours still succeed the past,
And growing always new, must always last.

(1750)

Questions for Discussion and Reading

Close Reading

1. What is the meaning of the tribute in the first twelve lines of the poem? How does it contrast with the rest of the poem?
2. Describe the rhythm of the poem. Is there a pattern of work-rest-work-rest, or does the poem reflect a growing weariness on the part of the threshers?
3. How is the master of the harvest depicted in this poem? What is his relationship with the speaker?

Critical and Creative Reading

4. Is there any comfort in the speaker's realization that a thresher's labor is never complete? Are any jobs that are worth doing ever really complete?
5. Why does the speaker react negatively to his master's postharvest feast toward the end of the poem?
6. What inspires the threshers to work as hard as they do?

Connections to Other Readings

7. Compare the tension between hard work and producing art in this poem and in Rebecca Harding Davis's story "Life in the Iron-Mills."
8. Read Mary Collier's response to "The Thresher's Labour" ("The Woman's Labour," immediately following). If Duck were to respond again to Collier, what would he say? Try writing a response in heroic couplets, the form Duck and Collier use (lines of ten syllables each, with end rhyme).

[5]*Sisyphus:* Because he angered the gods, Sisyphus was doomed to a punishment that involved rolling a boulder up a mountain, watching it roll back down, and rolling it back up again for eternity.

9. Compare the job of a reaper or thresher in this poem and in Wordsworth's "The Solitary Reaper." Does Duck have more credibility than Wordsworth simply because he is a thresher in this poem? Does Wordsworth seem naïve by comparison? Whose poem is better?

Mary Collier

The Woman's Labour

To Mr. Stephen Duck

Mary Collier (1688?–1762) was a working-class poet whose reputation rests largely on her response to Stephen Duck's poem "The Thresher's Labour." She apparently did not make much money from her poetic endeavor, even though it reached three editions. She was working as a charwoman, a domestic female laborer who performed odd jobs, when she encountered and memorized Duck's poems. Although her response to Duck was well recognized in her lifetime, it receded into obscurity until scholars unearthed it in the 1970s, and it is frequently published, as it is here, alongside Duck's poem.

Immortal Bard! thou Fav'rite of the Nine!
Enrich'd by Peers, advanc'd by CAROLINE!
Deign to look down on One that's poor and low,
Remembring you yourself was lately so;
Accept these Lines: Alas! what can you have
From her, who ever was, and's still a Slave?
No Learning ever was bestow'd on me;
My Life was always spent in Drudgery:
And not alone; alas! with Grief I find,
It is the Portion of poor Woman-kind.
Oft have I thought as on my Bed I lay,
Eas'd from the tiresome Labours of the Day,
Our first Extraction from a Mass refin'd,
Could never be for Slavery design'd;
Till Time and Custom by degrees destroy'd
That happy State our Sex at first enjoy'd.
When Men had us'd their utmost Care and Toil,
Their Recompence was but a Female Smile;
When they by Arts or Arms were render'd Great,
They laid their Trophies at a Woman's Feet;
They, in those Days, unto our Sex did bring
Their Hearts, their All, a Free-will Offering;
And as from us their Being they derive,
They back again should all due Homage give.

Jove[1] once descending from the Clouds, did drop
In Show'rs of Gold on lovely *Danae*'s[2] Lap;
The sweet-tongu'd Poets, in those generous Days,
Unto our Shrine still offer'd up their Lays:
But now, alas! that Golden Age is past,
We are the Objects of your Scorn at last.
And you, great DUCK, upon whose happy Brow
The Muses seem to fix the Garland now,
In your late *Poem* boldly did declare
Alcides[3] Labours can't with your's compare;
And of your annual Task have much to say,
Of Threshing, Reaping, Mowing Corn and Hay;
Boasting your daily Toil, and nightly Dream,
But can't conclude your never-dying Theme,
And let our hapless Sex in Silence lie
Forgotten, and in dark Oblivion die;
But on our abject State you throw your Scorn,
And Women wrong, your Verses to adorn.
You of Hay-making speak a Word or two,
As if our Sex but little Work could do:
This makes the honest Farmer smiling say,
He'll seek for Women still to make his Hay;
For if his Back be turn'd, their Work they mind
As well as Men, as far as he can find.
For my own Part, I many a *Summer*'s Day
Have spent in throwing, turning, making Hay;
But ne'er could see, what you have lately found,
Our Wages paid for sitting on the Ground.
'Tis true, that when our Morning's Work is done,
And all our Grass expos'd unto the Sun,
While that his scorching Beams do on it shine,
As well as you, we have a Time to dine:
I hope, that since we freely toil and sweat
To earn our Bread, you'll give us Time to eat.
That over, soon we must get up again,
And nimbly turn our Hay upon the Plain;
Nay, rake and row it in, the Case is clear;
Or how should Cocks in equal Rows appear?
But if you'd have what you have wrote believ'd,
I find, that you to hear us talk are griev'd:
In this, I hope, you do not speak your Mind,

[1]*Jove:* The chief god in Roman mythology (equivalent to Zeus in Greek mythology).
[2]*Danae:* In Greek mythology, Zeus impregnated the childless Danae, who gave birth to Perseus.
[3]*Alcides:* Another name for Hercules.

For none but *Turks*, that ever I could find,
Have Mutes to serve them, or did e'er deny
Their Slaves, at Work, to chat it merrily.
Since you have Liberty to speak your Mind,
And are to talk, as well as we, inclin'd,
Why should you thus repine, because that we,
Like you, enjoy that pleasing Liberty?
What! would you lord it quite, and take away
The only Privilege our Sex enjoy?

When Ev'ning does approach, we homeward hie,
And our domestic Toils incessant ply:
Against your coming Home prepare to get
Our Work all done, our House in order set;
Bacon and *Dumpling* in the Pot we boil,
Our Beds we make, our Swine we feed the while;
Then wait at Door to see you coming Home,
And set the Table out against you come:
Early next Morning we on you attend;
Our Children dress and feed, their Cloaths we mend;
And in the Field our daily Task renew,
Soon as the rising Sun has dry'd the Dew.

When Harvest comes, into the Field we go,
And help to reap the Wheat as well as you;
Or else we go the Ears of Corn to glean;
No Labour scorning, be it e'er so mean;
But in the Work we freely bear a Part,
And what we can, perform with all our Heart.
To get a Living we so willing are,
Our tender Babes into the Field we bear,
And wrap them in our Cloaths to keep them warm,
While round about we gather up the Corn;
And often unto them our Course do bend,
To keep them safe, that nothing them offend:
Our Children that are able, bear a Share
In gleaning Corn, such is our frugal Care.
When Night comes on, unto our Home we go,
Our Corn we carry, and our Infant too;
Weary, alas! but 'tis not worth our while
Once to complain, or *rest at ev'ry Stile;*
We must make haste, for when we Home are come,
Alas! we find our Work but just begun;
So many Things for our Attendance call,
Had we ten Hands, we could employ them all.
Our Children put to Bed, with greatest Care

We all Things for your coming Home prepare:
You sup, and go to Bed without delay,
And rest yourselves till the ensuing Day;
While we, alas! but little Sleep can have,
Because our froward Children cry and rave;
Yet, without fail, soon as Day-light doth spring,
We in the Field again our Work begin,
And there, with all our Strength, our Toil renew,
Till *Titan*'s golden Rays have dry'd the Dew;
Then home we go unto our Children dear,
Dress, feed, and bring them to the Field with care.
Were this your Case, you justly might complain
That Day nor Night you are secure from Pain;
Those mighty Troubles which perplex your Mind,
(*Thistles* before, and *Females* come behind)
Would vanish soon, and quickly disappear,
Were you, like us, encumber'd thus with Care.
What you would have of us we do not know:
We oft' take up the Corn that you do mow;
We cut the Peas, and always ready are
In ev'ry Work to take our proper Share;
And from the Time that Harvest doth begin,
Until the Corn be cut and carry'd in,
Our Toil and Labour's daily so extreme,
That we have hardly ever *Time to dream.*

The Harvest ended, Respite none we find;
The hardest of our Toil is still behind:
Hard Labour we most chearfully pursue,
And out, abroad, a Charing often go:
Of which I now will briefly tell in part,
What fully to declare is past my Art;
So many Hardships daily we go through,
I boldly say, the like *you* never knew.

When bright *Orion*[4] glitters in the Skies
In *Winter* Nights, then early we must rise;
The Weather ne'er so bad, Wind, Rain, or Snow,
Our Work appointed, we must rise and go;
While you on easy Beds may lie and sleep,
Till light does thro' your Chamber-windows peep.
When to the House we come where we should go,
How to get in, alas! we do not know:
The Maid quite tir'd with Work the Day before,

[4]*Orion:* A stellar constellation known as the hunter.

O'ercome with Sleep; we standing at the Door
Oppress'd with Cold, and often call in vain,
E're to our Work we can Admittance gain:
But when from Wind and Weather we get in,
Briskly with Courage we our Work begin;
Heaps of fine Linen we before us view,
Whereon to lay our Strength and Patience too;
Cambricks and Muslins, which our Ladies wear,
Laces and Edgings, costly, fine, and rare,
Which must be wash'd with utmost Skill and Care;
With Holland Shirts, Ruffles and Fringes too,
Fashions which our Fore-fathers never knew.
For several Hours here we work and slave,
Before we can one Glimpse of Day-light have;
We labour hard before the Morning's past,
Because we fear the Time runs on too fast.

At length bright *Sol* illuminates the Skies,
And summons drowsy Mortals to arise;
Then comes our Mistress to us without fail,
And in her Hand, *perhaps*, a Mug of Ale
To cheer our Hearts, and also to inform
Herself, what Work is done that very Morn;
Lays her Commands upon us, that we mind
Her Linen well, nor *leave the Dirt behind:*
Not this alone, but also to take care
We don't her Cambricks nor her Ruffles tear;
And *these* most strictly does of us require,
To save her Soap, and sparing be of Fire;
Tells us her Charge is great, nay furthermore,
Her Cloaths are fewer than the Time before.
Now we drive on, resolv'd our Strength to try,
And what we can, we do most willingly;
Until with Heat and Work, 'tis often known,
Not only Sweat, but Blood runs trickling down
Our Wrists and Fingers; still our Work demands
The constant Action of our lab'ring Hands.

Now Night comes on, from whence you have Relief,
But that, alas! does but increase our Grief;
With heavy Hearts we often view the Sun,
Fearing he'll set before our Work is done;
For either in the Morning, or at Night,
We piece the *Summer*'s Day with Candle-light.
Tho' we all Day with Care our Work attend,
Such is our Fate, we know not when 'twill end:

When Ev'ning's come, you Homeward take your Way,
We, till our Work is done, are forc'd to stay;
And after all our Toil and Labour past,
Six-pence or Eight-pence pays us off at last;
For all our Pains, no Prospect can we see
Attend us, but *Old Age* and *Poverty*.

The *Washing* is not all we have to do:
We oft change Work for Work as well as you.
Our Mistress of her Pewter cloth complain,
And 'tis our Part to make it clean again.
This Work, tho' very hard and tiresome too,
Is not the worst we hapless Females do:
When Night comes on, and we quite weary are,
We scarce can count what falls unto our Share;
Pots, Kettles, Sauce-pans, Skillets, we may see,
Skimmers and Ladles, and such Trumpery,
Brought in to make complete our Slavery.
Tho' early in the Morning 'tis begun,
'Tis often very late before we've done;
Alas! our Labours never know an End;
On Brass and Iron we our Strength must spend;
Our tender Hands and Fingers scratch and tear:
All this, and more, with Patience we must bear.
Colour'd with Dirt and Filth we now appear;
Your threshing *sooty Peas* will not come near.
All the Perfections Woman once could boast,
Are quite obscur'd, and altogether lost.

Once more our Mistress sends to let us know
She wants our Help, because the Beer runs low:
Then in much haste for Brewing we prepare,
The Vessels clean, and scald with greatest Care;
Often at Midnight, from our Bed we rise
At other Times, ev'n *that* will not suffice;
Our Work at Ev'ning oft we do begin,
And 'ere we've done, the Night comes on again.
Water we pump, the Copper we must fill,
Or tend the Fire; for if we e'er stand still,
Like you, when threshing, we a Watch must keep,
Our Wort boils over if we dare to sleep.

But to rehearse all Labour is in vain,
Of which we very justly might complain:
For us, you see, but little Rest is found;
Our Toil increases as the Year runs round.

While you to *Sysiphus*[5] yourselves compare,
With *Danaus' Daughters*[6] may claim a Share;
For while *he* labours hard against the Hill,
Bottomless Tubs of Water *they* must fill.

So the industrious Bees do hourly strive
To bring their Loads of Honey to the Hive;
Their sordid Owners always reap the Gains,
And poorly recompense their Toil and Pains.

(1760)

QUESTIONS FOR DISCUSSION AND WRITING

CLOSE READING

1. How does the speaker of the poem compare herself to the poet Duck? What connects them, and what separates them?
2. How does the speaker defend the female inclination to talk, the activity that Duck scorns in "The Thresher's Labour"?
3. In his poem Duck argues that a thresher's job is never done by examining the cycles of the harvest and the passage of a day and by comparing the threshers to the myth of Sisyphus, whose fate was to roll a boulder up a hill only to watch it roll down again. What methods does Collier use to argue that a woman's work is never done?

CRITICAL AND CREATIVE READING

4. Is Collier's poem an attempt to make Duck, and all men, notice women's work, honor women's work, or acknowledge that women work harder than they do? In other words, consider her tone: is she picking a fight with men?
5. Write a poetic exchange updated to the twenty-first century. Are the terms "men's work" and "women's work" outdated now, or could we have a similar exchange to the one advanced in Duck's and Collier's poems?
6. Try to put aside your opinions about whether men or women worked harder in the eighteenth century and focus on the imagery in each poem. Which poem is more convincing in its argument about the hard work done either by threshers or by women?

[5] *Sisyphus:* Because he angered the gods, Sisyphus was doomed to a punishment that involved rolling a boulder up a mountain, watching it roll back down again, and rolling it up again for eternity. (See line 281 in Duck's poem "The Thresher's Labor.")

[6] *Danaus' Daughters:* In Greek mythology, Danaus had fifty daughters (called the Danaides), who fled from Danaus's twin brother Aegyptus and his fifty sons. When Aegyptus and his sons arrived on Argos, Danaus gave them his fifty daughters to avoid a battle but instructed the daughters to kill their husbands. As punishment, the Danaides were forced to carry water in jugs that were actually sieves, so the water leaked out endlessly.

CONNECTIONS TO OTHER READINGS

7. Are the gender issues in Collier's poem also applicable to Ann Cummins's story "Where I Work," or is Cummins's story about something other than male and female work even though the narrator is a woman?
8. Examine gender roles in Rebecca Harding Davis's story "Life in the Iron-Mills." Does Davis's story bear out the arguments Collier makes, or do Hugh and Deb work equally hard?
9. Based on her essay "Professions for Women," how would Virginia Woolf respond to the exchange between Duck and Collier?

Joanna Baillie

Hay Making

Joanna Baillie (1762–1851) was known more for her plays than for her poetry, though she published a good deal of both in her long life. Born in Scotland, Baillie was on the outskirts of the movement known as Romanticism, represented also in the poem by William Wordsworth that follows "Hay Making." (See also the poems by Keats in Chapter 13, Coleridge in Chapter 15, and Wordsworth in Chapter 17.) Romanticism emphasized common, rustic members of the working class and sought to appreciate beauty in nature and the simplicity of human existence. The following poem is a good example of the Romantic sensibility, though it also has connections to the preceding two poems from the eighteenth century.

Upon the grass no longer hangs the dew;
Forth hies the mower, with his glittering scythe,
In snowy shirt bedight, and all unbraced,
He moves athwart the mead with sidling bend,
And lays the grass in many a swathey line:
In every field, in every lawn and meadow,
The rousing voice of industry is heard;
The haycock rises, and the frequent rake
Sweeps on the fragrant hay in heavy wreaths.
The old and young, the weak and strong, are there,
And, as they can, help on the cheerful work.
The father jeers his awkward half-grown lad,
Who trails his tawdry armful o'er the field,
Nor does he fear the jeering to repay.
The village oracle, and simple maid,

Jest in their turns and raise the ready laugh;
All are companions in the general glee;
Authority, hard-favoured, frowns not there,
Some, more advanced, raise up the lofty rick,
Whilst on its top doth stand the parish toast,
In loose attire, and swelling ruddy cheek.
With taunts and harmless mockery she receives
The tossed-up heaps from fork of simple youth,
Who, staring on her, takes his arm away,
While half the load falls back upon himself.
Loud is her laugh, her voice is heard afar:
The mower busied on the distant lawn,
The carter trudging on his dusty way,
The shrill sound know, their bonnets toss in air,
And roar across the field to catch her notice:
She waves her arm to them, and shakes her head,
And then renews her work with double spirit.
Thus do they jest and laugh away their toil
Till the bright sun, now past his middle course,
Shoots down his fiercest beams which none may brave.
The stoutest arm feels listless, and the swart
And brawny-shouldered clown begins to fail,
But to the weary, lo! there comes relief!
A troop of welcome children o'er the lawn
With slow and wary steps approach: some bear
In baskets oaten cakes or barley scones,
And gusty cheese and stoups of milk or whey.
Beneath the branches of a spreading tree,
Or by the shady side of the tall rick,
They spread their homely fare, and seated round,
Taste every pleasure that a feast can give.

(1820)

QUESTIONS FOR DISCUSSION AND WRITING

CLOSE READING

1. The poem does not employ end rhyme; does it use any metrical pattern? What is it, and what effect does it have?
2. What is the function of laughter within the poem?
3. The poem is not divided into stanzas. If you were to divide it into stanzas, where would you do so? What logic affects your decision?

CRITICAL AND CREATIVE READING

4. What forms of "cooperative work," if any, are prominent today?

5. Would work be more or less satisfying if it did not make people "weary"?
6. Consider the various ways people are connected to nature in this poem.

CONNECTIONS TO OTHER READINGS

7. William Wordsworth's poem "The Solitary Reaper" might be classified with this poem as examples of Romanticism in British poetry. Do the poems strike you as more alike or different in tone, form, and theme?
8. Compare this poem to Stephen Duck's "The Thresher's Labour," which describes the same kind of work. Do you respond differently to them?
9. The laborers in this poem seem happy and pleased with their work. Does the essay "Work and Its Contents" by Aristides sufficiently explain why they are happy?

William Wordsworth

The Solitary Reaper

William Wordsworth (1770–1850) is one of the most prominent poetic figures in English literary history. Along with Samuel Taylor Coleridge, he is at the center of the Romantic school of poetry, a group of poets including figures like William Blake, John Keats, Percy Bysshe Shelley, and Lord Byron, who derived inspiration from nature, visions, and solitary wanderers. (The preceding poem by Joanna Baillie is another example of Romantic poetry; see also the poems by Keats and Byron in Chapter 13, Coleridge in Chapter 15, and Wordsworth in Chapter 17.) The following poem reveals both a connection to and a distance from a solitary figure, a woman "reaping," or cutting grain.

Behold her, single in the field,
Yon solitary Highland Lass!
Reaping and singing by herself;
Stop here, or gently pass!
Alone she cuts and binds the grain,
And sings a melancholy strain;
O listen! for the Vale profound
Is overflowing with the sound.

No Nightingale did ever chaunt
More welcome notes to weary bands
Of travellers in some shady haunt,
Among Arabian sands:

A voice so thrilling ne'er was heard
In spring-time from the Cuckoo-bird,
Breaking the silence of the seas
Among the farthest Hebrides.

Will no one tell me what she sings?—
Perhaps the plaintive numbers flow
For old, unhappy, far-off things,
And battles long ago:
Or is it some more humble lay,
Familiar matter of to-day?
Some natural sorrow, loss, or pain,
That has been, and may be again?

Whate'er the theme, the Maiden sang
As if her song could have no ending;
I saw her singing at her work,
And o'er the sickle bending;—
I listened, motionless and still;
And, as I mounted up the hill,
The music in my heart I bore,
Long after it was heard no more.

(1805)

QUESTIONS FOR DISCUSSION AND WRITING

CLOSE READING

1. How does the speaker try to connect his vision of the solitary reaper to the larger world in both time and place?
2. What is the speaker's relationship with us, his audience? How does he invite us to enter his vision?
3. Most of the lines in the poem are eight syllables long. Locate those that are not and discuss their effect.

CRITICAL AND CREATIVE READING

4. Why doesn't the speaker ask the solitary reaper what she is singing about? More generally, why does he listen "motionless and still" and pass "gently" so as not to call attention to himself?
5. Look again at the third stanza, in which the speaker wonders whether the song is about something historical or something more "humble," more "familiar" to the singing woman. He never resolves this question: why does he raise it?
6. In the final stanza the speaker bears the Maiden's song in his heart. Based on a careful examination of the whole poem, do you interpret that to mean that

he shares her burden, that he feels some connection to her, or that her song has somehow saddened him? (If you have a different interpretation, feel free to argue it.)

Connections to Other Readings

7. Compare the insider's account of fieldwork in Stephen Duck's "The Thresher's Labour" to the outsider's account in this poem. How can you reconcile the two perspectives or find common ground between them? Would Duck be able to tell Wordsworth's speaker what the solitary reaper sings?
8. Is the speaker in Walt Whitman's poem "Sparkles from the Wheel" like Wordsworth's speaker in his attitude toward workers? Is their response to workers similar?
9. Compare the speaker's response to the solitary reaper's song with May's, Mitchell's, and Kirby's response to Hugh Wolfe's statue in Davis's story "Life in the Iron-Mills."

Walt Whitman

Sparkles from the Wheel

One of the most innovative and significant American poets, Walt Whitman (1819–1892) broke out of the conventions of poetry with a vengeance. His sprawling lines, lengthy catalogs, and affirmative spirit have inspired countless poets who followed him, notably the Beat poet Allen Ginsberg, whose debt to Whitman is clear. (See Ginsberg's poem "C'mon Pigs of Western Civilization Eat More Grease" in Chapter 17.) Whitman believed wholeheartedly in American principles such as democracy, which was important during the U.S. Civil War, a period that caused many Americans to doubt whether their country could be made whole again.

Where the city's ceaseless crowd moves on the livelong day,
Withdrawn I join a group of children watching, I pause aside with them.
By the curb toward the edge of the flagging,
A knife-grinder works at his wheel sharpening a great knife,
Bending over he carefully holds it to the stone, by foot and knee,
With measur'd tread he turns rapidly, as he presses with light but firm hand,
Forth issue then in copious golden jets,
Sparkles from the wheel.

The scene and all its belongings, how they seize and affect me,
The sad sharp-chinn'd old man with worn clothes and broad shoulder-band
  of leather,
Myself effusing and fluid, a phantom curiously floating, now here absorb'd
  and arrested,
The group, (an unminded point set in a vast surrounding,)
The attentive, quiet children, the loud, proud, restive base of the streets,
The low hoarse purr of the whirling stone, the light-press'd blade,
Diffusing, dropping, sideways-darting, in tiny showers of gold,
Sparkles from the wheel.

(1871)

Questions for Discussion and Writing

Close Reading

1. What is the effect of repeating the phrase "Sparkles from the wheel" at the end of each stanza and in the title? Is it meaningful that these are also the shortest lines in the poem?
2. Whitman does not use end rhyme in his poem; what poetic devices does he use, and to what effect?
3. Describe and discuss the tension in the poem between things in motion and things at rest.

Critical and Creative Reading

4. Why do children typically watch scenes like those described in Whitman's poem, while adults typically do not? How is it clear that Whitman's speaker is an adult, and how does he depict himself? Do poets need to see the world as children do?
5. Are the golden sparkles supposed to redeem the life of the knife-sharpener producing them (who appears "sad" and whose clothes are "worn")? If so, do the sparkles benefit the worker or only the poet and the children?
6. Write a poem from the point of view of the knife-sharpener describing the same scene Whitman describes. Consider what words he might use and how the form of the poem might be different.

Connections to Other Readings

7. The speaker of this poem says that the scene has the power to "seize and affect" him. Is he seized and affected the same way the speaker of Wordsworth's poem "The Solitary Reaper" is seized and affected by the singing, working maiden?
8. If you contrast this poem with Stephen Duck's "The Thresher's Labour," does it seem that Whitman is overlooking the effort expended by the knife-sharpener, or does he account for that effort?

9. Discuss whether the sparkles from the wheel in this poem operate the same way the korl statues operate in Davis's story "Life in the Iron-Mills."

Alfred, Lord Tennyson

Ulysses

One of the most popular and venerated British poets of the nineteenth century, Alfred, Lord Tennyson (1809–1892) succeeded William Wordsworth as poet laureate of England in 1850. Tennyson's popularity led him to be associated with the voice of the people, a poetic equivalent to the fiction writer Charles Dickens. Although his reputation following his death has been uneven, Tennyson earned his legacy through the hard work of painstaking revision. The following is one of his most enduring poems (along with "The Charge of the Light Brigade," included in Chapter 12). Its subject is Ulysses, the hero of Homer's epic *Odysseus*. After his many travels, battles, and the fall of Troy, Ulysses has returned home to reunite with his wife and his son Telemachus. This speech takes place after that reunion.

It little profits that an idle king,
By this still hearth, among these barren crags,
Matched with an aged wife, I mete and dole
Unequal laws unto a savage race,
That hoard, and sleep, and feed, and know not me.

I cannot rest from travel; I will drink
Life to the lees. All times I have enjoyed
Greatly, have suffered greatly, both with those
That loved me, and alone; on shore, and when
Through scudding drifts the rainy Hyades[1]
Vexed the dim sea. I am become a name;
For always roaming with a hungry heart
Much have I seen and known—cities of men
And manners, climates, councils, governments,
Myself not least, but honored of them all—
And drunk delight of battle with my peers,
Far on the ringing plains of windy Troy,[2]
I am a part of all that I have met;

[1]*Hyades:* A constellation of stars that were believed to bring rain.

[2]*Troy:* An ancient city-state in what is now northwestern Turkey. It is located on the Dardanelles, a narrow strait that separates Europe from the mainland of Asia. Ulysses (originally Odysseus in Homer's epics *The Iliad* and *The Odyssey*) was a Greek hero who conquered Troy and took ten years to return to his home island of Ithaca.

Yet all experience is an arch wherethrough
Gleams that untraveled world whose margin fades
Forever and forever when I move.
How dull it is to pause, to make an end,
To rust unburnished, not to shine in use!
As though to breathe were life! Life piled on life
Were all too little, and of one to me
Little remains; but every hour is saved
From that eternal silence, something more,
A bringer of new things; and vile it were
For some three suns to store and hoard myself,
And this gray spirit yearning in desire
To follow knowledge like a sinking star,
Beyond the utmost bound of human thought.

This is my son, mine own Telemachus,
To whom I leave the scepter and the isle—
Well-loved of me, discerning to fulfill
This labor, by slow prudence to make mild
A rugged people, and through soft degrees
Subdue them to the useful and the good.
Most blameless is he, centered in the sphere
Of common duties, decent not to fail
In offices of tenderness, and pay
Meet adoration to my household gods,
When I am gone. He works his work, I mine.

There lies the port; the vessel puffs her sail;
There gloom the dark, broad seas. My mariners,
Souls that have toiled, and wrought, and thought with me—
That ever with a frolic welcome took
The thunder and the sunshine, and opposed
Free hearts, free foreheads—you and I are old;
Old age hath yet his honor and his toil.
Death closes all; but something ere the end,
Some work of noble note, may yet be done,
Not unbecoming men that strove with Gods.
The lights begin to twinkle from the rocks;
The long day wanes; the slow moon climbs; the deep
Moans round with many voices. Come, my friends,
'Tis not too late to seek a newer world.
Push off, and sitting well in order smite
The sounding furrows; for my purpose holds
To sail beyond the sunset, and the baths
Of all the western stars, until I die.
It may be that the gulfs will wash us down;

It may be we shall touch the Happy Isles,[3]
And see the great Achilles, whom we knew.
Though much is taken, much abides; and though
We are not now that strength which in old days
Moved earth and heaven, that which we are, we are—
One equal temper of heroic hearts,
Made weak by time and fate, but strong in will
To strive, to seek, to find, and not to yield.

(1833)

Questions for Discussion and Writing

Close Reading

1. Note the places in the poem where the speaker is most aware of his audience and the places where he is most introspective. How do these two elements of his speech advance the poem's theme?
2. Speechmakers are fond of repeating words. Mark the places in the poem where Tennyson repeats words: what poetic effect does this repetition have?
3. What might the speaker mean when he says, "I am become a name" (line 11)?

Critical and Creative Reading

4. How does the speaker define a worthwhile life?
5. The speaker Ulysses seems to desire neither rest nor retirement. Do you admire him for his ambition, or pity him because he doesn't value leisure?
6. The speaker is a king, a leader. Do leaders generally have higher expectations that might prevent them from ever believing that their work is complete?

Connections to Other Readings

7. Consider the speaker's attitude in conjunction with Prince Hal's vacation from his kingly duties in Shakespeare's *I Henry IV*. You might want to put Ulysses and Hal in dialogue with one another regarding the duties of a leader.
8. Stephen Duck and Mary Collier, in their exchange "The Thresher's Labour" and "The Woman's Labour," also write of work that is never finished. Is Ulysses's attitude different here because his status is higher than the other speakers, or do all three essentially agree about the nature of work?
9. Discuss the status of leisure in "Ulysses" and in Washington Irving's story "Rip Van Winkle."

[3]*Happy Isles:* In Greek mythology, the Islands of the Blessed were believed to be populated with the heroes (such as Achilles in the next line) who became immortal after death.

Robert Frost

The Tuft of Flowers

Most students have encountered Robert Frost (1874–1963) before college, usually through one of his famous poems: "Stopping by Woods on a Snowy Evening" or "The Road Not Taken." This Pulitzer Prize recipient is one of America's most beloved poets, and the range of his talents is not necessarily encompassed by these two familiar poems, which merely give glimpses of the depth and darkness of his philosophical vision. Yet they do indicate a consistent theme in his works that is also evident in the following poem: we allow ourselves philosophical insight when we remove ourselves to natural settings and seek out moments of solitude.

I went to turn the grass once after one
Who mowed it in the dew before the sun.

The dew was gone that made his blade so keen
Before I came to view the leveled scene.

I looked for him behind an isle of trees;
I listened for his whetstone on the breeze.

But he had gone his way, the grass all mown,
And I must be, as he had been—alone,

"As all must be," I said within my heart,
"Whether they work together or apart."

But as I said it, swift there passed me by
On noiseless wing a bewildered butterfly,

Seeking with memories grown dim o'er night
Some resting flower of yesterday's delight.

And once I marked his flight go round and round,
As where some flower lay withering on the ground.

And then he flew as far as eye could see,
And then on tremulous wing came back to me.

I thought of questions that have no reply,
And would have turned to toss the grass to dry;

But he turned first, and led my eye to look
At a tall tuft of flowers beside a brook,

A leaping tongue of bloom the scythe had spared
Beside a reedy brook the scythe had bared.

The mower in the dew had loved them thus,
By leaving them to flourish, not for us,

Nor yet to draw one thought of ours to him,
But from sheer morning gladness at the brim.

The butterfly and I had lit upon,
Nevertheless, a message from the dawn,

That made me hear the wakening birds around,
And hear his long scythe whispering to the ground,

And feel a spirit kindred to my own;
So that henceforth I worked no more alone;

But glad with him, I worked as with his aid,
And weary, sought at noon with him the shade;

And dreaming, as it were, held brotherly speech
With one whose thought I had not hoped to reach.

"Men work together," I told him from the heart,
"Whether they work together or apart."

(1906)

Questions for Discussion and Writing

Close Reading

1. Why do you suppose Frost organized his poem in two-line stanzas? How else might he have organized it?
2. End rhyme is the most notable poetic device this poem uses. As you look closer, what other poetic devices are apparent, and how do they function?
3. What is the difference in context and meaning between the first time the speaker utters the line "Whether they work together or apart" (line 10) and the second time in the concluding line of the poem?

CRITICAL AND CREATIVE READING

4. List all the examples of failed communication in the poem. How does the speaker manage to have a kind of "conversation" without ever speaking with the mower?
5. Is the butterfly a necessary component of this poem?
6. Do we ever work alone, or is work always a communal activity? Use this poem to discuss that question.

CONNECTIONS TO OTHER READINGS

7. Discuss the communal aspects of work in "The Tuft of Flowers" and in Walt Whitman's "Sparkles from the Wheel."
8. Discuss communication in this poem and in William Wordsworth's "The Solitary Reaper."
9. Like the unnamed mower in this poem, Hugh in "Life in the Iron-Mills" creates art while he works. Are the situations comparable?

Philip Larkin

Toads
Toads Revisited

British poet Philip Larkin (1922–1985) wrote honestly and directly about life in London in the mid-twentieth century. While the speakers of his poems are often cynical and depressed, his poems have a quality of optimism in them, perhaps because of their bluntness. His subjects are human relationships and modern society. Work is a common subject, as is evident in the following pair of poems.

Toads

Why should I let the toad *work*
Squat on my life?
Can't I use my wit as a pitchfork
And drive the brute off?

Six days of the week it soils
With its sickening poison—
Just for paying a few bills!
That's out of proportion.

Lots of folk live on their wits:
Lecturers, lispers,
Losels, loblolly-men, louts—
They don't end as paupers;

Lots of folk live up lanes
With fires in a bucket,
Eat windfalls and tinned sardines—
they seem to like it.

Their nippers have got bare feet,
Their unspeakable wives
Are skinny as whippets—and yet
No one actually *starves.*

Ah, were I courageous enough
To shout *Stuff your pension!*
But I know, all too well, that's the stuff
That dreams are made on:

For something sufficiently toad-like
Squats in me, too;
Its hunkers are heavy as hard luck,
And cold as snow,

And will never allow me to blarney
My way of getting
The fame and the girl and the money
All at one sitting.

I don't say, one bodies the other
One's spiritual truth;
But I do say it's hard to lose either,
When you have both.

(1954)

Toads Revisited

Walking around in the park
Should feel better than work:
The lake, the sunshine,
The grass to lie on,

Blurred playground noises
Beyond black-stockinged nurses—
Not a bad place to be.
Yet it doesn't suit me,

Being one of the men
You meet of an afternoon:
Palsied old step-takers,
Hare-eyed clerks with the jitters,

Waxed-fleshed out-patients
Still vague from accidents,
And characters in long coats
Deep in the litter-baskets—

All dodging the toad work
By being stupid or weak.
Think of them!
Hearing the hours chime,

Watching the bread delivered,
The sun by clouds covered,
The children going home;
Think of being them,

Turning over their failures
By some bed of lobelias,
Nowhere to go but indoors,
No friends but empty chairs—

No, give me my in-tray,
My loaf-haired secretary,
My shall-I-keep-the-call-in-Sir:
What else can I answer,

When the lights come on at four
At the end of another year?
Give me your arm, old toad;
Help me down Cemetery Road.

(1962)

Questions for Discussion and Writing

Close Reading

1. What qualities of a toad make it a possible metaphor for work?
2. How would you describe the rhyme scheme of the poems?
3. What do the poems finally say about the "toad work"? Is it necessary, important, inevitable?

CRITICAL AND CREATIVE READING

4. In "revisiting" his topic and his metaphor in the second poem, does Larkin arrive at a similar conclusion? Does the speaker seem to have aged or changed in the time between the poems?
5. Can you think of another animal that could be used as a metaphor for work? How would the metaphor operate? Compare your ideas to Larkin's toad.
6. The speaker of "Toads Revisited" says that a life of leisure is not for him. Would you say he's typical or unusual in this sense?

CONNECTIONS TO OTHER READINGS

7. Would the narrator of Ann Cummins's short story "Where I Work" also describe work as a "toad"?
8. Use Aristides's argument about work to analyze the speaker of Larkin's poems.
9. How would Larkin's speaker explain Bartleby's refusal to work (or preference not to work) in Melville's story "Bartleby, the Scrivener"?

Theodore Roethke

Dolor

Theodore Roethke (1908–1963) was, like his contemporary and sometime friend Robert Lowell, a volatile person whose success seemed to be driven by a fierce determination to write, and to be recognized for it. Roethke was an accomplished poet who was always looking over his shoulder at his colleagues. While holding down various college teaching positions and writing poetry, he was given to bouts of reckless drinking and mood swings, probably a form of manic depression. His subject matter ranged considerably, though many of his most famous poems return to the setting of his youth in Michigan. The title of the following poem, "Dolor," is a synonym for intense sadness.

I have known the inexorable sadness of pencils,
Neat in their boxes, dolor of pad and paper-weight,
All the misery of manilla folders and mucilage,
Desolation in immaculate public places,
Lonely reception room, lavatory, switchboard,
The unalterable pathos of basin and pitcher,
Ritual of multigraph, paper-clip, comma,
Endless duplication of lives and objects.
And I have seen dust from the walls of institutions,

Finer than flour, alive, more dangerous than silica,
Sift, almost invisible, through long afternoons of tedium,
Dropping a fine film on nails and delicate eyebrows,
Glazing the pale hair, the duplicate grey standard faces.

(1948)

QUESTIONS FOR DISCUSSION AND WRITING

CLOSE READING

1. Where do you see alliteration in the poem? How does it affect your understanding of the poem?
2. Determine the poem's meter and consider how it is appropriate to the poem's subject.
3. Consider the speaker's word choice: why are words like "inexorable," "immaculate," and "institutions" in the poem? What other words strike you as unusual and significant choices?

CRITICAL AND CREATIVE READING

4. Where do human beings show up in the poem? Why are they placed where they are?
5. Would it have been possible for the speaker to have written a poem in the same setting that is exuberant? Can boxes of pencils, for instance, represent happiness rather than inexorable sadness? What would have to change for this to be true?
6. The speaker of this poem uses the phrases "I have known" (line 1) and "I have seen" (line 9) to establish his authority. (This is a familiar formula: see T. S. Eliot's "The Love Song of J. Alfred Prufrock" in Chapter 12.) How do you imagine this speaker's relationship to this workplace?

CONNECTIONS TO OTHER READINGS

7. Which poem is more optimistic: Roethke's "Dolor" or Larkin's "Toad"?
8. Compare the office setting of this poem and in Marge Piercy's "The Secretary Chant" and/or Herman Melville's "Bartleby, the Scrivener."
9. Is nature an important factor in worker satisfaction? Compare this poem to "The Thresher's Labour," "Hay Making," "The Solitary Reaper," or "Sparkles from the Wheel" in your response.

Marge Piercy

The Secretary Chant

Marge Piercy (b. 1936) is a prolific writer of both novels and poetry collections: she currently has published seventeen of each. From humble beginnings in Detroit, she attended college on scholarship at the University

of Michigan, then received an MA at Northwestern in Chicago. Her life has taken her to the East Coast: after a period of activism, especially in response to the Vietnam War, she has settled on Cape Cod, where she and her husband continue to write and to publish the works of others at a small literary publisher called Leap Frog Press. The following poem was published in 1973, at the height of a period of intense struggle for women's liberation.

....

My hips are a desk.
From my ears hang
chains of paper clips.
Rubber bands form my hair.
My breasts are wells of mimeograph ink.
My feet bear casters.
Buzz. Click.
My head is a badly organized file.
My head is a switchboard
where crossed lines crackle.
Press my fingers
and in my eyes appear
credit and debit
Zing. Tinkle.
My navel is a reject button.
From my mouth issue canceled reams.
Swollen, heavy, rectangular
I am about to be delivered
of a baby
Xerox machine.
File me under W
because I wonce
was
a woman.

(1973)

Questions for Discussion and Writing

Close Reading

1. Discuss the poet's use of onomatopoeia, the convention of using words that sound like what they describe.
2. Consider the tone of the poem: how does the speaker's voice and the length of her lines reinforce the poem's central argument?

3. The poem can be seen as a series of metaphors. How would the poem's impact have changed if the poet had used similes throughout?
4. How and where does the poem use alliteration?

CRITICAL AND CREATIVE READING

5. Why is the poem titled "The Secretary Chant" instead of "Secretary's Chant" or "A Secretary's Chant"? Why "chant"?
6. The poem ends with the word "woman": could the poem have been written about a man who was dehumanized by his workplace? What would have to change, and what would be lost or gained?
7. The position of "secretary" is perhaps different from the way it was perceived in the early 1970s. (Indeed, the title *secretary* is not as common as it was then.) Write a twenty-first-century update of this poem, or "chant," accounting for changes in the workplace. Given the gendered conclusion of the poem, you might consider whether you want to make your chant conform to a job that is either stereotypically male or stereotypically female.

CONNECTIONS TO OTHER READINGS

8. Use Virginia Woolf's essay "Professions for Women" to analyze "The Secretary Chant."
9. Compare the way office spaces dehumanize workers in "The Secretary Chant," Theodore Roethke's poem "Dolor," and Melville's story "Bartleby, the Scrivener."
10. Compare the notion of "women's work" in Mary Collier's poem "The Woman's Labour" and in "The Secretary Chant."

Philip Levine

What Work Is

Philip Levine (b. 1928) is the recipient of many awards for his sixteen volumes of poetry, including the Pulitzer Prize and the National Book Award. The son of Jewish immigrants in Detroit, Levine worked in automobile factories there until he was twenty-six, at which point he pursued an education and a career as a poet. The substance of much of his poetry is the memory of his working-class youth. He lives in New York City and California and teaches at New York University.

We stand in the rain in a long line
waiting at Ford Highland Park. For work.
You know what work is—if you're

old enough to read this you know what
work is, although you may not do it.
Forget you. This is about waiting,
shifting from one foot to another.
Feeling the light rain falling like mist
into your hair, blurring your vision
until you think you see your own brother
ahead of you, maybe ten places.
You rub your glasses with your fingers,
and of course it's someone else's brother,
narrower across the shoulders than
yours but with the same sad slouch, the grin
that does not hide the stubbornness,
the sad refusal to give in to
rain, to the hours wasted waiting,
to the knowledge that somewhere ahead
a man is waiting who will say, "No,
we're not hiring today," for any
reason he wants. You love your brother,
now suddenly you can hardly stand
the love flooding you for your brother,
who's not beside you or behind or
ahead because he's home trying to
sleep off a miserable night shift
at Cadillac so he can get up
before noon to study his German.
Works eight hours a night so he can sing
Wagner, the opera you hate most,
the worst music ever invented.
How long has it been since you told him
you loved him, held his wide shoulders,
opened your eyes wide and said those words,
and maybe kissed his cheek? You've never
done something so simple, so obvious,
not because you're too young or too dumb,
not because you're jealous or even mean
or incapable of crying in
the presence of another man, no,
just because you don't know what work is.

(1991)

Questions for Discussion and Writing

Close Reading

1. Discuss the tension between individuals and groups in this poem. Pay particular attention to the way the poet uses the pronoun "you."

2. Why is "waiting" such an important motif in this poem?
3. How does the idea of "knowing what work is" change from the beginning of the poem to the end?

CRITICAL AND CREATIVE READING

4. What connections exist between the words "work" and "love"?
5. In a paragraph, write an essay inspired by the beginning of this sentence: "Work is . . ." Then compare your definition of work to the definition implied in Levine's poem. What points of contact exist between your definitions?
6. Can a person ever understand what work is simply by reading about it, or must work always be experienced?

CONNECTIONS TO OTHER READINGS

7. Examine Aristides's essay "Work and Its Contents." Based on his essay, do you imagine that the speaker of Levine's poem enjoys work or not?
8. Stephen Duck's "The Thresher's Labour" is also a poem about the working-class experience. Do Duck's poem and Levine's both attempt to educate the reader in some way? In the same way?
9. How does manual labor affect workers? Use Whitman's poem "Sparkles from the Wheel" and Levine's poem in your response. (You might also use Davis's story "Life in the Iron-Mills" or Cummins's story "Where I Work.")

Seamus Heaney

Digging

When Seamus Heaney won the Nobel Prize for literature in 1995, he had long been the most prominent of the many great poets active in Ireland during the time known as "the Troubles." Heaney was born into a rural Catholic household in Northern Ireland in 1939. By the mid-1960s, Northern Ireland was embroiled in a brutal undeclared war between Catholic separatists and Protestant loyalists. (The six counties of Northern Ireland are officially part of the United Kingdom, separate from the Republic of Ireland in the south.) Though violence has abated somewhat in recent years, the divisions in Northern Irish society are deep and painful. Heaney emigrated from Northern Ireland to Dublin in the early 1970s and has divided his time since then between Dublin, Oxford, and Cambridge, Massachusetts, where he regularly teaches at Harvard University. His work is characterized by a sense of rootedness to his own history and to the ancestral history of Ireland. The following poem, "Digging," is the first poem in his first collection of poetry.

Between my finger and my thumb
The squat pen rests; snug as a gun.

Under my window, a clean rasping sound
When the spade sinks into gravelly ground;
My father, digging. I look down

Till his straining rump among the flowerbeds
Bends low, comes up twenty years away
Stooping in rhythm through potato drills
Where he was digging.

The coarse boot nestled on the lug, the shaft
Against the inside knee was levered firmly.
He rooted out tall tops, buried the bright edge deep
To scatter new potatoes that we picked
Loving their cool hardness in our hands.

By God, the old man could handle a spade.
Just like his old man.

My grandfather cut more turf in a day
Than any other man on Toner's bog.
Once I carried him milk in a bottle
Corked sloppily with paper. He straightened up
To drink it, then fell to right away

Nicking and slicing neatly, heaving sods
Over his shoulder, going down and down
For the good turf. Digging.

The cold smell of potato mould, the squelch and slap
Of soggy peat, the curt cuts of an edge
Through living roots awaken in my head.
But I've no spade to follow men like them.

Between my finger and my thumb
The squat pen rests.
I'll dig with it.

(1966)

Questions for Discussion and Writing

Close Reading

1. The first stanza uses a slant rhyme, and the second stanza uses both slant rhyme and true end rhyme. What happens to this pattern as the poem continues? How can you use the rhyme scheme to make sense of the poem?

2. What is the relationship between the speaker and his father and his grandfather? How does he establish the relationship? How does he feel about it?
3. What is the effect of repeating the phrase "The squat pen rests" in the first and last stanzas of the poem? Does the phrase have a different meaning at these two points?

CRITICAL AND CREATIVE READING

4. Compare the poet's digging to his father's digging.
5. Writing poetry and digging potatoes are very different types of work. Is everyone capable of both?
6. Consider the imagery in the poem that suggests *life:* what accounts for it? Why does Heaney use this imagery?

CONNECTIONS TO OTHER READINGS

7. Write an essay about the poetic observation of manual labor using the following poems: Baillie's "Hay Making," Wordsworth's "The Solitary Reaper," Whitman's "Sparkles from the Wheel," and Heaney's "Digging."
8. Compare outdoor labor to office work: you can consider almost all the poems in this chapter for this question.
9. Write about the relationship between fathers and sons in terms of work using Heaney's "Digging" and Shakespeare's *I Henry IV* as your primary texts.

Elizabeth Alexander

Blues

Elizabeth Alexander (b. 1962) has written in a variety of genres, including poetry, short stories, critical writing, and verse drama. Born in Harlem, New York City, Alexander received her undergraduate education at Yale, earned a master's degree from Boston University, and completed her formal education at the University of Pennsylvania. She has also had an extensive and impressive teaching career, and in addition to giving poetry readings, she is a frequent lecturer on African American literature and culture. Consider the many connotations of the word *blues* as you read the following poem.

I am lazy, the laziest
girl in the world. I sleep during
the day when I want to, 'til
my face is creased and swollen,

'til my lips are dry and hot. I
eat as I please: cookies and milk
after lunch, butter and sour cream
on my baked potato, foods that
slothful people eat, that turn
yellow and opaque beneath the skin.
Sometimes come dinnertime Sunday
I am still in my nightgown, the one
with the lace trim listing because
I have not mended it. Many days
I do not exercise, only
consider it, then rub my curdy
belly and lie down. Even
my poems are lazy. I use
syllabics instead of iambs,
prefer slant to the gong of full rhyme,
write briefly while others go
for pages. And yesterday,
for example, I did not work at all!
I got in my car and I drove
to factory outlet stores, purchased
stockings and panties and socks
with my father's money.

To think, in childhood I missed only
one day of school per year. I went
to ballet class four days a week
at four-forty-five and on
Saturdays, beginning always
with plie ending with curtsy.
To think, I knew only industry,
the industry of my race
and of immigrants, the radio
tuned always to the station
that said, Line up your summer
job months in advance. Work hard
and do not shame your family,
who worked hard to give you what you have.
There is no sin but sloth. Burn
to a wick and keep moving.

I avoided sleep for years,
up at night replaying
evening news stories about

nearby jailbreaks, fat people
who ate fried chicken and woke up
dead. In sleep I am looking
for poems in the shape of open
V's of birds flying in formation,
or open arms saying, I forgive you, all.

(1996)

Questions for Discussion and Writing

Close Reading

1. Consider the poet's "critique" of her "lazy" poems in the first stanza: does her assessment of her own poetry hold true in this poem? (You may need to consult "Chapter 5, Reading and Writing about Poetry," for some of the technical terms she uses.)
2. How do you understand line 42, "There is no sin but sloth," in relation to the rest of the poem?
3. Why does the speaker describe herself as a "girl" in line 2? Is she a "girl" as opposed to a "woman"?

Critical and Creative Reading

4. Separate the three stanzas of the poem and reread them. Following your reading of each stanza, write an honest essay assessing your response to the speaker. How does it change?
5. Why is the poem titled "Blues"?
6. Does the "lazy" behavior of the speaker as an adult seem to be a rebellion against her youth? What does the relationship between her adult self and her child self have to do with "forgiveness" in the poem's final line?

Connections to Other Readings

7. The speaker links her childhood work habits to those of "immigrants" (line 36). Compare her childhood "industry" to the work habits of the Welsh iron-mill workers in Davis's "Life in the Iron-Mills."
8. Discuss the notion of "sloth" or "laziness" in this poem and in Irving's story "Rip Van Winkle." Do you admire Rip and this speaker in any way? If so, do you admire them for the same reasons?
9. Write an essay discussing parent/child relationships relative to work in this poem and in Seamus Heaney's "Digging."

Drama

William Shakespeare *(1564–1616)*

The First Part of Henry the Fourth

Critics generally divide Shakespeare's plays into three categories: comedies, tragedies, and history plays. (It is also common to refer to a handful of "problem plays" that are not easily categorized.) *I Henry IV* is a history play, so called because it is inspired by events and characters from history. However, Shakespeare was a dramatist and poet, not a careful historian, and he uses history mainly as a backdrop for drama. The following play is part of a cycle of four plays: *Richard II, I Henry IV, 2 Henry IV,* and *Henry V.* At the end of the fourteenth century, Henry Hereford, known as Bullingbrook, returned from exile in France when his father (John of Gaunt) died. In Shakespeare's imagination and in history, King Richard II was weak and inefficient, and Bullingbrook eventually took advantage of the chaotic situation by forcing Richard II to abdicate his throne and then killing him in prison. Bullingbrook became King Henry IV, the monarch in this play whose power was secured in the decisive Battle of Shrewsbury (1403), which forms the climax in Act V.

Two other figures emerge as interesting, central characters in this play. The first is Henry IV's son, Prince "Hal," who famously decides to play hooky from his princely duties in favor of spending time among some shady tavern-dwellers, whose characteristic activities include drinking, stealing, and spending time with women of ill repute. The other notable figure is Sir John Falstaff, the leader of this band of rogues. Falstaff is a fat, notorious drunkard. He is a recurrent character in Shakespeare's plays because he can provide comic relief to tense situations and is a safe character for satire, so confident is he with his position in the world. Far from a subplot, the story surrounding Prince Hal and Falstaff is of primary importance in the play, particularly when we consider the theme of work. Here, as in many cases, "work" is tied to "duty." Before you begin reading, consider how you might react if you were born into a position of responsibility. If you cannot imagine yourself as royalty, make the circumstances more immediate: what if you were expected to take over the family business? How would you react to this mandate, especially once you reached adolescence?

DRAMATIS PERSONAE

King Henry the Fourth
Henry, Prince of Wales
sons to the King
Prince John of Lancaster

Earl of Westmerland
Sir Walter Blunt
Thomas Percy, Earl of Worcester
Henry Percy, Earl of Northumberland
Henry Percy, surnamed *Hotspur*, his son
Edmund Mortimore, Earl of March
Richard Scroop, Archbishop of York
Archibald, Earl of Douglas
Owen Glendower
Sir Richard Vernon
Sir John Falstaff
Sir Michael, of the household of the Archbishop of York
Edward Poins, gentleman-in-waiting to Prince Henry
Gadshill
Peto
Bardolph
Lady Percy, wife to Hotspur, and sister to Mortimer
Lady Mortimer, daughter to Glendower, and wife to Mortimer
Mistress Quickly, hostess of the Boar's Head Tavern in Eastcheap
Lords, *Officer*, *Sheriff*, *Vintner*, *Chamberlain*, *Ostler*, *Drawers*, two *Carriers*, *Travellers*, and *Attendants*

[Scene: England and Wales]

ACT I

Scene I

Enter the King [Henry], Lord John of Lancaster, Earl of Westmerland, [Sir Walter Blunt,] *with others.*

King: So shaken as we are, so wan with care,
Find we a time for frighted peace to pant
And breathe short-winded accents of new broils
To be commenc'd in stronds afar remote.
No more the thirsty entrance of this soil
Shall daub her lips with her own children's blood,
No more shall trenching war channel her fields,
Nor bruise her flow'rets with the armed hoofs
Of hostile paces. Those opposed eyes,
Which, like the meteors of a troubled heaven,

I.i. Location: London. The palace. 2 **Find we:** let us find. 3 **accents:** words.
3–4 **new . . . remote.** At the close of *Richard II* (V.vi.49–50) the newly crowned Henry IV, remorseful for the death of Richard, had promised to "make a voyage to the Holy Land / To wash this blood off from my guilty hand." 4 **stronds:** strands, shores.
5 **thirsty entrance:** parched mouth. 7 **trenching:** cutting 8–9 **armed . . . paces:** tread of armed horses in combat.

All of one nature, of one substance bred,
Did lately meet in the intestine shock
And furious close of civil butchery,
Shall now, in mutual well-beseeming ranks,
March all one way and be no more oppos'd
Against acquaintance, kindred, and allies.
The edge of war, like an ill-sheathed knife,
No more shall cut his master. Therefore, friends,
As far as to the sepulchre of Christ—
Whose soldier now, under whose blessed cross
We are impressed and engag'd to fight—
Forthwith a power of English shall we levy,
Whose arms were moulded in their mother's womb,
To chase these pagans in those holy fields,
Over whose acres walk'd those blessed feet
Which fourteen hundred years ago were nail'd
For our advantage on the bitter cross.
But this our purpose now is twelve month old,
And bootless 'tis to tell you we will go;
Therefore we meet not now. Then let me hear
Of you, my gentle cousin Westmerland,
What yesternight our Council did decree
In forwarding this dear expedience.

Westmerland: My liege, this haste was hot in question.
And many limits of the charge set down
But yesternight, when all athwart there came
A post from Wales loaden with heavy news,
Whose worst was that the noble Mortimer,
Leading the men of [Herfordshire] to fight
Against the irregular and wild Glendower,
Was by the rude hands of that Welshman taken,

---

12 **intestine:** internal. 13 **close:** hand-to-hand combat. 14 **mutual:** united for a common purpose. 18 **his:** its. 21 **impressed:** conscripted. **engag'd:** pledged. 22 **power:** force, army. 28 **twelve month old.** Actually, two years separated Richard II's death (1400) and the battle of Homildon (Shakespeare's Holmedon), news of which reaches the King at lines 52 ff. 29 **bootless:** useless. 30 **Therefore . . . now:** it is not for this purpose that we meet now. 31 **gentle cousin:** noble kinsman. 33 **dear expedience:** urgent undertaking. 34 **liege:** sovereign. **hot in question:** under urgent discussion. 35 **limits . . . down:** specific military responsibilities assigned. 36 **athwart:** across (the plans). 37 **post:** messenger. **heavy:** sad, depressing. 38 **Mortimer.** Shakespeare, like English historian Raphael Holinshed (d. 1580), had trouble keeping the Mortimers straight. By marrying (1368) Philippa, daughter of Lionel, Duke of Clarence, third son of Edward III, Edmund Mortimer, third Earl of March, raised his family to a place of great importance. In 1385 his son Roger, fourth Earl of March, was recognized by Richard II as heir presumptive to the throne. In the present scene Shakespeare confuses Glendower's captive Sir Edmund Mortimer (1376–?1409), Roger's younger brother, with Roger's son Edmund (1391–1425), fifth and last Earl of March, who had been named heir presumptive by Richard II in 1398 after the death of the fourth earl. 40 **irregular:** i.e., because he resorted to guerrilla warfare.

A thousand of his people butchered,
Upon whose dead corpse' there was such misuse,
Such beastly shameless transformation,
By those Welshwomen done as may not be
Without much shame retold or spoken of.

King: It seems then that the tidings of this broil
Brake off our business for the Holy Land.

Westmerland: This match'd with other did, my gracious lord,
For more uneven and unwelcome news
Came from the north, and thus it did import:
On Holy-rood day, the gallant Hotspur there,
Young Harry Percy, and brave Archibald,
That ever-valiant and approved Scot,
At Holmedon met,
Where they did spend a sad and bloody hour,
As by discharge of their artillery
And shape of likelihood the news was told;
For he that brought them, in the very heat
And pride of their contention did take horse,
Uncertain of the issue any way.

King: Here is [a] dear, a true industrious friend,
Sir Walter Blunt, new lighted from his horse,
Stain'd with the variation of each soil
Betwixt that Holmedon and this seat of ours;
And he hath brought us smooth and welcome news.
The Earl of Douglas is discomfited:
Ten thousand bold Scots, two and twenty knights,
Balk'd in their own blood, did Sir Walter see
On Holmedon's plains. Of prisoners, Hotspur took
Mordake Earl of Fife and eldest son

---

43 **corpse':** corpses. 44 **transformation:** mutilation. According to Holinshed (Bullough, IV, 182), "the shamefull villanie used by the Welsh-women towards the dead carcasses [of the English], was such, as honest eares would be ashamed to heare, and continent toongs to speake thereof." 48 **Brake:** broke. 49 **other:** i.e., other tidings. Actually, the battle at Homildon (or Humbleton) Hill in Northumberland (September 1402) occurred three months after Mortimer's capture by Glendower. 50 **uneven:** disturbing. 52 **Holy-rood day:** September 14. 53 **Young Harry Percy.** Although here and elsewhere (for example, III.ii.103) Shakespeare implies that Sir Henry Percy, eldest son of the first Earl of Northumberland, was a high-spirited youth, he was in fact thirty-eight years old in 1402, twenty-three years the senior of Prince Hal, his rival and presumed contemporary in this play. **brave Archibald:** Archibald Douglas (1369?–1424), fourth Earl of Douglas and first Duke of Touraine, a Scot noted for his valor. 58 **shape of likelihood:** apparent probability. 59 **them:** i.e., the news. 60 **pride:** height. 62 **true industrious:** truly devoted. 69 **Balk'd:** heaped up in balks or ridges. 71 **Mordake.** Murdac Stewart, son of Robert Stewart, first Earl of Albany and "governor" of Scotland. Shakespeare's erroneously calling him the son of Archibald Douglas results from the faulty punctuation in Holinshed (Bullough, IV, 183): "of prisoners among other were these, Mordacke earle of Fife, son to the governour Archembald earle Dowglas, which in the fight lost one of his eies, Thomas erle of Murrey, Robert earle of Angus (and as some writers have) the earles of Atholl & Menteith, with five hundred other of meaner degrees."

To beaten Douglas, and the Earl of Athol,
Of Murray, Angus, and Menteith.
And is not this an honorable spoil?
A gallant prize? Ha, cousin, is it not?

Westmerland: In faith,
It is a conquest for a prince to boast of.

King: Yea, there thou mak'st me sad, and mak'st me sin
In envy that the Lord Northumberland
Should be the father to so blest a son—
A son who is the theme of honor's tongue,
Amongst a grove the very straightest plant,
Who is sweet Fortune's minion and her pride,
Whilst I, by looking on the praise of him,
See riot and dishonor stain the brow
Of my young Harry. O that it could be prov'd
That some night-tripping fairy had exchang'd
In cradle-clothes our children where they lay,
And call'd mine Percy, his Plantagenet!
Then would I have his Harry and he mine.
But let him from my thoughts. What think you, coz,
Of this young Percy's pride? The prisoners
Which he in this adventure hath surpris'd
To his own use he keeps, and sends me word
I shall have none but Mordake Earl of Fife.

Westmerland: This is his uncle's teaching; this is Worcester,
Malevolent to you in all aspects,
Which makes him prune himself, and bristle up
The crest of youth against your dignity.

King: But I have sent for him to answer this;
And for this cause a while we must neglect
Our holy purpose to Jerusalem.
Cousin, on Wednesday next our Council we
Will hold at Windsor, so inform the lords.
But come yourself with speed to us again,
For more is to be said and to be done
Than out of anger can be uttered.

Westmerland: I will, my liege. *Exeunt.*

---

82 **plant:** tree. 83 **minion:** darling. 87 **Some . . . fairy.** It was popularly believed that defective children were "changelings" left by fairies in exchange for babies whom they had abducted. 89 **Plantagenet:** family name of the English royal family. 91 **from:** go from. **coz:** cousin, i.e., kinsman. 93 **surpris'd:** captured. 94 **To . . . use:** i.e., for purpose of ransom. 95 **none but Mordake.** Although Hotspur could legitimately hold the other prisoners he had taken, the law of arms required that Murdac, being of royal blood, be surrendered to the King. 97 **Malevolent . . . aspects:** i.e., habitually hostile (a metaphor from astrology). 98 **Which:** i.e., Worcester's "teaching." **prune:** preen, trim (a term from falconry). 101 **neglect:** put aside. 107 **uttered:** said in public.

A scene from *The First Part of Henry the Fourth.*

Scene II

Enter Prince of Wales *and* Sir John Falstaff.

Falstaff: Now, Hal, what time of day is it, lad?

Prince: Thou art so fat-witted with drinking of old sack, and unbuttoning thee after supper, and sleeping upon benches after noon, that thou hast forgotten to demand that truly which thou wouldest truly know. What a devil hast thou to do with the time of the day? unless hours were cups of sack, and minutes capons, and clocks the tongues of bawds, and dials the signs of leaping-houses, and the blessed sun himself a fair hot wench in flame-color'd taffata; I see no reason why thou shouldst be so superfluous to demand the time of the day.

Falstaff: Indeed you come near me now, Hal, for we that take purses go by the moon and the seven stars, and not by Phoebus, he, "that wand'ring knight so fair." And I prithee, sweet wag, when thou art a

---

I.ii. Location: London. Prince Henry's house. 3 **sack:** dry Spanish wine. 8 **dials:** clocks. 9 **leaping-houses:** brothels. 10 **taffata:** taffeta (often worn by prostitutes). 14 **seven stars:** constellation of the Pleiades. 15–16 **Phoebus . . . fair.** Falstaff identifies Phoebus, the sun-god or knight of the sun, with the knight errant ("wand'ring knight") of a popular romance. 16 **wag:** rogue.

king, as, God save thy Grace—Majesty I should say,
for grace thou wilt have none—

Prince: What, none?

Falstaff: No, by my troth, not so much as will serve to
be prologue to an egg and butter.

Prince: Well, how then? Come, roundly, roundly.

Falstaff: Marry, then, sweet wag, when thou art king,
let not us that are squires of the night's body be call'd
thieves of the day's beauty. Let us be Diana's
foresters, gentlemen of the shade, minons of the moon,
and let men say we be men of good government, being
govern'd, as the sea is, by our noble and chaste mistress
the moon, under whose countenance we steal.

Prince: Thou sayest well, and it holds well too, for
the fortune of us that are the moon's men doth ebb and
flow like the sea, being govern'd, as the sea is, by the
moon. As, for proof, now: a purse of gold most
resolutely snatch'd on Monday night and most dis-
solutely spent on Tuesday morning; got with
swearing "Lay by," and spent with crying "Bring in";
now in as low an ebb as the foot of the ladder, and by
and by in as high a flow as the ridge of the gallows.

Falstaff: By the Lord, thou say'st true, lad. And is not
my hostess of the tavern a most sweet wench?

Prince: As the honey of Hybla, my old lad of the
castle. And is not a buff jerkin a most sweet robe of
durance?

Falstaff: How now, how now, mad wag? What, in thy
quips and thy quiddities? What a plague have I to do
with a buff jerkin?

Prince: Why, what a pox have I to do with my
hostess of the tavern?

Falstaff: Well, thou hast call'd her to a reckoning many
a time and oft.

Prince: Did I ever call for thee to pay thy part?

Falstaff: No, I'll give thee thy due, thou hast paid all
there.

---

18 **grace:** virtue, sense of propriety. 20 **troth:** faith. 21 **prologue . . . butter:** i.e., a short grace before a skimpy meal. 22 **roundly:** directly. 23 **Marry:** indeed (originally the name of the Virgin Mary used as an oath). 25–26 **Diana's foresters:** i.e., thieves (Diana being the moon-goddess). 26 **minions:** darlings. 27 **government:** behavior. 29 **countenance:** (1) face; (2) protection, patronage. 30 **holds well:** is apt. 36 **Lay by:** hands up. 37 **ladder:** i.e., to the gallows. 41 **Hybla:** region of Sicily noted for its honey. 41–42 **old . . . castle:** (1) cant phrase for roisterer; (2) an allusion to Sir John Oldcastle, the name that Shakespeare originally intended for Falstaff. 42 **buff jerkin:** leather jacket (often worn by jailers). 42–43 **of durance:** (1) durable, serviceable; (2) of imprisonment. 45 **quiddities:** subtle jests. 49 **reckoning:** settling of the bill.

Prince: Yea, and elsewhere, so far as my coin would stretch, and where it would not, I have us'd my credit.

Falstaff: Yea, and so us'd it that, were it not here apparent that thou art heir apparent—But I prithee, sweet wag, shall there be gallows standing in England when thou art king? and resolution thus fubb'd as it is with the rusty curb of old father antic the law? Do not thou, when thou art king, hang a thief.

Prince: No, thou shalt.

Falstaff: Shall I? O rare! By the Lord, I'll be a brave judge.

Prince: Thou judgest false already. I mean thou shalt have the hanging of the thieves, and so become a rare hangman.

Falstaff: Well, Hal, well, and in some sort it jumps with my humor as well as waiting in the court, I can tell you.

Prince: For obtaining of suits?

Falstaff: Yea, for obtaining of suits, whereof the hangman hath no lean wardrobe. 'Sblood, I am as melancholy as a gib cat or a lugg'd bear.

Prince: Or an old lion, or a lover's lute.

Falstaff: Yea, or the drone of a Lincolnshire bagpipe.

Prince: What sayest thou to a hare, or the melancholy of Moor-ditch?

Falstaff: Thou hast the most unsavory [similes] and art indeed the most comparative, rascalliest, sweet young prince. But, Hal, I prithee trouble me no more with vanity; I would to God thou and I knew where a commodity for good names were to be bought. An old lord of the Council rated me the other day in the street about you, sir, but I mark'd him not, and yet he talk'd very wisely, but I regarded him not, and yet he talk'd wisely, and in the street too.

Prince: Thou didst well, for wisdom cries out in the streets, and no man regards it.

Falstaff: O, thou hast damnable iteration, and art indeed able to corrupt a saint. Thou hast done much

---

60 **resolution:** i.e., the valor of thieves. **fubb'd:** fobbed, thwarted. 61 **antic:** clown, buffoon. 64 **brave:** fine. 69–70 **in . . . humor:** in some ways it suits my temperament. 71 **suits:** petitions (but Falstaff plays on another sense: the clothing of an executed person that was claimed by the hangman). 73 **'Sblood:** by God's (Christ's) blood. 74 **gib cat:** tomcat. **lugg'd:** led (as with a chain). 77 **hare:** i.e., because of its melancholy appearance. 78 **Moor-ditch:** open sewer or drainage ditch outside the walls of London. 80 **comparative:** i.e., given to (unflattering) comparisons. 83 **commodity:** supply. 84 **rated:** berated. 88–89 **wisdom . . . it.** An echo of Proverbs 1:23, 24. 90 **iteration:** i.e., trick of repeating biblical texts (with a satirical twist).

harm upon me, Hal, God forgive thee for it? Before I
knew thee, Hal, I knew nothing, and now am I, if a
man should speak truly, little better than one of the
wicked. I must give over this life, and I will give
it over. By the Lord, and I do not, I am a villain,
I'll be damn'd for never a king's son in Christendom.

Prince: Where shall we take a purse to-morrow, Jack?

Falstaff: 'Zounds, where thou wilt, lad, I'll make one,
an' I do not, call me villain and baffle me.

Prince: I see a good amendment of life in thee,
from praying to purse-taking.

Falstaff: Why, Hal, 'tis my vocation, Hal, 'tis no sin
for a man to labor in his vocation.

Enter Poins.

Poins! Now shall we know if Gadshill have set a
match. O, if men were to be sav'd by merit, what hole
in hell were hot enough for him? This is the most
omnipotent villain that ever cried "Stand!" to a true man.

Prince: Good morrow, Ned.

Poins: Good morrow, sweet Hal. What says
Monsieur Remorse? What says Sir John Sack and
Sugar? Jack, how agrees the devil and thee about thy
soul that thou soldest him on Good Friday last, for a
cup of Madeira and a cold capon's leg?

Prince: Sir John stands to his word, the devil shall
have his bargain, for he was never yet a breaker of
proverbs. He will give the devil his due.

Poins: Then art thou damn'd for keeping thy word
with the devil.

Prince: Else he had been damn'd for cozening the
devil.

Poins: But, my lads, my lads, to-morrow morning
by four a' clock early, at Gadshill, there are
pilgrims going to Canterbury with rich offerings, and
traders riding to London with fat purses. I have
vizards for you all; you have horses for yourselves.
Gadshill lies to-night in Rochester. I have bespoke

---

96 **and:** if. 100 **'Zounds:** by God's (Christ's) wounds. **make one:** be one of the party.
101 **an':** and, i.e., if. **baffle:** disgrace (literally, deprive a perjured knight of his rank).
106 **Gadshill:** the name of one of the thieves. 106–7 **set a match:** planned a robbery.
109 **true:** honest. 115 **Good Friday:** i.e., the most solemn of fast days.
117 **stands to:** keeps. 119 **his due:** i.e., Falstaff's soul. 122 **cozening:** cheating.
125 **Gadshill:** hill near Rochester on the road from London to Canterbury, notorious for its robberies. 128 **vizards:** masks. 129 **lies:** lodges.

supper to-morrow night in Eastcheap. We may do it as secure as sleep. If you will go, I will stuff your purses full of crowns; if you will not, tarry at home and be hang'd.

Falstaff: Hear ye, Yedward, if I tarry at home and go not, I'll hang you for going.

Poins: You will, chops?

Falstaff: Hal, wilt thou make one?

Prince: Who, I rob? I a thief? Not I, by my faith.

Falstaff: There's neither honesty, manhood, nor good fellowship in thee, nor thou cam'st not of the blood royal, if thou darest not stand for ten shillings.

Prince: Well then, once in my days I'll be a mad-cap.

Falstaff: Why, that's well said.

Prince: Well, come what will, I'll tarry at home.

Falstaff: By the Lord, I'll be a traitor then, when thou art king.

Prince: I care not.

Poins: Sir John, I prithee leave the Prince and me alone, I will lay him down such reasons for this adventure that he shall go.

Falstaff: Well, God give thee the spirit of persuasion and him the ears of profiting, that what thou speakest may move and what he hears may be believ'd, that the true prince may (for recreation sake) prove a false thief, for the poor abuses of the time want countenance. Farewell, you shall find me in Eastcheap.

Prince: Farewell, the latter spring! Farewell, All-hallown summer! [*Exit Falstaff.*]

Poins: Now, my good sweet honey lord, ride with us to-morrow. I have a jest to execute that I cannot manage alone. Falstaff, [Bardolph, Peto], and Gadshill shall rob those men that we have already way-laid; yourself and I will not be there; and when they have the booty, if you and I do not rob them, cut this head off from my shoulders.

Prince: How shall we part with them in setting forth?

Poins: Why, we will set forth before or after them and appoint them a place of meeting, wherein it is at

---

130 **Eastcheap:** thoroughfare in London, site of the tavern of line 40. 136 **chops:** fat-face. 141 **royal.** With a pun on *royal* = a gold coin worth ten shillings. **stand for:** (1) make a fight for; (2) be worth. 156 **want countenance:** lack encouragement (from men of rank like the Prince). 158 **latter spring:** i.e., old man with youthful impulses. 158–59 **All-hallown summer:** i.e., Indian summer. All-hallows (or All Saints') Day is November 1. 163–64 **waylaid:** set an ambush for.

our pleasure to fail; and then will they adventure
upon the exploit themselves, which they shall have no
sooner achiev'd but we'll set upon them.

Prince: Yea, but 'tis like that they will know us by
our horses, by our habits, and by every other appointment to be ourselves.

Poins: Tut, our horses they shall not see—I'll tie
them in the wood; our vizards we will change after we
leave them; and, sirrah, I have cases of buckrom for
the nonce, to immask our noted outward garments.

Prince: Yea, but I doubt they will be too hard for us.

Poins: Well, for two of them, I know them to be
as true-bred cowards as ever turn'd back; and for the
third, if he fight longer than he sees reason, I'll for-
swear arms. The virtue of this jest will be the
incomprehensible lies that this same fat rogue will tell
us when we meet at supper, how thirty at least he
fought with, what wards, what blows, what extremities
he endur'd, and in the reproof of this lives the jest.

Prince: Well, I'll go with thee. Provide us all
things necessary, and meet me to-morrow night in
Eastcheap, there I'll sup. Farewell.

Poins: Farewell, my lord. *Exit Poins.*

Prince: I know you all, and will a while uphold
The unyok'd humor of your idleness,
Yet herein will I imitate the sun,
Who doth permit the base contagious clouds
To smother up his beauty from the world,
That when he please again to be himself,
Being wanted, he may be more wond'red at
By breaking through the foul and ugly mists
Of vapors that did seem to strangle him.
If all the year were playing holidays,
To sport would be as tedious as to work;
But when they seldom come, they wish'd for come,
And nothing pleaseth but rare accidents.
So when this loose behavior I throw off
And pay the debt I never promised,
By how much better than my word I am,

---

175 **habits:** clothes. 175–76 **appointment:** accoutrement. 179 **sirrah:** customarily a form of address to an inferior; here, a term of comradeship. 179–80 **cases . . . nonce:** garments of buckram (stiff, coarse cloth) suitable for the occasion. 180 **noted:** well-known. 181 **doubt:** fear. **too hard:** i.e., too many. 189 **wards:** postures of defense, parries. 190 **reproof:** disproof. 196 **unyok'd . . . idleness:** undisciplined tendency of your frivolity. 198 **contagious:** noxious (because fogs were thought to breed pestilence). 200 **That:** so that. 201 **wanted:** missed. 207 **rare accidents:** exceptional events.

By so much shall I falsify men's hopes,
And like bright metal on a sullen ground,
My reformation, glitt'ring o'er my fault,
Shall show more goodly and attract more eyes
Than that which hath no foil to set it off.
I'll so offend, to make offense a skill,
Redeeming time when men think least I will. *Exit.*

Scene III

Enter the King, Northumberland, Worcester, Hotspur, Sir Walter Blunt, *with others.*

King: My blood hath been too cold and temperate,
Unapt to stir at these indignities,
And you have found me, for accordingly
You tread upon my patience; but be sure
I will from henceforth rather be myself,
Mighty and to be fear'd, than my condition,
Which hath been smooth as oil, soft as young down,
And therefore lost that title of respect
Which the proud soul ne'er pays but to the proud.

Worcester: Our house, my sovereign liege, little deserves
The scourge of greatness to be us'd on it,
And that same greatness too which our own hands
Have holp to make so portly.

Northumberland: My lord—

King: Worcester, get thee gone, for I do see
Danger and disobedience in thine eye.
O, sir, your presence is too bold and peremptory,
And majesty might never yet endure
The moody frontier of a servant brow.
You have good leave to leave us. When we need
Your use and counsel, we shall send for you.

[Exit Worcester.]

---

211 **hopes:** expectations. 212 **sullen ground:** dark background. 215 **foil:** thin sheet of metal set behind a jewel to enhance its brilliance. 216 **to:** as to. **skill:** i.e., something good and clever. 217 **Redeeming time:** making up for misspent time.

I.iii. Location: London. The palace. 2 **Unapt:** slow. 3 **found me:** i.e., found me so mild. 5 **myself:** i.e., my kingly self. 6 **my condition:** my (naturally mild) disposition. 10 **Our house:** i.e., the Percy family, which had thrown its powerful support to Bullingbrook on his return from exile. Worcester was Northumberland's brother and thus Hotspur's uncle. 13 **holp:** helped. **portly:** stately. 16 **Danger:** defiance. 17 **peremptory:** imperious. 19 **moody frontier:** i.e., frowning forehead.

You were about to speak.
Northumberland: Yea, my good lord.
Those prisoners in your Highness' name demanded,
Which Harry Percy here at Holmedon took,
Were, as he says, not with such strength denied
As is delivered to your Majesty.
Either envy, therefore, or misprision
Is guilty of this fault, and not my son.
Hotspur: My liege, I did deny no prisoners,
But I remember, when the fight was done,
When I was dry with rage and extreme toil,
Breathless and faint, leaning upon my sword,
Came there a certain lord, neat, and trimly dress'd,
Fresh as a bridegroom, and his chin new reap'd
Show'd like a stubble-land at harvest-home.
He was perfumed like a milliner,
And 'twixt his finger and his thumb he held
A pouncet-box, which ever and anon
He gave his nose and took't away again,
Who therewith angry, when it next came there,
Took it in snuff—and still he smil'd and talk'd:
And as the soldiers bore dead bodies by,
He call'd them untaught knaves, unmannerly,
To bring a slovenly unhandsome corse
Betwixt the wind and his nobility.
With many holiday and lady terms
He questioned me, amongst the rest demanded
My prisoners in your Majesty's behalf.
I then, all smarting with my wounds being cold,
To be so pest'red with a popinjay,
Out of my grief and my impatience
Answer'd neglectingly, I know not what—
He should, or he should not—for he made me mad
To see him shine so brisk and smell so sweet,
And talk so like a waiting-gentlewoman
Of guns, and drums, and wounds, God save the mark!
And telling me the sovereignest thing on earth
Was parmaciti for an inward bruise,

---

25 **strength:** vehemence. 26 **delivered:** reported. 27 **envy:** malice. **misprision:** misunderstanding. 34 **chin new reap'd:** i.e., beard freshly clipped. 35 **Show'd:** looked. 38 **pouncet-box:** pomander, perfume box. 40 **Who:** which (i.e., his nose). 41 **Took . . . snuff:** (1) snuffed it up; (2) was offended. **still:** continually. 44 **corse:** corpse. 46 **many . . . terms:** much dainty and effeminate language. 47 **questioned:** prattled to. **the rest:** other things. 50 **popingjay:** popinjay, parrot. 51 **grief:** pain. 52 **neglectingly:** without considering. 56 **God . . . mark:** God forbid. 57 **sovereignest thing:** most efficacious remedy. 58 **parmaciti:** ointment made of spermaceti or whale sperm.

And that it was great pity, so it was,
This villainous saltpetre should be digg'd
Out of the bowels of the harmless earth,
Which many a good tall fellow had destroyed
So cowardly, and but for these vile guns
He would himself have been a soldier.
This bald unjointed chat of his, my lord.
I answered indirectly, as I said,
And I beseech you, let not his report
Come current for an accusation
Betwixt my love and your high Majesty.

Blunt: The circumstance considered, good my lord,
What e'er Lord Harry Percy then had said
To such a person, and in such a place,
At such a time, with all the rest retold,
My reasonably die, and never rise
To do him wrong, or any way impeach
What then he said, so he unsay it now.

King: Why, yet he doth deny his prisoners,
But with proviso and exception,
That we at our own charge shall ransom straight
His brother-in-law, the foolish Mortimer,
Who, on my soul, hath willfully betray'd
The lives of those that he did lead to fight
Against that great magician, damn'd Glendower,
Whose daughter, as we hear, that Earl of March
Hath lately married. Shall our coffers then
Be emptied to redeem a traitor home?
Shall we buy treason? and indent with fears,
When they have lost and forfeited themselves?
No, on the barren mountains let him starve;
For I shall never hold that man my friend

---

62 **tall:** brave. 63 **but:** except. 65 **bald:** trivial. 68 **Come current:** be accepted as valid. 71 **had:** may have. 75 **impeach:** discredit. 76 **so:** provided that. 78 **But . . . exception:** unless on the condition. 79 **charge:** expense. **straight:** immediately. 80 **brother-in-law.** Hotspur's wife Elizabeth (called Kate in this play) was the sister of Roger, fourth Earl of March, and of Sir Edmund Mortimer (who married Glendower's daughter). 83 **magician:** Following Mortimer's capture, reports Holinshed (Bullough, IV, 182–83), Henry himself led an expedition to take Glendower, but the Welshman "conveied himself out of the waie, into his knowen lurking places, and (as was thought) through art magike, he caused such foule weather of winds, tempest, raine, snow, and haile to be raised, for the annoiance of the kings armie, that the like had not been heard of." 84–85 **Whose . . . married.** Once Mortimer had been captured, says Holinshed (Bullough, IV, 184), he, "whether for irkesomnesse of cruell captivitie, or feare of death, or for what other cause, it is uncerteine, agreed to take part with Owen [Glendower], against the king of England, and tooke to wife the daughter of the said Owen." 87 **indent with fears:** i.e., come to terms with persons who have given us cause to fear them.

Whose tongue shall ask me for one penny cost
To ransom home revolted Mortimer.

Hotspur: Revolted Mortimer!
He never did fall off, my sovereign liege,
But by the chance of war; to prove that true
Needs no more but one tongue for all those wounds,
Those mouthed wounds, which valiantly he took,
When on the gentle Severn's sedgy bank,
In single opposition hand to hand,
He did confound the best part of an hour
In changing hardiment with great Glendower.
Three times they breath'd and three times did they drink,
Upon agreement, of swift Severn's flood,
Who then affrighted with their bloody looks,
Ran fearfully among the trembling reeds,
And hid his crisp head in the hollow bank,
Blood-stained with these valiant combatants.
Never did bare and rotten policy
Color her working with such deadly wounds,
Nor never could the noble Mortimer
Receive so many, and all willingly.
Then let not him be slandered with revolt.

King: Thou dost belie him, Percy, thou dost belie him;
He never did encounter with Glendower.
I tell thee,
He durst as well have met the devil alone
As Owen Glendower for an enemy.
Art thou not asham'd? But, sirrah, henceforth
Let me not hear you speak of Mortimer.
Send me your prisoners with the speediest means,
Or you shall hear in such a kind from me
As will displease you. My Lord Northumberland:
We license your departure with your son.
Send us your prisoners, or you will hear of it.

Exit King *[with* Blunt *and* Train*]*.

Hotspur: And if the devil come and roar for them,
I will not send them. I will after straight

---

92 **revolted:** rebellious. 97 **mouthed:** gaping. 100 **confound:** consume.
101 **changing hardiment:** matching valor. 102 **breath'd:** stopped to get their breath.
106 **crisp head:** curled head, i.e., rippled surface. 108 **policy:** cunning, trickery.
112 **revolt:** i.e., accusation of rebellion. 113 **belie:** not tell the truth about.

And tell him so, for I will ease my heart,
Albeit I make a hazard of my head.

Northumberland: What? drunk with choler? Stay, and pause
a while.
Here comes your uncle.

Enter Worcester.

Hotspur: Speak of Mortimer!
'Zounds, I will speak of him, and let my soul
Want mercy if I do not join with him.
Yea, on his part I'll empty all these veins,
And shed my dear blood drop by drop in the dust,
But I will lift the down-trod Mortimer
As high in the air as this unthankful king,
As this ingrate and cank'red Bullingbrook.

Northumberland: Brother, the King hath made your nephew mad.

Worcester: Who strook this heat up after I was gone?

Hotspur: He will, forsooth, have all my prisoners,
And when I urg'd the ransom once again
Of my wive's brother, then his cheek look'd pale,
And on my face he turn'd an eye of death,
Trembling even at the name of Mortimer.

Worcester: I cannot blame him: was not he proclaim'd
By Richard, that dead is, the next of blood?

Northumberland: He was, I heard the proclamation.
And then it was when the unhappy king
(Whose wrongs in us God pardon!) did set forth
Upon his Irish expedition;
From whence he intercepted did return
To be depos'd, and shortly murdered.

Worcester: And for whose death we in the world's wide mouth
Live scandaliz'd and foully spoken of.

Hotspur: But soft, I pray you, did King Richard then
Proclaim my brother Edmund Mortimer
Heir to the crown?

Northumberland: He did, myself did hear it.

Hotspur: Nay, then I cannot blame his cousin king,
That wish'd him on the barren mountains starve.
But shall it be that you, that set the crown
Upon the head of this forgetful man,

---

126 **after straight:** go after him at once. 129 **choler:** anger. 132 **Want:** lack. 133 **on his part:** in his behalf. 137 **cank'red:** malignant. 140 **forsooth:** indeed. 142 **wive's:** wife's. 147–50 **I . . . expedition.** Shakespeare again confuses the Mortimers; see note to I.i.38. 149 **Whose . . . us:** i.e., the wrongs that we did to him (by supporting Bullingbrook). 151 **intercepted:** interrupted (by Bullingbrook's return from exile). 154 **scandaliz'd:** defamed.

And for his sake wear the detested blot
Of murtherous subornation—shall it be
That you a world of curses undergo,
Being the agents or base second means,
The cords, the ladder, or the hangman rather?
O, pardon me that I descend so low
To show the line and the predicament
Wherein you range under this subtile king?
Shall it for shame be spoken in these days,
Or fill up chronicles in time to come,
That men of your nobility and power
Did gage them both in an unjust behalf
(As both of you—God pardon it!—have done)
To put down Richard, that sweet lovely rose,
And plant this thorn, this canker, Bullingbrook?
And shall it in more shame be further spoken,
That you are fool'd, discarded, and shook off
By him for whom these shames ye underwent?
No, yet time serves wherein you may redeem
Your banish'd honors and restore yourselves
Into the good thoughts of the world again;
Revenge the jeering and disdain'd contempt
Of this proud king, who studies day and night
To answer all the debt he owes to you
Even with the bloody payment of your deaths.
Therefore I say—

Worcester: Peace, cousin, say no more.
And now I will unclasp a secret book,
And to your quick-conceiving discontents
I'll read you matter deep and dangerous,
As full of peril and adventurous spirit
As to o'erwalk a current roaring loud
On the unsteadfast footing of a spear.

Hotspur: If he fall in, good night, or sink or swim.
Send danger from the east unto the west,
So honor cross it from the north to south,
And let them grapple. O, the blood more stirs
To rouse a lion than to start a hare!

Northumberland: Imagination of some great exploit
Drives him beyond the bounds of patience.

---

162 **detested:** detestable. 163 **murtherous subornation:** inciting to murder. 168 **predicament:** category. 169 **range:** i.e., are classified. 173 **gage:** pledge. **them both:** i.e., nobility and power. 176 **canker:** (1) wild rose; (2) ulcer. 183 **disdain'd:** disdainful. 185 **answer:** discharge. 189 **to . . . discontents:** i.e., to you, who in your disaffecton will be quick to understand me. 191 **adventurous:** adventurous. 194 **he:** i.e., the man attempting such a crossing. **good . . . swim:** i.e., he's done for, whether he sinks or stays afloat (for a time). 196 **So:** provided that. 200 **patience:** self-control.

Hotspur: By heaven, methinks it were an easy leap,
To pluck bright honor from the pale-fac'd moon,
Or dive into the bottom of the deep,
Where fadom-line could never touch the ground,
And pluck up drowned honor by the locks,
So he that doth redeem her thence might wear
Without corrival all her dignities;
But out upon this half-fac'd fellowship!
Worcester: He apprehends a world of figures here,
But not the form of what he should attend.
Good cousin, give me audience for a while.
Hotspur: I cry you mercy.
Worcester: Those same noble Scots
That are your prisoners—
Hotspur: I'll keep them all!
By God, he shall not have a Scot of them,
No, if a Scot would save his soul, he shall not!
I'll keep them, by this hand.
Worcester: You start away,
And lend no ear unto my purposes.
Those prisoners you shall keep.
Hotspur: Nay, I will; that's flat.
He said he would not ransom Mortimer,
Forbade my tongue to speak of Mortimer,
But I will find him when he lies asleep,
And in his ear I'll hollow "Mortimer!"
Nay,
I'll have a starling shall be taught to speak
Nothing but "Mortimer," and give it him
To keep his anger still in motion.
Worcester: Hear you, cousin, a word.
Hotspur: All studies here I solemnly defy,
Save how to gall and pinch this Bullingbrook,
And that same sword-and-buckler Prince of Wales,
But that I think his father loves him not
And would be glad he met with some mischance,
I would have him poisoned with a pot of ale.
Worcester: Farewell, kinsman! I'll talk to you
When you are better temper'd to attend.

---

206 **redeem:** rescue. 207 **corrival:** partner. 208 **half-fac'd:** thin, meagre. **fellowship:** i.e., sharing of honors. 209 **apprehends:** seizes on. **figures:** figures of speech (an allusion to Hotspur's highly figurative language). 210 **attend:** be intent upon. 212 **cry you mercy:** beg your pardon. 228 **studies:** concerns, pursuits. **defy:** renounce. 230 **sword-and-buckler.** Like the vulgar "pot of ale" in line 233, an allusion to the Prince's disreputable associates, for in Shakespeare's time swords and bucklers were used only by the lowest class of soldiers.

Northumberland: Why, what a wasp-stung and impatient fool
Art thou to break into this woman's mood,
Tying thine ear to no tongue but thine own!
Hotspur: Why, look you, I am [whipt] and scourg'd with rods,
Nettled and stung with pismires, when I hear
Of this vile politician, Bullingbrook.
In Richard's time—what do you call the place?—
A plague upon it, it is in Gloucestershire—
'Twas where the madcap duke his uncle kept—
His uncle York—where I first bow'd my knee
Unto this king of smiles, this Bullingbrook—
'Sblood!
When you and he came back from Ravenspurgh—
Northumberland: At Berkeley castle.
Hotspur: You say true.
Why, what a candy deal of courtesy
This fawning greyhound then did proffer me!
"Look when his infant fortune came to age"
And "gentle Harry Percy" and "kind cousin"—
O, the devil take such cozeners!—God forgive me!
Good uncle, tell your tale—I have done.
Worcester: Nay, if you have not, to it again,
We will stay your leisure.
Hotspur: I have done, i' faith.
Worcester: Then once more to your Scottish prisoners:
Deliver them up without their ransom straight,
And make the Douglas' son your only mean
For powers in Scotland, which, for divers reasons
Which I shall send you written, be assur'd
Will easily be granted. [*To* Northumberland.] You, my lord, Your son in Scotland being thus employed,
Shall secretly into the bosom creep

---

240 **pismires:** ants. 241 **vile politician:** contemptible schemer. 244 **kept:** resided. 245–46 **where . . . Bullingbrook.** See *Richard II,* II.iii. 248 **Ravenspurgh:** Ravenspur, at the mouth of the Humber in Yorkshire, where Henry landed on his return from exile. 251 **candy deal:** sugary lot. 253–54 **Look . . . cousin.** See *Richard II,* II.iii.45–49. 255 **cozeners:** cheats (with obvious pun). 258 **stay your leisure:** wait until you have time to listen. 260 **Deliver them up:** liberate them. **straight:** at once. 261 **the Douglas' son:** i.e., Murdac Stewart. See note to I.i.71. Then as now the head of a prominent Scottish family was designated by his surname preceded by the definite article. 261–62 **mean For powers:** agent for raising troops.

Of that same noble prelate well belov'd,
The Archbishop.

Hotspur: Of York, is it not?

Worcester: True, who bears hard
His brother's death at Bristow, the Lord Scroop.
I speak not this in estimation,
As what I think might be, but what I know
Is ruminated, plotted, and set down,
And only stays but to behold the face
Of that occasion that shall bring it on.

Hotspur: I smell it. Upon my life, it will do well.

Northumberland: Before the game is afoot thou still let'st slip.

Hotspur: Why, it cannot choose but be a noble plot.
And then the power of Scotland, and of York,
To join with Mortimer, ha?

Worcester: And so they shall.

Hotspur: In faith, it is exceedingly well aim'd.

Worcester: And 'tis no little reason bids us speed,
To save our heads by raising of a head,
For bear ourselves as even as we can,
The King will always think him in our debt,
And think we think ourselves unsatisfied,
Till he hath found a time to pay us home.
And see already how he doth begin
To make us strangers to his looks of love.

Hotspur: He does, he does, we'll be reveng'd on him.

Worcester: Cousin, farewell! No further go in this
Than I by letters shall direct your course.
When time is ripe, which will be suddenly,
I'll steal to Glendower and Lord Mortimer,
Where you and Douglas and our powers at once,
As I will fashion it, shall happily meet
To bear our fortunes in our own strong arms,
Which now we hold at much uncertainty.

Northumberland: Farewell, good brother, we shall thrive, I trust.

Hotspur: Uncle, adieu! O, let the hours be short,
Till fields, and blows, and groans applaud our sport!

Exeunt.

268 **The Archbishop:** Richard le Scrope or Scroop (1350?–1405), one of the most prominent of the Percies' allies in their insurrection. In line 271 Shakespeare repeats Holinshed's error in calling him the brother, instead of the cousin, of William Scroop, Earl of Wiltshire.
270 **bears hard:** greatly resents. 271 **Bristow:** Bristol.
272 **estimation:** (mere) conjecture. 276 **occasion:** opportunity. 278 **thou . . . slip:** you always loose the dogs. 282 **aim'd:** planned. 284 **head:** army. 285 **even:** prudently, carefully. 286 **him:** himself. 288 **home:** fully. 294 **suddenly:** soon.
296 **powers at once:** united forces. 302 **fields:** battlefields.

ACT II

Scene I

Enter a Carrier *with a lantern in his hand.*

1. Carrier: Heigh-ho! an' it be not four by the day, I'll be hang'd. Charles' wain is over the new chimney, and yet our horse not pack'd. What, ostler!

Ostler [*Within.*]: Anon, anon.

1. Carrier: I prithee, Tom, beat Cut's saddle, put a few flocks in the point. Poor jade is wrung in the withers, out of all cess.

Enter another Carrier.

2. Carrier: Peas and beans are as dank here as a dog, and that is the next way to give poor jades the bots. This house is turn'd upside down since Robin ostler died.

1. Carrier: Poor fellow never joy'd since the price of oats rose, it was the death of him.

2. Carrier: I think this be the most villainous house in all London road for fleas. I am stung like a tench.

1. Carrier: Like a tench? by the mass, there is ne'er a king christen could be better bit than I have been since the first cock.

2. Carrier: Why, they will allow us ne'er a jordan, and then we leak in your chimney, and your chamber-lye breeds fleas like a loach.

1. Carrier: What, ostler! come away and be hang'd! come away.

2. Carrier: I have a gammon of bacon and two razes of ginger, to be deliver'd as far as Charing-cross.

1. Carrier: God's body, the turkeys in my pannier are quite starv'd. What, ostler! A plague on thee! hast

---

II.i. Location: Rochester. An innyard.

1 **by the day:** in the morning. 2 **Charles' wain:** Charlemagne's wagon, i.e., the constellation of the Great Bear (*Ursa Major*). 3 **horse:** horses. 4 **Anon:** at once, i.e., coming. 6 **flocks . . . point:** tufts of wool in the pommel (to make it more comfortable for the horse). 6 **Poor . . . withers:** the nag is chafed (by the saddle) along the ridge between its shoulders. **cess:** measure. 9 **next:** nearest, i.e., quickest. 10 **bots:** intestinal worms. 14 **house:** inn. 15 **tench:** spotted fish. 17 **king christen:** Christian king. 18 **first cock:** i.e., midnight. 19 **jordan:** chamber pot. 20 **chamber-lye:** urine. 21 **like a loach:** i.e., as fast as a loach (a kind of fish) spawns loaches. 22 **come away:** come along, hurry up. 24 **gammon of bacon:** ham. **razes:** roots. 25 **Charing-cross:** village between London and Westminster.

thou never an eye in thy head? Canst not hear? And 'twere not as good deed as drink to break the pate on thee, I am a very villain. Come, and be hang'd! hast no faith in thee?

Enter Gadshill.

Gadshill: Good morrow, carriers, what's a' clock?

[*1.*] *Carrier:* I think it be two a' clock.

Gadshill: I prithee lend me thy lantern, to see my gelding in the stable.

1. Carrier: Nay, by God, soft, I know a trick worth two of that, i' faith.

Gadshill: I pray thee lend me thine.

2. Carrier: Ay, when, canst tell? Lend me thy lantern, quoth he! Marry, I'll see thee hang'd first.

Gadshill: Sirrah carrier, what time do you mean to come to London?

2. Carrier: Time enough to go to bed with a candle, I warrant thee. Come, neighbor Mugs, we'll call up the gentlemen. They will along with company, for they have great charge. *Exeunt* [*Carriers*].

Gadshill: What ho! chamberlain!

Enter Chamberlain.

Chamberlain: At hand, quoth pick-purse.

Gadshill: That's even as fair as—at hand, quoth the chamberlain; for thou variest no more from picking of purses than giving direction doth from laboring: thou layest the plot how.

Chamberlain: Good morrow, Master Gadshill. It holds current that I told you yesternight: there's a franklin in the Wild of Kent hath brought three hundred marks with him in gold. I heard him tell it to one of his company last night at supper, a kind of auditor, one that hath abundance of charge too—God knows what. They are up already, and call for eggs and butter. They will away presently.

28–30 **And . . . thee:** if it were not as good to clout you on the head as to take a drink. 39 **Ay . . . tell:** i.e., never. 45–46 **They . . . charge:** they will want to travel in a group because of the valuables they are carrying. 47 **chamberlain:** servant who tended the rooms of an inn. 48 **At . . . pick-purse:** here I am right beside you, as the pickpocket said. 49 **fair:** apt. Inn servants were notoriously dishonest. 50–52 **thou . . . how:** i.e., you stand in the same relation to pickpockets as a foreman does to workmen, for you make the plans that others carry out. 53–54 **holds current:** proves to be true. 54 **that:** what. 55 **franklin:** small landowner. **Wild:** Weald (forest). 55–56 **three hundred marks:** two hundred pounds. 57 **auditor:** accountant. 60 **presently:** at once.

Gadshill: Sirrah, if they meet not with Saint Nicholas' clerks, I'll give thee this neck.

Chamberlain: No, I'll none of it, I pray thee keep that for the hangman, for I know thou worshippest Saint Nicholas as truly as a man of falsehood may.

Gadshill: What talkest thou to me of the hangman? If I hang, I'll make a fat pair of gallows; for if I hang, old Sir John hangs with me, and thou knowest he is no starveling. Tut, there are other Troyans that thou dream'st not of, the which for sport sake are content to do the profession some grace, that would (if matters should be look'd into) for their own credit sake make all whole. I am join'd with no foot land-rakers, no long-staff sixpenny strikers, none of these mad mustachio purple-hu'd malt-worms, but with nobility and tranquility, burgomasters and great oney'rs, such as can hold in, such as will strike sooner than speak, and speak sooner than drink, and drink sooner than pray; and yet, 'zounds, I lie, for they pray continually to their saint, the commonwealth, or rather, not pray to her, but prey on her, for they ride up and down on her, and make her their boots.

Chamberlain: What, the commonwealth their boots? Will she hold out water in foul way?

Gadshill: She will, she will, justice hath liquor'd her. We steal as in a castle, cock-sure; we have the receipt of fern-seed, we walk invisible.

Chamberlain: Nay, by my faith, I think you are more beholding to the night than to fern-seed for your walking invisible.

Gadshill: Give me thy hand. Thou shalt have a share in our purchase, as I am a true man.

Chamberlain: Nay, rather let me have it as you are a false thief.

61–62 **Saint Nicholas' clerks:** highwaymen. In Elizabethan slang St. Nicholas was regarded as the patron of thieves. 63 **I'll . . . it:** i.e., I don't want your neck. 69 **Troyans:** Trojans, i.e., roisterers. 71 **profession:** i.e., robbery. 73 **join'd:** associated. **foot land-rakers:** footpads. 74 **long-staff sixpenny strikers:** those who, armed only with cudgels, will rob a man of sixpence; i.e., petty thieves. 74–75 **mad . . . malt-worms:** topers whose mustaches are stained with ale. 76 **oney'rs:** ones (?). 77 **hold in:** retain secrets. 82 **boots:** booty. 84 **hold . . . way:** keep one dryshod in muddy roads, i.e., protect one. 85 **liquor'd:** (1) greased; (2) bribed. 86 **as . . . castle:** i.e., in security (with an allusion to Sir John Oldcastle, the name originally given to Falstaff in this play). 87 **receipt of fern-seed:** procedure for finding fern-seed, which, almost invisible itself, was thought to confer invisibility on whoever carried it. 89 **beholding:** beholden, indebted. 92 **purchase:** booty. **true:** honest.

Gadshill: Go to, *homo* is a common name to all men. Bid the ostler bring my gelding out of the stable. Farewell, you muddy knave. [*Exeunt.*]

SCENE II

Enter Prince, Peto, *and* [Bardolph, *with*] Poins [*following just behind*].

Poins: Come, shelter, shelter! I have remov'd Falstaff's horse, and he frets like a gumm'd velvet.

Prince: Stand close. [*They retire.*]

Falstaff: Poins! Poins, and be hang'd! Poins!

Prince [*Coming forward*]: Peace, ye fat-kidney'd rascal! what a brawling dost thou keep!

Falstaff: Where's Poins, Hal?

Prince: He is walk'd up to the top of the hill, I'll go seek him. [*Retires.*]

Falstaff: I am accurs'd to rob in that thieve's company. The rascal hath remov'd my horse, and tied him I know not where. If I travel but four foot by the squier further afoot, I shall break my wind. Well, I doubt not but to die a fair death for all this, if I scape hanging for killing that rogue. I have forsworn his company hourly any time this two and twenty years, and yet I am bewitch'd with the rogue's company. If the rascal have not given me medicines to make me love him, I'll be hang'd. It could not be else, I have drunk medicines. Poins! Hal! a plague upon you both! Bardolph! Peto! I'll starve ere I'll rob a foot further. And 'twere not as good a deed as drink to turn true man and to leave these rogues, I am the veriest varlet that ever chew'd with a tooth. Eight yards of uneven ground is threescore and ten miles afoot with me, and the stony-hearted villains know it well enough. A plague upon it when thieves cannot be true one to another! [*They whistle.*] Whew! a plague upon you all! Give me my horse, you rogues, give me my horse, and be hang'd!

---

95 **homo:** man. Gadshill implies that a generic term, without such adjectives as *true* or *false*, will suffice. 97 **muddy:** stupid.

II.ii. Location: The highway near Gadshill.

2 **frets:** (1) complains; (2) frays. **gumm'd:** stiffened with gum. 3 **close:** concealed. 6 **keep:** keep up. 10 **thieve's:** thief's. 12 **squier:** square, foot rule. 14 **for:** despite. 18 **medicines:** potions.

Prince [*Coming forward*]: Peace, ye fat-guts, lie down. Lay thine ear close to the ground, and list if thou canst hear the tread of travellers.

Falstaff: Have you any levers to lift me up again, being down? 'Sblood, I'll not bear my own flesh so far afoot again for all the coin in thy father's exchequer. What a plague mean ye to colt me thus?

Prince: Thou liest, thou art not colted, thou art uncolted.

Falstaff: I prithee, good prince—Hal!—help me to my horse, good king's son.

Prince: Out, ye rogue! shall I be your ostler?

Falstaff: Hang thyself in thine own heir-apparent garters! If I be ta'en, I'll peach for this. And I have not ballads made on you all and sung to filthy tunes, let a cup of sack be my poison. When a jest is so forward, and afoot too! I hate it.

Enter Gadshill.

Gadshill: Stand.

Falstaff: So I do, against my will.

Poins [*Coming forward with Bardolph and Peto*]: O, 'tis our setter, I know his voice.

Bardolph: What news?

Gadshill: Case ye, case ye, on with your vizards. There's money of the King's coming down the hill, 'tis going to the King's exchequer.

Falstaff: You lie, ye rogue, 'tis going to the King's tavern.

Gadshill: There's enough to make us all.

Falstaff: To be hang'd.

Prince: Sirs, you four shall front them in the narrow lane; Ned Poins and I will walk lower. If they scape from your encounter, then they light on us.

Peto: How many be there of them?

Gads: Some eight or ten.

Falstaff: 'Zounds, will they not rob us?

Prince: What, a coward, Sir John Paunch?

Falstaff: Indeed I am not John of Gaunt, your grandfather, but yet no coward, Hal.

Prince: Well, we leave that to the proof.

---

37 **colt:** trick. 39 **uncolted:** i.e., deprived of your horse. 43–44 **heir-apparent garters.** An allusion to the Order of the Garter, in which the Prince, as heir apparent, had been installed as a knight. 44 **peach:** turn informer. 46–47 **is so forward:** goes so far. 51 **setter.** See note to I.ii.106–7. 53 **Case ye:** mask yourselves. 58 **make us all:** i.e., make our fortunes. 67 **John of Gaunt.** A punning allusion to Hal's thinness (on which see II.iv.244–48). John of Gaunt was so called from his birthplace, Ghent in Flanders. 69 **proof:** test.

Poins: Sirrah Jack, thy horse stands behind the hedge; when thou need'st him, there thou shalt find him. Farewell, and stand fast.

Falstaff: Now cannot I strike him, if I should be hang'd.

Prince [*Aside*]: Ned, where are our disguises?

Poins [*Aside*]: Here, hard by. Stand close.

[Exeunt Prince *and* Poins.*]*

Falstaff: Now, my masters, happy man be his dole, say I, every man to his business.

Enter the Travellers.

[*1.*] *Traveller:* Come, neighbor, the boy shall lead our horses down the hill. We'll walk afoot a while, and ease our legs.

Thieves: Stand!

Travellers: Jesus bless us!

Falstaff: Strike! down with them! cut the villains' throats! Ah, whoreson caterpillars! bacon-fed knaves! they hate us youth. Down with them! fleece them!

[*1.*] *Traveller:* O, we are undone, both we and ours for ever!

Falstaff: Hang ye, gorbellied knaves, are ye undone? No, ye fat chuffs, I would your store were here! On, bacons, on! What, ye knaves, young men must live! You are grandjurors, are ye? We'll jure ye, faith. *Here they rob them and bind them. Exeunt.*

Enter the Prince *and* Poins *[in buckram].*

Prince: The thieves have bound the true men. Now could thou and I rob the thieves and go merrily to London, it would be argument for a week, laughter for a month, and a good jest for ever.

Poins: Stand close, I hear them coming.

Enter the Thieves *again.*

Falstaff: Come, my masters, let us share, and then to horse before day. And the Prince and Poins be not two arrant cowards, there's no equity stirring. There's no more valor in that Poins than in a wild duck.

---

76 **happy . . . dole:** i.e., may each man be fortunate; good luck to you. *Dole* = that which is dealt (by fate). 84 **caterpillars:** parasites. 88 **gorbellied:** potbellied. 89. **chuffs:** misers. **your store:** all your possessions. 90 **bacons:** fat men. 91 **grandjurors:** i.e., affluent citizens (eligible for jury duty). 93 **true:** honest. 95 **argument:** topic of conversation. 100 **equity:** judgment, discrimination.

Prince: Your money!

As they are sharing, the Prince *and* Poins *set upon them; they all run away, and* Falstaff, *after a blow or two, runs away too, leaving the booty behind them.*

Poins: Villains!

Prince: Got with much ease. Now merrily to horse.
The thieves are all scattered, and possess'd with fear
So strongly that they dare not meet each other;
Each takes his fellow for an officer.
Away, good Ned. Falstaff sweats to death,
And lards the lean earth as he walks along.
Were't not for laughing, I should pity him.

Poins: How the fat rogue roar'd! *Exeunt.*

SCENE III

Enter Hotspur *solus, reading a letter.*

Hotspur: "But, for mine own part, my lord, I could be well contented to be there, in respect of the love I bear your house." He could be contented: why is he not then? In the respect of the love he bears our house: he shows in this, he loves his own barn better than he loves our house. Let me see some more. "The purpose you undertake is dangerous"—why, that's certain. 'Tis dangerous to take a cold, to sleep, to drink, but I tell you, my lord fool, out of this nettle, danger, we pluck this flower, safety. "The purpose you undertake is dangerous, the friends you have nam'd uncertain, the time itself unsorted, and your whole plot too light for the counterpoise of so great an opposition." Say you so, say you so? I say unto you again, you are a shallow, cowardly hind, and you lie. What a lack-brain is this! By the Lord, our plot is a good plot as ever was laid, our friends true and constant: a good plot, good friends, and full of expectation; an excellent plot, very good friends. What a frosty-spirited rogue is this! Why, my Lord of York commends the plot and the general course of the action. 'Zounds, and I were now by this rascal, I could brain him with his lady's fan. Is there not my father, my uncle, and myself? Lord Edmund Mortimer, my Lord of York, and Owen Glendower?

---

109 **lards:** bastes.

II.iii. Location: Warkworth Castle (stronghold of the Percies in Northumberland). o.s.d. **solus:** alone. 3 **house:** family. **He.** The writer of the letter is never identified. 12 **unsorted:** unsuitable. 21 **Lord of York:** i.e., Archbishop Scroop.

is there not besides the Douglas? have I not all their letters to meet me in arms by the ninth of the next month? and are they not some of them set forward already? What a pagan rascal is this! an infidel! Ha, you shall see now in very sincerity of fear and cold heart will he to the King, and lay open all our proceedings. O, I could divide myself and go to buffets, for moving such a dish of skim-milk with so honorable an action! Hang him! let him tell the King: we are prepar'd. I will set forward to-night.

Enter his Lady.

How now, Kate? I must leave you within these two hours.

Lady: O my good lord, why are you thus alone?
For what offense have I this fortnight been
A banish'd woman from my Harry's bed?
Tell me, sweet lord, what is't that takes from thee
Thy stomach, pleasure, and thy golden sleep?
Why dost thou bend thine eyes upon the earth,
And start so often when thou sit'st alone?
Why hast thou lost the fresh blood in thy cheeks,
And given my treasure and my rights of thee
To thick-ey'd musing and curst melancholy?
In thy faint slumbers I by thee have watch'd,
And heard thee murmur tales of iron wars,
Speak terms of manage to thy bounding steed,
Cry "Courage! to the field!" And thou hast talk'd
Of sallies and retires, of trenches, tents,
Of palisadoes, frontiers, parapets,
Of basilisks, of cannon, culverin,
Of prisoners' ransom, and of soldiers slain,
And all the currents of a heady fight;
Thy spirit within thee hath been so at war,
And thus hath so bestirr'd thee in thy sleep,
That beads of sweat have stood upon thy brow,
Like bubbles in a late-disturbed stream,
And in thy face strange motions have appear'd,
Such as we see when men restrain their breath
On some great sudden hest. O, what portents are these?

---

29 **pagan:** unbelieving. 30 **very:** veritable. 32 **divide . . . buffets:** split in two and have a boxing-match with myself (cf. "I could kick myself"). 41 **stomach:** appetite. 47 **faint:** light. 49 **manage:** manège, horsemanship. 52 **palisadoes:** stakes set for defense. **frontiers:** ramparts. 53 **basilisks:** heavy ordnance. **culverin:** light ordnance. 55 **heady:** headlong. 62 **hest:** behest, command.

Some heavy business hath my lord in hand,
And I must know it, else he loves me not.

Hotspur: What ho!

[Enter Servant.*]*

Is Gilliams with the packet gone?

Servant: He is, my lord, an hour ago.

Hotspur: Hath Butler brought those horses from the sheriff?

Servant: One horse, my lord, he brought even now.

Hotspur: What horse? Roan? a crop-ear, is it not?

Servant: It is, my lord.

Hotspur: That roan shall be my throne.
Well, I will back him straight. O *Esperance!*
Bid Butler lead him forth into the park.

[Exit Servant.*]*

Lady: But hear you, my lord.

Hotspur: What say'st thou, my lady?

Lady: What is it carries you away?

Hotspur: Why, my horse, my love, my horse.

Lady: Out, you mad-headed ape!
A weasel hath not such a deal of spleen
As you are toss'd with. In faith,
I'll know your business, Harry, that I will.
I fear my brother Mortimer doth stir
About his title, and hath sent for you
To line his enterprise, but if you go—

Hotspur: So far afoot, I shall be weary, love.

Lady: Come, come, you paraquito, answer me
Directly unto this question that I ask.
In faith, I'll break thy little finger, Harry,
And if thou wilt not tell me all things true.

Hotspur: Away,
Away, you trifler! Love, I love thee not,
I care not for thee, Kate. This is no world
To play with mammets and to tilt with lips.
We must have bloody noses and crack'd crowns,
And pass them current too. God's me, my horse!
What say'st thou, Kate? What wouldst thou have with me?

---

63 **heavy:** (1) weighty; (2) sorrowful. 71 **Esperance:** Hope (the motto of the house of Percy). 78 **spleen:** nervous energy, impulsiveness. 82 **title:** claim to the throne. 83 **line:** support. 92 **mammets:** dolls (like you). 94 **pass them current:** cause them to circulate as legal tender, i.e., give them in exchange. Hotspur is playing on two senses of *crowns:* (1) heads; (2) coins worth five shillings. Cracked coins were not normally accepted as currency. **God's me:** God save me.

Lady: Do you not love me? do you not indeed?
Well, do not then, for since you love me not,
I will not love myself. Do you not love me?
Nay, tell me if you speak in jest or no.

Hotspur: Come, wilt thou see me ride?
And when I am a' horseback, I will swear
I love thee infinitely. But hark you, Kate,
I must not have you henceforth question me
Whither I go, nor reason whereabout.
Whither I must, I must, and to conclude,
This evening must I leave you, gentle Kate.
I know you wise, but yet no farther wise
Than Harry Percy's wife; constant you are,
But yet a woman, and for secrecy,
No lady closer, for I well believe
Thou wilt not utter what thou dost not know,
And so far will I trust thee, gentle Kate.

Lady: How! so far?

Hotspur: Not an inch further. But hark you, Kate,
Whither I go, thither shall you go too;
To-day will I set forth, to-morrow you.
Will this content you, Kate?

Lady: It must of force. *Exeunt.*

[Scene IV]

Enter Prince *and* Poins.

Prince: Ned, prithee come out of that fat room,
and lend me thy hand to laugh a little.

Poins: Where hast been, Hal?

Prince: With three or four loggerheads amongst
three or four score hogsheads. I have sounded the
very base-string of humility. Sirrah, I am sworn
brother to a leash of drawers, and can call them all by
their christen names, as Tom, Dick, and Francis.
They take it already upon their salvation, that though
I be but Prince of Wales, yet I an the king of
courtesy, and tell me flatly I am no proud Jack like
Falstaff, but a Corinthian, a lad of mettle, a good boy

---

101 **a':** on. 104 **whereabout:** about what. 109 **for:** as for.
117 **of force:** of necessity.

II.iv. Location: London. The Boar's Head Tavern in Eastcheap.

1 **fat:** vat (?) or stuffy (?). 4 **loggerheads:** blockheads. 7 **leash:** set of three. **drawers:** tapsters (who sometimes invited favored guests to have their drinks in the cellar). 11 **Jack:** fellow. 12 **Corinthian:** gay blade.

(by the Lord, so they call me!), and when I am King of England I shall command all the good lads in Eastcheap. They call drinking deep, dyeing scarlet, and when you breathe in your watering, they cry "hem!" and bid you play it off. To conclude, I am so good a proficient in one quarter of an hour, that I can drink with any tinker in his own language during my life. I tell thee, Ned, thou hast lost much honor that thou wert not with me in this action. But, sweet Ned—to sweeten which name of Ned, I give thee this pennyworth of sugar, clapp'd even now into my hand by an under-skinker, one that never spake other English in his life than "Eight shillings and sixpence," and "You are welcome," with this shrill addition, "Anon, anon, sir! Score a pint of bastard in the Half-moon," or so. But, Ned, to drive away the time till Falstaff come, I prithee do thou stand in some by-room, while I question my puny drawer to what end he gave me the sugar, and do thou never leave calling "Francis," that his tale to me may be nothing but "Anon." Step aside, and I'll show thee a [president].

[Exit Poins.*]*

Poins [Within.]: Francis!
Prince: Thou art perfect.
[*Poins*] [*Within.*]: Francis!

Enter Drawer [Francis].

Francis: Anon, anon, sir. Look down into the Pomgarnet, Ralph.
Prince: Come hither, Francis.
Francis: My lord?
Prince: How long hast thou to serve, Francis?
Francis: Forsooth, five years, and as much as to—
Poins [*Within.*]: Francis!
Francis: Anon, anon, sir.
Prince: Five year! by'r lady, a long lease for the clinking of pewter. But, Francis, darest thou be so

---

15 **dyeing scarlet.** Perhaps an allusion to the complexion of hard drinkers. 16 **breathe . . . watering:** stop for breath while drinking. 17 **play:** drink. 23 **sugar.** Used to sweeten certain wines, especially sack. 24 **under-skinker:** waiter's assistant. 27 **Anon:** at once, coming. **Score:** i.e., chalk up, charge. **bastard:** sweet Spanish wine. 27–28 **Half-moon.** Rooms in inns were often given special names. 30 **puny:** inexperienced. 33 **president:** precedent, example. 38 **Pomgarnet:** Pomegranate, another room in the tavern. 45 **by'r lady:** by Our Lady (i.e., the Virgin).

valiant as to play the coward with thy indenture, and show it a fair pair of heels and run from it?

Francis: O Lord, sir, I'll be sworn upon all the books in England, I could find in my heart—

Poins [*Within.*]: Francis!

Francis: Anon, sir.

Prince: How old art thou, Francis?

Francis: Let me see—about Michaelmas next I shall be—

Poins [*Within.*]: Francis!

Francis: Anon, sir. Pray stay a little, my lord.

Prince: Nay, but hark you, Francis: for the sugar thou gavest me, 'twas a pennyworth, was't not?

Francis: O Lord, I would it had been two!

Prince: I will give thee for it a thousand pound. Ask me when thou wilt, and thou shalt have it.

Poins [*Within.*]: Francis!

Francis: Anon, anon.

Prince: Anon, Francis? No, Francis; but tomorrow, Francis; or, Francis, a' Thursday; or indeed, Francis, when thou wilt. But, Francis!

Francis: My lord?

Prince: Wilt thou rob this leathern-jerkin, crystal-button, not-pated, agate-ring, puke-stocking, caddis-garter, smooth-tongue, Spanish-pouch—

Francis: O Lord, sir, who do you mean?

Prince: Why then your brown bastard is your only drink! for look you, Francis, your white canvas doublet will sully. In Barbary, sir, it cannot come to so much.

Francis: What, sir?

Poins [*Within.*]: Francis!

Prince: Away, you rogue, dost thou not hear them call?

Here they both call him; the drawer stands amazed, not knowing which way to go.
Enter Vintner.

Vintner: What, stand'st thou still, and hear'st such a calling? Look to the guests within. [*Exit* Francis.]

---

47 **indenture:** apprentice's contract (which was normally for seven years). 49 **books:** i.e., Bibles. 54 **Michaelmas:** September 29. 69–71 **Wilt . . . pouch.** The Prince describes Francis' master, the vintner. 70 **not-pated:** close-cropped. **puke:** dark woollen. **caddis:** worsted. 71 **Spanish:** of Spanish leather. 74–75 **your . . . sully:** your costume (as an apprentice) will get dirty (in Barbary), i.e., you'd better stay here. 75 **it:** i.e., sugar. 79 s.d. **amazed:** thoroughly confused.

My lord, old Sir John with half a dozen more are at the door, shall I let them in?

Prince: Let them alone awhile, and then open the door. [*Exit* Vintner.] Poins!

Poins [*Within.*]: Anon, anon, sir.

Enter Poins.

Prince: Sirrah, Falstaff and the rest of the thieves are at the door; shall we be merry?

Poins: As merry as crickets, my lad. But hark ye, what cunning match have you made with this jest of the drawer? Come, what's the issue?

Prince: I am now of all humors that have show'd themselves humors since the old days of goodman Adam to the pupil age of this present twelve a' clock at midnight.

[Enter Francis *hurrying across the stage with wine.]*

What's a' clock, Francis?

Francis: Anon, anon, sir. [*Exit.*]

Prince: That ever this fellow should have fewer words than a parrot, and yet the son of a woman! His industry is up stairs and down stairs, his eloquence the parcel of a reckoning. I am not yet of Percy's mind, the Hotspur of the north, he that kills me some six or seven dozen of Scots at a breakfast, washes his hands, and says to his wife, "Fie upon this quiet life! I want work." "O my sweet Harry," says she, "how many hast thou kill'd to-day?" "Give my roan horse a drench," says he, and answers, "Some fourteen," an hour after; "a trifle, a trifle." I prithee call in Falstaff. I'll play Percy, and that damn'd brawn shall play Dame Mortimer his wife. "*Rivo!*" says the drunkard. Call in ribs, call in tallow.

Enter Falstaff, *[*Gadshill, Bardolph, *and* Peto, Francis *following with wine].*

Poins: Welcome, Jack, where hast thou been?

Falstaff: A plague of all cowards, I say, and a vengeance too! marry and amen! Give me a cup of sack,

---

90–91 **what . . . issue:** i.e., what's the point of your teasing the servant. 92–95 **I . . . midnight:** i.e., as a consequence of my foolery with the servant I am now in the mood for anything. 93 **goodman:** occupational title for a farmer or yeoman. 94 **pupil:** youthful. 101 **parcel . . . reckoning:** items of a bill. 107 **drench:** medicinal drink. 110 **brawn:** pig. 111 **Rivo:** reveller's exclamation (of uncertain origin and meaning). 114 **of:** on.

boy. Ere I lead this life long, I'll sew nether-stocks, and mend them and foot them too. A plague of all cowards! Give me a cup of sack, rogue. Is there no virtue extant? *He drinketh.*

Prince: Didst thou never see Titan kiss a dish of butter, pitiful-hearted Titan, that melted at the sweet tale of the sun's? If thou didst, then behold that compound.

Falstaff: You rogue, here's lime in this sack too. There is nothing but roguery to be found in villainous man, yet a coward is worse than a cup of sack with lime in it. A villainous coward! Go thy ways, old Jack, die when thou wilt; if manhood, good manhood, be not forgot upon the face of the earth, then am I a shotten herring. There lives not three good men unhang'd in England, and one of them is fat and grows old, God help the while! a bad world, I say. I would I were a weaver, I could sing psalms, or any thing. A plague of all cowards, I say still.

Prince: How now, wool-sack, what mutter you?

Falstaff: A king's son! If I do not beat thee out of thy kingdom with a dagger of lath, and drive all thy subjects afore thee like a flock of wild geese, I'll never wear hair on my face more. You, Prince of Wales!

Prince: Why, you whoreson round man, what's the matter?

Falstaff: Are not you a coward? Answer me to that; and Poins there?

Poins: 'Zounds, ye fat paunch, and ye call me coward, by the Lord, I'll stab thee.

Falstaff: I call thee coward! I'll see thee damn'd ere I call thee coward, but I would give a thousand pound I could run as fast as thou canst. You are straight enough in the shoulders, you care not who sees your back. Call you that backing of your friends? A plague upon such backing! give me them that will face me. Give me a cup of sack. I am a rogue if I drunk to-day.

Prince: O villain, thy lips are scarce wip'd since thou drunk'st last.

---

116 **nether-stocks:** stockings. 119 **virtue:** manliness. 120 **Titan:** the sun. 121 **that:** i.e., the butter. 123 **compound:** melting butter, i.e., Falstaff. 124 **lime.** Sometimes used as an additive to wine to increase its sparkle. 130 **shotten herring:** (as thin as) a herring that has spawned. 132 **the while:** in these (bad) times.
133 **sing psalms.** Elizabethan weavers, many of whom were immigrants from the Low Countries and dissenters, were notorious for psalm-singing. 137 **dagger of lath:** wooden stick (commonly used by the Vice, the mischievously comic stock character in morality plays).

Falstaff: All is one for that. [*He drinketh.*] A plague of all cowards, still say I.

Prince: What's the matter?

Falstaff: What's the matter! There be four of us here have ta'en a thousand pound this day morning.

Prince: Where is it, Jack? where is it?

Falstaff: Where is it? taken from us it is: a hundred upon poor four of us.

Prince: What, a hundred, man?

Falstaff: I am a rogue if I were not at half-sword with a dozen of them two hours together. I have scap'd by miracle. I am eight times thrust through the doublet, four through the hose, my buckler cut through and through, my sword hack'd like a hand-saw—*ecce signum!* I never dealt better since I was a man, all would not do. A plague of all cowards! Let them speak; if they speak more or less than truth, they are villains and the sons of darkness.

[*Prince.*] Speak, sirs, how was it?

[*Gadshill.*] We four set upon some dozen—

Falstaff: Sixteen at least, my lord.

[*Gadshill.*] And bound them.

Peto: No, no, they were not bound.

Falstaff: You rogue, they were bound, every man of them, or I am a Jew else, an Ebrew Jew.

[*Gadshill.*] As we were sharing, some six or seven fresh men set upon us—

Falstaff: And unbound the rest, and then come in the other.

Prince: What, fought you with them all?

Falstaff: All? I know not what you call all, but if I fought not with fifty of them, I am a bunch of radish. If there were not two or three and fifty upon poor old Jack, then am I no two-legg'd creature.

Prince: Pray God you have not murd'red some of them.

Falstaff: Nay, that's past praying for, I have pepper'd two of them. Two I am sure I have paid, two rogues in buckrom suits. I tell thee what, Hal, if I tell thee a lie, spit in my face, call me horse. Thou knowest my old ward: here I lay, and thus I bore my point. Four rogue in buckrom let drive at me—

---

155 **All . . . that:** i.e., no matter. 164 **at half-sword:** i.e., at close quarters. 167 **hose:** breeches. **buckler:** shield. 169 **ecce signum:** behold the proof. **dealt:** i.e., fought. 179 **Ebrew:** Hebrew. 183 **other:** others. 192 **paid:** i.e., killed. 194 **horse:** i.e., a stupid animal. 195 **ward:** parry. **lay:** stood.

Prince: What, four? Thou saidst but two even now.

Falstaff: Four, Hal, I told thee four.

Poins: Ay, ay, he said four.

Falstaff: These four came all afront, and mainly thrust at me. I made me no more ado but took all their seven points in my target, thus.

Prince: Seven? why, there were but four even now.

Falstaff: In buckrom?

Poins: Ay, four in buckrom suits.

Falstaff: Seven, by these hilts, or I am a villain else.

Prince: Prithee let him alone, we shall have more anon.

Falstaff: Dost thou hear me, Hal?

Prince: Ay, and mark thee too, Jack.

Falstaff: Do so, for it is worth the list'ning to. These nine in buckrom that I told thee of—

Prince: So, two more already.

Falstaff: Their points being broken—

Poins: Down fell their hose.

Falstaff: Began to give me ground; but I follow'd me close, came in, foot and hand, and with a thought seven of the eleven I paid.

Prince: O monstrous! eleven buckrom men grown out of two.

Falstaff: But, as the devil would have it, three misbegotten knaves in Kendal green came at my back and let drive at me, for it was so dark, Hal, that thou couldest not see thy hand.

Prince: These lies are like their father that begets them, gross as a mountain, open, palpable. Why, thou clay-brain'd guts, thou knotty-pated fool, thou whoreson, obscene, greasy tallow-catch—

Falstaff: What, art thou mad? art thou mad? is not the truth the truth?

Prince: Why, how couldst thou know these men in Kendal green when it was so dark thou couldst not see thy hand? Come, tell us your reason; what sayest thou to this?

Poins: Come, your reason, Jack, your reason.

Falstaff: What, upon compulsion? 'Zounds, and I were at the strappado, or all the racks in the world, I would

---

200 **afront:** abreast. **mainly:** powerfully. 202 **target:** shield. 206 **these hilts:** i.e., the pommel, haft, etc. of a sword (a common oath). **villain:** i.e., no gentleman. 214 **points:** sword points (but Poins takes the word in a second sense: tagged laces for holding garments together). 217 **with a thought:** as quick as thought. 222 **Kendal:** town in Westmorland noted for its textiles. 226 **gross:** obvious. 227 **knotty-pated:** thick-headed. 228 **tallow-catch:** tallow-tub. 237 **strappado:** a form of torture.

not tell you on compulsion. Give you a reason on compulsion? if reasons were as plentiful as blackberries, I would give no man a reason upon compulsion, I.

Prince: I'll be no longer guilty of this sin. This sanguine coward, this bed-presser, this horse-back-breaker, this huge hill of flesh—

Falstaff: 'Sblood, you starveling, you [eel-]skin, you dried neat's tongue, you bull's pizzle, you stock-fish! O for breath to utter what is like thee! you tailor's yard, you sheath, you bowcase, you vile standing tuck—

Prince: Well, breathe a while, and then to it again, and when thou hast tir'd thyself in base comparisons, hear me speak but this—

Poins: Mark, Jack.

Prince: We two saw you four set on four and bound them, and were masters of their wealth. Mark now how a plain tale shall put you down. Then did we two set on you four, and with a word, outfac'd you from your prize, and have it, yea, and can show it you here in the house; and, Falstaff, you carried your guts away as nimbly, with as quick dexterity, and roar'd for mercy, and still run and roar'd, as ever I heard bull-calf. What a slave art though to hack thy sword as thou hast done, and then say it was in fight! What trick? what device? what starting-hole? canst thou now find out to hide thee from this open and apparent shame?

Poins: Come, let's hear, Jack, what trick hast thou now?

Falstaff: By the Lord, I knew ye as well as he that made ye. Why, hear you, my masters, was it for me to kill the heir-apparent? Should I turn upon the true prince? Why, thou knowest I am as valiant as Hercules; but beware instinct—the lion will not touch the true prince. Instinct is a great matter; I was now a coward on instinct. I shall think the better of myself, and thee, during my life; I for a valiant lion, and thou for a true prince. But by the Lord, lads, I am glad you have the money. Hostess, clap to the doors! Watch to-night, pray to-morrow. Gallants, lads, boys, hearts of gold, all the titles of good fellowship

---

239 **reasons.** Pronounced *raisins* (hence the pun with *blackberries*). 242 **sanguine:** ruddy. 245 **neat's:** ox's. 245 **stock-fish:** dried cod. 248 **tuck:** rapier. 256 **with a word:** to be brief. **outfac'd:** frightened, bluffed. 263 **starting-hole:** refuge, loophole; i.e., excuse. 264 **apparent:** obvious.

come to you! What, shall we be merry, shall we have a play extempore?

Prince: Content, and the argument shall be thy running away.

Falstaff: Ah, no more of that, Hal, and thou lovest me!

Enter Hostess.

Hostess: O Jesu, my lord the Prince!

Prince: How now, my lady the hostess! what say'st thou to me?

Hostess: Marry, my lord, there is a nobleman of the court at door would speak with you. He says he comes from your father.

Prince: Give him as much as will make him a royal man, and send him back again to my mother.

Falstaff: What manner of man is he?

Hostess: An old man.

Falstaff: What doth gravity out of his bed at midnight? Shall I give him his answer?

Prince: Prithee do, Jack.

Falstaff: Faith, and I'll send him packing. *Exit.*

Prince: Now, sirs, by'r lady, you fought fair, so did you, Peto, so did you, Bardolph. You are lions too, you ran away upon instinct, you will not touch the true prince, no, fie!

Bardolph: Faith, I ran when I saw others run.

Prince: Faith, tell me now in earnest, how came Falstaff's sword so hack'd?

Peto: Why, he hack'd it with his dagger, and said he would swear truth out of England but he would make you believe it was done in fight, and persuaded us to do the like.

Bardolph: Yea, and to tickle our noses with speargrass to make them bleed, and then to beslubber our garments with it and swear it was the blood of true men. I did that I did not this seven year before, I blush'd to hear his monstrous devices.

Prince: O villain, thou stolest a cup of sack eighteen years ago, and wert taken with the manner, and ever since thou hast blush'd extempore. Thou hadst

---

281 **argument:** subject. 290–91 **as much . . . man:** i.e., 3s. 4d., the difference between a noble (6s. 8d.) and a royal (10s.). 291 **send . . . mother:** i.e., get rid of him permanently. The Prince's mother, Mary de Bohun, had died in 1394. 298 **fair:** well. 306 **swear . . . England:** i.e., vanquish truth by the force of his lies. **but he would:** if he did not. 312 **that . . . not:** what I hadn't done. 315 **taken . . . manner:** caught in the act.

fire and sword on thy side, and yet thou ran'st away; what instinct hadst thou for it?

Bardolph: My lord, do you see these meteors? do you behold these exhalations? [*Pointing to his own face.*]

Prince: I do.

Bardolph: What think you they portend?

Prince: Hot livers and cold purses.

Bardolp Choler, my lord, if rightly taken.

Enter Falstaff.

Prince: No, if rightly taken, halter. Here comes lean Jack, here comes bare-bone: How now, my sweet creature of bombast, how long is't ago, Jack, since thou sawest thine own knee?

Falstaff: My own knee? When I was about thy years, Hal, I was not an eagle's talent in the waist, I could have crept into any alderman's thumb-ring. A plague of sighing and grief, it blows a man up like a bladder. There's villainous news abroad. Here was Sir John Bracy from your father; you must to the court in the morning. That same mad fellow of the north, Percy, and he of Wales that gave Amamon the bastinado and made Lucifer cuckold and swore the devil his true liegeman upon the cross of a Welsh hook—what a plague call you him?

Poins: O, Glendower.

Falstaff: Owen, Owen, the same; and his son-in-law Mortimer, and old Northumberland, and that sprightly Scot of Scots, Douglas, that runs a' horseback up a hill perpendicular—

Prince: He that rides at high speed and with his pistol kills a sparrow flying.

Falstaff: You have hit it.

Prince: So did he never the sparrow.

---

317 **fire.** An allusion to Bardolph's ruddy complexion, the subject of the jests and pun that follow. 319, 320 **meteors, exhalations:** i.e., the red blotches and carbuncles on Bardolph's face. 322 **portend:** threaten, presage (continuing the astronomical imagery of *meteors* and *exhalations*). 323 **Hot . . . purses:** i.e., livers inflamed by liquor and purses emptied to pay for it. 324 **Choler . . . taken:** i.e., my fiery complexion, if properly understood, indicates a choleric temperament (which makes me quick to anger and dangerous).

325 **No . . . halter:** i.e., no, if you're arrested as you deserve, you'll get the hangman's noose. Behind *halter* lies a pun on *choler* and *collar.* 327 **bumbast:** bombast, cotton padding. 330 **talent:** talon. 334 **Sir John Bracy.** Apparently unhistorical. 336 **Amamon:** the name of a fiend. 337 **bastinado:** beating on the soles of the feet. **made Lucifer cuckold:** i.e., gave Lucifer his horns (the sign of a cuckold). 338 **liegeman:** subject.

338–39 **Welsh hook:** pike with a curved blade.

Falstaff: Well, that rascal hath good mettle in him, he will not run.

Prince: Why, what a rascal art thou then, to praise him so for running!

Falstaff: A' horseback, ye cuckoo, but afoot he will not budge a foot.

Prince: Yes, Jack, upon instinct.

Falstaff: I grant ye, upon instinct. Well, he is there too, and one Mordake, and a thousand blue-caps more. Worcester is stol'n away to-night. Thy father's beard is turn'd white with the news. You may buy land now as cheap as stinking mack'rel.

Prince: Why then, it is like, if there come a hot June and this civil buffeting hold, we shall buy maiden-heads as they buy hobnails, by the hundreds.

Falstaff: By the mass, lad, thou sayest true, it is like we shall have good trading that way. But tell me, Hal, art not thou horrible afeard? Thou being heir-apparent, could the world pick thee out three such enemies again as that fiend Douglas, that spirit Percy, and that devil Glendower? Art thou not horribly afraid? Doth not thy blood thrill at it?

Prince: Not a whit, i' faith, I lack some of thy instinct.

Falstaff: Well, thou wilt be horribly chid to-morrow when thou comest to thy father. If thou love me, practice an answer.

Prince: Do thou stand for my father and examine me upon the particulars of my life.

Falstaff: Shall I? Content. This chair shall be my state, this dagger my sceptre, and this cushion my crown.

Prince: Thy state is taken for a join'd-stool, thy golden sceptre for a leaden dagger, and thy precious rich crown for a pitiful bald crown!

Falstaff: Well, and the fire of grace be not quite out of thee, now shalt thou be mov'd. Give me a cup of sack to make my eyes look red, that it may be thought I have wept, for I must speak in passion, and I will do it in King Cambyses' vein.

Prince: Well, here is my leg.

Falstaff: And here is my speech. Stand aside, nobility.

---

357 **blue-caps:** blue bonnets, i.e., Scots. 362 **hold:** continue. 370 **thrill:** run cold. 378 **state:** chair of state, i.e., throne. 380 **join'd-stool:** stool of joiner's work. 382 **bald crown:** bald pate. 386 **in passion:** with deep emotion. 387 **in . . . vein:** i.e., in a style of ludicrous and old-fashioned rant (like that of Thomas Preston's *Cambyses*, an early Elizabethan play). 388 **leg:** elaborate bow.

Hostess: O Jesu, this is excellent sport, i' faith!
Falstaff: Weep not, sweet queen, for trickling tears are vain.
Hostess: O, the father, how he holds his countenance!
Falstaff: For God's sake, lords, convey my [tristful] queen,
For tears do stop the flood-gates of her eyes.
Hostess: O Jesu, he doth it as like one of these harlotry players as ever I see!
Falstaff: Peace, good pint-pot, peace, good ticklebrain. Harry, I do not only marvel where thou spendest thy time, but also how thou art accompanied; for though the camomile, the more it is trodden on, the faster it grows, [yet] youth, the more it is wasted, the sooner it wears. That thou art my son I have partly thy mother's word, partly my own opinion, but chiefly a villainous trick of thine eye, and a foolish hanging of thy nether lip, that doth warrant me. If then thou be son to me, here lies the point: why being son to me, art thou so pointed at? Shall the blessed sun of heaven prove a micher and eat blackberries? a question not to be ask'd. Shall the son of England prove a thief and take purses? a question to be ask'd. There is a thing, Harry, which thou hast often heard of, and it is known to many in our land by the name of pitch. This pitch (as ancient writers do report) doth defile, so doth the company thou keepest; for, Harry, now I do not speak to thee in drink, but in tears; not in pleasure, but in passion; not in words only, but in woes also. And yet there is a virtuous man whom I have often noted in thy company, but I know not his name.
Prince: What manner of man, and it like your Majesty?
Falstaff: A goodly portly man, i' faith, and a corpulent, of a cheerful look, a pleasing eye, and a most noble carriage, and as I think, his age some fifty, or, by'r lady, inclining to threescore; and now I remember me, his name is Falstaff. If that man should be

---

392 **holds his countenance:** keeps a straight face. 393 **convey:** escort hence. **tristful:** sorrowful. 395–96 **harlotry:** knavish. 397 **ticklebrain:** strong drink. 400 **camomile:** plant of the aster family. 405 **warrant:** assure. 407 **pointed at:** i.e., in derision and disapproval. 408. **micher:** truant. 409 **England:** i.e., the King of England. 413 **ancient writers.** For one, the writer of the Apocryphal book Ecclesiasticus (13:1). 416 **passion:** sorrow. 422 **portly:** stately, imposing. **corpulent:** full-fleshed.

lewdly given, he deceiveth me; for, Harry, I see virtue in his looks. If then the tree may be known by the fruit, as the fruit by the tree, then peremptorily I speak it, there is virtue in that Falstaff; him keep with, the rest banish. And tell me now, thou naughty varlet, tell me, where hast thou been this month?

Prince: Dost thou speak like a king? Do thou stand for me, and I'll play my father.

Falstaff: Depose me? If thou dost it half so gravely, so majestically, both in word and matter, hang me up by the heels for a rabbit-sucker or a poulter's hare.

Prince: Well, here I am set.

Falstaff: And here I stand. Judge, my masters.

Prince: Now, Harry, whence come you?

Falstaff: My noble lord, from Eastcheap.

Prince: The complaints I hear of thee are grievous.

Falstaff: 'Sblood, my lord, they are false.—Nay, I'll tickle ye for a young prince, i' faith.

Prince: Swearest thou, ungracious boy? henceforth ne'er look on me. Thou art violently carried away from grace, there is a devil haunts thee in the likeness of an old fat man, a tun of man is thy companion. Why dost thou converse with that trunk of humors, that bolting-hutch of beastliness, that swoll'n parcel of dropsies, that huge bombard of sack, that stuff'd cloak-bag of guts, that roasted Manningtree ox with the pudding in his belly, that reverent Vice, that grey Iniquity, that father ruffian, that vanity in years? Wherein is he good, but to taste sack and drink it? wherein neat and cleanly, but to carve a capon and eat it? wherein cunning, but in craft? wherein crafty, but in villainy? wherein villainous, but in all things? wherein worthy, but in nothing?

Falstaff: I would your Grace would take me with you. Whom means your Grace?

---

427 **lewdly given:** wickedly inclined. 428–29 **If . . . by the fruit.** See Matthew 12:33. 429 **peremptorily:** decisively. 431–32 **naughty varlet:** ill-behaved boy. 437 **rabbit-sucker:** unweaned rabbit. **poulter's:** poulterer's. 438 **set:** seated (i.e., on the "throne"). 443–44 **I'll . . . prince:** I'll play the role of a young prince so as to delight you. 445 **ungracious:** graceless. 449 **converse:** associate. **humors:** secretions in the body, diseases. 450 **bolting-hutch:** miller's bin. 451 **bombard:** large leathern vessel. 452 **Manningtree:** town in Essex, a region noted for fat oxen. 453 **pudding:** stuffing. **Vice:** mischievously comic stock character in morality plays who served chiefly as a "misleader of youth" (lines 462–63). *Iniquity* (line 454) is another name for him. 456 **cleanly:** adroit, dextrous. 457 **cunning:** skillful. 460 **take . . . you:** i.e., go more slowly (so I can keep up with you).

Prince: That villainous abominable misleader of youth, Falstaff, that old white-bearded Sathan.

Falstaff: My lord, the man I know.

Prince: I know thou dost.

Falstaff: But to say I know more harm in him than in myself, were to say more than I know. That he is old, the more the pity, his white hairs do witness it, but that he is, saving your reverence, a whoremaster, that I utterly deny. If sack and sugar be a fault, God help the wicked! If to be old and merry be a sin, then many an old host that I know is damn'd. If to be fat be to be hated, then Pharoah's [lean] kine are to be lov'd. No, my good lord, banish Peto, banish Bardolph, banish Poins, but for sweet Jack Falstaff, kind Jack Falstaff, true Jack Falstaff, valiant Jack Falstaff, and therefore more valiant, being as he is old Jack Falstaff, banish not him thy Harry's company, banish not him thy Harry's company—banish plump Jack, and banish all the world.

Prince: I do, I will.

[A knocking heard. Exeunt Hostess, Francis, *and* Bardolph.*]*
Enter Bardolph *running.*

Bardolph: O my lord, my lord, the sheriff with a most monstrous watch is at the door.

Falstaff: Out, ye rogue, play out the play, I have much to say in the behalf of that Falstaff.

Enter the Hostess.

Hostess: O Jesu, my lord, my lord!

Prince: Heigh, heigh! the devil rides upon a fiddle-stick. What's the matter?

Hostess: The sheriff and all the watch are at the door, they are come to search the house. Shall I let them in?

Falstaff: Dost thou hear, Hal? Never call a true piece of gold a counterfeit. Thou art essentially made, without seeming so.

---

469 **saving your reverence:** i.e., excuse me for using an offensive term.
473 **Pharaoh's lean kine.** See Genesis 41:1–4. 483 **watch:** body of constables.
487–88 **the devil . . . fiddlestick:** i.e., the Hostess is going to report some astounding event.
491–93 **Never . . . so.** A much disputed passage. Perhaps Falstaff means that the Prince should not turn him—a true piece of gold—over to the law as a counterfeit coin, for Hal himself, despite misleading appreciates, is a true prince (*essentially made*).

Prince: And thou a natural coward, without instinct.
Falstaff: I deny your major. If you will deny the
sheriff, so, if not, let him enter. If I become not a cart
as well as another man, a plague on my bringing up!
I hope I shall as soon be strangled with a halter as
another.
Prince: Go hide thee behind the arras, the rest walk
up above. Now, my masters, for a true face and good
conscience.
Falstaff: Both which I have had, but their date is out,
and therefore I'll hide me. [*Exit.*]
Prince: Call in the sheriff.

[Exeunt all except the Prince *and* Peto.*]*
Enter Sheriff *and the* Carrier.

Now, Master Sheriff, what is your will with me?
Sheriff: First, pardon me, my lord. A hue and cry
Hath followed certain men unto this house.
Prince: What men?
Sheriff: One of them is well known, my gracious lord,
A gross fat man.
Carrier: As fat as butter.
Prince: The man I do assure you is not here,
For I myself at this time have employ'd him.
And, sheriff, I will engage my word to thee
That I will by to-morrow dinner-time
Send him to answer thee, or any man,
For any thing he shall be charg'd withal,
And so let me entreat you leave the house.
Sheriff: I will, my lord. There are two gentlemen
Have in this robbery lost three hundred marks.
Prince: It may be so. If he have robb'd these men,
He shall be answerable, and so farewell.
Sheriff: Good night, my noble lord.
Prince: I think it is good morrow, is it not?
Sheriff: Indeed, my lord, I think it be two a' clock.

Exit [with Carrier*].*

Prince: This oily rascal is known as well as Paul's.
Go call him forth.

---

495 **major:** major premise. 495–96 **deny the sheriff:** i.e., refuse to admit him.
496 **cart:** i.e., hangman's cart. 500 **arras:** tapestry wall-hangings. 501 **true:** honest.
515 **engage:** pledge. 518 **withal:** with. 525 **good morrow:** i.e., past midnight.
527 **Paul's:** St. Paul's Cathedral.

Peto: Falstaff!—Fast asleep behind the arras, and snorting like a horse.

Prince: Hark how hard he fetches breath. Search his pockets. [*He searcheth his pocket, and findeth certain papers.*] What hast thou found?

Peto: Nothing but papers, my lord.

Prince: Let's see what they be. Read them.

[*Peto.*] [*Reads.*]
Item, a capon . . . . . 2s. 2d.
Item, sauce . . . . . 4d.
Item, sack, two gallons . . . 5s. 8d.
Item, anchoves and sack after supper . 2s. 6d.
Item, bread . . . . . ob.

[*Prince.*] O monstrous! but one half-pennyworth of bread to this intolerable deal of sack! What there is else, keep close, we'll read it at more advantage. There let him sleep till day. I'll to the court in the morning. We must all to the wars, and thy place shall be honorable. I'll procure this fat rogue a charge of foot, and I know his death will be a march of twelve score. The money shall be paid back again with advantage. Be with me betimes in the morning, and so good morrow, Peto.

Peto: Good morrow, good my lord. *Exeunt.*

[ACT III]

[Scene I]

Enter Hotspur, Worcester, Lord Mortimer, Owen Glendower.

Mortimer: These promises are fair, the parties sure,
And our induction full of prosperous hope.

Hotspur: Lord Mortimer, and cousin Glendower,
Will you sit down?
And uncle Worcester—a plague upon it!
I have forgot the map.

---

539 **anchoves:** anchovies. 540 **ob.:** obolus; here, halfpenny. 543 **close:** secret. 543–44 **more advantage:** a more opportune time. 547 **charge of foot:** command of a troop of infantry. 547–48 **death . . . score:** i.e., a march of 240 yards will kill him. 549 **advantage:** interest.

III.i. Location: Wales. Glendower's castle. (Holinshed places the events of this scene in the house of the Archdeacon of Bangor [see the note to lines 71–78], but the Archdeacon is not present in the scene and Glendower acts throughout as host.)
2 **induction:** beginning. **prosperous hope:** hope of prospering.

Glendower: No, here it is.
Sit, cousin Percy, sit, good cousin Hotspur,
For by that name as oft as Lancaster
Doth speak of you, his cheek looks pale, and with
A rising sigh he wisheth you in heaven.
Hotspur: And you in hell, as oft as he hears
Owen Glendower spoke of.
Glendower: I cannot blame him. At my nativity
The front of heaven was full of fiery shapes
Of burning cressets, and at my birth
The frame and huge foundation of the earth
Shak'd like a coward.
Hotspur: Why, so it would have done
At the same season if your mother's cat had
But kitten'd, though yourself had never been born.
Glendower: I say the earth did shake when I was born.
Hotspur: And I say the earth was not of my mind,
If you suppose as fearing you it shook.
Glendower: The heavens were all on fire, the earth did
tremble.
Hotspur: O then the earth shook to see the heavens on
fire,
And not in fear of your nativity.
Diseased nature oftentimes breaks forth
In strange eruptions; oft the teeming earth
Is with a kind of colic pinch'd and vex'd
By the imprisoning of unruly wind
Within her womb, which, for enlargement striving,
Shakes the old beldame earth, and topples down
Steeples and moss-grown towers. At your birth
Our grandam earth, having this distemp'rature,
In passion shook.
Glendower: Cousin, of many men
I do not bear these crossings. Give me leave
To tell you once again that at my birth
The front of heaven was full of fiery shapes,
The goats ran from the mountains, and the herds
Were strangely clamorous to the frighted fields.
These signs have mark'd me extraordinary,
And all the courses of my life do show
I am not in the roll of common men.
Where is he living, clipt in with the sea

8 **Lancaster:** i.e., King Henry. 14 **front:** forehead. 15 **cressets:** fire-baskets mounted on poles; here, meteors. 30 **enlargement:** release. 31 **beldame:** grandmother, aged woman. 34 **passion:** pain. 35 **crossings:** contradictions. 43. **clipt in with:** enclosed by.

That chides the banks of England, Scotland, Wales,
Which calls me pupil or hath read to me?
And bring him out that is but woman's son
Can trace me in the tedious ways of art,
And hold me pace in deep experiments.

Hotspur: I think there's no man speaks better Welsh.
I'll to dinner.

Mortimer: Peace, cousin Percy, you will make him
mad.

Glendower: I can call spirits from the vasty deep.

Hotspur: Why, so can I, or so can any man,
But will they come when you do call for them?

Glendower: Why, I can teach you, cousin, to command
The devil.

Hotspur: And I can teach thee, coz, to shame the devil
By telling truth: tell truth and shame the devil.
If thou have power to raise him, bring him hither,
And I'll be sworn I have power to shame him hence.
O, while you live, tell truth and shame the devil!

Mortimer: Come, come, no more of this unprofitable
chat.

Glendower: Three times hath Henry Bullingbrook made
head
Against my power; thrice from the banks of Wye
And sandy-bottom'd Severn have I sent him
Bootless home and weather-beaten back.

Hotspur: Home without boots, and in foul weather too!
How scapes he agues, in the devil's name?

Glendower: Come, here is the map. Shall we divide our
right
According to our threefold order ta'en?

Mortimer: The Archdeacon hath divided it
Into three limits very equally:
England, from Trent and Severn hitherto,
By south and east is to my part assign'd;
All westward, Wales beyond the Severn shore,

---

45 **read to:** i.e., taught. 47 **trace . . . art:** follow me in the laborious ways of magic. 48 **hold me pace:** keep up with me. **deep:** occult. 49 **better Welsh:** i.e., more boastfully and incomprehensibly. 52 **vasty deep:** lower world. 63 **made head:** raised a force. 64 **power:** armed followers. 66 **Bootless:** without advantage, i.e., unsuccessful. 69 **right:** rightful possessions. 71–78 **The Archdeacon . . . Trent.** According to Holinshed (Bullough, IV, 185), the revels "by their deputies in the house of the archdeacon of Bangor, divided the realme amongst them, causing a tripartite indenture to be made and sealed with their seales, by the covenants whereof, all England from Severne and Trent, south and eastward, was assigned to the earle of March: all Wales, & the lands beyond Severne westward, were appointed to Owen Glendouer: and all the remnant from Trent northward, to the lord Persie." 72 **limits:** regions defined by a boundary. 73 **hitherto:** to this point.

And all the fertile land within that bound,
To Owen Glendower; and, dear coz, to you
The remnant northward lying off from Trent.
And our indentures tripartite are drawn,
Which being sealed interchangeably
(A business that this night may execute),
To-morrow, cousin Percy, you and I
And my good Lord of Worcester will set forth
To meet your father and the Scottish power,
As is appointed us, at Shrewsbury.
My father Glendower is not ready yet,
Nor shall we need his help these fourteen days.
Within that space you may have drawn together
Your tenants, friends, and neighboring gentlemen.

Glendower: A shorter time shall send me to you, lords,
And in my conduct shall your ladies come,
From whom you now must steal and take no leave,
For there will be a world of water shed
Upon the parting of your wives and you.

Hotspur: Methinks my moi'ty, north from Burton
here,
In quantity equals not one of yours.
See how this river comes me cranking in,
And cuts me from the best of all my land
A huge half-moon, a monstrous [cantle] out.
I'll have the current in this place damm'd up,
And here the smug and silver Trent shall run
In a new channel fair and evenly.
It shall not wind with such a deep indent,
To rob me of so rich a bottom here.

Glendower: Not wind? It shall, it must, you see it doth.

Mortimer: Yea, but
Mark how he bears his course, and runs me up
With like advantage on the other side,
Gelding the opposed continent as much
As on the other side it takes from you.

Worcester: Yea, but a little charge will trench him here,
And on this north side win this cape of land,
And then he runs straight and even.

---

79 **our . . . drawn:** our agreement is now drawn up in triplicate. 86 **father:** i.e., father-in-law. 91 **conduct:** escort. 95 **moi'ty:** share. 97 **cranking:** winding. 99 **cantle:** piece, segment. 101 **smug:** smooth. 102 **fair and evenly:** i.e., in a straight course. 104 **bottom:** valley. 109 **Gelding . . . continent:** cutting off from the opposite bank. 111 **charge:** expense.

Hotspur: I'll have it so, a little charge will do it.
Glendower: I'll not have it alt'red.
Hotspur: Will not you?
Glendower: No, nor you shall not.
Hotspur: Who shall say me nay?
Glendower: Why, that will I.
Hotspur: Let me not understand you then,
Speak it in Welsh.
Glendower: I can speak English, lord, as well as you,
For I was train'd up in the English court,
Where being but young I framed to the harp
Many an English ditty lovely well,
And gave the tongue a helpful ornament,
A virtue that was never seen in you.
Hotspur: Marry,
And I am glad of it with all my heart.
I had rather be a kitten and cry mew
Than one of these same metre ballet-mongers.
I had rather hear a brazen canstick turn'd,
Or a dry wheel grate on the axle-tree,
And that would set my teeth nothing an edge,
Nothing so much as mincing poetry.
'Tis like the forc'd gait of a shuffling nag.
Glendower: Come, you shall have Trent turn'd.
Hotspur: I do not care. I'll give thrice so much land
To any well-deserving friend;
But in the way of bargain, mark ye me,
I'll cavil on the ninth part of a hair.
Are the indentures drawn? Shall we be gone?
Glendower: The moon shines fair, you may away by
night.
I'll haste the writer, and withal
Break with your wives of your departure hence.
I am afraid my daughter will run mad,
So much she doteth on her Mortimer. *Exit.*
Mortimer: Fie, cousin Percy, how you cross my father!

---

120 **For . . . court.** According to Holinshed (Bullough, IV, 180), Glendower "was first set to studie the lawes of the realme, and became an utter barrester, or an apprentise of the law (as they terme him) and served king Richard at Flint castell, when he was taken by Henrie duke of Lancaster, though other have written that he served this king Henry the fourth, before he came to atteine the crowne, in roome of an esquier." 123 **gave . . . ornament:** i.e., not only adorned the words with music but also enriched the language with poetry. 124 **virtue:** accomplishment. 128 **ballet:** ballad. 129 **canstick turn'd:** candlestick turned on a lathe. 133 **shuffling:** hobbled. 141 **withal:** also. 142 **Break with:** inform.

Hotspur: I cannot choose. Sometime he angers me
With telling me of the moldwarp and the ant,
Of the dreamer Merlin and his prophecies,
And of a dragon and a finless fish,
A clip-wing'd griffin and a moulten raven,
A couching lion and a ramping cat,
And such a deal of skimble-skamble stuff
As puts me from my faith. I tell you what:
He held me last night at least nine hours
In reckoning up the several devils' names
That were his lackeys. I cried "hum," and "well, go to,"
But mark'd him not a word. O, he is as tedious
As a tired horse, a railing wife,
Worse than a smoky house. I had rather live
With cheese and garlic in a windmill, far,
Than feed on cates and have him talk to me
In any summer house in Christendom.

Mortimer: In faith, he is a worthy gentleman,
Exceedingly well read, and profited
In strange concealments, valiant as a lion,
And wondrous affable, and as bountiful
As mines of India. Shall I tell you, cousin?
He holds your temper in a high respect,
And curbs himself even of his natural scope
When you come 'cross his humor, faith, he does.
I warrant you, that man is not alive
Might so have tempted him as you have done,
Without the taste of danger and reproof.
But do not use it oft, let me entreat you.

Worcester: In faith, my lord, you are too willful-blame,
And since your coming hither have done enough
To put him quite besides his patience.

146–53 **Sometimes . . . faith.** According to Holinshed (Bullough, IV, 185), the rebels laid their plans "through a foolish credit given to a vaine prophesie, as though king Henrie was the moldwarpe, cursed of Gods owne mouth, and they three were the dragon, the lion, and the woolfe, which should divide this realme between them. Such in the deviation (saith *Hall*) and not divination of those blind and fantasticall dreames of the Welsh prophesiers."
147 **moldwarp:** mole. 148 **Merlin:** famous prophet and magician of Arthurian legend.
150 **griffin:** fabulous beast, half lion and half eagle. 151 **couching, ramping:** parodies of the heraldic terms *couchant* (lying down with the head raised) and *rampant* (rearing).
152 **skimble-skamble:** nonsensical. 153 **puts . . . faith:** i.e., kills my confidence (in Glendower). 155 **several:** various. 161 **cates:** delicacies. 164 **profited:** proficient.
165 **concealments:** occult arts. 169 **scope:** freedom of speech. 172 **tempted:** irritated. 175 **willful-blame:** willfully to blame.

You must needs learn, lord, to amend this fault;
Though sometimes it show greatness, courage, blood—
And that's the dearest grace it renders you—
Yet oftentimes it doth present harsh rage,
Defect of manners, want of government,
Pride, haughtiness, opinion, and disdain,
The least of which haunting a nobleman
Loseth men's hearts and leaves behind a stain
Upon the beauty of all parts besides,
Beguiling them of commendation.

Hotspur: Well, I am school'd: good manners be your speed!
Here come our wives, and let us take our leave.

Enter Glendower *with the* Ladies.

Mortimer: This is the deadly spite that angers me:
My wife can speak no English, I no Welsh.

Glendower: My daughter weeps, she'll not part with you,
She'll be a soldier too, she'll to the wars.

Mortimer: Good father, tell her that she and my aunt Percy
Shall follow in your conduct speedily.

Glendower *speaks to her in Welsh, and she answers him in the same.*

Glendower: She is desperate here, a peevish self-will'd harlotry,
One that no persuasion can do good upon.

The lady speaks in Welsh.

Mortimer: I understand thy looks. That pretty Welsh
Which thou pourest down from these swelling heavens
I am too perfect in, and but for shame,
In such a parley should I answer thee.

The Lady *again in Welsh.*

I understand thy kisses, and thou mine,
And that's a feeling disputation,
But I will never be a truant, love,

---

179 **blood:** spirit. 180 **dearest grace:** main distinction. 181 **present:** indicate. 182 **government:** self-control. 183 **opinion:** self-conceit. 186 **all parts besides:** all other (good) qualities. 187 **Beguiling:** depriving. 188 **be your speed:** give you success. 190 **spite:** vexation. 193 **she'll to:** she wants to go to. 194 **my aunt Percy:** i.e., Hotspur's wife, who was actually the sister, not the aunt, of Glendower's son-in-law. See notes to I.i.38, I.iii.80. 196 **She . . . harlotry:** she is hopeless on this point, a willful hussy. 198 **That pretty Welsh:** your language, i.e., your tears. 200 **perfect in:** well acquainted with. 201 **In . . . parley:** i.e., by weeping. 203 **a feeling disputation:** i.e., an exchange of sentiments, not of language.

Till I have learn'd thy language, for thy tongue
Makes Welsh as sweet as ditties highly penn'd,
Sung by a fair queen in a summer's bow'r,
With ravishing division, to her lute.

Glendower: Nay, if you melt, then will she run mad.

The Lady *speaks again in Welsh.*

Mortimer: O, I am ignorance itself in this!

Glendower: She bids you on the wanton rushes lay you down,
And rest your gentle head upon her lap,
And she will sing the song that pleaseth you,
And on your eyelids crown the god of sleep,
Charming your blood with pleasing heaviness,
Making such difference 'twixt wake and sleep
As is the difference betwixt day and night
The hour before the heavenly-harness'd team
Begins his golden progress in the east.

Mortimer: With all my heart I'll sit and hear her sing.
By that time will our book, I think, be drawn.

Glendower: Do so,
And those musicians that shall play to you
Hang in the air a thousand leagues from hence,
And straight they shall be here. Sit and attend.

Hotspur: Come, Kate, thou art perfect in lying down.
Come, quick, quick, that I may lay my head in thy lap.

Lady P: Go, ye giddy goose. *The music plays.*

Hotspur: Now I perceive the devil understands Welsh,
And 'tis no marvel he is so humorous.
By'r lady, he is a good musician.

Lady P: Then should you be nothing but musical,
for you are altogether govern'd by humors. Lie still,
ye thief, and hear the lady sing in Welsh.

Hotspur: I had rather hear Lady, my brach, howl in Irish.

Lady P: Wouldst thou have thy head broken?

Hotspur: No.

Lady P: Then be still.

Hotspur: Neither, 'tis a woman's fault.

Lady P: Now God help thee!

---

208 **division:** embellishment. 211 **wanton:** luxurious, comfortable. 215 **heaviness:** drowsiness. 221 **book:** i.e., the "indentures tripartite" of line 79. 229–30 **Now . . . humorous:** i.e., since the devil understands Welsh (which is incomprehensible), it's no wonder that he's so whimsical (*humorous*). 233 **humors:** whims. 235 **brach:** bitch. 240 **Neither . . . fault:** I won't be silent either, for that's a woman's trait (and I'm a man).

Hotspur: To the Welsh lady's bed.
Lady P: What's that?
Hotspur: Peace, she sings.

Here the Lady *sings a Welsh song.*

Hotspur: Come, Kate, I'll have your song too.
Lady P: Not mine, in good sooth.
Hotspur: Not yours, in good sooth! Heart, you swear
like a comfit-maker's wife: "Not you, in good sooth,"
and "as true as I live," and "as God shall mend me,"
and "as sure as day";
And givest such sarcenet surety for thy oaths
As if thou never walk'st further than Finsbury.
Swear me, Kate, like a lady as thou art,
A good mouth-filling oath, and leave "in sooth,"
And such protest of pepper-gingerbread,
To velvet-guards and Sunday-citizens.
Come sing.
Lady P: I will not sing.
Hotspur: 'Tis the next way to turn tailor, or be
redbreast teacher. And the indentures be drawn,
I'll away within these two hours, and so come in when
ye will. *Exit.*
Glendower: Come, come, Lord Mortimer, you are as
slow
As hot Lord Percy is on fire to go.
By this our book is drawn, we'll but seal,
And then to horse immediately.
Mortimer: With all my heart. *Exeunt.*

[Scene II]

Enter the King, Prince of Wales, *and others.*
King: Lords, give us leave, the Prince of Wales
and I
Must have some private conference, but be near at
hand,
For we shall presently have need of you.

Exeunt Lords.

---

246 **sooth:** truth. 247 **Heart:** by God's (Christ's) heart. 248 **comfit-maker's:** confectioner's. 251 **sarcenet:** i.e., flimsy, insubstantial (from the name of a very fine, soft material made of silk). 252 **Finsbury:** district much frequented by London citizens and their families. Hotspur implies that his wife's genteel and colorless language makes her sound like a burgher's wife. 255 **such . . . pepper-gingerbread:** i.e., such namby-pamby protestations. 256 **velvet-guards:** velvet trimmings such as citizens' wives wore on their Sunday finery. 259 **next:** quickest. **tailor.** A trade noted for singing.
III.ii. Location: London. The palace.

I know not whether God will have it so
For some displeasing service I have done,
That in his secret doom, out of my blood
He'll breed revengement and a scourge for me;
But thou dost in thy passages of life
Make me believe that thou art only mark'd
For the hot vengeance, and the rod of heaven,
To punish my mistreadings. Tell me else,
Could such inordinate and low desires,
Such poor, such bare, such lewd, such mean attempts,
Such barren pleasures, rude society,
As thou art match'd withal and grafted to,
Accompany the greatness of thy blood,
And hold their level with thy princely heart?

Prince: So please your Majesty, I would I could
Quit all offenses with as clear excuse
As well as I am doubtless I can purge
Myself of many I am charg'd withal;
Yet such extenuation let me beg
As in reproof of many tales devis'd,
Which oft the ear of greatness needs must hear
By smiling pick-thanks and base newsmongers,
I may for some things true, wherein my youth
Hath faulty wand'red and irregular,
Find pardon on my true submission.

King: God pardon thee! yet let me wonder, Harry,
At thy affections, which do hold a wing
Quite from the flight of all thy ancestors.
Thy place in Council thou hast rudely lost,
Which by thy younger brother is supplied,

---

6 **doom:** judgment. 8 **passages:** actions. 12 **inordinate:** unsuitable (for one of your rank). 13 **lewd:** base, vulgar. 15 **withal:** with. 17 **hold their level:** i.e., maintain their appeal and force. 19 **Quit:** clear myself of. 20 **doubtless:** certain. 23 **reproof:** disproof. 25 **pick-thanks:** busybodies, flatterers. Shakespeare may have got the word from Holinshed (Bullough, IV, 195), who, incidentally, dates the King's reproof of and reconciliation with his wayward son after the battle of Shrewsbury: "Thus were the father and the sonne reconciled, betwixt whom the said pickthanks had sowne division, insomuch that the sonne upon a vehement conceit of unkindnesse sproong in the father, was in the waie to be worne out of favour. Which was the more likelie to come to passe, by their informations that privilie charged him with riot and other uncivill demeanor un-seemelie for a prince." **newsmongers:** talebearers. 28 **submission:** confession. 30 **affections:** inclinations. **hold a wing:** pursue a course. 32–33 **Thy . . . supplied.** An allusion to the apocryphal story—apparently first told by Sir Thomas Elyot in *The Governor* (1531)—of one of the Prince's most flamboyant escapades. In Holinshed's account (Bullough, IV, 280), "to hie offense of the king his father, he had with his fist striken the cheefe justice [Sir William Gascoigne] for sending one of his minions (upon desert) to prison, when the justice stoutlie commanded himself also streict to ward, & he (then prince) obeied. The king after expelled him out of his privie councell, banisht him the court, and made the duke of Clarence (his younger brother) president of councell in his steed." Shakespeare treats the escapade more fully in *2 Henry IV,* V.ii. **rudely:** by violence.

And art almost an alien to the hearts
Of all the court and princes of my blood;
The hope and expectation of thy time
Is ruin'd, and the soul of every man
Prophetically do forethink thy fall.
Had I so lavish of my presence been,
So common-hackney'd in the eyes of men,
So stale and cheap to vulgar company,
Opinion, that did help me to the crown,
Had still kept loyal to possession,
And left me in reputeless banishment,
A fellow of no mark nor likelihood.
By being seldom seen, I could not stir
But like a comet I was wond'red at,
That men would tell their children, "This is he";
Others would say, "Where, which is Bullingbrook?"
And then I stole all courtesy from heaven,
And dress'd myself in such humility
That I did pluck allegiance from men's hearts,
Loud shouts and salutations from their mouths,
Even in the presence of the crowned King.
Thus did I keep my person fresh and new,
My presence, like a robe pontifical,
Ne'er seen but wond'red at, and so my state,
Seldom but sumptuous, show'd like a feast,
And wan by rareness such solemnity.
The skipping King, he ambled up and down,
With shallow jesters, and rash bavin wits,
Soon kindled and soon burnt, carded his state,
Mingled his royalty with cap'ring fools,
Had his great name profaned with their scorns,
And gave his countenance, against his name,
To laugh at gibing boys, and stand the push
Of every beardless vain comparative,
Grew a companion to the common streets,
Enfeoff'd himself to popularity,
That, being daily swallowed by men's eyes,

36 **time:** time of life, i.e., youth. 40 **common-hackney'd:** cheapened, vulgarized. A hackney is a horse kept for hire. 42 **Opinion:** i.e., public opinion. 43 **Had:** would have. **possession:** the possessor, i.e., Richard II. 57 **state:** i.e., appearance on state occasions. 59 **wan:** won. 61 **bavin:** brushwood, kindling. 62 **carded:** mixed (and so adulterated), a term from cloth-making. **state:** royal status. 65 **gave . . . name:** lent his authority, to the jeopardy of his kingly title. 66–67 **stand . . . comparative:** tolerate the impertinent witticisms of every beardless youth. 69 **Enfeoff'd:** sold, surrendered. 70 **That:** so that.

They surfeited with honey and began
To loathe the taste of sweetness, whereof a little
More than a little is by much too much.
So when he had occasion to be seen,
He was but as the cuckoo is in June,
Heard, not regarded; seen, but with such eyes
As, sick and blunted with community,
Afford no extraordinary gaze,
Such as is bent on sunlike majesty
When it shines seldom in admiring eyes;
But rather drows'd and hung their eyelids down,
Slept in his face and rend'red such aspect
As cloudy men use to their adversaries,
Being with his presence glutted, [gorg'd], and full.
And in that very line, Harry, standest thou,
For thou hast lost thy princely privilege
With vile participation. Not an eye
But is a-weary of thy common sight,
Save mine, which hath desir'd to see thee more,
Which now doth that I would not have it do,
Make blind itself with foolish tenderness.

Prince: I shall hereafter, my thrice-gracious lord,
Be more myself.

King: For all the world
As thou art to this hour was Richard then
When I from France set foot at Ravenspurgh,
And even as I was then is Percy now.
Now by my sceptre, and my soul to boot,
He hath more worthy interest to the state
Than thou the shadow of succession.
For of no right, nor color like to right,
He doth fill fields with harness in the realm,
Turns head against the lion's armed jaws,
And being no more in debt to years than thou,
Leads ancient lords and reverend bishops on
To bloody battles and to bruising arms.
What never-dying honor hath he got
Against renowned Douglas! whose high deeds,
Whose hot incursions and great name in arms,

---

77 **community:** familiarity. 82 **aspect:** look. 83 **cloudy:** sullen. 87 **participation:** fellowship. 90 **that:** that which. 91 **foolish tenderness:** i.e., tears. 98 **more . . . state:** a better claim to the throne. 99 **shadow:** i.e., because your intrinsic merits are so slight. 100 **color:** pretext. 101 **harness:** (men in) armor. 102 **Turns head:** leads an army. 103 **being . . . thou.** See note to I.i.53. 107 **renowmed:** renowned.

Holds from all soldiers chief majority
And military title capital
Through all the kingdoms that acknowledge Christ.
Thrice hath this Hotspur, Mars in swathling clothes,
This infant warrior, in his enterprises
Discomfited great Douglas, ta'en him once,
Enlarg'd him and made a friend of him,
To fill the mouth of deep defiance up,
And shake the peace and safety of our throne.
And what say you to this? Percy, Northumberland,
The Archbishop's grace of York, Douglas, Mortimer,
Capitulate against us, and are up.
But wherefore do I tell these news to thee?
Why, Harry, do I tell thee of my foes,
Which art my nearest and dearest enemy?
Thou that art like enough, through vassal fear,
Base inclination, and the start of spleen,
To fight against me under Percy's pay,
To dog his heels and curtsy at his frowns,
To show how much thou art degenerate.

Prince: Do not think so, you shall not find it so,
And God forgive them that so much have sway'd
Your Majesty's good thoughts away from me!
I will redeem all this on Percy's head,
And in the closing of some glorious day
Be bold to tell you that I am your son,
When I will wear a garment all of blood,
And stain my favors in a bloody mask,
Which wash'd away shall scour my shame with it.
And that shall be the day, when e'er it lights,
That this same child of honor and renown,
This gallant Hotspur, this all-praised knight,
And your unthought-of Harry chance to meet.
For every honor sitting on his helm,
Would they were multitudes, and on my head
My shames redoubled! For the time will come
That I shall make this northren youth exchange
His glorious deeds for my indignities.
Percy is but my factor, good my lord,
To engross up glorious deeds on my behalf;

---

109 **majority:** supremacy. 110 **capital:** preeminent. 112 **swathing:** swaddling. 115 **Enlarg'd:** freed. 120 **Capitulate:** combine. **up:** i.e., in arms. 123 **dearest:** (1) best beloved; (2) direst. 124 **like:** likely. **vassal:** slavish. 125 **start of spleen:** fit of caprice and ill temper. 136 **favors:** features. 138 **lights:** dawns. 145 **northren:** northern. 147 **factor:** agent. 148 **engross:** gather, amass.

And I will call him to so strict account
That he shall render every glory up,
Yea, even the slightest worship of his time,
Or I will tear the reckoning from his heart.
This in the name of God I promise here,
The which if he be pleas'd I shall perform,
I do beseech your Majesty may salve
The long-grown wounds of my intemperance.
If not, the end of life cancels all bands,
And I will die a hundred thousand deaths
Ere break the smallest parcel of this vow.

King: A hundred thousand rebels die in this.
Thou shalt have charge and sovereign trust herein.

[Enter Blunt.*]*

How now, good Blunt? thy looks are full of speed.

Blunt: So hath the business that I come to speak of.
Lord Mortimer of Scotland hath sent word
That Douglas and the English rebels met
The eleventh of this month at Shrewsbury.
A mighty and a fearful head they are,
If promises be kept on every hand,
As ever off'red foul play in a state.

King: The Earl of Westmerland set forth to-day,
With him my son, Lord John of Lancaster,
For this advertisement is five days old.
On Wednesday next, Harry, you shall set forward,
On Thursday we ourselves will march. Our meeting
Is Bridgenorth. And, Harry, you shall march
Through Gloucestershire; by which account,
Our business valued, some twelve days hence
Our general forces at Bridgenorth shall meet.
Our hands are full of business, let's away,
Advantage feeds him fat while men delay. *Exeunt.*

---

151 **worship:** honor. **time:** time of life, i.e., youth. 156 **intemperance:** dissolute behavior. 157 **bands:** bonds, debts. 159 **parcel:** part. 161 **charge:** command of troops, i.e., a commission. 164 **Mortimer of Scotland:** i.e., George Dunbar, the Scottish Earl of the "March," or border, whom Shakespeare confuses with Edmund, Earl of March. 167 **head:** army. 171 **John of Lancaster:** Prince John, third son of Henry IV. 172 **advertisement:** information. 174 **meeting:** meeting place, rendezvous. 175 **Bridgenorth:** town on the Severn River southeast of Shrewsbury. 177 **Our business valued:** the time necessary for our business being considered. 180 **Advantage . . . fat:** i.e., opportunity grows lazy. **him:** himself.

[SCENE III]

Enter Falstaff *and* Bardolph.

Falstaff: Bardolph, am I not fall'n away vilely since this last action? do I not bate? do I not dwindle? Why, my skin hangs about me like an old lady's loose gown; I am wither'd like an old apple-john. Well, I'll repent, and that suddenly, while I am in some liking. I shall be out of heart shortly, and then I shall have no strength to repent. And I have not forgotten what the inside of a church is made of, I am a peppercorn, a brewer's horse. The inside of a church! Company, villainous company, hath been the spoil of me.

Bardolph: Sir John, you are so fretful you cannot live long.

Falstaff: Why, there is it. Come sing me a bawdy song, make me merry. I was as virtuously given as a gentleman need to be, virtuous enough: swore little, dic'd not above seven times—a week, went to a bawdy-house not above once in a quarter—of an hour, paid money that I borrow'd—three or four times, liv'd well and in good compass, and now I live out of all order, out of all compass.

Bardolph: Why, you are so fat, Sir John, that you must needs be out of all compass, out of all reasonable compass, Sir John.

Falstaff: Do thou amend thy face, and I'll amend my life. Thou art our admiral, thou bearest the lantern in the poop, but 'tis in the nose of thee. Thou art the Knight of the Burning Lamp.

Bardolph: Why, Sir John, my face does you no harm.

Falstaff: No, I'll be sworn, I made as good use of it as many a man doth of a death's-head or a *memento mori.* I never see thy face but I think upon hell-fire and Dives that liv'd in purple; for there he is in his robes, burning, burning. If thou wert any way given to virtue, I would swear by thy face; my oath should be "By this fire, that['s] God's angel." But thou

---

III.iii. Location: The Boar's Head Tavern.
1 **fall'n away:** shrunk. 2 **this last action:** i.e., the robbery at Gadshill. **bate:** grow thin. 4 **apple-john:** kind of apple that could be kept a long time and was eaten after its skin had become shrivelled. 5 **suddenly:** at once. 5–6 **in some liking:** (1) in good condition; (2) in the mood. 9 **a brewer's horse:** i.e., decrepit. 14 **given:** inclined. 19 **compass:** moderation. 22 **compass:** circumference, expanse. 25 **admiral:** flagship. 30–31 **memento mori:** reminder of death (e.g., a skull engraved on a seal ring). 32 **Dives:** in Jesus' parable about the beggar Lazarus, "a certain rich man" who went to hell. See Luke 16:19–31. 35 **By . . . angel.** Perhaps an echo of Exodus 3:2.

art altogether given over, and wert indeed, but for the light in thy face, the son of utter darkness. When thou ran'st up Gadshill in the night to catch my horse, if I did not think thou hadst been an *ignis fatuus* or a ball of wildfire, there's no purchase in money. O, thou art a perpetual triumph, an everlasting bonfire light! Thou hast sav'd me a thousand marks in links and torches, walking with thee in the night betwixt tavern and tavern; but the sack that thou hast drunk me would have bought me lights as good cheap at the dearest chandler's in Europe. I have maintain'd that salamander of yours with fire any time this two and thirty years, God reward me for it!

Bardolph: 'Sblood, I would my face were in your belly!

Falstaff: God-a-mercy, so should I be sure to be heart-burnt.

[Enter Hostess.*]*

How now, Dame Partlet the hen? have you inquir'd yet who pick'd my pocket?

Hostess: Why, Sir John, what do you think, Sir John? Do you think I keep thieves in my house? I have search'd, I have inquir'd, so has my husband, man by man, boy by boy, servant by servant. The [tithe] of a hair was never lost in my house before.

Falstaff: Ye lie, hostess, Bardolph was shav'd, and lost many a hair, and I'll be sworn my pocket was pick'd. Go to, you are a woman, go.

Hostess: Who, I? No, I defy thee. God's light, I was never call'd so in mine own house before.

Falstaff: Go to, I know you well enough.

Hostess: No, Sir John, you do not know me, Sir John. I know you, Sir John, you owe me money, Sir John, and now you pick a quarrel to beguile me of it. I bought you a dozen of shirts to your back.

Falstaff: Dowlas, filthy dowlas. I have given them away to bakers' wives, they have made bolters of them.

Hostess: Now as I am a true woman, holland of eight shillings an ell. You owe money here besides, Sir John,

---

36 **given over:** i.e., to wickedness. 39 **ignis fatuus:** will-o'-the-wisp. 40 **wildfire:** fireworks. 41 **triumph:** torchlight procession. 42 **links:** torches. 45 **as good cheap:** as cheap. 47 **salamander:** fabulous lizard believed to live in fire. 52 **Dame Partlet:** traditional name for a hen. Falstaff alludes to the Hostess' agitation and flutter. 57 **tithe:** tenth part. 69 **Dowlas:** kind of coarse linen. 70 **bolters:** cloths for sifting flour. 71 **holland:** fine linen. 72 **ell:** a measurement of 45 inches.

for your diet and by-drinkings, and money lent you, four and twenty pound.

Falstaff: He had his part of it, let him pay.

Hostess: He? alas, he is poor, he hath nothing.

Falstaff: How? poor? Look upon his face; what call you rich? Let them coin his nose, let them coin his cheeks. I'll not pay a denier. What, will you make a younker of me? Shall I not take mine ease in mine inn but I shall have my pocket pick'd? I have lost a seal-ring of my grandfather's worth forty mark.

Hostess: O Jesu, I have heard the Prince tell him, I know not how oft, that that ring was copper!

Falstaff: How? the Prince is a Jack, a sneak-up. 'Sblood, and he were here, I would cudgel him like a dog if he would say so.

Enter the Prince marching, [with Peto,] and Falstaff meets him playing upon his truncheon like a fife.

How now, lad? is the wind in that door, i' faith? must we all march?

Bardolph: Yea, two and two, Newgate fashion.

Hostess: My lord, I pray you hear me.

Prince: What say'st thou, Mistress Quickly? How doth thy husband? I love him well, he is an honest man.

Hostess: Good my lord, hear me.

Falstaff: Prithee let her alone, and list to me.

Prince: What say'st thou, Jack?

Falstaff: The other night I fell asleep here behind the arras and had my pocket pick'd. This house is turn'd bawdy-house, they pick pockets.

Prince: What didst thou lose, Jack?

Falstaff: Wilt thou believe me, Hal, three or four bonds of forty pound a-piece, and a seal-ring of my grand-father's.

Prince: A trifle, some eight-penny matter.

Hostess: So I told him, my lord, and I said I heard your Grace say so; and, my lord, he speaks most vilely of you, like a foul-mouth'd man as he is, and said he would cudgel you.

Prince: What, he did not?

Hostess: There's neither faith, truth, nor womanhood in me else.

---

73 **by-drinkings:** drinks between meals. 79 **denier:** French copper coin of little value. 80 **younker:** novice, greenhorn. 85 **Jack:** rascal. **sneak-up:** sneak. 90 **Newgate:** a London prison.

Falstaff: There's no more faith in thee than in a stew'd prune, nor no more truth in thee than in a drawn fox, and for womanhood, Maid Marian may be the deputy's wife of the ward to thee. Go, you thing, go.

Hostess: Say, what thing? what thing?

Falstaff: What thing? why, a thing to thank God on.

Hostess: I am no thing to thank God on, I would thou shouldst know it. I am an honest man's wife, and setting thy knighthood aside, thou art a knave to call me so.

Falstaff: Setting thy womanhood aside, thou art a beast to say otherwise.

Hostess: Say, what beast, thou knave, thou?

Falstaff: What beast? why, an otter.

Prince: An otter, Sir John, why an otter?

Falstaff: Why? she's neither fish nor flesh, a man knows not where to have her.

Hostess: Thou art an unjust man in saying so. Thou or any man knows where to have me, thou knave, thou!

Prince: Thou say'st true, hostess, and he slanders thee most grossly.

Hostess: So he doth you, my lord, and said this other day you ought him a thousand pound.

Prince: Sirrah, do I owe you a thousand pound?

Falstaff: A thousand pound, Hal? a million, thy love is worth a million; thou owest me thy love.

Hostess: Nay, my lord, he call'd you Jack, and said he would cudgel you.

Falstaff: Did I, Bardolph?

Bardolph: Indeed, Sir John, you said so.

Falstaff: Yea, if he said my ring was copper.

Prince: I say 'tis copper. Darest thou be as good as thy word now?

Falstaff: Why, Hal! thou knowest, as thou art but man, I dare, but as thou art Prince, I fear thee as I fear the roaring of the lion's whelp.

Prince: And why not as the lion?

112–13 **stew'd prune:** i.e., bawd. Stewed prunes were commonly associated with brothels. 113 **drawn:** i.e., out of its hole (and seeking to trick its pursuers). 114–15 **Maid . . . thee:** i.e., compared to you, Maid Marian—a disreputable character in Robin Hood ballads and May-games—was a model of propriety. 120 **setting . . . aside:** disregarding your rank. 128 **where . . . her:** i.e., how to take her. In lines 129–30 the Hostess, repeating the phrase, stumbles on an unflattering double-entendre. 134 **ought:** owed.

Falstaff: The King himself is to be fear'd as the lion. Dost thou think I'll fear thee as I fear thy father? Nay, and I do, I pray God my girdle break.

Prince: O, if it should, how would thy guts fall about thy knees! But, sirrah, there's no room for faith, truth, nor honesty in this bosom of thine; it is all fill'd up with guts and midriff. Charge an honest woman with picking thy pocket! Why, thou whoreson, impudent, emboss'd rascal, if there were any thing in thy pocket but tavern-reckonings, memorandums of bawdy-houses, and onc poor pennyworth of sugar-candy to make thee long-winded—if thy pocket were enrich'd with any other injuries but these, I am a villain. And yet you will stand to it, you will not pocket up wrong. Art thou not asham'd?

Falstaff: Dost thou hear, Hal? Thou knowest in the state of innocency Adam fell, and what should poor Jack Falstaff do in the days of villainy? Thou seest I have more flesh than another man, and therefore more frailty. You confess then you pick'd my pocket?

Prince: It appears so by the story.

Falstaff: Hostess, I forgive thee. Go make ready breakfast; love thy husband, look to thy servants, cherish thy guesse. Thou shalt find me tractable to any honest reason; thou seest I am pacified still. Nay, prithee be gone. [*Exit* Hostess.] Now, Hal, to the news at court for the robbery, lad, how is that answer'd?

Prince: O, my sweet beef, I must still be good angel to thee. The money is paid back again.

Falstaff: O, I do not like that paying back, 'tis a double labor.

Prince: I am good friends with my father and may do any thing.

Falstaff: Rob me the exchequer the first thing thou doest, and do it with unwash'd hands too.

Bardolph: Do, my lord.

Prince: I have procur'd thee, Jack, a charge of foot.

Falstaff: I would it had been of horse. Where shall I find one that can steal well? O for a fine thief, of the age of two and twenty or thereabouts! I am hei-

---

157 **emboss'd:** swollen. **rascal:** lean, inferior deer. 161 **injuries:** things whose loss would be an injury to you (with a play on the phrase *pocket up injuries* = swallow insults). 172 **guesse:** guests. 173 **still:** always. 176 **answer'd:** settled. 184 **with unwash'd hands:** i.e., hastily. 186 **charge of foot:** command of a company of infantry.

nously unprovided. Well, God be thank'd for these
rebels, they offend none but the virtuous. I laud them,
I praise them.

Prince: Bardolph!

Bardolph: My lord?

Prince: Go bear this letter to Lord John of Lancaster,
To my brother John; this to my Lord of Westmerland.

[Exit Bardolph.]

Go, Peto, to horse, to horse, for thou and I
Have thirty miles to ride yet ere dinner-time.

[Exit Peto.]

Jack, meet me to-morrow in the Temple Hall
At two [a'] clock in the afternoon;
There shalt thou know thy charge, and there receive
Money and order for their furniture.
The land is burning, Percy stands on high,
And either we or they must lower lie. [*Exit.*]

Falstaff: Rare words! brave world! Hostess, my
breakfast, come!
O, I could wish this tavern were my drum! [*Exit.*]

ACT IV

[Scene I]

[*Enter* Hotspur, Worcester, *and* Douglas.]

Hotspur: Well said, my noble Scot! If speaking truth
In this fine age were not thought flattery,
Such attribution should the Douglas have
As not a soldier of this season's stamp
Should go so general current through the world.
By God, I cannot flatter, I do defy
The tongues of soothers, but a braver place

190 **unprovided:** ill equipped (for the campaign). 199 **Temple Hall:** hall of the Inner Temple, one of the Inns of Court that housed the legal societies of London.
202 **furniture:** equipment. 206 **I . . . drum.** A disputed passage. Perhaps Falstaff means merely that he would rather continue to take his ease at the inn than go to the wars.

IV.i. Location: The rebel camp near Shrewsbury.
3 **attribution:** tribute. 4 **stamp:** coinage. 7 **soothers:** flatterers.

In my heart's love hath no man than yourself.
Nay, task me to my word, approve me, lord.

Douglas: Thou art the king of honor.
No man so potent breathes upon the ground
But I will beard him.

Enter one [a Messenger*] with letters.*

Hotspur: Do so, and 'tis well.—
What letters hast thou there?—I can but thank you.

Messenger: These letters come from your father.

Hotspur: Letters from him! Why comes he not himself?

Messenger: He cannot come, my lord, he is grievous sick.

Hotspur: 'Zounds! how has he the leisure to be sick
In such a justling time? Who leads his power?
Under whose government come they along?

Messenger: His letters bears his mind, not I, my [lord].

Worcester: I prithee tell me, doth he keep his bed?

Messenger: He did, my lord, four days ere I set forth,
And at the time of my departure thence
He was much fear'd by his physicians.

Worcester: I would the state of time had first been whole
Ere he by sickness had been visited,
His health was never better worth than now.

Hotspur: Sick now? droop now? This sickness doth infect
The very life-blood of our enterprise,
'Tis catching hither, even to our camp.
He writes me here, that inward sickness—
And that his friends by deputation could not
So soon be drawn, nor did he think it meet
To lay so dangerous and dear a trust
On any soul remov'd, but on his own.
Yet doth he give us bold advertisement
That with our small conjunction we should on,
To see how fortune is dispos'd to us,
For, as he writes, there is no quailing now,
Because the King is certainly possess'd

---

9 **task:** challenge. **approve:** test. 12 **But . . . him:** but that I will defy him. 18 **justling:** turbulent. **power:** troops. 19 **government:** command. 24 **fear'd:** feared for. 25 **state of time:** times. **whole:** sound, healthy. 27 **better worth:** more important. 30 **catching hither:** contagious as far away as this. 32 **by deputation:** through deputies. 33 **drawn:** mustered. 34 **dear:** significant. 35 **remov'd:** i.e., less intimately involved. 36 **advertisement:** advice. 37 **conjunction:** allied force.

Of all our purposes. What say you to it?
Worcester: Your father's sickness is a maim to us.
Hotspur: A perilous gash, a very limb lopp'd off—
And yet, in faith, it is not; his present want
Seems more than we shall find it. Were it good
To set the exact wealth of all our states
All at one cast? to set so rich a main
On the nice hazard of one doubtful hour?
It were not good, for therein should we read
The very bottom and the soul of hope,
The very list, the very utmost bound
Of all our fortunes.
Douglas: Faith, and so we should,
Where now remains a sweet reversion,
We may boldly spend upon the hope of what
[Is] to come in.
A comfort of retirement lives in this.
Hotspur: A rendezvous, a home to fly unto,
If that the devil and mischance look big
Upon the maidenhead of our affairs.
Worcester: But yet I would your father had been here.
The quality and hair of our attempt
Brooks no division. It will be thought
By some that know not why he is away
That wisdom, loyalty, and mere dislike
Of our proceedings kept the Earl from hence,
And think how such an apprehension
May turn the tide of fearful faction,
And breed a kind of question in our cause.
For well you know we of the off'ring side
Must keep aloof from strict arbitrement,
And stop all sight-holes, every loop from whence
The eye of reason may pry in upon us.
This absence of your father's draws a curtain
That shows the ignorant a kind of fear
Before not dreamt of.
Hotspur: You strain too far.
I rather of his absence make this use:
It lends a lustre and more great opinion,

---

40 **possess'd:** informed. 44 **want:** absence. 46 **set . . . states:** i.e., stake the whole of our resources. 47 **main:** stake. 48 **nice:** delicate. 51 **list:** limit. 53 **reversion:** future prospects, expectation. 56 **comfort of retirement:** refuge to fall back on. 58 **big:** threatening. 59 **maidenhead:** i.e., early phase. 61 **hair:** fiber, nature. 62 **Brooks:** permits. 64 **mere:** outright. 67 **fearful faction:** timorous support. 69 **off'ring:** attacking. 70 **strict arbitrement:** scrupulous inspection. 71 **loop:** loophole. 73 **draws:** draws aside. 77 **opinion:** renown.

A larger dare to our great enterprise,
Than if the Earl were here, for men must think,
If we without his help can make a head
To push against a kingdom, with his help
We shall o'erturn it topsy-turvy down.
Yet all goes well, yet all our joints are whole.

Douglas: As heart can think. There is not such a word
Spoke of in Scotland as this term of fear.

[Enter Sir Richard Vernon.*]*

Hotspur: My cousin Vernon, welcome, by my soul!

Vernon: Pray God my news be worth a welcome, lord.
The Earl of Westmerland, seven thousand strong,
Is marching hitherwards, with him Prince John.

Hotspur: No harm. What more?

Vernon: And further, I have learn'd,
The King himself in person is set forth,
Or hitherwards intended speedily,
With strong and mighty preparation.

Hotspur: He shall be welcome too. Where is his son,
The nimble-footed madcap Prince of Wales,
And his comrades, that daff'd the world aside
And bid it pass?

Vernon: All furnish'd, all in arms;
All plum'd like estridges, that with the wind
Bated like eagles having lately bath'd,
Glittering in golden coats like images,
As full of spirit as the month of May,
And gorgeous as the sun at midsummer;
Wanton as youthful goats, wild as young bulls.
I saw young Harry with his beaver on,
His cushes on his thighs, gallantly arm'd,
Rise from the ground like feathered Mercury,
And vaulted with such ease into his seat
As if an angel [dropp'd] down from the clouds
To turn and wind a fiery Pegasus,
And witch the world with noble horsemanship.

Hotspur: No more, no more! worse than the sun in March,
This praise doth nourish agues. Let them come!
They come like sacrifices in their trim,

---

80 **make a head:** raise an army. 83 **joints:** limbs.
92 **intended:** i.e., intended to come. 96 **daff'd:** thurst. 97 **furnish'd:** equipped.
98 **estridges:** ostriches. 99 **Bated:** beat their wings (a term from falconry).
103 **Wanton:** frolicsome. 104 **beaver:** helmet. 105 **cushes:** cuisses, armor for the thighs. 107 **seat:** saddle. 109 **wind:** wheel. **Pegasus:** winged horse of ancient myth. 112 **agues:** fevers (thought to result from vapors drawn by the sun). 113 **trim:** finery.

And to the fire-ey'd maid of smoky war
All hot and bleeding will we offer them.
The mailed Mars shall on his [altar] sit
Up to the ears in blood. I am on fire
To hear this rich reprisal is so nigh,
And yet not ours. Come let me taste my horse,
Who is to bear me like a thunderbolt
Against the bosom of the Prince of Wales.
Harry to Harry shall, hot horse to horse,
Meet and ne'er part till one drop down a corse.
O that Glendower were come!

Vernon: There is more news:
I learn'd in Worcester, as I rode along,
He [cannot] draw his power this fourteen days.

Douglas: That's the worst tidings that I hear of [yet].

Worcester: Ay, by my faith, that bears a frosty sound.

Hotspur: What may the King's whole battle reach unto?

Vernon: To thirty thousand.

Hotspur: Forty let it be!
My father and Glendower being both away,
The powers of us may serve so great a day.
Come let us take a muster speedily.
Doomsday is near, die all, die merrily.

Douglas: Talk not of dying, I am out of fear
Of death or death's hand for this one half year.

Exeunt.

Scene II

Enter Falstaff, Bardolph.

Falstaff: Bardolph, get thee before to Coventry; fill me a bottle of sack. Our soldiers shall march through; we'll to Sutton Co'fil' to-night.

Bardolph: Will you give me money, captain?

Falstaff: Lay out, lay out.

Bardolph: This bottle makes an angel.

---

114 **fire-ey'd maid:** i.e., Bellona, goddess of war. 116 **mailed:** armored. 118 **reprisal:** prize. 119 **taste:** test. 123 **corse:** corpse. 125 **Worcester:** cathedral city on the Severn River south of Shrewsbury. 126 **draw his power:** assemble his troops. 129 **battle:** army. 135 **out of:** free from.

IV.ii. Location: A public road near Coventry.

3 **Sutton Co'fil':** Sutton Coldfield, a town in Warwickshire. 5 **Lay out:** i.e., pay for it yourself.
6 **makes an angel:** i.e., brings your debt to ten shillings. An angel was a gold coin stamped with the figure of the archangel Michael.

Falstaff: And if it do, take it for thy labor, and if it make twenty, take them all, I'll answer the coinage. Bid my lieutenant Peto meet me at town's end.

Bardolph: I will, captain, farewell. *Exit.*

Falstaff: If I be not asham'd of my soldiers, I am a sous'd gurnet. I have misus'd the King's press damnably. I have got, in exchange of a hundred and fifty soldiers, three hundred and odd pounds. I press me none but good householders, [yeomen's] sons, inquire me out contracted bachelors, such as had been ask'd twice on the banes, such a commodity of warm slaves, as had as lieve hear the devil as a drum, such as fear the report of a caliver worse than a struck fowl or a hurt wild duck. I press'd me none but such toasts-and-butter, with hearts in their bellies no bigger than pins' heads, and they have bought out their services; and now my whole charge consists of ancients, corporals, lieutenants, gentlemen of companies—slaves as ragged as Lazarus in the painted cloth, where the glutton's dogs lick'd his sores, and such as indeed were never soldiers, but discarded unjust servingmen, younger sons to younger brothers, revolted tapsters, and ostlers trade-fall'n, the cankers of a calm world and a long peace, ten times more dishonorable ragged than an old feaz'd ancient: and such have I, to fill up the rooms of them as have bought out their services, that you would think that I had a hundred and fifty totter'd prodigals lately come from swine-keeping, from eating draff and husks. A mad fellow met me on the way and told me I had unloaded all the gibbets and press'd the dead bodies. No eye hath seen such scarecrows. I'll not march through Coventry with them, that's flat. Nay, and the villains march wide betwixt the legs, as if they

---

8 **answer the coinage:** i.e., be responsible for whatever money the purchases "make." 12 **sous'd gurnet:** pickled fish. **press:** warrant for conscripting. 14 **press:** conscript. 16 **contracted:** engaged to be married. 17 **banes:** banns, i.e., public announcements, repeated on three successive Sundays, of a projected marriage. 17–18 **commodity . . . slaves:** lot of comfort-loving fellows. 18 **lieve:** lief. 19 **caliver:** musket. **struck:** wounded. 22–23 **bought . . . services:** i.e., bribed me to let them off. 23 **charge:** troop. 24 **ancients:** ensigns, i.e., standard-bearers. 24–25 **gentlemen of companies:** gentlemen—but not officers—who had volunteered for military service. 25 **Lazarus.** See note to III.iii.32. 25–26 **painted cloth:** cheap wall-hangings. 28 **unjust:** dishonest. 29 **revolted:** runaway. **trade-fall'n:** unemployed. 31 **feaz'd ancient:** tattered flag. 34 **totter'd:** tattered. **prodigals.** See Luke 15:11 ff. 35 **draff:** swill.

had gyves on, for indeed I had the most of them out of prison. There's not a shirt and a half in all my company, and the half shirt is two napkins tack'd together and thrown over the shoulders like a herald's coat without sleeves; and the shirt, to say the truth, stol'n from my host at Saint Albons, or the red-nose innkeeper of Daventry. But that's all one, they'll find linen enough on every hedge.

Enter the Prince, Lord of Westmerland.

Prince: How now, blown Jack? how now, quilt?

Falstaff: What Hal? how now, mad wag? What a devil dost thou in Warwickshire? My good Lord of Westmerland, I cry you mercy! I thought your honor had already been at Shrewsbury.

Westmerland: Faith, Sir John, 'tis more than time that I were there, and you too, but my powers are there already. The King, I can tell you, looks for us all, we must away all night.

Falstaff: Tut, never fear me, I am as vigilant as a cat to steal cream.

Prince: I think, to steal cream indeed, for thy theft hath already made thee butter. But tell me, Jack, whose fellows are these that come after?

Falstaff: Mine, Hal, mine.

Prince: I did never see such pitiful rascals.

Falstaff: Tut, tut, good enough to toss, food for powder, food for powder; they'll fill a pit as well as better. Tush, man, mortal men, mortal men.

Westmerland: Ay, but, Sir John, methinks they are exceeding poor and bare, too beggarly.

Falstaff: Faith, for their poverty, I know not where they had that, and for their bareness, I am sure they never learn'd that of me.

Prince: No, I'll be sworn, unless you call three fingers in the ribs bare. But, sirrah, make haste, Percy is already in the field. *Exit.*

Falstaff: What, is the King encamp'd?

Westmerland: He is, Sir John. I fear we shall stay too long.

Falstaff: Well,

---

41 **gyves:** fetters, leg-irons. 46 **Saint Albons:** St. Albans, town north of London. 47 **Daventry:** town in Northamptonshire. **that's all one:** i.e., no matter. 48 **hedge.** Where linen was spread to dry. 49 **blown:** swollen. 55 **powers:** troops. 57 **must away:** must march. 58 **fear:** worry about. 65 **toss:** i.e., on a pike. 73–74 **three fingers:** i.e., several layers of fat. A finger, used as a measurement, was three-fourths of an inch.

To the latter end of a fray and the beginning of a feast
Fits a dull fighter and a keen guest. *Exeunt.*

SCENE III

[Enter Hotspur, Worcester, Douglas, Vernon.*]*

Hotspur: We'll fight with him to-night.
Worcester: It may not be.
Douglas: You give him then advantage.
Vernon: Not a whit.
Hotspur: Why say you so? Looks he not for supply?
Vernon: So do we.
Hotspur: His is certain, ours is doubtful.
Worcester: Good cousin, be advis'd, stir not to-night.
Vernon: Do not, my lord.
Douglas: You do not counsel well,
You speak it out of fear and cold heart.
Vernon: Do me no slander, Douglas. By my life,
And I dare well maintain it with my life,
If well-respected honor bid me on,
I hold as little counsel with weak fear
As you, my lord, or any Scot that this day lives.
Let it be seen to-morrow in the battle
Which of us fears.
Douglas: Yea, or to-night.
Vernon: Content.
Hotspur: To-night, say I.
Vernon: Come, come, it may not be. I wonder much,
Being men of such great leading as you are,
That you foresee not what impediments
Drag back our expedition. Certain horse
Of my cousin Vernon's are not yet come up.
Your uncle Worcester's horses came but to-day,
And now their pride and mettle is asleep,
Their courage with hard labor tame and dull,
That not a horse is half the half of himself.
Hotspur: So are the horses of the enemy
In general journey-bated and brought low.
The better part of ours are full of rest.
Worcester: The number of the King exceedeth our.
For God's sake, cousin, stay till all come in.

IV.iii. Location: The rebel camp near Shrewsbury.
3 **supply:** reinforcements. 10 **well-respected:** well-considered (in contrast to Hotspur's bravado). 17 **leading:** leadership. 19 **expedition:** (speedy) progress. **horse:** cavalry. 26 **journey-bated:** weary from travel. 28 **our:** our number. 29 s.d. **parley:** trumpet call sounded to request a conference.

The trumpet sounds a parley.
Enter Sir Walter Blunt.

Blunt: I come with gracious offers from the King,
If you vouchsafe me hearing and respect.

Hotspur: Welcome, Sir Walter Blunt; and would to God
You were of our determination!
Some of us love you well, and even those some
Envy your great deservings and good name,
Because you are not of our quality,
But stand against us like an enemy.

Blunt: And God defend but still I should stand so,
So long as out of limit and true rule
You stand against anointed majesty.
But to my charge. The King hath sent to know
The nature of your griefs, and whereupon
You conjure from the breast of civil peace
Such bold hostility, teaching his duteous land
Audacious cruelty. If that the King
Have any way your good deserts forgot,
Which he confesseth to be manifold,
He bids you name your griefs, and with all speed
You shall have your desires with interest
And pardon absolute for yourself and these
Herein misled by your suggestion.

Hotspur: The King is kind, and well we know the King
Knows at what time to promise, when to pay.
My father and my uncle and myself
Did give him that same royalty he wears,
And when he was not six and twenty strong,
Sick in the world's regard, wretched and low,
A poor unminded outlaw sneaking home,
My father gave him welcome to the shore;
And when he heard him swear and vow to God
He came but to be Duke of Lancaster,
To sue his livery and beg his peace,
With tears of innocency and terms of zeal,
My father, in kind heart and pity mov'd,
Swore him assistance, and perform'd it too.
Now when the lords and barons of the realm
Perceiv'd Northumberland did lean to him,

---

33 **of our determination:** i.e., on our side. 35 **Envy:** begrudge. 36 **quality:** party.
38 **defend:** forbid. 39 **limit . . . rule:** i.e., the bounds of honest conduct.
51 **suggestion:** (evil) prompting. 62 **sue his livery:** claim his inheritance. **beg his peace:** i.e., from King Richard. 63 **terms of zeal:** i.e., declarations of loyalty. 65 **perform'd it:** i.e., fulfilled his oath.

The more and less came in with cap and knee,
Met him in boroughs, cities, villages,
Attended him on bridges, stood in lanes,
Laid gifts before him, proffer'd him their oaths,
Gave him their heirs as pages, followed him
Even at the heels in golden multitudes.
He presently, as greatness knows itself,
Steps me a little higher than his vow
Made to my father, while his blood was poor,
Upon the naked shore at Ravenspurgh,
And now forsooth takes on him to reform
Some certain edicts and some strait decrees
That lie too heavy on the commonwealth,
Cries out upon abuses, seems to weep
Over his [country's] wrongs, and by this face,
This seeming brow of justice, did he win
The hearts of all that he did angle for;
Proceeded further—cut me off the heads
Of all the favorites that the absent King
In deputation left behind him here,
When he was personal in the Irish war.

Blunt: Tut, I came not to hear this.

Hotspur: Then to the point.
In short time after, he depos'd the King,
Soon after that, depriv'd him of his life,
And in the neck of that, task'd the whole state;
To make that worse, suff'red his kinsman March
(Who is, if every owner were well plac'd,
Indeed his king) to be engag'd in Wales,
There without ransom to lie forfeited;
Disgrac'd me in my happy victories,
Sought to entrap me by intelligence,
Rated mine uncle from the Council-board,
In rage dismiss'd my father from the court,
Broke oath on oath, committed wrong on wrong,
And in conclusion drove us to seek out
This head of safety, and withal to pry
Into his title, the which we find
Too indirect for long continuance.

---

68 **with . . . knee:** with cap in hand and on bended knee, i.e., deferentially. 70 **lanes:** rows. 73 **golden:** resplendent. 74 **knows itself:** comes to recognize its power. 76 **blood:** spirit. 79 **strait:** strict. 82 **face:** pretense. 88 **personal:** personally engaged. 92 **in . . . that:** immediately thereafter. **task'd:** taxed. 94 **if . . . plac'd:** i.e., if everyone occupied his proper station. 95 **engag'd:** held as hostage. 96. **forfeited:** unclaimed, unredeemed. 97 **happy:** fortunate. 98 **intelligence:** espionage. 99 **Rated:** scolded. 103 **head of safety:** army for security. **withal:** moreover. 104 **title:** i.e., to the throne.

Blunt: Shall I return this answer to the King?
Hotspur: Not so, Sir Walter; we'll withdraw a while.
Go to the King, and let there be impawn'd
Some surety for a safe return again,
And in the morning early shall mine uncle
Bring him our purposes. And so farewell.
Blunt: I would you would accept of grace and love.
Hotspur: And may be so we shall.
Blunt: Pray God you do. [*Exeunt.*]

[Scene IV]

Enter Archbishop of York, Sir Michael.

Archbishop: Hie, good Sir Michael, bear this sealed brief
With winged haste to the Lord Marshal,
This to my cousin Scroop, and all the rest
To whom they are directed. If you knew
How much they do import, you would make haste.
Sir Michael: My good lord,
I guess their tenor.
Archbishop: Like enough you do.
To-morrow, good Sir Michael, is a day
Wherein the fortune of ten thousand men
Must bide the touch; for, sir, at Shrewsbury,
As I am truly given to understand,
The King with mighty and quick-raised power
Meets with Lord Harry; and I fear, Sir Michael,
What with the sickness of Northumberland,
Whose power was in the first proportion,
And what with Owen Glendower's absence thence,
Who with them was a rated sinew too,
And comes not in, overrul'd by prophecies,
I fear the power of Percy is too weak
To wage an instant trial with the King.
Sir Michael: Why, my good lord, you need not fear,
There is Douglas and Lord Mortimer.

---

108 **impawn'd:** pledged.
IV.iv. Location: York. The Archbishop's palace.
o.s.d. **Sir Michael.** Apparently unhistorical.
1 **brief:** letter. 2 **Lord Marshal:** i.e., Thomas Mowbray, third Duke of Nottingham, son of the Thomas Mowbray of *Richard II* whose quarrel with Bullingbrook led to the exile of both men. He would of course be hostile to the House of Lancaster. 3 **my cousin Scroop:** perhaps the Scroop (presumably Sir Stephen) of *Richard II.* III.ii.91 ff. 10 **bide the touch:** withstand the test (as when gold is tested by the touchstone). 15 **in . . . proportion:** i.e., larger than that of his associates. 17 **rated sinew:** i.e., a force on which they thought they could rely. 20 **wage:** risk. **instant:** immediate.

Archbishop: No, Mortimer is not there.
Sir Michael: But there is Mordake, Vernon, Lord Harry Percy,
And there is my Lord of Worcester, and a head
Of gallant warriors, noble gentlemen.
Archbishop: And so there is; but yet the King hath drawn
The special head of all the land together:
The Prince of Wales, Lord John of Lancaster,
The noble Westmerland, and warlike Blunt,
And many moe corrivals and dear men
Of estimation and command in arms.
Sir Michael: Doubt not, my lord, they shall be well oppos'd.
Archbishop: I hope no less, yet needful 'tis to fear,
And to prevent the worst, Sir Michael, speed;
For if Lord Percy thrive not, ere the King
Dismiss his power he means to visit us,
For he hath heard of our confederacy,
And 'tis but wisdom to make strong against him.
Therefore make haste. I must go write again
To other friends, and so farewell, Sir Michael.
Exeunt.

[ACT V]

[SCENE I]

Enter the King, Prince of Wales, Lord John of Lancaster, Sir Walter Blunt, Falstaff.

King: How bloodily the sun begins to peer
Above yon bulky hill! the day looks pale
At his distemp'rature.
Prince: The southren wind
Doth play the trumpet to his purposes,
And by his hollow whistling in the leaves
Foretells a tempest and a blust'ring day.
King: Then with the losers let it sympathize,
For nothing can seem foul to those that win.

The trumpet sounds.

---

25 **head:** troop. 31 **moe corrivals:** more associates. **dear:** valued. 35 **prevent:** forestall. 37 **visit:** i.e., attack.

V.i. Location: The King's camp near Shrewsbury.
3 **his distemp'rature:** i.e., the sun's abnormal appearance. **southren:** southern.
4 **trumpet:** trumpeter. 7 **sympathize:** accord.

Enter Worcester *[and* Sir Richard Vernon*]*.

How now, my Lord of Worcester? 'tis not well
That you and I should meet upon such terms
As now we meet. You have deceiv'd our trust,
And made us doff our easy robes of peace,
To crush our old limbs in ungentle steel.
This is not well, my lord, this is not well.
What say you to it? Will you again unknit
This churlish knot of all-abhorred war?
And move in that obedient orb again
Where you did give a fair and natural light,
And be no more an exhal'd meteor,
A prodigy of fear, and a portent
Of broached mischief to the unborn times?

Worcester: Hear me, my liege.
For mine own part, I could be well content
To entertain the lag end of my life
With quiet hours; for I protest
I have not sought the day of this dislike.

King: You have not sought it, how comes it then?

Falstaff: Rebellion lay in his way, and he found it.

Prince: Peace, chewet, peace!

Worcester: It pleas'd your Majesty to turn your looks
Of favor from myself and all our house,
And yet I must remember you, my lord,
We were the first and dearest of your friends.
For you my staff of office did I break
In Richard's time, and posted day and night
To meet you on the way, and kiss your hand,
When yet you were in place and in account
Nothing so strong and fortunate as I.
It was myself, my brother, and his son,
That brought you home, and boldly did outdare
The dangers of the time. You swore to us,
And you did swear that oath at Doncaster,

---

17 **obedient orb:** (customary) sphere of obedience. 19 **exhal'd meteor.** It was believed that meteors were formed of vapors drawn up from the earth (*exhal'd*) by the sun. 20 **prodigy of fear:** terrifying omen. 21 **broached:** set going. 24 **entertain:** pass. 29 **chewet:** jackdaw, i.e., chatterer. 32 **remember:** remind. 34–35 **For . . . time.** See *Richard II*, II.iii.26–28. 38 **Nothing:** by no means. 42 **Doncaster:** town in Yorkshire. According to Holinshed (Bullough, III, 398), when Bullingbrook reached Doncaster, on his march from Ravenspur, "the earle of Northumberland, and his sonne, sir Henrie Persie, wardens of the marches against Scotland, with the earle of Westmerland, came unto him, where he sware unto those lords that he would demand no more, but the lands that were to him descended by inheritance from his father, and in right of his wife."

That you did nothing purpose 'gainst the state,
Nor claim no further than your new-fall'n right,
The seat of Gaunt, dukedom of Lancaster.
To this we swore our aid. But in short space
It rain'd down fortune show'ring on your head,
And such a flood of greatness fell on you,
What with our help, what with the absent King,
What with the injuries of a wanton time,
The seeming sufferances that you had borne,
And the contrarious winds that held the King
So long in his unlucky Irish wars
That all in England did repute him dead;
And from this swarm of fair advantages
You took occasion to be quickly wooed
To gripe the general sway into your hand,
Forgot your oath to us at Doncaster,
And being fed by us you us'd us so
As that ungentle gull, the cuckoo's bird,
Useth the sparrow; did oppress our nest,
Grew by our feeding to so great a bulk
That even our love durst not come near your sight
For fear of swallowing; but with nimble wing
We were enforc'd for safety sake to fly
Out of your sight and raise this present head,
Whereby we stand opposed by such means
As you yourself have forg'd against yourself
By unkind usage, dangerous countenance,
And violation of all faith and troth
Sworn to us in your younger enterprise.

King: These things indeed you have articulate,
Proclaim'd at market-crosses, read in churches,
To face the garment of rebellion
With some fine color that may please the eye
Of fickle changelings and poor discontents,
Which gape and rub the elbow at the news
Of hurly-burly innovation;
And never yet did insurrection want
Such water-colors to impaint his cause,

---

44 **new-fall'n:** recently inherited. 50 **injuries:** abuses. 51 **sufferances:** sufferings. 57 **gripe:** seize. 60 **ungentle gull:** rude nestling. 63 **our love:** we who loved you. 64 **swallowing:** i.e., being swallowed. 69 **unkind usage:** unnatural treatment. **dangerous:** threatening. 70 **troth:** truth. 72 **articulate:** stated in articles. 74 **face:** trim. 76 **changelings:** turncoats. **discontents:** malcontents. 77 **rub the elbow:** i.e., hug themselves with pleasure. 78 **innovation:** rebellion. 80 **water-colors:** i.e., thin excuses.

Nor moody beggars, starving for a time
Of pell-mell havoc and confusion.

Prince: In both your armies there is many a soul
Shall pay full dearly for this encounter,
If once they join in trial. Tell your nephew
The Prince of Wales doth join with all the world
In praise of Henry Percy. By my hopes,
This present enterprise set off his head,
I do not think a braver gentleman,
More active, valiant, or more valiant, young,
More daring or more bold, is now alive
To grace this latter age with noble deeds.
For my part, I may speak it to my shame,
I have a truant been to chivalry,
And so I hear he doth account me too;
Yet this before my father's Majesty:
I am content that he shall take the odds
Of his great name and estimation,
And will, to save the blood on either side,
Try fortune with him in a single fight.

King: And, Prince of Wales, so dare we venture thee,
Albeit considerations infinite
Do make against it. No, good Worcester, no,
We love our people well, even those we love
That are misled upon your cousin's part,
And, will they take the offer of our grace,
Both he and they and you, yea, every man
Shall be my friend again, and I'll be his.
So tell your cousin, and bring me word
What he will do. But if he will not yield,
Rebuke and dread correction wait on us,
And they shall do their office. So be gone;
We will not now be troubled with reply.
We offer fair, take it advisedly.

Exit Worcester *[with* Vernon*]*.

Prince: It will not be accepted, on my life.
The Douglas and the Hotspur both together
Are confident against the world in arms.

---

81 **moody:** sullen, disaffected. 83 **both:** i.e., the King's and the rebels'. 88 **This . . . head:** not counting his part in this rebellion. 89 **braver:** nobler. 98 **estimation:** renown. 100 **single fight.** The Prince's challenge was apparently Shakespeare's own invention. 102 **Albeit:** although.

King: Hence therefore, every leader to his charge,
For on their answer will we set on them,
And God befriend us as our cause is just!

Exeunt. Manent Prince, Falstaff.

Falstaff: Hal, if thou see me down in the battle and bestride me, so; 'tis a point of friendship.
Prince: Nothing but a Colossus can do thee that
friendship. Say thy prayers, and farewell.
Falstaff: I would 'twere bed-time, Hal, and all well.
Prince: Why, thou owest God a death. [*Exit.*]
Falstaff: 'Tis not due yet, I would be loath to pay him
before his day. What need I be so forward with him
that calls not on me? Well, 'tis no matter, honor pricks
me on. Yea, but how if honor prick me off when
I come on? how then? Can honor set to a leg? No.
Or an arm? No. Or take away the grief of a wound?
No. Honor hath no skill in surgery then? No. What
is honor? A word. What is in that word honor?
What is that honor? Air. A trim reckoning!
Who hath it? He that died a' Wednesday. Doth he
feel it? No. Doth he hear it? No. 'Tis insensible
then? Yea, to the dead. But will['t] not live with the
living? No. Why? Detraction will not suffer it.
Therefore I'll none of it, honor is a mere scutcheon.
And so ends my catechism. *Exit.*

[SCENE II]
Enter Worcester, Sir Richard Vernon.

Worcester: O no, my nephew must not know, Sir
Richard,
The liberal and kind offer of the King.
Vernon: 'Twere best he did.
Worcester: Then are we all [undone];
It is not possible, it cannot be,
The King should keep his word in loving us.
He will suspect us still, and find a time
To punish this offense in other faults.
Supposition all our lives shall be stuck full of eyes,

122 **so:** good. 126 **death:** with a homophonic pun on *debt.* 132 **grief:** pain.
135 **trim reckoning:** neat total. 137 **insensible:** imperceptible to the senses.
140 **scutcheon:** heraldic device exhibited at funerals, on coaches, etc.
V.ii. Location: A plain near the rebel camp.
6 **still:** always. 8 **Supposition:** suspicion.

For treason is but trusted like the fox,
Who never so tame, so cherish'd and lock'd up,
Will have a wild trick of his ancestors.
Look how we can, or sad or merrily,
Interpretation will misquote our looks,
And we shall feed like oxen at a stall,
The better cherish'd, still the nearer death.
My nephew's trespass may be well forgot,
It hath the excuse of youth and heat of blood,
And an adopted name of privilege,
A hare-brain'd Hotspur, govern'd by a spleen.
All his offenses live upon my head
And on his father's. We did train him on,
And his corruption being ta'en from us,
We as the spring of all shall pay for all.
Therefore, good cousin, let not Harry know,
In any case, the offer of the King.

Vernon: Deliver what you will, I'll say 'tis so.
Here comes your cousin.

Enter Percy *[Hotspur and* Douglas*]*.

Hotspur: My uncle is return'd,
Deliver up my Lord of Westmerland.
Uncle, what news?

Worcester: The King will bid you battle presently.

Douglas: Defy him by the Lord of Westmerland.

Hotspur: Lord Douglas, go you and tell him so.

Douglas: Marry, and shall, and very willingly.

Exit Douglas.

Worcester: There is no seeming mercy in the King.

Hotspur: Did you beg any? God forbid!

Worcester: I told him gently of our grievances,
Of his oath-breaking, which he mended thus,
By now forswearing that he is forsworn.
He calls us rebels, traitors, and will scourge
With haughty arms this hateful name in us.

Enter Douglas.

Douglas: Arm, gentlemen, to arms! for I have thrown
A brave defiance in King Henry's teeth,

---

10 **never so:** however. 11 **wild trick:** i.e., trace of the characteristic wildness.
18 **adopted . . . privilege:** i.e., a nickname (Hotspur) that sanctions rash behavior.
19 **spleen:** irrational impulse. 21 **train:** lure (into rebellion). 23 **spring:** source.
26 **Deliver:** report. 28 **Deliver up:** release. **Westmerland.** The hostage mentioned at IV.iii.108–9. 30 **presently:** at once. 42 **brave:** haughty.

And Westmerland, that was engag'd, did bear it,
Which cannot choose but bring him quickly on.

Worcester: The Prince of Wales stepp'd forth before the King,
And, nephew, challeng'd you to single fight.

Hotspur: O would the quarrel lay upon our heads,
And that no man might draw short breath to-day
But I and Harry Monmouth! Tell me, tell me,
How show'd his tasking? seem'd it in contempt?

Vernon: No, by my soul, I never in my life
Did hear a challenge urg'd more modestly,
Unless a brother should a brother dare
To gentle exercise and proof of arms.
He gave you all the duties of a man,
Trimm'd up your praises with a princely tongue,
Spoke your deservings like a chronicle,
Making you ever better than his praise
By still dispraising praise valued with you,
And which became him like a prince indeed,
He made a blushing cital of himself,
And chid his truant youth with such a grace
As if he mast'red there a double spirit
Of teaching and of learning instantly
There did he pause, but let me tell the world,
If he outlive the envy of this day,
England did never owe so sweet a hope,
So much misconstrued in his wantonness.

Hotspur: Cousin, I think thou art enamored
On his follies. Never did I hear
Of any prince so wild a liberty.
But be he as he will, yet once ere night
I will embrace him with a soldier's arm
That he shall shrink under my courtesy.
Arm, arm with speed! and, fellows, soldiers, friends,
Better consider what you have to do
Than I, that have not well the gift of tongue,
Can lift your blood up with persuasion.

Enter a Messenger.

Messenger: My lord, here are letters for you.

Hotspur: I cannot read them now.
O gentlemen, the time of life is short!

---

43 **engag'd:** held as hostage. 50 **tasking:** challenge. 52 **urg'd:** presented. 54 **proof:** test. 55 **duties:** due merits. 59 **dispraising:** disparaging, discounting. **valued:** compared. 61 **cital:** impeachment. 64 **instantly:** simultaneously. 66 **envy:** malice. 67 **owe:** own. 71 **so . . . liberty:** such reckless dissipation.

To spend that shortness basely were too long
If life did ride upon a dial's point,
Still ending at the arrival of an hour.
And if we live, we live to tread on kings,
If die, brave death, when princes die with us!
Now for our consciences, the arms are fair
When the intent of bearing them is just.

*Enter another [*Messenger*].*

[2.] *Messenger:* My lord, prepare, the King comes on apace.

Hotspur: I thank him that he cuts me from my tale,
For I profess not talking; only this—
Let each man do his best, and here draw I
A sword, whose temper I intend to stain
With the best blood that I can meet withal
In the adventure of this perilous day.
Now *Esperance! Percy!* and set on.
Sound all the lofty instruments of war,
And by that music let us all embrace,
For, heaven to earth, some of us never shall
A second time do such a courtesy.

Here they embrace [and exeunt].

[Scene III]

The trumpets sound. The King enters with his power [*and passes over*].
Alarm to the battle. Then enter
Douglas *and* Sir Walter Blunt.

Blunt: What is thy name, that in battle thus
Thou crossest me? What honor dost thou seek
Upon my head?

Douglas: Know then, my name is Douglas,
And I do haunt thee in the battle thus
Because some tell me that thou art a king.

Blunt: They tell thee true.

Douglas: The Lord of Stafford dear to-day hath bought
Thy likeness, for in stead of thee, King Harry,

---

83 **dial's point:** clock's hand. 84 **Still . . . hour:** i.e., lasting only for an hour.
87 **for:** as for. **fair:** just. 99 **heaven to earth:** heaven wagered against earth.

V.iii. Location: Scene continues.
o.s.d. **power:** army. **Alarm:** trumpet signal to advance.

This sword hath ended him. So shall it thee,
Unless thou yield thee as my prisoner.

Blunt: I was not born a yielder, thou proud Scot,
And thou shalt find a king that will revenge
Lord Stafford's death.

They fight. Douglas *kills* Blunt.
Then enter Hotspur.

Hotspur: O Douglas, hadst thou fought at Holmedon
thus,
I never had triumph'd upon a Scot.

Douglas: All's done, all's won, here breathless lies the King.

Hotspur: Where?

Douglas: Here.

Hotspur: This, Douglas? No, I know this face full well.
A gallant knight he was, his name was Blunt,
Semblably furnish'd like the King himself.

Douglas: [A] fool go with thy soul, whither it goes!
A borrowed title hast thou bought too dear.
Why didst thou tell me that thou wert a king?

Hotspur: The King hath many marching in his coats.

Douglas: Now by my sword, I will kill all his coats;
I'll murder all his wardrop, piece by piece,
Until I meet the King.

Hotspur: Up and away!
Our soldiers stand full fairly for the day. [*Exeunt.*]

Alarm. Enter Falstaff *solus.*

Falstaff: Though I could scape shot-free at London, I fear the shot here, here's no scoring but upon the pate. Soft, who are you? Sir Walter Blunt. There's honor for you! Here's no vanity! I am as hot as molten lead, and as heavy too. God keep lead out of me! I need no more weight than mine own bowels. I have led my ragamuffins where they are pepper'd; there's not

---

10 **yield thee:** surrender yourself. 13 **Lord Stafford's death.** According to Holinshed (Bullough, IV, 190–91), Hotspur and Douglas, intent on killing the King, "gave such a violent onset upon them that stood about the kings standard, that slaieng his standard-bearer sir Walter Blunt, and overthrowing the standard, they made slaughter of all those that stood about it, as the earle of Stafford, that daie made by the king constable of the realme, and diverse other." 21 **Semblably furnish'd:** similarly armed and dressed (to serve as a decoy). 22 **A fool . . . goes:** i.e., may the opprobrious epithet "fool" be attached to you, wherever you're going. 25 **The King . . . coats.** A common strategem. 27 **wardrop:** wardrobe. 29 **stand . . . day:** i.e., seem to be upon the point of victory. 30 **shot-free:** i.e., without paying the shot, or tavern bill. 31 **scoring:** cutting (with a pun on scoring one's bill by making notches on a stick). 33 **vanity:** trifling.

three of my hundred and fifty left alive, and they are for the town's end, to beg during life. But who comes here?

Enter the Prince.

Prince: What, stands thou idle here? Lend me thy sword.
Many a nobleman lies stark and stiff
Under the hoofs of vaunting enemies,
Whose deaths are yet unreveng'd. I prithee lend me thy sword.

Falstaff: O Hal, I prithee give me leave to breathe a while. Turk Gregory never did such deeds in arms as I have done this day. I have paid Percy, I have made him sure.

Prince: He is indeed, and living to kill thee. I prithee lend me thy sword.

Falstaff: Nay, before God, Hal, if Percy be alive, thou gets not my sword, but take my pistol, if thou wilt.

Prince: Give it me. What? is it in the case?

Falstaff: Ay, Hal, 'tis hot, 'tis hot. There's that will sack a city.

The Prince *draws it out, and finds it to be a bottle of sack.*

Prince: What, is it a time to jest and dally now?

He throws the bottle at him. Exit.

Falstaff: Well, if Percy be alive, I'll pierce him. If he do come in my way, so; if he do not, if I come in his willingly, let him make a carbonado of me. I like not such grinning honor as Sir Walter hath. Give me life, which if I can save, so; if not, honor comes unlook'd for, and there's an end. [*Exit.*]

[Scene IV]

Alarm: Excursions. Enter the King, *the* Prince *[wounded]*, Lord John of Lancaster, Earl of Westmerland.

---

38 **town's end:** i.e., the city gate (where beggars congregated). 45 **Turk:** stock title for a merciless person. **Gregory:** perhaps Pope Gregory VII, who was famous for his valor. 46 **paid:** settled with, i.e., killed. 47 **made him sure:** made sure of him. 48 **He is:** i.e., he is sure (to be alive and dangerous). 56 **pierce.** Pronounced *perse.* 58 **carbonado:** meat slashed for broiling.

V.iv. Location: Scene continues.
o.s.d. **Excursions:** sallies, sorties.

King: I prithee,
Harry, withdraw thyself, thou bleedest too much.
Lord John of Lancaster, go you with him.
Lancaster: Not I, my lord, unless I did bleed too.
Prince: I beseech your Majesty make up,
Lest your retirement do amaze your friends.
King: I will do so.
My Lord of Westmerland, lead him to his tent.
Westmerland: Come, my lord, I'll lead you to your tent.
Prince: Lead me, my lord? I do not need your
help,
And God forbid a shallow scratch should drive
The Prince of Wales from such a field as this,
Where stain'd nobility lies trodden on,
And rebels' arms triumph in massacres!
Lancaster: We breathe too long. Come, cousin West-
merland,
Our duty this way lies; for God's sake come.

[Exeunt Prince John *and* Westmerland.*]*

Prince: By God, thou hast deceiv'd me, Lancaster,
I did not think thee lord of such a spirit.
Before, I lov'd thee as a brother, John,
But now I do respect thee as my soul.
King: I saw him hold Lord Percy at the point,
With lustier maintenance than I did look for
Of such an ungrown warrior.
Prince: O, this boy
Lends mettle to us all! *Exit.*

[Enter Douglas.*]*

Douglas: Another king? they grow like Hydra's
heads.
I am the Douglas, fatal to all those
That wear those colors on them. What art thou
That counterfeit'st the person of a king?
King: The King himself, who, Douglas, grieves at
heart
So many of his shadows thou hast met
And not the very King. I have two boys

---

5 **make up:** advance. 6 **amaze:** dismay. 13 **stain'd:** (1) soiled with battle; (2) disgraced. 15 **breathe:** pause for breath. 22 **lustier maintenance:** more valiant endurance. 25 **Hydra:** in Greek mythology, a many-headed monster that grew two new heads for each one struck off. Holinshed (Bullough, IV, 191) reports that Douglas "slue sir Walter Blunt, and three other, apparelled in the kings sute and clothing, saieng: I marvell to see so many kings thus suddenlie arise one in the necke of an other." 27 **those colors:** i.e., colors of the King's coat of arms. 30 **shadows:** likenesses. 31 **the very King:** the King himself.

Seek Percy and thyself about the field,
But seeing thou fall'st on me so luckily,
I will assay thee, and defend thyself.

Douglas: I fear thou art another counterfeit,
And yet in faith thou bearest thee like a king.
But mine I am sure thou art, whoe'er thou be,
And thus I win thee.

They fight; the King *being in danger, enter* Prince of Wales.

Prince: Hold up thy head, vile Scot, or thou art like
Never to hold it up again! The spirits
Of valiant Shirley, Stafford, Blunt are in my arms.
It is the Prince of Wales that threatens thee,
Who never promiseth but he means to pay.

They fight: Douglas *flieth.*

Cheerly, my lord, how fares your Grace?
Sir Nicholas Gawsey hath for succor sent,
And so hath Clifton. I'll to Clifton straight.

King: Stay and breathe a while.
Thou hast redeem'd thy lost opinion,
And show'd thou mak'st some tender of my life
In this fair rescue thou hast brought to me.

Prince: O God, they did me too much injury
That ever said I heark'ned for your death.
If it were so, I might have let alone
The insulting hand of Douglas over you,
Which would have been as speedy in your end
As all the poisonous potions in the world,
And sav'd the treacherous labor of your son.

King: Make up to Clifton, I'll to Sir Nicholas
Gawsey. *Exit* King.

Enter Hotspur.

Hotspur: If I mistake not, thou art Harry Monmouth.

Prince: Thou speak'st as if I would deny my name.

Hotspur: My name is Harry Percy.

Prince: Why then I see
A very valiant rebel of the name.
I am the Prince of Wales, and think not, Percy,
To share with me in glory any more.

---

32 **Seek:** who seek. 34 **assay:** challenge. 41, 45, 46 **Shirley, Gawsey, Clifton.** Holinshed (Bullough, IV, 191) mentions "sir Hugh Shorlie," "sir Nicholas Gausell," and "sir John Clifton" as notable casualties of the battle of Shrewsbury. 44 s.d. **They . . . flieth.** Holinshed (Bullough, IV, 191) records the tradition that the King was struck down by Douglas but does not assign his rescue to the Prince, saying only that the King "was raised." 48 **opinion:** reputation. 49 **mak'st . . . of:** hast some regard for. 54 **insulting:** exulting.

Two stars keep not their motion in one sphere,
Nor can one England brook a double reign
Of Harry Percy and the Prince of Wales.

Hotspur [*Nor*]: shall it, Harry, for the hour is come
To end the one of us, and would to God
Thy name in arms were now as great as mine!

Prince: I'll make it greater ere I part from thee,
And all the budding honors on thy crest
I'll crop to make a garland for my head.

Hotspur: I can no longer brook thy vanities.

They fight.

Falstaff: Well said, Hal! to it, Hal! Nay, you shall find
no boy's play here, I can tell you.

Enter Douglas; *he fighteth with* Falstaff. *He* [Falstaff] *falls down as if he were dead [and exit* Douglas*]. The Prince killeth* Percy.

Hotspur: O Harry, thou hast robb'd me of my youth!
I better brook the loss of brittle life
Than those proud titles thou hast won of me.
They wound my thoughts worse than thy sword my flesh.
But thoughts, the slaves of life, and life, time's fool,
And time, that takes survey of all the world,
Must have a stop. O, I could prophesy,
But that the earthy and cold hand of death
Lies on my tongue. No, Percy, thou art dust,
And food for— [*Dies.*]

Prince: For worms, brave Percy. Fare thee well, great heart!
Ill-weav'd ambition, how much art thou shrunk!
When that this body did contain a spirit,
A kingdom for it was too small a bound,
But now two paces of the vilest earth
Is room enough. This earth that bears [thee] dead
Bears not alive so stout a gentleman.
If thou wert sensible of courtesy,
I should not make so dear a show of zeal;
But let my favors hide thy mangled face,
And even in thy behalf I'll thank myself

---

66 **brook:** endure. 83 **I could prophesy.** Dying men were thought to have the gift of prophecy. 86 s.d. **Dies.** Holinshed (Bullough, IV, 191) does not credit the Prince with Hotspur's death, saying merely that those loyal to the King, "incouraged by his doings, fought valiantlie, and slue the lord Persie, called sir Henrie Hotspurre." 93 **stout:** brave. 95 **make . . . zeal:** i.e., express my admiration so freely. 96 **favors:** scarves, gloves, plumes, or the like (with which the Prince covers Hotspur's "mangled face").

For doing these fair rites of tenderness.
Adieu, and take thy praise with thee to heaven!
Thy ignominy sleep with thee in the grave,
But not remembʼred in thy epitaph!

He spieth Falstaff *on the ground.*

What, old acquaintance! could not all this flesh
Keep in a little life? Poor Jack, farewell!
I could have better sparʼd a better man.
O, I should have a heavy miss of thee
If I were much in love with vanity!
Death hath not strook so fat a deer to-day,
Though many dearer, in this bloody fray.
Embowellʼd will I see thee by and by,
Till then in blood by noble Percy lie.

Exit. Falstaff *riseth up.*

Falstaff: Embowellʼd! if thou embowel me to-day, Iʼll give you leave to powder me and eat me too to-morrow. ʼSblood, ʼtwas time to counterfeit, or that hot termagant Scot had paid me scot and lot too. Counterfeit? I lie, I am no counterfeit. To die is to be a counterfeit, for he is but the counterfeit of a man who hath not the life of a man; but to counterfeit dying, when a man thereby liveth, is to be no counterfeit, but the true and perfect image of life indeed. The better part of valor is discretion, in the which better part I have savʼd my life. ʼZounds, I am afraid of this gunpowder Percy though he be dead. How if he should counterfeit too and rise? By my faith, I am afraid he would prove the better counterfeit. Therefore Iʼll make him sure, yea, and Iʼll swear I killʼd him. Why may not he rise as well as I? Nothing confutes me but eyes, and nobody sees me. Therefore, sirrah [*stabbing him*], with a new wound in your thigh, come you along with me. *He takes up* Hotspur *on his back.*

Enter Prince *[and]* John of Lancaster.

Prince: Come, brother John, full bravely hast thou
fleshʼd
Thy maiden sword.

---

106 **vanity:** frivolity. 109 **Embowellʼd:** disembowelled (for embalming). 112 **powder:** salt. 114 **termagent:** violent. 114 **scot and lot:** completely. 120 **part:** quality. 130 **fleshʼd:** initiated (with the first taste of blood).

Lancaster: But soft, whom have we here?
Did you not tell me this fat man was dead?

Prince: I did, I saw him dead,
Breathless and bleeding on the ground. Art thou alive?
Or is it fantasy that plays upon our eyesight?
I prithee speak, we will not trust our eyes
Without our ears: thou art not what thou seem'st.

Falstaff: No, that's certain, I am not a double man; but if I be not Jack Falstaff, then am I a Jack. There is Percy [*throwing the body down*]. If your father will do me any honor, so; if not, let him kill the next Percy himself. I look to be either earl or duke, I can assure you.

Prince: Why, Percy I kill'd myself, and saw thee dead.

Falstaff: Didst thou? Lord, Lord, how this world is given to lying! I grant you I was down and out of breath, and so was he, but we rose both at an instant and fought a long hour by Shrewsbury clock. If I may be believ'd, so; if not, let them that should reward valor bear the sin upon their own heads. I'll take it upon my death, I gave him this wound in the thigh. If the man were alive and would deny it, 'zounds, I would make him eat a piece of my sword.

Lancaster: This is the strangest tale that ever I heard.

Prince: This is the strangest fellow, brother John.
Come bring your luggage nobly on your back.
For my part, if a lie may do thee grace,
I'll gild it with the happiest terms I have.

A retrait is sounded.

The trumpet sounds retrait, the day is our.
Come, brother, let us to the highest of the field,
To see what friends are living, who are dead.

Exeunt [Prince *and* Lancaster].

Falstaff: I'll follow, as they say, for reward. He that rewards me, God reward him! If I do grow great, I'll grow less, for I'll purge and leave sack, and live cleanly as a nobleman should do. *Exit.*

---

138 **double man:** (1) spectre; (2) two men. 139 **Jack:** rascal. 157 **grace:** credit. 158 s.d. **retrait:** retreat, trumpet signal to withdraw. 159 **our:** ours. 160 **highest:** highest point. 164 **purge:** (1) take laxatives (to reduce); (2) purge my sins, i.e., repent.

[Scene V]

The trumpets sound. Enter the King, Prince of Wales, Lord John of Lancaster, Earl of Westmerland, *with* Worcester *and* Vernon prisoners.

King: Thus ever did rebellion find rebuke.
Ill-spirited Worcester, did not we send grace,
Pardon, and terms of love to all of you?
And wouldst thou turn our offers contrary?
Misuse the tenor of thy kinsman's trust?
Three knights upon our party slain to-day,
A noble earl, and many a creature else
Had been alive this hour,
If like a Christian thou hadst truly borne
Betwixt our armies true intelligence.

Worcester: What I have done my safety urg'd me to;
And I embrace this fortune patiently,
Since not to be avoided it falls on me.

King: Bear Worcester to the death and Vernon too.
Other offenders we will pause upon.

[Exeunt Worcester *and* Vernon guarded.*]*

How goes the field?

Prince: The noble Scot, Lord Douglas, when he saw
The fortune of the day quite turn'd from him,
The noble Percy slain, and all his men
Upon the foot of fear, fled with the rest,
And falling from a hill, he was so bruis'd
That the pursuers took him. At my tent
The Douglas is; and I beseech your Grace
I may dispose of him.

King: With all my heart.

Prince: Then, brother John of Lancaster, to you
This honorable bounty shall belong.

V.v. Location: The command post of the King.

2 **grace:** assurance of favor. 3 **terms of love:** expressions of friendship. 5 **Misuse . . . trust:** i.e., abuse Hotspur's confidence in you (as emissaries). 10 **intelligence:** information. 12 **patiently:** tranquilly. 15 **pause upon:** reflect about. 20 **Upon . . . fear:** fleeing in terror. 21–22 **falling . . . him.** According to Holinshed (Bullough, IV, 191), "the earle of Dowglas, for hast, falling from the crag of an hie mounteine, brake one of his cullions [testicles], and was taken, and for his valiantnesse, of the king frankelie and freelie delivered." 24 **dispose of him:** decide what to do with him. 26 **honorable bounty:** gracious assignment.

Go to the Douglas, and deliver him
Up to his pleasure, ransomless and free.
His valors shown upon our crests to-day
Have taught us how to cherish such high deeds
Even in the bosom of our adversaries.

Lancaster: I thank your Grace for this high courtesy,
Which I shall give away immediately.

King: Then this remains, that we divide our
power.
You, son John, and my cousin Westmerland
Towards York shall bend you with your dearest speed,
To meet Northumberland and the prelate Scroop,
Who, as we hear, are busily in arms.
Myself and you, son Harry, will towards Wales,
To fight with Glendower and the Earl of March.
Rebellion in this land shall lose his sway,
Meeting the check of such another day,
And since this business so fair is done,
Let us not leave till all our own be won. *Exeunt.*

(1598)

Questions for Discussion and Writing

Close Reading

1. How does Prince Henry (Hal) justify the time he spends with Falstaff and the other thieves and drunkards at the tavern?
2. How does King Henry IV respond to his son Hal's behavior?
3. What is Hotspur's plan? Why does it fail?

Critical and Creative Reading

4. Although Falstaff is a foil to King Henry IV, he is a kind of mentor to Prince Hal, as well as a leader within his circle. What does a comparison of Falstaff and King Henry reveal about both characters and about their place in the drama?
5. Note all the references to time. Why is time important?
6. Do you approve or disapprove of Prince Hal's plan to live among the lowly before taking on his kingly duties? What are the benefits and potential drawbacks of this plan?

---

27 **deliver:** release. 33 **give away:** i.e., inform Douglas of. 34 **power:** army.
36 **dearest:** most zealous. 43 **fair:** successfully.

Connections to Other Readings

7. Consider the role of kings in this play and in Tennyson's poem "Ulysses."
8. In Washington Irving's story "Rip Van Winkle," Rip, like Hal, shirks his expected duties, yet both characters are admired and necessary in their social group. Consider the way "avoidance of labor" and "avoidance of duty" function in these two works, and draw a conclusion about the two characters. (Ruth Prawer Jhabvala's story "The Interview" might also help you develop this question.)
9. In Aristides's essay "Work and Its Contents," a key concept for enjoying one's work is to regard it as an evolution of play. If Hal's time with Falstaff and Company is Hal's playtime, is there any evidence that he will be able to preserve that playful element once he has returned to his prescribed "job" as heir to the throne?

Essays

Virginia Woolf

Professions for Women

Known primarily for her experimental novels such as *Mrs. Dalloway* and *To the Lighthouse* and for her long essay *A Room of One's Own,* Virginia Woolf (1882–1941) is one of the most important, influential writers of the twentieth century. She was a member of the "Bloomsbury Group" of writers and thinkers who helped usher in the modern age in England. She was also the cofounder, with her husband Leonard Woolf, of the Hogarth Press, an important publisher responsible for the first English translation of Sigmund Freud's works and the poetry of T. S. Eliot. Woolf's writing combines the sophistication of British intellectualism with the desire to accomplish something new, modern, and experimental. "Professions for Women," originally read as a paper to the Women's Service League, advances some of the ideas Woolf explores in *A Room of One's Own,* a powerful work too lengthy to include here.

When your secretary invited me to come here, she told me that your Society is concerned with the employment of women and she suggested that I might tell you something about my own professional experiences. It is true I am a woman; it is true I am employed; but what professional experiences have I had? It is difficult to say. My profession is literature; and in that profession there are fewer experiences for women than in any other, with the exception of the stage—fewer, I mean, that are peculiar to women. For the road was cut many years ago—by

Fanny Burney, by Aphra Behn, by Harriet Martineau, by Jane Austen, by George Eliot[1]—many famous women, and many more unknown and forgotten, have been before me, making the path smooth, and regulating my steps. Thus, when I came to write, there were very few material obstacles in my way. Writing was a reputable and harmless occupation. The family peace was not broken by the scratching of a pen. No demand was made upon the family purse. For ten and sixpence one can buy paper enough to write all the plays of Shakespeare—if one has a mind that way. Pianos and models, Paris, Vienna and Berlin, masters and mistresses, are not needed by a writer. The cheapness of writing paper is, of course, the reason why women have succeeded as writers before they have succeeded in the other professions.

But to tell you my story—it is a simple one. You have only got to figure to yourselves a girl in a bedroom with a pen in her hand. She had only to move that pen from left to right—from ten o'clock to one. Then it occurred to her to do what is simple and cheap enough after all—to slip a few of those pages into an envelope, fix a penny stamp in the corner, and drop the envelope into the red box at the corner. It was thus that I became a journalist; and my effort was rewarded on the first day of the following month—a very glorious day it was for me—by a letter from an editor containing a cheque for one pound ten shillings and sixpence. But to show you how little I deserve to be called a professional woman, how little I know of the struggles and difficulties of such lives, I have to admit that instead of spending that sum upon bread and butter, rent, shoes and stockings, or butcher's bills, I went out and bought a cat—a beautiful cat, a Persian cat, which very soon involved me in bitter disputes with my neighbours.

What could be easier than to write articles and to buy Persian cats with the profits? But wait a moment. Articles have to be about something. Mine, I seem to remember, was about a novel by a famous man. And while I was writing this review, I discovered that if I were going to review books I should need to do battle with a certain phantom. And the phantom was a woman, and when I came to know her better I called her after the heroine of a famous poem, The Angel in the House. It was she who used to come between me and my paper when I was writing reviews. It was she who bothered me and wasted my time and so tormented me that at last I killed her. You who come of a younger and happier generation may not have heard of her—you may not know what I mean by the Angel in the House.[2] I will describe her as shortly as I can. She was intensely sympathetic. She was immensely charming. She was utterly unselfish. She excelled in the difficult arts of family life. She sacrificed herself daily. If there was chicken, she took the leg; if there was a draught she sat in it—in short she was so constituted that she never had a mind or a wish of her own, but preferred to sympathize always with the minds and wishes of others. Above all—I need not say

[1]*George Eliot:* Woolf is referring to female authors who preceded her, including Mary Ann Evans (1819–1880), a female Victorian novelist who published under a male pseudonym, George Eliot.

[2]*Angel in the House:* A poem by Coventry Patmore (1823–1896) published between 1854 and 1862.

it—she was pure. Her purity was supposed to be her chief beauty—her blushes, her great grace. In those days—the last of Queen Victoria—every house had its Angel. And when I came to write I encountered her with the very first words. The shadow of her wings fell on my page; I heard the rustling of her skirts in the room. Directly, that is to say, I took my pen in hand to review that novel by a famous man, she slipped behind me and whispered: "My dear, you are a young woman. You are writing about a book that has been written by a man. Be sympathetic; be tender; flatter; deceive; use all the arts and wiles of our sex. Never let anybody guess that you have a mind of your own. Above all, be pure." And she made as if to guide my pen. I now record the one act for which I take some credit to myself, though the credit rightly belongs to some excellent ancestors of mine who left me a certain sum of money—shall we say five hundred pounds a year?—so that it was not necessary for me to depend solely on charm for my living. I turned upon her and caught her by the throat. I did my best to kill her. My excuse, if I were to be had up in a court of law, would be that I acted in self-defence. Had I not killed her she would have killed me. She would have plucked the heart out of my writing. For, as I found, directly I put pen to paper, you cannot review even a novel without having a mind of your own, without expressing what you think to be the truth about human relations, morality, sex. And all these questions, according to the Angel in the House, cannot be dealt with freely and openly by women; they must charm, they must conciliate, they must—to put it bluntly—tell lies if they are to succeed. Thus, whenever I felt the shadow of her wing or the radiance of her halo upon my page, I took up the inkpot and flung it at her. She died hard. Her fictitious nature was of great assistance to her. It is far harder to kill a phantom than a reality. She was always creeping back when I thought I had despatched her. Though I flatter myself that I killed her in the end, the struggle was severe; it took much time that had better have been spent upon learning Greek grammar; or in roaming the world in search of adventures. But it was a real experience; it was an experience that was bound to befall all women writers at that time. Killing the Angel in the House was part of the occupation of a woman writer.

But to continue my story. The Angel was dead; what then remained? You may say that what remained was a simple and common object—a young woman in a bedroom with an inkpot. In other words, now that she had rid herself of falsehood, that young woman had only to be herself. Ah, but what is "herself"? I mean, what is a woman? I assure you, I do not know. I do not believe that you know. I do not believe that anybody can know until she has expressed herself in all the arts and professions open to human skill. That indeed is one of the reasons why I have come here—out of respect for you, who are in process of showing us by your experiments what a woman is, who are in process of providing us, by your failures and successes, with that extremely important piece of information.

But to continue the story of my professional experiences. I made one 5
pound ten and six by my first review; and I bought a Persian cat with the proceeds. Then I grew ambitious. A Persian cat is all very well, I said; but a Persian cat is not enough. I must have a motor car. And it was thus that I became

a novelist—for it is a very strange thing that people will give you a motor car if you will tell them a story. It is a still stranger thing that there is nothing so delightful in the world as telling stories. It is far pleasanter then writing reviews of famous novels. And yet, if I am to obey your secretary and tell you my professional experiences as a novelist, I must tell you about a very strange experience that befell me as a novelist. And to understand it you must try first to imagine a novelist's state of mind. I hope I am not giving away professional secrets if I say that a novelist's chief desire is to be as unconscious as possible. He has to induce in himself a state of perpetual lethargy. He wants life to proceed with the utmost quiet and regularity. He wants to see the same faces, to read the same books, to do the same things day after day, month after month, while he is writing, so that nothing may break the illusion in which he is living—so that nothing may disturb or disquiet the mysterious nosings about, feelings round, darts, dashes and sudden discoveries of that very shy and illusive spirit, the imagination. I suspect that this state is the same both for men and women. Be that as it may, I want you to imagine me writing a novel in a state of trance. I want you to figure to yourselves a girl sitting with a pen in her hand, which for minutes, and indeed for hours, she never dips into the inkpot. The image that comes to my mind when I think of this girl is the image of a fisherman lying sunk in dreams on the verge of a deep lake with a rod held out over the water. She was letting her imagination sweep unchecked round every rock and cranny of the world that lies submerged in the depths of our unconscious being. Now came the experience, the experience that I believe to be far commoner with women writers than with men. The line raced through the girl's fingers. Her imagination had rushed away. It had sought the pools, the depths, the dark places where the largest fish slumber. And then there was a smash. There was an explosion. There was foam and confusion. The imagination had dashed itself against something hard. The girl was roused from her dream. She was indeed in a state of the most acute and difficult distress. To speak without figure she had thought of something, something about the body, about the passions which it was unfitting for her as a woman to say. Men, her reason told her, would be shocked. The consciousness of what men will say of a woman who speaks the truth about her passions had roused her from her artist's state of unconsciousness. She could write no more. The trance was over. Her imagination could work no longer. This I believe to be a very common experience with women writers—they are impeded by the extreme conventionality of the other sex. For though men sensibly allow themselves great freedom in these respects, I doubt that they realize or can control the extreme severity with which they condemn such freedom in women.

These then were two very genuine experiences of my own. These were two of the adventures of my professional life. The first—killing the Angel in the House—I think I solved. She died. But the second, telling the truth about my own experiences as a body, I do not think I solved. I doubt that any woman has solved it yet. The obstacles against her are still immensely powerful—and yet they are very difficult to define. Outwardly, what is simpler than to write books?

Outwardly, what obstacles are there for a woman rather than for a man? Inwardly, I think, the case is very different; she has still many ghosts to fight, many prejudices to overcome. Indeed it will be a long time still, I think, before a woman can sit down to write a book without finding a phantom to be slain, a rock to be dashed against. And if this is so in literature, the freest of all professions for women, how is it in the new professions which you are now for the first time entering?

Those are the questions that I should like, had I time, to ask you. And indeed, if I have laid stress upon these professional experiences of mine, it is because I believe that they are, though in different forms, yours also. Even when the path is nominally open—when there is nothing to prevent a woman from being a doctor, a lawyer, a civil servant—there are many phantoms and obstacles, as I believe, looming in her way. To discuss and define them is I think of great value and importance; for thus only can the labour be shared, the difficulties be solved. But besides this, it is necessary also to discuss the ends and the aims for which we are fighting, for which we are doing battle with these formidable obstacles. Those aims cannot be taken for granted; they must be perpetually questioned and examined. The whole position, as I see it—here in this hall surrounded by women practising for the first time in history I know not how many different professions—is one of extraordinary interest and importance. You have won rooms of your own in the house hitherto exclusively owned by men. You are able, though not without great labour and effort, to pay the rent. You are earning your five hundred pounds a year. But this freedom is only a beginning; the room is your own, but it is still bare. It has to be furnished; it has to be decorated; it has to be shared. How are you going to furnish it, how are you going to decorate it? With whom are you going to share it, and upon what terms? These, I think are questions of the utmost importance and interest. For the first time in history you are able to ask them; for the first time you are able to decide for yourselves what the answers should be. Willingly would I stay and discuss those questions and answers—but not tonight. My time is up; and I must cease.

(1942)

Questions for Discussion and Writing

Close Reading

1. Paraphrase the concept of "The Angel in the House" in Woolf's experience, and describe what you think she means by the sentence "Had I not killed her she would have killed me."
2. According to Woolf, what does it take to be a writer besides the activity of "moving a pen from left to right"?
3. How does Woolf use the metaphor of a fisherman to describe the creative process of a novelist?

Critical and Creative Reading

4. Woolf tells her audience that they might not be familiar with the concept of "The Angel in the House," a Victorian figure of female domesticity. More than half a century after this essay was written, can you point to any similar figures in contemporary society? Who are they, how would you name them, and how do they affect career choices by women (or, if your figure is male, men)?
5. Woolf begins by talking about her profession, writing, but she suggests that the women who are entering other new professions for the first time have many other "phantom[s] to be slain." How might this be interpreted? What phantoms still exist for women workers?
6. Woolf admits that she began her profession with some privilege (an inherited stipend) and that her desire to become a novelist as opposed to a reviewer grew from her desire to buy cars rather than cats. Do you feel that this class privilege and materialism affect the message of the essay?

Connections to Other Readings

7. Discuss the writing of "literature" as a profession in this work and in Aristides's essay "Work and Its Contents."
8. What types of "phantoms" might exist for the narrator of Ann Cummins's "Where I Work"? Does Woolf's argument about "professions for women" also apply to "jobs for women" as described in this story? (The same question could be applied to Marge Piercy's poem "The Secretary Chant.")
9. Consider Woolf's essay alongside Mary Collier's poem "The Woman's Labour." Do they make similar arguments about women and working? You might also consider which author argues more persuasively.

Aristides

Work and Its Contents

Although his name makes him sound like an ancient Greek scribe, "Aristides" is actually the pen name for Joseph Epstein (b. 1937), a professor and essayist who was also editor of *The American Scholar* from 1975 to 1997. During that time he contributed a number of humorous and insightful essays to the journal, including the following essay, "Work and Its Contents," which first appeared in 1982. Note the way Aristides (also a professor of literature) balances personal experience with his reading of essays and other literature.

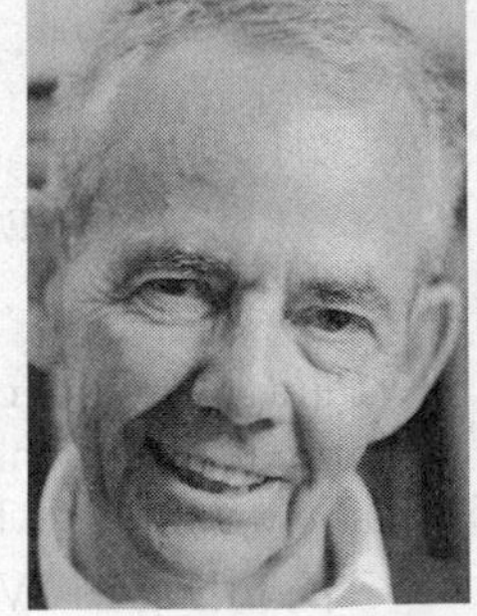

"Comes another Depression," said my father, as he noted the patch of grass I missed in the center of our small back lawn, the weeds I forgot to pull up next to the fence, and the uneven edges I left along the pavement, "it's guys like you they fire first." I haven't yet been fired, but then neither have we had a major Depression. "If you work for a man for a dollar an hour," my father used to say, "always give that man at least a dollar and a quarter of effort." But my first job, at age thirteen, was that of a delivery and stock boy at Sanders Pharmacy and paid sixty cents an hour and was so excruciatingly boring—I mostly dusted bottles—that my problem was how to find a way to give Mr. Sanders even twenty cents an hour in honest effort.

When I was growing up my father gave me a good deal of advice about work that I could neither use nor quite shake off. But, then, what you have to know about my father is that he himself was a Herculean worker, a six-day-a-week, never-look-at-the-clock man until his recent retirement at seventy-five. Perhaps an anecdote will give you something of the flavor of his work habits. My father once told me, in complaint about a man who worked for him, that for fifteen years this man had come to work at 8:30 on the dot, which was the precise time his business opened. "You would think that once," my father said, "just once he would be early." "Dad," I said, "please don't tell that story to anyone else." But now I see that I have told it for him.

My father also used to say, over and over as it seemed to me then, "If you don't like your work, you're in real trouble." He began to tell me this when I was perhaps eleven or twelve, and I only came to know it was true when I was in my late twenties. Until then, work was work, a necessary evil, though not so evil as all that, something to fill the hours between sleeping and enjoying myself. "Work is the curse of the drinking classes," said Oscar Wilde, which is a remark I would once have found more amusing than I do now. Today I must own that I subscribe to the less witty, indeed not witty at all, but vaguely moralizing strain of Thomas Carlyle, who in *Past and Present* wrote: "Blessed is he who has found his work; let him ask no other blessedness." If I did needlepoint, I should stitch that on my pillowcase and sleep on it, exhausted after a good day's work.

Not everyone, I realize, shares this taste for work. Far from it—so far that I sometimes think that the world is divided between those who work so they can live and those who live chiefly so they can work. I make this sound more black-and-white, either-or, one-way-or-the-other than it truly is. But the fact is, in my experience, some of the most forlorn people I know are those who haven't found their work: people of artistic temperament who have no art to practice, leaders without followers, serious men and women with nothing serious to do. On the other side, people who have found their work can seem, while at work, creatures of great dignity, even beauty. "A man blowing a trumpet successfully is a rousing spectacle," noted the Welsh writer Rhys Davies in one of his short stories. And so, too, is a man or woman working at anything he or she loves.

5 Contemporary novelists have tended to banish the subject of work from their books, though work, both in its dreary and in its glorious aspects, has been of great significance in so many novels of the past. One thinks of poor Oliver Twist slaving away at the blacking factory; of Clyde Griffiths, his head full of dreams, working as a bellboy in Kansas City and on the assembly line at his uncle's shirt-collar factory in Lycurgus, New York; of the figure of Levin, in

Anna Karenina,[1] sweating joyously as he works in the fields with his peasants, stopping from time to time under the blazing sun for a swig of kvass; of the seamen in so many tales and novels of Melville and Conrad going about doing ship's work—scrubbing down the decks, lashing up the mizzenmast—and working together to fight off typhoons and other seagoing disasters. And finally one thinks of prisoner Ivan Denisovich, of his long day's work done under the worst possible conditions of cold, hunger, and fear, from which he emerges, in Solzhenitsyn's novel, with simple but hugely impressive dignity. In the novels of Solzhenitsyn[2] a true sense of and love for work comes through, and part of Solzhenitsyn's distaste for politics is that it is the enemy of work. As the engineer Ilya Isakovich Arkhangorodsky says in *August 1914:*

> "On one side—the Black Hundreds: on the other—the Red Hundreds! And in the middle"—he formed his hands into the shape of a ship's keel—"a dozen people who want to pass through to get on with a job of work! Impossible!" He opened his hands and clapped them together. "They are crushed—flattened!"

I was put in mind of the place of work in our lives, and in the general scheme of society, by an essay in a fairly recent issue of *Harper's* (December 1982) entitled "Dirty Work Should Be Shared" by Michael Walzer. The argument of Professor Walzer's essay, though its general line is conveyed by its title, is a bit blurry. Professor Walzer wishes that there weren't so much drudgery, so much hard, unpleasant, ungratifying, ill-rewarded work in the world. Like Oscar Wilde, from whose "The Soul of Man Under Socialism" he quotes, he would have "all unintellectual labor, all monotonous, dull labor, all labor that deals with dreadful things and involves unpleasant conditions . . . . be done by machinery." Yet Professor Walzer knows this cannot be so, and that it is not soon likely to be so. But being an equalitarian, he yearns for a rearrangement of institutions, a readjustment of conditions, an alteration of names and attitudes whereby the burden of what he terms "dirty work" in society can be more equally shared than it is now. "Hence the question," he writes, "in a society of equals, who will do the dirty work? And the necessary answer is that, at least in some partial and symbolic sense, we all should do it." Exactly, or even roughly, how we should do it he does not say. Professor Walzer does, though, discuss such things as worker ownership of garbage collection firms, arrangements for work sharing in Israeli kibbutzim, the old French institution of the corvée (a form of labor for the state). But in the end he hasn't a solution and concludes not with a bang but with a whimper of exhortation: "Society's worst jobs should not be the exclusive business of a pariah class, powerless, dishonored, underpaid."

When one begins to talk about work in connection with power, honor, and payment, one steps onto a verdant field of quicksand. The world's work is, after

[1]*Oliver Twist:* The protagonist of Charles Dickens's (1812–1870) novel *Oliver Twist* (1839); Clyde Griffiths is the main character of Theodore Dreiser's (1871–1945) *An American Tragedy* (1925); *Anna Karenina* was written by Leo Tolstoy (1828–1910) and published in 1877.

[2]*Alexandr Solzhenitsyn:* A novelist (b. 1918) who was exiled from his native Russia (then the Soviet Union) and who won the Nobel prize in 1970. He returned to Russia after the collapse of the Soviet Union.

all, only rarely paid for commensurately with its worth. This is a problem compounded by the fact that commensurability between work and wages is never an easy thing to determine, especially if one hopes to pay for work according to what one construes to be its social usefulness. If the job of determining such wages were mine, I should lower the wages paid for some work and raise those now paid for other, and some I should leave pretty much as they are. For example, I tend to doubt that the quality of policemen would become greatly improved if the job paid vastly more money, yet I have a hunch that the quality of doctors and lawyers might rise if they were paid less.

I used to hear the argument made fairly regularly that teachers are greatly underpaid, and at some point in this argument someone would inevitably say, "Why even garbage collectors make more!" As someone in favor of better education—a courageous stand for me to take, don't you think?—this argument always made me a trifle edgy. I thought that garbage collectors deserved more. For one thing, teachers are usually teachers by choice, while garbage collectors collect garbage for want of anything better to do. For another, a good teacher is rather rare, but who knows a bad garbage collector? But if we are going to talk about the underpaid, what about that national treasure, that lonely yet proud figure, on whose shoulders so much of the quality of a country's culture depends—I speak of course of that splendid and stalwart chap, the essayist.

As an equalitarian, Professor Walzer, if I read him aright, would have teacher, garbage collector, and essayist earning roughly equal salaries (a true leg up, by the way, for the essayist). He would also like them, I gather, to be equally honored and equally powerful. He argues against the degradation of certain kinds of work—I am not sure anyone is arguing for it—and wants a society in which there will be "no more bowing and scraping, fawning and toadying, no more fearful trembling; no more high-and-mightiness." Somehow, I must here confess, I find myself not so much unsympathetic as uninterested in Professor Walzer's proposals. I am not sure, for example, that sycophancy is built into specific jobs. A duke can be more fawning to a powerful prince than a washroom attendant to a United States senator; some of the worst snobs I have ever seen in action have been waiters. Nor do the teacher, the garbage collector, and the essayist bow and scrape, fawn and toady before one another—or, for that matter, before anyone (unless it is in the nature of the individual to do so). I am not aware, either, that one causes fearful trembling in the others. No, it seems to me that they greet one another the way most people do who work at very different jobs—with a lively and only slightly muted incomprehension.

But, then, the difference in point of view between Professor Walzer and me 10
is vast. As a social theorist of sorts, he likes to come at things at a fairly high level of generality, while the points he attempts to make seem to me of interest only when they are treated on a much lower level of generality. He feels he knows why certain social classes bog down in dreary work; I am more interested in how it is and what it took for so many members of these classes to have been able to climb out successfully. He is sure much modern work is degrading; I am more impressed with the competence, dignity, and ingenuity that people apply to difficult jobs. He begins his observations with a yearning for equality; I begin mine

yearning to understand how even one person—I, for example—came to do what he does.

Professor Walzer feels that perhaps dirty work "should be done by society's only legitimate proletariat—the proletariat of the young." There is, if I may say so, something a touch goofy about referring to the young generally as "proletariat"—Workers of the world unite! You have nothing to lose but your sneakers!—for it gives yet another abstract twist to a word that has by now almost completely lost its relation to reality. Still, it is true that the young do get a goodly share of society's worst jobs; or at least they used to. I know I had my share of these jobs when young, and each time I would set out on another one, my father would say, "It can't hurt you. It's good experience." It took me a while to understand that the term "good experience" was my father's artful euphemism for "bad job."

Of these bad jobs, as I say, I had my share. Most of the "good experience" of my youth served to convince me of my incompetence. I found that I grew bored quickly, and could not very well sustain, on my first job, a false interest in dusting drugstore stock for the duration of my two- or three-hour shifts at Sanders Pharmacy. I tried out as a golf caddy; this was during the time before golf carts and when clubs were not yet called by number but still had such names as mashie niblick—names that seemed to me more appropriate for canned vegetables. But one had to be out of the house by five in the morning to get in two full rounds, which, at age thirteen, I found difficult to do, so I quit, thus proving to myself that I was not a person of much perseverance. ("Quitters never win," said my father.) My first year in high school I worked as a food bagger in one of the first supermarkets in our neighborhood, a place called Hillman's. Milk still came in bottles, and the reason I recall this so vividly is that milk bottles seemed to break through so many of my bags before the women carrying them were able to get up the marble stairs leading out of the store. Although for some reason I wasn't fired, it wasn't long before I was out searching for fresh "good experience."

By now I was convinced that I had a short attention span, little perseverance (or, as the moralizers put it, "stick-to-it-iveness"), and wasn't very good with my hands. Yet onward, ever onward, substituting for a month for a classmate, I next worked as a busboy in a neighborhood Chinese restaurant. The neighborhood was predominantly Jewish, and the man who ran the restaurant, though Chinese, had begun to look a little Jewish himself, in the odd way that people have of absorbing into themselves their surrounding atmosphere. (The most notable example is that of people who begin to resemble their dogs.) I cleared dishes, poured the remains of tea over the Formica-topped tables, swabbing the mess up with a damp cloth, and scraped off the dishes in the tumult of chopping, frying, and Chinese language in the kitchen. After the restaurant closed—during the middle of the week, roughly at 8:30—the staff could eat, limitlessly, anything they wished, with the exception of shrimp dishes. At that time—I was then fourteen—it was Chinese shrimp dishes almost exclusively that I liked, and so I ate scarcely anything at all. Through the mechanism psychologists call "overcompensation," I continue to try to make up for this youthful folly.

But that summer I began the best job of my life—that of ball boy for a nearby university tennis coach and teaching professional. My job was to tote out a large box of used balls, which the pro would use to demonstrate strokes—backhand, forehand, volley, and three kinds of serve—to his pupils. During the lesson I would shag the loose balls and return them to the box. I would also sometimes throw balls to the pro, a great gruff but very gentle fat man, who would thwack them back across the net. On occasion I would demonstrate a stroke or a serve. Mostly, though, I shagged balls.

The pay was poor—it barely covered the expenses of my travel and courtside soda pop intake—but the benefits bountiful. These included unlimited free court time and a modest discount on equipment. I would hang around the courts all day long, working two, at most three, hours a day, the remainder of the time playing with people whose partners didn't show up or were late, or filling in as a fourth for doubles. The courts were clay, of a light copperish color, from which loose clay dust turned one's shoes and tennis balls lightly beige. The sun shone down, the days stretched out. A taut tennis net, a clean white ball, and pow—and life, as Mr. Khayyám's *Rubáiyát* has it, was "paradise enow."[3] The lesson this job taught, if on a very rudimentary level, was that work was best when it was combined with play.

This was a lesson reinforced by working with my father, which I began to do when I was sixteen years old and had acquired a driver's license. Although he then owned a business in partnership with another man, my father was this business's chief salesman, and my job was to drive him to cities anywhere from a hundred to four hundred miles away, where he would call on customers: I also lugged his sample cases, and sometimes wrote up his orders. My father, it occurs to me, was then exactly my age now.

I wish Arthur Miller had met my father before he wrote his lumpy and mawkish play about Willy Loman.[4] My father was not only very good at what he did, but he seemed to enjoy it all immensely. "Now this is a very popular item," he would say to a customer. "I know a man who bought an enormous quantity of it—me!" Here was a man having a very good time while at work.

"What do you think," my father would ask, at six o'clock at the end of a day on which we had set out at four-thirty in the morning to drive two hundred miles. "What do you think—should we spend the night here or have a nice dinner and try to make it back home tonight?" For slow readers allow me to say that the correct answer was "have a nice dinner and try to make it back home tonight." And this we would do. Some days we would put in eighteen or twenty hours. I would usually sleep long the following morning. My father would be down at (as he called it) "the place" well before it opened for business. I love my work now, but I think my father must have loved his even more.

Love is not something one reads much about in connection with work. Quite the reverse, in fact. Ten or so years ago Studs Terkel assembled a book of

[3]*The Rubáiyát of Omar Khayyám:* A poem by British Victorian poet Edward Fitzgerald (1809–1883) based on the poetry of twelfth-century Persian astronomer Omar Khayyám.

[4]*Willy Loman:* A character in Arthur Miller's (1915–2005) *Death of a Salesman* (1949).

interviews that he called *Working*, which turned out to be a clanging best-seller and which begins on this cheery note:

> This book, being about work, is, by its very nature, about violence—to the spirit as well as to the body. It is about ulcers as well as accidents, about shouting matches as well as fistfights, about nervous breakdowns as well as kicking the dog around. It is, above all (or beneath all), about daily humiliations. To survive the day is triumph enough for the walking wounded among the great many of us.

But then Studs Terkel's is the conventional anti-capitalist view of work. He 20
is a man who sees capitalist conspiracies everywhere, the way the old John Birchers used to see Communist conspiracies. He has a syndicated interview show on FM radio, and on this show his idea of a fine time is to interview someone who has written about some fresh piece of big-business skulduggery. It might be an interview with a man who has written a book about, say, IBM having recently acquired the Gerber baby food company, and he has discovered that the plumbing connected to the urinals in the executive washroom at IBM leads directly to the assembly line at the Gerber baby food factory, and . . . "That's right, Studs, it's as bad as you think."

Although there is much tough work in the world, some of it done under grueling and some of it under grinding conditions, I doubt that the picture of work conveyed by a tricked-up book like *Working* is anywhere near accurate as a picture of how most people regard their work. True, many people have been cornered by circumstances into work they would not have chosen if their freedom of choice had been wider: many people find themselves under bosses or supervisors who are stupid or petty tyrants: and many others long to work at something other than what they work at now. Yet many more people, my guess is, feel the need and the stimulus and the satisfaction of their work—and for these people not to work, quite apart from the money that work provides, is a kind of slow death. When on television one hears the unemployed interviewed, there is, naturally enough, much talk of bills piling up and of financial worry generally; but at another level one can grasp a deeper demoralization—their feeling, now that they are deprived of work, of uselessness.

Other people's work often looks fairly interesting to me, or seems to have oddly interesting virtues. Apart from jobs for which I am altogether unfitted—lion tamer, say, or brain surgeon, or ship's captain—there are only two jobs for which I feel a strong antipathy. One is working in a bank, which involves too much detail for my taste and the additional difficulty of spending my days handling other people's money, which would not exactly plant roses in my cheeks. The other job I should not like to have is that of clergyman, especially today when values are so scrumptiously scrambled and the prospects of making a dignified appeal for faith so slim. Yet T. S. Eliot, I note, much preferred working in the international department of Lloyd's Bank in London to teaching; and many women in almost all the modern Western religions feel somewhat put down because they are not permitted to work at the job I wouldn't touch with a ten-foot pulpit.

When I was an adolescent I never had the best jobs: these included construction worker, which paid very well, built up muscles, and withal seemed very manly; or copyboy on a major metropolitan daily, which put one on the periphery of interesting events; or lifeguard, which, along with giving one an opportunity to acquire that most ephemeral of the world's possessions, a nice tan, set one in a fine position to meet girls. But neither did I have the worst jobs: these included setting pins in a bowling alley, which in those days paid ten cents a line and gave one an opportunity for so many uninteresting and extremely painful injuries; and selling shoes, especially women's shoes, which could try the patience of a glacier and often paid no commission, except 1 percent on polish and laces.

I had middling jobs. My last two years in high school I sold costume jewelry on Saturdays and during Christmas holidays downtown in what must have been one of the first of this country's discount stores. During the time I was there, two veterans of carnival life worked the costume jewelry concession with me. The first was Art, a man in his late forties, with pomaded black hair, who sweated heavily in all seasons. "Hold down the fort, kid," he would say, ducking out for ten or fifteen minutes, his breath, on return, areek with booze. He was a fumbling man who had confident views, particularly on contemporary sexual mores, which, though often amusing, seemed to me even then wildly erroneous. Then there was Fritz, an Englishman who referred to all other Englishmen as limeys. He had the accent of a man of some cultivation, and on the cheap cigarette lighters, lockets, and identification bracelets we sold he engraved names and initials with a grand artistic flourish. He was a fine companion, filled with stories of traveling round the world, in all a decent sort, though at the time very much down on his uppers. He would sometimes borrow a few dollars from me, which he always repaid. Fritz, too, was a boozer, not a nipper but a binger. He would miss work for two or three days, then come in as if nothing were amiss, his same good, gentle self. For reasons never known to me, and perhaps not to himself, he was not to be one of the world's winners.

By the time I had my first factory job, I was in college, which is to say that 25
I knew for certain, if I hadn't already known it earlier, that I would not work at a labor job permanently. I was a visitor there, a tourist on the payroll. The factory made phonograph needles. It had no assembly line; instead most of the people, the majority of them women, worked at long tables. I worked in the receiving department. My job was to unload trucks, but not enough trucks came in to merit my working full-time at this, so I put in part of my time organizing and filing boxes of labels, which was heartily boring. But I also sat around a lot, schmoozing away with the head of the receiving room, a middle-aged man named Steve, who was extremely efficient at covering over the fact that he was exceedingly lazy. We were often joined by two brothers-in-law, Italians of fine high spirits, who were the factory's maintenance crew. Both were small men, and one of them might technically have been a dwarf. Well under five-feet tall with a large head, long arms, and big hands, he was courageous in his mischief, sometimes ducking out to one of the factory's upper

floors, where behind packing cases he might take a nap of two full hours' duration. The brothers-in-law appeared to use the factory as a place to hang out during the day. Their real life was elsewhere. Their true speciality was fixing up old cars, which they would sell for a few hundred bucks profit. Then they would buy another, and start fixing it up.

At the factory it was known that I was a college student, which was problematic. It was the first inkling I had of the separation between those whose lives revolve around books and those whose lives don't. I didn't want the separation made any greater than it needed to be, so instead of saying that I was studying such things as literature, history, and philosophy, I claimed I was thinking of going to medical school. This turned out to be a mistake. More than once the brothers-in-law wanted to know if I needed any dead cats for purposes of dissection, and I was sure that one day I would have to bring a dead cat home on the bus in a shopping bag. Worse still, Steve and other people round the plant came to me for medical advice, some of it, I fear, rather intimate in nature.

Many people at the factory told me to be sure to return to school, saying that they regretted not having had the opportunity to go themselves. Yet their lives did not seem to me either dreary or dreadful. On coffee breaks to the lunchroom their talk was what most talk is about: the economy, the previous day's no-hitter or the pennant race, the bowling league being formed for the fall, their kids, I recall each afternoon standing in line to punch out. The working day did some people in; others indomitable, were not in the least done in. Not at all. Work, I thought then, is neither intrisically dignified nor undignified; it is the people doing the work who give it its character. There are people who can make the creation of poetry or leadership of a large university or corporation seem loathsome, and then there are people who can make the job of porter or waitress seem a good and useful thing.

The most impressive man I encountered in the army was a training sergeant named Andrew Atherton, who in private life had been a soda jerk in St. Louis; the most intelligent person in many academic departments in universities is the secretary. Nothing, really, so surprising in this. Nearly a century ago Henry James noted the common occurrence of "imbeciles in great places, people of sense in small." Although few people actually work in Henry James novels, James knew a great deal about work and its special benefits. After the rude failure of his play *Guy Domville* on the London stage, James, it will be recalled, slipped into a blue funk. The only way out of it, as he himself recognized, was work. Writing to his friend William Dean Howells, James recounted his depression and its antidote:

> The sense of being utterly out of it weighed me down, and I asked myself what the future would be. All these melancholies were qualified indeed by one redeeming reflection—the sense of how little for a good while past (for reasons very logical, but accidental and temporary), I had been producing. I *did* say to myself, "Produce again—produce; produce better than ever, and all will yet be well.

And he did. And it was.

The restorative effects of work seem to be beyond doubt. Being out of work, for so many, is the surest path to self-loathing. The loss of work isn't only the loss of wages but the loss of an organizing principle in life. Blocked writers are but one example of the phenomenon. But one needn't turn to the arts for examples. Some years ago, when I had not yet produced enough work to be allowed to consider myself a writer, I underwent roughly a five-week period of unemployment. I was married and had children, and the sense of not producing for them diminished me in my own eyes, which is, I suppose, not surprising. What did surprise me, though, was that during this time jobs I would not formerly even have considered for myself suddenly came to seem highly possible, interesting, attractive even. Driving a bus, for one, or selling men's clothes, for another. Leisure enforced, I found, was no leisure at all, so I took no pleasure in my free time. At one point, just to be doing something, I attempted to sell newspaper subscriptions over the telephone; I rarely made more at this than seven or eight dollars for three hours' work—a figure so demoralizing that after less than a week of it, I quit. I walked around envying people who had jobs to go to. Unemployment had made me feel useless, utterly hopeless. I recognize that this doesn't compare with any sort of serious tragedy, or even with any sort of serious unemployment, but I nonetheless cannot recall when I felt quite so sorry for myself. At other difficult times in my life, at least I could throw myself into my work.

For a great many people TGIF (Thank God It's Friday) is a serious slogan, 30
but then for a great many others so is TGIM (Thank God It's Monday). As a TGIM man, I think work has gotten a bad rep—and a bum rap—in recent years. Consider the word "workaholic," whose implicit meaning is drunk on work. Or consider the term "Protestant ethic," which began as an explanation for the economic behaviour of a historical people but which today exists almost solely as a pejorative term applied to people who are thought to take their work too much in earnest. Those Protestants Max Weber described in his famous essay may or may not have been welcome in heaven for their hard work, but they surely could have spent their days worse—pool-side, let us say, at Caesar's Palace or at Esalin. I am neither Protestant nor quite a workaholic, but I have known many moments when work seemed to me a more pleasurable prospect than being with very good friends. Toward the end of two or three weeks of even a splendid vacation, I have longed to read my mail, to sit at my desk, to slip into harness.

Once one has acquired skills, it seems a waste not to use them. Strike, I say, even when the iron is merely warm. A career passes so quickly. ("Careerist" is another pejorative word.) Someone once said, cleverly in my view, that every career has five stages, which may be denoted thus: (1) Who is Aristides? (2) Get me Aristides. (3) We need someone like Aristides. (4) What we need is a young Aristides. (5) Who is Aristides? Am I now at stage 3, or getting close to stage 4? When I consider these stages, and how quickly one passes from one to the next, I think perhaps it is best to strike even before the iron is plugged in.

Life is short, and work life shorter. At many jobs, age works against one. Much work is, as the sociologists have it, age-specific. Certain jobs are more than a touch unseemly beyond a certain age: lifeguard, movie reviewer, gigolo, television anchor-man or anchor-woman (unless you happen to have one of those granitic Cronkitic faces). The jobs I work at—writing, editing, teaching—though one can go at them for quite a spell, nonetheless all have about them a sense of a prime period, after which one does not figure to get better. Some writers, most famously Yeats, found their true prime in their old age, but most do not get better as they get older. Editors beyond a certain period tend to lose their touch and their passion. And teachers, perhaps from having been allowed to hold the floor for so long before a captive audience, not infrequently grow spiritually gaseous and mentally gaga. When I think of these possibilities, it occurs to me to strike even without an iron.

H. L. Mencken, himself a hard and highly efficient worker, says somewhere that it is probably a fine idea for a person to change jobs every ten or so years. Without consciously setting out to do so, I seem to have been following this plan. The last time I changed jobs was roughly eight years ago, when, in my late thirties, I began teaching at a university. The chance to mold minds, the opportunity for lively exchanges of ideas, the pleasures of virtuous friendships with the young, all these are doubtless among the possible rewards of teaching. But what attracted me were the spacious margins of leisure—or, to put it less grandly, the time-off seemed terrific. My view of the job then coincides with that held by my barber now. Often, in order to beat the rush of customers that gathers in his shop in the afternoon, I will go in for a haircut at nine or nine-thirty in the morning. Flapping the sheet over me, he will usually say, with a barely perceptible smile in which I think I have espied envy mingling with the faintest contempt, "Through for the day, Professor?"

I still think the leisure offered by university teaching is impressive. Yet while working at it, the job often seems oddly enervating. Perhaps it has to do with the pressures of intellectual performance—of being "on," in several of the complicated senses of that simple word. Perhaps it has to do with working too exclusively among the young, which can be a sharp reminder that young is, most clearly, what one no longer is. Perhaps it is the element of repetition, for teaching is one of those jobs in which, as one grows older, one's responsibilities do not increase. Perhaps it has to do with the fact that, in teaching, the sense of intellectual progress, in one's students and in oneself, is often unclear, and teaching is never more tiring than when the sense of intellectual progress is absent.

Still, teaching has it moments, and these come in various forms: exhilaration, surprising intellectual discovery, appreciation for things one felt confident went unnoticed. Yet of the jobs I do, teaching is the one I approach with a tinge of fear. I shall hold back on a quotation from Kierkegaard here, but even after seven years on the job I often walk into classrooms slightly tremulous. Colleagues have told me that they continue to do so after thirty or more years of teaching. What is there to be fearful of? Of being boring? Of seeming boobish? Of, somehow, blowing it? I do, after all, know more than my students—at least most of the time I do. Yet the touch of fear is still usually there, and the troubling thing is that I tend to teach worse when it isn't.

I imagine fear has salubrious effects on other kinds of work. The stage fright of action is of course well enough known. So, too, are those butterflies in the stomachs of even the most fearsome athletes before games. Do trial lawyers feel fear? I should hope that airline pilots feel a bit of it. I should hope, too, that surgeons feel fear, but fear, in their case, that stops well short of trembling. I don't mean to exaggerate the benefits of fear; a little of it, e.a. I have found, goes a long way.

So, in connection with work, does play. Good work often involves play, an element of fooling around even while doing the most serious things. Fortunate are those people is a position to transform their work into play. Artists are often able to do so. But I have seen fine waitresses and businessmen do it, too. The most fortunate people of all, though, are those for whom the line between work and play gets rubbed out, for whom work is pleasure and pleasure is in work. I may be one of those people. Strange. When I was a child I never dreamed of doing any particular kind of work, for none especially attracted me. I wished merely to be rich and respected, in a general way. Rich I am not; whether I am respected is not for me to say; but, because of the joy I am able to take in my work, I feel myself luckier than any child could have dreamed. Now, if only I could shake this feeling that, comes another Depression, it's guys like me they fire first.

(1982)

Questions for Discussion and Writing

Close Reading

1. Why does Aristides examine the issue of work in novels, contemporary and classic?
2. What is the author's argument with Michael Walzer, author of "Dirty Work Should Be Shared"?
3. Summarize with specific examples the way Aristides's essay illustrates his idea that "good work often involves play."

Critical and Creative Reading

4. At the beginning of the essay the author contrasts his youthful self with his father, a superworker who always put in more time and effort than a job required. Does the author fully come around to his father's philosophy about work?
5. Make a list of the best jobs as they are described or suggested in Aristides's essay; then compare them with the lists your classmates have made. Would you add other jobs to the list that do not fit the author's criteria?
6. Do you think that Americans like work more than they are willing to admit? Is our national slogan "TGIF," or is it "TGIM" (Thank God It's Monday)?

Connections to Other Readings

7. According to Philip Levine's poem "What Work Is," does Aristides know what work is?
8. Discuss Aristides's argument with Michael Walzer's essay "Dirty Work Should Be Shared" in conjunction with Rebecca Harding Davis's story "Life in the Iron-Mills."
9. Discuss the way writers regard the manual labor of others in this essay and in the poems by Wordsworth, Whitman, Heaney, and/or Frost.

Considering Art: Industry and Idleness

The discussion below references art reproduced on color insert pages 17 and 18.

Visual images of work inevitably raise questions in the viewer's mind. What is the artist saying about work, or what questions about work is he or she raising? Which types of work are valued within a particular culture, and which are not, and why? What is the relationship between repetitive tasks (such as cleaning, caretaking, child rearing, and physically taxing forms of manual labor) and creative or artistic work? Visual images do not merely reflect an imbalance that exists "out there" in the culture. They participate in privileging some forms of work over others and in forming social attitudes toward individuals based on their profession or occupation.

***Self-Portrait in Iron* (see color insert p. 17).** In *Self-Portrait in Iron* (1980), American artist G. G. Kopilak (b. 1942) paints a **still life** that functions as a self-portrait of both the artist at work and of the housewife who abandons or ignores the housework to paint. An unplugged iron rests on a man's striped shirt, and its shiny metal reflects the artist's gaze back to her. Here the domestic sphere has been transformed from the realm of repeated, unpaid, anonymous, and undervalued women's work to the productive and creative space of the studio.

***The Poet Reclining* (see color insert p. 17).** Prior to the First World War, the Russian Jewish painter Marc Chagall (1887–1985) lived in the close-knit bohemian community of expatriate artists in the Paris neighborhood of Montparnasse. During what he thought would be a three-month vacation to his native Belarus, war broke out and he was unable to return to Paris. During this time, he met his wife, Bella (they married in 1915), and his daughter Ida was born. He did not return to Paris until 1923. When he painted *The Poet Reclining* (1915), Chagall had just wed Bella and had taken a honeymoon in the Russian countryside. He depicts himself reclining in a dreamy, poetic state of solitude and reverie, surrounded by fir trees, farm animals, and a lilac sky. He seems both in touch with his native, idyllic landscape and isolated from the art world by distance and a war that was then being fought on Russian soil.

***Work* (see color insert p. 18).** American painter Edmund M. Ashe (1867–1941) has no illusions about the heroic nature of modern labor in his painting *Work* (1939–1942). Ashe often represents the daily grinding social conditions of manual labor in the context of Pennsylvania's steel, coal, and petroleum industries. Like many social realists who painted during the Depression, his bleak, harsh, aggressive realism makes it clear that this sort of work grinds down bodies and wears out minds. In this gritty view of working class life, a muscular worker (whose sensitive face belies the mind-numbing exhaustion of his job) heads back down into the pit in an ominous setting that looks almost postapocalyptic.

***The News Room* (see color insert p. 18).** Painter of folksy Americana Jane Wooster Scott (b. 1939) creates a nostalgic image of American industriousness in *The News Room* (1969). Like good worker ants, the newsroom employees scurry through the close confines of their environment, exuding an air of productiveness and shared purpose. The space of this frenetic and cluttered office has clearly been divided according to the sorts of work going on and their varying degrees of importance. Wooster Scott has been successful with this style of painting, which is deliberately naïve and mimics the look of folk art.

Questions about the Art

1. How does using the surface of an iron, rather than a mirror, change the meaning of the artist's reflection?
2. What are we to make of the idleness and his body posture of the "poet" in Chagall's painting?
3. Compare the treatment of men's bodies in the paintings by Chagall and Ashe.
4. Compare the ways that space is treated in *The Poet Reclining* and in *The News Room.*
5. In all four images, how do the artists indicate the identities of the people they depict?

Connecting Art and Literature

1. Discuss the mood of the workplace as depicted in Theodore Roethke's poem, "Dolor," Marge Piercy's poem, "The Secretary's Chant," and Wooster Scott's painting, *The News Room.*
2. Consider the artist-as-worker in Chagall's painting along with the poem "Blues" and "Digging" by Elizabeth Alexander and Seamus Heaney.
3. According to the speaker of Philip Levine's poem "What Work Is," which of the four artists whose work is represented here best knows what work is?

Common Characters

The "Rags-to-Riches" Figure

Part of our collective willingness to work hard is our collective desire to succeed, economically and socially. One of the ideas underpinning this chapter is that hard work, in the right circumstances, does "pay off," and you do not have to look far to see evidence of that idea all around you. Hard work might not always lead to happiness, but many people hope that it leads to prosperity (which they hope will lead, in turn, to happiness).

In America, especially in the eighteenth and nineteenth centuries when Americans were coming to terms with their national identity, the idea that a hard worker could go from "rags to riches" was a pervasive myth. Benjamin Franklin's

Title page from Horatio Alger's story "Ragged Dick."

Film still from Charlie Chaplin's *The Gold Rush* (1925).

Autobiography is one of the most familiar illustrations of this myth. In the nineteenth century young readers consumed the works of Horatio Alger (1832–1899), whose novels and stories were based on this idea. Alger wrote scores of these stories, over a hundred in all; their formulaic nature did not seem to bother readers. In *Ragged Dick*, one of the most frequently studied Alger novels today, the protagonist advances from a street kid who shines shoes to "a young gentleman on the way to fame and fortune," as his friend describes him. He does this through a combination of hard work and good luck: being in the right place at the right time, and impressing influential people.

This Common Characters section contains three poems and a short story, each representing a more complex and nuanced approach to the "rags-to-riches" theme than is expressed in Alger's works. The first two poems are by the late-nineteenth- and early-twentieth-century poets Thomas Hardy (1840–1928: see also "At Tea" in Chapter 14) and Edwin Arlington Robinson (1869–1935). Hardy's poem "The Ruined Maid" addresses the fate of a "ruined" woman, that is, one who has lost her virginity before marriage. Robinson's poem, which was adopted as a popular song by Simon and Garfunkel in the mid-1960s, takes as its subject a wealthy, respectable man about town, described by a member of the working class. The third poem, by Anne Sexton (1928–1974), was written more recently, in 1971. It directly confronts the children's story "Cinderella" about a working girl who wins the favor of the prince. The story in this section, "Success Story" by Russell Banks (b. 1940), centers on a young man who drops out of college to embark on a series of jobs that only he takes seriously.

Edward Arlington Robinson *(1869–1935)*

Richard Cory

Whenever Richard Cory went down town,
We people on the pavement looked at him:
He was a gentleman from sole to crown,
Clean favored, and imperially slim.

And he was always quietly arrayed,
And he was always human when he talked;
But still he fluttered pulses when he said,
"Good-morning," and he glittered when he walked.

And he was rich,—yes, richer than a king,—
And admirably schooled in every grace:
In fine, we thought that he was everything,
To make us wish that we were in his place.

So on we worked, and waited for the light,
And went without the meat, and cursed the bread;
And Richard Cory, one calm summer night,
Went home and put a bullet through his head.

(1897)

Thomas Hardy *(1840–1928)*

The Ruined Maid

O 'Melia, my dear, this does everything crown!
"Who could have supposed I should meet you in Town?
And whence such fair garments, such prosperi-ty?"—
"O didn't you know I'd been ruined?" said she.

—"You left us in tatters, without shoes or socks,
Tired of digging potatoes, and spudding up docks;
And now you've gay bracelets and bright feathers three!"
"Yes: that's how we dress when we're ruined," said she.

—"At home in the barton you said 'thee' and 'thou,'
And 'thik oon', and 'theäs oon', and 't'other'; but now
Your talking quite fits 'ee for high compa-ny !"—
"Some polish is gained with one's ruin," said she.

—"Your hands were like paws then, your face blue and bleak
But now I'm bewitched by your delicate cheek,
And your little gloves fit as on any la-dy!"—
"We never do work when we're ruined," said she.

—"You used to call home-life a hag-ridden dream,
And you'd sigh, and you'd sock; but at present you seem
To know not of megrims or melancho-ly!"—
"True. One's pretty lively when ruined," said she.

—"I wish I had feathers, a fine sweeping gown,
And a delicate face, and could strut about Town!"—
"My dear—a raw country girl, such as you be,
Cannot quite expect that. You ain't ruined," said she.

(1866)

Anne Sexton *(1928–1974)*

Cinderella

You always read about it:
the plumber with twelve children
who wins the Irish Sweepstakes.
From toilets to riches.
That story.

Or the nursemaid,
some luscious sweet from Denmark
who captures the oldest son's heart.
From diapers to Dior.
That story.

Or a milkman who serves the wealthy,
eggs, cream, butter, yogurt, milk,

the white truck like an ambulance
who goes into real estate
and makes a pile.
From homogenized to martinis at lunch.

Or the charwoman
who is on the bus when it cracks up
and collects enough from the insurance.
From mops to Bonwit Teller.[1]
That story.

Once
the wife of a rich man was on her deathbed
and she said to her daughter Cinderella:
Be devout. Be good. Then I will smile
down from heaven in the seam of a cloud.
The man took another wife who had
two daughters, pretty enough
but with hearts like blackjacks.
Cinderella was their maid.
She slept on the sooty hearth each night
and walked around looking like Al Jolson.[2]
Her father brought presents home from town,
jewels and gowns for the other women
but the twig of a tree for Cinderella.
She planted that twig on her mother's grave
and it grew to a tree where a white dove sat.
Whenever she wished for anything the dove
would drop it like an egg upon the ground.
The bird is important, my dears, so heed him.

Next came the ball, as you all know.
It was a marriage market.
The prince was looking for a wife.
All but Cinderella were preparing
and gussying up for the big event.
Cinderella begged to go too.
Her stepmother threw a dish of lentils
into the cinders and said: Pick them
up in an hour and you shall go.
The white dove brought all his friends;
all the warm wings of the fatherland came,

[1]*Bonwit Teller:* A fashionable retail department store.

[2]*Al Jolson:* Al Jolson (1886–1950) was a popular white singer and actor who appeared in blackface, or heavy black makeup designed to make him look African American, in the first nonsilent film *The Jazz Singer* (1927).

and picked up the lentils in a jiffy.
No, Cinderella, said the stepmother,
you have no clothes and cannot dance.
That's the way with stepmothers.
Cinderella went to the tree at the grave
and cried forth like a gospel singer:
Mama! Mama! My turtledove,
send me to the prince's ball!
The bird dropped down a golden dress
and delicate little gold slippers.
Rather a large package for a simple bird.
So she went. Which is no surprise.
Her stepmother and sisters didn't
recognize her without her cinder face
and the prince took her hand on the spot
and danced with no other the whole day.

As nightfall came she thought she'd better
get home. The prince walked her home
and she disappeared into the pigeon house
and although the prince took an axe and broke
it open she was gone. Back to her cinders.

These events repeated themselves for three days.
However on the third day the prince
covered the palace steps with cobbler's wax
and Cinderella's gold shoe stuck upon it.
Now he would find whom the shoe fit
and find his strange dancing girl for keeps.
He went to their house and the two sisters
were delighted because they had lovely feet.
The eldest went into a room to try the slipper on
but her big toe got in the way so she simply
sliced it off and put on the slipper.
The prince rode away with her until the white dove
told him to look at the blood pouring forth.
That is the way with amputations.
They don't just heal up like a wish.
The other sister cut off her heel
but the blood told as blood will.
The prince was getting tired.
He began to feel like a shoe salesman.
But he gave it one last try.
This time Cinderella fit into the shoe
like a love letter into its envelope.
At the wedding ceremony

the two sisters came to curry favor
and the white dove pecked their eyes out.
Two hollow spots were left
like soup spoons.

Cinderella and the prince
lived, they say, happily ever after,
like two dolls in a museum case
never bothered by diapers or dust,
never arguing over the timing of an egg,
never telling the same story twice,
never getting a middle-aged spread,
their darling smiles pasted on for eternity.
Regular Bobbsey Twins.[3]
That story.

(1971)

[3]*Bobbsey Twins:* A series of novels for children popular throughout the twentieth century and characterized by an idealized vision of reality.

Russell Banks *(b. 1940)*

Success Story

After high school, I attended an Ivy League college for less than one term. A year later, I was married and living in central Florida. This was 1958 and '59. General Dwight Eisenhower was our President, and Dr. Fidel Castro, hunkered down in the mountain passes southeast of Havana, was getting praised for his integrity and good looks by *Time* magazine and *Reader's Digest.*

I'd been a whiz kid in high school, rewarded for it with an academic scholarship. In this Ivy League school, however, among the elegant, brutal sons of the captains of industry, I was only that year's token poor kid, imported from a small New Hampshire mill town like an exotic herb, a dash of mace for the vichyssoise. It was a status that perplexed and intimidated and finally defeated me, so that, after nine weeks of it, I fled in the night.

Literally. On a snowy December night, alone in my dormitory room (they had not thought it appropriate for me to have a roommate, or no one's profile matched mine), I packed my clothes and few books into a canvas duffle, waited until nearly all the lights on campus were out, and sneaked down the hallway, passed through the service entrance, and walked straight down the hill from the eighteenth-century cut-stone dormitories and classroom buildings to the wide boulevard below, where huge, neoclassical fraternity houses lounged beneath high, ancient elms. At the foot of the hill, I turned south and jogged through unplowed snow, shifting my heavy duffle from one shoulder to the other every twenty or thirty yards, until I passed out of the valley town into darkness and found myself walking through a heavy snowstorm on a winding, narrow road.

A month later—with the holidays over and my distraught mother and bewildered younger brother and sister, aunts, uncles, and cousins, all my friends and neighbors and high school teachers, as well as the dean and director of admissions at the Ivy League college, convinced that I not only had ruined my life but may have done something terrible to theirs, too—I turned up in St. Petersburg, Florida, with seven dollars in my pocket, my duffle on my shoulder, and my resolve to join Castro in the Sierra Maestra seriously weakening.

5 I'd spent Christmas and New Year's at home, working days and nights as a salesman in a local men's clothing store, trying hard to behave as if nothing had happened. My mother seemed always to be red-eyed from weeping, and my friends from high school treated me coolly, distantly, as if I had dropped out of college because of a social disease. In some ways, my family was a civic reclamation project—the bright and pretty children and pathetic wife of a brute who, nearly a decade ago, had disappeared into the northern woods with a woman from the post office, never to be heard from again. As the oldest male victim of this abandonment, I was expected by everyone who knew the story to avenge the crime, mainly by making myself visibly successful, by rising above my station, and in that paradoxical way show the criminal how meaningless his crime had been. For reasons I was only dimly aware of, my story was important to everyone.

Leaving them behind, then, abandoning my fatherless family in a tenement and my old friends and the town I had been raised in, was an exquisite pleasure, like falling into bed and deep sleep after having been pushed beyond exhaustion. Now, I thought the morning I left—stepping onto the ramp to Route 93 in Catamount, showing my thumb to the cars headed south—*now* I can start to dream my own dreams, not everyone else's.

The particular dream of joining Castro died easily. It started dying the moment I got out of the big, blue Buick sedan with Maryland plates that had carted me straight through all the way from Norfolk, Virginia, to Coquina Key in St. Petersburg, where the elderly man who drove the car had a "fiancée," he told me, with a suite in the Coquina Key Hotel.

"You, you're a smart kid," he said to me, as I slid from the car and hauled out my duffle from the back. "You'll do all right here. You'll catch on." He was a ruddy, white-haired man with a brush cut that he liked to touch with the flat of his hand, as if patting a strange dog, "Forget Cuba, though. No sense getting yourself killed for somebody else's country." He was a retired U.S. Army captain, named Knox, "like the fort," he'd said, and he gave advice as if he expected it to be taken. "Kid like you," he said, peering across at me from the driver's seat, "smart, good-looking, good personality, you can make a million bucks here. This place," he said, looking warmly around him at the marina, the palm trees, the acres of lawn, the flashy bougainvillea blossoms, the large new cars with out-of-state plates, the tall, pink Coquina Key Hotel with the dark red canopy leading from the street to the front entrance, "this place is *made* for a kid like you!"

"Yeah. Well, I got plenty of time for that." I took a step away from the car, and Knox leaned farther across the front seat. I said to him, "I don't need to make a pile of money just yet."

"No? How much you got?"

"Not much. Enough." I lifted my duffle to my shoulder and gave the man a wave.

"If you don't need money, kid, what *do* you need, then?"

"Experience, I guess." I tried to smile knowingly.

"Listen. I've been coming down here every goddamned winter for eight years now, ever since I retired. I've *got* experience, and lemme tell you, this place is gonna be a boom town. It already is. All these old people from the North, and there's gonna be more of 'em, son, not less, and all of 'em got money to spend, and here you are on the ground floor. I'd give all my experience for your youth. Son, forget Cuba. Stay in St. Pete, you'll be a millionaire before you're twenty-five."

I was sorry now that I'd told Knox the truth back in Virginia, when he'd asked me where I was going. I'd said Cuba, and he'd laughed and asked why, and I had tried to tell him, but all I could say was that I wanted to help the Cuban people liberate themselves from a cruel and corrupt dictator. We both knew how that sounded, and neither of us had spoken of Cuba again, until now.

I stepped away from the car to the curb. "Well, thanks. Thanks for the advice. And the ride. Good meeting you," I said.

He called me by my name. I hadn't thought he'd caught it. "Look, if you need some help, just give me a call," he said and stuck a small white card out the window on the passenger's side.

I took the card and read his first name, Dewey, his address back in Chevy Chase, Maryland, and a post office box here in St. Petersburg. "Thanks," I said.

"I stay at the hotel," Knox said, nodding toward the high, pink, stuccoed building. "With my fiancée. Her name's Sturgis, Bea Sturgis. Bea's here all the time, year round. Nice woman. Give a call anytime."

"I'm okay," I said. "Really. I know what I'm doing."

He smiled. "No," he said. "You don't." Then he waved good-bye, dropped the Buick into gear, and moved off slowly toward the hotel garage.

It was not quite nine in the morning, and it was already hot. I peeled off my jacket, tied it to the duffle, and strolled across the street to the park by the marina and sat down on a bench facing the street. Behind me, charter fishing boats and yachts rocked tenderly against the narrow dock, where pelicans perched somberly on the bollards. Across the street, men and women in short-sleeved, pastel-colored blouses and shirts and plaid Bermuda shorts drifted in and out of the hotel. New cars and taxis and limousines drove people by and let people off and picked people up. A light breeze riffled quietly through the royal palm trees that lined the street. Everyone and everything belonged exactly where it was.

I was suddenly hungry and realized that I hadn't eaten since the night before at a Stuckeys in North Carolina. A few minutes passed, and then I saw Knox emerge from the parking garage at the left of the hotel and walk briskly along the sidewalk toward the hotel, his gaze straight ahead of him, businesslike.

He reached the canopy, turned under it, and entered the building, nodding agreeably to the doorman as he passed through the glass doors to the dark, cool interior.

I stood up slowly, grabbed my duffle, crossed the street, and followed him.

I never saw Knox again. I called him from the house phone in the lobby, and 25
he laughed and called the manager, who met me at the front desk and gave me a note to take to the concierge, who put me to work that very day as a furniture mover.

I was the youngest and the healthiest of a gang of seven or eight men who set up tables and chairs for meeting rooms and convention halls, decorated ballrooms for wedding receptions, moved pianos from one dining room to another, dragged king-sized mattresses from suite to suite, unloaded supplies from trucks, delivered carts of dirty linen to the basement laundry, lugged sofas, lamps, cribs, and carpets from one end of the hotel to the other. Paid less than thirty dollars a week for six ten-hour days a week, we worked staggered shifts and were on call seven days a week, twenty-four hours a day. We were given room and board and ate in a bare room off the hotel kitchen with the dishwashers and slept two to a tiny, cell-like room in a cinder-block dormitory behind the hotel.

Most of the kitchen help was black and went home, or somewhere, at night. We furniture movers were to a man white and, except for me, over forty, terminally alcoholic, physically fragile, and itinerant. It took me a few days to realize that we were all a type of migrant worker, vagrants, wanderers down from the cold cities and railroad yards of the North, and that the day after payday most of this week's crew would be gone, replaced the next day by a new group of men, who, a week later, would leave, too, for Miami, New Orleans, or Los Angeles. No one else wanted our jobs, and we couldn't get any other. We were underpaid, overworked, and looked down upon by chambermaids, elevator operators, and doormen. Like certain plumbing tools, we were not thought to exist until we were needed.

Even so, less than two weeks into this line of work, I decided to succeed at it. Which was like deciding to succeed at being a prisoner of war, deciding to become a *good* prisoner of war. I believed that I could become so good at moving furniture that I'd be irreplaceable and shortly thereafter would be made boss of the furniture movers, and then my talent for organization, my affection for the hotel, and the warmth of my personality would be recognized by the concierge, who would promote me, would make me his assistant, and from there I'd go on to concierge itself, then assistant manager, until, before long, why not *manager?* In the distant future, I saw a chain of hotels linking every major city on the Gulf of Mexico (a body of water I had not actually seen yet) that I would control from a bank of telephones here on my desk in St. Petersburg at the Coquina Key, which, since it was where I got my start, would become the central jewel in my necklace of hotels and resorts, my diadem, a modest man's point of understandable pride. I would entertain world leaders here—Dr. Fidel Castro, President Dwight Eisenhower, Generalissimo Chiang Kai-shek. People would congratulate me for having dropped out of an Ivy League college after less than one term, and my mother and brother and sister would now realize the wisdom of my decision, and friends from high school would call me up, begging for jobs in one of my many hotels. Late at night, lying in my narrow bunk, my temporary roommate snoring in the bunk below, I imagined testimonial dinners at which I would single out my old friend Dewey Knox from Chevy Chase. He'd be seated alongside his lady, Bea Sturgis, at the head table, just beyond the mayor of St. Petersburg and the governor of Florida. "It all started with Knox," I'd say. "He told me this place was made for a guy like me, and he was right!"

Furniture movers came and went, but I stayed. The fourth person in five weeks with whom I shared my grim cell was named Bob O'Neil, from Chicago, and when he found out that I'd been a furniture mover at the Coquina Key for longer than a month, he told me I was crazy. I'd come back from setting up a VFW luncheon in the Oleander Room, hoping to sneak a few hours' sleep, as I'd been up most of the night before, taking down the tables and chairs and cleaning up the hall after an all-state sports award banquet. My previous roommate, Fred from Columbus, a fat, morosely silent man whose hands trembled while he read religious tracts, which he wordlessly passed on to me, had got his first week's pay two days before and had taken off for Phoenix, he said, where his sister lived.

My new roommate, when I arrived, had already claimed the bottom bunk 30
and removed my magazines and was now lying stretched out on it. I closed the door, and he sat up, stuck out his hand, and introduced himself. "Hi," he said, "I'm Bob, and I'm an alcoholic." He was in his early or late forties; it was hard to tell which. His face was broad and blotched, with broken veins crisscrossing his cheeks and large red nose. He was bright-eyed and had a cheerful, loose mouth and a wash of thin, sandy-gray hair.

I removed his open, nearly empty, cardboard suitcase from the only chair in the room and sat down. I said, "How come you tell people you're an alcoholic, Bob?" and he explained that he was required to by Alcoholics Anonymous, which he said he had joined just yesterday, after years of considering it.

"That's what you *got* to say," he said. "You got to admit to the world that you're an alcoholic. Put it right out there. First step to recovery, kid."

"How long before you're cured?" I asked. "And don't have to go around introducing yourself like that?"

"Never," he said. "Never. It's like . . . a condition. Like diabetes or your height. I'm allergic to booze, to alcohol. Simple as that."

"So you can't touch the stuff?" 35

"Right. Not unless I want to die." He swung his feet around to the floor and lit a cigarette. "Smoke?"

"No, thanks," I said. "The bottom bunk's mine."

"You're kidding me," he said, smiling broadly. "Look at you—what're you, eighteen? Twenty?"

"Eighteen. Almost nineteen."

"Eighteen. Right. And here I am, an old, sick man, an alcoholic, and you can 40
jump up there like a pole vaulter. And you're saying that bottom bunk's yours." He sighed, coughed, lay back down, and closed his eyes. "You're right. It's yours."

"No, go ahead. I'll sleep on top."

"No, no, no! You're right, you got here before me. First come, first served. That's the law of the land. I understand, kid."

I climbed up the rickety ladder at the end of the bunk and flung myself face-forward onto the bed.

"You sure you don't mind?" he asked, sticking his head out and peering up at me.

"No."

"How long you been here, anyhow?"

"Little over five weeks," I said. More than half as long as I went to college, I noticed.

"Five weeks!" He laughed and told me I was crazy, said it in a high, amused voice. "Well," he said, yawning, "you must be getting real good at it."

"Yeah."

Nobody worked these jobs more than a week or at the most two, he explained. "You're like a prisoner, never see the light of day, never make enough money to make a difference in your life, so what you gotta do, you just gotta get your pay and leave. Get the hell out. Find a place or a job that does make a difference. Smart, good-looking kid like you," he said, "you can do better than this. This is America, for Christ's sake. You can do real good for yourself. How much money you got saved up?"

"Not much. Little over sixty bucks."

"Well, there you go," he said, as if presenting a self-evident truth.

I thanked him for the advice, explained that I was tired and needed sleep. I was on the night shift that week and had been told to fill in for a guy who'd left the morning crew, something that was happening with increasing frequency, which I had taken as a sure sign of imminent success.

Over the next few days, whenever we talked, which was often, as he was garrulous and I was lonely, we talked about Bob's alcoholism and my refusal to take his advice, which was to leave the hotel immediately, rent a room in town, get a job in a restaurant or a store, where people could see me, as Bob explained, because, according to him, I had the kind of face people trusted. "An *honest* face," he said, as if it communicated more than merely a commitment to telling the truth, as if intelligence, reliability, sensitivity, personal cleanliness, and high ambition all went with it. "You got an *honest* face, kid. You should get the hell out there in the real world, where you can *use* it."

For my part, I advised him to keep going to his AA meetings, which he said he did. He was tempted daily to drink, I knew, by the flask toters in our crew, and often he'd come into the room trembling, on the verge of tears, and he'd grab me by the shoulders and beg me not to let him do it. "Don't let me give in, kid! Don't let the bastards get to me. Talk to me, kid," he'd beg, and I'd talk to him, remind him of all he'd told me—his broken marriages, his lost jobs, his penniless wanderings between Florida and Chicago, his waking up sick in filthy flophouses and panhandling on street corners—until at last he'd calm down and feel a new determination to resist temptation. I could see that it was hard on him physically. He seemed to be losing weight, and his skin, despite the red blotches and broken veins, had taken on a dull gray pallor, and he never seemed to sleep. We were both on the night shift that week, and all day long, except when he went out for what he said were his AA meetings, I'd hear him in the bunk below, tossing his body from side to side in the dim afternoon light as he struggled to fall asleep, eventually giving up, lighting a cigarette, going out for a walk, returning to try and fail again.

One afternoon, a few days before his first payday, he reached up to my bunk and woke me. "Listen, kid, I can't sleep. Loan me a couple bucks, willya? I got to go get a bottle." His voice was unusually firm, clear. He'd made a decision.

"Bob, don't! You don't want that. Stick it out."

"Don't lecture me, kid, just loan me a coupla bucks." This time he was giving me an order, not making a request.

I looked into his eyes for a few seconds and saw my own stare back. "No," I said and turned over and went defiantly to sleep.

When I woke, it was growing dark, and I knew I'd almost missed supper, so 60
I rushed from the room and down the long tunnel that connected the dormitory to the hotel kitchen, where the night dishwashers and furniture movers were already eating. Bob wasn't there, and no one had seen him.

"He's working tonight!" I said. "He's got to work tonight!"

They shrugged and went on eating. No one cared.

A half dozen rooms on the fourteenth floor were being painted, and we spent the night moving furniture out and storing it in the basement, and there was a chamber of commerce breakfast that we had to set up in the Crepe Myrtle Room. By the time I got back to my room, it was daylight. Bob was there, sound asleep in the bottom bunk.

I looked around the room, checked the tin trash can, even peered into the dresser drawers, but found no bottle. He heard me and rolled over and watched.

"Lookin' for something?" 65

"You know what."

"A bottle?"

"Yeah. Sure."

"Sorry, kid."

"You didn't drink?" 70

"Nope." He sat up and smiled. He looked rested for the first time, and his color had returned. He lit a cigarette. "Nope, I didn't break. Close, though," he said, his blue eyes twinkling, and he held his thumb and index finger a pencil width apart. "Close."

I grinned, as if his triumph were mine. "You really got through it, huh? What'd you do? Where were you all night?"

"Right here. While you were working, I was sleeping like a baby. I got back here late from the AA meeting. It was a long one, and I was burnt, man. So I just told 'em I was sick, they could dock my pay, and then I came back here and slept the night away."

"Wow! That's great!" I shook his hand. "See, man, that's what I've been telling you! You got to keep going to those AA meetings!"

He smiled tolerantly, rubbed out his cigarette, and lay back down. I pulled 75
off my shirt and trousers, climbed up to my bed, and when I heard Bob snoring, I fell asleep.

That afternoon, when I woke, Bob was gone again. I got down from my bed and noticed that his cardboard suitcase was gone, too. His drawer in the dresser was empty, and when I looked into the medicine cabinet above the tiny sink in the corner, I saw that he'd taken his shaving kit. He'd moved out.

I was confused and suddenly, unexpectedly, sad. I stood in front of the mirror and shaved, the first time in three days, and tried to figure it all out—Bob's alcoholism, which did indeed seem as much a part of him as his height or the color of his eyes, and my caring about it; his persistent advice to me, and mine to him; his vain dream of not drinking, my dream of . . . what? Success? Forgiveness? Revenge? Somehow, Bob and I were alike, I thought, especially now that he had fled from the hotel. The thought scared me. It was the first time since that snowy night I left the college on the hill that I'd been scared.

I wiped off the scraps of shaving cream, washed my razor, and opened the cabinet for my bottle of Aqua Velva. Gone. A wave of anger swirled around me and passed quickly on. I sighed. Oh, what the hell, let him have it. The man left without even one week's pay; a morning splash of aftershave would make him feel successful for at least a minute or two. The rest of the day he'll feel like what he is, I thought, a failure.

I picked up my shirt and pants and slowly got dressed, when, leaning down to tie my shoe, I saw the pale blue bottle in the tin trash can between the dresser and the bed. I reached in, drew it out, and saw that it was empty.

Chucking it back, as if it were a dead animal, I looked around the gray room, 80
and I saw its pathetic poverty for the first time—the spindly furniture, the bare cinder-block walls and linoleum floor, the small window that faced the yellow-brick side of the parking garage next door. Knox's blue Buick was probably still parked there. I looked at my half dozen paperback books on the dresser—mysteries, a Stendhal novel, an anthology of *Great American Short Stories*— and my papers, a short stack of letters from home, a sketchbook, a journal I was planning to write in soon. I'd brought it for Cuba. Then I pulled my old canvas duffle out from under the bed and began shoving clothes inside.

I rented a room from an old lady who owned a small house off Central Avenue in downtown St. Petersburg, a quiet neighborhood of bungalows and tree-lined streets that was beginning to be devoured at the edges by glass-and-concrete buildings housing condominiums, insurance companies, and banks. The room was small, but bright and clean, in the back off the kitchen, with its own bathroom and separate entrance. With the room went kitchen privileges, but I would have to eat in my bedroom. There were strict house rules that I eagerly agreed to: no visitors, by which I knew she meant women; no smoking; no drinking. I'd been meaning to give up smoking anyhow, and since the only way I could drink was more or less illegally, it seemed more or less a luxury to me. Especially after Bob O'Neil. As for women in my room, based on my experience so far, the old lady might as well have said no Martians.

"I'm a Christian," she said, "and this is a Christian home." Her name was Mrs. Treworgy. She was tiny, half my size, and pink—pink hair, pink skin, pink rims around her watery eyes.

"I'm a Christian too," I assured her.

"What church?"

I hesitated. "Methodist?"

She smiled, relieved, and told me where the nearest Methodist church was located; not far, as it turned out. She herself was a Baptist, which meant that she had to walk ten blocks each way on Sundays. "But the preaching's worth it," she said. "And our choir is much better than the Methodist choir."

"I'm sure."

"Maybe you'd like to come with me some Sunday."

"Oh, yes, I would," I said. "But I'll probably try the Methodist church first. You know, it being what I'm used to and all." What I was used to was sleeping till noon on Sundays, and before that, back when my mother made me go, dozing through mass.

"Yes, of course." Then she asked for the first and last months' rent in advance. Eighty dollars.

"All I've got to my name is sixty-seven dollars," I said and confessed, as if to a crime, that I had just quit my job at the Coquina Key Hotel and briefly described the conditions there, as if they were extenuating circumstances. "It was a very . . . unsavory atmosphere," I said, looking at the floor of her living room. The room was small, crowded with large, dark furniture and portraits of Jesus, close-ups and long shots, seated by a rock at prayer and ascending like Superman into heaven.

She looked at me carefully. "You have an honest face," she pronounced. "And I'm sure you'll find a new job right away. Whyn't you just pay me the first month's rent, forty dollars, and we'll go from there."

"Oh, thank you, Mrs. Treworgy. Thank you. And you wait," I said, "I'll have a job by tomorrow!"

Which I did. Following at last the advice of my ex-roommate Bob O'Neil, I applied for a job where I could be seen, as a menswear salesman at the fashionable downtown Maas Brothers Department Store. On the application form, however, under hobbies, I wrote "drawing and painting" and was instead hired to work in the Display Department as an assistant window trimmer.

The Display Department was located in the basement of the large, modern building, and as an assistant I was expected to build and paint the backdrops for the interior and window displays designed and installed by a tall, thin, Georgia man named, appropriately, Art, and a bulky, middle-aged, black-haired woman named Sukey, who wore turquoise and silver Indian jewelry and hand-printed muumuus. Art was an agreeable man in his forties who'd worked in advertising in Atlanta until a decade ago, when his ulcers erupted and sent him to the hospital for the third time in one year, after which he'd quit and moved to Florida. He popped antacid tablets all day, and his mouth was perpetually dry and white-lipped, but he joked and smiled easily, teased Sukey for her artistic pretensions, me for my youth and ignorance, and Ray, the obese, bald sign painter, for his weight and baldness.

It was a cheerful, easygoing place, especially after the Coquina Key Hotel, and I enjoyed the work, which was not difficult. I built lightweight wood frames, usually four feet by eight feet, covered them with colored paper or foil, painted screens and backdrops, cleaned brushes and swept the floor of the shop. Afternoons, I delivered signs for Ray to the department heads upstairs, ate lunch with the salespeople and the rest of the staff in the company cafeteria on the first floor, and after work went out for beers with Art, Sukey, and Ray, and then walked whistling back to my room at Mrs. Treworgy's, where, after supper, I drew pictures, usually somber self-portraits, read, and prepared to write in my journal.

I turned nineteen that spring, and there were pink, white, and yellow hibiscus blossoms everywhere and sweet-smelling jasmine, oleander, and poinciana trees in bloom. Palm trees fluttered in the warm breezes off the Gulf, and tamarind trees clacked their long dark pods, while citrus trees in backyards produced huge, juicy oranges for the plucking. I wore short-sleeved shirts, light cotton trousers, sandals, and felt my body gradually cease cringing from the remembered New England cold and begin to expand and move out to meet this strange new world. I was tanned and well fed, muscular and extremely healthy, and my mind, naturally, began turning obsessively to thoughts of women.

Even though it was only a respite, for the first time since the previous December I felt free of guilt for having failed at life without having first tried to succeed. Freed from such a complex, burdensome guilt, I was trapped instantly by lust. Not ordinary lust, but late-adolescent, New England virginal lust, lust engendered by chemistry crossed with curiosity, lust with no memory to restrain and train it, lust that seeks not merely to satisfy and deplete itself, but to avenge itself as well. For the first time in my life, I seemed to be happy and consequently wanted only to make up for lost time and lost opportunities, to get even with all those Catholic schoolgirls who'd said, "Stop," and I stopped, all those passionate plunges frozen in agonizing positions in midair over car seats, sofas, daybeds, carpeted living room floors, beach blankets, and hammocks, all those semen-stained throw pillows on the asbestos tile floors of pine-paneled basement dens. This was lust with a vengeance.

The male of the species ceased to exist. Walking to work in the morning, I saw only women and girls getting on and off buses, stepping from parked cars, long brown legs drawing skirts tightly against tender thighs, blouses whose sole function seemed to be to draw my attention to breasts. At lunch in the cafeteria, I looked watery-eyed and swollen across the food counter at the black women, the first I'd seen up close, all shades of brown and black, from pale gold and coffee to maple red and mahogany, their dark eyes looking straight through me, as if I were invisible, and when I tried to smile, to be seen, and now and then succeeded, I quickly dropped my eyes and moved down the line to the cash register, where, as I paid, I searched the cafeteria for the girl who'd been standing next to me in line, a salesgirl I'd once heard talking to Sukey in the basement shop about eye makeup and had watched from then on every chance I got, always from a safe distance, however, as she had strawberry blond, wavy, shoulder-length hair that made my hands open and close involuntarily, large green eyes that made my lips dry out, a soft Southern accent that made my breath come in tiny packets.

It was as if my awareness of my surroundings were determined by a glandular condition. After work, I sat with Art, Sukey, and Ray in the bar on the corner across from the store, and while they spoke to one another and to me, I watched, like a panther about to pounce, the girls from the store, watched them smoke their cigarettes and talk, slender wrists flicking, gold bracelets catching light and bouncing it through smoke off the walls, moist red lips nipping at the air, parting for white teeth, pink wet tongues, little cries of laughter. I began to wonder what Sukey looked like under her throat-to-ground muumuu and pictured hot loaves of flesh. Delivering signs for Ray to swimwear on the second floor, I rode the escalator up from the first and sniffed the air eagerly and caught the scent of perfume, lipstick, shaved underarms, and nearly tripped at the top. I went to church with Mrs. Treworgy, got lost watching the teenage girls in the choir, and as we left I inadvertently crossed myself, which I knew Protestants did not do, though I told Mrs. Treworgy that we Methodists sometimes did. I was invited by Art to have dinner with him and his wife, and throughout the meal wondered how Art would take it if I had a brief love affair with his dark, bouffant-haired wife, who asked me if people from New England really did say, "Pahk the cah in Hahvahd Yahd," and if so, why didn't I talk that way? I told her they did and I did, and for the rest of the evening I did. 100

To save myself from abject humiliation and worse, I did what men usually do in this situation. I went back to guilt and became obsessed with my work. I decided to succeed in this new trade, to become the best assistant window trimmer that had ever worked at Maas Brothers. It was time, I decided, for me to make my move. In my room at night, I drew window displays—anything to keep my mind and hands busy at the same time. Some of the designs were for windows that exhibited spring dresses, but more often they portrayed less agitating merchandise, like air conditioners, men's shoes, lawn mowers, and lamps. Many of them were inventive and well-drawn designs that the next day I left lying around Art's workbench and Sukey's easel, even leaving my pad open next to Ray's brushes when I went upstairs for his midmorning snack. I figured that once I was permitted to design and install my own window, my talent would be recognized and I'd be promoted. On my way. With a new kid hired to replace me as assistant, Art or Sukey would be moved to the larger store in Tampa or shifted to the Maas Brothers about to open in Miami. I'd follow a few years later, only to pass them by, moving swiftly up the ladder of window trimming to where the only moves left would be horizontal, into management, vice president in charge of advertising, and on up from there.

Then it happened. One morning in May, I came whistling cheerfully into the shop, as was my habit, and Art called me aside and said that there was going to be a fashion show in swimwear that afternoon and they needed a tropical-island floor display right away. "Sukey and me're all tied up getting them damned Memorial Day windows done," he drawled. "Whyn't you-all try your hand on the tropical island?"

"Why, sure," I said. I flipped open my sketchbook. "What've you got in mind, Art? I'll work up some sketches."

"Just some kind of backdrop, some grass or sand, a mannequin in a swimsuit, maybe a coupla colored spots. You can do it. I seen your drawings lying around. Now's your opportunity to show us what you can do on your own." He smiled down at me and winked.

I made my sketches, a four-by-eight-foot panel with broad streaks of rose, 105
silver, and orange to signify a tropical sunset, three or four long palm fronds on the upper left corner of the panel, and two women, one standing, looking mournfully out to sea, her hands at her eyes, as if watching eagerly for her lover's return, the other seated, resigned to his absence, contemplating the pink and white gauze blossoms that I planned to scatter over the earth. The two faces of Penelope, thought, waiting for Odysseus, me.

I cut two-by-fours for the frame, instead of the usual one-by-twos, nailed them together with eightpenny nails, cross-braced it horizontally and vertically, cut and nailed on plywood triangles to square the corners, and covered both sides with tautly drawn metallic paper, stapling back and hiding the seams neatly, so that, finished, it resembled nothing so much as a solid block of sea blue steel. They'll use this panel for years, I gloated, and indeed, when I stood the panel up, it was like a well-made house, an oak tree, a piece of public sculpture that would outlive the culture that had produced it.

The others went up to lunch, but I stayed down in the shop, painting streaks of cloud and sunlight on my panel. "Don't fuss with that thing too long now," Art called back. "You got to have that display done and installed by two. The fashion show starts up at two."

"No sweat!" I hollered. I had everything I needed out and arranged neatly before me: the two mannequins, wigs, one blond, one brunette, gauze blossoms, palm fronds, colored spots and extension cords, and the tools I'd need to set them up—hammer, screwdriver, screws, and angle iron to fasten the panel to the island, tape, staple gun, and so on. All I needed now was the bathing suits.

I telephoned swimwear from Art's office. One of the salesgirls answered, and instantly, though she said nothing more than "Swimwear," I recognized the voice. Two notes, and I knew the entire tune. It was the girl I'd overheard talking to Sukey about eye makeup, the strawberry blond I'd studied from a distance in the cafeteria, the green-eyed beauty in the crowd at whom I'd aimed my hunter's gaze from the corner booth after work.

I cleared my throat and stammered that I needed a pair of bathing suits for 110
the fashion show display.

"Okay," she sang. "We're trying on bathing suits right now, for the show and all, so whyn't you come on up and just pick out what you-all want?"

"Sure, fine. Sure, that's great, a great idea. Ah . . . who'll I ask for? What's your name?"

"Eleanor," she said, and the word rose in my mind like an elegant seabird against a silver moon over dark Caribbean waters.

"Sure. Fine. Eleanor, then. Okay, then . . ."

"G'bye," her voice chimed in my ear. 115

I put down the phone and decided to take my panel to the second floor right away, to set it up first and then see which bathing suits matched the colors of my sunset before I made my selection. It was surprisingly heavy. In fact, I could barely lift it. I tipped it, got leverage, lifted, and carried the panel out of the shop, ducking at the door to keep it from scraping, and managed to get it all the way up the wide stairs from the basement to the first floor, before I had to stop and rest a minute. The store was jammed with lunch-hour shoppers, women mostly, many of whom gazed with what I took to be admiration at my blue panel, which I now regarded as very nearly a work of art.

The escalators were located at the center of the large, crowded floor, where the ceiling swooped and opened up to reveal the second floor as a kind of mezzanine. I could see young women strolling about in bathing suits up there, bare shoulders, naked arms and legs, bare feet, pink arches, toes.

I hefted my panel, got it balanced, and moved carefully through the throng of shoppers to the escalator and got in line. By the time I stepped onto the metal stairs, the panel had grown heavy again, so I set it down, placing one corner on the step. I peered around it and up and caught a glimpse of the girl named Eleanor, wearing a two-piece bathing suit, blood red it was, and very revealing, for in that instant I saw that she had large, high breasts, and a navel, my God, a female navel—when I noticed something falling lightly past my face like sprinkles of dust. I heard a loud, grinding noise from overhead, screams from below, and debris started falling all about me. I looked up and saw that the top edge of my panel was digging a trench into the ceiling, a gouge that ripped away plaster, wires, pipes, and tubes, and the higher we rode on the escalator, my panel and I, the deeper into the ceiling it dug, relentlessly, as if with rage, while women above and below me, pushing and grabbing one another in fear, shrieked and ran to escape falling chunks of ceiling.

I let go of the panel, but it held there, rigid, like a plow blade, jammed now between the metal tread of the escalator and the ceiling above, which curved lower and lower as we neared the second floor, until the ceiling was almost low enough for me to reach up and touch, when the top of the panel ground against the reinforced-concrete floor of the mezzanine itself, and promptly the metal stair began to give. The panel, however, refused to give. It creaked, bowed a little, but it held. The escalator kept on moving, while the noise level rose—screams, shouts, cries for help, falling debris, wood grinding against concrete, metal bending under wood—until, at last, the ceiling curved up and away from the stairwell, and my panel sprung free, rising like a mainsail, floating over the rail, and tumbling onto the adjacent down escalator, where people ran in horror as it bounced heavily end over end toward glass counters filled with cosmetics, notions, jewelry, perfumes.

120 Up above, still riding the escalator, I watched with almost scientific detachment as the stair, bent by the panel into a shallow V, neared the slot in the floor where the stairs in front of it one by one flattened neatly and slid away I saw the bent stair hit the slot, felt the whole escalator beneath my feet buckle and jump, heard the motor grind on stubbornly, until at last it stopped.

All the electricity in the building had gone off. We were in a dusky haze, as if after a terrorist's attack. It was silent, with smoke and dust hovering in the air. A chunk of rubble rolled into a corner. Water splashed aimlessly from a broken pipe. A fluorescent light fixture held by a single wire broke loose and fell to the floor. A woman sobbed. A mother called her child.

I was at the top of the stairs, facing swimwear. Before me stood several girls in bathing suits, their hands fisted in horror before open mouths, their eyes wild with fear. One or two wept quietly. I saw the girl named Eleanor among them, and I turned and ran blindly back down the way I had just ridden to the top, leaping over rubble and shoving my way past terrified shoppers, stunned men in business suits, janitors, salesgirls, crunching over broken glass toward the door and away from the crowd that had emerged from the cafeteria, past a white-faced Art and Sukey, and out, finally, to the street. My chest heaved furiously, my ears rang, and still I ran, charging through traffic without looking, as fire trucks and police cars with sirens wailing pulled up at the store.

I was in a small park, walking slower and slower along a white crushed-stone pathway that curved around flower beds. There were live oak trees overhead with Spanish moss hanging down, and small birds flitted in and out of the pale green leaves. Finally, I stopped. I sat down on a bench and put my head in my hands. I believed that my life had all but ended. I was wrapped entirely in shame, as if in a shroud. It was a new feeling, a horrible one, for it surrounded me, enveloping my mind and body totally.

There was no way out of it. In those few moments in the park in St. Petersburg, immolated by endless shame, I was every man who had failed, who had run out on job, family, children, friends—who had run out on *opportunity*. I was Bob O'Neil, drunk and lying about it in Florida; I was my father, silent and withdrawn in northern New Hampshire. I was the boy who went up the hill and then, inexplicably, turned around and came back empty-handed. I was Little Boy Blue asleep with his horn, while the sheep roamed the meadow, and the cows ate the corn. I was ashamed for all of us, every one.

Then, gradually, I felt the presence of a hand on my shoulder. I sat up and turned and followed the delicate, white hand on my shoulder out to a woman's arm. It was Eleanor's, and her green eyes were filled with pity, endless pity that matched perfectly my endless shame. She was wearing the dark red bathing suit that I had loved, and she reached forward and placed her naked arms around my chest and laid her head on my shoulder. I smelled her hair, felt her smooth skin against mine.

We stayed like that for a long time, I on the bench, she standing behind me, both of us weeping silently, me in shame and she in pity, until it was almost dark. And that is how I met my first wife, and why I married her.

(1986)

THE "RAGS-TO-RICHES" FIGURE: QUESTIONS FOR DISCUSSION AND WRITING

1. Compare the mill owner Kirby in "Life in the Iron-Mills" to Richard Cory in Robinson's poem: does anything explain their different fates, if we believe they have different fates? Is Richard Cory's fate more surprising than Hugh Wolfe's fate in Davis's story?

2. Discuss notions of respectability in the three poems in this section.
3. Why is Banks's story entitled "Success Story," given what would seem a colossal (if somewhat humorous) failure at its end?
4. Discuss "women's work" in Joanna Baillie's "The Woman's Labour," Marge Piercy's "The Secretary Chant," Virginia Woolf's "Professions for Women," and Anne Sexton's "Cinderella."
5. Does the conventional "rags-to-riches" story imply happiness? How do these four works connect "riches" and "happiness"? Can you go from "rags-to-riches" and still be happy?
6. Discuss the story of Cinderella in conjunction with Thomas Hardy's poem "The Ruined Maid" and Anne Sexton's poem "Cinderella." If your instructor requires research, this topic might lead to a good paper, as versions of the "Cinderella" story exist in many cultures.

Considering Art: Rags to Riches

The discussion below references art reproduced on color insert pages 19 and 20.

In visual terms, an allegory is an image that stands for something other than simply itself. Allegorical language allows us to say one thing and mean another; to explain internal truths by reference to external appearances, to express abstract ideas in a down-to-earth manner. In seventeenth-century Holland, it was common for artists to paint allegorical images that had moralizing messages. Although these works look naturalistic on first glance, they would have been understood as using very readable pictorial conventions. Godfried Schalcken (1643–1706) and several other painters from the city of Leiden were renowned for painstaking and meticulous attention to detail and for the smoothness of their painted surfaces. Many of their references came from popular sayings, proverbs, and emblem books that warned of the dangers of foolishness, greed, and the shortness of transitory pleasures. Images of scales were commonly read as allusions to the weighing of souls in the last judgment but could equally refer to the process of decision making and weighing options.

***Allegory of Virtues and Riches* (see color insert p. 19).** In Schalcken's *Allegory of Virtues and Riches* (1667), a young woman weighs jewels and a small bird in a hand-held scale. Surprisingly, the piled up jewels cannot tip the balance. Unless the viewer knows that this is an allegorical image, it makes little sense. The bird was a common metaphor for virtue and true love, a theme that is underlined by the embracing cherubs that are depicted as if carved on the stone ledge below her elbow. Her scales are tipping in the direction of love in spite of the strings of pearls that she adds to the weighty lot. The woman's downcast eyes and the sad expression of the cupid above her shoulder may indicate that she has sacrificed or compromised her virtue to attain this material wealth. But all may not be lost: the contrast between the crying and embracing cupids may suggest that the woman is still in the process of weighing her options and working out her dilemma.

***The Ladder of Fortune* (see color insert p. 20).** There is much less interpretive ambiguity in the popular print, *The Ladder of Fortune* published in 1875 by the printmaking firm owned by Nathaniel Currier (1813–1888) and James Merritt Ives (1824–1895). Its subject is an allegorical form for the American work ethic, a metaphor that originates in the writings of Benjamin Franklin. The instructional subtitle of this image is that "industry and morality bring solid rewards; idle schemes and speculations yield poverty and ruin." Although many hopeful workers gather to climb the virtuous rungs of industry, temperance, prudence, integrity, economy, punctuality, courage, and perseverance, the vices of gambling, swindling, betting, stock trading, and, surprisingly, labor strikes attract their own crowds. The desired fruits of virtue will come to those who earn them through honest work rather than by chance or trickery. The American dream of overcoming adversity in a land of equal opportunity has for centuries encouraged hard-working men and women to strive for these same fruits. Currier and Ives prints were an inexpensive and widespread form of popular culture. From 1835 to 1907, the printmakers published over a million hand-colored lithographs that depicted a wide range of scenes from American life.

Questions about the Art

1. How are visual oppositions (such as right and left, up and down) used in these images to represent opposing choices?
2. What knowledge or visual literacy do they assume on the part of the viewer?
3. How has the ladder remained a metaphor of the route to success in the United States? Is hard work all it takes, or is this mobility for all a nostalgic myth?
4. In *The Ladder of Fortune*, who is the assumed viewer? Who is left out of this version of the working world? In whose interest are these values instilled?

Connecting Art and Literature

1. Discuss the role of gender in the "Rags-to-Riches" theme as it applies to "The Ruined Maid" by Thomas Hardy, "Cinderella" by Anne Sexton, and Godfried Schalacken's *Allegory of Virtues and Riches.*
2. Compare the moral of "Ragged Dick" to the one implied in "The Ladder of Fortune."
3. How might the Currier and Ives print apply to the values of the Trickster Figure in Chapter 14?

Chapter 17

Greed, Gluttony, and Generosity

Imagine someone walking into your room and asking you if he or she can have one of your possessions, perhaps your iPod, your laptop, a treasured piece of art or clothing, or your billfold full of cash. You reply: "Of course not. It's mine." We all have a disturbing tendency to want nice things and to feel possessive of those things we have. Once we have what we think we want, we still want more, especially if we live in a democracy in which we are bombarded with advertisements. Legend says that when a reporter asked John D. Rockefeller, the richest man in the world at the time, how much money is enough, he responded, "It's always just a little more than you have." There seems to be no limit to what a person wants to have, and no way that our desires can be completely fulfilled.

Rockefeller was acknowledging that people are greedy and acquisitive, not prone to sharing or contentedly living within their means. The fact that children have difficulty learning how to share suggests that generosity does not come easily to human beings. Although children eventually figure out that no one will play with them if they don't learn to share their toys, how many of us really believe that it is better to give than to receive? Sharing is hard, and giving is even harder. Tax season is rarely regarded as a joyous time. Most people walk by panhandlers, ignoring or resisting their pleas for a handout. Charities and other philanthropic organizations often have trouble raising funds, despite the worthiness of their causes. Once we are in possession of something—particularly money—most of us want to hold onto it for our own purposes, even if only to show it off.

To a certain extent, our culture rewards greed by idolizing those who acquire and maintain wealth. Although people call firefighters and soldiers "heroes," they rarely wait in line for their autographs. Professional athletes and movie stars are as much admired for their millionaire lifestyle as for their talents. Whatever we may think of Donald Trump and Martha Stewart, most of us envy their ability to amass large fortunes. Some people who have made immense amounts of money, like Bill Gates and Oprah Winfrey, are known for giving away millions to support good causes. At the same time, we are still fascinated by their extravagant lifestyles.

From *Winnie-the-Pooh* by A. A. Milne (1926).

What if the thing that is craved, acquired, and consumed in great amounts is not money or material possessions, but food and drink? What is the relation between greed and gluttony? Both involve a desire for more than is needed for survival, a failure to recognize reasonable boundaries, and a self-indulgent attempt to fill a "bottomless pit." However, while greed is sometimes viewed as part of the Puritan work ethic—a positive force that motivates people to work hard and to make something of their lives, to be "clever" or "productive"—gluttony is often linked with the pleasure principle and viewed more critically. Although a rich and indulgent meal is a guilty pleasure and relatively harmless, it can come to stand for a hedonistic approach to life that is wasteful or damaging to self and society. In this view, both the greedy and the gluttonous lack control and a concern for others and for the consequences of their actions. The greedy pursue and pile up too much money for selfish aims, often ignoring ethical concerns. The gluttonous consume too much food and drink, ignoring thoughts of the productive future for the sensual pleasures of the moment. Both are overly wrapped up in the self and see only their own narrow perspectives.

This chapter presents characters and poetic speakers who seek a middle ground between self-indulgence and self-denial, often unsuccessfully. In O. Henry's famous Christmas love story, "The Gift of the Magi," a married couple sacrifice their favorite possessions for one another, and the wife finds herself in "hysterical tears" when she realizes what she has done. In Tobias Wolff's story, "The Rich Brother," a financially successful man is bound by ties of kinship to a more generous but maddeningly hapless brother. Each must learn to take from and give to the other. Other characters struggle to be generous when they would rather be greedy or discover almost by accident the pleasure of giving. The stories by W. W. Jacobs and D. H. Lawrence associate the desire for wealth with tragedy. Gish Jen's story "In the American Society" uses humor to address the difficulties of assimilating into a wealthy country.

Walter Crane, *Midas's Daughter Turned to Gold* (1892).

In the drama for this chapter, Molière's *The Miser*, the main character, Harpagon (the miser) does not seek a middle ground and instead is willing to sacrifice his children's happiness to his own greed.

Allen Ginsberg makes gluttony revolting in his poem "C' mon Pigs of Western Civilization Eat More Grease," as does William Matthews in "The Bear at the Dump." For other poets, like William Carlos Williams in "This Is Just to Say," a little self-indulgence can be a life-affirming treat. Some of the works in this chapter, such as Natalia Ginzburg's essay "The Little Virtues" and Diane Wakoski's poem "The Greed That Is Not Greed," express a complex attitude toward greed. The poems by Pablo Neruda, William Wordsworth, and César Vallejo are troubled by the notion that people desire more than they need, whereas Arthur Hugh Clough's poem "Le Diner" seems to accept that idea. The

Common Characters section at the end of the chapter focuses on the figure of the gambler, someone who is willing to risk a great deal in the hope of a big payoff. As you read all these works, consider where you might position yourself between self-indulgent and self-denying, greedy and generous, and drawn to risk and averse to risk.

Fiction

W. W. Jacobs

The Monkey's Paw

William Wymar Jacobs (1863–1943) was the son of a London dockworker. In his fiction about life at sea, he drew on his memories of sailors and dockworkers. A prolific author of novels and short stories, Jacobs chronicled the lives of the British working classes with a humorist's touch. He also wrote a number of macabre tales, including the famous and much-anthologized horror story "The Monkey's Paw," which first appeared in the September 1902 issue of *Harper's Monthly*. It has been successfully adapted for both stage and film. The power of the story partially lies in the fact that the Whites are a completely unremarkable family with modest ambitions. As you read the story, consider the degree to which the Whites bring about the destruction of their family.

I

Without, the night was cold and wet, but in the small parlor of Lakesnam Villa the blinds were drawn and the fire burned brightly. Father and son were at chess, the former, who possessed ideas about the game involving radical changes, putting his king into such sharp and unnecessary perils that it even provoked comment from the white-haired old lady knitting placidly by the fire.

"Hark at the wind," said Mr. White, who, having seen a fatal mistake after it was too late, was amiably desirous of preventing his son from seeing it.

"I'm listening," said the latter, grimly surveying the board as he stretched out his hand. "Check."

"I should hardly think that he'd come to-night," said his father, with his hand poised over the board.

"Mate," replied the son. 5

"That's the worst of living so far out," bawled Mr. White, with sudden and unlooked-for violence; "of all the beastly, slushy, out-of-the-way places to live in, this is the worst. Pathway's a bog, and the road's a torrent. I don't know what people are thinking about. I suppose because only two houses on the road are let, they think it doesn't matter."

"Never mind, dear," said his wife, soothingly; "perhaps you'll win the next one."

Mr. White looked up sharply, just in time to intercept a knowing glance between mother and son. The words died away on his lips, and he hid a guilty grin in his thin gray beard.

"There he is," said Herbert White, as the gate banged to loudly and heavy footsteps came towards the door.

The old man rose with hospitable haste, and opening the door, was heard condoling with the new arrival. The new arrival also condoled with himself, so that Mrs. White said, "Tut, tut!" and coughed gently as her husband entered the room, followed by a tall burly man, beady of eye and rubicund of visage.

"Sergeant-Major Morris," he said, introducing him.

The sergeant-major shook hands, and taking the proffered seat by the fire, watched contentedly while his host got out whiskey and tumblers and stood a small copper kettle on the fire.

At the third glass his eyes got brighter, and he began to talk, the little family circle regarding with eager interest this visitor from distant parts, as he squared his broad shoulders in the chair and spoke of strange scenes and doughty deeds, of wars and plagues and strange peoples.

"Twenty-one years of it," said Mr. White, nodding at his wife and son. "When he went away he was a slip of a youth in the warehouse. Now look at him."

"He don't look to have taken much harm," said Mrs. White, politely.

"I'd like to go to India myself," said the old man, "just to look round a bit, you know."

"Better where you are," said the sergeant-major, shaking his head. He put down the empty glass, and sighing softly, shook it again.

"I should like to see those old temples and fakirs[1] and jugglers," said the old man. "What was that you started telling me the other day about a monkey's paw or something, Morris?"

"Nothing," said the soldier, hastily. "Leastways nothing worth hearing."

"Monkey's paw?" said Mrs. White, curiously.

"Well, it's just a bit of what you might call magic, perhaps," said the sergeant-major, off-handedly.

His three listeners leaned forward eagerly. The visitor absent-mindedly put his empty glass to his lips and then set it down again. His host filled it for him.

"To look at," said the sergeant-major, fumbling in his pocket, "it's just an ordinary little paw, dried to a mummy."

He took something out of his pocket and proffered it. Mrs. White drew back with a grimace, but her son, taking it, examined it curiously.

[1]*fakir:* A term commonly used to describe a street dweller with magical powers or the ability to perform superhuman tricks; traditionally refers to Sufi or Indian ascetics.

"And what is there special about it?" inquired Mr. White as he took it from his son, and having examined it, placed it upon the table.

"It had a spell put on it by an old fakir," said the sergeant-major, "a very holy man. He wanted to show that fate ruled people's lives, and that those who interfered with it did so to their sorrow. He put a spell on it so that three separate men could each have three wishes from it."

His manner was so impressive that his hearers were conscious that their light laughter jarred somewhat.

"Well, why don't you have three, sir?" said Herbert White, cleverly.

The soldier regarded him in the way that middle age is wont to regard presumptuous youth. "I have," he said, quietly, and his blotchy face whitened.

"And did you really have the three wishes granted?" asked Mrs. White.

"I did," said the sergeant-major, and his glass tapped against his strong teeth.

"And has anybody else wished?" inquired the old lady.

"The first man had his three wishes, yes," was the reply. "I don't know what the first two were, but the third was for death. That's how I got the paw."

His tones were so grave that a hush fell upon the group.

"If you've had your three wishes, it's no good to you now, then, Morris," said the old man at last. "What do you keep it for?"

The soldier shook his head. "Fancy, I suppose," he said, slowly. "I did have some idea of selling it, but I don't think I will. It has caused enough mischief already. Besides, people won't buy. They think it's a fairy-tale, some of them, and those who do think anything of it want to try it first and pay me afterwards."

"If you could have another three wishes," said the old man, eying him keenly, "would you have them?"

"I don't know," said the other. "I don't know."

He took the paw, and dangling it between his front finger and thumb, suddenly threw it upon the fire. White, with a slight cry, stooped down and snatched it off.

"Better let it burn," said the soldier, solemnly.

"If you don't want it, Morris," said the old man, "give it to me."

"I won't," said his friend, doggedly. "I threw it on the fire. If you keep it, don't blame me for what happens. Pitch it on the fire again, like a sensible man."

The other shook his head and examined his new possession closely. "How do you do it?" he inquired.

"Hold it up in your right hand and wish aloud," said the sergeant-major, "but I warn you of the consequences."

"Sounds like the *Arabian Nights*," said Mrs. White, as she rose and began to set the supper. "Don't you think you might wish for four pairs of hands for me?"

Her husband drew the talisman from his pocket, and then all three burst into laughter as the sergeant-major, with a look of alarm on his face, caught him by the arm.

"If you must wish," he said, gruffly, "wish for something sensible."

Mr. White dropped it back into his pocket, and placing chairs, motioned his friend to the table. In the business of supper the talisman was partly forgotten, and afterwards the three sat listening in an enthralled fashion to a second installment of the soldier's adventures in India.

"If the tale about the monkey paw is not more truthful than those he has been telling us," said Herbert, as the door closed behind their guest, just in time for him to catch the last train, "we sha'n't make much out of it."

"Did you give him anything for it, father?" inquired Mrs. White, regarding 50
her husband closely.

"A trifle," said he, coloring slightly. "He didn't want it, but I made him take it. And he pressed me again to throw it away."

"Likely," said Herbert, with pretended horror. "Why, we're going to be rich, and famous, and happy. Wish to be an emperor, father, to begin with; then you can't be henpecked."

He darted round the table, pursued by the maligned Mrs. White armed with an antimacassar.

Mr. White took the paw from his pocket and eyed it dubiously. "I don't know what to wish for, and that's a fact," he said, slowly. "It seems to me I've got all I want."

"If you only cleared the house, you'd be quite happy, wouldn't you?" said 55
Herbert, with his hand on his shoulder. "Well, wish for two hundred pounds, then; that'll just do it."

His father, smiling shamefacedly at his own credulity, held up the talisman, as his son, with a solemn face somewhat marred by a wink at his mother, sat down at the piano and struck a few impressive chords.

"I wish for two hundred pounds," said the old man, distinctly.

A fine crash from the piano greeted the words, interrupted by a shuddering cry from the old man. His wife and son ran towards him.

"It moved," he cried, with a glance of disgust at the object as it lay on the floor. "As I wished, it twisted in my hands like a snake."

"Well, I don't see the money," said his son as he picked it up and placed it on 60
the table, "and I bet I never shall."

"It must have been your fancy, father," said his wife, regarding him anxiously.

He shook his head. "Never mind, though; there's no harm done, but it gave me a shock all the same."

They sat down by the fire again while the two men finished their pipes. Outside, the wind was higher than ever, and the old man started nervously at the sound of a door banging upstairs. A silence unusual and depressing settled upon all three, which lasted until the old couple rose to retire for the night.

"I expect you'll find the cash tied up in a big bag in the middle of your bed," said Herbert, as he bade them good-night, "and something horrible squatting up on top of the wardrobe watching you as you pocket your ill-gotten gains."

II

In the brightness of the wintry sun next morning as it streamed over the breakfast 65
table Herbert laughed at his fears. There was an air of prosaic wholesomeness

about the room which it had lacked on the previous night, and the dirty, shrivelled little paw was pitched on the sideboard with a carelessness which betokened no great belief in its virtues.

"I suppose all old soldiers are the same," said Mrs. White. "The idea of our listening to such nonsense! How could wishes be granted in these days? And if they could, how could two hundred pounds hurt you, father?"

"Might drop on his head from the sky," said the frivolous Herbert.

"Morris said the things happened so naturally," said his father, "that you might if you so wished attribute it to coincidence."

"Well, don't break into the money before I come back," said Herbert as he rose from the table. "I'm afraid it'll turn you into a mean, avaricious man, and we shall have to disown you."

His mother laughed, and following him to the door, watched him down the road, and returning to the breakfast table, was very happy at the expense of her husband's credulity. All of which did not prevent her from scurrying to the door at the postman's knock, nor prevent her from referring somewhat shortly to retired sergeant-majors of bibulous habits when she found that the post brought a tailor's bill.

"Herbert will have some more of his funny remarks, I expect, when he comes home," she said as they sat at dinner.

"I dare say," said Mr. White, pouring himself out some beer; "but for all that, the thing moved in my hand; that I'll swear to."

"You thought it did," said the old lady, soothingly.

"I say it did," replied the other. "There was no thought about it; I had just— What's the matter?"

His wife made no reply. She was watching the mysterious movements of a man outside, who, peering in an undecided fashion at the house, appeared to be trying to make up his mind to enter. In mental connection with the two hundred pounds, she noticed that the stranger was well dressed and wore a silk hat of glossy newness. Three times he paused at the gate, and then walked on again. The fourth time he stood with his hand upon it, and then with sudden resolution flung it open and walked up the path. Mrs. White at the same moment placed her hands behind her, and hurriedly unfastening the strings of her apron, put that useful article of apparel beneath the cushion of her chair.

She brought the stranger, who seemed ill at ease, into the room. He gazed furtively at Mrs. White, and listened in a preoccupied fashion as the old lady apologized for the appearance of the room, and her husband's coat, a garment which he usually reserved for the garden. She then waited as patiently as her sex would permit for him to broach his business, but he was at first strangely silent.

"I—was asked to call," he said at last, and stooped and picked a piece of cotton from his trousers. "I come from 'Maw and Meggins.'"

The old lady started. "Is anything the matter?" she asked, breathlessly. "Has anything happened to Herbert? What is it? What is it?"

Her husband interposed. "There, there, mother," he said, hastily. "Sit down, and don't jump to conclusions. You've not brought bad news, I'm sure, sir," and he eyed the other wistfully.

"I'm sorry—" began the visitor.

"Is he hurt?" demanded the mother.

The visitor bowed in assent. "Badly hurt," he said, quietly, "but he is not in any pain."

"Oh, thank God!" said the old woman, clasping her hands. "Thank God for that! Thank —"

She broke off suddenly as the sinister meaning of the assurance dawned upon her and she saw the awful confirmation of her fears in the other's averted face. She caught her breath, and turning to her slower-witted husband, laid her trembling old hand upon his. There was a long silence.

"He was caught in the machinery," said the visitor at length in a low voice.

"Caught in the machinery," repeated Mr. White in a dazed fashion, "yes."

He sat staring blankly out at the window, and taking his wife's hand between his own, pressed it as he had been wont to do in their old courting days nearly forty years before.

"He was the only one left to us," he said, turning gently to the visitor. "It is hard."

The other coughed, and rising, walked slowly to the window. "The firm wished me to convey their sincere sympathy with you in your great loss," he said, without looking round. "I beg that you will understand I am only their servant and merely obeying orders."

There was no reply; the old woman's face was white, her eyes staring, and her breath inaudible; on the husband's face was a look such as his friend the sergeant might have carried into his first action.

"I was to say that Maw and Meggins disclaim all responsibility," continued the other. "They admit no liability at all, but in consideration of your son's service they wish to present you with a certain sum as compensation."

Mr. White dropped his wife's hand, and rising to his feet, gazed with a look of horror at his visitor. His dry lips shaped the words, "How much?"

"Two hundred pounds," was the answer.

Unconscious of his wife's shriek, the old man smiled faintly, put out his hands like a sightless man, and dropped, a senseless heap, to the floor.

III

In the huge new cemetery, some two miles distant, the old people buried their dead, and came back to a house steeped in shadow and silence. It was all over so quickly that at first they could hardly realize it, and remained in a state of expectation as though of something else to happen—something else which was to lighten this load, too heavy for old hearts to bear.

But the days passed, and expectation gave place to resignation—the hopeless resignation of the old, sometimes miscalled apathy. Sometimes they hardly exchanged a word, for now they had nothing to talk about, and their days were long to weariness.

It was about a week after that that the old man, waking suddenly in the night, stretched out his hand and found himself alone. The room was in darkness, and the sound of subdued weeping came from the window. He raised himself in bed and listened.

"Come back," he said, tenderly. "You will be cold."

"It is colder for my son," said the old woman, and wept afresh.

The sound of her sobs died away on his ears. The bed was warm, and his eyes heavy with sleep. He dozed fitfully, and then slept until a sudden wild cry from his wife awoke him with a start.

"The monkey's paw!" she cried, wildly. "The monkey's paw!"

He started up in alarm. "Where? Where is it? What's the matter?"

She came stumbling across the room towards him. "I want it," she said, quietly. "You've not destroyed it?"

"It's in the parlor, on the bracket," he replied, marvelling. "Why?"

She cried and laughed together, and bending over, kissed his cheek.

"I only just thought of it," she said, hysterically. "Why didn't I think of it before? Why didn't you think of it?"

"Think of what?" he questioned.

"The other two wishes," she replied, rapidly. "We've only had one."

"Was not that enough?" he demanded, fiercely.

"No," she cried, triumphantly; "we'll have one more. Go down and get it quickly, and wish our boy alive again."

The man sat up in bed and flung the bedclothes from his quaking limbs. "Good God, you are mad!" he cried, aghast.

"Get it," she panted; "get it quickly, and wish— Oh, my boy, my boy!"

Her husband struck a match and lit the candle. "Get back to bed," he said, unsteadily. "You don't know what you are saying."

"We had the first wish granted," said the old woman, feverishly; "why not the second?"

"A coincidence," stammered the old man.

"Go and get it and wish," cried the old woman, and dragged him towards the door.

He went down in the darkness, and felt his way to the parlor, and then to the mantel-piece. The talisman was in its place, and a horrible fear that the unspoken wish might bring his mutilated son before him ere he could escape from the room seized upon him, and he caught his breath as he found that he had lost the direction of the door. His brow cold with sweat, he felt his way round the table, and groped along the wall until he found himself in the small passage with the unwholesome thing in his hand.

Even his wife's face seemed changed as he entered the room. It was white and expectant, and to his fears seemed to have an unnatural look upon it. He was afraid of her.

"Wish!" she cried, in a strong voice.

"It is foolish and wicked," he faltered.

"Wish!" repeated his wife.

He raised his hand. "I wish my son alive again."

The talisman fell to the floor, and he regarded it shudderingly. Then he sank trembling into a chair as the old woman, with burning eyes, walked to the window and raised the blind.

He sat until he was chilled with the cold, glancing occasionally at the figure of the old woman peering through the window. The candle end, which had burnt below the rim of the china candlestick, was throwing pulsating shadows on the ceiling and walls, until, with a flicker larger than the rest, it expired. The old man, with an unspeakable sense of relief at the failure of the talisman, crept back to his bed, and a minute or two afterwards the old woman came silently and apathetically beside him.

Neither spoke, but both lay silently listening to the ticking of the clock. A stair creaked, and a squeaky mouse scurried noisily through the wall. The darkness was oppressive, and after lying for some time screwing up his courage, the husband took the box of matches, and striking one, went down stairs for a candle.

At the foot of the stairs the match went out, and he paused to strike another, and at the same moment a knock, so quiet and stealthy as to be scarcely audible, sounded on the front door.

The matches fell from his hand. He stood motionless, his breath suspended until the knock was repeated. Then he turned and fled swiftly back to his room, and closed the door behind him. A third knock sounded through the house.

"*What's that?*" cried the old woman, starting up.

"A rat," said the old man in shaking tones— "a rat. It passed me on the stairs."

His wife sat up in bed listening. A loud knock resounded through the house.

"It's Herbert!" she screamed. "It's Herbert!"

She ran to the door, but her husband was before her, and catching her by the arm, held her tightly.

"What are you going to do?" he whispered hoarsely.

"It's my boy; it's Herbert!" she cried, struggling mechanically. "I forgot it was two miles away. What are you holding me for? Let go. I must open the door."

"For God's sake don't let it in," cried the old man, trembling.

"You're afraid of your own son," she cried, struggling. "Let me go. I'm coming, Herbert; I'm coming."

There was another knock, and another. The old woman with a sudden wrench broke free and ran from the room. Her husband followed to the landing, and called after her appealingly as she hurried down stairs. He heard the chain rattle back and the bottom bolt drawn slowly and stiffly from the socket. Then the old woman's voice, strained and panting.

"The bolt," she cried loudly. "Come down. I can't reach it."

But her husband was on his hands and knees groping wildly on the floor in search of the paw. If he could only find it before the thing outside got in. A perfect fusillade of knocks reverberated through the house, and he heard the scraping of a chair as his wife put it down in the passage against the door. He heard the creaking of the bolt as it came slowly back, and at the same moment he found the monkey's paw, and frantically breathed his third and last wish.

The knocking ceased suddenly, although the echoes of it were still in the 140
house. He heard the chair drawn back and the door opened. A cold wind rushed up the staircase, and a long loud wail of disappointment and misery from his wife gave him courage to run down to her side, and then to the gate beyond. The street lamp flickering opposite shone on a quiet and deserted road.

(1902)

Questions for Discussion and Writing

Close Reading

1. Contrast the humble setting of the Whites' home to the exotic origins of the paw. How does the setting contribute to the story's effect?
2. Why do the Whites wish for money? Why do you think they refuse to listen to the sergeant-major's warning?
3. Identify the foreshadowing in the story's opening pages. How does Jacobs prepare you for the story's grisly end?
4. Why does Mrs. White persist in wanting to bring her dead son back to life? Do you fault her for this wish?

Critical and Creative Reading

5. How sympathetic are you toward the Whites? Would you make a similar wish if given the chance? Do you consider the Whites greedy?
6. Why doesn't Sergeant-Major Morris explain more clearly the dangers of the paw? Is he partially to blame for what happens? Do you think Morris has himself been a victim of the paw's magic?
7. How might this story be different if the Whites had wished for something more extravagant: a mansion, wealth, jewels? How would your response to the characters' fates be different?

Connections to Other Readings

8. Discuss the role of luck and fate in "The Monkey's Paw" and in D. H. Lawrence's "The Rocking Horse Winner."
9. Compare the concluding "twists" in "The Monkey's Paw" and in O. Henry's "The Gift of the Magi." How do the authors both prepare you for these endings and surprise you with them?
10. Abraham Cowley's essay "Of Avarice" discusses the personal dangers of falling prey to avarice. Do you think the Whites exemplify Cowley's argument? Why or why not?

O. Henry

The Gift of the Magi

The American short story writer O. Henry (born William Sydney Porter in 1862) knew something of the poverty he depicts in his most famous short story, "The Gift of the Magi." After a career as a journalist, he was convicted of embezzlement and spent three years in prison, where he began writing to support his daughter. After his release he changed his name and became a successful short story writer. His works are best known for their surprise endings. Until his death in 1910, O. Henry published prolifically, tallying up over six hundred short stories and ten collections in his lifetime. His literary success was not matched by personal happiness, and he battled alcoholism, depression, and a failed marriage in his final years. Given even a slight notion of these circumstances, does this famous story seem idealized or fantastic?

One dollar and eighty-seven cents. That was all. And sixty cents of it was in pennies. Pennies saved one and two at a time by bulldozing the grocer and the vegetable man and the butcher until one's cheeks burned with the silent imputation of parsimony that such close dealing implied. Three times Della counted it. One dollar and eighty-seven cents. And the next day would be Christmas.

There was clearly nothing to do but flop down on the shabby little couch and howl. So Della did it. Which instigates the moral reflection that life is made up of sobs, sniffles, and smiles, with sniffles predominating.

While the mistress of the home is gradually subsiding from the first stage to the second, take a look at the home. A furnished flat at $8 per week. It did not exactly beggar description, but it certainly had that word on the lookout for the mendicancy squad.

In the vestibule below was a letter-box into which no letter would go, and an electric button from which no mortal finger could coax a ring. Also appertaining thereunto was a card bearing the name "Mr. James Dillingham Young."

The "Dillingham" had been flung to the breeze during a former period of 5
prosperity when its possessor was being paid $30 per week. Now, when the income was shrunk to $20, though, they were thinking seriously of contracting to a modest and unassuming D. But whenever Mr. James Dillingham Young came home and reached his flat above he was called "Jim" and greatly hugged by Mrs. James Dillingham Young, already introduced to you as Della. Which is all very good.

Della finished her cry and attended to her cheeks with the powder rag. She stood by the window and looked out dully at a gray cat walking a gray fence in a gray backyard. Tomorrow would be Christmas Day, and she had only $1.87 with which to buy Jim a present. She had been saving every penny she could for months, with this result. Twenty dollars a week doesn't go far. Expenses had been greater than she had calculated. They always are. Only $1.87 to buy a present for Jim. Her Jim. Many a happy hour she had spent planning for something nice for him. Something fine and rare and sterling—something just a little bit near to being worthy of the honor of being owned by Jim.

There was a pier glass between the windows of the room. Perhaps you have seen a pier glass in an $8 flat. A very thin and very agile person may, by observing his reflection in a rapid sequence of longitudinal strips, obtain a fairly accurate conception of his looks. Della, being slender, had mastered the art.

Suddenly she whirled from the window and stood before the glass. Her eyes were shining brilliantly, but her face had lost its color within twenty seconds. Rapidly she pulled down her hair and let it fall to its full length.

Now, there were two possessions of the James Dillingham Youngs in which they both took a mighty pride. One was Jim's gold watch that had been his father's and his grandfather's. The other was Della's hair. Had the queen of Sheba lived in the flat across the airshaft, Della would have let her hair hang out the window some day to dry just to depreciate Her Majesty's jewels and gifts. Had King Solomon been the janitor, with all his treasures piled up in the basement, Jim would have pulled out his watch every time he passed, just to see him pluck at his beard from envy.

So now Della's beautiful hair fell about her rippling and shining like a 10
cascade of brown waters. It reached below her knee and made itself almost a garment for her. And then she did it up again nervously and quickly. Once she faltered for a minute and stood still while a tear or two splashed on the worn red carpet.

On went her old brown jacket; on went her old brown hat. With a whirl of skirts and with the brilliant sparkle still in her eyes, she fluttered out the door and down the stairs to the street.

Where she stopped the sign read: "Mme. Sofronie. Hair Goods of All Kinds." One flight up Della ran, and collected herself, panting. Madame, large, too white, chilly, hardly looked the "Sofronie."

"Will you buy my hair?" asked Della.

"I buy hair," said Madame. "Take yer hat off and let's have a sight at the looks of it."

Down rippled the brown cascade. 15

"Twenty dollars," said Madame, lifting the mass with a practised hand.

"Give it to me quick," said Della.

Oh, and the next two hours tripped by on rosy wings. Forget the hashed metaphor. She was ransacking the stores for Jim's present.

She found it at last. It surely had been made for Jim and no one else. There was no other like it in any of the stores, and she had turned all of them inside out. It was a platinum fob chain simple and chaste in design, properly proclaiming its value by substance alone and not by meretricious ornamentation—as all good things should do. It was even worthy of The Watch. As soon as she saw it she knew that it must be Jim's. It was like him. Quietness and value—the description applied to both. Twenty-one dollars they took from her for it, and she hurried home with the 87 cents. With that chain on his watch Jim might be properly anxious about the time in any company. Grand as the watch was, he sometimes looked at it on the sly on account of the old leather strap that he used in place of a chain.

20 When Della reached home her intoxication gave way a little to prudence and reason. She got out her curling irons and lighted the gas and went to work repairing the ravages made by generosity added to love. Which is always a tremendous task, dear friends—a mammoth task.

Within forty minutes her head was covered with tiny, close-lying curls that made her look wonderfully like a truant schoolboy. She looked at her reflection in the mirror long, carefully, and critically.

"If Jim doesn't kill me," she said to herself, "before he takes a second look at me, he'll say I look like a Coney Island chorus girl. But what could I do—oh! what could I do with a dollar and eighty-seven cents?"

At 7 o'clock the coffee was made and the frying-pan was on the back of the stove hot and ready to cook the chops.

Jim was never late. Della doubled the fob chain in her hand and sat on the corner of the table near the door that he always entered. Then she heard his step on the stair away down on the first flight, and she turned white for just a moment. She had a habit of saying a little silent prayer about the simplest everyday things, and now she whispered: "Please God, make him think I am still pretty."

25 The door opened and Jim stepped in and closed it. He looked thin and very serious. Poor fellow, he was only twenty-two—and to be burdened with a family! He needed a new overcoat and he was without gloves.

Jim stopped inside the door, as immovable as a setter at the scent of quail. His eyes were fixed upon Della, and there was an expression in them that she could not read, and it terrified her. It was not anger, nor surprise, nor disapproval, nor horror, nor any of the sentiments that she had been prepared for. He simply stared at her fixedly with that peculiar expression on his face.

Della wriggled off the table and went for him.

"Jim, darling," she cried, "don't look at me that way. I had my hair cut off and sold because I couldn't have lived through Christmas without giving you a present. It'll grow out again—you won't mind, will you? I just had to do it. My hair grows awfully fast. Say 'Merry Christmas!' Jim, and let's be happy. You don't know what a nice—what a beautiful, nice gift I've got for you."

"You've cut off your hair?" asked Jim, laboriously, as if he had not arrived at that patent fact yet even after the hardest mental labor.

30 "Cut it off and sold it," said Della. "Don't you like me just as well, anyhow? I'm me without my hair, ain't I?"

Jim looked about the room curiously.

"You say your hair is gone?" he said, with an air almost of idiocy.

"You needn't look for it," said Della. "It's sold, I tell you—sold and gone, too. It's Christmas Eve, boy. Be good to me, for it went for you. Maybe the hairs of my head were numbered," she went on with sudden serious sweetness, "but nobody could ever count my love for you. Shall I put the chops on, Jim?"

Out of his trance Jim seemed quickly to wake. He enfolded his Della. For ten seconds let us regard with discreet scrutiny some inconsequential object in the other direction. Eight dollars a week or a million a year—what is the difference? A mathematician or a wit would give you the wrong answer. The magi brought valuable gifts, but that was not among them. This dark assertion will be illuminated later on.

Jim drew a package from his overcoat pocket and threw it upon the table. 35

"Don't make any mistake, Dell," he said, "about me. I don't think there's anything in the way of a haircut or a shave or a shampoo that could make me like my girl any less. But if you'll unwrap that package you may see why you had me going a while at first."

White fingers and nimble tore at the string and paper. And then an ecstatic scream of joy; and then, alas! a quick feminine change to hysterical tears and wails, necessitating the immediate employment of all the comforting powers of the lord of the flat.

For there lay The Combs—the set of combs, side and back, that Della had worshipped long in a Broadway window. Beautiful combs, pure tortoise shell, with jewelled rims—just the shade to wear in the beautiful vanished hair. They were expensive combs, she knew, and her heart had simply craved and yearned over them without the least hope of possession. And now, they were hers, but the tresses that should have adorned the coveted adornments were gone.

But she hugged them to her bosom, and at length she was able to look up with dim eyes and a smile and say: "My hair grows so fast, Jim!"

And then Della leaped up like a little singed cat and cried, "Oh, oh!" 40

Jim had not yet seen his beautiful present. She held it out to him eagerly upon her open palm. The dull precious metal seemed to flash with a reflection of her bright and ardent spirit.

"Isn't it a dandy, Jim? I hunted all over town to find it. You'll have to look at the time a hundred times a day now. Give me your watch. I want to see how it looks on it."

Instead of obeying, Jim tumbled down on the couch and put his hands under the back of his head and smiled.

"Dell," said he, "let's put our Christmas presents away and keep 'em a while. They're too nice to use just at present. I sold the watch to get the money to buy your combs. And now suppose you put the chops on."

The magi,[1] as you know, were wise men—wonderfully wise men—who 45
brought gifts to the Babe in the manger. They invented the art of giving Christmas presents. Being wise, their gifts were no doubt wise ones, possibly bearing the privilege of exchange in case of duplication. And here I have lamely related to you the uneventful chronicle of two foolish children in a flat who most unwisely sacrificed for each other the greatest treasures of their house. But in a

[1]*magi:* Plural of *magus* (from Latin, via Greek and Persian); refers to a tribe from ancient Media that was absorbed into the Persian empire five centuries before the Christian era and that was responsible for ceremonies such as funerals. The term commonly refers to the three wise men from the Bible who traveled to the site of Jesus's birth to offer gifts of gold, frankincense, and myrrh.

last word to the wise of these days let it be said that of all who give gifts these two were the wisest. Of all who give and receive gifts, such as they are wisest. Everywhere they are wisest. They are the magi.

(1906)

Questions for Discussion and Writing

Close Reading

1. Why do the Youngs consider shortening the "Dillingham" of Jim's middle name to "D." when their financial situation grows worse? What does this tell you about the couple?
2. What details does O. Henry use to convey the Youngs' poverty? How happy or unhappy are the two at the opening of the story?
3. How does O. Henry prepare the reader for the story's final "twist"?

Critical and Creative Reading

4. The narrator describes Della and Jim as "two foolish children in a flat who most unwisely sacrificed for each other the greatest treasures of their house. But in a last word to the wise of these days let it be said that of all who give gifts these two were the wisest." Do you think these characters are "wise," or are they "foolish children"?
5. In what way is the sacrifice of this couple like the gifts the wise men gave to the Christ child in the Bible? Why do you think O. Henry chose this title for his story?
6. Examine the gender roles in this story. Does the story challenge or reinforce stereotypes of masculinity and femininity? Why do you think O. Henry focuses more on Della's sacrifice than on Jim's?
7. Do you agree with the statement that "life is made up of sobs, sniffles, and smiles, with sniffles predominating"? What does it say about the speaker's perspective?
8. This story is set at Christmas time. Even if you do not celebrate Christmas, you are no doubt inundated with talk of the "Christmas spirit" around the holidays. How does this story embody this "Christmas spirit"? Do you think that people actually experience this "spirit" around the holidays?

Connections to Other Readings

9. A number of stories and poems in this chapter have overt or implicit religious references and messages. Choose two, including this one. What is the role of religion in encouraging generosity and discouraging greed? Why do you think religious references are more common in this chapter than in, say, the chapter on love and lust?
10. Analyze this story as a response to Hugh Clough's poem, "Le Dîner."
11. Discuss the notion of sacrifice in this story and in Tobias Wolff's "The Rich Brother." Does true generosity always require sacrifice?

D. H. Lawrence

The Rocking Horse Winner

David Herbert Lawrence (1885–1930) certainly knew what it was like to grow up in a household like the one depicted in this story, in which everyone feels the lack of money. He was the son of a coalminer whose more educated mother resented her husband's working-class background. Writing fiction was a way for Laurcnce to escape the drudgery of his father's life. He left England after World War I and traveled throughout southern Europe and the United States. His works include the sexually explicit and thus controversial *Lady Chatterley's Lover* (1928) and the semi-autobiographical *Sons and Lovers* (1913). "The Rocking Horse Winner" raises the question of "luck" in achieving prosperity and encourages us to consider whether people make their own luck.

There was a woman who was beautiful, who started with all the advantages, yet she had no luck. She married for love, and the love turned to dust. She had bonny children, yet she felt they had been thrust upon her, and she could not love them. They looked at her coldly, as if they were finding fault with her. And hurriedly she felt she must cover up some fault in herself. Yet what it was that she must cover up she never knew. Nevertheless, when her children were present, she always felt the centre of her heart go hard. This troubled her, and in her manner she was all the more gentle and anxious for her children, as if she loved them very much. Only she herself knew that at the centre of her heart was a hard little place that could not feel love, no, not for anybody. Everybody else said of her: "She is such a good mother. She adores her children." Only she herself, and her children themselves, knew it was not so. They read it in each other's eyes.

There were a boy and two little girls. They lived in a pleasant house, with a garden, and they had discreet servants, and felt themselves superior to anyone in the neighbourhood.

Although they lived in style, they felt always an anxiety in the house. There was never enough money. The mother had a small income, and the father had a small income, but not nearly enough for the social position which they had to keep up. The father went into town to some office. But though he had good prospects, these prospects never materialized. There was always the grinding sense of the shortage of money, though the style was always kept up.

At last the mother said: "I will see if I can't make something." But she did not know where to begin. She racked her brains, and tried this thing and the other, but could not find anything successful. The failure made deep lines come into her face. Her children were growing up, they would have to go to school. There must be more money, there must be more money. The father, who was always very handsome and expensive in his tastes, seemed as if he never would be able to do anything worth doing. And the mother, who had a great belief in herself, did not succeed any better, and her tastes were just as expensive.

And so the house came to be haunted by the unspoken phrase: There must be more money! There must be more money! The children could hear it all the time, though nobody said it aloud. They heard it at Christmas, when the expensive and splendid toys filled the nursery. Behind the shining modern rocking horse, behind the smart doll's-house, a voice would start whispering: "There must be more money! There must be more money!" And the children would stop playing, to listen for a moment. They would look into each other's eyes, to see if they had all heard. And each one saw in the eyes of the other two that they too had heard. "There must be more money! There must be more money!"

It came whispering from the springs of the still-swaying rocking horse, and even the horse, bending his wooden, champing head, heard it. The big doll, sitting so pink and smirking in her new pram, could hear it quite plainly, and seemed to be smirking all the more self-consciously because of it. The foolish puppy, too, that took the place of the Teddy bear, he was looking so extraordinarily foolish for no other reason but that he heard the secret whisper all over the house: "There must be more money!"

Yet nobody ever said it aloud. The whisper was everywhere, and therefore no one spoke it. Just as no one ever says: "We are breathing!" in spite of the fact that breath is coming and going all the time.

"Mother," said the boy Paul one day, "why don't we keep a car of our own? Why do we always use uncle's, or else a taxi?"

"Because we're the poor members of the family," said the mother.

"But why are we, mother?"

"Well—I suppose," she said slowly and bitterly, "it's because your father has no luck."

The boy was silent for some time.

"Is luck money, mother?" he asked, rather timidly.

"No, Paul. Not quite. It's what causes you to have money."

"Oh!" said Paul vaguely. "I thought when Uncle Oscar said filthy lucker, it meant money."

"Filthy lucre does mean money," said the mother. "But it's lucre, not luck."

"Oh!" said the boy. "Then what is luck, mother?"

"It's what causes you to have money. If you're lucky you have money. That's why it's better to be born lucky than rich. If you're rich, you may lose your money. But if you're lucky, you will always get more money."

"Oh! Will you? And is father not lucky?"

"Very unlucky, I should say," she said bitterly.

The boy watched her with unsure eyes.

"Why?" he asked.

"I don't know. Nobody ever knows why one person is lucky and another unlucky."

"Don't they? Nobody at all? Does nobody know?"

"Perhaps God. But He never tells."

"He ought to, then. And aren't you lucky either, mother?"

"I can't be, if I married an unlucky husband."

"But by yourself, aren't you?"

"I used to think I was, before I married. Now I think I am very unlucky indeed."

"Why?"

"Well—never mind! Perhaps I'm not really," she said.

The child looked at her, to see if she meant it. But he saw, by the lines of her mouth, that she was only trying to hide something from him.

"Well, anyhow," he said stoutly, "I'm a lucky person."

"Why?" said his mother, with a sudden laugh.

He stared at her. He didn't even know why he had said it.

"God told me," he asserted, brazening it out.

"I hope He did, dear!" she said, again with a laugh, but rather bitter.

"He did, mother!"

"Excellent!" said the mother, using one of her husband's exclamations.

The boy saw she did not believe him; or, rather, that she paid no attention to his assertion. This angered him somewhat, and made him want to compel her attention.

He went off by himself, vaguely, in a childish way, seeking for the clue to "luck." Absorbed, taking no heed of other people, he went about with a sort of stealth, seeking inwardly for luck. He wanted luck, he wanted it, he wanted it. When the two girls were playing dolls in the nursery, he would sit on his big rocking horse, charging madly into space, with a frenzy that made the little girls peer at him uneasily. Wildly the horse careered, the waving dark hair of the boy tossed, his eyes had a strange glare in them. The little girls dared not speak to him.

When he had ridden to the end of his mad little journey, he climbed down and stood in front of his rocking horse, staring fixedly into its lowered face. Its red mouth was slightly open, its big eye was wide and glassy-bright.

"Now!" he would silently command the snorting steed. "Now, take me to where there is luck! Now take me!"

And he would slash the horse on the neck with the little whip he had asked Uncle Oscar for. He knew the horse could take him to where there was luck, if only he forced it. So he would mount again, and start on his furious ride, hoping at last to get there. He knew he could get there.

"You'll break your horse, Paul!" said the nurse.

"He's always riding like that! I wish he'd leave off!" said his elder sister Joan.

But he only glared down on them in silence. Nurse gave him up. She could make nothing of him. Anyhow he was growing beyond her.

One day his mother and his Uncle Oscar came in when he was on one of his furious rides. He did not speak to them.

"Hallo, you young jockey! Riding a winner?" said his uncle.

"Aren't you growing too big for a rocking horse? You're not a very little boy any longer, you know," said his mother.

But Paul only gave a blue glare from his big, rather close-set eyes. He would speak to nobody when he was in full tilt. His mother watched him with an anxious expression on her face.

At last he suddenly stopped forcing his horse into the mechanical gallop, and slid down.

"Well, I got there!" he announced fiercely, his blue eyes still flaring, and his sturdy long legs straddling apart.

"Where did you get to?" asked his mother.

"Where I wanted to go," he flared back at her. 55

"That's right, son!" said Uncle Oscar. "Don't you stop till you get there. What's the horse's name?"

"He doesn't have a name," said the boy.

"Gets on without all right?" asked the uncle.

"Well, he has different names. He was called Sansovino last week."

"Sansovino, eh? Won the Ascot. How did you know his name?" 60

"He always talks about horse races with Bassett," said Joan.

The uncle was delighted to find that his small nephew was posted with all the racing news. Bassett, the young gardener, who had been wounded in the left foot in the war and had got his present job through Oscar Cresswell, whose batman[1] he had been, was a perfect blade of the "turf." He lived in the racing events, and the small boy lived with him.

Oscar Cresswell got it all from Bassett.

"Master Paul comes and asks me, so I can't do more than tell him, sir," said Bassett, his face terribly serious, as if he were speaking of religious matters.

"And does he ever put anything on a horse he fancies?" 65

"Well—I don't want to give him away—he's a young sport, a fine sport, sir. Would you mind asking him yourself? He sort of takes a pleasure in it, and perhaps he'd feel I was giving him away, sir, if you don't mind."

Bassett was serious as a church.

The uncle went back to his nephew, and took him off for a ride in the car. "Say, Paul, old man, do you ever put anything on a horse?" the uncle asked.

The boy watched the handsome man closely. 70

"Why, do you think I oughtn't to?" he parried.

"Not a bit of it! I thought perhaps you might give me a tip for the Lincoln."

The car sped on into the country, going down to Uncle Oscar's place in Hampshire.

"Honour bright?" said the nephew.

"Honour bright, son!" said the uncle. 75

"Well, then, Daffodil."

"Daffodil! I doubt it, sonny. What about Mirza?"

"I only know the winner," said the boy. "That's Daffodil."

"Daffodil, eh?"

There was a pause. Daffodil was an obscure horse comparatively. 80

"Uncle!"

"Yes, son?"

"You won't let it go any further, will you? I promised Bassett."

"Bassett be damned, old man! What's he got to do with it?"

[1]*batman:* A valet to a cavalry officer.

"We're partners. We've been partners from the first. Uncle, he lent me my first five shillings, which I lost. I promised him, honour bright, it was only between me and him; only you gave me that ten-shilling note I started winning with, so I thought you were lucky. You won't let it go any further, will you?"

The boy gazed at his uncle from those big, hot, blue eyes, set rather close together. The uncle stirred and laughed uneasily.

"Right you are, son! I'll keep your tip private. Daffodil, eh? How much are you putting on him?"

"All except twenty pounds," said the boy. "I keep that in reserve."

The uncle thought it a good joke.

"You keep twenty pounds in reserve, do you, you young romancer? What are you betting, then?"

"I'm betting three hundred," said the boy gravely. "But it's between you and me, Uncle Oscar! Honour bright?"

The uncle burst into a roar of laughter.

"It's between you and me all right, you young Nat Gould,"[2] he said, laughing. "But where's your three hundred?"

"Bassett keeps it for me. We're partners."

"You are, are you! And what is Bassett putting on Daffodil?"

"He won't go quite as high as I do, I expect. Perhaps he'll go a hundred and fifty."

"What, pennies?" laughed the uncle.

"Pounds," said the child, with a surprised look at his uncle. "Bassett keeps a bigger reserve than I do."

Between wonder and amusement Uncle Oscar was silent. He pursued the matter no further, but he determined to take his nephew with him to the Lincoln races.

"Now, son," he said, "I'm putting twenty on Mirza, and I'll put five for you on any horse you fancy. What's your pick?"

"Daffodil, uncle."

"No, not the fiver on Daffodil!"

"I should if it was my own fiver," said the child.

"Good! Good! Right you are! A fiver for me and a fiver for you on Daffodil."

The child had never been to a race meeting before, and his eyes were blue fire. He pursed his mouth tight, and watched. A Frenchman just in front had put his money on Lancelot. Wild with excitement, he flayed his arms up and down, yelling "Lancelot! Lancelot!" in his French accent.

Daffodil came in first, Lancelot second, Mirza third. The child, flushed and with eyes blazing, was curiously serene. His uncle brought him four five-pound notes, four to one.

"What am I to do with these?" he cried, waving them before the boy's eyes.

"I suppose we'll talk to Bassett," said the boy. "I expect I have fifteen hundred now; and twenty in reserve; and this twenty."

His uncle studied him for some moments.

[2]*Nat Gould:* A famous British gambler of the 1920s.

"Look here, son!" he said. "You're not serious about Bassett and that fifteen hundred, are you?"

"Yes, I am. But it's between you and me, uncle. Honour bright!"

"Honour bright all right, son! But I must talk to Bassett."

"If you'd like to be a partner, uncle, with Bassett and me, we could all be partners. Only, you'd have to promise, honour bright, uncle, not to let it go beyond us three. Bassett and I are lucky, and you must be lucky, because it was your ten shillings I started winning with . . ."

Uncle Oscar took both Bassett and Paul into Richmond Park for an afternoon, and there they talked.

"It's like this, you see, sir," Bassett said. "Master Paul would get me talking about racing events, spinning yarns, you know, sir. And he was always keen on knowing if I'd made or if I'd lost. It's about a year since, now, that I put five shillings on Blush of Dawn for him—and we lost. Then the luck turned, with that ten shillings he had from you, that we put on Singhalese. And since that time, it's been pretty steady, all things considering. What do you say, Master Paul?"

"We're all right when we're sure," said Paul. "It's when we're not quite sure that we go down."

"Oh, but we're careful then," said Bassett.

"But when are you sure?" smiled Uncle Oscar.

"It's Master Paul, sir," said Bassett, in a secret, religious voice. "It's as if he had it from heaven. Like Daffodil, now, for the Lincoln. That was as sure as eggs."

"Did you put anything on Daffodil?" asked Oscar Cresswell.

"Yes, sir, I made my bit."

"And my nephew?"

Bassett was obstinately silent, looking at Paul.

"I made twelve hundred, didn't I, Bassett? I told uncle I was putting three hundred on Daffodil."

"That's right," said Bassett, nodding.

"But where's the money?" asked the uncle.

"I keep it safe locked up, sir. Master Paul he can have it any minute he likes to ask for it."

"What, fifteen hundred pounds?"

"And twenty! and forty, that is, with the twenty he made on the course."

"It's amazing!" said the uncle.

"If Master Paul offers you to be partners, sir, I would, if I were you; if you'll excuse me," said Bassett.

Oscar Cresswell thought about it.

"I'll see the money," he said.

They drove home again, and sure enough, Bassett came round to the garden-house with fifteen hundred pounds in notes. The twenty pounds reserve was left with Joe Glee, in the Turf Commission deposit.

"You see, it's all right, uncle, when I'm sure! Then we go strong, for all we're worth. Don't we, Bassett?"

"We do that, Master Paul."

"And when are you sure?" said the uncle, laughing.

"Oh, well, sometimes I'm absolutely sure, like about Daffodil," said the boy; "and sometimes I have an idea; and sometimes I haven't even an idea, have I, Bassett? Then we're careful, because we mostly go down."

"You do, do you! And when you're sure, like about Daffodil, what makes you sure, sonny?"

"Oh, well, I don't know," said the boy uneasily. "I'm sure, you know, uncle; that's all."

"It's as if he had it from heaven, sir," Bassett reiterated.

"I should say so!" said the uncle.

But he became a partner. And when the Leger was coming on, Paul was "sure" about Lively Spark, which was a quite inconsiderable horse. The boy insisted on putting a thousand on the horse, Bassett went for five hundred, and Oscar Cresswell two hundred. Lively Spark came in first, and the betting had been ten to one against him. Paul had made ten thousand.

"You see," he said, "I was absolutely sure of him."

Even Oscar Cresswell had cleared two thousand.

"Look here, son," he said, "this sort of thing makes me nervous."

"It needn't, uncle! Perhaps I shan't be sure again for a long time."

"But what are you going to do with your money?" asked the uncle.

"Of course," said the boy, "I started it for mother. She said she had no luck, because father is unlucky, so I thought if I was lucky, it might stop whispering."

"What might stop whispering?"

"Our house. I hate our house for whispering."

"What does it whisper?"

"Why—why"—the boy fidgeted—"why, I don't know. But it's always short of money, you know, uncle."

"I know it, son, I know it."

"You know people send mother writs, don't you, uncle?"

"I'm afraid I do," said the uncle.

"And then the house whispers, like people laughing at you behind your back. It's awful, that is! I thought if I was lucky . . ."

"You might stop it," added the uncle.

The boy watched him with big blue eyes that had an uncanny cold fire in them, and he said never a word.

"Well, then!" said the uncle. "What are we doing?"

"I shouldn't like mother to know I was lucky," said the boy.

"Why not, son?"

"She'd stop me."

"I don't think she would."

"Oh!"—and the boy writhed in an odd way—"I don't want her to know, uncle."

"All right, son! We'll manage it without her knowing."

They managed it very easily. Paul, at the other's suggestion, handed over five thousand pounds to his uncle, who deposited it with the family lawyer, who was then to inform Paul's mother that a relative had put five thousand pounds into his hands, which sum was to be paid out a thousand pounds at a time, on the mother's birthday, for the next five years.

"So she'll have a birthday present of a thousand pounds for five successive years," said Uncle Oscar. "I hope it won't make it all the harder for her later."

Paul's mother had her birthday in November. The house had been "whispering" worse than ever lately, and, even in spite of his luck, Paul could not bear up against it. He was very anxious to see the effect of the birthday letter, telling his mother about the thousand pounds.

When there were no visitors, Paul now took his meals with his parents, as he was beyond the nursery control. His mother went into town nearly every day. She had discovered that she had an odd knack of sketching furs and dress materials, so she worked secretly in the studio of a friend who was the chief "artist" for the leading drapers. She drew the figures of ladies in furs and ladies in silk and sequins for the newspaper advertisements. This young woman artist earned several thousand pounds a year, but Paul's mother only made several hundreds, and she was again dissatisfied. She so wanted to be first in something, and she did not succeed, even in making sketches for drapery advertisements.

She was down to breakfast on the morning of her birthday. Paul watched her face as she read her letters. He knew the lawyer's letter. As his mother read it, her face hardened and became more expressionless. Then a cold, determined look came on her mouth. She hid the letter under the pile of others, and said not a word about it.

"Didn't you have anything nice in the post for your birthday, mother?" said Paul.

"Quite moderately nice," she said, her voice cold and absent.

She went away to town without saying more.

But in the afternoon Uncle Oscar appeared. He said Paul's mother had had a long interview with the lawyer, asking if the whole five thousand could be advanced at once, as she was in debt.

"What do you think, uncle?" said the boy.

"I leave it to you, son."

"Oh, let her have it, then! We can get some more with the other," said the boy.

"A bird in the hand is worth two in the bush, laddie!" said Uncle Oscar.

"But I'm sure to know for the Grand National; or the Lincolnshire; or else the Derby. I'm sure to know for one of them," said Paul.

So Uncle Oscar signed the agreement, and Paul's mother touched the whole five thousand. Then something very curious happened. The voices in the house suddenly went mad, like a chorus of frogs on a spring evening. There were certain new furnishings, and Paul had a tutor. He was really going to Eton, his father's school, in the following autumn. There were flowers in the winter, and a blossoming of the luxury Paul's mother had been used to. And yet the voices in the house, behind the sprays of mimosa and almond blossom, and from under the piles of iridescent cushions, simply trilled and screamed in a sort of ecstasy: "There must be more money! Oh-h-h, there must be more money. Oh, now,

now-w! Now-w-w—there must be more money—more than ever! More than ever!"

It frightened Paul terribly. He studied away at his Latin and Greek with his tutors. But his intense hours were spent with Bassett. The Grand National had gone by: he had not "known," and had lost a hundred pounds. Summer was at hand. He was in agony for the Lincoln. But even for the Lincoln he didn't "know" and he lost fifty pounds. He became wild-eyed and strange, as if something were going to explode in him.

"Let it alone, son! Don't you bother about it!" urged Uncle Oscar. But it was as if the boy couldn't really hear what his uncle was saying.

"I've got to know for the Derby! I've got to know for the Derby!" the child reiterated, his big blue eyes blazing with a sort of madness.

His mother noticed how overwrought he was.

"You'd better go to the seaside. Wouldn't you like to go now to the seaside, instead of waiting? I think you'd better," she said, looking down at him anxiously, her heart curiously heavy because of him.

But the child lifted his uncanny blue eyes.

"I couldn't possibly go before the Derby, mother!" he said. "I couldn't possibly!"

"Why not?" she said, her voice becoming heavy when she was opposed. "Why not? You can still go from the seaside to see the Derby with your Uncle Oscar, if that's what you wish. No need for you to wait here. Besides, I think you care too much about these races. It's a bad sign. *My* family has been a gambling family, and you won't know till you grow up how much damage it has done. But it has done damage. I shall have to send Bassett away, and ask Uncle Oscar not to talk racing to you, unless you promise to be reasonable about it; go away to the seaside and forget it. You're all nerves!"

"I'll do what you like, mother, so long as you don't send me away till after the Derby," the boy said.

"Send you away from where? Just from this house?"

"Yes," he said, gazing at her.

"Why, you curious child, what makes you care about this house so much, suddenly? I never knew you loved it."

He gazed at her without speaking. He had a secret within a secret, something he had not divulged, even to Bassett or to his Uncle Oscar.

But his mother, after standing undecided and a little bit sullen for some moments, said:

"Very well, then! Don't go to the seaside till after the Derby, if you don't wish it. But promise me you won't let your nerves go to pieces. Promise you won't think so much about horse racing and *events*, as you call them!"

"Oh, no," said the boy casually. "I won't think much about them, mother. You needn't worry. I wouldn't worry, mother, if I were you."

"If you were me and I were you," said his mother, "I wonder what *we* should do!"

"But you know you needn't worry, mother, don't you?" the boy repeated.

"I should be awfully glad to know it," she said wearily.

"Oh, well, you can, you know. I mean, you ought to know you needn't worry," he insisted.

"Ought I? Then I'll see about it," she said.

Paul's secret of secrets was his wooden horse, that which had no name. Since he was emancipated from a nurse and a nursery-governess, he had had his rocking horse removed to his own bedroom at the top of the house.

"Surely, you're too big for a rocking horse!" his mother had remonstrated.

"Well, you see, mother, till I can have a real horse, I like to have some sort of animal about," had been his quaint answer.

"Do you feel he keeps you company?" she laughed.

"Oh, yes! He's very good, he always keeps me company, when I'm there," said Paul.

So the horse, rather shabby, stood in an arrested prance in the boy's bedroom.

The Derby was drawing near, and the boy grew more and more tense. He hardly heard what was spoken to him, he was very frail, and his eyes were really uncanny. His mother had sudden seizures of uneasiness about him. Sometimes, for half-an-hour, she would feel a sudden anxiety about him that was almost anguish. She wanted to rush to him at once, and know he was safe.

Two nights before the Derby, she was at a big party in town, when one of her rushes of anxiety about her boy, her first-born, gripped her heart till she could hardly speak. She fought with the feeling, might and main, for she believed in common sense. But it was too strong. She had to leave the dance and go downstairs to telephone to the country. The children's nursery-governess was terribly surprised and startled at being rung up in the night.

"Are the children all right, Miss Wilmot?"

"Oh, yes, they are quite all right."

"Master Paul? Is he all right?"

"He went to bed as right as a trivet. Shall I run up and look at him?"

"No," said Paul's mother reluctantly. "No! Don't trouble. It's all right. Don't sit up. We shall be home fairly soon." She did not want her son's privacy intruded upon.

"Very good," said the governess.

It was about one o'clock when Paul's mother and father drove up to their house. All was still. Paul's mother went to her room and slipped off her white fur coat. She had told her maid not to wait up for her. She heard her husband downstairs, mixing a whisky-and-soda.

And then, because of the strange anxiety at her heart, she stole upstairs to her son's room. Noiselessly she went along the upper corridor. Was there a faint noise? What was it?

She stood, with arrested muscles, outside his door, listening. There was a strange, heavy, and yet not loud noise. Her heart stood still. It was a soundless noise, yet rushing and powerful. Something huge, in violent, hushed motion. What was it? What in God's name was it? She ought to know. She felt that she knew the noise. She knew what it was.

Yet she could not place it. She couldn't say what it was. And on and on it went, like a madness.

Softly, frozen with anxiety and fear, she turned the door handle.

The room was dark. Yet in the space near the window, she heard and saw something plunging to and fro. She gazed in fear and amazement.

Then suddenly she switched on the light, and saw her son, in his green pyjamas, madly surging on the rocking horse. The blaze of light suddenly lit him up, as he urged the wooden horse, and lit her up, as she stood, blonde, in her dress of pale green and crystal, in the doorway.

"Paul!" she cried. "Whatever are you doing?"

"It's Malabar!" he screamed, in a powerful, strange voice. "It's Malabar."

His eyes blazed at her for one strange and senseless second, as he ceased urging his wooden horse. Then he fell with a crash to the ground, and she, all her tormented motherhood flooding upon her, rushed to gather him up.

But he was unconscious, and unconscious he remained, with some brain-fever. He talked and tossed, and his mother sat stonily by his side.

"Malabar! It's Malabar! Bassett, Bassett, I know it! It's Malabar!"

So the child cried, trying to get up and urge the rocking horse that gave him his inspiration.

"What does he mean by Malabar?" asked the heart-frozen mother.

"I don't know," said the father stonily.

"What does he mean by Malabar?" she asked her brother Oscar.

"It's one of the horses running for the Derby," was the answer.

And, in spite of himself, Oscar Cresswell spoke to Bassett, and himself put a thousand on Malabar: at fourteen to one.

The third day of the illness was critical: they were waiting for a change. The boy, with his rather long, curly hair, was tossing ceaselessly on the pillow. He neither slept nor regained consciousness, and his eyes were like blue stones. His mother sat, feeling her heart had gone, turned actually into a stone.

In the evening, Oscar Cresswell did not come, but Bassett sent a message, saying could he come up for one moment, just one moment? Paul's mother was very angry at the intrusion, but on second thought she agreed. The boy was the same. Perhaps Bassett might bring him to consciousness.

The gardener, a shortish fellow with a little brown moustache, and sharp little brown eyes, tiptoed into the room, touched his imaginary cap to Paul's mother, and stole to the bedside, staring with glittering, smallish eyes, at the tossing, dying child.

"Master Paul!" he whispered. "Master Paul! Malabar come in first all right, a clean win. I did as you told me. You've made over seventy thousand pounds, you have; you've got over eighty thousand. Malabar came in all right, Master Paul."

"Malabar! Malabar! Did I say Malabar, mother? Did I say Malabar? Do you think I'm lucky, mother? I knew Malabar, didn't I? Over eighty thousand pounds! I call that lucky, don't you, mother? Over eighty thousand pounds! I knew, didn't I know I knew? Malabar came in all right. If I ride my horse till I'm sure, then I tell you, Bassett, you can go as high as you like. Did you go for all you were worth, Bassett?"

"I went a thousand on it, Master Paul." 240

"I never told you, mother that if I can ride my horse, and get there, then I'm absolutely sure—oh, absolutely! Mother, did I ever tell you? I'm lucky."

"No, you never did," said the mother.

But the boy died in the night.

And even as he lay dead, his mother heard her brother's voice saying to her: "My God, Hester, you're eighty-odd thousand to the good and a poor devil of a son to the bad. But, poor devil, poor devil, he's best gone out of a life where he rides his rocking horse to find a winner."

(1933)

Questions for Discussion and Writing

Close Reading

1. To what does Paul's mother attribute the family's lack of money? How accurate is her assessment of Paul's father?
2. The mother in this story is clearly a bitter woman. How responsible is she for the story's outcome? How sympathetic are you with her? What details in the story make you feel as you do?
3. How does Paul's character change in the course of the story? In what ways is he a typical child? In what ways does he seem more like an adult?
4. How is this story an example of irony?

Critical and Creative Reading

5. How does Lawrence play with the words "filthy lucre" and "filthy luck"? Are luck and money the same in this story? Are they both inherently "filthy"?
6. What is your response to the story's end, in which Paul's uncle claims that the boy is "best gone out of a life where he rides his rocking horse to find a winner"? In your opinion, is Paul better off dead than having to grow up in this family?
7. Although this story represents an extreme case, how typical do you think Paul's family is? Do most parents convey an anxiety about money to their children? In your opinion, how much should children be told about their family's financial situation?

Connections to Other Readings

8. How does Paul's family exemplify an overconcern with the "little virtues" as defined by Natalia Ginzburg?
9. Compare Paul's mother with Harpagon in *The Miser*. What price do they pay for their obsession with money?
10. Consider this story in conjunction with the Common Characters section at the end of the chapter on the gambler figure. How is the subject of gambling treated in this story?

Tobias Wolff

The Rich Brother

Tobias Wolff (b. 1945) is perhaps best known for his 1989 memoir *This Boy's Life*, which was made into a film starring Robert Deniro and a young Leonardo Dicaprio. That work tells the story of Wolff's troubled childhood at the hands of an abusive stepfather. Wolff escaped his difficulties at home and at school by serving in the U.S. Army in Vietnam, an experience he wrote about in his 1996 memoir, *In Pharoah's Army: Memories of a Lost War*. After returning from his tour of duty, he graduated from Oxford University and received an MA from Stanford, and he has since become an influential writer of fiction and nonfiction. "The Rich Brother" appears in his short story collection *Back in the World* (1985). It explores one of the oldest conflicts of all time, sibling rivalry, and revisits the question in the Bible that Cain asked God after killing his brother Abel: "Am I my brother's keeper?"

There were two brothers, Pete and Donald.

Pete, the older brother, was in real estate. He and his wife had a Century 21 franchise in Santa Cruz. Pete worked hard and made a lot of money, but not any more than he thought he deserved. He had two daughters, a sailboat, a house from which he could see a thin slice of the ocean, and friends doing well enough in their own lives not to wish bad luck on him. Donald, the younger brother, was still single. He lived alone, painted houses when he found the work, and got deeper in debt to Pete when he didn't.

No one would have taken them for brothers. Where Pete was stout and hearty and at home in the world, Donald was bony, grave, and obsessed with the fate of his soul. Over the years Donald had worn the images of two different Perfect Masters around his neck. Out of devotion to the second of these he entered an ashram in Berkeley, where he nearly died of undiagnosed hepatitis. By the time Pete finished paying the medical bills Donald had become a Christian. He drifted from church to church, then joined a pentecostal community that met somewhere in the Mission District to sing in tongues and swap prophecies.

Pete couldn't make sense of it. Their parents were both dead, but while they were alive neither of them had found it necessary to believe in anything. They managed to be decent people without making fools of themselves, and Pete had the same ambition. He thought that the whole thing was an excuse for Donald to take himself seriously.

5 The trouble was that Donald couldn't content himself with worrying about his own soul. He had to worry about everyone else's, and especially Pete's. He handed down his judgments in ways that he seemed to consider

subtle: through significant silence, innuendo, looks of mild despair that said, *Brother, what have you come to?* What Pete had come to, as far as he could tell, was prosperity. That was the real issue between them. Pete prospered and Donald did not prosper.

At the age of forty Pete took up sky diving. He made his first jump with two friends who'd started only a few months earlier and were already doing stunts. They were both coked to the gills when they jumped but Pete wanted to do it straight, at least the first time, and he was glad that he did. He would never have used the word *mystical*, but that was how Pete felt about the experience. Later he made the mistake of trying to describe it to Donald, who kept asking how much it cost and then acted appalled when Pete told him.

"At least I'm trying something new," Pete said. "At least I'm breaking the pattern."

Not long after that conversation Donald also broke the pattern, by going to live on a farm outside of Paso Robles. The farm was owned by several members of Donald's community, who had bought it and moved there with the idea of forming a family of faith. That was how Donald explained it in the first letter he sent. Every week Pete heard how happy Donald was, how "in the Lord." He told Pete that he was praying for him, he and the rest of Pete's brothers and sisters on the farm.

"I only have one brother," Pete wanted to answer, "and that's enough." But he kept this thought to himself.

In November the letters stopped. Pete didn't worry about this at first, but 10
when he called Donald at Thanksgiving Donald was grim. He tried to sound upbeat but he didn't try hard enough to make it convincing. "Now listen," Pete said, "you don't have to stay in that place if you don't want to."

"I'll be all right," Donald answered.

"That's not the point. Being all right is not the point. If you don't like what's going on up there, then get out."

"I'm all right," Donald said again, more firmly. "I'm doing fine."

But he called Pete a week later and said that he was quitting the farm. When Pete asked him where he intended to go, Donald admitted that he had no plan. His car had been repossessed just before he left the city, and he was flat broke.

"I guess you'll have to stay with us," Pete said. 15

Donald put up a show of resistance. Then he gave in. "Just until I get my feet on the ground," he said.

"Right," Pete said. "Check out your options." He told Donald he'd send him money for a bus ticket, but as they were about to hang up Pete changed his mind. He knew that Donald would try hitchhiking to save the fare. Pete didn't want him out on the road all alone where some head case could pick him up, where anything could happen to him.

"Better yet," he said, "I'll come and get you."

"You don't have to do that. I didn't expect you to do that," Donald said. He added, "It's a pretty long drive."

"Just tell me how to get there." 20

But Donald wouldn't give him directions. He said that the farm was too depressing, that Pete wouldn't like it. Instead, he insisted on meeting Pete at a service station called Jonathan's Mechanical Emporium.

"You must be kidding," Pete said.

"It's close to the highway," Donald said. "I didn't name it."

"That's one for the collection," Pete said.

The day before he left to bring Donald home, Pete received a letter from a man who described himself as "head of household" at the farm where Donald had been living. From this letter Pete learned that Donald had not quit the farm, but had been asked to leave. The letter was written on the back of a mimeographed survey form asking people to record their response to a ceremony of some kind. The last question said:

What did you feel during the liturgy?
a) Being
b) Becoming
c) Being and Becoming
d) None of the Above
e) All of the Above

Pete tried to forget the letter. But of course he couldn't. Each time he thought of it he felt crowded and breathless, a feeling that came over him again when he drove into the service station and saw Donald sitting against a wall with his head on his knees. It was late afternoon. A paper cup tumbled slowly past Donald's feet, pushed by the damp wind.

Pete honked and Donald raised his head. He smiled at Pete, then stood and stretched. His arms were long and thin and white. He wore a red bandanna across his forehead, a T-shirt with a couple of words on the front. Pete couldn't read them because the letters were inverted.

"Grow up," Pete yelled. "Get a Mercedes."

Donald came up to the window. He bent down and said, "Thanks for coming. You must be totally whipped."

"I'll make it." Pete pointed at Donald's T-shirt. "What's that supposed to say?"

Donald looked down at his shirt front. "Try God. I guess I put it on backwards. Pete, could I borrow a couple of dollars? I owe these people for coffee and sandwiches."

Pete took five twenties from his wallet and held them out the window.

Donald stepped back as if horrified. "I don't need that much."

"I can't keep track of all these nickels and dimes," Pete said. "Just pay me back when your ship comes in." He waved the bills impatiently. "Go on—take it."

"Only for now." Donald took the money and went into the service station office. He came out carrying two orange sodas, one of which he gave to Pete as he got into the car. "My treat," he said.

"No bags?"

"Wow, thanks for reminding me," Donald said. He balanced his drink on the dashboard, but the slight rocking of the car as he got out tipped it onto the passenger's seat, where half its contents foamed over before Pete could snatch it up again. Donald looked on while Pete held the bottle out the window, soda running down his fingers.

"Wipe it up," Pete told him. "Quick!"

"With what?"

Pete stared at Donald. "That shirt. Use the shirt."

Donald pulled a long face but did as he was told, his pale skin puckering against the wind.

"Great, just great," Pete said. "We haven't even left the gas station yet."

Afterwards, on the highway, Donald said, "This is a new car, isn't it?"

"Yes. This is a new car."

"Is that why you're so upset about the seat?"

"Forget it, okay? Let's just forget about it."

"I said I was sorry."

Pete said, "I just wish you'd be more careful. These seats are made of leather. That stain won't come out, not to mention the smell. I don't see why I can't have leather seats that smell like leather instead of orange pop."

"What was wrong with the other car?"

Pete glanced over at Donald. Donald had raised the hood of the blue sweatshirt he'd put on. The peaked hood above his gaunt, watchful face gave him the look of an inquisitor.

"There wasn't anything wrong with it," Pete said. "I just happened to like this one better."

Donald nodded.

There was a long silence between them as Pete drove on and the day darkened toward evening. On either side of the road lay stubble-covered fields. A line of low hills ran along the horizon, topped here and there with trees black against the grey sky. In the approaching line of cars a driver turned on his headlights. Pete did the same.

"So what happened?" he asked. "Farm life not your bag?"

Donald took some time to answer, and at last he said, simply, "It was my fault."

"What was your fault?"

"The whole thing. Don't play dumb, Pete. I know they wrote to you." Donald looked at Pete, then stared out the windshield again.

"I'm not playing dumb."

Donald shrugged.

"All I really know is they asked you to leave," Pete went on. "I don't know any of the particulars."

"I blew it," Donald said. "Believe me, you don't want to hear the gory details."

"Sure I do," Pete said. He added, "Everybody likes the gory details."

"You mean everybody likes to hear how someone else messed up."

"Right," Pete said. "That's the way it is here on Spaceship Earth."

Donald bent one knee onto the front seat and leaned against the door so that he was facing Pete instead of the windshield. Pete was aware of Donald's scrutiny. He waited. Night was coming on in a rush now, filling the hollows of the land. Donald's long cheeks and deep-set eyes were dark with shadow. His brow was white. "Do you ever dream about me?" Donald asked.

"Do I ever dream about you? What kind of a question is that? Of course I don't dream about you," Pete said, untruthfully.

"What do you dream about?"

"Sex and money. Mostly money. A nightmare is when I dream I don't have any."

"You're just making that up," Donald said.

Pete smiled.

"Sometimes I wake up at night," Donald went on, "and I can tell you're dreaming about me."

"We were talking about the farm," Pete said. "Let's finish that conversation and then we can talk about our various out-of-body experiences and the interesting things we did during previous incarnations."

For a moment Donald looked like a grinning skull; then he turned serious again. "There's not that much to tell," he said. "I just didn't do anything right."

"That's a little vague," Pete said.

"Well, like the groceries. Whenever it was my turn to get the groceries I'd blow it somehow. I'd bring the groceries home and half of them would be missing, or I'd have all the wrong things, the wrong kind of flour or the wrong kind of chocolate or whatever. One time I gave them away. It's not funny, Pete."

Pete said, "Who did you give the groceries to?"

"Just some people I picked up on the way home. Some fieldworkers. They had about eight kids with them and they didn't even speak English—just nodded their heads. Still, I shouldn't have given away the groceries. Not all of them, anyway. I really learned my lesson about that. You have to be practical. You have to be fair to yourself." Donald leaned forward, and Pete could sense his excitement. "There's nothing actually wrong with being in business," he said. "As long as you're fair to other people you can still be fair to yourself. I'm thinking of going into business, Pete."

"We'll talk about it," Pete said. "So, that's the story? There isn't any more to it than that?"

"What did they tell you?" Donald asked.

"Nothing."

"They must have told you something."

Pete shook his head.

"They didn't tell you about the fire?" When Pete shook his head again Donald regarded him for a time, then said, "I don't know. It was stupid. I just completely lost it." He folded his arms across his chest and slumped back into the corner. "Everybody had to take turns cooking dinner. I usually did tuna casserole or spaghetti with garlic bread. But this one night I thought I'd do something different, something really interesting." Donald looked sharply at Pete. "It's all a big laugh to you, isn't it?"

"I'm sorry," Pete said.

"You don't know when to quit. You just keep hitting away." 85

"Tell me about the fire, Donald."

Donald kept watching him. "You have this compulsion to make me look foolish."

"Come off it, Donald. Don't make a big thing out of this."

"I know why you do it. It's because you don't have any purpose in life. You're afraid to relate to people who do, so you make fun of them."

"Relate," Pete said softly. 90

"You're basically a very frightened individual," Donald said. "Very threatened. You've always been like that. Do you remember when you used to try to kill me?"

"I don't have any compulsion to make you look foolish, Donald—you do it yourself. You're doing it right now."

"You can't tell me you don't remember," Donald said. "It was after my operation. You remember that."

"Sort of." Pete shrugged. "Not really."

"Oh yes," Donald said. "Do you want to see the scar?" 95

"I remember you had an operation. I don't remember the specifics, that's all. And I sure as hell don't remember trying to kill you."

"Oh yes," Donald repeated, maddeningly. "You bet your life you did. All the time. The thing was, I couldn't have anything happen to me where they sewed me up because then my intestines would come apart again and poison me. That was a big issue, Pete. Mom was always in a state about me climbing trees and so on. And you used to hit me there every chance you got."

"Mom was in a state every time you burped," Pete said. "I don't know. Maybe I bumped into you accidentally once or twice. I never did it deliberately."

"Every chance you got," Donald said. "Like when the folks went out at night 100
and left you to baby-sit. I'd hear them say good night, and then I'd hear the car start up, and when they were gone I'd lie there and listen. After a while I would hear you coming down the hall, and I would close my eyes and pretend to be asleep. There were nights when you would stand outside the door, just stand there, and then go away again. But most nights you'd open the door and I would hear you in the room with me, breathing. You'd come over and sit next to me on the bed—you remember, Pete, you have to—you'd sit next to me on the bed and pull the sheets back. If I was on my stomach you'd roll me over. Then you would lift up my pajama shirt and start hitting me on my stitches. You'd hit me as hard as you could, over and over. And I would just keep lying there with my eyes closed. I was afraid that you'd get mad if you knew I was awake. Is that strange or what? I was afraid that you'd get mad if you found out that I knew you were trying to kill me." Donald laughed. "Come on, you can't tell me you don't remember that."

"It might have happened once or twice. Kids do those things. I can't get all excited about something I maybe did twenty-five years ago."

"No maybe about it. You did it."

Pete said, "You're wearing me out with this stuff. We've got a long drive ahead of us and if you don't back off pretty soon we aren't going to make it. You aren't, anyway."

Donald turned away.

"I'm doing my best," Pete said. The self-pity in his own voice made the 105
words sound like a lie. But they weren't a lie! He was doing his best.

The car topped a rise. In the distance Pete saw a cluster of lights that blinked out when he started downhill. There was no moon. The sky was low and black.

"Come to think of it," Pete said, "I did have a dream about you the other night." Then he added, impatiently, as if Donald were badgering him, "A couple of other nights too. I'm getting hungry," he said.

"The same dream?"

"Different dreams. I only remember one of them well. There was something wrong with me, and you were helping out. Taking care of me. Just the two of us. I don't know where everyone else was supposed to be."

Pete left it at that. He didn't tell Donald that in this dream he was blind. 110

"I wonder if that was when I woke up," Donald said. He added, "I'm sorry I got into that thing about my scar. I keep trying to forget it but I guess I never will. Not really. It was pretty strange, having someone around all the time who wanted to get rid of me."

"Kid stuff," Pete said. "Ancient history."

They ate dinner at a Denny's on the other side of King City. As Pete was paying the check he heard a man behind him say, "Excuse me, but I wonder if I might ask which way you're going?" and Donald answer, "Santa Cruz."

"Perfect," the man said.

Pete could see him in the fish-eye mirror above the cash register: a red 115
blazer with some kind of crest on the pocket, little black moustache, glossy black hair combed down on his forehead like a Roman emperor's. A rug, Pete thought. Definitely a rug.

Pete got his change and turned. "Why is that perfect?" he asked.

The man looked at Pete. He had a soft ruddy face that was doing its best to express pleasant surprise, as if this new wrinkle were all he could have wished for, but the eyes behind the aviator glasses showed signs of regret. His lips were moist and shiny. "I take it you're together," he said.

"You got it," Pete told him.

"All the better, then," the man went on. "It so happens I'm going to Santa Cruz myself. Had a spot of car trouble down the road. The old Caddy let me down."

"What kind of trouble?" Pete asked. 120

"Engine trouble," the man said. "I'm afraid it's a bit urgent. My daughter is sick. Urgently sick. I've got a telegram here." He patted the breast pocket of his blazer.

Pete grinned. Amazing, he thought, the old sick daughter ploy, but before he could say anything Donald got into the act again. "No problem," Donald said. "We've got tons of room."

"Not that much room," Pete said.

Donald nodded. "I'll put my things in the trunk."

"The trunk's full," Pete told him. 125

"It so happens I'm traveling light," the man said. "This leg of the trip anyway. In fact I don't have any luggage at this particular time."

Pete said, "Left it in the old Caddy, did you?"

"Exactly," the man said.

"No problem," Donald repeated. He walked outside and the man went with him. Together they strolled across the parking lot, Pete following at a distance. When they reached Pete's car Donald raised his face to the sky, and the man did the same. They stood there looking up. "Dark night," Donald said.

"Stygian," the man said. 130

Pete still had it in mind to brush him off, but he didn't do that. Instead he unlocked the door for him. He wanted to see what would happen. It was an adventure, but not a dangerous adventure. The man might steal Pete's ashtrays but he wouldn't kill him. If Pete got killed on the road it would be by some spiritual person in a sweatsuit, someone with his eyes on the far horizon and a wet Try God T-shirt in his duffel bag.

As soon as they left the parking lot the man lit a cigar. He blew a cloud of smoke over Pete's shoulder and sighed with pleasure. "Put it out," Pete told him.

"Of course," the man said. Pete looked into the rearview mirror and saw the man take another long puff before dropping the cigar out the window. "Forgive me," he said. "I should have asked. Name's Webster, by the way."

Donald turned and looked back at him. "First name or last?"

The man hesitated. "Last," he said finally. 135

"I know a Webster," Donald said. "Mick Webster."

"There are many of us," Webster said.

"Big fellow, wooden leg," Pete said.

Donald gave Pete a look.

Webster shook his head. "Doesn't ring a bell. Still, I wouldn't deny the connection. Might be one of the cousinry." 140

"What's your daughter got?" Pete asked.

"That isn't clear," Webster answered. "It appears to be a female complaint of some nature: Then again it may be tropical." He was quiet for a moment, and added: "If indeed it *is* tropical, I will have to assume some of the blame myself. It was my own vaulting ambition that first led us to the tropics and kept us in the tropics all those many years, exposed to every evil. Truly I have much to answer for. I left my wife there."

Donald said quietly, "You mean she died?"

"I buried her with these hands. The earth will be repaid, gold for gold."

"Which tropics?" Pete asked. 145

"The tropics of Peru."

"What part of Peru are they in?"

"The lowlands," Webster said.

Pete nodded. "What's it like down there?"

"Another world," Webster said. His tone was sepulchral. "A world better imagined than described." 150

"Far out," Pete said.

The three men rode in silence for a time. A line of trucks went past in the other direction, trailers festooned with running lights, engines roaring.

"Yes," Webster said at last, "I have much to answer for."

Pete smiled at Donald, but Donald had turned in his seat again and was gazing at Webster. "I'm sorry about your wife," Donald said.

"What did she die of?" Pete asked.

"A wasting illness," Webster said. "The doctors have no name for it, but I do." He leaned forward and said, fiercely, "*Greed.*" Then he slumped back against his seat. "My greed, not hers. She wanted no part of it."

Pete bit his lip. Webster was a find and Pete didn't want to scare him off by hooting at him. In a voice low and innocent of knowingness, he asked, "What took you there?"

"It's difficult for me to talk about."

"Try," Pete told him.

"A cigar would make it easier."

Donald turned to Pete and said, "It's okay with me."

"All right," Pete said. "Go ahead. Just keep the window rolled down."

"Much obliged." A match flared. There were eager sucking sounds.

"Let's hear it," Pete said.

"I am by training an engineer," Webster began. "My work has exposed me to all but one of the continents, to desert and alp and forest, to every terrain and season of the earth. Some years ago I was hired by the Peruvian government to search for tungsten in the tropics. My wife and daughter accompanied me. We were the only white people for a thousand miles in any direction, and we had no choice but to live as the Indians lived—to share their food and drink and even their culture."

Pete said, "You knew the lingo, did you?"

"We picked it up." The ember of the cigar bobbed up and down. "We were used to learning as necessity decreed. At any rate, it became evident after a couple of years that there was no tungsten to be found. My wife had fallen ill and was pleading to be taken home. But I was deaf to her pleas, because by then I was on the trail of another metal—a metal far more valuable than tungsten."

"Let me guess," Pete said. "Gold?"

Donald looked at Pete, then back at Webster.

"Gold," Webster said. "A vein of gold greater than the Mother Lode itself. After I found the first traces of it nothing could tear me away from my search—not the sickness of my wife nor anything else. I was determined to uncover the vein, and so I did—but not before I laid my wife to rest. As I say, the earth will be repaid."

Webster was quiet. Then he said, "But life must go on. In the years since my wife's death I have been making the arrangements necessary to open the mine. I could have done it immediately, of course, enriching myself beyond measure, but I knew what that would mean—the exploitation of our beloved Indians, the brutal destruction of their environment. I felt I had too much to atone for already." Webster paused, and when he spoke again his voice was dull and rushed, as if he had used up all the interest he had in his own words. "Instead I drew up a program for returning the bulk of the wealth to the Indians themselves. A kind of trust fund. The interest alone will allow them to secure their ancient lands and rights in perpetuity. At the same time, our investors will be rewarded a thousandfold. Two-thousandfold. Everyone will prosper together."

"That's great," Donald said. "That's the way it ought to be."

Pete said, "I'm willing to bet that you just happen to have a few shares left. Am I right?"

Webster made no reply.

"Well?" Pete knew that Webster was on to him now, but he didn't care. The 175
story had bored him. He'd expected something different, something original, and Webster had let him down. He hadn't even tried. Pete felt sour and stale. His eyes burned from cigar smoke and the high beams of road-hogging truckers. "Douse the stogie," he said to Webster. "I told you to keep the window down."

"Got a little nippy back here."

Donald said, "Hey, Pete. Lighten up."

"Douse it!"

Webster sighed. He got rid of the cigar.

"I'm a wreck," Pete said to Donald. "You want to drive for a while?" 180

Donald nodded.

Pete pulled over and they changed places.

Webster kept his counsel in the back seat. Donald hummed while he drove, until Pete told him to stop. Then everything was quiet.

Donald was humming again when Pete woke up. Pete stared sullenly at the road, at the white lines sliding past the car. After a few moments of this he turned and said, "How long have I been out?"

Donald glanced at him. "Twenty, twenty-five minutes." 185

Pete looked behind him and saw that Webster was gone. "Where's our friend?"

"You just missed him. He got out in Soledad. He told me to say thanks and good-bye."

"Soledad? What about his sick daughter? How did he explain her away?" Pete learned over the seat. Both ashtrays were still in place. Floor mats. Door handles.

"He has a brother living there. He's going to borrow a car from him and drive the rest of the way in the morning."

"I'll bet his brother's living there," Pete said. "Doing fifty concurrent life 190
sentences. His brother and his sister and his mom and his dad."

"I kind of liked him," Donald said.

"I'm sure you did," Pete said wearily.

"He was interesting. He'd been places."

"His cigars had been places, I'll give you that."

"Come on, Pete." 195

"Come on yourself. What a phony."

"You don't know that."

"Sure I do."

"How? How do you know?"

Pete stretched. "Brother, there are some things you're just born knowing. What's the gas situation?"

"We're a little low."

"Then why didn't you get some more?"

"I wish you wouldn't snap at me like that," Donald said.

"Then why don't you use your head? What if we run out?"

"We'll make it," Donald said. "I'm pretty sure we've got enough to make it. You didn't have to be so rude to him," Donald added.

Pete took a deep breath. "I don't feel like running out of gas tonight, okay?"

Donald pulled in at the next station they came to and filled the tank while Pete went to the men's room. When Pete came back, Donald was sitting in the passenger's seat. The attendant came up to the driver's window as Pete got in behind the wheel. He bent down and said, "Twelve-fifty-five."

"You heard the man," Pete said to Donald.

Donald looked straight ahead. He didn't move.

"Cough up," Pete said. "This trip's on you."

Donald said, softly, "I can't."

"Sure you can. Break out that wad."

Donald glanced up at the attendant, then at Pete. "Please," he said. "Pete, I don't have it anymore."

Pete took this in. He nodded, and paid the attendant.

Donald began to speak when they left the station but Pete cut him off. He said, "I don't want to hear from you right now. You just keep quiet or I swear to God I won't be responsible."

They left the fields and entered a tunnel of tall trees. The trees went on and on. "Let me get this straight," Pete said at last. "You don't have the money I gave you."

"You treated him like a bug or something," Donald said.

"You don't have the money," Pete said again.

Donald shook his head.

"Since I bought dinner, and since we didn't stop anywhere in between, I assume you gave it to Webster. Is that right? Is that what you did with it?"

"Yes."

Pete looked at Donald. His face was dark under the hood but he still managed to convey a sense of remove, as if none of this had anything to do with him. "Why?" Pete asked. "Why did you give it to him?" When Donald didn't answer, Pete said, "A hundred dollars. Gone. Just like that. I *worked* for that money, Donald."

"I know, I know," Donald said.

"You don't know! How could you? You get money by holding out your hand."

"I work too," Donald said.

"You work too. Don't kid yourself, brother."

Donald leaned toward Pete, about to say something, but Pete cut him off again.

"You're not the only one on the payroll, Donald. I don't think you understand that. I have a family."

"Pete, I'll pay you back."

"Like hell you will. A hundred dollars!" Pete hit the steering wheel with the palm of his hand. "Just because you think I hurt some goofball's feelings. Jesus, Donald."

"That's not the reason," Donald said. "And I didn't just *give* him the money."

"What do you call it, then? What do you call what you did?"

"I *invested* it. I wanted a share, Pete." When Pete looked over at him Donald nodded and said again, "I wanted a share."

Pete said, "I take it you're referring to the gold mine in Peru."

"Yes," Donald said.

"You believe that such a gold mine exists?"

Donald looked at Pete, and Pete could see him just beginning to catch on. "You'll believe anything," Pete said. "Won't you? You really will believe anything at all."

"I'm sorry," Donald said, and turned away.

Pete drove on between the trees and considered the truth of what he had just said—that Donald would believe anything at all. And it came to him that it would be just like this unfair life for Donald to come out ahead in the end, by believing in some outrageous promise that would turn out to be true and that he, Pete, would reject out of hand because he was too wised up to listen to anybody's pitch anymore except for laughs. What a joke. What a joke if there really was a blessing to be had, and the blessing didn't come to the one who deserved it, the one who did all the work, but to the other.

And as if this had already happened Pete felt a shadow move upon him, darkening his thoughts. After a time he said, "I can see where all this is going, Donald."

"I'll pay you back," Donald said.

"No," Pete said. "You won't pay me back. You can't. You don't know how. All you've ever done is take. All your life."

Donald shook his head.

"I see exactly where this is going," Pete went on. "You can't work, you can't take care of yourself, you believe anything anyone tells you. I'm stuck with you, aren't I?" He looked over at Donald. "I've got you on my hands for good."

Donald pressed his fingers against the dashboard as if to brace himself. "I'll get out," he said.

Pete kept driving.

"Let me out," Donald said. "I mean it, Pete."

"Do you?"

Donald hesitated. "Yes," he said.

"Be sure," Pete told him. "This is it. This is for keeps."

"I mean it."

"All right. You made the choice." Pete braked the car sharply and swung it to the shoulder of the road. He turned off the engine and got out. Trees loomed on both sides, shutting out the sky. The air was cold and musty. Pete took

Donald's duffel bag from the back seat and set it down behind the car. He stood there, facing Donald in the red glow of the taillights. "It's better this way," Pete said.

Donald just looked at him.

"Better for you," Pete said.

Donald hugged himself. He was shaking. "You don't have to say all that," he told Pete. "I don't blame you."

"Blame me? What the hell are you talking about? Blame me for what?"

"For anything," Donald said.

"I want to know what you mean by blame me."

"Nothing. Nothing, Pete. You'd better get going. God bless you."

"That's it," Pete said. He dropped to one knee, searching the packed dirt with his hands. He didn't know what he was looking for; his hands would know when they found it.

Donald touched Pete's shoulder. "You'd better go," he said.

Somewhere in the trees Pete heard a branch snap. He stood up. He looked at Donald, then went back to the car and drove away. He drove fast, hunched over the wheel, conscious of the way he was hunched and the shallowness of his breathing, refusing to look at the mirror above his head until there was nothing behind him but darkness.

Then he said, "A hundred dollars," as if there were someone to hear.

The trees gave way to fields. Metal fences ran beside the road, plastered with windblown scraps of paper. Tule fog hung above the ditches, spilling into the road, dimming the ghostly halogen lights that burned in the yards of the farms Pete passed. The fog left beads of water rolling up the windshield.

Pete rummaged among his cassettes. He found Pachelbel's Canon[1] and pushed it into the tape deck. When the violins began to play he leaned back and assumed an attentive expression as if he were really listening to them. He smiled to himself like a man at liberty to enjoy music, a man who has finished his work and settled his debts, done all things meet and due.

And in this way, smiling, nodding to the music, he went another mile or so and pretended that he was not already slowing down, that he was not going to turn back, that he would be able to drive on like this, alone, and have the right answer when his wife stood before him in the doorway of his home and asked, Where is he? Where is your brother?

(1985)

Questions for Discussion and Writing

Close Reading

1. Why are Pete and Donald always at odds with each another? Do you agree with Pete when he suggests that it comes down to prosperity? Based on textual evidence, what else might be at the root of their conflicts?

[1]*Pachelbel's Canon:* Johann Pachelbel (1653–1706) was a German Baroque composer. The *Canon* is his most famous piece, and its soothing, familiar theme and variation are often played at weddings.

2. Why does Pete have a hard time stifling his laughter at Donald and at Webster? What does that say about his character? Do you fault Pete for laughing in these situations?
3. What is the significance of the brothers' dreams about one another? What do these dreams suggest about their relationship?

CRITICAL AND CREATIVE READING

4. Both Donald and Pete can be exasperating characters: Pete is self-involved and judgmental, while Donald is, in Pete's words, a taker, unwilling or unable to help himself. Where do your sympathies lie in this story? Are you sympathetic with Pete's willingness to bail his brother out of one disaster after another, or are you more sympathetic with Donald's quest to understand "the fate of his soul"? Who, in your opinion, is the better person?
5. According to the Old Testament of the Bible, God asks Cain where his brother is, and Cain replies with the line "Am I my brother's keeper?" How does this story try to answer that question? Should Pete continue to take care of his brother? Could Donald be said to be *his* brother's keeper as well? If so, in what way does he take care of Pete?
6. Based on your own experiences with your siblings or your observations of other people and their siblings, do you think Wolff's depiction of the relationship between Donald and Pete is realistic? Why or why not?

CONNECTIONS TO OTHER READINGS

7. In what way does this story exemplify the theme of Wordsworth's poem "The World Is Too Much with Us"?
8. Think about generosity in terms of one's duties to one's siblings in this story and in James Baldwin's story "Sonny's Blues" in the Common Characters section at the end of Chapter 15.

Gish Jen

In the American Society

Gish Jen (b. 1955) is the daughter of parents who immigrated to the United States from Shanghai, China. She earned a BA from Harvard and a master's of fine arts in writing from the University of Iowa. Her works include three novels (*Typical American*, 1991; *Mona in the Promised Land*, 1996; and *The Love Wife*, 2004), as well as a number of short stories. The following story, "In the American Society," examines the themes of greed and generosity in the context of the immigrant experience: Chinese society and American society prove to be two separate realms, and Ralph Chang, the protagonist of the story, wants to make both of them his own.

In His Own Society

When my father took over the pancake house, it was to send my little sister Mona and me to college. We were only in junior high at the time, but my father believed in getting a jump on things. "Those Americans always saying it," he told us. "Smart guys thinking in advance." My mother elaborated, explaining that businesses took bringing up, like children. They could take years to get going, she said, years.

In this case, though, we got rich right away. At two months we were breaking even, and at four, those same hotcakes that could barely withstand the weight of butter and syrup were supporting our family with ease. My mother bought a station wagon with air conditioning, my father an oversized, red vinyl recliner for the back room; and as time went on and the business continued to thrive, my father started to talk about his grandfather and the village he had reigned over in China—things my father had never talked about when he worked for other people. He told us about the bags of rice his family would give out to the poor at New Year's, and about the people who came to beg, on their hands and knees, for his grandfather to intercede for the more wayward of their relatives. "Like that Godfather in the movie," he would tell us as, his feet up, he distributed paychecks. Sometimes an employee would get two green envelopes instead of one, which meant that Jimmy needed a tooth pulled, say, or that Tiffany's husband was in the clinker again.

"It's nothing, nothing," he would insist, sinking back into his chair. "Who else is going to take care of you people?"

My mother would mostly just sigh about it. "Your father thinks this is China," she would say, and then she would go back to her mending. Once in a while, though, when my father had given away a particularly large sum, she would exclaim, outraged, "But this here is the U—S—of—A!"—this apparently having been what she used to tell immigrant stock boys when they came in late.

5 She didn't work at the supermarket anymore; but she had made it to the rank of manager before she left, and this had given her not only new words and phrases, but new ideas about herself, and about America, and about what was what in general. She had opinions, now, on how downtown should be zoned; she could pump her own gas and check her own oil; and for all she used to chide Mona and me for being "copycats," she herself was now interested in espadrilles, and wallpaper, and most recently, the town country club.

"So join already," said Mona, flicking a fly off her knee.

My mother enumerated the problems as she sliced up a quarter round of watermelon: There was the cost. There was the waiting list. There was the fact that no one in our family played either tennis or golf.

"So what?" said Mona.

"It would be waste," said my mother.

10 "Me and Callie can swim in the pool."

"Plus you need that recommendation letter from a member."

"Come *on*," said Mona. "Annie's mom'd write you a letter in *sec*."

My mother's knife glinted in the early summer sun. I spread some more newspaper on the picnic table.

"*Plus* you have to eat there twice a month. You know what that means." My mother cut another, enormous slice of fruit.

15 "No, I *don't* know what that means," said Mona.

"It means Dad would have to wear a jacket, dummy," I said.

"Oh! Oh! Oh!" said Mona, clasping her hand to her breast. "Oh! Oh! Oh! Oh! Oh!"

We all laughed: my father had no use for nice clothes, and would wear only ten-year-old shirts, with grease-spotted pants, to show how little he cared what anyone thought.

"Your father doesn't believe in joining the American society," said my mother. "He wants to have his own society."

20 "So go to dinner without him." Mona shot her seeds out in long arcs over the lawn. "Who cares what he thinks?"

But of course we all did care, and knew my mother could not simply up and do as she pleased. For in my father's mind, a family owed its head a degree of loyalty that left no room for dissent. To embrace what he embraced was to love; and to embrace something else was to betray him.

He demanded a similar sort of loyalty of his workers, whom he treated more like servants than employees. Not in the beginning, of course. In the beginning all he wanted was for them to keep on doing what they used to do, and to that end he concentrated mostly on leaving them alone. As the months passed, though, he expected more and more of them, with the result that for all his largesse, he began to have trouble keeping help. The cooks and busboys complained that he asked them to fix radiators and trim hedges, not only at the restaurant, but at our house; the waitresses that he sent them on errands and made them chauffeur him around. Our head waitress, Gertrude, claimed that he once even asked her to scratch his back.

"It's not just the blacks don't believe in slavery," she said when she quit.

My father never quite registered her complaint, though, nor those of the others who left. Even after Eleanor quit, then Tiffany, then Gerald, and Jimmy, and even his best cook, Eureka Andy, for whom he had bought new glasses, he remained mostly convinced that the fault lay with them.

25 "All they understand is that assembly line," he lamented. "Robots, they are. They want to be robots."

There *were* occasions when the clear running truth seemed to eddy, when he would pinch the vinyl of his chair up into little peaks and wonder if he was doing things right. But with time he would always smooth the peaks back down; and when business started to slide in the spring, he kept on like a horse in his ways.

By the summer our dishboy was overwhelmed with scraping. It was no longer just the hashbrowns that people were leaving for trash, and the service was as bad as the food. The waitresses served up French pancakes instead of German, apple juice instead of orange, spilt things on laps, on coats. On the Fourth of July some green-horn sent an entire side of fries slaloming down a lady's *massif centrale.* Meanwhile in the back room, my father labored through articles on the economy.

"What is housing starts?" he puzzled. "What is GNP?"

Mona and I did what we could, filling in as busgirls and bookkeepers and, one afternoon, stuffing the comments box that hung by the cashier's desk. That was Mona's idea. We rustled up a variety of pens and pencils, checked boxes for an hour, smeared the cards up with coffee and grease, and waited. It took a few days for my father to notice that the box was full, and he didn't say anything about it for a few days more. Finally, though, he started to complain of fatigue; and then he began to complain that the staff was not what it could be. We encouraged him in this—pointing out, for instance, how many dishes got chipped—but in the end all that happened was that, for the first time since we took over the restaurant, my father got it into his head to fire someone. Skip, a skinny busboy who was saving up for a sportscar, said nothing as my father mumbled on about the price of dishes. My father's hands shook as he wrote out the severance check; and he spent the rest of the day napping in his chair once it was over.

As it was going on midsummer, Skip wasn't easy to replace. We hung a sign in the window and advertised in the paper, but no one called the first week, and the person who called the second didn't show up for his interview. The third week, my father phoned Skip to see if he would come back, but a friend of his had already sold him a Corvette for cheap.

Finally a Chinese guy named Booker turned up. He couldn't have been more than thirty, and was wearing a lighthearted seersucker suit, but he looked as though life had him pinned: his eyes were bloodshot and his chest sunken, and the muscles of his neck seemed to strain with the effort of holding his head up. In a single dry breath he told us that he had never bussed tables but was willing to learn, and that he was on the lam from the deportation authorities.

"I do not want to lie to you," he kept saying. He had come to the United States on a student visa, had run out of money, and was now in a bind. He was loath to go back to Taiwan, as it happened—he looked up at this point, to be sure my father wasn't pro-KMT[1]—but all he had was a phony social security card and a willingness to absorb all blame, should anything untoward come to pass.

"I do not think, anyway, that it is against law to hire me, only to be me," he said, smiling faintly.

Anyone else would have examined him on this, but my father conceived of laws as speed bumps rather than curbs. He wiped the counter with his sleeve, and told Booker to report the next morning.

"I will be good worker," said Booker.

"Good," said my father.

"Anything you want me to do, I will do."

My father nodded.

Booker seemed to sink into himself for a moment. "Thank you," he said finally. "I am appreciate your help. I am very, very appreciate for everything." He reached out to shake my father's hand.

[1]*KMT*: Kuomintang, a right-leaning political party in the Republic of China on Taiwan that advocates unifying China and Taiwan.

My father looked at him. "Did you eat today?" he asked in Mandarin.

Booker pulled at the hem of his jacket.

"Sit down," said my father. "Please, have a seat."

My father didn't tell my mother about Booker, and my mother didn't tell my father about the country club. She would never have applied, except that Mona, while over at Annie's, had let it drop that our mother wanted to join. Mrs. Lardner came by the very next day.

"Why, I'd be honored and delighted to write you people a letter," she said. Her skirt billowed around her.

"Thank you so much," said my mother. "But it's too much trouble for you, and also my husband is . . . ."

"Oh, it's no trouble at all, no trouble at all. I tell you." She leaned forward so that her chest freckles showed. "I know just how it is. It's a secret of course, but you know, my natural father was Jewish. Can you see it? Just look at my skin."

"My husband," said my mother.

"I'd be honored and delighted," said Mrs. Lardner with a little wave of her hands. "Just honored and delighted."

Mona was triumphant. "See, Mom," she said, waltzing around the kitchen when Mrs. Lardner left. "What did I tell you? 'I'm just honored and delighted, just honored and delighted.'" She waved her hands in the air.

"You know, the Chinese have a saying," said my mother. "To do nothing is better than to overdo. You mean well, but you tell me now what will happen."

"I'll talk Dad into it," said Mona, still waltzing. "Or I bet Callie can. He'll do anything Callie says."

"I can try, anyway," I said.

"Did you hear what I said?" said my mother. Mona bumped into the broom closet door. "You're not going to talk anything; you've already made enough trouble." She started on the dishes with a clatter.

Mona poked diffidently at a mop.

I sponged off the counter. "Anyway," I ventured. "I bet our name'll never even come up."

"That's if we're lucky," said my mother.

"There's all these people waiting," I said.

"Good," she said. She started on a pot.

I looked over at Mona, who was still cowering in the broom closet. "In fact, there's some black family's been waiting so long, they're going to sue," I said.

My mother turned off the water. "Where'd you hear that?"

"Patty told me."

She turned the water back on, started to wash a dish, then put it back down and shut the faucet.

"I'm sorry," said Mona.

"Forget it," said my mother. "Just forget it."

Booker turned out to be a model worker, whose boundless gratitude translated into a willingness to do anything. As he also learned quickly, he soon knew not only how to bus, but how to cook, and how to wait table, and how to keep the books. He fixed the walk-in door so that it stayed shut, reupholstered the torn seats in the dining room, and devised a system for tracking inventory. The only stone in the rice was that he tended to be sickly; but, reliable even in illness, he would always send a friend to take his place. In this way we got to know Ronald, Lynn, Dirk, and Cedric, all of whom, like Booker, had problems with their legal status and were anxious to please. They weren't all as capable as Booker, though, with the exception of Cedric, whom my father often hired even when Booker was well. A round wag of a man who called Mona and me *shou hou*—skinny monkeys—he was a professed non-smoker who was nevertheless always begging drags off of other people's cigarettes. This last habit drove our head cook, Fernando, crazy, especially since, when refused a hit, Cedric would occasionally snitch one. Winking impishly at Mona and me, he would steal up to an ashtray, take a quick puff, and then break out laughing so that the smoke came rolling out of his mouth in a great incriminatory cloud. Fernando accused him of stealing fresh cigarettes too, even whole packs.

"Why else do you think he's weaseling around in the back of the store all the time," he said. His face was blotchy with anger. "The man is a frigging thief."

Other members of the staff supported him in this contention and joined in on an "Operation Identification," which involved numbering and initialing their cigarettes—even though what they seemed to fear for wasn't so much their cigarettes as their jobs. Then one of the cooks quit; and rather than promote someone, my father hired Cedric for the position. Rumors flew that he was taking only half the normal salary, that Alex had been pressured to resign, and that my father was looking for a position with which to placate Booker, who had been bypassed because of his health.

The result was that Fernando categorically refused to work with Cedric.

"The only way I'll cook with that piece of slime," he said, shaking his huge tattooed fist, "is if it's his ass frying on the grill."

My father cajoled and cajoled, to no avail, and in the end was simply forced to put them on different schedules.

The next week Fernando got caught stealing a carton of minute steaks. My father would not tell even Mona and me how he knew to be standing by the back door when Fernando was on his way out, but everyone suspected Booker. Everyone but Fernando, that is, who was sure Cedric had been the tip-off. My father held a staff meeting in which he tried to reassure everyone that Alex had left on his own, and that he had no intention of firing anyone. But though he was careful not to mention Fernando, everyone was so amazed that he was being allowed to stay that Fernando was incensed nonetheless.

"Don't you all be putting your bug eyes on me," he said. "*He's* the frigging crook." He grabbed Cedric by the collar.

Cedric raised an eyebrow. "Cook, you mean," he said.

At this Fernando punched Cedric in the mouth; and the words he had just uttered notwithstanding, my father fired him on the spot.

With everything that was happening, Mona and I were ready to be getting out of the restaurant. It was almost time: the days were still stuffy with summer, but our window shade had started flapping in the evening as if gearing up to go out. That year the breezes were full of salt, as they sometimes were when they came in from the East, and they blew anchors and docks through my mind like so many tumbleweeds, filling my dreams with wherries and lobsters and grainy-faced men who squinted, day in and day out, at the sky. It was time for a change, you could feel it; and yet the pancake house was the same as ever. The day before school started my father came home with bad news.

"Fernando called police," he said, wiping his hand on his pant leg.

My mother naturally wanted to know what police; and so with much coughing and hawing, the long story began, the latest installment of which had the police calling immigration, and immigration sending an investigator. My mother sat stiff as whalebone as my father described how the man summarily refused lunch on the house and how my father had admitted, under pressure, that he knew there were "things" about his workers.

"So now what happens?"

My father didn't know. "Booker and Cedric went with him to the jail," he said. "But me, here I am." He laughed uncomfortably.

The next day my father posted bail for "his boys" and waited apprehensively 80
for something to happen. The day after that he waited again, and the day after that he called our neighbor's law student son, who suggested my father call the immigration department under an alias. My father took his advice; and it was thus that he discovered that Booker was right: it was illegal for aliens to work, but it wasn't to hire them.

In the happy interval that ensued, my father apologized to my mother, who in turn confessed about the country club, for which my father had no choice but to forgive her. Then he turned his attention back to "his boys."

My mother didn't see that there was anything to do.

"I like to talking to the judge," said my father.

"This is not China," said my mother.

"I'm only talking to him. I'm not give him money unless he wants it." 85

"You're going to land up in jail."

"So what else I should do?" My father threw up his hands. "Those are my boys."

"Your boys!" exploded my mother. "What about your family? What about your wife?"

My father took a long sip of tea. "You know," he said finally. "In the war my father sent our cook to the soldiers to use. He always said it—the province comes before the town, the town comes before the family."

"A restaurant is not a town," said my mother. 90

My father sipped at his tea again. "You know, when I first come to the United States, I also had to hide-and-seek with those deportation guys. If people did not helping me, I'm not here today."

My mother scrutinized her hem.

After a minute I volunteered that before seeing a judge, he might try a lawyer.

He turned. "Since when did you become so afraid like your mother?"

I started to say that it wasn't a matter of fear, but he cut me off. 95

"What I need today," he said, "is a son."

My father and I spent the better part of the next day standing in lines at the immigration office. He did not get to speak to a judge, but with much persistence he managed to speak to a judge's clerk, who tried to persuade him that it was not her place to extend him advice. My father, though, shamelessly plied her with compliments and offers of free pancakes until she finally conceded that she personally doubted anything would happen to either Cedric or Booker.

"Especially if they're 'needed workers,'" she said, rubbing at the red marks her glasses left on her nose. She yawned. "Have you thought about sponsoring them to become permanent residents?"

Could he do that? My father was overjoyed. And what if he saw to it right away? Would she perhaps put in a good word with the judge?

She yawned again, her nostrils flaring. "Don't worry," she said. "They'll get a fair hearing."

My father returned jubilant. Booker and Cedric hailed him as their savior, their Buddha incarnate. He was like a father to them, they said; and laughing and clapping, they made him tell the story over and over, sorting over the details like jewels. And how old was the assistant judge? And what did she say?

That evening my father tipped the paperboy a dollar and bought a pot of mums for my mother, who suffered them to be placed on the dining room table. The next night he took us all out to dinner. Then on Saturday, Mona found a letter on my father's chair at the restaurant.

> Dear Mr. Chang,
>
> You are the grat boss. But, we do not like to trial, so will runing away now. Plese to excus us. People saying the law in America is fears like dragon. Here is only $140. We hope some day we can pay back the rest bale. You will getting intrest, as you diserving, so grat a boss you are. Thank you for every thing. In next life you will be burn in rich family, with no more pancaks.
>
> Yours truley,
Booker + Cedric

In the weeks that followed my father went to the pancake house for crises, but otherwise hung around our house, fiddling idly with the sump pump and boiler in an effort, he said, to get ready for winter. It was as though he had gone into retirement, except that instead of moving south, he had moved to the basement. He even took to showering my mother with little attentions, and to calling her "old girl," and when we finally heard that the club had entertained all the applications it could for the year, he was so sympathetic that he seemed more disappointed than my mother.

II. In the American Society

Mrs. Lardner tempered the bad news with an invitation to a bon voyage "bash" she was throwing for a friend of hers who was going to Greece for six months.

"Do come," she urged. "You'll meet everyone, and then, you know, if things open up in the spring . . ." She waved her hands.

My mother wondered if it would be appropriate to show up at a party for 105
someone they didn't know, but "the honest truth" was that this was an annual affair. "If it's not Greece, it's Antibes," sighed Mrs. Lardner. "We really just do it because his wife left him and his daughter doesn't speak to him, and poor Jeremy just feels so *unloved*."

She also invited Mona and me to the goings on, as "*demi*-guests" to keep Annie out of the champagne. I wasn't too keen on the idea, but before I could say anything, she had already thanked us for so generously agreeing to honor her with our presence.

"A pair of little princesses, you are!" she told us. "A pair of princesses!"

The party was that Sunday. On Saturday, my mother took my father out shopping for a suit. As it was the end of September, she insisted that he buy a worsted rather than a seersucker, even though it was only ten, rather than fifty percent off. My father protested that it was as hot out as ever, which was true—a thick Indian summer had cozied murderously up to us—but to no avail. Summer clothes, said my mother, were not properly worn after Labor Day.

The suit was unfortunately as extravagant in length as it was in price, which posed an additional quandary, since the tailor wouldn't be in until Monday. The salesgirl, though, found a way of tacking it up temporarily.

"Maybe this suit not fit me," fretted my father. 110

"Just don't take your jacket off," said the salesgirl.

He gave her a tip before they left, but when he got home refused to remove the price tag.

"I like to asking the tailor about the size," he insisted.

"You mean you're going to *wear* it and then *return* it?" Mona rolled her eyes.

"I didn't say I'm return it," said my father stiffly. "I like to asking the tailor, 115
that's all."

The party started off swimmingly, except that most people were wearing bermudas or wrap skirts. Still, my parents carried on, sharing with great feeling the complaints about the heat. Of course my father tried to eat a cracker full of shallots and burnt himself in an attempt to help Mr. Lardner turn the coals of the barbeque; but on the whole he seemed to be doing all right. Not nearly so well as my mother, though, who had accepted an entire cupful of Mrs. Lardner's magic punch, and seemed indeed to be under some spell. As Mona and Annie skirmished over whether some boy in their class inhaled when he smoked, I watched my mother take off her shoes, laughing and laughing as a man with a beard regaled her with navy stories by the pool. Apparently he had been stationed in the Orient and remembered a few words of Chinese, which made my mother laugh still more. My father excused himself to go to the men's room then drifted back and weighed anchor at the hors d'oeuvres table, while my mother sailed on to a group of women, who tinkled at length over the clarity of her complexion. I dug out a book I had brought.

Just when I'd cracked the spine, though, Mrs. Lardner came by to bewail her shortage of servers. Her caterers were criminals, I agreed; and the next thing I knew I was handing out bits of marine life, making the rounds as amiably as I could.

"Here you go, Dad," I said when I got to the hors d'oeuvres table.

"Everything is fine," he said.

I hesitated to leave him alone; but then the man with the beard zeroed in on him, and though he talked of nothing but my mother, I thought it would be okay to get back to work. Just that moment, though, Jeremy Brothers lurched our way, an empty, albeit corked, wine bottle in hand. He was a slim, well-proportioned man, with a Roman nose and small eyes and a nice manly jaw that he allowed to hang agape.

"Hello," he said drunkenly. "Pleased to meet you."

"Pleased to meeting you," said my father.

"Right," said Jeremy. "Right. Listen. I have this bottle here, this most recalcitrant bottle. You see that it refuses to do my bidding. I bid it open sesame, please, and it does nothing." He pulled the cork out with his teeth, then turned the bottle upside down.

My father nodded.

"Would you have a word with it please?" said Jeremy. The man with the beard excused himself. "Would you please have a goddamned word with it?"

My father laughed uncomfortably.

"Ah!" Jeremy bowed a little. "Excuse me, excuse me, excuse me. You are not my man, not my man at all." He bowed again and started to leave, but then circled back. "Viticulture is not your forte, yes I can see that, see that plainly. But may I trouble you on another matter? Forget the damned bottle." He threw it into the pool, and winked at the people he splashed. "I have another matter. Do you speak Chinese?"

My father said he did not, but Jeremy pulled out a handkerchief with some characters on it anyway, saying that his daughter had sent it from Hong Kong and that he thought the characters might be some secret message.

"Long life," said my father.

"But you haven't looked at it yet."

"I know what it says without looking." My father winked at me.

"You do?"

"Yes, I do."

"You're making fun of me, aren't you?"

"No, no, no," said my father, winking again.

"Who are you anyway?" said Jeremy.

His smile fading, my father shrugged.

"*Who are you?*"

My father shrugged again.

Jeremy began to roar. "This is my party, *my party*, and I've never seen you before in my life." My father backed up as Jeremy came toward him. "*Who are you? WHO ARE YOU?*"

Just as my father was going to step back into the pool, Mrs. Lardner came running up. Jeremy informed her that there was a man crashing his party.

"Nonsense," said Mrs. Lardner. "This is Ralph Chang, who I invited extra especially so he could meet you." She straightened the collar of Jeremy's peach-colored polo shirt for him.

"Yes, well, we've had a chance to chat," said Jeremy.

She whispered in his ear; he mumbled something; she whispered something more.

"I do apologize," he said finally. 145

My father didn't say anything.

"I do." Jeremy seemed genuinely contrite. "Doubtless you've seen drunks before, haven't you? You must have them in China."

"Okay," said my father.

As Mrs. Lardner glided off, Jeremy clapped his arm over my father's shoulders. "You know, I really am quite sorry, quite sorry."

My father nodded. 150

"What can I do, how can I make it up to you?"

"No thank you."

"No, tell me, tell me," wheedled Jeremy. "Tickets to casino night?" My father shook his head. "You don't gamble. Dinner at Bartholomew's?" My father shook his head again. "You don't eat." Jeremy scratched his chin. "You know, my wife was like you. Old Annabelle could never let me make things up—never, never, never, never, never."

My father wriggled out from under his arm.

"How about sport clothes? You are rather overdressed, you know, excuse me 155
for saying so. But here." He took off his polo shirt and folded it up. "You can have this with my most profound apologies." He ruffled his chest hairs with his free hand.

"No thank you," said my father.

"No, take it, take it. Accept my apologies." He thrust the shirt into my father's arms. "I'm so very sorry, so very sorry. Please, try it on."

Helplessly holding the shirt, my father searched the crowd for my mother.

"Here, I'll help you off with your coat."

My father froze. 160

Jeremy reached over and took his jacket off. "Milton's, one hundred twenty-five dollars reduced to one hundred twelve-fifty," he read. "What a bargain, what a bargain!"

"Please give it back," pleaded my father. "Please."

"Now for your shirt," ordered Jeremy.

Heads began to turn.

"Take off your shirt." 165

"I do not take orders like a servant," announced my father.

"Take off your shirt, or I'm going to throw this jacket right into the pool, just right into this little pool here." Jeremy held it over the water.

"Go ahead."

"One hundred twelve-fifty," taunted Jeremy. "One hundred twelve . . ."

My father flung the polo shirt into the water with such force that part of it 170
bounced back up into the air like a fluorescent fountain. Then it settled into a soft heap on top of the water. My mother hurried up.

"You're a sport!" said Jeremy, suddenly breaking into a smile and slapping my father on the back. "You're a sport! I like that. A man with spirit, that's what you are. A man with panache. Allow me to return to you your jacket." He handed it back to my father. "Good value you got on that, good value."

My father hurled the coat into the pool too. "We're leaving," he said grimly. "Leaving!"

"Now, Ralphie," said Mrs. Lardner, bustling up; but my father was already stomping off.

"Get your sister," he told me. To my mother: "Get your shoes."

"That was *great*, Dad," said Mona as we walked down to the car. "You were *stupendous*."

"Way to show 'em," I said.

"What?" said my father offhandedly.

Although it was only just dusk, we were in a gulch, which made it hard to see anything except the gleam of his white shirt moving up the hill ahead of us.

"It was all my fault," began my mother.

"Forget it," said my father grandly. Then he said, "The only trouble is I left those keys in my jacket pocket."

"Oh *no*," said Mona.

"Oh no is right," said my mother.

"So we'll walk home," I said.

"But how're we going to get into the *house*," said Mona.

The noise of the party churned through the silence.

"Someone has to going back," said my father.

"Let's go to the pancake house first," suggested my mother. "We can wait there until the party is finished, and then call Mrs. Lardner."

Having all agreed that that was a good plan, we started walking again.

"God, just think," said Mona. "We're going to have to *dive* for them."

My father stopped a moment. We waited.

"You girls are good swimmers," he said finally. "Not like me."

Then his shirt started moving again, and we trooped up the hill after it, into the dark.

(1991)

Questions for Discussion and Writing

Close Reading

1. What various forms of generosity does Ralph demonstrate in the first part of the story? Do they all lead to the same end?
2. How is "the law" bent, broken, or violated throughout the story?
3. Why doesn't Callie's mother tell Ralph about her desire to join the country club?

Critical and Creative Reading

4. If you owned a restaurant that primarily hired immigrant workers, would you conduct business differently than Ralph Chang conducts it in this story? Does it make any difference that they are immigrant workers?
5. What is the relationship between the two parts of this story? Why does Jen structure the story this way?
6. If sending your kids to college, owning a successful business, dressing in expensive clothes, and joining the local country club are ways of showing you have "made it" in American society, what does it say that Ralph subscribes to only the first two of these status symbols?

Connections to Other Readings

7. Ralph buys a cheap suit with the intention of returning it after the pool party; is he miserly in the same way Harpagon is miserly in Moliere's play *The Miser*?
8. Discuss the theme of giving in this story and in O. Henry's "The Gift of the Magi" and/or Tobias Wolff's "The Rich Brother."
9. Compare the values of Western society and of American society in "In the American Society" and in Allen Ginsberg's poem "C'mon Pigs of Western Civilization Eat More Grease."

Poetry

William Wordsworth

The World Is Too Much with Us

Together with his friend Samuel Taylor Coleridge (see headnote for "The Rime of the Ancient Mariner, Chapter 15), William Wordsworth (1770–1850) changed the nature of poetry. In 1798, the two friends reissued their small book of poems, *Lyrical Ballads*, with a famous "Preface" in which Wordsworth outlined his definition of poetry and the poet. Rather than a great bard existing apart from the "real" world, Wordsworth asserts that a poet is merely "a man speaking to men," and as such, can move common readers with observations of everyday people, places, and things. Although Wordsworth is most often associated with the Romantic Movement in England, he was poet laureate during the Victorian period, possibly the peak of his fame. While "The World Is Too Much with Us" was written in 1807, contemporary readers are likely to recognize his description of people who waste their lives "getting and spending." (See also Wordsworth's poem "The Solitary Reaper" in Chapter 16 and the author illustration there.)

The world is too much with us; late and soon,
Getting and spending, we lay waste our powers:
Little we see in Nature that is ours;
We have given our hearts away, a sordid boon!
This Sea that bares her bosom to the moon;
The winds that will be howling at all hours,
And are up-gathered now like sleeping flowers;
For this, for every thing, we are out of tune;
It moves us not.—Great God! I'd rather be
A Pagan suckled in a creed outworn;
So might I, standing on this pleasant lea,
Have glimpses that would make me less forlorn;
Have sight of Proteus[1] rising from the sea;
Or hear old Triton[2] blow his wreathèd horn.

(1807)

Questions for Discussion and Writing

Close Reading

1. According to the speaker, what is wrong with the world in which he lives?
2. How does "getting and spending" equate with "wast[ing] our powers"?
3. What do you think the speaker means by "the world"? Why, in the context of the poem, is this connotation of the word ironic?

Critical and Creative Reading

4. What is the function of the "pagan" references in the poem? What advantage did the pagans like the ancient Greeks have over Wordsworth's contemporaries, in the speaker's opinion?
5. Do you agree with the speaker that "getting and spending" makes one insensitive to nature?
6. Wordsworth writes, "Little we see in Nature that is ours." What does he mean? Do you think his criticism applies more or less to people today?

Connections to Other Readings

7. In Tobias Wolff's short story "The Rich Brother," both brothers could be said to be, in Wordsworth's words, "out of tune." Which one do you think Wordsworth would be more critical of? Has he, as Wordsworth fears, "given [his] heart away"?

[1]*Proteus:* In Greek mythology, an early god of the sea who became Poseidon's son. His name has become synonymous with someone or something that is flexible or changeable.

[2]*Triton:* Another son of Poseidon in Greek mythology who blew on a conch shell to either raise or calm the ocean waves.

Arthur Hugh Clough

Le Dîner

Arthur Hugh Clough (1819–1861) was an earnest Victorian who devoted his life to seeking religious "truth." After an excellent education in England's exclusive public school system (similar to "private" schools in the United States), he rejected a prestigious fellowship when it meant he would have to be ordained in the Anglican religion. He left the Anglican Church and temporarily found the answers he was looking for with the Unitarians, but he eventually rejected them also for their dogmatism. As a political radical, he traveled in support of liberal causes abroad and spent the last decade of his life lobbying with Florence Nightingale for medical reforms. While his spiritual struggles were profound and his dedication to his causes sincere, he did not lack irony or wit, as we see here in "Le Dîner."

Come along, 'tis the time, ten or more minutes past,
And he who came first had to wait for the last;
The oysters ere this had been in and been out;
Whilst I have been sitting and thinking about
  How pleasant it is to have money, heigh-ho!
  How pleasant it is to have money.

A clear soup with eggs; *voilà tout*;[1] of the fish
The *filets de sole* are a moderate dish
A la Orly, but you're for red mullet, you say:
By the gods of good fare, who can question to-day
  How pleasant it is to have money, heigh-ho!
  How pleasant it is to have money.

After oysters, sauterne; then sherry; champagne,
Ere one bottle goes, comes another again;
Fly up, thou bold cork, to the ceiling above,
And tell to our ears in the sound that they love
  How pleasant it is to have money, heigh-ho!
  How pleasant it is to have money.

[1]*voilà tout:* There you are (French).

I've the simplest of palates; absurd it may be,
But I almost could dine on a *poulet-au-riz*,[2]
Fish and soup and omelette and that—but the deuce—
There were to be woodcocks, and not *Charlotte Russe!*
  So pleasant it is to have money, heigh-ho!
  So pleasant it is to have money.

Your Chablis is acid, away with the Hock,
Give me the pure juice of the purple Médoc:
St Peray is exquisite; but, if you please,
Some Burgundy just before tasting the cheese.
  So pleasant it is to have money, heigh-ho!
  So pleasant it is to have money.

As for that, pass the bottle, and damn the expense,
I've seen it observed by a writer of sense,
That the labouring classes could scarce live a day,
If people like us didn't eat, drink, and pay.
  So useful it is to have money, heigh-ho!
  So useful it is to have money.

One ought to be grateful, I quite apprehend,
Having dinner and supper and plenty to spend,
And so suppose now, while the things go away,
By way of a grace we all stand up and say
  How pleasant it is to have money, heigh-ho!
  How pleasant it is to have money.

(1861)

Questions for Discussion and Writing

Close Reading

1. What is the effect of the repeated final lines of each stanza? What do you make of the switch from "pleasant" to "useful" in stanza 6?
2. From the biblical reference in line 2 (echoing Christ's promise that "the first shall be last" in the kingdom of heaven), to the "gods of good fare" in stanza 2, to the "grace" in the final stanza, Clough means us to consider the religious implications of the poem's subject. How are these religious references ironic?
3. What kind of person is the speaker? What poetic features reveal his character?

[2]*poulet-au-riz:* Chicken with rice (French).

CRITICAL AND CREATIVE READING

4. What does the speaker's reference to "the labouring classes" tell us about his worldview? Do you hear similar comments today?
5. Clough lists symbols of wealth in Victorian society, such as good food and good wine. If the poem were written today, what might be included in the list of "pleasant" things that money can buy? What does the difference between your list and Clough's suggest about the nature of contemporary society?
6. Clough's attitude toward his speaker is clearly ironic. We are meant to judge the speaker and people like him for their sense of entitlement and complacency. To some degree, do you also envy the speaker? In other words, how "pleasant" and "useful" is it to have money?
7. How does the speaker's language reflect his social class? Do you think this poem is as much about class as about money? What is the difference?

CONNECTIONS TO OTHER READINGS

8. How might the speaker's "gratitude" and good manners be considered examples of "the little virtues" as explained by Natalia Ginzburg in her essay?
9. The tone and language of "Le Dîner" and Allen Ginsberg's "C'mon Pigs of Western Civilization Eat More Grease" could not be more different, yet their subjects are similar. How does each poem express a critique of wealthy complacency and its effect on the less fortunate? Compare and contrast their methods.

William Carlos Williams

This Is Just to Say

The poetry of William Carlos Williams (1883–1963) is known for its evocation of everyday American life. Unlike many of his American contemporaries, like the poets T. S. Eliot and Ezra Pound, Williams turned away from European values and culture and sought to give his work a distinctly American quality. Williams's output as a writer was impressive, especially considering that he had a busy career as a medical doctor in Rutherford, New Jersey. His works include the five-volume epic, *Paterson* (1963). In the following short poem, Williams exemplifies the Imagism for which he and Pound were known. Note how he conveys the qualities of the plums in a few words.

I have eaten
the plums
that were in
the icebox

and which
you were probably
saving
for breakfast

Forgive me
they were delicious
so sweet
and so cold

(1934)

Questions for Discussion and Writing

Close Reading

1. What is the relationship between the title and the poem? Do you see the title as part of the poem? Is this the title you would have chosen? If not, what would you have chosen instead?
2. What is the speaker's tone? Do you think he really wants "forgiveness"? How much does he appear to regret eating the plums?
3. Whom do you think the speaker is addressing? Based on the subtle evidence offered, how would you characterize the relationship between the "I" and the "you" of the poem?

Critical and Creative Reading

4. How appealing does Williams make the plums? Would you have been tempted to eat them? Write your own version of "This Is Just to Say" in which you describe food that you are tempted to eat even though someone else is saving it for himself or herself.
5. Does the speaker seem gluttonous or greedy? What is your reaction to this unapologetic enjoyment of food?

Connections to Other Readings

6. Compare the pleasures of forbidden eating in this poem to M. F. K. Fisher's "chocolate orgy" in "Young Hunger."
7. How might Barbara Ras respond to Williams's poem, based on her poem "You Can't Have It All"?

César Vallejo

Translated by James Wright

Our Daily Bread

Born in 1892 in Peru, César Vallejo was an experimental poet whose defiant verses were influenced by the three months he spent as a political prisoner in Lima. His second book, *Trilce* (1922), made Vallejo a major figure in the Latin American Vanguardist movement, although he left Peru in the 1920s for France and Spain. He was persecuted for his Socialist views and died in exile in Paris in 1938. Although he remained a controversial figure even after his death–his country refused to accept his body for burial–he remains an inspirational figure among revolutionaries for his commitment to artistic activism and for his years of suffering for his cause.

(for Alejandro Gamboa)

Breakfast is drunk down . . . Damp earth
of the cemetery gives off the fragrance of the precious blood.
City of winter . . . the mordant crusade
of a cart that seems to pull behind it
an emotion of fasting that cannot get free!

I wish I could beat on all the doors,
and ask for somebody; and then
look at the poor, and, while they wept softly,
give bits of fresh bread to them.
And plunder the rich of their vineyards
with those two blessed hands
which blasted the nails with one blow of light,
and flew away from the Cross!

Eyelash of morning, you cannot lift yourselves!
Give us our daily bread,
Lord . . . !

Every bone in me belongs to others;
and maybe I robbed them.
I came to take something for myself that maybe
was meant for some other man;
and I start thinking that, if I had not been born,

another poor man could have drunk this coffee.
I feel like a dirty thief . . . Where will I end?

And in this frigid hour, when the earth
has the odor of human dust and is so sad,
I wish I could beat on all the doors
and beg pardon from someone,
and make bits of fresh bread for him
here, in the oven of my heart . . . !

(1918)

Questions for Discussion and Writing

Close Reading

1. The title refers to a line from one of the most common Christian prayers, "The Lord's Prayer": "Give us this day our daily bread." How does this reference to Christian faith affect your reading of the poem? Does the title make the poem more or less revolutionary?
2. The poem opens with images of death. How does Vallejo link the hunger in his land to the death of Christ?
3. According to Vallejo, who is responsible for poverty? How does the speaker feel about his own role in the suffering of the poor?

Critical and Creative Reading

4. Bread has symbolic significance beyond its literal function as an important staple food: it is slang for "money," and it also represents the body of Christ for many Christians, two seemingly opposite associations. What different meanings of the word "bread" does Vallejo connote in his poem? What kind of bread is baked in "the oven of [the] heart"?
5. Why do you think the speaker feels the need to "beg pardon from someone"? From whom might he ask for forgiveness?
6. Can you identify with Vallejo's feelings of being a "dirty thief" merely for having been born? Are you ever struck with a sense of the injustice of a world in which some have so much and some so little simply because of accidents of birth? If so, what did you do?

Connections to Other Readings

7. Contrast the speakers in this poem and in Hugh Clough's "Le Dîner." Are the themes of the poems similar?
8. What kinds of "virtues," to use Natalia Ginzburg's term, does the speaker in the poem advocate? How does this poem support Ginzburg's contention that the great virtues are not necessarily conducive to self-preservation?

9. What qualities does the character of Donald in Tobias Wolff's "The Rich Brother" share with the speaker in this poem?

Pablo Neruda

Translated by Ben Belitt

The Beggars

Chilean poet Pablo Neruda (1904–1973) is one of the most prominent poets of the twentieth century. Although his poems cover a broad range of subjects, he is perhaps most noted as a poetic spokesman for the peasants of Latin America and throughout the world. After beginning his career as a diplomat, he became a leftist in the 1930s and joined the Communist Party in the 1940s. He was elected to the Chilean senate during that decade and forced to leave his native country as a political exile until he returned in 1953. His poetry remained socially conscious throughout his career, which culminated in his reception of the Nobel Prize for literature in 1971, two years before his death. Note the tone of the following poem, "The Beggars," which was published midway through Neruda's career in 1950.

By the cathedrals, clotting
the walls, they deploy
with their bundles, their black looks, their limbs,
ripped tins of provender,[1]
the livid increase of the gargoyles;
beyond, on the obdurate
unction of stone
they nurture a gutter-flower, the flower
of legitimized plague, in migrations.

The park has its paupers
like its trees of extortionate
foliage and root-forms:
at the garden's margin, the slave,
like a sink at the verge of humanity,

[1]*provender:* Food, or provisions.

content with his tainted dissymmetry
supine by the broom of his dying.

Though charity bury them
in the pit of their pestilence,
they suffice for the human condition: they prefigure us.
Our wisdom is this: to trample them under,
to harry the breed in the sties of contempt,
servility's creatures, wearing servility's livery—
we may show them our bootsoles
or interpret their lack in the order of nature.
American panhandlers, '48's
offspring, grandsons
of church doors, I do not commend you.
I will not invest you with ivory usages,
the rhetorists' figure, monarchical beards,
or explain you away with a book, like the others.

I efface you, and hope—
who never will enter my discipline's love,
neither you nor your pieties, nor pass to my pity.
I exile your dust from the earth
and those who contrived you to soil
a contemptible image—
till metals remake you
and you issue and blaze like a blade.

(1950)

Questions for Discussion and Writing

Close Reading

1. What is the setting of this poem? How is it significant?
2. What is the relationship between the pronouns in this poem ("I," "they/them," "you," "we")?
3. Make two lists: the words in the poem that signify something temporary and the words that signify things that attempt to be permanent. How might these two lists lead to an analysis of the poem's themes?

Critical and Creative Reading

4. Ask a significant number of people what their attitude is toward "beggars." (You might come up with a few questions, such as "Do you ever give them money? Are you afraid of them? Do you pity them? Do you resent them?") Compare your findings to the attitude expressed in Neruda's poem.

5. What do you suppose the speaker means in line 19: "they suffice for the human condition: they prefigure us"?
6. In lines 25 and 26, the speaker refers to "'48's offspring." (The original is "hijo del año / 1948.") Research the history of the year 1948 to make sense of that allusion.

CONNECTIONS TO OTHER READINGS

7. Compare this poem to César Vallejo's "Our Daily Bread" in terms of religious imagery and the notion of giving as a Christian ideal.
8. Use Natalia Ginzburg's essay "The Little Virtues" to evaluate the speaker of this poem.

Diane Wakoski

The Greed That Is Not Greed

Diane Wakoski (b. 1937) was born and educated in California; she moved from there to New York City and has spent the last three decades in Michigan, teaching at Michigan State and writing. She has published more than three dozen collections of poetry and three books of criticism, collected in the volume *Toward a New Poetry* (1980). The following poem is part of a volume entitled *The Collected Greed: Parts 1–13*, published in 1984. In the preface to this collection she mentions Robert Kelly, another poet who, like Wakoski, is sometimes associated with the "deep image school" of poetry, which used surreal exploratory imagery. Both Wakoski and Kelly departed from this school: in this collection she says she wants to do something different, something "taboo." She writes, "I decided I wanted to write a long, preachy, didactic poem, using personal and trivial details, names of people, and even gossipy hearsay. I wanted to pontificate about life, to moralize, and yet somehow to write a poem which would have a nobility to it." Although she envisioned the poem in four parts, it ended up having thirteen, and she was not even certain that she was finished with the subject when the book was published in 1984.

(a poem with no universals, with very personal histories & exploring a subject mentioned by Robert Kelly)

Rarely do I let myself
  write, mentioning real names or places.
  But in discussing the matter of greed,

I, always slightly overweight according to *Vogue* standards
and living in the richest country in the world,
would not be fairly using the material at hand
were I not to speak of my experiences.
Robert Kelly is overweight.
I do not believe that it is greed that makes him eat
too much,
but hunger.
He probably does not eat much more than George Washington
who was about the same height (6′ 4″),
but his body makes fat out of the food.
In my original concept of greed,
I judged anything in excess to be a result of greed.
Kelly pointed out that this is not strictly
true.
Greed is motivated by deprivation & resultant pettiness.
Many things done in excess by one man's standard
are only the norm
by another's.
If I were to require a 350 pound man to eat my daily diet,
I would starve him.
And once you accept this,
you accept the concept of the variable norm.
The Variable Norm.
Once it is variable
who is to say it is a standard any longer?

Over a period of years
having been a somewhat social person
I have definitely seen many acts of greed.
An act out of a desire of excess
that leads to a man's debasement
is greed.
Having 2 wives
if it divides your house
your mind
or your loyalties
is an act of greed. But generosity
would not necessarily
have a better result. The greed, perhaps,
is not in having 2 women
but in having 2 who cannot live in the same house with peace
or 2 whom you do not love equally, thus giving hurt to one,
or 2 because of habit or convenience,
not because 1 will not be enough,
or 2 because you cannot tell one to go away.

But supply and demand are vicious forces,
making a man wallow when there is plenty
and cry when there's not enough.
The ungreedy eats the same every day,
saving the plenty to augment the sparse.
In any area where you've conquered supply and demand
you've conquered greed.
For instance, Diane, the wife of the Hawk's Well Head,
who told me she'd never pay $30 for a dress
because whether she were rich or poor, it seemed like
the wrong price.
Some of the richest men
walk around from year to year
with a fixed idea of how much something should cost.
And with that stability
they are seldom at the mercy
of their fortunes.
In matters of money
at least
they have no greed.

Every time I think of greed,
I think of the bitterness it causes,
of what it takes away from others,
how it destroys some balance
that we are all trying to set up.
Putting one thing above all others
usually results in some form of greed.
It is true that we usually look at our one obsession in life
as a right, because we are willing to
sacrifice other parts of our life for it;
but there is no such thing as self-sacrifice
without hurting others.
Only a complete hermit and orphan can say
that by following his greedy obsession to be alone
he is hurting or depriving no one.
We are social creatures;
all our actions reflect back to others.

Rarely do I express my hostilities
without also defending the person
I feel anger towards.
Sometimes defending him more than
he would himself.
I feel that to express anger
without also giving mitigating circumstances

or explanations
is a greed. And that greed destroys
the greedy.
My anger with Carol Bergé
that beautiful black orchid of the Chelsea
for her poison pen letter to me
in December 1967 telling me that I am too aggressive (Blaming it,
of course, on some poor constellation in the sky which happened
to harbor the sun when I was born)
has made me so angry
that I constantly find it necessary to say nice things about her
even when no one else wants to.

It is a choice of greeds, sometimes.
When I would rather like everyone than hate anyone.
But there is a greed which is not greed. It is the desire to have,
to know, to experience, be,
everything,
so that you can share it, possess it with the world.
Desire
for the purpose of control or
excluding others
or of total ownership
is greed
whether motivated out of extreme need
or sheer petulance.
The effect can only debase the spirit.
Clayton Eshleman is often accused of being greedy for power.
He edits a literary magazine;
he has deep political commitments;
he left his wife in a very unsympathetic manner
because of a desire to shape his life differently than he could living
in her presence.
He, like Kelly, is not greedy for power.
He suffers from the greed which is not greed.
The greed to know everything,
to be everything,
to say everything.
But it is a desire to be complete with the world
and there accompanies it
a willingness to share all,
to include all,
to give all.
  Provided he / they are given all.
That demand
          to be given all
yes, it is a greed.

But a greed that in the long run
is not
greed;
perhaps if sustained long enough,
carried far enough
becomes
greatness.

Telling Ted Berrigan,
as a point of honor or integrity
(and beware of the users of that last word,
the breeding of self-righteousness)
that I don't like his poems,
is an act of greed on my part.
His life is as honest as anyone's.
His poems are as important to him
as mine are to me.
He has a different style
a different way of life
a different set of values
but whereas I don't like his poems any less
than I like the poems of lots of other poets,
I don't like the way he treats his wife,
and so I put him down publicly.
It is a sign of rotten moral greed
to be so frugal with approval.
The greed of a man who can genuinely like everyone,
maybe just because they're human beings,
is the greed that is not greed.
Do not confuse this with wanting everyone to like you.

Kelly has a talent of giving
that, even with the best of intentions,
few others could show.
Perhaps it is that he has the language
to communicate to everyone.
Most of my friends are good people
as well as good poets
in my judgment.
None of them are greed-less
but most are intelligent
and know what their greed is
and how to compensate for it.
Jerome Rothenberg is greedy for peace & harmony
having lived all the centuries of the Jew's persecution
in his mind.
David Antin is greedy for authority on every subject.

Jackson Mac Low is greedy to write every poem at least once, try every idea.
Armand Schwerner to unite science and art.
Rochelle Owens to say every swear word and have every erotic experience.
Jack Anderson to make everything unusual.
Paul Blackburn to be able to talk to anyone, on any level, & communicate.

Everyone has his own greed
and suffers from it. It stops being greed
when it is understood
and compensated for. When it leads to
a greater product
a fullness
otherwise not there.
The greed that is not greed
benefits others,
even while destroying some part of you.

Lonely poets. We need to be alone to think.
Our hallucinations creep up on us
and scare us into company. We talk.
We tell everything we dreamed or felt,
what we saw in the dark,
the stone breathing,
the trees pulling our hair.

Lying poets. Making up stories
to exonerate ourselves,
to hide the greed.
It is not necessary.

Young children don't hide their needs.
They don't hide desire either.
The greed that is not greed
goes one step beyond the scratch in the phonograph record,
the spot that repeats over & over,
cannot get beyond itself.
The man who acknowledges his ill
that he needs more than the norm or more than others allow
and who takes it, in the face of all accusations,
but gives it back with interest.
He is the great man. The man who
takes greed beyond greed.

(1984)

QUESTIONS FOR DISCUSSION AND WRITING

CLOSE READING

1. Paraphrase Wakoski's definition of this particular kind of greed "that is not greed." What is it? What isn't it?
2. What is the concept of "the variable norm"? How is it illustrated in the poem, and why is it so important to the poem's themes?
3. Like other late-twentieth-century experimental poems, "The Greed That Is Not Greed" does not seem to conform to classical poetic form. What are the poetic features of this poem, and how do they work? In other words, what makes it a poem?
4. What is the relationship between "greed" and "greatness" in the poem?

CRITICAL AND CREATIVE READING

5. Consider the possible applications of the speaker's assertion that "supply and demand are vicious forces."
6. Self-sacrifice seems to be a noble gesture, the opposite of greed. How do you understand Wakoski's speaker's assertion that "there is no such thing as self-sacrifice / without hurting others"?
7. The poet begins the poem with an expression of her own poetic conventions: "Rarely do I let myself / write, mentioning real names or places." Why does she resist her own method of writing for this particular poem? In other words, how does the subject dictate the nature of her method? Why couldn't she write in nonspecific terms about this particular subject?

CONNECTIONS TO OTHER READINGS

8. Discuss the form of "The Greed That Is Not Greed" along with two other poems written within a decade of it—Ginsberg's "C'mon Pigs of Western Civilization Eat More Grease" and Ai's "Greed." What can you say about the style and subject of these three poets?
9. Wakoski distinguishes between greed and hunger in the first stanza. Discuss the differences between these two words here and in M. F. K. Fisher's essay "Young Hunger."
10. According to her preface to *The Collected Greed*, Wakoski originally envisioned that each poem would contain "a presiding metaphor in the form of a cold-blooded animal or creature that symbolized the kind of greed on which I was going to focus in that part." Ignoring "cold-blooded," compare the greed evident in this poem to the greed discussed in William Matthews's poem "The Bear at the Dump." Are the two types of greed the same? If not, what animal might serve as a metaphor for the type of greed in Wakoski's poem?

Barbara Ras

You Can't Have It All

The poetry of Barbara Ras (b. 1949) has earned numerous awards. Since the 1998 publication of her first collection, *Bite Every Sorrow*, which won the 1997 Walt Whitman Award, she has received the Ascher Montandon Award, the Kate Tufts Discovery Award, and a number of other honors. Her writing is informed by her travels to Latin America, and she is the editor of a collection of Costa Rican fiction, *Costa Rica: A Traveler's Literary Companion* (1994). Born in Massachusetts, she currently lives in Athens, Georgia. Her poem "You Can't Have It All" suggests that, in fact, we can have an awful lot if we just take the time to appreciate it.

But you can have the fig tree and its fat leaves like clown hands
gloved with green. You can have the touch of a single eleven-year-old finger
on your cheek, waking you at one a.m. to say the hamster is back.
You can have the purr of the cat and the soulful look
of the black dog, the look that says, If I could I would bite
every sorrow until it fled, and when it is August,
you can have it August and abundantly so. You can have love,
though often it will be mysterious, like the white foam
that bubbles up at the top of the bean pot over the red kidneys
until you realize foam's twin is blood.
You can have the skin at the center between a man's legs,
so solid, so doll-like. You can have the life of the mind,
glowing occasionally in priestly vestments, never admitting pettiness,
never stooping to bribe the sullen guard who'll tell you
all roads narrow at the border.
You can speak a foreign language, sometimes,
and it can mean something. You can visit the marker on the grave
where your father wept openly. You can't bring back the dead,
but you can have the words *forgive* and *forget* hold hands
as if they meant to spend a lifetime together. And you can be grateful
for makeup, the way it kisses your face, half spice, half amnesia, grateful
for Mozart, his many notes racing one another towards joy, for towels
sucking up the drops on your clean skin, and for deeper thirsts,
for passion fruit, for saliva. You can have the dream,
the dream of Egypt, the horses of Egypt and you riding in the hot sand.
You can have your grandfather sitting on the side of your bed,
at least for a while, you can have clouds and letters, the leaping

of distances, and Indian food with yellow sauce like sunrise.
You can't count on grace to pick you out of a crowd
but here is your friend to teach you how to high jump,
how to throw yourself over the bar, backwards,
until you learn about love, about sweet surrender,
and here are periwinkles, buses that kneel, farms in the mind
as real as Africa. And when adulthood fails you,
you can still summon the memory of the black swan on the pond
of your childhood, the rye bread with peanut butter and bananas
your grandmother gave you while the rest of the family slept.
There is the voice you can still summon at will, like your mother's,
it will always whisper, you can't have it all,
but there is this.

(1997)

QUESTIONS FOR DISCUSSION AND WRITING

CLOSE READING

1. In addition to not being able to "have it all," what other things does the poem tell us we can't do?
2. How adequate are the compensations in life for not being able to have it all, according to Ras? What do the compensations she lists have in common, if anything? What do you know about the speaker based on her list of things you *can* have?
3. What does it mean to "bite every sorrow"? Do you see this as a positive or a negative action?

CRITICAL AND CREATIVE READING

4. Ras talks about the power of memory "when adulthood fails you." What kinds of circumstances do you think might be implied by that phrase? Why would memories of childhood provide a remedy under those circumstances?
5. Write a poem or essay in which you write about the things in your life that compensate for not being able to "have it all." Compare and contrast your list to Ras's. What do these compensations say about you?
6. What do you think people mean when they talk about "having it all"? Is the desire to have it all a greedy or gluttonous impulse, or is it human nature? Do you think the poem's speaker wants to "have it all"? Compare yourself to the speaker in this regard.
7. The speaker suggests that people should be grateful for thirsts and for dreams—for wanting things even if they do not get them. How does this notion go against common wisdom about desire?

CONNECTIONS TO OTHER READINGS

8. Compare this poem to the ideas in Natalia Ginzburg's "The Little Virtues." What do both works have in common?

9. O'Henry's "The Gift of the Magi" also suggests that there are more important things than "having it all." How might the characters in that story describe the things they *can* have?

Allen Ginsberg

C'mon Pigs of Western Civilization Eat More Grease

Allen Ginsberg's first book of poems, *Howl and Other Poems* (1956), spoke to a generation of young, disaffected Americans with its angry yet lyrical lines. Along with the novelist Jack Kerouac, Ginsberg (1926–1997) was a leading figure in America's Beat Generation, a group of outcasts and intellectual bohemians whose writing favored uninhibited expression over artist revision. (See also Gregory Corso's poem "Marriage" in Chapter 12.) Ginsberg was an activist as well as an artist, and one of his major subjects was the soulless materialism of American culture. In the following poem, written in 1993, Ginsberg links America's gluttonous consumption of food to its imperialism. Allen Ginsberg died in 1997. If he were alive today, how would he assess America?

Eat Eat more marbled Sirloin more Pork'n
  gravy.
Lard up the dressing, fry chicken in
  boiling oil
Carry it dribbling to gray climes, snowed with
  salt,
Little lambs covered with mint roast in racks
  surrounded by roast potatoes wet with
  buttersauce,
Buttered veal medallions in creamy saliva,
  buttered beef, by glistening mountains
  of french fries
Stroganoffs in white hot sour cream, chops
  soaked in olive oil,
surrounded by olives, salty feta cheese, followed
  by Roquefort & Bleu & Stilton
  thirsty
for wine, beer Cocacola Fanta Champagne
  Pepsi retsina arak whiskey
  vodka

Agh! Watch out heart attack, pop more
  angina pills
order a plate of Bratwurst, fried frankfurters,
couple billion Wimpys', MacDonald burgers
  to the moon & burp!
Salt on those fries! Boil onions
  & breaded mushrooms even zucchini
  in deep hot Crisco pans—Hot Dog!
Forget greenbeans, everyday a few carrots,
  a mini big spoonful of salty rice'll
  do, make the plate pretty;
throw in some vinegar pickles, briney sauerkraut
  check yr. cholesterol, swallow a pill
and order a sugar Cream donut, pack 2 under
  the size 44 belt

Pass out in the vomitorium come back cough
  up strands of sandwich still chewing
  pastrami at Katz's delicatessen
Back to central Europe & gobble Kielbasa
  in Lódź
swallow salami in Munich with beer, Liverwurst
on pumpernickel in Berlin, greasy cheese in
  a 3 star Hotel near Syntagma,[1] on white
  bread thick-buttered
Set an example for developing nations, salt,
  sugar, animal fat, coffee tobacco Schnapps
Drop dead faster! Make room for
  Chinese guestworkers with alien soybean
  curds green cabbage & rice!
Africans Latins with rice beans & calabash can
  stay thin & crowd in apartments for working
  class foodfreaks—

Not like western cuisine rich in protein
  cancer heart attack hypertension sweat
  bloated liver & spleen megaly[2]
Diabetes & stroke—monuments to carnivorous
  civilizations
presently murdering Belfast
  Bosnia Cypress Ngorno Karabach Georgia
mailing love letter bombs in

[1]*Syntagma:* A square in Athens.
[2]*spleen megaly:* Usually *splenomegaly*: enlargement of the spleen.

Vienna or setting houses afire
  in East Germany—have another coffee,
  here's a cigar.
And this is a plate of black forest chocolate cake,
  you deserve it.

(1993)

Questions for Discussion and Writing

Close Reading

1. The foods Ginsberg describes are not, in and of themselves, disgusting. How does Ginsberg render them completely unappetizing?
2. In what way does Ginsberg suggest that America is "set[ting] an example for developing nations"? How does this differ from the example Americans tend to see themselves as setting?
3. How is the poem's final line, "you deserve it," ironic? What does the speaker seem to think America deserves?

Critical and Creative Reading

4. Ginsberg is clearly assigning a moral value to gluttony. According to Ginsberg's speaker, what is wrong with this consumption? How does Ginsberg imply a connection between the gluttony of "Western Civilization" and the problems of the developing world?
5. What is the poem's tone? Cite specific passages. Do you share Ginsberg's attitude toward Western civilization? Why or why not?
6. Do you think Ginsberg is targeting all of Western culture or just the wealthy? What evidence supports your view?
7. Go to your school cafeteria or to a local restaurant and record your observations. (You might also compare an upscale restaurant to a fast-food eatery.) Do the menus and eating habits of the diners support Ginsberg's argument about American consumption?

Connections to Other Readings

8. Compare the tone, images, and theme in this poem to that of William Matthews's "The Bear at the Dump."
9. How does Verna, the speaker in Ai's poem, "Greed," exemplify the kind of excess that Ginsberg is critiquing in this poem?
10. Contrast the tone of this poem to the tone of William Carlos Williams's "This Is Just to Say."

Ai

Greed

Ai was born in 1947 and grew up in the southwestern United States. Since the publication of her first book, *Cruelty,* in 1973, Ai (a word that means "love" in Japanese) has won numerous honors and awards, including the American Book Award from the Before Columbus Foundation and the Lamont Poetry Award of the Academy of American Poets. Her 1999 collection, *Vice*, won the National Book Award for Poetry. The following selection comes from Ai's book *Greed* (1993), a volume of dramatic monologues that explore the effects of greed on several fictional personae as well as on the American character more generally. While Ai has experimented with other poetic forms, she is known for her use of the dramatic monologue, about which she says, "I feel that the dramatic monologue was the form in which I was born to write and I love it as passionately, or perhaps more passionately, than I have ever loved a man."

I was named after my daddy, Vern,
but I was like my mama,
though I'd never admit it, until now.
Before she settled down,
she traveled from town to town
on the roller derby circuit
for the Texas Tornadoes.
Sometimes I went with her.
She always knew how to make me happy.
She'd take me to the nearest hot dog stand
and tell the man,
"Give Verna the works."
She was a big-boned farm girl with flame-red hair
and with the smallest, most delicate feet.
She had to have her skates made specially
and even then, she had to fill them in
with wads of cotton.
I looked like her, but I had daddy's feet,
wide, flat, and reliable.
I wore cowboy boots, a cowboy hat and jeans,
and I was high school rodeo queen of '75.
I learned to drive a tractor, brand cattle
and spit, after I took a bit of chaw.

The boys admired me and asked me out,
but I didn't trust them. They talked too much,
but Russ, the Viet Nam vet,
who drove the school bus was fine for me,
though all in all I'd have to say I wasn't half the girl
I could have been.

A wild mother sometimes makes a cautious child,
who takes the safest path to her destination.
In my case, it was a savings and loan bank,
where at nineteen, I sank
into the routine of being secretary
to Mr. Joe Bob Merriweather,
the president and decent, churchgoing family man.

My change of life began in '82,
when money started pouring in here
like heavy rain through a leaky roof.
All we had to do was set out buckets anyplace
and we would catch a mess of money.
I was polishing my nails lunch time one day,
when a man sailed in the door
and asked me for a date.
Just then, Joe Bob came out
and without a glance at me said, "Boy, she's taken."
After that, we were making love
at least three times a week,
sometimes across the desk
or in the backseat of his Pontiac.
He wasn't that good at it,
but he tried and I was grateful
just to be at his side,
when all his deals paid off.
Then he bought a Rolls.
He partied with politicians and whores,
until word got back to his wife
and she threatened to slit off a piece
of you know what.
After that, he thought he'd better quit it with me too,
so he bought me a sable coat from SAKS JANDEL.

He wished me well
and I sat at my desk, reading the *Wall Street Journal.*
I dabbled in real estate with my latest raise.
I was making one hundred thousand dollars a year,
plus monthly bonus,

and Joe Bob was clearing millions,
building condos, financed through his S & L,
hiw own contractors, and just plain old-fashioned kickbacks.
We were riding the crest of deregulations wave.
The S & L was like a building without foundation.
How could it stand
longer than a man's imagination?
We were drowning in the illusion of money.
We couldn't be saved.
But that was later.
For a while, I slaved for him,
but then I thought I'd work for my own benefit.
I told mama how he'd used me like I was a slut
he could tip when he got done.
All she said was, "You're just like me.
I could skate all right,
but I couldn't pick men worth a damn.
Your father's a fine example.
You have the brains, the looks.
What took you so long to get what you want?"
I told Joe Bob I'd tell his wife about us.
I said, "Pleading won't get you anywhere.
You're a betting man.
Take out the cards
and deal this hand."
When I went in my own office at last, I cried,
then poured a glass of champagne,
opened a box of Godiva chocolates,
and put my feet up on the desk.

The rest of the time, I learned the trade.
I stayed out of Joe Bob's way and he out of mine.
In time, I had my clients too, a few deals
that added up to two million dollars
in my personal account,
but you know, it didn't amount to much
without love,
which I didn't know was coming
in the form of Bubba Taylor.
Yes, love and hate were waiting in his arms.
He was a charming scoundrel,
who found a way to get my money
that was just setting like a laying hen on eggs.
When he got between my legs,
I was begging for destruction
and it came a mere six months to the day

after I met him.
He robbed me is what he did.
I admit I gave him access to my accounts.
He was my fiancé, wasn't he?
He disappeared just like he'd come
and I had to start over,
only now the government was cracking down
on what it once had ballyhooed
as the way to turn around the banking industry
and free it from the controls
it had enacted in the first place.
Ronald Reagan and his bunch threw out the rules,
but did not go down on the ship of fools,
when it foundered. We did
and we took a lot of people with us.
The unsold real estate piled up—
apartment buildings, condos, homes, and office towers.
Loans in default.

We ought to have known it couldn't last,
but we were past all reasoning.
We had to keep the money moving back and forth
to cover up the fact
that Santa Claus's sack was empty.

Joe Bob took off for parts unknown
and I went home to Abilene,
but not for long.
I was called back to Dallas to testify.
Joe Bob was tried and sentenced to twenty-five years
minimum security, reduced to three,
and when I finished my spiral down
the chain of lies,
I took up keeping books
at Clem's West Side Auto Supply.
They claim the S & L's are getting bailed out,
though it sounds like some of the same shenanigans
are going on at RTC.
They're moving money into other bottomless pockets,
behind the screen of fixing things.
The whole country's on the edge of insolvency,
but I am watching from the sidelines now
like a drunk who's pledged to stay off the bottle,
but the ledge where I'm standing is so narrow.
I could fall back in the fire,

where the money's burning like desire,
only with much more intensity.
Finally, mama and me moved to Vegas,
where I cocktail-waitress at the Sands
and each paycheck I tell the man
at the craps table,
let it ride, until it hurts.

(1993)

Questions for Discussion and Writing

Close Reading

1. How does Verna's upbringing influence her decision to work in a bank and try to amass wealth?
2. The poem describes the financial rise and fall of the 1980s, in which the slogan "Greed is good," from a speech made in the movie *Wall Street*, echoed the words of a real-life white-collar criminal. How much does Verna attribute her mistakes to the spirit of the times? To what degree does that explain her actions, in your opinion? What other motives do you see for Verna making the mistakes she did?
3. What is the significance of the poem's final line, "let it ride, until it hurts"? Why do you think Verna is embracing a philosophy that essentially destroyed her life? Do you think that she regrets her decisions?

Critical and Creative Reading

4. Verna sets out to distance herself from her mother. To what degree is she more like her mother than she thinks? In what ways is she different? Who is the more appealing character?
5. What is at the root of Verna's greed? In addition to money, how important are power and sex to her? What motivates her most?
6. What do you think of Verna's decision to testify against Joe Bob? Is she as guilty as he is? Who used whom more in their relationship? Does each, in your opinion, get what he or she deserves?

Connections to Other Readings

7. Compare Ai's description of Verna's activities to those of "the bear at the dump" in William Matthews's poem.
8. How does Verna represent the worst aspects of America as described in Allan Ginsberg's "C'mon Pigs of Western Civilization Eat More Grease"?

William Matthews

The Bear at the Dump

William Matthews (1942–1997) was born in Ohio and earned degrees from Yale University and the University of North Carolina. He published numerous collections of poetry during his lifetime, and some have been published posthumously. His book *Time & Money* (1995) won the National Book Critics Circle Award. He served as member and chair of the Literature Panel of the National Endowment for the Arts and won numerous grants and fellowships. In "The Bear at the Dump," the speaker is repulsed by the gluttony of a bear that makes its way through the refuse of a landfill. Matthews's depiction of the bear implies a criticism of human consumption as well.

Amidst the too much that we buy and throw
away and the far too much we wrap it in,
the bear found a few items of special
interest—a honeydew rind, a used tampon,
the bone from a leg of lamb. He'd rock back
lightly onto his rear paws and slash
open a plastic bag, and then his nose—
jammed almost with a surfeit of rank
and likely information, for he would pause—
and then his whole dowsing snout would
insinuate itself a little way
inside. By now he'd have hunched his weight
forward slightly, and then he'd snatch it back,
trailed by some tidbit in his teeth. He'd look
around. What a good boy am he.
The guardian of the dump was used
to this and not amused. "He'll drag that shit
every which damn way," he grumbled
who'd dozed and scraped a pit to keep that shit
where the town paid to contain it.
The others of us looked and looked. "City
folks like you don't get to see this often,"
one year-round resident accused me.
Some winter I'll bring him down to learn
to love a rat working a length of subway
track. "Nope," I replied. Just then the bear
decamped for the woods with a marl of grease

and slather in his mouth and on his snout,
picking up speed, not cute (nor had he been
cute before, slavering with greed, his weight
all sunk to his seated rump and his nose stuck
up to sift the rich and fetid air, shaped
like a huge, furry pear), but richly
fed on the slow-simmering dump, and gone
into the bug-thick woods and anecdote.

(1995)

Questions for Discussion and Writing

Close Reading

1. Note Matthews's choice of words to describe the bear's actions: "slash," "jammed," "dowsing," "insinuate," "slavering." How do these words affect our reaction to the bear's gluttony? Do we need to be told that the bear was "not cute"? Do you find gluttony in all its forms this repulsive?
2. Matthews tells us that the bear chooses "a honeydew rind, a used tampon, / the bone from a leg of lamb"—three items that have nothing in common except that they were discarded by humans. What does this variety of selected items suggest about the bear's appetite? How do these details contribute to the overall tone of the poem?
3. The speaker is described as a city-dweller who is vacationing in a more rural area. What do you make of his comparison of the bear to the rat "working a length of subway track"? What do the bear and the rat have in common? What is the attitude of the year-round resident who refers to "city folks"? What does the speaker's comment about the rat suggest about his attitude toward that resident?
4. What does the speaker mean when he describes the bear as having "gone into the bug-thick woods and anecdote"?

Critical and Creative Reading

5. What is the speaker saying about the relationship between mankind and the scavengers who rely on our waste? Are we like the bear in our buying and throwing away "too much"? Do you think Matthews is comparing human beings to the bear (and the rat), or is he contrasting the disgusting habits of animals to the more savory ones of people who pay to contain their garbage in dumps?
6. Why does the bear look around with an air of self-satisfaction? What is the speaker's response to the bear's attitude of "what a good boy am he"? How do you know?
7. If you were witnessing this scene, would you have the same attitude as the speaker? Might you find the bear "cute"? Why or why not?

8. Do you agree with Matthews that as human beings we buy and throw away "far too much"? If so, why do you think we do that? Are we simply gluttonous and wasteful, or is there another explanation this behavior?

CONNECTIONS TO OTHER READINGS

9. Compare the bear's gluttony to the appetite described in M. F. K. Fisher's "Young Hunger." Is youthful hunger as all-engrossing as that of the ravenous bear?
10. Do the appetites of this bear resemble the avarice of Abraham Cowley's metaphorical ostrich or chough? Explain.

Drama

Molière

Translated by Charles Heron Wall

The Miser (L'Avare)

Molière was born Jean-Baptiste Poquelin in 1622, the son of a well-to-do Parisian merchant with a position in the royal court. He received his law degree in 1642, but he soon turned to the theater, first as an actor, then as director, and—most famously—as playwright. After a rocky start in the business, his theater company came under the patronage of the royal family and his troupe became the official entertainers for the court of Louis XIV. Although his comedies were widely popular with both the public and the king, Molière made many enemies by satirizing influential politicians and the church. After his death in 1673, the church refused to allow him burial on sacred ground until the king intervened. *The Miser*, first performed in 1668 with the playwright acting the title role, is a classic example of a Molière comedy.* The many misunderstandings and double entendres are laugh-out-loud funny, and Harpagon, the central character, is both vile and ridiculous. His vanity and the extreme nature of his avarice make him a classic satirical figure: at sixty, he believes any young woman would be more attracted to him than to a younger man, and his greed is so all-consuming that he will gladly be rid of his daughter to any man who will take her without a dowry. In the end, he is left alone with his gold.

*This play was acted for the first time on September 9, 1668. In it, Molière has borrowed from Plautus and has imitated several other authors, but he far surpasses them in the treatment of his subject. The picture of the miser, in whom love of money takes the place of all natural affections, who not only withdraws from family intercourse but considers his children as natural enemies, is finely drawn, and renders Molière's *Miser* altogether more dramatic and moral than those of his predecessors. Molière acted the part of Harpagon.—[Translator's note.]

PERSONS REPRESENTED

Harpagon, *father to* Cléante, *in love with* Marianne
Cléante, Harpagon's *son, lover to* Marianne
Valére, *son to* Anselme, *and lover to* Élise
Anselme, *father to* Valére *and* Marianne
Master Simon, *broker*
Master Jacques, *cook and coachman to* Harpagon
La Fléche, *valet to* Cléante
Brindavoine, *and* La Merluche, *lackeys to* Harpagon
A Magistrate *and his* Clerk
Élise, *daughter to* Harpagon
Marianne, *daughter to* Anselme
Frosine, *an intriguing woman*
Mistress Claude, *servant to* Harpagon

The scene is at Paris, *in* Harpagon's *house.*

ACT I

SCENE I. VALÈRE, ÉLISE

Valère: What, dear Élise! you grow sad after having given me such dear tokens of your love; and I see you sigh in the midst of my joy! Can you regret having made me happy? and do you repent of the engagement which my love has forced from you?

Élise: No, Valère, I do not regret what I do for you; I feel carried on by too delightful a power, and I do not even wish that things should be otherwise than they are. Yet, to tell you the truth, I am very anxious about the consequences; and I greatly fear that I love you more than I should.

Valère: What can you possibly fear from the affection you have shown me?

Élise: Everything; the anger of my father, the reproaches of my family, the censure of the world, and, above all, Valère, a change in your heart! I fear that cruel coldness with which your sex so often repays the too warm proofs of an innocent love.

Valère: Alas! do not wrong me thus; do not judge of me by others. Think me capable of everything, Élise, except of falling short of what I owe to you. I love you too much for that; and my love will be as lasting as my life!

Élise: Ah! Valère, all men say the same thing; all men are alike in their words; their actions only show the difference that exists between them.

Valère: Then why not wait for actions, if by them alone you can judge of the truthfulness of my heart? Do not suffer your anxious fears to mislead you, and to wrong me. Do not let an unjust suspicion destroy the happiness which is to me dearer than life; but give me time to show you by a thousand proofs the sincerity of my affection.

Élise: Alas! how easily do we allow ourselves to be persuaded by those we love. I believe you, Valère; I feel sure that your heart is utterly incapable of deceiving me, that your love is sincere, and that you will ever remain faithful to me. I will no longer doubt that happiness is near. If I grieve, it will only be over the difficulties of our position, and the possible censures of the world.

Valère: But why even this fear?

Élise: Oh, Valère! if everybody knew you as I do, I should not have much to fear. I find in you enough to justify all I do for you; my heart knows all your merit, and feels, moreover, bound to you by deep gratitude. How can I forget that horrible moment when we met for the first time? Your generous courage in risking your own life to save mine from the fury of the waves; your tender care afterwards; your constant attentions and your ardent love, which neither time nor difficulties can lessen! For me you neglect your parents and your country; you give up your own position in life to be a servant of my father! How can I resist the influence that all this has over me? Is it not enough to justify in my eyes my engagement to you? Yet, who knows if it will be enough to justify it in the eyes of others? and how can I feel sure that my motives will be understood?

Valère: You try in vain to find merit in what I have done; it is by my love alone that I trust to deserve you. As for the scruples you feel, your father himself justifies you but too much before the world; and his avarice and the distant way in which he lives with his children might authorise stranger things still. Forgive me, my dear Élise, for speaking thus of your father before you; but you know that, unfortunately, on this subject no good can be said of him. However, if I can find my parents, as I fully hope I shall, they will soon be favourable to us. I am expecting news of them with great impatience; but if none comes I will go in search of them myself.

Élise: Oh no! Valère, do not leave me, I entreat you. Try rather to ingratiate yourself in my father's favour.

Valère: You know how much I wish it, and you can see how I set about it. You know the skilful manoeuvres I have had to use in order to introduce myself into his service; under what a mask of sympathy and conformity of tastes I disguise my own feelings to please him; and what a part I play to acquire his affection. I succeed wonderfully well, and I feel that to obtain favour with men, there are no better means than to pretend to be of their way of thinking, to fall in with their maxims, to praise their defects, and to applaud all their doings. One need not fear to overdo it, for however gross the flattery, the most cunning are easily duped; there is nothing so impertinent or ridiculous which they will not believe, provided it be well seasoned with praise. Honesty suffers, I acknowledge; but when we have need of men, we may be allowed without blame to adapt ourselves to their mode of thought; and if we have no other hope of success but through such stratagem, it is not after all the fault of those who flatter, but the fault of those who wish to be flattered.

Élise: Why do you not try also to gain my brother's goodwill, in case the servant should betray our secret?

Jean Vilar and Catherine de Seynes in *The Miser,* Paris, 1962.

Valère: I am afraid I cannot humour them both. The temper of the father is so different from that of the son that it would be difficult to be the confidant of both at the same time. Rather try your brother yourself; make use of the love that exists between you to enlist him in our cause. I leave you, for I see him coming. Speak to him, sound him, and see how far we can trust him.

Élise: I greatly fear I shall never have the courage to speak to him of my secret.

SCENE II. CLÉANTE, ÉLISE

Cléante: I am very glad to find you alone, sister. I longed to speak to you and to tell you a secret.

Élise: I am quite ready to hear you, brother. What is it you have to tell me?

Cléante: Many things, sister, summed up in one word—love.

Élise: You love?

Cléante: Yes, I love. But, before I say more, let me tell you that I know I depend on my father, and that the name of son subjects me to his will; that it would be wrong to engage ourselves without the consent of the authors of our being; that heaven has made them the masters of our affections, and that it is our duty not to dispose of ourselves but in accordance to their wish; that their judgment is not biased by their being in love themselves; that they are, therefore, much more likely not to be deceived by appearances, and to judge better what is good for us; that we ought to trust their experience rather than the passion which blinds us; and that the rashness of youth often carries us to the very brink of dangerous abysses. I know all this, my sister, and I tell it you to spare you the trouble of saying it to me, for my love will not let me listen to anything, and I pray you to spare me your remonstrances.

Élise: Have you engaged yourself, brother, to her you love?

Cléante: No, but I have determined to do so; and I beseech you once more not to bring forward any reason to dissuade me from it.

Élise: Am I such a very strange person, brother?

Cléante: No, dear sister; but you do not love. You know not the sweet power that love has upon our hearts; and I dread your wisdom.

Élise: Alas! my brother, let us not speak of my wisdom. There are very few people in this world who do not lack wisdom, were it only once in their lifetime; and if I opened my heart to you, perhaps you would think me less wise than you are yourself.

Cléante: Ah! would to heaven that your heart, like mine. . . .

Élise: Let us speak of you first, and tell me whom it is you love.

Cléante: A young girl who has lately come to live in our neighbourhood, and who seems made to inspire love in all those who behold her. Nature, my dear sister, has made nothing more lovely; and I felt another man the moment I saw her. Her name is Marianne, and she lives with a good, kind mother, who is almost always ill, and for whom the dear girl shows the greatest affection. She waits upon her, pities and comforts her with a tenderness that would touch you to the very soul. Whatever she undertakes is done in the most charming way; and in all her actions shine a wonderful grace, a most winning gentleness, an adorable modesty, a . . . ah! my sister, how I wish you had but seen her.

Élise: I see many things in what you tell me, dear brother; and it is sufficient for me to know that you love her for me to understand what she is.

Cléante: I have discovered, without their knowing it, that they are not in very good circumstances, and that, although they live with the greatest care, they have barely enough to cover their expenses. Can you imagine, my sister, what happiness it must be to improve the condition of those we love; skilfully to bring about some relief to the modest wants of a virtuous family? And think what grief it is for me to find myself deprived of this great joy through the avarice of a father, and for it to be impossible for me to give any proof of my love to her who is all in all to me.

Élise: Yes, I understand, dear brother, what sorrow this must be to you.

Cléante: It is greater, my sister, than you can believe. For is there anything more cruel than this mean economy to which we are subjected? this strange penury in which we are made to pine? What good will it do us to have a fortune if it only comes to us when we are not able to enjoy it; if now to provide for my daily maintenance I get into debt on every side; if both you and I are reduced daily to beg the help of tradespeople in order to have decent clothes to wear? In short, I wanted to speak to you that you might help me to sound my father concerning my present feelings; and if I find him opposed to them, I am determined to go and live elsewhere with this most charming girl, and to make the best of what Providence offers us. I am trying everywhere to raise money for this purpose; and if your circumstances, dear sister, are like mine, and our father opposes us, let us both leave him, and free ourselves from the tyranny in which his hateful avarice has for so long held us.

Élise: It is but too true that every day he gives us more and more reason to regret the death of our mother, and that. . . .

Cléante: I hear his voice. Let us go a little farther and finish our talk. We will afterwards join our forces to make a common attack on his hard and unkind heart.

SCENE III. HARPAGON, LA FLÈCHE

Harpagon: Get out of here, this moment; and let me have no more of your prating. Now then, be gone out of my house, you sworn pickpocket, you veritable gallows' bird.

La Flèche [*aside*]: I never saw anything more wicked than this cursed old man; and I truly believe, if I may be allowed to say so, that he is possessed with a devil.

Harpagon: What are you muttering there between your teeth?

La Flèche: Why do you send me away?

Harpagon: You dare to ask me my reasons, you scoundrel? Out with you, this moment, before I give you a good thrashing.

La Flèche: What have I done to you?

Harpagon: Done this, that I wish you to be off.

La Flèche: My master, your son, gave me orders to wait for him.

Harpagon: Go and wait for him in the street, then; out with you; don't stay in my house, straight and stiff as a sentry, to observe what is going on, and to make your profit of everything. I won't always have before me a spy on all my affairs; a treacherous scamp, whose cursed eyes watch all my actions, covet all I possess, and ferret about in every corner to see if there is anything to steal.

La Flèche: How the deuce could one steal anything from you? Are you a man likely to be robbed when you put every possible thing under lock and key, and mount guard day and night?

Harpagon: I will lock up whatever I think fit, and mount guard when and where I please. Did you ever see such spies as are set upon me to take note of everything I do? [*Aside*] I tremble for fear he should suspect something of my money. [*Aloud*] Now, aren't you a fellow to give rise to stories about my having money hid in my house?

La Flèche: You have some money hid in your house?

Harpagon: No, scoundrel! I do not say that. [*Aside*] I am furious! [*Aloud*] I only ask if out of mischief you do not spread abroad the report that I have some?

La Flèche: Oh! What does it matter whether you have money, or whether you have not, since it is all the same to us?

Harpagon [*raising his hand to give* La Flèche *a blow*]: Oh! oh! You want to argue, do you? I will give you, and quickly too, some few of these arguments about your ears. Get out of the house, I tell you once more.

La Flèche: Very well; very well. I am going.

Harpagon: No, wait; are you carrying anything away with you?

La Flèche: What can I possibly carry away?

Harpagon: Come here, and let me see. Show me your hands.

La Flèche: There they are.

Harpagon: The others.

La Flèche: The others?

Harpagon: Yes.

La Flèche: There they are.

Harpagon [*pointing to* La Flèche's *breeches*]: Have you anything hid in here?

La Flèche: Look for yourself.

Harpagon [*feeling the knees of the breeches*]: These wide knee-breeches are convenient receptacles of stolen goods; and I wish a pair of them had been hanged.

La Flèche [*aside*]: Ah! how richly such a man deserves what he fears, and what joy it would be to me to steal some of his. . . .

Harpagon: Eh?

La Flèche: What?

Harpagon: What is it you talk of stealing?

La Flèche: I say that you feel about everywhere to see if I have been stealing anything.

Harpagon: And I mean to do so too. [*He feels in* La Flèche's *pockets*].

La Flèche: Plague take all misers and all miserly ways!

Harpagon: Eh? What do you say?

La Flèche: What do I say?

Harpagon: Yes. What is it you say about misers and miserly ways?

La Flèche: I say plague take all misers and all miserly ways.

Harpagon: Of whom do you speak?

La Flèche: Of misers.

Harpagon: And who are they, these misers?

La Flèche: Villains and stingy wretches!

Harpagon: But what do you mean by that?

La Flèche: Why do you trouble yourself so much about what I say?

Harpagon: I trouble myself because I think it right to do so.

La Flèche: Do you think I am speaking about you?

Harpagon: I think what I think; but I insist upon your telling me to whom you speak when you say that.

La Flèche: To whom I speak? I am speaking to the inside of my hat.

Harpagon: And I will, perhaps, speak to the outside of your head.

La Flèche: Would you prevent me from cursing misers?

Harpagon: No; but I will prevent you from prating and from being insolent. Hold your tongue, will you?

La Flèche: I name nobody.

Harpagon: Another word, and I'll thrash you.

La Flèche: He whom the cap fits, let him wear it.

Harpagon: Will you be silent?

La Flèche: Yes; much against my will.

Harpagon: Ah! ah!

La Flèche [*showing* Harpagon *one of his doublet pockets*]: Just look, here is one more pocket. Are you satisfied?

Harpagon: Come, give it up to me without all that fuss.

La Flèche: Give you what?

Harpagon: What you have stolen from me.

La Flèche: I have stolen nothing at all from you.

Harpagon: Are you telling the truth?

La Flèche: Yes.

Harpagon: Good-bye, then, and now you may go to the devil.

La Flèche [*aside*]: That's a nice way of dismissing anyone.

Harpagon: I leave it to your conscience, remember!

SCENE IV. HARPAGON [ALONE]

This rascally valet is a constant vexation to me; and I hate the very sight of the good-for-nothing cripple. Really, it is no small anxiety to keep by one a large sum of money; and happy is the man who has all his cash well invested, and who needs not keep by him more than he wants for his daily expenses. I am not a little puzzled to find in the whole of this house a safe hiding-place. Don't speak to me of your strong boxes, I will never trust to them. Why, they are just the very things thieves set upon!

SCENE V. HARPAGON

Élise and Cléante are seen talking together at the back of the stage.

Harpagon [*thinking himself alone*]: Meanwhile, I hardly know whether I did right to bury in my garden the ten thousand crowns which were paid to me yesterday. Ten thousand crowns in gold is a sum sufficiently. . . . [*Aside, on perceiving* Élise *and* Cléante *whispering together*] Good heavens! I have betrayed myself; my warmth has carried me away. I believe I spoke aloud while reasoning with myself. [*To* Cléante *and* Élise] What do you want?

Cléante: Nothing, father.

Harpagon: Have you been here long?

Élise: We have only just come.

Harpagon: Did you hear . . . ?

Cléante: What, father?

Harpagon: There . . . !

Cléante: What?
Harpagon: What I was just now saying.
Cléante: No.
Harpagon: You did. I know you did.
Élise: I beg your pardon, father, but we did not.
Harpagon: I see well enough that you overheard a few words. The fact is, I was only talking to myself about the trouble one has nowadays to raise any money; and I was saying that he is a fortunate man who has ten thousand crowns in his house.
Cléante: We were afraid of coming near you, for fear of intruding.
Harpagon: I am very glad to tell you this, so that you may not misinterpret things, and imagine that I said that it was I who have ten thousand crowns.
Cléante: We do not wish to interfere in your affairs.
Harpagon: Would that I had them, these ten thousand crowns!
Cléante: I should not think that. . . .
Harpagon: What a capital affair it would be for me.
Cléante: There are things. . . .
Harpagon: I greatly need them.
Cléante: I fancy that. . . .
Harpagon: It would suit me exceedingly well.
Élise: You are. . . .
Harpagon: And I should not have to complain, as I do now, that the times are bad.
Cléante: Dear me, father, you have no reason to complain; and everyone knows that you are well enough off.
Harpagon: How? I am well enough off! Those who say it are liars. Nothing can be more false; and they are scoundrels who spread such reports.
Élise: Don't be angry.
Harpagon: It is strange that my own children betray me and become my enemies.
Cléante: Is it being your enemy to say that you have wealth?
Harpagon: Yes, it is. Such talk and your extravagant expenses will be the cause that some day thieves will come and cut my throat, in the belief that I am made of gold.
Cléante: What extravagant expenses do I indulge in?
Harpagon: What! Is there anything more scandalous than this sumptuous attire with which you jaunt it about the town? I was remonstrating with your sister yesterday, but you are still worse. It cries vengeance to heaven; and were we to calculate all you are wearing, from head to foot, we should find enough for a good annuity. I have told you a hundred times, my son, that your manners displease me exceedingly; you affect the marquis terribly, and for you to be always dressed as you are, you must certainly rob me.
Cléante: Rob you? And how?
Harpagon: How should I know? Where else could you find money enough to clothe yourself as you do?

Cléante: I, father? I play; and as I am very lucky, I spend in clothes all the money I win.

Harpagon: It is very wrong. If you are lucky at play, you should profit by it, and place the money you win at decent interest, so that you may find it again some day. I should like to know, for instance, without mentioning the rest, what need there is for all these ribbons with which you are decked from head to foot, and if half a dozen tags are not sufficient to fasten your breeches. What necessity is there for anyone to spend money upon wigs, when we have hair of our own growth, which costs nothing. I will lay a wager that, in wigs and ribbons alone, there are certainly twenty pistoles spent, and twenty pistoles brings in at least eighteen livres six sous eight deniers[1] per annum, at only eight per cent interest.

Cléante: You are quite right.

Harpagon: Enough on this subject; let us talk of something else. [*Aside, noticing* Cléante *and* Élise, *who make signs to one another*] I believe they are making signs to one another to pick my pocket. [*Aloud*] What do you mean by those signs?

Élise: We are hesitating as to who shall speak first, for we both have something to tell you.

Harpagon: And I also have something to tell you both.

Cléante: We wanted to speak to you about marriage, father.

Harpagon: The very thing I wish to speak to you about.

Élise: Ah! my father!

Harpagon: What is the meaning of that exclamation? Is it the word, daughter, or the thing itself that frightens you?

Cléante: Marriage may frighten us both according to the way you take it; and our feelings may perhaps not coincide with your choice.

Harpagon: A little patience, if you please. You need not be alarmed. I know what is good for you both, and you will have no reason to complain of anything I intend to do. To begin at the beginning. [*To* Cléante] Do you know, tell me, a young person, called Marianne, who lives not far from here?

Cléante: Yes, father.

Harpagon: And you?

Élise: I have heard her spoken of.

Harpagon: Well, my son, and how do you like the girl?

Cléante: She is very charming.

Harpagon: Her face?

Cléante: Modest and intelligent.

Harpagon: Her air and manner?

Cléante: Perfect, undoubtedly.

Harpagon: Do you not think that such a girl well deserves to be thought of?

Cléante: Yes, father.

---

[1]*pistoles, livres, sous, deniers:* French monetary units.

Harpagon: She would form a very desirable match?
Cléante: Very desirable.
Harpagon: That there is every likelihood of her making a thrifty and careful wife.
Cléante: Certainly.
Harpagon: And that a husband might live very happily with her?
Cléante: I have not the least doubt about it.
Harpagon: There is one little difficulty; I am afraid she has not the fortune we might reasonably expect.
Cléante: Oh, my father, riches are of little importance when one is sure of marrying a virtuous woman.
Harpagon: I beg your pardon. Only there is this to be said: that if we do not find as much money as we could wish, we may make it up in something else.
Cléante: That follows as a matter of course.
Harpagon: Well, I must say that I am very much pleased to find that you entirely agree with me, for her modest manner and her gentleness have won my heart; and I have made up my mind to marry her, provided I find she has some dowry.
Cléante: Eh!
Harpagon: What now?
Cléante: You are resolved, you say . . . ?
Harpagon: To marry Marianne.
Cléante: Who? you? you?
Harpagon: Yes, I, I, I. What does all this mean?
Cléante: I feel a sudden dizziness, and I must withdraw for a little while.
Harpagon: It will be nothing. Go quickly into the kitchen and drink a large glass of cold water, it will soon set you all right again.

Scene VI. Harpagon, Élise

Harpagon: There goes one of your effeminate fops, with no more stamina than a chicken. That is what I have resolved for myself, my daughter. As to your brother, I have thought for him of a certain widow, of whom I heard this morning; and you I shall give to Mr. Anselme.
Élise: To Mr. Anselme?
Harpagon: Yes, a staid and prudent man, who is not above fifty, and of whose riches everybody speaks.
Élise [*curtseying*]: I have no wish to marry, father, if you please.
Harpagon [*imitating* Élise]: And I, my little girl, my darling, I wish you to marry, if you please.
Élise [*curtseying again*]: I beg your pardon, my father.
Harpagon [*again imitating* Élise]: I beg your pardon, my daughter.
Élise: I am the very humble servant of Mr. Anselme, but [*curtseying again*], with your leave, I shall not marry him.
Harpagon: I am your very humble servant, but [*again imitating* Élise] you will marry him this very evening.
Élise: This evening?

Harpagon: This evening.
Élise [*curtseying again*]: It cannot be done, father.
Harpagon [*imitating* Élise]: It will be done, daughter.
Élise: No.
Harpagon: Yes.
Élise: No, I tell you.
Harpagon: Yes, I tell you.
Élise: You will never force me to do such a thing
Harpagon: I will force you to it.
Élise: I had rather kill myself than marry such a man.
Harpagon: You will not kill yourself, and you will marry him. But did you ever see such impudence? Did ever any one hear a daughter speak in such a fashion to her father?
Élise: But did ever anyone see a father marry his daughter after such a fashion?
Harpagon: It is a match against which nothing can be said, and I am perfectly sure that everybody will approve of my choice.
Élise: And I know that it will be approved of by no reasonable person.
Harpagon [*seeing* Valère]: There is Valère coming. Shall we make him judge in this affair?
Élise: Willingly.
Harpagon: You will abide by what he says?
Élise: Yes, whatever he thinks right, I will do.
Harpagon: Agreed.

SCENE VII. VALÈRE, HARPAGON, ÉLISE

Harpagon: Valère, we have chosen you to decide who is in the right, my daughter or I.
Valère: It is certainly you, Sir.
Harpagon: But have you any idea of what we are talking about?
Valère: No; but you could not be in the wrong; you are reason itself.
Harpagon: I want to give her tonight, for a husband, a man as rich as he is good; and the hussy tells me to my face that she scorns to take him. What do you say to that?
Valère: What do I say to it?
Harpagon: Yes?
Valère: Eh! eh!
Harpagon: What?
Valère: I say that I am, upon the whole, of your opinion, and that you cannot but be right; yet, perhaps, she is not altogether wrong; and. . . .
Harpagon: How so? Mr. Anselme is an excellent match; he is a nobleman, and a gentleman too; of simple habits, and extremely well off. He has no children left from his first marriage. Could she meet with anything more suitable?
Valère: It is true. But she might say that you are going rather fast, and that she ought to have at least a little time to consider whether her inclination could reconcile itself to. . . .

Harpagon: It is an opportunity I must not allow to slip through my fingers. I find an advantage here which I should not find elsewhere, and he agrees to take her without dowry.

Valère: Without dowry?

Harpagon: Yes.

Valère: Ah! I have nothing more to say. A more convincing reason could not be found; and she must yield to that.

Harpagon: It is a considerable saving to me.

Valère: Undoubtedly; this admits of no contradiction. It is true that your daughter might represent to you that marriage is a more serious affair than people are apt to believe; that the happiness or misery of a whole life depends on it, and that an engagement which is to last till death ought not to be entered into without great consideration.

Harpagon: Without dowry!

Valère: That must of course decide everything. There are certainly people who might tell you that on such occasions the wishes of a daughter are no doubt to be considered, and that this great disparity of age, of disposition, and of feelings might be the cause of many an unpleasant thing in a married life.

Harpagon: Without dowry!

Valère: Ah! it must be granted that there is no reply to that; who in the world could think otherwise? I do not mean to say but that there are many fathers who would set a much higher value on the happiness of their daughter than on the money they may have to give for their marriage; who would not like to sacrifice them to their own interests, and who would, above all things, try to see in a marriage that sweet conformity of tastes which is a sure pledge of honour, tranquility and joy; and that. . . .

Harpagon: Without dowry!

Valère: That is true; nothing more can be said. Without dowry. How can anyone resist such arguments?

Harpagon [*aside, looking towards the garden*]: Ah! I fancy I hear a dog barking. Is anyone after my money? [*To* Valère] Stop here, I'll come back directly.

SCENE VIII. ÉLISE, VALÈRE

Élise: Surely, Valère, you are not in earnest when you speak to him in that manner?

Valère: I do it that I may not vex him, and the better to secure my ends. To resist him boldly would simply spoil everything. There are certain people who are only to be managed by indirect means, temperaments averse from all resistance, restive natures whom truth causes to rear, who always kick when we would lead them on the right road of reason, and who can only be led by a way opposed to that by which you wish them to go. Pretend to comply with his wishes; you are much more likely to succeed in the end, and. . . .

Élise: But this marriage, Valère?

Valère: We will find some pretext for breaking it off.

Élise: But what pretext can we find if it is to be concluded tonight?

Valère: You must ask to have it delayed, and must feign some illness or other.

Élise: But he will soon discover the truth if they call in the doctor.

Valère: Not a bit of it. Do you imagine that a doctor understands what he is about? Nonsense! Don't be afraid. Believe me, you may complain of any disease you please, the doctor will be at no loss to explain to you from what it proceeds.

SCENE IX. HARPAGON, ÉLISE, VALÈRE

Harpagon [*alone, at the farther end of the stage*]: It is nothing, thank heaven!

Valère [*not seeing* Harpagon]: In short, flight is the last resource we have left us to avoid all this; and if your love, dear Élise, is as strong as. . . . [*Seeing* Harpagon] Yes, a daughter is bound to obey her father. She has no right to inquire what a husband offered to her is like, and when the most important question, "without dowry," presents itself, she should accept anybody that is given her.

Harpagon: Good; that was beautifully said!

Valère: I beg your pardon, Sir, if I carry it a little too far, and take upon myself to speak to her as I do.

Harpagon: Why, I am delighted, and I wish you to have her entirely under your control. [*To* Élise] Yes, you may run away as much as you like. I give him all the authority over you that heaven has given me, and I will have you do all that he tells you.

Valère: After that, resist all my expostulations, if you can.

SCENE X. HARPAGON, VALÈRE

Valère: I will follow her, Sir, if you will allow me, and will continue the lecture I was giving her.

Harpagon: Yes, do so; you will oblige me greatly.

Valère: She ought to be kept in with a tight hand.

Harpagon: Quite true, you must. . . .

Valère: Do not be afraid; I believe I shall end by convincing her.

Harpagon: Do so, do so. I am going to take a short stroll in the town, and I will come back again presently.

Valère [*going towards the door through which* Élise *left, and speaking as if it were to her*]: Yes, money is more precious than anything else in the world, and you should thank heaven that you have so worthy a man for a father. He knows what life is. When a man offers to marry a girl without a dowry, we ought to look no farther. Everything is comprised in that, and "without dowry" compensates for want of beauty, youth, birth, honour, wisdom, and probity.

Harpagon: Ah! the honest fellow! he speaks like an oracle. Happy is he who can secure such a servant!

ACT II

SCENE I. CLÈANTE, LA FLÈCHE

Clèante: How now, you rascal! where have you been hiding? Did I not give you orders to . . . ?

La Flèche: Yes, Sir, and I came here resolved to wait for you without stirring, but your father, that most ungracious of men, drove me into the street in spite of myself, and I well nigh got a good drubbing into the bargain.

Clèante: How is our affair progressing? Things arc worse than ever for us, and since I left you, I have discovered that my own father is my rival.

La Flèche: Your father in love?

Clèante: It seems so; and I found it very difficult to hide from him what I felt at such a discovery.

La Flèche: He meddling with love! What the deuce is he thinking of? Does he mean to set everybody at defiance? And is love made for people of his build?

Clèante: It is to punish me for my sins that this passion has entered his head.

La Flèche: But why do you hide your love from him?

Clèante: That he may not suspect anything, and to make it more easy for me to fall back, if need be, upon some device to prevent this marriage. What answer did you receive?

La Flèche: Indeed, Sir, those who borrow are much to be pitied, and we must put up with strange things when, like you, we are forced to pass through the hands of the usurers.

Clèante: Then the affair won't come off?

La Flèche: Excuse me; Mr. Simon, the broker who was recommended to us, is a very active and zealous fellow, and says he has left no stone unturned to help you. He assures me that your looks alone have won his heart.

Clèante: Shall I have the fifteen thousand francs which I want?

La Flèche: Yes, but under certain trifling conditions, which you must accept if you wish the bargain to be concluded.

Clèante: Did you speak to the man who is to lend the money?

La Flèche: Oh! dear no. Things are not done in that way. He is still more anxious than you to remain unknown. These things are greater mysteries than you think. His name is not by any means to be divulged, and he is to be introduced to you today at a house provided by him, so that he may hear from yourself all about your position and your family; and I have not the least doubt that the mere name of your father will be sufficient to accomplish what you wish.

Clèante: Particularly as my mother is dead, and they cannot deprive me of what I inherit from her.

La Flèche: Well, here are some of the conditions which he has himself dictated to our go-between for you to take cognisance of, before anything is begun.

"Supposing that the lender is satisfied with all his securities, and that the borrower is of age and of a family whose property is ample, solid, secure, and free from all incumbrances, there shall be drawn up a good and correct bond before as honest a notary as it is possible to find, and who for this purpose shall be chosen by the lender, because he is the more concerned of the two that the bond should be rightly executed."

Clèante: There is nothing to say against that.

La Flèche: "The lender, not to burden his conscience with the least scruple, does not wish to lend his money at more than five and a half per cent."

Clèante: Five and a half per cent? By Jove, that's honest! We have nothing to complain of,

La Flèche: That's true.

"But as the said lender has not in hand the sum required, and as, in order to oblige the borrower, he is himself obliged to borrow from another at the rate of twenty per cent., it is but right that the said first borrower shall pay this interest, without detriment to the rest; since it is only to oblige him that the said lender is himself forced to borrow."

Clèante: The deuce! What a Jew! what a Turk we have here! That is more than twenty-five per cent.

La Flèche: That's true; and it is the remark I made. It is for you to consider the matter before you act.

Clèante: How can I consider? I want the money, and I must therefore accept everything.

La Flèche: That is exactly what I answered.

Clèante: Is there anything else?

La Flèche: Only a small item.

"Of the fifteen thousand francs which are demanded, the lender will only be able to count down twelve thousand in hard cash; instead of the remaining three thousand, the borrower will have to take the chattels, clothing, and jewels, contained in the following catalogue, and which the said lender has put in all good faith at the lowest possible figure."

Clèante: What is the meaning of all that?

La Flèche: I'll go through the catalogue:—

"Firstly: —A fourpost bedstead, with hangings of Hungary lace very elegantly trimmed with olive-coloured cloth, and six chairs and a counterpane to match; the whole in very good condition, and lined with soft red and blue shot-silk. Item: —the tester of good pale pink Aumale serge, with the small and the large fringes of silk."

Clèante: What does he want me to do with all this?

La Flèche: Wait.

"Item: —Tapestry hangings representing the loves of Gombaud and Macée. Item: —A large walnut table with twelve columns or turned legs, which draws out at both ends, and is provided beneath with six stools."

Clèante: Hang it all! What am I to do with all this?

La Flèche: Have patience.

"Item: —Three large matchlocks inlaid with mother-of-pearl, with rests to correspond. Item: —A brick furnace with two retorts and three receivers, very useful to those who have any taste for distilling."

Clèante: You will drive me crazy.

La Flèche: Gently!

"Item: —A Bologna lute with all its strings, or nearly all. Item: —A pigeon-hole table and a draught-board, and a game of mother goose, restored from the Greeks, most useful to pass the time when one has nothing to do. Item: —A lizard's skin, three feet and a half in length, stuffed with hay, a pleasing curiosity to hang on the ceiling of a room. The whole of the above-mentioned articles are really worth more than four thousand five hundred francs, and are reduced to the value of a thousand crowns through the considerateness of the lender."

Clèante: Let the plague choke him with his considerateness, the wretch, the cut-throat that he is! Did ever anyone hear of such usury? Is he not satisfied with the outrageous interest he asks that he must force me to take, instead of the three thousand francs, all the old rubbish which he picks up. I shan't get two hundred crowns for all that, and yet I must bring myself to yield to all his wishes; for he is in a position to force me to accept everything, and he has me, the villain, with a knife at my throat.

La Flèche: I see you, Sir, if you'll forgive my saying so, on the high-road followed by Panurge[2] to ruin himself—taking money in advance, buying dear, selling cheap, and cutting your corn while it is still grass.

Clèante: What would you have me do? It is to this that young men are reduced by the accursed avarice of their fathers; and people are astonished after that, that sons long for their death.

La Flèche: No one can deny that yours would excite against his meanness the most quiet of men. I have not, thank God, any inclination gallows-ward, and among my colleagues whom I see dabbling in various doubtful affairs, I know well enough how to keep myself out of hot water, and how to keep clear of all those things which savour ever so little of the ladder; but to tell you the truth, he almost gives me, by his ways of going on, the desire of robbing him, and I should think that in doing so I was doing a meritorious action.

Clèante: Give me that memorandum that I may have another look at it.

Scene II. Harpagon, Mr. Simon

Cléante *and* La Flèche *at the back of the stage.*

Mr. Simon: Yes, Sir; it is a young man who is greatly in want of money; his affairs force him to find some at any cost, and he will submit to all your conditions.

---

[2]*Panurge:* A crafty, cowardly character in François Rabelais's sixteenth-century satire *Gargantua and Pantagruel.*

Harpagon: But are you sure, Mr. Simon, that there is no risk to run in this case? and do you know the name, the property, and the family of him for whom you speak?

Mr. Simon: No; I cannot tell you anything for certain, as it was by mere chance that I was made acquainted with him; but he will tell you everything himself, and his servant has assured me that you will be quite satisfied when you know who he is. All I can tell you is that his family is said to be very wealthy, that he has already lost his mother, and that he will pledge you his word, if you insist upon it, that his father will die before eight months are passed.

Harpagon: That is something. Charity, Mr. Simon, demands of us to gratify people whenever we have it in our power.

Mr. Simon: Evidently.

La Flèche [*aside to* Cléante, *on recognising* Mr. Simon]: What does this mean? Mr. Simon talking with your father!

Clèante [*aside to* La Flèche]: Has he been told who I am, and would you be capable of betraying me?

Mr. Simon [*to* Cléante *and* La Flèche]: Ah! you are in good time! But who told you to come here? [*To* Harpagon] It was certainly not I who told them your name and address; but I am of opinion that there is no great harm done; they are people who can be trusted, and you can come to some understanding together.

Harpagon: What!

Mr. Simon [*showing* Cléante]: This is the gentleman who wants to borrow the fifteen thousand francs of which I have spoken to you.

Harpagon: What! miscreant! is it you who abandon yourself to such excesses?

Clèante: What! father! is it you who stoop to such shameful deeds?

Mr. Simon *runs away, and* La Flèche *hides himself.*

SCENE III. HARPAGON, CLÈANTE

Harpagon: It is you who are ruining yourself by loans so greatly to be condemned!

Clèante: So it is you who seek to enrich yourself by such criminal usury!

Harpagon: And you dare, after that, to show yourself before me?

Clèante: And you dare, after that, to show yourself to the world?

Harpagon: Are you not ashamed, tell me, to descend to these wild excesses, to rush headlong into frightful expenses, and disgracefully to dissipate the wealth which your parents have amassed with so much toil.

Clèante: Are you not ashamed of dishonouring your station by such dealings, of sacrificing honour and reputation to the insatiable desire of heaping crown upon crown, and of outdoing the most infamous devices that have ever been invented by the most notorious usurers?

Harpagon: Get out of my sight, you reprobate; get out of my sight!

Clèante: Who is the more criminal in your opinion: he who buys the money of which he stands in need, or he who obtains, by unfair means, money for which he has no use?

Harpagon: Begone, I say, and do not provoke me to anger. [*Alone*] After all, I am not very much vexed at this adventure; it will be a lesson to me to keep a better watch over all his doings.

SCENE IV. FROSINE, HARPAGON

Frosine: Sir.

Harpagon: Wait a moment, I will come back and speak to you. [*Aside*] I had better go and see a little after my money.

SCENE V. LA FLÈCHE, FROSINE

La Flèche [*without seeing* Frosine]: The adventure is most comical. Hidden somewhere he must have a large store of goods of all kinds, for the list did not contain one single article which either of us recognised.

Frosine: Hallo! is it you, my poor La Flèche? How is it we meet here?

La Flèche: Ah! ah! it is you, Frosine; and what have you come to do here?

Frosine: What have I come to do? Why! what I do everywhere else, busy myself about other people's affairs, make myself useful to the community in general, and profit as much as I possibly can by the small talent I possess. Must we not live by our wits in this world? and what other resources have people like me but intrigue and cunning?

La Flèche: Have you, then, any business with the master of this house?

Frosine: Yes. I am transacting for him a certain small matter for which he is pretty sure to give me a reward.

La Flèche: He give you a reward! Ah! ah! Upon my word, you will be 'cute if you ever get one, and I warn you that ready money is very scarce hereabouts.

Frosine: That may be, but there are certain services which wonderfully touch our feelings.

La Flèche: Your humble servant; but as yet you don't know Harpagon. Harpagon is the human being of all human beings the least humane, the mortal of all mortals the hardest and closest. There is no service great enough to induce him to open his purse. If, indeed, you want praise, esteem, kindness, and friendship, you are welcome to any amount; but money, that's a different affair. There is nothing more dry, more barren, than his favour and his good grace, and "give" is a word for which be has such a strong dislike that he never says "I give," but "I lend, you a good morning."

Frosine: That's all very well; but I know the art of fleecing men. I have a secret of touching their affections by flattering their hearts, and of finding out their weak points.

La Flèche: All useless here. I defy you to soften, as far as money is concerned, the man we are speaking of. He is a Turk on that point, of a Turkishness to drive anyone to despair, and we might starve in his presence and never a peg would he stir. In short, he loves money better than reputation, honour, and virtue, and the mere sight of anyone making demands upon his purse sends him into convulsions; it is like striking him in a vital place, it is piercing him to the heart, it is like tearing out his very bowels! And if . . . But here he comes again; I leave you.

Scene VI. Harpagon, Frosine

Harpagon [*aside*]: All is as it should be. [*To* Frosine] Well, what is it, Frosine?

Frosine: Bless me, how well you look! You are the very picture of health.

Harpagon: Who? I?

Frosine: Never have I seen you looking more rosy, more hearty.

Harpagon: Are you in earnest?

Frosine: Why! you have never been so young in your life; and I know many a man of twenty-five who looks much older than you do.

Harpagon: And yet, Frosine, I have passed threescore.

Frosine: Threescore! Well, and what then? You don't mean to make a trouble of that, do you? It's the very flower of manhood, the threshold of the prime of life.

Harpagon: True; but twenty years less would do me no harm, I think.

Frosine: Nonsense! You've no need of that, and you are of a build to last out a hundred.

Harpagon: Do you really think so?

Frosine: Decidedly. You have all the appearance of it. Hold yourself up a little. Ah! what a sign of long life is that line there straight between your two eyes!

Harpagon: You know all about that, do you?

Frosine: I should think I do. Show me your hand. Dear me, what a line of life there is there!

Harpagon: Where?

Frosine: Don't you see how far this line goes?

Harpagon: Well, and what does it mean?

Frosine: What does it mean? There . . . I said a hundred years; but no, it is one hundred and twenty I ought to have said.

Harpagon: Is it possible?

Frosine: I tell you they will have to kill you, and you will bury your children and your children's children.

Harpagon: So much the better! And what news of our affair?

Frosine: Is there any need to ask? Did ever anyone see me begin anything and not succeed in it? I have, especially for matchmaking, the most wonderful talent. There are no two persons in the world I could not couple together; and I believe that, if I took it into my head, I could make the Grand Turk marry the Republic of Venice. But we had, to be sure, no such difficult thing to achieve in this matter. As I know the ladies very well, I told them every particular about you; and I acquainted the mother with your intentions towards Marianne since you saw her pass in the street and enjoy the fresh air out of her window.

Harpagon: What did she answer . . . ?

Frosine: She received your proposal with great joy; and when I told her that you wished very much that her daughter should come tonight to assist at the marriage contract which is to be signed for your own daughter, she assented at once, and entrusted her to me for the purpose.

Harpagon: You see, Frosine, I am obliged to give some supper to Mr. Anselme, and I should like her to have a share in the feast.

Frosine: You are quite right. She is to come after dinner to pay a visit to your daughter; then she means to go from here to the fair, and return to your house just in time for supper.

Harpagon: That will do very well; they shall go together in my carriage, which I will lend them.

Frosine: That will suit her perfectly.

Harpagon: But I say, Frosine, have you spoken to the mother about the dowry she can give her daughter? Did you make her understand that under such circumstances she ought to do her utmost and to make a great sacrifice? For, after all, one does not marry a girl without her bringing something with her.

Frosine: How something! She is a girl who will bring you a clear twelve thousand francs a year?

Harpagon: Twelve thousand francs a year?

Frosine: Yes! To begin with, she has been nursed and brought up with the strictest notions of frugality. She is a girl accustomed to live upon salad, milk, cheese, and apples, and who consequently will require neither a well served up table, nor any rich broth, nor your everlasting peeled barley; none, in short, of all those delicacies that another woman would want. This is no small matter, and may well amount to three thousand francs yearly. Besides this, she only cares for simplicity and neatness; she will have none of those splendid dresses and rich jewels, none of that sumptuous furniture in which girls like her indulge so extravagantly; and this item is worth more than four thousand francs per annum. Lastly, she has the deepest aversion to gambling; and this is not very common nowadays among women. Why, I know of one in our neighbourhood who lost at least twenty thousand francs this year. But let us reckon only a fourth of that sum. Five thousand francs a year at play and four thousand in clothes and jewels make nine thousand; and three thousand francs which we count for food, does it not make your twelve thousand francs?

Harpagon: Yes, that's not bad; but, after all, that calculation has nothing real in it.

Frosine: Excuse me; is it nothing real to bring you in marriage a great sobriety, to inherit a great love for simplicity in dress, and the acquired property of a great hatred for gambling?

Harpagon: It is a farce to pretend to make up a dowry with all the expenses she will not run into. I could not give a receipt for what I do not receive; and I must decidedly get something.

Frosine: Bless me! you will get enough; and they have spoken to me of a certain country where they have some property, of which you will be master.

Harpagon: We shall have to see to that. But, Frosine, there is one more thing that makes me uneasy. The girl is young, you know; and young people generally like those who are young like themselves, and only care for the society of the young. I am afraid that a man of my age may not exactly suit her taste, and that this may occasion in my family certain complications that would in nowise be pleasant to me.

Frosine: Oh, how badly you judge her! This is one more peculiarity of which I had to speak to you. She has the greatest detestation to all young men, and only likes old people.

Harpagon: Does she?

Frosine: I should like you to hear her talk on that subject; she cannot bear at all the sight of a young man, and nothing delights her more than to see a fine old man with a venerable beard. The oldest are to her the most charming, and I warn you beforehand not to go and make yourself any younger than you really are. She wishes for one sixty years old at least; and it is not more than six months ago that on the very eve of being married she suddenly broke off the match on learning that her lover was only fifty-six years of age, and did not put on spectacles to sign the contract.

Harpagon: Only for that?

Frosine: Yes; she says there is no pleasure with a man of fifty-six; and she has a decided affection for those who wear spectacles.

Harpagon: Well, this is quite new to me.

Frosine: No one can imagine how far she carries this. She has in her room a few pictures and engravings, and what do you imagine they are? An Adonis, a Cephalus, a Paris, an Apollo? Not a bit of it! Fine portraits of Saturn, of King Priam, of old Nestor, and of good father Anchises[3] on his son's shoulders.

Harpagon: That's admirable. I should never have guessed such a thing; and I am very pleased to hear that she has such taste as this. Indeed had I been a woman, I should never have loved young fellows.

Frosine: I should think not. Fine trumpery indeed, these young men, for any one to fall in love with. Fine jackanapes and puppies for a woman to hanker after. I should like to know what relish anyone can find in them?

Harpagon: Truly; I don't understand it myself, and I cannot make out how it is that some women dote so on them.

Frosine: They must be downright idiots. Can any one be in his senses who thinks youth amiable? Can those curly-pated coxcombs be men, and can one really get attached to such animals?

Harpagon: Exactly what I say every day! With their effeminate voices, their three little bits of a beard turned up like cat's whiskers, their tow wigs, their flowing breeches and open breasts!

---

[3]*Adonis . . . Anchises:* The first set of mythological characters are handsome young lovers; the second set are older men.

Frosine: Yes; they are famous guys compared with yourself. In you we see something like a man. There is enough to satisfy the eye. It is thus that one should be made and dressed to inspire love.

Harpagon: Then you think I am pretty well?

Frosine: Pretty well! I should think so; you are charming, and your face would make a beautiful picture. Turn round a little, if you please. You could not find anything better anywhere. Let me see you walk. You have a well-shaped body, free and easy, as it should be, and one which gives no sign of infirmity.

Harpagon: I have nothing the matter to speak of, I am thankful to say. It is only my cough, which returns from time to time.

Frosine: That is nothing, and coughing becomes you exceedingly well.

Harpagon: Tell me, Frosine, has Marianne seen me yet? Has she not noticed me when I passed by?

Frosine: No; but we have had many conversations about you. I gave her an exact description of your person, and I did not fail to make the most of your merit, and to show her what an advantage it would be to have a husband like you.

Harpagon: You did right, and I thank you very much for it.

Frosine: I have, Sir, a small request to make to you. I am in danger of losing a lawsuit for want of a little money [Harpagon *looks grave*], and you can easily help me with it, if you have pity upon me. You cannot imagine how happy she will be to see you. [Harpagon *looks joyful.*] Oh! how sure you are to please her, and how sure that antique ruff of yours is to produce a wonderful effect on her mind. But, above all, she will be delighted with your breeches fastened to your doublet with tags; that will make her mad after you, and a lover who wears tags will be most welcome to her.

Harpagon: You send me into raptures, Frosine, by saying that.

Frosine: I tell you the truth, Sir; this lawsuit is of the utmost importance for me. [Harpagon *looks serious again.*] If I lose it, I am for ever ruined; but a very small sum will save me. I should like you to have seen the happiness she felt when I spoke of you to her. [Harpagon *looks pleased again.*] Joy sparkled in her eyes while I told her of all your good qualities; and I succeeded, in short, in making her look forward with the greatest impatience to the conclusion of the match.

Harpagon: You have given me great pleasure, Frosine, and I assure you I. . . .

Frosine: I beg of you, Sir, to grant me the little assistance I ask of you. [Harpagon *again looks grave.*] It will put me on my feet again, and I shall feel grateful to you for ever.

Harpagon: Good-bye; I must go and finish my correspondence.

Frosine: I assure you, Sir, that you could not help me in a more pressing necessity.

Harpagon: I will see that my carriage is ready to take you to the fair.

Frosine: I would not importune you so if I were not compelled by necessity.

Harpagon: And I will see that we have supper early, so that nobody may be ill.

Frosine: Do not refuse me the service; I beg of you. You can hardly believe, Sir, the pleasure that. . . .

Harpagon: I must go; somebody is calling me. We shall see each other again by and by.

Frosine [*alone*]: May the fever seize you, you stingy cur, and send you to the devil and his angels! The miser has held out against all my attacks; but I must not drop the negotiation; for I have the other side, and there, at all events, I am sure of a good reward.

ACT III

SCENE I. HARPAGON, CLÉANTE, ÉLISE, VALÈRE, DAME CLAUDE [*HOLDING A BROOM*], MASTER JACQUES, LA MERLUCHE, BRINDAVOINE

Harpagon: Here, come here, all of you; I must give you orders for by and by, and arrange what each one will have to do. Come nearer, Dame Claude; let us begin with you. [*Looking at her broom.*] Good; you are ready armed, I see. To you I commit the care of cleaning up everywhere; but, above all, be very careful not to rub the furniture too hard, for fear of wearing it out. Besides this, I put the bottles under your care during supper, and if any one of them is missing, or if anything gets broken, you will be responsible for it, and pay it out of your wages.

Jacques [*aside*]: A shrewd punishment that.

Harpagon [*to* Dame Claude]: Now you may go.

SCENE II. HARPAGON, CLÉANTE, ÉLISE, VALÈRE, MASTER JACQUES, BRINDAVOINE, LA MERLUCHE

Harpagon: To you, Brindavoine, and to you, La Merluche, belongs the duty of washing the glasses, and of giving to drink, but only when people are thirsty, and not according to the custom of certain impertinent lackeys, who urge them to drink, and put the idea into their heads when they are not thinking about it. Wait until you have been asked several times, and remember always to have plenty of water.

Jacques [*aside*]: Yes; wine without water gets into one's head.

La Merluche: Shall we take off our smocks, Sir?

Harpagon: Yes, when you see the guests coming; but be very careful not to spoil your clothes.

Brindavoine: You know, Sir, that one of the fronts of my doublet is covered with a large stain of oil from the lamp.

La Merluche: And I, Sir, that my breeches are all torn behind, and that, saving your presence. . . .

Harpagon [*to* La Merluche]: Peace! Turn carefully towards the wall, and always face the company. [*To* Brindavoine, *showing him how he is to hold his hat*

before his doublet, to hide the stain of oil] And you, always hold your hat in this fashion when you wait on the guests.

SCENE III. HARPAGON, CLÉANTE, ÉLISE, VALÈRE, MASTER JACQUES

Harpagon: As for you, my daughter, you will look after all that is cleared off the table, and see that nothing is wasted: this care is very becoming to young girls. Meanwhile get ready to welcome my lady-love, who is coming this afternoon to pay you a visit, and will take you off to the fair with her. Do you understand what I say?

Élise: Yes, father.

SCENE IV. HARPAGON, CLÉANTE, VALÈRE, MASTER JACQUES

Harpagon: And you, my young dandy of a son to whom I have the kindness of forgiving what happened this morning, mind you don't receive her coldly, or show her a sour face.

Cléante: Receive her coldly! And why should I?

Harpagon: Why? why? We know pretty well the ways of children whose fathers marry again, and the looks they give to those we call stepmothers. But if you wish me to forget your last offence, I advise you, above all things, to receive her kindly, and, in short, to give her the heartiest welcome you can.

Cléante: To speak the truth, father, I cannot promise you that I am very happy to see her become my stepmother; but as to receiving her properly, and as to giving her a kind welcome, I promise to obey you in that to the very letter.

Harpagon: Be careful you do, at least.

Cléante: You will see that you have no cause to complain.

Harpagon: You will do wisely.

SCENE V. HARPAGON, VALÈRE, MASTER JACQUES

Harpagon: Valère, you will have to give me your help in this business. Now, Master Jacques, I kept you for the last.

Jacques: Is it to your coachman, Sir, or to your cook you want to speak, for I am both the one and the other?

Harpagon: To both.

Jacques: But to which of the two first?

Harpagon: To the cook.

Jacques: Then wait a minute, if you please.

Jacques takes off his stable-coat and appears dressed as a cook.

Harpagon: What the deuce is the meaning of this ceremony?

Jacques: Now I am at your service.

Harpagon: I have engaged myself, Master Jacques, to give a supper tonight.

Jacques [*aside*]: Wonderful!

Harpagon: Tell me, can you give us a good supper?
Jacques: Yes, if you give me plenty of money.
Harpagon: The deuce! Always money! I think they have nothing else to say except money, money, money! Always that same word in their mouth, money! They always speak of money! It's their pillow companion, money!
Valère: Never did I hear such an impertinent answer! Would you call it wonderful to provide good cheer with plenty of money? Is it not the easiest thing in the world? The most stupid could do as much. But a clever man should talk of a good supper with little money.
Jacques: A good supper with little money?
Valère: Yes.
Jacques [*to* Valère]: Indeed, Mr. Steward, you will oblige me greatly by telling me your secret, and also, if you like, by filling my place as cook; for you keep on meddling here, and want to be everything.
Harpagon: Hold your tongue. What shall we want?
Jacques: Ask that of Mr. Steward, who will give you good cheer with little money.
Harpagon: Do you hear? I am speaking to you, and expect you to answer me.
Jacques: How many will there be at your table?
Harpagon: Eight or ten; but you must only reckon for eight. When there is enough for eight, there is enough for ten.
Valère: That is evident.
Jacques: Very well, then; you must have four tureens of soup and five side dishes; soups, entrées. . . .
Harpagon: What! do you mean to feed a whole town?
Jacques: Roast. . . .
Harpagon [*clapping his hand on* Master Jacques' *mouth*]: Ah! Wretch! you are eating up all my substance.
Jacques: Entremêts. . . .
Harpagon [*again putting his hand on* Jacques' *mouth*]: More still?
Valère [*to* Jacques]: Do you mean to kill everybody? And has your master invited people in order to destroy them with over-feeding? Go and read a little the precepts of health, and ask the doctors if there is anything so hurtful to man as excess in eating.
Harpagon: He is perfectly right.
Valère: Know, Master Jacques, you and people like you, that a table overloaded with eatables is a real cut-throat; that, to be the true friends of those we invite, frugality should reign throughout the repast we give, and that according to the saying of one of the ancients,[4] "We must eat to live, and not live to eat."
Harpagon: Ah! How well the man speaks! Come near, let me embrace you for this last saying. It is the finest sentence that I have ever heard in my life: "We must live to eat, and not eat to live." No; that isn't it. How do you say it?

---

[4]*one of the ancients*: Valère is referring to Socrates.

Valère: That we must eat to live, and not live to eat.

Harpagon [*to* Master Jacques]: Yes. Do you hear that? [*To* Valère] Who is the great man who said that?

Valère: I do not exactly recollect his name just now.

Harpagon: Remember to write down those words for me. I will have them engraved in letters of gold over the mantel-piece of my dining-room.

Valère: I will not fail. As for your supper, you had better let me manage it. I will see that it is all as it should be.

Harpagon: Do so.

Jacques: So much the better; all the less work for me.

Harpagon [*to* Valère]: We must have some of those things of which it is not possible to eat much, and that satisfy directly. Some good fat beans, and a pâté well stuffed with chestnuts.

Valère: Trust to me.

Harpagon: Now, Master Jacques, you must clean my carriage.

Jacques: Wait a moment; this is to the coachman. [Jacques *puts on his coat.*] You say. . . .

Harpagon: That you must clean my carriage, and have my horses ready to drive to the fair.

Jacques: Your horses! Upon my word, Sir, they are not at all in a condition to stir. I won't tell you that they are laid up, for the poor things have got nothing to lie upon, and it would not be telling the truth. But you make them keep such rigid fasts that they are nothing but phantoms, ideas, and mere shadows of horses.

Harpagon: They are much to be pitied. They have nothing to do.

Jacques: And because they have nothing to do, must they have nothing to eat? It would be much better for them, poor things, to work much and eat to correspond. It breaks my heart to see them so reduced; for, in short, I love my horses; and when I see them suffer, it seems as if it were myself. Every day I take the bread out of my own mouth to feed them; and it is being too hard-hearted, Sir, to have no compassion upon one's neighbour.

Harpagon: It won't be very hard work to go to the fair.

Jacques: No, Sir. I haven't the heart to drive them; it would go too much against my conscience to use the whip to them in the state they are in. How could you expect them to drag a carriage? They have not even strength enough to drag themselves along.

Valère: Sir, I will ask our neighbour, Picard, to drive them; particularly as we shall want his help to get the supper ready.

Jacques: Be it so. I had much rather they should die under another's hand than under mine.

Valère: Master Jacques is mightily considerate.

Jacques: Mr. Steward is mightily indispensable.

Harpagon: Peace.

Jacques: Sir, I can't bear these flatteries, and I can see that, whatever this man does, his continual watching after the bread, wine, wood, salt, and candles, is done but to curry favour and to make his court to you. I am indignant to see it all; and I am sorry to hear every day what is said of you; for, after all, I have a certain tenderness for you; and, except my horses, you are the person I like most in the world.

Harpagon: And I would know from you, Master Jacques, what it is that is said of me.

Jacques: Yes, certainly, Sir, if I were sure you would not get angry with me.

Harpagon: No, no; never fear.

Jacques: Excuse me, but I am sure you will be angry.

Harpagon: No, on the contrary, you will oblige me. I should be glad to know what people say of me.

Jacques: Since you wish it, Sir, I will tell you frankly that you are the laughing-stock of everybody; that they taunt us everywhere by a thousand jokes on your account, and that nothing delights people more than to make sport of you, and to tell stories without end about your stinginess. One says that you have special almanacks printed, where you double the ember days and vigils, so that you may profit by the fasts to which you bind all your house; another, that you always have a ready-made quarrel for your servants at Christmas time or when they leave you, so that you may give them nothing. One tells a story how not long since you prosecuted a neighbour's cat because it had eaten up the remainder of a leg of mutton; another says that one night you were caught stealing your horses' oats, and that your coachman,—that is the man who was before me,—gave you, in the dark, a good sound drubbing, of which you said nothing. In short, what is the use of going on? We can go nowhere but we are sure to hear you pulled to pieces. You are the butt and jest and byword of everybody; and never does anyone mention you but under the names of miser, stingy, mean, niggardly fellow and usurer.

Harpagon [*beating* Jacques]: You are a fool, a rascal, a scoundrel, and an impertinent wretch.

Jacques: There, there! Did not I know how it would be? You would not believe me. I told you I should make you angry if I spoke the truth?

Harpagon: Learn how to speak.

SCENE VI. VALÈRE, MASTER JACQUES

Valère [*laughing*]: Well, Master Jacques, your frankness is badly rewarded, I fear.

Jacques: S'death! Mr. Upstart, you who assume the man of consequence, it is no business of yours as far as I can see. Laugh at your own cudgelling when you get it, and don't come here and laugh at mine.

Valère: Ah! Master Jacques, don't get into a passion, I beg of you.

Jacques [*aside*]: He is drawing in his horns. I will put on a bold face, and if he is fool enough to be afraid of me, I will pay him back somewhat. [*To* Valère] Do you know, Mr. Grinner, that I am not exactly in a laughing humour, and that if you provoke me too much, I shall make you laugh after another fashion. [Jacques *pushes* Valère *to the farther end of the stage, threatening him.*]

Valère: Gently, gently.

Jacques: How gently? And if it does not please me to go gently?
Valère: Come, come! What are you about?
Jacques: You are an impudent rascal.
Valère: Master Jacques. . . .
Jacques: None of your Master Jacques here! If I take up a stick, I shall soon make you feel it.
Valère: What do you mean by a stick? [*Drives back* Jacques *in his turn.*]
Jacques: No; I don't say anything about that.
Valère: Do you know, Mr. Conceit, that I am a man to give you a drubbing in good earnest?
Jacques: I have no doubt of it.
Valère: That, after all, you are nothing but a scrub of a cook?
Jacques: I know it very well.
Valère: And that you don't know me yet?
Jacques: I beg your pardon.
Valère: You will beat me, you say?
Jacques: I only spoke in jest.
Valère: I don't like your jesting, and [*beating* Jacques] remember that you are but a sorry hand at it.
Jacques [*alone*]: Plague take all sincerity; it is a bad trade. I give it up for the future, and will cease to tell the truth. It is all very well for my master to beat me; but as for that Mr. Steward, what right has he to do it? I will be revenged on him if I can.

SCENE VII. *MARIANNE, FROSINE, MASTER JACQUES*

Frosine: Do you know if your master is at home?
Jacques: Yes, he is indeed; I know it but too well.
Frosine: Tell him, please, that we are here.

SCENE VIII. *MARIANNE, FROSINE*

Marianne: Ah! Frosine, how strange I feel, and how I dread this interview!
Frosine: Why should you? What can you possibly dread?
Marianne: Alas! can you ask me? Can you not understand the alarms of a person about to see the instrument of torture to which she is to be tied.
Frosine: I see very well that to die agreeably, Harpagon is not the torture you would embrace; and I can judge by your looks that the fair young man you spoke of to me is still in your thoughts.
Marianne: Yes, Frosine; it is a thing I do not wish to deny. The respectful visits he has paid at our house have left, I confess, a great impression on my heart.
Frosine: But do you know who he is?
Marianne: No, I do not. All I know is that he is made to be loved; that if things were left to my choice, I would much rather marry him than any other, and

that he adds not a little to the horrible dread that I have of the husband they want to force upon me.

Frosine: Oh yes! All those dandies are very pleasant, and can talk agreeably enough, but most of them are as poor as church mice; and it is much better for you to marry an old husband, who gives you plenty of money. I fully acknowledge that the senses somewhat clash with the end I propose, and that there are certain little inconveniences to be endured with such a husband; but all that won't last; and his death, believe me, will soon put you in a position to take a more pleasant husband, who will make amends for all.

Marianne: Oh, Frosine! What a strange state of things that, in order to be happy, we must look forward to the death of another. Yet death will not fall in with all the projects we make.

Frosine: You are joking. You marry him with the express understanding that he will soon leave you a widow; it must be one of the articles of the marriage contract. It would be very wrong in him not to die before three months are over. Here he is himself.

Marianne: Ah! dear Frosine, what a face!

Scene IX. Harpagon, Marianne, Frosine

Harpagon [*to* Marianne]: Do not be offended, fair one, if I come to you with my glasses on. I know that your beauty is great enough to be seen with the naked eye; but, still, it is with glasses that we look at the stars, and I maintain and uphold that you are a star, the most beautiful and in the land of stars. Frosine, she does not answer, star, it seems to me, shows no joy at the sight of me.

Frosine: It is because she is still quite awe-struck, and young girls are always shy at first, and afraid of showing what they feel.

Harpagon [*to* Frosine]: You are right. [*To* Marianne] My pretty darling, there is my daughter coming to welcome you.

Scene X. Harpagon, Élise, Marianne, Frosine

Marianne: I am very late in acquitting myself of the visit I owed you.

Èlise: You have done what I ought to have done. It was for me to have come and seen you first.

Harpagon: You see what a great girl she is; but ill weeds grow apace.

Marianne [*aside to* Frosine]: Oh, what an unpleasant man!

Harpagon [*to* Frosine]: What does my fair one say?

Frosine: That she thinks you perfect.

Harpagon: You do me too much honour, my adorable darling.

Marianne [*aside*]: What a dreadful creature!

Harpagon: I really feel too grateful to you for these sentiments.

Marianne [*aside*]: I can bear it no longer.

SCENE XI. HARPAGON, MARIANNE, ÉLISE, CLÉANTE, VALÈRE, FROSINE, BRINDAVOINE

Harpagon: Here is my son, who also comes to pay his respects to you.

Marianne [*aside to* Frosine]: Oh, Frosine! what a strange meeting! He is the very one of whom I spoke to you.

Frosine [*to* Marianne]: Well, that is extraordinary.

Harpagon: You are surprised to see that my children can be so old; but I shall soon get rid of both of them.

Cléante [*to* Marianne]: Madam, to tell you the truth, I little expected such an event; and my father surprised me not a little when he told me today of the decision he had come to.

Marianne: I can say the same thing. It is an unexpected meeting; and I certainly was far from being prepared for such an event.

Cléante: Madam, my father cannot make a better choice, and it is a great joy to me to have the honour of welcoming you here. At the same time, I cannot say that I should rejoice if it were your intention to become my stepmother. I must confess that I should find it difficult to pay you the compliment; and it is a title, forgive me, that I cannot wish you to have. To some this speech would seem coarse, but I feel that you understand it. This marriage, Madam, is altogether repugnant to me. You are not ignorant, now that you know who I am, how opposed it is to all my own interests, and with my father's permission I hope you will allow me to say that, if things depended on me, it would never take place.

Harpagon [*aside*]: What a very impertinent speech to make; and what a confession to make to her!

Marianne: And as my answer, I must tell you that things are much the same with me, and that, if you have any repugnance in seeing me your stepmother, I shall have no less in seeing you my stepson. Do not believe, I beg of you, that it is of my own will that this trouble has come upon you. I should be deeply grieved to cause you the least sorrow, and unless I am forced to it by a power I must obey, I give you my word that, I will never consent to a marriage which is so painful to you.

Harpagon: She is right. A foolish speech deserves a foolish answer. I beg your pardon, my love, for the impertinence of my son. He is a silly young fellow, who has not yet learnt the value of his own words.

Marianne: I assure you that he has not at all offended me. I am thankful, on the contrary, that he has spoken so openly. I care greatly for such a confession from him, and if he had spoken differently, I should feel much less esteem for him.

Harpagon: It is very kind of you to excuse him thus. Time will make him wiser, and you will see that his feelings will change.

Cléante: No, father, they will never change; and I earnestly beg of you, Madam, to believe me.

Harpagon: Did ever anybody see such folly? He is becoming worse and worse.

Cléante: Would you have me false to my inmost feelings?

Harpagon: Again! Change your manners, if you please.

Cléante: Very well, since you wish me to speak differently. Allow me, Madam, to take for a moment my father's place; and forgive me if I tell you that I never saw in the world anybody more charming than you are; that I can understand no happiness to equal that of pleasing you, and that to be your husband is a glory, a felicity, I should prefer to the destinies of the greatest princes upon earth. Yes, Madam, to possess you is, in my mind, to possess the best of all treasures; to obtain you is all my ambition. There is nothing I would not do for so precious a conquest, and the most powerful obstacles. . . .

Harpagon: Gently, gently, my son, if you please.

Cléante: These are complimentary words which I speak to her in your name.

Harpagon: Bless me! I have a tongue of my own to explain my feelings, and I really don't care for such an advocate as you. . . . Here, bring us some chairs.

Frosine: No; I think it is better for us to go at once to the fair, in order to be back earlier, and have plenty of time for talking.

Harpagon [*to* Brindavoine]: Have the carriage ready at once.

SCENE XII. HARPAGON, MARIANNE, ÉLISE, CLÉANTE, VALÈRE, FROSINE

Harpagon [*to* Marianne]: I hope you will excuse me, my dear, but I forgot to order some refreshments for you, before you went out.

Cléante: I have thought of it, father, and have ordered to be brought in here some baskets of China oranges, sweet citrons, and preserves, which I sent for in your name.

Harpagon [*aside, to* Valère]: Valère!

Valère [*aside, to* Harpagon]: He has lost his senses!

Cléante: You are afraid, father, that it will not be enough? I hope, Madam, that you will have the kindness to excuse it.

Marianne: It was by no means necessary.

Cléante: Did you ever see, Madam, a more brilliant diamond than the one my father has upon his finger?

Marianne: It certainly sparkles very much.

Cléante [*taking the diamond off his father's finger*]: You must see it near.

Marianne: It is a beautiful one; it possesses great lustre.

Cléante [*steps before* Marianne, *who wants to restore it*]: No, Madam, it is in hands too beautiful; it is a present my father gives you.

Harpagon: I?

Cléante: Is it not true, father, that you wish her to keep it for your sake?

Harpagon [*aside, to his son*]: What?

Cléante [*to* Marianne]: A strange question indeed! He is making me signs that I am to force you to accept it.

Marianne: I would not. . . .

Cléante [*to* Marianne]: I beg of you. . . . He would not take it back.

Harpagon [*aside*]: I am bursting with rage!

Marianne: It would be. . . .

Cléante [*still hindering* Marianne *from returning it*]: No; I tell you, you will offend him.

Marianne: Pray. . . .

Cléante: By no means.

Harpagon [*aside*]: Plague take. . . .

Cléante: He is perfectly shocked at your refusal.

Harpagon [*aside, to his son*]: Ah! traitor!

Cléante [*to* Marianne]: You see he is in despair.

Harpagon [*aside, to his son, threatening him*]: You villain!

Cléante: Really, father, it is not my fault. I do all I can to persuade her to accept it; but she is obstinate.

Harpagon [*in a rage, aside to his son*]: Rascal!

Cléante: You are the cause, Madam, of my father scolding me.

Harpagon [*aside, with the same looks*]: Scoundrel!

Cléante [*to* Marianne]: You will make him ill; for goodness' sake, hesitate no longer.

Frosine [*to* Marianne]: Why so much ceremony? Keep the ring, since the gentleman wishes you to.

Marianne [*to* Harpagon]: I will keep it now, Sir, in order not to make you angry, and I shall take another opportunity of returning it to you.

SCENE XIII. HARPAGON, MARIANNE, ÉLISE, VALÈRE, FROSINE, BRINDAVOINE

Brindavoine: Sir, there is a gentleman here who wants to speak to you.

Harpagon: Tell him that I am engaged, and that I cannot see him today.

Brindavoine: He says he has some money for you.

Harpagon [*to* Marianne]: Pray, excuse me; I will come back directly.

SCENE XIV. HARPAGON, MARIANNE, ÉLISE, CLÉANTE, FROSINE, LA MERLUCHE

La Merluche [*comes in running, and throws* Harpagon *down*]: Sir. . . .

Harpagon: Oh! he has killed me.

Cléante: What's the matter, father? Have you hurt yourself?

Harpagon: The wretch must have been bribed by some of my debtors to break my neck.

Valère [*to* Harpagon]: There is nothing serious.

La Merluche [*to* Harpagon]: I beg your pardon, Sir; I thought I had better run fast to tell you. . . .

Harpagon: What?

La Merluche: That your two horses have lost their shoes.

Harpagon: Take them quickly to the smith.

Cléante: In the meantime, father, I will do the honours of the house for you, and take this lady into the garden, where lunch will be brought.

SCENE XV. HARPAGON, VALÈRE

Harpagon: Valère, look after all this; and take care, I beseech you, to save as much of it as you can, so that we may send it back to the tradesman again.

Valère: I will.

Harpagon [*alone*]: Miscreant! do you mean to ruin me?

ACT IV

SCENE I. CLÉANTE, MARIANNE, ÉLISE, FROSINE

Cléante: Let us come in here; we shall be much better. There is no one about us that we need be afraid of, and we can speak openly.

Élise: Yes, Madam, my brother has told me of the love he has for you. I know what sorrow and anxiety such trials as these may cause, and I assure you that I have the greatest sympathy for you.

Marianne: I feel it a great comfort in my trouble to have the sympathy of a person like you, and I entreat you, Madam, ever to retain for me a friendship so capable of softening the cruelty of my fate.

Frosine: You really are both very unfortunate not to have told me of all this before. I might certainly have warded off the blow, and not have carried things so far.

Cléante: What could I do? It is my evil destiny which has willed it so. But you, fair Marianne, what have you resolved to do? What resolution have you taken?

Marianne: Alas! Is it in my power to take any resolution? And, dependent as I am, can I do anything else except form wishes?

Cléante: No other support for me in your heart? Nothing but mere wishes? No pitying energy? No kindly relief? No active affection?

Marianne: What am I to say to you? Put yourself in my place, and judge what I can possibly do. Advise me, dispose of me, I trust myself entirely to you, for I am sure that you will never ask of me anything but what is modest and seemly.

Cléante: Alas! to what do you reduce me when you wish me to be guided entirely by feelings of strict duty and of scrupulous propriety.

Marianne: But what would you have me do? Even if I were, for you, to divest myself of the many scruples which our sex imposes on us, I have too much regard for my mother, who has brought me up with great tenderness, for me to give her any cause of sorrow. Do all you can with her. Strive to win her. I give you leave to say and do all you wish; and if anything depends upon her knowing the true state of my feelings, by all means tell her what they are; indeed I will do it myself if necessary.

Cléante: Frosine, dear Frosine, will you not help us?

Frosine: Indeed, I should like to do so, as you know. I am not naturally unkind. Heaven has not given me a heart of flint, and I feel but too ready to help when I see young people loving each other in all earnestness and honesty. What can we do in this case?

Cléante: Try and think a little.

Marianne: Advise us.

Élise: Invent something to undo what you have done.

Frosine: Rather a difficult piece of business. [*To* Marianne] As far as your mother is concerned, she is not altogether unreasonable and we might succeed in making her give to the son the gift she reserved for the father. [*To* Cléante] But the most disheartening part of it all is that your father is your father.

Cléante: Yes, so it is.

Frosine: I mean that he will bear malice if he sees that he is refused, and he will be in no way disposed afterwards to give his consent to your marriage. It would be well if the refusal could be made to come from him, and you ought to try by some means or other to make him dislike you, Marianne.

Cléante: You are quite right.

Frosine: Yes, right enough, no doubt. That is what ought to be done; but how in the world are we to set about it? Wait a moment. Suppose we had a somewhat elderly woman with a little of the ability which I possess, and able sufficiently well to represent a lady of rank, by means of a retinue made up in haste, and of some whimsical title of a marchioness or viscountess, whom we would suppose to come from Lower Brittany.[5] I should have enough power over your father to persuade him that she is a rich woman, in possession, besides her houses, of a hundred thousand crowns in ready money; that she is deeply in love with him, and that she would marry him at any cost, were she even to give him all her money by the marriage contract. I have no doubt he would listen to the proposal. For certainly he loves you very much, my dear, but he loves money still better. When once he has consented to your marriage, it does not signify much how he finds out the true state of affairs about our marchioness.

Cléante: All that is very well made up.

Frosine: Leave it to me; I just remember one of my friends who will do beautifully.

Cléante: Depend on my gratitude, Frosine, if you succeed. But, dear Marianne, let us begin, I beg of you, by gaining over your mother; it would be a great deal accomplished if this marriage were once broken off. Make use, I beseech you, of all the power that her tenderness for you gives you over her. Display without hesitation those eloquent graces, those all-powerful charms, with which Heaven has endowed your eyes and lips; forget not, I beseech you, those sweet persuasions, those tender entreaties, those loving caresses to which, I feel, nothing could be refused.

Marianne: I will do all I can, and will forget nothing.

---

[5]*lower Brittany:* Region in the northwest peninsula of France. This region, geographically isolated and settled by Celtic people, would have been considered uncivilized by Molière's sophisticated French audience. Marchioness and Viscountess are minor aristocratic titles.

SCENE II. HARPAGON, MARIANNE, ÉLISE, FROSINE

Harpagon [*aside, and without being seen*]: Ah! ah! my son is kissing the hand of his intended stepmother, and his intended stepmother does not seem much averse to it! Can there be any mystery in all this?

Élise: Here comes my father.

Harpagon: The carriage is quite ready, and you can start when you like.

Cléante: Since you are not going, father, allow me to take care of them.

Harpagon: No, stop here; they can easily take care of themselves, and I want you.

SCENE III. HARPAGON, CLÉANTE

Harpagon: Well, now, all consideration of stepmother aside, tell me what do you think of this lady?

Cléante: What I think of her?

Harpagon: Yes, what do you think of her appearance, her figure, her beauty and intelligence?

Cléante: So, so.

Harpagon: But still?

Cléante: To tell you the truth, I did not find her such as I expected. Her manner is that of a thorough coquette, her figure is rather awkward, her beauty very middling, and her intelligence of the meanest order. Do not suppose that I say this to make you dislike her; for if I must have a stepmother, I like the idea of this one as well as of any other.

Harpagon: You spoke to her just now, nevertheless. . . .

Cléante: I paid her several compliments in your name, but it was to please you.

Harpagon: So then you don't care for her?

Cléante: Who? I? Not in the least.

Harpagon: I am sorry for it, for that puts an end to a scheme which had occurred to me. Since I have seen her here, I have been thinking of my own age; and I feel that people would find fault with me for marrying so young a girl. This consideration had made me determine to abandon the project, and as I had demanded her in marriage, and had given her my promise, I would have given her to you if it were not for the dislike you have for her.

Cléante: To me?

Harpagon: To you.

Cléante: In marriage?

Harpagon: In marriage.

Cléante: It is true she is not at all to my taste; but, to please you, father, I will bring myself to marry her, if you please.

Harpagon: If I please! I am more reasonable than you think. I don't wish to compel you.

Cléante: Excuse me! I will make an attempt to love her.

Harpagon: No, no; a marriage cannot be happy where there is no love.

Cléante: That, my father, will, perhaps, come by and by, and it is said that love is often the fruit of marriage.

Harpagon: No, it is not right to risk it on the side of the man, and there are some troublesome things I don't care to run the chance of. If you had felt any inclination for her, you should have married her instead of me, but as it is, I will return to my first intention and marry her myself.

Cléante: Well, father, since things are so, I had better be frank with you, and reveal our secret to you. The truth is that I have loved her ever since I saw her one day on the promenade. I intended to ask you today to let me marry her, and I was only deterred from it because you spoke of marrying her, and because I feared to displease you.

Harpagon: Have you ever paid her any visits?

Cléante: Yes, father.

Harpagon: Many?

Cléante: Yes; considering how long we have been acquainted.

Harpagon: You were well received.

Cléante: Very well, but without her knowing who I was; and that is why Marianne was so surprised when she saw me today.

Harpagon: Have you told her of your love, and of your intention of marrying her?

Cléante: Certainly, and I also spoke a little to the mother on the subject.

Harpagon: Did she kindly receive your proposal for her daughter?

Cléante: Yes, very kindly.

Harpagon: And does the daughter return your love?

Cléante: If I can believe appearances, she is certainly well disposed towards me.

Harpagon [*aside*]: Well! I am very glad to have found out this secret; it is the very thing I wanted to know. [*To his son*] Now, look here, my son, I tell you what. You will have, if you please, to get rid of your love for Marianne, to cease to pay your attentions to a person I intend for myself, and to marry very soon the wife I have chosen for you.

Cléante: So, father, it is thus you deceive me! Very well, since things are come to such a pass, I openly declare to you that I shall not give up my love for Marianne. No! understand that henceforth there is nothing from which I shall shrink in order to dispute her with you; and if you have on your side the consent of the mother, perhaps I shall have some other resources left to aid me.

Harpagon: What, rascal! You dare to trespass on my grounds?

Cléante: It is you who trespass on mine. I was the first.

Harpagon: Am I not your father, and do you not owe me respect?

Cléante: There are things in which children are not called upon to pay deference to their fathers; and love is no respector of persons.

Harpagon: My stick will make you know me better.

Cléante: All your threatenings are nothing to me.

Harpagon: You will give up Marianne?

Cléante: Never!

Harpagon: Bring me my stick. Quick, I say! my stick!

Scene IV. Harpagon, Cléante, Master Jacques

Jacques: Hold! hold! Gentlemen, what does this mean? What are you thinking of?

Cléante: I don't care a bit for it.

Jacques [*to* Cléante]: Ah! Sir, gently.

Harpagon: He dares to speak to me with such impudence as that!

Jacques [*to* Harpagon]: Ah! Sir, I beg of you.

Cléante: I shall keep to it.

Jacques [*to* Cléante]: What! to your father?

Harpagon: Let me do it.

Jacques [*to* Harpagon]: What! to your son? To me it's different.

Harpagon: I will make you judge between us, Master Jacques, so that you may see that I have right on my side.

Jacques: Willingly. [*To* Cléante] Go a little farther back.

Harpagon: There is a young girl I love and want to marry, and the scoundrel has the impudence to love her also, and wants to marry her in spite of me.

Jacques: Oh! he is wrong.

Harpagon: Is it not an abominable thing to see a son who does not shrink from becoming the rival of his father? And is it not his bounden duty to refrain from interfering with my love?

Jacques: You are quite right; stop here, and let me go and speak to him.

Cléante [*to* Master Jacques, *who comes near him*]: Very well; if he wants to make you a judge between us, I have no objection. I care little who it is, and I don't mind referring our quarrel to you.

Jacques: You do me great honour.

Cléante: I am in love with a young girl who returns my affection, and who receives kindly the offer of my heart; but my father takes it into his head to disturb our love by asking her in marriage.

Jacques: He certainly is wrong.

Cléante: Is it not shameful for a man of his age to think of marrying? I ask you if it is right for him to fall in love? and ought he not now to leave that to younger men?

Jacques: You are quite right; he is not serious; let me speak a word or two to him. [*To* Harpagon] Really, your son is not so extravagant as you think, and is amenable to reason. He says that he is conscious of the respect he owes you, and that he only got angry in the heat of the moment. He will willingly submit to all you wish if you will only promise to treat him more kindly than you do, and will give him in marriage a person to his taste.

Harpagon: Ah! tell him, Master Jacques, that he will obtain everything from me on those terms, and that, except Marianne, I leave him free to choose for his wife whomsoever he pleases.

Jacques: Leave that to me. [*To* Cléante] Really, your father is not so unreasonable as you make him out to me; and he tells me that it is your violence which irritated him. He only objects to your way of doing things, and is quite ready to grant you all you want, provided you will use gentle means and will give him the deference, respect, and submission that a son owes to his father.

Cléante: Ah! Master Jacques, you can assure him that if he grants me Marianne, he will always find me the most submissive of men, and that I shall never do anything contrary to his pleasure.

Jacques [*to* Harpagon]: It's all right; he consents to what you say.

Harpagon: Nothing could be better.

Jacques [*to* Cléante]: It's all settled; he is satisfied with your promises.

Cléante: Heaven be praised!

Jacques: Gentlemen, you have nothing to do but to talk quietly over the matter together; you are agreed now, and yet you were on the point of quarrelling through want of understanding each other.

Cléante: My poor Jacques, I shall be obliged to you all my life.

Jacques: Don't mention it, Sir.

Harpagon: You have given me great pleasure, Master Jacques, and deserve a reward. [Harpagon *feels in his pocket,* Jacques *holds out his hand, but* Harpagon *only pulls out his handkerchief, and says,*] Go; I will remember it, I promise you.

Jacques: I thank you kindly, Sir.

SCENE V. HARPAGON, CLÉANTE

Cléante: I beg your pardon, father, for having been angry.

Harpagon: It is nothing.

Cléante: I assure you that I feel very sorry about it.

Harpagon: I am very happy to see you reasonable again.

Cléante: How very kind of you so soon to forget my fault.

Harpagon: One easily forgets the faults of children when they return to their duty.

Cléante: What! you are not angry with me for my extravagant behaviour?

Harpagon: By your submission and respectful conduct you compel me to forget my anger.

Cléante: I assure you, father, I shall for ever keep in heart the remembrance of all your kindness.

Harpagon: And I promise you that, in future, you will obtain all you like from me.

Cléante: Oh, father! I ask nothing more; it is sufficient for me that you give me Marianne.

Harpagon: What?

Cléante: I say, father, that I am only too thankful already for what you have done, and that when you give me Marianne, you give me everything.

Harpagon: Who talks of giving you Marianne?

Cléante: You, father.

Harpagon: I?

Cléante: Yes.

Harpagon: What! is it not you who promised to give her up?

Cléante: I! give her up?

Harpagon: Yes.
Cléante: Certainly not.
Harpagon: Did you not give up all pretensions to her?
Cléante: On the contrary, I am more determined than ever to have her.
Harpagon: What, scoundrel! again?
Cléante: Nothing can make me change my mind.
Harpagon: Let me get at you again, wretch!
Cléante: You can do as you please.
Harpagon: I forbid you ever to come within my sight.
Cléante: As you like.
Harpagon: I abandon you.
Cléante: Abandon me.
Harpagon: I disown you.
Cléante: Disown me.
Harpagon: I disinherit you.
Cléante: As you will.
Harpagon: I give you my curse.
Cléante: I want none of your gifts.

SCENE VI. CLÉANTE, LA FLÈCHE

La Flèche [*leaving the garden with a casket*]: Ah! Sir, you are just in the nick of time. Quick! follow me.
Cléante: What is the matter?
La Flèche: Follow me, I say. We are saved.
Cléante: How?
La Flèche: Here is all you want.
Cléante: What?
La Flèche: I have watched for this all day.
Cléante: What is it?
La Flèche: Your father's treasure that I have got hold of.
Cléante: How did you manage it?
La Flèche: I will tell you all about it. Let us be off. I can hear him calling out.

SCENE VII. HARPAGON, FROM THE GARDEN, RUSHING IN WITHOUT HIS HAT, AND CRYING

Thieves! thieves! assassins! murder! Justice, just heavens! I am undone; I am murdered; they have cut my throat; they have stolen my money! Who can it be? What has become of him? Where is he? Where is he hiding himself? What shall I do to find him? Where shall I run? Where shall I not run? Is he not here? Who is this? Stop! [*To himself, taking hold of his own arm*] Give me back my money, wretch. . . . Ah . . . ! it is myself. . . . My mind is wandering, and I know not where I am, who I am, and what I am doing. Alas! my poor money! my poor money! my dearest friend, they have bereaved me of thee; and since thou art gone, I have lost my support, my consolation, and my joy. All is ended for me, and I have nothing more to do in the world! Without thee it is impossible for me to live. It is all over with me; I can bear it no longer. I am dying; I am dead; I am buried. Is there nobody who will call me from the dead, by restoring my dear money to me, or by telling me who has taken it? Ah! what is it you say? It is no one. Whoever has committed the deed must have watched carefully for his opportunity, and must have chosen the very moment when I was talking with my miscreant of a son. I must go. I will demand justice, and have the whole of my house put to the torture—my maids and my valets, my son, my daughter, and myself too. What a crowd of people are assembled here! Everyone seems to be my thief. I see no one who does not rouse suspicion in me. Ha! what are they speaking of there? Of him who stole my money? What noise is that up yonder? Is it my thief who is there? For pity's sake, if you know anything of my thief, I beseech you to tell me. Is he hiding there among you? They all look at me and laugh. We shall see that they all have a share in the robbery. Quick! magistrates, police, provosts, judges, racks, gibbets, and executioners. I will hang everybody, and if I do not find my money, I will hang myself afterwards.

ACT V

SCENE I. HARPAGON, A POLICE OFFICER

Officer: Leave that to me. I know my business. Thank Heaven! this is not the first time I have been employed in finding out thieves; and I wish I had as many bags of a thousand francs as I have had people hanged.

Harpagon: Every magistrate must take this affair in hand; and if my money is not found, I shall call justice against justice itself.

Officer: We must take all needful steps. You say there was in that casket . . . ?

Harpagon: Ten thousand crowns in cash.

Officer: Ten thousand crowns!

Harpagon: Ten thousand crowns.

Officer: A considerable theft.

Harpagon: There is no punishment great enough for the enormity of the crime; and if it remain unpunished, the most sacred things are no longer secure.

Officer: In what coins was that sum?

Harpagon: In good louis d'or and pistoles of full weight.

Officer: Whom do you suspect of this robbery?

Harpagon: Everybody. I wish you to take into custody the whole town and suburbs.

Officer: You must not, if you trust me, frighten anybody, but must use gentle means to collect evidence, in order afterwards to proceed with more rigour for the recovery of the sum which has been taken from you.

Scene II. Harpagon, The Police Officer, Master Jacques

Jacques [*at the end of the stage, turning back to the door by which he came in*]: I am coming back. Have his throat cut at once; have his feet singed; put him in boiling water, and hang him up to the ceiling.

Harpagon: What! Him who has robbed me?

Jacques: I was speaking of a sucking pig that your steward has just sent me; and I want to have it dressed for you after my own fancy.

Harpagon: This is no longer the question; and you have to speak of something else to this gentleman.

Officer [*to* Jacques]: Don't get frightened. I am not a man to cause any scandal, and matters will be carried on by gentle means.

Jacques [*to* Harpagon]: Is this gentleman coming to supper with you?

Officer: You must, in this case, my good man, hide nothing from your master.

Jacques: Indeed, Sir, I will show you all I know, and will treat you in the best manner I possibly can.

Officer: That's not the question.

Jacques: If I do not give as good fare as I should like, it is the fault of your steward, who has clipped my wings with the scissors of his economy.

Harpagon: Rascal! We have other matters to talk about than your supper; and I want you to tell me what has become of the money which has been stolen from me.

Jacques: Some money has been stolen from you?

Harpagon: Yes, you rascal! And I'll have you hanged if you don't give it me back again.

Officer [*to* Harpagon]: Pray, don't be hard upon him. I see by his looks that he is an honest fellow, and that he will tell you all you want to know without going to prison. Yes, my friend, if you confess, no harm shall come to you, and you shall be well rewarded by your master. Some money has been stolen from him, and it is not possible that you know nothing about it.

Jacques [*aside*]: The very thing I wanted in order to be revenged of our steward. Ever since he came here, he has been the favourite, and his advice is the only one listened to. Moreover, I have forgotten neither the cudgelling of today nor. . . .

Harpagon: What are you muttering about there?

Officer [*to* Harpagon]: Leave him alone. He is preparing himself to satisfy you; I told you that he was an honest fellow.

Jacques: Sir, since you want me to tell you what I know, I believe it is your steward who has done this.

Harpagon: Valère?

Jacques: Yes.

Harpagon: He who seemed so faithful to me!

Jacques: Himself. I believe that it is he who has robbed you.

Harpagon: And what makes you believe it?

Jacques: What makes me believe it?

Harpagon: Yes.

Jacques: I believe it . . . because I believe it.

Officer: But you must tell us the proofs you have.

Harpagon: Did you see him hanging about the place where I had put my money?

Jacques: Yes, indeed. Where was your money?

Harpagon: In the garden.

Jacques: Exactly; I saw him loitering about in the garden; and in what was your money?

Harpagon: In a casket.

Jacques: The very thing. I saw him with a casket.

Harpagon: And this casket, what was it like? I shall soon see if it is mine.

Jacques: What it was like?

Harpagon: Yes.

Jacques: It was like . . . like a casket.

Officer: Of course. But describe it a little, to see if it is the same.

Jacques: It was a large casket.

Harpagon: The one taken from me is a small one.

Jacques: Yes, small if you look at it in that way; but I call it large because of what it contains.

Harpagon: And what colour was it?

Jacques: What colour?

Officer: Yes.

Jacques: Of a colour . . . of a certain colour. . . . Can't you help me to find the word?

Harpagon: Ugh!

Jacques: Red; isn't it?

Harpagon: No, grey.

Jacques: Ha! yes, reddish-grey! That's what I meant.

Harpagon: There is no doubt about it, it's my casket for certain. Write down his evidence, Sir! Heavens! whom can we trust after that? We must never swear to anything, and I believe now that I might rob my own self.

Jacques [*to* Harpagon]: There he is coming back, Sir; I beg of you not to go and tell him that it was I who let it all out, Sir.

SCENE III. HARPAGON, THE POLICE OFFICER, VALÈRE, MASTER JACQUES

Harpagon: Come, come near, and confess the most abominable action, the most horrible crime, that was ever committed.

Valère: What do you want, Sir?

Harpagon: What, wretch! you do not blush for shame after such a crime?

Valère: Of what crime do you speak?

Harpagon: Of what crime I speak? Base villain, as if you did not know what I mean! It is in vain for you to try to hide it; the thing is discovered, and I have just heard all the particulars. How could you thus abuse my kindness, introduce yourself on purpose into my house to betray me, and to play upon me such an abominable trick?

Valère: Sir, since everything is known to you, I will neither deny what I have done nor will I try to palliate it.

Jacques [*aside*]: Oh! oh! Have I guessed the truth?

Valère: I intended to speak to you about it, and I was watching for a favourable opportunity; but, as this is no longer possible, I beg of you not to be angry, and to hear my motives.

Harpagon: And what fine motives can you possibly give me, infamous thief?

Valère: Ah! Sir, I do not deserve these names. I am guilty towards you, it is true; but, after all, my fault is pardonable.

Harpagon: How pardonable? A premeditated trick, and such an assassination as this!

Valère: I beseech you not to be so angry with me. When you have heard all I have to say, you will see that the harm is not so great as you make it out to be.

Harpagon: The harm not so great as I make it out to be! What! my heart's blood, scoundrel!

Valère: Your blood, Sir, has not fallen into bad hands. My rank is high enough not to disgrace it, and there is nothing in all this for which reparation cannot be made.

Harpagon: It is, indeed, my intention that you should restore what you have taken from me.

Valère: Your honour, Sir, shall be fully satisfied.

Harpagon: Honour is not the question in all this. But tell me what made you commit such a deed?

Valère: Alas! do you ask it?

Harpagon: Yes, I should rather think that I do.

Valère: A god, Sir, who carries with him his excuses for all he makes people do: Love.

Harpagon: Love?

Valère: Yes.

Harpagon: Fine love that! fine love, indeed! the love of my gold!

Valère: No, Sir, it is not your wealth that has tempted me, it is not that which has dazzled me; and I swear never to pretend to any of your possessions, provided you leave me what I have.

Harpagon: In the name of all the devils, no, I shall not leave it to you. But did anyone ever meet with such villainy! He wishes to keep what he has robbed me of!

Valère: Do you call that a robbery?

Harpagon: If I call that a robbery? A treasure like that!

Valère: I readily acknowledge that it is a treasure, and the most precious one you have. But it will not be losing it to leave it to me. I ask you on my knees to leave in my possession this treasure so full of charms; and if you do right, you will grant it to me.

Harpagon: I will do nothing of the kind. What in the world are you driving at?

Valère: We have pledged our faith to each other, and have taken an oath never to forsake one another.

Harpagon: The oath is admirable, and the promise strange enough!

Valère: Yes, we are engaged to each other for ever.

Harpagon: I know pretty well how to disengage you, I assure you of that.

Valère: Nothing but death can separate us.

Harpagon: You must be devilishly bewitched by my money.

Valère: I have told you already, Sir, that it is not self-interest which has prompted me to what I have done. It was not that which prompted my heart; a nobler motive inspired me.

Harpagon: We shall hear presently that it is out of Christian charity that he covets my money! But I will put a stop to all this, and justice, impudent rascal, will soon give me satisfaction.

Valère: You will do as you please, and I am ready to suffer all the violence you care to inflict upon me, but I beg of you to believe, at least, that if there is any harm done, I am the only one guilty, and that your daughter has done nothing wrong in all this.

Harpagon: I should think not! It would be strange, indeed, if my daughter had a share in this crime. But I will have that treasure back again, and you must confess to what place you have carried it off.

Valère: I have not carried it off, and it is still in your house.

Harpagon [*aside*]: O my beloved casket! [*To* Valère] My treasure has not left my house?

Valère: No, Sir.

Harpagon: Well, then, tell me, have you taken any liberties with . . . ?

Valère: Ah! Sir, you wrong us both; the flame with which I burn is too pure, too full of respect.

Harpagon [*aside*]: He burns for my casket!

Valère: I had rather die than show the least offensive thought: I found too much modesty and too much purity for that.

Harpagon [*aside*]: My cash-box modest!

Valère: All my desires were limited to the pleasures of sight, and nothing criminal has profaned the passion those fair eyes have inspired me with.

Harpagon [*aside*]: The fair eyes of my cash-box! He speaks of it as a lover does of his mistress.

Valère: Dame Claude knows the whole truth, and she can bear witness to it.

Harpagon: Hallo! my servant is an accomplice in this affair?

Valère: Yes, Sir, she was a witness to our engagement; and it was after being sure of the innocence of my love that she helped me to persuade your daughter to engage herself to me.

Harpagon: Ah! [*Aside*] Has the fear of justice made him lose his senses? [*To* Valère] What rubbish are you talking about my daughter?

Valère: I say, Sir, that I found it most difficult to make her modesty consent to what my love asked of her.

Harpagon: The modesty of whom?

Valère: Of your daughter; and it was only yesterday that she could make up her mind to sign our mutual promise of marriage.

Harpagon: My daughter has signed a promise of marriage?

Valère: Yes, Sir, and I have also signed.
Harpagon: O heavens! another misfortune!
Jacques [*to the* Officer]: Write, Sir, write.
Harpagon: Aggravation of misery! Excess of despair! [*To the* Officer] Sir, discharge your duty, and draw me up an indictment against him as a thief and a suborner.
Jacques: As a thief and a suborner.
Valère: These are names which I do not deserve, and when you know who I am. . .

Scene IV. Harpagon, Élise, Marianne, Valère, Frosine, Master Jacques, The Police Officer

Harpagon: Ah! guilty daughter! unworthy of a father like me! is it thus that you put into practice the lessons I have given you? You give your love to an infamous thief, and engage yourself to him without my consent! But you shall both be disappointed. [*To* Élise] Four strong walls will answer for your conduct in the future; [*to* Valère] and good gallows, impudent thief, shall do me justice for your audacity.
Valère: Your anger will be no judge in this affair, and I shall at least have a hearing before I am condemned.
Harpagon: I was wrong to say gallows; you shall be broken alive on the wheel.
Èlise [*kneeling to her father*]: Ah! my father, be more merciful, I beseech you, and do not let your paternal authority drive matters to extremes. Do not suffer yourself to be carried away by the first outburst of your anger, but give yourself time to consider what you do. Take the trouble of inquiring about him whose conduct has offended you. He is not what you imagine, and you will think it less strange that I should have given myself to him, when you know that without him you would long ago have lost me for ever. Yes, father, it is he who saved me from the great danger I ran in the waters, and to whom you owe the life of that very daughter who. . . .
Harpagon: All this is nothing; and it would have been much better for me if he had suffered you to be drowned rather than do what he has done.
Èlise: My father, I beseech you, in the name of paternal love, grant me. . . .
Harpagon: No, no. I will hear nothing, and justice must have its course.
Jacques [*aside*]: You shall pay me for the blows you gave me.
Frosine: What a perplexing state of affairs!

Scene V. Anselme, Harpagon, Élise, Marianne, Frosine, Valère, The Police Officer, Master Jacques

Anselme: What can have happened, Mr. Harpagon? You are quite upset.
Harpagon: Ah, Mr. Anselme, you see in me the most unfortunate of men; and you can never imagine what vexation and disorder is connected with the contract you have come to sign! I am attacked in my property; I am attacked in my honour; and you see there a scoundrel and a wretch who

has violated the most sacred rights, who has introduced himself into my house as a servant in order to steal my money, and seduce my daughter.

Valère: Who ever thought of your money about which you rave?

Harpagon: Yes; they have given each other a promise of marriage. This insult concerns you, Mr. Anselme; and it is you who ought to be plaintiff against him, and who at your own expense ought to prosecute him to the utmost, in order to be revenged.

Anselme: It is not my intention to force anybody to marry me, and to lay claim to a heart which has already bestowed itself; but as far as your interests are concerned, I am ready to espouse them as if they were my own.

Harpagon: This is the gentleman, an honest commissary, who has promised that he will omit nothing of what concerns the duties of his office. [*To the* OFFICER, *showing* VALÈRE] Charge him, Sir, as he ought to be, and make matters very criminal.

Valère: I do not see what crime they can make of my passion for your daughter, nor the punishment you think I ought to be condemned to for our engagement; when it is known who I am. . . .

Harpagon: I don't care a pin for all those stories, and the world is full, nowadays, of those pretenders to nobility, of those impostors, who take advantage of their obscurity and deck themselves out insolently with the first illustrious name that comes into their head.

Valère: Know that I am too upright to adorn myself with a name which is not mine, and that all Naples can bear testimony to my birth!

Anselme: Softly! Take care of what you are about to say. You speak before a man to whom all Naples is known, and who can soon see if your story is true.

Valère [*proudly putting on his hat*]: I am not the man to fear anything; and if all Naples is known to you, you know who was Don Thomas d'Alburci.

Anselme: Certainly; I know who he is, and few people know him better than I do.

Harpagon: I care neither for Don Thomas nor Don Martin. [*Seeing two candles burning, he blows one out.*]

Anselme: Have patience and let him speak; we shall soon know what he has to say of him.

Valère: That it is to him that I owe my birth.

Anselme: To him?

Valère: Yes.

Anselme: Nonsense; you are laughing. Try and make out a more likely story, and don't pretend to shelter yourself under such a piece of imposture.

Valère: Consider your words better before you speak; it is no imposture, and I say nothing here that I cannot prove.

Anselme: What! You dare to call yourself the son of Don Thomas d'Alburci?

Valère: Yes, I dare to do so; and I am ready to maintain the truth against anyone, who ever he may be.

Anselme: This audacity is marvellous. Learn to your confusion that it is now at least sixteen years ago since the man of whom you speak died in a shipwreck at sea with his wife and children, when he was trying to save their lives from the cruel persecutions which accompanied the troubles at Naples,[6] and which caused the banishment of several noble families.

Valère: Yes; but learn to your confusion that his son, seven years of age, was, with a servant, saved from the wreck by a Spanish vessel, and that this son is he who now speaks to you. Learn that the captain of that ship, touched with compassion at my misfortune, loved me; that he had me brought up as his own son, and that the profession of arms has been my occupation ever since I was fit for it; that lately I heard that my father is not dead, as I thought he was; that, passing this way to go and find him out, an accident, arranged by heaven, brought to my sight the charming Élise; that the sight of her made me a slave to her beauty, and that the violence of my love and the harshness of her father made me take the resolution to come into his house disguised as a servant, and to send some one else to look after my parents.

Anselme: But what other proofs have you besides your own words that all this is not a fable based by you upon truth.

Valère: What proofs? The captain of the Spanish vessel; a ruby seal which belonged to my father; an agate bracelet which my mother put upon my arm; and old Pedro, that servant who was saved with me from the wreck.

Marianne: Alas! I can answer here for what you have said; that you do not deceive us; and all you say clearly tells me that you are my brother.

Valère: You my sister!

Marianne: Yes, my heart was touched as soon as you began to speak; and our mother, who will be delighted at seeing you, often told me of the misfortunes of our family. Heaven spared us also in that dreadful wreck; but our life was spared at the cost of our liberty, for my mother and myself were taken up by pirates from the wreck of our vessel. After ten years of slavery a lucky event gave us back to liberty, and we returned to Naples, where we found all our property sold, and could hear no news of our father. We embarked for Genoa, where my mother went to gather what remained of a family estate which had been much disputed. Leaving her unjust relatives, she came here, where she has lived but a weary life.

Anselme: O heaven! how wonderful are thy doings, and how true it is that it only belongs to thee to work miracles! Come to my arms, my children, and share the joy of your happy father!

Valère: You are our father?

Marianne: It was for you that my mother wept?

Anselme: Yes, my daughter; yes, my son; I am Don Thomas d'Alburci, whom heaven saved from the waves, with all the money he had with him, and who, after sixteen years, believing you all dead, was preparing, after long journeys, to seek the consolations of a new family in marrying a gentle and virtuous woman. The little security there was for my life in Naples has made me abandon the idea of returning there, and having found the means of selling what I had, I settled here under the name of Anselme. I wished to forget the sorrows of a name associated with so many and great troubles.

---

[6]*troubles at Naples:* Refers to seventeenth-century Italian unrest characterized by class conflict.

Harpagon [*to* Anselme]: He is your son?
Anselme: Yes.
Harpagon: That being so, I make you responsible for the ten thousand crowns that he has stolen from me.
Anselme: He steal anything from you!
Harpagon: Yes.
Valère: Who said so?
Harpagon: Master Jacques.
Valère [*to* Master Jacques]: You say that?
Jacques: You see that I am not saying anything.
Harpagon: He certainly did. There is the officer who has received his deposition.
Valère: Can you really believe me capable of such a base action?
Harpagon: Capable or not capable, I must find my money.

SCENE VI. HARPAGON, ANSELME, ÉLISE, MARIANNE, CLÉANTE, VALÈRE, FROSINE, THE POLICE OFFICER, MASTER JACQUES, LA FLÈCHE

Clèante: Do not grieve for your money, father, and accuse any one. I have news of it, and I come here to tell you that if you consent to let me marry Marianne, your money will be given back to you.
Harpagon: Where is it?
Clèante: Do not trouble yourself about that. It is in a safe place, and I answer for it; everything depends on your resolve. It is for you to decide, and you have the choice either of losing Marianne or your cash-box.
Harpagon: Has nothing been taken out?
Clèante: Nothing at all. Is it your intention to agree to this marriage, and to join your consent to that of her mother, who leaves her at liberty to do as she likes?
Marianne [*to* Cléante]: But you do not know that this consent is no longer sufficient, and that heaven has given me back a brother [*showing* Valère], at the same time that it has given me back a father [*showing* Anselme]; and you have now to obtain me from him.
Anselme: Heaven, my dear children, has not restored you to me that I might oppose your wishes. Mr. Harpagon, you must be aware that the choice of a young girl is more likely to fall upon the son than upon the father. Come, now, do not force people to say to you what is unnecessary, and consent, as I do, to this double marriage.
Harpagon: In order for me to be well advised, I must see my casket.
Clèante: You shall see it safe and sound.
Harpagon: I have no money to give my children in marriage.
Anselme: Never mind, I have some; do not let this trouble you.
Harpagon: Do you take upon yourself to defray the expenses of these two weddings?
Anselme: Yes, I will take this responsibility upon myself. Are you satisfied?
Harpagon: Yes, provided you order me a new suit of clothes for the wedding.

Anselme: Agreed! Let us go and enjoy the blessings this happy day brings us.

Officer: Stop, Sirs, stop; softly, if you please. Who is to pay me for my writing?

Harpagon: We have nothing to do with your writing.

Officer: Indeed! and yet I do not pretend to have done it for nothing.

Harpagon [*showing* Master Jacques]: There is a fellow you can hang in payment!

Jacques: Alas! what is one to do? I receive a good cudgelling for telling the truth, and now they would hang me for lying.

Anselme: Mr. Harpagon, you must forgive him this piece of imposture.

Harpagon: You will pay the officer then?

Anselme: Let it be so. Let us go quickly, my children, to share our joy with your mother!

Harpagon: And I to see my dear casket.

(1668)

Questions for Discussion and Writing

Close Reading

1. Why does Valère pretend to agree with Harpagon about his plans for his daughter?
2. How does Frosine manipulate both Harpagon and Marianne?
3. Why does Master Jacques resent Valère's mistreatment of him more than Harpagon's? What larger issues of class does his situation raise?
4. Cite some examples of Harpagon's miserliness. Which examples strike you as being strictly comic? Which ones are part of a larger social critique? How does Molière blend the two in his play?

Critical and Creative Reading

5. What is your response to the character of Valère? Do you see him as opportunistic and violent or charming and witty? How does Molière prepare his audience early in the play for Valère's true identity?
6. The comic ending in which Valère and Marianne discover their relationship and find their father is obviously unrealistic. Does the artificiality detract from the play's conclusion? Without this ending, could the play be a tragedy? Imagine a different ending for the play.
7. Do you sympathize with Harpagon at any point during the play? If so, when? If not, how does Molière draw the character of a lonely, unloved man and make him unsympathetic?
8. Do any of the characters in the play care for Harpagon? How do you know?

Connections to Other Readings

9. The play details the relationship between love and money. Compare and contrast how the same issue is addressed and resolved in O'Henry's "The Gift of the Magi." Do you think the lovers in *The Miser* would be prepared to make the kinds of sacrifices made in O'Henry's story?

Essays

Abraham Cowley

Of Avarice

In his *Lives of the Poets*, Samuel Johnson sums up the critical reputation of Abraham Cowley as one that "has been at one time too much praised, and too much neglected at another." Born in England in 1618, Cowley published his first book of poetry, *Poetical Blossoms*, at the age of fifteen. He went on to publish plays and essays as well as poetry throughout his life and was part of the metaphysical school of poets, along with his contemporaries John Donne and Andrew Marvell. He lived in exile in France during the Puritan Revolution and died in 1667, leaving his greatest work, the epic *Davideis*, unfinished. In this essay, "Of Avarice," Cowley distinguishes between different types of greed, all potentially harmful to the self and others.

There are two sorts of avarice: the one is but of a bastard kind, and that is, the rapacious appetite of gain; not for its own sake, but for the pleasure of refunding it immediately through all the channels of pride and luxury: the other is the true kind, and properly so called; which is a restless and unsatiable desire of riches, not for any farther end or use, but only to hoard, and preserve, and perpetually increase them. The covetous man, of the first kind, is like a greedy ostrich, which devours any metal; but it is with an intent to feed upon it, and in effect it makes a shift to digest and excern it. The second is like the foolish chough,[1] which loves to steal money only to hide it. The first does much harm to mankind; and a little good too, to some few: the second does good to none; no, not to himself. The first can make no excuse to God, or angels, or rational men, for his actions: the second can give no reason or colour, not to the devil himself, for what he does; he is a slave to Mammon,[2] without wages. The first makes a shift to be beloved; ay, and envied, too, by some people: the second is the universal object of hatred and contempt. There is no vice has been so pelted with good sentences, and especially by the poets, who have pursued it with stories and fables, and allegories, and allusions; and moved, as we say, every stone to fling at it: among all which, I do not remember a more fine and gentleman-like correction than that which was given it by one line of Ovid:[3]

[1]*chough:* A large bird, a member of the crow family.

[2]*Mammon:* Wealth (Hebrew). It connotes the worship of the "false god" of wealth.

[3]*Ovid:* Ovid (43 BC–AD 17) was a Roman poet who wrote *Metamorphoses*.

Desunt luxuriæ multa, avaritiæ omnia.
Much is wanting to luxury, all to avarice.

To which saying, I have a mind to add one member, and tender it thus;

Poverty wants some, luxury many, avarice all things.

Somebody says of a virtuous and wise man, "that having nothing, he has all:" this is just his antipode, who, having all things, yet has nothing. He is a guardian eunuch to his beloved gold: "audivi eos amatores esse maximos, sed nil potesse." They are the fondest lovers but impotent to enjoy.

And, oh, what man's condition can be worse
Than his, whom plenty starves, and blessings curse;
The beggars but a common fate deplore,
The rich poor man's emphatically poor.

I wonder how it comes to pass, that there has never been any law made against him: against him, do I say? I mean, for him: as there are public provisions made for all other mad-men: it is very reasonable that the king should appoint some persons (and I think the courtiers would not be against this proposition) to manage his estate during his life (for his heirs commonly need not that care): and out of it to make it their business to see, that he should not want alimony befitting his condition, which he could never get out of his own cruel fingers. We relieve idle vagrants, and counterfeit beggars; but have no care at all of these really poor men, who are (methinks) to be respectfully treated, in regard of their quality. I might be endless against them, but I am almost choaked with the superabundance of the matter; too much plenty impoverishes me, as it does them.

(c. 1665)

Questions for Discussion and Writing

Close Reading

1. According to Cowley, what are the two sorts of avarice?
2. Why does Cowley seem to pity men who "have all things"?
3. How seriously do you think Cowley is when he suggests passing a law against avarice? What argument does he use to justify such a law?

Critical and Creative Reading

4. Cowley compares his two types of avarice to an ostrich and a chough (a crowlike bird). How effective are these comparisons in helping you understand the distinctions between the two terms? Can you think of other, perhaps more contemporary, metaphors that might work as well?

5. Do you agree with Cowley's description of the man who, "having all things, yet has nothing"? Give an example from your own experience or from the news.
6. What do you make of Cowley's suggestion that people who suffer from avarice should not be allowed to manage their own estates? How might a legal intervention benefit such people?

CONNECTIONS TO OTHER READINGS:

7. Compare the thesis of this essay to William Wordsworth's ideas in "The World Is Too Much with Us."

M. F. K. Fisher

Young Hunger

Although Mary Frances Kennedy Fisher (1908–1992) was born in Michigan, the years she spent living in France as a young adult shaped the writing for which she became famous. Her first book, *Serve It Forth* (1937), introduced a new kind of food writing by a woman—part essay, part storytelling, part cookbook. Although her writing was not limited to works about eating, she wrote about the pleasures of the table with an unapologetic enthusiasm. Her 1942 book, *How to Cook a Wolf*, was written during a period in American history in which most cookbooks and "lifestyle" books were teaching women how to cut back and make do with less at the table. Instead, Fisher reminded her readers of the pleasures of feasting. In this essay, "Young Hunger," Fisher recalls the intensity of youthful appetite and suggests that older people would do well to remember the longings (both physical and psychological) of young people. Her description of the buttery waffle gives the reader a taste of Fisher's signature style of food writing.

It is very hard for people who have passed the age of, say, fifty to remember with any charity the hunger of their own puberty and adolescence when they are dealing with the young human animals who may be frolicking about them. Too often I have seen good people helpless with exasperation and real anger upon finding in the morning that cupboards and iceboxes have been stripped of their supplies by two or three youths—or even *one*—who apparently could have eaten four times their planned share at the dinner table the night before.

Such avidity is revolting, once past. But I can recall its intensity still; I am not yet too far from it to understand its ferocious demands when I see a fifteen-year-old boy wince and whiten at the prospect of waiting politely a few more hours for food, when his guts are howling for meat-bread-candy-fruit-cheese-milkmilk milk—ANYTHING IN THE WORLD TO EAT.

I can still remember my almost insane desperation when I was about eighteen and was staying overnight with my comparatively aged godparents. I had come home along from France in a bad continuous storm and was literally concave with solitude and hunger. The one night on the train seemed even rougher than those on board ship, and by the time I reached my godparents' home I was almost lightheaded.

I got there just in time for lunch. It is clear as ice in my mind: a little cup of very weak chicken broth, one salted cracker, one-half piece of thinly sliced toast, and then, ah then, a whole waffle, crisp and brown and with a piece of beautiful butter melting in its middle—which the maid deftly cut into four sections! One section she put on my godmother's plate. The next *two*, after a nod of approval from her mistress, she put on mine. My godfather ate the fourth.

5 There was a tiny pot of honey, and I dutifully put a dab of it on my piggish portion, and we all nibbled away and drank one cup apiece of tea with lemon. Both my godparents left part of their waffles.

It was simply that they were old and sedentary and quite out of the habit of eating amply with younger people: a good thing for them, but pure hell for me. I did not have the sense to explain to them how starved I was—which I would not hesitate to do now. Instead I prowled around my bedroom while the house slumbered through its afternoon siesta, wondering if I dared sneak to the strange kitchen for something, anything, to eat, and knowing I would rather die than meet the silent, stern maid or my nice, gentle little hostess.

Later we walked slowly down to the village, and I was thinking sensuously of double malted ice-cream sodas at the corner drugstore, but there was no possibility of such heaven. When we got back to the quiet house, the maid brought my godfather a tall glass of exquisitely rich milk, with a handful of dried fruit on the saucer under it, because he had been ill; but as we sat and watched him unwillingly down it, his wife said softly that it was such a short time until dinner that she was sure I did not want to spoil my appetite, and I agreed with her because I was young and shy.

When I dressed, I noticed that the front of my pelvic basin jutted out like two bricks under my skirt: I looked like a scarecrow.

Dinner was very long, but all I can remember is that it had, as *pièce de résistance*, half of the tiny chicken previously boiled for broth at luncheon, which my godmother carved carefully so that we should each have a bit of the breast and I, as guest, should have the leg, after a snippet had been sliced from it for her husband, who liked dark meat too.

10 There were hot biscuits, yes, the smallest I have ever seen, two apiece under a napkin on a silver dish. Because of them we had no dessert: it would be too rich, my godmother said.

We drank little cups of decaffeinized coffee on the screened porch in the hot Midwestern night, and when I went up to my room I saw that the maid had left a large glass of rich malted milk beside my poor godfather's bed.

My train would leave before five in the morning, and I slept little and unhappily, dreaming of the breakfast I would order on it. Of course when I finally saw it all before me, twinkling on the Pullman silver dishes, I could eat very little, from too much hunger and a sense of outrage.

I felt that my hosts had been indescribably rude to me, and selfish and conceited and stupid. Now I know that they were none of these things. They had simply forgotten about any but their own dwindling and cautious needs for nourishment. They had forgotten about being hungry, being young, being . . .

In an essay by Max Beerbohm[1] about hosts and guests, the tyrants and the tyrannized, there is a story of what happened to him once when he was a schoolboy and someone sent him a hamper that held, not the usual collection of marmalade, sardines, and potted tongue, but twelve whole sausage-rolls.

15 "Of sausage-rolls I was particularly fond," he says. He could have dominated all his friends with them, of course, but "I carried the box up to my cubicle, and, having eaten two of the sausage-rolls, said nothing that day about the other ten, nor anything about them when, three days later, I had eaten them all—all, up there, alone."

What strange secret memories such a tale evokes! Is there a grown-up person anywhere who cannot remember some such shameful, almost insane act of greediness of his childhood? In recollection his scalp will prickle, and his palms will sweat, at the thought of the murderous risk he may have run from his outraged companions.

When I was about sixteen, and in boarding-school, we were allowed one bar of chocolate a day, which we were supposed to eat sometime between the sale of them at the little school book-store at four-thirty and the seven o'clock dinner gong. I felt an almost unbearable hunger for them—not for one, but for three or four or five at a time, so that I should have *enough,* for once, in my yawning stomach.

I hid my own purchases for several days, no mean trick in a school where every drawer and cupboard was inspected, openly and snoopingly too, at least twice a week. I cannot remember now how I managed it, with such lack of privacy and my own almost insurmountable hunger every afternoon, but by Saturday I had probably ten chocolate bars—my own and a few I had bribed my friends who were trying to lose weight to buy for me.

I did not sign up for any of the usual weekend debauchery such as a walk to the village drugstore for a well-chaperoned double butterscotch and pecan sundae. Instead I lay languidly on my bed, trying to look as if I had a headache and pretending to read a very fancy book called, I think, *Martin Pippin in the Apple Orchard*, until the halls quieted.

20 Then I arranged all my own and my roommate's pillows in a voluptuous pile, placed so that I could see whether a silent housemotherly foot stood outside the swaying monk's-cloth curtain that served as a door (to cut down our libidinous chitchat, the school board believed), and I put my hoard of Hersheys discreetly under a fold of the bedspread.

I unwrapped their rich brown covers and their tinfoil as silently as any prisoner chipping his way through a granite wall, and lay there breaking off the

[1]*Max Beerbohm*: Max Beerbohm (1872–1956) was an English parodist.

rather warm, rubbery, delicious pieces and feeling them melt down my gullet, and reading the lush symbolism of the book; and all the time I was hot and almost panting with the fear that people would suddenly walk in and see me there. And the strange thing is that nothing would have happened if they had!

It is true that I had more than my allotted share of candy, but that was not a crime. And my friends, full of their Saturday delights, would not have wanted ordinary chocolate. And anyway I had much more than I could eat, and was basically what Beerbohm calls, somewhat scornfully, "a host" and not "a guest": I loved to entertain people and dominate them with my generosity.

Then why was I breathless and nervous all during that solitary and not particularly enjoyable orgy? I suppose there is a Freudian explanation for it, or some other kind. Certainly the experience does not make me sound very attractive to myself. Even the certainty of being in good company is no real solace.

(1946)

Questions for Discussion and Writing

Close Reading

1. The narrator thinks her godparents are "rude" when she is eighteen, but she changes her mind as she writes about them years later. To what does she attribute the paltry amount of food they offered her? What do you think about their role as hosts?
2. What does the Max Beerbohm anecdote on page 1414 suggest about the appetites of youth? Do you think Beerbolm behaved gluttonously?
3. What does Fisher make of her reasons for hoarding the chocolate bars at her boarding school? What do you make of them?

Critical and Creative Reading

4. Referring to her godparents, Fisher excuses them because, she says, "They had forgotten about being hungry, being young, being . . ." What do these ellipses represent? What other longings do older people forget from their youth? Do you agree with Fisher's assessment of the way the old regard the young?
5. Fisher uses sensual and even sexual language to describe her "orgy" with the chocolate bars. What is the relationship between hunger and sexual desire? Do you agree that these two appetites are similar?
6. How does Fisher use contrasting images to highlight the difference between deprivation and plenty? Cite one or two particularly effective descriptions.
7. Do you agree with this essay's thesis, that young people have stronger appetites than older people? If so, how do you account for that difference?

Connections to Other Readings

8. How does the hunger described in this essay compare to the types of "avarice" described by Abraham Cowley? Is hunger, even gluttonous hunger, a more positive quality than avarice?

Natalia Ginzburg

Translated by Dick Davis

The Little Virtues

Natalia Levi was born in Palermo, Italy, in 1916 and grew up in an intellectual household in Turin where her father and his friends met frequently to discuss their opposition to the fascist leadership of Benito Mussolini. Her father, brothers, and later her husband, Leone Ginzburg, were arrested for their socialist views. Leone Ginzburg was eventually tortured and killed by the Nazis. Natalia Ginzburg went on to a prolific career as an editor, translator, and author of plays, novels, essays, and memoirs. She was also elected to the Italian Parliament in 1983. *The Little Virtues,* published in 1962, argues that parents should teach their children the "great virtues," ones that might go against their immediate self-interest. As you read, you might consider which types of virtues you think our culture emphasizes to children through television shows and movies. Ginzburg died in 1991.

As far as the education of children is concerned I think they should be taught not the little virtues but the great ones. Not thrift but generosity and an indifference to money; not caution but courage and a contempt for danger; not shrewdness but frankness and a love of truth; not tact but love for one's neighbour and self-denial; not a desire for success but a desire to be and to know.

Usually we do just the opposite; we rush to teach them a respect for the little virtues, on which we build our whole system of education. In doing this we are choosing the easiest way, because the little virtues do not involve any actual dangers, indeed they provide shelter from Fortune's blows. We do not bother to teach the great virtues, though we love them and want our children to have them; but we nourish the hope that they will spontaneously appear in their consciousness some day in the future, we think of them as being part of our instinctive nature, while the others, the little virtues, seem to be the result of reflection and calculation and so we think that they absolutely must be taught.

In reality the difference is only an apparent one. The little virtues also arise from our deepest instincts, from a defensive instinct; but in them reason speaks, holds forth, displays its arguments as the brilliant advocate of self-preservation. The great virtues well up from an instinct in which reason does not speak, an instinct that seems to be difficult to name. And the best of us is in that silent instinct, and not in our defensive instinct which harangues, holds forth and displays its arguments with reason's voice.

Education is only a certain relationship which we establish between ourselves and our children, a certain climate in which feelings, instincts and thoughts can flourish. Now I believe that a climate which is completely pervaded by a respect for the little virtues will, insensibly, lead to cynicism or to a fear of life. In themselves the little virtues have nothing to do with cynicism or a fear of life, but taken together, and without the great virtues, they produce an atmosphere that leads to those consequences. Not that the little virtues are in themselves contemptible; but their value is of a complementary and not of a substantial kind; they cannot stand by themselves without the others, and by themselves and without the others they provide but meagre fare for human nature. By looking around himself a man can find out how to use the little virtues—moderately and when they are necessary—he can drink them in from the air, because the little virtues are of a kind that is common among men. But one cannot breathe in the great virtues from the surrounding air, and they should be the basis of our relationship with our children, the first foundation of their education. Besides, the great can also contain the little, but by the laws of nature there is no way that the little can contain the great.

In our relationships with our children it is no use our trying to remember 5
and imitate the way our parents acted with us. The time of our youth and childhood was not one of little virtues; it was a time of strong and sonorous words that little by little lost all their substance. The present is a time of cold, submissive words beneath which a desire for reassertion is perhaps coming to the surface. But it is a timid desire that is afraid of ridicule. And so we hide behind caution and shrewdness. Our parents knew neither caution nor shrewdness and they didn't know the fear of ridicule either: they were illogical and incoherent but they never realized this; they constantly contradicted themselves but they never allowed anyone to contradict them. They were authoritarian towards us in a way that we were quite incapable of being. Strong in their principles, which they believed to be indestructible, they reigned over us with absolute power. They deafened us with their thunderous words: a dialogue was impossible because as soon as they suspected that they were wrong they ordered us to be quiet: they beat their fists on the table and made the room shake. We remember that gesture but we cannot copy it. We can fly into a rage and howl like wolves, but deep in our wolf's howl there lies a hysterical sob, the hoarse bleating of a lamb.

And so we have no authority; we have no weapons. Authority in us would be a hypocrisy and a sham. We are too aware of our own weakness, too melancholy and insecure, too conscious of our illogicality and incoherence, too conscious of our faults; we have looked within ourselves for too long and seen too many things there. And so as we don't have authority we must invent another kind of relationship.

In these days, when a dialogue between parents and their children has become possible—possible though always difficult, always complicated by mutual prejudices, bashfulness, inhibitions—it is necessary that in this dialogue we show ourselves for what we are, imperfect, in the hope that our children will not resemble us but be stronger and better than us.

As we are all moved in one way or another by the problem of money, the first little virtue that it enters our heads to teach our children is thrift. We give them a moneybox and explain to them what a fine thing it is to save money instead of spending it, so that after a few months there will be lots of money, a nice little hoard of it; and how good it is not to give in to the wish to spend money so that in the end we can buy something really special. We remember that when we were children we were given a similar moneybox; but we forget that money, and a liking for saving it, were much less horrible and disgusting things when we were children than they are today; because the more time passes the more disgusting money becomes. And so the moneybox is our first mistake. We have installed a little virtue into our system of education.

That innocent-looking moneybox made of earthenware, in the shape of a pear or an apple, stays month after month in our children's room and they become used to its presence; they become used to the money saved inside it, money which in the dark and in secret grows like a seed in the womb of the earth; they like the money, at first innocently, as we like anything—plants and little animals for example—that grows because we take care of it; and all the time they long for that expensive something they saw in a shop window and which they will be able to buy, as we have explained to them, with the money they have saved up. When at last the moneybox is smashed and the money is spent, the children feel lonely and disappointed; there is no longer any money in their room, saved in the belly of the apple, and there isn't even the rosy apple any more; instead there is something longed for from a shop window, something whose importance and price we have made a great fuss about, but which, now that it is in their room, seems dull and plain and ordinary after so much waiting and so much money. The children do not blame money for this disappointment, but the object they have bought; because the money they have lost keeps all its alluring promise in their memories. The children ask for a new moneybox and for more money to save, and they give their thoughts and attention to money in a way that is harmful to them. They prefer money to things. It is not bad that they have suffered a disappointment; it is bad that they feel lonely without the company of money.

We should not teach them to save, we should accustom them to spending 10
money. We should often give children a little money, small sums of no importance, and encourage them to spend it immediately and as they wish, to follow some momentary whim; the children will buy some small rubbishy toy which they will immediately forget as they will immediately forget money spent so quickly and thoughtlessly, and for which they have no liking. When they find the little rubbishy toy—which will soon break—in their hands they will be a bit disappointed but they will quickly forget the disappointment, the rubbishy toy and the money; in fact they will associate money with something momentary and silly, and they will think that money is silly, as it is right that they should think whilst they are children.

It is right that in the first years of their life children should live in ignorance of what money is. Sometimes this is impossible, if we are very poor; and sometimes it is difficult because we are very rich. All the same when we are very poor and money is strictly a matter of daily survival, a question of life or death, then it turns itself before the baby's eyes into food, coal or blankets so quickly that it is unable to harm his spirit. But if we are so-so, neither rich nor poor, it is not difficult to let a child live during its infancy unaware of what money is and unconcerned about it. And yet it is necessary, not too soon and not too late, to shatter this ignorance; and if we have economic difficulties it is necessary that our children, not too soon and not too late, become aware of this, just is it is right that they will at a certain point share our worries with us, the reasons for our happiness, our plans and everything that concerns the family's life together. And we should get them used to considering the family's money as something that belongs to us and to them equally, and not to us rather than to them; or on the other hand we can encourage them to be moderate and careful with the money they spend, and in this way the encouragement to be thrifty is no longer respect for a little virtue, it is not an abstract encouragement to respect something which is in itself not worth our respect, like money, rather it is a way of reminding the children that there isn't a lot of money in the house; it encourages them to think of themselves as adult and responsible for something that involves us as much as them, not something particularly beautiful or pleasant but serious, because it is connected with our daily need. But not too soon and not too late; the secret of education lies in choosing the right time to do things.

Being moderate with oneself and generous with others; this is what is meant by having a just relationship with money, by being free as far as money is concerned. And there is no doubt that it is less difficult to educate a child so that he has such a sense of proportion, such a freedom, in a family in which money is earned and immediately spent, in which it flows like clear spring water and practically does not exist as money. Things become complicated where money exists and exists heavily, where it is a leaden stagnant pool that stinks and gives off vapours. The children are soon aware of the presence of this money in the family, this hidden power which no one ever mentions openly but to which the parents refer by means of complicated and mysterious names when they are talking among themselves with a leaden stillness in their eyes and a bitter curl to their lips; money which is not simply kept in a desk drawer but which accumulates who knows where and which can at any moment be sucked back into the earth, disappearing for ever and swallowing up both house and family. In families like this the children are constantly told to spend money grudgingly, every day the mother tells them to be careful and thrifty as she gives them a few coins for their tram fare; in their mother's gaze there is that leaden preoccupation and on her forehead there is that deep wrinkle which appears whenever money is discussed; there is the obscure fear that all the money will dissolve into nothing and that even those few coins might signify the first dust of a mortal and sudden collapse. The children in families like this often go to school in threadbare clothes and worn-out shoes and they have to pine for a long time, and sometimes in vain, for a bicycle or a camera, things which some of their friends who are certainly poorer than they are have had for a quite a while. And then when they are given the bicycle they want the present is accompanied by severe orders not to damage it, not to lend such a magnificent object—which has cost a great deal of money—to anyone. In such a house admonitions to save money are constant and insistent—school books are usually bought second-hand, and exercise books at a cheap supermarket. This happens partly because the rich are often mean, and because they think they are poor, but above all because mothers in rich families are—more or less subconsciously—afraid of the consequences of money and try to protect their children by surrounding them with the lie of simple habits, even making them grow accustomed to little instances of privation. But there is no worse error than to make a child live in such a contradiction; everywhere in the house money talks its unmistakeable language; it is there in the china, in the furniture, in the heavy silverware, it is there in the comfortable journeys, in the luxurious summer holidays, in the doorman's greeting, in the servants' rituals; it is there in his parents' conversation, it is the wrinkle on his father's forehead, the leaden perplexity in his mother's gaze; money is everywhere, untouchable perhaps because it is so fragile, It is something he is not allowed to joke about, a sombre god to whom he can only turn in a whisper, and to honour this god, so as not to disturb its mournful immobility, he has to wear last year's overcoat that has got too small, learn his lessons from books that are in tatters and falling to pieces, and amuse himself with a country bumpkin's bicycle.

If we are rich and want to educate our children so that they have simple habits it must in that case be made very clear that all the money saved by following such simple habits is to be spent, without any hint of meanness, on other people. Such habits mean only that they are not greed or fear but a simplicity that has—in the midst of wealth—been freely chosen. A child from a rich family will not learn moderation because they have made him wear old clothes, or because they have made him eat a green apple for tea, or because they deny him a bicycle he has wanted for a long time; such moderation in the midst of wealth is pure fiction, and fictions always lead to bad habits. In this way he will only learn to be greedy and afraid of money. If we deny him a bicycle which he wants and which we could buy him we only prevent him from having something that it is reasonable a boy should have, we only make his childhood less happy in the name of an abstract principle and without any real justification. And we are tacitly saying to him that money is better than a bicycle; on the contrary he should learn that a bicycle is always better than money.

The true defence against wealth is not a fear of wealth—of its fragility and of the vicious consequences that it can bring—the true defence against wealth is an indifference to money. There is no better way to teach a child this indifference than to give him money to spend when there is money—because then he will learn to part with it without worrying about it or regretting it. But, it will be said, then the child will be used to having money and will not be able to do without it; if tomorrow he is not rich, what is he to do? But it is easier not to have money once we have learnt to spend it, once we have learnt how quickly it runs through our hands; and it is easier to learn to do without money when we are thoroughly familiar with it than when we have paid it the homage of our reverence and fear throughout our childhood, than when we have sensed its presence all around us and not been allowed to raise our eyes and look it in the face.

As soon as our children begin to go to school we promise them money as 15
a reward if they do well in their lessons. This is a mistake. In this way we mix money—which is an ignoble thing—with learning and the pleasure of knowledge, which are admirable and worthy things. The money we give our children

should be given for no reason; it should be given indifferently so that they will learn to receive it indifferently; but it should be given not so that they learn to love it, but so that they learn not to love it, so that they realize its true nature and its inability to satisfy our truest desires, which are those of the spirit. When we elevate money into a prize, a goal, an object to be striven for, we give it a position, an importance, a nobility, which it should not have in our children's eyes. We implicitly affirm the principle—a false one—that money is the crowning reward for work, its ultimate objective. Money should be thought of as a wage of work, not its ultimate objective but its wage—that is, its legitimate recognition; and it is clear that the scholastic work of children cannot have a wage. It is a small mistake—but a mistake—to offer our children money in return for domestic services, for doing little chores. It is a mistake because we are not our children's employers; the family's money is as much theirs as it is ours; those little services and chores should be done without reward, as a voluntary sharing in the family's life. And in general I think we should be very cautious about promising and providing rewards and punishments. Because life rarely has its rewards and punishments; usually sacrifices have no reward, and often evil deeds go unpunished, at times they are even richly rewarded with success and money. Therefore it is best that our children should know from infancy that good is not rewarded and that evil goes unpunished; yet they must love good and hate evil, and it is not possible to give any logical explanation for this.

We usually give a quite unwarranted importance to our children's scholastic performance. And this is nothing but a respect for the little virtue "success." It should be enough for us that they do not lag too far behind the others, that they do not fail their exams; but we are not content with this; we want success from them, we want them to satisfy our pride. If they do badly at school or simply not as well as we would wish, we immediately raise a barrier of nagging dissatisfaction between us and them; when we speak to them we assume the sulky, whining tone of someone complaining about an insult. And then our children become bored and distance themselves from us. Or we support them in their complaints that the teachers have not understood them and we pose as victims with them. And every day we correct their homework, and study their lessons with them. In fact school should be from the beginning the first battle which a child fights for himself, without us; from the beginning it should be clear that this is his battlefield and that we can give him only very slight and occasional help there. And if he suffers from injustice there or is misunderstood it is necessary to let him see that there is nothing strange about this, because in life we have to expect to be constantly misunderstood and misinterpreted, and to be victims of injustice; and the only thing that matters is that we do not commit injustices ourselves. We share the successes and failures of our children because we love them, but just as much and in the same way that they, little by little as they grow up, share our successes and failures, our joys and anxieties. It is not true that they have a duty to do well at school for our sake and to give the best of their skills to studying. Once we have started them in their lessons, their duty is simply to go forward. If they wish to spend the best of their skills on things outside school—collecting

Coleoptera[1] or learning Turkish—that is their business and we have no right to reproach them, or to show that our pride has been hurt or that we feel dissatisfied with them. If at the moment the best of their skills do not seem to be applied to anything, then we do not have the right to shout at them very much in that case either; who knows, perhaps what seems laziness to us is really a kind of daydreaming and thoughtfulness that will bear fruit tomorrow. If it seems they are wasting the best of their energies and skills lying on the sofa reading ridiculous novels or charging around a football pitch, then again we cannot know whether this is really a waste of energy and skill or whether tomorrow this too will bear fruit in some way that we have not yet suspected. Because there are an infinite number of possibilities open to the spirit. But we, the parents, must not let ourselves be seized by a terror of failure. Our remonstrances must be like a squall of wind or a sudden storm—violent, but quickly forgotten—and not anything that could upset the nature of our relationship with our children, that could muddy its clarity and peace. We are there to console our children if they are hurt by failure; we are there to give them courage if they are humiliated by failure. We are also there to bring them down a peg or two when success has made them too pleased with themselves. We are there to reduce school to its narrow, humble limits; it is not something that can mortgage their future, it is simply a display of offered tools, from which it is perhaps possible to choose one which will be useful tomorrow.

What we must remember above all in the education of our children is that their love of life should never weaken. This love can take different forms, and sometimes a listless, solitary, bashful child is not lacking in a love of life, he is not overwhelmed by a fear of life, he is simply in a state of expectancy, intent on preparing himself for his vocation. And what is a human being's vocation but the highest expression of his love of life? And so we must wait, next to him, while his vocation awakens and takes shape. His behaviour can be like that of a mole, or of a lizard that holds itself still and pretends to be dead but in reality it has detected the insect that is its prey and is watching its movements, and then suddenly springs forward. Next to him, but in silence and a little aloof from him, we must wait for this leap of his spirit. We should not demand anything; we should not ask or hope that he is a genius or an artist or a hero or a saint; and yet we must be ready for everything; our waiting and our patience must compass both the possibility of the highest and the most ordinary of fates.

A vocation, an ardent and exclusive passion for something in which there is no prospect of money, the consciousness of being able to do something better than others, and being able to love this thing more than anything else—this is the only, the unique way in which a rich child can completely escape being conditioned by money, so that he is free of its claims; so that he feels neither the pride nor the shame of wealth when he is with others. He will not even be conscious of what clothes he is wearing, or of the clothes around him, and tomorrow he will be equal to any privation because the one hunger and thirst within him will be his own passion which will have devoured everything futile and provisional and divested him of every habit learnt in childhood, and which alone will rule his spirit. A vocation is man's one true wealth and salvation.

[1]*Coleoptera:* An order of insects that includes beetles.

What chance do we have of awakening and stimulating in our children the birth and development of a vocation? We do not have much; however there is one way open to us. The birth and development of a vocation needs space, space and silence, the free silence of space. Our relationship with our children should be a living exchange of thoughts and feelings, but it should also include deep areas of silence: it should be an intimate relationship but it must not violently intrude on their privacy; it should be a just balance between silence and words. We must be important to our children and yet not too important; they must like us a little, and yet not like us too much—so that it does not enter their heads to become identical to us, to copy us and the vocation we follow, to seek our likeness in the friends they choose throughout their lives. We must have a friendly relationship with them, and yet we must not be too friendly with them otherwise it will be difficult for them to have real friends with whom they can discuss things they do not mention to us. It is necessary that their search for friends, their love-life, their religious life, their search for a vocation, be surrounded by silence and shadows, so that they can develop separately from us. But then, it will be said, our intimacy with our children has been reduced to very little. But in our relationships with them all these things—their religious life, their intellectual life, their emotional life, their judgement of other human beings—should be included as it were in summary form; for them we should be a simple point of departure, we should offer them the springboard from which they make their leap. And we must be there to help them, if help should be necessary; they must realize that they do not belong to us, but that we belong to them, that we are always available, present in the next room, ready to answer every possible question and demand as far as we know how to.

And if we ourselves have a vocation, if we have not betrayed it, if over the 20
years we have continued to love it, to serve it passionately, we are able to keep all sense of ownership out of our love for our children. But if on the other hand we do not have a vocation, or if we have abandoned it or betrayed it out of cynicism or a fear of life, or because of mistaken parental love, or because of some little virtue that exists within us, then we cling to our children as a shipwrecked mariner clings to a tree trunk; we eagerly demand that they give us back everything we have given them, that they be absolutely and inescapably what we wish them to be, that they get out of life everything we have missed; we end up asking them for all the things which can only be given to us by our own vocation; we want them to be entirely our creation, as if having once created them we could continue to create them throughout their whole lives. We want them to be entirely our creation, as if we were not dealing with human beings but with products of the spirit. But if we have a vocation, if we have not denied or betrayed it, then we can let them develop quietly and away from us, surrounded by the shadows and space that the development of a vocation, the development of an existence, needs. This is perhaps the one real chance we have of giving them some kind of help in their search for a vocation—to have a vocation ourselves, to know it, to love it and serve it passionately; because love of life begets a love of life.

(1962)

Questions for Discussion and Writing

Close Reading

1. How does Ginzburg differentiate between "little" and "great" virtues?
2. According to Ginzburg, why should parents encourage children to spend, rather than save, money? Do you agree with her reasoning?
3. What does Ginzburg have to say about offering children rewards and punishments? How do these ideas defy conventional wisdom about raising children?

Critical and Creative Reading

4. Consider Ginzburg's examples of "little virtues." How might each of them be helpful in ensuring self-preservation? Do you think Ginzburg is too dismissive of these "little virtues"? How large a role do you think these little virtues should play in a child's education?
5. Ginzburg suggests that learning the "little virtues" may interfere with a child's "love of life." Do you agree or disagree? How do you think a "love of life" can best be taught?
6. Discuss Ginzburg's concept of "vocation." What is the difference between a vocation and a career? Do you agree with Ginzburg that "a vocation is man's one true wealth and salvation"? How many people truly find their vocation in life?

Connections to Other Readings

7. How does Molière's play *The Miser* connect to Ginzburg's discussion about money and thrift?
8. Analyze the brothers in Tobias Wolff's story "The Rich Brother." Which brother represents for you "the little virtues"? Which brother possesses a "vocation"? Does Wolff seem to share Ginzburg's opinion of the relative merit of having little virtues versus having a vocation?

Considering Art: Greed, Gluttony, and Generosity

The discussion below references art reproduced on color insert pages 21 and 22.

***Gluttony* (see color insert p. 21).** Contemporary printmaker and illustrator Annie Bissett (b. 1955) creates a humorous image of the bottomless appetite of *Gluttony* (2005). The simplified form of this figure is achieved by printing each color from a separate carved block. She notes that "gluttony (or greed or addiction) is an all-consuming desperate craving that can never be satisfied. It's a state of mind that ruins my ability to see beauty or abundance and it fosters anger (I said GIVE me some!) and resentment (Why does everyone else have more than me?). I know of no better antidote for this state of mind than to honestly answer the simple question, 'What are three things I'm grateful for?' I'm grateful for the person who taught me that question" (http://www.anniebissett.com/Gluttony.htm).

***St. Francis Giving His Cape* (see color insert p. 21).** In *St. Francis Giving His Cape* (1296), famed early Italian Renaissance artist Giotto di Bondone (1266–1337) paints a scene from the life of the saint that exemplifies his rejection of the material world. Francesco di Bernardone was born into a wealthy family in the town of Assisi. In his youth, according to his biographers, he lived a somewhat decadent life in the company of sons of local nobles. When he was a young man, Francis met a poor soldier on a road; the man asked him for alms and even though his friends mocked him, he gave him all he had including the clothes on his back. That night, he had his first vision: he dreamed of a floating castle with fluttering flags. By degrees, he would renounce the pleasures and possessions of world and embrace a life of poverty. This is a narrative image from a cycle of **fresco** paintings in the Basilica of San Francesco d'Assisi. It depicts one of the many legendary tales that grew up around his life. He is accredited with many doing many acts of extreme generosity and compassion and experiencing life-altering illnesses and visions, nursing outcasts like lepers, wrestling with his own demons and receiving the miraculous marks of the stigmata. Francis was canonized as a saint two years after his death in 1226. Franciscan monks follow his example and reject worldly pleasures and comforts and emphasize their role of teaching and helping the poor, not amassing wealth or building cathedrals. Giotto worked in Padua and Florence and attained an unprecedented degree of fame during his lifetime that has never diminished. Typical of early Renaissance painting, the landscape setting rises up in the background rather than receding in **perspective**. The principle characters of the tale are aligned in the seemingly shallow space of the foreground. Color is simple and gives the image great clarity. The figures have a small amount of **modeling** that lends them a degree of volume.

***Shelf Life* (see color insert p. 22).** *Shelf Life* (2005) is an assemblage of everyday items by James Hopkins (b. 1976). On six bracketed shelves, books, records, musical instruments, clocks, and boxes have been arranged to appear, from a distance, in the shape of a skull. The items on the shelf thus read as a still life with the theme of the transitory nature of life and worldly pleasures. In art of the seventeenth centuries, paintings sometimes had the theme of *Vanitas*, or the vanity of passing pleasures. The skull is a traditional symbol of mortality, and still lifes with skulls are termed "memento mori" images. This Latin phrase (which means "remember that you are mortal" or "remember your death") is a reminder that life is short and you can't take it with you.

Questions about the Art

1. How would you depict the possessions that you consider unnecessary or all-consuming?
2. What contemporary figures come to mind as examples of generosity?

Connecting Art and Literature

1. Discuss the connection between the accumulation of wealth and the inevitability of death in James Hopkins's "Shelf Life" and in Molière's play *The Miser.*
2. In Giotto di Bondone's painting *St. Francis Giving His Cape* and in O. Henry's story "The Gift of the Magi," generosity and self-sacrifice make ordinary people saintly, or better than human. Consider the virtue of generosity as "saintly" in both works.
3. Compare the depiction of gluttony in Annie Bisset's print *Gluttony* to the poems by Allen Ginsberg and William Matthews.

Common Characters

The Gambler

America is ambivalent about gambling. While no one admires the gambling addict who loses the family savings at a roulette table in Las Vegas, anyone who invests in the stock market is taking a large risk. The subject of legalized gambling is constantly debated: your state may get some of its revenue from lottery scratch tickets, taxes on horse racing, or compromises made with the owners of Native American casinos. (Such revenue has been called "the poor man's tax.")

American acceptance of gambling appears to be a matter of degrees. Most adults don't mind a little friendly wager on the Super Bowl or a handful of friends gathered around a poker table on a Saturday night, but the same

Fools Gambling, from *The Ship of Fools* by Sebastian Brant, woodcut attributed to the Haintz-Nar-Meister (1494).

Trading floor on the New York Stock Exchange.

people are wary of the casino culture of Las Vegas, Atlantic City, or (in recent years) the Internet. It's fun to win the office pool on the NCAA basketball tournament in March; it's pathetic to lose your life's savings because you can't control yourself. When does gambling become a social ill? Gambling is associated with other supposed vices in American culture: scantily clad women offer free drinks to gamblers in the hopes of altering their judgment. Casinos are well aware of the weaknesses of their clientele. The cliché is that the "house" always wins, which means that the naïve gambler loses. But nobody forced the little guy to open up his wallet.

The dream that fuels all gamblers is that they can beat the house, or beat the odds. Seasoned gamblers or champion poker players pride themselves on their ability to bluff, or wear cool expressions when they look at their cards. These people believe that they are stronger than the forces of fate, that they can win even when the "cards are stacked" or the "dice are loaded." We are familiar with stories of gamblers taking absurd risks; a whole tradition of stories deals with people gambling away their life savings, but also of gambling away their souls. The most famous of these stories involves a character named Faust (made famous in dramas by Christopher Marlowe and Johann Wolfgang von Goethe) who strikes a bargain with the Devil himself. This story has found its way into many cultures; in the 1970s a country rock hit by the Charlie Daniels Band has the Devil betting against the soul of a local boy over who can play the fiddle better.

Although we may believe that gambling is ultimately sinful, how do we react to a character such as Fleur in Louise Erdrich's story included here ("Raspberry Sun / Fleur"), in which the gambling character seems to have extraordinary, even supernatural, luck? What do we make of the vibrancy associated with gambling in the poems by Charles Baudelaire and Stuart Dischell? What composite portrait can we paint of gamblers based on the visual images here: does a little risk-taking make life more exciting?

Charles Baudelaire *(1821–1867)*

Translated by Richard Howard

The Gamblers

They sit in shabby armchairs, ancient whores
with eyebrows painted over pitiless eyes,
simpering so that the garish gems they wear
jiggle at their withered powdered ears.

Around the green felt, lipless faces loom
or colorless lips and toothless jaws, above
feverish fingers that cannot lie still
but fumble in empty pockets, trembling breasts;

under the dirty ceilings and a row
of dusty chandeliers, the low-hung lamps
sway over famous poets' shadowed brows,
the sweat of which they come to squander here;

this hideous pageant passed before my eyes
as if a nightmare picked out each detail:
I saw myself in a corner of that hushed den
watching it all, cold, mute—and envious!

envying the stubborn passion of such men,
the deadly gaiety of those old whores—
all blithely trafficking, as I looked on,
in honor or beauty—whatever they could sell!

Horrible, that I should envy these
who rush to recklessly into the pit,
each in his frenzy ravenous to prefer
pain to death, and hell to nothingness!

(1868)

Stuart Dischell *(b. 1954)*

Days of Me

When people say they miss me,
I think how much I miss me too,
Me, the old me, the great me,
Lover of three women in one day,
Modest me, the best me, friend
To waiters and bartenders, hearty
Laugher and name rememberer,
Proud me, handsome and hirsute
In soccer shoes and shorts
On the ball fields behind MIT,
Strong me in a weightbelt at the gym,
Mutual sweat dripper in and out
Of the sauna, furtive observer
Of the coeducated and scantily clad,
Speedy me, cyclist of rivers,
Goose and peregrine falcon
Counter, all season venturer,
Chatterer-up of corner cops,
Groundskeepers, mothers with strollers,
Outwitter of panhandlers and bill
Collectors, avoider of levies, excises,
Me in a taxi in the rain,
Pressing my luck all the way home.

That's me at the dice table, baby,
Betting come, little Joe, and yo,
Blowing the coals, laying thunder,
My foot on top a fifty dollar chip
Some drunk spilled on the floor,
Dishonest me, evener of scores,
Eager accepter of the extra change,
Hotel towel pilferer, coffee spoon
Lifter, fervent retailer of others'
Humor, blackhearted gossiper,
Poisoner at the well, dweller
In unsavory detail, delighted sayer
Of the vulgar, off course belier
Of the true me, empiric builder
Newly haircutted, stickerer-up
For pals, jam unpriser, medic
To the self-inflicted, attorney

To the self-indicted, petty accountant
And keeper of the double books,
Great divider of the universe
And all its forms of existence
Into its relationship to me,
Fellow trembler to the future,
Thin air gawker, apprehender
Of the frameless door.

(2003)

Louise Erdrich *(b. 1954)*

Raspberry Sun (Fleur)

The first time she drowned in the cold and glassy waters of Matchimanito, Fleur Pillager was only a child. Two men saw the boat tip, saw her struggle in the waves. They rowed over to the place she went down, and jumped in. When they lifted her over the gunwales, she was cold to the touch and stiff, so they slapped her face, shook her by the heels, worked her arms and pounded her back until she coughed up lake water. She shivered all over like a dog, then took a breath. But it wasn't long afterward that those two men disappeared. The first wandered off and the other, Jean Hat, got himself run over by his own surveyor's cart.

It went to show, the people said. It figured to them all right. By saving Fleur Pillager, those two had lost themselves.

The next time she fell in the lake, Fleur Pillager was fifteen years old and no one touched her. She washed on shore, her skin a dull dead gray, but when George Many Women bent to look closer, he saw her chest move. Then her eyes spun open, clear black agate, and she looked at him. "You take my place," she hissed. Everybody scattered and left her there, so no one knows how she dragged herself home. Soon after that we noticed Many Women changed, grew afraid, wouldn't leave his house and would not be forced to go near water or guide the mappers back into the bush. For his caution, he lived until the day that his sons brought him a new tin bathtub. Then the first time he used it he slipped, got knocked out, and breathed water while his wife stood in the other room frying breakfast.

Men stayed clear of Fleur Pillager after the second drowning. Even though she was good-looking, nobody dared to court her because it was clear that Misshepeshu, the water man, the monster, wanted her for himself. He's a devil, that one, love hungry with desire and maddened for the touch of young girls, the strong and daring especially, the ones like Fleur.

Our mothers warn us that we'll think he's handsome, for he appears with 5
green eyes, copper skin, a mouth tender as a child's. But if you fall into his arms, he sprouts horns, fangs, claws, fins. His feet are joined as one and his skin, brass scales, rings to the touch. You're fascinated, cannot move. He casts

a shell necklace at your feet, weeps gleaming chips that harden into mica on your breasts. He holds you under. Then he takes the body of a lion, a fat brown worm, or a familiar man. He's made of gold. He's made of beach moss. He's a thing of dry foam, a thing of death by drowning, the death a Chippewa cannot survive.

Unless you are Fleur Pillager. We all knew she couldn't swim. After the first time, we thought she'd keep to herself, live quiet, stop killing men off by drowning in the lake. We thought she would keep the good ways. But then, after the second return, and after old Nanapush nursed her through the sickness, we knew that we were dealing with something much more serious. Alone out there, she went haywire, out of control. She messed with evil, laughed at the old women's advice and dressed like a man. She got herself into some half-forgotten medicine, studied ways we shouldn't talk about. Some say she kept the finger of a child in her pocket and a powder of unborn rabbits in a leather thong around her neck. She laid the heart of an owl on her tongue so she could see at night, and went out, hunting, not even in her own body. We know for sure because the next morning, in the snow or dust, we followed the tracks of her bare feet and saw where they changed, where the claws sprang out, the pad broadened and pressed into the dirt. By night we heard her chuffing cough, the bear cough. By day her silence and the wide grin she threw to bring down our guard made us frightened. Some thought that Fleur Pillager should be driven from the reservation, but not a single person who spoke like that had the nerve. And finally, when people were just about to get together and throw her out, she left on her own and didn't come back all summer. That's what I'm telling about.

During those months, when Fleur lived a few miles south in Argus, things happened. She almost destroyed that town.

When she got down to Argus in the year of 1913, it was just a grid of six streets on either side of the railroad depot. There were two elevators, one central, the other a few miles west. Two stores competed for the trade of the three hundred citizens, and three churches quarreled with one another for their souls. There was a frame building for Lutherans, a heavy brick one for Episcopalians, and a long narrow shingle Catholic church. This last had a slender steeple, twice as high as any building or tree.

No doubt, across the low flat wheat, watching from the road as she came near on foot, Fleur saw that steeple rise, a shadow thin as a needle. Maybe in that raw space it drew her the way a lone tree draws lightning. Maybe, in the end, the Catholics are to blame. For if she hadn't seen that sign of pride, that slim prayer, that marker, maybe she would have just kept walking.

But Fleur Pillager turned, and the first place she went once she came into 10
town was to the back door of the priest's residence attached to the landmark church. She didn't go there for a handout, although she got that, but to ask for work. She got that too, or we got her. It's hard to tell which came out worse, her or the men or the town, although as always Fleur lived.

The men who worked at the butcher's had carved about a thousand carcasses between them, maybe half of that steers and the other half pigs, sheep, and game like deer, elk, and bear. That's not even mentioning the chickens, which were beyond counting. Pete Kozka owned the place, and employed three men: Lily Veddar, Tor Grunewald, and Dutch James.

I got to Argus through Dutch. He was making a mercantile delivery to the reservation when he met my father's sister Regina, a Puyat and then a Kashpaw through her first husband. Dutch didn't change her name right off, that came later. He never did adopt her son, Russell, whose father lived somewhere in Montana now.

During the time I stayed with them, I hardly saw Dutch or Regina look each other in the eye or talk. Perhaps it was because, except for me, the Puyats were known as a quiet family with little to say. We were mixed-bloods, skinners in the clan for which the name was lost. In the spring before the winter that took so many Chippewa, I bothered my father into sending me south, to the white town. I had decided to learn the lace-making trade from nuns.

"You'll fade out there," he said, reminding me that I was lighter than my sisters. "You won't be an Indian once you return."

"Then maybe I won't come back," I told him. I wanted to be like my mother, 15
who showed her half-white. I wanted to be like my grandfather, pure Canadian. That was because even as a child I saw that to hang back was to perish. I saw through the eyes of the world outside of us. I would not speak our language. In English, I told my father we should build an outhouse with a door that swung open and shut.

"We don't have such a thing upon our house." He laughed. But he scorned me when I would not bead, when I refused to pock my fingers with quills, or hid rather than rub brains on the stiff skins of animals.

"I was made for better," I told him. "Send me down to your sister." So he did. But I did not learn to thread and work the bobbins and spools. I swept the floors in a butcher shop, and cared for my cousin Russell.

Every day I took him to the shop and we set to work—sprinkled fresh sawdust, ran a hambone across the street to a customer's beanpot or a package of sausage to the corner. Russell took the greater share of orders, worked the harder. Though young, he was fast, reliable. He never stopped to watch a cloud pass, or a spider secure a fly with the same quick care as Pete wrapped a thick steak for the doctor. Russell and I were different. He never sat to rest, never fell to wishing he owned a pair of shoes like those that passed on the feet of white girls, shoes of hard red leather decorated with cut holes. He never listened to what those girls said about him, or imagined them doubling back to catch him by the hand. In truth, I hardly rinsed through the white girls' thoughts.

That winter, we had no word from my family, although Regina asked. No one knew yet how many were lost, people kept no track. We heard that wood could not be sawed fast enough to build the houses for their graves, and there were so few people strong enough to work, anyway, that by the time they got around to it the brush had grown, obscuring the new-turned soil, the marks of burials. The priests tried to discourage the habit of burying the dead in trees, but the ones they dragged down had no names to them, just scraps of their belongings. Sometimes in my head I had a dream I could not shake. I saw my sisters and my mother swaying in the branches, buried too high to reach, wrapped in lace I never hooked.

20 I tried to stop myself from remembering what it was like to have companions, to have my mother and sisters around me, but when Fleur came to us that June, I remembered. I made excuses to work next to her, I questioned her, but Fleur refused to talk about the Puyats or about the winter. She shook her head, looked away. She touched my face once, as if by accident, or to quiet me, and said that perhaps my family had moved north to avoid the sickness, as some mixed-bloods did.

I was fifteen, alone, and so poor-looking I was invisible to most customers and to the men in the shop. Until they needed me, I blended into the stained brown walls, a skinny big-nosed girl with staring eyes.

From this, I took what advantage I could find. Because I could fade into a corner or squeeze beneath a shelf I knew everything: how much cash there was in the till, what the men joked about when no one was around, and what they did to Fleur.

Kozka's Meats served farmers for a fifty-mile radius, both to slaughter, for it had a stockpen and chute, and to cure the meat by smoking it or spicing it in sausage. The storage locker was a marvel, made of many thicknesses of brick, earth insulation, and Minnesota timber, lined inside with wood shavings and vast blocks of ice cut from the deepest end of Matchimanito, hauled down from the reservation each winter by horse and sled.

A ramshackle board building, part killing shed, part store, was fixed to the low square of the lockers. That's where Fleur worked. Kozka hired her for her strength. She could lift a haunch or carry a pole of sausages without stumbling, and she soon learned cutting from Fritzie, a string-thin blond who chain-smoked and handled the razor-edged knives with nerveless precision, slicing close to her stained fingers. The two women worked afternoons, wrapping their cuts in paper, and Fleur carried the packages to the lockers. Russell liked to help her. He vanished when I called, took none of my orders, but I soon learned that he could always be found alongside Fleur's hip, one hand gently pinching a fold of her skirt, so delicately that she could pretend not to notice.

25 Of course, she did. She knew the effect she had on men, even the very youngest of them. She swayed them, sotted them, made them curious about her habits, drew them close with careless ease and cast them off with the same indifference. She was good to Russell, it is true, even fussed about him like a mother, combed his hair with her fingers, and scolded me for kicking or teasing him.

Fleur poked bits of sugar between Russell's lips when we sat for meals, skimmed the cream from the jar when Fritzie's back was turned and spooned it in into his mouth. For work, she gave him small packages to carry when she and Fritzie piled cut meat outside the locker's heavy doors, opened only at five P.M. each afternoon, before the men ate supper.

Sometimes Dutch, Tor, and Lily stayed at the lockers after closing, and when they did Russell and I stayed too, cleaned the floors, restoked the fires in the front smokehouse, while the men sat around the squat, cold cast-iron stove spearing slats of herring onto hardtack bread. They played long games of poker, or cribbage on a board made from the planed end of a salt crate. They talked. We ate our bread and the ends of sausages, watched and listened, although there wasn't much to hear since almost nothing ever happened in Argus. Tor was married, Dutch lived with Regina, and Lily read circulars. They mainly discussed the auctions to come, equipment, or women.

Every so often, Pete Kozka came out front to make a whist, leaving Fritzie to smoke her cigarettes and fry raised donuts in the back room. He sat and played a few rounds but kept his thoughts to himself. Fritzie did not tolerate him talking behind her back, and the one book he read was the New Testament. If he said something, it concerned weather or a surplus of wheat. He had a good-luck talisman, the opal-white lens of a cow's eye. Playing rummy, he rubbed it between his fingers. That soft sound and the slap of cards was about the only conversation.

Fleur finally gave them a subject.

Her cheeks were wide and flat, her hands large, chapped, muscular. Fleur's shoulders were broad and curved as a yoke, her hips fishlike, narrow. An old green dress clung to her waist, worn thin where she sat. Her glossy braids were like the tails of animals, and swung against her when she moved, deliberately, slowly in her work, held in and half-tamed. But only half. I could tell, but the others never noticed. They never looked into her sly brown eyes or noticed her teeth, strong and sharp and very white. Her legs were bare, and since she padded in beadworked moccasins they never saw that her fifth toes were missing. They never knew she'd drowned. They were blinded, they were stupid, they only saw her in the flesh.

And yet it wasn't just that she was a Chippewa, or even that she was a woman, it wasn't that she was good-looking or even that she was alone that made their brains hum. It was how she played cards.

Women didn't usually play with men, so the evening that Fleur drew a chair to the men's table there was a shock of surprise.

"What's this," said Lily. He was fat, with a snake's pale eyes and precious skin, smooth and lily-white, which is how he got his name. Lily had a dog, a stumpy mean little bull of a thing with a belly drum-tight from eating pork rinds. The dog was as fond of the cards as Lily, and straddled his barrel thighs through games of stud, rum poker, *vingt-un.* The dog snapped at Fleur's arm that first night, but cringed back, its snarl frozen, when she took her place.

"I thought," she said, her voice soft and stroking. "you might deal me in."

There was a space between the lead bin of spiced flour and the wall where Russell and I just fit. He tried to inch toward Fleur's skirt, to fit against her. Who knew but that he might have brought her luck like Lily's dog, except I sensed we'd be driven away if the men noticed us and so I pulled him back by the suspenders. We hunkered down, my arm around his neck. Russell smelled of caraway and pepper, of dust and sour dirt. He watched the game with tense interest for a minute or so, then went limp, leaned against me, and dropped his mouth wide. I kept my eyes open, saw Fleur's black hair swing over the chair, her feet solid on the boards of the floor. I couldn't see on the table where the cards slapped, so after they were deep in their game I pressed Russell down and raised myself in the shadows, crouched on a sill of wood.

I watched Fleur's hands stack and riffle, divide the cards, spill them to each player in a blur, rake and shuffle again. Tor, short and scrappy, shut one eye and squinted the other at Fleur. Dutch screwed his lips around a wet cigar.

"Gotta see a man," he mumbled, getting up to go out back to the privy. The others broke, left their cards, and Fleur sat alone in the lamplight that glowed in a sheen across the push of her breasts. I watched her closely, then she paid me a beam of notice for the first time. She turned, looked straight at me, and grinned the white wolf grin a Pillager turns on its victims, except that she wasn't after me.

"Pauline there," she said. "How much money you got?"

We had all been paid for the week that day. Eight cents was in my pocket.

"Stake me." She held out her long fingers. I put the coins on her palm and then I melted back to nothing, part of the walls and tables, twined close with Russell. It wasn't long before I understood something that I didn't know then. The men would not have seen me no matter what I did, how I moved. For my dress hung loose and my back was already stooped, an old woman's. Work had roughened me, reading made my eyes sore, forgetting my family had hardened my face, and scrubbing down bare boards had given me big, reddened knuckles.

When the men came back and sat around the table, they had drawn together. They shot each other small glances, stuck their tongues in their cheeks, burst out laughing at odd moments, to rattle Fleur. But she never minded. They played their *vingt-un*, staying even as Fleur slowly gained. Those pennies I had given her drew nickels and attracted dimes until there was a small pile in front of her.

Then she hooked them with five card draw, nothing wild. She dealt, discarded, drew, and then she sighed and her cards gave a little shiver. Tor's eye gleamed, and Dutch straightened in his seat.

"I'll pay to see that hand," said Lily Veddar.

Fleur showed, and she had nothing there, nothing at all.

Tor's thin smile cracked open, and he threw in his hand too.

"Well, we know one thing," he said, leaning back in his chair, "the squaw can't bluff."

With that I lowered myself into a mound of swept sawdust and slept. I woke during the night, but none of them had moved yet so I couldn't either. Still later, the men must have gone out again, or Fritzie come to break the game, because I was lifted, soothed, cradled in a woman's arms and rocked to quiet that I kept my eyes shut while Fleur rolled first me, then Russell, into a closet of grimy ledgers, oiled paper, balls of string, and thick files that fit beneath us like a mattress.

The game went on after work the next evening. Russell slept, I got my eight cents back five times over, and Fleur kept the rest of the dollar she'd won for a stake. This time they didn't play so late, but they played regular, and then kept going at it. They stuck with poker, or variations, for one solid week and each time Fleur won exactly one dollar, no more and no less, too consistent for luck.

By this time, Lily and other men were so lit with suspense that they got Pete to join the game. They concentrated, the fat dog tense in Lily Veddar's lap, Tor suspicious, Dutch stroking his huge square brow, Pete steady. It wasn't that Fleur won that hooked them in so, because she lost hands too. It was rather that she never had a freak deal or even anything above a straight. She only took on her low cards, which didn't sit right. By chance, Fleur should have gotten a full or a flush by now. The irritating thing was she beat with pairs and never bluffed, because she couldn't, and still she ended each night with exactly one dollar. Lily couldn't believe, first of all, that a woman could be smart enough to play cards, but even if she was, that she would then be stupid enough to cheat for a dollar a night. By day I watched him turn the problem over, his lard-white face dull, small fingers probing at his knuckles, until he finally thought he had Fleur figured as a bit-time player, caution her game. Raising the stakes would throw her.

More than anything now, he wanted Fleur to come away with something but a dollar. Two bits less or ten more, the sum didn't matter just so he broke her streak.

Night after night she played, won her dollar, and left to stay in a place that only Russell and I knew about. Fritzie had done two things of value for Fleur. She had given her a black umbrella with a stout handle and material made to shed water, and also let her board on the premises. Every night, Fleur bathed in the slaughtering tub, then slept in the unused brick smokehouse behind the lockers, a windowless place tarred on the inside with scorched fats. When I brushed against her skin I noticed that she smelled of the walls, rich and woody, slightly burnt. Since that night she put me in the closet, I was no longer jealous or afraid of her, but followed her close as Russell, closer, stayed with her, became her moving shadow that the men never noticed, the shadow that could have saved her.

August, the month that bears fruit, closed around the shop and Pete and Fritzie left for Minnesota to escape the heat. A month running, Fleur had won thirty dollars and only Pete's presence had kept Lily at bay. But Pete was gone now, and one payday, with the heat so bad no one could move but Fleur, the men sat and played and waited while she finished work. The cards sweat, limp in their fingers, the table was slick with grease, and even the walls were warm to the touch. The air was motionless. Fleur was in the next room boiling heads.

Her green dress, drenched, wrapped her like a transparent sheet. A skin of lakeweed. Black snarls of veining clung to her arms. Her braids were loose, half unraveled, tied behind her neck in a thick loop. She stood in steam, turning skulls through a vat with a wooden paddle. When scraps boiled to the surface, she bent with a round tin sieve and scooped them out. She'd filled two dishpans.

"Ain't that enough now?" called Lily. "We're waiting." The stump of a dog trembled in his lap, alive with rage. It never smelled me or noticed me above Fleur's smoky skin. The air was heavy in the corner, and pressed Russell and me down. Fleur sat with the men.

"Now what do you say?" Lily asked the dog. It barked. That was the signal for the real game to start.

"Let's up the ante," said Lily, who had been stalking this night for weeks. He had a roll of money in his pocket. Fleur had five bills in her dress. Each man had saved his full pay that the bank officer had drawn from the Kozkas' account.

"Ante a dollar then," said Fleur, and pitched hers in. She lost, but they let her scrape along, a cent at a time. And then she won some. She played unevenly, as if chance were all she had. She reeled them in. The game went on. The dog was stiff now, poised on Lily's knees, a ball of vicious muscle with its yellow eyes slit in concentration. It gave advice, seemed to sniff the lay of Fleur's cards, twitched and nudged. Fleur was up, then down, saved by a scratch. Tor dealt seven cards, three down. The pot grew, round by round, until it held all the money. Nobody folded. Then it all rode on one last card and they went silent. Fleur picked hers up and drew a long breath. The heat lowered like a bell. Her card shook, but she stayed in.

Lily smiled and took the dog's head tenderly between his palms.

"Say Fatso," he said, crooning the words. "You reckon that girl's bluffing?"

The dog whined and Lily laughed. "Me too," he said. "Let's show." He 60
tossed his bills and coins into the pot and then they turned their cards over.

Lily looked once, looked again, then he squeezed the dog like a fist of dough and slammed it on the table.

Fleur threw out her arms and swept the money close, grinning that same wolf grin that she'd used on me, the grin that had them. She jammed the bills inside her dress, scooped the coins in waxed white paper that she tied with string.

"Another round," said Lily, his voice choked with burrs. But Fleur opened her mouth and yawned, then walked out back to gather slops for the big hog that was waiting in the stockpen to be killed.

The men sat still as rocks, their hands spread on the oiled wood table. Dutch had chewed his cigar to damp shreds, Tor's eye was dull. Lily's gaze was the only one to follow Fleur. Russell and I didn't breathe. I felt them gathering, saw Dutch's veins, the ones in his forehead that stood out in anger. The dog rolled off the table and curled in a knot below the counter, where none of the men could touch him.

Lily rose and stepped to the closet of ledgers where Pete kept his private 65
stock. He brought back a bottle, uncorked and tipped it between his fingers. The lump in his throat moved, then he passed it on. They drank, steeped in the whiskey's fire, and planned with their eyes things they couldn't say aloud.

When they left, I grabbed Russell by the arm, dragged him along. We followed, hid in the clutter of broken boards and chicken crates beside the stockpen, where the men settled. Fleur could not be seen at first, and then the moon broke and showed her, slipping cautiously along the rough board chute with a bucket in her hand. Her hair fell wild and coarse to her waist, and her dress was a floating patch in the dark. She made a pig-calling sound, rang the tin pail lightly against the wood, paused suspiciously. But too late. In the sound of the ring Lily moved, fat and nimble, stepped right behind Fleur and put out his creamy hands. Russell strained forward and I stopped his mouth with both fists before he yelled. At Lily's first touch, Fleur whirled and doused him with the bucket of sour slops. He pushed her against the big fence and the package of coins split, went clinking and jumping, winked against the wood. Fleur rolled over once and vanished into the yard.

The moon fell behind a curtain of ragged clouds, and Lily followed into the dark muck. But he tripped, pitched over the huge flank of the pig, who lay mired to the snout, heavily snoring. Russell and I sprang from the weeds and climbed the boards of the pen, stuck like glue. We saw the sow rise to her neat, knobby knees, gain her balance and sway, curious, as Lily stumbled forward. Fleur had backed into the angle of splintered wood just beyond and when Lily tried to jostle past, the sow raised her powerful neck and suddenly struck, quick and hard as a snake. She plunged at Lily's thick waist and snatched a mouthful of shirt. She lunged again, caught him lower so that he grunted in pained surprise. He seemed to ponder, breathing deep. Then he launched his huge bulk in a swimmer's dive.

The sow screamed as his body smacked over hers. She rolled, striking out with her knife-sharp hooves and Lily gathered himself upon her, took her foot-long face by the ears, and scraped her snout and cheeks against the trestles of the pen. He hurled the sow's tight skull against an iron post, but instead of knocking her dead, he woke her from her dream.

She reared, shrieked, and then he squeezed her so hard that they leaned into each other and posed in a standing embrace. They bowed jerkily, as if to begin. Then his arms swung and flailed. She sank her black fangs into his shoulder, clasping him, dancing him forward and backward through the pen. Their steps picked up pace, went wild. The two dipped as one, box-stepped, tripped one another. She ran her split foot through his hair. He grabbed her kinked tail. They went down and came up, the same shape and then the same color until the men couldn't tell one from the other in that light and Fleur was able to vault the gates, swing down, hit gravel.

The men saw, yelled, and chased her at a dead run to the smokehouse. And Lily too, once the sow gave up in disgust and freed him. That is when I should have gone to Fleur, saved her, thrown myself on Dutch the way Russell did once he unlocked my arms. He stuck to his stepfather's leg as if he'd been flung there. Dutch dragged him for a few steps, his leg a branch, then cuffed Russell off and left him shouting and bawling in the sticky weeds. I closed my eyes and put my hands on my ears, so there is nothing more to describe but what I couldn't block out: those yells from Russell, Fleur's hoarse breath, so loud it filled me, her cry in the old language and our names repeated over and over among the words.

The heat was still dense the next morning when I entered slowly through the side door of the shop. Fleur was gone and Russell slunk along the woodwork like a beaten dog. The men were slack-faced, hungover. Lily was paler and softer than ever, as if his flesh had steamed on his bones. They smoked, took pulls off a bottle. It wasn't yet noon. Russell disappeared outside to sit by the stock gate, to hold his own knees and rock back and forth. I worked awhile, waiting shop and sharpening steel. But I was sick, I was smothered, I was sweating so hard that my hands slipped on the knives and I wiped my fingers clean of the greasy touch of the customers' coins. Lily opened his mouth and roared once, not in anger. There was no meaning to the sound. His terrier dog, sprawled limp beside his foot, never lifted its head. Nor did the other men.

They didn't notice when I stepped outdoors to call Russell. And then I forgot the men because I realized that we were all balanced, ready to tip, to fly, to be crushed as soon as the weather broke. The sky was so low that I felt the weight of it like a door. Clouds hung down, witch teats, a tornado's green-brown cones, and as I watched, one flicked out and became a delicate probing thumb. Even as Russell ran to me, the wind blew suddenly, cold, and then came blinding rain.

Inside, the men had vanished and the whole place was trembling as if a huge hand was pinched at the rafters, shaking it. We ran straight through, screaming for Dutch or for any of them. Russell's fingers were clenched in my skirt. I shook him off once, but he darted after and held me close in terror when we stopped. He called for Regina, called for Fleur. The heavy doors of the lockers, where the men had surely taken shelter without us, stood shut. Russell howled. They must have heard him, even above the driving wind, because the two of us could hear, from inside, the barking of that dog. A moment, and everything went still. We didn't dare move in that strange hush of suspension. I listened, Russell too. Then we heard a cry building in the wind, faint at first, a whistle and then a shrill scream that tore through the walls and gathered around the two of us, and at last spoke plain.

It was Russell, I am sure, who first put his arms on the bar, thick iron that was made to slide along the wall and fall across the hasp and lock. He strained and shoved, too slight to move it into place, but he did not look to me for help. Sometimes, thinking back, I see my arms lift, my hands grasp, see myself dropping the beam into the metal grip. At other times, the moment is erased. But always I see Russell's face the moment after, as he turned, as he ran for the door—a peaceful look of complicit satisfaction.

Then the wind plucked him. He flew as though by wires in the seat of his trousers, with me right after, toward the side wall of the shop that rose grand as a curtain, spilling us forward as the building toppled.

Outside, the wind was stronger, a hand held against us. We struggled forward. The bushes tossed, rain battered, the awning flapped off a storefront, the rails of porches rattled. The odd cloud became a fat snout that nosed along the earth and sniffled, jabbed, picked at things, sucked them up, blew apart, rooted around as if it was following a certain scent, then stopped behind us at the butcher shop and bored down like a drill.

I pitched head over heels along the dirt drive, kept moving and tumbling in such amazement that I felt no fear, past Russell, who was lodged against a small pine. The sky was cluttered. A herd of cattle flew through the air like giant birds, dropping dung, their mouths opened in stunned bellows. A candle, still lighted, blew past, and tables, napkins, garden tools, a whole school of drifting eyeglasses, jackets on hangers, hams, a checkerboard, a lampshade, and at last the sow from behind the lockers, on the run, her hooves a blur, set free, swooping, diving, screaming as everything in Argus fell apart and got turned upside down, smashed, and thoroughly wrecked.

Days passed before the town went looking for the men. Lily was a bachelor, after all, and Tor's wife had suffered a blow to the head that made her forgetful. Understandable. But what about Regina? That would always remain a question in people's minds. For she said nothing about her husband's absence to anyone. The whole town was occupied with digging out, in high relief because even though the Catholic steeple had been ripped off like a peaked cap and sent across five fields, those huddled in the cellar were unhurt. Walls had fallen, windows were demolished, but the stores were intact and so were the bankers and shop owners who had taken refuge in their safes or beneath their cash registers. It was a fair-minded disaster, no one could be said to have suffered much more than the next, except for Kozka's Meats.

When Pete and Fritzie came home, they found that the boards of the front building had been split to kindling, piled in a huge pyramid, and the shop equipment was blasted far and wide. Pete paced off the distance the iron bathtub had been flung, a hundred feet. The glass candy case went fifty, and landed without so much as a cracked pane. There were other surprises as well, for the back rooms where Fritzie and Pete lived were undisturbed. Fritzie said the dust still coated her china figures, and upon her kitchen table, in the ashtray, perched the last cigarette she'd put out in haste. She lit and finished it, looking through the window. From there, she could see that the old smokehouse Fleur had slept in was crushed to a reddish sand and the stockpens were completely torn apart, the rails stacked helter-skelter. Fritzie asked for Fleur. People shrugged. Then she asked about the others, and suddenly, the town understood that three men were missing.

There was a rally of help, a gathering of shovels and volunteers. We passed 80
boards from hand to hand, stacked them, uncovered what lay beneath the pile of jagged two-by-fours. The lockers, full of meat that was Pete and Fritzie's investment, slowly came into sight, still intact. When enough room was made for a man to stand on the roof, there were calls, a general urge to hack through and see what lay below. But Fritzie shouted that she wouldn't allow it because the meat would spoil. And so the work continued, board by board, until at last the solid doors of the freezer were revealed and people pressed to the entry. It was locked from the outside, someone shouted, wedged down, a tornado's freak whim. Regina stood in the crowd, clutching Russell's collar, trying to hold him against her short, tough body. Everyone wanted to be the first to enter, but only Russell and I were quick enough to slip through beside Pete and Fritzie as they shoved into the sudden icy air.

Pete scraped a match on his boot, lit the lamp Fritzie held, and then the four of us stood in its circle. Light glared off the skinned and hanging carcasses, the crates of wrapped sausages, the bright and cloudy blocks of lake ice, pure as winter. The cold bit into us, pleasant at first, then numbing. We stood there for a moment before we saw the men, or more rightly, the humps of fur, the iced and shaggy hides they wore, the bearskins they had taken down and wrapped about themselves. We stepped closer and Fritzie tilted the lantern beneath the flaps of fur into their faces. The dog was there, perched among them, heavy as a doorstop. The three had hunched around a barrel where the game was still laid out, and a dead lantern and an empty bottle too. But they had thrown down their last hands and hunkered tight, clutching one another, knuckles raw from beating at the door they had also attacked with hooks. Frost stars gleamed off their eyelashes and the stubble of their beards. Their faces were set in concentration, mouths open as if to speak some careful thought, some agreement they'd come to in each other's arms.

Only after they were taken out and laid in the sun to thaw did someone think to determine whether they were all entirely dead, frozen solid. That is when Dutch James's faint heartbeat was discovered.

Power travels in the bloodlines, handed out before birth. It comes down through the hands, which in the Pillagers are strong and knotted, big, spidery and rough, with sensitive fingertips good at dealing cards. It comes through the eyes, too, belligerent, darkest brown, the eyes of those in the bear clan, impolite as they gaze directly at a person.

In my dreams, I look straight back at Fleur, at the men. I am no longer the watcher on the dark sill, the skinny girl.

The blood draws us back, as if it runs through a vein of earth. I left Argus, left Russell and Regina back there with Dutch. I came home and, except for talking to my cousins, live a quiet life. Fleur lives quiet too, down on Matchimanito with her boat. Some say she married the water man, Misshepeshu, or that she lives in shame with white men or windigos, or that she's killed them all. I am about the only one here who ever goes to visit her. That spring, I went to help out in her cabin when she bore the child, whose green eyes and skin the color of an old penny have made more talk, as no one can decide if the child is mixed blood or what, fathered in a smokehouse, or by a man with brass scales, or by the lake. The girl is bold, smiling in her sleep, as if she knows what people wonder, as if she hears the old men talk, turning the story over.

It comes up different every time, and has no ending, no beginning. They get the middle wrong too. They only know they don't know anything.

(1986)

The Gambler: Questions for Discussion and Writing

1. In Erdrich's story, trace the supernatural elements that supposedly protect Fleur.
2. Pauline, the narrator of Erdrich's story, is close to the story's action; is she involved in the action in any way, or is she simply an innocent bystander?
3. Compare the way the speakers of Baudelaire's poem and Dischell's poem regard themselves.
4. Where is the viewer positioned in each of the paintings included here? Are we invited to participate in the gambling scene or to judge it?
5. Gambling on the Internet has been identified as a social problem in recent years; consider whether the scenes depicted in the literature and paintings in this section are different from Internet gambling.
6. Write an editorial either for or against legalizing gambling throughout the United States (not only in Las Vegas, Atlantic City, on Native American reservations, or offshore). Use the material in this section to support your argument.
7. Use Natalia Ginzburg's definition of "little virtues" to argue whether or not gambling is a "little vice" based on the materials in this section.
8. J. Alfred Prufrock, the narrator of T. S. Eliot's famous poem "The Love Song of J. Alfred Prufrock" (Chapter 12), is the opposite of a risk-taker. Compare him to the speakers of the poems by Dischell and Baudelaire in

terms of their willingness to take risks, and evaluate them accordingly: who is the most self-satisfied?

9. Using any of the selections from this chapter that are about greed, would you say that the gamblers in this section are universally motivated by greed, or does gambling differ from greed?

Considering Art: The Gambler

The discussion below references art reproduced on color insert pages 23 and 24.

Gambling involves opening oneself up to chance operations and the random nature of luck. Artists often try to carefully manage the outcome of their artworks, but some have used random, accidental or chance happenings as artistic processes. Many of our cultural heroes are risk takers who come out on top, but one person's adventurousness is another's foolish behavior.

***Snowboarding Sequence* (see color insert p. 23).** The extreme sports adrenaline addict tries to balance the thrill of risk and the skill of control. *Snowboarding Sequence* (2007), photographed by Dave Lehl (b. 1975), transforms a wild moment into a highly controlled image. The perilous leap of the snowboarder is caught by stop action photography that breaks his leap over the void into a series of eight moments in time. What would read as a blur to the eye in real time is suspended in a silent, tidy arc. When photography was a recent invention in the mid-nineteenth century, artists and scientists became interested in it as a tool for the exploration of visual perception. French photographer Etienne-Jules Marey (1830–1904) developed and patented "chronophotography" in which a series of images of a moving body were shot on the same photographic negative. Marey's explorations anticipated cinematic representations of movement in time. Lehl's digital image borrows from this earlier method for its dynamic visual effects, even though it would be simple to make a video recording of the jump and play it back in slow motion.

***Doubledown* (see color insert p. 23).** Scottish painter Stuart Luke Gatherer (b. 1971) often makes modern urban characters the subject matter of his paintings. His painstakingly detailed oil painting technique is rooted in historical modes of representing theatrical narratives, whether historical or biblical, using dramatic lighting and moody shadow. *Doubledown* (2004) brings together a cast of young urban types gather at the blackjack table, watching with bated breath as the uncertain gambler raises the stakes of his bet, basing his wager on only one upturned card. The blond dealer stands between us and him, her black jacket ominously alluding to the power of chance.

***Businessman on Branching Path* (see color insert p. 24).** Each decision leads to a different future, suggests *Businessman on Branching Path* (n.d.), a royalty-free image from the Getty Images agency. Such an image is not owned by the artist (Greg Hargreaves) or designer who created it: it is sold to an image bank, which then licenses it for publication. It might be used to illustrate a variety of subjects and appear in multiple formats such as print journals and on websites. Images like this are assumed to speak for themselves, but in fact their interpretations hinge on the cultural background of the viewer.

Questions about the Art

1. Compare the difference of taking a bodily risk versus a monetary risk in these images. Do the artists seem to celebrate their characters or to criticize them?
2. What risks do these artists seem to be taking in their images? Do these images seem to have any chance or random elements? How does the time and skill involved in making their images contibute to the final outcome?
3. How much risk is the businessman taking in his life's journey? Does he truly have options? How do the color and design of this graphic give this image emotional associations? Does this image remind you of other kinds of images? Where might you expect to find this image reproduced? To make what kind of point?
4. Compare the way that the images deal with movement in time and represent or imply multiple moments or outcomes.

Connecting Art and Literature

1. In the *Snowboarding Sequence*, a physical gamble is broken up into separate sequences. How would you divide Louise Erdrich's Fleur in a similar way? Do you see a "point of no return" in the story similar to the snowboarder's leap?
2. Compare in tone in *Doubledown* to that of Baudelaire's poem? How does each artist seem to feel about gambling?
3. Which work that you have read from this textbook would you illustrate with *Businessman on Branching Path?* Write an essay in which you explain your decision.

Glossary of Terms: Literature and Art History

act A main division in a play, sometimes further divided into scenes.

allegory A work of literature in which characters and actions are meant to represent something else that exists in reality. Allegories are usually extended *narratives* (in poetry or prose) in which characters are named for their characteristics (for example, "faith"). Readers can thus read allegories on two levels—as the interactions in the text and as the ideas they represent in the world outside the text.

alliteration The repetition of the first sound of several words within a *line* or a sentence (for example, "lovely lady"). Alliteration connects or unifies words that are grouped together.

allusion A figure of speech within a work of literature that refers to a work, *character,* or historical event outside the work. Writers often allude to mythological, biblical, or literary works to expand their range of meaning.

annotation A note taken in the margins of a text or on a separate sheet of paper. Formal annotation is often used to explain or comment on a work.

antagonist The *character* or force that opposes the *protagonist* in a work of literature.

argument An opinion-based analysis of a subject that is supported by evidence.

assonance Especially in poetry, the repetition of vowel sounds in words that are close to one another (for example, "a brave lady"). Like *alliteration,* assonance unifies or connects words, and the two can work in conjunction with one another.

audience The readers of a text or the spectators of a performance.

author The person who writes a text, as distinct from the *narrator.*

avant-garde The first division or vanguard of the army that goes first into battle. Its initial use in art criticism (1825) implied that artists were socially progressive leaders in society. By the early twentieth century, the meaning of the term had shifted to imply that artists were disengaged from contemporary life, created art that was innovative on its own terms, and that battled conventions only within the world of art.

back story See *exposition.*

ballad A *narrative* poem that has its origins in song.

belletristic essay A short, meditative essay that gives the impression of an eloquent person thinking out loud. Also known as a "reflective essay."

blank verse Unrhymed verse composed in iambic pentameter. The plays of Shakespeare, along with other major works of the English Renaissance, are largely written in blank verse.

body The part of a paper between the *introduction* and the *conclusion.* The body is composed of an undetermined number of paragraphs that follow one another in a logical manner.

brainstorming A part of the writing process in which a writer jots down words or phrases as they come to mind, with the goal of making connections and generating ideas for an essay.

catharsis According to Aristotle, the purging of pity and fear that accompanies the experience of watching tragic drama.

character A person who participates in a *narrative* or drama. "Flat characters" are fairly one-dimensional, while "round characters" are more fully developed. "Stock characters" are familiar types repeatedly used in drama.

climax The point in a *narrative* at which the *conflict* is most intense. It is usually followed by the *denouement*, or resolution.

comedy A work of literature with a happy ending, usually involving a marriage and the restoration of the social order.

composition The composition of a work of art refers to the arrangement of its lines, shapes and colors. The way in which the artist composes an image includes a consideration of proportions, movement, patterns and visual rhythms and the way in which the depicted elements relate to one another to form a pictorial whole.

conclusion The end of an essay or literary work.

conflict The source of tension in a *narrative;* can be between *characters*, between one character and an outside force, or between two forces within a character (internal dilemma).

connotation The suggested meaning of a word in *context*. The opposite of *denotation*.

consonance The repetition of similar consonant sounds in words that are close to one another but have different vowel sounds (for example, "spit spot").

context The biographical, historical, or thematic issues that surround an essay or literary work.

couplet A pair of *rhymed* lines in a poem.

denotation The literal meaning of a word. The opposite of *connotation*.

denouement The resolution of the *conflict* within a *narrative* work. This French word implies an "unraveling" of the "knot" that has been tied throughout the work; it is used most frequently when criticizing drama.

descriptive essay An essay that focuses on an *author*'s observations and that gives attention to detail rather than to the author's interpretation of his or her observations.

dialogue A speech between two or more *characters* in a work of literature.

diction An *author*'s choice of words. Styles of diction can be formal or informal, allusive or concrete.

elegy A poem written in memory and in honor of someone who is dead.

epic A classical form of *narrative* poetry (that is, a story in verse). Epics are typically long, center on the exploits of a hero, and are narrated in an elevated style.

epigram A short (often two-line), witty poem.

evidence Support for ideas and claims made in a paper. Evidence might include direct quotations from a text or materials from secondary sources (research).

explication A detailed, close analysis of a work of literature.

expressionism A visual style that is characterized by simplified, often distorted forms and by symbolic, rather than imitative, uses of color. Expressionism puts a priority on subjective emotion, spirituality, and psychological states and distrusts rationality, ideal forms, and the things that can be seen with the eye or proved by science.

exposition The part of a *narrative* that provides background information. Also called the *back story*.

expository essay An essay that is designed to inform the reader.

fable A short story, often involving animals, that is told to illustrate a larger point.

figurative language A type of language that compares one thing to another directly (*simile*) or indirectly (*metaphor*). The opposite of literal language.

flashback The depiction of a past event that is embedded in the current action of a *narrative* work such as a story or play.

foot The basic unit of rhythm in a poem. Includes a stressed syllable and one or two unstressed syllables. See also *meter.*

foreshadowing The clues that anticipate an event in a *narrative*.

free verse Verse that does not have an identifiable *meter* or *rhyme* but that contains other poetic elements.

freewriting A type of writing (often done before beginning a formal draft) in which a writer spontaneously notes thoughts "freely" to tap into potential ideas. Ideas generated during a freewriting exercise can later be organized into an essay.

fresco A painting technique that was developed in ancient Rome and was used throughout the Mediterranean area. Pigments are traditionally applied to wet plaster which caused them to permanently bond with the surface.

genre A category or type of literature. The major genres of literature are fiction, poetry, drama, and essays, but the term can also apply to smaller categories within these larger genres, such as *tragedy, comedy,* pastoral, *lyric*, or *epic*. In art history, the terms *genre images* and *genre scenes* mean scenes drawn from everyday life rather than from historical, biblical, or mythological narratives.

haiku A three-line poem with seventeen syllables (five in the first line, seven in the second, five in the third). The haiku is an ancient Japanese form.

heroic couplet In poetry, a rhyming *couplet* that follows the pattern of iambic pentameter.

illusionism A style of painting that uses highly skilled techniques to mimic the surface appearances of things in the real world and thereby blur the distinction between the actual and the represented.

imagery A form of *figurative language* in which an idea is depicted in visually suggestive language.

introduction The opening paragraph(s) of an essay. A good introduction signals the content, *tone*, and *argument* of a work of writing.

irony The use of a word to convey a meaning that is the opposite of what is explicitly stated; also, the use of a *tone* or attitude that is the opposite of what the text literally states.

line The basic structural division of a poem, composed of *feet*.

literature Written or oral texts, often composed with careful attention to language and form. Although the definition of literature is often debated, literature is usually considered texts that are especially worthy of analysis. While literature does not need to be difficult, it is generally complex enough to reward careful reading.

lyric A poem characterized by personal ideas, emotions, or observations and usually uttered by a single speaker.

metaphor A figure of speech that indirectly compares the qualities of one thing with another (for example, "My love is a rose"). See also *simile*.

meter In poetry, meter refers to the number of syllables in each *line* and the recurrent patterns they follow. See also *foot*.

mise en scène The complete *setting* of a film or play, including characters, *background*, and lighting.

modern art The art that was produced in Europe and North America from 1850 to 1950. This artwork frequently takes modern life as its subject matter or reflects on the language of art itself rather than referring to the outside world.

modeling A method that is used by artists to suggest that a figure has three-dimensional volume. Artists use shading and contour lines to achieve this optical effect.

monologue A long speech by a single *character* in a play.

moral The lesson of a work of literature, sometimes stated explicitly.

narrative A work of literature (either prose or poetry) that tells a story.

narrative essay An essay that tells a story.

narrator The speaker in a *narrative*, the figure or voice that tells the story.

naturalism A style in art in which an artist tries to observe and accurately imitate the world of visual appearances.

ode A *lyric* poem that attempts to address a difficult philosophical subject, usually by using a serious *tone* and formal *diction*.

Orientalism An eighteenth-century European style of art in which artists portrayed peoples of the Middle East and North Africa as more exotic, sensual, primitive, or natural than the average urban European.

outline An organizing device that helps writers plan an essay. In classic form, it features headings and subheadings.

oxymoron A surprising juxtaposition of two opposite words or terms.

palette The surface on which an artist mixes paint. The term also is used to refer to the range of colors used by an artist.

parody A poem that imitates another poem, generally by following the same form, *rhyme* scheme, or *meter* as the original poem.

persona A literary mask assumed by the *author* of a work of literature. It is a critical error to equate the author with his or her persona. For instance, in T. S. Eliot's poem "The Love Song of J. Alfred Prufrock," we know from the title that Eliot has created a persona distinct from himself to act as the speaker of the poem.

perspective A Western convention for depicting objects in space. By using lines that converge at the horizon, an artist visually suggests that some items in the two-dimensional image are closer to the eye of the viewer than others.

persuasive essay An essay that advances an *argument* that expresses an *author*'s opinion and that attempts to convince the reader to adopt that opinion.

plot The events or actions in a *narrative*.

point of view The *narrator*'s perspective in a story. When the narrator is a *character*, the story is told in the "first person." When the narrator is not a character or participant, the story is told in the "third person." More rarely, the story can be told in the "second person," when the point of view belongs to "you," the reader.

primitivism A style of modern art that emulates the forms found in folk art, children's art, and the art of some non-Western cultures. The simplified forms of primitivism became an important formal strategy for modern artists.

protagonist The main *character* of a work of literature. Although sometimes called the "hero" or "heroine," a protagonist is not necessarily heroic and might be the story's villain (or "antihero").

quatrain A four-line *stanza*.

rebuttal A refutation of an *argument*. In an essay, it can show how the opposition's potential disagreements are weak or invalid.

revision The process of improving your work by "looking again" at a draft and making changes.

rhetoric The art of persuasive communication.

rhyme A sound pattern shared by two words, often occurring at the end of two *lines* of poetry ("end rhyme"). If rhyme occurs in the middle of a line, it is called "internal rhyme." If the rhyme is imperfect, it is called "slant rhyme."

rising action The part of a *narrative* that introduces the *characters* and issues (or *conflicts*) of a story.

satire A mode of literature that attempts to expose and weaken a powerful and corrupt institution through humor or ridicule.

scale A relative relationship of size or proportion. Scale refers to the relative proportions or dimensions among objects represented.

setting The place and time in which a *narrative* occurs.

simile A direct comparison between two things (often using the word *like* or *as*) (for example, "My love is like a rose"). See also *metaphor.*

social realism An artistic style that was popular in the United States and Mexico in the 1930s and that was concerned with raising the consciousness of the viewer to the modern social conditions of the working class and poor in urban and rural areas. Instead of realizing reality, social realists frequently sought out subjects that they hoped would shock the viewing public into taking action to correct societal ills.

soliloquy In a play, a speech directed at the *audience* that represents a *character*'s inner thoughts.

sonnet A fourteen-line poem that follows a particular pattern of *lines* and *rhymes*. In Italian (Petrarchan) sonnets, the first eight lines generally introduce a problem, and the final six lines resolve the problem. In Elizabethan (Shakespearean) sonnets, three sets of four-line *stanzas* conclude with a two-line *couplet*. Sonnets often advance an *argument*.

stanza Italian for "room": a grouping of *lines* in a poem.

still life The representation of an arrangement of objects or inanimate natural forms, such as fruit or flowers.

summary A condensed recapitulation of a written text.

surrealism An international artistic and literary movement that began in Paris in 1924 and that aimed to merge everyday consciousness with the unconscious world of dreams and thereby to achieve a superior form of reality.

symbol A thing that stands for something else in a work of literature.

syntax The arrangement of words within a sentence.

Technicolor A product name that was given to one of the earliest and most widespread methods of color cinematography. This system was invented in 1922 and was perfected in the films *The Wizard of Oz* and *Gone with the Wind*, which both debuted in 1939.

tempera A paint that uses a water-soluble medium such as egg yolk to bind its mineral pigments. It produces clear pure colors and has a flat rather than transparent appearance on the surface of the painting.

tercet A three-line *stanza*.

theme The main idea of a text. Although the theme can be stated directly, in literature it is usually implied.

thesis The *theme* of a *persuasive essay*, usually explicitly stated.

tone The mood of a work of literature.

tragedy In the classical sense, a work of drama in which the downfall of a great person is occasioned by his or her own actions or *character* flaws and produces an emotional *catharsis* (feelings of pity and fear) in the *audience*. In a more contemporary sense, a tragedy can be any work with an unhappy conclusion.

transition In an essay, a device that allows a paragraph to flow easily into the next paragraph. Transitional phrases or sentences are logical links that demonstrate the relationship of ideas and the progression from earlier ideas to later ones.

unreliable narrator A *narrator* whom readers cannot fully trust because of his or her unspoken involvement in the story.

validity A measure of how informed, thoughtful, creative, and substantial an *argument* is in an essay.

Victorian era The period of the reign of Great Britain's Victoria (1819–1901). Her reign (1837–1901) coincided with the height of the industrial revolution and the expansion of the British empire overseas (she became empress of India in 1876). The artistic style associated with this era (for example, in architecture and furniture) tends to be one of massive proportions, with a great deal of heavy or elaborate ornamentation.

villanelle A nineteen-line poem organized into six *stanzas* with a specific pattern of *rhyme* and the repetition of certain *lines*.

voice The *tone* and *persona* of an essay, which indicate the perspective of the *author*.

Works Cited A list of the works that a writer has mentioned in an essay. The Works Cited list appears at the end of the essay and includes full bibliographic information for each reference.

Credits

TEXT CREDITS

Ai. "Greed." From *Greed* by Ai. Copyright © 1993 by Ai. Used by permission of W. W. Norton & Company, Inc.

Akutagawa, Ryunosuke. "Kesa and Morito." From *Rashomon and Other Stories* by Ryunosuke Akutagawa, translated by Takashi Kojima. Copyright 1952 by Liveright Publishing Corporation. Used by permission of Liveright Publishing Corporation.

Alexander, Elizabeth. "Blues." From *Body of Life* by Elizabeth Alexander, published by Tia Church Press. Copyright © 1996 by Elizabeth Alexander. Reprinted by permission of the author. Elizabeth Alexander is the author of four books of poems, most recently *American Sublime*. She teaches at Yale University.

Aristides (Joseph Epstein). "Work and Its Contents." From *The American Scholar*, Volume 52, No. 3, Summer 1983. Copyright © 1983 by the author.

Auden, W. H. "Musée des Beaux Arts." From *Collected Poems* by W. H. Auden. Copyright 1940 and renewed 1968 by W. H. Auden. Used by permission of Random House, Inc. "The Unknown Citizen." From *Collected Poems* by W. H. Auden. Copyright © 1976 by Edward Mendelson, William Meredith, and Monroe K. Spears, Executors of the Estate of W. H. Auden. Used by permission of Random House, Inc.

Baldwin, James. "Sonny's Blues." From *Going to Meet the Man*, published by Vintage Books. Copyright © 1957 by James Baldwin. Copyright renewed. Originally published in *Partisan Review*. Used by arrangement with the James Baldwin Estate.

Banks, Russell. "Success Story." From *The Angel of the Roof: Stories* by Russell Banks. Copyright © 2000 by Russell Banks. Reprinted by permission of HarperCollins Publishers.

Baudelaire, Charles. "The Gamblers." From *Les Fleurs du Mal* by Charles Baudelaire. Translated from the French by Richard Howard. Reprinted by permission of David R. Godine, Publisher, Inc. Copyright © 1982 by Richard Howard.

Beattie, Ann. "Weekend." From *Secrets and Surprises* by Ann Beattie. Copyright © 1976, 1977, 1978 by Ann Beattie. Used by permission of Random House, Inc.

Camus, Albert. "The Guest." From *Exile and the Kingdom*, translated by Justin O'Brien. Copyright © 1957, 1958 by Alread A. Knopf. Used by permission of Alfred A. Knopf, a division of Random House, Inc.

Carew, Thomas. "A Rapture." From *Exile and the Kingdom* by Albert Camus, translated by Justin O'Brien. Copyright © 1957, 1958 by Alfred A. Knopf. Used by permission of Alfred A. Knopf, a division of Random House, Inc.

Carver, Raymond. "Jerry and Molly and Sam." From *Will You Please Be Quiet, Please?* Copyright © 1976–1988 by Raymond Carver; 1989 to present by Tess Gallagher. Used by permission of Tess Gallagher. Reprinted by permission of International Creative Management, Inc.

Colette. "The Other Wife." From *The Collected Stories of Colette* edited by Robert Phelps and translated by Matthew Ward. Translation copyright © 1983 by Farrar, Straus and Giroux, Inc. Reprinted by permission of Farrar, Straus and Giroux, LLC.

Corso, Gregory. "Marriage." From *Mindfield: New and Selected Poems.* Copyright © 1989 by Gregory Corso. Appears by permission of the publisher, Thunder's Mouth Press, a Division of Avalon Publishing Group, Inc.

Cullen, Countee. "Yet I Do Marvel." Copyright held by Amistad Research Center, Tulane University. Administered by Thompson and Thompson, Brooklyn, NY.

Cummins, Ann. "Where I Work." From *Red Ant House: Stories* by Ann Cummins. Copyright © 2003 by Ann Cummins. Reprinted by permission of Houghton Mifflin Company. All rights reserved.

Dickinson, Emily. "Mine Enemy is growing old," "Much Madness is divinest Sense," "Tell all the Truth but tell it slant," and "Wild Nights—Wild Nights!" are reprinted by permission of the publishers and the Trustees of Amherst College from *The Poems of Emily Dickinson*, Thomas H. Johnson, ed. Cambridge, Mass.: The Belknap Press of Harvard University Press. Copyright © 1951, 1955, 1979, 1983 by the President and Fellows of Harvard College.

Dischell, Stuart. "Days of Me." From *Dig Safe* by Stuart Dischell. Copyright © 2003 by Stuart Dischell. Used by permission of Penguin, a division of Penguin Group (USA) Inc.

Dove, Rita. "Courtship." From *Thomas and Beulah*, Carnegie Mellon University Press. Copyright © 1986 by Rita Dove. Reprinted by permission of the author.

Dubus, Andre. "Killings." From *Selected Stories* by Andre Dubus. Copyright © 1980 by Andre Dubus. Reprinted by permission of David R. Godine, Publisher, Inc.

Epstein, Joseph. "Work and Its Contents." From *The American Scholar*, 52, no. 3 (Summer 1983). Copyright © by the author.

Epstein, Julius J., Philip G. Epstein, and Howard Koch. Excerpt from *Casablanca*, screenplay by Julius and Philip Epstein and Howard Koch, in *Casablanca: Script and Legend, The Fiftieth Anniversary Edition* by Howard Koch, 1992. Copyright © 1943, Warner Bros./Turner Entertainment Co., care of Licensing Corporation of America. Reprinted by permission of The Overlook Press.

Erdrich, Louise. "Raspberry Sun (Fleur). From *Tracks* by Louise Erdrich. Copyright © 1988 by Louise Erdrich. Reprinted by permission of Henry Holt and Company, LLC.

Euripides. "Medea." Translated by E. P. Coleridge, 1910. Retrieved from <http://gutenberg.org.>

Fitzgerald, F. Scott. "Babylon Revisited." From *The Short Stories of F. Scott Fitzgerald*, edited by Matthew J. Bruccoli. Reprinted with the permission of Scribner, an imprint of Simon & Schuster Adult Publishing Group. Copyright 1931 by The Curtis Publishing Company. Copyright renewed © 1959 by Frances Scott Fitzgerald Lanahan.

Fisher, M. F. K. "Young Hunger." From *As They Were* by M. F. K. Fisher. Copyright © 1955, 1961, 1979, 1981, 1982 by M. F. K. Fisher. Used by permission of Alfred A. Knopf, a division of Random House, Inc.

Frost, Robert. "Fire and Ice" and "The Tuft of Flowers." From *The Poetry of Robert Frost* edited by Edward Connery Lathem. Copyright 1969 by Henry Holt and Company. Reprinted by permission of Henry Holt and Company, LLC.

Gilbert, Jack. "Failing and Flying." From *Refusing Heaven: Poems* by Jack Gilbert. Copyright © by Jack Gilbert, 2005. Used by permission of Alfred A. Knopf, a division of Random House, Inc.

Ginsberg, Allen. "C'mon Pigs of Western Civilization Eat More Grease." From *Selected Poems 1947–1995* by Allen Ginsberg. Copyright © 1996 by Allen Ginsberg. Reprinted by permission of HarperCollins Publishers.

Ginzburg, Natalia. "The Little Virtues." From *The Little Virtues* by Natalia Ginzburg, published by Seaver Books, New York. Originally published in Italian under the title *Le Piccole Virtu*. Copyright © 1962 by Giulio Einaudi, editore s.p.a. Translation copyright © 1985 by Dick Davis.

Giovanni, Nikki. "Woman." From *Cotton Candy on a Rainy Day* by Nikki Giovanni. Copyright © 1978 by Nikki Giovanni. Reprinted by permission of HarperCollins Publishers.

Glück, Louise. "The Mountain." From *The Triumph of Achilles from the First Four Books of Poems* by Louise Glück. Copyright 1968, 1971, 1972, 1973, 1974, 1975, 1976, 1977, 1978, 1979, 1980, 1985, 1995 by Louise Glück. Reprinted by permission of HarperCollins Publishers.

Greenbaum, Jessica. "Sonnets for the Autobiographical Urban Dweller." First published in *Salamander*, a magazine for poetry, fiction, and memoirs, 2005.

Halperin, Mark. "The Escape." From *Time as Distance*. Copyright 2001 by Mark Halperin. Reprinted by permission of New Issues Poetry & Prose.

Hamilton, Edith. "A Great Adventure." From *Mythology* by Edith Hamilton. Copyright © 1942 by Edith Hamilton, copyright © renewed 1969 by Dorian Fielding Reid and Doris Fielding Reid. By permission of Little, Brown and Co.

Hamilton, Virginia. "Little Girl and Buh Rabby." From *Her Stories: African-American Folk Tales, Fairy Tales and True Tales* told by Virginia Hamilton. Scholastic Inc./Blue Sky Press. Copyright © 1995 by Virginia Hamilton. Reprinted by permission.

Heaney, Seamus. "Digging." From *Opened Ground: Selected Poems 1966–1996* by Seamus Heaney. Copyright © 1998 by Seamus Heaney. Reprinted by permission of Farrar, Straus and Giroux, LLC.

Hesford, Walter. Excerpt from "Literary Contexts of 'Life in the Iron-Mills.'" Reprinted by permission of the author.

Hughes, Langston. "Theme for English B" copyright © 1994 by The Estate of Langston Hughes; "The Weary Blues" copyright © 1994 by The Estate of Langston Hughes; "Harlem (2)" copyright 1951 by Langston Hughes. From *The Collected Poems of Langston Hughes* by Langston Hughes, edited by Arnold Rampersad with David Roessel, associate editor. Used by permission of Alfred A. Knopf, a division of Random House, Inc.

Hughes, Sheila Hassell. "Between Bodies of Knowledge There Is a Great Gulf Fixed: A Liberationalist Reading of Class and Gender in 'Life in the Iron-Mills.'" *American Quarterly* 49, no. 1 (1997), 113–137. Copyright © The American Studies Association. Reprinted with permission of The Johns Hopkins University Press.

Hurston, Zora Neale. "Sweat." From *The Complete Stories* by Zora Neale Hurston. Introduction copyright © 1995 by Henry Louis Gates, Jr. and Sieglinde Lemke. Compilation copyright © 1995 by Vivian Bowden, Lois J. Hurston Gaston, Clifford Hurston, Lucy Ann Hurston, Winifred Hurston Clark, Zora Mack Goins, Edgar Hurston, Sr., and Barbara Hurston Lewis. Afterword and bibliography copyright © 1995 by Henry Louis Gates, Jr. "Sweat" was originally published in *Fire,* November 1926. Reprinted by permission of HarperCollins Publishers.

Jackson, Shirley. "The Lottery." From *The Lottery* by Shirley Jackson. Copyright © 1948, 1949 by Shirley Jackson. Copyright © renewed 1976, 1977 by Laurence Hyman, Barry Hyman, Mrs. Sarah Webster and Mrs. Joanne Schnurer. Reprinted with the permission of Farrar, Straus and Giroux, LLC.

Jen, Gish. "In the American Society." From *Who's Irish?* by Gish Jen, published in 1999 by Alfred A. Knopf. First published in *Southern Review*. Copyright © 1986 by Gish Jen. Reprinted by permission of the author.

Jhabvala, Ruth Prawer. "The Interview." From *Out of India* by Ruth Prawer Jhabvala. Copyright © 1976, 1986 by Ruth Prawer Jhabvala. Reprinted by permission of HarperCollins Publishers.

Kincaid, Jamaica. "Girl." From *At the Bottom of the River* by Jamaica Kincaid. Copyright © 1983 by Jamaica Kincaid. Reprinted by permission of Farrar, Straus and Giroux, LLC.

King, Martin Luther. "Letter from Birmingham Jail." Reprinted by arrangement with The Heirs to the Estate of Martin Luther King Jr., care of Writers House as agent for the proprietor, New York. Copyright 1963 Martin Luther King Jr., copyright renewed 1991 Coretta Scott King.

Kingston, Maxine Hong. "No Name Woman." From *The Woman Warrior* by Maxine Hong Kingston. Copyright © 1975, 1976 by Maxine Hong Kingston. Used by permission of Alfred A. Knopf, a division of Random House, Inc.

Kinnell, Galway. "It All Comes Back." From *Strong Is Your Hold: Poems* by Galway Kinnell. Copyright © 2006 by Galway Kinnell. Reprinted by permission of Houghton Mifflin Company. All rights reserved.

Kwasny, Melissa. "Deception." *Ploughshares*, 32, no. 1 (Spring 2005). Lee et al., eds. Reprinted by permission of the author.

Lahiri, Jhumpa. "This Blessed House." From *Interpreter of Maladies* by Jhumpa Lahiri. Copyright © 1999 by Jhumpa Lahiri. Reprinted by permission of Houghton Mifflin Company. All rights reserved.

Larkin, Philip. "Toads." From *The Less Deceived* by Philip Larkin. Copyright © 1955 by Philip Larkin. By permission of The Marvell Press, England and Australia. "Toads Revisited." From *Collected Poems* by Philip Larkin. Copyright © 1988, 1989 by the Estate of Philip Larkin. Reprinted by permission of Farrar, Straus and Giroux, LLC.

Lasseter, Janice Milner. "The Censored and Uncensored Literary Lives of 'Life in the Iron-Mills.'" From *Legacy: A Journal of American Women Writers,* 20, nos. 1–2 (2003). Copyright © 2003 by the University of Nebraska Press. Reprinted by permission of the University of Nebraska Press.

Lawrence, D. H. "The Rocking Horse Winner." From *Complete Short Stories of D. H. Lawrence* by D. H. Lawrence. Copyright 1933 by the Estate of D. H. Lawrence, copyright renewed 1961 by Angelo Ravagli and C. M. Weekley, Executors of the Estate of Frieda Lawrence. Used by permission of Viking Penguin, a division of Penguin Group (USA) Inc.

Levine, Philip. "What Work Is." From *What Work Is* by Philip Levine. Copyright © 1992 by Philip Levine. Used by permission of Alfred A. Knopf, a division of Random House, Inc.

Long, David. "Morphine." Originally published in *The New Yorker,* August 8, 1989. Reprinted by permission of Brick House Literary Agents.

Luke. "The Parable of the Lost Son." From the Gospel According to Luke, chapter 15, verses 11–32, *The Holy Bible: Today's New International Version, TNIV*. Copyright © 2001, 2005 by International Bible Society. Used by permission of International Bible Society. All rights reserved worldwide.

MacLeish, Archibald. "Ars Poetica." From *Collected Poems 1917–1982* by Archibald MacLeish. Copyright © 1985 by The Estate of Archibald MacLeish. Reprinted by permission of Houghton Mifflin Company. All rights reserved.

Matthews, William. "The Bear at the Dump." From *Search Party: Collected Poems of William Matthews.* Copyright © 2004 by Sebastian Matthews and Stanley Plumly. Reprinted by permission of Houghton Mifflin Company. All rights reserved.

McKenzie, Elizabeth. "Stop That Girl." From *Stop That Girl* by Elizabeth McKenzie. Copyright © 2005 by Elizabeth McKenzie. Used by permission of Random House, Inc.

Melville, Herman. "Bartleby, the Scrivener: A Tale of Wall Street."

Millay, Edna St. Vincent. "What Lips My Lips Have Kissed." From *Collected Poems,* HarperCollins. Copyright © 1923, 1951 by Edna St. Vincent Millay and Norma Millay Ellis. All rights reserved. Reprinted by permission of Elizabeth Barnett, literary executor.

Minot, Susan. "Lust." Copyright © 1989 by Susan Minot. Reprinted by permission of Houghton Mifflin Company. All rights reserved.

Mitchell, Joni. "Amelia." Words and music by Joni Mitchell. Copyright © 1976 (renewed) Crazy Crow Music. All rights administered by Sony/Atv Music Publishing, 8 Music Square West, Nashville, TN 37203. All rights reserved. Used by permission of Alfred Publishing Co., Inc.

Molière. "The Miser." Retrieved from <http://www.gutenberg.org>.

Mukherjee, Bharati. "The Tenant." Copyright © 1988 by Bharati Mukherjee. Used by permission of Grove / Atlantic, Inc.

Nelson, Marilyn. "Minor Miracle." From *The Fields of Praise*, published by Louisiana State University Press. Copyright © 1997 by Marilyn Nelson. Reprinted by permission of Louisiana State University Press.

Neruda, Pablo. "The Beggars." From *Selected Poems* by Pablo Neruda. Copyright © 1961 by Grove Press, Inc. Used by permission of Grove/Atlantic, Inc.

Olds, Sharon. "Sex without Love." From *The Dead and the Living* by Sharon Olds. Copyright © 1987 by Sharon Olds. Used by permission of Alfred A. Knopf, a division of Random House, Inc.

Orwell, George. "Shooting an Elephant." From *Shooting an Elephant and Other Essays* by George Orwell. Copyright 1950 by Sonia Brownell Orwell and renewed 1978 by Sonia Pitt-Rivers. Reprinted by permission of Harcourt, Inc.

Ousmane, Sembene. "Her Three Days." From *Tribal Scars and Other Stories* (Portsmouth, NH: Heinemann, 1974). Reprinted by permission of Samba Gadjigo.

Ovid. "The Story of Daedalus and Icarus." From *Metamorphoses* by Ovid, translated by Rolfe Humphries, Indiana University Press, 1955, pp. 187–189. Reprinted by permission of Indiana University Press.

Parker, Dorothy. "The Little Old Lady in Lavender Silk." From *The Portable Dorothy Parker* by Dorothy Parker, edited by Marion N. Meade. Copyright © 1928, copyright renewed 1956 by Dorothy Parker. Used by permission of Viking Penguin, a division of Penguin Group (USA) Inc.

Paz, Octavio. "Two Bodies." *Early Poems 1935–1955*. Bloomington: Indiana University Press, 1973. Reprinted by permission of Indiana University Press.

Piercy, Marge. "The Secretary Chant." From *Circles on the Water* by Marge Piercy. Copyright © 1982 by Marge Piercy. Used by permission of Alfred A. Knopf, a division of Random House, Inc.

Pound, Ezra. "In a Station in the Metro." From *Personae* by Ezra Pound. Copyright © 1926 by Ezra Pound. Reprinted by permission of New Directions Publishing Corp.

Pritchett, V. S. "A Story of Don Juan." From *The Pritchett Century* by V. S. Pritchett. Copyright © 1997 by The Estate of V. S. Pritchett. Used by permission of Modern Library, a division of Random House, Inc.

Proulx, E. Annie. "On the Antler." From *Heart Songs and Other Stories* by E. Annie Proulx. Reprinted with the permission of Scribner, an imprint of Simon & Schuster Adult Publishing Group. Copyright © 1988, 1995 by E. Annie Proulx. All rights reserved.

Randall, Dudley. "Ballad of Birmingham." From *Cities Burning*. Reprinted by permission of the Dudley Randall Estate.

Ras, Barbara. "You Can't Have It All." From *Bite Every Sorrow* by Barbara Ras. Published by Louisiana State University Press, 1998. Copyright © 1997 by Barbara Ras. Reprinted by permission of Louisiana State University Press.

Rifaat, Alifa. "Another Evening at the Club." From *Distant View of a Minaret and Other Stories* (African Writers Series No. 271), Heinemann. Translated by Denys Johnson-Davies. Reprinted by permission of Denys Johnson-Davies.

Roethke, Theodore. "Dolor." From *Collected Poems of Theodore Roethke* by Theodore Roethke. Copyright 1943 by Modern Poetry Association, Inc. Used by permission of Doubleday, a division of Random House, Inc.

Rushdie, Salman. "The Prophet's Hair." From *East, West: Stories* by Salman Rushdie. Copyright © 1994 by Salman Rushdie. Used by permission of Pantheon Books, a division of Random House, Inc.

Schlosser, S. E. "Brer Rabbit Meets a Tar Baby." Used with permission of S. E. Schlosser and AmericanFolklore.net. Copyright 2006. All rights reserved.

Sexton, Anne. "Cinderella." From *Transformations* by Anne Sexton. Copyright © 1971 by Anne Sexton. Reprinted by permission of Houghton Mifflin Company. All rights reserved.

Shakespeare, William. *The First Part of Henry the Fourth.* "My Love Is as a Fever Longing Still" (Sonnet 147). "My Mistress' Eyes Are Nothing Like the Sun" (Sonnet 130). "When My Love Swears That She Is Made of Truth"(Sonnet 138).

Shepard, Reginald. "Icarus on Fire Island." From *Wrong* by Reginald Sheperd. Copyright © 1999. Reprinted by permission of the University of Pittsburgh Press.

Silver, Andrew. "'Unnatural Unions': Picturesque Travel, Sexual Politics, and Working-Class Representation in 'A Night under Ground' and 'Life in the Iron-Mills.'" From *Legacy: A Journal of American Women Writers*, 20, nos. 1–2 (2003). Copyright © 2003 by the University of Nebraska Press. Reprinted by permission of the Universtiy of Nebraska Press.

Soyinka, Wole. *Death and the King's Horseman.* Copyright © 1975 by Wole Soyinka. Used by permission of W. W. Norton & Company, Inc.

Tan, Amy. "Rules of the Game." From *The Joy Luck Club* by Amy Tan. Copyright © 1989 by Amy Tan. Used by permission of G. P. Putnam's Sons, a division of Penguin Group (USA) Inc.

Thomas, Dylan. "Do Not Go Gentle into That Good Night." From *The Poems of Dylan Thomas.* Copyright © 1952 by Dylan Thomas. Reprinted by permission of New Directions Publishing Corp.

Trethewey, Natasha. "Letter Home." From *Bellocq's Ophelia.* Copyright 2002 by Natasha Trethewey. Reprinted with the permission of Graywolf Press, Saint Paul, Minnesota.

Updike, John. "A & P." From *Pigeon Feathers and Other Stories* by John Updike. Copyright © 1962 and renewed 1990 by John Updike. Used by permission of Alfred A. Knopf, a division of Random House, Inc. "Wife-Wooing." From *Pigeon Feathers and Other Stories* by John Updike, copyright © 1962 and renewed 1990 by John Updike. Used by permission of Alfred A. Knopf, a division of Random House, Inc.

Vowell, Sarah. "Take the Cannoli." From *Take the Cannoli* by Sarah Vowell. Copyright © 2000 by Sarah Vowell. Reprinted with the permission of Simon & Schuster Adult Publishing Group. All rights reserved.

Wakoski, Diane. "The Greed That Is Not Greed" From *The Collected "Greed"* by Diane Wakoski. Reprinted by permission of David R. Godine, Publisher, Inc. Copyright © Diane Wakoski.

Walker, Alice. "Everyday Use." From *In Love and Trouble: Stories of Black Women.* Copyright © 1973 and renewed 2001 by Alice Walker. Reprinted by permission of Harcourt, Inc.

Walker, Margaret. "Since 1619." *For My People*, foreword by Stephen Vincent Benet (New Haven: Yale University Press, 1942). Reprinted by permission.

Weldon, Fay. "Inspector Remorse." From *A Hard Time to Be a Father* (New York: Bloomsbury, 1998, 1999), pp. 105–113. Reprinted by permission of Bloomsbury.

Wilbur, Richard. "Lying." From *New and Collected Poems.* Copyright © 1988 by Richard Wilbur, reprinted by permission of Harcourt, Inc.

Williams, Tennessee. *Cat on a Hot Tin Roof.* Copyright © 1954, 1955, 1971, 1975 by The University of the South. Reprinted by permission of New Directions Publishing Corp.

Williams, William Carlos. "This Is Just to Say." From *Collected Poems: 1909–1939*, volume 1. Copyright © 1938 by New Directions Publishing Corp. Reprinted by permission of New Directions Publishing Corp.

Wolff, Tobias. "The Rich Brother." From *Back in the World.* Copyright © 1985 by Tobias Wolff. Reprinted by permission of International Creative Management, Inc.

Wong, Nellie. "Mama, Come Back." From *The Death of the Long Steam Lady.* Copyright © 1984 by Nellie Wong. Reprinted with the permission of West End Press, Albuquerque, New Mexico.

Woolf, Virginia. "Professions for Women." From *The Death of the Moth and Other Essays* by Virginia Woolf. Copyright 1942 by Harcourt, Inc. and renewed 1970 by Marjorie T. Parsons, Executrix, reprinted of the publisher.

Yoki, Mori. "Spring Storm." From *The Mother of Dreams.* Published by Kodansha International Ltd. © 1989. Reprinted by permission.

PHOTO CREDITS

Chapter 1: page 9, © Mario Tama/Getty Images.
Chapter 4: page 66, Courtesy of Sarah Himberger.
Chapter 5: page 83, AP/Wide World Photos; page 89, *Play de Blues* by Aaron Douglas, 1926, offset lithograph, 16 x 11.5 inches. Art & Artifacts Division, Schomburg Center for Research in Black Culture, The New York Public Library, Astor, Lenox and Tilden Foundations; page 90, Courtesy of Kristin Seabolt.
Chapter 6: page 98, © Jose Fuste Raga/Corbis; page 99, © Adrian Arbib/Corbis, page 100, © Adam Woolfitt/Corbis; page 118, Courtesy of Darryl Holliday.
Chapter 7: page 128, Courtesy of Lacey Perkins.
Chapter 8: page 134, © Bettmann/Corbis; page 139, © Sunset Boulevard/Corbis; page 145, Courtesy of Jinyeda Tapia.
Chapter 11: page 186, © Bettmann/Corbis; page 201, Courtesy of George Scala III.
Chapter 12: page 212, From *The Hobbit*, illustrations © 1984 by Oak, Ash and Thorn Ltd. Illustration used with permission of Michael Hague, www.michaelhague.com; page 213, © Blue Lantern Studio/Corbis; page 214, © Corbis; page 225, AP/Wide World Photos; page 233, © Bettmann/Corbis; page 243, © Brian Snyder/Reuters/Corbis; page 244, by permission of the Houghton Library, Harvard University. bMS Am 1793.1; page 250, © Jeremy Bembaron/Corbis Sygma; page 252, © Marc Brasz/Corbis; page 261, Courtesy of Elizabeth McKenzie; page 270, The Granger Collection, New York; page 273, © Hulton-Deutsch Collection/Corbis; page 274, Dante Charles Gabriel Rossetti (1828–1882), Frontispiece of *Goblin Market and Other Poems* (1862) (litho), British Library, London, UK, © British Library Board. All rights reserved / The Bridgeman Art Library International; page 288, © Bettmann/Corbis; page 291, The Granger Collection, New York; page 292, by permission of the Houghton Library, Harvard University. bMS Am 1118.3 (151d) © The President and Fellows of Harvard College; page 293, © Hulton-Deutsch Collection/Corbis; page 295, © Bettmann/Corbis; page 300, © Hulton-Deutsch Collection/Corbis; page 302, © Hulton-Deutsch Collection/Corbis; page 304, © Christopher Felver/Corbis; page 308, © Ira Wyman/Corbis Sygma; page 309, Robert Hubner, WSU Photo Services, Washington State University; page 360, © Bettmann/Corbis; page 377, © Bettmann/Corbis; page 383, BookPeople in Austin, Texas; photographer Frank Arnold; page 391, © The Bridgeman Art Library/Getty Images; page 397, © Hulton-Deutsch Collection/Corbis.
Chapter 13: page 405, © Bettmann/Corbis; page 436, Kyodo News; page 437, © Asian Art & Archaeology, Inc./Corbis; page 446, © Reagan Louie; page 458, AP/Wide World Photos; page 466, The Granger Collection, New York; page 468, © Michael Nicholson/Corbis; page 472, © Hulton-Deutsch Collection/Corbis; page 477, © Hulton-Deutsch Collection/Corbis; page 479, © Bettmann/Corbis; page 485, © Hulton-Deutsch Collection/Corbis; page 486, © Bettmann/Corbis; page 489, © Bettmann/Corbis; page 490, AP/Wide World Photos; page 492, © Christopher Felver/Corbis; page 493, © Tim Wright/Corbis; page 495, © Bettman/Corbis; page 496, © Bettmann/Corbis; page 497, © Bettmann/Corbis; page 569, © Stefano Bianchetti/Corbis; page 573, © Bettmann/Corbis; page 582, © Stock Montage/SuperStock; page 583, © Bettmann/Corbis; page 584, The Granger Collection, New York.
Chapter 14: page 640, The Granger Collection, New York; page 641, Tad Lauritzen Wright, *String of Lies*, acrylic on canvas, 48" x 60" (2005); page 641, Fisk University Franklin Library's Special Collections; page 651, AP/Wide World Photos; page 662, Montana and Heather Long; page 678, © Christopher Felver/Corbis; page 690, © Sopphie Bassouls/Corbis Sygma; page 700, Kyodo News; page 713, © Corbis; page 714, © Bettmann/Corbis; page 716, © Corbis; page 718, AP/Wide World Photos; page 720, © Oscar White/Corbis; page 723, Courtesy of Mark Halperin; page 725, Courtesy of Jessica Greenbaum, photo by Avigail Schimmel; page 726, Courtesy of Melissa Kwasny; page 728, © John Rou Photography; page 730, © Bettmann/Corbis; page 732, © Bettmann/Corbis; page 777, AP/Wide World Photos; page 789, © Swim Ink 2, LLC/Corbis; page 790, © Archivo Iconografico, S.A./Corbis; page 797, © Bettmann/Corbis; page 807, © Bettmann/Corbis.
Chapter 15: page 814, Paramount/The Kobal Collection; page 815, © The New Yorker Collection 1988, William Hamilton from cartoonbank.com. All rights reserved; page 815, © Corbis; 822, © Bettmann/Corbis; page 833, © Corbis; page 843, © Bettmann/Corbis; page 859, © Caroline Penn/Corbis; page 870, © Marc McAndrews/Getty Images; page 882, AP/Wide World Photos; page 896, © Rune Hellestad/Corbis; page 903, © Hulton-Deutsch Collection/Corbis; page 904,

© Michael Nicholson/Corbis; page 926, © Corbis; page 927, Courtesy of Margaret Walker Alexander National Research Center at Jackson State University; page 930, Department of Special Collections, Davidson Library, University of California, Santa Barbara; page 933, AP/Wide World Photos; page 935, © Christopher Felver/Corbis; page 937, The Granger Collection, New York; page 939, Paramount/The Kobal Collection; page 941, © ArenaPal / Topham / The Image Works; page 964, © Bettmann/Corbis; page 966, © Flip Schulke/Corbis; page 967, © Bettmann/Corbis; page 982, © Historical Picture Archive/Corbis.

Chapter 16: page 1018, © Daniel Nevins/Superstock; page 1019, The Granger Collection, New York; page 1022, The Granger Collection, New York; page 1033, Courtesy of Janice Lasseter; page 1034, © Corbis; page 1035, © Corbis; page 1061, © Corbis; page 1089, © Bernard Gotfryd/Getty Images; page 1098, Photo courtesy of Ann Cummins; photo by Steve Willis; page 1105, © Mary Evans Picture Library / The Image Works; page 1120, The Granger Collection, New York; page 1122, © Bettmann/Corbis; page 1124, © Corbis; page 1131, © Topham / The Image Works; page 1134, © Bettmann/Corbis; page 1136, AP/Wide World Photos; page 1137, © Christopher Felver/Corbis; page 1139, © Christopher Felver/Corbis; page 1141, Courtesy of Graywolf Press; photo by Michael Marsland; page 1144, © Archivo Iconografico, S.A./Corbis; page 1149, © Robbie Jack/Corbis; page 1235, © Hulton-Deutsch Collection/Corbis; page 1240, Robert Birnbaum, Duende Publishing; page 1254, © Corbis; page 1255, United Artists / The Kobal Collection.

Chapter 17: page 1278, From A. A. Milne, *Winnie-the-Pooh*, illustrated by E. H. Shepard, copyright 1926 by E. P. Dutton, renewed 1954 by A. A. Milne. Used by permission of www.penguin.com. All rights reserved; page 1279, © British Library / HIP / Art Resource, NY; page 1280, National Portrait Gallery, London; page 1289, The Granger Collection, New York; page 1294, © Bettmann/Corbis; page 1306, © J. J. Guillen / epa / Corbis; page 1319, © Steve Liss / Time Life Pictures / Getty Images; page 1333, The Granger Collection, New York; page 1335, © Pach Brothers/Corbis; page 1337, Courtesy of Shearsman Books; photo by Juan Domingo Córdoba, 1929; page 1339, © Bettmann/Corbis; page 1341, Courtesy of Diane Wakoski; photo by Robert Turney; page 1348, Anna Zoë Rucker; page 1350, © Hulton-Deutsch Collection/Corbis; page 1353, © Christopher Felver / Corbis; page 1358, AP / Wide World Photos; page 1360, © Gianni Dagli Orti/Corbis; page 1363, © Lipnitzki / Roger-Viollet / The Image Works; page 1410, © British Library / HIP / The Image Works; page 1412, Courtesy of Lescher & Lescher, Ltd., photo © Thomas Victor; page 1416, © C. Vaterra / SV-Bilderdienst / The Image Works; page 1427, The Art Archive; page 1428, © James Leynse/Corbis.

Index of Terms

Index of Authors and Titles

Contents of *Connections* Arranged by Chronology

Early Writings and Oral Tradition

1500 to 1800: Shakespeare and Renaissance Literature

Early Nineteenth Century: From Restoration to Romanticism

Late Nineteenth Century: Realism and the Movement toward Modernism

1910 to 1945: The Age of Modernism